D1567574

THE INDIANA COMPANION TO TRADITIONAL CHINESE LITERATURE

(Volume 2)

THE
Indiana Companion
TO
Traditional
Chinese Literature
(Volume 2)

WILLIAM H. NIENHAUSER, JR.
Editor and Compiler

CHARLES HARTMAN
Associate Editor

SCOTT W. GALER
Assistant Editor

INDIANA UNIVERSITY PRESS • BLOOMINGTON & INDIANAPOLIS

This volume is dedicated to my teachers:

Friedrich A. Bischoff, Wu-chi Liu,
Irving Yucheng Lo, and Peter Olbricht.

This book is a publication of

Indiana University Press
601 North Morton Street
Bloomington, Indiana 47404-3797 USA

http://www.indiana.edu/~iupress

Telephone orders 800-842-6796
Fax orders 812-855-7931
Orders by e-mail iuporder@indiana.edu

The paper used in this publication meets the minimum requirements of American National Standard for Information Sciences—Permanence of Paper for Printed Library Materials, ANSI Z39.48-1984.

Manufactured in the United States of America

Library of Congress Cataloging-in-Publication Data
Main entry under title:

The Indiana companion to traditional Chinese Literature.

  Bibliography: p.
  Includes indexes.
  Contents: pt. 1. Essays. — pt. 2. Entries
  1. Chinese literature—Bio-bibliography. 2. Chinese
literature—History and criticism—Addresses, essays, lectures.
I. Nienhauser, William H. Jr.
Z3108.L5153 1985 [PL2264] 895.1'09 83-49511
ISBN 0-253-32983-3 (v. 1 : alk. paper). — ISBN 0-253-33456-X (v. 2 : alk. paper)

1 2 3 4 5 03 02 01 00 99 98

Contents

Preface

This book, it seems, began with the inertia from the first volume of the *Indiana Companion to Traditional Chinese Literature*. It also originated with my colleagues and students, especially those in the graduate History of Chinese Literature classes over the years. But it must have originally taken its impetus from the classes I had at Indiana University and Bonn University in the late 1960s and 1970s, from the lectures of my teachers, Friedrich A. Bischoff, Wu-chi Liu, Irving Yucheng Lo, and Peter Olbricht. This second volume of the *Indiana Companion* is, therefore, dedicated to them.

The first volume of the *Indiana Companion* has been a fixture in the introductory graduate courses at the University of Wisconsin. For this reason, revisions of errors and additions to the bibliographies began as soon as the text was available in early 1986. The desire to correct the minor errors and typos we found led to a Second Revised Edition in Taiwan (Taipei: SMC Publishing Co. 南天, 1988). I want to thank again those colleagues who contributed to the list of 500 errata corrected in that Taiwan edition: Wang Ch'iu-kuei 王秋桂, Robert Joe Cutter, Silvio Vita, Ch'an Chiu-ming 陳照明, Wei Te-wen 魏德文 (my Taiwan publisher and friend), and especially Glen Dudbridge who followed up his review of the book (*TLS,* 9 May 1986) with a long list of errata. These original 500 errata have recently been conflated with another list prepared by William Schultz and form the basis of the "Errata and Corrigenda" appended to this second volume. To my knowledge Bill Schultz is the only person who has read volume one cover to cover. I am most grateful to him. An important correction made in the Revised Taiwan Edition which I do not want to be lost in an appendix was the addition of George Kao's name and key (GK) to the "List of Contributors" in volume one.

After the publication of the Taiwan Edition in 1988, the errata were put away in a drawer and the updated bibliographic lists began to interest me more. That same year (1988) some of these lists were edited and published as the *Bibliography of Selected Western Works on T'ang Dynasty Literature* (Taipei: Center for Chinese Studies, 1988). Later, these bibliographies became lengthy enough that I began to contemplate a second volume of the *Indiana Companion*. At first I envisioned only a bibliographic update. But there were a few left-over entries from the first volume and reviewers had made a number of useful suggestions for additional entries. Moreover, by 1990 memories of the difficulties of organizing the contributions of nearly two-hundred colleagues for the first volume had began to fade. Besides, I was convinced that my mentor in all attempts at publishing over the past fifteen years, John Gallman, Director of Indiana University Press, would dissuade me from the idea of a second volume. To my surprise, John's response to my inquiries in early 1996 was encouraging and enthusiastic.

My longtime colleague and friend Charles Hartman was equally supportive and agreed to serve again as associate editor for the volume. Besides continued advice, Charles has been a careful reader of both the entries and some of the bibliographies of this second volume. He also contributed two entries. With Charles willing to help, I began to write to colleagues and to enlist them in the project. Within a short period of time more than twenty colleagues agreed to help. By the end of 1996 there were thirty-two contributors who eventually wrote sixty-three new entries. This was a carefully picked group. They were attentive to deadlines and guidelines and produced some excellent, innovative entries within a period of a little more than a year.

These entries are on average fifty-percent longer than those in volume one. Many treat generals topics such as *Erh-t'ung wen-hsüeh* (Children's Literature), Late-Ch'ing fiction, Literary Chinese, *Pao-chüan,* Printing and Circulation, *tzu-shu* or *tzu-tien,* and *Wu-hsia hsiao-shuo.* An effort has been made to incorporate more Chinese characters (for cross-referenced authors and works, for example). Finally, a number of entries include translations and Chinese texts of works that illustrate a claim or argument.

The sixty-three entries are not concentrated in any era. Nearly a third deal with subjects in the pre-T'ang period. Four entries relate to the T'ang, ten are on Sung subjects, fifteen on the Ming, and about the same number treat topics associated with the Ch'ing.

Each entry, as in the first volume, presents basic information followed by a tripartite bibliography which lists editions, translations (into English, French, German, Japanese and occasionally other languages), and studies.

The sections of bibliographic updates which follow that of the new entries do not claim to present every title published since the first volume. They generally include works from 1984 (when the bibliographies in volume one left off) through 1996, with some items for 1997 and 1998 included as well. For entries with a number of studies, we have tried to select only the most important (primarily monographs and articles by well-known authors or those which appeared in well-known journals). For subjects which are less explored, we tried to incorporate most of what we have found. When we could not locate one part of a bibliographic item (like the page numbers), we often included an incomplete bibliographic reference as long as it seemed that the information provided was sufficient to allow the reader to locate that item. None of the essays or entries in volume one of the *Indiana Companion* were listed in these bibliographic updates.

Turning to human resources, a special note of gratitude is due W. L. Idema of Leiden University. During the compilation of the first volume, I met with a group of more than a dozen European scholars in Germany to discuss the scope of the project and the design of the essays and entries. Wilt was as instrumental in making this European Workshop a success as he was tireless in his suggestions on the manuscript as it developed. For this second volume he has again been a generous benefactor, lending me the extensive bibliography which was the basis for that in his *A Guide to Chinese Literature* (coauthored with Lloyd Haft; Ann Arbor: Center for Chinese Studies, University of Michigan, 1997) and suggesting extensive additions to the updated bibliographies for both Popular Literature and Drama (see below). Other scholars who assisted with the bibliographic updates include: Stephen F. Teiser and Neil Schmid (Buddhist literature), Robert E. Hegel (fiction), Haun Saussy and Pauline Yu (literary criticism), Victor H. Mair (popular literature), Thomas Hahn and Franciscus Verellen (Taoist literature), Kang-i Sun Chang and Ellen Widmer (women's literature). Ronald Egan and William Schultz added items to the bibliographies of several entries. Finally, the students in my classes at the University of Wisconsin have been consistently supportive. Among this later group several deserve special mention.

First and foremost is Scott W. Galer. Scott is listed as the assistant editor, but he actually wore many hats. Without him the book could not have been completed. He not only read and helped revise the manuscript several times, but also was instrumental in organizing, typing, revising, formatting and printing it. He did the name and title indexes to the new entries. Scott was also the person who was able to steady the editorial sloop in the rough waters of the last few months of reading and revising the text.

These last few months also proofed the patience and scholarship of several other valuable assistants: Cao Weiguo 曹衛國, Bruce Knickerbocker, and Keiko Oda 小田惠子. Besides contributing two entries, Weiguo was in charge of the J-L section of the bibliographic updates for the entries and undertook various other tasks, such as answering my own questions regarding various original texts. Weiguo was also determined to find updated bibliographic listings for each of the over five-hundred entries in volume one and nearly succeeded in doing so. Bruce Knickerbocker handled the M-Y bibliographic updates as well as the "List of Chinese and Japanese Publishers." He also worked on whatever portion of the manuscript needed immediate attention and did so with care and good cheer. With Burton Watson's admonitions concerning the first volume in mind, we enlisted the aid of Keiko Oda, a graduate student in Japanese linguistics at the University of Wisconsin who has studied Chinese. Ms. Oda joined us late, but worked diligently and long to romanize and type most of the Japanese bibliographic entries. She also helped brighten the drudgery involved in editing the lengthy bibliographies. Su Zhi 蘇晰 provided fresh eyes to carefully check bibliographic items in the library in recent weeks. Yamanaka Emi 山中惠美 assisted with typing the Japanese materials. Several of these students are my advisees. Watching them grow in many ways (without growing tired!) during the compilation of this book has been one of the great pleasures of the past year.

These bibliographies had been organized and expanded earlier by Bruce, Scott, Weiguo, and J. Michael Farmer. Mike also set up, and for a long time maintained, the computer system on which we typeset this volume. He also helped with advice on dozens of questions regarding the production of camera-ready copy and still found time to contribute two entries.

I am also grateful to the Pacific Cultural Foundation and the Graduate School of the University of Wisconsin for supporting related research that contributed to the compilation of this book. Work on the bibliographies in Berlin (summer 1997) was generously funded by the Alexander von Humboldt-Stiftung. Thanks to the Stiftung and to Dr. Hartmut Walravens and Dr. Cordula Gumbrecht of the Staatsbibliothek-Berlin for sharing their knowledge about recent European scholarship. Klaus Stermann enabled us to find housing at the FU–Berlin. Professor Wolfgang Kubin once again made a sojourn in Germany possible by helping with practical matters and by visiting me in Berlin to offer sound advice on the project. During his sojourn in Madison this winter, he has cheered our editorial group and continued to offer advice. Thanks is also owed to those who prepared the trip to Japan and Hawaii from which I just returned. My stay in Japan was harmoniously orchestrated by Professor Kawai Kôzô 川合康三. He lent his expertise, access to libraries in Kyoto and Tokyo, and his own excellent collection of books during my stay. Moreover, he has offered advice on Japanese publications throughout this project. In Hawaii another former teacher, Bart Mathias, gave counsel on Korean sources. My colleague, John Wallace, lent his experience in negotiating the practical aspects of Tokyo today.

During the compilation of the bibliographies, Tai-loi Ma 馬泰來 (then at the University of Chicago) answered tens of queries. Lu Zongli 呂宗力 has been a regular source of information on the publishing industry in China. Kawai Kôzô 川合康三 gave similarly valuable commentary on Japanese publications. Teresa Nealon, Administrative Secretary of the Department of East Asian Languages and Literature, University of Wisconsin, Madison, advised on a number of practical matters and kept the cash strings untangled.

I would be remiss were I not to thank John Gallman and his staff once again. This is the fourth book I have published with Indiana University Press and the staff there seems to provide better guidance each time. John "Zig" Zeigler and others have assisted and advised us for months, tirelessly explaining what might be done to enhance the contents and appearance of the text.

In closing, I need to thank those tireless reviewers of the first volume who helped inspire and shape the second. To assist them in future endeavors, I should note that we now have two entries on the poet Ku Ch'un 顧春 (1799–after 1876): in this second volume she is found under Ku Ch'un, but is listed under her *hao* as Ku T'ai-ch'ing 顧太清 in volume one. This duplication was by design, since the approach and comments of the two authors seemed complementary.

Finally, I want to thank my family. Although my daughter and son were not around to sort and stack file-cards this time, their children—my grandchildren—managed on more than one occasion to rearrange various materials in my study—always with a positive result (I have my eye on them for volume three). My wife, Judith, is certainly disappointed that she was not involved in the day-to-day production of this volume as she was with the original, but she remains the keeper of the psychic keys and the chair of the goodwill and good luck that somehow seems to surround these ventures.

Lacking some such ties to volume one, this second volume of *The Indiana Companion to Traditional Literature* is to a certain extent an independent work. It presents more than sixty new entries on important authors, texts, styles, and groups from traditional Chinese literature. Yet the numerous cross-references to volume one, the bibliographies intended to update their counterparts in the original *Indiana Companion,* and the list of errata for the first volume suggest that volumes one and two would best be consulted together. Towards this end, Indiana University Press is reissuing the first volume concurrently with this sequel.

William H. Nienhauser, Jr.
Madison, 21 March 1998

List of Contributors

Alan Berkowitz, Swarthmore College
Cao Weiguo 曹衛國, University of Wisconsin, Madison
Chen Bingmei 陳冰梅, University of Wisconsin, , Madison
Chen Zhi 陳致, The National University of Singapore
Scott Cook, Grinnell College
Robert Joe Cutter, University of Wisconsin, Madison
William Dolby, University of Edinburgh
Glen Dudbridge, Oxford University
J. Michael Farmer, University of Wisconsin, Madison
Grace C. Fong, McGill University
Beata Grant, Washington University
John Christopher Hamm, University of California-Berkeley
Charles Hartman, The University at Albany
Robert E. Hegel, Washington University
Hsiung Ping-chen 熊秉真, Institute of Modern History, Academia Sinica
W. L. Idema, Leiden University
Karl S. Y. Kao 高辛勇, Hong Kong University of Science and Technology
André Lévy, University of Bordeaux
Irving Yucheng Lo
Lu Zongli 呂宗力, Hong Kong University of Science and Technology
Janet Lynn-Kerr, Valparaiso University
Victor H. Mair, University of Pennsylvania
William H. Nienhauser, Jr., University of Wisconsin, Madison
Jonathan Pease, Portland State University
Timoteus Pokora, Prague
Jui-lung Su, The National University of Singapore
Franciscus Verellen, EFEO
David W. Wang, Columbia University
Ellen Widmer, Wesleyan University
Ernst Wolff
Yenna Wu, University of California-Riverside
Michelle Yeh, University of California

A Note on Using This Book

Most of what was said in the "Note on Using This Book" in volume one of the *Indiana Companion to Traditional Chinese Literature* applies to this volume. As in the first volume, asterisks following a name or title–Han Yü 韓愈 (768-824)*–indicate cross references. One asterisk, as here, refers the reader to an entry on Han Yü in volume one; two asterisks, as in "Shen Ya-chih 沈亞知 (781-832)**"–mean the entry on Shen Ya-chih is included in this second volume. (In this volume, unlike volume one, Chinese characters and dates are given for a cross-referenced author.)

One major difference in this volume is that original works (or excerpts of such works), along with the original texts, are presented in some entries to help illustrate a style or technique.

Chinese and Japanese journals are cited by romanization only throughout the entries and bibliographic updates. Complete titles, with Chinese and Japanese, are found in the "List of Chinese and Japanese Journals."

Official titles are given in the following form: "administrator (*chih* 知)." The translations are generally based on Charles O. Hucker, *A Dictionary of Official Titles in Imperial China* (Stanford: Stanford University Press, 1985).

The three indexes (name, title and subject) are keyed to the New Entries only.

The bibliographic updates are not intended to be complete. They include most works from 1984 (when the bibliographies for volume one left off) through 1996, with some items from 1997 and 1998 also listed. For entries with a number of studies, we have tried to select only monographs and articles by well-known scholars which appeared in standard journals. For subjects that are less studied, we were more catholic in our selection. We included partial bibliographic entries as long as sufficient information was provided to allow the reader to locate the item. Other instructions on using this book can be found in the brief notes before the updated bibliographies for the essays and entries below.

Abbreviations

annot.	–	annotator
c.	–	century
ca.	–	*circa*
comm.	–	commentator
coll.	–	collator
comp.	–	compiler
ed.	–	editor
fl.	–	*floruit*
rev. ed.	–	revised editions
trans.	–	translator
transl.	–	translation

List of Chinese and Japanese Journals

This list is intended to give the Chinese or Japanese characters for all journals cited in the bibliographies by romanized titles only. Abbreviations and full references for Western journals can be found in "Oft-cited Works" below.

A

Ajia Afurika bunpô kenkyû　アジアアフリカ文法研究

B

Bungaku kenkyû 文学研究

C

Che-hsüeh yen-chiu 哲學研究
Cheng-chou Ta-hsüeh hsüeh-pao 鄭州大學學報
Cheng-ta hsüeh-pao 政大學報
Ch'eng-te Shih-chuan hsüeh-pao 承德師專學報
Ch'eng-tu Shih-chuan Hsüeh-pao 成都師專學報
Chi-lin Ta-hsüeh She-hui K'o-hsüeh hsüeh-pao　吉林大學社會科學學報
Ch'i-Lu hsüeh-k'an 齊魯學刊
Chiang-hai hsüeh-k'an 江海學刊
Chiang-han lun-t'an　江漢論壇
Chiang-hsi Chiao-yü Hsüeh-yüan hsüeh-pao　江西教育學院學報
Chiang-hsi hsüeh-k'an 江西學刊
Chiang-su Chiao-yü Hsüeh-yüan hsüeh-pao 江蘇教育學院學報
Chikushi Jokakuen Tanki Daigaku kiyo　筑紫女学園短期大学紀要
Chin-ling hsüeh-pao 金陵學報
Chin-tai Chung-kuo fu-nü shih yen-chiu 近代中國婦女史研究
Chin-yang hsüeh-k'an 晉陽學刊
Ch'ing-hai she-hui k'o-hsüeh 青海社會科學
Ch'ing-t'ung shih-tai 青銅時代
Ch'iu shih　求是
Chûbun kenkyû shûkan 中文研究集刊
Chûgoku bungaku hô 中国文学報
Chûgoku bungaku ronshû 中国文学論集
Chûgoku bunka 中国文化
Chûgoku Chûsei bungaku kenkyû 中國中世文學研究
Chûgoku koten gikyoku ronshû　中国戯曲論集
Chûgoku koten shôsetsu kenkyû dôtai　中国古典小説研究動態
Chûgoku shibun ronsô　中国詩文論叢
Chûgokugakushi　中国学誌
Chûgoku–Shakai to bunka　中国ーー社会と文化
Chung-ch'ing Shih-yüan hsüeh-pao 重慶師院學報
Chung-chou hsüeh-k'an 中州學刊
Chung-hua hsüeh-yüan 中華學苑

Chung-hua wen-hua fu-hsing yüeh-kan 中華文化復興月刊
Chung-hua wen-shih lun-ts'ung, 中華文史論叢
Chung-kuo hsiao-shuo yen-chiu ts'ung-k'an 中國小説研究叢刊
Chung-kuo ku-tien wen-hsüeh lun-ts'ung 中國古典文學論叢
Chung-kuo Li Po yen-chiu shang 中國李白研究上
Chung-kuo she-hui k'o-hsüeh 中國社會科學
Chung-kuo shih yen-chiu 中國史研究
Chung-kuo tao-chiao 中國道教
Chung-kuo wen-che yen-chiu chi-k'an 中國文哲研究集刊
Chung-kuo wen-che yen-chiu t'ung-hsün 中國文哲研究通訊
Chung-kuo wen-hsüeh yen-chiu ts'ung-k'an 中國文學研究叢刊
Chung-kuo Yin-yüeh Hsüeh-yüan hsüeh-pao, ch'uan-k'an hao 中國音樂學院學報
Chung-kuo yü-wen 中國語文
Chung-pao 中報
Chung-wai wen-hsüeh 中外文學
Chung-yang Hsüeh-shu Yen-chiu-so chi-yao 中央學術研究所紀要
Chung-yang t'u-shu-kuan kuan-k'an 中央圖書館館刊
Chûtetsu bungaku kaihô 中哲文学会報

D

Daitô Bunka Daigaku Kiyô-Jimbun Kagaku 大東文化大学紀要——人文科学

F

Fu-chien lun-t'an 福建論壇
Fu-chou shih-chuan hsüeh-pao 福州師大學報
Fu-jen hsüeh chih 輔仁學誌
Fu-jen kuo-wen hsüeh-pao 輔仁國文學報
Fu-ta Chung-yen-suo hsüeh-k'an 輔大中研所學刊
Fu-tan hsüeh-pao 復旦學報
Fu-yang Shih-yüan hsüeh-pao 阜陽師院學報

G

Gakurin 学林

H

Han-hsüeh Yen-chiu 漢學研究
Hanazono Daigaku Bungakubu kenkyû kiyô 花園大学文学部研究紀要
Hang-chou Shih-yüan hsüeh-pao 杭州師院學報
Hiroshima Daigaku Bungakubu kiyô 広島大学文学部紀要
Ho-nan Ta-hsüeh hsüeh-pao 河南大學學報
Ho-pei hsüeh-k'an, 河北學刊
Ho-pei Shih-fan Ta-hsüeh hsüeh-pao 河北師范大學學報
Ho-pei Shih-yüan hsüeh-pao 河北師院學報
Hokkaidô Kyôiku Daigaku kiyô, Jimbun kagaku 北海道教育大学紀要人文科学
Hôsei Daigaku Kyôyôbu kiyô jimbun-kagakuhen 法制大学教養部紀要人文科学編
Hsi-ch'ü yen-chiu 戲曲研究
Hsi-pei Shih-ta hsüeh-pao 西北師大學報
Hsi-pei Ta-hsüeh hsüeh-pao 西北大學學報
Hsia-men Ta-hsüeh hsüeh-pao 廈門大學學報
Hsiang-kang Chung-wen Ta-hsüeh Chung-kuo Wen-hua Yen-chiu-so hsüeh-pao 香港中文大學
    中國文化研究所學報

Hsiao-shuo tsung-mu t'i-yao 小說總目提要
Hsien-ning Shih-chuan hsüeh-pao 咸寧師專學報
Hsin Ya hsüeh-pao 新亞學報
Hsin-yang Shih-fan Hsüeh-yüan hsüeh-pao 信陽師範學院學報
Hsing-ta chung-wen hsüeh-pao 興大中文學報
Hsü-ch'ang Shih-chuan hsüeh-pao 許昌師專學報
Hsü-chou Shih-fan Hsüeh-yüan hsüeh-pao 徐州師範學院學報
Hsü-chou Shih-yüan hsüeh-pao 徐州師院學報
Hsüeh-feng 學衡
Hsüeh-lin man-lu 學林漫錄
Hsüeh-shu lun-t'an 學術論壇
Hsüeh-shu yen-chiu 學術研究
Hsüeh-shu yen-chiu ts'ung-k'an 學術研究叢刊
Hsüeh-shu yüeh-k'an 學術月刊
Hsüeh-wen tsa-chih 學文雜誌
Hua-chung Shih-fan Ta-hsüeh hsüeh-pao 華中師範大學學報
Hua-kuo 華國
Hua-nan Shih-fan Ta-hsüeh hsüeh-pao 華南師範大學學報

I

I-wen chih 藝文誌

J

Jen-wen tsa-chih 人文雜誌
Jimbun kenkyû 人文研究
Joshidai bungaku 女子大文学

K

K'ung Meng yüeh-k'an 孔孟月刊
Kangakkai zasshi 漢学会雑誌
Kansai Daigaku Chûgoku Bungakkai Kiyô 関西大学中国文学会紀要
Kobe Gaidai ronsô 神戸外大論叢
Ku-chi cheng-li yen-chiu hsüeh-k'an 古籍整理研究學刊
Ku-kung wen-wu yüeh-k'an 故宮文物月刊
Ku-tai wen-hsüeh li-lun yen-chiu 古代文學理論研究
Ku-tien wen-hsüeh chih-shih 古典文學知識
Kuang-chou jih-pao 廣州日報
Kuang-ming jih-pao 光明日報
Kuei-chou she-hui k'o-hsüeh 貴州社會科學
Kuei-chou Ta-hsüeh hsüeh-pao 貴州大學學報
Kuei-chou wen-shih ts'ung-k'an 貴州文史叢刊
Kuo-li Cheng-chih Ta-hsüeh hsüeh-pao 國立政治大學學報
Kuo-li Chung-yang Ta-hsüeh Wen-hsüeh-yüan yüan-k'an 國立中央大學文學院院刊
Kuo-li pien-i kuan kuan k'an 國立編譯館館刊
Kuo-li T'ai-wan Ta-hsüeh Li-shih-hsüeh-hsi hsüeh-pao 國立台灣大學歷史學系學報
Kuo-wen yüeh-k'an 國文月刊
Kyûshû Chûgoku gakkaihô 九州中国学会報

L

Lan-chou hsüeh-k'an 蘭州學刊
Li-shih chiao-hsüeh wen-t'i 歷史教學問題
Li-shih hsüeh 歷史學

Liao-ning Chiao-yü Hsüeh-yüan Hsüeh-pao 遼寧教育學院學報
Liao-ning Kuang-po Tien-shih Ta-hsüeh hsüeh-pao 遼寧廣播電視大學學報
Liao-ning Ta-hsüeh hsüeh-pao 遼寧大學學報
Lo-yang Shih-fan Hsüeh-yüan hsüeh-pao 洛陽師範學院學報

M

Mimei 未名
Min Shin bungaku gengo kenkyûkai kaihô 明清文学言語研究会会報
Min-chien wen-i chi-k'an 民間文藝集刊
Ming Ch'ing hsiao-shuo lun-ts'ung 明清小説論叢
Ming Ch'ing hsiao-shuo yen-chiu 明清小説研究
Ming-tso hsin-shang 名作欣賞

N

Nagoya Daigaku Chûgoku gogaku bungaku ronshu 名古屋大学中国語学文学論集
Nan-ching Shih-ta hsüeh-pao 南京師大學報
Nan-ching Ta-hsüeh hsüeh-pao 南京大學學報
Nan-k'ai Ta-hsüeh hsüeh-pao 南開大學學報
Nan-yang Ta-hsüeh hsüeh-pao 南洋大學學報
Nihon Ajia gengo bunka kenkyû 日本アジア言語文化研究
Nihon Chûgoku Gakkai hô 日本中国学会報
Ning-hsia Chiao-yü Hsüeh-yüan hsüeh-pao 寧夏教育學院學報
Nippon Chûgoku Gakkaihô 日本中国学会報
Nishô 二松

O

Ochanomizu Joshi Daigaku Jinbun Kagaku kiyô お茶の水女子大学人文科学紀要
Ôtani gakuhô 大谷學報

P

Pei-ching She-hui K'o-hsüeh 北京社會科學
Pei-ching Shih-fan Hsüeh-yüan hsüeh-pao 北京師範學院學報
Pei-ching Shih-ta hsüeh-pao 北京師大學報
Pei-ching Ta-hsüeh hsüeh-pao 北京大學學報
Pei-fang lun-tsung 北方論叢

R

Ryûkoku Daigaku Bukkyô Bunka Kenkyûjo kiyô 龍谷大学仏教文化研究所紀要

S

Saga Daigaku Kyôyôbu kenkyû kiyô 佐賀大学教養部研究紀要
Shan-hsi Shih-ta hsüeh-pao (Che-hsüeh she-hui k'o-hsüeh) 山西師大學報哲學社會科學
Shan-hsi Ta-hsüeh hsüeh-pao (Che-hsüeh) 山西大學學報哲學
Shan-tungTa-hsüeh hsüeh-pao 山東大學學報
Shang-hai Chiao-yü Hsüeh-yüan hsüeh-pao 上海教育學院學報
Shang-hai Shih-fan Hsüeh-yüan hsüeh-pao 上海師範學院學報
Shanghai Shih-fan Ta-hsüeh hsüeh-pao 上海師範大學學報
She-hui k'o-hsüeh chan-hsien 社會科學戰線
She-hui k'o-hsüeh chi-k'an 社會科學輯刊
Shibun 斯文
Shih-hsüeh nien-pao 史學年報

Shih-hsüeh yüeh-k'an wu 史學月刊物 (Chengchow 鄭州)
Shih-huo yüeh-k'an (fu-k'an) 食貨月刊（復刊）
Shih-ta hsüeh-pao 師大學報
Shu-mu chi-k'an 書目季刊
Shukan Toyogaku 集刊東洋学
Ssu-ch'uan Shih-yüan hsüeh-pao 四川師院學報
Ssu-ch'uan Ta-hsüeh hsüeh-pao 四川大學學報
Ssu-ch'uan Ta-hsüeh hsüeh-pao ts'ung-k'an 四川大學學報叢刊
Ssu-ch'uan Ta-hsüeh hsüeh-pao ts'ung-k'an (Yen-chiu-sheng lun-wen hsüan-k'an) 四川大學學報叢刊（研究生論文選刊）
Ssu-chüan Shih-fan Ta-hsüeh hsüeh-pao 四川師範大學學報
Ssu-hsiang chan-hsien 思想戰線
Su-chou Ta-hsüeh hsüeh-pao 蘇州大學學報

T
Ta-hua wan-pao 大華晚報
T'ai-chung Shang-chuan hsüeh-pao 台中商專學報
T'ai-nan Shih-yüan hsüeh-pao 台南師院學報
T'ai-ta chung-wen hsüeh-pao 台大中文學報
Tan-chiang hsüeh-pao 淡江學報
T'ang-tai wen-hsüeh lun-ts'ung 唐代文學論叢
T'ang-tu hsüeh-k'an 唐都學刊
Tao-chiao wen-hua yen-chiu 道教文化研究
Tenri Daigaku gakuhô 天理大学学報
Tien-chin Shih-ta hsüeh-pao 天津師大學報
Tôhô shûkyô 東京宗教
Tôhoku Gakuin Daigaku ronshû–Ippan kyôiku 東北学院大学論集一般教育
Tôkyô shinagaku hô 東京支那学報
Tôyô bunka 東洋文化
Tôyô bunka (Mukyûkai) 東洋文化（無窮会）
Tôyô bunka gakka nenpô 東洋文化学科年報
Tôyô gakuhô 東洋学報
Tôyôgaku 東洋学
Tu-shu 讀書
Tun-huang-hsüeh chi-k'an 敦煌學輯刊
Tung-hai hsüeh-pao 東海學報
T'ung-hua Shih-yüan hsüeh-pao 通化師院學報
Tung-nan wen-hua 東南文化
Tung-wu Wen-shih Hsüeh-pao 東吳文史學報

W
Wayô kokubun kenkyû 和洋国文研究
Wen Hsien 文獻
Wen i li-lun yen-chiu 文藝理論研究
Wen shih che 文史哲
Wen shih hsüeh-pao 文史學報
Wen-hsien 文獻
Wen-hsüeh i-ch'an 文學遺產
Wen-hsüeh i-ch'an hsüan-chi 文學遺產選集
Wen-hsüeh p'ing-lun 文學評論
Wen-hsüeh tsa-chih 文學雜誌

Wen-i li-lun yen-chiu 文藝理論研究
Wen-shih chi-lin 文史集林
Wen-shih chih-shih 文史知識
Wen-shih p'ing-lun 文史評論
Wen-shih 文史
Wen-shih-che 文史哲
Wen-shih-che hsüeh-pao 文史哲學報
Wu-han Ta-hsüeh hsüeh-pao 武漢大學學報

Y
Yamagata Daigaku kiyô 山形大学紀要
Yamagata Daigaku kiyô–Jinbun kagaku 山形大学紀要――人文科学
Yang-chou shih-yüan hsüeh-pao 揚州師院學報
Yang-chou shih-yüan hsüeh-pao: She-k'o-pan 揚州師院學報，社科版
Yen-ch'eng Shih-chuan hsüeh-pao 鹽城師專學報
Yen-t'ai Shih-fan Hsüeh-yüan hsüeh-pao 煙台師範學院學報
Yin-shan hsüeh-k'an 陰山學刊
Yu-shih hsüeh-chih 幼獅學誌

Z
Zengaku kenkyû 禅学研究

List of Chinese and Japanese Publishers

A

An-huei Chiao-yü Ch'u-pan-she 安徽教育出版社
An-huei Jen-min Ch'u-pan-she 安徽人民出版社
An-huei Wen-i Ch'u-pan-she 安徽文藝出版社
Asahi Shinbunsha 朝日新聞社
Ashi Shobô 葦書房

B

Benseisha 勉誠社

C

Ch'ang-an Ch'u-pan-she 長安出版社
Ch'ang-chiang Wen-i 長江文藝出版社
Ch'ao-hua Ch'u-pan-she 朝華出版社
Che-chiang Jen-min Ch'u-pan-she 浙江人民出版社
Che-chiang Ku-chi Ch'u-pan-she 浙江古籍出版社
Che-chiang Wen-i Ch'u-pan-she 浙江文藝出版社
Cheng-chih Ta-hsüeh 政志大學
Cheng-chung Shu-chü Ku-fen Yu-hsien Kung-ssu 正中書局股份有限公司
Ch'eng-tu K'o-chi Ta-hsüeh Ch'u-pan-she 成都科技大學出版社
Ch'eng-tu Ku-chi Shu-tien 成都古籍書店
Ch'eng-wen Ch'u-pan-she Yu-hsien Kung-ssu 成文出版社有限公司
Chi-lin Chiao-yü Ch'u-pan-she 吉林教育出版社
Chi-lin Mei-shu Ch'u-pan-she 吉林美術出版社
Chi-lin Ta-hsüeh Ch'u-pan-she 吉林大學出版社
Chi-lin Wen-shih Ch'u-pan-she 吉林文史出版社
Chi-lin Wen-hsüeh Ch'u-pan-she 吉林文學出版社
Ch'i-Lu Shu-she 齊魯書社
Chi-nan Ch'u-pan-she 濟南出版社
Chi-nan Shan-tung Wen-i Ch'u-pan-she 濟南山東文藝出版社
Chi-nan Ta-hsüeh Ch'u-pan-she 暨南大學出版社
Chia-hsin Shui-ni Kung-ssu Wen-hsu Chi-chin Hui 嘉新水泥公司文化基金會
Chiang-hsi Chiao-yü Ch'u-pan-she 江西教育出版社
Chiang-hsi Jen-min Ch'u-pan-she 江西人民出版社
Chiang-su Chiao-yü Ch'u-pan-she 江蘇教育出版社
Chiang-su Ku-chi Ch'u-pan-she 江蘇古籍出版社
Chiang-su Kuang-ling Ku-chi K'o-yin-she 江蘇廣陵古籍刻印社
Chiang-su Wen-i Ch'u-pan-she 江蘇文藝出版社
Chiao-yü K'o-hsüeh Ch'u-pan-she 教育科學出版社
Chiao-yü-pu 教育部
Chieh-fang-chün Ch'u-pan-she 解放軍出版社
Chih-shih Ch'u-pan-she 知識出版社
Chikuma Shobô 筑摩書房
Chin-hsiu Ch'u-pan Shih-yeh Ku-fen Yu-hsien Kung-ssu 錦繡出版事業股份有限公司
Chin-jih Chung-kuo Ch'u-pan-she 今日中國出版社
Ch'in-ch'in Wen-hua Shih-yeh Kung-ssu 親親文化事業公司

Ching-chi Jih-pao Ch'u-pan-she 經濟日報出版社
Ching-sheng Wen-wu Kung-ying Ku-fen Yu-hsien Kung-ssu 驚聲文物供應股份有限公司
Chü-liu T'u-shu Yu-hsien Kung-ssu 巨流圖書有限公司
Ch'ing-hai Jen-min Ch'u-pan-she 青海人民出版社
Ch'ing-tao Ch'u-pan-she 青島出版社
Chûgoku Shoten 中国書店, Fukuoka
Ch'un Wen-hsüeh Ch'u-pan-she 純文學出版社
Ch'un-feng Wen-i Ch'u-pan-she 春風文藝出版社
Ch'un-ming Ch'u-pan-she 純明學出版社
Ch'ün-yü T'ang Ch'u-pan Shih-yeh Kung-ssu 群玉堂出版事業公司
Chung-chou Ku-chi Ch'u-pan-she 中州古籍出版社
Chung-chou Shu-hua-she 中州書畫社
Chung-hua ch'üan-kuo t'u-shu-kuan ku-chi wen-hsien chen-pen hui-k'an 中華全國圖書館古
　　籍文獻珍本會刊
Chung-hua Shu-chü 中華書局
Chung-hua Wen-hua Fu-hsing Yün-tung Tsung-hui 中華文化復興運動總會
Chung-kung Kung-jen Ch'u-pan-she 中共工人出版社
Chung-kuo Chan-wang Ch'u-pan-she 中國展望出版社
Chung-kuo Cheng-chih Ch'u-pan-she 中國政志出版社
Chung-kuo Ch'ing-nien Ch'u-pan-she 中國青年出版社
Chung-kuo Ch'ü-i Ch'u-pan-she 中國曲藝出版社
Chung-kuo Fu-nü Ch'u-pan-she 中國婦女出版社
Chung-kuo Hsi-chü Ch'u-pan-she 中國戲劇出版社
Chung-kuo Hsüeh-she 中國書社
Chung-kuo Hua-ch'iao Ch'u-pan-she 中國華橋出版社
Chung-kuo ISBN Ch'u-pan-she 中國華 ISBN 出版社
Chung-kuo Jen-min Ta-hsüeh Ch'u-pan-she 中國人民大學出版社
Chung-kuo Kuang-po Tien-shih Ch'u-pan-she 中國廣播電視出版社
Chung-kuo Kuang-po Tien-t'ai Ch'u-pan-she 中國廣播電臺出版社
Chung-kuo Kuo-chi Kuang-po Ch'u-pan-she 中國國際廣播出版社
Chung-kuo Kung-jen Ch'u-pan-she 中國工人出版社
Chung-kuo Lü-yu Ch'u-pan-she 中國旅游出版社
Chung-kuo Min-chien Wen-i Ch'u-pan-she 中國民間文藝出版社
Chung-kuo Min-chien Wen-i Yen-chiu Hui Hu-pei Fen-hui 中國民間文藝研究會湖北分會
Chung-kuo Shang-yeh Ch'u-pan-she 中國商業出版社
Chung-kuo She-hui Ch'u-pan-she 中國社會出版社
Chung-kuo She-hui K'o-hsüeh Ch'u-pan-she 中國社會科學出版社
Chung-kuo She-hui K'o-hsüeh-yüan 中國社會科學院
Chung-kuo Shih-pao 中國時報
Chung-kuo Shu-chi Ch'u-pan-she 中國書籍出版社
Chung-kuo Shu-tien 中國書店
Chung-kuo Ta Pai-k'e Ch'üan-shu Ch'u-pan-she 中國大百科全書出版社
Chung-kuo Wen-hsüeh Ch'u-pan-she 中國文學出版社
Chung-kuo Wen-hua Ta-hsüeh 中國文化大學
Chûng-kuo Wen-lien Ch'u-pan Kung-ssu 中國文聯出版公司
Chung-kuo Wen-shih Ch'u-pan-she 中國文史出版社
Chung-shan Ta-hsüeh 中山大學出版社
Chung-wen Ta-hsüeh 中文大學
Chung-yang Yen-chiu Yüan, Chung-kuo Wen-che Yen-chiu So 中央研究院，中國文哲研究
　　所
Chung-yang Yen-chiu Yüan, Li-shih Yü-yen Yen-chiu So 中央研究院，歷史語言研究所
Chung-yüan Nung-min Ch'u-pan-she 中原農民出版社

Ch'ung-ch'ing Ch'u-pan-she 重慶出版社
Chûô Kôronsha 中央公論社

D

Daitô Bunka Daigaku 東方文化大学
Daitô　Shuppansha 東方出版社
Daizô Shuppan 大蔵出版
Dôhôsha 同朋社, Kyoto

F

Fa-jen Wen-hua She 發人文畫社
Fu-chi Wen-hua T'u-shu Yu-hsien Kung-ssu 福記文化圖書有限公司
Fu-chien Chiao-yü Ch'u-pan-she 福建教育出版社
Fu-chien Jen-min Ch'u-pan-she 福建人民出版社
Fu-jen Ta-hsüeh Ch'u-pan-she 輔仁大學出版社
Fu-tan Ta-hsüeh Ch'u-pan-she 复旦大學出版社
Fu-wen Shu-chü 复文書局
Fu-wen T'u-shu Kung-ssu 复文圖書公司
Fuji Shuppan 不二出版

G

Gakushû Kenkyûsha 学習研究社

H

Ha-erh-pin Ch'u-pan-she 哈爾濱出版社
Hai-hsia Wen-i Ch'u-pan-she 海峽文藝出版社
Hai-nan Kuo-chi Hsin-wen Ch'u-pan Chung-hsin 海南國際新聞出版中心
Hai-t'ien Ch'u-pan-she 海天出版社
Hai-yang Ch'u-pan-she 海洋出版社
Hakuteisha 白帝社
Hakutsuru Bijutsukan 白鶴美術館, Kobe
Han-ching Wen-hua Shih-yeh 漢京文化書業
Han-hsüeh Yen-chiu Chung-hsin 漢學研究中心
Han-mei T'u-shu Yu-hsien Kung-ssu 漢美圖書有限公司
Han-yü Ta-tzu-tien Ch'u-pan-she 漢語大詞典出版社
Hang-chou Ta-hsüeh Ch'u-pan-she 杭州大學出版社
Hei-lung-chiang Jen-min Ch'u-pan-she 黑龍江人民出版社
Heibonsha 平凡社
Hirakawa Shuppansha 平河出版社
Ho-hai Ta-hsüeh Ch'u-pan-she 河海大學出版社
Ho-nan Chiao-yü Ch'u-pan-she 河南教育出版社
Ho-nan Ta-hsüeh Ch'u-pan-she 河南大學出版社
Ho-pei Chiao-yü Ch'u-pan-she 河北教育出版社
Ho-pei Jen-min Ch'u-pan-she 河北人民出版社
Ho-pei Ta-hsüeh Ch'u-pan-she 河北大學出版社
Hokkaidô Kyôiku Daigaku 北海道教育大学
Hôyû Shoten 朋友書店
Hsi-pei Ta-hsüeh Ch'u-pan-she 西北大學出版社
Hsia-men Ta-hsüeh Ch'u-pan-she 廈門大學出版社
Hsiang-kang Cheng-chih Ch'u-pan-she 香港政治出版社
Hsiao-hsüeh-sheng Tsa-chih-she 小學生雜誌社

Hsiao-yüan Ch'u-pan-she Yu-hsien Kung-ssu 曉園出版社有限公司
Hsien-tai Ch'u-pan-she 現代出版社
Hsien-tai Chiao-yü Ch'u-pan-she 現代教育出版社
Hsin-chiang Jen-min Ch'u-pan-she 新疆人民出版社
Hsin-hsing Shu-chü Yu-hsien Kung-ssu 新興書局有限公司
Hsin-hua Ch'u-pan-she 新華出版社
Hsin-tu Hsien Yang Sheng-an Tan-ch'en Wu-pai Chou-nien Li-tao Hsiao-tsu 新都楊升庵誕
    辰五百周年紀歷道小組
Hsin-wen-feng Ch'u-pan-she Ku-fen Yu-hsien Kung-ssu 新文豐出版社股份有限公司
Hsüeh-hai Ch'u-pan-she Ku-fen Yu-hsien Kung-ssu 學海豐出版社股份有限公司
Hsüeh-lin Ch'u-pan-she 學林出版社
Hsüeh-sheng Shu-chü 學生書局
Hsüeh-yüan Ch'u-pan-she 學苑出版社
Hu-nan Ch'u-pan-she 湖南出版社
Hu-nan Chiao-yü Ch'u-pan-she 湖南教育出版社
Hu-nan Jen-min Ch'u-pan-she 湖南人民出版社
Hu-nan Mei-shu Ch'u-pan-she 湖南美術出版社
Hu-nan Wen-i Ch'u-pan-she 湖南文藝出版社
Hu-pei Chiao-yü Ch'u-pan-she 湖北教育出版社
Hu-pei Jen-min Ch'u-pan-she 湖北人民出版社
Hua-ch'eng Ch'u-pan-she 花城出版社
Hua-cheng Shu-chü Yu-hsien Kung-ssu Ch'u-pan-she 華正書局有限公司出版社
Hua-chung Li-kung Ta-hsüeh Ch'u-pan-she 華中理工大學出版社
Hua-chung Shih-fan Ta-hsüeh Ch'u-pan-she 華中師範大學出版社
Hua-feng Shu-chü 華風書局
Hua-hsia Ch'u-pan-she 華夏出版社
Hua-ling Ch'u-pan-she 華齡出版社
Hua-shan Wen-i Ch'u-pan-she 華山文藝出版社
Hua-tung Shih-fan Ta-hsüeh Ch'u-pan-she 華東師範大學出版社
Hua-i Ch'u-pan-she 華藝出版社
Huang-ho Wen-i Ch'u-pan-she 黃河文藝出版社
Huang-shan Shu-she 黃山書社
Huang-shan Wen-i Ch'u-pan-she 黃山文藝出版社
Hung-fan Shu-tien 洪範書店
Hung-yeh Shu-chü Yu-hsien Kung-ssu 宏業書局有限公司

I
Ibundo Shoten 彙文堂, Kyoto
I-chün Ch'u-pan-she 益群出版社
Iwanami Shoten 岩波書店
I-wen Yin-shu-kuan 藝文印書館.

J
Jen-min Ch'u-pan-she 人民出版社
Jen-min Chung-kuo Ch'u-pan-she 人民中國出版社
Jen-min Jih-pao Ch'u-pan-she 人民日報出版社
Jen-min Wen-hsüeh Ch'u-pan-she 人民文學出版社
Jen-min Yin-yüeh Ch'u-pan-she 人民音樂出版社

K
Kadokawa Shoten 角川書店
K'ai-ming Shu-tien 開明書店

Kan-su Jen-min Ch'u-pan-she 甘肅人民出版社
Kan-su Min-tsu Ch'u-pan-she 甘肅人族出版社
K'ang-ch'iao Ch'u-pan Shih-yeh Kung-ssu 康橋出版事業公司
Kao-hsiung Fu-wen T'u-shu Ch'u-pan-she 高雄复文圖書出版社
K'ao-cheng Ch'u-pan-she 考正出版社
Kazama Shoin 笠間書院
Keisô Shobô 勁草書局
Kembun Shuppan 研文出版
Kenkyû Shuppan 研究出版
Kindai Bungeisha 近代文芸社
Kôdansha 講談社
K'o-hsüeh Chi-shu Wen-hsien Ch'u-pan-she 科學技術文獻出版社
Kokusho Kankôkai 国書刊行会
Ku-tien Wen-hsüeh Ch'u-pan-she 古典文學出版社
Kuang-chiao-ching Ch'u-pan-she 廣角鏡出版社
Kuang-hsi Chiao-yü Ch'u-pan-she 廣西教育出版社
Kuang-hsi Jen-min Ch'u-pan-she 廣西人民出版社
Kuang-hsi Shih-fan Ta-hsüeh Ch'u-pan-she 廣西師範大學出版社
Kuang-ming Jih-pao Ch'u-pan-she 光明日報出版社
Kuang-tung Jen-min Ch'u-pan-she 廣東人民出版社
Kuang-tung Kao-teng Chiao-yü Ch'u-pan-she 廣東高等教育出版社
Kuang-tung Lü-yu Ch'u-pan-she 廣東旅游出版社
Kuang-wen Shu-chü 廣文書局
Kuei-chou Jen-min Ch'u-pan-she 貴州人民出版社
Kuei-chou Min-tsu Ch'u-pan-she 貴州民族出版社
Kuo-chi Wen-hua Ch'u-pan Kung-ssu 國際文化出版公司
Kuo-chia Ch'u-pan-she 國家出版社
Kuo-li Chung-yang T'u-she-kuan 國立中央圖書館
Kuo-li Ku-kung Po-wu-kuan 國立故宮博物館
Kuo-li Pien-i-kuan Fan-kung Ch'u-pan-she 國立編譯館反攻出版社
Kuo-li Shih-fan Ta-hsüeh Yen-chiu So 國立師範大學研究所
Kuo-li T'ai-wan Ta-hsüeh Ch'u-pan Weiyüan Hui 國立臺灣大學出版委員會
Kuo-wen T'ien-ti Tsa-chih 國文天地雜誌
Kyûko Shoin 汲古書院
Kyûshû Daikgaku Bungakubu 九州大学文学部

L
Lan-chou Ku-chi Shu-tien 蘭州古籍書店
Lan-chou Ta-hsüeh Ch'u-pan-she 蘭州大學出版社
Li-chiang Ch'u-pan-she 漓江出版社
Li-jen Shu-chü 立人書局
Li-jen Wen-chiao Ch'u-pan-she 立人文教出版社
Li-ming Wen-hua Shih-yeh Ku-fen Yu-hsien Kung-ssu 黎明文化事業股份有限公司
Li-wen Wen-hua Ch'u-pan-she 立文文化出版社
Liao-ning Chiao-yü Ch'u-pan-she 遼寧教育出版社
Liao-ning Jen-min Ch'u-pan-she 遼寧人民出版社
Liao-ning Ta-hsüeh Ch'u-pan-she 遼寧大學出版社
Liao-ning Ta-hsüeh, Chung-wen Hsi 遼寧大學，中文系
Liao-Shen Shu-she 遼沈書社
Lien-cheng Ch'u-pan-she 聯正出版社
Lien-ching Ch'u-pan Shih-yeh Ku-fen Yu-hsien Kung-ssu 聯經初版事業有限公司

Ling-nan Hsüeh-yüan 岭南學院
Lü-yu Chiao-yü Ch'u-pan-she 旅游教育出版社
Lung-yün Ch'u-pan-she 龍韻出版社

M
Man-t'ien-hsing Erh-t'ung Shih-k'an-she 滿天星兒童詩刊社
Meiji Shoten 明治書院
Meitoku Shuppansha　明德出版社
Ming-lun Ch'u-pan-she 明倫出版社
Ming-sheng Pao She 民生報社
Ming-t'ien Ch'u-pan-she 明天出版社
Ming-wen Shu-chü Ku-fen Yu-hsien Kung-ssu 明文書局股份有限公司
Misuzu Shobô みすず書房
Mokujisha 木耳社
Mu-to Ch'u-pan-she 木鐸出版社

N
Nan-ching Ta-hsüeh Ch'u-pan-she 南京大學出版社
Nan-hai Ch'u-pan-she 南海出版社
Nan-k'ai Ta-hsüeh Ch'u-pan-she 南開大學出版社
Nan-t'ien Shu-chü Yu-hsien Kung-ssu 南天書局有限公司
Nei-meng-ku Chiao-yü Ch'u-pan-she 內蒙古教育出版社
Nei-meng-ku Jen-min Ch'u-pan-she 內蒙古人民出版社
Ning-hsia Jen-min Ch'u-pan-she 寧夏人民出版社

P
Pa-Shu Shu-she, Chengtu　巴蜀書社
Pai-hua Wen-i Ch'u-pan-she 百花文藝出版社
Pai-hua-chou Wen-i Ch'u-pan-she 百花洲文藝出版社
Pao-wen T'ang Shu-tien 寶文堂書店
Pei-ching Ch'u-pan-she 北京出版社
Pei-ching Ku-chi Ch'u-pan-she 北京古籍出版社
Pei-ching Kuang-po Hsüeh-yüan Ch'u-pan-she 北京廣播學院出版社
Pei-ching Shih-fan Hsüeh-yüan 北京師範學院
Pei-ching Shih-fan Ta-hsüeh Ch'u-pan-she 北京師範大學出版社
Pei-ching Shih-yüeh Wen-i Ch'u-pan-she 北京十月文藝出版社
Pei-ching Ta-hsüeh Ch'u-pan-she 北京十月文藝出版社
Pei-ching Yen-shan Ch'u-pan-she 北京燕山出版社
Pei-fang Wen-i Ch'u-pan-she 北方文藝出版社
Pei-yüeh Wen-i Ch'u-pan-she 北岳文藝出版社

R
Ryûkei Shosha 竜渓書舎
Ryûkoku Daigaku Bukkyô Bunka Kenkyûjo 竜谷大学仏教文化研究所

S
San Ch'in Ch'u-pan-she 三秦出版社
San-huan Ch'u-pan-she 三環出版社
San-lien Shu-tien 三聯書店
San-min Shu-chü Yu-hsien Kung-ssu 三民書局有限公司
Sanseidô　三省堂

Satsuki Shobô 五月書房
Shan-hsi Chiao-yü Ch'u-pan-she 陝西教育出版社
Shan-hsi Jen-min Ch'u-pan-she 陝西人民出版社
Shan-hsi Jen-min Chiao-yü Ch'u-pan-she 陝西人民教育出版社
Shan-hsi Shih-fan Ta-hsüeh Ch'u-pan-she 陝西師範大學出版社
Shan-t'ou Ta-hsüeh Ch'u-pan-she 汕頭大學出版社
Shan-tung Chiao-yü Ch'u-pan-she 山東教育出版社
Shan-tung Ta-hsüeh Ch'u-pan-she 山東大學出版社
Shan-tung Wen-i Ch'u-pan-she 山東文藝出版社
Shan-tung Yu-i Shu-she 山東友誼書社
Shang-hai Jen-min Ch'u-pan-she 上海人民出版社
Shang-hai Jen-min Mei-shu Ch'u-pan-she 上海人民美術出版社
Shang-hai Ku-chi Ch'u-pan-she 上海古籍出版社
Shang-hai She-hui K'o-hsüeh Yüan Ch'u-pan-she 上海社會科學院出版社
Shang-hai Shu-hua Ch'u-pan-she 上海書畫出版社
Shang-hai Shu-tien 上海書店
Shang-hai T'ung-chi Ta-hsüeh Ch'u-pan-she 上海同濟大學出版社
Shang-hai T'zu-shu Ch'u-pan-she 上海辭書出版社
Shang-hai Wen-hua Ch'u-pan-she 上海文化出版社
Shang-hai Wen-hua I-shu Ch'u-pan-she 上海文化藝術出版社
Shang-hai Wen-i Ch'u-pan-she 上海文藝出版社
Shang-ting Wen-hua Ch'u-pan-she 商鼎文化出版社
Shang-wu Yin-shu-kuan 商務印書館
Shao-nien Erh-t'ung Ch'u-pan-she 少年兒童出版社
She-hui K'o-hsüeh Wen-hsien Ch'u-pan-she 社會科學文獻出版社
Shih-chieh Shu-chü 世界書局
Shih-pao (Chung-kuo Shih-pao) 中國時報
Shih-pao Wen-hua Ch'u-pan Ch'i-yeh Yu-hsien Kung-ssu 時報文化出版企業有限公司
Shih-tai Wen-i Ch'u-pan-she 時代文藝出版社
Shih-yüeh Wen-i Ch'u-pan-she 北京十月文藝出版社
Shin Jimbutsu Ôraisha 新人物往来社
Shinchôsha 新潮社
Shou-tu Shih-fan Ta-hsüeh Ch'u-pan-she 首都師範大學出版社
Shou-tu T'u-shu-kuan 首都圖書館
Shu-mu Wen-hsien Ch'u-pan-she 書目文獻出版社
Shuang-t'i Kuo-chi Shih-wu Yu-hsien Kung-ssu 雙笛國際事務有限公司
Shûeisha 集英社
Shui-niu Ch'u-pan-she Yu-hsien Kung-ssu 水牛出版社有限公司
Shunjûsha 春秋社
Sôbunsha 創文社
Ssu-ch'uan Ch'u-pan-she 四川出版社
Ssu-ch'uan Jen-min Ch'u-pan-she 四川人民出版社
Ssu-ch'uan Sheng She-hui K'o-hsüeh Yüan 四川省社會科學院
Ssu-ch'uan Ta-hsüeh Ch'u-pan-she 四川大學出版社
Ssu-ch'uan Tz'u-shu Ch'u-pan-she 四川辭書出版社
Ssu-ch'uan Wen-i Ch'u-pan-she 四川文藝出版社
Sung-kao Shu-she 松高書社

T
Ta-an Ch'u-pan-she 大安出版社
Ta-lien Ch'u-pan-she 大連古籍出版社
Taishûkan Shoten 大修館書店

T'ai-p'ing Shu-chü 太瓶書局
T'ai-wan Hsüeh-sheng Shu-chü 臺灣學生書局
T'ai-wan Kuo-yü Shu-chü 臺灣國語書局
T'ai-wan Shang-wu Yin-shu-kuan 臺灣商務印書館
T'ai-wan Sheng Wen-hsien Wei-yüan Hui 臺灣省文獻委員會
T'ai-wan Ta-hsüeh 臺灣大學
Takahashi Jôhô 高橋情報
Tang-an Ch'u-pan-she 檔案出版社
Tang-tai Chung-kuo Ch'u-pan-she 當代中國出版社
Tao-hsiang Ch'u-pan-she 稻鄉出版社
Ti-ch'iu Ch'u-pan-she 地球出版社
T'ien-chin Chiao-yü Ch'u-pan-she 天津教育出版社
T'ien-chin Jen-min Ch'u-pan-she 天津人民出版社
T'ien-chin Ku-chi Ch'u-pan-she 天津古籍出版社
T'ien-chin She-hui K'o-hsüeh Yüan Ch'u-pan-she 天津社會科學院出版社
T'ien-chin Ta-hsüeh Ch'u-pan-she 天津大學出版社
T'ien-i Ch'u-pan-she 天一出版社
Ting-wen Shu-chü Ku-fen Yu-hsien Kung-ssu 鼎文書局股份有限公司
Tôhô Shoten 東方書店
Tôkai Daigaku Shuppankai 東海大学出版会
Tôkyô Daigaku Bungakubu 東京大学文学部
Tôkyô Daigaku Tôyô Bunkajo Fuzoku Tôyôgaku Bunken Sentâ 東京大学東方文化所附属東
　　洋文献センタ
Tôkyô Daigaku Tôyô Bunka Kenkyûjo 　東京大学東方文化研究所
Tôyô Bunka Daigaku 東方文化大学
Ts'e-hui Ch'u-pan-she 測繪出版社
Ts'e-hui K'o-ta Ch'u-pan-she 測繪科大出版社
Tso-chia Ch'u-pan-she 作家出版社
Tsung-ch'ing T'u-shu Ch'u-pan Yu-hsien Kung-ssu 宗青圖書初版有限公司
Tu Fu Yen-chiu Hsüeh-k'an Pien-chi-pu 杜甫研究學刊編輯部
T'uan-chieh Ch'u-pan-she 團結出版社
Tun-huang Wen-i Ch'u-pan-she 敦煌文藝出版社
Tun-huang Yen-chiu Yüan 敦煌研究院
Tung-fang Wen-hua Shu-chü 東方文化書局
Tung-fang Ch'u-pan-she 東方出版社
Tung-hai Ta-hsüeh 東海大學
Tung-i Ch'u-pan-she 東益出版社
Tung-pei Shih-fan Ta-hsüeh Ch'u-pan-she 東北師範大學出版社
Tung-sheng Ch'u-pan Shih-yeh Yu-hsien Kung-ssu 東昇初版事業有限公司
Tung-ta T'u-shu Ku-fen Yu-hsien Kung-ssu 東大圖書股份有限公司
Tung-wu Ta-hsüeh 東吳大學
Tzu-chin-ch'eng Ch'u-pan-she 紫禁城出版社

W
Wai-wen Ch'u-pan-she 外文出版社
Wan-chüan-lou T'u-shu Kung-ssu 萬卷樓圖書公司
Waseda Daigaku Shuppanbu 早稻田大学出版部
Wen-che So, Chung-yang Yen-chiu Yüan 文哲所，中央研究院
Wen-chien Hui 文件會
Wen-chin Ch'u-pan-she 文津出版社
Wen-hai Ch'u-pan-she Yu-hsien Kung-ssu 文海出版社有限公司

Wen-hsüeh Ku-chi K'an-hang-she 文學古籍刊行社
Wen-hsüeh Ch'u-pan-she 文學出版社
Wen-hua I-shu Ch'u-pan-she 文化藝術出版社
Wen-hua Ta-hsüeh 文化大學
Wen-lien Ch'u-pan-she 文聯出版社
Wen-sheng Shu-chü Ku-fen Yu-hsien Kung-ssu 文笙書局股份有限公司
Wen-shih-che Ch'u-pan-she Yu-hsien Kung-ssu 文史哲出版社有限公司
Wen-wu Ch'u-pan-she 文物出版社
Wen-yu Ch'u-pan-she 文友出版社
Wu-chou Wang An-shih Yen-chiu Hui 吳州王安石研究會
Wu-han Ch'u-pan-she 武漢出版社
Wu-han Ta-hsüeh Ch'u-pan-she 武漢大學出版社
Wu-nan T'u-shu Kung-ssu 五南圖書公司

Y
Ya-t'ai T'u-shu Ch'u-pan-she 亞太圖書出版社
Yen-shan Ch'u-pan-she 燕山出版社
Yü-ching Shu-hui 玉京書會
Yu-shih Wen-hua Shih-yeh Kung-ssu 幼獅文化事業公司
Yü-wen Ch'u-pan-she 語文出版社
Yüan-liu Ch'u-pan-she 遠流出版社
Yüeh-lu Shu-she 岳麓書社
Yün-ch'en Wen-hua Shih-yeh Ku-fen yu-hsien Kung-ssu 允晨文化事業股份有限公司
Yün-nan Jen-min Ch'u-pan-she 雲南人民出版社

Oft-Cited Works

This list includes both journals and books. The abbreviations used throughout this volume are on the left, the complete citations on the right.

AF	*Altorientalische Forschungen.*
AM	*Asia Major.*
AO	*Archiv Orientálni.*
AS	*Asiatische Studien.*
Bol, *"This Culture of Ours"*	Peter K. Bol. *"This Culture of Ours": Intellectual Transitions in T'ang and Sung China.* Stanford: Stanford University Press, 1992.
BSOAS	*Bulletin of the School of Oriental and African Studies (University of London)*
Chang, "Ming and Qing Anthologies"	Kang-i Sun Chang. "Ming and Qing Anthologies of Women's Poetry and Their Selection Strategies." In *Writing Women in Late Imperial China.* Ellen Widmer and Kang-i Sun Chang, eds. Stanford: Stanford University Press, 1997.
Chaves, *Later Chinese Poetry*	Jonathan Chaves. *The Columbia Book of Later Chinese Poetry: Yüan, Ming and Ch'ing Dynasties (1279-1911).* New York: Columbia University Press, 1986.
China Under Jurchen Rule	Hoyt Cleveland Tillman and Stephen H. West, eds. *China Under Jurchen Rule, Essays on Chin Intellectual and Cultural History.* Albany: SUNY Press, 1995.
CLEAR	*Chinese Literature: Essays, Articles, Reviews.*
Ch'üan Sung shih	*Ch'üan Sung shih* 全宋詩. 25v. Pei-ching Ta-hsüeh, Ku-wen-hsien Yen-chiu So, eds. Peking: Pei-ching Ta-hsüeh, 1991-1995.
Ch'üan Sung tz'u	*Ch'üan Sung tz'u* 全宋詞. 5v. T'ang Kuei-chang 唐圭璋, ed. Shanghai: Chung-hua, 1965.
Ch'üan Sung-wen	*Ch'üan Sung wen* 全宋文. Tseng Tsao-chuang 曾棗莊 and Liu Lin 劉琳, eds. 50v. Chengtu: Pa-Shu Shu-she, 1988–1994.
Ch'üan T'ang shih	*Ch'üan T'ang shih* 全唐詩. 12v. Rpt. Taipei: Ming-lun, 1971.
Ch'üan T'ang shih so-yin	*Ch'üan T'ang shih so-yin* 全唐詩索引. Luan Kuei-ming 欒貴明 *et al.*, ed. Peking: Hsien-tai, 1990- .
Ch'üan T'ang wen	*Ch'üan T'ang wen* 全唐文. 20v. + 1v. Index. Taipei: Wen-yu, 1972.
CRI	*China Review International*
Demiéville, *Anthologie*	Demiéville, Paul, ed. *Anthologie de la poésie chinoise classique.* Paris: Gallimard, 1962.
DMB	L. Carrington Goodrich and Chaoying Fang, eds. *Dictionary of Ming Biography 1368-1644.* 2v. New

York: Columbia University Press, 1976.

Early Chinese Texts	Michael Loewe. *Early Chinese Texts, A Bibliographic Guide.* Berkeley: The Society for the Study of Early China and the Institute of East Asian Studies, University of California, 1993.
EC	*Early China*
ECCP	Arthur W. Hummel, ed. *Emminent Chinese of the Ch'ing Period (1644-1912).* 2v. Washington, D.C.: United States Government Printing Office, 1943; rpt. Taipei: Ch'eng-wen Publishing Company, 1967.
Forke, *Dichtungen*	Forke, Alfred. *Dichtungen T'ang-und-Sung-zeit aus dem Chinesischen metrisch übertragen.* Veröffentlichungen des Seminars für Sprache und Kultur Chinas an der Hamburgischen Universität, Numbers 3 and 4. Hamburg: Friederichsen, de Gruyter and Co., 1929.
Frankel, *The Flowering Plum*	Hans H. Frankel. *The Flowering Plum and the Palace Lady: Interpretations of Chinese Poetry.* New Haven and London: Yale University Press, 1976.
Frodsham, *Anthology*	J. D. Frodsham, with the collaboration of Ch'eng Hsi. *An Anthology of Chinese Verse, Han Wei Chin and the Northern and Southern Dynasties.* Oxford: The Clarendon Press, 1967.
Fu, *T'ang-tai*	Fu Hsüan-ts'ung 傅璇琮 et al., ed. *T'ang-tai wen-hsüeh yen-chiu* 唐代文學研究. Kuei-lin Kuang-hsi Shih-fan Ta-hsüeh, 1990.
Hartman, *Han Yü*	Hartman, Charles. *Han Yü and the Search for T'ang Unity.* Princeton: Princeton University Press, 1986.
Hefte-	*Hefte für Ostasiatische Literatur.*
HJAS	*Harvard Journal of Asiatic Studies.*
Hsu, *Anthologie*	Hsu, S. N. *Anthologie de la littérature chinoise des origines à nos jours.* Paris: Librairie Delagrave, 1933.
Hsü Fu-kuan	Hsü Fu-kuan 徐復觀. *Liang Han ssu-hsiang shih* 兩漢思想史. 3v. Rpt. Taipei: Hsüeh-sheng, 1993 (1979).
JA	*Journal asiatique..*
JAS	*Journal of Asian Studies.*
JAOS	*Journal of the American Oriental Society.*
JCP	*Journal of Chinese Philosophy.*
JCR	*Journal of Chinese Religion.*
JOSA	*Journal of the Oriental Society of Australia.*
JSYS	*Journal of Sung-Yuan Studies.*
Kao, *Chinese Classical Tales*	Karl S. Y. Kao, ed. *Classical Chinese Tales of the Supernatural and the Fantastic, Selections from the Third to the Tenth Century.* Bloomington: Indiana University Press, 1985.
Klöpsch, *Faden*	Klöpsch, Volker. *Die seidene Faden: Gedichte der Tang.*

	Frankfurt am Main: Insel, 1991. A complete translation of the *T'ang-shih san-pai-shou*.*
Knechtges, *Wen xuan*	David. R. Knechtges. *Wen xuan or Selections of Refined Literature. Volume 1: Rhapsodies on Metropolises and Capitals.* Princeton: Princeton University Press, 1982. *Volume 2: Rhapsodies on Sacrifices, Hunting, Travel, Sightseeing, Palaces and Halls, Rivers and Seas.* Princeton: Princeton University Press, 1987. *Volume 3: Rhapsodies on Natural Phenomena, Birds and Animals, Aspirations and Feelings, Sorrowful Laments, Literature, Music and Passions.* Princeton: Princeton University Press, 1996.
Landau, *Beyond Spring*	Julie Landau, trans. *Beyond Spring, Tz'u Poems of the Sung Dynasty.* New York: Columbia University Press, 1994.
Liu, *Lyricists*	Liu, James J. Y. *Major Lyricists of the Northern Sung.* Princeton: Princeton University Press, 1974.
Liu and Lo, *Sunflower Splendor*	Wu-chi Liu and Irving Yucheng Lo, eds. *Sunflower Splendor, Three Thousand Years of Chinese Poetry.* Garden City, New York: Anchor Press/ Doubleday, 1975.
Liu-ch'ao wen	*Ch'üan Shang-ku San-tai, Ch'in, Han, San-kuo, Liu-ch'ao wen* 全上古三代秦漢三國六朝文. Yen K'o-chün 嚴可均 (1762-1843), ed. 4v. + 1v. Index. Rpt. Kyoto: Chûgoku Shuppansha, 1975.
Loewe, *Early Chinese Texts*	Michael Loewe, ed. *Early Chinese Texts: A Bibliographic Guide.* Berkeley: The Society for the Study of Early China and The Institute of East Asian Studies, University of California, 1993.
Lu, *Nan-pei-ch'ao shih*	Lu, Ch'in-li 逯欽立, ed. *Hsien-Ch'in Han, Wei Chin, Nan-pei-ch'ao shih* 先秦漢魏晉韓南北朝詩. 3v. Peking: Chung-hua, 1983.
Ma and Lau, *Traditional Chinese Stories*	Y. W. Ma and Joseph S. M. Lau, eds. *Traditional Chinese Stories: Themes and Variations.* New York: Columbia University Press, 1978.
Margouliès, *Anthologie raisonnée*	Georges Margouliès. *Anthologie raisonnée de la littérature chinoise.* Paris: Payot, 1948.
McCraw, *Chinese Lyricists*	McCraw. David R. *Chinese Lyricists of the Seventeenth Century.* Honolulu: University of Hawaii Press, 1990.
MS	*Monumenta Serica.*
MSOS	*Mitteilungen des Seminars für Orientalische Sprachen* (Berlin).
Nachrichten	*Nachrichten der Gesellschaft für Natur- und Völkerkunde Ostasiens/Hamburg.*
Pai-san	Chang P'u 張溥 (1602–1641), comp. *Han Wei Liu-ch'ao Pai-san ming-chia chi* 漢魏六朝百三名家集. 5v. Taipei, 1963.
Pai-pu	*Pai-pu ts'ung-shu chi-ch'eng* 百部叢書集成.

PFEH	*Papers on Far Eastern History*
RBS	*Revue bibliographique de sinologie*
Republican China	Howard L. Boorman, ed. *Biographical Dictionary of Republican China.* 5v. New York: Columbia University Press, 1967-69.
Six Dynasties Poetry	Kang-i Sun Chang. *Six Dynasties Poetry.* Princeton: Princeton University Press, 1986.
Strassberg, *Inscribed Landscapes*	Richard E. Strassberg. *Inscribed Landscapes, Travel Writing from Imperial China.* Berkeley: University of California Press, 1994.
Ssu-k'u	*Ssu-k'u ch'üan-shu* 四庫全書.
SPPY	*Ssu-pu pei-yao*四部備要.
SPTK	*Ssu-pu ts'ung-k'an* 四部叢刊.
SUNY	State University of New York
T'ang-jen hsiao-shuo	*T'ang-jen hsiao-shuo* 唐人小説. Wang Pi-chiang 汪辟疆, ed. Rpt. Shanghai: Shang-hai Ku-chi, 1978.
THHP	*Ts'ing-hua hsüeh-pao* 清華學鮑 *(Ts'ing-hua Journal of Chinese Studies).*
TkR	*Tamkang Review*
TP	*T'oung pao.*
TS	*T'ang Studies*
TSCC	*Ts'ung-shu chi-ch'eng* 叢書集成.
TT + number	*Tao-tsang* fascicle number.
Waiting for the Unicorn	Irving Yucheng Lo and William Schultz, eds. *Waiting for the Unicorn: Poems and Lyrics of China's Last Dynasty, 1644-1911.* Bloomington: Indiana University Press, 1986.
Waley, *The Temple*	Arthur Waley. *The Temple and Other Poems.* London: Allen & Unwin, 1923.
Watson, *Earlier Chinese Poetry*	Burton Watson. *The Columbia Book of Chinese Poetry from Early Times to the Thirteenth Century.* New York: Columbia University Press, 1984.
Watson, *Chinese Rhyme-Prose*	Burton Watson. *Chinese Rhyme-Prose, Poems in the Fu Form from the Han and Six Dynasty Periods.* New York: Columbia University Press, 1971.
Wen-hsüan	Hsiao T'ung 蕭統, ed. *Wen-hsüan* 文選. Taipei: Hua-cheng, 1982.
Wen-lin	*Wen-lin: Studies in the Chinese Humanities* II, ed. Tse-tsung Chow. Madison and Hong Kong: Department of East Asian Languages and Literature, University of Wisconsin-Madison and N.T.T. Chinese Language research Center, Institute of Chinese Studies, The Chinese University of Hong Kong, 1989,
Widmer and Chang, *Writing Women*	Ellen Widmer and Kang-i Sun Chang, eds. *Writing Women in Late Imperial China.* Stanford: Stanford University Press, 1997.
Wieger, *La Chine*	Leon Wieger. *La Chine à travers les ages.* Hien-hien, 1920.
Yu, *Voices*	Yu, Pauline. *Voices of the Song Lyric in China.* Berkeley: University of California Press, 1994.

Major Chinese Dynasties and Periods

Hsia 夏	*ca.* 2100–*ca.* 1600 B.C.
Shang 商	*ca.* 1600–*ca.* 1028 B.C.
Chou 周	*ca.* 1027–*ca.* 256 B.C.
Western Chou 西周	*ca.* 1027–771 B.C.
Eastern Chou 東周	*ca.* 770–256 B.C.
Spring and Autumn 春秋	722–468 B.C.
Warring States 戰國	403–221 B.C.
Ch'in 秦	221–207 B.C.
Han 漢	206 B.C.–A.D. 220
Former Han 前漢	206 B.C.–A.D. 8
Latter Han 後漢	A.D. 25–220
Hsin 新	A.D. 9–25
Three Kingdoms 三國	220–265
Wei 魏	220–265
Shu 蜀	221–263
Wu 吳	222–280
Six Dynasties 六朝	
(Wu 吳, Eastern Chin 東晉, Liu Sung 劉宋,	
Southern Ch'i 南齊, Southern Liang 南梁,	
and Southern Ch'en 南陳)	222–589
Chin 晉	265–420
Western Chin 西晉	265–317
Eastern Chin 東晉	317–420
Southern Dynasties 南朝	420–589
Former (Liu) Sung 劉宋	420–479
Southern Ch'i 南齊	479–502
Southern Liang 南梁	502–557
Southern Ch'en 南陳	557–589
Northern Dynasties 北朝	386–581
Northern Wei 北魏	386–534
Eastern Wei 東魏	534–550
Western Wei 西魏	535–577
Northern Ch'i 北齊	550–577
Northern Chou 北周	557–581
Sui 隋	581–618
T'ang 唐	618–907
Five Dynasties 五代	907–960
Liao 遼	916–1125
Sung 宋	960–1279
Northern Sung 北宋	960–1126
Southern Sung 南宋	1127–1279
Chin (Jurchen) 金	1115–1234
Yüan 元	1260–1368
Ming 明	1368–1644
Ch'ing 清	1644–1911

THE INDIANA COMPANION TO
TRADITIONAL CHINESE LITERATURE

(Volume 2)

Chang Lei 張耒 (*tzu*, Wen-ch'ien 文潛, also known as K'o-shan 柯山, Wan-ch'iu Hsien-sheng 宛丘先生, Ch'iao-chün Hsien-sheng 譙郡先生, Yu-shih 右史 and Lung-ko 龍閣, 1054–1114) was born in Huai-yin 淮陰 prefecture of Ch'u-chou 楚州 (in modern Kiangsu). He grew up under a Northern Sung government which was troubled both economically and militarily. Chang Lei became involved in the factionalism of the Sung court before he even began his political career. While still preparing for the examinations, he wrote to Su Shih's 蘇軾 (1037–1101)* younger brother, Su Ch'e 蘇轍 (1039–1112),* in part to exploit his own growing reputation for being well versed in the history of his own dynasty. When he passed the *chin-shih* examination in 1073, not yet twenty years old, he was already identified with the Sus.

Since the New Party which the Sus opposed held sway until the end of Emperor Shen-tsung's 神宗 reign (1068–1086), Chang Lei held only provincial posts until he was recommended by Fan Ch'un-jen 范純仁, the son of Fan Chung-yen 范仲淹 (989–1052), in 1086 to be Proofreader of the Imperial Library (*Mi-shu-sheng cheng-tzu* 秘書省正字). He held a variety of literary posts in the Imperial Library and Office of History thereafter and further associated himself with Ch'ao Pu-chih 晁補之 (1053–1110), Ch'in Kuan 秦觀 (1049–1100)** and Huang T'ing-chien 黃庭堅 (1045–1105)* who also served in the San-Kuan 三館 (Three Institutes–i.e., the Chao-wen Kuan 昭文館 (Institute for the Glorification of Literature), Chi-hsien Tien 集賢殿 (Academy of Scholarly Worthies) and Shih Kuan 史館 (Office of History). The four of them came to be known as the *Su-men Ssu Hsüeh-shih* 蘇門四學士 (Four Scholars at Su Shih's Gate). Thus Chang Lei's political career, as well as those of the other three, was in part dependent on Su's political fortune. In the early years of the Shao-sheng 紹聖 reign period (1094–1098), the revival of the New Party realized the worst nightmare of Su Shih and the other conservatives. As Su Shih was denounced and exiled from one trivial provincial post to another, Chang Lei shared Su's misfortune. In 1094, he asked to be delegated to a provincial post and was appointed to be Administrator (*chih* 知) of Jun-chou 潤州 (modern Kiangsu).

Thereafter, he was demoted repeatedly, moving from Jun-chou to become Administrator of Hsüan-chou 宣州 (modern Anhwei) and then Wine Tax Supervisor (*chiu-shui* 酒稅) of Huang-chou 黃州 (modern Hupei). In the early years of Emperor Hui-tsung 徽宗 (r. 1101–1126), Chang Lei was once reinstated as Controller-general (*t'ung-p'an* 通判) of the Huang-chou, Yen-chou 兗州 (modern Shantung), Administrator of Ying-chou 潁州 (in modern Anhwei) and Ju-chou 汝州 (in modern Honan). However, this transient revival of his political life did not last long.

Because he openly mourned Su Shih's death (1101), Chang Lei was demoted once again to be Administrative Aide (*pieh-chia* 別駕) of Fang-chou 房州 (modern Hupei), then transferred to Huang-chou again. In this third sojourn in Huang-chou, Chang Lei lived at the foot of Mount K'o 柯, which is reflected in the names later used to designate some collections of his works. During this stay at Huang-chou, he was also temporarily assigned to guard the Ming-tao 明道 Temple; at this time he wrote his *Ming-tao tsa-chih* 明道雜誌 (Clarifying the *Tao* Miscellany), a collection of biographical entries on unusual happenings, historical figures, and contemporary men of distinction. In 1102, the Su brothers and many other conservatives including Chang Lei were blacklisted as 'factionalists of Yüan-yu' 元祐 (1086–1094) since they had held power during this era which had policies directly opposed to those then current. Their names were engraved on a stone tablet in order to

1

hold them perpetually at fault. But in 1106 the tablet was destroyed and Chang Lei was freed from his exile in Huang-chou. He moved to Ch'en-chou and lived in reclusion, dying in poverty and illness eight years later.

Since his first acquaintance with the Su brothers in his teens, Chang had modeled himself after Su Shih both politically and intellectually. Among the four disciples of Su Shih, his *shih*-poetry is considered second only to that of Huang T'ing-chien. His *tz'u*, though only six pieces are extant, were rated by contemporaries as nearly as good as those by Ch'in Kuan. Like the other three disciples, Chang Lei borrowed his literary principles from Su Shih. He was primarily concerned with the direct depiction of reality and the exposure of principles of things (*li* 理). Incidents and situations of common life provide the subject matter for most of his poems. Like Su Shih, he advocated a straightforward means of expression.

Chang Lei's corpus can be seen as a continuation of the poetry and poetics of Po Chü-i 白居易 (772–846)* and his followers. Thus his verse shares strengths and weaknesses with Po's work; his emphasis on depicting the actual lives of people, in lucid and simple poetic language, on occasion led his style into a crude rhetoric which invited criticism from later scholars. But Chang Lei certainly felt this risk justified in his attempt to stem what he saw as an overly developed aestheticism in the late T'ang and early Sung eras.

In prose, Chang Lei adhered to the tenets of the ancient-style which Ou-yang Hsiu 歐陽修 (1007–1072)* and Su Shih championed. Despite his commitment to the style which produced great works from the pens of his mentors, his prose (nearly three hundred pieces are extant) including biographies, anecdotes, letters, prefaces and postscripts, epigraphs, and rhapsodies, met with only moderate contemporary success. His "Shu Han

T'ui-chih chih chuan hou" 書韓退之傳後 (Postscript on the Biography of Han T'ui-chih) and his essays on Ssu-ma Ch'ien 司馬遷 (145–*ca.* 86 B.C.),* Ssu-ma Hsiang-ju 司馬相如 (179–117 B.C.),* Han Hsin 韓信, Han Yü 韓愈 (768–824)* and others exemplify his interest in historical figures and his ability to convey his own political ideas through them. He also composed fiction and miscellaneous writings. Two biographies display his imagination and literary skills: that of Lady Bamboo ("Chu Fu-jen chuan" 竹夫人傳), is an allegory in the style of Han Yü's pseudo-biographies, whereas that on Jen Ch'ing 任青 depicts the peculiarities of a man of the lower social strata.

Editions and References

Chang Yu-shih wen-chi 張右史文集. 60 *chüan*. SPPY.

Chu fu-jen chuan 竹夫人傳. 1 *chüan*. In *Hsiang-yen ts'ung-shu* 香豔叢書.

Ch'üan Sung shih, 20:1155-1187.13027-13420.

Ch'üan Sung tz'u, 1:592-594.

K'o-shan chi 柯山集. T'ien Yü-fan 田毓璠 ed. 50 *chüan*. Kuang-ya Shu-chü 廣雅書局 edition. Supplemented by Lu Hsin-yüan 陸心源 (1834–1894), comp. *K'o-shan chi pu* 柯山集補 in 12 *chüan*, anonymous ed. "Hsü shih-i" 續拾移 *chüan*, and Shao Tsu-t'ao 邵祖燾 "Chang Wen-ch'ien Hsien-sheng Nien-p'u" 張文潛先生年譜 [A Chronicle of Chang Wen-ch'ien]. 1929.

Li, I-an 李逸安, Sun T'ung-hai 孫通海, and Fu Hsin 傅信, eds. *Chang Lei chi* 張耒集. Peking: Chung-hua, 1990. A modern critical edition with excellent front and back matter (biography, information on editions, etc., including Shao Tsu-t'ao 邵祖燾 "Chang Wen-ch'ien Hsien-sheng nien-p'u" 張文潛先生年譜 [A Chronicle of Chang Wen-ch'ien].

Ming-tao tsa-chih 明道雜誌. 1 *chüan*. In *Ts'ung-shu chi-ch'eng* 叢書集成.

Wan-ch'iu t'i-pa 宛丘題跋. 1 *chüan*. In *Chin-tai mi-shu* 津逮祕書, *Ts'ung-shu chi-ch'eng ch'u-pien* 叢書集成初編.

Wu, Fu-chu 吳福助. "*K'o-shan tz'u* chiao-chu" 柯山詞校注. In *Ch'ing-chu Jui-an Lin*

Ching-i Hsien-sheng liu-chih tan-ch'en lun-wen chi 慶祝瑞安林景伊先生六秩誕辰論文集, Taipei: Cheng-chih Ta-hsüeh, Chung-kuo Wen-hsüeh Yen-chiu-so 政治大學中國文學研究所, 1969, 2391-2402.

Translations

Demiéville, *Anthologie,* p. 357.
Hsu, *Anthologie,* p. 203.
Wieger, Leon. *La Chine à travers les ages: hommes et choses.* Sienhsien (Hokienfu): Impr. de la Mission Catholique, 1920, pp. 231-32.

Studies

Bol, Peter K. "A Literati Miscellany and Sung Intellectual History: the Case of Chang Lei's *Ming-tao tsa-chih.*" *JSYS* 25 (1995):121-151.
Huang, Chen-yün 黃震雲. "Ch'in Kuan te tsu-nien ho Chang Lei te chi-kuan sheng-tsu nien" 秦觀的卒年和張耒的籍貫生卒年. *Ch'ing-hai Shih-fan Ta-hsüeh hsüeh-pao* 青海師範大學學報 1984.4.
Sung Biographies, 1:20-23
Liu, Nai-ch'ang 劉乃昌. "Su-men Ssu-hsüeh-shih chih-i, Chang Lei" 蘇門四學士之一, 張耒. *Ku-tien wen-hsüeh chih-shih* 1990.1: 79-83.
Lung, Yü-sheng 龍榆生. "Su-men Ssu-hsüeh-shih Tz'u" 蘇門四學士詞. *Wen-hsüeh* 文學 2 (1934).
Yü, Pei-shan 于北山. "Lüeh-lun Chang Lei shih te ssu-hsiang yü i-shu" 略論張耒詩的思想與藝術. *Huai-yin Shih-chuan hsüeh-pao* 淮陰師專學報 1981.4.

Chen Zhi
The National University of Singapore

Chang Yen 張炎 (*tzu* Shu-hsia 叔夏, *hao* Yü-t'ien 玉田, 1248-1320?) is, along with Chou Mi 周密 (1232-1299 or 1308)* and Wang I-sun 王沂孫 (1240- 1290),* one of three major late Sung *tz'u* poets who witnessed the end of Sung and the subsequent Mongol occupation of China. His family traced its origins to the beginning of the Southern Sung when the general Chang Chün 張俊 (1086-1154) accepted a mansion in Lin-an and enormous wealth in return for the surrender of his private army to government control and his support for the policy of peaceful coexistence with the Jurchen Chin dynasty in the North. The family soon applied this wealth and status toward cultural pursuits in the capital. Chang Chün's great-grandson, and the great-grand-father of Chang Yen, was Chang Tzu 張鎡 (1153-after 1211), a noted poet, painter, and arbiter of aesthetic issues. Chang's Cassia Retreat, an enormous villa constructed in the suburbs north of Lin-an, contained over eighty pavilions, halls, bridges, and ponds where Chang and his colleagues engaged in a *récherché* pursuit of the ultimate in elegant living.

The Mongol invasions brought this world to a violent end. In retaliation for his mistreatment of two Mongol envoys, the Mongols in 1276 executed Chang Ju 張濡, Chang Yen's grandfather, and confiscated the family property. Chang Yen, then aged 28, continued to live in Lin-an where he associated with other writers loyal to the Sung cause. In 1279, he was among fourteen poets who gathered in Shao-hsing to mourn the desecration of the Sung royal tombs (including the tomb of his ancestor Chang Chün), in a series of thirty-six highly allusive *tz'u* poems. These works are both a culmination of the Southern Sung *tz'u* style and a lament for the passing of the world that produced it. He continued to reside sporadically in Lin-an, traveling often in search of patronage. He made a long trip North to the Mongol capital in 1290-91 in search of literary work, but frustration and homesickness soon brought him South again. He continued his travels with scholars such as Shu Yüeh-hsiang 舒岳祥 (1219-1298) and Tai Piao-yüan 戴表元 (1244-1310). The latter has left a vivid portrait of Chang Yen in these years (translated in Lin Shuen-fu, *Transformation,* pp. 195-7—see *Studies* below), a perpetual exile wandering in search of a lost world, recording his impressions and memories in his *tz'u* lyrics. Chang Yen, whose family had once supported large numbers of itinerant artists and writers, ended his own life, in the words of Lin Shuen-fu, "the last recluse-artist."

About three hundred of Chang Yen's *tz'u* survive along with a major theoretical and technical treatise on *tz'u* poetry called the *Tz'u-yüan* 詞源, which was probably completed toward the end of his life. A recent study has divided this corpus into the following topical subgroups: love poetry, poetry written on the West Lake, poetry written on the northern journey, poems in description of objects (*yung-wu tz'u* 詠物詞), and poetry of reclusion. There is a remarkable degree of stylistic consistency in Chang Yen's lyrics, and this consistency, in turn, accords with the principles of *tz'u* composition set forth in the *Tz'u-yüan*. The first part of the *Tz'u-yüan* is concerned exclusively with musical issues, and this emphasis underscores Chang Yen's insistence that there be perfect accord between the music and the lyrics of the *tz'u.* Chang paid great attention to the musical quality of his *tz'u*, and Tai Piao-yüan's account of him describes the striking effect of hearing Chang Yen sing his own songs. Second, Chang stressed that *tz'u* must be "elegant and proper" (*ya erh cheng* 雅而正). Following the example of the Northern Sung masters who first sought to bring the gravity of *shih* poetry to the lyric, lyric diction was not to be based on the vernacular but upon the vocabulary of T'ang poetry. And just as raw language was to be avoided, so raw sentiment was also devalued as vulgar. Valued were suggestion, obliqueness, and craft, the earlier "heroic mode" (see *Hao-fang p'ai* 豪放派**) of writers like Hsin Ch'i-chi 辛棄疾 (1140–1207)* being rejected as too direct. Third, Chang Yen promoted a quality he called "transparency" (*ch'ing-k'ung* 清空), which

advocated the liberal use of "empty words" or "lead-segments" that helped to coordinate music and text by providing for textual fluidity and syntactical flexibility. The end result was to make the language of the lyric "come alive" without being vulgar. With this last quality, Chang Yen sought to place his verse in a tradition that ran through Chiang K'uei 姜夔 (*ca.* 1155–1221)* back to the Northern Sung masters and to retreat slightly from the dense allegorical structures of late Sung *tz'u* poets such as Wu Wen-ying 吳文英 (*ca.* 1200–*ca.* 1260).*

Editions and References:

Chang, Shu-ch'iung 張淑瓊, ed. *Chang Yen* 張炎. *T'ang-Sung tz'u hsin-shang* 唐宋詞新賞, v. 15. Taipei: Ti-ch'iu, 1990. A semi-popular anthology with extensive annotation and paraphrases.

Cheng, Meng-chin 鄭孟津 and Wu P'ing-shan 吳平山. *Tz'u-yüan chieh-chien* 詞源解箋. Hangchow: Che-chiang Ku-chi, 1990. An exhaustive study of the first chapter of the *Tz'u-yüan*.

Ch'üan Sung tz'u, 5:3463-3523.

Hsia, Ch'eng-t'ao 夏丞燾 and Ts'ai Sung-yün 蔡嵩雲, eds. *Tz'u-yüan chu Yüeh-fu chih-mi chien-shih* 詞源注樂府指迷箋釋. Peking: Jen-min Wen-hsüeh, 1981.

Shan-chung pai-yün tz'u 山中白雲詞. 8 *chüan.* *SPPY* edition.

For details on other editions see Jao Tsung-i 饒宗頤, *Tz'u chi k'ao* 詞籍考, Hong Kong: Hong Kong University Press, 1963, pp. 259-61 and Etienne Balazs and Yves Hervouet, *A Sung Bibliography,* Hong Kong: Chinese University Press, pp. 472-73, 78.

Tz'u-yüan 詞源. 2 *chüan. SPPY* edition.

Translations

Dutton, Helen Wiley. *Secrets Told in the Bamboo Grove.* Peking: The French Bookstore, 1940, pp. 33 and 36.

Mair, *Anthology,* p. 348.

Studies

Ch'en, Hsüeh-hua 陳雪華. "Yü-t'ien tz'u yen-chiu chi chiao-tu" 玉田詞研究及校讀, *Tz'u-hsüeh chi-k'an* 詞學集刊, 1966: 272-

538.

Feng, Yüan-chün 馮沅君. *Chang Yü-t'ien* 張玉田. Pei-p'ing: P'u-she, 1928.

Yang, Hai-ming 楊海明. *Chang Yen tz'u yen-chiu* 張炎詞研究. Tsinan: Ch'i-Lu Shu-she, 1989. A comprehensive, "life and works" study.

Although there is no full-length study of Chang Yen in a Western language, Shuen-fu Lin, *The Transformation of the Chinese Lyrical Tradition: Chiang K'uei and Southern Sung Tz'u Poetry* (Princeton: Princeton University Press, 1978) and Grace S. Fong, *Wu Wenying and the Art of Southern Song Ci Poetry* (Princeton: Princeton University Press, 1987) both contain material on Chang Yen.

Charles Hartman
The University at Albany

Ch'en San-li 陳三立 (*tzu,* Po-yen 伯嚴; San-yüan 散原; 1852–1937), a talented and influential poet of the late Ch'ing, and also a noted essayist of the T'ung-ch'eng 桐城 School,* was the acknowledged leader of the so-called "T'ung-Kuang Style" 同光體 poetry ("T'ung" refers to the reign of the emperor T'ung-chih 同治, 1862–74, and "Kuang" the reign of emperor Kuang-hsü 光緒, 1875–1908) and the person most responsible for the resurgence of Sung poetry, which remained the dominant influence in China for the next three quarters of a century (until the start of the Sino-Japanese War in 1937).

Ch'en San-li was born in I-ning 義寧 (modern Hsiu-shui 秀水, Kiangsi) to a family of scholar-officials. His father, Ch'en Pao-chen 陳寶箴 (1831–1900) was a forward-looking official who, as Governor of Hunan, carried out a modernization program in an effort to make it a model province. Ch'en San-li obtained his *chin-shih* degree in 1886, and after a short stint as a junior official in the Board of Revenue in Peking, joined his father's staff as an aide and involved himself in every significant aspect of his father's administration. Joining them were such prominent intellectuals as Chang Chih-tung 張之洞 (1837–1909), Liang Ch'i-ch'ao 梁啟超 (1873–1929),* T'an Ssu-t'ung 譚嗣同 (1865–1908), and Huang Tsun-hsien 黃遵憲 (1848–1905).* But when the coup d'etat of 1898 spelled an end to the Hundred Days' Reform Movement 百日政變, both father and son were cashiered from government service. His father was implicated in the movement because he had recommended to the court four of the six martyrs executed for treason.

After a period of banishment, Ch'en San-li devoted his life entirely to literature. He lead a roaming life, spending most of his time in the south, including extended stays in Shanghai and Nanking. But is was the disastrous events of 1898, together with the national humiliation which China suffered at the hands of Japan, Russia, and other European powers in the nineties and during the Boxer Rebellion of 1900, which imbued his poetry with a strong sense of reality and a deep melancholy and resonance. His success as a poet won him the respect of his peers and younger contemporaries, leading to a revival of the *Chiang-hsi shih-p'ai* (江西詩派),* and particularly of the Sung poet Huang T'ing-chien 黃庭堅 (1045–1105),* the idol of the T'ung-Kuang poets.

The "Chiang-hsi School of Poetry" denotes a style of verse which originated with such Sung poets as Huang T'ing-chien, Ch'en Shih-tao 陳師道 (1052–1102),* and Ch'en Yü-i 陳與義 (1090–1139).* One poet worshipped by all members of the school was Tu Fu 杜甫 (721–770),* and next to him Han Yü 韓愈 (768–824).* Poetry-writing, according to this school, begins with an exhaustive study of the ancients, such as Tu Fu, which allowed the student to absorb their skills and imitate them creatively. This process was described by Huang T'ing-chien as "transmuting iron into gold with a touch" (*tien t'ieh ch'eng chin* 點鐵成金) and "snatching the embryo and changing the bones" (*t'o-t'ai huan-ku* 脱胎換骨). By "creative imitation" Huang meant that the poet must strike out in new directions and never shun unusual words —or even "raw words" (*ying-yü* 硬語). He must also base his observations on concrete things or events and pay attention to the thought-content of a poem. Diction (*tzu* 字), Huang argued, must be "refined" or "smelted" (*lien* 煉) as though by fire, and the strategy for a given line must be thought out beforehand, and strictly governed by regulations (*fa* 法).

Actually, a generation before Ch'en San-li's time, Sung poetry had already gained favor with several poets such as Ho Shao-chi 何紹基 (1799–1873), Wei Yüan 魏源 (1794–1857), and Cheng Chen 鄭珍 (1806–1864).* But what the T'ung-Kuang poets did was to elevate the rank of Huang T'ing-chien to that formerly reserved for Tu Fu and Han Yü, while advocating a new way of writing poetry by emulating the ancients. In this regard, Ch'en wielded such an influence that, in a book entitled *Kuang-Hsüan shih-t'an tien-chiang lu* 光宣詩壇點將錄 (An Honor Roll of Poets of the Kuang[-hsü] and Hsüan[-t'ung] Reigns) by Wang Pi-chiang 汪辟疆 [Wang Kuo-yüan 汪國垣, 1887–1966], Ch'en was rated the foremost poet among a "band" of 108 individuals. (Each poet was likened to a "general,"or one of the heroic characters in the novel *Shui-hu chuan* 水滸傳,* Ch'en San-li was compared to Sung Chiang 宋江, thereby heading the honor roll.)

Just as this emphasis on the technical perfection of verse was trumpeted in Sung times as an antidote to the heavy reliance on ornate and allusive language of the Hsi-k'un 西崑* poets, Ch'en San-li's insistence on the use of realistic, sometimes even strange, diction to describe ordinary events was actually a call to depart from the critical theory of "spirit and tone" (*shen-yün* 神韻), as championed by Wang Shih-chen 王士禎 (1634–1711)* earlier in the dynasty.

As pointed out by Kuo Shao-yü 郭紹虞 (1893–1984) and others, Ch'en San-li's critical tenets also owe much to the "flesh texture" (*chi-li* 肌理) theory of Weng Fang-kang 翁方綱 (1733–1818).

Put into practice, such a theory "translates," for instance, into a poem such as Ch'en's description of a journey by boat on a moonlit night ("Shih-i yüeh shih-ssu yeh fa Nan-ch'ang yüeh-chiang chou hsing, Ssu-shou chih erh" 十一月十四夜發南昌月江舟行，四首之二, revised from a version in *Waiting for the Unicorn*, p. 350):

> The dew's breath is like tiny insects,
> The force of the waves is like a bull
>   *couchant,*
> Bright moon is like a cocoon of
>   white silk,
> My boat on the river is enwrapped
>   therein.

露氣如微蟲，波勢如臥牛，
明月如繭素，裹我江上舟。

In this quatrain of twenty words the poet employs three extravagant, if not bizarre, similes, but what particularly catches the reader's attention is the word *kuo* 裹, "to wrap" or "to envelope." This word had never before been associated with "moonlight" in poetry. The result is a kind of "cragginess" or "severity" (denoted by the word *ch'iao* 峭) of diction, deliberately achieved and yet leaving no trace of the poet's deliberateness. This approach adheres closely to what is regarded by the Chiang-hsi poets as the highest achievement in poetry, the so-called "unregulated" or "unconventional" style (*ao-t'i* 拗體).

Ch'en San-li's success in writing this kind of poetry won enthusiastic endorsement from many contemporaries, such as Shen Tseng-chih 沈曾植 (1850–1922), Fan Tang-shih 范當世 (1854–1904), Mo Yu-chih 莫友芝 (1811–1871), and the poet-critic Ch'en Yen 陳衍 (1856–1937), as well as from his followers, such as

Cheng Hsiao-hsü 鄭孝胥 (1860–1938), Ch'en Pao-shen 陳寶琛 (1848–1935), Li Hsüan-kung 李宣龔 (1876–1966?), and Tseng K'o-tuan 曾克耑 (1900–?). The last five poets were all natives of Fukien, where the influence of the T'ung-Kuang School was particularly strong.

Ch'en San-li was fortunate in being survived not only by a sizeable group of talented younger contemporaries but also by sons, all of whom excelled in poetry and scholarship. The eldest, Ch'en Heng-k'o 陳衡恪 (1876–1923), composed some poems which a critic claimed were indistinguishable from those of his father; Heng-k'o was also a painter and an art historian. The best known of Ch'en San-li's five sons, however, was Ch'en Yin-k'o 陳寅恪 (1890–1969), an eminent Sanskrit scholar, authority on Buddhism, and literary historian whose death during the Cultural Revolution had a devastating impact on modern Chinese scholarship.

Editions and References
San-yüan ching-she shih 散原精舍詩 (Poems from the San-yüan Studio); *San-yüan ching-she shih pieh-chi* 散原精舍詩別集 (Supplemental Poems from the San-yüan Studio). Shanghai: Commercial Press, 1909 and 1922 respectively; both reprinted in 1 volume as *San-yüan ching-she shih* 詩 (Taipei: Taiwan Commercial Press, 1962).
San-yüan ching-she wen-chi 文集 (Prose Writings from the San-yüan Studio). Shanghai: Chung-hua Book Company, 1949; rpt. Taipei, 1961.
San-yüan ching-she shih-chi 散原精舍詩集 (Collected Poems from the San-yüan Studio). Taipei: Taiwan Commercial Press, 1961. A reproduction of Ch'en San-li's poems written from 1909 to 1926 in his own calligraphy.

Translations
Waiting for the Unicorn, pp. 350-2.

Studies
Ch'ien, Chi-po 錢基博. "Ch'en San-li." In Ch'ien's *Hsien-tai Chung-kuo wen-hsüeh*

shih 現代中國文學史. 4th ed. Shanghai, 1936; rpt. Hong Kong: Lung-men, 1965, pp. 209-245. An overview of Ch'en San-li and the school of poets which attached itself to him, chiefly Ch'en Yen 陳衍 and Cheng Hsiao-hsü 鄭孝胥, both from Foochow.
Ch'ien, Chung-lien 錢仲聯. *Ming-Ch'ing shih-wen yen-chiu ts'ung-k'an* 明清詩文研究叢刊. First series. Soochow: Chiang-su Shih-yüan, 1982, pp. 188-96 (three separate articles on Ch'en San-li, Ch'en Yen, and the T'ung-Kuang Style).
___. "Lun T'ung-Kuang t'i" 論同光體. In his *Meng-t'iao-an Ch'ing-tai wen-hsüeh lun-chi* 夢苕庵清代文學論集.Tsinan: Ch'i-Lu Shu-she, 1963, pp. 111-34.
Republican China, I:225-8.

Irving Yucheng Lo

Ch'eng-kung Sui 成公綏 (231–273, *tzu,* Tzu-an 子安), was from Pai-ma 白馬 prefecture in the Eastern Commandery 東郡 (east of modern Hua 滑 county, Honan). He was an accomplished scholar and poet of the Western Chin, best known for his *fu* 賦 (prose-poems, rhapsodies).* His biography in the "Wen-yüan" 文苑 (Garden of Literati) section of the *Chin shu* 晉書 (92:2371-75) is almost entirely taken up by complete versions of two of his *fu,* and little information is provided about his life. He is described almost iconographically as showing great intelligence when young and being well-read in the classical literature. Although growing up in impoverished circumstances, he strove not for riches and fame, but for personal quietude. We are told that his poetic writings were polished, yet he did not seek to make them known. They were not highly regarded until they came to the attention of Chang Hua 張華 (232–300),* who recommended Ch'eng-kung in 255 to serve as erudite (*po-shih* 博士) in the Wei 魏 Ministry of Ceremony (*T'ai-ch'ang* 太常) to which he himself had recently been appointed. Other information tells that despite

Ch'eng-kung Sui's talent in writing, especially of *fu,* he had a severe speech impediment that compelled him to respond to rapid questions in writing. After entering official service, Ch'eng-kung Sui later served for a time (probably *ca.* 260–62) as Assistant in the Palace Library (*Mi-shu lang* 秘書郎), rising to the position of vice director (*ch'eng* 丞). Between August 264–February 268, Ch'eng-kung, then commandant of cavalry (*ch'i tu-wei* 騎都尉), assisted in the large-scale revision of the corpus of laws and penal codes undertaken by a commission of fourteen persons under the supervision of Chia Ch'ung 賈充 (217–282); this would become the code of laws for the Chin, whose rule began in February, 266. In 269, as Attendant Gentleman in the Secretariat (*Chung-shu shih-lang* 中書侍郎), Ch'eng-kung was commanded along with Chang Hua and others to compose dynastic ritual hymns for use in imperial ceremonies; Ch'eng-kung's extant compositions include a suite of fifteen songs to be sung at dawn convocations, and one song toasting to the emperor's longevity. Ch'eng-kung Sui spent nearly all his career associated with the court; his highest office was that of chief compiler (*chu-tso lang* 著作郎). His one posting outside the capital was as Prefect (*ling* 令) of Ch'ang-an (章安) in Lin-hai 臨海 commandery (about 40 miles southeast of modern Lin-hai County, Chekiang), where it is said that he composed a "Yün fu" 雲賦 (*Fu* on Clouds) while gazing at the river from his offices atop the Ch'ih-lan 赤欄 Bridge. The collected literary works of Ch'eng-kung Sui, amounting to ten *chüan,* were intact at least through the T'ang.

Previous to his first official appointment under the Wei, Ch'eng-kung Sui had composed a eulogy for Ssu-ma I 司馬懿 (178–251); grandfather of the first Chin emperor), and a *fu* on the crow (inspired when the auspicious bird nested at his residence). It is likely that he had also by then composed his ambitious "T'ien Ti fu" 天地賦 (*Fu* on Heaven and Earth), one of the two *fu* contained in his biography. Ch'eng-kung composed this *fu* because no one before him had undertaken to extol in writing the splendor of the cosmos. It is a tightly woven composite of astrological, geographical, and mythological lore. The other piece contained in his biography is his "Hsiao fu" 嘯賦 (*Fu* on Whistling), a description in musical terms of the mystical Taoist breathing technique *hsiao* 嘯. This is the most celebrated of Ch'eng-kung Sui's writings, and was chosen for inclusion in the *Wen-hsüan* 文選* (*chüan* 18). Ch'eng-kung may have composed this *fu ca.* 263, during a stint in the secretariat. The piece blends a flowing description of the *hsiao*'s melodic sound, with the lore associated with the art of whistling. While Ch'eng-kung himself apparently experimented with the arcane technique, he probably modeled the protagonist of his *fu* on the most renowned whistling adept of his time, Sun Teng 孫登. Sun lived as a recluse in the Su-men 蘇門 Mountains, not far from Ch'eng-kung's home in modern Honan, and has been immortalized by the often related anecdote in which Juan Chi 阮籍 (210–263)* encounters Sun's mystical, majestic whistle. While only the two *fu* contained in Ch'eng-kung's biography in the *Chin shu* have been preserved intact, portions or quotations are extant for twenty-two others that he composed. Among other topics, he wrote about musical instruments, the Yellow River, the writing brush, birds, flora, and insects. Ch'eng-kung Sui was widely praised by his contemporaries (especially by Chang Hua) and later literati for the excellence of his *fu.* Lu Yün 陸雲 (262–301),** a younger contemporary, wrote to his brother Lu Chi 陸機 (261–301)* that while Chi's literary prose was superior to that of Ch'eng-kung Sui, his *fu* were not. And Liu Hsieh 劉勰 (*ca.* 465–*ca.* 522) in his *Wen-hsin tiao-lung* 文

心雕龍* also cited Ch'eng-kung's *fu* as having made significant contributions to the genre. Nevertheless, by the end of the Ming most of Ch'eng-kung's compositions were no longer extant, and Chang P'u 張溥 (1602–1641), compiler of the remains of Cheng-kung's works, commented that he preferred the prefaces to Cheng-kung's *fu* to the *fu* themselves. In addition to *fu* and ritual hymns, parts of a number of compositions on a variety of topics also exist; among others, these contain a piece on clerical script (which properly should be considered a *fu*), a treatise on the money god, praises to the chrysanthemum, an admonition to fire, five poems, and a piece in the popular genre known as "Sevens" (see *Ch'i* 七**).

Editions and References

Ch'eng-kung Tzu-an chi 成公子安籍. In *Pai-san* (*chüan* 21).
Liu-ch'ao wen, 59:1a-10b
Lu, *Nan-pei-ch'ao shih*, 1:584-585; 2:823-824.

Translations

Knechtges, *Wen xuan*, 3:314-323.
Mair, *Anthology*, pp. 429-434.
von Zach, *Anthologie*, 1:258-261.

Alan Berkowitz
Swarthmore College

ch'i 七 (sevens) is a designation for a genre initiated by Mei Ch'eng's 枚乘 (d. 141 B.C.)* "Ch'i fa" 七發 (Seven Stimuli). All of the *ch'i* pieces of later generations without exception are modeled on Mei's work. The 'Seven Stimuli" is constructed in the form of a dialogue between a guest from the state of Wu 吳 and a prince of the state of Ch'u 楚, a well-known convention in the *fu** tradition. The poem opens with the prince suffering an illness resulting from his extravagant life at court. A persona of Mei Ch'eng himself who was a native of the Wu area, the guest appears to have a deep understanding of medi-

cine and volunteers to diagnose the prince. Like a doctor, the guest first inquires of the prince's condition and then gives a detailed description of his symptoms and their causes. He points out that long-term overindulgence in physical comfort is the major source of the prince's illness. He cautions that the prince cannot be cured by herb, cauterization, or acupuncture, but only by listening to the "essential words and marvelous doctrines" 要言妙道 of the sages. After the prince agrees to his suggestion, the guest proceeds to present six most fascinating allurements in the world, including the best zither music, gustatory delicacies, thoroughbred horses, a journey to a scenic spot accompanied by most learned men of letters and the most beautiful ladies, a royal hunt, and a spectacular view of the tidal bore of the Ch'ü-chiang 曲江 (modern Yangchow, Kiangsu) River.

At the end of the elaborate description of each enticement, the guest asks the prince if he is able to rise from his sickbed to enjoy it. The answer is of course always negative since the prince feels powerless to carry out such activities. However, after he hears about the sixth enticement—the tidal bore—signs of recovery suddenly appear on his face. This critical step prepares him for the seventh and the last enticement, the "essential words and marvelous doctrines" which eventually heal him. It is interesting that Mei Ch'eng pours all his eloquence into the previous six enticements, while summarily treating the "marvelous doctrines" by merely referring to the sages who uttered them: Confucius, Mencius, Chuang-tzu, Yang Chu 楊朱, Mo-tzu, and other Taoist philosophers.

The most conspicuous rhetorical aspect of the "Seven Stimuli" is the "extended doubled persuasion" (see Knechtges and Swanson in *Studies* below). On the one hand, the guest points out that the prince must temper his own immoderation in sensual pleasures to remove the root of illness, while on the other hand, he uses these same sensual pleasures as enticements to persuade the prince. Given two alternatives, the prince must chose but one. As soon as he chooses the first, he is cured. Similar techniques were employed in the *Chan-kuo ts'e* 戰國策.*

In terms of form—a "seven"—Mei Ch'eng's work is the earliest extant example. Although some pieces had earlier been entitled *ch'i* (sevens) or *chiu* 九 (nines), they differ from Mei's "Sevens." For example, the "Ch'i-chien" 七諫 (Seven Remonstrances), the "Chiu-huai" 九懷 (Nine Regrets), and the "Chiu-t'an" 九歎 (Nine Laments) collected in the *Ch'u-tz'u* 楚辭* all used numbers in their titles. However, these works all consisted of seven or nine independent piece, and were not holistically organized works like the "sevens."

Rather than tracing their origins to these numerical titles, the *ch'i* seems to be related to the *fu* 賦. In his *Wen-hsin tiao-lung* 文心雕龍,* Liu Hsieh 劉勰 (*ca.* 465–*ca.* 522) treats the *ch'i* together with the *tui-wen* 對問 and *lien-chu* 連珠 in the chapter on "miscellaneous writings" (*tsa-wen* 雜文) The three genres are all influenced by the *fu.* The "Seven Stimuli" reveals its connection with the epideictic *fu* through its dialogue framework, numerous parallelisms, descriptive binomes (both alliterative and rhyming), extensive cataloguing, and hyperbole. Each enticement provides a perfect arena for the author to display his literary skill. The descriptions of the zither music and the tidal bore in the "Seven Stimuli" are so extraordinary that they became a model for many *yung-wu* 詠物 pieces of later periods. Furthermore, the "Sevens" share an identical purpose with many of the Han epideictic rhapsodies: persuasion. In the Han, the representative *fu*-writers, Ssu-ma Hsiang-ju 司馬相如 (*ca.* 179–117 B.C.)* and Yang Hsiung 揚雄 (53 B.C.–A.D. 18),* whose works are representative of the long *fu* tradition, always aimed to persuade the ruler in their rhapsodies. In the *ch'i,* the authors without exception structure their work around a debate between two fictional characters, one of whom tries to persuade the other. Thus, the *ch'i* should be considered a subgenre of the *fu.*

Over time the "Sevens" underwent transformations in form and theme. Originally intended to admonish a ruler to abandon his extravagant life-style, in later periods it became a common theme for an eloquent speaker to attempt to persuade a wise man in retirement to enter officialdom. Chang Heng's 張衡 (78–139)* "Ch'i-pien" 七辯 (Seven Debates), Ts'ao Chih's 曹植 (192–232)* "Ch'i-ch'i" 七啟 (Seven Inspirations), and Chang Hsieh's 張協 (d. 307) "Ch'i-ming" 七命 (Seven Counsels) are the most famous examples of this type of *ch'i.* In all of these works, the protagonist is always a recluse who decides to withdraw from the dusty world. The persuader is someone who is reluctant to see a talented man remain unemployed and detached from the court. He tries to present six kinds of worldly pleasure in order to rouse the hermit to reenter officialdom. But the first six enticements are usually fruitless, the critical moment always occurring in the seventh in which the persuader presents the ideal political world created by a (the current) sagacious Emperor. It is this last enticement of political perfection that convinces the recluse. Accordingly, the *ch'i* pieces in this category eulogize the current Emperor and his court. Since during the Han era many *fu* were meant to eulogize the ruler, this is another example of the ties between the two forms.

Throughout the Six Dynasties, although the seven allurements in *ch'i* may have varied, music, food, wine, women, weapons, horses, hunting, architecture, and worldly accomplishment were the usual subjects. In the T'ang and Sung, the *ch'i* underwent further transformation. Yüan Chieh 元結 (719–772)* employs the title in his 'Ch'i pu-ju" 七不如 (Seven I Am No Better Than), but totally overthrows *ch'i* conventions by claiming that he is no better than seven things: a child, sleeping at night, illness, drunkenness, silence, absence of desire, and plants. It is a completely personal piece that skillfully uses the *ch'i* structure. Another creative example is Liu Tsung-yüan's 柳宗元 (773–819)* "Chin wen" 晉問 (Asking about the Chin). Although not titled a *ch'i,* the seven answers to the guest's question in the essay resembles the conventional *ch'i* form. This piece is based on a dialogue between Mr. Liu 柳 the host, and Master Wu 吳, the guest. The seven passages described by Mr. Liu include Chin's 晉 geography/topography, advanced metallurgy, great thoroughbreds, rich forests, abundant fish, fresh salt, and the impressive accomplishments of Duke Wen 文 of the Chin (r. 636–628 B.C.). Liu thereby uses the Chin to refer to his contemporary government and Chin's strong points to imply his hopes for the T'ang regime.

In the Sung, Ch'ao Pu-chih 晁補之 (1053–1110) seems to have been inspired by Liu Tsung-yüan to write a "Ch'i-shu" 七述 (Seven Narrations), seven lengthy passages portraying the famed landscape and distinguished personages of Hangchow. Ch'ao's work turns about the earlier convention of opposing reclusion to eulogize the pleasures of the eremitic life in Hangchow. Wang Ying-lin's 王應麟 (1223–1296)* "Ch'i-kuan" 七觀 (Seven Spectacles) takes this a step further, turning the recluse into a persuader himself. In "Seven Spectacles," Mr. Tung-kuo 東郭 successfully convinces the young, rich Mr. Nan-chou 南州 to become one of his disciples. Interestingly, one of the "spectacles" Wang describes is the philosophy of Neo-Confucian masters such as Chou Tun-i 周敦頤 (1017–1073) and Chu Hsi 朱熹 (1130–1200).

The only *ch'i* author in the Ming is Chin Shih 金寔 who wrote the "Han-mo Lin ch'i-keng" 翰墨林七更 (Seven Changes in the Forest of Brushes and Ink). The seven items depicted are elegant music, chess, calligraphy, painting, writing in general, the essays of the Eight Masters of T'ang and Sung, and the Confucian Classics. By this time the genre, following general literary trends, had become a piece written by literati for literati.

The Ch'ing dynasty saw several notable *ch'i,* including Huang Tsung-hsi's 黃宗羲 (1610–1695)* "Ch'i-kuai" 七怪 (Seven Bizarre Things), Ling T'ing-k'an 凌廷堪 "Ch'i-chieh" 七戒 (Seven Warnings), Hung Liang-chi 洪亮吉 (1746–1809)* "Ch'i-chao" 七招 (Seven Summons). Huang's satirical piece takes the form of an essay that deals with seven corrupt practices among scholars. Ling's work harkens back to Wang Ying-lin's "Seven Spectacles." This rhapsodic essay, based on a conversation between two scholars, elaborates a series of fields of scholarship (calligraphy and painting, refined literature, human nature, economy, and historiography) before finally focusing on the exegesis of the Confucian Classics. Hung combined the "Chao hun" 招魂 (Summons of the Soul) and "Ta chao" 大招 (The Great Summons) from the *Ch'u-tz'u* 楚辭* with the "Sevens." He created a fictional character, Master Vacuous (K'ung-t'ung 空同主人) whose soul leaves his body, while his friend Sir Foolish (Yü-kung 愚公) climbs up a mountain to summon it back. Sir Foolish displays the usual five enticements–wine, delicacies, women, etc.–to little effect. His sixth allure is a demonstration that the current government encourages scholarship and there are specialists in all the classics, histories, and major works of literature. Suddenly the soul of Master Vacuous appears. The piece culminates as usual in its final allurement when Sir Foolish presents the erudite scholars he knows personally and their achievements. With this, the soul returns to the body of Master Vacuous.

The history of the "Sevens" is impressive—this minor genre survived nearly two millennia. Its enduring life span must be related to its form which leaves much freedom for the writer's imagination. Indeed, in each era were writers who modified the original form of the "Seven Stimuli" to create their own "sevens," thereby demonstrating as well the tendency for different genres (especially minor genres) to influence each other by sharing conventions and/or structures.

Translations

Frankel, *The Flowering Plum,* pp. 186-211.

Mair, Victor H. *Mei Cherng's "Seven Stimuli" and Wang Bor's "Pavilion of King Teng," Chinese Poems for Princes. Studies in Asian Thought and Religion,* V. 11. Lewiston, New York: The Edwin Mellen Press, 1988.

von Zach, *Anthologie,* 2:607-17.

Studies

Fujiwara, Takashi 藤原尚. "'Shichihatsu' no shûji ni tsuite—sono rizumu to tenko" 七發の修辭について—そのリズムと典故. In *Obi Hakushi koki kinen Chûgoku bungaku ronshû* 小尾博士古稀記中国文学論集念. Tokyo: Kyûko Shoin, 1983, pp. 39-55.

Ho, Kenneth P. H. "The Seven Stimuli of Mei Sheng," *The Chu Hai Journal* 11 (1980), pp. 205-16.

Hsü, Shih-ying 許世瑛. "Mei Ch'eng 'Ch'i fa' yü ch'i mo-ni-che" 枚乘七發與其摹擬者, *Ta-lu tsa-chih* 6.8 (1953): 11-17. The most comprehensive survey of the *ch'i* pieces.

Knechtges, David R. and Jerry Swanson. "Seven Stimuli for the Prince: The *Ch'i-fa* of Mei Cheng," *Monumenta Serica* 29 (1970-71): 99-116.

Scott, John. *Love and Protest.* London: Rapp and Whiting, 1972, pp. 36-48.

Wu, Hsiao-ju 吳小如. "Mei Ch'eng 'Ch'i fa' Li Shan chu ting-pu" 枚乘七發李善注訂補. *Wen-shih* 2 (April 1963):129-37.

Yü, Kuan-ying 余冠英. "Ch'i-fa chieh-shao" 七發介紹, *Wen-hsüeh chih-shih* 10 (1959): 19-20.

Jui-lung Su
The National University of Singapore

Ch'in Kuan 秦觀 (*tzu,* Shao-yu 少游, earlier *tzu,* T'ai-hsü 太虛, *hao* Han-kou chü-shih 邗溝居士, also Huai-hai chü-shih 淮海居士, 1049–1100), is invariably defined in the public imagination by something that almost certainly never happened: his having loved and married "Su Hsiao-mei" 蘇小妹, the little sister of his friend Su Shih 蘇軾 (1037–1101).* Although it is only a legend, probably from a Ming opera, the story dramatizes two facts: that Ch'in Kuan was part of the celebrated circle of poets who surrounded Su Shih, and that his talents found their best use in *tz'u** lyrics of sentiment and romance. No matter how painstakingly scholars try to rehabilitate him as a serious political thinker and poetic chronicler of a genteel nation threatened by conquest, it is his carefully delineated, erotically charged yet decorous *tz'u* which have captivated most readers since his time. His strengths in other literary areas were of the sort that equipped him to produce extra power whenever he turned to writing *tz'u.* If Northern Sung literature began as a contest between extreme ornamentation (Hsi-k'un poetry–see *Hsi-k'un ch'ou-ch'ang chi* 西崑酬唱集*) and extreme plainness (Liu K'ai 柳開, 947–1000,** Wang Yü-ch'eng 王禹偁, 954–1001,* and others); and if the next stage was dominated by three generations of writers who knew how to be ornamental when it was seemly, but leaned toward plainness and utility (Fan Chung-yen 范仲淹, 989–1052,* Ou-yang Hsiu 歐陽修, 1007–1072,* Wang An-shih 王安石, 1021–1086,* and Su Shih), then Ch'in Kuan seems to have been part of a newer generation who still valued the plainness but did not cling to it, and allowed more florid emotion into their verse and prose.

Ch'in was born at Kiukiang, when his father was en route to a government post. His home was at Kao-yu 高郵, north of Yangchow on the Grand Canal. As a young man he probably supervised the family farm, and may have labored with his own hands. He lost his father at age 14 *sui*, married a local girl, Hsü Wen-mei 徐文美, at 19 *sui*, all the while studying for the examinations. He read avidly from the arts of war during his early twenties, a time during which the prime minister Wang An-shih was promoting his New Policies, among them a redirecting of the civil-service examinations from poetry and scholar-ship to the analysis of actual state affairs. Ch'in Kuan, steeped in *shih***and *fu,** retrained himself to write in the new style, but did not completely accept the new orthodoxy. He had good connect-ions among moderate conservative thinkers. One of them, Sun Chüeh 孫覺 (1028–1090), who along with Ch'in's father had been a student of Hu Yüan 胡瑗 (993–1059), helped introduce Ch'in to Su Shih as early as 1074, when Ch'in was only 26 *sui* and Su only 39. Ch'in also went on outings with Su Shih's friend Ts'an-liao-tzu 參寥子, and exchanged dozens of poems with the socially prominent Ch'eng Shih-meng 程師孟 (*tzu,* Kung-p'i 公闢, *fl.* 1062–1082). But he stayed in Kao-yu for most of his first 33 years. In 1082, at 34 *sui,* he failed the *chin-shih,* then took the long route home, visiting Su Shih in exile at Huang-chou. When Su came out of exile two years later, he enthusiastically recom-mended Ch'in Kuan to Wang An-shih, who read and praised Ch'in's writing samples, but was already retired and not much immediate use to him.

Ch'in's career, which started at 37 *sui* and lasted only fifteen years, coincided with the anti-reform party's headiest triumphs and harshest losses, as Wang An-shih's New Policies met their demise and subsequent resurrection. Ch'in obtained the *chin-shih* in 1085, the year in which the reformist Emperor Shen-tsung 神宗 (r. 1068–1085) died and the new Prime Minister Ssu-ma Kuang 司馬光 (1019–1086) began to replace the entire program with his conservative agenda. This was the Yüan-yu 元祐 reign (1086–1093) of the boy emperor Che-tsung 哲宗 under the Dowager Empress, and Ch'in belonged to the dominant "Yüan-yu Faction" 元祐黨 named for that era, perhaps as much by fate as by choice. Assigned to Ts'ai-chou 蔡州 (modern Ju-nan 汝南 in southern Honan), he did not have a chance to join the restoration juggernaut in the capital until 1087, when Su Shih recommended him for the prestigious, rarely-offered *Hsien-liang-fang-cheng* (賢良方正, "Worthy, Frank and Proper") decree examination which had made Su a celebrity twenty-six years earlier. Su probably guided Ch'in in the writing of his fifty examination essays, which still survive and are considered good. But Ch'in did not pass, and returned to Ts'ai-chou. The conservatives themselves were split: being Su Shih's protege meant that Ch'in was treated as one of the "Shu 蜀 Faction" within the conservative movement, and thus subject to harass-ment by Ssu-ma Kuang's followers in the "Loyang Faction." In 1090, Ch'in was summoned to a palace library position, in 1091 promoted to proof-reader, only to be impeached from that rank by Loyang-party censors. Fierce protests by Su Ch'e 蘇轍 (1039–1112)* and others kept Ch'in from being further demoted or sent away. By 1093, Su Shih, Huang T'ing-chien 黃庭堅 (1045–1105),* Ch'ao Pu-chih 晁補之 (1053–1110), Chang Lei 張耒 (1054–1114)** and Ch'in Kuan all served in the capital simultaneously for the first and only time; these *Su-men Ssu Hsüeh-shih* 蘇門四學士 (Four Scholars at Su Shih's Gate) became an actual group. Ch'en Shih-tao 陳師道 (1052–1102),* who had long been one of Ch'in's staunch boosters, is often listed as a fifth disciple. This was a group bound by friendship and spiritual affinity; as writers they were too diverse to be a literary school. That year they faced a common threat, greater than that from the other conservatives: when the Empress Dowager died and Che-tsung 哲宗 (r. 1086–1100) took over the government himself, the regime reactivated the reform policies, led this time by vindictive zealots. Purges began in 1094. "Su's Scholars" were all sent away as punishment for various misdeeds, Ch'in Kuan first assigned to Hangchow, then Ch'u-chou 處州 farther south, then Ch'en-chou 郴州 (Hunan) in 1096, where he wrote an ode to the God of the Tung-t'ing Lake and poems to Ch'ang-sha courtesans; next came Heng-chou 橫州 (Kwangsi) in 1097, which inspired the *tz'u* "Tsui-hsiang ch'un" 醉鄉春 (Spring in the Land of Drink); finally the dreaded Lei-chou 雷州 (southern Kwangtung) in 1099, where he drafted his own funeral song and corresponded with Su Shih, who was across the water on Hainan Island in the deepest exile of all the Yüan-yu officials. In 1100, when Hui-tsung 徽宗 took the throne and began calling back the exiles, Su Shih stopped at Lei-chou on his way north and saw Ch'in for the last time. Ch'in died that fall, it is said in a drunken doze; Su died the next year. Ch'in was rehabilitated posthumously in 1102, but in 1103 the tide shifted, his name was inscribed on the infamous stone slab as one of 128 Yüan-yu Partisans, and his works were banned. These names were not cleared again until 1130, under the Southern Sung.

Ch'in Kuan's *shih,* numbering over 400, sort themselves roughly into three stages. Poetry from before he held office tends to appear in bursts of travel pieces, often written in conjunction with poems by his companions. His career in Ts'ai-chou and the capital produced an appropriate mix of socially-aware and merely social verse. But the truly extraordinary pieces are the few dozen from his exile, complex because they combine a dark awareness of how serious his plight was, along with what seems to have been a genuine love for the landscape, fragrances and customs of the tropical south. Few other poets have written as evocatively about Kwangtung as Ch'in did.

His stirring prose, admired during his lifetime, is less agile and surprising than that of his mentor Su Shih, and is not read as often. Without question, it is Ch'in's *tz'u* that will keep him famous. Ch'en Shih-tao supposedly said that while Su Shih wrote *tz'u* as if they were *shih,* Ch'in wrote *shih* that resembled *tz'u.* Although that has been considered a backhanded compliment for Ch'in, if it was a compliment at all, and he has many *shih* for which it is not true, it can help us understand how he approached the writing of verse in general. His *tz'u* offer titanic emotions veiled only partially by the nuanced language. He favored the short *hsiao-ling* 小令 over the longer *man-tz'u* 慢詞 that Liu Yung 柳永 (987–1053)* had used with such power, and his style is *Wan-yüeh* 婉約 (Delicate Restraint)** rather than Su Shih's *Hao-fang* 豪放 (Heroic and Unrestricted)**; but one could say that Ch'in wrote *hsiao-ling* on a monumental scale similar to the best quatrains, or that his style was *Wan-yüeh* "with muscle." The hushed thrill of the urban demimonde pervades his lyrics. He wrote of dreams throughout his life. His moods—sunny, petulant, bleak, flip, nostalgic—vary even more than those in Su Shih's lyrics, and, unlike supposedly typical Sung poets, he seldom presents overt opinions. Instead he marshals the little words, chooses verbs meticulously, and guides the alert reader through minute twists of tone and mental rhythms. He is a master at laying down conclusions just strong enough to let the flavor waft past the final line. And, as with his *shih,* one can sense his *tz'u* maturing in theme and technique, from the fully-conscious, verb-bedecked "Hills wipe the thinnest of clouds / Sky sticks to withered grasses. . . ." (山抹微雲，天黏衰草), which opens an early "Man-t'ing fang" 滿庭芳 about parting lovers, down to the equally focused but far more somber second half of the "Tsui hsiang ch'un" 醉鄉春 written on a clammy spring day deep in exile: ". . . Gentle smiles: final distillation from the Earth God's jug / Are what that half-split coconut ladled up for you and me. / I found I was toppling. / Lunged in panic toward the bed – / For broad and spacious is the Land of Drink, unlike the little universe of men" (社甕釀成微笑，半缺椰瓢共舀。覺傾倒，急投床，醉鄉廣大人間小).

Critics have worried that Ch'in Kuan's writing is not manly enough. Yüan Hao-wen 元好問 (1190–1257)* defined the issue when he wrote of Ch'in's "female diction" (*fu-jen yü* 婦女語) and "women's verse" (*nü-lang shih* 女郎詩)—phrases that haunt Ch'in Kuan studies to this day, abetted sometimes by the Su Hsiao-mei legend. Even Ch'in's sympathizers often point out overly subtle weak spots which they feel his many passages of vigorous prose and sober ancient-style *shih* do not entirely make up for. His life-long involvement with women of the "Blue Houses" —including during every stage of his career and banishment—though it gave his *tz'u* passion, authenticity, and indeed their very reason for being, does not help posterity place him as high in the pantheon as his talent might warrant, and his disappointing official resumé diminishes him next to Su Shih or Ou-yang Hsiu. It is largely his political sincerity, manifested in his essays on statecraft, that spares him from suffering Liu Yung's talented-wastrel reputation. But Ch'en Shih-tao's affectionate "Introduction to Ch'in Shao-yu's New Courtesy Name" ("Ch'in Shao-yu tzu hsü" 秦少游字序) points the way to a useful perspective about Ch'in's character, by linking Ch'in to the unquestionably manly Tu Mu 杜牧 (803–852),* who almost three centuries before had also poured out his heart in Yangchow pleasure-palaces, mastered the old military writings, and dreamed of saving the country. Ch'in emulated Tu Mu most of his life, interrupted only by a period of frustration and regret when he changed his *tzu* to Shao-yu in honor of the Later Han recluse Ma Shao-yu 馬少游, who had stayed on the family estate cultivating the art of contentment while his cousins fought the wars far away. Ch'en Shih-tao understood how Ch'in might feel frustrated, living as a *de facto* recluse with no advanced degree, under an incompatible regime; Ch'en agreed that continuing to stay out of public life was an honorable option. But it was by far the easier option: so easy that a Ma Shao-yu, simply muddling through a recluse's existence, had achieved more glory than Tu Mu ever attained with all his wit in the worldly arena, simply because Tu's activist path inevitably offered more chances to stumble. Ch'en was right that Ch'in Kuan's talent would soon pull him back onto that activist path, but was wrong in predicting that Ch'in's career would outshine Tu Mu's. Factional struggles set Ch'in back just as they had Tu. But with both men, struggling for success only to meet with failure seems to have brought greater depth to their already complex minds. Depth and complexity, of course, are exactly what literature needs, and they pervade Ch'in Kuan's poetry. Exact labels for his other qualities will vary from one era to the next.

Editions and References

Ch'üan Sung shih, 18:1053-1068.12063-12158.

Ch'üan Sung tz'u, 1:454-486.

Huai-hai chi 淮海集. *SPTK* and *SPPY* editions contain all works including *tz'u.* Serviceable but unannotated, and collation is superseded by Hsü P'ei-chün's editions.

Huai-hai chi chien-chu 淮海集箋注. Hsü P'ei-chün 徐培均, annot. 3v. Shanghai: Shanghai Ku-chi, 1994. This and the next work used together constitute the most definitive edition to date, and the only complete annotated collection of Ch'in's works. Introductory essays, biographical and critical materials make these works even more useful.

Huai-hai chü-shih ch'ang-tuan chü 淮海居士長短句. Hsü P'ei-chün, annot. Shanghai: Shang-hai Ku-chi, 1985. Most complete collection of Ch'in's *tz'u,* annotated with biographical material and thorough discussion of textual history; appends a chronology of Ch'in's *tz'u.*

Huai-hai chü-shih ch'ang-tuan chü. Rpt. Hong Kong: Longman, 1965. Facsimile of Sung edition printed at Kao-yu.

Huai-hai tz'u chien-chu 淮海詞箋注. Yang Shih-ming 楊士明, annot. Chengtu: Ssuch'uan Jen-min, 1984.

"Huai-hai shih-chu, fu tz'u chiao-chu" 淮海詩注，附詞校注. Hsü Wen-chu 徐文助, annot. In *T'ai-wan Shih-ta kuo-wen chi-k'an* (1968.6): 1-194.

Ts'an shu 蠶書. 1 *chüan.* Treatise on silkworms, attributed to Ch'in Kuan, but possibly written by one of his sons. Most accessible edition may be in *Chih-pu-tsu Chai ts'ung-shu* 知不足齋叢書.

Translations

Liu, *Lyricists,* pp. 99-120.
Mair, *Anthology,* p. 329-332.
Strassberg, *Inscribed Landscapes,* pp. 199-204.

Studies

Chin, Shih-ch'iu 金實秋. *Ch'in Kuan yen-chiu tzu-liao* 秦觀研究資料. Tientsin: T'ien-chin Ku-chi, 1988.

Chiu, Chai 疚齋. "Huai-hai chi-chien ch'ang-pien" 淮海集箋長編, *T'ung-sheng yüeh-k'an* 3.9 (1943.11): 1-28.

Chu, Te-ts'ai 朱德才. "Ch'in Shao-yu ti 'Fu-ya kuei-tsung'"秦少游的復雅歸宗, *Wen-shih-che* 178 (1987.1): 55-61.

Hsü, P'ei-chün 徐培均. "Ch'in Kuan tz'u nien-piao" 秦觀詞年表, in *Huai-hai Chü-shih ch'ang-tuan chü* 淮海居士長短句. Shanghai: Shang-hai Ku-chi, 1985.

Advocates a different set of dates (1049-1105) for Ch'in Kuan.

Josephs, Hilary. "The Tz'u of Ch'in Kuan (1049–1100)." Unpublished Ph. D. dissertation, Harvard University, 1973.

Liang, Jung-jo 梁容若. "Ch'in Kuan ti sheng-p'ing yü chu-tso" 秦觀的生平與著作, *Shu ho jen* 210 (May, 1973): 5-8.

Lin, Yutang 林語堂. "Su Hsiao-mei wu ch'i jen k'ao" 蘇小妹無其人考, *Chung-yang jih-pao fu-k'an* (March 26, 1952). Also Chuang Lien 莊練, "Kuan-yü Su Hsiao-mei" 關於蘇小妹, in Ibid. (January 29, 1969), and Lin Yutang, "Ta 答 Chuang Lien 'Kuan-yü Su Hsiao-mei," Ibid. (February 5, 1969).

Nakata, Yûjirô 中田勇次郎. "Shin Waikai shibun nenpô" 秦淮海詩文年譜, *Shina-gaku* 10 (1942): 399-436.

Wang, Ch'u-jung 王初蓉. "Ch'in Shao-yu Hsien-sheng nien-p'u" 秦少游先生年譜, *Chung-hua hsüeh-yüan* 2 (1968): 136-168.

Wang, Pao-chen 王保珍. *Ch'in Shao-yu yen-chiu* 秦少游研究. Taipei: Hsüeh-hai, 1977.

Yü, Chao-i 于肇怡. "Ch'in Kuan yü Huang T'ing-chien" 秦觀與黃庭堅, *Wen-hsüeh shih-chieh* 36 (1962.12): 60-66.

Jonathan Pease
Portland State University

Chiu-seng t'i 九僧體 (Nine Monks Style) is the name given to the poetic style which continued the so-called "Late T'ang Style" in the Five Dynasties and early Sung dynasty, especially in the works of the "Nine Monks." "Late T'ang Style" is a misleading label, since by it these poets meant the verse of a number of rather minor ninth-century poets like Chia Tao 賈島 (779–843)* and Yao Ho 姚合 (775–*ca.* 845), and not the poetics of major late-T'ang poets such as Li Shang-yin 李商隱 (*ca.* 813–858) and Tu Mu 杜牧 (803–852).*

This style can first be seen in the writings of two poets of the Five Dynasties, Liu Tung 劉洞 and Hsia Pao-sung 夏寶松, both recluses at Mount Lu 廬. During the early Sung, those fond of this style include P'an Lang 潘閬 (*d.* 1009), Wei Yeh 魏野 (960–1019), Lin

Pu 林逋 (967–1028), Chung Fang 種放 (956–1015), Lu San-chiao 魯三交 in addition to the Nine Monks.

Although lists may vary, Chou Hui 周輝 (b. 1126) records their names in his *Ch'ing-po tsa-chih* 清波雜誌 as: Hsi-chou 希晝 of Chien-nan 劍南 (modern Szechwan), Pao-hsien 保暹 of Chin-hua 金華 (in Chekiang), Wen-chao 文兆 of Nan-yüeh 南越 (southern part of modern Chekiang), Hsing-chao 行肇 of T'ien-t'ai 天台 (Chekiang), Chien-chang 簡長 of Wo-chou 沃州 (in modern Hopei), Wei-feng 惟鳳 of Ch'ing-ch'eng 青城 (in Szechwan), Yü-chao 宇昭 from Chiang-tung 江東 (modern Kiangsu), Huai-ku 懷古 from O-mei 峨眉 (Szechwan), and Hui-ch'ung 惠崇 (d. 1018) from Huai-nan 淮南 (modern Anhwei); but there is virtually no biographical information on any of these poets.

What is known about them is primarily drawn from their verse. Although the original collection of their poetry, compiled by Ch'en Ch'ung 陳充 (*fl.* 1004–1007), *Chiu-seng shih* 九僧詩 (Poems of the Nine Monks) was lost sometime during the Sung dynasty, in 1712 Mao I 毛扆 (1640–after 1712) found a manuscript version of the text and printed it (as a Chi-ku Ko 汲古閣 edition; there is a modern reprint–see "Editions" below). The 134 poems found therein bear out what we learn of the Nine Monk's poetry in an anecdote recorded by Ou-yang Hsiu 歐陽修 (1007–1072)* in his *Liu-i shih-hua* 六一詩話. There it is maintained that in the early years of the Hsien-p'ing 咸平 reign period (998–1004), Hsü Tung 許洞 (970–1011, *chin-shih* 1000) gathered the Nine Monks to improvise some poems. But Hsü demanded that the participants refrain from using the following words in their compositions: *shan* 山 "mountain," *shui* 水 "water," *feng* 風 "wind," *yün* 雲 "clouds," *chu* 竹 "bamboo," *shih* 石 "stones," *hua* 花 "flowers," *ts'ao* 草 "grasses," *hsüeh* 雪 "snow," *shuang* 霜 "frost," *hsing* 星 "stars," *yüeh* 月 "moon,"

and *ch'in* 禽 "birds." As a result, none of the nine monks were able to write a single line.

Although this story is certainly apocryphal, it illustrates some of the restrictions which marked their verse and helps to define further the style. Generally speaking, the Nine Monks inherited from Chia Tao the tendency to focus on a conventional landscape featuring many of the objects cited by Hsü Tung above. Their repetition of similar diction and tone produced many insipid works, such as the following poem by Hui-ch'ung:

The early moon gone before the dawn,
The colors of the night are endless.
I stand alone on an autumn river bank,
Viewing the cold stars rolled in windy
    waves.

初月不到曉，夜色何冥冥。
獨立秋江上，風波卷寒星。

Hui-ch'ung is also supposed to have a painter of some talent, but he was unable to paint anything but miniature landscapes. In an age of masters who painted huge works, his achievements in the world of art may serve as a metaphor for the role of the Nine Monks in early Sung verse.

Editions and References

Sheng-Sung Chiu-seng shih 聖宋九僧詩. In Li Chih-ting 李之鼎, comp. *Sung-jen Chi* 宋人集, Nan-ch'eng Li-shih I-ch'iu-kuan 南城李氏宜秋館, 1921, v. 48.

Studies

Chang, I 張毅. *Sung-tai wen-hsüeh ssu-hsiang shih* 宋代文學思想史. Peking: Chung-hua, 1995, pp. 42-52.

Ch'en, Chih-o 陳植鍔. "Shih-lun Wang Yü-ch'en yü Sung-ch'u shih-feng" 試論王禹偁與宋初詩風, *Social Sciences in China*, 14 (1982): 131-54.

Hsiung, Li-hui 熊黎輝. "Lun Sung-ch'u shih-t'an" 論宋初詩壇. *She-hui k'o-hsüeh chan-hsien*, 56 (1991): 310-6.

Kurata, J. *et al.* "Wei Yeh," "Lin Pu," and

"P'an Lang" in *Sung Biographies,* pp. 1186-87, 613-15, and 816-18, respectively.

Liang, K'un 梁昆. "Wan T'ang p'ai" 晚唐派. In *Sung shih p'ai-pieh lun* 宋詩派別論. Changsha: Shang-wu Yin-shu-kuan, 1938.

Wang, Tseng-pin 王增斌. "Sung-ch'u wan-T'ang shih-p'ai lun-kao" 宋初晚唐詩派論稿, *Shan-hsi Ta-hsüeh hsüeh-pao* 53 (1991): 22-27.

Yin, Kung-hung 尹恭弘. "Lun Sung-ch'u te chu-yao shih-feng" 論宋初的主要詩風. In *Chung-kuo ku-tien wen-hsüeh lun-ts'ung* 2 (1985): 87-103.

Chen Zhi
The National University of Singapore

Ch'ü-lü 曲律 (*Song rules*) by Wang Chi-te 王驥德 (d. 1623)* is the earliest known extensive analytical study and systematically organized single body of critical comment on the poetry, language, prosody, phonetics, music and other aspects of both southern and northern styles of dramatic and non-dramatic songs and plays. In 4 folios, divided into 40 sections, and running to over 130 closely printed pages in a recent edition, it provides brief but compact and stimulating monographs on such topics as "tune-titles," "tonal meter," "rhyme," "parallelism" "dialogue" and "comic interludes," and is characterized by well-informed confidence and directness of opinion and clarity of presentation. Even when the author's opinions seem open to challenge, they are valuable as a strong statement of how an ancient scholar, poet and playwright of high repute viewed China's dramatic, musical and poetic history. The work has a preface dated 1625 by the celebrated playwright and story-writer Feng Meng-lung 馮夢龍 (1574–1646),* who terms himself his pupil. Wang's own preface is dated 1610, which shows that the book was many years being drafted or polished before its final version was attained. Both prefaces make it clear that he wrote in full awareness of earlier classics of drama criticism, song and phonology and was reacting to them, as indeed, we see from his ensuing writing, he was to more contemporary published theorizations. He also wrote a *Nan-tz'u cheng-yün* 南詞正韻 (Standard rhymes for southern songs), no longer extant.

Wang was a student of the famous dramatist Hsü Wei 徐渭 (1521–1593)* and a friend of the eminent recluse *ch'ü*-poet Sun Ju-fa 孫如法 (late sixteenth–early seventeenth c. A.D.), and, himself a playwright of both *tsa-chü**and *ch'uan-ch'i**styles, also annotated *Hsi-hsiang chi** and *P'i-p'a chi* (see Kao Ming*). In addition he has a collection of non-dramatic *ch'ü, Fang-chu Kuan yüeh-fu* 方諸館樂府 (Lays of the Square Moonlight Water-Scooper Lodge). So he was able to bring his considerable creative dramatic and poetic experience to bear in this wide-ranging treatise.

Wang foreshadowed many of Li Yü's 李漁 (1611–1680)* views on plot-structure and related topics, promoting a conscious and disciplined control of language and composition, and was a pioneer in this aspect of drama criticism.

Traditionally, the songs of Chinese drama have been much more esteemed than their intervening speech. In another innovative approach, Wang championed the raising of the status of the speech, boldly and iconoclastically declaring that its complexities are no less than those of song. Moreover, he urged in powerful terms the mixture of Naturalness (*pen-se* 本色) with the adornment of refined literary language (*wen-tz'u* 文辭). He used an informative system of three grades to assess the value of dramatic writing, placing works which combined both the refined and Natural or common first, the Ornate ones second, and those that were neither refined nor Natural third. Any with entirely Natural lyrics do not come into his rankings, which is remarkable considering his close personal connection with Shen Ching

沈璟 (1553–1610),* a strong partisan and practitioner of Naturalness. He accorded importance, too, to the element of comedy in drama performance.

Yet with regard to content and treatment of ideas, he has a traditional, view, lauding *P'i-p'a chi* 琵琶記 (The Lute; see Kao Ming 高明, *ca.* 1305-*ca.* 1370*) for its morality and condemning *Pai-yüeh t'ing* 拜月亭 (Moon-worship Pavilion; see *Ssu-ta ch'uan-ch'i* 四大傳奇*) for its "proclaiming of lewdness." In this judgement was a foretaste of the puritanical moralizers of subsequent centuries. While asserting that a playwright needs to study widely, he also warned against pedantry and the flaunting of learning in the writing of plays. This echoes some of Hsü Wei's statements. He acknowledged what he saw as the superior professionalism of Yüan *tsa-chü* plays over the *ch'uan-ch'i* plays of the Ming, whereas Ming playwrights, he claimed, were only concerned with preparations for their careers, for their farming, or for domestic pursuits.

Heir to Shen Ching's musical and prosodic theories, Wang was nevertheless broader and more flexible in his views. He was also influenced by Sun Ju-fa in these aspects, and later learned much from the eminent dramatist T'ang Hsien-tsu 唐顯祖 (1550–1616).*

The complexity of Wang's views was not confined to technical matters. He rightly sought to link the detail to vaster ideas and human conditions. Seeing the fading of T'ang *shih,** Sung *tz'u** and Yüan *ch'ü** as coinciding with the downfalls of those dynasties, he worried that the demise of the southern-style *ch'ü* was also in the offing, and thus mourned this decline as a sign of his own dynasty was in decay.

He showed insight in consciously appreciating the immense skills required for the creation of humorous poetry, and perceived the high value of deadpan comedy in acting, whereby "without any change in vocal or facial expression the accomplished joker can make people collapse with laughter." He saw comedy as desirable, even essential, for drama, while at the same time warning of the danger that a dramatist's contrivedly dragging in comic episodes will "give one goose-pimples." Humorous song, he argued, should make a virtue of "turning common language into elegance."

Section 37 discusses role-type categories, which he calls *pu-se* 部色, and is one of the earliest surviving full and mature examinations of this essential characteristic of traditional Chinese drama; this disquisition is particularly useful for juxtaposing northern and southern dramatic terminology. He claimed to have seen versions of Yüan dramas with details of costuming and props attached to specific role-type categories, but he may well be talking about earlier Ming dynasty plays or editions.

Elsewhere he showed scepticism regarding Ming versions of Yüan plays and *ch'ü*. In a key summary of the survival of the plays and songs in his own day, he deplored the book-marts' "giving false authorship attributions for the sake of profit, and even assigning ancient persons' names to our contemporary songs in order to cheat present-day society."

Wang's views are often stated with an adamant and lucid authority that is pleasantly striking, but they are sometimes open to challenge. His scornful castigation in Section 7 of Chou Te-ch'ing 周德清 (1277-1355), the prime phonologist of early *ch'ü*, as a "shallow scholar" (*ch'ien-shih* 淺士) is one example of this. Criticizing another major early dramatic and prosodic theorist, Chu Ch'üan 朱權 (1378–1448),* at the same time, he attacked Chou for supposed flaws in his rhyme-tables, accused him of dialectal errors, and petulantly complained, "It was all right for Te-ch'ing to alter the *shih*-rhymes of such great men of old as Shen Yüeh 沈約 (441–513)* and after, but nowadays we are not allowed to alter a single one of that mountain yokel's rhymes, and, what is more, present-day singers have been perhaps quite deeply led astray by Te-ch'ing."

Stricturing some of Chou's remarks on tonal meter as "especially ridiculous," he mentioned that Shen Ching thought to write a new rhyme-book but died before achieving that aim, while he himself opposed Chou so as to support southern songs, this having motivated him to produce his *Nan-tz'u cheng-yün.*

Wang came from Chekiang in "southerly" China. His criticisms here confuse two issues: Chou's accuracy, and whether Chou should still be used as a standard for *ch'ü* composition in the late Ming. It was probably irritation at the latter that stirred him to opposition. Chou had never claimed to set up standards for *shih* rhymes, simply to describe *ch'ü* language as it was during the early heyday of that genre.

With surprisingly vehemence Wang advocated that the use of musical modes in drama should closely adhere to the moods and emotions of the plot. As an ideal, such a matching has much to be said for it, but in practice has always proven difficult to implement, and even in musicological theory difficult to justify with any clarity.

Concerning allusion, Wang is on firmer ground. He encapsulates an excellent principle for this salient aspect of Chinese literature, adopting a sensibly relativistic rather than partisan approach, and asserting that "Fondness for using allusion fails in too much piling up of allusions, while having no allusions fails in being too dry and bleak." He also maintained that "the excellence of songs lies neither in their using of allusions nor in their not using allusions," here meaning that what produces excellence is the exceptionally appropriate use of allusion.

Editions and References
Ch'ü-lü 曲律. Original printed edition of

1625.
Lü-yin T'ang 綠蔭堂, Soochow; 1689 reprint edition included in the *Chih-hai* 指海 collection (Part 7) of Ch'ien Hsi-tso 錢熙 祚 (d. 1844), printed by Mr. Ch'ien of Chin-shan 金山錢氏 between 1821-1850.
Chi, Fo-t'o 姬佛陀, *Hsüeh-hai ts'ung-pien* 學 海叢編.Shanghai: Ts'ang-sheng Ming-chih Ta-hsüeh 倉聖明智大學, 1916.
Chung-kuo Hsi-ch'ü Yen-chiu Yüan 中國戲 曲言究院, comp. *Chung-kuo ku-tien hsi-ch'ü lun-chu chi-ch'eng* 中國古典戲曲論箸 集成. Peking: Chung-kuo Hsi-chü, 1959, 4:45-191.

Studies

Chou, I-pai 周貽白. *Hsi-ch'ü yen-ch'ang lun-chu chi-shih* 戲曲演唱論箸集釋. Peking, 1962, pp. 67-111.
Hsia, Hsieh-shih 夏寫時. "Wang Chi-te" 王 驥德, in Chung-kuo Ta Pai-k'o Ch'üan-shu Tsung Pien-chi Wei-yüan-hui 中國 大百科全書總編輯委員會, ed. *Chung-kuo ta pai-k'o ch'üan-shu: Hsi-ch'ü ch'ü-i* 中國 大百科全書：戲曲曲藝. Peking: Chung-kuo Ta Pai-k'o Ch'üan-shu Ch'u-pan-she, pp. 402-403.
Lo, K'ang-lieh 羅慷烈. "Ch'ü-chin shu-cheng" 曲禁疏證, in *Tz'u-ch'ü lun-kao* 詞 曲論稿. Hong Kong, 1977, pp. 303-405.
Yao, Shu-i 么疏儀. "Wang Chi-te" 王驥德, in *Chung-kuo Ta Pai-k'o Ch'üan-shu: Chung-kuo wen-hsüeh* 中國文學. Chung-kuo Ta Pai-k'o Ch'üan-shu Tsung Pien-chi Wei-yüan-hui, ed. Peking: Chung-kuo Ta Pai-k'o Ch'üan-shu Ch'u-pan-she, pp. 887-888.

William Dolby
University of Edinburgh

Chuang Tzu 莊子 is the most important pre-Ch'in text for the study of Chinese literature. The literary worth of the *Chuang Tzu* may be measured in two respects: 1. its own intrinsic merit as a monument of ancient Chinese literature, and 2. its impact upon writers from the Han period up to the present day. In both respects, the *Chuang Tzu* is peerless.

It is customary to view the *Chuang*

Tzu primarily as a religious or philosophical text, and there is no doubt that it has these dimensions. In the all-consuming preoccupation with questions of religion and philosophy, however, the fact that the *Chuang Tzu* is one of the greatest works in the entire tradition of Chinese literature is frequently overlooked.

One of the most noteworthy features of the *Chuang Tzu* is its utterly unique quality of inventiveness. The author's fondness for anecdotes, allegories, parables, and fables was totally unprecedented and remained without parallel until the arrival of Buddhism in China centuries later. Indeed, the impish irreverence (e.g., the Way is to be found in excrement and urine) of Master Chuang anticipates the spirit of Zen by more than a millennium. So *sui generis* is the *Chuang Tzu* that the question of its origins in Chinese culture must be seriously confronted. It has always been assumed that the *Chuang Tzu* is a purely Chinese text, but there are a sufficient quantity of Indo-European mythological, yogic, philosophical, rhetorical, and other aspects to warrant a full-scale investigation of its international linkages. Until such an investigation is carried out intensively, however, the cosmopolitan dimensions of the *Chuang Tzu* can only be raised as a tantalizing possibility. In the meantime, we must remain less than content with a review of the known textual history, contents, and influence of this remarkable book.

The *Chuang Tzu* is commonly attributed to Chuang Chou 莊周, a Warring States figure who is supposed to have lived in the state of Sung between around the time of King Hui of Liang 梁惠王(370–319 B.C.) and King Hsüan of Ch'i齊宣王 (319–301 B.C.). His dates are usually given roughly as 369–286 B.C. While it is likely that a historical personage known as Chuang Chou may well have composed portions of the text, it is impossible that he could have written the entire book because of the internal contradictions, repetitions, and stylistic discrepancies with which it is riddled, not to mention the detached, retrospective manner with which Chuang Chou is described in the final chapter. It is preferable, then, not to think of the *Chuang Tzu* as the integral product of a single author, but rather as an anthology which has undergone a prolonged process of accretion and redaction. To describe the *Chuang Tzu* as an anthology, however, is by no means to deny the role of the individual who was responsible for its core chapters and whose creative genius served as the chief inspiration for the book which presumably bears his name. Even the imitative, slipshod, and lackluster portions of the text are clearly responding—each in its own way—to the scintillating brilliance that suffuses its heart. Thus, when we speak of Master Chuang's thought or language, we are referring to the guiding spirit of the central chapters and to other portions of the text animated by that spirit. The safest policy is to refer whenever possible to specific passages of the book and to think of Master Chuang as the collective personality around which they are grouped.

Although Ssu-ma Ch'ien's "biography" in *chüan* 63 of the *Shih-chi* 史記* asserts that the writings of Master Chuang totalled over 100,000 graphs and a 52-chapter version of the text survived as late as the fourth century, the sole extant recension, which was established by Kuo Hsiang 郭象 (d. 312), consists of 33 chapters. These may be listed as follows: 1. Hsiao-yao yu 逍遙遊 (Carefree Wandering), 2. Ch'i wu lun 齊物論 (On the Equality of Things), 3. Yang sheng chu 養生主 (Essentials for Nurturing Life), 4. Jen-chien shih 人間世 (The Human World), 5. Te ch'ung fu 德充符 (Symbols of Integrity Fulfilled), 6. Ta tsung shih 大宗師 (The Great Ancestral Teacher), 7. Ying ti wang

應帝王 (Responses for Emperors and Kings), 8. P'ien-mu 駢拇 (Webbed Toes), 9. Ma-t'i 馬蹄 (Horses' Hooves), 10. Ch'ü ch'ieh 胠篋 (Ransacking Coffers), 11. Tsai yu 在宥 (Preserving and Accepting), 12. T'ien-ti 天地 (Heaven and Earth), 13. T'ien-tao 天道 (The Way of Heaven), 14. T'ien-yün 天運 (Heavenly Revolutions), 15. K'o i 刻意 (Ingrained Opinions), 16. Shan hsing 繕性 (Mending Nature), 17. Ch'iu shui 秋水 (Autumn Floods), 18. Chih-lo 至樂 (Ultimate Joy), 19. Ta sheng 達生 (Understanding Life), 20. Shan mu 山木 (The Mountain Tree), 21. T'ien-tzu Fang 田子方 (Sir Square Field), 22. Chih Pei-yu 知北遊 (Knowledge Wanders North), 23. Keng-sang Ch'u 庚桑楚 (Keng-sang Ch'u), 24. Hsü Wu-kuei 徐無鬼 (Ghostless Hsü), 25. Tse-yang 則陽 (Sunny), 26. Wai-wu 外物 (External Things), 27. Yü-yen 寓言 (Metaphors), 28. Jang wang 讓王 (Abdicating Kingship), 29. Tao Chih 盜跖 (Robber Footpad), 30. Shuo chien 說劍 (Discoursing on Swords), 31. Yü-fu 漁父 (An Old Fisherman), 32. Lieh Yü-k'ou 列禦寇 (Lieh Yü-k'ou), 33. T'ien-hsia 天下 (All Under Heaven).

The thirty-three chapters of Kuo Hsiang's recension of the *Chuang Tzu* are divided into *Nei-p'ien* 內篇 (Inner Chapters)—the first seven), *Wai-p'ien* 外篇 (Outer Chapters—the next fifteen), and *Tsa-p'ien* 雜篇 (Miscellaneous Chapters —the last eleven). The seven *Inner Chapters* are generally regarded as more or less closely reflecting the thought and mode of expression of Master Chuang, whereas the *Outer Chapters* and *Miscellaneous Chapters* include extraneous materials and even some blatantly contradictory passages. There are, nonetheless, portions of the latter two sections that come close to equalling the grandeur of the *Inner Chapters* (e.g., the magnificent dialogue between the Overlord of the Northern Sea and the Earl of the Yellow River in Chapter 17). As such, when general statements about the *Chuang Tzu* are made, they normally refer to the *Inner Chapters* and those parts of the *Outer Chapters* and *Miscellaneous Chapters* that are compatible with them.

The main themes of the *Inner Chapters* are an advocacy of creative spontaneity, the relativity of all things, transcendent knowledge, following nature, equanimity toward life and death, the usefulness of uselessness, and the blessings of emptiness and nonexistence. Although these are weighty, abstract subjects, Master Chuang employs metaphors and similes, humor and satire to enliven his treatment of them. It is Master Chuang's surpassing wit that makes reading his discussions of such profound topics not only palatable but supremely pleasurable and stimulating. Furthermore, not only does his prose possess a poetic quality of its own, many passages are actually written in rhymed poetry which has gone largely unrecognized until recently.

As one early example of the extraordinary literary influence of the *Chuang Tzu*, we may cite Chia I's 賈誼 (200–168 B.C.)* "Fu niao fu" 鵬鳥賦 (Rhapsody on An Owl). The rhapsody relates how once, when Chia I was living in semi-exile in the southern region of Ch'ang-sha, an owl flew into his house. According to southern folklore, this was an evil omen and was thought to presage the death of the master of the house. Troubled, Chia I sought consolation in the teachings of Master Chuang. While he does not mention it by name, nine out of fifty-four lines (one-sixth of the total) in the rhapsody (the first of this genre whose authorship and date are reasonably certain) derive directly from the *Chuang Tzu*. In comparison, two lines of the rhapsody may be said to derive from the *Tao Te Ching* 道德經 and one other line occurs both in the *Huai-nan Tzu* 淮南子 and in the *Lü-shih ch'un-ch'iu* 呂氏春秋.

From Chia I, Sung Yü 宋玉, Ssu-ma Hsiang-ju 司馬相如 (179–117 B.C.),* and Ssu-ma Ch'ien 司馬遷 (145–*ca.* 86)*

22

onward, virtually all major Chinese writers were influenced by the majestic language and self-mocking unconventionality of the *Chuang Tzu*. Many of China's finest poets, such as Juan Chi 阮籍 (210–263),* T'ao Ch'ien 陶潛 (365–427),* Li Po 李白 (701–762),* Su Shih 蘇軾 (1037–1101),* and Lu Yu 陸游 (1125–1210),* were deeply imbued with the ideas and artistry of the *Chuang Tzu*. Some of them explicitly acknowledged their debt to Master Chuang in essays like "[Ta] Chuang lun" [達]莊論 (A Discourse on [Summing up] the *Chuang Tzu*) by Juan Chi, "Chuang Tzu lun" 莊子論 (A Discourse on the *Chuang Tzu*) by Wang An-shih 王安石 (1021–1086),* and "Chuang Tzu tz'u-t'ang chi" 莊子祠堂記 (A Record of the Memorial Shrine of Master Chuang) by Su Shih.

Nearly every chapter of the *Chuang Tzu* contains fables and allegories. Many of them, such as that about Cloud General 雲將 and Vast Obscurity 鴻蒙 in Chapter 11, seem to have been made up by the author, while others, such as that about the enormous P'eng 鵬 bird in Chapter 1, are taken from myths that now exist only in fragments or have disappeared altogether. Still other tales are concocted by having historical figures such as Confucius say and do whatever the author pleases.

There are a few rather long and somewhat complex accounts, such as that about Master Lieh and the magus in Chapter 7, that about the music of the Yellow Emperor in Chapter 14, and that about Robber Footpad which takes up the first part of Chapter 29. The structure of most tales in the anthology is simple, however, and they usually consist of but a single incident or episode (e.g., Lickety and Split drilling seven holes in Wonton at the end of Chapter 7 or Master Chuang beating on a basin when his wife dies [second story in Chapter 18]).

The authors of other pre-Ch'in texts such as the *Mencius*, *Lü shih ch'un-ch'iu*,

Han Fei Tzu 韓非子, and *Chan-kuo ts'e* 戰國策* also used allegories to express their thought, but the allegories of Master Chuang are different from theirs in several respects: they are the rule rather than the exception, they are not restricted by reality, they are charged with emotion, and they are invariably witty. Whereas his contemporaries used allegories only occasionally and usually adopted them from history, legend, folk tales, or proverbial wisdom, Master Chuang frequently devised his allegories out of thin air. Thus, although the status of mature fiction may not be claimed for the *Chuang Tzu*, either in whole or in part, because its underlying intent is the exposition of ideas and because the scope of its narratives is limited, a fictional impulse is nonetheless present. To be sure, some of the lengthier and more complicated allegories in the *Chuang Tzu* come close to being short stories in that their characters are clearly delineated (without being fully developed), subtle emotions are conveyed, and dialogue and other elements of fiction are employed. The *Chuang Tzu*'s imaginative creation of fictitious characters in an allegorical setting would not be matched again until the anomalous tales of the Six Dynasties period (*chih-kuai* 志怪*) and the classical short stories of the T'ang (*ch'uan-ch'i* 傳奇).*

Master Chuang frequently gives vent to sheer whimsy, as in his romp through evolution at the end of Chapter 18: "The spittle of the dried surplus bones becomes a misty spray and the misty spray becomes mother of vinegar. Midges are born from mother of vinegar; yellow whirligigs are born from fetid wine; blindgnats are born from putrid slimebugs. When goat's-queue couples with bamboo that has not shooted for a long time, they produce greenies. The greenies produce panthers; panthers produce horses; horses produce men; and men return to the wellsprings of nature." There are passages in the *Chuang*

Tzu which read like Jabberwocky or Joyce: "'In pits there are pacers; around stoves there are tufties. Fulgurlings frequent dust piles inside the door; croakers and twoads hop about in low-lying places to the northeast; spillsuns frequent low-lying places to the north-west. In water there are nonimagoes; on hills there are scrabblers; on mountains there are unipedes; in the wilds there are will-o'-the-wisps; and in marshes there are bendcrooks'" (Chapter 19, Section 6). So enamored of Master Chuang were later scholars that they wrote learned annotations which tried valiantly to make scholarly sense of his playful nonsense.

Relying on his fertile imagination and matchless mastery of language, Master Chuang peopled the pages of his text with the quirkiest characters this side of bedlam: Mad Stammerer, Lipless Clubfoot Scattered, Fancypants Scholar, Sir Plow, and a man who fancies that his left arm will turn into a rooster, his right arm will turn into a crossbow, and his buttocks will become cartwheels,

At several places in the text, Master Chuang affects the trappings of logic and reasoning, but turns them on their head or reduces them to absurdity to show the limitations of rationality and knowledge. Sometimes he adopts a pattern of reasoning that is curiously reminiscent of Socratic or Platonic dialogues in Greek philosophy (e.g., his celebrated argument with Hui Shih about the joy of fishes which closes Chapter 17), while the paradoxes of Hui Shih in the final section of the book are strikingly like those of Zeno of Elea. Elsewhere, as in the famous butterfly dream which closes Chapter 2, there is little or no argumentation but rather a fluid meditation on the various states of transformation.

Some of the most outstanding features of Chuang Chou's writing style are pointed out in the *Chuang Tzu* itself: "With absurd expressions, extravagant words, and unbounded phrases, he often gave rein to his whims but was not presumptuous and did not look at things from one angle only. Believing that all under heaven were sunk in stupidity and could not be talked to seriously, he used impromptu words for his effusive elaboration, quotations for the truth, and metaphors for breadth" (Chapter 33). Chapter 27 ("Metaphors"), perhaps the most difficult in the book, probes the question of language itself. The problem it addresses is how to convey ideas, sentiments, and meanings effectively through an inadequate medium. The chapter begins with a discussion of the effectiveness of metaphors, which work nine times out of ten, moves on to a consideration of quotations, which are said to be effective seven times out of ten, and then opines that the most effective form of language is "impromptu words" (*chih-yen* 卮言, frequently translated more literally as "goblet words"), which may be thought of as language that is uttered unconsciously and unpremeditatedly: "Impromptu words pour forth every day and harmonize within the framework of nature. Consequently, there is effusive elaboration so that they may live out their years. Without speech, there is equality. Equality plus speech yields inequality; speech plus equality yields inequality. Therefore, it is said, 'Speak nonspeech.' If you speak nonspeech, you may speak till the end of your life without ever having spoken. If till the end of your life you do not speak, you will never have failed to speak." In the final analysis, Master Chuang's attitude toward language is best exemplified by the unforgettable metaphor with which he closes Chapter 27: "A fish-trap is for catching fish; once you've caught the fish, you can forget about the trap. A rabbit-snare is for catching rabbits; once you've caught the rabbit, you can forget about the snare. Words are for catching ideas; once you've caught the idea, you can forget about the words. Where can I find a person who knows how to forget about words so that I can have a few words with him?"

Tributes were paid to Master Chuang as a writer even by those who were indifferent or opposed to his philosophy. Thus, Kuo Hsiang, in his preface to the *Chuang Tzu*, declared that "the reason Master Chuang was the foremost of all the early thinkers despite not being ranked among the classics" 其所以不經而為百家之冠 was because of his inimitable style. Lu Hsün, the greatest Chinese writer of the twentieth century, exclaimed in his *Han wen-hsüeh shih kang-yao* 漢文學史綱要 (An Outline of Sinitic Literature) that the reason no other work by any of the late Chou thinkers could stand before the *Chuang Tzu* was because of its incomparable literary excellence.

In the richness of his vocabulary, the agility of his prose, the subtlety of his poetry, and the breadth of his conception, Master Chuang's skill as a writer was unmatched by any other author of his age. The overwhelming effect of the *Chuang Tzu* upon the Chinese literary tradition, and through the literary tradition upon Chinese culture as a whole, is still operative today.

Editions and References

Ch'en, Ku-ying 陳鼓應. *Chuang Tzu chin chu chin i* 莊子今注今譯 (A Modern Annotation and Translation of the *Chuang Tzu*). Peking: Chung-hua, 1983. A slightly revised reprinting of the edition published in 2v. by Taiwan Commercial Press in 1975.

Ch'ien, Mu 錢穆. *Chuang Tzu tsuan chien* 莊子纂箋 (A Compilation of Notes on the *Chuang Tzu*). Taipei: San-min, 1974; 4th rev. and enlarged ed. (1951).

Chuang Tzu tz'u-tien 莊子詞點. Wang Shih-shun 王世舜 and Han Mu-chün 韓慕君, eds. Tsinan: Shan-tung Chiao-yü, 1993.

A Concordance to the Chuang Tzu 莊子引德. Rpt. Taipei: Chinese Materials and Research Aids Service Center, Inc., 1966. *Harvard-Yenching Institute Sinological Index Series*, Supplement #20.

Han, Mu-chün 韓慕龜 *et al.,* eds. *Lao Chuang tz'u-tien* 老莊詞典. Tsinan: Shan-tung Chiao-yü, 1993.

Hsieh, Hsiang-hao 謝祥皓. *Chuang Tzu tao-tu* 莊子導讀. Chengtu: Pa-Shu Shu-she, 1988.

Kuo, Ch'ing-fan 郭慶藩 (1844-1896), comp. *Chuang Tzu chi shih* 莊子集釋 (Collected Annotations on the *Chuang Tzu*). 4v. Peking: Chung-hua, 1961.

Wang, Hsien-ch'ien 王先謙 (1842-1918). *Chuang Tzu chi-chieh* 莊子集解. Shen Hsiao-huan 沈嘯寰, ed. and coll. Peking: Chung-hua, 1987. *Hsin-pien chu-tzu chi-ch'eng, Ti-i chi.*

Translations

Akatsuka, Kiyoshi 赤塚忠. *Sôshi* 莊子 (Chuang Tzu). *Zenshaku kanbun taikei* 全釈漢文大系 (Fully Interpreted Chinese Literature Series), V. 16-17. Tokyo: Shûeisha, 1974–1977.

Fung, Yu-lan. *Chuang-tzu: A New Selected Translation with an Exposition of the Philosophy of Kuo Hsiang* Peking: Foreign Languages Press, 1989; originally published by Commercial Press, 1931.

Giles, Herbert A. *Chuang Tzu: Taoist Philosopher and Chinese Mystic.* London: George Allen & Unwin, 1926, 2nd rev. ed.; originally published 1889.

Graham, A. C. *Chuang-tzu: The Seven Inner Chapters and other writings from the book Chuang-tzu.* London: George Allen and Unwin, 1981.

Legge, James. *The Texts of Taoism.* 2v. In *The Sacred Books of the East,* ed. F. Max Müller, v. XXXIX-XL. Oxford: Oxford University Press, 1891; rpt. New York: Dover, 1962.

Mair, Victor H. *Wandering on the Way: Early Taoist Tales and Parables of Chuang Tzu.* New York: Bantam Books, 1994; Honolulu: University of Hawaii Press, 1997.

Watson, Burton. *The Complete Works of Chuang Tzu.* New York: Columbia University Press, 1968.

Studies

Chuang-tzu yen-chiu 莊子研究. Shanghai: Fu-tan Ta-hsüeh, 1986. Contains 40 studies given at a conference.

Graham, A. C. "Chuang-tzu and the Rambling Mode." In T. C. Lai, ed., *The*

Art and Profession of Translation. Hong Kong: Hong Kong Translation Society, 1976, pp. 61-77.

___. "How Much of *Chuang Tzu* Did Chuang Tzu Write?" In the author's *Studies in Chinese Philosophy and Philosophical Literature.* Albany: State University of New York Press, 1990; originally published in Singapore, 1986, pp. 283-321.

Huang-shan Wen-hua Shu-yüan 黃山文化書院, ed. *Chuang Tzu yü Chung-kuo wen-hua* 莊子與中國文化 (Chuang Tzu and Chinese Culture). Hofei: An-hui Jen-min, 1990.

Kjellberg, Paul and Philip J. Ivanhoe, ed. *Essays on Skepticism, Relativism, and Ethics in the "Zhuangzi."* Albany: State University of New York Press, 1996. The "Bibliography" (pp. 215-225) "is intended to be a comprehensive survey of sources for *Zhuangzi* studies in Western languages" (also includes many modern Chinese studies and a few Japanese works).

Liu, Hsiao-kan 流笑敢. *Classifying the "Zhuangzi" Chapters.* Ann Arbor: Center for Chinese Studies, University of Michigan, 1994. A translation by William E. Savage of the first three chapters of the author's *Chuang Tzu che-hsüeh chi ch'i yen-pien* 莊子哲學及其演變. Peking: Chung-kuo She-hui K'o-hsüeh Ch'u-pan-she, 1988; 2nd printing, 1993.

Mair, Victor H., ed. *Chuang-tzu: Composition and Interpretation.* A Symposium Issue of the *Journal of Chinese Religions,* 11 (Fall, 1983).

___, ed. *Experimental Essays on Chuang-tzu.* Asian Studies at Hawaii, 29. Honolulu: University of Hawaii Press, 1983 and later reprints.

___. "Introduction and Notes for a Complete Translation of the *Chuang Tzu.*" *Sino-Platonic Papers,* 48 (September, 1994).

___. "Wandering in and through the *Chuang-tzu.*" In Mair, ed., *Chuang-tzu: Composition and Interpretation,* pp. 106-117.

Rand, Christopher C. "Chuang Tzu: Text and Substance." In Mair, ed., *Chuang-tzu: Composition and Interpretation,* pp. 5-58.

Robinet, I. "Une lecture du *Zhuangzi,*" *Études chinoises* 15 (1996): 109-158.

Roth, Harold. "Who Compiled the *Chuang Tzu?*" In Henry Rosemont, Jr., ed. *Chinese Texts and Philosophical Contexts: Essays Dedicated to Angus C. Graham.* La Salle, Illinois: Open Court, 1991, pp. 79-128.

Victor H. Mair
University of Pennsylvania

Erh-nü ying-hsiung chuan 兒女英雄傳 ("A Tale of Tender-hearted Heroes" is but one of several translations suggested by the prologue) stands out among the great number of Ch'ing novels as having several unusual features. It grafts a Chinese chivalric story, featuring a female knight, to a modified version of the scholar-beauty romance (see *Ts'ai-tzu chia-jen hsiao-shuo**). Like *Hung-lou-meng,** but to a lesser extent, it is "encyclopedic" for its inclusion of a wide range of Chinese cultural topics in its narrative. A modern reader weary of the lack of narrative innovation in traditional Chinese fiction will also find in this text refreshing instances of metafictional reflexivity and an imaginative play with storytelling conventions.

The author of the novel, Wen K'ang 文康, came from a prominent Manchu family of the Bordered Red Banner. Born in the last decade of the eighteenth century, probably in the year 1798, he is believed to have died sometime after 1865, but no later than 1877. He spent his early official career in the Court of Colonial Affairs (理藩院), and the local gazetteers indicate he was made Circuit Intendant of the Military Defense Circuit of Tientsin (天津兵略道) in 1842–43 and then Assistant Sub-Prefect (通判) in Anhwei sometime later. There were indications that he was appointed at one time as Imperial Agent to Tibet (駐藏大臣) but did not take up this post due to "ill health." Like Ts'ao Hsüeh-ch'in 曹雪芹 (*ca.* 1715–1763),* Wen K'ang hailed from a family which had rendered important service to the throne and his novel is to some extent autobiographical.

The successes of the father and son of the An family in the exams as described in the novel, especially the son's swift advancements in officialdom, however, have been seen by critics as a "wishful projection" on the part of the author. Wen K'ang's official appointments were made as hereditary rewards, not a result of his own efforts in civil service examinations, and his sons are believed to have fared no better in this respect.

The novel consists of forty chapters preceded by a prologue. Composed mainly of a dream scene, the prologue is given mostly to presenting the overall thematic outlook of the novel. The action of the main text can roughly be divided into two parts. The first begins with the story of An Hsüeh-hai 安學海, a Bannerman of the Plain Yellow Chinese Banner, who passed the provincial exams late in life and was appointed to a local post in Huai-an 淮安. A Confucian scholar of great personal integrity, he refused to bribe his superior official, and as a consequence was implicated for having failed in the floods-control duty and put under arrest. His seventeen-year old son An Chi 安驥, brought up sequestered and inexperienced with life, traveled from Peking to Huai-an with the redemption money. On the way, he almost lost his life at a temple but was saved by a girl who called herself Shih-san Mei 十三妹, or Thirteenth Sister. A girl with superhuman martial prowess, Thirteenth Sister had been hiding away in the countryside with her aged mother awaiting a chance to avenge the death of her father, who had died from the machinations of a powerful minister at court. At the temple she also rescued Chang Chin-feng 張金鳳. Slightly younger than Thirteenth Sister but with an uncommon resemblance to her, Chang was a country girl who had also been kidnapped by the evil monk. Then and there Thirteenth Sister arranged a betrothal between Chang and An Chi before sending them on their way again.

The plot of this part is basically that of a *Wu-hsia hsiao-shuo* 武俠小説* novel; it constructs a perilous situation and then arranges its resolution through the interference of a chivalrous stranger. But instead of a young lady 'in distress,' as usually is the case, it is a young man who is in need of help here, while the altruistic savior is a female. The portrayal of Thirteenth Sister—with her superhuman martial skills, her shrouded origin, and her mysterious mission—constitutes the main interest of the narrative in this part.

After the reunion of young An Chi with his parents and the release of the father from his bondage, the family set out in search of Thirteenth Sister to express their gratitude. This task led them to the villa of the retired military man, Teng Chiu-kung 鄧九公, who was also in debt to Thirteenth Sister and now was acting as her guardian. After revealing to her that the man who killed her father had already been put to death by imperial order, An Hsüeh-hai proceeded to dissuade Thirteenth Sister, now known by her real name as Ho Yü-feng 何玉鳳, from her original plan to become a nun and had her marry his son An Chi (as a second wife). After the marriage An Chi successfully passed the examinations and rose rapidly in the bureaucracy. The story concludes with An Hsüeh-hai taking a trip to Shantung to visit Teng Chiu-kung, with whom he had formed a fast friendship, for the occasion of the latter's nineteenth birthday. The visit was cut short by the devastating news of his son's appointment to a distant post in Mongolia. But all ends well as An Chi was eventually re-appointed to Shantung as Inspector of Customs and Morals, and the narrative stops at the point where he was to embark on his journey to this office.

The subject matter of this part of the novel, then, is largely domestic and civil, as opposed to the 'martial' subject of the first part. And the portrayal of the young hero An Chi has also changed. Ridiculously inexperienced and timid when he first took to the road, he is shown to have matured here. Now in his own element in the arena of civil-service examinations, he is confident and excels in what he has been trained to do—display his literary talents and self-possessing manners which impress even the Emperor. But the center stage in this second part is shared by his father, who glows in his son's success and whose personality dominates many of the scenes.

The novel has the explicit intention of promoting Confucian values based on 'human relations' (*lun-ch'ang* 倫常), making all of its important characters agents of this concept and its plot a manifestation of how Confucian ethics will prevail and all the virtuous will be rewarded. The prologue chapter has a clear thematic function with its explanation of the significance of the term *erh-nü ying-hsiung*. *Erh-nü* is a metonymy for all the 'tender-hearted' and thus represents also all the emotive qualities or feelings (cf. *erh-nü ch'ing-ch'ang* 情長) that range from affectionate attachments between parents and children to romantic passion and human compassion in general. The term *ying-hsiung* likewise refers to both the 'heroic figures' and the active qualities associated with them—heroism, valiance, bravery. These sentiments and qualities are said to be nothing but the manifestations of "heavenly principle" (*tien-li* 天理) and "human feelings" (*jen-ch'ing* 人情), the enactments of which supposedly make saints and sages out of the ordinary people. In the socio-political contexts of Chinese culture, they become the grounds for the Confucian virtues (especially loyalty and filial piety) which the book celebrates. Thirteenth Sister fits the epithet in that as a typical *erh-nü* person of the 'weaker (tender)' sex, she also embodies the heroic, valiant qualities normally associated with men.

But the epithet is meant to apply to most other characters in the book as well, their conduct being a manifestation of these sentiments and principles. Fore-most among them are of course An Hsüeh-hai and his son; but a character like Teng Chiu-kung, a man of the martial profession who still possesses a child-like temperament at age ninety, for example, is apparently also an *erh-nü ying-hsiung*.

Because of the prominent role of Thirteenth Sister, the novel has recently drawn attention from scholars for its implications in gender studies. From this perspective, the featuring of a female knight as a central character presents a reversal in both the gender and the character roles as traditionally conceived. In spite of this unconventionality, conservative values still reign in the book. The potentially subversive figure of the female knight is assimilated into the Confucian order when Thirteenth Sister is turned into an exemplary daughter-in-law in the An family. On the other hand, female superiority portrayed in the novel has been seen as a 'correction' of male weakness, with Thirteenth Sister serving as a beneficial catalyst for the transformation of An Chi into a mature individual able to assume the role as the head of the polygynous sub-household in the family. In this relation, the novel's showcasing of characters with different cultural backgrounds (Manchu and Han), who are connected in a variety of ways and interact in diverse situations, may also be studied for its ethnico-political implications.

In addition to these thematic dimensions, the novel exhibits many features that are of linguistic, socio-cultural, and narratorial interests. One of the things about this text that scholars have often noted is its language: Wen K'ang writes in standard Pekinese of his day. To the linguists, this mid-nineteenth-century work has served for the study of how Mandarin evolved from the Ch'ing to the present, just as comparisons of its linguistic features with expressions in *Hung-lou meng* 紅樓夢* have helped with the mapping of the dialect's earlier evolution. Wen K'ang's text also shows a richness in its coverage of a great number of social and cultural phenomena. It contains a goodly array of learned cultural references such as the demonstration of the prognostic use of the *Book of Changes,* the ingenious exposition of a passage from the Confucian *Analects,* and a scientific explanation of the lunar and solar eclipses. Some of the incidents in the narrative no doubt were added for the purpose of capturing particular social practices and customs of the author's time: common prostitutes and enter- tainers plying their trades in the roadside inn, notorious society figures patronizing actresses in theater boxes, and adept larcenists tricking unwary victims at the temple fair. Court intrigues are revealed in an embedded story that An Hsüeh-hai tells about the rise and fall of the enemy of Thirteenth Sister's family; through the description of the elder An's failure in office, the narrator reveals the corruption of the bureaucracy at many levels. But one of the best known of various sociocultural practices represented in the narrative, valuable for the under- standing of Ch'ing literati culture, is the detailed account of the civil-service examinations at the provincial, capital, and court levels. The entire process is engagingly described as An Ch'i experiences it—in his preparation with a mock exam at home, his sitting for three sessions in a sequestered booth, his appearance at the Emperor's ranking of the finalists, the subsequent rituals of paying homage to teachers, and the triumphant return home.

For all its reflection of social realities, Wen K'ang's novel, like many other Ch'ing novels, is essentially 'rhetorical' in nature. The overall design of its action is modeled not on real life, but on the literary motifs of the chivalric and scholar-beauty genres (including a motif of 'paired objects' represented by a bow and an inkstone). The second half of the novel contains little action, as discursive felicities are meant to sustain narrative interest. In this sense, inconsequential incidents are often introduced to serve as occasions for locutionary displays and equally improbable situations are created as excuses for ingenious rationalizations. Both the characters' speeches and the narrator's interpolations proffer the pleasure of verbal art. The characters usually speak in an individualized style: Auntie T'ung's 佟舅太太 idioms, spiced with Manchu phrases, have been singled out by critics for their expressiveness. But it is An Hsüeh-hai, as head of the family, who presides over these scenes of non-action with his discursive eloquence. His speech *is* speech-act and it is through his words that he makes himself an embodiment of Confucian ethics. His persuasion of Thirteenth Sister which causes her to renounce her vow of celibacy, for instance, is a tour de force of argumentative skills (in which Chang Chin-feng also takes part). This episode, as it exemplifies the author's ability to create narrative tension and suspense by introducing inconsequential complications, also functions to under- score the theme that discursive force is more than a match for 'martial' prowess. The 'rhetorical' nature of this novel may be seen in its carefully planned events, creating the impression of a 'well- wrought' novel. Many details, seemingly irrelevant at first mention, turn out to have a narrative function later on. Some elements, improbable from a realistic point of view, are made plausible by the narrator's suasive force.

For a reader attentive to narratorial issues, Wen K'ang's text is interesting for its traits of metafiction, its self- reflexivity, and its conscious play with narrative conventions. From the outset, the text makes explicit its adoption of the model of oral storytelling by positing a narrator (styled Tung-hai Wu-liao-weng 東海吾了翁) who is ostensibly relating the story based on a text written by an author styled Yen-pei Hsien-jen (燕北閑人,The Idler from the North of Yen), while allowing himself the possibility for digression or diversion. Beyond the use of the conventional 'storyteller's phrases' and the like, the 'simulated oral context' has been explored further for new narrative possibilities. In the course of his story, the narrator stops often to comment not only on the contents of the narrative, but also on the techniques of storytelling, providing explanations about the esthetics of the structure and using traditional critical concepts (e.g., the flow of the 'vein and rhythm') to justify the arrangement of events. The narrator himself divides the story into five sections and points out that each is centered on one or two characters. In addition to the "author" and the "narrator," the characters here at times also comment on the structure of the narrative, arguing about how their action may affect the story and pondering whether they should do this or that. This phenomenon of characters taking part in the design of the narrative seems a most striking form of self-reflexivity (cf. Brecht; but compare this also with a performer's easy shift between the roles of the character and the commentator in the performing prosemetric genres such as *p'ing-t'an* 評彈). In addition, Wen K'ang's text also endeavors to add new varieties to conventional devices. To the traditional method of creating suspense by having a character *whispering* his or her plan of action to another, for instance, Wen K'ang offers a variation with a scene where characters engage in a "conversation by brush" (*pi t'an* 筆談) and pass information to each other *silently*. This has the effect of keeping the reader in suspense as he/she is unable to enter

the fiction world physically to see what transpires in the "conversation."

Metafictional self-reflection can be seen here both in the intra-textual and inter-textual manner. As a character created out of the mold of a literary motif, Thirteenth Sister has been compared by the narrator himself to earlier literary figures. The reader also knows that the motif of "a swordswoman hiding incognito awaiting a chance to avenge the wrong done to her family" is derived from tales like "Ts'ui Shen-ssu" 崔慎思 of the T'ang and "The Female Knight-errant" 俠女 of *Liao-chai chih-i* 聊齋志異,* while "the rescue of a man from peril by a swordswoman" can be found in the story of Wei Shih-i-niang 韋十一娘 of *P'ai-an ching-ch'i* 拍案驚奇 (see Ling Meng-chu*). In a sense, Wen K'ang's novel as a whole could be considered to have been composed in dialogic response to the *Hung-lou meng*; it makes express comparisons of its own plot and characters to those of the latter novel, professing a 'correction' to Ts'ao Hsüeh-ch'in's unflattering portrayals of Pao-yü and the Chia family and his novel's pessimist outlook in general. There are also intriguing cases of intra-textual references by way of 'retelling' of events in different narrative forms. The corrupt official T'an Erh-yin 談爾音, for example, uses the performing verse genre of *tao-ch'ing* 道情 to comment on his own life when he is reduced to beggary after being indicted. And An Hsüeh-hai's composition of a *sheng-chuan* 生傳, a biography whose subject is still alive, for Teng Chiu-kung, is an instance of a re-representation of a character's life, forming an inner narrative within the main narrative. This retelling is, moreover, carried out not without bias in the selection and modification of the 'facts,' yet it is openly presented for everyone to see. Thus, while Wen K'ang (or Yen-pei Hsien-jen) relates the story of the chivalric Thirteenth Sister in response to the supposedly skewed form of scholar-beauty romance, An Hsüeh-hai shapes his text within the Confucian concept of a martial hero.

Fashioned largely from the existing motifs and genres, *Erh-nü ying-hsiung chuan* has in turn exerted influences on later literature. Besides inspiring two sequels (*Hsü Erh-nü ying-hsiung chuan* 續兒女英雄傳 [A Sequel to *Tender-hearted Heroes*] and *Tsai-hsü Erh-nü ying-hsiung chuan* 再續 [Another Sequel to *Tender-hearted Heroes*]), the story of Thirteenth Sister has been adapted into dramas and retold in oral performances. She is believed to have influenced the conception of Kuan Hsiu-ku 關秀姑 in Chang Hen-shui's 張恨水, *T'i-hsiao yin-yüan* 啼笑姻緣.

Editions and References

Erh-nü ying-hsiung chuan 兒女英雄傳. Incomplete version in 39 chapters. Manuscript, n.d., Peking Library.

Erh-nü ying-hsiung chuan. Peking: Chü-chen-t'ang 聚珍堂, 1878. Edition with commentary by Tung Hsün 董恂 (1807–1892). Peking: Chü-chen-t'ung, 1880.

Erh-nü ying-hsiung chuan. Commentary by Tung Hsün. Prefaces by Tung-hai Wu-liao-weng 東海吾了翁, Kuan-chien-wo-chai 觀鑒我齋, and Ma Ts'ung-shan 馬從善. Shanghai: Fei-ying-kuan 蜚英館, 1888.

Erh-nü ying-hsiung chuan. Wang Yüan-fang 汪原放, ed. Punctuated, based on 1888 ed. Additional preface by Hu Shih 胡適 (1891–1962). Shanghai: Ya-tung T'u-shu-kuan 亞東圖書館, 1925.

Erh-nü ying-hsiung chuan. Sung-i 松頤, collator and annotator. Peking: Jen-min Wen-hsüeh, 1983. Several useful appendices including an annotated list of Manchu expressions. The best modern edition.

Translations

Bestaux, Eugène. *La cavalière noire*. Paris: Calmann-Lévy, 1956.

Kuhn, Franz. *Die schwarze Reiterin, "Erh-nü ying-hsiung chuan."* Zürich: Manesse-Verlag, 1954.

Povert' o novych gerojach (Hsin erh-nü ying-hsiung chuan). Moscow: Izdat. Inostr. Liter., 1951.

Shapiro, Sidney. *Daughters and Sons*. Peking: Foreign Languages Press, 1979.

Studies

Epstein, Maram. "Beauty Is the Beast: The Dual Face of Woman in Four Ch'ing Novels." Unpublished Ph. D. dissertation, Princeton University, 1992, especially, pp. 272-319.

Hou, Chien 侯健, "*Erh-nü ying-hsiung chuan shih-p'ing*" 兒女英雄傳試評 (An Attempt at the Appraisal of *Erh-nü ying-hsiung chuan*." In his *Chung-kuo hsiao-shuo pi-chiao yen-chiu* 中國小説比較研究 (Comparative Studies of Chinese Fiction). Taipei: Tung-ta, 1983, pp. 55-73.

Liao, Ch'iung-yüan 廖瓊媛. "*Erh-nü ying-hsiung chuan chih hsia-i yen-chiu*" 兒女英雄傳之俠義研究 (A Study of Knight-errantry and Altruism as seen in *Erh-nü ying-hsiung chuan*). Unpublished M.A. thesis, Tung-hai University, 1985.

McMahon, Keith. *Misers, Shrews, and Polygamists*. Durham and London: Duke University Press, 1995, pp. 265-282.

Mi, Sung-i 彌松頤. "*Erh-nü ying-hsiung chuan tso-che Wen K'ang chi ch'i chia-shih*" 兒女英雄傳作者文康及其家世 (Wen K'ang the Author of *Erh-nü ying-hsiung chuan* and the History of His Family). *Wen-hsien* 18 (1983): 21-29.

P'eng, Ts'ai-chu 彭彩珠. "Wen K'ang yü *Erh-nü ying-hsiung chuan*" 文康與兒女英雄傳. Unpublished M.A. thesis, Wen-hua Ta-hsüeh, Taipei, 1986.

Wang, Wei-k'ang 王偉康. "Lun *Erh-nü ying-hsiung chuan* ssu-hsiang nei-yün te fu-tsa-hsing" 兒女英雄傳思想內蘊複雜性 (On the complexity of the thought of *Erh-nü ying-hsiung chuan*), *Yang-chou shih-yüan hsüeh-pao: She-k'o-pan* (1992): 17-21.

Karl S. Y. Kao
Hong Kong University of Science and Technology

Erh-t'ung wen-hsüeh 兒童文學 (children's literature) in traditional China, not unlike its counterparts elsewhere, is an ill-defined and little studied subject. This is not to say that there was a dearth of children's literature in traditional China. Abundant historical references and biographical data attest to literary creations produced *for* the (direct and indirect) consumption of children, centered *around* young protagonists (thus stimulating popularity among the youngest section of the population), and, in the case of rhymes and verses, literary expressions may have been circulated *by* children. Taken together, these works produced for, around, of, even by children, though not an exclusively juvenile phenomenon, relate in various ways to the experience of childhood and represent a significant aspect of traditional literature.

Categorically speaking, works intended for children belong to two large groups: the pedagogical (those produced for teaching purposes) and the non-pedagogical (products from other daily-life activities or for amusement). The various *tzu-shu* 字書 (character books) or *meng-shu* 蒙書 (children's primers) represented two important kinds of instruction materials for beginners that existed at least since the Han dynasty and increased rapidly after the Sung period. The *Chi-chiu p'ien* 急就篇 (Words in Haste; 2016 characters in 32 sections written in seven-word couplets) attributed to Shih Yu 史游 (first century A.D.) is the single surviving example of the 10 titles listed as "primary learning" (*hsiao-hsüeh* 小學) materials in "Bibliographic Treatise" of the *Han-shu* (see Pan Ku*). The contemporary standard required young men beginning their careers to master 9000 characters. Thus anything less than a quarter that number was a sheer initiation. The rhymed-verse style of such works guaranteed their easy oral transmission. They quickly spread on the village level. Later, counterparts such as the *Ch'ien-tzu wen* 千字文 (One-thousand Character Text; 1000 characters in 125 four-word couplets) compiled by Chou Hsing-ssu 周興嗣 (early 6th century), the *Pai-chia hsing* 百家姓 (One-hundred Surnames; a 568-character text in four-word couplets which presents 509 surnames) from an anonymous ninth-century author, and the *San-tzu ching* 三字經 (The Three-character Classic, 1140 characters in three-word couplets) attributed to Wang Ying-lin 王應麟 (1223–1296),* were the best known and most popular of these children's primers. Bibliographic information suggests, however, that many more in their rank were produced and circulated for one period of time or another. The twentieth-century discovery among the Tun-huang documents of one such item entitled *K'ai-meng yao-hsün* 開蒙要訓 (Key Advice for Beginners, in 1400 words of four-word couplets) presents an important example of a once widely used Six-dynasty text. The reference to the "San, Pai, Ch'ien" 三百千 (that is, *San-tzu ching, Pai-chia hsing,* and *Ch'ien-tzu wen*) as the standard primers was a late-imperial recognition of a long-standing situation. A nineteenth-century local bookshop owner reported he sold over ten-thousand copies of these three books in a year.

Although not of a high literary quality themselves, as time passed the character books paid increasing attention to content and style. Their audience, which had been a mix of adult beginners of various social strata early on, also changed. From the thirteenth century onward, paralleling a significant expansion in elementary learning, production of these primer was reoriented to suit the interest of a sizable new, younger audience. The words became simpler, and classical references, abstruse terms, and complicated and difficult characters were avoided. Several traits of these character books deserve attention here. First, they made up an important part of the "literary" experience of Chinese children. Second, they were composed in three-word, four-word, or five-word rhymed phrases, gearing them towards easy memorization and oral transmission. Finally, these word books formed a foundation for the pre-modern Chinese literary world, providing material for popular literature and a shared repertoire for a wide range of popular literary productions. The *Ch'ien-tzu wen,* for example, influenced not only the formulation and syntax of technical manuals, catalogues, and indexing systems, but also puns, jokes, dialogues in novels, stories, and dramatic plots well into the twentieth century.

Closely related in nature, but slightly 'advanced' in content, was the corpus of works of "Meng-hsüeh" 蒙學 (Beginners' Study) that grew rapidly after the Sung dynasty. These works could be divided into four groups: (1) moral dicta, such as Chu Hsi's 朱熹 (1130–1200) *Tung-meng hsü-chih* 童蒙須知 (Essential Knowledge for School Children); (2) simple renditions of encyclopedic knowledge such as *Ming-wu meng-ch'iu* 名物蒙求 (Beginner's Guide to Names and Things); (3) history in rhymed verses such as Ch'en Li's 陳樂 (1252–1334) *Li-tai meng-ch'iu* 歷代蒙求 (Beginner's Guide to History, from the Yüan), Ch'eng Teng-chi's 程登吉 *Yu-hsüeh hsü-chih* 幼學須知 (Essential Knowledge for Elementary Learning; 33 *chüan*) from the Ming which was adapted to become *Yu-hsüeh ku-shih ch'iung-lin* 幼學故事瓊林 (A Collection of Valuable Stories for Elementary Learning), or Hsiao Liang-yu's 蕭良有 *Meng-yang ku-shih* 蒙養故事 (Stories to Nourish Beginners) which became *Lung-wen pien-ying* 龍文鞭影 (Fine Historical Texts for Quick Mastery); and (4) poetry readers for children such as the *Hsün-meng shih pai-shou* 訓蒙詩百首 (One-hundred Poems for Beginners) and *T'ang-shih san-pai shou* 唐詩三百首 (Three-hundred Poems of the T'ang)* were prepared primarily for pedagogical purposes. But like the character books they were not entirely devoid of literary quality and formed an important part of a younger reader's intellectual development. The readers in history and poetry, moreover, sprang from the same pool of material which later produced many stories and lyrics for children.

Children also absorbed other instructional literature including various clan or family instructional manuals (*p'u-hsün* 譜訓 or *chia-hsün* 家訓). Copies of *Chu Po-lu chih-chia ko-yen* 朱柏廬治家格言 (Proverbial Sayings for Household Management from Chu Po-lu), for instance, was held in countless family halls beginning in late-imperial times and were something that children of the gentry, the merchants, the artisans, and even some of the peasants were expected to memorize. However, these texts cannot be considered literature produced primarily for children.

Readers in history and biography adapted for youth were an important subgenre of children's literature. Ch'en Li's *Li-tai meng-ch'iu* (mentioned above) is a good example. It is an account of Chinese history from its earliest mythical period to the author's Yüan dynasty, rendered in four-word rhymed verses. In title and concept, the book follows the tradition of the T'ang-dynasty reader, *Meng-ch'iu* 蒙求 (Beginner's Guide; also in four-word verse) by Li Han 李瀚 (*fl.* early 8th c.). *Li-tai meng-ch'iu,* however, was written in a much simpler style using simpler characters in order to appeal to the increased numbers of readers of school age (rather than older beginners). After an introduction on heaven, earth and the people, *Li-tai meng-ch'iu* traces Chinese history from the Hsia dynasty to the Yüan, mentioning each dynasty's founding and final rulers as well as those who achieved fame in between, explaining their deeds, and commenting on their successes and failures. The *Chien-lüeh* 鑒略 (Simple Historical Examples), later called *Wu-tzu chien* 五字鑒 (Historical Examples in Five-word [Phrases]), authored by Li T'ing-chi 李廷機 (*chin-shih* 1583) of the Ming, put a general history in five-word rhymed verse. Tsou Sheng-mai 鄒聖脈 expanded and annotated the *Yu-hsüeh hsü-chih* (33 *chüan*) by Ch'eng Teng-chi to produce a popular children's reader, *Yu-hsüeh ku-shih ch'iung-lin* 幼學故事瓊林 (A Fine Garden of Inspiring Precedents for Young Students; 4 *chüan*). Hsiao Liang-yu's 蕭良有 *Meng-yang ku-shih* 蒙養故事 (Inspiring Precedents for the Raising of Children; Wan-li [1573–1619] era) also put history into four-word verses. A revision of Hsiao's work by the Anhwei schoolteacher Yang Ch'en-cheng 楊臣諍 became a widely circulated history for young readers during the Ch'ing dynasty entitled *Lung-wen pien-ying*. Yang's book treats history according to major themes and important events, rather than the usual rise and fall of dynasties. The tradition of producing simple histories in rhymed verse for children continued well into the nineteenth century. Pao Tung-li's 鮑東里 mid-nineteenth-century *Shih-chien chieh-yao pien-tu* 史鑒節要便讀 (A Handy Reader of Historical Examples in Outline Form; 16,000 characters) was one of the last works in this tradition.

Collections of short tales prepared for young children began to appear in the late sixteenth century and early seventeenth century. Although it is impossible to conclude that earlier works in the popular and oral traditions were intended exclusively for adults, the emergence of these specialized stories is important because it marks the earliest belletristic literature for children. Three of the most popular collections suffice as examples. The *Hsin-k'o lien-tui pien-meng ch'i-pao ku-shih ta-ch'üan* 新刻聯對便蒙七寶故事大全 (A Newly Printed Collection of Literary Couplets with Seven Treasuries of Stories for Made Easy for Beginners; 20 *chüan*) compiled by Wu Tao-ming 吳道明 contains 1623 entries (though the book-leaf claimed over 3000). It is an encyclopedic introduction to objects, phenomena, flora, fauna, numbers, colors, clothes, foods, and so forth. Each entry is headed

by a four-word verse, followed by a section of stories which illustrate the history of the term. The prefaces explains that this is in the tradition of classical instructional materials and is aimed at children at the beginning level and their teachers. The phrases *pien-meng* 便蒙 "made easy for beginners" and *lien-tui* 聯對 "literary couplets" in the title indicate the importance given to initiating students in the vital art of "rhyming" and "making couplets"–a vital step in basic literary training. The author, like many authors of similar works, spent his life as a village schoolteacher. Old legends, famous biographies and significant examples from the classics, the histories, and other sources are the basis for the thousands of tales included. The wood-block illustrations that grace each page of the 1604 edition must also have attracted young readers.

The *Hsin-chüan chu-shih ku-shih pai-mei* 新鐫註釋故事白眉 (Annotated Stories from White Eyebrows on Newly Cut Woodblocks) attributed to a certain Hsü Kuan-jih 許貫日 from Kiangnan, contains 2366 tales in 10 *chüan*. These stories are arranged under 26 categories, each headed by a four-word proverbial phrase and an explanatory, base story. According to the preface, these tales were collected from those which the author "happened to have heard or read" (*wen-wen chien-chien* 聞聞見見). He hoped to use them to open the minds of those who were still illiterate. The preface also makes clear that this was but one of countlessly similar works that were flooding the children's book market at the time.

Teng Pai-cho's 鄧百拙 *Ching-hsüan huang-mei ku-shih* 精選黃眉故事 (A Fine Selection of Yellow Eyebrow Stories) appeared shortly after Hsü Kuan-chih's and was clearly modeled on Hsü's work (Teng expresses the hope in his preface that his work will outsell Hsü's). The 1826 stories were arranged under 33 categories in 10 *chüan* and introduced (again according to the preface) "stories old and new" intended for young children. The four-word headings which preceded each short narrative were said to have been culled from the classics, histories and other miscellaneous works.

Many legends, novels, myths and even dramatic works provided material for or were adapted for children. But until very late in the imperial era, there seems to have been no mythology created exclusively for children. On the other hand, young readers shared with the wider population a large appetite for retellings of any tale. Thus, adaptation of stories from the Classics, from early histories, and from vernacular literature itself, were common. Those stories in which natural forces, animals or plants were anthropomorphized were most popular. The plots were easy to follow, the characters heroic, providing clear moral implications. The tale of Hou I shooting down nine of the ten suns ("Hou I she jih" 侯羿射日) was often the lead story in a collection, whereas love stories about Taoist goddesses (*hsien-nü* 仙女) or the well-known saga of the Herder Boy (Niu-lang 牛郎) and Weaver Maid (Chih-nü 織女), probably because of their complicated narratives and adult concerns, were consigned to the back of the book. Three accounts were extremely popular: excerpts from the story of Mu-lien rescuing his mother from hell ("Mu-lien chiu mu" 目蓮救母), No-cha's battle with the sea spirits ("No-cha nao-hai" 哪吒鬧海), and Monkey's disrupting Heaven ("Wu-k'ung nao T'ien-kung 悟空鬧天宮). All three deal with children (even Mu-lien is portrayed here in his role as a son) or childlike characters and show their potential for rebellion or resistance—a theme which seemed popular with the young audience. The powerful impact of these stories in their oral as well as literary incarnations had on children and childhood is attested in late imperial biographies and reminiscences.

Lastly, there are a large number of rhymes, songs, ditties and miscellaneous verse that were either prepared for children or reputed to be composed by them. These works can be classified under three headings according to their background and nature. First were the special poetry collections or nursery rhymes intended for the children's enjoyment. *Hsün-meng shih pai-shou* and *T'ang-shih san-pai-shou* (see above) are the best known, but other collections of simplified poems of various genres (*ku-shih* 古詩, *chüeh-chü* 絕句, *lü-shih* 律詩, etc.—see *shih*⁸) also flooded the late-imperial children's book market. Poems with a limited number of basic characters, simple tropes, and lively images—i.e., those considered of interest for a youthful audience—were selected. In addition to choosing such poems from existing collections, a second type of children's verse was the new poetry written especially for children. The best known collections of such verse was the trilogy of *Hsiao-erh yü* 小兒語 (Verses for Children), *Nü hsiao-erh yü* 女小兒語 (Verses for Girls), and *Hsü Hsiao-erh yü* 續小兒語 (More Verses for Children) written by the father-son pair of Lü Te-sheng 呂得勝 and Lü K'un 呂坤 in the sixteenth century. Most of these works presented "appropriate" material for children and were designed to have a positive moral impact on their readers. A third type were the poems which were purely didactic in nature, such as the eighty-four works included in P'eng Chi-kuang's 彭繼光 *T'ung-ko yang-cheng* 童歌養正 (Children's Songs for Moral Rectification).

Given the long-standing interest in initiating and enhancing children's appreciation of rhymed literature, it was not unusual for educated Chinese youngsters to be composing their own simple poems at an early age. Late imperial manuals like the anonymous *Chin-pi ku-shih* 金壁故事 (Golden Wall

Tales), Chü Wan-yü's 車萬育 *Sheng-lü ch'i-meng* 聲律啟蒙 (Introduction to Rhymes and Phonetics), *Hsün-meng p'ien-chü* 訓蒙駢句 (Parallel Verses for Beginners), or *Li-weng tui-yün* 笠翁對韻 (Li-weng's Book of Rhymes and Couplets; attributed to Li Yü's 李漁 [1611–1680]*) were convenient aids for daily drills. Individual biographies contain random poems said to come from the mouths or brushes of literary boys and girls at an early age. Although some are clearly child-like in tone and puerile in language, the authenticity of such works is difficult to verify. Collections of children's poetry, moreover, were rare. The Sung genius Wang Chu 汪洙 is said to have composed thirty-four five-word *chüeh-chü* at age nine; these works were collected in his *Sheng-t'ung shih* 神童詩 (Poems by a Child Prodigy), but the didactic sentiments and mature emotions contained in them are not what one would expect from a nine-year-old boy. Nevertheless, the representation of the "child's voice" in traditional Chinese literature is a subject which deserves further exploration.

Other than poems written for children by adults and those few verses they wrote themselves, a third group of songs and rhymes may be considered children's lyrics: folksongs for children. Common sense and the popularity of children's verse in the twentieth century suggest that children in traditional China could hardly have lived in a world without songs. Documentary evidence has shown that lyrics and verses centering around children's lives often appeared in a "freer" style which disregarded some of the prosodic niceties. Over two hundred *t'ung-yao* 童謠 or "children's rhymes" can be culled from the twenty-four dynastic histories, but since these works normally survived because they contained a political connotation or social message, it is doubtful whether they had much to do with the world of children, although they may have been chanted by young and old alike. Whatever the case, these works feature simple, rustic diction and oral characteristics. Late imperial compilations of varied verse also contain a fair number of examples said to be children's songs. Yang Shen's 楊慎 (1488–1559)* *Ku-chin yao-yen* 古今謠諺 (Rhymes and Proverbs, Past and Present) includes 123 *t'ung-ko* 童歌 (children's songs) from ancient times to the sixteenth century. Shih Meng-lan's 史夢蘭 *Ku-chin feng-yao shih-i* 古今風謠拾遺 (A Collection of Rhymes and Lyrics, Past and Present, Previously Lost) contained 75; and Tu Wen-lan's 杜文瀾 (1815–1881) *Ku yao-yen* 古謠諺 (Old Rhymes and Proverbs) had 200. It seems that songs from the "younger folk" were prevalent in the towns and villages of traditional China. If nothing else, these were the disturbingly "nonsensical" activities that prefaces of didactic works like *Hsiao-erh yü* vowed to eradicate and replace. Late nineteenth-century and early-twentieth-century inventories of popular rhymes and children's verses from many regions and provinces preserved a sizable number of these works, many of which had an undaunted folk character and an attractive childlike tone. "Action songs" such as those sung while bathing, going to sleep, comforting an infant, or playing games, as well as more literary verses shaped by verbal competition or matching, evolved naturally around the lives of children. Some may suggest traces of reworking, but others appear relatively free of an editorial hand. A fraction of these poems have accompanying tunes (these were true children's "songs"), while the majority existed as lyric-texts only (called *t'u-ko* 徒歌, "plain verse").

Aside from literature for children and by children, there was also a considerable corpus of works *about* children. Many literary genres included narratives about the lives and experiences of child protagonists. *San-yen* 三言 (see Feng Meng-lung 馮夢龍, 1574–

1646*), *Erh-p'o* 二拍 (see Ling Meng-ch'u 凌濛初, 1580–1644*) and *Liao-chai chih-i* 聊齋志異 (Strange Stories from the Leisure Studio)* contain a number of these portraits of children. These representations of the very young are another aspect of the interplay of children, childhood and literature in traditional Chinese society.

From educational materials such as character books and primers, to potted histories and biographies, to adaptations of legends, myths, and fables, to poetry, rhymes and songs, a wide range of literary works for, about, and by children existed in traditional China. They are not only an important part of the traditional literary activity, but also a vital source for authors, scholars, and readers interested in traditional history and culture. Moreover, when a new generation of authors ushered in the modern Chinese children's literature movement (1921-1927), this was the indigenous heritage that supplied them with material and inspiration, on the one hand, and defined the line of their revolt and departure, on the other.

Editions and References

Ch'en, Ch'un 陳淳 (Sung dynasty). *Ching-hsüeh ch'i-meng* 經學啟蒙. Mss. edition collated by Mr. Chiang 蔣 of the Hsi-pu 西圃.

Ch'eng, Teng-chi 程登吉 (Ming dynasty). *Yu-hsüeh hsü-chih* 幼學須知 (Essential Knowledge for Elementary Learning). 33 *chüan*. Wu-pen T'ang 務本堂 edition (1842).

Cheng, I-wei 鄭以偉, ed. *Chin-pi ku-shih* 金璧故事 (Golden Wall Tales). Shanghai: Shang-hai Ku-chi, 1990. Photolithic reprint of a Wan-li 萬曆 era (1573–1619) edition printed by the Huang-chih Chai 黃直齋 of the Chi-i T'ang 集義堂.

Chou, Hsing-ssu 周興嗣 (early 6th century). *Ch'ien-tzu wen* 千字文 (One-thousand Character Text). Tsinan: Shan-tung Yu-i, 1989.

Chü, Wan-yü 車萬育 (Ch'ing dynasty). *Sheng-lü ch'i-meng* 聲律啟蒙 (Introduction to Rhymes and Phonetics). Changsha: Yüeh-li, 1987.

Fang, Feng-ch'en 方逢辰 (1221-1291). *Ming-wu meng-ch'iu* 名物蒙求. In Chu Sheng 朱升 (1299–1371), *Hsiao Ssu-shu* 小四書. 5 *ch.* Fu-chien Fan-shu, 1872.

Hsiao, Liang-yu 蕭良有 (Ming dynasty). *Lung-wen pien-ying* 龍文鞭影 (Fine Historical Texts for Quick Mastery). Yang Ch'eng-cheng 楊臣諍 (Ch'ing dynasty), ed. Taipei: Te-chih, 1967. This work is Yang Ch'eng-cheng revision of Hsiao's original *Meng-yang ku-shih* 蒙養故事.

Li, Yü 李漁 (1611–1680). *Li Weng tui-yün* 李翁對韻 (Li Weng's Book of Rhymes and Couplets). Changsha: Yüeh-li, 1987.

Lü, Te-sheng 呂得勝 (Ch'ing dynasty). *Hsiao-erh yü* 小兒語 (Verses for Children). Shanghai: Shang-wu, 1936. Based on the *I-hai chu-ch'en* 藝海珠塵 edition.

Pai-chia hsing 百家姓. Tsinan: Shan-tung Yu-i, 1989.

Shih, Meng-lan 史夢蘭 (Ch'ing dynasty). *Ku-chin feng-yao shih-i* 古今風謠拾遺 (A Collection of Rhymes and Lyrics, Past and Present, Previously Lost). Printed edition from the T'ung-chih 同治 era (1862-1874).

Shih, Yu 史游 (2nd c. A.D.) *Chi-chiu p'ien* 急就篇. Yen Shih-ku 顏師古 (581–645), comm. Shanghai: Shang-hai Shu-tien, 1984. Reprint of a Ming-manuscript version held by Han-fen Lou 涵芬樓 (Shanghai).

Teng, Pai-cho 鄧百拙, ed. and comp. *Ching-hsüan huang-mei ku-shih* 精選黃眉故事 (A Fine Selection of Yellow Eyebrow Stories). Preface dated 1616; Ching-chi T'ang 經濟堂 ed.

Tu, Wen-lan 杜文瀾 (1815–1881). *Ku yao-yen* 古謠諺 (Old Rhymes and Proverbs). Taipei: Shih-chieh, 1960.

Wang, Ying-ling 王應麟 (1223–1296). *San-tzu ching* 三字經. Tsinan: Shan-tung Yu-i, 1989.

Wu, Tao-ming 吳道明. *Hsin-k'o lien-tui pien-meng ch'i-pao ku-shih ta-ch'üan* 新刻對聯便蒙七寶故事大全 (A Newly Printed Collection of Literary Couplets with Seven Treasuries of Stories for Beginners). 20 *ch'üan*. A 1604 reprints.

Yang, Shen 楊慎 (1488–1559).* *Ku-chin yao-yen* 古今謠諺 (Rhymes and Proverbs, Past and Present). Taipei: Shang-wu Yin-shu-kuan, 1976.

Translations

Giles, Herbert A. *San tzu ching: Elementary Chinese.* 2nd ed., rev. Rpt. Taipei: Literature House, 1964.

Julien, Stanislas (1797–1873). *Institutio prima linguae sinicae; San-tseu king. . . Trium litterarum liber a Wang-Pe-heo. . . compositus; sinicum textum adjecta 214 clavium tabula ed. et in latinum vertit.* Paris: B. Duprant, 1864.

Malan, Solomon Caesar (1812–1894). *The Three-fold San-tsze-King, or, the Trilateral Classic of China.* London: D. Nutt, 1856.

des Michels, Abel. *Tam tu kinh; ou, Le livre des phrases de trois caracteres. Avec le grand commentaire du Vuong tan thang. Texte, transcription annamite et chinoise, explication litterale et traduction complète.* Paris: E. Leroux, 1882.

Ogawa, Tamaki 小川環樹 and Kida Akiyoshi 木田章義. *Chûkai Senjibun* 注解千字文. 2v. Tokyo: Iwanami, 1984.

Watson, Burton. *Meng Ch'iu: Famous Episodes from Chinese History and Legend.* Tokyo: Kodansha, 1979. Transl. of a Japanese edition, Hayakawa Mitsusaburô, ed. (*Môgyu.* 2v. Tokyo: Meiji Shoin 1973); useful introduction and translator's note.

Studies

Ch'en, Cheng-chih 陳正治. *Chung-kuo erh-ko yen-chiu* 中國兒歌研究. Taipei: Ch'in-ch'in Wen-hua, 1985.

Ch'en, T'ien-shui 陳天水. *Chung-kuo ku-tai shen-hua* 中國古代神話. Taipei: Ch'ün-yü T'ang, 1988.

Chang, Sheng-yü 張聖瑜. *Erh-t'ung wen-hsüeh yen-chiu* 中國兒童文學研究. Shang-hai: Shang-wu, 1920.

Cheng, Kuang-chung 鄭光中. *Yu-erh wen-hsüeh* 幼兒文學. Chengtu: Shao-nien Erh-t'ung, 1988.

Chiang, Feng 蔣風, ed. *Chung-kuo hsien-tai erh-t'ung wen-hsüeh shih 1917–1927* 中國現代兒童文學史 1917–1927. Shih-chia-chuang: Shao-nien Erh-t'ung, 1987.

Chu, Chieh-fan 朱介凡. *Chung-kuo erh-ko* 中國兒歌. Taipei: Ch'un Wen-hsüeh, 1978.

Han, Hsi-to 韓錫鐸. *Chung-hua meng-hsüeh chi-ch'eng* 中華蒙學集成. Shenyang: Liao-ning Chiao-yü, 1993.

Hsü, Shou-t'ao 徐守濤. *Erh-t'ung shih lun* 兒童詩論. Pingtung: Tung-i, 1979.

Hui-t'u t'ung-yao ta-kuan 繪圖童謠大觀.

Taipei: Kuang-wen, 1977.

Ko, Lin 葛琳. *Erh-t'ung wen-hsüeh–chuang-tso yü hsin-shang* 兒童文學一創作與欣賞. Taipei: K'ang-ch'iao, 1980.

Lei, Ch'iao-yün 雷僑雲. *Chung-kuo erh-t'ung wen-hsüeh yen-chiu* 中國兒童文學研究. Taipei: Hsüeh-sheng, 1988.

___. *Tun-huang erh-t'ung wen-hsüeh* 敦煌兒童文學. Taipei: Hsüeh-sheng, 1985.

Li, Ching-chiang 林景江. *Chung-kuo ko min-tsu min-chien wen-hsüeh chi-ch'u* 中國各民族民間文學基礎. Tsilin: Hsin-hua, 1986.

Lin, Chung-lung 林鍾隆. *Ah Hui te hsin* 阿輝的心. Taichung: Man-t'ien-hsing, 1965.

___. *Yüeh kuang-kuang* 月光光. Chung-li: T'ai-wang Kuo-yü, n.d.

Lin, Liang 林良. *Erh-t'ung tu-wu yen-chiu Ti-erh chi–T'ung-hua yen-chiu* 兒童讀物研究第二輯一童化研究. Taipei: Hsiao-hsüeh-sheng, 1966.

Lin, Wen-pao 林文寶. *Erh-t'ung shih-ko yen-chiu* 兒童詩歌研究. Taitung: Privately published, 1995.

Su, Shang-yao 蘇尚耀. *Erh-t'ung wen-hsüeh ku-shih hsüan-chi* 兒童文學故事選集. Taipei: Yu-shih Wen-hua, 1989.

Sun, Ch'ing-feng 孫晴峰. *Hsiao feng* 小紅. Taipei: Min-sheng Pao, 1989.

T'an, Ta-hsien 譚達先. *Chung-kuo min-chien t'ung-hua yen-chiu* 中國民間童話研究. Taipei: Shang-wu, 1988.

___. *Chung-kuo min-chien yü-yen yen-chiu* 中國民間寓言研究. Taipei: Shang-wu, 1988.

Ts'ai, Shang-chih 蔡尚志. *Erh-t'ung ku-shih yüan-li* 兒童故事原理. Taipei: Wu-nan, 1992.

Wu, Ting 吳鼎. *Erh-t'ung wen-hsüeh yen-chiu* 兒童文學研究. Taipei: Yüan-liu, 1980.

Yin, Shih-lin 尹世霖. *Chung-kuo erh-ko i-ch'ien shou* 中國兒歌一千首. Tsinan: Ming-t'ien, 1988.

Hsiung Ping-chen 熊秉真
Institute of Modern History, Academia Sinica

Fan Yeh 范曄 (*tzu* Wei-tsung 蔚宗, 398–446) was a great historian and skillful writer. Born into a gentry family from Shun-yang 順陽 (modern Nei-hsiang 內鄉, or Hsi-ch'uan 淅川, in Hopei), several of his close relatives had distinguished themselves in government service and scholarship. His grandfather, Fan Ning 范寧 (339–401), Prefect of Yü-hang 餘杭 County and Governor of Yü-chang 豫章 Commandery during the Eastern Chin dynasty (317–420), was well known for promoting canonical learning, for encouraging the establishment of Confucian schools at the provincial level, and for writing what was later recognized as the standard commentary on *Ku-liang chuan* 穀梁傳. His father, Fan T'ai 范泰 (355–428), a senior minister of the Eastern Chin and an extensively learned scholar, was fond of drinking, careless of social niceties, and paid little heed to his administrative duties. Yet he was the one of the important supporters of Liu Yü 劉裕 (356-422), who later founded the Liu-Sung dynasty (420–479). Fan Yeh, the fourth son of Fan T'ai, was adopted by his uncle, Fan Hung-chih 范弘之, an Erudite at the Imperial Academy during the Chin. He thereby inherited the title of marquis from his uncle, but his own father remained his main influence.

Fan Yeh received extensive canonical and historiographical training in his youth, and showed talent in music, calligraphy and belles lettres. His biography in the *Sung-shu* 宋書 (69:1819-33) mentions that he played the *p'i-p'a* well and could compose new tunes. His musical talent even impressed Emperor Wen 文 of the Sung (r. 424–453). Fan Yeh began his official career on Liu Yü's staff at the end of the Eastern Chin. For most of his career, however, Fan served under Liu I-k'ang 劉義康, the Liu-Sung Prince of P'eng-ch'eng 彭城 and a younger brother of Emperor Wen, whose power extended beyond his fief to the capital. By 432 he had been appointed to a high position in the personnel division of the Imperial Secretariat. During that year, however, Fan Yeh committed the indiscretion of drinking to excess, which his father had certainly done many times, on the eve

of the burial of Liu I-k'ang's mother. He was then exiled to the post of Governor of Hsüan-ch'eng 宣城 (modern Anhwei). Thanks to the interruption of his official career in the capital and his frustration with politics in general, Fan Yeh began during these years to compile the great work of his life, the *Hou Han shu* 後漢書 (History of the Later Han).

From the late 430s onward, Fan Yeh received a series of promotions that eventually restored him to the court, where he seems to have won the favor of Emperor Wen. He was eventually appointed to influential posts: Commander of the Imperial Guard on the Left (*Tso-wei chiang-chün* 左衛將軍) and Supplier to the Heir Apparent (*T'ai-tzu chan-shih* 太子詹事). Then in 445 a plot to install Liu I-k'ang on the throne was exposed. The plot had been organized by K'ung Hsi-hsien 孔熙先, with whom Fan Yeh had close personal associations, and Hsieh Tsung 謝綜, Fan's nephew. Although he concealed what he knew of the plot, Fan was named one of the ringleaders by disgruntled colleagues. After an investigation conducted by the emperor himself, Fan Yeh was publicly executed on 23 January 446.

His major legacy was the *Hou Han shu*, a history in 120 *chüan* covering the period 25–220 A.D. It is one of the few privately compiled dynastic histories to be recognized as one of the "official histories" 正史. The work consists of ten *chüan* of annals (*pen-chi* 本紀), eighty *chüan* of biographies (*lieh-chuan* 列傳), and thirty *chüan* of treatises (*chih* 志). Although Fan Yeh intended to compile various treatises to complement all those that Pan Ku wrote for the *Han-shu*, he could not accomplish this goal, perhaps due to the unexpected incident that cut short his natural life. The thirty *chüan* of treatises now attached to the *Hou Han shu* are actually from Ssu-ma Piao's 司馬彪 (240–306) *Hsü Han-shu* 續漢書, a work no longer extant. Ssu-ma's treatises have regularly circulated together with Fan Yeh's work since the eleventh century.

Fan Yeh lived two-hundred years after the end of the Later Han. He was neither eyewitness to the events of the period, nor did he have access to original, official documents. Nonetheless, he was able to make thorough use of all sources available to him: there were already a number of precedent works of Later Han history, mostly written by Chin-dynasty historians, which Fan Yeh could have consulted. In addition to Ssu-ma Piao's *Hsü Han-shu*, there were several works with the title *Hou Han shu* (by Hsieh Ch'eng 謝承, Hsieh Ch'en 謝沈, Yüan Shan-sung 袁山松, and Liu I-ch'ing 劉義慶 [403-444; see *Shih-shuo hsin-yü* 世說新語 (New Account of Tales of the World)*]), three titled *Hou Han chi* 後漢紀 (by Yüan Hung 袁宏, Hsüeh Ying 薛瑩 and Chang Fan 張璠), in addition to Chang Ying's 張瑩 *Hou Han nan-chi* 後漢南紀 and Hua Chiao's 華嶠 *Hou Han shu*. In addition, there was the chronological history of the Later Han, *Tung-kuan Han-chi* 東觀漢記 compiled by numerous Later Han historians, that has been the basis for all accounts of the Later Han. These works in total contain more than nine-hundred *chüan*, providing abundant data on the history of the period that would have made Fan Yeh's task easier. It seems he primarily utilized the *Tung-kuan Han-chi* and Hua Chiao's *Hou Han shu*. Although Fan was dependent on earlier histories for the factual details in his annals and biographies, he developed his own historiographical principles and has shown his own unique style in the combination of these materials and the compilation of his history. This is evident in the organization and arrangement of the biographies in the *Hou Han shu* is clearly influenced by ethical concerns. More attention was given to the representative individuals of various types who were influential in the period rather than to those who held high position or social status. A state chancellor with no unusual characteristics would merit only a short notice (if any at all), while a hermit possessed with ethical courage would often be treated in a lengthy biography. Although Fan Yeh was not the first to devote a chapter in a dynastic history to a particular group of persons, he followed precedents in Hsieh Ch'eng's *Hou Han shu* and Ssu-ma Piao's *Hsü Han-shu* to create more collective biographies than all the then existing "official histories"; examples include those accounts of partisans (*tang-ku* 黨錮), eunuchs (*huan-che* 宦者), literati (*wen-yüan* 文苑), independent spirits (*tu-hsing* 獨行), magicians and physicians (*fang-shu* 方術), hermits (*i-min* 逸民), and female exemplars (*lieh-nü* 列女). Biographies of some of these types of individuals (for example, magicians and physicians—usually called *fang-shih* 方士) found in the early dynastic histories such as the *Shih-chi* 史記, *Han-shu* 漢書, and *Hou Han shu,* contain vivid and imaginative writing, but were based primarily on non-official sources, such as *pieh-chuan* 別傳 (independent biography) and *chih-kuai* 志怪.* Thus Fan Yeh's choice to emphasize such figures more than his predecessors produced, first, many colorful narratives of immortals and *fang-shih*, prophecies and strange phenomena, and, second, a series of comments critical of his indulging his own interests in the occult to the point that some of his narratives in the *Hou Han shu* were "unorthodox" (*pu-ching* 不經).

Although Fan Yeh was probably dependent on factual details from his various probable sources and this dependence must have made the composition of *Hou Han shu* to some extent a mechanical task, Fan's narrative style is striking and deserves comment. Fan often rephrased the sources he drew upon, and probably rewrote them as well. The overall impression his narrative prose makes, according to Ronald Egan (see *Studies* below) differs from that of the previous Later Han histories. The more carefully chosen language, the denser and more interesting diction, and the stronger rhythms (Egan, pp. 346-380) distinguish the style of *Hou Han shu* from all earlier accounts of the era. Fan Yeh himself took most pride in the sections of his *Hou Han shu* that were not the mere narration of events; that is, in the *hsü* 序 (introductions), *lun* 論 (discussions), and *tsan* 贊 (eulogies), which contain his summaries of major developments and his evaluations of policies. In these essays Fan Yeh speaks most clearly in his own voice. The essays are characterized by a careful structure and strong, well-considered opinions. The language itself is rich, contributing to Fan Yeh's reputation as a parallel prose (*p'ien-t'i wen* 駢體文)* stylist and helping to establish this kind of writing as the standard mode for all narrative in subsequent eras. Intelligent use of rhythm, parallel construction, and innovative language, however, helps to distinguish Fan Yeh's literary style from that of his contemporaries and has enforced the power of his writing. As Egan points out, "Fan Yeh developed a new style of narrative prose, one that was influenced by certain contemporary trends, but which can lay claim to excellencies all its own" (p. 380). Fan Yeh surely also benefited greatly not only from the plentiful data in the precedent Later Han histories, but also from their stylistic techniques. For instance, several discussions in Fan's *Hou Han shu* were copied entirely or part from Hua Chiao's *Hou Han shu.* Current scholarly opinion recognizes that Fan Yeh's work, though the last of the histories to treat the Later Han, epitomizes the achievements of its predecessors. This situation was enhanced as Fan's *Hou Han shu* completely supplanted all earlier histories of the Later Han except for Yüan Hung's *Hou Han-chi.*

Other historical and belletristic works by Fan Yeh, including the *Han-shu tsuan* 漢書纘 (eighteen *chüan*), a collected works (in fifteen *chüan*), some *lu* 錄 (records, one *chüan*), and the *Pai-kuan chieh-tz'u* 百官階次 (one *chüan*), are no longer extant. More of Fan Yeh's historical essays were included in the *Wen-hsüan* 文選*than those by any other historian. A few more essays can be found in the Yen K'o-chün's 嚴可均 (1762–1843) *Ch'üan [Liu] Sung wen* 全[劉]宋文 (see *Ch'üan Shang-ku San-tai Ch'in Han San-kuo Liu-ch'ao wen* 全上古三代秦漢三國六朝文*). Early praise for Fan Yeh's writing skill can be found in *Shih p'in* 詩品 (An Evaluation of Poetry)* by Chung Jung 鍾嶸 (*ca.* 465–518) and *Shih-t'ung* 史通 (Generalities on History) by Liu Chih-chi 劉知幾 (661–721).*

Editions and References

Chang, Shun-hui 張舜徽. *Hou Han shu tzu-tien* 後漢書詞典. Tsinan: Shan-tung Chiao-yü, 1994.
Chou, T'ien-yu 周天游, comm. *Pa chia Hou Han shu chi-chu* 八家後漢書輯注. Shanghai: Shang-hai Ku-chi, 1986.
Go Kansho goi shûsei 後漢書語彙集成 (Index to Historical Terms in the Standard History of the Later Han). 3v. Kyoto, 1960-62.
Hou Han shu 後漢書. *Po-na* edition. Rpt. Taipei, 1968.
Hou Han shu. 12v. Peking: Chung-hua, 1965. A punctuated, critical edition.
Hou Han shu chi chu-shih tsung-ho yin-te 後漢書及注釋總合引得 (Combined Indices to the Standard History of the Later Han). Rpt. Taipei: Ch'eng-wen, 1966. *Harvard-Yenching Institute Sinological Index Series* 41.
*Hou Han shu tz'u-tien*後漢書. Chang Shun-hui 張舜徽, ed. Tsinan: Shan-tung Chiao-yü, 1994.
Li, Yü-min 李裕民. *Hou Han shu jen-ming so-yin* 後漢書人名索引. Peking: Chung-hua, 1979.
Liu-ch'ao wen 六朝文, 3:2518-2519.
Shih, Chih-mien 施之勉. *Hou Han shu chi-chieh pu* 後漢書集解補. Taipei, 1982.
Wong, Fook-luen 黃福鑾, ed. *Hou Han shu so-yin* 後漢書人名索引. Hong Kong, 1971.
Wang, Hsien-ch'ien 王先謙 (1842-1918),

comm. *Hou Han shu chi-chieh* 後漢書集解. Changsha, 1915; rpt. Taipei, 1955.

Translations

de Crespigny, Rafe. *Portents of Protest in the Later Han Dynasty.* Canberra: Australian National University Press, 1976.

DeWoskin, Kenneth J. *Doctors, Diviners, and Magicians of Ancient China: Biographies of Fang-shih.* New York: Columbia University Press, 1983. Translates *Fang-shih* 方士 biographies from *Hou Han shu.*

Goodrich, Chauncey S. "Two Chapters in the Life of an Empress of the Later Han," *HJAS* 25(1965): 165-77.

Honda, Wataru 本田済. *Kansho, Go Kansho, Sangoku shi retsudensen* 漢書後漢書三国志列伝選. Tokyo: Heibon-sha, 1969. Includes translations of 14 biographies from the *Hou Han shu.*

Mansvelt-Beck, B. J. *The Treatise of Later Han, Their Author, Sources, Contents and Place in Chinese Historiography.* Leiden: E. J. Brill, 1990.

Young, Gregory. *Three Generals of Later Han.* Canberra: Faculty of Asian Studies, Australian National University, 1984. Translation of Chapter 65.

Studies

Bielenstein, Hans. "Prolegomena on the Historiography of the *Hou Han Shu,*" in "The Restoration of the Han Dynasty, I," *BMFEA* 26 (1954): 1-81[209].

Chang, Shu-tsu 張術祖. "Fan Wei-tsung nien-p'u" 范蔚宗年譜, *Shih-hsüeh nien-pao* 3.2 (1940).

Chao, Chih-han 趙志漢 and Lin Chien-ming 林劍鳴. "Fan Yeh," in Ch'en Ch'ing-ch'üan 陳清泉 and Su Shuang-pi 蘇霜碧 *et al., Chung-kuo shih-hsüeh-chia p'ing-chuan* 中國史學家評傳. Chengchow: Chung-chou Ku-chi, 1985, pp. 184-209.

Egan, Ronald C. "The Prose Style of Fan Yeh," *HJAS* 39 (1979): 339-401.

Gardiner, K. H. J. "The *Hou-Han-shu* as a Source for the Early Expansion of Koguryô," *MS* 28(1969): 148-87.

Lin, Li-o 林麗娥. "Fan Yeh chih wen-hsüeh chi ch'i shih-lun" 范曄之文學及其論. Unpublished M. A. thesis, National Cheng-chih University (Taiwan), 1982.

Shen, Li-hsün 沈麗薰. "Fan Wei-tsung te shih-hsüeh" 范蔚宗的史學. Unpublished M. A. thesis, Tung-hai University (Taiwan), 1972.

Sung, Wen-min 宋文民. *Hou Han shu k'ao-shih* 後漢書考釋. Shanghai, 1995.

Wang, Yün-hsi 王運熙. "Fan Yeh *Hou Han shu* te hsü-lun" 范曄後漢書的序論, *Wen-hsüeh i-ch'an tseng-k'an* 10(1966): 52-65.

Wu, Shu-p'ing 吳樹平. "Ch'in Han shih shih-liao" 秦漢史史料. In Ch'en Kao-hua 陳高華, Ch'en Chih-ch'ao 陳智超 *et al. Chung-kuo ku-tai-shih shih-liao hsüeh* 中國古代史史料學. Peking: Pei-ching Ch'u-pan-she, 1983, pp. 104-109.

Lu Zongli 呂宗力
Hong Kong University of Science and Technology

Hao-fang p'ai 豪放派 (School of the Heroic and Unrestricted) was a term used by Ming and later *tz'u* 詞* critics to depict a lyrical style begun by Su Shih 蘇軾 (1037–1101)* and realized by Hsin Ch'i-chi 辛棄疾 (1140–1207),* his contemporaries, and his followers. The *Hao-fang p'ai* was a reaction to the limitations in subject matter, the sentimental tone, and the elevated diction of the *tz'u* composers of the Late T'ang. These Late T'ang lyricists had depicted an extravagant, indulgent life-style, were preoccupied with sentiment, especially romantic love and the depiction of feminine beauty, and preferred exquisite, ornamented language.

Before Su Shih only Liu Yung 柳永 (987–1053)* had striven to broaden the subject matter of the *tz'u* and to write in a more colloquial language about the lives and feelings of a broader cross-section (although primarily urban) of the populace. Liu also adopted many new tunes, longer than the conventional ones, which were later called *man-tz'u* 慢詞 (slow or extended lyrics–see *tz'u**). Liu's efforts also marked the first significant change in the development of the literati lyric.

Although Su Shih left a multi-faceted legacy, his *tz'u* works have deservedly drawn a great deal of attention.

Disregarding the prosodic and stylistic conventions of his era, Su Shih displayed a straightforward manner of expression in his lyrics. Although Fan Chung-yen 范仲淹 (989–1052)* and Wang An-shih 王安石 (1021–1086)* also attempted a new, freer style in their tz'u, it was Su Shih whose lyrics were successful in breaking away from the gentility and delicacy of what was then tz'u convention. For the first time he brought techniques of shih-poetry and even prose writing into the tz'u genre. The Ming critics conceived this as a Hao-fang Style, in contrast to the conventional Wan-yüeh 婉約 Style (see Wan-yüeh p'ai**). Among the more than 300 pieces of his extant tz'u preserved in Tung-p'o yüeh-fu 東坡樂府, the free revelation of personal feelings and experiences dominates.

Although traditionally Hsin Ch'i-chi is credited with taking the Hao-fang tendency the next step beyond Su Shih, the Jurchen also played a role in this literary development. Their capture of the Sung capital Pien-liang 汴梁 (modern K'ai-feng 開封, Honan) and the subsequent apprehension of Emperor Hui 徽 (r. 1101–1125) in 1126 stimulated the patriotism of Sung loyalists. Some lyricists, such as Li Kang 李綱 (d. 1140), Chao Ting 趙鼎 (1085–1147), Hu Ch'üan 胡銓 (1102–1180), Li Kuang 李光 (1078–1159), Chang Yüan-kan 張元幹 (1091–1161), Ch'en Yü-i 陳與義 (1090–1138),* Yüeh Fei 岳飛 (1103–1141), Lü Pen-chung 呂本中 (fl. 1119) and Chu Tun-ju 朱敦儒 (1080/1–ca. 1175) had already attempted to interweave patriotic themes into their tz'u, a genre formerly confined to the roomscapes of private life. To be sure, many of these "poets" were primarily known as patriotic or political figures. Nevertheless, their works had some influence on Hsin Ch'i-chi and his friends. These latter poets also used lyrics to record their hopes for a political or military career, their meditations on history, their travels, or merely to

respond to a friend. In terms of literary skill, Hsin and his colleagues Chang Hsiao-hsiang 張孝祥 (1132–1169), Liu Kuo 劉過 (1154–1206), Ch'en Liang 陳亮 (1143–1194)* and Liu K'o-chuang 劉克莊 (1187–1269)* displayed the talent and maturity necessary for literary historians to take note of the appearance of a new style.

The emergence of these Hao-fang poets was, however, also related to ideology, to personality types. Sung literati were all faced with the frustration of trying to cultivate their own moral character while serving a government they often viewed as amoral. Many reacted by withdrawing from the political arena, some even from society. Others attempted to effect change, convinced that their ethical superiority and administrative talent could make a difference. The Hao-fang lyricists inevitably belonged to the latter group. They carried over into their lyrics an unconstrained conception of art, a broadened scenic vision, a sonorous tone, and a fluid narrative technique. The Ming critic Yang T'ing-chih 楊廷芝 sums up their attitude best: "Hao means that I can subjugate the whole world, and fang means that nothing can confine me." 豪則我可蓋乎世，放則物無可羈乎我。

This heroic manner naturally inspired and influenced a number of admirers and imitators, especially in the later years of the Southern Sung dynasty. Liu Ch'en-weng 劉辰翁 (1232–1297)* was best known for his adoption of Hsin's style, but some lyricists better known for their aestheticism and sensuality, such as Chang Yen 張炎 (1248–1320)** occasionally wrote hao-fang pieces. In the late-seventeenth century, following the virtual disappearance of the genre during the Ming dynasty, a group of lyricists in Yang-hsien 陽羨 (modern I-hsing 宜興, Kiangsu) led by Ch'en Wei-sung 陳維崧 (1626–1682)* revived the Hao-fang Style and were known as the Yang-hsien *p'ai* (Yang-hsien School), a rival to the two other major lyric schools, Che-hsi 浙西* and Ch'ang-chou 常州.*

The term *hao-fang* was initially used to refer to a heroic and unbridled character. In the *Chiu T'ang shu* 舊唐書 (190C:5053), Liu Hsü 劉昫 described Li Po's 李白 (701–762)* unrestrained and natural nature as *'hao-fang."* Ssu-k'ung T'u 司空圖 (837–908),* the author of the *Erh-shih-ssu shih-p'in* 二十四詩品, first applied *hao-fang* to a literary style. Su Shih, ironically, was the first person to label a lyric *"hao-fang,"* criticizing a friend's lyrics in a letter for being too *hao-fang* (heroic, or in this context "bold," and unrestrained). There may, therefore, have been a discrepancy between Su Shih's lyric theory and his actual creative practice.

Despite the liberating effect of the *Hao-fang p'ai* on the *tz'u,* many lyricists and literary critics still maintained there should be a stylistic and thematic distinction between the *tz'u* and conventional *shih*-poetry. Ch'ao Pu-chih 晁補之 (1053–1110) and Li Ch'ing-chao 李清照 (1084–*ca.* 1151)* had criticized Su Shih for his deviation from the prosaic rules of the *tz'u,* asserting that the poetics of the *tz'u* and the *shih* should not be confused. From Ch'ao and Li onward, the lyricists of the *Hao-fang p'ai,* were criticized for their lack of concern about the music, metrical patterns, and stylistic restrictions of the *tz'u.* By the late Ch'ing, *tz'u* critics like Ch'en T'ing-cho 陳廷焯 (1853–1892) and Wang Kuo-wei 王國維 (1877–1927) deplored the *Hao-fang* lyricists for their transgression of the rules. For these critics, *tz'u* had an original identity (*pen-se* 本色) integrally related to delicacy (*wan-chuan* 婉轉), subtlety (*ching-li* 精麗), implicitness (*yün-chi* 蘊籍), profundity (*shen-hui* 深回) and evocation (*hsing-chi* 興寄).The *Hao-fang* Style was a generic deflection (*pien* 變) of this ideal.

Although modern scholars of the lyric like Wu Shih-ch'ang 吳世昌 have questioned the validity of the division of the *tz'u* into *Hao-fang* and *Wan-yüeh* schools, because the Sung lyricists never divided themselves into or pictured themselves as members of any "school," the distinction seems useful in tracing the history of the genre from the modern perspective.

Editions and References

Li, Ch'in-yin 李勤印, ed. *Hao-fang tz'u-p'ai hsüan-chi* 豪放詞派選集. Peking: Pei-ching Shih-fan Hsüeh-yüan, 1993.

Wang, Shuang-ch'i 王雙啟, ed. *Li-tai hao-fang tz'u-hsüan* 歷代豪放詞選. Kweiyang: Kuei-chou Jen-min, 1984.

Studies

Chang, Kang-i Sun. *The Evolution of the Chinese Tz'u Poetry.* Princeton: Princeton University Press, 1980.

Chang, Wei 張澂. "Chia-hsüan Wan-yüeh tz'u lun" 稼軒婉約詞論. *Hua-tung Shih-fan Ta-hsüeh hsüeh-pao,* 2, 1994: 77-83.

Chou, Sheng-wei 周聖偉. "Nan-Sung Hao-fang tz'u-p'ai hsing-ch'eng te yüan-yin" 南宋豪放詞派形成的原因, *Tz'u hsüeh,* 2 (1983): 132-149.

Kao, Chien-chung 高建中. "Hao-fang, Wan-yüeh yü cheng-pien" 豪放，婉約與正變, *Tz'u hsüeh,* 2 (1983): 150-53.

Lin, Shuen-fu. "The Formation of a Distinct Generic Identity for *Tz'u.*" In Yu, *Voices,* pp. 3-29.

Liu, Chi-ts'ai 劉繼才. "Lun Hao-fang *Tz'u* te hsing-ch'eng yü fa-chan" 論豪放詞的形成與發展. In *T'ang-Sung shih tz'u lun-kao* 唐宋詩詞論稿. Shenyang: Liao-ning Jen-min, 1987, pp. 236-53.

Liu, Nai-ch'ang 劉乃昌. "Hao-fang yü hsieh-lü" 豪放與協律, *Tz'u hsüeh* 1983.2: 125-31.

Liu, *Major Lyricists.*

Lung, Mu-hsün 龍沐勛. "Su-Hsin *Tz'u*-p'ai chih yüan-yüan liu-pien" 蘇辛詞派之淵源流變, *Wen-shih ts'ung-k'an* 1.6 (1933): 1-16.

Wang, Chi-ssu 王季思. "*Tz'u* te cheng-pien" 詞的正變. In *Yü-lun-hsüan ku-tien wen-hsüeh lun-chi* 玉輪軒古典文學論集. Peking: Chung-hua, 1982, pp. 287-294.

Wu, Hsiang-chou 吳湘洲. "Chien-kuo i-lai Hao-fang *tz'u* yen-chiu shu-p'ing" 建國以來豪放詞研究述評. *Ta-lien Ta-hsüeh Shih-yüan hsüeh-pao* 1988.3.

Wu, Shih-ch'ang 吳世昌. "Sung *tz'u* chung te Hao-fang P'ai yü Wan-yüeh P'ai" 宋辭中的豪放派與婉約派. In *Lo-yin Shih hsüeh-shu lun-chu* 羅音室學述論著. Peking: Chung-kuo Wen-lien, 1991, pp. 121-36.

Yang, Yu-shan 楊有山. "Wan-yüeh yü hao-fang: '*pen-se*' *tz'u* yü '*shih hua*' *tz'u*' 婉約與豪放一本色詞與詩化詞. *Kuei-yang Shih-fan Hsüeh-yüan hsüeh-pao* 1994.3: 72-76.

Chen Bingmei
University of Wisconsin, Madison

Ho Hsün 何遜 (*tzu,* Chung-yen 仲言, *ca.* 468–*ca.* 518) came from a scholarly family and was well-known for his poetic genius since his childhood. He was the great-grandson of the illustrious renaissance scholar of the Liu Sung period, Ho Ch'eng-t'ien 何承天 (370–447), a historian, a scientist, and an astronomer. His erudition made him a consultant to Emperor Wen 文 (r. 424–453), Liu I-lung 劉義隆 (407–453). However, his descendants did not fare well. The Ho family originally came from T'an 郯 (modern T'an-ch'eng 郯城, Shantung), but during the Chin dynasty they moved to Chen-chiang 鎮江 (modern Kiangsu) where Ho Hsün grew up. Hsün's grandfather, Ho I 何翼, and father, Ho Hsün 何珣, were not gifted, though they both occupied minor offices. By Hsün's generation, his family was in decline. Like his great-grandfather, Hsün showed poetic talent in his youth. At the age of nineteen, he became a *hsiu-ts'ai* 秀才 (cultivated talent). His examination questions (*tui-tse* 對策) attracted the attention of the famous poet, Fan Yün 范雲 (451–503), who became his lifelong friend. They often exchanged poems and, when Fan passed away in 503, Ho composed a poem to lament him.

Ho Hsün became still more renowned for his poetry because of his association with Fan Yün and Shen Yüeh 沈約 (441–513).* The foremost writer among contemporary literary circles, Shen Yüeh, also highly praised Ho's poetry. He claimed that even after reading it three times in a day, he still could not put down Ho's poetry. Despite appreciation from prominent poets of his time, Ho was not successful in his official career, probably because of his humble background. He served under the Prince of Chien-an 建安 from about 507 to 510 as record-keeper (*chi-shih* 記室), a title that was applied to him in later generations. During this period, he wrote many landscape poems. Later he served under the Prince of An-ch'eng 安成 as a military adjutant and Secretary of the Bureau of Waterways and Irrigation (*Shui-pu lang* 水部郎). This later became one of the designations used to title some collections of Ho Hsün's work. The Prince of Chien-an recommended him to Hsiao Yen 蕭衍, Emperor Wu 武 of Liang 梁 (r. 502–549), but for some unknown reason, Ho never gained imperial favor. It seems that Emperor Wu purposefully ignored and rejected talented men from lowly families. Both Liu Chün 劉峻 (*ca.* 462–521)** and Wu Chün 吳均 (469–520),* who came from families in decline, suffered the same treatment. Blocked in his career, Ho Hsün continued to move among the Liang princes until the end of his life.

After Ho Hsün's death, Wang Seng-ju 王僧孺 (465–522) gathered his works and compiled a collection. As noted above, however, Ho's poetry had already gained a great deal of attention while he was alive. Fan Yün praised him as follows: "As for contemporary men of letters, when they try to be straightforward, they appear plain; when they try to be ornate, they become vulgar. The only one who can achieve a balance between these two is Ho Hsün." Hsiao I 蕭繹 (508–554) also attempted to assess Ho among his contemporaries, concluding that Shen Yüeh was prolific and excellent, while Hsieh T'iao 謝朓 (464–499)* and Ho Hsün were less productive but equally good. Ho's collection circulated in the North only ten years after his death and won immediate recognition and popularity there.

Ho's collection includes imitations of ancient *yüeh-fu* 樂府,* personal poems to friends and colleagues, miscellaneous poems on seasonal thoughts and palace themes, and linked verse (*lien-chü* 聯句**). However, the two major topics of Ho Hsün's poetry are farewell scenes and landscapes. He was often separated from his family and friends as he moved from one minor post to another. His poetry is a fusion of his life and poetic genius. Ho was also the most skilled landscape poet of his time after Hsieh T'iao. But because of his different background and career, Ho's landscape poetry is very different from Hsieh's. First, Ho tends to affect the landscape with his own feelings, while Hsieh's landscape is usually independent of personal emotion. For example, Hsieh T'iao may describe a lively and cheerful landscape while the speaker in the poem feels melancholy. But in Ho's poems the landscape normally appears gloomy and dismal because he is usually depressed. Secondly, Hsieh includes descriptions of the capital and its palaces in his poetry, whereas Ho never sets such imposing objects in his scenes. What Ho aims to describe is the melancholy and desolation he experiences in his travels. The season is often set in autumn and the time late in the day. Ho prefers to delineate dark scenes rather than scenic panorama, in place of palaces, to describe a overgrown tombs in the wild (as Yen Ts'ai-p'ing argues–see "Studies" below). Ho's "Yü Hu Hsing-an yeh-pieh" 與胡興安夜別 (Parting from Hu Hsing-an in the Evening) is typical:

> As host I return in my carriage,
> While the traveler stays on his boat.
> I think of the joy of the party mat,
> Now turned to two places of
>   melancholy.
> The dew wets the grass around the

cold pool,
> The moon shines in the lucid stream   of the Huai.
> I embrace the regret of this new
>   parting,
> Alone with the autumn in the old
>   garden.

居人行轉軾，客子暫維舟。
念此一筵笑，分為兩地愁。
露濕寒塘草，月映清淮流。
方抱新離恨，獨守故園秋。

Ho Hsün's poetic works, like those of Hsieh T'iao, are representative of the *Yung-ming* 永明 Style (named after the verse of the eponymous reign period, 483–493). His poetic language is replete with original images, elegant phrases, and harmonious auditory effects. Traditionally, Ho has been considered a poet who made a great contribution to the development of what later became T'ang regulated verse. Tu Fu 杜甫 (712–770)* praised both Ho and Yin K'eng 陰鏗 (*fl.* 560) for their well-wrought poetic lines. Thus Ho was meticulous not only in his choice of words, but also in structuring the rhyme and tonal patterns. According to the modern scholar, Li Chin-hsing, Ho was one of the few poets during the Ch'i dynasty who paid heed to rhyme scheme and tonal patterns. Li lists several features of Ho Hsün's use of rhyme and tones in his poetry. First, although it had been conventional since the Han for *yüeh-fu* poetry to contain repeated rhymes, Ho often changed the rhyme in his *yüeh-fu* imitations. Compared to most poets of the era, he was more particular about diversifying the rhyme in a poem. Secondly, poets during this period usually did not distinguish characters from the *keng* 庚 and *keng* 耕 or *ch'ing* 清 and *ch'ing* 青 rhyme groups. In the Liu Sung dynasty, only Hsieh Chuang 謝莊 (421–466), who was knowledgeable about rhymes, treated the *ch'ing* 青 group rhyme words as a separate group. In the Ch'i, only Ho

46

Hsün, Wang Chien 王儉 (452–489), Hsieh T'iao, and Shen Yüeh distinguished these groups. Thirdly, the first line in Ho's poetry usually does not carry a rhyme. In addition, the statistics show that Ho often used four tones in a single line in order to create a special auditory effect. Sometimes each line of a poem contains four characters of different tones. In many eight-line poems each of the odd lines ends with a character of different tone. This reveals the main concern of the *Yung-ming* Poets: the distribution of four tones in a single line and a couplet. Ho seems to have been strict about tonal patterns. Fourthly, in his quatrain and eight-line poems, Ho often adopts oblique rhymes, a practice most common in ancient poetry. This indicates that Ho, though he tried to regulate tonal patterns, was still prone to old practices of employing rhyme (see Li Chin-hsing, under "Studies," below).

In addition to tonal patterns, the formal and stylistic features of Ho's poetry also include the use of binomes and *tieh-tzu* 疊字 (repetition of the same character). The binomes Ho used are normally formed by repeating the same graph and often appear at the beginning or the end of a line. They are either descriptive or onomatopoeic binomes, often arranged in parallel. The high frequency of these binomes indicates Ho's rhetorical inclinations. The *tieh-tzu* are repeated characters that interlock two phrases or two sentences such as the following lines from Ho's "Jih-hsi wang chiang shan tseng Yü Ssu-ma" 日夕望江山贈魚司馬 (For Assistant Yü, Written while Gazing at Mountains and Rivers in the Sunset): "Pen City is belted by Pen River, / And the Pen River winds like a belt" 溢城帶溢水，溢水縈如帶. This technique was commonly found in folk ballads and is similar to the "incremental repetition" of English and German ballads; it was also employed by numerous T'ang poets.

Ho Hsün not only excelled in poetry

but also in parallel prose (*p'ien-t'i wen* 駢體文*). His "Wei Heng-shan Hou yü fu shu" 為衡山侯與婦書 (A Letter to Marquis Heng-shan's Wife on behalf of the Marquis) is anthologized in almost every parallel-prose collection. Furthermore, the "Ch'i-chao" 七召 (Seven Summons–see *Ch'i* 七**), though of dubious authorship, is traditionally attributed to him because its exquisite language resembles Ho's style.

A large number of Ho's quatrains and eight-line poems are similar to the *chüeh-chü* 絕句 and *lü-shih* 律詩 (see *shih* 詩*) in the T'ang in terms of their tonal patterns. These strict and regulated patterns are typical of the Ch'i and Liang poets, who were obsessed with the tonal distribution within a couplet, even though the mature form of the regulated verse, with its interlocking tonal pattern of four couplets, did not come into existence until the T'ang. Ho Hsün should be recognized as one of the most talented poets in his time and a forerunner whose works greatly contributed to the final crystallization of regulated verse in the T'ang.

Editions and References
Ho Shui-pu chi 何水部集. *SPPY*.
Hao, Li-ch'üan 郝立權. *Ho Shui-pu shih-chu* 何水部詩注. Tsinan: Ch'i-Lu Ta-hsüeh, 1937.
Ho Hsün chi 何遜集. Peking: Chung-hua, 1980. A modern punctuated edition.
Liu, Ch'ang 劉暢, ed. and comm. *Ho Hsün chi-chu* 何遜集注. *Han-Wei Liu-ch'ao wen-shih ts'ung-shu* 漢魏六朝文史叢書. Tientsin: T'ien-chin Ku-chi, 1988.
Li, Po-ch'i 李伯齊, ed. and comm. *Ho Hsün chi chiao-chu* 何遜集校注. Tsinan: Ch'i-Lu Shu-she, 1989.
Lu, *Nan-pei-ch'ao shih*, 2:1678-1714..

Studies
Chang, Chung-kang 張忠綱. "Ho Hsün" 何遜. *Chung-kuo li-tai chu-ming wen-hsüeh-chia p'ing-chuan* 中國歷代著名文學家評傳, v. 1, pp. 615-622.
Li, Chin-hsing 李金星. *Ho Hsün yen-chiu* 何遜研究. Taipei: Hua-shih, 1982. This is

the most comprehensive study of the formal features of Ho Hsün's poetry.

Numaguchi, Masaru 沼口勝 "Ka Son no 'Ryûsaku Hyaku itsu tai' no shi ni tsuite" 何遜の'聊作百一体の詩'について," *Kambun-Gakkai-kaihô* 34 (1975): 13-25.

Obi, Kôichi 小尾郊一. *Chûgoku bungaku ni arawareta shizen to shizenkan* 中国文学に現われた自然の自然観. Tokyo: Iwanami, 1962.

Ts'ao, Tao-heng 曹道衡. "Ho Hsün san t'i" 何遜三題, *Chung-hua wen-shih lun-ts'ung* 4 (1983); rpt. in Ts'ao's *Chung-ku wen-hsüeh-shih lun-wen-chi* 中古文學史論文集, pp. 409-13.

___. "Ho Hsün sheng-tsu nien wen-t'i shih-t'an" 何遜生卒年問題試探, *Wen-shih* 24 (1985), 219-23; rpt. in Ts'ao's *Chung-ku wen-hsüeh shih lun-wen-chi* 中古文學史論文集. Peking: Chung-hua, 1986, pp. 401-8.

Yamada, Hideo 山田英雄. "Ka Son no shifû" 何遜の詩風. *Nagoya Daigaku Bungakubu kenkyû ronshû* 55 (1972).

Yen, Ts'ai-p'ing 閻采平. *Ch'i-Liang shih-ko yen-chiu* 齊梁詩歌研究. Peking: Pei-ching Ta-hsüeh, 1994, pp. 141-149.

Jui-lung Su
The National University of Singapore

Hou Chih 侯芝 (other name Ju-chih 如芝, studio name Hsiang-yeh Ko 香葉閣; 1764–1829) was the daughter of *chin-shih* Hou Hsüeh-shih 侯學詩 and the wife of *chü-jen* Mei Ch'ung 梅沖, a disciple of Yüan Mei 袁枚 (1716–1798).* As both her father and her husband lived in the Nanking area, she was a lifelong resident of that city. Her father was not sympathetic to female learning, but her cousin Hou Yün-chin 侯雲錦 saw that she learned to read at an early age. Yün-chin's support was a mainstay of Hou Chih's writing career. In her married life Hou was poor but happy and gave birth to several sons. Hou Yün-chin was the tutor of all of her children, including a daughter, Mei Shu-i 梅淑儀, also a writer, and a son, Mei Tseng-liang 梅曾亮, who became a prominent disciple of Yao Nai 姚乃 (1732–1815).

Hou's health was never good, and in 1794 her condition worsened. Too ill to assume household duties, she returned to the habit of reading and writing, which she had set aside since childhood. Hou Yün-chin and her various brothers saw to it that her works were circulated to women writers in the Kiangnan area. Although they never came to Yüan Mei's attention, they were widely respected among men and women alike for their erudition, remarkable in a woman, and for their Confucian tone.

Approximately fifteen years after she first became ill, Hou turned away from poetry and began writing *t'an-tz'u* 彈詞.* Her name is of interest today because of her contributions to this form. The editor of the first published version of Ch'en Tuan-sheng's 陳端生 (1751–1796?)* *Tsai-sheng yüan* 再生緣 (1821), Hou is also credited with editorial or authorial work on four other titles: *Chin-shang hua* 錦上花 (1813), *Chin-kuei chieh* 金閨傑 (1824, a revised version of *Tsai-sheng yüan*), *Tsai-tsao t'ien* 再造天 (preface 1826, pub. 1828) and *Yü-ch'uan yüan* 玉釧緣. *Yü-ch'uan yüan* survives in a re-edition only; all that is known about its date of publication is that Hou worked on it before she published *Tsai-sheng yüan.* This one learns from the 1821 preface to *Tsai-sheng yüan,* which mentions her other titles and further asserts that Hou had been working on *t'an-tz'u* for about ten years.

To critics of the May Fourth era, Hou's contribution to *t'an-tz'u* was not entirely positive. This is especially because of her work on *Tsai-sheng yüan,* which sought to curb the feminist (and in Hou's view unfilial) leanings of the heroine, Meng Li-chün 孟麗君. From a contemporary perspective, it might be deemed fortunate that Hou's version was snatched from her hands by publishers before she was willing to part with it (this according to her preface to *Chin-kuei chieh,* Hou's more proper Confucian

48

revision of the story).

One mystery in this picture is the apparent contradiction between Hou's firmly Confucian principles, which should have kept her in ladylike seclusion, and her interactions with publishers. The most likely resolution of this mystery lies in the person of Hou Yün-chin, who furthered her interest in letters on many other occasions and helped to circulate her work outside the home. It is also quite apparent that Hou herself was ambitious, despite the manifest import of her writing, which encourages the view that "lack of learning in a woman is a virtue."

Hou's last published *t'an-tz'u* came out in 1828, the year before her death. At this point, her thoughts turned back to poetry, for she is said to have derived comfort in her final illness from Hou Yün-chin's successful effort to publish her poems. Yün-chin's plan to turn out a second posthumously published volume was apparently never realized. As she herself had predicted, *t'an-tz'u* provided a more reliable vehicle to fame. Were it not for her work in this medium, neither Hou's life nor her long career as a poet would be studied today.

Editions and References

Hou, Chih, ed. *Chin-shang hua* 錦上花. 1813).

___. *Chin-kuei chieh* 津閨傑 (a revised version of *Tsai-sheng yüan*). 1824.

___. *Tsai-tsao t'ien* 再造天 (preface 1826, pub. 1828).

___. *Yü-ch'uan yüan* 玉釧緣.

Wang, Yü 王豫, ed. *Ch'ün-ya chi* 群雅集. First collection, Preface 1807; second collection, Preface 1811; especially the edition in the Naikaku Bunko, with the attached collections *Ai-lan hsüan shih-hsüan* 愛蘭軒詩選 (by Wang Ch'iung 王瓊 and others).

Studies

Chen, Yin-k'o 陳寅恪. "Lun *Tsai-sheng yüan* 論再生緣," in *Han-liu T'ang chi* 寒柳堂集. Shanghai: Shang-hai Ku-chi, 1980.

Fa-shih-shan 法式善. *Wu-men shih-hua* 梧門詩話, in Shen Yün-lung 沈雲龍, ed., *Chin-tai Chung-kuo shih-liao tsung-k'an hsü-pien* 近代中國史料叢刊續編 20, v. 198. Taipei: Wen-hai, 1975.

Hou, Chih. Preface to Chiang Chu 江珠, *Hsiao-wei-mo shih-chi* 小維摩詩集. Nanking: blocks cut by Liu Wen-k'uei Chia 劉文奎家 and published in 1811 (now in Peking Library).

Hu, Shih-ying 乎士瑩. "*T'an-tz'u* nü tso-chia Hou Chih hsiao-chuan 彈詞女作家侯芝小傳," *Wen-hsien* 15 (1983): 87-93.

Hu, Siao-chen. "Literary *Tanci*: A Woman's Tradition of Narrative in Verse." Unpublished Ph. D. dissertation, Harvard University, 1994.

Hu, Wen-k'ai 胡文楷. *Li-tai fu-nü chu-tso k'ao* 歷代婦女著作考. Rev. ed., Shanghai: Shang-hai Ku-chi, 1985, p. 411.

Lo, Ch'i-lan 駱綺蘭. *T'ing-ch'iu Kuan kuei-chung t'ung-jen-chi* 聽秋館閨中同仁記. Preface 1797, in Nanking Library

Ellen Widmer
Wesleyan University

Hsia Wan-ch'un 夏完淳 (original *ming,* Fu 復, *hao,* Ts'un-ku 存古 "Preserving the Ancient" or Hsiao-yin 小隱 "The Lesser Hermit," 1631–1647) gained fame as a child prodigy who became a poet-patriot following the fall of the Ming dynasty. His subsequent fame may not have rivaled that of Wen T'ien-hsiang 文天祥 (1236–1283) following the collapse of the Sung, but his martyr's death became a rallying cry among latter-day intellectuals like Kuo Mo-jo 郭沫若 (1892–1978) and Liu Ya-tzu 柳亞子 (1887–1958) during the Sino-Japanese War (1937–1945).

Native of Hua-t'ing 華亭 in Sung-chiang 松江 prefecture (near Shanghai), Hsia Wan-ch'un (his given name means "perfection of purity") grew up in a literary family; his father, Hsia Yün-i 夏允彝 (1596–1645), was a leading poet-intellectual of the Yangtze Region. Greatly influenced by Chang P'u 張溥 (1602–1641), who founded the Fu-she

復社 (Restoration Society), the elder Hsia became the founder of the Chi-she 幾社 (Origin of Change Society). Another member of this group was Ch'en Tzu-lung 陳子龍 (1608–1647),* who also became Hsia Wan-ch'un's teacher.

Hsia Wan-ch'un's literary prowess as a child was recognized early by many of his older contemporaries. The noted scholar Ch'en Chi-ju 陳繼儒 (1558–1639) met Hsia, then a child of five *sui*, in 1635 when he himself was seventy-eight-years old. After testing the child's knowledge of the classics, he wrote a poem hailing Hsia Wan-ch'un as a "child prodigy" (*t'ung-shen* 童神).

The poet Ch'ien Ch'ien-i 錢謙益 (1582–1664),* who met Hsia three years later, addressed a poem to him entitled "Tseng Hsia T'ung-tzu Tuan-ko" 贈夏童子端哥 (Sent to the Child Hsia Tuan-ko) in which he testified ardently to the child's knowledge of books and his great eloquence. In short, Hsia Wan-ch'un was acknowledged to be a child genius.

Besides his literary gifts, Hsiao Wan-ch'un inherited genes included a commitment to "loyalist" (i.e., anti-Manchu) and Confucian values. When a descendent of the Ming royal house, Chu Yu-sung 朱由崧 (d. 1645), was proclaimed the Hung-kuang emperor in Nanking in 1644, several centers of resistance against the Ch'ing sprang up in the Yangtze delta region. One such center was Sung-chiang, under the command of Wu I 吳易 (sometimes given as Wu Yang 吳易, 1612–1646). Wu's "Righteous Army" found an ally in a student of Hsia Yün-i's, Wu Chih-k'uei 吳志葵, who commanded a naval detachment on Lake T'ai. Both father and son served as advisers on Wu's staff. After a military campaign to capture Soochow in 1645 ended in defeat, the elder Hsia refused to flee south; in an act of penance, he drowned himself in the Sung River on the seventeenth day of the ninth month–but not before he had completed a prose account of his experiences under the Southern Ming, entitled *Hsing-ts'un lu* 幸存錄 (A Record of Being Lucky to Have Survived), and biographies of two of his fellow-resisters.

After the death of his father, Wu I's resistance efforts continued with the advice of both Hsia Wan-ch'un and Ch'en Tzu-lung, his teacher. Unfortunately, in the spring of 1647 a misadventure involving the Sung-chiang commander, Wu Sheng-chao 吳勝兆 (who had been persuaded by Ch'en to switch his allegiance to the Ming cause) ended in failure; Ch'en drowned himself while being held prisoner on a boat. His death was a blow to Hsia Wan-ch'un comparable to that of his father's a year and a half earlier.

Later in the same year, Hsia Wan-ch'un was suspected as the author of a memorial addressed to the Prince of Lu 魯, Chu I-hai 朱以海 (1618–62), then acting as regent, whose court was located in Shao-hsing. This followed the capture of a spy named Hsieh Yao-wen 謝堯文. Along with forty-two other prisoners, Hsia Wan-ch'un was executed on the nineteenth day of the ninth month in 1647. He was only seventeen *sui*. Disagreement dominates contemporary accounts of where he was captured, how he became involved in the conspiracy, where he met his death, and what his last words were. His life had already become a legend before he met his death at age sixteen. In 1775 the Ch'ing court conferred upon him the posthumous honorific of "Chieh-min" 節愍 (Inviolable and Compassionate).

Perhaps the most dramatic episode related to the martyrdom of Hsia Wan-ch'un was his trial. It was presided over by Hung Ch'eng-ch'ou 洪承疇 (1593–1665), the newly created (1645) Pacificator of Kiangnan, was a former high official of the Ming who had rendered significant service to his new masters as a military commander. To a Han Chinese, such a person was undoubtedly viewed as an arch-traitor. In fact, Hung was later listed in the official history of the dynasty as someone who served two masters (*erh-ch'en* 貳臣). It is said that when Hsia Wan-ch'un was brought before Hung, the latter made some effort to mitigate Hsia's offense on account of his age, but Hsia refused this offer of leniency. Instead, he castigated Hung by stating that the real Hung was an upright official who had met a martyr's death, and therefore the person conducting the trial was only an imposter. Such a confrontation between a master collaborator and a defiant patriot is, of course, fraught with irony and some comicality. Not surprisingly, therefore, Kuo Mo-jo in 1943 turned this episode into the central act of a four-act dramatization of Hsia Wan-ch'un's capture and death, entitled *Nan-kuan ts'ao* 南冠草 (A Prisoner's Weeds). In a biographical supplement to the play, and elsewhere, Kuo also offered profuse apologies for the poet's old-fashioned loyalty, since Hsia had earlier referred to the peasant leader Li Tzu-ch'eng 李自成 (1606–45) as a "great traitor" (*ta ni* 大逆). Clearly, Kuo was willing to put aside his proletarian sympathies here for the higher good of arousing nationalistic fervor.

Literary works that have survived Hsia Wan-ch'un's death consist of both prose and poetry. The best-known of the former is the "Ta ai fu" 大哀賦 (The Great Lamentation: A Prose-poem) which he wrote in the autumn of 1646. Obviously modeled after the famous sixth-century masterpiece "Ai Chiang-nan fu" 哀江南賦 (Lament for the South: A Prose-poem) of Yü Hsin 庾信 (513–581),* it follows its predecessor in offering a grand sweep of history (beginning with the Wan-li 萬曆 reign period, 1573–1619) and by giving vent to the poet's personal sorrow caused by calamitous events. It is a passionate and moving statement, characterized by an excessive use of allusions and oblique references. Even a modern edition of the work, fully annotated and published in 1993, is not able to identify all the allusions.

Hsia Wan-ch'un's juvenilia (a collection known as *Tai-ju chi* 代乳集 [A Substitute for Mother's Milk], written at age nine) is no longer extant). Posthumous collections include *Yü-fan chi* 玉樊集 (Collection from the Studio of Jade Girth, 1644–45), and *Hsia Nei-shih chi* 夏內史集 (The Collection of Secretariat-Director Hsia, 1646–47)–both containing discourses, imaginary conversations, edicts, and letters. Another prose work consisting of two parts, "An Outline of the Southern Capital" (*Nan-tu ta-lüeh* 南都大略) and "Miscellanies of the Southern Capital" (*Nan-tu tsa-chi* 南都雜記), contains an objective assessment of personalities and events at the Southern Ming court, collectively known as the *Hsü Hsing-ts'un lu* 續幸存錄 (Sequel to a Record of Being Lucky to Have Survived; a continuation of his father's work).

Hsia Wan-ch'un's poetic œuvre was written in a variety of metrical forms. In addition to twelve *fu* and two *sao* 騷, he wrote a little over three hundred *shih*-poems; about half are written in the *yüeh-fu* 樂府 or *ku-shih* 古詩 style, the other half are *chin-t'i* 今體 (modern-style) poems. Some of his early *yüeh-fu* were obviously meant to be imitations or literary exercises, such as "Ballad of a Beautiful Women" (*Yen-ko hsing* 艷歌行). While he would occasionally write poems in the T'ang style like the series of eight entitled "Spring Meditations" (*Ch'un hsing* 春興; which recall, of course, Tu Fu's "Autumn Meditations" [*Ch'iu hsing* 秋興]), his poetry shows greater affinity with some of the Six Dynasties poets such as Juan Chi 阮藉 (210–263)* or Hsi K'ang 嵇康 (223–262).* A pervasive sense of melancholy and defiance characterize most of his work. But even in this generally imitative mode, one can often glimpse an original mind. For example, in depicting the two ancient recluses Po I 伯夷 and Shu Ch'i 叔齊, men who chose to eat thorn-fern in the mountains rather than the grain of the

Chou dynasty (which had replaced their own Yin dynasty) and thus eventually starved to death, he wrote:

In those days, there were plenty of the
    unruly people left,
So why head for the Western Hills to
    gather thorn-fern by yourselves?

當時尚有頑民在，何事西山獨采薇。
("Yung-shih tsa-ch'eng k'ou-hao" 詠史雜
成口號)

The phrase "unruly people" (wan-min 頑民) carries the connotation of "the ungovernable" or "the unenlightened" and is ironic here since it supports a rather unconventional view of the Confucian ideal of eremitism.

What constitutes the more poignant and significant portion of Hsia Wan-ch'un's verse are those poems that document his life and career, at home and in an army camp. There are also those elegiac pieces written about a rather large group of his family members, or relatives, friends, teachers, and colleagues, whose death or martyrdom he mourned. While in prison, besides letters addressed to his mother and to his wife, he also wrote some modern-style poems which made up Nan-kuan ts'ao. Taken from a series of eighteen quatrains written on the death of his brother-in-law, Ch'ien Hsi 錢熙 (ca. 1620–46), the poem reads:

'Tis a pity that after death one's features
    fade with time,
Yet the same undiminished tenderness
    as if you were still among the living.
In a dream, alone with grief, I knew you
    to be dead;
Now since waking, I find you in my
    memory suddenly alive.

可憐沒後久銷形，猶是生前未盡情。
夢里對愁知已沒；醒來回想忽如生。

A more spontaneous or authentic voice of grief is hard to find in the poetry of any period.

While Hsia Wan-ch'un's shih-poetry tends in the main to represent the personal utterances of the poet, his tz'u or lyrics, numbering forty-four, treat conventional themes but embody the qualities of wan-yüeh 婉約 (delicacy and restraint–see Wan-yüeh p'ai 婉約派**). His style echoes more the Sung lyricists Ch'in Kuan 秦觀 (1049–1100)** and Li Ch'ing-chao 李清照 (1084–ca. 1151)* than that of Su Shih 蘇軾 (1037–1101)* or Hsin Ch'i-chi 辛棄疾 (1140-1207).* It won high praise from the modern critic K'uang Chou-i 況周頤 (1859–1926) who included Hsia along with Ch'en Tzu-lung, P'eng Sun-i 彭孫貽 (fl. 1637), and Wang Fu-chih 王夫之 (1619–1692)* as the four best lyricists of the Ming dynasty. Only in their works, K'uan wrote, can be found both "grace (o-na 婀娜) and "virility" (kang-chien 剛健), qualities which, he felt, exemplified the best of the feng 風 and sao 騷 tradition.

Editions and References

Ta-ai fu 大哀賦. H. T. Wang 王學曾, annotator. Stuttgart: Privately Printed, 1993.

Hsia Wan-ch'un chi ch'ien-chiao 夏完淳集箋校. Pai Chien 白堅, ed. Shanghai: Ku-chi, 1991. Virtually a variorum edition which appends all relevant material on the life of Hsia Wan-ch'un.

Studies

Ho, Chen-ch'iu 何振球 and Yüan Hsüeh-hung 袁雪洪. "Hsia Wan-ch'un ho t'a te Nan-kuan ts'ao" 夏完淳和他的南冠草. In Ch'ien Chung-lien 錢仲聯, ed., Ming-Ch'ing shih-wen yen-chiu ts'ung-k'an 明清詩文研究叢刊, Series 1 (1982): 19-25.

Kuo, Mo-jo 郭沫若, ed. Nan-kuan ts'ao 南冠草. Rpt. Peking: Jen-min Wen-hsüeh, 1979 (Chungking, 1944); also in Kuo Mo-jo ch'üan-chi 郭沫若全集. Peking: Jen-min Wen-hsüeh, 1986, VII: 305-457.

Liu, Yao-tzu 柳亞子 (1887-1958). Huai-chiu chi 懷舊集 (Remembering the Past). Shanghai: Keng-yün, 1947. The first full-length biography of the poet (pp. 211-53).

Irving Yucheng Lo

Hsing-shih yin-yüan chuan 醒世姻緣
傳 (Marriage As Retribution, Awakening
the World) is the most important novel
from seventeenth-century China. Primarily known for its depiction of a
henpecked husband and his termagant
wife and concubine, it is actually an
insightful social satire. Its one-hundred
chapters portray more than two-hundred
fictional characters and present a broad
social panorama: from quotidian life in
Shantung towns as well as in the capital,
to darker scenes of torture, murder,
courtrooms, prisons, natural disasters,
famines, and even cannibalism. A masterpiece focusing on domestic life and
gender relationships, it demonstrates the
influence of *Chin P'ing Mei* 金瓶梅 (The
Golden Lotus,* published *ca.* 1617) and
in turn influenced the writing of *Hung-lou
meng* 紅樓夢 (The Dream of the Red
Chamber,* *ca.* 1760). Its satirical portrayal of different walks of life also had
an impact on *Ju-lin wai-shih* 儒林外史
(The Scholars,* *ca.* 1750) and late Ch'ing
satire. It thus fills a gap in scholarship
on Chinese fiction, bridging sixteenth-
century and eighteenth-century vernacular classics.

The novel's authorship and exact date
are still in question. It was written under
the pseudonym Hsi-Chou Sheng 西周
生 (Scholar of Western Chou), and
collated by Jan-li Tzu 燃藜子 (Master of
Burning Pigweed). At the end of some
chapters, there are comments written by
Ko Shou-chih 葛受之. In the first
foreword, Huan-pi Chu-jen 環碧主人
(The Master of the Surrounding Green)
calls the novel *Yin-yüan ch'i-chuan* 姻緣
奇傳 (A Strange Account of Marriage
Destinies), while Tung-ling Hsüeh-tao-
jen 東嶺學道人 (Taoist Student of the
Eastern Peak) tells us in the second
foreword that the novel was originally
entitled *E yin-yüan* 惡姻緣 (Bad Marriage
Destinies) before he changed it to *Hsing-
shih yin-yüan chuan* with the intention of
"awakening the world."

Judging from the diction, the author

was either a native of Shantung or
someone who had resided there long
enough to master its dialect. Hu Shih
胡適 (1891–1962) and a number of other
modern scholars attributed the authorship to P'u Sung-ling 蒲松齡 (1640–
1715)*; other scholars proposed Ting
Yao-k'ang 丁耀亢 (*ca.* 1599–*ca.* 1669);
still others put forth Chia Fu-hsi 賈鳧西
(1589–1675). Based on circumstantial
evidence and uses of common language
and theme, attributing authorship to
these three Shantung writers remains
inconclusive.

A copy of *Hsing-shih yin-yüan chuan* is
recorded among the entries for the year
1728 in the *Hakusai shomoku* 舶載書目,
a catalogue of Chinese books imported
into Japan. Sun K'ai-ti 孫楷第 established
the novel's earliest possible date as 1628
based on internal evidence. Therefore,
some scholars argue for a late Ming
composition, while others for the early
Ch'ing. No sufficient internal or external
evidence exists to prove either contention. However, a recent discovery of
a letter written by Chou Tsai-chün 周在
濬 around 1681 mentioning a novel titled
E yin-yüan suggests that the novel must
have been written, and even published,
by 1681.

Hsing-shih yin-yüan chuan has an
original plot which, though seemingly
haphazard and episodic, is actually
carefully designed and tightly structured.
The first twenty-two chapters focus on
the Ch'ao 晁 family's fortune, decline,
and incipient revival in Wu-ch'eng 武
城 (modern Shantung). Through
networking and good luck, a poor school
teacher named Ch'ao Ssu-hsiao 晁思孝
passes a qualifying examination,
becomes a magistrate, and grows rich.
Avaricious and corrupt, Ch'ao Ssu-hsiao
is promoted to the position of prefect
after bribing the powerful eunuch Wang
Chen 王振 with the help of two actors,
Liang 梁 and Hu 胡. When the Mongols,
led by Esen 也先, invade the northern
territory (1449), Ch'ao Ssu-hsiao

attempts to resign in order to save his own skin. The Cheng-t'ung 正統 emperor (r. 1436–1449), failing in his military campaign, is captured by the Mongols. Ch'ao Ssu-hsiao is eventually impeached and dies soon after taking a young maidservant as a concubine.

Ch'ao Ssu-hsiao's misconduct is outdone by the worse behavior of his wastrel son, Ch'ao Yüan 晃源. Out hunting one day, Ch'ao Yüan shoots and kills a fox fairy who had taken refuge under his horse. After taking the actress-prostitute Chen-ko 珍哥 as a concubine, Ch'ao Yüan begins mistreating his wife, Madame Chi 計. Falsely accused by Chen-ko of adultery, Madame Chi commits suicide. Her family brings suit against Ch'ao Yüan and Chen-ko, resulting in Chen-ko's imprisonment. Ch'ao Yüan also persecutes Liang and Hu, depriving them of their possessions. The impoverished actors become monks and later play an important role in the spiritual redemption of Ch'ao Yüan's reincarnation. Ch'ao Yüan eventually dies at the hand of a cobbler whom he had cuckolded.

Contrasted with the avarice and cruelty of father and son is the benevolence of Madam Ch'ao. Unable to restrain her husband and son from committing evil during their lives, she nevertheless sets about remedying their errors after their deaths. She returns the belongings to Liang and Hu, as well as to others from whom her husband and son had seized property; shares her family property with the Ch'ao clan members, who had attempted to dispossess her; and reciprocates generosities received in the past. Monk Liang is so grateful to Madam Ch'ao that he wills himself to death so as to be reborn as her son and thus repay her kindness. He is born to Ch'ao Ssu-hsiao's concubine and called Ch'ao Liang 晃梁.

The remaining 78 chapters branch off into two tales, the tale of the Ch'aos and the tale of the Ti 狄 family, which converge in the last chapter. The tale of the Ch'aos continues in 13 separate chapters. After committing adulteries and escaping from prison with her final paramour, Chen-ko is caught and dies after being tortured in a courtroom. Madam Ch'ao survives many hardships, including clan conflict, blackmail, and a lawsuit, but lives to be 104. As a reward for her virtue, Ch'ao Liang brings her much happiness through his devotion, his harmonious marriage, and his help in doing good works such as famine relief. After her death, Madam Ch'ao becomes a goddess and continues to protect people from calamities.

The tale of the Tis, which dominates the second part of the novel, features a symmetrical inversion of the account of Ch'ao Yüan, with major victims and victimizers reversing roles through rebirth to even out old scores. Ti Hsi-ch'en 狄希陳, the reincarnation of Ch'ao Yüan born in Ming-shui 明水 (modern Shantung), is disobedient, mischievous, and semi-literate. He becomes a licentiate through cheating in the examinations and good luck and a National University student by purchasing the status. Having already had an affair with a singsong girl, he marries the sixteen-year-old Hsüeh Su-chieh 薛素姐. Once married to Su-chieh, the reincarnation of the fox spirit, Hsi-ch'en begins to suffer her torments. Su-chieh's many perversions bring shame to the otherwise respectable households of the Hsüehs and the Tis. She defies her parents and her in-laws, causing them to die of rage. After her father-in-law's death, she attempts to drive away his concubine along with Hsi-ch'en's half-brother, but Hsi-ch'en secretly finds shelter for them.

Hsi-ch'en is temporarily released from Su-chieh's clutches when he goes to Peking to attend the University. On his second visit to Peking, Hsi-ch'en falls in love with T'ung Chi-chieh 童寄姐 (the reincarnation of Madame Chi) and marries her without Su-chieh's knowledge. Turning ferocious after marriage, Chi-chieh mistreats her husband and tortures a maidservant Chen-chu 珍珠 (the reincarnation of Chen-ko) to death. Hsi-ch'en assumes the post of Registrar in Chengtu, accompanied by Chi-chieh. The furious Su-chieh soon follows. Due to marital problems, Hsi-ch'en has to resign from his post and returns to northern China.

Chapter 100 relates Hsi-ch'en's final release from torments and his spiritual redemption. One day Su-chieh shoots an arrow at Hsi-ch'en, but an eminent monk (the former actor Hu) appears, saving him as well as enlightening him. Hsi-ch'en meets Ch'ao Liang, is informed of his former guilt, and repents. After Hsi-ch'en has taken Buddhist vows to abstain from killing and has chanted the *Vajracchedikâ* (*Chin-kang ching* 金剛 經, or the *Diamond Sutra*) many times, Su-chieh dies and Chi-chieh reforms. Hsi-ch'en then leads a happy life with Chi-chieh and their two sons until he dies peacefully at age 87.

The author creates an intricate plot and watertight closure for his didactic agenda. Underscoring the importance of marital relationships, he explains that a marriage is harmonious or infelicitous depending on one's karma in a previous life. If one person victimized another and the victim could not retaliate in a former life, then they will be matched as man and wife in this life. Only when reborn as the former victimizer's wife can the victim take full revenge.

The author's core teaching combines Confucian benevolence (*pu-jen chih hsin* 不忍之心, "the commiserating heart") with Buddhist compassion. He admonishes his readers to revere life; be selfless and charitable; observe Confucian morality; commit no evil; and carry out their duties in society. To convey his cautionary message, he carefully maps out the workings of retribution, karma, and rebirth, demonstrating that all characters receive

their just punishments and rewards in the end. Within the seemingly rigid framework of reincarnation, however, there remain possibilities for change. Some characters improve their fates through self-cultivation and charity, emphasizing the author's belief in individual moral responsibility and human effort over determinism.

Although the main story is set between the 1440s and 1490s, the author obviously intends it as a vehicle for voicing concerns about his own society of the late Ming and possibly early Ch'ing. As indicated by his pseudonym, the author feels nostalgia for Western Chou, a Confucian golden age. In Chapters 23-24 he depicts, albeit allegorically, a utopia in the pristine Ming-shui of the early Ming (*ca.* 1368–1436). However, with a sense of devolution, he proceeds to demonstrate in Chapters 25-29 the gradual degradation of Ming-shui into a dystopia, the breakdown of social order, and Heaven's sending a devastating flood as a warning.

Through his depiction of perversions, inverted hierarchies, and the spinelessness of Ti Hsi-ch'en and other male characters, the author conveys his scorn for the irresponsible, albeit educated, elite of his day. He uses the episode about the Mongols' capture of the emperor—possibly reflecting the Manchu conquest of China in 1644—as a political backdrop for the family drama and social dysfunction, as well as a means of communicating his anxiety about China's fate. However, the author intersperses rays of hope amidst despair by having some competent and incorruptible scholar-officials carry out justice. Hsi-ch'en's eventual reform and good end also signal the author's optimism.

The novel's satire does not focus exclusively on cowed husbands and ferocious wives. Its various targets include: avarice (*t'an* 貪), wrath (*ch'en*

嗔), foolishness (*ch'ih* 癡), jealousy (*tu* 妒), as well as excesses in alcohol, sex, wealth, anger—all human evils particularly abhorred by Buddhists; deviant social practices such as the inversion of marital and social hierarchies and the transgression of class boundaries and proper human relationships; debased systems and institutions such as the civil-service examinations, the National University, official recruitment, and jurisprudential process; and specific types of characters such as corrupt or incompetent officials, unethical or semi-literate scholars, irresponsible teachers, gullible wastrels and patrons, greedy craftsmen, deceitful servants, sycophants, phonies, and quacks.

The author's favorite technique for satire is to deflate the degenerates by contrasting them with their moral superiors. The incompetent and corrupt Ch'ao Ssu-hsiao becomes even more ridiculous when juxtaposed with his learned and honorable secretary Hsing Kao-men 邢皋門, while the inept Ti Hsi-ch'en is doubly laughable when compared with his able aide, Chou Ching-yang 周景楊. Successful satire is also achieved through mimetic portrayals of characters and scenes employing humor, punning, exaggeration, burlesque, slapstick, and parody. Obviously familiar with earlier drama and fiction criticism, the author makes extensive use of such narrative techniques as foreshadowing, echoing, and interweaving to heighten the overall dramatic effect.

Humorous and entertaining, the novel's tremendous appeal results from its characterization and language. Despite his didactic intent, the author strives to individualize characters of the same profession (e.g., officials, cooks, wet-nurses, matchmakers), and of the same general type (e.g., dominant women and lustful men). He creates a number of well-rounded and memorable characters, demonstrating psychological insight. For example, Madam Ch'ao starts out as an ordinary human being with common weaknesses—a doting mother who fails to discipline her son—before becoming a saintly figure who imparts saving grace. Su-chieh's hatred of Hsi-ch'en is fated, but the motives and circumstances leading to her outbursts are often depicted in human and understandable terms. By juxtaposing characters who share similarities and differences, such as Ch'ao Liang and Ti Hsi-ch'en, or Su-chieh and Chi-chieh, the author highlights the complexities of each.

The vividness of characterization must be attributed to the novel's colorful and lively language. A master of the colloquial idiom, the author enlivens the dialogues with a liberal dose of folk sayings, proverbs, post-pause expressions (*hsieh-hou yü* 歇後語), jokes, and curse words, carefully capturing the rhythm and cadence of the Shantung dialect. His skillful use of the vernacular also results from his erudition. Freely drawing from earlier poetry, drama, fiction, prose and anecdotal literature, he subjects his sources to a fresh and often parodic use.

Its allegorical and satirical aspects notwithstanding, the novel impresses the readers with its realism. The author's profound insight into lives at different social strata and in different regions enables him to create a strong sense of verisimilitude. Precisely because the novel is so rich in ethnographic details, Hu Shih hails it as an indispensable sourcebook on the social, economic, and institutional history of seventeenth-century China. It contributes much to social history, enhancing, in particular, understanding of popular culture and beliefs.

Despite remarkable achievements in fictional imagination and poetics, the novel suffered relative neglect by literary critics until the 1980s when new editions were published in both China and Taiwan. The majority of Chinese scholarship has focussed on issues of authorship and dating, although scholars in recent years have begun to study other aspects as well. With only its first twenty chapters translated into English in 1995, the novel is still little known in the West. A linguistic, literary, and sociocultural treasure-trove, the novel will reward future scholarship.

Editions and References

Ch'ung-ting Hsing-shih yin-yüan chuan 重訂醒世姻緣傳. Preface by Huan-pi Chu-jen 環碧主人 dated in the year *hsin-ch'ou* 辛丑 (1661?). Blockprint edition by T'ung-te T'ang 同德堂; copy in Harvard-Yenching Library.

Ch'ung-ting Hsing-shih yin-yüan chuan. Preface by Huan-pi Chu-jen dated in the year *wu-tzu* 戊子. Blockprint edition published by Huai-te T'ang 懷德堂; now in Shantung Provincial Library.

Hsing-shih yin-yüan chuan. 3v. Chou Pin 周斌 and Tseng Sheng-ming 曾生明, eds. Peking: Jen-min Chung-kuo, 1993. Modern typeset, expurgated edition.

Hsing-shih yin-yüan chuan. 3v. Hsü Pei-wen 徐北文, ed. Tsinan: Ch'i-Lu Shu-she, 1980. Modern typeset, expurgated edition.

Hsing-shih yin-yüan chuan. 3v. Huang Su-ch'iu 黃肅秋, annot. Shanghai; Shang-hai Ku-chi, 1981. Modern typeset, expurgated edition. Reprints Hu Shih's "*Hsing-shih yin-yüan chuan* k'ao-cheng" 考證 (1935).

Hsing-shih yin-yüan chuan. Peking: Wen-hsüeh Ku-chi K'an-hsing-she, 1988. Reprint of the T'ung-te T'ang edition supplemented with material from the 1870 blockprint edition.

Hsing-shih yin-yüan chuan. Shanghai: Shang-hai Ku-chi, 1990. Reprint of the T'ung-te T'ang edition. Preface by Yüan Shih-shuo 袁釋碩.

Ch'ung-ting Ming-ch'ao Yin-yüan ch'üan chuan 重訂明朝姻緣全傳. Blockprint edition, 1870. Same frontmatter as in *hsin-ch'ou* year edition; copies in Peking University Library, Keiô University Library, and Harvard-Yenching Library.

For detailed information on editions see

Yenna Wu, "Marriage Destinies," pp. 284-96, and *"Hsing-shih yin-yüan chuan* ti pan-pen wen-t'i."

Translations

Dudbridge, Glen. "Women Pilgrims to T'ai Shan: Some Pages from a Seventeenth-Century Novel," in Susan Naquin and Chün-fang Yü, eds. *Pilgrims and Sacred Sites in China*. Berkeley: University of California Press, 1992, pp. 39-64. Translation of Chapters 68-69.

Nyren, Eve Alison. *The Bonds of Matrimony: Hsing-shih Yin-yüan Chuan, A Seventeenth-Century Chinese Novel (Volume One)*. Lewiston, N.Y.: Mellen, 1995. Translation of the first 20 chapters.

Wang, Chi-chen. "Marriage as Retribution," *Renditions* 17 & 18 (1982): 46-94. Partial translation and summaries of the first 20 chapters.

Studies

Arita, Tadahiro 有田忠弘. "*Seisei innen den no kotoba*" 醒世姻緣伝のことば, *Ryûkoku Daigaku Bukkyô Bunka Kenkyûjo kiyô* 14 (1975): 19-28.

Berg, Daria. "The *Xingshi yinyuan zhuan:* A Study of Utopia and the Perception of the World in Seventeenth-century Chinese Discourse." Unpublished Ph. D. dissertation, University of Oxford, 1994.

Chang, Ch'ing-chi 張清吉. *Hsing-shih yin-yüan chuan hsin-k'ao* 醒世姻緣傳新考. Honan, 1991.

Chua, Siewteen. "Die Probleme im *Hsing-shih yin-yüan* und seine literarische Stellung." Unpublished Ph. D. dissertation, Ludwig-Maximilians Universität, 1966.

Dudbridge, Glen. "A Pilgrimage in Seventeenth-century Fiction: T'ai-shan and the *Hsing-shih yin-yüan chuan*," *TP* 77.4-5 (1991): 226-252.

Fan, Pen Chen. "Vivifying the Vernacular: Language Games in *Xingshi Yinyuan Zhuan*," *JCLTA* 30.1 (1995): 17-33.

Hsü, Fu-ling 徐復嶺. *Hsing-shih yin-yüan chuan tso-che ho yü-yen k'ao-lun* 醒世姻緣傳作者和語言考論. Tsinan: Ch'i-Lu Shu-she, 1993.

Hsü, Shuo-fang 徐朔方. "Lun *Hsing-shih yin-yüan chuan* i chi t'a ho *Chin P'ing Mei* ti kuan-hsi" 論醒世姻緣傳以及它和金瓶梅

的關係. In *She-hui k'o-hsüeh chan-hsien* 2 (1986): 278-297.

Kôsaka, Jun'ichi 香坂順一. "*Seisei innen* no sakusha no kotoba" 醒世姻緣の作者のことば, *Min Shin bungaku gengo kenkyûkai kaihô* 5 (1964): 22-38.

Li, Yung-hsiang 李永祥. "*P'u Sung-ling yü Hsing-shih yin-yüan chuan*" 蒲松齡與醒世姻緣傳, *Chung-hua wen-shih lun-ts'ung* 1 (1984): 163-176.

Liu, Chieh-p'ing 劉階平. "*Hsing-shih yin-yüan chuan* ti tso-che Hsi-Chou Sheng k'ao-i" 醒世姻緣傳的作者疑問, *Shu-mu chi-k'an* 10.2 (1976): 3-10.

Liu, Ts'un-yan. "Introduction: 'Middlebrow' in Perspective," *Renditions* 17 & 18 (1982): 1-40, esp., pp. 6-11.

Matsuda, Shigeo 松田茂夫. "*Seisei innen den* no hanashi" 醒世姻緣伝の話. In his *Chûgoku no shôsetsu* 中国の小説. Tokyo, 1948.

Plaks, Andrew H. "After the Fall: *Hsing-shih yin-yüan chuan* and the Seventeenth-Century Chinese Novel," *HJAS* 45.2 (Dec. 1985): 543-580.

Ts'ao, I-ping 曹亦冰. *Lin Lan Hsiang ho Hsing-shih yin-yüan-chuan* 林蘭香和醒世姻緣傳. Shenyang: Liao-ning Chiao-yü, 1992.

Wu, Yenna (吳燕娜). "The Anti-hero in the *Xingshi yinyuan zhuan*" *JCLTA* 28.3 (1993): 17-34.

___. "From History to Allegory: Surviving Famine in the *Xingshi yinyuan zhuan*," *Chinese Culture* 38.4 (December 1997): 87-120.

___. "*Hsing-shih yin-yüan chuan* ti pan-pen wen-t'i" 的版本問題, *Chung-wai wen-hsüeh* 17.2 (1988): 97-107.

___. "Marriage Destinies to Awaken the World: A Literary Study of *Xingshi yinyuan zhuan*." Unpublished Ph. D. dissertation, Harvard University, 1986.

___. "Repetition in *Xingshi yinyuan zhuan*," *HJAS* 51.1 (1991): 55-87.

Yenna Wu
University of California, Riverside

Hsü Yüan-tuan 徐元端 (*fl.* eighteenth century), whose school name is Yen-hsiang 延香, is also known as "Master Yen-hsiang" 延香主人. Like many distinguished women poets in the Ch'ing period, she came from the prosperous region south of the Yangtze. A native of Yangchow (modern Kiangsu province), Hsü was the daughter of Hsü Shih-lin 徐石麟 and wife of a scholar named Fan 范. She left behind two volumes of poetry, entitled *Hsiu-hsien chi* 繡閑集 (A Collection of Poems Written during Pauses from Embroidery) and *Fen-lien hsin yung* 粉奩新詠 (New Songs from the Powder Case), respectively. She was well-known in her time for her *tz'u* lyrics in the Northern Sung mode.

When we compare Hsü with other women poets in late imperial China, there are probably more similarities than differences. For instance, the titles of women's individual collections often contain words like "embroidery," "embroidery studio," and "powder and rouge." These images evoke the idea that the authors write poetry in their spare time from embroidery and other tasks expected of women. Although such titles are not to be taken literally, they do suggest that the women are fully aware of the gender difference in the production and reception of poetry. That they see themselves as "poetesses" and write, for the most part, a certain kind of poetry suggests both modesty and self-imposed limitations.

It is not surprising then that, given the limitations under which they wrote, traditional women's poetry can by and large be categorized under the subgenre of "moods in the boudoir" (*kuei-ch'ing* 閨情). Typically, a poem is set in a lady's chamber, from which the woman poet observes, whether it is the interiors of her room (e.g., the bed, painted screens, dressing table, lamps), the garden (e.g. flowers and plants, butterflies and birds), or a more distant vista (e.g., rivers and mountains). The observation leads her to expresses her feelings, often as they relate to a romantic or marital situation, such as the parting from and longing for a loved one. Further, because the subject matter of the subgenre is predominantly love or especially lovesickness, poets often employ the image of spring to express their feelings. Often, the waiting for the arrival of spring symbolizes the return of the loved one; spring scenes are a painful reminder of the absent loved one and unfulfilled love; and the passage of spring evokes the fading away of youth and beauty.

All of these characteristics can be seen in Hsü's work. However, she succeeds in adding an individual touch to her poems of "moods in the boudoir" as the following example, "Nan-hsiang tzu: Ch'un-ch'ing" 南鄉子：春情 (Spring Mood: To the Tune of 'Southern Hometown'), illustrates:

> Sitting alone, I count the days till his return.
> In the depth of flowering shrubs,
>   sun's shadow is low.
> I pace back and forth, searching for
>   a good line,
> My chin in my hand—
> There is no other topic than spring
>   melancholy.
>
> I lean on the railing in the west of
>   the adorned boudoir.
> Sweet green grass covers the old
>   riverbank.
> I still remember when he left,
> We couldn't part—
> A wine shop's banner flapped by
>   [fluttering] red-apricot flowers.

> 默坐數歸期
> 華影重重日影低
> 無計徘徊
> 思好句支頤
> 除卻春愁沒個題
>
> 閑倚畫樓西
> 芳草青青失舊堤
> 猶記當時
> 人分處依依
> 紅杏華邊卓酒旗

Like many written by women, this poem expresses the unmitigated sadness of a wife waiting for her husband's return.

Several images recurrent in this subgenre appear here: the spring scene, a woman "sitting alone," "pacing back and forth," "leaning on the railing," and reminiscing about a happier time. What distinguishes the poem from numerous others like it are: first, Hsü's description of herself in line three not only as a woman but also as a poet; and second, the vivid description of the parting scene in the last two lines.

The line: "I pace back and forth, searching for a good line" is a rather unusually self-conscious assertion of one's role as a poet in a *kuei-ch'ing* poem. The line reminds readers of such eminent male predecessors as Tu Fu 杜甫 (712–770)* and Chia Tao 賈島 (779–843),* who wrote about the painstaking process of poetic creation. Through this kind of association, the gender difference commonly accepted by traditional women poets seems to be suspended temporarily. For one moment, Hsü sees her as much a poet (not just a poetess) in her own right as a pining wife. Not only is there no contradiction between these two roles, but in fact the first enhances the second. Hard as she tries to think of a good line of poetry, she cannot escape from the thought of her husband and ends up writing a poem about him. (The connection between poetry writing and conjugal love is also seen in another lyric, "Ch'ung-tieh chin" 重疊金：春恨 [Spring Regrets: To the Tune of 'Layered Gold'] where Hsü laments: "Writing new poems—alas, no one matches them" 新題遍無人和詩.)

The last two lines of the poem recreate the parting scene, where Hsü saw her husband off at a wine shop in spring. The concluding image of the shop's banner fluttering in the wind, as if flapped by apricot blossoms, is both original and suggestive. Apricot blossoms blown about by the wind take on the active role of an agent, when in fact they, like the banner, are a passive receiver of the

59

wind. Such rendering transfers human attributes to the inanimate flowers. Like Hsü, the flowers are so distressed on the sad occasion that they toss and tumble, thus causing the banner to flutter in the air. The flapping banner and the flying petals mingle and seem inseparable, just as the couple about to part at the wine shop.

There are other significant details in the poem under discussion. For instance, the contrast between the past and the present enhances the sense of loss and sadness. Also, the use of green grass covering the old riverbank reminds readers of the poem "Yin-ma Ch'ang-ch'eng k'u hang" 飲馬長城窟行 (Lines on Letting My Horse Drink at the Waterhole by the Great Wall) by Ts'ai Yung 蔡邕 (133–192)* of the Eastern Han, which begins with: "Green is the grass by the riverbank, / Never ending I think of the distant one." The parallel between the flourishing wild grass and the never-ending thoughts of the loved one appears repeatedly in traditional poetry.

Together, the features noted above make "Spring Melancholy: To the Tune of 'Southern Hometown'" a superior poem. It is no wonder that it was praised by the critic Ch'en T'ing-cho 陳廷焯 as reminiscent of Li Ch'ing-chao 李清照 (1084–*ca.* 1151),* the preeminent woman poet in the Chinese tradition. Hsü's poetry reveals a sensitive mind and an adroit synthesis of traditional images and motifs. Although her work is still very much within the tradition of "feminine" poetry, its depth of feeling and occasional original imagery render it memorable.

Editions and References
Hsiu-hsien chi 繡閑集 (A Collection of Poems Written during Pauses from Embroidery). Collected in v. 7 of *Hsiao-T'an-luan Shih hui-k'o kuei-hsiu tz'u* 小檀欒室彙刻閨秀詞. Hsü Nai-ch'ang 徐乃昌, ed. 1896.
Fen-lien hsin yung 粉奩新詠 (New Songs from the Powder Case), cited in *Chung-kuo li-tai ts'ai-nü shih-ko chien-shang tz'u-tien* 中國

歷代才女詩歌鑒賞辭典. Cheng Kuang-i 鄭光儀, ed. Peking: Chung-kung Kung-jen, 1991, p. 1656.

Michelle Yeh
University of California, Davis

Huan T'an 桓譚 (*tzu,* Chün-shan 君山, *ca.* 43 B.C.–*ca.* A.D. 28) was a many-sided personality: a Confucian official, critical thinker, musician, astronomer, specialist in mechanics and other sciences, keen observer of magical practices, a poet, a literary critic, a disciple and friendly critic of Yang Hsiung 揚雄 (53 B.C.–A.D. 18),* and a contemporary and opponent of Liu Hsin 劉歆 (50 B.C.–A.D. 23).* His father was Prefect of Imperial Musicians (*T'ai-yüeh ling* 太樂令), and Huan T'an was first a Gentleman of Imperial Carriages (*Feng-chü lang* 奉車郎), then (12–7 B.C.) Prefect of the Bureau of Music (*Yüeh-fu ling* 樂府令). After the abolition of the Bureau and dismissal of Huan and his 440 fellow employees because they adhered to "unorthodox music" (*su-yüeh* 俗樂), he became a Gentleman again. From A.D. 2–6 he controlled plans for the regulation of the Yellow River; his support for Wang Mang on a mission in A.D. 7 brought him an inferior aristocratic title. Between 9–*ca.* 20 he was a Grandee of the Director of Music (*Chang-yüeh Tai-fu* 掌樂大夫) and a libationer (*chi-chiu* 祭酒) Expounding the *Yüeh ching* 樂經 (Classic of Music). After having witnessed the death of Yang Hsiung and Wang Mang, he received an inferior post due to his fame and recommendation; but in 26 he had a new clash with critics because he performed the "frivolous" new music (*hsin sheng* 新聲) liked by Emperor Kuang-wu 光武 (r. 25–57). Huan T'an became famous due to his three critical memorials. He frankly claimed that prognostication texts (*ch'an wei* 懺緯) were contrary to the Classics, although he knew that Emperor Kuang-wu believed he had obtained the throne partly on the basis of such texts. Having escaped the death sentence, Huan T'an died on the way to his new post (in modern Anhwei; see also *Hou Han shu* 28A: 955-962).

Huan T'an's only book is *Hsin lun* 新論 (New Treatise) in 16 chapters (13 of them divided in to two parts, in all 29 *chüan*). The last chapter, "Ch'in tao" 琴道 (The Way of the Zither, also known as "Ch'in ts'ao" 琴操 [Principles of the Zither], perhaps originally an independent work), had to be finished by Pan Ku 班固 (32–92).* Nothing is known of his other work on music, *Yüeh yüan-ch'i* 樂元起 (Origins of Music). *Hsin lun* was probably lost after the T'ang and its 203 fragments do not at all represent the size of the original text, which might have equalled that of the *Lun-heng* 論衡 (see Wang Ch'ung 王充 (27–ca. 97).** Some fragments of Huan T'an's other writings exist, including the "Wang-hsien fu" 望仙賦 (*Fu* on Gazing after Immortals), originating evidently from his *T'an chi* 譚集 in 5 *chüan*. No more disputable is his authorship of the essay "Hsing-shen" 形神 (Body and Spirit) dealing exhaustively and in an accomplished form with the inevitability of death, the impossibility of artificially prolonging life, and acknowledging at the same time the usefulness of applying oneself to some hygienic practices. The figure of candle and flame, as representative of body and mind, is used.

As for Huan's major work, the titles of some chapters show the spirit of *Hsin lun:* "Observing Evidence" (*Chien cheng* 見徵), "Reprimanding Wrong" (*Ch'ien fei* 譴非), "Dispersing Obscurantism" (*Ch'u pi* 祛蔽) "Correcting the Classics" (*Cheng ching* 正經) etc. *Lun-heng* has similar chapter titles and Wang Ch'ung showed a high respect for Huan T'an.

Due to the fragmentary state of the text and the habit of Huan T'an to propose first a statement he disagrees with, some of his statements may be interpreted as contradictory or as a change of a former standpoint. In fact, the larger fragments show that he was a skeptical naturalistic philosopher and political critic, basing himself both on his personal experience from the upheavals during three dynasties and upon his observation of natural phenomena. Like Wang Ch'ung he knew many books, but formulated his own judgments. Huan T'an described practices of Taoists and magicians in order to evaluate their psycho-physiological methods. He applied this dialectical approach even to the *hsiao-shuo* 小説* stories which, according to him, were not fully reliable, but contained matters of use for daily life. Similarly, he promoted the "free," amusing music regularly oppressed by the ceremonial music. In this way he tried to contribute to the autonomy of culture.

Editions and References

Huan, T'an 桓譚. *Hsin lun* 新論. Shanghai: Ku-chi, 1977.
Huan Tzu Hsin lun 桓子新論 (Master Huan's New Treatise). In *Ch'üan Hou Han wen*, 12.7a-10a and the Chapters 13-15 in Yen K'o-chün. Much better than the following.
Huan Tzu Hsin-lun. In *Wen-Ching T'ang ts'ung-shu* 問經堂叢書. Sun P'ing-i 孫馮翼, ed. Also in *SPPY*.

Translation

Pokora, Timoteus. *Hsin-lun (New Treatise) and Other Writings by Huan T'an (43 B.C.-28 A.D.), An Annotated Translation with Index.* Ann Arbor: Center for Chinese Studies, 1975. Includes also studies.

Studies

Chung, Chao-p'eng 鍾肇鵬. "*Hsin lun 'Hsing-shen' te tso-che ying tuan-kuei Huan T'an* 新論形神的作者應斷歸桓譚, *Jen-wen tsa-chih* 1959.2: 34-36.
___. "Huan T'an ho Wang Ch'ung" 桓譚和王充, *Chiang-hsi hsüeh-k'an* 1963.5: 40-43.
Narita, Nirao 成田衡. "Kan Tan no tetsugaku" 桓譚の哲学, *Kangakkai zasshi* 5.3 (1937): 1-12.

Pokora, Timoteus. "Huan T'an's '*Fu* on Looking for the Immortals,'" *AO* 28 (1960): 353-67.

___. "The Life of Huan T'an," *AO* 31 (1963): 1-79, 521-576.

___. "Two Answers to Professor Moriya Mitsuo," *AO* 28 (1960): 353-67.

Timoteus Pokora
Prague

Huan-hsi yüan-chia 歡喜冤家 (Antagonists in Love) is a collection of twenty-four stories on the common theme of love turning into hatred, so that many belong to the "sex and crime" type. In fact, half of them carry over motives from the *San-yen/Erh-p'o* 三言/二拍 collections of Feng Meng-lung 馮夢龍 (1574–1646)* and Ling Meng-ch'u 凌濛初 (1580–1644).* The pseudonym of the author, Hsi-hu Yü-yin Chu-jen 西湖漁隱主人 (The Master who Fishes and Lives Reclusively on West Lake), points to a Hangchow writer, perhaps Kao I-wei 高一葦, who also wrote two late Ming *ch'uan-ch'i* (romances)* and dealt with the same publisher, Shan-shui Lin 山水鄰. The preface is dated October 1640.

Though rather explicit, the author avoids lengthy sexual descriptions and uses the vernacular language with a pleasant fluency. A typical story is the third, "Li Yüeh-hsien ko-ai chiu fu" 李月仙割愛救夫 (Li Yüeh-hsien Gives Up What She Treasures to Save Her Husband). The protagonist is Wang Wen-fu 王文夫, a young scholar. Although barely twenty, he has already lost his parents, his wife, and his child and lives together with Chang Pi-ying 章必英, the son of his father's friends. At twenty five he remarries Li Yüeh-hsien. To support his new wife, Wang travels about selling herbs. While Wang is out, Chang Pi-ying seduces Li Yüeh-hsien's maid and then Li herself. Later, Chang accompanies Wang on one of his trips and pushes him into a river, taking Wang's money and returning home. But Wang does not drown and has Chang arrested. Chang is tried and sentenced to death, but through bribes gains his freedom and has Wang Wen-fu arrested on trumped-up charges. Impoverished, Li Yüeh-hsien is forced to agree to a "marriage proposal" from an unknown suitor who turns out to be none other than Chang Pi-ying. Finally, Li is able to inform the authorities of this entire, complicated series of events and the tale ends "happily" with Wang's release and Chang's execution.

Though repeatedly prohibited, the book survived in more than a dozen editions under several different titles; the earliest is *T'an-huan pao* 貪歡報 (Retribution of Concupiscence) and the latest the *San, Ssu Hsü* 三四續 (Third and Fourth Sequels) to the *Chin-ku ch'i-kuan* 今古奇觀 (Wonders of the Present and Past).* In the *Shôsetsu jiui* 小説字匯, a Japanese lexicon of spoken Chinese (preface 1784), the book is listed by its original title of *Huan-hsi yüan-chia*.

Editions and References
Huan-hsi yüan-chia. Shan-shui Lin 山水鄰, 1640. The version in the Tokyo Tôyôbunka Sôkôdô 東京東洋文化双紅堂 Library is illustrated (half-page illustrations for each story).
Hsin-chüan hui-t'u Ku-pen Huan-hsi yüan-chia 新鐫繪圖古本歡喜冤家. Shang-hsin T'ing 賞心亭. 8 *chüan*. In the British Museum.
No modern edition.

Translations
Lanselle, Rainier. *Le Poisson de jade et l'épingle au phénix, douze contes chinoise du XVIIe siècle*. Paris: Gallimard, 1987. Numbers 4, 8, 10 and 15.

Studies
Chung-kuo ku-tai hsiao-shuo pai-k'o ch'üan-shu 中國古代小說百科全書. Peking: Hsin-hua, 1993, p. 181.
Hanan, Patrick. *The Chinese Vernacular Story*. Cambridge, Mass.: Harvard University Press, 1981, p. 161. Brief critical comment.

Hsiao, Hsiang-k'ai 蕭相愷. *"Huan-hsi yüan-chia,"* in *Hsiao-shuo tsung-mu t'i-yao*, pp. 245-48. A description of the text history followed by summaries of the stories.

Lévy, André. *Le Conte en langue vulgaire du XVIIe siècle*. Paris: Institut des Hautes Études Chinoises, 1981, pp. 94-5 and 368-71. Brief critical comment.

André Lévy
University of Bordeaux

I-p'ien ch'ing 一片情 (Expanse of Passion or Expanse of Love) is an anonymous collection of fourteen pieces from an author making liberal use of Hangchow's colloquialisms, published in 1644 or slightly later. In contrast to earlier erotic fiction, the work testifies to the high level reached at the time by Chinese narrative craft: the stories are woven from a fertile imagination into a fluent spoken language. Most of them deal with humble strata of society, perhaps because ribald comedy calls for the low mimetic mode. They go beyond the conventions of the genre in conceding to women strong sexual urges which justify many a crafty trick.

For example, the second story, "Shao Hsia-tzu chin-t'ing yin-sheng" 邵瞎子近聽淫聲 (The Blindman Hsia from Nearby Listens to the Sounds of Lascivity) involves a blind fortune-teller named Shao 邵. Shao's business flourishes and a neighbor offers the blind man his daughter, Hsiu-yüeh 羞月, in marriage. After the ceremony, the handicapped husband takes many precautions to protect his new wife's virtue, but she is soon carrying on an affair virtually under his nose. Shao detects the sounds of lovemaking, however, and catches the lovers *in flagrante*. Finally, he decides to allow his wife to remarry.

Though surviving in a single copy of a later, early Ch'ing edition, the book may have had a fairly large cloaked circulation as it is mentioned in the *Shôsetsu jiui* 小説字彙, a Japanese lexicon of spoken Chinese with a preface dated 1784, as well as on the list of forbidden books promulgated in 1868 by Ting Jih-ch'ang 丁日昌 (1823–1882). Several stories have been taken over into the collection of eight pieces entitled *Pa-tuan chin* 八斷錦, a book also on Ting Jih-ch'ang's list.

Editions and References

I-p'ien ch'ing. A complete, printed edition with a preface; Tokyo Tôyôbunka Sôkôdô 東京東洋文化双紅堂 Library.

I-p'ien ch'ing. Found in the Chung-yang Mei-shu-yüan 中央美術院 (Peking). Only three chapters (of the original fourteen) remain; Wu Hsiao-lin (see Studies below) believes this was originally a selected edition.

Translations

Lanselle, Rainier. *Le Poisson de jade et l'épingle au phénix, douze contes chinoise du XVIIe siècle*. Paris: Gallimard, 1987. (Numbers 9 and 12.)

Lévy, André. *Tout pour l'amour*. Arles: Ph. Picquier, 1996 (The remaining 12 pieces).

Studies

Chung-kuo ku-tai hsiao-shuo pai-k'o ch'üan-shu 中國古代小説百科全書. Peking: Hsin-hua, 1993, pp. 674-75.

Hanan, Patrick. *The Chinese Vernacular Story*. Cambridge, Mass.: Harvard University Press, 1981, p. 162. Brief critical comment.

Lévy, André. *Le Conte en langue vulgaire du XVIIe siècle*. Paris: Institut des Hautes Études Chinoises, 1981, pp. 374-5. Brief critical comment.

Wu, Hsiao-lin 吳小林. "I-p'ien ch'ing," in *Hsiao-shuo tsung-mu t'i-yao*, p. 240. Gives a detailed description of the edition in Peking along with summaries of the three stories it contains.

André Lévy
University of Bordeaux

I-wen chih 藝文志 (Records of Classical and Other Literature) are bibliographic chapters in the Chinese dynastic histories, particularly in the twenty-four *cheng-shih* 正史, "official" or "standard histories," acknowledged as such in an imperial compilation of 1739 (cf. C. S. Gardner, *Chinese Traditional Historiography,* p. 97). The character *i* 藝 in *I-wen chih* stands for "classics;" the Han scholar Chia I 賈誼 (200–168 B.C.),* for instance, names the "six *i*" as the *Book of Poetry,* the *Book of History,* the *Book of Changes,* the *Spring and Autumn Annals* and the *Book of Music* (Chia I, *Hsin shu* 新書, "Liu shu" 六術 chapter; cf. also Chang Ping-lin 章炳麟 (1868–1936),* *Kuo-hsüeh lüeh shuo* 國學略説, "Hsiao-hsüeh lüeh shuo" 小學略説 chapter: "Confucian scholars of the Han understood the six *i* to be classics.").

Only six of the standard dynastic histories have bibliographic chapters. Of these, the *Han shu* 漢書 (History of the Han) *Hsin T'ang shu* 新唐書 (New T'ang History), *Sung shi* 宋史 (History of the Sung) and *Ming shih* 明史 (History of the Ming) use the term *i-wen chih,* while two, the *Sui shu* 隋書 (History of the Sui) and *Chiu T'ang shu* 舊唐書 (Old T'ang History), use the synonymous term *ching-chi chih* 經籍志. However, *i-wen chih* has become an accepted fixed term, used in so late a history as the *Ch'ing-shih kao* 清史稿 of 1927–28, although this work has never been recognized as one of the standard histories.

The value of these bibliographic chapters is very obvious; they provide reliable information on the entire literature available at a certain period of history. In their prefaces and postscripts they offer valuable information on the development and fate of book collections, genres, and on genre classification in China. Indirectly, they remind "of the size and variety of literature by that time, vastly bigger and more varied than the scanty survivals we handle today would lead us to suppose" (E. R. Hughes, "Concerning the Importance and Reliability of the *I-wen chih,*" p. 175).

The most remarkable *I-wen chih* is the prototype, Chapter 30 of the *Han shu,* the dynastic history of the Former Han, due to its volume and great antiquity. The *Han shu* was compiled mainly by Pan Ku 班固 (32–92),* with others contributing to its completion and final form (cf. O. B. van der Sprenkel, *Pan Piao, Pan Ku, and the Han History* [Canberra: Australian National University, 1964]). The actual booklist in this *I-wen chih* is preceded by a preface in which Pan Ku gives a short history of book collecting, leading up to the works of the imperial librarians Liu Hsiang 劉向 (77B.C.?–6?)* and Liu Hsin 劉歆 (50 B.C.–A.D. 23).* Liu Hsiang compiled the *Pieh lu* 別錄 (Separate Records), a classified catalog of all books available to him, and his son Liu Hsin compiled the *Ch'i lüeh* 七略 (Seven Summaries), presumably commentaries on groups of books. Both these works were lost, possibly already at the end of the T'ang dynasty. However, Pan Ku states in his introduction that he edited these works of the Liu's "in preparing this [the *Han shu* "I-wen chih"] list of books." A full translation of Pan Ku's "Introduction" may be found in James Legge's "Prolegomena" (*Chinese Classics,* I:7), and a partial translation in Gardener's *Historiography,* p. 33. From the mentioned statement by Pan Ku and from the structure and substance of the booklet, it is generally assumed that Pan Ku's *I-wen chih* reproduces, in full or slightly edited, the works of Liu Hsiang and Liu Hsin.

The *Han-shu* "I-wen chih" consist of a Preface and six sections which are headed: (1) "Liu i lüeh" 六藝略 (The Six Classics), (2) "Chu tzu lüeh" 諸子略 (Philosophers of Various Schools), (3) "Shih fu lüeh" 詩賦略 (Rhapsody and *Shih* Poetry), (4) "Ping-shu lüeh" 兵書略 (Military Science), (5) "Shu-shu lüeh" 術數略 (Divination), (6) "Fang chi lüeh" 方技略 (Medical Science and Pharmacopeia). Each of the six sections is provided with an explanatory, or summarizing postscript. The six post-scripts together are assumed to have originally constituted the "Chi lüeh" 輯略 (General Summary), the first of Liu Hsin's *Seven Summaries,* which Pan Ku mentions in his Preface but of which there is otherwise no trace in the "I-wen chih."

The postscript to Section 3, "Rhapsody and *Shih* Poetry," is a short exposé on poetry, partly historical and partly critical. It ends with a quotation from the second chapter of the *Fa yen* 法言 by Yang Hsiung 揚雄 (53 B.C.-A.D. 18),* "The poetry of the *Book of Odes* was beautiful by upholding [moral] principles. The poetry of the *tz'u* 辭 poets was beautiful by its voluptuousness. If the Confucians would have used the *fu* style of poetry [with its serious political and moral purposes], Chia I would have 'reached the hall [achieved well] and Ssu-ma Hsiang-ju would have 'entered the chamber' [achieved excellence]. Oh, that they should not have used it." (For a full, alternative translation of the Postscript, see Helmut Wilhelm, "The Scholar's Frustration," pp. 312-313, in "Studies" below).

Each of the six "I-wen chih" sections is furthermore subdivided; there are thirty-eight such subdivisions. For instance, Section 3, "*Fu* and *Shih* Poetry," is divided into five groups. The criteria for this group are not altogether clear. The difference is obvious between the *fu* of groups 1-4, on the one hand, and the *ko shih* 歌詩 (songs and *shih* poetry) of the last group, but the reasons for subdividing the *fu* into four groups is difficult to explain. The last group of *fu,* designated as *tsa fu* 雜賦 (sundry *fu)* seems to contain poems for which no authorship could be established, while the preceding three *fu* groups are (with very few exceptions) by single identifiable authors. As to groups 1 to 3, there is neither a chronological order, nor an apparent generic difference, although the prominent names that head each

group may have suggested that. If that is the case, the first group, headed by Ch'ü Yüan 屈原 (*ca.* 340–278 B.C.),* would contain only *sao* 騷 type, the second group only *fu* of the sort Lu Chia 陸賈 (*ca.* 228–*ca.* 140 B.C.) wrote, and the third group only Sun Ch'ing 孫卿 type *fu.* Although there must be great differences in perception and sensitivity to poetic nuances between then contemporary readers and modern scholars, it is still difficult to reconcile that Group 1 contains such heterogeneous poets as Ch'ü Yüan, the exponent of the elegiac *sao,* as well as Mei Sheng 枚乘 (d. 141 B.C.)* and Ssu-ma Hsiang-ju 司馬相如 (179–117 B.C.),* exponents of the verbose, over-descriptive *fu* from the time of its ultimate development in the mid-late second century B.C. It may therefore appear more plausible that Pan Ku grouped his *fu* authors by their importance, based on his own judgment, or the judgment of the time. Classification in this manner was not uncommon among Chinese literary critics, as, for instance, in the well-known *Shih-p'in* 詩品 (Evaluation of Poetry)* by Chung Jung 鍾嶸 (*ca.* 465–518). This would also well explain why we find the most famous names in Group 1, and why so many more poems of groups 2 and 5 were lost, namely for the reason that they were poems of less appreciated and less respected poets.

The *Han-shu* "I-wen chih" is also noteworthy for presenting the first Chinese book classification, Liu Hsin's *Ch'i lüeh* system, adopted by Pan Ku. This system was later gradually superseded by the *Ssu pu* 四部 (Four Departments) system originated by Hsün Hsü 荀勖 (231–189 B.C.). The four departments, which Hsün Hsü in his *Chung ching* 中經 (Books for the Inner Place Secretariat) merely called *chia* 甲, *i* 乙, *ping* 丙, and *ting* 丁(equivalent to our A, B, C, and D) were later clearly identified as *ching* 經 (classics), *shih* 史 (histories), *tzu* 子 (various philosophers), and *chi* 集 (belles lettres). This classification found its first significant application in the *Sui shu* "Ching-chi chih" 隋書經籍志, the bibliographic chapter in the History of the Sui Dynasty.

The *Sui shu* "Ching-chi chih" is next to Pan Ku's bibliography the most important historical bibliography, again in view of the early periods it covers and the rich material it discloses. It forms Chapters 32-35 of the *Sui-shu*, but its bibliographical data had originally been prepared for the Liang, Ch'en, Chou, Ch'i as well as the Sui dynastic histories. The essay-type postscripts to the various subsections are therefore of great historical interest, as they cover so much more than merely Sui texts and Sui history.

By following the *Ssu pu* classification, the *Sui shu* "Ching-chi chih" divides the four main divisions into many subdivisions. However, the literature section shows only three subdivisions, with the rather incongruous distribution of: the *Ch'u tz'u* section—10 items, *Pieh chi* 別集 (Collections of Individuals' Works)—437 items, and *Tsung chi* 宗集 (Anthologies by Periods of Genres)—107 items.

The Preface of the "Ching-chi chih" delves into the history of the production and collection of written records. It also adduces a great amount of data on the tragic destruction of books by revolutions, wars, and, in one instance, through the hazards of water transportation. It also indicates that original booklists had been purged so as not to show shallow (*ch'ien* 淺) or vulgar (*su* 俗) items that would not be beneficial to moral cultivation. As a somewhat reluctant afterthought, the bibliography ends with a historical description and bibliography of Taoism and Buddhism, rather meager if compared, for instance, with the 2,257 works listed in the catalog *Sui chung ching mu-lu* 隋眾經目錄 by the Sui monk Fa-ching 法經 in 594 A.D., which is a better testimonial to the significance of Buddhism in the era under review.

The two T'ang dynastic histories both had booklists, the *Chiu T'ang shu* list titled "Ching-chi chih" and the *Hsin T'ang shu* list called "I-wen chih." The introduction to the *Chiu T'ang shu* "Ching-chi chih," as well as its postscript, gives a short historical résumé of book collecting, book cataloguing, and the deplorable losses incurred in the various insurrections during and at the end of the dynasty. In the early K'ai-ch'eng 開成 era (836–840) the "Four Departments" (i.e., the imperial library) counted 56,476 *chüan* said to have fallen victim to the rebellion led by Huang Ch'ao 黃巢 (d. 884). The introduction mentions several T'ang scholars who had collaborated in earlier booklists, in particular Wu Chiung 毋煚 of the K'ai-yüan 開元 (713–742) era, and quotes from their introductory and explanatory essay. As it stands, the "Ching-chi chih" of the *Chiu T'ang shu,* therefore, reflects the holdings of the imperial library at the height of the K'ai-yüan era. The list is arranged by *Ssu pu* classification. The fourth department, the *chi* 集, is subdivided into three sections: *Ch'u tz'u* 楚詞, *pieh chi* 別集, and *tsung chi* 總集. The *Hsin T'ang shu* "I-wen chih" presents a much more comprehensive list of T'ang books because it also includes post-K'ai-yüan items, such as the works of Li Po 李白 (701–762),* Tu Fu 杜甫 (712–770),* Han Yü 韓愈 (768–824),* and Liu Tsung-yüan 柳宗元 (773–819).* A comparison of the two T'ang booklists can be found in *T'ang-shu Ching-chi I-wen ho-chih* 唐書經籍藝文合志 (Shanghai: Shang-wu Yin-shu-kuan, 1956).

The *Sung shih* 宋史, compiled 1342–45 with the Mongol T'o T'o 脫脫 (1314–1355) as chief editor, is generally faulted for its many errors and omissions. However, its bibliographic section, the "I-wen chih," provides substantial information. Its introduction gives statistical data on library holdings, recounts the many mishaps to libraries, and ends listing 9,819 items in 119,792

66

chüan. The arrangement is again by the *Ssu pu* system, which by then appears to be widely accepted as standard. It is interesting that the *chi* 集 section has an additional subsection, *wen shih* 文史 (literary history and criticism), apparently due to the abundant *shih hua* 詩話 (poetry talks)* produced during Sung times.

The *Ming shih* 明史 (History of the Ming), prepared under the supervision of Chang T'ing-yü 張廷玉 (1672–1755) and published in 1739, gives in its bibliographic section, the "I-wen chih," a comprehensive listing of Ming publications, based on an earlier booklist by Huang Yü-chi 黃虞稷 (1629-1691). This is a break with the tradition of including publications of all earlier dynasties in previous "I-wen chih." Moreover, there are numerous omissions probably due to the literary censorship by the Ch'ing emperors (cf. L. C. Goodrich, *The Literary Inquisition of Ch'ien-lung* [Baltimore: Waverly Press, 1935]). The Manchu *index expurgatorius* listed 2,320 books for total destruction and 345 or partial suppression. Note-worthy in the *Ming shih* "I-wen chih" is the large number of *fang-chih* 方志 (local gazetteers) in its "Ti-li 地理 Section" and the listing of the *Yung-lo ta-tien* 永樂大典 of 22,900 *chüan* in Subsection 10, "Lei-shu" 類書 (Encyclopedias)* of the *Tzu* 子 Section.

Apart from the above-named "i-wen chih" in the standard histories, there are many more booklists calling themselves "i-wen chih" or "ching-chi chih" in non-standard historical or bibliographic works, for instance, the *Hou Han shu* "I-wen chih" 後漢書藝文志 (Bibliographic Chapter to the History of the Latter Han) prepared by Ssu-ma Piao 司馬彪 (*ca.* 246–*ca.* 306) of the Chin dynasty, or the "I-wen chih" in the *Ch'ing shih kao* 清史稿 prepared under the chairmanship of Chao Erh-sun 趙爾巽 and published 1927–28. Information on these booklists may be obtained from Liang Tzu-han

梁子涵, *Chung-kuo li-tai shu-mu tsung-lu* 中國歷代書目總錄 (Comprehensive Booklists Throughout China's History; Taipei: Chung-hua Wen-hua Ch'u-pan Shih-yeh Wei-yüan-hui, 1955).

References

I-wen chih erh-shih-chung tsung-ho yin-te 藝文志二十種綜合引得 (Combined Indices to Twenty Historical Bibliographies). Hung Yeh 洪業, ed. 4v. Rpt. Taipei: Chinese Materials and Research Aids Service Center, 1966.

There are also numerous supplements to the dynastic-history bibliographies in the *Erh-shih-wu shih pu-pien* 二十五史補編 (6v.; Shanghai: Shang-wu Yin-shu-kuan, 1936-37).

Studies

Ch'en, Kuo-ch'ing 陳國慶, ed. *Han shu "I-wen chih" chu-shih hui-pien* 漢書藝文志注釋彙編. Peking: Chung-hua, 1983.

Ch'en, Teng-yüan 陳登原. *Ku-chin tien-chi chü san k'ao* 古今典籍聚散考. Shanghai: Shang-wu, 1936.

Gardner, Charles Sidney. *Chinese Traditional Historiography.* Cambridge, Mass., Harvard University Press, 1958.

Hsü, Shih-ying 許世瑛. *Chung-kuo mu-lu-hsüeh shih* 中國目錄學史. Ta ei: Chung-hua Wen-hua Ch'u-pan Shih-yeh Wei-yüan-hui, 1954.

Hughes, E. R. "Concerning the Importance and Reliability of the *I-wen chih,*" *Mélanges Chinois et Bouddhiques,* 6 (1938-39): 175-182,

Koh, Thong-ngee [Hsü T'ung-i 許統義]. "The Beginning of Chinese Bibliography: A Study of the Record of Literature in the History of the Former Han Dynasty." *Ts'e fu, The Chinese Repository* 7/8 (Spring/Summer 1964): 26-41; 9/10 (Fall/Winter 1964): 1-26.

Kôzen, Hiroshi 興膳宏 and Kawai Kôzô 川合康三. *Zui sho "Keiseki shi" shôkô* 隋書経籍志詳考. Tokyo: Iwanami, 1995.

Suzuki, Yoshijirô 鈴木由次郎. *Kanjo Geimon-shi* 漢書芸文志. Tokyo: Meitoku, 1968. The introduction traces the history of "I-wen chih."

Wilhelm, Helmut. "The Scholar's Frustration, Notes on a Type of *Fu,*" in John

Fairbank, ed. *Chinese Thought and Institutions.* Chicago: University of Chicago Press, 1957, pp. 312-13.

Wilkinson, Endymion. "Dynastic Bibliographies," in *The History of Imperial China; A Research Guide.* Cambridge, Mass.: East Asian Research Center, Harvard University, 1973, p. 88.

Ernst Wolff

Ku Ch'un 顧春 (*tz'u,* Tzu-ch'un 子春, *hao,* T'ai-ch'ing 太清, 1799–after 1876), or Ku T'ai-ch'ing as she is more commonly known, though generally regarded as one of the foremost women poets of the late-Ch'ing period, has left little definitive information about her family background and early childhood. It has been suggested by many scholars that she was the grand-daughter of O Ch'ang 鄂昌 (*chü-jen* 1724), nephew of the Manchu statesman and poet, O-erh-t'ai 鄂爾泰 (1680–1745). O Ch'ang, who was then serving as the Provincial Governor of Kwangsi province, was forced to commit suicide in 1755 because of his association with the poet and official Hu Chung-tsao 胡鍾藻, who in that same year was executed for allegedly having written poems containing anti-Manchu sentiments. Following this incident, the family quickly slid into poverty and disgrace, which is perhaps why the daughter born to O Ch'ang's son in 1799 was entrusted to a family surnamed Ku 顧. The Ku family—it is unclear whether they were Manchu or Chinese—were very likely bondservants of the household of Mien-i 綿億 (1764–1815), a grandson of the Ch'ien-lung emperor, which is how Ku T'ai-ch'ing eventually became the concubine of one of Mien-i's son's, I-hui 奕繪 (1799–1838).

Whatever her origins, it is clear that Ku's relationship with I-hui was one of considerable intellectual and emotional compatibility. I-hui, who was the same age as Ku, was not only a prince, but also a poet, calligrapher, architect and collector of antiquities, all of which interests Ku fully shared. Just one of many examples of their compassionate connection is Ku's literary sobriquet T'ai-ch'ing 太清, which she chose to match that of I-hui which was T'ai-su 太素. Similarly, the titles of their collected works and many of their poems were also purposefully matched. The fact that I-hui's legal wife had died young no doubt contributed to the harmony of the relationship between I-hui and Ku T'ai-ch'ing, a relationship which resulted in seven children. However, this seemingly idyllic life came to an abrupt end when I-hui died in 1838 leaving the fate of Ku T'ai-ch'ing and her children in the hands of I-hui's son by his deceased first wife, who inherited both his father's title and his wealth. Ku and her children were expelled from the family home and forced to fend for themselves. Thus her later life was one of considerable hardship and suffering, although she single-handedly raised her children and successfully married them off. Ku T'ai-ch'ing seems to have lost her eyesight in 1875, and although we know she was still alive in 1876, there is no trace of her after that year.

Ku T'ai-ch'ing's extant œuvre is one of the largest we have for a woman poet of this period—it consists of nearly one-thousand *shih** and *tz'u** poems in two collections. Her collection of *shih* poetry, entitled *T'ien-yu ko chi* 天游閣集, was first published in 1908 by Mao Kuang-sheng 冒光生 (b. 1873); her *tz'u* are contained in the *Tung-hai yü ko* 東海漁歌, printed in 1913 by the poet K'uang Chou-i 況周頤 (1859–1926), one of the most important figures in the late Ch'ing and early Republican *tz'u* revival. A number of the prefaces to these collections were written by well-known poets of the day, all of whom held Ku in high esteem and greatly admired her poetic talent. The well-known poet Kung Tzu-chen 龔自珍 (1792–1841)* was one of these poetic admirers, although there is but little basis to the speculation that not only was he Ku's lover, but that he was poisoned by I-hui because of this supposed relationship. She also had a large circle of women friends with whom she would take excursions and exchange poetry and letters. Among her poems we also find verses dedicated to women poets and artists from an earlier time, such as the Sung poet Li Ch'ing-chao 李清照 (1084–*ca.* 1151)* and the Ming loyalist writer and teacher Wang Tuan-shu 王端淑 (1620–*ca.* 1701).** What is striking about her work, in fact, is the ease with which she addresses both her male and female friends; the poetic authority with which she draws inspiration from both male and female poets who preceded her; and the extent to which she uses poetic images, language, allusions and themes, not because they necessarily fit the traditional expectations of "women's poetry," but rather because they suited her self-expressive or communicative intent.

Although Ku was skilled at writing both *shih* and *tz'u*, she is best known for her *tz'u*, and her relatively simple, unadorned style has often been compared to that of the famous Sung lyric poets, Chou Pang-yen 周邦彥 (1056–1121)* and Chiang K'uei 姜夔 (1155?–1235?).* She is also often referred to as the female counterpart to Na-lan Hsing-te 納蘭性德 (1655–1685),* generally considered to be a master of the *tz'u* form and one of the leading poets of his time, although it is unclear whether this pairing was made on the basis of their common Manchu background or their poetic talent. K'uang Chou-i expresses his opinion that she ranks first among the women poets of her time. There is no question, however, that Ku has yet to receive the study and the full appreciation she deserves.

A large percentage of Ku T'ai-ch'ing's poems were written for particular occasions—inscriptions for paintings,

epigraphs of poetry collections, farewell and epistolary poems, and poems written to commemorate visits or excursions of one kind or another. A great many of her poems, for instance, were written as inscriptions to paintings–both she and I-hui were avid collectors and connoisseurs, and Ku was herself a noted painter. Unlike many of her late-Ch'ing contemporaries, she appears to have been particularly fond of the rather austere paintings of the Yüan-dynasty painter Ni Tsan 倪瓚 (1301–1374) as well as the bold and often idiosyncratic works of the late-Ming artist T'ang Yin 唐寅 (1470–1523). Ku T'ai-ch'ing's own poems share some of the characteristics of these painters' works, tending towards the straightforward, unadorned and descriptive rather than the artful, allusive and obscure, philosophical rather than sentimental. In this, and it can be seen especially in her *tz'u* poems, she clearly modeled herself on the style and spirit of Su Shih 蘇軾 (1037–1101).* Her poems are often deceptively simple: K'uang Chou-i, for instance, notes that while there is nothing strikingly unique or outstanding about her poetic style, the general "atmosphere" of her poems is extraordinary. He also praises her talent at writing verse that is descriptive of tangible objects–flowers, paintings, scenery–but which is "neither clinging nor detached" (*pu t'ieh pu t'o* 不帖不脱).

The detailed prefaces to many of Ku T'ai-ch'ing's poems also afford us a glimpse of the remarkably full social, intellectual and artistic life that she led, especially during her time with I-hui. If read carefully between the lines, they also provide a hint of the deeply-felt frustrations of women artists and poets such as Ku, women who took full advantage of their talent and education, but still found themselves painfully constrained by traditional notions of female possibility which, although increasingly questioned and tested, still remained firmly in place.

Editions and References

Ku, T'ai-ch'ing 顧太清. *T'ien-yu Ko chi: Ku T'ai-ch'ing shih tz'u* 天游閣集：顧太清詩詞. Li Shu-t'ien 李澍田, ed. Rpt. Changchun: Chi-lin Wen-shih, 1989.

Ku, Ch'un 顧春. *T'ien-you Ko chi* 天游閣集. In *Feng-yü Lou ts'ung-shu* 風雨樓叢書.

___. *Tung-hai yü ko* 東海漁歌. Mss. copy in 6 *chüan*. Osaka.

___. *Tung-hai yü ko (chüan 2 only)*. In *Tzu-hsüeh chi-k'an*. Lung Mu-hsiang, ed. 3v. (1933–36); 1:2 (1933): 152-66.

___. *Tung-hai yü ko*. In *Feng-yü Lou ts'ung-shu*. Teng Shih 鄧實, ed. N.p.: Hsün-te Teng-shih, 1910–1911, 58v., v. 33.

Translations

Waiting for the Unicorn, pp. 83-86.

Studies

Wu, Kuang-pin 吳光濱. *Ku T'ai-ch'ing yen-chiu chi Tung-hai yu-ko chien chi* 顧太清研究集東海漁歌箋注. Taipei: T'ien-i, 1975. See also the "Ku T'ai-ch'ing" entry in the first volume of the *Indiana Companion to Traditional Chinese Literature,* p. 492.

Beata Grant
Washington University

Kuang-i chi 廣異記 (The Great Book of Marvels) was a collection of tales of the strange and supernatural compiled by Tai Fu 戴孚, who graduated as *chin-shih* in 757. This is known from the collection's original preface by Ku K'uang 顧況 *(ca. 725–ca. 814),** an important document for the history of *chih-kuai* 志怪* literature as perceived during the T'ang. Tai Fu began his career in court as collator (*chiao-shu lang* 校書郎) and ended it with a post in Jao-chou 饒州; he died at 57 *sui* some time after 780. Neither his collected literary works (in 20 *chüan*) nor his *Kuang-i chi* (20 *chüan*) survive in transmission, but the latter has been largely reconstructed from quotations in *T'ai-p'ing kuang-chi* 太平廣記* and other Sung sources.

The *Kuang-i chi* succinctly reports tales as they came to the notice of an official serving in the provinces during the 760s and 770s (the Chekiang region is particularly richly represented). It stands out among *chih-kuai* collections from this period for its catholic range of interest, betraying no religious or intellectual bias beyond the *chih-kuai* author's traditional commitment against scepticism. There is a strong preoccupation with the dead returning through possessions, haunt-ings, activity in coffins, matings, and revival after underworld visits. Other common themes include rewards for *sûtra* piety (stressing the *Vajracchedikâ);* interaction with gods and their temple cults; dreams, omens, premonitions, cures; interaction with animals, particularly foxes, tigers and snakes, involving afflictions, possessions and transformations.

In the *Kuang-i chi* these familiar themes are often presented with a close historical particularity which reveals a range of religious behavior spread through T'ang society from top to bottom. Since the focus in time is so closely restricted to Tai Fu's own career, there is scope for setting this social panorama within a historical context. It is characterized throughout by a lay-man's, and in ritual matters even a consumer's, viewpoint, creating a per-spective on religious behavior quite distinct from the priestly traditions of Buddhism and Taoism, as it is from the policies and doctrines of state Confu-cianism.

Editions and References

Fang, Shih-ming 方詩銘, ed. *Ming-pao chi, Kuang-i chi* 冥報記，廣異記. Peking: Chung-hua, 1992.

Translations

Dudbridge, Glen. *Religious Experience and Lay Society in T'ang China, a Reading of Tai Fu's Kuang-i Chi* Cambridge: Cambridge University Press, 1995. Appendix details selected translations given in this and the following works:

Groot, J.J.M. de. *The Religious System of China.*

6v. Leiden: E. J. Brill, 1892–1910.

Hammond, Charles E. "An Excursion in Tiger Lore," *AM*, 3rd Series, 4 (1991): 84-100.

Kao, Karl S.Y. *Classical Chinese Tales of the Supernatural and the Fantastic*, Bloomington: Indiana University Press, 1985, pp. 241-3.

Lévi, Jean. "Les fonctionnaires et le divin: luttes de pouvoirs entre divinités et administrateurs dans les contes des Six Dynasties et des Tang," *Cahiers d'Extrême-Asie* 2 (1986): 81-110.

Schafer, Edward. *The Golden Peaches of Samarkand, a Study of T'ang Exotics* Berkeley and Los Angeles: University of California Press, 1963.

___. *The Vermilion Bird, T'ang Images of the South.* Berkeley and Los Angeles: University of California Press, 1967.

Wieger, Léon. *Folk-lore chinois moderne.* Ho-chien fu: Mission Catholique, 1909, rep. Farnborough: Gregg, 1969.

Studies

Dudbridge, *Religious Experience* (see "Translations" above).

Tu, Te-ch'iao 杜德橋 [Glen Dudbridge]. *"Kuang-i chi* ch'u-t'an" 廣異記初探. *Hsin Ya hsüeh-pao* 15 (1986), 395-414.

Uchiyama, Chinari 内山知也. "Chū Tō shoki no shōsetsu–*Kōiki* o chūshin to shite" 中唐初期の小説―廣異記を中心として. In *Kaga Hakushi taikan kinen, Chūgoku bunshi tetsugaku ronshū* 加賀博士退官記念、中国文史哲学論集. Tokyo: Kodansha, 1979, pp. 527-41.

Wu, Hsiu-feng 吳秀鳳. *"Kuang-i chi* yen-chiu" 廣異記研究. Unpublished M.A. thesis, Fu-jen University, Taiwan, 1986.

Glen Dudbridge
The University of Oxford

Kuo P'u 郭璞 (*tzu*, Ching-ch'un 景純, 276–324), exemplifies the ancient, obvious yet often overlooked idea that factual knowledge is an essential part of wisdom. Of the myriads of facts that he spent his life collecting, he seems to have been most drawn to geography, portents, and odd phenomena from throughout the universe. He approached that knowledge with a diviner's instinct, preserving information regardless of whether or not there were clues to what it meant. It is said that he was trained by an "Elder Kuo" who left him a blue sack of secrets. This collecting of far-flung lore marks him as a successor to the Ch'ü Yüan 屈原 (340?–278 B.C.)* who compiled the "T'ien wen" 天問 (Heavenly Questions), the same Ch'ü Yüan who celebrated a riotous mandala of "Far Roaming" in the "Yüan yu" 遠遊. Wise men in that tradition served kings not only as advisors but soothsayers, basing their advice on encyclopedic knowledge that kings seldom had the time or talent to amass. It was in this way that Ch'ü Yüan the adept merged with Ch'ü Yüan the martyred minister: Ch'ü the minister, whose wisdom was not enough to sway the king, sadly proclaimed his loyalty in the "Li sao" 離騷, then "Left Tribulation Behind" through suicide—or, as some have read it, through transcendence into an Immortal realm which was his true spiritual and intellectual home. It is no coincidence that Kuo P'u annotated Ch'ü Yüan's works. And he further partook of Ch'ü's tradition when he strove to serve the nation, wrote of its grandeur, and complained, in lush imagery, of his struggle to make a difference.

He has been called the most skillful writer of the refugee generation: later than Tso Ssu 左思 (*ca.* 253-*ca.* 307),* P'an Yüeh 潘岳 (247–300),* and Lu Chi 陸機 (261–303),* who lived entirely under the Western Chin's lethally volatile Loyang regime, but earlier than the Southern-raised T'ao Ch'ien 陶潛 (365–427),* or Hsieh Ling-yün 謝靈運 (385–433).* From his home at Wen-hsi 聞喜 in Hotung 河東 (modern Shansi), between 307 and 310 Kuo led several dozen families of relatives and intimates on a trek through the Huai region, Yangchow and eventually to Chien-yeh 建業 (soon to become Chien-k'ang 建

康, the Southern capital–modern Nanking), joining what would become almost a million refugees who abandoned the north with its disintegrating ruling house, barbarian conquerors, starvation and even cannibalism. Kuo's official career began on the road, when at Hsüan-ch'eng 宣城 (now part of Anhwei), probably in 311 he joined the staff of Prefect Yin Yu 殷祐. Kuo went with Yin to a new posting at Chien-yeh, where the chancellor Wang Tao 王導 (276–339) frequently recruited him for advice. Kuo served the Eastern Chin court after its founding in 317 under Emperor Yüan, attaining the title of Secretarial Court Gentleman (*Shang-shu lang* 尚書郎). In 323, he started to serve the energetic young Emperor Ming, but was soon commandeered by Wang Tao's cousin, the warlord Wang Tun 王敦 (266-324), who had captured the prime minister-ship and by 324 was plotting a run for the throne. Kuo prognosticated, to Wang Tun's face (correctly, it turned out), that if Wang tried his usurpation he would fail and die. When the wrathful, ailing Wang asked Kuo "And what is to be the length of *your* life?" (says the story), Kuo answered, "It shall end this day before day has ended!" Wang Tun had him killed then and there, at age 49.

As a writer, Kuo is best known for his "Yu-hsien shih" 遊仙詩 (Poems of Roaming in the Immortal), and his "Chiang fu" 江賦 (Yangtze River Rhapsody). The rhapsody, a paean to the Southland and the river as its life force, was clearly intended to celebrate the Chin state in its reborn Southern glory. Magnificent and learned though it is, the "Chiang fu" does not break poetic ground in the way that Kuo's "Yu-hsien" poems do. Immortals have played various roles in poetry, most prominent being that of a metaphor by which the poet can lament the realities around him, or embody a longing that the world be happier. The "Yu-hsien" poems of Ts'ao

Chih 曹植 (192–232),* from the previous dynasty, are usually considered to be that metaphorical kind or even to have been written as sheer recreation–it is generally accepted that Ts'ao did not believe in Immortals. Kuo P'u's ten surviving "Yu-hsien" pieces present a range of tones, including the clarity of Ts'ao Chih and the throbbing understatement of Juan Chi 阮籍 (210–263)* (as in Juan's "Yung huai shih" 詠懷詩 #35). Kuo's superworldly beings can be seen as symbols of success, and also as symbols of how wise it can be to reject the pursuit of that same success. But most striking in Kuo's pieces is his view of the transcendent realm itself: his sparkling surfaces, studded with images of back-slapping sky-flyers straight out of Taoist legend, shine brightest in the third of the series, the poem most often antholo-gized and has been distinctively trans-lated in Ezra Pound's *Cathay*. This is the Kuo P'u of the famous "rainbow brush" (*wu-se pi* 五色筆) which would so haunt Chiang Yen 江淹 (444–505)* that he lost his talent after dreaming that Kuo had lent him the brush but then came to take it back. Kuo's radiant style may have been an exercise not only in repre-senting his imagination but in depicting *reality*, as he seems to have believed that Immortals existed; yet his defiant death, the risks he took with his career, and some anecdotes about his reckless physi-cal appetites, indicate that he was not interested in wasting time to seek al-chemical or magical ways to become immortal himself. He sought *knowledge*, even of the unseen, but held few hopes that he could change fate. That combin-ation of attitudes makes all the more stirring his use of Immortals as signposts toward something better, whether mental or physical, than the madness that engulfs so much of humanity.

Surviving prose includes Kuo's bold memorials, mostly warnings about harsh government, inspired by sunspots, dark miasmas or other signs. His piece "K'o ao" 客傲 (A Stranger Sneered), reminiscent of Han essays by Tung-fang Shuo 東方朔 (154–93 B.C.), Yang Hsiung 揚雄 (53 B.C.–A. D. 18 A.D.),* and Pan Ku 班固 (32–92)* defends Kuo's worth as a mere diviner in the face of an imaginary visitor who smirks at his lack of achievement. Overall, his prose indicates that he was genuinely concerned for his country, and frustrated at the indignity of being pressured to use such prodigious learning to prognosticate for the bullies and upstarts who dotted the Eastern Chin political landscape, even as they lumped him together in their minds with charlatan sorcerers such as Jen Ku 任谷, whom Kuo bitterly attacked in a message to the throne.

More aesthetically striking to the modern ear than his eloquent prose are Kuo's works in four-character lines, in particular his "Praises" for sets of illustrations to the *Erh-ya* and *Shan-hai-ching* 山海經* (*"Erh-ya* t'u-tsan" 爾雅圖贊, *"Shan-hai-ching* t'u-tsan" 山海經圖贊), included in his prose works although in fact they are six-line verses. With a cool pithiness, he lightly summarizes topics ranging from "The Tripod" (鼎) and "The Flounder" (比目魚), to "Ghost Grass" (鬼草) and "The Land of the Long-Armed People" (長臂國). The same quiet wit appears also in many of his doggerel-like divination rhymes, some in lines of four characters and some in seven, most of which come to us in the remaining fragments of his *I tung lin* 易洞林, a memoir of divinations that he made or phenomena he heard about, beginning with how the *Classic of Changes* helped him plan his escape route to the South. This work, while perhaps not strictly literature, is a rare example of Chin autobiography, and despite being fragmentary and perhaps not entirely Kuo's writing, in some ways it gives a more balanced impression than his official biography in the *Chin shu* 晉書 (72:1899-1910). While the historians repeat tales about Kuo conjuring beans into tiny red-coated men (as part of a ruse to obtain a concubine cheaply), or summoning a strange ape to revive a general's dead horse mouth-to-mouth, the *Tung-lin* shows Kuo taking hexagram readings in the standard way, curing diseases with rabbit meat, and commenting cautiously that he did not know whether a report of a dragon being born was true or not.

Some of Kuo's thought may be gleaned from his esoteric works (assuming they are his), and even from his annotations to such works as the *Ch'u-tz'u* 楚辭,* *Shan-hai ching* 山海經,* *Mu T'ien-tzu chuan* 穆天子傳,* *Erh-ya* 爾雅 and *Fang-yen* 方言, and to Ssu-ma Hsiang-ju's 司馬相如 (179–117 B.C.)* massive "Shang-lin fu" 上林賦 and "Tzu-hsü fu" 子虛賦. One might learn more about Kuo and his generation, including what must have been a searing collective refugee experience, by examining him in the light of his friendship with Kan Pao 干寶 (*fl.* 320) and his contrasts with Kan Pao's friend, the alchemist-adept Ko Hung 葛洪 (283–343),* who *did* advocate literal Immortality and whom Kuo seems not to have known personally, although the *Chin shu* places his biography with Kuo's. Despite his occult training, Kuo seems to have been more "Confucian" than "Taoist" in those areas that he considered most important. He embodied the patriotically death-defying side of Confucius' heritage, but was also willing to examine "the strange, the strong, depraved and supernatural" (怪力亂神), from which Confucius had abstained.

A final dimension: Kuo is a folk hero. His hagiography, which asserts that his corpse disappeared and he became an Immortal, appears in the *Shen-hsien chuan* 神仙傳,* *Lieh-hsien chuan* 列仙傳,* and numerous Taoist sources, while his divination secrets are advertised to this day in the backs of magazines almost as frequently as those of Chu-ko Liang 諸葛亮 (181–234). There being indications that this fame began while Kuo was still alive, he could serve as an interesting study of the role of legend and notoriety among poets and scholars before the age of print.

Editions and References

(1) Literary works:

Hsien Ch'in Han Wei Chin Nan-pei-ch'ao shih, 2:862-869. Surviving verse.

Liu-ch'ao wen, Chin section, *ch*. 120-123. Most surviving prose, including the "T'u-tsan" for the *Erh-ya* and *Shan-hai ching*.

Lu, *Nan-pei-ch'ao shih*, 2:862-870.

Wen-hsüan. Best edition of the "Chiang fu" (*ch*. 12) and 7 of the 10 complete "Yu hsien shih" (*ch*. 21).

(2) Esoteric or doubtful works:

Hsüan-chung chi 玄中記. Notes about exotica. Reconstructed text, remotely attributable to Kuo P'u. Punctuated edition in *Ts'ung-shu chi-ch'eng*.

I tung-lin 易洞林. Incomplete, reconstructed text, likely authentic at least in part. Best-organized edition seen is in Ma Kuo-han 馬國翰 (1794-1857), ed. *Yü-han shan-fang chi i-shu* 玉函山房輯佚書, 78.52a-68a.

Tsang shu 葬書. Book of geomancy related to burial. Seems largely intact, but difficult to be sure if it is actually the same *Tsang-shu* that Kuo P'u wrote. Two good, thoroughly annotated editions: (Yüan dynasty) Wu Ch'eng 吳澂, ed., Cheng Mi 鄭謐, annot. *Ti-li tsang-shu chi-chu* 地理葬書集註, in *Hsü Chin-hua ts'ung-shu* 續金華叢書; (modern) Kao Hsing-ch'üan 高星權, Kao Shih-ming 高視明, annot. *Tsang-ching chu-shu* 葬經註疏, in *Tsang-hsüeh* 葬學 series. Shanghai: Privately printed, 1936.

Yü-chao shen-ying chen-ching 玉照神應真經. Attribution to Kuo is speculative. Hsü Tzu-p'ing 徐子平, annot. In *Ku-chin t'u-shu chi-ch'eng* (Po-wu hui-pien, I-shu tien, 565 *chüan*, Hsing-ming pu hui-k'ao) 古今圖書集城(博物彙編, 藝術典565卷, 星命部彙考).

Translations

Knechtges, *Wen xuan*, 2:321-352.

Mair, *Anthology*, pp. 176-177.

Studies

Ch'eng, Ch'ien-fan 程千帆. "Kuo Ching-ch'un Ts'ao Yao-pin yu-hsien shih pien-i" 郭景純曹堯賓遊仙詩辨異, in his *Ku-shih k'ao-so* 古詩考索. Shanghai: Ku-chi, 1984,

pp. 296-307.

Ching, Shu-hui 景蜀慧. "Kuo P'u 'Yu-hsien shih' yü Wei-Chin hsüan-hsüeh" 郭璞遊仙詩與魏晉玄學, *Ssu-ch'uan Ta-hsüeh hsüeh-pao ts'ung-k'an (Yen-chiu-sheng lun-wen hsüan-k'an)* 28 (1985.5): 16-26.

Funatsu, Tomihiko 船津富彦. "Kaku Haku no Yûsenshi no tokushitsu ni tsuite" 郭璞の遊仙詩の特質について, *Tôkyô shina-gaku hô* 10 (June, 1964): 53-70.

Kôzen, Hiroshi 興膳宏. "Shijin to shite no Kaku Haku" 詩人としての郭璞, *Chûgoku bungaku hô* 19 (Oct. 1963): 17-67; English summary, ii-iii.

Morita, Shinnosuke 森田慎之助. "Kaku Haku ni okeru shijin no ummei" 郭璞における詩人の運命, *Kyûshû Chûgoku gakkaihô* 7 (1961): 47-63.

Pease, Jonathan. "Kuo P'u's Life and Five-colored Rhymes (An 'Immortal' Chin-dynasty Writer and Diviner, 276-324)." Unpublished M.A. thesis, University of Washington, 1980.

Sasake, Yasuko 佐竹保子. "Yûsenshi no keifu–Sô Hi kara Kaku Haku made" 遊仙詩の系譜一曹丕から郭璞まで, *Tôhoku Gakuin Daigaku ronshû–Ippan kyôiku* 83/84 (1986): 101-165.

Weng, Shih-hua 翁世華. "Kuo P'u Ch'u-tz'u-chu i-wen shih-pu" 郭璞楚辭註佚文拾補. In *Nan-yang Ta-hsüeh hsüeh-pao* 6 (1972): 122-130. On the fragments of Kuo's *Ch'u-tz'u* annotations.

Yu, Hsin-li 游信利. "Kuo P'u nien-p'u ch'u-kao" 郭璞年譜初稿, *Chung-hua hsüeh-yüan* 10 (1972.9): 79-110.

——. "Kuo P'u yu-hsien shih ti yen-chiu" 郭璞遊仙詩的研究, *Kuo-li Cheng-chih Ta-hsüeh hsüeh-pao* 32 (1975.12), 91-120.

——. "Kuo P'u cheng-chuan" 郭璞正傳, *Kuo-li Cheng-chih Ta-hsüeh hsüeh-pao* 33 (1976.5): 123-151.

Jonathan Pease
Portland State University

Late-Ch'ing fiction refers to the fictional narratives which appeared from the end of the Opium War (1844) to the fall of the Ch'ing dynasty (1911). This period witnessed changes in writing, printing, and reading fiction in a multitude of ways unknown to previous generations. The changes culminated at the turn-of-the-century, when the enlightened elite elevated fiction to the highest generic position in the hierarchy of literature and the public found in fiction a major solution to their desire for both entertainment and information. For these reasons, late-Ch'ing fiction studies since the May Fourth era have focused mostly on the era from the Hundred Days Reform of 1898 to 1911. Recent scholarship, however, has questioned such a limited view of the period and has expanded the range of late-Ch'ing studies to include the second half of the nineteenth century.

Fiction appeared as an integral part of the new publishing medium, the newspaper, as early as the 1870s. The front pages of *Shen-pao* 申報 (1872–1949), one of the earliest Chinese newspapers, often highlighted reports that combined both journalistic relevance and fictional imagination. The monthly literary supplement of *Shen-pao, Ying-huan so-chi* 瀛寰瑣記 (Random Sketches of the World), routinely put narrative fiction side by side with other, more prestigious genres such as essays and poetry. By 1892, fiction had become such a popular genre that it commanded a venue of its own. Under the auspices of Han Pang-ch'ing 韓邦慶 (1856–1894), himself an established novelist, *Hai-shang ch'i-shu* 海上奇書 (Wonderbook of Shanghai, 1892–94) appeared as the first modern Chinese fiction magazine.

In the meantime, fiction also found new territory in tabloids dedicated to *yu-hsi* 遊戲 (recreation) and *hsiao-hsien* 消閒 (pastimes). Most of the thirty-two tabloids that have been identified, such as *Chih-nan pao* 指南報 (News about Pleasure Quarters) and *Yu-hsi pao* 遊戲報 (News about Recreation), carried fiction. Both Wu Chien-jen 吳趼人 (1866–1910)* and Li Po-yüan 李伯元 (1867–1906),* two of the most important late-Ch'ing writers, started their careers

as editors of and regular contributors to these tabloids. While selected works in classical Chinese, such as Hsüan Ting's 宣鼎 (1832–1880) voluminous *Yeh-yü ch'iu-teng lu* 夜雨秋燈錄 (Writings Done on Rainy Nights under the Autumn Lamp, 1895), were still appreciated by elite readers, it was vernacular fiction that won increasing popularity, to the point where intellectuals such as Yen Fu 嚴復 (1853–1921)* and Liang Ch'i-ch'ao 梁啟超 (1873–1929)* advocated the vernacular form of fiction (and drama) as the only way to renovate the Chinese mentality.

In the wake of literati advocacy of fiction in the late 1890s, an estimated two thousand or more works of fiction were written and circulated in various forms. Only half this number, one thousand or so, have been recovered. These works, mostly written in the vernacular, can be assigned to a wide range of genres, from detective fiction to science fantasy, from erotic escapades to didactic utopias, and from chivalric cycles to revolutionary romances. More than thirty presses specialized in publishing fiction, and at least twenty-one literary periodicals appeared with *hsiao-shuo* or fiction as part of their titles. The most famous four are *Hsin hsiao-shuo* 新小説 (New Fiction, 1902–1906), *Hsiu-hsiang hsiao-shuo* 繡像小説 (Illustrated Fiction, 1903–1906), *Hsiao-shuo yüeh-pao* 小説月報 (All-story Monthly, 1906–1908), and *Hsiao-shuo lin* 小説林 (Fiction Grove, 1907–1908).

This is a period in which Western fiction was introduced to China in various forms of translation. Based on the catalogue of late-Ch'ing fiction compiled by Ah Ying 阿英 (Ch'ien Hsing-t'un 錢杏邨, 1900–1977), one of the pioneers of late-Ch'ing fiction studies, mainland Chinese scholars have identified at least 479 creations and 628 translations. The Japanese scholar Tarumoto Teruo, drawing on a different method of counting, concludes that, between 1840 and 1911, there appeared at least 1016 kinds of fiction translation. Charles Dickens and Alexandre Dumas fils, Victor Hugo and Leo Tolstoy, among others, were warmly welcomed by readers, while works by A. Conan Doyle, H. Rider Haggard, and Jules Verne remained the top three bestsellers.

The practice of translation at this time, however, was such a loosely defined vocation that it necessarily included paraphrasing, rewriting, truncating, translation relays, and restyling. Lin Shu 林紓 (1852–1924),* the most productive popular translator of the time, was responsible for introducing to China writers from William Shakespeare to Alexandre Dumas fils. Lin never had any training in foreign languages, but with the assistance of friends, he translated, or rewrote, more than 170 works into ornate classical Chinese. With Yen Fu, Liang Ch'i-ch'ao, and Lin Shu as their respective examples, scholars such as Benjamin Schwartz, C. T. Hsia, and Leo Lee long ago noted that late-Ch'ing translators employed their works to serve emotive and ideological goals inconceivable to the original authors, and, moreover, that these translators' witting and unwitting misinterpretations of the originals generated spontaneous alternative versions of the modern. As a form of human communication, translation is always already overdetermined by historical contingency. And late-Ch'ing translators played as free with the texts of the modern as late-Ch'ing novelists did with the texts of tradition.

Chinese fictional renovation was already under way when Western and Japanese texts began to appear in Chinese form. When *Tang-k'ou chih* 蕩寇志 (Quell the Bandits, 1853) became the target of propaganda warfare during the Taiping Rebellion, alternately banned by the rebels and promoted by the Ch'ing government, it was re-inducting the novel into the service of Chinese political warfare; when *P'in-hua pao-chien* 品花寶鑑 (A Mirror for Judging Flowers, 1849) brought the aesthetics of female impersonation to · bear on heterosexual romantic conventions, it was re-engendering Chinese sexual subjectivity. Almost all major classic Chinese novels, from *Shui-hu chuan* 水滸傳* to *Hung-lou meng* 紅樓夢,* appear as their parodic doubles at this time. The late Ch'ing, as a *fin-de-siècle* period, is both decadent and decadent, engaged in cacophonous retuning of the traditional harmonies.

Furthermore, the discovery and late-Ch'ing publication of two eccentric mid-Ch'ing works, Shen Fu's 沈復 (1762–after 1803) lyrical autobiography *Fu-sheng liu-chi* 浮生六記 (Six Sketches from My Floating Life) and Chang Nan-chuang's 張南莊 (*fl.* 1880) ghostly satire *Ho tien* 何典 (What Sort of Book Is This?), in 1877 and 1879 respectively, showed two additional ways of narrating subjective and social realities. *Ho tien,* in particular, distinguished itself by using dialect--in this case, the Wu dialect--as part of its realistic effect. It flaunted the colloquial mannerisms embedded in traditional vernacular fiction and anticipated the next generation's experiments with linguistic local color. By the time Yen Fu and Liang Ch'i-ch'ao proposed reforms in the manner of Japanese and Western novels (respectively in 1897 and 1898), Chinese fictional convention had shown every sign of disintegrating and reinventing itself. The advent of various foreign models compounded rather than initiated this complex phenomenon; it thrust the whole late-Ch'ing practice of fiction into the cross-cultural and inter-lingual dialogue we know as *modernity.*

Studies of late-Ch'ing fiction started as early as the 1910s. Hu Shih 胡適 (1891–1962), for example, made brief comments on *Kuan-ch'ang hsien-hsing chi* 官場現形記 (Exposure of Officialdom; see Li Pao-chia*) and *Erh-shih-nien mu-tu chih kuai-hsien chuang* 二十年目睹之怪

現狀 (Eyewitness Reports on Strange Things from the Past Twenty Years; see Wu Wo-yao*) in "Wen-hsüeh kai-liang ch'u-i" 文學改良芻議 (A Proposal of Literary Reform, 1917). Hu Shih's meticulous research on novels such as *Lao Ts'an yu-chi* 老殘遊記 (The Travels of Lao Ts'an, 1906; see Liu E*), *San-hsia wu-i* 三俠五義* (Three Knights-Errant and Five Sworn Brothers, 1879), and *Hai-shang-hua lieh-chuan* 海上花列傳 (Sing-Song Girls of Shanghai, 1894) enlarged the view as to the social and cultural contexts in which the works were produced. In his introduction to late-Ch'ing fiction in his lecture series as well as in *Chung-kuo hsiao-shuo shih-lüeh* 中國小說史略 (A Brief History of Chinese Fiction, 1935), Lu Hsün's 魯迅 (1881–1936) was the first to map out the directions of late-Ch'ing fiction in thematic terms. The categories of late-Ch'ing fiction named by Lu Hsün-–*hsia-hsieh hsiao-shuo* 狹邪小説 (novels about prostitutes), *kung-an hsia-i hsiao-shuo* 公案俠義小説 (novels of adventure and detection), and *ch'ien-tse hsiao-shuo* 譴責小説 (novels of exposure)-–have been used by scholars for over half a century.

Ah Ying's *Wan-Ch'ing hsiao-shuo shih* 晚清小説史 (A History of Late-Ch'ing Fiction, 1937) is perhaps the most comprehensive and influential study of late-Ch'ing fiction as seen on the eve of the Second World War. He provides abundant information regarding the political circumstances, socioeconomic motivations, and ideological factors that gave rise to late-Ch'ing fiction. In his *Hsiao-shuo hsien-t'an* 小説閒談 (Idle Talks on Fiction) series, Ah Ying wrote extensively about works he discovered or took personal interest in. A leftist ideologue, Ah Ying made it clear that the most important virtue of late-Ch'ing fiction lay in its reflection of a society on the eve of revolutionary change, its critique of social evil, and its propagation of progressive ideals. To this list of studies of late-Ch'ing fiction one should also add works by modern scholars such as Chao Ching-shen 趙景深, K'ung Ling-ching 孔令境, Liu Ta-chieh 劉大杰 (1904–1977), and others.

Although scholars agree that late-Ch'ing fiction represents one of the most drastic changes in Chinese narrative tradition, they are quite ambivalent about its aesthetic achievement. Their criticisms fall mostly in the following three areas. First, arising in the shadow of late-Ming to mid-Ch'ing fiction, after the peak of classical Chinese narrative, late-Ch'ing fiction displays an aesthetic inferiority in terms of both formal expertise and thematic sophistication. Second, motivated by contemporary socio-political forces, late-Ch'ing fiction writers of fiction have been criticized by modern humanists for tending to ignore the broader context of "human" experience, of which socio-political turmoil is only a part. Alternatively, Marxist critics have berated late-Ch'ing fiction for not having enough foresight and courage to show socio-political turmoil leading to freedom and revolution, despite writers' increasing awareness of the relation between writing and national destiny. Whether too political or not political enough, late-Ch'ing fiction is seen as handicapped by its superficial grasp of social reality, a flaw that in turn affects its artistic merit.

Finally, because of its artistic crudity and historical/ideological short-sightedness, late-Ch'ing fiction is said to have contributed little to the formation of truly modern Chinese fiction. For all the translations of Western and Japanese literature available in the marketplace, and writers' efforts at honing their skills on foreign models, late-Ch'ing fiction retains firm links to traditional fiction. Modern Chinese fiction could not arise until writers finally mastered the narrative devices, thematic topoi, and image repertory of the West. Late-Ch'ing fiction is thus a momentary diversion preceding the arrival of the next great beginning—namely, the May Fourth literary revolution.

Based on these observations, late-Ch'ing fiction conventionally begins with Yen Fu and Hsia Tseng-yu's 夏曾佑 (1886–1924) "Pen-kuan fu-yin shuo-pu yüan-ch'i" 本館附印說部緣起 (Announcing Our Intention to Publish a Supplementary Fiction Section, 1897), arguably the first piece of criticism to affirm the social function of fiction in modern times. In response to Yen and Hsia's view of fiction, Liang's "I-yin cheng-chih hsiao-shuo hsü" 譯印政治小說序 (Foreword to Our Series of Political Novels in Translation, 1898) introduced the political novel, a genre Liang believed responsible for the success of the Japanese Restoration, as the type of fiction that would most benefit China.

Liang's promotion of the political novel was later substantiated by his founding of *Hsin hsiao-shuo* and the publication of the inaugural essay, "Lun hsiao-shuo yü ch'ün-chih chih kuan-hsi" 論小說與群治之關係 (On the Relation between Fiction and Ruling the Public) and his own novel, *Hsin Chung-kuo wei-lai chi* 新中國未來記 (The Future of New China), in 1902. The essay opens with the famous passage that affirms the didactic role of fiction and its positive political and moral consequences, and concludes that to renovate morality, religion, manners, learning and the arts of China, one "must first renovate fiction . . . Why? It is because fiction exercises a power of incalculable magnitude over mankind." Similar statements can also be found in essays by contemporary literati like T'ao Yu-tseng 陶佑曾 (1886–1927), Wang Chung-ch'i 王鍾麒 (1880–1913), Su Man-shu 蘇曼殊 (1884–1918), and numerous magazine and newspaper editorials. Although critics such as Huang Mo-hsi 黃摩西 (1866–1913) and Hsü Nien-tz'u 徐念慈 (1875–1908) had already voiced skepticism in the heyday of the "new fiction" fever, the conviction that fiction could and should serve as the foremost medium of enlightenment was apparently endorsed by the then-elite and by literary historians ever since.

This account of the "rise of new fiction" has continually been challenged in recent years as a result of shifted critical paradigms and discoveries of new materials. Motivated by the discourse of enlightenment and revolution, conventional May Fourth scholars credit the "new fiction" as the sole late-Ch'ing contribution to literary modernization. But it is a rare piece of "new fiction" that hasn't been "contaminated" by undesirable genres. A quick glance at the oeuvre of late Ch'ing shows that, for every item of desirable "new fiction," there appear all too many undesirable counter-examples, works later to be called depravity novels, *hei-mu* 黑幕 (literally, "black screen") novels, chivalric romance, fantasy, and so forth. The target audience of "new fiction" was the general public; yet according to the estimation of Hsü Nien-tz'u, Liang Ch'i-ch'ao's contemporary, the common people constituted no more than ten percent of its total readership. Moreover, Liang never finished his own model of new fiction, *Hsin Chung-kuo wei-lai chi;* the novel starts with a promising scene about the strength and prosperity of future China, only to come to a sudden halt after Chapter 5. In picturing the development of late-Ch'ing fiction, one should always be alert to the gap between what the writers and critics thought they had achieved and what they really did, what the elite expected their readers to like and what their readers actually read.

Liang Ch'i-ch'ao's prestige as the champion theoretician has also been reassessed in the face of the increasing appeal of works by Wang Kuo-wei 王國維 (1877–1927),* a scholar of classical literature and a conservative royalist who committed suicide for the Ch'ing in the Republican era. Of Wang's critical studies the best known is his 1904 treatise on the classic novel *Hung-lou meng.*

Inspired by Schopenhauer, Nietzsche, and Kant, Wang sees in the Chinese romance a most compelling dramatization of the eternal tension between desire and the object of desire, between human suffering and the sublimation of that suffering in art. He fits Western theories into a radical reading of Chinese classics, thus adding a new, Chinese dimension to what we understand as modern criticism. Liang Ch'i-ch'ao brandishes the banner of "new fiction," but the core of his literary conception is old Confucian didacticism. Wang Kuo-wei recommends classical Chinese fiction, but at the center of his literary thought is something very new.

In practice, traditional scholarship on the late-Ch'ing has mostly concentrated on the "four great novelists," Liu E 劉鶚 (1857–1909),* Wu Chien-jen, Li Po-yüan, and Tseng P'u 曾樸 (1872–1935).* Each is credited with one of the "four great novels of the late Ch'ing." Liu E's *Lao Ts'an yu-chi* 老殘遊記 (The Travels of Lao Ts'an, 1906) features a traveling literatus-doctor, Lao Ts'an, through whose lonely adventures within natural and human landscapes, his wanderings amid different social milieux, and his debates with friends on political and philosophical issues, a fresco of late-Ch'ing society is presented. Wu Chien-jen's *Erh-shih-nien mu-tu chih kuai-hsien chuang* (1910), deals with a young man's initiation into a society devoid of any moral scruples and his subsequent withdrawal from it. The novel appeals to readers, nevertheless, more as a grotesque parade of clowns, impostors, buffoons, and frauds, all reveling in a world turned upside down. Equally farcical in scope and sarcastic in tone is Li Po-yüan's *Kuan-chang hsien-hsing chi* (1905), a novel ridiculing the late-Ch'ing officialdom where bribery, mismanagement, and the buying and selling of posts are routine. Tseng P'u's *Nieh-hai hua* 孽海花 (A Flower in the Sea of Sins, 1905) recounts the last three decades of late-

Ch'ing history from the angle of the merry adventures of Sai Chin-hua 賽金花 (1874–1936), a courtesan best remembered for her marriage to the scholar-diplomat Hung Chün 洪鈞 (1840–1893) and her alleged liaison with the German field-marshal Count Waldersee (1832–1904), the commander-in-chief of the Allied Occupation Forces in Peking after the Boxer Rebellion.

All four of these novels, as Lu Hsün would have it, fall into the category of *ch'ien-tse hsiao-shuo,* or novels which expose and chastise social malaise. By stressing these novels' capacity to reflect and criticize reality, critics in the vein of Lu Hsün call attention to the moral bearings of late-Ch'ing writers, and as such these critics reveal their fixation on the May Fourth discourse of critical realism, which is uncannily indebted to Liang Ch'i-ch'ao's reactionary criteria for the "new fiction." Against such an approach, recent studies have provided more independent views of the novels. Accordingly, *Lao Ts'an yu-chi* is more noticeable for its expression of subjective, lyrical sensibilities and its inquiry into the terms of legal justice and poetic justice. Both *Kuan-chang hsien-hsing chi* and *Erh-shih-nien mu-tu chih kuai-hsien chuang* draw attention to the experiments of late-Ch'ing writers with the effect of the real in either grotesque or fantastic terms. And *Nieh-hai hua* sheds important light on late-Ch'ing male imagination of the dialectic between eroticism and politics. The eminence of "the great four novels" has also obscured other equally noticeable achievements by writers such as Wu Chien-jen and Li Po-yüan. Unlike Liu E and Tseng P'u, whose reputations were each based on a single work, Wu and Li were versatile, prolific writers, with long lists of novels to their credit. In particular, Li Po-yüan's *Wen-ming hsiao-shih* 文明小史 (Modern Times, 1905) provides one of the most poignant portraits of China's frustrated and hilarious experiences in confrontation with modern imports from the West. Wu Chien-jen's *Hsin Shih-t'ou chi* 新石頭記 (The New Story of the Stone, 1905) represents an intricate parody of Ts'ao Hsüeh-ch'in's* *Shih-t'ou chi,* or *Hung-lou meng* 紅樓夢,* in recourse to the newly acquired mode of science fiction. Wu's *Hen-hai* 恨海 (Sea of Regret, 1906) reinterprets the *ts'ai-tzu chia-jen* 才子佳人 or "scholar-beauty" convention (see *Ts'ai-tzu chia-jen hsiao-shuo*) against the late-Ch'ing historical background, there-by anticipating the rise of modern Chinese sentimental discourse.

Beyond the generic boundaries of the "four great novels," one encounters a panoply of works ranging from detective fiction to science fantasy, from erotic escapades to didactic utopias. These works experimented with a wide range of narrative formats unknown to writers of previous ages; ironically enough, they would find few successors in the decades immediately following. Most noticeable are works along the lines of science fantasy. A mixture of both western models of science fiction and the indigenous legacy of fantasy, science fantasy once won enormous popularity among readers with its wide spectrum of subjects: the adventure in utopia or dystopia, the flight to the moon or the sun, the odyssey among the stars or planets, and the expedition to the center of the earth or the bottom of the sea. In Huang-chiang Tiao-sou's 荒江釣叟 (The Old Man Who Fishes the Deserted River, identity otherwise unknown) *Yüeh-ch'iu chih-min-ti* 月球殖民地 (Moon Colony, 1904), Chinese emigrants at the turn of the century are seen as trying to sail to the moon in balloons. In Hsü Nien-tz'u "Hsin Fa-lo Hsien-sheng t'an" 新法螺先生譚 (New Account of Mr. Windbag, 1905), a story modeled after the German legend of Baron Münchhausen, Mr. Windbag takes an adventure to outer space and lands on Venus and Mars. In Pi-ho-kuan Chu-jen's 碧荷館主人 (Master of the Azure-

lotus Lodge, identity otherwise unknown) *Hsin chi-yüan* 新紀元 (New Era, 1908), China emerges as the superpower of the year 2000 after launching a world war against the nations of Europe. By imagining and inscribing the incredible and the impractical, late-Ch'ing writers were setting forth the terms for China's modernization project, both as a new political agenda and as a new national myth.

Finally, breaking away from the limited time span constituted by the four great novels and the last decade of the Ch'ing dynasty, recent scholarship has looked more carefully into works produced in the second half of the nineteenth century and drawn a more complicated picture of late Ch'ing fiction. Han Pang-ch'ing's *Hai-shang-hua lieh-chuan,* a panoramic presentation of life in the Shanghai pleasure quarters, investigates to chilling depth the moral and psychological consequences of courtesans' lives. It signals the final triumph of indigenous realism before imported realism became the canon of modern Chinese narrative. Wei Hsiu-jen's 魏秀仁 (Wei Tzu-an 魏子安, 1819–1874) *Hua-yüeh hen* 花月痕 (Traces of Flower and Moon, 1858), develops a maudlin romance aesthetic that inculcates linkages between love, death, and tears, prefiguring the sentimental strain of modern Chinese *Yüan-yang hu-tieh* 鴛鴦蝴蝶 (Mandarin Ducks and Butter-flies) fiction. Ch'en Sen's 陳森 (ca. 1796– ca. 1870) *P'in-hua pao-chien* 品花寶鑑 (A Precious Mirror for Judging Flowers, 1849), allegedly the initiator of a whole chain of late-Ch'ing stories about prostitution, describes the liaisons between female impersonators and their patrons. It parades and parodies the conventions of Chinese erotic and sentimental fiction and posits them in the new light of gendered subjectivity and desire.

Shih Yü-k'un's 石玉崑 (1810–1871) *San-hsia wu-i* (1879),* based on the storytelling cycle about the adventures of the imperial judge-investigator, Pao Kung 包公 (Judge Pao), with the assistance of a group of chivalric knights-errant, won tremendous popularity among late-Ch'ing audiences. The novel has been denounced as obsolete for its advocacy of feudal issues such as loyalty, sworn brotherhood, and heroic self-sacrifice. But close reading indicates that it served as the unlikely model for progressive writers when the time came for them to imagine such "modern" virtues as patriotism, revolutionary fraternity, and humanist altruism. Wen K'ang's 文康 (ca. 1798–1872) *Erh-nü ying-hsiung chuan* 兒女英雄傳 (A Tale of Lovers and Heroes, 1872), casts a nostalgic look at the declining system of Confucian values and chivalric codes. Yü Wan-ch'un's 俞萬春 (1794–1849) *Tang k'ou-chih,* a critical rewriting of *Shui-hu chuan,* intensifies the ambiguous political ideology of loyalism in the original novel. Written over a long period from the 1820s to the post-Opium War era, the novel anachronistically rehearses the new debates over imperial mandate versus popular will, Western military technology versus Chinese military prowess.

One more word about the dispute over the formal inefficacy of late-Ch'ing fiction. Few readers will want to deny that a kind of degradation happens to the grammar of Ch'ing narrative: redundancies in plotting, shallowness in characterization, and fragmentation in structure. This was a time many literati made fiction-writing their sole profession, but they were a group of most "unprofessional" writers: they hurried to get their stories into print but rarely finished them; they pursued one new international topic after another, only to expose their deep-seated parochialism; they fabricated, plagiarized, and sensationalized their materials; they reached into every social stratum for realistic data, but ended up with an idiosyncratic display of bias and perversity. Granting all these flaws, one must recognize that in late-Ch'ing fiction, familiar conventions and canons are made strange, and decorums parodically humbled. Late-Ch'ing writers have also been described as incapable of grasping Western models and thus inevitably failing to reach the threshold of the modern. Their May Fourth successors did grasp, acquire, and impose a Western model (nineteenth-century realism), and in so doing pulled China back from the threshold of the modern. Like the moderns, the late Ch'ing relentlessly appropriated, mocked, and misrepresented the old conventions, in ways that would have been exciting and new to the West, had they not been suppressed.

Lu Hsün once observed, of the changing style of the courtesan novel, that "at its first stage, it fails due to an excess of praise (for the courtesan life). . . at its last stage, it fails due to an excess of condemnation (of it)." Lu Hsün's words can be used to describe other genres of late-Ch'ing fiction as well. Praising or condemning, exaggerating or trivializing their subjects, late-Ch'ing writers cannot resist the impulse to transgress limits, to ornament a convention till it becomes a heavy-handed parody of itself. The tendency of late-Ch'ing writers to play with conventions is especially evident in the way they parody classic novels. Almost all major Chinese novels, from *Hsi-yu chi* * to *Feng-shen pang* 封神榜, find one or more rewritings and sequels at this time. Because of its tremendous popularity, *Hung-lou meng* was rewritten as a homosexual romance (*P'in-hua pao-chien* 1849), a brothel adventure (*Ch'ing-lou meng* 青樓夢 [The Dream of the Green Chamber, 1878]), a science utopia (*Hsin Shih-t'ou-chi* 新石頭記 [The New Story of the Stone]), and a novel with the same title about overseas students (*Hsin Shih-t'ou chi* [The New Story of the Stone, 1909–also identical in title with the novel by Wu Chien-jen], by Nan-wu yeh-man 南武野蠻 [The Wild Barbarian from Nan-wu]).

This libertinism is seen not merely in the writers' choice of linguistic and narrative models, but also in their attitude toward the discursive restraints handed down from the past. Some writers are so familiar with the conventions that they can play with them to the point of creating a chiasmatic replica, a hallucinatory mimicry. Thus Liu E's *Lao Ts'an yu-chi* inverts the tenor of the court-case novel (*kung-an hsiao-shuo* 公案小說) by declaring that corrupt judges may be hateful, but incorruptible judges are even more hateful; Li Po-yüan's *Kuan-chang hsien-hsing chi* suggests that incorruptible governmental officials are no more virtuous than prostitutes who call themselves virgins; Wu Chien-jen's *Erh-shih-nien mu-tu chih kuai-hsien chuang* likens the human world to that of goblins, fox spirits, and demons; Tseng P'u's *Nieh-hai-hua* endorses the myth of China saved from the invading armies of the West by a prostitute.

Austere critics of the late-Ch'ing and the May Fourth period have not been able to appreciate the libertinism in late-Ch'ing fiction except negatively, by deploring it. Few of them have thought about the possibility that late-Ch'ing fiction had a different kind of aesthetic. In the early 1980s, the Czech scholar Milena Doležzelová took on the task, investigating a formalist typology of late-Ch'ing fiction. She proposed "string-like novels" and "novels of cycles" as the binding structural rules of the period. From a different angle and a few years later, the modern-Chinese scholar Chen Pingyuan [Ch'en P'ing-yüan] 陳平原 presented a newly complicated picture of the way in which late-Ch'ing writers responded to their literary heritage and Western inventions. Contrary to the idea that this was a period of stagnation or mere "transition," Chen argues that late-Ch'ing fiction writers drew material from

both the "noble" genres—such as the lyric, the political treatise, oratory, and essays, and the petty genres, such as anecdotes, sketches, jokes, travelogues, memoirs, and diaries—and incorporated them into their new discourse.

At a time when the Western models of the modern had not become a totem and certain more obvious Chinese traditions had not become a taboo, when "serious" writers were not overwhelmed by their moral obligations and "frivolous" writers were allowed to express their own peculiar "obsession with China," late-Ch'ing fiction made itself a marketplace where a full polyphony of human voices could clamor and be heard. When reading works of the period, therefore, one must continually ask oneself whether they are *fin-de-siècle* spectacles, entropic signs of a moribund creativity, or provocations of the modern, delineating the trajectories of a twentieth-century Chinese narrative discourse that can only now be fully realized. In any case, without a conscious decision to appreciate how wayward, perverse, or "inappropriate" these works can be, one would have missed entirely one of the most radical, and most "creative," periods in Chinese literary history.

Editions and References

Ah Ying 阿英, ed. *Wan-Ch'ing wen-hsüeh ts'ung-ch'ao, hsiao-shuo chüan* 晚清文學叢鈔, 小說卷. 4v. Rpt. Taipei: Hsüeh-sheng, 1975. One of the earliest collections of late-Ch'ing fiction.

___. *Hsiao-shuo hsien-t'an ssu-chung* 小說閒談四種. Shanghai: Shang-hai Ku-chi, 1985. An overview of sources and editions of late-Ch'ing fiction.

Chen, P'ing-yüan 陳平原 [Chen Pingyuan] and Hsia Hsiao-hung [Xia Xiaohong] 夏小虹, eds. *Erh-shih shih-chi chung-kuo hsiao-shuo li-lun tzu-liao, ti-i-chüan, 1897–1916,* 二十世紀中國小說理論資料，第一卷 1897–1916. Peking: Pei-ching Ta-hsüeh, 1989.

Chung-kuo chin-tai hsiao-shuo ta-hsi 中國近代小說大系. 27v. by 1996. Nanchang:

Chiang-hsi Jen-min, 1988–. Both well-known and obscure texts included.

Chung-kuo chin-tai wen-hsüeh ta-hsi 中國近代文學大系. 13v. by 1996. Shanghai: Shanghai Shu-tien, 1990–. Published in four genres: fiction, poetry, translation, and prose.

Tarumoto, Teruo 樽本照雄, ed. *Shinben Seimatsu Minsho shôsetsu mokuroku* 新編清末民初小説目録. Osaka: Shinmatsu Shosetsu Kenkyûkai, 1997. The most thorough bibliography of late-Ch'ing fiction to date, with more than two-thousand entries.

Wan-Ch'ing hsiao-shuo ta-hsi 晚清小説大系. 37v. Taipei: Kuang-ya, 1984. A comprehensive collection of major works.

Wu, Chien-jen 吳趼人. *Wo-fo Shan-jen wen-chi* 我佛山人文及. 8 v. Lu Shu-tu 廬叔度, ed. Canton: Hua-ch'eng, 1989. The most comprehensive collection of Wu Chien-jen's works to date.

Translations

Hanan, Patrick. *The Sea of Regret: Two Turn-of-the-Century Chinese Romantic Novels.* Honolulu: University of Hawaii Press, 1995.

Liu, Ts'un-yan, ed. *Chinese Middlebrow Fiction: From the Ch'ing and Early Republican Eras.* Hong Kong: The Chinese University Press, 1984.

Shadick, Harold. *The Travels of Lao Ts'an.* Ithaca: Cornell University Press, 1959.

Studies

Ah, Ying 阿英. *Wan-Ch'ing hsiao-shuo shih* 晚清小説史. Rpt. Hong Kong: T'ai-p'ing, 1966.

Ch'en, P'ing-yüan 陳平原 [Chen Pingyuan]. *Erh-shih shih-chi Chung-kuo hsiao-shuo shih: 1897–1916* 二十世紀中國小説史: 1897–1916. Peking: Pei-ching Ta-hsüeh, 1989.

___. *Chung-kuo hsiao-shuo hsü-shih mo-shih te chuan-pien* 中國小説敍世模式之轉變. Taipei: Chiu-ta, 1990.

Cheng, Stephen H. "Flowers of Shanghai and the Late Ch'ing Courtesan Novels." Unpublished Ph. D. dissertation, Harvard University, 1979.

Dolezelová-Velingerová, Milena, ed. *The Chinese Novel at the Turn of the Century.* Toronto: University of Toronto Press, 1980.

Fang, Cheng-yao 方正耀. *Wan-Ch'ing hsiao-shuo yen-chiu* 晚清小説研究. Shanghai: Hua-tung Shih-ta, 1991.

Gálik, Márian. *Milestones in Sino-Western Literary Confrontation (1898–1979).* Wiesbaden: Otto Harrassowitz, 1986.

Hsia, C. T. "The Travels of Lao Ts'an: An Exploration of Its Art and Meaning." *THHP* 7.2 (1969): 40-66.

___. "Yen Fu and Liang Ch'i-ch'ao as Advocates of New Fiction," in *Chinese Approaches to Literature,* pp. 221-257.

Huters, Theodore. "A New Way of Writing: The Possibilities of Literature in Late Qing China, 1895–1908," *Modern China,* 14.3 (1988): 243-276.

___. "From Writing to Literature: The Development of Late Qing Theories of Prose," *HJAS* 47.1 (1987): 51-96.

K'ang, Lai-hsin 康來新. *Wan-Ch'ing hsiao-shuo li-lun yen-chiu* 晚清小説理論研究. Taipei: Ta-an, 1986.

Kuo, Yen-li 郭延禮. *Chung-kuo chin-tai wen-hsüeh fa-chan-shih* 中國近代文學發展史. Tsinan: Shan-tung Chiao-yü, 1990.

Lai, Fang-ling 賴芳伶. *Ch'ing-mo hsiao-shuo yü she-hui cheng-chih pien-ch'ien* 清末小説與政治變遷. Taipei: Ta-an, 1994.

Lancashire, Douglas. *Li Po-yüan.* Boston: Twayne, 1981.

Li, Peter. *Tseng P'u.* Boston: Twayne, 1980.

Lin, Ming-te 林明德, ed. *Wan-Ch'ing hsiao-shuo yen-chiu* 晚清小説研究. Taipei: Lien-ching, 1988.

Lu, Hsün. *A Brief History of Chinese Fiction.* Trans. Yang Hsien-yi and Gladys Yang. Rpt. Peking: Foreign Language Press, 1976.

Semanov, V. I. *Lu Xun and His Predecessors.* Trans. Charles Alber. Armonk: M.E. Sharpe, 1980.

Wang, Chün-nien 王俊年 [Wang Junnian]. *Chung-kuo chin-tai wen-hsüeh lun-wen chi: 1919–1949, Hsiao-shuo chüan* 中國近代文學論文集，1919–1949 小説卷. Peking: Chung-kuo She-hui K'o-hsüeh, 1988.

Wang, David Der-wei. *Fin-de-siècle Splendor: Repressed Modernities of Late Qing Fiction, 1849–1911.* Stanford: Stanford University Press, 1997.

Wei, Shao-ch'ang 魏紹昌 [Wei Shaochang], ed. *Li Po-yüan yen-chiu tzu-liao* 李伯元研究資料. Shanghai: Jen-min Wen-hsüeh, 1962.

___. *Wu Chien-jen yen-chiu tzu-liao* 吳趼人研

究資料. Shanghai: Ku-chi, 1981.

___. *Nieh-hai hua tzu-liao* 孽海花資料. Shanghai: Ku-chi, 1982.

Yeh, Catherine V. "Zeng P'u's *Nie-hai hua* as a Political Novella: A World Genre in a Chinese Form." Unpublished Ph. D. dissertation, Harvard University, 1990.

Yeh, Chia-ying 葉嘉瑩. *Wang Kuo-wei chi ch'i wen-hsüeh p'i-p'ing* 王國維及其文學批評. Taipei: Yüan-liu, 1983.

Yüan, Chin 袁進. *Chung-kuo hsiao-shuo te chin-tai pien-ko* 中國小說的近代變革. Peking: Chung-kuo She-hui K'o-hsüeh, 1992.

David D. W. Wang
Columbia University

Li E 厲鶚 (*tzu,* T'ai-hung 太鴻, *hao,* Fan-hsieh 樊榭, 1692–1752), a native of Ch'ien-t'ang 錢塘 (modern Hangchow), rose from poverty to become a widely-respected man of letters. In the *Ssu-k'u ch'üan-shu tsung-mu* 四庫全書總目 (see Chi Yün*) Li E's name was listed as historian, local gazetteer, essayist, poet (of *shih,** *tz'u** and *ch'ü**), scholar, and compiler.

Born into a poor family and orphaned early, for many years Li E made his living as a tutor before he passed the *chü-jen* 舉人 examination in 1720. Unfortunately, however, owing either to personal temperament or circumstances not of his making, he could proceed no further in seeking official advancement through examinations for which he had been recommended.

Li E placed a greater value on his antiquarian instincts and scholarship than on worldly success. One year when he was passing through Tientsin on his way to the capital to wait for an appointment, he became the house-guest of the bibliophile-scholar Cha Wei-jen 查為仁 (1694–1749), son of the wealthy salt-merchant Cha Li 查禮 (1715–1783), at the Chas' famous library-villa, Shui-hsi Chuang 水西莊. There he discovered that Cha Wei-jen was working on annotated edition of Chou Mi's 周密 (1232–1299 or 1308)* lyrics, *Chüeh-miao hao-tz'u* 絕妙好詞 (Best of the Best Lyrics; *ca.* 1290). This slim volume contains Chou Mi's own selection of works by 132 lyricists from Chang Hsiao-hsiang 張孝祥 (1129–1166) to Ch'iu Yüan 仇遠 (b. 1247), an anthology having historical interest perhaps second only to Tseng Tsao's 曾慥 (*fl.* 1147) *Yüeh-fu ya-tz'u* 樂府雅詞 (Elegant Songs from the Music Bureau). Li E immediately joined forces with Cha and together they completed, in 1749, an annotated edition of this compilation, known as the *Chüeh-miao hao-tz'u chien* 絕妙好詞箋 (An Annotated Best of the Best Lyrics) which was printed in 1750.

Though Li E often proved himself to be a discerning critic when it came to specific words or lines, even the Ssu-k'u editors found him to be over-indulgent, and sometimes irrelevant, in citing anecdote after anecdote having nothing to do with a poem. For example, in the case of a famous lyric by Hsin Ch'i-chi 辛棄疾 (1140–1207)* written to the tune "Chu Ying-t'ai chin" 祝英臺近 and beginning "Halving the precious hairpin,/At Peach-leaf Ferry" 寶釵分／桃葉渡, Li E cited the anecdote found in Chang Tuan-i's 張端義 (*fl.* 1235) *Kuei-erh chi* 貴耳集 to the effect that Hsin wrote this lyric to express his displeasure at a woman in his service, née Lü, the daughter of a prominent official. According to Teng Kuang-ming 鄧廣銘 and other modern scholars, this story is entirely without foundation (see p. 85 in Teng's *Chia-hsüan tz'u pien-nien chien-chu* 稼軒詞編年箋注).

Nevertheless, Li E was widely recognized as the most erudite person of his day with respect to *shih** and *tz'u** poetry of the Sung dynasty. Another major opus of his is the *Sung-shih chi-shih* 宋詩紀事 (Recorded Occasions in Sung Poetry), with a preface dated 1746. This monumental work was modeled after Chi Yu-kung's 計有功 (*fl.* 1126) *T'ang-shih chi-shih* 唐詩紀事 (Recorded

Occasions in T'ang Poetry),* a valuable source for the study of T'ang poets and poems. And like his other annotated *tz'u* anthology, this, too, was completed by Li with the aid of another vast personal library named the *Ts'ung-shu Lou* 叢書樓 (The Loft of Collectanea), which was the collection of Ma Yüeh-kuan 馬曰琯 (1688–1766) and Ma Yüeh-lu 馬曰璐 (1697–1766), two bibliophiles from Yangchow. For the compilation of this work, Li E claimed in the preface to having consulted works by 3,812 authors. The final result, however, was far from perfect. According to the notice in the *Ssu-k'u ch'üan-shu tsung-mu,* there are numerous repetitions and factual errors as well as poems cited without anecdotes and anecdotes told without poems. The work, thought, was still applauded for the compiler's "extreme diligence" (*yung-li ch'in i* 用力勤矣).

Li E's antiquarian interests embraced several diverse fields, including geography, history and art. Because Hangchow, his native place, had been the capital of the Southern Sung, he was especially keen in preserving historical anecdotes about various famous sites in the city which had not been recorded in earlier gazetteers. Besides the *Tung-ch'eng tsa-chi* 東城雜記 (Miscellanies of the Eastern City), in 1744 he emended an account of the famous Buddhist temple, Yün-lin Ssu 雲林寺, under the title *Tseng-hsiu Yün-lin ssu-chih* 增修雲林寺志. A more ambitious work is his *Liao-shih shih-i* 遼史拾遺 (Supplements to the History of the Liao), for which he had consulted over three-hundred titles. He viewed his labor of love as an equal to P'ei Sung-chih's 裴松之 (372–451) annotations to Ch'en Shou's 陳壽 (233–297) *San-kuo chih* 三國志 (A History of the Three Kingdoms). In addition, Li E was also the author of the *Nan-Sung hua-yüan lu* 南宋畫院錄 (A History of the [Imperial] Painting Academy of the Southern Sung), which contained biographical accounts of ninety-six

artists of the Southern Sung, including all the famous painters of the time, such as Li T'ang 李唐 (*ca.* 1050–after 1130), Ma Yüan 馬遠 (*fl.* 1180–1230), Liu Sung-nien 劉松年 (late 12th century), and Hsia Kuei 夏圭 (*fl.* 1190–1230).

Li E's own belletristic writings consist of two *chüan* of dramatic verse (*ch'ü*ʔ), nine *chüan* of prose, nine *chüan* of lyrics (*tz'u*), and twenty *chüan* of *shih*–all contained in his *Fan-hsieh Shan-fang chi* 樊謝山房集 (The Collection of Fan-hsieh Mountain Studio), its continuation (*Hsü-chi* 續集), and supplemental series (*Chi-wai chi* 集外集). As a poet, Li E lived up to his name as a leader of the Chekiang School, or more precisely the *Che-hsi tz'u-p'ai* 浙西詞派 (Western Chekiang School of Lyrics),* continuing the work started by Cha Shen-hsing 查慎行 (1650–1727)* in *shih*-poetry and by Chu I-tsun 朱彝尊 (1629–1709)* in the lyric.

Li E's *shih*-poetry contains a good deal of landscape poetry, and it has been remarked that there is not a single famous scenic spot in his beloved city of Hangchow for which he did not write a poem. In the best of his verse, there is often an ethereal quality which may have stemmed from his successful juxtaposition of the abstract and the concrete. For example, in "A Moonlit Night at Ling-yin Temple" 靈隱寺月夜 we read:

Atop crowded peaks the moon
  shines;
Amid jumbled leaves a stream flows.
One lamp sets all motion to rest.
The lone sound of a chime empties
  the Four Skies.

月在眾峰頂;/泉流亂葉中。
一燈群動息;/孤磬四天空。

(The last phrase probably refers to the Four Heavens of the deva kings or it could simply mean "the sky in all four directions.") Lines like these imbue his poetry with an air of quiet beauty. Frequently, though, betraying his

85

penchant for scholarship, Li E would deliberately introduce into his lines some obscure words or allusions. Chu Tse-chieh 朱則杰, the author of a recent history of Ch'ing poetry (*Ching shih shih* 清詩史 [Nanking: Chiang-su Ku-chi, 1992]) claims Li's poetry intentionally blends erudition and etherealness (p. 234).

Certainly it was Li E's immense knowledge that led him to join with six fellow natives of Hangchow—Shen Chia-ch'e 沈嘉轍, Wu Cho 吳焯, Ch'en Chih-kuang 陳芝光, Fu Tseng 符曾, Chao Yü 趙昱, and Chao Hsin 趙信—to undertake the creation of a new anthology. Each of the seven authors was to write a hundred poems on lost anecdotes they had collected about Hangchow, and then to provide a note at the end of each poem as elucidation. This collection of seven-hundred poems was published under the title of *Nan-Sung tsa-shih shih* 南宋雜事詩 (Poems on Miscellaneous Events of the Southern Sung Dynasty). Such a work, according to the *Ssu-k'u ch'üan-shu tsung-mu* 四庫全書總目 (see Chi Yün*) editors, is valuable only as a source book for anecdotes, not as a work of poetic merit. Li E clearly enjoyed playing his game both ways: he unearthed old myths and legends as a means to elucidate ancient poetry and also wrote new poems which incorporated (and thereby preserved) similar stories from the past.

Li E followed Chu I-tsun 朱彝尊 (1629–1709)* in his admiration for Chang Yen 張炎 (1248–*ca.* 1320)** and Chiang K'uei 姜夔 (*ca.* 1155–1221) and for their *ch'ing-k'ung* 清空 (pure and spare) style, a style meant to create the impression of delicacy and etherealness in a poem. As Chang Yen and Chiang K'uei attempted to reverse the trend toward direct boastful expressions admired so much in the works of Su Shih 蘇軾 (1037–1101)* and Hsin Ch'i-chi, so Chu I-tsun had attempted to counter the influence of Ch'en Wei-sung's 陳維崧 (1626–1682)* heroic verse. Another example of this style can be seen in a famous line of his, which reads: 雨洗秋濃人淡–literally: "rain/wash/autumn/lush/people/pale" (from his "Written Following Rain at the Lake after the Fifteenth of the Seventh Month" 七月既望湖上雨後作). Following the reading of the word *jen* 人 as the persona of the poem, which could be rendered as either "she" or "I," Shirleen S. Wong has translated this line as "Autumn ablaze with colors after rain, but paler she looks" (*Waiting for the Unicorn,* p. 175). One could also take *ch'iu* 秋 (autumn) as the object of the verb *hsi* 洗 (to wash away); similarly, *jen* 人 could also be the object of the same verb. The contrast between *nung* 濃 (fullness, lush) and *tan* 淡 (insipid, flavorless, faded, light-colored) heightens the mood of dejection. Therefore, another translation might read: "Rain has drenched autumn's lush colors as well as a paler me." Here it is the rain which drained the color of the persona's cheeks as it did the colors of autumn, thereby leaving her but a shadow of her former self. In this way, Li E enlivened this Che-hsi tradition with lyrics he believed adhered to the standards of Chang Yen and Chiang K'uei and also assured his own place in the literary tradition.

Editions and References
Li E. *Fan-hsieh Shan-fang chi* 樊榭山房集. 10 *chüan. Hsü-chi* 續集, 10 *chüan. Wen-chi* 文集, 8 *chüan. Chi-wai shih* 集外詩, 8 *chüan.* Miscellaneous, 1 *chüan. SPTK.*

Translations
Waiting for the Unicorn, pp. 172-7.

Studies
Chang, Wei-p'ing 張維屏. *Kuo-ch'ao shih-jen cheng-lüeh ch'u-pien* 國朝詩人徵略初編. *Chüan* 22. In *Ch'ing-tai chuan-chi ts'ung-k'an* 清代傳記叢刊. V. 21, pp. 733-40.
Chu, Tse-chieh 朱則杰. *Ch'ing shih shih* 清詩史. Nanking: Chiang-su Ku-chi, 1992, pp. 231-6.

ECCP, pp. 454-5.

Ho, Kuang-chung 賀光中. *Lun Ch'ing tz'u* 論清詞. Singapore: Tung-fang Hsüeh-hui, 1958, pp. 69-81.

Wang, Chung 汪中. *Ch'ing-tz'u chin-ch'üan* 清詞金荃. Taipei: Hsüeh-sheng, 1965, pp. 64-70.

Yen, Ti-ch'ang 嚴迪昌. *Ch'ing tz'u shih* 清詞史. Nanking: Chiang-su Ku-chi, 1990, pp. 312-23.

Irving Yucheng Lo

Li Kuan 李觀 (*tzu,* Yüan-pin 元賓, 766–794) is best known as a prose writer whose life and ideals paralleled those of Li Ho 李賀 (791–817)* and for his friendship with Han Yü 韓愈 (768–824).* Li was born in Soochow to a family originally from Lung-hsi 隴西 (modern Kansu). It has been argued that he was a nephew of the essayist Li Hua 李華 (*ca.* 715–*ca.* 774),* but this seems to have been an incorrect attribution. In 782 at 18 *sui* he was recommended as a provincial candidate for the national examinations, but stayed in Soochow, presumably for further study. Several of his works mention his devotion to books and wide reading. It was perhaps for this reason that he claimed not to have made any close friends until he went to the capital.

Arriving in Ch'ang-an in 790–seven years after he had first been made a provincial candidate–he described his wonderment with the city: "In the days of the first month, I set myself up with the landlord of an inn, saw the imperial palace with its twin gatetowers stretching to the sky, craning my neck as I went back and forth, as if I had trod through the dust to stop at the heights of the Five Sacred Mountains" (*Ch'üan T'ang wen,* 533:6859). Shortly thereafter he began to prepare for the examinations by attempting to find a patron: "In the days of the second month, I took my incomparable writings to several well known gentlemen, hoping they would carefully read them and perceive their truth .... But when I went to see them, their gates were shut" (*Ibid.*). Although he was unsuccessful in the examinations of 790, he continued to seek influential friends (about a fourth of his prose pieces are letters appealing to potential sponsors).

Perhaps through these appeals Li Kuan was able to enter the State University (Kuo-tzu chien 國子監) and study there for a time. The *T'ang chih yen* 唐摭言 claims he was at the Kuang-wen Tien 廣文殿 (Hall of Broad Writings). After his failure in 790, Li was encouraged by the selection of Tu Huang-shang 杜黃裳 (*ca.* 738–808) as examiner the following year. Tu had a reputation for honesty and Li Kuan was brimming with confidence, as can be seen in his "Yeh Fu-tzu Miao wen" 謁夫子廟文 (On Visiting the Confucian Temple), probably written about this time:

> Among those who have carried down the Confucian teachings through the ages, I, this clan-descendant of the Lung-hsi Lis, have rectified my phrases as a means of purification and, holding up this purified object in offering, reverently present it to you.

The "purified object" was of course Li Kuan's essay.

After failing the examination in 790, as did fellow students Liu Tsung-yüan 柳宗元 (773–819)* and Liu Yü-hsi 劉禹錫 (772–842),* he seems to have lived on in what he described as impoverished circumstances, failing again in 791, but continuing to study, write and seek a patron. Li shows in numerous letters that he was clearly under the influence of the *fu-ku* 復古 "returning to antiquity" school of writers, the most famous of whom was Han Yü. In 792, therefore, those talented young writers in this group must have been buoyed by the news that Lu Chih 陸贄 (754–805)* would examine them, assisted by Liang Su 梁蕭 (753–793)* and Ts'ui Yüan-han 崔元翰 (*ca.* 725–795), both *fu-ku* advocates. In the spring of that year, apparently still with no patron, Li Kuan attained the fifth rank on the list of successful *chin-shih* graduates, above Han Yü and several other notable T'ang figures who passed that year. Because of the subsequent fame of the 792 graduates in literature and politics (five became chief ministers), and in part because of the reputations of the examiners themselves, this group soon became collectively known as the Lung-hu Pang 龍虎榜 (Dragons and Tigers List).

Shortly after passing the examinations, Han Yü and Li Kuan exchanged poems. In Han's verse he compares himself to the gigantic mythical fish *k'un* 鯤 and Li Kuan to the *p'eng* 鵬 (roc) bird which measures over a thousand miles across its back. Li Kuan was also close to another fellow-graduate, Feng Su 馮宿 (767-836). Li and Feng shared geographical backgrounds, too—Feng was also a Southerner (from Wu-chou 婺州, modern Chekiang). In a poem Li wrote for Feng, probably in the winter before their success, he reveals his state of mind (*Ch'üan T'ang shih*, 319:3596):

> Presented to Feng Su
> From the cold city-wall I ascend to the
>   plains of Ch'in,
> A wanderer with thoughts flying in the
>   wind.
> Black clouds cut off the view of a
>   myriad miles,
> Hunting fires burn from their midst.
> Into the dark void steams a long trail of
>   smoke,
> Only the killing air will not disperse.
> Pieces of ice interlock—stones about to
>   split;
> The winds crazed—mountains seem to
>   sway.
> These days no hearts steadfast as the
>   green pines,
> But I alone will not wither and fade.

寒城上秦原，游子意飄飄。
黑雲截萬里，獵火從中燒。
陰空烝長煙，殺氣獨不銷。
冰交十可裂，風疾山如搖。
時無青松心，顧我獨不凋。

Aside from avowing his loyalty to Feng Su, the poem discloses Li Kuan's pessimism about contemporary society and politics. It also exhibits the "harsh diction" (*se* 澀) reminiscent of the poetic style usually associated with Han Yü and Meng Chiao 孟郊 (751–814).*

Li Kuan's prose prior to 792 embodies the contradiction of employing a haughty, intransigent style to express his requests for assistance in his career—this interspersed with references to his own moral superiority. Despite passing the more advanced examination of *Po-hsüeh Hung-tz'u* 博學宏辭 (Vast Erudition and Grand Exposition, designed to assist in the placement of recent *chih-shih* graduates) later that spring, ranking second of four candidates, Li Kuan seems to have won few friends in the government. Meng Chiao's "Tseng Li Kuan" 贈李觀 (Presented to Li Kuan) suggests on the contrary that his success in the examinations aroused jealousy. Nevertheless, he was offered the post of *T'ai-tzu chiao-shu-lang* 太子校書郎 (Gentleman in Charge of Collating Books for the Heir Apparent), a sinecure often given to recent graduates who displayed literary talent. Li Kuan seems to have been disappointed with this appointment and went home to Soochow during the summer of 792. On his return to Ch'ang-an later that year he suggests (in works such as "Shang Chia P'u-yeh shu" 上賈僕射書 [Letter to Vice Director (of the Department of State) Chia]; *Ch'üan T'ang wen*, 534:6874) that he was still not employed. Often ill during his years in the capital, his health deteriorated in 793 and he died the following year. Han Yü wrote an epitaph which praised Li Kuan's literary talents and his moral behavior.

Li's literary reputation today is based on four poems (of an original thirty) and about fifty works of prose. This may seem an insignificant corpus, but it is a larger number of works than either Han Yü or Liu Tsung-yüan had written by their late twenties and presents a broad spectrum of genres and subjects. Moreover, although clearly infused with the Confucian spirit of *fu-ku,* works like Li Kuan's "T'ung Ju Tao shuo" 通儒道説 (Discourse on the Compatibility of Confucianism and Taoism; *Ch'üan T'ang wen,* 535:6885) reveal an eclectic mind which might have added another dimension to mid-T'ang thought, had Li lived longer.

Despite admiration from peers and success in the examinations, Li Kuan seems never to have found contentment. His "Chiao nan shuo" 交難説 (Discourse on the Difficulty of Making Friends; *Ch'üan T'ang wen,* 535:6885) reveals the paradoxical approach he took to life, and the mood in which he undoubtedly faced his too-early death:

> In ancient times men regarded it unsound not to have friends. Thus friends are something you must have... . . Making friends is difficult. A casual union based on profit leads to indignation and loud cursing. I often admonish myself not to recklessly speak of making friends. How much more does this apply to the men of today, who truly suffer from the poison of snakes and lizards. For this reason, I keep to myself, and grieve for the lonely spider [in his web].

Editions and References
Ch'üan T'ang shih, 319:3596-3597.
Ch'üan T'ang wen, 532-535:6845-6893.
Li Yüan-pin wen-chi wen-pien 李元賓文集文編. 3 *chüan. Wai-pien* 外編 . 2 *chüan. Hsü-pien* 續編 . 1 *chüan.* In *T'ang-jen san-chia chi* 唐人三家集. Ch'in Yin-fu 秦因復 (1760-1843), ed. 1818.
Li Yüan-pin wen-pien 李元賓文編. 3 *chüan. Wai-pien.* 2 *chüan. Ssu-k'u.*

Translations
Nienhauser, William H., Jr. "Among Dragons and Tigers: Li Guan (766-794) and His Role in the Late 8th Century Literary Scene," *Proceedings of the 2nd International Sinological Conference, Sect. on Lit..* Taipei: Academia Sinica, 1988, 1:243-87.

Studies
Lo, Lien-t'ien 羅聯添. *Han Yü yen-chiu* 韓愈研究. Taipei: Hsüeh-sheng, 1977, pp. 138-40.
Nienhauser, "Among Dragons and Tigers" (see *Translations* above).

William H. Nienhauser, Jr.
University of Wisconsin, Madison

Lien-chu 連珠 (literally, "strung pearls") is a highly embellished genre, characterized by ornate language, rich allusions, balanced analogies, and parallelism, that often deals with political persuasion. Structurally, the basic *lien-chu* consists of an octet, a set of eight lines in four couplets. One *lien-chu* title could contain from one to fifty octets. Usually each octet begins with the same stock expression, *ch'en-wen* 臣聞 ("Your subject has heard" or "I have heard"). It is a kind of anaphora, a rhetorical device that repeats the same word or phrase in order to display a sense of emphasis. The fourth and eighth lines rhyme.

The *lien-chu* were first composed during the Eastern Han dynasty. It underwent a series of transformations and finally became standardized in the Chin dynasty. Lu Chi's 陸機 (261–303)* fifty "Yen lien-chu" 演連珠 (Strung Pearls Expanded) is considered the most standard form of this genre. The thirteenth piece reads (modified from Jenny Tu-li Teng's translation—see "Studies"):

> Your subject has heard that:
> When the keen eye (of heaven—the sun) overlooks the clouds,
> It cannot penetrate and shine through.
> When the bright uncut jade is covered with dirt,
> It cannot shed its rays.
> This is why
> The enlightened and sagacious ruler
> Has the burden of being blocked from the truth;

The talented and outstanding
officials
Often embrace the sorrow of
missing the proper time.

臣聞
    利眼臨雲，不能垂照；
    朗璞蒙垢，不能吐輝。
是以
    明哲之君，時有蔽壅之累。
    俊乂之臣，屢抱後時之悲。

The concise and aphoristic language of the style is clear: the four- and six-syllable parallel lines, and the analogies derived from natural phenomena. Its reasoning is similar to the syllogism. It begins with the primary premise based on a natural event (the sun obscured by clouds), moves to the minor premise of human causality (jade is traditionally used to describe a person's virtue), and concludes with the political consequence necessarily resulting from the two premises. Thematically, it is typical of the *lien-chu* to offer political advice from the point of view of a subject. Lu Chi's example here is typical.

However, as the form of the genre underwent changes through different dynasties, so did its theme and content. The stock phrase "Your subject has heard" was changed to "I have heard" (*kai wen* 蓋聞), which designates a general voice. In the Six Dynasties, some writers expanded on its conventional theme of political persuasion to express their own personal feelings. For example, Yü Hsin's 庾信 (513–581)* "Ni lien-chu" 擬連珠 (Imitating the "Strung Pearls") expresses his lament over the total destruction of the Liang dynasty, while Hsiao Kang 蕭綱 (503–551) composed "Pei-yu lien-chu" 被幽連珠 ("Strung Pearls" while Imprisoned) to convey his mournful thoughts, while he was incarcerated by Hou Ching 侯景 (503–552). Liu Ch'ien 劉潛 (484–550) wrote two "Yen-t'i lien-chu" 艷體連珠 ("Strung Pearls" in Amorous Style) in which he speaks through the persona of a palace

lady. This poem shows the interaction of the *lien-chu* and palace-style poetry (see *Kung-t'i shih* 宮體詩*). Nevertheless, these works all sustain the basic structure of the standard *lien-chu*. In the Ming and Ch'ing, the *lien-chu* gradually became irregular in style. Liu Chi's 劉基 (1311–1375)* works contain two-, three-, four-, and six-syllable lines. The great Ch'ing parallel-prose master, Hung Liang-chi 洪亮吉 (1746–1809),* employs the genre to present his views on literature. Throughout the history of Chinese literature, the development and expansion of the *lien-chu,* both in its form and subject matter, continued. More-over, in many genres of the Six Dynasties standard *lien-chu* lines are found, such as in *fu* 賦 (rhapsody),* *yüeh-fu** poetry, inscriptions, eulogies, memorials, commands, and edicts. For example, Lu Chi in his "Hao-shih fu" 豪士賦 (Rhapsody on the Valiant Prince) employed pure *lien-chu* lines. This indicates that the *lien-chu* crossed its generic boundaries to influence other genres; *lien-chu* could therefore refer both to works of an independent genre as well as to a style adopted by authors of other literary forms.

The strict parallelism of the *lien-chu* also contributed to the formation of the *p'ien-t'i wen* 駢體文 (parallel prose).* In the Han dynasty, none of the *fu* were written according to the strict prosody of parallel prose. The earliest genuine parallel prose is Pan Ku's 班固 (32–92)* *lien-chu* in which every sentence is structured on parallelism. This sort of rigid prosody became a stylistic convention of *lien-chu* first, subsequently influencing the development of mature parallel prose.

The most controversial issue regarding the *lien-chu* is its origin. The majority of the Six Dynasties critics agree that it originated with Yang Hsiung 揚雄 (53 B.C.–A.D. 18),* since he wrote the earliest piece bearing the title *lien-chu*. Both Shen Yüeh 沈約 (441–513)* and Liu Hsieh 劉勰 (*ca.* 465–522)* champion this view. The second view, based on Fu Hsüan's 傅玄 (217–278)* preface to his own pieces, points out that the genre flourished during Emperor Chang's 章 reign (r. 76–88). The third opinion, represented by Yang Shen 楊慎 (1488–1559)* and based on a passage from the *Pei-shih* 北史 (27:978), claims that *lien-chu* originated from the *Han-fei-tzu* 韓非子. Yang's claim involves equating the *lien-chu* mentioned in the *Pei-shih* with the passages in the "Ch'u shui" 儲説 (Collected Persuasions) in the *Han-fei-tzu*. The fourth view comes from Sun Te-ch'ien 孫德謙 (1869–1935) who believes that the *Teng-hsi-tzu* 鄧析子, which is closely related to legalist tradition and deals with the techniques of ruling, should be the origin of the *lien-chu*. But the *Teng-hsi-tzu,* characterized by effective argument and eloquence, has been shown to be a forgery which is not a pre-Ch'in work. The fifth proposal, upheld by the modern scholar, Yamada Katumi 山田勝美, connects the origin of *lien-chu* to the *Yen-t'ieh lun* 鹽鐵論 (Discourses on Salt and Iron) by Huan K'uan 桓寬 (*fl.* 73 B.C.).

The problem of origin will never be completely solved. It is undeniable that Yang Hsiung was the first writer who employed *lien-chu* as a title for a literary piece, though its style may not totally conform to that of later *lien-chu* pieces. At the same time, we find that many passages from the pre-Ch'in masters, such as *Tso-chuan* 左傳,* *Kuo-yü* 國語,* *Chan-kuo-ts'e* 戰國策,* *Lao-tzu* 老子, *Mo-tzu* 墨子, etc., resemble the *lien-chu* in their style and argument. However, none of them possesses the conventions and form of the *lien-chu*. A genre forms slowly and often originates from more than one source. The rhetorical techniques and the pattern of arguments of all the pre-Ch'in rhetorical literature should be recognized as precedents of the *lien-chu*. Yang Hsiung wrote one of the earliest *lien-chu,* but it could not be considered a typical piece (in the sense that Lu Chi's

were). During Emperor Chang's reign writers like Pan Ku, Chia K'uei 賈逵 (30–101), and Fu I 傅毅 (?–89) began to compose *lien-chu* pieces at the command of the Emperor and the basis for the genre was laid.

The second critical issue concerning the *lien-chu* is its relationship with *fu,* with which it shares some features. First, they both contain an oratory framework, though in *fu* two characters are usually present while in *lien-chu* there are only monologues. Second, both deal with political advice and aim to persuade the ruler. In his *Wen-hsin tiao-lung* 文心雕龍,* Liu Hsieh never argues that *lien-chu* is a sub-genre of the *fu,* but he places it together with the *ch'i* 七 (sevens)** and *tui-wen* 對問 (responses to questions), both of which were derived from the *fu,* in the chapter of "Tsa-wen" 雜文 (Miscellaneous Writings). Third, most *lien-chu* authors such as Yang Hsiung and Pan Ku were also *fu* writers. However, differences separate the two genres: the language of the *lien-chu* is extremely epigrammatic and regulated, that of the *fu* not as consistently so. *Fu* appear more diffusive and irregular: the number of characters in each line could vary from three to nine while the standard *lien-chu* consist of four- and six-syllable lines. Whereas those who composed *fu* often try to hide their intention behind ornate language and only reveal it indirectly at the end of their works, *lien-chu* writers were straightforward and explicit in presenting their political advice. Thus although it is unlikely that *lien-chu* developed directly from the *fu,* both genres must have been strongly influenced by the same corpus of rhetorical literature in the pre-Ch'in period.

Studies

Liao, Wei-ch'ing 廖蔚卿. "Lun Lien-chu t'i ti hsing ch'eng" 論連珠體的形成, *Yu-shih hsüeh-chih* 15.2 (1978): 15-59.

—. "Lun Han-Wei Liu-ch'ao lien-chu t'i ti i-shu chi ch'i ying-hsiang" 論漢魏六朝連珠體的藝術及其影響. In *T'ai Ching-nung*

Hsien-sheng Pa-shih shou-ch'ing lun-wen chi 臺靜農先生八十壽慶論文集. Taipei: Lien-ching, 1981, pp. 443-90.

Shen, Hai-yen 沈海燕. "Lien-chu t'i shih-lun" 連珠體試論, *Wen-hsüeh i-ch'an* 4 (1985): 31-41.

Teng, Jenny Tu-li. "The Genre of *Lien-chu.*" Unpublished Ph. D. dissertation, University of Washington, 1985.

Yokoyama, Hiroshi 橫山宏. "Riku Yu *renju shokô*" 陸瑜連珠小考, *Chûgoku bungaku hô* 22 (1968): 1-27.

___, ed. "Rekidai *renju shû*, Part I" 歷代連珠集, *Tenri Daigaku gakuhô* 85 (1973): 33-64.

___. "Rekidai *renju shû*, Part II," *Joshidai bungaku* 27 (1976): 51-55.

___. "Rekidai *renju shû*, Part III," *Joshidai bungaku* 28 (1977): 39-51.

Jui-lung Su
The National University of Singapore

Literary Chinese is the usual English name for the language in which the majority of traditional Chinese literature is written. The corresponding Chinese terms–*ku-tai Han-yü* 古代漢語 or "ancient Chinese" in the Peoples Republic of China and *wen-yen* 文言 or "patterned/elegant language," an older expression still used on Taiwan–both in their own way emphasize the distinction between literary Chinese and the modern vernacular: literary Chinese is essentially pre-modern written Chinese. The often stated parallel between the relationship of Latin to the modern Romance vernaculars and the relationship of literary Chinese to modern Chinese is valid in some respects. There is, however, an important difference. Although there was always a mutual, flexible relationship between literary Chinese and the historical Chinese vernaculars, literary Chinese did not evolve from and was never based upon a popular vernacular, such as was Latin during the Roman Empire.

There is no agreed upon periodization for the literary Chinese language. Some terms in current use are "pre-classical" to describe the language before Confucius (551–479 B.C.) and "classical" to describe the important formative period between Confucius and the Ch'in unification in 221 B.C. "Early Middle Chinese" and "Late Middle Chinese" refer to the language about 600 and 800 A.D. respectively, although these distinctions are based largely on phonological rather than morphological changes.

The earliest surviving form of Chinese, the Shang oracle bones from about 1,300 B.C., already employs a technical language whose character and function is essentially hieratic and political. In short, although we know virtually nothing about spoken Shang speech, it seems clear that the written language of the oracle bones already represents a highly stylized and specialized subset of general language use. This earliest written language derives its special character not only from its ritual context but also because it was the exclusive domain of a hereditary class of bureaucratic technicians charged with divination and record keeping. The bronze inscriptions of the Western Chou period, as well as the earliest portions of the *Classic of Changes* (*I-ching*), the *Classic of Documents* (*Shu-ching*), and the *Classic of Poetry* (*Shih-ching*)–the foundational texts of the Chinese cultural tradition–continue this specialized, hieratic language use. This situation did not change until Confucius, who was born into this hereditary group of language custodians, expanded the content and style of written language. Despite three thousand years of change and shifting usage, literary Chinese retained its original character as a refined, technical language whose mastery and use marked its writers as a cultural and political class distinct from speakers of the vernaculars.

There are two major reasons for the

dominance and persistence of literary Chinese over this long period of time: first, the character of the Chinese written graph, and second, the close relationship between the literary language and the structure of political power in China. As is well-known, Chinese graphs, although they represent the sounds of spoken words—and probably always did—have no inherently fixed pronunciation other than by recognized convention. The graphs do not record, as alphabetic writing systems do, the phonology of a specific moment in the history of the spoken language. The same graph can be read and "pronounced" with equal validity in any number of Chinese vernaculars at any moment in historical time, or in Japanese, Korean, or Vietnamese. An important consequence of this feature is that, although the grammar of older texts may become increasingly arcane, their pronunciations were periodically updated and so never became phonologically archaic as Chaucer has now become for speakers of English. Modern Chinese readers of T'ang poetry, for example, read the grammar and vocabulary of the original texts but pronounce the graphs in modern readings that would be incomprehensible to the original audience. This unique, "update" feature of Chinese graphs enabled the creation and persistence of a literary and cultural canon whose remarkable longevity provided the lexical and grammatical standards for literary Chinese.

Second, to the extent that successive governments in China supported the core of this traditional canon, they also supported literary Chinese. Beginning in the seventh century A.D., state-sponsored civil-service examinations increasingly regulated access to the highest government positions. These examinations established a cultural and literary curriculum whose criteria served to standardize many aspects of the written language. On the phonological level, the pronunciation of the capital became the "official" pronunciation of the graphs for examination purposes, and this pronunciation formed the basis for a bureaucratic koine—the *kuan-hua* 官話 or "Mandarin" of later times—that served as a vehicle for spoken communication between officials who often spoke mutually unintelligible vernaculars. Although there has been much scholarship on the effect of examination culture on poetry and belles-lettres, most rank and file officials put greater value on the ability to compose an array of bureaucratic prose documents in an elegant and correct style. There is thus a close and natural connection between literary and "documentary" Chinese, and many of the traditional Chinese prose genres exhibit a distinctive tension between the bureaucratic need to conform to mandated standards and the artistic need for greater self-expression in personal communications. Finally, the examination system meant that matters of vocabulary and style were closely regulated political issues. Submission of an examination response written in a politically unapproved style was a sure guarantee of failure and could even be interpreted as a sign of political dissent.

By far the greatest influence of the examinations on the literary language, however, was the creation of a homogenous educational base for the cultural elite. The curriculum required that students memorize large sections of the traditional canon and their commentaries, usually before the student could properly comprehend the texts. Later, as the teacher explained the memorized texts and as words and phrases gradually acquired significance, the student began his own first efforts at composition by imitating the vocabulary and syntax of this memorized corpus rather than drawing upon the reservoir of his own spoken speech. It is in this sense that the written language of China is quintessentially "literary" and relates to but does not derive from the vernacular. Prescriptive grammars and dictionaries were unnecessary, since all the student needed to know in the way of grammatical patterns and definitions was, theoretically, already in his head. Necessary study guides were rather rhyme-books, which listed the current, "official" pronunciation of the graphs, and phrase books that reorganized the memorization corpus into searchable two-graph phrases and provided not definitions, but citations to the original sources for examples of usage. Such books could be used both as pedagogical short-cuts and as aids for weaker memories. The greatest of these, the *Rhymed Repository of Girded Literature* (*P'ei-wen yün-fu* 佩文韻府) completed by government order in 1711, remains the single most useful traditional reference work for the study of works written in literary Chinese.

Although the particular literary corpus for memorization varied over time, its essential core remained steady enough to ensure that all students acquired a basic vocabulary and collection of grammatical precedents for syntax. These shared basics enabled writers to compose with a fair knowledge of the literary and educational background of their readers. This knowledge in turn accounts for the intimate, "in-group" atmosphere of traditional Chinese literature (especially before the development of printing in the Sung) where most compositions were addressed to known and often named readers. On the other hand, at the highest levels of attainment, the literary process was cumulative and conservative. Subsequent to language standardization under the Ch'in (221–206 B.C.), the unchanging written form of the Chinese graphs insured that nothing was ever irretrievably lost from the tradition. The daring or playful or subversive writer could always tap an obscure corner of the canon for an unusual graph or allusion to challenge and test his reader. One might argue that those who wrote with Chinese graphs were able to place greater, legitimate challenges before a readership with a decent prospect of meeting those challenges than were writers in alphabetic languages where phonological change constantly truncated the beginning of the canon. This feature, in turn, accounts for the often pedantic and game-like competitiveness of much traditional literature, especially poetry.

In spite of the many static and conservative qualities of literary Chinese, one should by no means ignore the importance of the constant interplay between literary Chinese and the vernaculars. Some modern scholars believe that part of the revolutionary program of Confucius was the incorporation of vernacular elements into the writing system, and these scholars argue that the *Analects* represents the spoken speech of the period. Whatever the case may be, there is no doubt that the incorporation of popular literary forms continually enriched the canon of traditional Chinese literature. In fact, virtually all of the major Chinese poetic genres began as popular verse forms that were gradually adopted and adapted by literati practitioners whose writings in these genres then became part of the canon of literary Chinese expression. Because this canon was continually edited and reworked to value "elegance," signs of the early traces of this process have usually disappeared. Occasionally, however, chance archaeological discoveries yield startling evidence of this process of transition from vernacular to literary status. The recovery early in this century of the medieval cave-library at Tun-huang, for example, has revealed the semi-literary, T'ang "pre-history" of the *tz'u* 詞* or "song-lyric poetry" that subsequently flourished in the Sung dynasty. The same library also revealed the only surviving examples of *pien-wen* 變文 or "transformation texts," a popular narrative genre whose generous examples of T'ang vernacular have since enabled scholars to detect colloquial formulations in the T'ang poetry of the period. Such admissions of the colloquial and their absorption into standard literary usage account partially for progressive changes and evolving styles of literary Chinese usage. The *ku-wen yün-tung* 古文運動* or "ancient literature" movement of the mid-T'ang, for example, promoted a return to the literary style of classical antiquity, but in fact utilized colloquial diction and rhythm to create what was essentially a new style of prose.

In speaking of the "canon" of traditional Chinese literature as a repository for examples of literary Chinese usage, we speak actually of two canons whose interaction and combination defined the essence of what it meant to be educated in traditional Chinese. The so-called "Confucian canon" was codified and provided with commentaries in the Han dynasty (206 B.C.–A. D. 220), and this corpus, despite important changes in focus and commentarial tradition, remained at the center of orthodox Chinese literary education until modern times. But to this core there was often added a more flexible, more contemporary "literary" canon of writings, the acquisition of which was thought to provide a final, aesthetic embellish to the often tedious preparation of the primary canon. For example, during the T'ang dynasty (618–907), the sixth-century *Wen-hsüan* 文選 * constituted the major work in this secondary canon. The *Wen-hsüan* was not a formal part of the examination curriculum, yet its mastery was equally as important to a successful performance as that of the primary Confucian texts. Formal and informal arbiters of Chinese literary taste argued incessantly about the value and composition of this

secondary canon. Such arguments usually concerned the proper relationship between the primary canon and subsequent literary forms whose language was often more vernacular and whose content was often less concerned with Confucian values. The shifting results of this discourse determined what it meant to be educated in literary Chinese at any given moment in Chinese history. But some portion of the central, primary core always remained to provide continuity.

It is probable that the perception of greater interaction between vernacular and literary Chinese during the later imperial period (Yüan through Ch'ing) results simply from the greater amount of surviving literary material from these more recent periods. In virtually all cases, however, the more "vernacularized" writings from these periods, Yüan drama and the various forms of Ming and Ch'ing fiction, are the conscious product of literati effort. Conservative scholars objected to these efforts to add to the traditional canon, not only because of the often popular origins of the subject matter, but also because such additions enlarged and diluted (and in a sense also polluted) the traditional pedagogical memorization corpus, thus decreasing and endangering the cultural cohesiveness of the educational elite. Only with the demise of the examination system in 1905 and the subsequent end of traditional education were these works fully admitted into the canon of traditional Chinese literature. In truth, works such as the great full-length novels of the sixteenth century straddle a linguistic middle-ground. Their authors were literati traditionally trained in literary Chinese who were writing, often anonymously, for similarly trained colleagues; and a solid grounding in literary Chinese is necessary to read these works. At the same time, a desire for innovation and verisimilitude also drove the authors to experiment with

95

using Chinese graphs to record the vernacular, even though a consensus on how to record any true Chinese vernacular did not develop until the twentieth century, when the old *kuan-hua* of the Ch'ing mandarins was adopted to write the vernacular of Peking.

P. Angelo Zottoli's five-volume *Cursus litteraturae sinicae,* a textbook published in the 1870s and 1880s to furnish Jesuit missionaries an introduction to Chinese language and literature, offers an orthodox, pre-modern view of the relationship between this primary and secondary canon. The first volume, subtitled *Lingua familiaris,* introduces Chinese graphs, then proceeds to extracts from Yüan drama, the *Chin-ku ch'i-kuan* 今古奇觀, and the *San-kuo chih yen-i* 三國志演義.* Described as being written in "a common and low style" (*vulgaris aut humilis stylus*), Zottoli presents these works as part of Chinese "vulgar" literature but not part of the educational canon. This begins in volume two, subtitled *Studium classicorum,* with the *San-tzu ching* 三字經, the *Ch'ien-tzu wen* 千字文 (late imperial primers for beginning students—see *Erh-t'ung wen-hsüeh* 兒童文學**), and the complete *Four Books.* Volume three, *Studium canonicorum,* contains the complete *Shih-ching,* * *Shu-ching,* most of the *I-ching,* and extracts from the *Li-chi* and *Ch'un-ch'iu.* Volume four is largely devoted to the *Tso-chuan,* * classical *ku-wen* texts, and a collection of various epistolary models. Volume five explains and rehearses the requirements of *pa-ku-wen* 八股文,* the late imperial examination-essay format, and concludes with samples of *shih* poetry, *fu,* * and *tz'u.* This curriculum in fact replicates the orthodox view of a late Ch'ing literatus on the proper repertory of literary Chinese works: the Confucian canon is the basic foundation for examination preparation and composition, to which medieval poetry and prose were later added as a secondary,

final refinement. And the range of quotations in the *P'ei-wen yün-fu* mirrors this view: coverage of the classics is virtually complete, there is a generous sampling of medieval prose and *shih* poetry, but seldom a quotation from *tz'u* poetry, fiction, or drama.

Given the long and complex history of literary Chinese, it would be difficult to isolate a full range of rhetorical features common to the all forms and periods of the language. But two that stand out are allusion and parallelism. The traditional composition process of crafting previously digested bits of language into new works virtually guaranteed that all new texts were to some extant and in some sense intertextual. Quotations in literary Chinese come in many degrees and nuances, and their continual manipulation (done in the full view and with the hopefully full understanding of the intended reader) accounts for much of the rhetorical structure and appeal of the literary masters of the medieval period. For example, a Sung critic wrote approvingly of the T'ang masters that every graph in their writings had a "source" and disapprovingly of his contemporaries that they were no longer learned enough to recognize these intertextual connections. In fact, during this period, experimentations in recording the vernacular were often the only recourse for authors, such as Po Chü-i 白居易 (772–846)* and Liu Yü-hsi 劉禹錫 (772–842),* who wished to write upon occasion without allusion.

Parallelism pervades most compositions in literary Chinese and can affect any level of the text. It can be a major principle ordering the presentation of entire themes and arguments, as in the *pa-ku-wen.* In *p'ien-wen* 駢文* or "parallel prose" it orders the syntax of each distich in the composition. In *lü-shih* 律詩 or "regulated verse" it orders the rhythmic alternation of contrasting tone values for each graph in the couplet. And a relaxed, more fluid syntactical parallelism is often present even in *ku-wen* compositions, a prose style that originally arose in opposition to "parallel prose." Parallel structures, especially those that operated at the sentence or phrase level of the text, were popular with Chinese literati because the recurring rhymes and patterns made texts easier to memorize. But parallelism is in fact a fundamental feature of the Chinese spoken language itself, and vernacular works also manifest a wide array of rhetorical effects based on parallelism.

Although few modern scholars retain the ability to write with ease in the traditional Chinese literary genres, literary Chinese continues today to be a major influence on both written and spoken communication. Modern Chinese written by educated speakers often contains large amounts of syntax and vocabulary that derives from the literary Chinese corpus rather than from spoken speech.

Studies

Bodde, Derk. "Punctuation: Its Use in China and Elsewhere," *RO* XLVII.2 (1991): 15-23.

Harbsmeier, Christoph. *Aspects of Classical Chinese Syntax*. London and Malmo: Curzon Press, 1981.

Karlgren, Bernhard. *The Chinese Language, An Essay on Its Nature and History*. New York: Ronald Press, 1949.

Norman, Jerry. *Chinese*. Cambridge and New York: Cambridge University Press, 1988. See especially chapters 1-4.

Pulleyblank, Edwin G. *Outline of Classical Chinese Grammar*. Vancouver: University of British Columbia Press, 1995.

Ramsey, S. Robert. *The Languages of China*. Princeton: Princeton University Press, 1987. See "Chapter 7: History," pp. 116-42.

Wang, Li 王力. *Han-yü shih-kao* 漢語史稿. 3v. Peking: K'o-hsüeh-yüan, 1957–58.

___, ed. *Ku-tai Han-yü* 古代漢語. 4v. Peking: Chung-hua, 1962.

Charles Hartman
The University at Albany

Liu Chün 劉峻 (Original *ming,* Fa-hu 法虎 or Fa-wu 法武, *tzu,* Hsiao-piao 孝標, *ca.* 462–521) was the second son of Liu T'ing 劉珽, who occupied the position of chamberlain for Shih-hsing 始興 in the Liu Sung period. Although Liu was born in Mo-ling 秣陵 (modern Chiang-ning 江寧, Kiangsu), he was a native of P'ing-yüan 平原 (modern P'ing-yüan, Shantung). When Ch'ing-chou 青州 (Shantung) was invaded by the Northern Wei in 469, he was abducted as a slave and taken to Chung-shan 中山 (modern Ting-hsien 定縣, Hopei). Fortunately, a wealthy man named Liu Pao 劉寶 redeemed him and taught him how to read and write. At the age of eleven, his family became so poor that both he and his mother were forced to enter a Buddhist temple as a monk and a nun. His relation with Buddhism is also evidenced by the fact that he helped Chi-chia-yeh 吉迦夜 record the translation of the *sûtra Fo-shuo ta-fang kuang-p'u-sa shih-ti ching* 佛說大方廣菩薩十地經. Despite living in extreme destitution, he remained a studious and voracious reader who would stay up all night reading by a hemp torch. Ts'ui Wei-tsu's 崔慰祖 nickname for Liu was "Shu yin" 書淫 (Bibliomaniac or Crazy about Books) because whenever Liu heard about an unusual book, he would try to go to the capital to borrow it. His diligence made him one of the most learned men of his times.

Liu could not return to the South until 486 during the Yung-ming 永明 era (483-94) when literature flourished under the patronage of the Ch'i 齊 princes. By then he already spent over sixteen years under the Northern Wei. On returning to the South, his career as an official was never smooth. At first, he sought to join the staff of Prince Ching-ling 竟陵, Hsiao Tzu-liang 蕭子良 (460–494), but was rejected by one of Hsiao's senior officers. Later, he took the lowly position of a penal officer. In 502 when Hsiao Yen 蕭衍 (464–549), Emperor Wu 武 of the

97

Liang, ascended to the throne, Liu Chün was already forty years old and did not fare better. He was summoned to the court to collate and edit texts in the imperial archives.

Hsiao Yen, who gathered numerous literati in his court, was famous for his personal interest and talent in poetry. However, Liu was never one of the Emperor's favorite courtiers, probably because of his straightforward character. A well-known anecdote displays Liu's unyielding and unsociable personality. Once Hsiao Yen asked his literary entourage to write down as many allusions as possible to brocade quilts. When everyone present declared that all the allusions on this subject had been exhausted, Liu casually asked for brush and ink and jotted down more than ten additional references. Everyone in the court was astonished, but the Emperor was completely displeased by this show of bravado and erudition. It was probably because of this sort of behavior that Liu never won the imperial favor. Finally, Liu decided to retire to Mount Tzu-yen 紫巖山 (known today as Mount Chin-hua 金華山) in Tung-yang東陽 (modern Chekiang) to teach and write until the end of his life.

In terms of scholarship, Liu Chün is most famous for his erudite commentary on the *Shih-shuo hsin-yü* 世說新語* in which he cited more than 160 documents to explain the text. Rather than emphasizing the glossing of obscure words and expressions, his commentary focuses on quoting a great variety of sources to elucidate each event. Thus, his commentary preserves many historical sources that are no longer available. He also compiled one of the earliest compendia called *Lei-yüan* 類苑 (The Garden of Diverse Topics) which unfortunately has not survived. Another scholarly contribution was his annotation of Lu Chi's 陸幾 (261–303)* "Yen lien-chu" 演連珠 (Strung Pearls Expanded–see *Lien-chu***) preserved

intact in the *Wen-hsüan* 文選.* Without his commentary, it would extremely difficult to understand Lu Chi's highly polished style.

In the history of Chinese literature, Liu Chün is better known as an excellent writer of parallel prose than as a poet. He has only four extant poems and his poetic style clearly shows a strong influence from the language of the *fu* 賦.* Two of his verses depict landscapes, one was written on the border theme, and the other on his dwelling in the mountains. The quality of these pieces suggests Liu should have been a superb poet. Unfortunately, his poetic corpus did not survive. The parallel prose collection has attracted most critical attention. Of all his works, the "Tzu-hsü" 自序 (Autographical Essay) is the most personal and moving piece. In the essay, Liu compares himself to Feng Yen 馮衍 (*ca.* 1–*ca.* 76) of the Eastern Han dynasty who was rejected by Emperor Kuang-wu 光武 (r. 25–57) because of his former alliance with Liu Hsüan 劉玄 (d. 25), the Emperor's major opponent. He notes that both he and Feng met with failure politically despite their talent and ambition. Both married shrewish wives. Although Feng once found glory on the battlefield, Liu would remain obscure and unhappy through-out his life. Feng had a son, but Liu himself has no children to continue his family line. Feng was physically strong, but Liu weak and sickly. Finally, Feng's name would be passed down to posterity, but Liu feared that he would be buried like autumn grass, unknown to future generations. As proof that Liu was overly pessimistic, this essay served as a model for a subsequent autobiographical essay by Wang Chung 汪中 (1743–1794).

Liu Chün was also a master of the *lun* 論 (discourse) genre. That two of his *lun* were collected in the *Wen hsüan* attests to his achievement, even more impressive because they were written in parallel prose, a style that imposes tremendous restrictions on the writer. The first is the "Pien-ming lun" 辯命論 (Discourse on Fate) which argues that everything is controlled by fate: life and death, nobility and low birth, prosperity and poverty, order and disorder, and fortune and misfortune. These are given by Heaven and cannot be altered. Kings and princes do not achieve their enterprise simply because of their power and ability, but because their destiny is prescribed by Heaven. Their rise in the world is evident even if the controller behind these events is not. But heavenly fate can neither be predicted nor explained. Men of wisdom and virtue like Wu Tzu-hsü 伍子胥 (d. 484 B.C.) and Ch'ü Yüan 屈原 (340?–278 B.C.)* were afflicted with grief and pain because one's merits are not related to one's success. In this piece, Liu tries to reconcile his own fate, concluding that as a Confucian scholar he must continue his moral cultivation, despite his fated obscurity.

His second *lun* is the "Kuang Chüeh-chiao lun" 廣絕交論 (An Expanded Discourse on Severing Friendship). As its title and preface indicate, it is a sequel to Chu Mu's 朱穆 (100–163) "Chüeh-chiao lun" 絕交論 (Discourse on Sever-ing Friendship). The piece was actually triggered by Jen Fang's 任昉 (460–508)* friends who showed complete indif-ference towards the poverty of Jen's family after Jen passed away. In it Liu lists five types of false friendships: those based on power, commiseration, wealth, connection, and profit. He concludes that all five types are equally unfortunate and disastrous, and ends in an admonition to future generations to hide in mountains because any friendship only brings pain and affliction.

Although Liu Chün's literary corpus does not include any *fu,* he was undoubtedly a skilled rhapsodist. His monumental "Shan-chü chih" 山居志 (Record on Dwelling in the Mountains) bears resemblance to *fu* in all aspects except its title. This piece, written during the last stage of his life, harkens back the famous "Shan-chü fu" 山居賦 (Rhapsody on Dwelling in the Mountains) by Hsieh Ling-yün 謝靈運 (385–433)* and depicts both the geographical and the cultural landscapes of Mount Chin-hua where he had retired.

In general, Liu Chün's literary achievement lies in his parallel prose. Many parallel prose writers indulged themselves in the ornate parallelism of the style and were unable to project their own character in their works. But in spite of the limitations of this particular style, Liu was able to make his own personality and character felt. His language is full of individual flavor and strength, as it reveals his considerable erudition and literary talent.

Editions and References

Chang, P'u 張溥. *Liu Hu-ts'ao chi* 劉戶曹集. *Han-Wei Liu-ch'ao pai-san-chia chi* 漢魏六朝百三家集. Ming edition.

Lo, Kuo-wei 羅國威, comm. *Liu Hsiao-piao chi chiao-chu* 劉孝標集校注. Shanghai: Shang-hai Ku-chi, 1988. The best modern critical edition.

Studies

Matsuoka, Eiji 松岡栄志. "Ryû Shun 'Sansei shi'–Bukkyô e no kyori" 劉峻山棲志—仏教への距離, *Tôyô bunka* 70 (1990): 81-113.

Morino, Shigeo 森野繁夫. "Ryû Kôhyô ten" 劉孝標伝. In *Obi Hakushi taikyû kinen Chûgoku bungaku ronshû* 小尾博士退休記念中国文学論集. Tokyo, 1976, pp. 339-362.

Wakatsuki, Toshihirei 若槻俊秀. "Ryû Kôhyô no 'Henmeiron' ni tsuite" 劉孝標の辯命論について, *Ôtani gakuhô* 56.1 (1976).

Yang, Wei-hsien 楊位先. "Liu Hsiao-piao yen-chiu" 劉孝標研究. Unpublished M.A. Thesis, National Taiwan University, 1971.

Jui-lung Su
The National University of Singapore

Liu K'ai 柳開 (original *tzu*, Chung-t'u 仲塗; original name, Chien-yü 肩愈 or Hsiao-yü 肖愈; later *tzu*, Shao-hsien 紹先 or Shao-yüan 紹元; *hao*, Tung-chiao yeh-fu 東郊野夫, Pu-wang Hsien-sheng 補亡先生; 947–1000) was a forerunner of the "ancient-style prose movement" (*ku-wen yün-tung* 古文運動)* of the Northern Sung dynasty. A native of Ta-ming 大名 (modern Hopei), he claimed to be a descendent of Liu Tsung-yüan 柳宗元 (773–819).* His father was Liu Ch'eng-han 柳承翰, a scholar who served as a low-ranking official during the transition period between the Five Dynasties and Northern Sung. In his childhood, Liu K'ai traveled with his father, who held local official posts here and there. Once when he was only thirteen, a bandit entered his house, frightening everyone. Liu K'ai alone kept his head, picked up a sword, and drove the man away. At seventeen, he obtained Han Yü's 韓愈 (768–824)* works. Fascinated with Han's *ku-wen* style, he re-named himself Chien-yu ("Shouldering Han Yü's Cause") and changed his *tzu* to Shao-hsien ("Continuing the Predecessor"), indicating he was to carry on the undertaking of his ancestor, Liu Tsung-yüan, the other major T'ang-dynasty *ku-wen* writer. Thus Liu K'ai was the first person in the Sung dynasty to call attention to these two important T'ang ancient-style essayists.

In his early twenties, Liu K'ai remained in the Ta-ming area, styling himself Tung-chiao Yeh-fu (Rustic of Eastern Suburban). He wrote a *Yeh shih* 野史 (Unofficial History), in ninety *p'ien*. Soon after, he turned his attention to Wang T'ung 王通 (584–617) and, in imitation of Wang's continuation of the Classics, tried to compose pieces to fill in the lost portions of the *Shih ching* 詩經 (Classic of Poetry) and the *Shu ching* 書經 (Classic of Documents) which were collected in *Pu wang p'ien* 補亡篇 (Pieces to Fill in the Gaps). In recognition of this achievement, he called himself Pu-

wang Hsien-sheng (Master Fill-in-the-Gaps). Later, he again changed his name to K'ai 開 ("To Open Up") and his *tzu* to Chung-t'u ("On the Right Way," *k'ai* and *chung-t'u* also match *t'ung* and *chung-yen* 仲淹, Wang T'ung's name and *tzu,* respectively). According to his own explanation, this showed he wanted to open the Way of the ancient sages and worthies for the present. It also indicated he was no longer satisfied with merely following the example of Han Yü and tried to learn directly from Confucius. By taking the Six Classics as a model, his writings gradually distanced themselves from those of Han Yü.

In order to promote *ku-wen*, Liu K'ai began to associate with other literati who had similar interests. Among his friends was Fan Kao 范杲. Referred to in tandem as "Liu and Fan," both men became famous for their predilection for ancient writing and ancient learning. Liu K'ai sent his writings and letters to Wang Hu 王祜 (924–987), a high-ranking official and then the prefect of Ta-ming, and won the latter's appreciation.

Although he was a man of letters, Liu K'ai was gallant and generous by nature and loved to associate with stalwart and heroic men. Several anecdotes tell how he gave away all he had when encountering someone in need of help. Because of this people compared him to Kuo Chen 郭震 (656-713), a T'ang scholar who was noted for similarly chivalrous conduct. Liu K'ai's heroic deeds may have helped him pass the *chin-shih* examination. One source relates that Liu K'ai failed several times in the examinations because of his *ku-wen* style. But when in 973 he was recommended as "a heroic scholar" (*ying-hsiung chih shih* 英雄之士) the emperor summoned him and granted him the degree by a special dispensation. Two years later, he was assigned to a minor official post in the provinces. From then on, he served mostly as a prefect in various places. On several occasions, he displayed his valor by pacifying local bandits or rebels. In the late 980s (probably 986), he sent a memorial to the emperor, asking to be sent to the border to fight against the Khitan. As a result, the emperor decided to appoint scholars with literary talents to places traditionally run by military men, and he was accordingly made Commissioner for Fostering Propriety (*Ch'ung-i-shih* 崇儀使).

Many of Liu K'ai's works have been lost. After Liu K'ai's death, although his disciple Chang Ching 張景 (970–1018) collected ninety-six pieces and compiled the *Ho-tung Hsien-sheng chi* 河東先生集 (The Collected Works of Master Ho-tung). Neither the *Yeh shih* nor *Pu wang p'ien* are extant. Almost all of the extant prose is written in the "ancient-prose style." Five of his poems are also extant. His well-known "Sai-shang ch'ü" 塞上曲 (Song from the Border) depicted the frontier scenery so vividly that it became the basis for a number of contemporary paintings.

In the early Sung, the dominate prose style was *shih-wen* 時文 (current prose), a type of *p'ien-t'i wen* 駢體文 (parallel prose).* Liu K'ai criticized this type of prose because it emphasized verbal beauty over content. Liu believed contemporaries in their labored and ornate style were unable to effect any didactic purport. Their works were flashy, but without substance. Therefore, his major effort was to oppose current style and revive "the ancient Way" (*ku-tao* 古道). As he wrote, "If I were to adopt the literary style of the current age, how could I instruct the commoners?... If one intended to practice the Way of the ancients but follow the writing of contemporaries, it would be just like someone who wanted to cross the sea riding on a thoroughbred horse. How could that be done?"

In keeping with the models set by Han Yü and Liu Tsung-yüan, Liu K'ai wrote some works which employed a classical style to express opinions which often transcended accepted opinion; his "Tai Wang Chao-chün hsieh Han-ti shu" 代王昭君謝漢帝疏 (Memorial Written for Wang Chao-ch'un Taking Leave of the Han Emperor)," in which Liu reinterprets the famous story of the palace lady being sent off to marry a Tartar prince, may serve as an example. Here Liu fictively speaks through the persona of Wang Chao-chün to explain that far from resenting her arranged marriage, she realizes that she has an opportunity few women have to secure the security and prosperity of the empire through her own actions.

His choice of genres also reflects the influence the T'ang *ku-wen* masters had on him. He wrote four *shuo* 説, two *chuan* 傳 (biographies), three *lun* 論 (essays), and three *chi* 記 (records). His "Hsü shih shuo" 續師説 (Continuing the Discourse on Teachers) was a sequel to Han Yü's "Shih shuo" 師説 (Discourse on Teachers). Two autobiographies, titled "Tung-chiao Yeh-fu chuan" 東郊野夫傳 (Biography of the Rustic Fellow in the Eastern Suburbs) and "Pu-wang Hsien-sheng chuan" 補亡先生傳 (Biography of Mr. Fill-in-the-Gaps), create a literary persona for himself and contain much about his own ideas of "ancient-style prose."

Liu also wrote *yu-chi* 游記 (see *yu-chi wen-hsüeh* 游記文學 [travel-record literature]*) in the manner of Liu Tsung-yüan such as his "Yu T'ien-p'ing Shan chi" 游天平山記 (A Record of Travelling on Plain of Heaven Mountain). These pieces, although incorporating some of the features which distinguished Liu Tsung-yüan's records such as elegant depictions of the scenery and interesting figures of speech, do not attempt the speculative conclusions which made the T'ang master's works famous.

Despite crafted pieces such as these, many people would not accept Liu K'ai's attempts at reform, calling him "insane and absurd" (*ch'ih-wang* 痴妄). Liu K'ai wrote his famous letter "Ying tse" 應責 (Response to Criticism) to defend himself and express his ideas about *ku-wen*: "You criticize me because I am fond of *ku-wen*. What do you mean when you say *ku-wen*? Now, *ku-wen* does not aim at the diction being so harsh and the language being so demanding that others will have difficulty reading or reciting it. Rather, it aims to make the ancient principles its own and the lofty its intent, to determine the length [of a work] according to what one has to say, to create a structure in response to change, and to conduct affairs as the ancients did. This is called *ku-wen*." Liu K'ai also emphasized the relationship between ancient style and ancient thought, i.e., the Confucian Way: "My Way is the Way of Confucius, Mencius, Yang Hsiung 揚雄 (53 B.C.–A. D. 18), and Han Yü. My writing is the writing of Confucius, Mencius, Yang Hsiung, and Han Yü." In raising these ideas, Liu K'ai considered himself to be the true heir to the sages of the past and the spokesman for the ancient Way. He was obviously influenced by Han Yü, who first created the notion of an orthodox Confucian "succession of the Way" (*tao-t'ung* 道統) in his "Yüan Tao" 原道 (Essentials of the Way) and who claimed that "writing is to carry out the Way" (*wen i kuan tao* 文以貫道).

Despite criticism from many contemporaries, a number of scholars gradually began to follow Liu K'ai's lead by writing *ku-wen*. Eventually they formed a small literary group. Liu K'ai's ideas about *ku-wen* also had a historical dimension, providing the theoretical background for the Sung *Ku-wen* Movement. His praise of Han Yü, his emphasis on the ancient Way were both echoed and amplified by subsequent *ku-wen* writers. In addition to his emphasis on ancient style, Liu K'ai stressed ancient thought, and his study of Confucian Classics also shaped the Classics learning of the Sung dynasty.

Despite his impact during his lifetime, Liu K'ai's prose was often criticized by later scholars as dry and difficult to read. It is possible that in fighting against parallel prose, Liu K'ai went to another extreme, paying too much attention to the didactic function of the writing and neglecting its artistic value. It was not until Ou-yang Hsiu 歐陽修 (1007–1072)* began to attach importance to aesthetic and moral values in his writings that Sung *ku-wen* could mature and flourish.

Editions and References
Ch'üan Sung wen, 3:562-721.
Ho-tung Hsien-sheng chi 河東先生集. *SPTK*. 16 *chüan;* 15 *chüan* of Liu K'ai's works and 1 *chüan* of his *hsing-chuang* 行狀 written by a disciple.
Ho-tung Hsien-sheng chi. 16 *chüan.* 3v. in *Wu-shih ts'ung-shu t'ang ch'ao-pen* 吳氏叢書堂抄本 of the Ming dynasty. This is the earliest extant Mss. copy.
Ho-tung Hsien-sheng chi. 16 *chuan.* In *San Sung jen chi* 三宋人集.

Translations
Strassberg, *Inscribed Landscapes*, pp. 151-55.

Studies
Bol, *This Culture of Ours,* pp. 162-165.
Chang, I 張毅. *Sung-tai wen-hsüeh ssu-hsiang shih* 宋代文學思想史. Peking: Chung-hua, 1995, pp. 32-37.
Chin, Ch'i-hua 金啟華. "Pei Sung shih-wen ko-hsin san hsien-ch'ü lüeh-shu" 北宋詩文革新三先驅略述, *Chiang-hai hsüeh-k'an* 1992.5: 153-56.
Chin, Chung-shu 金中樞. *Sung-tai hsüeh-shu ssu-hsiang yen-chiu* 宋代學術思想研究. Taipei: Yu-shih Wen-hua, 1989, pp. 58-62, 182-97.
Chu, Ching-hua 朱靖華. "Liu K'ai" in *Chung-kuo li-tai chu-ming wen-hsüeh-chia p'ing-chuan hsü-pien erh* 中國歷代著名文學家評傳續編貳 Lü, Hui-chuan 呂彗鵑 *et al.* eds. Tsinan: Shan-tung Chiao-yü, 1988, pp. 1-19.
Chu, Kuo-neng 朱國能. "Liu K'ai chi-ch'i chu-shu yen-chiu" 柳開及其著述研究. Unpublished Ph.D. dissertation, University of Hong Kong, 1992.

Chu, Shang-shu 祝尚書. "Liu K'ai nien-p'u" 柳開年譜, in *Sung-tai wen-hua yen-chiu* 宋代文化研究, v. 3, Chengtu: Ssu-ch'uan Ta-hsüeh, 1993, pp. 113-47.

____. *Pei-Sung ku-wen yün-tung fa-chan shih* 北宋古文運動發展史. Chengtu: Pa-shu Shu-she, 1995, pp. 11-46.

Egan, Ronald C. *The Literary Works of Ou-yang Hsiu (1007–72).* Cambridge: Cambridge University Press,1984, pp. 14-16.

Ho, P'ei-hsiung 何沛雄. "Liu K'ai yü Sung-tai ku-wen yün-tung" 柳開與宋代古文運動, *Shu-mu chi-k'an* 82.4: 24-31.

Kurata, J. "Liu K'ai," in *Sung Biographies*, pp. 645-48.

Li, K'o-feng 李可風. "Liu K'ai wen-chi pan-pen k'ao-lüeh" 柳開文集版本考略, *Wen-hsien* 33: 226-230.

Weiguo Cao
University of Wisconsin, Madison

Liu K'un 劉琨 (*tzu,* Yüeh-shih 越石, 270–318) was a poet-statesman of the mid-Chin dynasty, noted for his emotional verse lamenting the chaos of the age. From Wei-ch'ang 魏昌 in the state of Chung-shan 中山國 (modern Hopei), Liu was descended from a branch of the Han imperial family. His immediate ancestors held high office during the Han dynasty. As a youth, Liu K'un was recognized for his refinement and talent, and also gained a reputation for his bravery and heroics. As a young man, Liu K'un fell into the orbit of Chia Mi 賈謐 (d. 300), nephew of the Empress Chia, director of the palace library in Lo-yang, and a powerful patron of the arts. This circle, including noted men of letters such as Shih Ch'ung 石崇 (249–300), Ou-yang Chien 歐陽建 (d. 300), Lu Chi 陸機 (261–303)* and Lu Yün 陸雲 (262–303),** as well as Liu K'un's own brothers, was known as the "Twenty-four Friends" 二十四友. At the age of twenty-seven, he took his first official position, rapidly advancing through a series of offices and ranks. During the insurrection of the eight princes (*ca.* 290–306), he supported Emperor Hui 惠 (r. 290–307), and was subsequently made governor of Ping 并 province. After the fall of Lo-yang in 311, Liu K'un remained in Ping, and was placed in charge of Ping, Chi 冀, and Yu 幽 provinces. In the north, he was actively engaged in attempts to restore the Chin court to Lo-yang. In 316, Liu K'un allied with the governor of Chi 薊, Tuan P'i-ti 段匹磾 (n.d.) to protect the northern provinces from attack. The following year, he submitted a memorial to the throne encouraging Ssu-ma Jui 司馬睿 (Emperor Yüan 元, r. 317–323) to take the throne (see *Wen-hsüan, chüan* 37) at Chien-yeh 建業 (modern Nanking). Later that year, Liu was defeated by Shih Lo 石勒 (274–333), and in 318, he was detained and killed by his former ally, Tuan. Liu's biography is found in *Chin shu* (62.1679-1702).

Liu K'un left some seventeen works and fragments in a variety of prose genres. Among this body are four memorials (*piao* 表); four memoranda (*chien* 牋); seven letters (*shu* 書); one oath (*meng* 盟); and one dirge (*lei* 誄). The two most notable examples are Liu's "Ch'üan-chin Yüan-ti piao" 勸進元帝表 (Memorial Urging the Succession of Emperor Yüan, in *Wen-hsüan, chüan* 37) and "Yü Tuan P'i-ti meng-wen" 與段匹磾盟文 (Oath with Tuan P'i-ti, in *I-wen lei-chü, chüan* 33). In his *Wen-hsin tiao-lung* 文心雕龍,* Liu Hsieh 劉勰 (*ca.* 465–*ca.* 520) praises both of these works. Regarding Liu's "Oath with Tuan P'i-ti," Liu Hsieh says, "the iron oath of Liu K'un possesses spirit so subtly moving that it even affected the sleet and frost." Liu Hsieh praised his memorial urging Emperor Yüan be put on the throne as follows: "The memorial by Liu K'un beseeching [Emperor Yüan] to assume the throne [is] clear and straightforward, excelling in [its] narrative account."

Liu K'un's extant poetic corpus is small but highly regarded by traditional critics. Four pieces are all that remain of his poetic works. Throughout Liu's poetry, themes of loyalty and despair reflect the turbulent age in which he lived and wrote. His most famous poem, "Fu-feng ko" 扶風歌 (Song of Fu-feng, collected in *chüan* 28 of *Wen-hsüan, chüan* 43 of the *I-wen lei-chü,* and *chüan* 84 of *Yüeh-fu shih-chi)* was written in the fall of 307 as Liu was leaving Lo-yang to take up his post as governor of the famine-plagued area of Ping. The poem, written in the *yüeh-fu** style, expresses Liu's feelings of regret about the turmoil of the age as he left the capital for the northern frontier. On a personal level, Liu also laments the separation from his home and family that he was then facing. Despite the hardships at hand, Liu K'un draws solace by relating his situation to that faced by Confucius and later, the Han general Li Ling 李陵 (d. 74 B.C.), illustrating the theme of loyalty during times of distress. Two of the remaining pieces in Liu K'un's poetic works are from an exchange between Liu and aide-de-camp Lu Ch'en 盧諶 (n.d.). Like the "Song of Fu-feng," Liu's "Ta Lu Ch'en" 答盧諶 ("Reply to Lu Ch'en") and "Ch'ung tseng Lu Ch'en" 重贈盧諶 ("Again Presented to Lu Ch'en," both in *Wen-hsüan* 28 and *I-wen lei-chü chüans* 31 and 8), express feelings of gloom and despair regarding the chaotic age. In "Reply to Lu Ch'en," Liu K'un mourns the decline of the Chin dynasty, and laments his own weakness and inability to remedy the situation. Both poems also contain admonishment and encouragement to Liu's younger friend. All three of these pieces rely heavily on classical allusions—generally to anecdotes about loyal officials under duress. Additionally, they are rich in lyric expression of Liu's own sadness and frustration. The authorship of the final poem included in Liu K'un's extant works, "Hu-chieh nien shih-wu" 胡姬年十五 (Fifteen-year-old Barbarian Concubine, in *Yüeh-fu shih-chi, chüan* 63) has come under some scrutiny from traditional and modern scholars. Some claim the poem is the

work of another Liu K'un of the Liang 梁 dynasty. However, Kuo Mao-ch'ien's 郭茂倩 (*fl.* 12th c.) *Yüeh-fu shih-chi* 樂府詩集 (Collection of Music-Bureau Poems),* the editors of the *Ssu-k'u ch'üan-shu tsung-mu t'i-yao* 四庫全書總目提要, and Ting Fu-pao's 丁福保 (1874–1952) *Chüan Chin shih* 全晉詩 all attribute authorship to Liu K'un of Chin. The poem in question is a short work in the *yüeh-fu* style that laments the fate of a beautiful young barbarian (*hu* 胡) servant girl, fated to wait upon the arrogant and conceited in a tavern. Like Liu's other poetic works, this piece captures an air of darkness and despair.

Traditional Chinese critics have generally praised Liu K'un's poetry for its vigor and emotion. In his chapter on literary talent, Liu Hsieh wrote, "The works of Liu K'un are characterized by grace and vigor, effervescing with spirit." Chung Jung's 鍾嶸 (*ca.* 465–518) *Shih-p'in* 詩品* praised Liu's poetry as being in the spirit of Wang Ts'an, and being from immortal realms. Chung also recognized Liu's works as capturing the emotion of his chaotic times, and being filled with words of feeling and regret. The critic Yüan Hao-wen 元好問 (1190–1257)* compared Liu K'un to Ts'ao Chih 曹植 (192–232),* saying, "Ts'ao Chih and Liu K'un were like roaring tigers, creating a wind. Within the four seas, there was no one who could match these two heroes."

In addition to the praise given to Liu by traditional literary critics, he was also honored by later Chinese poets. Pao Chao 鮑照 (*ca.* 414–466)* paid homage by writing a companion to Liu's own "Song of Fu-feng." Chiang Yen 江淹 (444–505)* composed a piece with Liu as his subject. During the T'ang, literary masters Wang Wei 王維 (701–761),* Li Po 李白 (701–762),* and Tu Fu 杜甫 (712–770)* all wrote poems either referring directly to Liu K'un or borrowing from Liu's own poetry. Perhaps the Southern Sung poet Lü Yu

陸游 (1125–1210)* put it best, "After Liu K'un died, there were no rare gentlemen; Alone listening to the wild cock, tears soaking his garment" 劉琨死後無奇士, 獨聽野雞淚滿衣.

Editions and References

Chao, T'ien-jui 趙天瑞, ed. *Liu K'un chi* 劉琨集. Tientsin: T'ien-chin Ku-chi, 1996.

Liu-ch'ao wen, 108:2078-2083 (prose).

I-wen lei-chü 藝文類聚. Peking: Chung-hua, 1965, 43:773; 13:249; 33:589; 26:480; and 31:551.

Lu, *Nan-pei-ch'ao shih,* 2:849-853.

Pai-san, 2:49-70.

Wen-hsüan, 25:355-357 and 28:408.

Yüeh-fu shih-chi 樂府詩集. Shanghai: Shang-hai Ku-chi, 1993, 63:555; 84:714.

Translations

Frodsham, *Anthology,* pp. 76-77.

Knechtges, David R. "Liu K'un: Memorial Urging the Succession," *Renditions* 33/34 (1990): 102-111.

von Zach, *Anthologie,* 1:412-417, 511-512.

Studies

Chang, Ping-hsin 張並新. "Wan-chu pei-liang te shih-lu ying-hsiung—Liu K'un" 萬緒悲涼的失路英雄, *Ku-tien wen-hsüeh chih-shih* 1991.5: 77-84.

Fang, Pu-ho 方步和. "Ho-i pai-lien-kang hua-wei yao-chih jou: Lun Liu K'un 'Ch'ung-tseng Lu Ch'en' chi ch'i-t'a" 何意百煉剛化為繞指柔：論劉琨＜重贈盧諶＞詩及其他, *Shan-tung Ta-hsüeh hsüeh-pao,* 1985.1.

Hsü, Jen-fu 徐仁甫. "Liu K'un 'Ta Lu Ch'en' chieh" 劉琨答盧諶解, "Liu K'un 'Ch'ung-tseng Lu Ch'en' chieh" 劉琨重贈盧諶解, and "Liu K'un 'Fu-feng ko' chieh" 劉琨扶風歌解, in *Ku-shih pieh-chieh* 古詩別解. Peking: Chung-hua, 1984, pp. 171-172, 172-173 and 172-173.

Ku, Nung 顧農. "Kuan-yü Liu K'un yü Lu Ch'en te tseng-ta shih" 關於劉琨 與盧諶贈答詩, *Ho-pei Shih-fan Ta-hsüeh hsüeh-pao,* 1993.4: 43-48.

Li, Ching-ch'i 李景琦. "Ying-hsiung shih-lu, k'ang-k'ai pei-ko—tu Liu K'un 'Ch'ung-tseng Lu Ch'en'" 英雄失路 慷慨悲歌：讀劉琨＜重贈盧諶＞, *Wen-shih chih-shih,* 1994.2: 32-35.

Liu, Wen-chung 劉文忠. "Lu Chen, Liu K'un tseng-ta shih k'ao-pien" 盧諶劉 琨贈答詩考辨, *Wen-shih-che,* 1988.2: 89-91.

Yün, Chung 允中. "K'ang-k'ai pei-ko te ai-kuo ying-hsiung" 慷慨悲歌的愛國 英雄, *Wen-shih chih-shih,* 1985.2: 77-81.

J. Michael Farmer
University of Wisconsin, Madison

Liu Mien 柳冕 (*tzu,* Ching-shu 敬 叔, d. *ca.* 805) was a scholar-official with a strong interest in ritual who enjoyed good close relations with many of the most important literary figures at the end of the eighth century. He used these ties to advocate the *Fu-ku* 復古 (Return to Antiquity) and *Ku-wen* 古文 (Ancient Prose)* movements.

The Lius were a family of scholar-officials from P'u-chou 蒲州 (modern Yung-chi 永濟 county in Shansi). Liu's father, Liu Fang 柳芳 (*ca.* 710–*ca.* 785), was a noted genealogist and historian who had worked with Wei Shu 韋述 (d. 757). He was involved in a number of important projects in the 750s and 760s and the author of the influential *Kuo shih* 國史 (History of the State, completed 759–760). Liu Mien's predilection for *ku-wen* can probably be traced to Liu Fang, who passed the *chin-shih* in 735 together with Li Hua 李華 (ca. 715–*ca.* 774)* and Hsiao Ying-shih 蕭穎士 (717–758)* under the examiner Sun T'i 孫逖 (*fl.* 735), a scholar who rejected the rote memorization of passages and commentary from the Chinese Classics in favor of the careful study and discussion of the canon.

There is no record of Liu Mien taking the *chin-shih* or any of the other examinations. He began his career in the College of Assembled Worthies (Chi-hsien Yüan 集賢院) and worked as a collator in the Office of History. In 780, Liu Mien was sent to the provinces to take up a minor post in Pa-chou 巴州, because of his friendship with the financial doyen Liu Yen 劉晏 (d. 780) who had just fallen from power. In 785 he was recalled to the capital as Erudite in the Court of Imperial Sacrifices (*T'ai-ch'ang Po-shih* 太常博士). It was in this position that he became embroiled in the controversy over royal burial and the appropriate type of mourning (this controversy was part of a larger discussion of ritual which often occupied the court in the late eighth century—see his biographies—*Chiu T'ang shu*, 149:4030-32; *Hsin T'ang shu*, 132:4537-38). After having been transferred to Director of the Board of Civil Office (*Li-pu Lang-chung* 吏部郎中) and spending a rather lengthy period at court, he was again appointed to provincial posts, rising to Civil Governor of Fu-chien (*Fu-chien Kuan-ch'a Shih* 復福建觀察使) in the early ninth century. Recalled in 805, he died en route to the capital.

Liu Mien is best known to modern readers through the lengthy discussion of his prose and prose theories in Liu Ta-chieh's 劉大杰 (1904–1977) standard *Chung-kuo wen-hsüeh fa-chan shih* 中國文學發展史 (A History of the Development of Chinese Literature). Liu Ta-chieh devotes almost as much space to Liu Mien as he does to Liu Tsung-yüan 柳宗元 (773–819),* and emphasizes the importance Liu Mien gave to expressing the Tao in literature. Indeed, the fourteen prose writings remaining from what was once certainly a larger collection reveal two important literary contributions: (1) Liu Mien stresses the importance of the Tao in literature and outlines a history of literature which closely follows the Confucian tradition, thereby preparing

the way for the theories of Han Yü 韓愈 (768–824)* and other *fu-ku* authors of the ninth century; (2) Liu Mien seems to have spread the *ku-wen* gospel more than most writers through an active correspondence with some of the most influential literary figures of the 780s and 790s, men who were patrons or advisors to Han Yü and his associates, including P'ei Tu 裴度 (765–839), Ch'üan Te-yü 權德輿 (759–818), Tu Yu 杜佑 (735–812), and Chang Chien-feng 張建封 (735–800).

Liu wrote none of the genres that typify the writings of the later *ku-wen* masters (*chuan* 傳, *shuo* 説, *lun* 論, etc.), but his five extant letters which discuss various aspects of literature and its history are important pieces of literary criticism. Although he disparaged his own prose style, these letters present strong arguments in a cogent style. An excerpt from his letter to Chang Chien-feng reveals many of the problems that continued to trouble *ku-wen* writers through the end of the T'ang (*Ch'üan T'ang wen*, 527:6792):

> Literary writings are rooted in moral teachings and civilizing transformations expressed according to one's emotions and nature. Rooted in moral teachings and civilizing transformations was the Way of Yao and Shun; expressed according to their emotions and nature were the words of the sages. Since the deaths of kings Ch'eng 成 and K'ang 康 [at the start of the Chou dynasty], the music of the laudes has ceased, the *sao* 騷 poets began to compose, licentious beauty arose, and literary writings and moral teachings separated into two. Those who were not adequate produced literary writings by force, thus they did not understand the Way of the superior man; those who understood the Way of the superior man, were ashamed by their literary writings. To write and to understand the Way—these two things are difficult to unite. To unite them is the task of the grandly superior man.

Liu Mien here presents the

contradiction he and many subsequent *ku-wen* writers faced: literature was a personal thing, "expressed according to one's emotions and nature," but it was also meant to be combined with politics, to serve society. The difficulty of combining literary skills and Confucian didacticism eluded all but a few (such as Han Yü), leading to the bifurcation of these writers into two schools of *ku-wen* in the late ninth century, one stressing Tao, the other *wen* 文 (literary skills).

Liu's letter to Lu Ch'ün 盧群 (742–800) reiterates the role of the superior man (*chün-tzu* 君子) in literature, which he touched on above, and also explains the relationship between literature and government (*Ch'üan T'ang wen,* 527: 6790)::

> Literature arises from emotions, emotions arise from sorrow and joy, sorrow and joy arise from order and chaos. Therefore, when the superior man is moved by sorrow and joy to compose literary writings, he thereby comes to understand the root of order and chaos.

Finally, in his letter to Tu Yu, Liu Mien applies some of his ideas to the development of early Chinese literature (*Ch'üan T'ang wen,* 527:6788):

> The writings of today and the writings of antiquity differ in how they establish their meaning. Why is this? The writers of antiquity, according to whether the government was ordered or chaotic, were moved to sorrow or joy; according to whether they felt sorrow or joy, they came to chant or sing; according to whether they chanted or sang, engendered comparisons and stimuli. For this reason when the Greater Elegentiae were composed, the Royal Way flourished, when the Lesser Elegentiae were composed, the Royal Way was damaged, and when the Elegentiae became the Odes, the Royal Way was in decline, and when poems like those in the [Classic of] Poetry were no longer composed, the Royal Grace was exhausted. As for the sorrowful laments of Ch'ü Yüan and Sung Yü, who because of their thoughts were exiled and yet did not rebel, they are all the sounds of a kingdom about to perish.

Although there is some repetition in the themes and language of these letters, the multifarious subjects and daring arguments expressed in them suggest that Liu Ta-chieh's assessment of Liu Mien as the most important precursor to Han Yü and Liu Tsung-yüan has considerable merit.

Editions and References
Ch'üan T'ang wen, 527:6783-94.

Studies
Bol, Peter K. *"This Culture of Ours,"* pp. 144-45.
Liu Ta-chieh's 劉大杰 (1904–1977). *Chung-kuo wen-hsüeh fa-chan shih* 中國文學發展史 (A History of the Development of Chinese Literature). Rpt. of 1957 edition; Hong Kong: Ku-wen Shu-chü, 1964, v. 2, pp. 10-11
McMullen, David L. *State and Scholars in T'ang China.* Cambridge: Cambridge University Press, 1988, pp. 246-247.

William H. Nienhauser, Jr.
University of Wisconsin, Madison

Liu Shih 柳是 (*tzu,* Ju-shih 如是; 1618–1664), was born in Kiangsu province, in either what is today Chia-hsing 嘉興 or Wu-chiang 吳江, but little is known about her early life. Ch'en Yin-k'o 陳寅恪, who has written a three-volume biography of her life (1980), tells us that she began life as a maidservant by the name of Yang Ai 楊愛 in the courtesan's quarters, but soon became the concubine of retired prime minister Chou Tao-teng 周道登 who provided her with her first literary and poetic training. Harassed by members of Chou's household jealous of her beauty and talent, she set out on her own and in 1632 moved to Sung-chiang 宋江—an important cultural center during the late Ming. It is from this time on that Liu

Shih—under various different names and sobriquets—began to become famous for her literary and artistic talents. She associated widely with a great number of poets, artists and other literati, in particular the Ming loyalist-poet Ch'en Tzu-lung 陳子龍 (1608–1647)* with whom she lived until 1635 when she was forced to leave by Ch'en's jealous wife. Liu Shih's association with Ch'en was poetically very fruitful—she was instrumental in helping him establish the Yün-chien 雲間 School of tz'u* revival and he in turn encouraged her to publish her own poetry. Her first collection of shih* poems (prefaced by Ch'en Tzu-lung) and entitled Wu-yin Ts'ao 戊寅草, was published in 1638, followed a year later by a collection of tz'u poems, Hu-shang ts'ao 湖上草.

In 1640 Liu Shih's life took yet another turn, due in large part to her own initiative. In the eleventh month of that year, Liu Shih went to the home of the famous literary scholar-official Ch'ien Ch'ien-i 錢謙益 (1582–1664)* in Ch'ang-shu 常熟 and introduced herself. By the following month she was living with him and a year later they were married; although Ch'ien was already married, from the beginning he treated Liu as his legal first-wife rather than as a concubine. Ch'ien was sixty years old and Liu Shih just a little over twenty, but they were in many ways perfectly matched. It was Ch'ien Ch'ien-i, a lay Buddhist, who gave her the name Liu Shih or Liu Ju-shih, from the phrase "ju-shih wo-wen" 如是我聞 (thus I have heard) which is the opening phrase of Buddhist scriptures. In 1643, Ch'ien built a library, the Chiang-yün Lou 絳雲樓, where the couple worked together on the Ch'ien's anthology of Ming poetry, Lieh-ch'ao shih-chi 列朝詩集. Liu Shih assumed responsibility for the fourth section of this anthology, which was devoted to women's poetry (including her own), not only editing them but probably doing much of the scholarly and critical annotation as well. After a fire destroyed the Chiang-yün Lou, the symbol of a "compassionate marriage" built on common literary and aesthetic concerns, Liu Shih turned increasingly to her Buddhist religious practice and took tonsure the year before Ch'ien died. After Ch'ien's death in 1663, the forty-six-year-old Liu Shih found herself pressured by his relatives for money and, in order to shame them into providing for her stepson as well as the daughter she had borne Ch'ien, she hanged herself.

Although Liu Shih probably shared the loyalist sentiments of both Ch'en Tzu-lung and Ch'ien Ch'ien-i (the Lieh-ch'ao shih-chi was banned during the Ch'ien-lung emperor's reign), her own poetry was more romantic than political. Its romanticism was, however, by no means conventional: a striking example is Liu Shih's "Nan Lo-shen fu" 男洛神賦 (Fu on the Male God of River Lo), addressed to her lover Ch'en Tzu-lung, in which she boldly reverses traditional gender roles and assumes the voice of a woman courting a male river-god. Liu's romanticism can be seen with particular clarity in her tz'u or song-lyrics, the poetic genre traditionally associated with the courtesan class and which, together with Ch'en Tzu-lung, she helped to revive. Liu modeled herself after the Sung lyricist Ch'in Kuan 秦觀 (1049–1100)** whose romantic verses expressed various types of passion, including the heroic, an emphasis on genuine love or ch'ing 情 rather than mere coquetry or conventionality, and a respect for courtesans and women in general.

Liu Shih's importance in the literary history of late-Ming China is not restricted to her two slender volumes of poetry. Her personal struggles to raise her own status from that of a lowly courtesan to the wife of one of the most eminent scholars of his time is reflected in her attempts at raising the level of courtesan poetry in general. Thus, in her section of Ch'ien Ch'ien-i's *Lieh-ch'ao shih chi*, she made a point of including a significant number of poems by major courtesan poets such as Wang Wei 王微 (*ca.* 1600–*ca.* 1647) and Ching P'ien-p'ien 景翩翩 (*fl.* late 16th c.). She by no means ignored the more "respectable" gentry women, but she did tend to select those who wrote poems on overtly romantic themes, and in so doing she consciously tried to blur the traditional boundaries between courtesan and gentry women.

Editions and References

Liu, Shih 柳是. *Liu Ju-shih shih-chi* 柳如是詩文集. N.p., n.d. Chekiang Library.

___. *Liu Ju-shih shih wen-chi* 柳如是詩集. Rpt. Peking: Chung-hua Ch'üan-kuo T'u-shu-kuan Ku-chi Wen-hsien Chen-pen Hui-k'an, 1996.

___, ed., *Lieh-ch'ao shih-chi kuei-chi* 列朝詩集閨集. In *Lieh-ch'ao shih-chi* 列朝詩集. Ch'ien Ch'ien-i 錢謙益, ed. N.p., completed 1649, printed 1652?

___. *Wu-yin ts'ao* 戊寅草. Preface by Ch'en Tzu-lung 陳子龍. N.p. 1638. Chekiang Library.

___. *Hu-shang ts'ao* 湖上草. In *Liu Ju-shih shih-chi*, pt. 2. N.p.: n.d. Chekiang Library.

___. *Liu Ju-shih ch'ih-tu* 柳如是尺牘. In *Liu Ju-shih shih-chi*, pt. 2. N.p.: n.d. Chekiang Library.

Translations

Chang, K'ang-I Sun. "Twenty Songs by Liu Shih." In *The Late-Ming Poet Ch'en Tzu-lung* (New Haven and London: Yale University Press, 1990), Appendix 2, pp. 123-126.

Mair, *Anthology,* p. 348.

Waiting for the Unicorn, pp. 83-86.

Studies

Ch'en, Yin-k'o 陳寅恪. *Liu Ju-shih pieh-chuan* 柳如是別傳. 3v. Shanghai: Shang-hai Ku-chi, 1980.

Chou, Fa-kao 周法高. *Ch'ien Mu-chai, Liu Ju-shih i-shih chi Liu Ju-shih yu kuan tzu-liao* 錢牧齊，柳如是佚詩及柳如是有關資料. Taipei: San-min, 1978.

___. *Liu Ju-shih shih k'ao* 柳如是事考. Taipei: San-min, 1978.

Chang, Kang-i Sun. *The Late-Ming Poet Ch'en Tzu-lung.* New Haven and London: Yale University Press, 1990.

___. "Liu Shih and Hsü Ts'an: Feminine or Feminist?" In Yu, *Voices,* pp. 169-190.

Beata Grant
Washington University

Lu Yün 陸雲 (*tzu,* Shih-lung 士龍, 262–303) was a descendant of a most prominent, noble family in the Three-Kingdoms state of Wu 吳. His grandfather Lu Hsün 陸遜 (183–245) was the Prime Minister of Wu and his father, Lu K'ang 陸抗 (202–274), was Minister of War. Born in Hua-t'ing 華亭 (modern Shanghai 上海), after fall of Wu in 280, Lu Yün and his elder brother Lu Chi 陸機 (261–303)* retreated to their estate there where they concentrated on study for over a decade. When Emperor Wu's 武 (r. 265–290) rule came to an end, Lu Yün, Lu Chi, and Ku Jung 顧榮 (*ca.* 260–*ca.* 322), who were known as the *San-chün* 三俊 (Three Talents), came to Loyang 洛陽. Chang Hua 張華 (232–300), Grand Master of Ceremonies, received the two brothers and was greatly impressed by their literary talent. It is said that originally Lu Chi would not let Lu Yün meet Chang Hua because Yün was prone to fits of laughter. Finally, when a meeting was arranged, Lu Yün burst out laughing when he saw Chang's beard tied up in silk strings. Nevertheless, Chang was impressed by Lu Yün's skill in conversation and recommended the two brothers to the court. Lu Yün was especially skilled in pure conversation (*ch'ing-t'an* 清談). His *Chin-shu* 晉書 biography (54:1481-88) records some of his witty repartees, testifying to his wit and learning. According to a legend, at first Yün was not familiar with mysterious learning (*hsüan-hsüeh* 玄學). One night he lost his way while traveling. Suddenly he saw a house in which he met a handsome young man who talked with him about the *Lao-tzu* 老子 all night. At dawn, he discovered that the young man was the ghost of Wang Pi 王弼 (226–249), a master of mysterious learning and a noted commentator on the *Lao-tzu*. From that time on, Lu Yün was a master versed in the *Lao-tzu*.

Through recommendations Yün first assumed the position of Drafter for the Heir Apparent and then was assigned to be District Magistrate for Chün-i 浚儀 (modern Kaifeng, Honan). Later he was transferred to the post of Chamberlain for Attendants under Prince Wu 吳. Lu Yün was a beloved magistrate who displayed kindness and sagacity to the people he governed. Unfortunately, the political climate during the Chin was extremely unstable and numerous literati became victims of power struggles. In 300, he two brothers lost their benefactor, Chang Hua, who was executed. Later both Lu brothers also lost their lives in the Insurrection of the Eight Princes (Pa-wang chih luan 八王之亂). In 302 Lu Yün joined Ssu-ma Ying's 司馬穎 staff as Chamberlain for the Capital of Ch'ing-ho 清河 (modern Hopei). In 303 he was appointed Commander of the Right to the Commander-in-chief while Lu Chi assumed the position of Chamberlain for the Capital of P'ing-yüan 平原 (modern P'ing-yüan, Shantung). During the war between Ssu-ma I 司馬乂 and Ssu-ma Ying, Lu Chi was made a general. Owing to strategic failures, Chi was defeated by Ssu-ma I and barely managed to escape himself. Meng Chiu 孟玖, a eunuch who had a feud with the Lu brothers, slandered them to Ssu-ma Ying. Like their patron Chang Hua and many other literati of the Chin, both the Lu brothers were mercilessly executed.

In politics as well as literature, Lu Yün is overshadowed by his elder brother Lu Chi. Although Chi is famous for his ornate and erudite language, some of his poems and *fu* are still read today.

Lu Yün's works, equally learned and polished, rarely caught the attention of modern or even ancient critics. His extant corpus includes seven *fu* 賦,* some thirty poems, eulogies, *sao* 騷, encomiums (*tsan* 贊), letters to his brothers, and memorials. Yün was a excellent *fu* writer. His "I-min fu" 逸民賦 (Rhapsody on the Cultivated Recluse) is one of the earliest *fu* on hermits and harkens back to the tradition initiated by Chang Heng's 張衡 (78–139) "Kuei-t'ien fu" 歸田賦 (Rhapsody on Returning to the Fields). Lu Yün's piece, however, seems to have been written to match Lu Chi's "Yu-jen fu" 幽人賦 (Rhapsody on the Hidden Man). The summons into reclusion (*chao-yin* 招隱) theme was popular during the Chin dynasty. This *fu,* written in that spirit, expresses Lu Yün's desire to withdraw from the dangerous political environment which eventually cost him his life. "Chou-lin fu" 愁霖賦 (Rhapsody on the Melancholy Caused by Torrential Rain) and "Hsi-chi fu" 喜霽賦 (Rhapsody Expressing Gladness on the Cease of Rain) are also devoted to contemporary, popular poetic topics. Most of Lu Yün's *fu* were written in the traditional *Sao-fu* 騷賦 style, consisting four and six-syllable lines or six-syllable lines ending with *hsi* 兮, reflecting a strong influence from the *Ch'u-tz'u* 楚辭.* Yün also wrote the "Chiu-min" 九愍 (Nine Laments) in imitation of the *chiu* pieces in the "Chiu-chang" 九章 (Nine Chapters). In its preface, he declares that he intends to follow the model set by the "Li sao" 離騷 (Encountering Sorrow); this was in keeping with the trend to imitate ancient works popular at this time. Besides works explicating labelled *fu*, Lu Yün's "Niu tse Chi-yu" 牛責季友 (The Ox Reprimands Chi-yu) is a humorous piece written in the style of a *fu*. In this vein he also composed *chao* 嘲 (taunts).

In *Shih-p'in* 詩品 (An Evaluation of Poetry),* Chung Jung 鍾嶸 (*ca.* 465–518) highly praises Lu Chi who occupies the first rank, while placing Lu Yün in the middle rank. In his *Wen-hsin tiao-lung* 文心雕龍* Liu Hsieh 劉勰 (*ca.* 465–*ca.* 520) points out that Lu Yün was concise and fresh, excelling at short pieces. But Lu Yün left few poems, most of which are written in four-syllable lines in response to official occasions. Thus Yün is often criticized for lacking personal feelings and for an extreme formalism. Yet there are also personal pieces written to his close friends and his brother, these are unusual because they were also composed in the then old fashioned four-syllable style. Lu Yün apparently had a strong preference for the *sao* and four-syllable line, suggesting that in addition to the *Ch'u-tz'u*, the *Shih-ching* 詩經* was also a major influence. The Lu brothers are among the best writers of the *ni-ku* 擬古 (imitating the ancients) movement. Lu Ch'i's imitations of the "Nineteen Ancient Poems" are greatly extolled by Chung Jung in his *Shih-p'in*. In a letter Lu Yün encouraged his brother Lu Chi to write a piece to emulate the "Chiu-ko" 九歌 (Nine Songs) and "Chiu-huai" 九懷 (Nine Regrets) in the *Ch'u tz'u* so that Chi could leave his name to posterity. In many ways Lu Yün's literary ideals belonged to the past. Even his use of the then more fashionable five-syllable poetry was primarily in imitation of earlier poems.

If Lu Yün's poetry has not drawn attention, his literary criticism has. Revealed in letters to his brother, it is one of the focal points of recent scholarship on literary concepts in medieval China. The principal concept of Yün's aesthetics is *ch'ing-sheng* 清省 (clear and concise–also in variants such as *ch'ing-miao* 清妙 [clear and remarkable], *ch'ing-hsin* 清新 [clear and fresh], *ch'ing-mei* 清美 [clear and beautiful], etc.). Although some critics like Liu Hsieh attributed Yün's preference for clarity to be an admission of his own lack of literary skills, this seems unwarranted. Lu Yün also argued that good literary works should possess unique ideas, stimulating allusions, and pay attention to auditory effects (including the effects of local dialects). He advised Lu Chi to trim some of his passages in order to achieve an ideal succinctness and clarity. Yün also emphasized the importance of true feelings–a writer should feel heavy-hearted before attempting a fare-well piece. Although he admits to have suffered from this fault himself as a younger writer, mature works such as his "Nine Laments," emulating the melancholy and sorrow of Ch'ü Yüan 屈原 (340?-278 B.C.),* adhere closely to his critical principles.

Lu Yün was a versatile poet capable of a variety of styles and genres. Although his modern reputation suffers from the general disinterest in the euphuistic works of the Six Dynasties, he occupies a significant position in the history of Chinese poetry and literary criticism.

Editions and References

Chang, P'u 張溥, ed. *Lu Ch'ing-ho chi* 陸清河集, *Han Wei Liu-ch'ao pai-san-chia chi.*

Huang, K'uei 黃葵, ed. *Lu Yün chi* 陸雲集. Peking: Chung-hua, 1988.

Lu Yün chi 陸雲集. *SPPY.*

Lu Shih-lung wen-chi 陸士龍文集. *SPTK.*

Studies

Hsiao, Hua-jung 肖華容. "Lu Yün 'ch'ing-sheng' ti mei-hsüeh kuan" 陸雲「清省」的美學觀, *Wen-shih-che* 1 (1982): 41-43.

Kamatani, Takeshi 釜谷武志. "Riku Un 'Ani e no shokan'–sono bungaku ron kôsatsu" 陸雲兄への書簡ーその文学論考察, *Chûgoku bungaku hô* 28 (1977): 1-31.

Liu, P'ing-shan 劉平山. "Sung-k'an *Lu Shih-lung wen-chi* t'i-pa chi" 宋刊陸士龍題跋記, *Hsüeh-feng* 1.4 (1930).

Satô, Toshiyuki 佐藤利行. *Riku Un kenkyû* 陸雲研究. Tokyo: Hakuteisha, 1990. Contains a comprehensive Japanese translation of all Lu Yün's letters.

Tai, Yen 戴燕. "Lu Yün ti 'yung-ssu k'un-jen' chi ch'i-t'a" 陸雲的「用思困人」及其他. *Chûgoku bungaku hô* 52 (1996): 23-36.

Ts'ao, Tao-heng 曹道衡. "Shih-lun Lu Chi Lu Yün ti 'Wei Ku Yen-hsien tseng-fu'" 試論陸機陸雲的〔為顧彥先贈婦〕, *Ho-pei Shih-yüan hsüeh-pao* 1 (1989): 81-86.

Ueki, Hisayuki 植木久行. "Rikuchô bunjin no besshû no ikkeitai—Riku Un shû no shigakuteki kôsatsu" 陸六朝文人の別集の一形態ー陸雲集の誌学的考察, *Nihon Chûgoku gakkai hô* 29 (1977): 76-90.

Jui-lung Su 蘇瑞隆
The National University of Singapore

Meng Ch'eng-shun 孟稱舜 (*tzu,* Tzu-jo 子若, Tzu-shih 子適, Tzu-sai 子塞, Wo-yün tzu 臥雲子, Hua-yü hsien-shih 花嶼仙史, Hua-yü Chu-jen 花嶼主人, 1598–1684) was one of the leading playwrights of the seventeenth century. He composed both *tsa-chü** and *ch'uan-ch'i** and also edited a major collection of Yüan and Ming *tsa-chü.*

Meng Ch'eng-shun hailed from Kuei-chi 會稽 (modern Shaohsing). His family belonged to the local elite and its wealth allowed the family to maintain its own operatic troupe. Meng Ch'eng-shun's father Meng Ying-lin 孟應麟 served for many years as an assistant-prefect in Shantung province, and also participated on occasion in the anti-Manchu campaigns of the Late Ming. Meng Ch'eng-shun's elder brother Meng Ch'eng-yao 孟稱堯 attained the *chü-jen* degree. Together with his brother, Meng Ch'eng-shun participated in the Restoration Society (Fu-she 復社) and in the Maple Society (Feng-she 楓社), but despite his many repeated attempts in the provincial examinations, he himself never advanced beyond the *sheng-yüan* degree until after the collapse of the Ming

dynasty. He vented his frustration over his lack of success in the examination system not only repeatedly and at length in his plays, but also in a lost collection of historical essays. Among his friends, one may note his fellow-townsman Ch'i Piao-chia 祁彪佳 (1602–1645), the famous painter Ch'en Hung-shou 陳洪綬 (1598–1652), and the playwright Cho Jen-yüeh 卓人月 (b. 1606).

Meng Ch'eng-shun had two sons, one of whom died in the course of the Ch'ing conquest of Southern China in 1645. Meng Ch'eng-shun obtained the *kung-sheng* degree in 1649 and thereupon served for some years as the Assistant Instructor of the Sung-yang 松陽 district school in Southern Chekiang. He made great efforts to restore the school following the devastations of the war years, but relinquished his post in 1656, after siding with the students in a conflict with the local authorities. Nothing is known about the last twenty years of his life.

Meng Ch'eng-shun started out on his career as a playwright by writing *tsa-chü*. Six titles are known, while five plays have been preserved. None of these five plays adheres strictly to the Yüan-time conventions as all of them reflect to a larger or lesser degree the influence of Southern-style drama. Three of Meng Ch'eng-shun's *tsa-chü* are more or less conventional love comedies. *Yen-erh-mei* 眼兒媚, perhaps Meng Ch'eng-shun's earliest venture in drama, is set in the Sung dynasty and deals with the love-affair of a young official and a courtesan: the lovers are temporarily separated by his superior but eventually reunited by his friend. The title of the play refers to the tune of a lyric the young man writes when he is separated from his beloved. *Hua-ch'ien i-hsiao* 花前一笑 (A Single Smile Before Flowers) is the earliest stage adaptation of the legendary love of the poet-painter T'ang Yin 唐寅 (1470-1524) for a slave girl who had caught his fancy by her single smile. While the legend tells that T'ang Yin sold himself as slave to the household to which she belonged in order to approach her, Meng Ch'eng-shun changed the status of the slave-girl to that of an adopted daughter and had T'ang Yin hire himself out to the family as a clerk. Meng Ch'eng-shun's version inspired his friend Cho Jen-yüeh to his adaptation of this story as *Hua-fang yüan* 花舫緣 (Flower-boat karma). Meng Ch'eng-shun's most successful romantic comedy was his dramatic adaptation of an anecdote form Meng Ch'i's 孟啟 (*fl.* 841–886) *Pen-shih-shih* 本詩事* (The Original Incidents of Poems), entitled "Ts'ui Hu yeh-chiang" 崔護謁漿 (Ts'ui Hu Asks for Refreshment). This very popular anecdote had been adapted for the stage as a *tsa-chü* already a number of times, but none of these versions has been preserved. Meng Ch'eng-shun's version consists of five acts, and has singing roles for both Ts'ui Hu and the heroine, whom is given the name of Yeh Ch'in-erh 葉蓁兒. The play is preserved in two editions, an earlier version entitled *T'ao hua jen-mien* 桃花人面 (Peach Blossoms and a Lady's Cheeks; included in Shen T'ai's *Sheng Ming tsa-chü* of 1629), and a later version, revised by the author himself and entitled *T'ao-yüan san-fang* 桃源三訪 (Three Visits to Peach Fountain; included in his *Ku-chin ming-chü ho-hsüan* 古今名劇合選 of 1633). Critics especially praise the suite of songs of the second act, in which the heroine vents her love longing.

The two remaining *tsa-chü* are of a rather different kind. His *Ssu-li t'ao-sheng* 死裡逃生 (Escape from Death) may well have been based on a contemporary court case. The middle-ranking capital official Yang Tsung-hsüan 楊宗玄 retires all by himself to a Buddhist monastery in the Western Hills in order to nurse an eye ailment. While there, he discovers by chance that his friend, the abbot Liao-yüan 了緣, abducts and rapes female devotees, who are kept prisoner in a detached building on the monastery grounds. When Liao-yüan discovers that he has been found out, he has Yang locked up in a small room and orders him to commit suicide. However, during the night Yang escapes and with the help of some charcoal sellers he manages to elude the pursuing monks. Once has arrived safely in the capital, he has the women freed and the abbot executed. The play is remarkable for its realistic presentation of a contemporary incident; it is a scathing indictment of all forms of hypocrisy and power abuse. *Ssu-li t'ao-sheng* also shows the strongest influence of southern music among Meng Ch'eng-shun's *tsa-chü*.

Meng's *Ts'an T'ang tsai-ch'uang* 殘唐再創 (The Restoration of the T'ang–as it is known in the version in Meng Ch'eng-shun's *Ku-chin ming-chü ho-hsüan*) is also entitled *Ying-hsiung ch'eng-pai* 英雄成敗 (Success and Failure of Heroes) in the earlier version in Shen T'ai's *Sheng Ming tsa-chü*. Both titles reflect the action of the play: during the reign of Emperor Hsi-tsung 僖宗 (r. 874–888), the court is dominated by the evil eunuch T'ien Ling-tzu 田令孜 and the state examinations are turned into a corrupt farce. While Huang Ch'ao 黃巢 reacts by rebelling against the government, Cheng T'ien 鄭畋 retires to the countryside, biding his time. Eventually he is called to court and succeeds both in defeating Huang Ch'ao and in punishing T'ien Ling-tzu (who never appears on stage). Contemporary commentators of the play point out in their marginal notes that Meng Ch'eng-shun wrote this play during the T'ien-ch'i 天啟 reign (1621–1627) and that it was directed against the evil machinations of the at that time all-powerful eunuch Wei Chung-hsien 魏忠賢 (1568–1627).

Meng Ch'eng-shun's interest in *tsa-chü* also led him to publish in 1633 a selection of fifty-six Yüan and Ming plays, under the collective title *Ku-chin ming-chü ho-hsüan* 古今名劇合選 (A Collective Selection of Famous Plays from Past and Present), including four of his own plays. It was divided into two equal sections, one of plays representing a "manly heroic" (*hao-fang* 豪放) style, and one plays representing a "feminine graceful" (*wan-yüeh* 婉約) style, in order to prove that Northern plays and music were not merely "manly heroic." The preface to this collection and the many marginal notes to the plays included establish Meng Ch'eng-shun as one of the most important drama critics of his time. As a follower of T'ang Hsien-tsu 湯顯祖 (1550-1617)* rather than Shen Ching 沈璟 (1553–1610),* he stressed naturalness of expression over metrical regularity and insisted on *ch'ing* 情 (love, emotion, passion) as the well-spring of human action. Actions that were based on sincere passion, he argued, could not but be virtuous.

Three *ch'uan-ch'i* plays by Meng Ch'eng-shun have been preserved. His most ambitious and most successful attempt in this genre is *Chiao Hung chi* 嬌紅記 (The Tale of Wang Chiao-niang 王嬌娘 and Fei-hung 飛紅) of 1636. This play in fifty scenes is an adaptation of a classical tale of the same title (also known as *Chiao Hung chuan* 嬌紅傳) by a certain Sung Yüan 宋遠 (*fl.* 1280). This classical tale of the tragic love affair of the girl Wang Chiao-niang and her cousin Shen Ch'un 申純 (complicated by the initial jealousy of her father's concubine Fei-hung) enjoyed a great popularity in Yüan and Ming times, and also during the early Ch'ing dynasty. Of the many adaptations for the stage as a *tsa-chü* only the early Ming version by Liu Tui 劉兌 (*fl.* 1383)* has survived; of an earlier version as *ch'uan-ch'i* only fragments have come down to us.

Meng Ch'eng-shun in his version of the story adheres closely to the classical tale but focuses on the relation between Wang Chiao-niang and Shen Ch'un, while limiting the role of Fei-hung. After Wang Chiao-niang and Shen Ch'un have fallen in love, Shen Ch'un has his parents repeatedly ask for a marriage. Wang Chiao-niang's father is opposed because a marriage of cousins is against the law; by the time he is willing to consent, a powerful local family comes and asks for her and he gives in to their pressure. Wang Chiao-niang now dies, heart-broken, and Shen Ch'un soon follows her in death. Only in the celestial realm is the couple briefly united.

Since the 1980s critics in the People's Republic have hailed *Chiao Hung chi* as one of China's finest tragedies; in the development of the Chinese theory of love, they have assigned the play an intermediary role between *Mu-tan t'ing** and *Hung-lou meng.** In their analyses of Wang Chiao-niang they stress the fact that she insists on selecting her own partner and that she would rather run the risk of breaking the formal rules of ritual than ending up with an unattractive husband. They also stress that the love between Wang Chiao-niang and Shen Ch'un is not "love at first sight" but develops gradually. In the case of Shen Ch'un, they highlight the fact that he places love above success in the examinations; moreover, in this play (unlike e.g. *Hsi hsiang chi** or *Mu-tan t'ing)* success in the examinations does not bring about a happy marriage and this is seen as a sign of increasing realism. Critics diverge in their evaluation of the final scene.

Meng Ch'eng-shun's two other remaining *ch'uan-chi* have attracted less attention. His *Erh Hsü chi* 二胥記 (The Tale of Wu Tzu-hsü and Shen Pao-hsü) in thirty scenes may be compared to his earlier *Ying-hsiung ch'eng-pai* as it contrasts once again two heroes in their reaction to corruption. The play is yet another stage adaptation of the legend of Wu Tzu-hsü 伍子胥 and his revenge on the kings of Ch'u. Wu Tzu-hsü, whose father and elder brother have been unjustly killed by King P'ing 平 of Ch'u, flees the country and later returns at the head of the troops of Wu. As King P'ing has died in the meantime and as his successor has fled, Wu Tzu-hsü has the corpse of King P'ing exhumed and has it whipped to pieces. However, this scene is only the final scene of the first *chüan* of the play and Wu Tzu-hsü is only played by the *wai*. The main hero of the play is Shen Pao-hsü 申包胥, who retires from court during the reign of King P'ing and vows to restore the state of Ch'u once Wu Tzu-hsü has had his revenge. Shen treks to the state of Ch'in and weeps for seven days and nights in front of the palace gate until the King of Ch'in promises him the troops he needs to drive the army of Wu from the territory of Ch'u and reinstate the young king. While Wu Tzu-hsü is presented as an exemplar of filial piety (*hsiao* 孝), Shen Pao-hsü appears as an exemplar of loyalty (*chung* 忠); the loyalty of Shen Pao-hsü is mirrored in the fidelity and chastity of his wife during his absence.

The prefaces of *Erh Hsü chi* are dated to 1643. Hsü Shuo-fang (see *Studies* below) has recently argued that the play actually must have been written in the second half of 1644 or in early 1645, because it reflects the military history of those years. He detects a parallel between Shen Pao-hsü and Wu San-kuei 吳三桂 (1612–1678), who had aligned himself with the Manchus in order to avenge the death of the Ch'ung-chen 崇禎 emperor (r. 1628–1644) and who was in contemporary sources compared to Shen Pao-hsü. On the other hand, one may note that the barbarian nature of the state of Wu is consistently stressed by our author. As some Chinese generals had gone over to the Manchus after having been treated unfairly by the Ming court, the play may well have been written as an expression of concern over the growing Manchu menace even before 1644. The prefaces to *Chen-wen chi* 貞文記 (The Chaste Poetess) are dated to 1643, too, but in this case there is stronger evidence for a later date of composition. From statements in the prefaces it is clear that Meng Ch'eng-shun wrote this play after he had served as an Assistant Instructor in Sung-yang. Most likely therefore the play dates from 1656 or 1657. The costs of the printing were borne by Meng's friends in Shaohsing and Nanking. As the play evinces an outspoken Ming loyalism, the dates of the prefaces most likely were doctored in order to avoid suspicion of the authorities. The subject of the play was provided by the life and death of Chang Yü-niang 張玉娘, a poetess of local renown in Sung-yang, who lived during the second half of the thirteenth century. Meng Ch'eng-shun also had her collection of poetry, *Lan-hsüeh chi* 蘭雪集 (Orchids and Snow) printed and had a shrine erected at her grave.

Meng Ch'eng-shun set the action of this play of thirty-five scenes in the very first years of the Yüan, when Sung loyalist resistance fighters still engage in incidental actions. While Wang Chiao-niang insisted on making her own choice of a partner, Chang Yü-niang insists on marrying her original fiancé Shen Ch'üan 沈佺, even though she has never seen him (and will never see him for the duration of the play). However, her parents want to renege on the marriage contract because the Shens have fallen on hard times. The action is further complicated because of the interference of a certain Wang Chüan 王娟, the son of a high court official, who enlists the help of the local officials to press his marriage proposal. This comes to nothing because the district magistrate is killed by the Sung-loyalist general Wang Yüan-i 王遠宜 in a suicide action when he is on his way to the Chang family house with the wedding presents on behalf of Wang Chüan. Shen Ch'üan dies from grief; Chang Yü-niang, her two servant girls and her parrot follow him in death shortly thereafter.

As in his other plays, Meng Ch'eng-shun made great effort to enliven the stage action by the insertion of bustling scenes. (*Chiao Hung chi* includes, for example, an elaborately described medium séance and *Erh Hsü chi* includes a scene in which Master Sun 孫子 trains the palace ladies of Wu in military drill). *Chen-wen chi* includes among others one scene featuring a dragon boat race and another portraying the various exorcistic performances of First Night. Most remarkable in this respect is perhaps Meng's handling of the examination scene in *Chen-wen chi*. In *ch'uan-ch'i* the examination scene usually provided an opportunity for broad farce, but Meng Ch'eng-shun gave it a new twist by elaborating on the (widespread but mistaken) belief that the Yüan dynasty selected its officials by dramatic song and therefore has the examination candidates perform a potted version of Hsü Wei's 徐渭 (1521–1593)* *Nü chuang-yüan* 女壯元 (The Female Top Graduate).

Editions and References:
Sheng Ming tsa-chü includes *T'ao-hua jen-mien, Ssu-li t'ao-sheng,* and *Ying-hsiung ch'eng-pai. Ku-chin ming-chü ho-hsüan* includes *T'ao-yüan san-fang, Hua-ch'ien i-hsiao, Ts'an T'ang tsai-ch'uang,* and *Yen-erh-mei. Yen-erh-mei* was also included in *Tsa-chü san-chi* 雜劇三集; *Ts'an T'ang tsai-ch'uang* was also included in *Ssu-ta-ch'ih ch'uan ch'i* 四大癡傳奇.
All five *tsa-chü* have been photomechanically reproduced in Ch'en Wan-nai 陳萬鼐. *Ch'üan Ming tsa-chü* 全明雜劇. Taipei: Ting-wen, 1979), v. 9, pp. 5191-5454. *Ku-chin ming-chü ho-hsüan* has been reproduced as part of *Ku-pen hsi-chü ts'ung-k'an ssu-chi* (1957).
Chiao Hung chi, Erh Hsü chi, and *Chen-wen chi* have been reproduced in *Ku-pen hsi-ch'ü ts'ung-k'an erh-chi* (1955).
An annotated edition of *T'ao-hua jen-mien* may be found in Chou I-pai 周貽白, annot., *Ming-jen tsa-chü hsüan* 明人雜劇選. Peking: Jen-min Wen-hsüeh, 1962, pp. 485-510. An annotated edition of *Chiao Hung chi* has been provided by Ou-yang Kuang 歐陽光: Meng Ch'eng-shun, *Chiao Hung chi,* annot. by Ou-yang Kuang. Shanghai: Shang-hai Ku-chi, 1988. For another modern edition of this

play, see Wang Chi-ssu 王季思, ed., *Chung-kuo shih-ta ku-tien pei-chü chi* 中國十大古典悲劇集, Shanghai: Shang-hai Wen-i, 1982, pp. 343-500.

Studies:
Cheng, Jun 鄭閏. "Meng Ch'eng-shun pu-k'ao san-tse 孟稱舜樸考三則," *Hsi-ch'ü yen-chiu* 17 (1985): 272-79.
Chu, Ying-hui 朱穎輝. "Meng Ch'eng-shun hsin-k'ao 孟稱舜新考," *Hsi-ch'ü yen-chiu* 6 (1982): 193-217.
___. "Meng Ch'eng-shun *Chiao Hung chi* ti pei-chü mei" 孟稱舜嬌紅記的悲劇美, *Hsi-ch'ü yen-chiu* 8 (1983): 142-53.
Hsiao, Shan-yin 蕭善因 and Chang Ch'üan-t'ai 張全太. "I-pen ch'eng-ch'ien ch'i-hou ti ai-ch'ing pei-chü: *Chiao Hung chi* ho Yüan-tai ssu-ta ai-ch'ing-chü ti pi-chiao fen-hsi" 一本承前啟後的愛情悲劇嬌紅記和元代四大愛情劇的比較分析, *Chung-hua hsi-ch'ü* 2 (1986): 244-65.
Hsieh, Po-liang 謝柏梁. *Chung-kuo pei-chü shih-kang* 中國悲劇史綱. Shanghai: Hsüeh-lin, 1993, pp. 146-50.
Hsü, Shuo-fang 許朔方. "Lun Meng Ch'eng-shun ti hsi-ch'ü ch'uang-tso 論孟稱舜的戲曲創作," *Hsi-ch'ü yen-chiu* 33 (1990): 55-76.
___. *Wan Ming ch'ü-chia nien-p'u* 晚明曲家年譜. Hangchow: Che-chiang Ku-chi, 1993, v. 2, pp. 539-72.
Hu, Hsü-wei 胡緒偉. "Meng Ch'eng-shun ti tsu-nien chi ch'i hou-jen" 孟稱舜的卒年及其後人, *Hsi-ch'ü yen-chiu* 26 (1988): 63-65.
Itô, Sohei 伊藤漱平. "Formation of the *Chiao-hung chi:* Its Change and Dissemination," *Acta Asiatica* 32 (1977): 73-95.
Lo Ch'iu-chao 羅秋昭. *Meng Ch'eng-shun chi ch'i hsi-ch'ü yen-chiu* 孟稱舜及其戲曲研究. Taipei: Ch'i-yeh, 1990.
Ou-yang, Kuang 歐陽光. "Meng Ch'eng-shun ho t'a ti *Chiao Hung chi*" 孟稱舜和他的嬌紅記, in *Ku-tai hsi-ch'ü ts'ung-lun* 古代戲曲叢論. Canton: Chung-shan Ta-hsüeh, 1983, pp. 77-86.
Shen, Yao. "Ming-mo ku-tien chü-lun ti hsin pien-chang, Meng Ch'eng-shun pien chü li-lun tsung-shu" 明末古典劇論的新編章, 孟稱舜編劇理論綜述, *Hsi-chü yen-chiu* (1983): 167-86.
Su, Chen-yüan 蘇振元. "Meng Ch'eng-shun ho-shih tso *Chen-wen chi* 孟稱舜何時作貞

116

文記," *Hsi-ch'ü yen-chiu* 47 (1993): 67-71.

Tseng, Yung-i 曾永義. *Ming tsa-chü kai-lun* 明雜劇概論. Taipei: Hsüeh-hai, 1979, pp. 333-42.

Wang, Richard G. "The Cult of Qing: Romanticism in the Late Ming Period and in the Novel *Jiao Hong Ji*," *Ming Studies* 33 (1994): 12-55.

Wu, Kuo-ch'in 吳國欽 . *Chung-kuo hsi-ch'ü shih man-hua* 中國戲曲史漫話. Shanghai: Shang-hai Wen-i, 1980, pp. 208-11.

W. L. Idema
Leiden University

Pao-chüan 寶卷 (precious scrolls) were a form of written vernacular religious literature which flourished between the fifteenth and the early-twentieth centuries in China. Composed in the popular *shuo-ch'ang* 説唱 (spoken-and-sung or "prosimetric literature"—see the "Popular Literature" essay*) form, *pao-chüan* were read and recited through-out China, attracting an audience geographically and socially diverse. Lay religious leaders, storytellers, entertainers, and pious individuals used *pao-chüan* to transmit a wide variety of religious teachings and records of ritual actions through stories, songs, and sermons. *Pao-chüan* also reflected and recorded the vital world of the popular arts. The name *pao-chüan* had become the standard term for this literature by the eighteenth century; prior to that time some texts bore an alternate title, the most common of which was *ching* 經 (scripture). The vast majority of extant *pao-chüan* were produced by woodblock printing or hand-copying. Many of these texts open with engravings of Buddhas, Bodhisattvas, and other deities and almost without exception they include an invocation to the gods to descend and listen to the text during its presentation; the length and complexity of these invocations depend on the style of the particular *pao-chüan*. *Pao-chüan* drew on Confucian, Taoist, Buddhist, and folk resources to shape their vision of the world and paths for salvific action within that world. They are a prime source for the study of both religious culture and popular literature in the Ming and Ch'ing dynasties.

Scholars have discerned two distinct types of *pao-chüan*: the scriptural texts and the narrative, or story-telling, ones. This distinction is useful, but should not be adhered to too strictly, since both types thrived within the larger arena of popular religious literature, borrowing verse, story lines, tune titles etc. from the other literature within this arena. The scriptural texts, which flourished from the fifteenth through the mid-eighteenth century, exhibit a close affiliation with and imitation of Buddhist and Taoist scriptures, ritual penance texts (*ch'an* 懺), and other texts of institutional worship. Imitating some Buddhist scriptures, for instance, they are divided symmetrically into volumes (*chüan* 卷), and further into chapters (*p'in* 品) or sections (*fen* 分). The opening invocations in these *pao-chüan* are generally lengthy. There is usually one to the emperor, then to various deities and spirits, culminating in an invitation for the gods to descend to hear the text recited. The invocations are frequently accompanied by instructions for ritual burning of incense. Again in imitation of some Buddhist and Taoist scriptures, each chapter generally follows a fixed order: first a section of prose in which the substance of the chapter is introduced, then a section of verse, or series of verse sections, in seven- and ten-character lines, in which the content is repeated. These verse sections feature *tsan* 讚 (hymns), which are generally in seven-character verse, with a loose rhyme at the end of each double-line and *chieh* 偈 (*gatha*) which may begin with two couplets in seven-character verse, then switch to ten character verse. The chapters may end with a tune, bearing a title (*ch'ü-p'ai* 曲牌). Names of benefactors and/or contributors are often printed at the close of the *pao-chüan* or of each volume.

Many of the early scriptural *pao-chüan* served as the sacred scriptures of a variety of popular religious groups operating chiefly in north China; they have also been called sectarian *pao-chüan* because of their association with these groups. Lumped under the title "White Lotus" (*Pai-lien* 白蓮), these groups promulgated a heterodox mytho-history, organized outside the purview of the authorities, and were linked to a series of uprisings in the north. Recent research has suggested that despite their heterodox status, these groups were not opposed to the Confucian tradition, but in fact transmitted lay Confucian values. They directed their criticism against immoral officials who oppressed the rural people and were fiercely competitive with clergy of other religious groups and institutions, notably other sectarian leaders and Buddhist monks.

In style, the early scriptural *pao-chüan* are written in simple classical Chinese interlarded with written vernacular language and including some use of words transliterated from Sanskrit. These *pao-chüan* educate their audience in religious doctrine, mythical history, ritual practices, and moral behavior and generally contain detailed descriptions of purgatory. The stories they include, usually a hagiography of a god or a patriarch, are short, and the narrative line is curtailed by the rigid symmetry of the chapter's design. Their teachings are understood to be divinely revealed to the group's patriarch. The structure of these revelations at times bear close similarity to that of popular Taoist works such as the *T'ai-p'ing ching* 太平經. The earliest extant *pao-chüan*, published in 1430, promulgates a three-stage Maitreyan mythology which became one cornerstone of the sectarian *pao-chüan* tradition. This mythology features a female deity, known as *Mu* 母 (Mother), *Tsu-mu* 祖母 (Matriarch), or *Lao-mu* 老

母 (Venerable Mother). In the later sectarian *pao-chüan*, this mother deity becomes identified with Amitabha (*Amitofo* 阿彌陀佛), ruler of the Western Paradise. She despatches various emissaries to save her suffering children, the human race, in the Eastern world. The fullest expression of the Mother mythology is found in the *Ku-fo t'ien-chen k'ao-cheng Lung-hua pao-ching* 古佛天真考證龍華寶經 (The Precious Scripture on the Dragon Flower, as Verified by the Old Buddha of Heavenly Purity) published in 1654. Another stream within these *pao-chüan* are the *Wu-pu liu-ts'e* 五部六冊 (Five Books in Six Volumes) published in 1509 by lay Buddhist Lo Ch'ing 羅清 (1442–1527) and which became the sacred scriptures for the *Wu-wei chiao* 無為教 (Religion of Non-action). Lo's *pao-chüan* are influenced by Ch'an teachings, and focus more on meditation. These two streams, the quietist and the three-stage mythology, are intertwined in most sectarian *pao-chüan* after 1550. After 1750, few scriptural *pao-chüan* appeared, and those that did were usually reprints of earlier texts.

The narrative *pao-chüan* emerged before 1500 and changed significantly after 1850, after which point we have come to call them the later narrative *pao-chüan*. The narrative *pao-chüan* are generally not divided into discrete sections; they consist of one sustained narrative interspersed with sermons. The content of the narratives appears to have been drawn from a variety of sources: *pien-wen* 變文 (transformation texts—see *Tun-huang wen-hsüeh* ʾ), Buddhist scriptures, folk legends, and popular stories. The invocation(s) and benediction(s) of narrative *pao-chüan* were brief in comparison to those found in the scriptural *pao-chüan*. A common invocation found in these *pao-chüan* reads:

> The [. . .] *pao-chüan* has just been
> opened,

The myriad Buddhas and Bodhisattvas have drawn near.
The Eight Departments of Heavenly Dragons have come to
   support and protect,
To ensure that the masses are forever without disaster.

The narrative *pao-chüan* did not generally include hymns, gathas, or sacred verses. Instead, they were punctuated by salutations to the Buddha or the Bodhisattvas. The salutations were usually expressed in the formulaic saying, "I devote myself entirely to [one of the Buddhas or Bodhisattvas]" (*namo* 南無. . . *fo* 佛 or *p'u-sa* 菩薩). The sermons, delivered by a god, patriarch, or avatar to the unsaved within the story, served as a vehicle for explaining the fundamental points of doctrine. The religious function of these *pao-chüan* has yet to fully clarified. Nonetheless, even *pao-chüan* which retell popular stories ground them in a ritual setting, calling first on the gods to descend and witness the presentation. Furthermore, they generally speak in terms of good and bad, which are not simply moral language, but the language of salvation in this literature.

The early (i.e., before 1850) narratives are long (more than one-hundred folio pages is not uncommon), contain many words transliterated from Sanskrit, and although primarily storytelling texts, also contain lengthy sermons which expound upon doctrine. Many of these narratives feature pious heroines who refuse to marry, or who insist on living a virtuous life within marriage, stirring up a great conflict in their families, but eventually bringing the family to reconciliation and salvation. There are also numerous early narratives which recount the life of a deity or religious figure. The early narrative *pao-chüan* are more closely identified with the Buddhist tradition and may have been sponsored by religious organizations in order to preach to the laity. One of the most well-known of these early narratives, the *Hsiang-shan*

pao-chüan 香山寶卷 [The Precious Scroll on Fragrant Mountain] takes pains to clarify its role as a popular text which expounds the shallow teachings of *yin-yüan* 因緣 (karmic destiny), which it argues, must be employed in order to reach the common person. These narratives educated their audience in the lay Buddhist path, with emphasis on the five lay vows (*wu-chieh* 五戒) and recitation of the name of the Buddha (*nien-fo* 念佛), but these practices are grounded within more widely accepted beliefs of Chinese popular religion, such as the law of retribution. They may exhibit a closer link to *pien-wen* than the scriptural *pao-chüan*, but this link has not yet been fully demonstrated.

The recitation of the early narratives is described or referred to in Chapters 39, 73, 74 and 82 of the *Chin-p'ing mei** as well as other sources. As far can be told, they were generally either read or recited by two people, often women, one to tell the story, the other to interject salutations to the appropriate Buddha or Bodhisattva. The presentation of the *pao-chüan* was often followed by a vegetarian meal. There is some evidence that presentation of these *pao-chüan* was an important religious activity for vegetarian societies and the like.

The overwhelming majority of the later narratives, of which a sizable number remain extant, were shorter and less ornate than those from the earlier period and incorporated fewer sermons into the story line. Most of these texts were produced in the Wu-dialect area around Shanghai from the mid-nineteenth through the early twentieth centuries. The later *pao-chüan* were part of, or at least thrived in tandem to, a large and sophisticated entertainment culture that included a broad variety of spoken-and-sung performed arts. They traded story lines with *t'an-tz'u* 彈詞 (plucking rhymes or strummed lyrics)* and possibly other forms of spoken-and-sung art. Several cast their stories in a dramatic form, identifying their characters by the familiar dramatic terms of *cheng* 正, *tan* 旦, and so forth.

The later narrative *pao-chüan* demonstrate a shift to what C. K. Yang has called "diffuse religion." They were not used by an organized group in religious worship, nor did they espouse a unique or obviously identifiable set of teachings. Instead, they were broadly conceived to fit into the larger, universal institutions of Chinese life, the family, the community, and the state. Unlike their earlier counterparts, the later *pao-chüan* did not feature stories of gods and patriarchs but instead related the life stories of ordinary men and women who managed to achieve salvation for themselves and their families. Their heroes and heroines provided the audience with a model of a virtuous but ordinary person achieving salvation. These later *pao-chüan* refer to the realms of Heaven and Hell metaphorically. Paradisal mountain-tops are treated as if they are divine regions and the mundane prison plays a similar role to the dungeons of Hell in earlier *pao-chüan*. The later *pao-chüan* are extremely vague about religious practice, often merely mentioning certain familiar religious paths without explaining or describing them in depth. Most of the later *pao-chüan* were produced for mass circulation by booksellers and independent publishers. Performed in a broad array of venues, from the public stage of the marketplace to the private home, they shared their audience with the other art forms of the day. Although the mode of production changed, the understanding of its significance did not: while hand copying a text was understood to bring merit to the individual copyist, producing a text commercially was understood to generate merit for the business or family which sponsored the printing.

Editions and References
Chang Hsi-shun 張希舜, P'u Wen-ch'i 濮文

起, Kao K'o 高可, and Sung Chün 宋軍, eds. *Pao-chuan ch'u-chi* 寶卷初集. 40v. T'aiyüan: Shan-hsi Jen-min, 1994. A reprint of 148 titles.

Studies

Ch'e, Hsi-lun 車錫倫. "Chung-kuo tsui-tsao te *pao-chüan*" 中國最早的寶卷, *Chung-kuo wen-che yen-chiu t'ung-hsün* 6.3 (September 1996): 45-52.

Cheng, Chen-to 鄭振鐸. "Fo-ch'ü hsü-lu" 佛曲敍錄 in *Chung-kuo wen-hsüeh yen-chiu* 中國文學研究. Shanghai: Shang-hai Shu-tien, 1934 and 1981.

Hu, Shih-ying 胡世瑩. *T'an-tz'u Pao-chüan shu-mu* 彈詞寶卷書目. Peking: Ku-tien Wen-hsüeh, 1957.

Johnson, David. "Mu-lien in *Pao-chüan:* The Performance Context and Religious Meaning of the *Yu-ming Pao-chüan.*" In Johnson, ed. *Ritual and Scripture in Chinese Popular Religion: Five Studies*. Berkeley: Chinese Popular Culture Project, 1994, pp. 55-103.

Kuan, Te-tung 關德棟. *"Pao-chüan man-lu"* 寶卷漫錄. In his *Ch'ü-i lun-chi* 曲藝論集. Shanghai: Chung-hua, 1960, pp. 19-39,

Kerr, Janet Lynn. "Precious Scrolls in Chinese Popular Religious Culture, V. I and II." Unpublished Ph.D. dissertation, University of Chicago, 1994.

Li, Shih-yü 理世瑜. *Pao-chüan tsung-lu* 寶卷總錄. Shanghai: Chung-hua, 1960. Still the most comprehensive bibliography; lists 653 titles in 1,487 editions.

Nadeau, Randall. "Genre Classifications of Chinese Popular Religious Literature: *Pao-chüan,*" *Journal of Chinese Religions* 21 (Fall 1993): 121-128. Provides a helpful table of classifications of *pao-chüan.*

___. "The Domestication of Precious Scrolls, The *Ssu-ming Tsao-chün pao-chüan,*" *JCR* 22 (1996): 23-50.

Overmyer, Daniel. *Precious Volumes: An Introduction to Chinese Sectarian Scriptures from the Sixteenth and Seventeenth Centuries* (forthcoming from Harvard University Press). A comprehensive study of the scriptural *pao-chüan.*

___. "Attitudes Toward the Ruler and State in Chinese Popular Religious Literature: Sixteenth and Seventeenth Century *Pao-chüan,*" *HJAS* 44 (Dec. 1984): 347-379.

___. "Values in Sectarian Literature: Ming

and Ch'ing *Pao-chüan.*" In *Popular Culture in Late Imperial China.* David Johnson *et al.,* eds. Berkeley: University of California Press, 1985, pp. 219-254.

Sawada, Mizuho 沢田瑞穂. *Zôho Hôkan no kenkyû* 増補宝巻の研究. Tokyo: Kokusho Kankôkai, 1975.

Janet Lynn Kerr 林珍
Valparaiso University

Pien erh ch'ai 弁而釵 (Wearing a Cap But Also Hairpins) is a collection of four lengthy stories, each told over five chapters. These pieces provide a defense for and illustration of male homosexuality under the four rubrics of *ch'ing chen* 情貞 "loyalty in love," *ch'ing hsia* 情俠 "heroism in love," *ch'ing lieh* 情烈 "martyrdom in love," and *ch'ing ch'i* 情奇 "marvels in love." The author's pen-name, Tsui Hsi-hu Hsin-yüeh Chu-jen 醉西湖心月主人 (The Master Who Is Drunk with the Moon in the Middle of West Lake), points to a Hangchow writer, the same who wrote another pornographic work with a similar structure of four stories in twenty chapters, the *I ch'un hsiang chih* 宜春香質. Nai-ho t'ien a-a tao-jen 奈何天呵呵道人 (The Man of the Way Who Exclaims at Heaven's Fecklessness) offers a brief comment following each chapter.

Although each of the stories differs in theme, "Ch'ing-hsia chi" 情俠記 (Records of Chivalry in Love) may serve as an example of the style and structure. "Ch'ing-hsia chi" depicts Chang Chi 張機 ,handsome and well versed in both the literary and martial arts. After he is seen to win first place in the *hsiu-ts'ai* examination, the scene shifts to a bandit group in the nearby mountains. One of their leaders, Wang Fei-pao 王飛豹, is a righteous man who had turned to banditry after he killed a eunuch who had arranged to steal his wife. When Wang fled to the mountains he took both his two daughters, now fully grown. After attacking Chang's hometown, Wang decides to surrender to the government. He then matched with some of the government generals who excel in martial arts. Wang defeats these generals one after another until he meets Chang. Chang is able to overcome not only Wang, but also his daughters. As a result, Wang gives his daughters to Chang in marriage.

Not only Wang, but also another onlooker, Chung T'u-nan 鐘圖南 was impressed by Chang's powerful display. Chung fell in love with Chang, got him drunk, and seduced him. At first Chang was enraged, but over time accepted Chung's love. Together the two men passed the *chü-jen* examination. The men then separated, both passing the *chin-shih* examination and winning official posts. When Chang led troops to put down a rebellion in Shansi where Chung was serving, they revived their former love affair. Both were rewarded by the emperor for their role in putting down the rebellion. Several years later, after they had retired, Chang and Chung united their families through marriage, and the two clans enjoyed good relations for generations.

Though quite explicit in some of the love scenes, the author avoids coarse ribaldry and adapts the colloquial language to a rather elegant style interspersed with poetry. The elegance of the presentation in *Pien erh ch'ai* may allow it to be considered the masterpiece of Chinese homosexual fiction.

Though repeatedly prohibited, the book survived in three or more copies of the same late Ming edition, which may be the first one, with fourteen artistic, full-page illustrations. Copies are available in Taipei (Central Library), Peking (National Library), and Washington, D.C. (Library of Congress).

Editions and References
There is no modern critical edition of this

text.

Pien erh ch'ai. Pi-keng Shan-fang 筆耕山房 edition. Missing the preface and postface. Illustrated with 30 woodblock prints.

Translations

Lévy, André. *Épingle de femme sous le bonnet viril, Chronique d'un loyal amour.* Paris: Mercure de France, 1997. Contains the first story.

Studies

Hanan, Patrick. *The Chinese Vernacular Story.* Cambridge: Harvard University Press, 1981, p. 162. Brief critical comment.

Hsiao, Hsiang-k'ai 蕭相愷. *"Pien erh ch'ai,"* in *Hsiao-shuo tsung-mu t'i-yao,* p. 240. Gives a detailed description of the edition in Peking along with summaries of the three stories it contains.

Chung-kuo ku-tai hsiao-shuo pai-k'o ch'üan-shu 中國古代小說百科全書. Peking: Hsin-hua, 1993, p. 14.

André Lévy
University of Bordeaux

Po t'i 白體 (Po [Chü-i 居易] Style; also known as the Po Hsiang-shan t'i 白香山體, the Po Lo-t'ien t'i 白樂天體) was one of two poetic "schools" which have been identified by later critics as dominating Early Sung verse (the other school was the Late-T'ang style). Fang Hui 方回 (1227–1306), for example, claimed the following poets, primarily from the Five Dynasties' states of Nan T'ang 南唐, Wu-Yüeh 吳越, and Hou Chou 後周, wrote in the Po Style: Hsü Hsüan 徐鉉 (917–992), Hsü K'ai 徐鍇 (920–974), Li Fang 李昉 (925–996), Wang Ch'i 王奇 (*fl.* 1006–1016) and Wang Yü-ch'eng 王禹偁 (954–1001)*; later critics expanded the list to include T'ien Hsi 田錫 (940–1003), Sung Po 宋白 (936–1012), Li Hang 李沆(947–1004) and Li Chih 李至 (948–1001).

The problem with the label "Po t'i" is that it actually applies to two very different types of poetry, both written by Po Chü-i. Early Po-Style poets like

Hsü Hsüan, who served the Southern T'ang as Secretariat Drafter (*Chung-shu she-jen* 中書舍人) and the early Sung as Left Official in the Chancellery (*Tso Ch'ang-shih* 左常侍), and Li Fang, who was Vice Director of the Secretariat (*Chung-shu shih-lang* 中書侍郎) at the Sung court, were high officials and they emulated the poetic exchanges between Po Chü-i and Yüan Chen 元稹 (779–831)* which became known as the Yüan-Po t'i 元白體 (Style of Yüan and Po) during the Yüan-ho 元和 reign (806–820; also referred to as the Yüan-ho Style). Their verse form was, in imitation of Po and Yüan, primarily modern-style poetry and their content was restricted to personal concerns and events of their daily lives.

Representative of their works is a poem entitled "Hsien-k'o" 仙客 (Guests from the Otherworld) written by Li Fang to exalt five cranes he had domesticated:

Born in incubation, divine birds with
    a specialness innate;
What person brought you to the
    capital,
Accordingly titled you the beautiful
    "guests from the otherworld?"
You should keep company the idle
    man at home.
Startling the dew, your autumn cries
    reach far beyond the clouds,
Standing alone on the sand your
    shadow in the cloudless night is
    solitary under the moon.
To verdant fields thousands of miles
    across you will finally return–
Don't sigh that for a time you must
    gather with barnyard fowl.

胎化仙禽性本殊, 何人攜爾到京都,
因加美號為仙客. 稱向閑庭伴野夫,
驚露秋聲雲外遠, 翹沙晴影月中孤.
青田萬里終歸去, 暫處雞群莫嘆吁.

The explicitness and simplicity of expression demonstrates the poet's inheritance of Po's aesthetic pursuits during the Yüan-ho reign.

Although the style of such poems was

simple, this remained a personal genre created by an "in-group," admission to which depended upon socio-political contacts. The most famous collection of this type of the Po Style was the *Han-lin ch'ou-ch'ang chi* 翰林酬唱集, including works by Hsü Hsüan, Li Fang, and T'ang Yüeh 湯悦 (*fl.* 975), Prime Minister of Southern T'ang. Li Fang and Li Chih also collected their exchanges into the *Erh Li ch'ang-ho chi* 二李唱和集. Works by Wang Yü-ch'eng and Feng K'ang 馮伉 (d. 1000) became *Shang-yü ch'ang-ho chi* 商于唱和集.

But Wang Yü-ch'eng was a transitional figure in this style, since he was interested in another aspect of Po Chü-i's legacy–the social content of many of his poems. Raised in a poor family and having grown up among the common people, he had more sympathy for the lower levels of society than any of the other poets in the Po School. Thus his work, especially after a demotion in 991, begins to encompass two types of poems which represent two types of poems Po Chü-i himself wrote, modern-style poems for exchange with friends and colleagues, and socially conscious pieces intended to point out problems among the common people. His series of *yüeh-fu* 樂府* written during the early 990s exemplify the latter type.

Following the composition of the *Hsi-k'un ch'ou-ch'ang chi* 西崑酬唱集 (Anthology of Poems Exchanged in the Hsi-k'un Archives)* in the early tenth century, the euphuistic style of verse associated with Li Shang-yin 李商隱 (*ca.* 813–858)* dominated the poetic stage and the Po School died out, although exchanges in poems later in the dynasty were sometimes seen as a continuation of its influence.

Editions and References

Hsü, Hsüan 徐鉉. *Hsü-kung wen-chi* 徐公文集. 30 *chüan*. Supplement, 1 *chüan*. Hsü Nai-ch'ang 徐乃昌, comp. *Chiao-k'an chi* 校刊記 (Editorial Notes), 1 *chüan*. SPPY.

Li, Fang 李昉 and Li Chih 李至. *Erh-Li ch'ang-ho chi* 二李唱和集. 1 *chüan*; Supplement, 1 *chüan*. Hsü Nai-ch'ang, comp. *Chiao-k'an chi* (Editorial Notes), 1 *chüan* SPPY.

Wang, Yü-ch'eng 王禹偁. *Hsiao-hsü chi* 小畜集. 30 *chüan* Supplement, 1 *chüan*. *Wu-ying Tien Chü-chen* 武英殿聚珍 edition.

Translations

Forke, *Dichtungen*, 3:105-6, 4:47-48.

Liu and Lo, *Sunflower Splendor,* pp. 306-307.

Margouliès, *Anthologie raisonnée*, pp. 144-45 and 223-24.

Watson, *Earlier Chinese Poetry*, p. 333.

Wieger, *La Chine*, p. 228.

Studies

Chang, Pai-shan 張白山. "Lun Sung shih liu-p'ai" 論宋詩流派. In Chang's *Sung shih san-lun* 宋詩散論. Shanghai: Shang-hai Ku-chi, 1983, pp. 28-63.

Chang, Shu-hui 張蜀蕙. "Shih-lun Erh-Li ch'ang-ho chi yü Po Lo-t'ien shih chih kuan-hsi" 試論二李唱和集與白樂天詩之關係, *Chung-hua Hsüeh-yüan,* 43 (1993.3): 181-204.

Ch'en, Chih-o 陳植鍔. "Shih-lun Wang Yü-ch'eng yü Sung-ch'u shih-feng" 試論王禹偁與宋初詩風. *Social Sciences in China*, 14 (1982): 131-54.

Ch'en, Yin-k'o 陳寅恪. *Yüan Pai shih chien-cheng kao* 元白詩箋證稿. Rpt. Shanghai: Shang-hai Ku-chi, 1978.

Hsiung, Li-hui 熊黎輝. "Lun Sung-ch'u shih-t'an" 論宋初詩壇. *She-hui k'o-hsüeh chan-hsien,* 56 (1991.10): 310-6, 256.

Hsü, Kuei 徐規. *Wang Yü-ch'eng shih-chi chu-tso pien-nien* 王禹偁世跡著作編年. Peking: Chung-kuo She-hui K'o-hsüeh, 1982.

Yin Kung-hung 尹恭弘. "Lun Sung-ch'u te chu-yao shih-feng" 論宋初的主要詩風. In Yin's *Chung-kuo ku-tien wen-hsüeh lun-ts'ung* 中國古典文學論叢, 2 (1985): 87-103.

Yoshikawa, Kôjirô. "A Transitional Period at the Beginning of the Northern Sung," *An Introduction to Sung Poetry.* Burton Watson, trans. Cambridge, Mass.: Harvard University Press, 1967, pp. 49-85.

Chen Zhi
The National University of Singapore

The **Printing and Circulation of Literary Materials** are closely interrelated subjects in traditional China. It is difficult to determine how books circulated before the invention of printing, given the paucity of information extant today. One can only speculate, although the interference of modern conceptions lends possible misinterpretations.

The Development of Books. Indeed, in early China even the concept of the *book* is illusive to some degree, the word *shu* 書 meaning "writing" in general (as in *shu-fa* 書法 or "calligraphy") rather than a particular, named collection having a fixed content. For example, during the Chou period when large portions of textual material were commonly memorized for recitation during polite or political discourse, anecdotes and fables, songs, and dialogues appear essentially unchanged under different titles in several later compilations. A case in point is the material shared by *Tso-chuan** and the *Kuo-yü.** Similarly, during the Six Dynasties period the great degrees of overlap in contents between the numerous collections of *chih-kuai** and *chih-jen* 志人 texts demonstrate that there was no clear-cut sense of proprietorship over material bestowed by having it connected with a particular title or the name of an individual compiler. While there was far less debate about the authorship of poetry from the Han period onward, different compilations of poets' collected works, like less formal writings, varied widely in their length and their contents. The relative rarity of multiple copies of any given "work" was exacerbated by a lack of specificity in terminology: the term used to describe the length of a text, *chüan* 卷 ("roll"), was at best imprecise in denoting content.

The term *chüan* is a legacy of early book materials. Silk had been the medium of choice for hand-copied books from antiquity, as were long strips of bamboo tied together with strings to form bundles. Bamboo was heavy, comparatively speaking, but it was far cheaper. Both media could be rolled up for storage or transportation. The invention of paper is conventionally attributed to a eunuch official of the Han; certainly it was in widespread use by the third century and may have been a factor in the advent of individual poets. Paper was relatively inexpensive, light in weight making it easy to transport, and easy to write on. It was the perfect medium for the preservation of literature. But it is easily flammable, which contributed to the loss of imperial and other collections of books on numerous occasions from the Han period onward. Even so, paper production grew ultimately to became an important industry in many parts of the Lower Yangtze Region and Southeast China during the Ming and Ch'ing.

The Development of Printing. Recitation from memory, the collection and copying of texts by hand–these were the primary methods of transmitting hard-to-find books before the T'ang. But handcopied books assuredly did circulate: there were bookshops in the Han capital, Lo-yang during the lifetime of the philosopher Wang Ch'ung 王充 (27–*ca.* 100)**; bookstores were common in other major cities as well by the T'ang period. Yüan Chen 元稹 (779–831)* and his friend Po Chü-i 白居易 (772–846)* complained that others were trading copies of their poems for wine in Ch'ang-an; surely theirs and other literary works were being sold in manuscript copies and as rubbings from stone engravings. Soon afterward it became popular to circulate letters by well-known writers. Many of the extant early hand-copied books are religious or historical, not literary, texts, however.

By the eighth century a technological

breakthrough was becoming appreciated: block printing Buddhist charms on paper allowed the efficient reproduction of hundreds, even thousands, of identical copies. These charms spread widely during the T'ang, and so did the idea of printing by this means—not only in China but throughout East Asia. The oldest extant printed book is the *Chin-kang po-je p'o-lo-mi ching* 金剛般若波羅密經 (The Diamond Sutra; Sanskrit: *Vajracchedikâ-prajña-pâramitâ-sûtra*) of 868 discovered in a Tun-huang 敦煌 cave early in the twentieth century. By the tenth century printing had been recognized as an important means to standardize the Confucian texts; through the early Sung period most printed books were produced either by religious or by administrative units.

The process of block printing is relatively simple and easy to learn. First the text is written out—or the illustration drawn, or the chart constructed—in a fair hand, usually on thin ruled paper. When proofreading is completed and all corrections made, the clean copy is pasted face downward on a smoothed wooden board (during the Ming the size of these printing blocks came to be standardized at about ten by twenty inches and half an inch thick). A skilled carver then cuts away all but the black lines to a depth of around one-eighth of an inch, leaving the characters in relief. After sanding to remove these shreds of paper the block can be inked. Each sheet of paper patted against it will receive an imprint of the text; the quality of the print depends on the precision with which the block was carved and inked, the amount of wear on the printing surface, and the care with which the impression was made. Only one surface of a sheet of thin book paper was printed by this means. An experienced printer could pull 1500 or more copies from the same block during a single day; a printing block might be able to produce thousands of copies before becoming so

worn as to need touching up with the knife. Since few books except religious texts ever needed to be printed in such large quantities, the same blocks could be stored for later use, sold to another publisher, or planed smooth and recarved with a different text. Hundreds of thousands of Ming and Ch'ing printing blocks still exist today; the largest collection in China is in Yangchow.

Several of the states that arose following the fall of the T'ang furthered the cause of printing, especially those states in modern Szechwan. Among the most influential among these productions was an early tenth-century printed edition of the *Wen-hsüan** that inspired officials there and in Lo-yang to print the entire Confucian canon. Soon after the establishment of the Sung capital in K'ai-feng the National Academy began the publishing of commentaries on the Classics, encyclopedias, and literary collections. This office also produced an edition of the *Shih-ch'i shih* 十七史 (Seventeen [Dynastic] Histories) between 994 and 1063. The block printing of Buddhist scriptures had begun during the T'ang; it continues to the present day, particularly in Nanking. Religious merit was the impetus behind the production of scriptures; the government served its own ends by ensuring that standard editions of the Confucian texts were available for the developing civil-service examinations. Various levels of government during the Ming were involved in the production of more popular materials as well, ranging from almanacs through books on chess and music to the novels *Shui-hu chuan** and *San-kuo chih yen-i.** By the Ch'ing period most government publications were produced by the central court; among the most noteworthy are the "Palace editions" of the Wu-ying Tien in Peking, some of which were printed using moveable type, a relatively expensive—hence uncommon—way to publish books.

The Growth of the Publishing "Industry." During the Sung period Szechwan was joined as an important center of book printing by Fukien. The latter was well suited for the development of the trade: bamboo and other raw materials were in ample supply; so, too, was labor as the area became more culturally developed, especially during the Southern Sung. Fukien quickly took the lead in producing commercial editions, their lower prices—produced in part by shortcuts in production quality and physical appearance of the books—bringing them success in book markets throughout the realm. The collected works of well-known writers, *lei-shu** for practical needs, and school primers made up the bulk of early Fukien editions. Yet as they became more numerous, the reputation of privately produced Fukien editions suffered because of their shoddy materials and workmanship, their many wrong or miswritten characters, and the possibility that the text had been truncated to reduce costs further. Even so, Fukien printers were enormously successful as family enterprises; the Yü 余 family of Chien-yang 建陽 were prominent for over 700 years.

The most commonly known Fukien editions are illustrated; the characteristic format was *shang-t'u hsia-wen* 上圖下文 (illustrations above, text below) used in numerous popular editions, especially fiction and plays. Early examples are the uniform set of *p'ing-hua** published in Chien-yang 1321–1323, although novels in similar format—most frequently having illustrations considerably lower in quality—began appearing in considerable numbers from around 1550. Presumably because of the popularity of these editions, and the financial success it entailed, craftsmen from Fukien made their way to the southern Ming capital, Chin-ling 金陵 (modern Nanking) where they began to produce books in similar format. As the center of the Kiangnan or lower Yangtze cultural cities, Nanking attracted literati from around the country —and wealthy merchants as well. Consequently more books were produced there during the Ming than in Fukien. Various Nanking publishing houses managed by members of the T'ang 唐 family, including the Fu-ch'un T'ang 富春堂 and the Shih-te T'ang 世德堂, produced large collections of *ch'uan-ch'i* plays* in illustrated editions. But the finest editions of the Ming were produced elsewhere, in Hangchow and Soochow, as talented block carvers and illustrators moved there from Hui-chou 徽州 (modern She-hsien 歙縣) in Anhwei. By the last few decades of the Ming, it was fashionable to print illustrations in books of all types; their finest examples share many features with the paintings of commercial artists of the period. Consequently the album of blockprinted illustrations became very popular; the most outstanding are illustrated anthologies of famous poems. In such editions especially, the interaction of the arts of the brush (reflected in carefully reproduced calligraphy and in finely detailed illustrations) must be considered integral parts of the total aesthetic experience afforded the reader of the literary work. This is particularly true in the album-anthologies approaching the standards of well-executed paintings that have poems inscribed on them. One such example is *T'ang shih hua-p'u* 唐詩畫譜 produced around 1600 by Huang Feng-ch'ih 黃鳳池, each illustration of which—in the style of a well known painter—is faced by a famous T'ang poem written in a fine hand and signed by a contemporary scholar of note.

Equal in importance to the commercial publishing houses were the efforts of individual literati to publish their own writings or those of their forebears, friends, or famous poets of the past. These private editions are known for their careful editing and proofreading as well as for the high quality of their paper, ink, and carving. Many are very attractive and were produced in limited quantities.

Although the production of books continued to grow rapidly during the Ch'ing period, their quality as aesthetic objects generally fell. This is a function of two factors. First, the commercial publishing industry had been severely damaged during the devastation wrought on the lower Yangtze cities during the Manchu conquest. But publishing recovered; probably the more far-reaching cause was the rapid growth of reading audiences and the attendant rise in the demand for popular reading materials. Ch'ing printing on the whole is thus characterized by ever more characters printed on ever smaller paper; even the quality of the paper declined, both in texture and in lightness of color as bamboo became the most common ingredient for paper making. Only the Manchu Court and the private literati printers continued to produce fine editions, which were avidly sought after by connoisseurs and collectors.

Court printers firmly established Peking as a leading center of the book trade during the Ch'ing period. Liu-li-ch'ang 琉璃廠, just outside the Front Gate of the city, was lined with curio shops and bookstores, a situation that renovators have tried to duplicate today. But the introduction of Western printing technology again shifted the focus of publishing to the coastal cities, particularly Shanghai, by the end of the nineteenth century. Lithographic printing quickly came to dominate the book trade there; books could be produced by lithography with small yet very detailed illustrations and with extremely small type. If the standardization and professionalization of woodblock printing was involved in the development of the novel during the Ming, surely lithography played a role in the explosive development of the novel once more during the last decades of Ch'ing rule. Likewise, China's periodical press began

at that time, as did the widespread modernization of its literature, resulting in the literary "revolutions" of the twentieth century.

The Persistence of Manuscript Editions. However, as book printing became ever more common from the late-sixteenth century onward, certain books continued to be circulated only in manuscript copies, presumably to insure that they were not available to large numbers of readers. Such books were private collections of poems, literati plays in the *ch'uan-ch'i** form that were intended more to be dramatized anthologies of verse than performable theatricals, and a few novels. Some books were copied by hand because printed copies could not be found; their production filled gaps in the collections of wealthy book collectors who could afford to hire a scribe. Like the plays, the works of fiction that circulated in manuscript were the artistically more complex works known generally as "literati novels," some of which had content that at least initially mitigated against wide circulation. A case in point is *Chin P'ing Mei** which was printed in 1618 (perhaps only after the author's death), although Yüan Hung-tao* and his brothers had circulated a copy nearly twenty years previously. During the Ch'ing period other novels circulated in manuscript; they include as extreme example *Ch'i-lu teng** by Li Lü-yüan (1707–1790) fully published only in 1980, *Ju-lin wai-shih** by Wu Ching-tzu (1701–1754) first published in 1803, *Yeh-sou p'u-yen* 野叟曝言 (An Old Rustic's Idle Talk) by Hsia Ching-ch'ü 夏敬渠 (1705–1787) published in 1881, and of course the greatest of novels *Hung-lou meng** by Ts'ao Hsüeh-ch'in (1715?–1763?),* of which a variety of manuscript editions circulated for three decades after the author's death until it was first published in 1792. These novelists, like the dramatists who wrote plays to be read rather than performed, were amateur writers; they did not support themselves with their pens, nor did they necessarily have access to the financial backing needed to print a lengthy text. Furthermore, they were produced for discerning and sophisticated readers, not the general reading audiences that supported the publishing industry from the late-sixteenth century onward. Thus as printing became common to the point of vulgarity, the circulation of intensely personal texts in manuscript format among very limited circles of acquaintances continued to serve the aesthetic purposes of the elite.

Calligraphic Styles of Printed Characters. Through the Sung period printed texts were made to resemble in appearance the style of one of three great T'ang period calligraphers, including Ou-yang Hsün 歐陽詢 (557–641, known for his early *lei-shu** entitled *Pei-t'ang shu-ch'ao* 北堂書抄, *ca.* 620). By the fifteenth century the model, both for court documents and for fine quality printed books, was the style of the talented painter Chao Meng-fu 趙孟頫 (1254–1322). But while this style with its curving lines and gracefully varied strokes was pleasing to the eye, it was difficult to carve quickly on a printing block. Consequently by the middle of the sixteenth century, most books were being printed in what was known as the *fang Sung-t'i* 方宋體 (square Sung) or *chiang-t'i tzu* 匠體字 (craftsman) style of characters. These narrow graphs, elongated from top to bottom, consist of regular straight lines that are relatively quick and easy to carve; they became the standard for the texts of nearly all published works; more attractive calligraphic styles being reserved for prefaces and title pages.

Book Illustrations. Even though the texts of Ming period printed books were less appealing visually, other changes during the Ming were to produce distinctive new achievements. The most obvious is the use of increasingly fine quality illustrations in books of nearly every kind; however, perhaps the greater contribution of the Ming was the enormous increase in book production, particularly of literary texts. Some early printed books, such as the Buddhist sutras, had customarily been illustrated while others, such as the Confucian classics, had not. The Sung period saw the production of a few books on technical subjects most easily explained through the use of illustrations; likewise, moralistic tracts designed for the less well educated also carried exemplary pictures. The *Mei-hua hsi-shen p'u* 梅花喜神譜 (The Plum: A Portrait Album, 1261) was unprecedented: it contains one-hundred illustrations with brief poetic commentaries and may well have served as the model for the blockprinted albums that became popular during the late Ming. Perhaps the most beautifully printed play was the 1640 edition of *Hsi-hsiang chi** printed by Min Ch'i-chi 閔奇伋 (1580–after 1661); Min utilized multiple printing blocks and dampened paper to produce striking polychromatic illustrations. Some of the finest illustrations in terms of design and execution appear in the collection of lyrics compiled by the Soochow poet and calligrapher Wang Chih-teng 王稺登 (1535–1612) entitled *Wu sao chi* 吳騷集 (A Collection of Songs from Wu [i.e., *tz'u**], 1614) and its sequel (printed in 1616). Several albums of illustrations of the central characters of *Shui-hu chuan* appeared; the most widely appreciated is the work of the professional artist Ch'en Hung-shou 陳洪綬 (Ch'en Lao-lien 陳老蓮, 1598–1652) with inscriptions by the scholar-official Wang Tao-k'un 汪道昆 published in 1653.

Editions produced during the Sung have been viewed as the most important ever since; extensive work on cataloguing extant books from this period has produced printed bibliographies in China and elsewhere and a growing on-line catalogue of Chinese rare books through the RLIN bibliographic network. Sung imprints are generally considered the standard by which the quality of all later editions are judged: Sung publishers were officially required to print their names on all of their imprints, presumably to encourage faithful reproduction of the books' real contents. They competed as well in making their books physically attractive; the calligraphy of various famous scholars was used as a model for their printed type. Likewise, many Sung period books carried one or more illustrations, a practice that was to contribute to the boom in publishing during the Ming period. The general regard among bibliophiles for Sung editions, especially as they became more and more rare, drove the prices for originals upward and, during the Ch'ing and modern periods, inspired the reprinting of many, either by woodblock or by more modern techniques.

Book Collecting. The advent of printing did not immediately produce an explosion in the number of books. As the late Ch'ing bibliophile Yeh Te-hui 葉德輝 (1864–1927) has pointed out:

From Sung and Yüan times scholars have been far more fortunate than the ancients in having access to books; in the Ch'ing dynasty those of the Ch'ien-lung (1736–1795), Chia-ch'ing (1796–1820), and later periods had an especially liberal share of this good fortune. At the end of the Five Dynasties (907–959) and the beginning of the Northern Sung (960–1127) even standard texts of the Classics and Histories seldom circulated in printed form; unless a man had great means, the collecting of books could not be thought of. Even after printed books came into being, there were no facilities for collecting them in one place; men of means themselves did not find it easy to search for and obtain them. The ancients gloried in having a peep at the palace library and reading the

books of "Lao's Collection." We nowadays, however, can obtain several voluminous sets in a single day, provided that we have the means at our command.

(Yeh Te-hui, "Bookman's Decalogue," p. 147; Achilles Fang's note 81, p. 166 [see the section in the bibliography entitled, "General Studies of Book Production, Collection, and Circulation," below], explains that Lao's Collection, 老氏藏, refers, by allusion to the *Hou Han shu* 後漢書, to books in the palace library.) While Yeh surely overstates the case, major private collections of literary materials became practical to assemble only in fairly recent times, from the late Ming period onward. Fortunately the bibliographies of major private collections remain; reprints of them can be found in all major library collections today. Several late-Ch'ing scholars and bibliophiles wrote extensively on book collecting and collections; in addition to Yeh Te-hui, perhaps the most outstanding is Yeh Ch'ang-chih 葉昌熾, whose *Ts'ang-shu chi-shih shih* 藏書紀事詩 was published in 1910.

Bookbinding. The Tun-huang *Diamond Sutra* had been bound in scroll format, its seven sheets of paper glued together end to end to form a continuous roll nearly sixteen feet in length. But this was a cumbersome format for any reader who did not wish to proceed systematically from its beginning to the end. By the Northern Sung period Ou-yang Hsiu* noticed that scroll mounted books were disappearing, a change that he applauded. By his time some books were bound in *ching-che-chuang* 經摺裝 (sutra-binding) by folding long sheets of paper accordion-style; a second format, *hu-tieh-chuang* 蝴蝶裝 (butterfly binding), utilized separate sheets of paper folded in the center with the text inward and glued to each other along the fold. While both allowed the book to lie flat while being read, there was a tendency for "butterfly bound" pages to fall out. Books bound in this second format were popular during the Yüan period and the early Ming. By the middle of the Ming, however, this format became nearly exclusively reserved for albums of printed pictures; most other books were produced utilizing the sewn back or *hsien-chuang* 線裝 (literally "string binding") format. This binding produces the flexible fascicles that became the standard until the twentieth century: such books can as easily lie flat for lengthy scrutiny as they can have their pages turned quickly for a fast skimming. Likewise, the presence of glue in stiff spine and "butterfly" bindings attracted insects to a far greater degree than did string-bound volumes, as Yeh Te-hui points out (Yeh Te-hui, p. 142). It may not be coincidental that relatively standard characters for easy reading, a binding format that accommodated any type of reading, and the popularity of vernacular fiction all appeared during the middle of the sixteenth century. String binding prevailed after the introduction of Western-style lithographic printing; books bound with hard covers in the European style began to be common only after the fall of the Ch'ing dynasty.

Important Bibliographical Studies:

Ah, Ying 阿英, comp. *Wan Ch'ing hsi-chü hsiao-shuo mu* 晚清戲劇小説目. Shanghai: Wen-i Lien-ho, 1954.

An, P'ing-ch'iu 安平秋 and Chang P'ei-heng 章培恆, eds. *Chung-kuo chin-shu ta-kuan* 中國禁書大觀. Shanghai: Shang-hai Wen-hua, 1990.

Ch'en, Po-hai 陳伯海 and Chu I-an 朱易安, comp. *T'ang shih shu-lu* 唐詩書錄. Tsinan: Ch'i-Lu Shu-she, 1988.

Chiang, Liang-fu 姜亮夫. *Ch'u-tz'u shu-mu wu-chung* 楚辭書目五種. Peking: Chung-hua, 1961.

Chung-kuo ku-chi shan-pen shu-mu 中國古籍善本書目. 5 Collections. Shanghai: Shang-hai Ku-chi, 1985-.

Chung-kuo t'u-shu wen-shih lun-chi 中國圖書文史論集. Taipei: Cheng-chung, 1991;
Peking: Hsien-tai, 1992. *Festschrift* for T. H. Tsien on his 80th birthday.

Denda, Akira 伝田章, comp. *Meikan Gen zatsugeki Seisô ki mokuroku* 明刊元雑劇西廂記目録. Tokyo: Tôkyô Daigaku Tôyô Bunka Kenkyûjo Fuzoku Tôyôgaku Bunken Sentâ, 1970.

Ho, Tz'u-chün 賀次君. *Shih-chi shu-lu* 史記書錄. Peking: Shang-wu, 1958.

Hu, Wen-pin 胡文彬. *Chin P'ing Mei shu-lu* 金瓶梅書錄. Shenyang: Liao-ning Jen-min, 1986.

Kuo-li Chung-yang T'u-shu-kuan Sung-pen t'u-lu 國立中央圖書館宋本圖録. Taipei: Chung-hua Ts'ung-shu Wei-yüan-hui, 1958.

Ma, T'i-chi 馬蹄疾, comp. *Shui-hu shu-lu* 水滸書錄. Shanghai: Ku-chi, 1986.

Ôtsuka, Hidetaka 大塚秀高. *Zôho Chûgoku tsûzoku shôsetsu shomoku* 増補中国通俗小説書目. Tokyo: Kyûko Shoin, 1987.

Shih, T'ing-k'ang 施廷鏞. *Chung-kuo ku-chi pan-pen kai-yao* 中國古籍板本概要. Tientsin: T'ien-chin Ku-chi, 1987.

Sun, K'ai-ti 孫楷第. *Hsi-ch'ü hsiao-shuo shu-lu chieh-t'i* 戲曲小説書錄解題. Peking: Jen-min Wen-hsüeh, 1990.

___. *Jih-pen Tung-ching so-chien Chung-kuo hsiao-shuo shu-mu* 日本東京所見中國小説書目. 1932. Rpt. Hong Kong: Shih-yung, 1967.

___. *Chung-kuo t'ung-su hsiao-shuo shu-mu* 中國通俗小説書目. Rev. edition, 1958. Rpt. Hong Kong: Shih-yung, 1967.

Ts'ui, Fu-chang 崔富章, ed. *Ch'u tz'u shu-mu wu-chung hsü-pien* 楚辭書目五種續編. Shanghai: Shang-hai Ku-chi, 1993.

Tu, Hsin-fu 杜信孚. *Ming-tai pan-k'o tsung-lu* 明代版刻綜録. Yangchow: Chiang-su Kuang-ling K'o-yin-she, 1983.

Wan, Man 萬曼. *T'ang-chi hsü-lu* 唐集敍録. Peking: Chung-hua, 1980.

Wang, Chung-min 王重民. *Chung-kuo shan-pen-shu t'i-yao* 中國善本書提要. Shanghai: Shang-hai Ku-chi, 1983.

___, comp. *A Descriptive Catalogue of Rare Chinese Books in the Library of Congress.* 2v. Washington, D.C.: Library of Congress, 1957.

Wu, Han 吳唅. *Chiang-Che tsang-shu-chia shih-lüeh* 江浙藏書家史略. Peking: Chung-hua, 1981. A dictionary of about 800 famous book collectors in Kiangsu and Chekiang.

Studies of Printers and Printing

Chang, Hsiu-min 張秀民. *Chung-kuo yin-shua shih* 中國印刷史. Shanghai: Shang-hai Jen-min, 1989.

Chia, Lucille. "Printing for Profit: The Commercial Publishers of Jianyang, Fujian (Song-Ming)." Unpublished Ph.D. dissertation, Columbia University, 1996.

Edgren, Sören, ed. *Chinese Rare Books in American Collections*. New York: China Institute in America, 1984.

Fang, P'in-kuang 方品光, ed. *Fu-chien pan-pen tz'u-liao hui-pien* 福建版本資料彙編. Mimeograph ed., Fu-chien Shih-fan Ta-hsüeh T'u-shu-kuan, 1979.

Hsiao, Tung-fa 蕭東發. "Chien-yang Yü-shih k'o-shu k'ao-lüeh" 建陽余氏刻書考略, *Wen-hsien* 21 (1984): 230-247; 22 (1984): 195-219; 23 (1985): 236-250.

———, "Ming-tai hsiao-shuo-chia, k'o-shu-chia Yü Hsiang-tou" 明代小説家刻書家余象斗, *Ming Ch'ing hsiao-shuo lun-ts'ung* 1986.4: 195-211.

Huang, Shang 黃裳. *Ch'ing-tai pan-k'o i-yü* 清代版刻一隅. Tsinan: Ch'i-Lu Shu-she, 1992.

Li, Chih-chung 李致忠. *Li-tai k'o-shu k'ao-shu* 歷代刻書考述. Chengtu: Pa-Shu Shu-she, 1989.

Martinique, Edward. *Chinese Traditional Bookbinding: A Study of its Evolution and Techniques*. Taipei: Chinese Materials Center, 1983.

Nagasawa, Kikuya 長沢規矩也. *Zukai Wa Kan insatsushi* 図解和漢印刷史. Tokyo: Kyûko Shoin, 1976. 2v.: *Kaisetsuhen* 解説編, *Zurokuhen* 図録編.

Tsien, Tsuen-hsuin 錢存訓. *Chung-kuo shu-chi, chih-mo chi yin-shua shih lun-wen chi* 中國書籍紙墨及印刷史論文集. Hong Kong: Chinese University Press, 1992.

———. *Paper and Printing*. Vol. V, Part I, of *Science and Civilisation in China*. Joseph Needham, ed. Cambridge, England: Cambridge University Press, 1985.

Twitchett, Denis. *Printing and Publishing in Medieval China*. New York: Frederic C. Beil, 1983. Ger. transl. (Hartmut Walravens, *Druckkunst und Verlagswesen im mittlealterlichen China*, Wiesbaden: Harrassowitz, 1994) appends Helwig Schmidt-Glintzer's "Die Authentizität der Handschrift und ihr Verlust durch die Einführung des Buckdrucks," pp. 82-103.

Wang, Chao-wen 王肇文. *Ku-chi Sung Yüan k'an-kung hsing-ming so-yin* 古籍宋元刊工姓明索引. Shanghai: Shang-hai Ku-chi, 1990.

Wei, Yin-ju 魏隱儒. *Chung-kuo ku-chi yin-shua shih* 中國古籍印刷史. Peking: Yin-shua Kung-yeh, 1984.

Widmer, Ellen. "The Huanduzhai of Hangzhou and Suzhou: A Study in Seventeenth-Century Publishing," *HJAS* 56.1 (1996): 77-122.

Wu, K. T. "Chinese Printing Under Four Alien Dynasties," *HJAS* 13 (1950): 447-523.

———. "Ming Printing and Printers," *HJAS* 7 (1942): 203-260.

General Studies of Book Production, Collecting, and Circulation

Brokaw, Cynthia. "Commercial Publishing in Late Imperial China: The Zou and Ma Family Businesses of Sibao, Fujian," *Late Imperial China* 17.1 (1996): 49-92.

Cherniack., Susan. "Book Culture and Textual Transmission in Sung China," *HJAS* 54 (1994): 5-125.

Chia, Lucille. "The Development of the Jianyang Book Trade, Song-Yuan." *Late Imperial China* 17.1 (1996): 10-48.

Drege, Jean-Pierre. *Les bibliothèques den Chine au temps des manuscrits (jusqu'au Xe siècle)*. Paris: École Française d'Extrême-Orient, 1991. *Publ. de l'EFEO*, CLXI.

Fu, Hsi-hua 傅惜華, ed. *Chung-kuo ku-tien wen-hsüeh pan-hua hsüan-chi* 中國古典文學版畫選集. 2v. Shanghai: Shang-hai Jen-min Mei-shu, 1981.

Han, Hsi-to 韓錫鐸 and Wang Ch'ing-yüan 王清原, eds. *Hsiao-shuo shu-fang lu* 小説書坊錄. Shenyang: Ch'un-feng, 1987.

Hegel, Robert E. *Reading Illustrated Fiction in Late Imperial China*. Stanford: Stanford University Press, 1997.

Kobayashi, Hiromitsu 小林宏光. *Chûgoku no hanga—Tôdai kara Seidai made* 中国の版画唐代から清代まで. Tokyo: Tôshindô 東信堂, 1995.

Lai, Hsin-hsia 來新夏. *Chung-kuo ku-tai t'u-shu shih-yeh shih* 中國古代圖書事業史. Shanghai: Shang-hai Jen-min, 1990.

Lee, Thomas H. C. "Books and Bookworms in Song China: Book Collection and the Appreciation of Books," *JSYS* 25 (1995): 193-218.

Li, Chih-chung 李致忠. *Chung-kuo ku-tai shu-chi shih* 中國古代書籍史. Peking: Wen-wu, 1985.

Mote, Frederick W. and Hung-lam Chu. *Calligraphy and the East Asian Book. The Gest Library Journal* 2.2 (Princeton University, 1988). Special issue.

Ôki, Yasushi 大木康. "Minmatsu Kônan ni okeru shuppan bunka no kenkyû" 明末江南における出版文化の研究, *Hiroshima Daigaku Bungakubu kiyô* 50.1 (1991): 1-175. Special issue.

Sun, Tien-ch'i 孫殿起. *Liu-li-ch'ang hsiao-chih* 琉璃廠小志. Peking: Pei-ching Ku-chi, 1982.

Swann, Nancy Lee. "Seven Intimate Library Owners," *HJAS* 1 (1936): 363-390.

Wang, Li-ch'i 王利器, comp. *Yüan Ming Ch'ing san-tai chin-hui hsiao-shuo hsi-ch'ü shih-liao* 元明清三代禁毀小説戲曲史料. Rev. ed., Shanghai: Shang-hai Ku-chi, 1981.

Wu, K. T. 吳光清. "Libraries and Book Collecting in China Before the Invention of Printing." *T'ien Hsia Monthly* 5.3 (1937): 237-260.

Yeh, Ch'ang-chih 葉昌熾. *Ts'ang-shu chi-shih shih* 藏書紀事詩. 1910; Rpt. Shanghai: Ku-tien Wen-hsüeh, 1958.

Yeh, Te-hui 葉德輝. "Bookman's Decalogue (*Ts'ang-shu shih-yüeh* 藏書十約), trans. Achilles Fang. *HJAS* 13 (1950): 132-173.

___. *Shu-lin ch'ing-hua* 書林清話. Changsha: Kuan-ku T'ang, 1920; Rpt. Taipei: Wen-shih-che, 1973.

Important Reproductions of Rare Editions

Cheng, Chen-to 鄭振鐸, comp. *Chung-kuo ku-tai pan-hua ts'ung-k'an* 中國古代版畫叢刊. 4v. Shang-hai: Ku-tien Wen-hsüeh, 1958. Rpt. Shanghai: Shang-hai Ku-chi, 1988.

Ch'ien, Ch'ien-i 錢謙益. Chi Chen-i 季振宜, comp. *Ch'üan T'ang shih kao-pen* 全唐詩稿本. 760 *chüan*. Protoreprinted, Taipei: Lien-ching, 1979.

Huang, Feng-ch'ih 黃鳳池. *T'ang shih hua-p'u* 唐詩畫譜. *Ca.* 1600. Rpt. Shanghai: Shang-hai Ku-chi, 1982.

Ku-pen hsi-ch'ü ts'ung-kan 古本戲曲叢刊. Series 1-9. Shanghai: Shang-wu, 1954–1958.

Ku-pen hsiao-shuo chi-ch'eng 故本小説集成. Shanghai: Shang-hai Ku-chi, 1990–1992.

Ming Ch'eng-hua shuo-ch'ang tz'u-hua ts'ung-k'an 明成畫説唱詞話叢刊, ed. Shanghai Museum. Peking: Wen-wu, 1979.

Sung-k'o Mei-hua hsi-shen p'u 宋刻梅花喜神譜. Sung Po-jen 宋伯仁, comp. Peking: Wen-wu, 1982.

Robert E. Hegel
Washington University

P'u Meng-chu 浦夢珠 (also known as Ho-shuang 合雙, late eighteenth century) has only a sequence of nine *tz'u*** lyrics to the tune of "Lin-chiang hsien" 臨江仙 (Immortal by the River) that are extant. What distinguishes P'u from most traditional women poets is that her extant work presents a fairly complete autobiographical account of her life as a professional embroiderer.

The first poem of the series goes back to P'u's early childhood, when she first started to learn embroidery. The embroidery stand was "as tall as I," and she was so small that she could not even tell the "four corners of the floral design" or figure out "how to get to the center" of the embroidery. However, the poem depicts more than P'u's initiation to the art of embroidery; it also suggests her innocence in matters of the heart: "I did not recognize mandarin ducks/And wondered why the other girls/Never tired of embroidering them in pairs."

The second poem continues the first. An adorable girl, P'u was praised for her silken hair and for being "clever and smart." The poem depicts a childhood scene in vivid details: playing games with siblings and relatives at night, "We shuttled among flower shadows–/Afraid that our clogs might be heard,/We climbed up the stairs in our stockings."

Although her age is unclear, in the third poem are suggestions of an awakening of romantic desires in a young woman. Quite innocently the poem depicts a boating episode. When she and her companions were about to board an "orchid boat" for a ride on a lake with lotus flowers, a gust of wind blew the boat to the lakeside. Understandably dispirited, P'u says: "I cared not to pick any purple water caltrops,/For I resented their endless silken fibers—/Their nature is to entangle you." "Silken fibers" is a common pun in traditional poetry: one homonym of "silk" (*ssu* 糸) means "thoughts" (ssu 思), especially thoughts of love (as in "*ch'ing-ssu*" 情思). It seems that P'u was already "entangled" in thoughts of love.

This is confirmed by poem number four, which begins with P'u "secretly praying to the Lover Stars on the Double-Seventh Eve." The allusion evokes the ancient folktale of Cowherd Boy and Weaver Maiden (personifications of Vega and Altair), who were forced to live apart and only allowed to be reunited once a year by crossing the Milky Way on the seventh night of the seventh lunar month. The reference suggests that P'u was in love and could not be with her lover.

The allusion to Cowherd Boy and Weaver Maiden sets the tragic tone for the rest of the sequence. Poem number five depicts how P'u was sent back by her husband's family to her parents' home "for no reason." The line "the handsome one's waist became trimmer," suggests that her husband was not responsible for abandoning her. Could it have been the mother-in-law who was not happy with P'u? Could P'u be a victim like Lan-chih in "K'ung-ch'üeh tung-nan fei" 孔雀東南飛 (Southeast the Peacock Flies)? The last lines of the poem make this interpretation a strong possibility: "The red wall cannot stop swallows from flying in pairs,/But I regret that they can't convey my sorrow—/They only know how to peck mud to build their nests." She went into her old bedroom, opened the gold-trimmed trunk and saw the "dust-covered light gown," a reminder of her youth that now seemed so long ago.

Poem number six describes what happened after P'u was sent home. First she became ill. Though later she recovered physically, she continued to be in a lonely and wretched state: "When it comes to herbs, I plant only Live-Alone,/As to flowers, I don't pluck Forget-Your-Sorrow." Contact with her husband seems to have been cut off completely, and she doubted that he would understand even if she could communicate with him.

The last three poems in the sequence are flashbacks to the days before and during her marriage to "the handsome one." Poem number seven depicts her putting on makeup, as she thought about the man she would soon marry: "They said the man has the beauty of fine jade." In a mood of anticipation, she was both happy and shy.

Number eight suggests the cause of the tragedy. According to the "inauspicious matchmaker," whom she overheard in her chamber, her future husband's horoscope showed that he was to have two wives. Probably because of P'u's humble origin (an embroiderer), she was chosen to be his concubine. "How was I to refute such nonsense?/Born an immortal, I cannot follow just any man." She would not be Emerald Liu, a girl from a poor family who later became the cherished concubine of Prince Ju-nan. However, the allusion also suggests that the prospect of marrying into a rich family might be the reason why her parents agreed to the match despite her protest.

The last poem describes the mistreatment that P'u had suffered at the hands of the first wife.

I remember the oars on the Lonely
    River,
Which in a hurry I mistook for peach
    roots;
And I mistook a muddy puddle for a
    grassy lawn.
The City of Madams was ten-feet high,
But it could not confine flourishing
    spring.

I was assigned an empty chamber to
    inhabit by myself.
Its embroidered carpet of green moss
    reminded me of the Long Gate
    Palace.
My name was changed; each time I
    heard it I frowned–
There is no evening rain,
So why the name Morning Cloud?

記得零丁江上棹，
匆匆誤作桃根.
竟將入溷作飄茵，
夫人城十丈，
圍不住穠春.
付與閒房教獨守，
苔衣繡似長門.
小名替改更愁聽，
不教行暮雨，
偏喚作朝雲?

The contrast between "coarse oars" and
"peach roots" and between "grassy lawn"
and "muddy puddle" suggest the adverse
circumstances the poet found herself in.
The second stanza depicts the solitary,
humiliating life that P'u was forced to
live. Separated from her husband, she
did not experience the love and
happiness that she had dreamed of. The
wry references to the Long Gate Palace,
where Consort Ch'en who fell out of
favor with Emperor Wu of the Han
dynasty, and to the romantic interlude
between the King of Ch'u and the
Goddess of Mount Wu, make a bitter
comment on her own situation: like
Consort Ch'en, she lives in isolation and
dejection, and she is worse off than the
Goddess of Mount Wu, because at least
the goddess got to experience intimate
love, however fleeting it may have been.
The second allusion also evokes Chao-
yün (Morning Cloud), Su Shih's 蘇軾
(1037–1101)* faithful concubine who
refused to leave the poet in exile. In
contrast, P'u's fate was more cruel.
    Despite its brevity, P'u Meng-chu's
sequence of nine lyrics to the tune of
"Immortal by the River" gives a moving
autobiographical account about a
talented, uncommon woman in late-
imperial China. With each of the poems
beginning with the phrase "I remember,"
the sequence delineates P'u's life from
early childhood through adolescence, to
womanhood. The narrative is characterized by a high degree of drama and
suspense through the employment of
such devices as flashbacks, indirection,
and recreation of lyrical moments.
Despite the paucity of her extant work,
P'u deserves to be recognized not only
as a talented poet, but also as a woman
of uncommon courage and dignity.

Editions and References
Hsü, Nai-ch'ang 徐乃昌, ed. and comp.
    *Hsiao-t'an luan-shih hui-k'o pai-chia kuei-
    hsiu tz'u* 小檀欒室彙刻百家閨秀詞. 1896
    (foreword dated 1904).

Translations
Anthology of Chinese Women Poets
    (forthcoming).

Michelle Yeh
University of California, Davis

    San-kuo chih 三國志 (Records of the
Three States) is one of the most important
of the standard dynastic histories. It is
traditionally linked with Ssu-ma Ch'ien's
司馬遷 (145–*ca.* 86 B.C.) *Shih-chi* 史記,
Pan Ku's 班固 (A.D. 32–92) *Han shu* 漢
書, and Fan Yeh's 范曄 (398–446) *Hou
Han shu* 後漢書 as one of the Four
Histories (*Ssu shih* 四史), an indication
of the high regard in which it has been
held. *San-kuo chih*, which pre-dates *Hou
Han shu*, is a crucial source of information
and documents on the late second and
third centuries, a time of tremendous
social, economic, and political change
and an age of high achievements in
literature, important developments in
religion, and prodigious military activity.
It has long had an powerful impact on
Chinese life through its influence on
storytelling, vernacular fiction, drama,
and religion. The book's appeal has also

extended beyond China to Japan and other lands.

Written by Ch'en Shou 陳壽 (233–297), a native of the Shu 蜀 region (modern Szechwan), the *San-kuo chih* is a history of the three separatist states of Wei 魏 (220–265), Wu 吳 (222–280), and Shu 蜀 (or Shu Han 蜀漢, 221–263) that were established as a result of the dissolution of the Han 漢 empire (206 B.C.–A.D. 220). The work is in the *chi chuan* 紀傳 (annals and biographies) format originated by Ssu-ma Ch'ien and adopted by Pan Ku. But unlike their earlier histories, *San-kuo chih* lacks *chih* 志 (or *shu* 書, treatises) and *piao* 表 (tables) and is entirely made up of annals of rulers and biographies of individuals and groups. Of the sixty-five *chüan* that comprise *San-kuo chih*, thirty are devoted to Wei, fifteen to Shu, and twenty to Wu. There are relatively few textual problems with the work, and there is no doubt that these are Chen's originals.

Precisely when the history was written is unclear, but it may have been completed sometime after 280, the year the Western Chin 西晉 (266–317) conquered Wu, and before 289, the year Hsün Hsü 荀勖 died. According to *Hua-yang kuo chih* 華陽國志 [Record of States South of Mount Hua], Hsün expressed criticism of the Wei section. Contemporaries like Chang Hua 張華 (232–300)* and Hsia-hou Chan 夏侯湛 (243–291) praised Ch'en and his history, as did later figures, including the literary critic and theorist Liu Hsieh 劉勰 (*ca.* 465–*ca.* 522). Even so, it was not long before a need for elaboration and explanation of the text was felt. Emperor Wen 文 (r. 424–453) of the Liu Sung 劉宋 dynasty (420–479) ordered P'ei Sung-chih 裴松之 (372–451) to write a commentary. The completed commentary was submitted to the throne on 8 September 429. P'ei's commentary augments the text by quoting other sources; collects divergent versions of events; points out errors in the text and the alternative accounts;

and includes Pei's own critiques of various inaccuracies in *San-kuo chih* and other texts, as well as of certain people and events. The Wei-Chin period was significant in the development of Chinese historiography, and this latter feature of P'ei's commentary is instructive for the insights it provides into that historiography. The commentary also includes a relatively small amount of glossarial material. Virtually all published editions of *San-kuo chih* include the commentary, which is perhaps as important as Ch'en's work itself as a repository of information on the age. Many scholars since at least the Sung dynasty have presumed that the commentary is much longer than the *San-kuo chih* proper, but this has recently been disproved. Each has well over 300,000 characters, with *San-kuo chih* being substantially longer than the commentary.

Despite the approbation *San-kuo chih* has generally received, it has also been criticized. Three early and perennial complaints levelled at Ch'en are his alleged demand of payment to include biographies of Ting I 丁儀 and Ting I 丁廙, his putative disregard for Chu-ko Liang's 諸葛亮 (181–234) talents due to a grudge he bore the Chu-ko family, and his treatment of Wei as the legitimate successor of the Han. The first two charges have been convincingly refuted by various Ch'ing-dynasty scholars, as well as modern scholars such as Miao Yüeh 繆鉞 and Rafe de Crespigny. It is true that Ch'en bestows legitimacy on Wei in various ways, most obviously by placing Wei first and designating his chapters on its rulers *chi* 紀 (annals). But it is hard to see how he could have done otherwise—he was a Chin official, and Chin claimed succession from Wei. A final important criticism of *San-kuo chih*—one that has some merit—is that Ch'en occasionally distorts matters his superiors may have found sensitive, but these instances must be considered on a case-by-case basis to understand the reason for such distortions. Suffice to say that while *San-kuo chih* has some shortcomings, as early as the late Six Dynasties Ch'en was already seen as an outstanding historian who succeeded under difficult circumstances in producing a valuable and credible history.

The most useful redactions of the work today are the punctuated Chunghua shu-chü edition and the *San-kuo chih chi-chieh* 三國志集解 edited by Lu Pi 盧 弼 (1876–1967). The Chung-hua shu-chü edition first appeared in 1962, with a revised edition coming out in 1982. There are numerous reprints, and it should be understood that these sometimes introduce minor changes, perhaps most often in punctuation. Lu Pi's work, modeled on Wang Hsiench'ien's 王先謙 (1842–1918) *Han shu puchu* 漢書補注 and *Hou Han shu chi-chieh* 後漢書集解, contains scholia by important earlier authorities on *San-kuo chih* and its commentary, along with Lu's own opinions.

There are complete translations of *San-kuo chih* into modern Chinese and Japanese, though only the one by Ts'ao Wen-chu 曹文柱 and others translates P'ei's commentary–some do not even include it. There is no complete translation in a Western language. The translator who has taken most broadly from the text is Achilles Fang, but since he was translating from *Tzu-chih t'ung-chien* 資治通鑑, not *San-kuo chih*, only when the two texts overlap, and in occasional notes, does he translate *San-kuo chih* passages. Fang does translate relevant sections of P'ei's commentary. Other works that translate individual biographies and other parts of *San-kuo chih* are diverse in nature, so only a few that are mainly translations are listed in the bibliography below. Finally, it should be noted that the text of *San-kuo chih*, like the rest of the standard histories, is available on the Academia Sinica web site.

Editions and References

Chang, Shun-hui 張舜徽, Ts'ui Shu-t'ing 崔 曙庭, and Wang Jui-ming 王瑞明, eds. *San-kuo chih tz'u-tien* 三國志辭典. Tsinan: Shan-tung Chiao-yü, 1992.

Ch'en, Shou. *San-kuo chih*. Peking: Chunghua, 1962.

Hung, Yeh 洪業 *et al.*, comps. *San-kuo chih chi P'ei chu tsung-ho yin-te* 三國治及裴注 綜合引得. HYISIS, no. 33. 1938. Reprint. Shanghai: Shang-hai Ku-chi, 1986.

Kao, Hsiu-fang 高秀芳 and Yang Chi-an 楊 濟安, comps. *San-kuo chih jen-ming so-yin* 三國志人名索引. Peking: Chung-hua, 1980.

Lu, Pi, ed. *San-kuo chih chi-chieh*. 1936. Rpt. Taipei: Han-ching Wen-hua Shih-yeh Yu-hsien Kung-ssu, 1981.

Nakabayashi, Shirô 中林史郎 and Watanabe Yoshihiro 渡邊義浩, eds. *Sangoku shi kenkyū yaochilan* 三國志研究要籍覽. Tokyo: Hsin-wu Ooraisha, 1996.

Miao, Yüeh, ed. *San-kuo chih hsüan-chu* 三國 志選注. 3v. Peking: Chung-hua, 1984.

Miao, Yüeh *et al. San-kuo chih tao-tu* 三國志 導讀. Cheng-tu: Pa-Shu Shu-she, 1988.

San-kuo chih so-yin 三國志索引. Taipei: Tat'ung, 1986.

Wang, T'ien-liang 王天良, comp. *San-kuo chih ti-ming so-yin* 三國志地名索引. Peking: Chung-hua, 1980.

Translations

Cutter, Robert Joe and William Gordon Crowell. *Empresses and Consorts: Translations from Chen Shou's Records of the Three States with Pei Songzhi's Commentary.* Honolulu: Univ. of Hawaii Press, 1998.

DeWoskin, Kenneth J. *Doctors, Diviners, and Magicians of Ancient China: Biographies of Fang-shih.* New York: Columbia University Press, 1983.

Fang, Achilles. *The Chronicle of the Three Kingdoms (220–265): Chapters 69–78 from the Tzu chih t'ung chien of Ssu-ma Kuang (1019–1086).* Glen W. Baxter, ed. 2v. Cambridge: Harvard University, 1965.

Imataka, Makoto 今鷹真, Inami Ritsuko 井 波律子 and Kominami Ichiro 小南一郎. *Sangoku shi* 三國志. 3v. Tokyo: Chikuma Shobô, 1977–1989.

Liu, Kuo-hui 劉國輝 *et al. San-kuo chih (hsientai wen pan)* 三國志 (現代文版). 2v. Peking: Hung-ch'i, 1992.

Lu, Chih-hsiao 路志霄 and Hai Ch'eng-jui 海呈瑞, eds. *San-kuo chih hsüan-i* 三國志選譯. Lanchow: Lan-chou Ta-hsüeh, 1989.

Su, Yüan-lei 蘇淵雷, ed. *San-kuo chih chin-chu chin-i* 三國志今注今譯. 3v. Changsha: Hu-nan Shih-fan Ta-hsüeh, 1992.

T'ien, Yü-ch'ing 田余慶 and Wu Shu-p'ing 吳樹平, eds. *San-kuo chih chin-i* 三國志今譯. Chengchow: Chung-chou Ku-chi, 1991.

Ts'ao, Wen-chu *et al. Pai-hua San-kuo chih* 白話三國志. 2v. Peking: Chung-yang Min-tsu Hsüeh-yüan, 1994.

T'ung, Ch'ao 童超, Chang Kuang-ch'in 張光勤, and Chang Sheng-ju 張盛如, eds. *San-kuo chih ching-hua chu-i* 三國志精華注譯. Peking: Pei-ching Kuang-po Hsüeh-yüan, 1993.

Wang, Ching-chih 王靜芝 *et al. Pai-hua San-kuo chih* 白話三國志. Taipei: Ho Lo T'u-shu, 1970.

Studies

Chang, Meng-lun 張孟倫. "P'ei Sung-chih *San-kuo chih chu* 裴松之三國志注. In *Chung-kuo li-shih wen-hsien yen-chiu chi-k'an* 中國歷史文獻研究集刊. Changsha: Yüeh-lu Shu-she, 1984, pp. 32–37

Ch'ien, Ta-chao 錢大昭 (1744–1813). *San-kuo chih pien-i* 三國志辨疑. In *Shih-hsüeh ts'ung-shu* 史學叢書 (*Pai-pu* edition).

Chou, I-liang 周一良. *Wei Chin Nan-pei ch'ao shih cha-chi* 魏晉南北朝史札記. Peking: Chung-hua, 1985.

de Crespigny, Rafe. *The Records of the Three Kingdoms* Centre of Oriental Studies Occasional Paper no. 9. Canberra: Australian National University Centre of Oriental Studies, 1970.

de Crespigny, Rafe, trans. *The Last of the Han, Being the Chronicle of the Years 181–220 A.D. as Recorded in Chapters 58–68 of the* Tzu-chih t'ung-chien *of Ssu-ma Kuang.* Centre of Oriental Studies Monograph 9. Canberra: Australian National University, 1969.

___. *To Establish Peace, Being the Chronicle of Later Han for the Years 189 to 220 AD as Recorded in Chapters 59 to 69 of the* Zizhi tongjian *of Sima Guang.* 2v. Asian Studies Monographs, new series no. 21. Canberra: Faculty of Asian Studies, Australian National University, 1996.

Cutter, Robert Joe. "The Death of Empress Zhen: Fiction and Historiography in Early Medieval China." *JAOS* 112 (1992): 577–583.

Cutter, Robert Joe and William G. Crowell. "On Translating Chen Shou's *San guo zhi*: Bringing Him Back Alive." In *Translating Chinese Literature.* Eugene Eoyang and Lin Yao-fu, eds. Bloomington: Indiana University Press, 1995, pp. 114–130.

Fang, Pei-ch'en 方北辰. "*San-kuo chih* piao-tien shang-ch'üeh" 三國志標點商榷. *Ssu-ch'uan Ta-hsüeh hsüeh-pao* 1987.1: 90–97.

Gardiner, K.H.J. "Standard Histories, Han to Sui." In *Essays on the Sources for Chinese History.* Donald D. Leslie, Colin Macerras, and Gungwu Wang, eds. Columbia: University of South Carolina Press, 1973.

Leban, Carl. "Ts'ao Ts'ao and the Rise of Wei: the Early Years." Unpublished Ph.D. dissertation, Columbia University, 1971.

Li, Ch'un-chiao 李純蛟. "*San-kuo chih* te li-shih ti-wei" 三國志的歷史地位. *Li-shih hsüeh* 1996.6: 53–58.

Liang, Chang-chü 梁章鉅 (1775–1849). *San-kuo chih p'ang-cheng* 三國志旁證. Taipei: I-wen Yin-shu-kuan, 1955.

Lu, Chien-jung 盧建榮. "P'ei Sung-chih li-shih p'ing-lun de ssu-hsiang ken-yüan—chien lun tsun ching ch'uan-t'ung te hui-ying" 裴松之歷史評論的思想根源一兼論尊經傳統的回應. In *Chung-kuo li-shih lun-wen chi* 中國歷史論文集. Taipei: Shang-wu Yin-shu-kuan, 1986, 1:493–517.

Lu, Yao-tung 逯耀東. "Pei Sung-chih yü Wei Chin shih-hsüeh p'ing-lun" 裴松之與魏晉史學評論. *Shih-huo yüeh-k'an (fu-k'an)* 15.3–4 (January 1985): 93–107.

___. "*San-kuo chih chu* yü P'ei Sung-chih *San-kuo chih tzu chu*" 三國志注與裴松之自注. In *Chung-kuo li-shih lun-wen chi,* 1:257–272.

Miao, Yüeh. "Chen Shou yü *San-kuo chih*" 陳壽與三國志. In *Chung-kuo shih-hsüeh shih lun chi* 中國史學史論集. Wu Tse 吳澤 and Yüan Ying-kuang 袁英光, eds. Shanghai: Jen-min, 1980, 1:313–322.

Shen, Chia-pen 沈家本 (1840–1913). *San-kuo chih chu so yin shu-mu* 三國志注所引書目. In *Ku shu-mu san chung* 古書目三種. Peking: Chung-hua, 1964.

___. *Chu shih so-yen* 諸史瑣言. 4v. Peking: Chung-hua, 1963.

Ts'ui, Shu-t'ing. *"San-kuo chih* pen-wen ch'üeh-shih to yü P'ei chu" 三國志本文 確實多于裴注. *Hua-chung Shih-fan Ta-hsüeh hsüeh-pao,* 1990.2: 122–126.

Wu, Chin-hua 吳金華. *San-kuo chih chiao-ku* 三國志校詁. Nanking: Chiang-su Ku-chi, 1990.

Yang, I-hsiang 楊翼驤. "P'ei Sung-chih yü *San-kuo chih chu*" 裴松之與三國志注. In Wu and Yüan, *Chung-kuo shih-hsüeh shih lun chi,* 1:323–346.

Robert Joe Cutter
University of Wisconsin, Madison

Shen Shan-pao 沈善寶 (1807–1862, *tzu,* Hsiang-p'ei 湘佩) was a native of Ch'ien-t'ang 錢塘, modern Hangchow in Chekiang province, an area known for its high concentration of educated and talented women in the Ch'ing. A prolific poet and critic, Shen left behind two substantial collections of *shih** poetry (over 1300 poems), a large collection of critical poetic biographies of women, and a small collection of *tz'u** (song lyrics).

In 1819, when Shen Shan-pao was twelve years old, her father committed suicide in Nanchang, Kiangsi, having been involved in some kind of power struggle in the local bureaucracy after serving for three years as the assistant department magistrate there. Her mother was left a widow with a brood of seven small children—five sons and two daughters, stranded in a strange land. It was not until a few years later that they were able to make their way back to Hangchow with help from relatives. This tragic and traumatic loss changed the course of Shan-pao's life and in many ways shaped her sense of self and direction. As a twelve-year old, she wrote a long pentasyllabic verse "Shu ai" 述哀 (Expressing my Grief) on this terrible occasion. The end of the poem brings together the expression of anger with that of strength and filial devotion and the awareness of the limitations of her gender:

My thoughts go to seek the sword of Wu,
And desire to learn the skill of the Chao
    girl.
To the left I'll stab my enemy's breast,
To the right I'll gouge out the slanderer's
    teeth.
I hate my constitution, weak as the grass,
With my hair unpinned, I am not a man.
But I must support my sick mother,
Weeping blood, her frame is almost
    destroyed.
If I were to die for my father's sake,
Who would bring my mother simple
    food?
Until the seas dry up and the shores
    change,
The mountains collapse and the earth
    disintegrates,
In deep grief I will hold onto this rending
    hate,
Which will be there for all eternity.
(*Hung-hsüeh Lou shih-hsüan ch'u-chi* 鴻雪樓
詩選初集, 1.2a-b)

Much of the information concerning Shen Shan-pao and her family comes from her collection of poetry the *Hung-hsüeh-lou shih-hsüan ch'u-chi* 鴻雪樓詩選初集 (The First Collection of the Pavilion of Geese and Snow), which consists of four *chüan* with over 480 titles of *shih* poems (over 500 poems), written between 1819 and 1835, and published in 1836. Because so much of Shen Shan-pao's poetry focused intensely on her personal life, it constitutes in fact her life writings.

In the diversity of women's poetic production during the Ch'ing, the quality and quantity of her poetry provides an exceptionally rich instance for study. In several respects, Shen Shan-pao's life and poetry provide interesting points of comparison with other women poets: (1) the form and significance of the structural organization of her *shih* collections, (2) the generic choices and thematic preoccupations of her poetry, (3) the self-representation which negotiates both the image of the filial daughter and the dedicated poet, and which decries the gendered restrictions she experiences, and (4) the life of physical and social mobility associated with her literary and artistic—one might say, "professional" career.

The *Hung-hsüeh-lou shih-hsüan ch'u-chi* does not merely take chronology as its structuring principle. Its meticulous year-by-year arrangement of the poems for each of the sixteen years effectively turns the collection into an autobiographical orchestration. Such a consciously chronological trajectory asks of the reader a different kind of reading process. Here, the collection is not conceived of as a repository of independent art pieces as such but as a statement of a person's recognition of the significance of her experiences and life phases, of her growth and development as a poet and as a daughter in a carefully marked temporal framework. Furthermore, she introduces and favors practices that inflect and accentuate the autobiographical aspect of her collection. These practices bear on the matter of generic and thematic choices, the insertion of interlineal and intra-textual prose commentaries, and the extensive use of prose prefaces particularly for poems of social interaction. Shen Shan-pao wrote extensively in both old and recent style *shih* poetry. Her style and language tend toward the narrative and heroic mode. In her old-style poetry, the strong sense of moral integrity and intense emotion often echoes Tu Fu 杜甫 (712–770).* She seems to have eschewed the delicate feminine mode of expression, negotiating instead a relatively masculine-heroic rhetoric. This is particularly evident in some of her *tz'u* lyrics in which she clearly manipulates the well-established convention of the masculine *hao-fang* 豪放** mode.

Leading an unusual life compared to most other gentry women, in youth Shen Shan-pao made extensive travels to sell her paintings and poetry to support her siblings and mother, who died while she was away on one of these trips. In 1837, she had her first collections, one of *shih* and one of *tz'u*, printed in Hangchow. She did not marry until thirty-one in 1838, a year after she had made a major move from Hangchow to Peking. She continued her active literary and social life after marriage, while fulfilling her responsibilities as the second wife to Wu Ling-yün 武凌雲, an official who was a widower with small children. In fact, she worked from 1842 to 1845 on the monumental biographical and critical collection of women's poetry, the *Ming-yüan shih-hua* 名媛詩話 (Poetry Talk on Notable Women) in twelve *chüan*. This work is the result of a woman critic's "feminist" motivation to gather and transmit the disparate efforts of countless women of the Ch'ing period—some renowned but many unknown—to voice their gender and inscribe their selves through the medium of poetry. Her means to this end was to incorporate their lives and poems into a printed text. At the same time, some of her own personal records and recollections are interspersed with the objective compilation of other women's poetry. Each entry is usually introduced by a brief biographical sketch before a selection of poems are reproduced, sometimes with and sometimes without Shen's comments. The form of the work, on the one hand, observes certain established conventional hierarchizations in anthologies of poetry such as placing the work of the "marginalized" groups—Buddhist and Taoist nuns, Korean women, and female ghosts and immortals—at the end of the collection, on the other hand, it also follows new shapes and contours that are guided by a "feminine" focus in that it traces the gendered experiences of the women whose works she records and writes about. There are thus meandering narratives of her meaningful friendships with some women which thread through different entries and short life histories of others whom Shen had come across in some way, through personal contact, correspondence, or hearsay. The first eight *chüan* of the *Ming-yüan shih-hua* were reprinted as a monograph by the Shanghai newspaper *Yü-yen pao* 寓言報 in the 1910s.

Shen was a respected poet and critic among her women friends and acquaintances. She edited and wrote critical comments on poetry manuscripts which were sent to her by the authors themselves or were brought to her attention by others. Shen also had another collection of her poetry printed which includes the entire first collection (*chüan* 1 to 4) and contains the sequel (*chüan* 5 to 15) to it (sole extant copy in the Chekiang Library). The poems in the sequel are also arranged by year, beginning from where the first collection left off when she left Hangchow for Peking in 1837 and ending with the year 1854 when she was accompanying her husband on his official post in the far northwest. This collection seems to have been hastily put together, for the last two *chüan* are reversed in chronological order. The date of the printing is also not recorded.

With the exception of a few journeys, Shen Shen-pao spent the latter half of her life in Peking. As seen in the occasions and subject of her poetry, female friendship became more than ever an important aspect of her social and emotional life. In this respect, she exemplified the value of friendship for many literary women of the Ch'ing. Shen continued to write epistolary poems to some of her women friends back in Hangchow, particularly the *tz'u* poet Wu Tsao 吳藻. In Peking, Shen became a close friend of another famous *tz'u* woman poet Ku T'ai-ch'ing 顧太清 (1799–after 1876; see Ku Ch'un 顧春**). Both their collections contain many of the poems they exchanged. They formed a poetry society with a number of other gentry women, mostly from the Kiangnan area, who sojourned in the capital while their male kin were on official assignment there. These women acted as inspirations to each other in writing.

According to a poem by Ku T'ai-ch'ing mourning her death, Shen Shen-pao apparently died in 1862, but the details of her last years, without any further extant self writings in poetry or prose, remain rather obscure.

Editions and References

Hung-hsüeh Lou shih-hsüan ch'u-chi 鴻雪樓詩選初集. Four *chüan*. Printed 1837. Copies in Peking, Shanghai, and Nanking Libraries.

Hung-hsüeh Lou shih-hsüan 鴻雪樓詩選. Fifteen *chüan*. Printed after 1854. Copy in Chekiang Library.

Hung-hsüeh Lou shih-hsüan ch'u-chi. Four *chüan*. 1924 type-set reprint. Copies in Peking, Shanghai, Nanking, and Chekiang libraries.

Hung-hsüeh-lou tz'u 鴻雪樓詞. In *Hsiao-t'an-luan-shih hui-k'o Kuei-hsiu tz'u* 小檀樂室彙刻閨秀詞.

Ming-yüan shih-hua 名媛詩話. Twelve *chüan*. Preface 1845. Copy in Peking University Library.

Ming-yüan shih-hua. Eight *chüan*. 1924 type-set reprint based on incomplete copy. Copies in Shanghai, Chekiang, and Hangchow University libraries.

Ming-yüan shih-hua. Four *chüan*. In *Ch'ing shih-hua fang-i ch'u-pien* 清詩話訪佚初編. Taipei: Hsin-wen-feng, 1987.

Translations

Anthology of Chinese Women Poets, forthcoming 1998.

Studies

Chao, Po-t'ao 趙伯陶. "*Hung-lou-meng ying te tso-che chi ch'i-t'a*," 紅樓夢影的作者及其他, *Hung-lou-meng hsüeh-k'an* 3 (1989): 243-251.

Fong, Grace S. "Engendering the Lyric: Her Image and Voice in Song." In *Voices of the Song Lyric in China*, pp. 107-144.

Grace S. Fong
McGill University

Shen Ya-chih 沈亞之 (*tzu,* Hsia-hsien 下賢, 781-832) was descended from the well-known Shen family of Wu-k'ang 武康 in Wu-hsing 吳興 which also produced the poet Shen Yüeh 沈約 (441–513)* and Ya-chih's cousin, Shen Chi-chi 沈即濟 (*ca.* 740–*ca.* 800),* a historian and writer of tales. Shen Ya-chih was distantly related to Tai-tsung's 代宗 (r. 762–779) Empress Shen, the mother of Te-tsung 德宗 (r. 779–805).

Shen seems to have be born, however, in Lung-chou 隴州 (modern Lung 隴 County in western Shensi– about 100 miles west-northwest of Ch'ang-an) where his father was stationed. Shortly after his birth his father passed away and the family returned to the southeast (he apparently had relatives both in Hangchow and Soochow). When the family moved back south, Shen may have remained in the capital with his uncle Shen Ch'uan-shih 沈傳師 (769-827). In 803 in his early twenties he arranged to take a concubine from a good family in Ch'ang-an: Lu Chin-lan 盧金蘭 (*tzu,* Chao-hua 昭華, 789-814) who had studied music and dance and bore Shen a son and a daughter. Sometime a bit earlier he had married a woman named Yao 姚. In 805 Shen returned to the southeast, taking wife and concubine with him.

For the next few years Shen presumably studied while living with relatives. Then in 809, Shen Ya-chih did two things that he would continue to do in later years. First, he stopped at a monastery in Hangchow and inquired about the history of a statue of the Buddha that was being moved; then he recorded the story that the monks told him ("I Fo chi" 移佛記 [Record of Moving the Buddha]; *Ch'üan T'ang wen* 736:9619). Throughout the rest of his life Shen would remain interested in listening to and recording stories. Second, he (with his wife and concubine) retraced the long route to Ch'ang-an where he was to take the *chin-shih*

examination the following spring. His subsequent years were also beset by arduous travel, as he searched for a position early in his career and later was called upon to move from one post to another.

In the spring of 810 and again in 811 Shen failed the *chin-shih* examination. During this period he met Li Ho 李賀 (791–817)* and Nan Cho 南卓 (?791-854), also candidates for the examinations. Frustrated with his lack of success, Shen left Ch'ang-an in the summer of 811 and went from Fu-chou 鄜州 (modern Fu 富 county in Shensi about 100 miles north of the capital) to Lo-yang and finally all the way to P'eng-ch'eng 彭成 (modern Hsü-chou 徐州 City in Kiangsu) in search of someone to sponsor him in the examinations. On this trip, possibly at Li Ho's suggestion, he seems to have met Han Yü 韓愈 (768–824),* who was in Lo-yang and who had been supportive of Li Ho's examination efforts. Shen later claimed to have been Han's disciple for over a decade.

After failing to pass the *chin-shih* in 812, Shen Ya-chih went home for a short time. Li Ho and Chia Tao 賈島 (779–843)* wrote poems seeing him off. Shen left his wife and concubine in Ch'ang-an and that winter returned to them in the capital. The following spring Shen did not take the examinations. Instead he went to Ching-chou 涇州 (modern Ching-ch'uan 涇川 county in west-central Shensi); that summer he was in Lu-chou 潞州 (modern Ch'ang-chih Shih 長治市 in Shansi). In 814 he again eschewed the examinations, travelling east along the Yellow River to Han-tan 邯鄲 and then south to his home region. On the return later that year he passed through Hua-chou 滑州 (modern Hua County in northeast Honan) and visited the military governor (*chieh-tu shih* 節度 使), Hsüeh P'ing 薛平 (d. 830), a well-connected scion of an old military family. Shen's concubine, and later his wife, died during this year.

In 815, with Ts'ui Ch'ün 崔群 (772-832), Han Yü's fellow-graduate, as examiner, Shen Ya-chih passed the *chin-shih* and joined the staff of Li Hui 李彙, the son of the Prince of Lin-huai 臨淮王, Li Kuang-pi 李光弼, as a record keeper (*chi-shih* 記室). Li Hui was married to one of Shen's cousins and had just been appointed Military Governor of Ching-yüan 涇原(in charge of the Ching-chou 涇州 area). During the early summer Li Hui entertained a group of his officials and guests with a story about a dream encounter his mentor, Hsing Feng 邢鳳, had enjoyed. In the dream he met a beautiful woman who exchanged poems with him. When he awoke and changed his clothes, he found the poems stuck in one of his sleeves. Then another guest told a similar story. The party agreed that these tales should be written down, so Shen fashioned them into an account of the storytelling that day and titled it "I-meng lu" 異夢錄 (Account of Dreams of the Extraordinary; *T'ang-jen hsiao-shuo*, pp. 160-161). This "account" was in keeping with Shen's idea that he was a historian first and foremost. The fact that he among the various literati present was allowed to write up the story shows that already at this time he had a reputation as a skilled story-writer. Li Hui had obviously provided a milieu in which Shen might have thrived; unfortunately, however, Li passed away later that summer (Shen wrote the memorial inscription for him), leaving Shen unemployed. He returned to Ch'ang-an shortly thereafter. A few months later Shen was in Lo-yang again; he stayed with Fang Shu-pao 房叔豹, a friend of Nan Cho. While in Lo-yang, he wrote "Piao Liu Hsün-lan" 表劉薰蘭 (In Praise of Liu Hsün-lan, *Ch'üan T'ang wen*, 738:9651), recording the story of how Fang's young concubine had persuaded him to give up drinking in favor of study. After a short stay with Fang, Shen passed through P'eng-ch'eng

and visited an old friend, Ts'ui Chü 崔莒 of Po-ling 博陵. Ts'ui had a concubine who was a talented singer named Yeh 葉 whom Shen had heard perform a few years earlier (probably in 811). When he asked about her on this visit, he discovered she had just died. Because Shen felt an account of her talent should be left for posterity, he depicted some events from her life in a piece called "Ko-che Yeh chi" 歌者葉記 (Record of the Singer, Yeh; *Ch'üan T'ang wen*, 736:9627-27). The piece is particularly interesting because it uses a traditional story about the ancient singer Ch'in Ch'ing 秦青 to introduce the account of Ms. Yeh, a technique not unlike the *ju-hua* 入話 in the *hua-pen* 話本* stories of later dynasties, and because the depiction of Yeh's life is cast in language very similar to that of *ch'uan-ch'i* tales.

From P'eng-ch'eng Shen Ya-chih went back to Hangchow. Early in 816 he visited Mount K'uai-chi 會稽 for a period of time, then decided to return to the capital. Passing through Shou-chou 壽州 (modern Shou County in Anhwei) he wrote a letter to the prefect, Li Wen-t'ung 李文通, seeking his aid in finding a position. Shen remained in Shou-chou for a time because the prefecture was embroiled in the revolt led by Wu Yüan-chi's 吳元濟 (d. 817).

Having returned to the capital, Shen visited Ch'i-chou 岐州 (near modern Feng-hsiang 鳳翔, about 70 miles west of Sian) and Lung-chou 隴州 (modern Lung County in west-central Shensi) during the summer of 817. The following year he travelled eastward almost as far as modern Shantung (to Ssu-shang 泗上 in extreme eastern Honan). Each of these visits was probably to enhance Shen's growing network of friends and possible patrons. His poem "Pien-chou ch'uan-hsing fu an-p'ang so-chien" 卞州船行賦岸傍所見 (Depicting What I See Along the Shore from a Moving Boat at Pien-chou,*Ch'üan T'ang shih*, 493:5579) was probably written on this trip:

Ancient trees in the early light have
    gone grey–
The autumn forest brushes the bank
    with fragrance.
Pearls of dew, the "spider's web" so
    fine,
Threads of gold, the "rabbit's hair" so
    long.
Autumn waves from time to time throw
    back in foam,
Startled fish of a sudden bump against
    the boat.
The milkweed's mist catches hold of
    green [willow] threads,
The sour jujube's fruit stitched into red
    sacks.
Riotous ears of grain wave like flying-
    squirrels' tails,
Protruding roots hang down like
    phoenix entrails.
I'm merely holding one washed foot–
Who says I could be compared to the
    Ts'ang-lang [poet]?

古木曉蒼蒼，秋林拂岸香。
露珠蟲綱細，金縷兔絲長。
秋浪時迴沫，驚鱗乍躅航。
蓬煙拈綠線，棘實綴紅囊。
亂穗搖鼯尾，出根挂鳳腸。
聊持一濯足，誰道比滄浪。

"Rabbit's hair" is a euphemistic name
for a plant which grows by winding up
a tree; "spider's web" may have a similar
reference. This type of imagery, along
with verses like "Riotous ears of grain
wave like flying-squirrels' tails, /
Protruding roots hang down like phoenix
entrails" reflect the difficult diction and
figurative language of Han Yü and his
disciples (Han Yü mentions the flying
squirrel three times in his extant poetry
and his line "Hugging the road the sparse
locust trees put forth their old roots" 夾
道疏槐出老根 may have been the basis
for the tenth line in Shen's poem). The
final couplet alludes to the author of the
Ch'u tz'u 楚辭,* Ch'ü Yüan 屈原 (*ca.*
340-278 B.C.),* and is Shen's attempt to
excuse his failure to find a position by
suggesting that he would not want to
serve a government as unenlightened as
that then in Ch'ang-an.

Also in 818 he learned from friends
of a story told in a *yüeh-fu* poem (or
poems) written by Wei Ao 韋敖. It
involved the love affair between a
"dragon-lady" and a young scholar and
has been compared to the more famous
story "Liu I chuan" 柳毅傳 by Li Ch'ao-
wei 李朝威 (*fl.* 800). Shen gave it the
title "Hsiang-chung yüan chieh" 湘中怨
解 (An Explanation of the Laments
written in Hsiang; *T'ang-jen hsiao-shuo,*
pp. 157-159), suggesting that the poems
he includes in his narrative may have
been those left by Wei Ao. Shen claims
that he composed his piece to match
"Yen-chung chih chih" 煙中之志 by his
friend Nan Cho (a version of this story
has been preserved in *Lü-ch'uang hsin-hua*
綠窗新話 (New Tales from the Green
Window).

    Yet another story came as the result
of a trip east from the capital Shen made
with his friends Li Pao 李褒 and Li Meng-
t'ung 劉蒙同 in 819. They stopped at
Pai-ma Chin 白馬津 (White Horse Ford,
near Hua-chou) before continuing east
along the Yellow River. He revisited
Hua-chou (Shen had been there earlier
in 814) and recorded an account he heard
from Liu Yüan-ting 劉元鼎 (*chin-shih*
789) about a knight-errant named Feng
Yen 馮燕 ("Feng Yen chuan" 馮燕傳,
T'ang-jen hsiao-shuo, pp. 165-168). Feng
had served the noted scholar and chief
minister, Chia Tan 賈耽 (730-805) when
the latter was military governor of the
area from 786-793. Feng was carrying
on an affair with the garrison
commander's wife. One day the man
came home from a drinking bout and
surprised the adulterous couple. Feng
hid behind a door and, when the husband
passed out, his wife made signs indicating
Feng should kill him. Feng was outraged
by her suggestion and killed her instead,
then fled. When he learned that the
husband had been charged with the
murder, her turned himself in. Chia Tan
oversaw the case and petitioned the
emperor to pardon Feng. A

proclamation was issued granting amnesty to all who had received the death penalty in Hua-chou. At the end of the story Shen Ya-chih added a personal "historian's comment" imitating the doyen of Chinese historians, Ssuma Ch'ien 司馬遷 (145-*ca.* 86 B.C.),* in which he praised Feng for his righteousness. These events may well have actually happened (Lu Hsün does not include the story in his *T'ang Sung ch'uan-ch'i chi* 唐宋傳奇集 suggesting he may have believed it was a record of a real incident), but in his adaptation of the story to create a moral tale Shen reveals a growing confidence in his narrative skills. The tale may also have been written to flatter a relative or associate of Chia Tan and thereby establish another possible connection for Shen in his search for a position.

For most of 820 Shen seems to have remained in Ch'ang-an. In the spring of 821 he passed an advanced placement examination and was probably appointed proofreader (*cheng-tzu* 正字) in the Secretariat (Mi-shu sheng 秘書省). Later that spring and again in 822 he visited local officials in Hua-chou 華州 (modern Hua County, 45 miles east of Sian) and Lung-chou, presumably still seeking advancement in his official position. In late summer of 822 he was made Commandant (*wei* 尉) of Li-yang 櫟楊 (25 miles northeast of modern Sian), a position he held for almost two years. Although this was a minor position, it left him close to the capital and to the contacts he had established.

In 824 he received a promotion to Assistant Military Training Commissioner (*Tu T'uan-lien fu-shih* 都團練副使) of Fu-chien 福建 and neighboring prefectures and sent to serve under the new Civilian Governor (*Kuan-ch'a shih* 觀察使) of Fu-chien, Hsü Hui 徐晦 (d. 838), with headquarters in Fu-chou 福州 (modern Foochow).

Sometime during this sojourn in the Southeast (Hsü Hui was recalled to court in the early autumn of 826 and Shen Ya-chih presumably returned to Ch'ang-an with him), Shen probably wrote two other "stories." The first, entitled "Hsi-tzu chuan" 喜子傳 (Biography of Hsi-tzu; *Ch'üan T'ang wen* 738:9649-50), recounts how Hsi-tzu, a concubine of a merchant named Liu Ch'eng 劉承, resisted the improper advances of Liu's neighbor, a Master Wei 韋. Wei then had Liu imprisoned on trumped up charges in order to lay claim to Hsi-tzu. She attempted to drown herself, but was saved by a passerby, and Liu was finally released. The story is set in 809 and was told to Shen by a Master Ch'eng 程. Shen wrote it down because he was impressed with Hsi-tzu's upright behavior. This conventional plot recalls a number of similar stories in Chinese literature, but may here have been superimposed upon an actual situation.

The second story, "Piao i-che Kuo Ch'ang" 表醫者郭常 (In Praise of the Medical Practitioner Kuo Ch'ang; *Ch'üan T'ang wen* 738:9651), tells of a physician who lived in Jao-chou 饒州 (near modern Po-yang 波陽 in Kiangsi) and who was so skilled that many foreigners trading in South China sought his advice. Once a merchant was seriously ill and could find no one who knew how to treat his illness. He offered Kuo a huge sum of money if he could save his life. Kuo cured the man but then refused the money because he thought giving up so much would cause the man to have a relapse and die. This kind of idealized biography with a comment appended much like an official biography was probably intended as a means of moral suasion. It finds antecedents in works like Liu Tsungyüan's 柳宗元 (773-819)* "Sung Ch'ing chuan" 宋清傳 (Biography of [the Druggist] Sung Ch'ing).

Shortly after returning to Ch'ang-an, probably with Hsü Hui's assistance, Shen was appointed aide to the royal scribe in the palace (*Tien-chung ch'eng yü-shih*

殿中丞御史) and subsequently palace attendant (*Nei shih feng* 內侍奉). Also in 827 Shen wrote "Ch'in meng chi" 秦夢記 (Record of a Dream of Ch'in; *T'ang-jen hsiao-shuo,* pp. 162-164, in which he records a dream he claims to have had upon setting out for Pin-chou 邠州 (modern Pin 彬 County in west-central Shensi, 65 miles northwest of Sian). Stopping at an inn not far from the capital the first night, Shen falls asleep and believes he wakes up in the state of Ch'in 秦 during the reign of Duke Mu 穆 (r. 659-621 B.C.). He is showered with favor by the duke, marries his daughter, and is truly living a dream life. After a year, however, his wife dies and he decides to return to his own country. After an elaborate description (complete with poems) of the farewell festivities, Shen is accompanied to the Han-ku 函谷 Pass where before he can say good-bye he wakes up. When Shen and his friend Ts'ui Chiu-wan 崔九萬 set out from the inn the next day, he tells Ts'ui about his dream. Ts'ui helps to interpret it by pointing out that the inn where they had stayed was very near the place where Duke Mu was buried over a millennium ago. This plot is also familiar—it resembles Li Kung-tso's 李公佐 (*ca.* 770-*ca.* 848)* "Nan-k'o T'ai-shou chuan" 南柯太守傳 (Account of the Governor of Southern Branch) and Shen Chi-chi's 沈既濟 (*ca.* 740-*ca.* 800)* "Chen-chung chi" 枕中記 (A Record of [Events] within a Pillow).

The year 828 was a watershed for Shen Ya-chih. After finally securing a position at court, events beyond his control adumbrated the end of his career and his life. In the early fall the Military Governor of Ho-pei Yen-huai 河北兗海, Liu T'ung-chieh 李同捷, rebelled. Shen was assigned (as an administrative assistant [*p'an-kuan* 判官]) to the staff of one of the generals, Po Ch'i 柏耆, sent to put down the rebellion. Po Ch'i had fought against the rebel Wu Yüan-chi under P'ei Tu 裴度 (765-839) and was determined to bring Liu to justice. In early 829 while a compromise plan calling for Li T'ung-chieh to surrender was being negotiated by other generals, Po Ch'i rushed into Li's camp, arrested the rebel leader, and set out for the capital with him. Upon learning of a plot to free Li en route to Ch'ang-an, Po Ch'i on his own authority executed Li T'ung-chieh. As a result Emperor Wen-tsung came under pressure from Po Ch'i's jealous colleagues, from other provincial satraps, and from a group of eunuchs allied with provincial forces to punish Po Ch'i and his staff. In late spring Shen was therefore exiled to become Commandant of Nan-k'ang 南康 (modern Nan-k'ang in southern Kiangsi). Chang Hu 張祜 (791-854) and Yin Yao-fan 殷堯藩 wrote poems to see him off. He spent three years in Nan-k'ang and then was transferred to Ying-chou 郢州 (modern Chung-hsiang 鍾祥 in Hupei) in 831 as revenue administrator (*ssu-hu ts'an-chün* 司戶參軍). Not long after his arrival in Ying-chou, Shen became ill and died.

Although he had a reputation as a poet in his own day (cited along with Wei Ying-wu 韋應物 (737-*ca.* 792)* and others in the preface to the literati chapter in the *Hsin T'ang shu* 新唐書 [New History of the T'ang], 201:5726), only two dozen of his poems remain today. What should interest the modern reader is the variety of narrative in Shen's corpus and the development of his narrative art that can be seen in his prose (80 pieces are extant). Shen began by reporting simple stories like his "Record of Moving the Buddha" (809), next adapted narratives in other genres like "An Explanation of the Laments written in Hsiang" (from *yüeh-fu;* 817), was then asked to record stories such as "Account of Dreams of the Extraordinary" (815), adapted popular tales like the "Account of Feng Yen" (819) to didactic purposes, and finally exercised his own unconscious or conscious creativity in works like "Account of a Dream of Ch'in" (827).

He also wrote allegories such as "I-niao lu" 宜鳥錄 (Account of the Bird of Propriety; undated; *Ch'üan T'ang wen* 737:9637-38) which show the influence of the *ku-wen* movement. His own narrative legacy may be seen to support both Lu Hsün's idea that T'ang *hsiao-shuo* marked the first consciously created fiction in China as well as the claim by modern critics (Pien Hsiao-hsüan 卞孝萱 and Glen Dudbridge, for example) that the *ch'uan-ch'i* genre was closely tied to politics and political expression.

Editions and References

Ch'üan T'ang-shih, 493:5578-84.

Ch'üan T'ang-shih wai-pien, 2:466. Two fragments.

Ch'üan T'ang-wen, 734-738:9585-9654.

Shen Hsia-hsien wen chi 沈下賢文集, 9 *chüan.* SPTK.

Ssu-k'u, 150:39b-41b.

T'ang-jen hsiao-shuo, pp. 157-168 (standard edition of "Hsiang-chung yüan chieh," "I-meng lu," "Ch'in-meng chi," and "Feng Yen chuan").

T'ang Sung san-wen hsüan-chu 唐宋散文選注. Shen Ping, comm. Taipei: Cheng-chung, 1968, p. 117. Lightly annotated version of "Pieh-ch'ien Ch'i-shan Ling Tsou Chün hsü" 別前岐山令鄒君序.

Yü, Chia-hsi 余嘉錫. "*Shen Hsia-hsien chi shih-erh chüan*" 沈下賢集十二卷." In Yü's *Ssu-k'u t'i-yao pien-cheng* 四庫提要辨證. Peking: Chung-hua, 1974, *chüan* 20, pp. 1294-96.

Translations

Hartman, *Han Yü,* p. 165 (excerpt from "Sung Hung Sun hsü" 送洪遜序 [Preface Seeing Off the Master Hung Sun])

Ma and Lau, *Traditional Chinese Stories,* pp. 50-51 ("Feng Yen chuan").

Kao, *Chinese Classical Tales,* pp. 205-08 ("Hsiang-chung yüan chieh").

Studies

Chang, Ch'üan-kung 張全恭. "T'ang wen-jen Shen Ya-chih sheng-p'ing" 唐文人沈亞之生平, *Wen-hsüeh,* 2.6(1934).

Ch'eng, I-chung 程毅中. "Shen Ya-chih chi ch'i 'Ch'in-meng chi'—T'ang-tai hsiao-

shuo so-chi" 沈亞之及其秦夢記—唐人小說瑣記, *T'ang-tai wen-hsüeh lun-ts'ung,* 5 (1984).

Fukunaga, Ichitaka 富永一登. "Chin Ashi no shidenteki sakuhin" 沈亜之の史伝的作品. In *Obi Hakushi taikyû kinen Chûgoku bungaku ronshû* 小尾博士退休記念中国文学論集. Tokyo, 1976.

Hu, Wan-ch'uan 胡萬川. "'Feng Yen chuan' chi ch'i hsiang-kuan hsi-lieh ku-shih te li-chieh" 馮燕傳及其相關系列故事的理解. In *Hsiao-shuo hsi-ch'ü yen-chiu* 小説戲曲研究. Taipei: Lien-ching, 1995.

Li, Chien-kuo 李劍國. *T'ang, Wu-tai chih-kuai ch'uan-ch'i hsü-lu* 唐五代志怪傳奇敍錄. Tientsin: Nan-k'ai Ta-hsüeh, 1993, v. 1, pp. 380-95 and 404-10. See especially the fine discussion of Shen's life, pp. 380-95.

Lin, Ch'en 林辰. "Lu Hsün yü T'ang-tai ch'uan-ch'i tso-chia Shen Ya-chih" 魯迅與唐代傳奇作家沈亞之, *Lu Hsün yen-chiu,* 2 (1984).

Liu, Yen 劉衍. "Shen Ya-chih yü Shen Tzu ming-pien" 沈亞之與沈子明辯, *Hu-nan Shih-yüan hsüeh-pao* 1983.2.

Lu, Hsün 魯迅. *Chung-kuo hsiao-shuo shih lüeh* 中國小説史略. Peking: Jen-min Wen-hsüeh, 1973 (rpt. of 1925), ch. 8, pp. 59-60.

Wang, Meng-ou 王夢鷗. "Shen Ya-chih chih sheng-p'ing chi ch'i hsiao-shuo" 沈亞之之生平及其小説. In Wang's *T'ang-jen hsiao-shuo yen-chiu* 唐人小説研究. Taipei: I-wen, 1973, v. 2, pp. 97-106.

Wu, Ch'i-ming 吳企名, annot. "Shen Ya-chih." In *T'ang ts'ai-tzu chuan chiao-chien* 唐才子傳校箋. Fu Hsüan-ts'ung 傅璇琮, ed. Peking: Chung-hua, 1990, v. 3, pp. 86-93. Excellent annotation.

Uchiyama, Chinari 內山知也. "Chin Ashi to 'Shinmuki' sono hoka ni tsuite" 沈亜之と秦夢記その他について. In Uchiyama, *Zui Tô shôsetsu kenkyû* 隋唐小説研究. Tokyo: Mokujisha, 1978, pp. 489-546.

———. "Chin Ashi to shôsetsu" 沈亜之と小説, *Chûgoku bungaku hô* 12(1960): 85-134.

Yang, Sheng-k'uan 楊勝寬. "*Ch'üan T'ang shih wai-pien* so shou Shen Ya-chih i-shih chüeh-chu te chen-wei wen-t'i" 全唐詩外編所收沈亞之逸句的真偽問題, *She-hui k'o-hsüeh* (Lan-chou), 1986.3: 82-84.

William H. Nienhauser, Jr.
University of Wisconsin, Madison

Shih Chieh 石介 (*tzu*, Shou-tao 守道 or Kung-ts'ao 公操, *hao*, Ts'u-lai Hsien-sheng祖徠先生, 1005–1045) was a pioneer in the early Sung *ku-wen* 古文 (ancient-prose style) movement* as well as a forerunner of the "Sung Learning." Born in Feng-fu 奉符 County of Yen-chou 兗州 (modern Shantung), his family had been peasants until his father, Shih Ping 石丙 (969–1040), found a low-ranking post in the local government (he became county prefect in his sixties).

In his youth Shih Chieh went to study in the provincial school of Ying-t'ien-fu 應天府 (modern Honan), which was then directed by Fan Chung-yen 范仲淹 (989–1052). Influenced by his teacher, he later became an adherent of Fan's reform policies. At that time he also traveled the Wei 魏 (modern Hopei) area, where the earlier *ku-wen* advocate Liu K'ai 柳開 (947–1000)** had been born, and wrote "Kuo Wei tung-chiao shih" 過魏東郊詩 (Poem on Passing the Eastern Suburbs of Wei), showing his admiration of Liu's writing. In 1030 he passed the *chin-shih* examination. From 1030 to 1038 Shih Chieh served as a local official in Yün-chou 鄆州 (modern Shantung) and Ying-t'ien-fu. During this period he made the acquaintance of Sun Fu 孫復 (992–1057), a scholar who had failed the *chin-shih* examinations four times and who upheld that literature should be the modern equivalent of Classics. Since both cherished a number of similar ideas, the two became life-long friends. Although Sun Fu then held no position, Shih Chieh wished he could rally others under Sun's leadership to combat *shih-wen* 時文 ("current prose," i.e. *p'ien-t'i-wen* 駢體文,* parallel prose), which he regarded as shallow and florid, and to restore the Way of ancient sages. In 1035, Shih Chieh established a lecture hall for Sun at T'ai-shan 泰山 and served him as a teacher. A number of their followers became engaged in writing *ku-wen* and studying the Classics. They formed a so-called "T'ai-shan School,"

which played a key role in the philosophical as well as the literary development of the Sung dynasty. Chu Hsi 朱熹 (1130–1200) later wrote, "It is surely good that Sun [Fu] and Shih [Chieh] suddenly appeared and enjoyed discovering the correct [or "orthodox"] principles. For ages there had not been men of such rank" (*Chu-tzu yü-lei* 朱子語類, *chüan 129*).

Another close friend was Ou-yang Hsiu 歐陽修 (1007–1072),* who passed the *chin-shih* examination the same year as Shih Chieh. On reading Shih Chieh's writing, Ou-yang Hsiu was impressed by the vehemence and straightforward-ness of its expressions. He was worried that such writing would easily incurred the criticism of petty men, thus he admonished Shih not to "criticize current events in an excessive manner" (*ti shih t'ai kuo* 詆時太過). Shih Chieh obviously neglected his advice, and this proved to be a fatal weakness in his official career. When he served as an educational official in Ying-t'ien-fu, he ordered that the images of Buddha and Taoist immortals be removed, allowing the worship only of the Confucian sages, although his immediate superior believed in Buddhism. In one of his letters, he criticized the emperor for being too fond of women; consequently, his promotion was blocked.

From 1038 to 1042, Shih Chieh was in mourning for his parents and stayed at Mount Ts'u-lai, where he taught the *Classic of Changes*. People thus called him the "Master of Ts'u-lai." In 1042, both Shih Chieh and Sun Fu were summoned to the capital to be Lecturers of the Directorate of Education (*Kuo-tzu-chien Chih-chiang* 國子監直講). At that time, due to the reform policies of Fan Chung-yen and Ou-yang Hsiu, the National University (*T'ai-hsüeh* 太學) flourished, the number of the students soaring from several dozen to several thousands. Shih availed himself of this opportunity and spared no effort in promoting *ku-wen*.

He proclaimed that those who wrote current prose would be condemned. Consequently the writing style of the time was altered, few students continuing to write current prose. Not satisfied with teaching only writing, Shih Chieh encouraged his students to discuss current state affairs. In 1043, Fan Chung-yen and others began to apply a series of reforms. Shih Chieh enthusiastically supported this move and wrote a poem titled "Ch'ing-li sheng-te sung" 慶曆聖德頌 (Hymn on the Sage Virtue of the Ch'ing-li Era [1041–1049]) which made his feelings clear. The poem obviously caused a great sensation at that time, considering the fact that Su Shih 蘇軾 (1037–1101),* then only a seven-year-old schoolboy in a remote area in Szechwan, was able to recite it. However, the consequences were disastrous. In the poem, Shih Chieh bluntly criticized Fan Chung-yen's political opponents, thereby inviting attack from other factions. The reforms were abolished soon afterwards, and Shih Chieh had to leave the court in 1044.

Besides current politics, another major theme of Shih Chieh's writing was the restoration of the orthodox tradition of Confucian Classics. This required him to combat Taoism and Buddhism, because they were heterodox by nature. He expressed this clearly in his "Chung-kuo lun" 中國論 (Discourse on the Central Kingdom): "I have heard that there was a giant who was called 'Buddha.' He came to the Central Kingdom from the West. There was a man of hoary brow who was called Tan 聃. He came to the Central Kingdom from the Hu 胡 . . . . each used his 'way' to alter the Way of the Central Kingdom." Although previously no record showed that Tan (i.e. Lao Tan or Lao-tzu) was from West, Shih Chieh deliberately distorted historical fact to strengthen his argument. According to Shih Chieh, the current-prose style was another evil because it focused only on superficial beauty and thereby kept people from seeing the essence of writing, that is, the Way of ancient sages.

Shih Chieh's prose writing also revealed his concerns about current affairs. His *T'ang chien* 唐鑑 (The T'ang as a Mirror, originally in five *chuan,* now available only in fragments) as well as a number of *lun* 論 (discourses) on major political figures of the T'ang discussed the success and failure of that dynasty's government, intending to make the current ruler take heed. His "Tse su-ts'an" 責素餐 (Criticizing Those Who Live Off Others) and "Lu wei-che yen" 錄微者言 (Record of the Words of a Humble Person) sympathized the lives of commoners, strongly criticizing those officials who failed to do their duty. Similarly, his "Cheng Yüan chuan" 鄭元傳 (Biography of Cheng Yüan) extolled the heroic and filial deeds of a commoner, who went deep into Khitan territory to retrieve his father's corpse. Ou-yang Hsiu summarizes Shih Chieh's writing as follows: once he felt impassioned, he wrote down his feelings. He praises or condemns without reservation. In his eloquent and forceful discussion, he talks freely about the whole span of ancient and modern events. His works may astound or even agitate the common people, but they nonetheless show the author's great strength and courage.

In his extant works, Shih Chieh has 144 poems, 64 in the ancient style (*ku-shih* 古詩). Like his prose, most of his poems are permeated with strong feelings. In his "Tu Shih An-jen hsüeh-shih shih" 讀石安仁學士詩 (Reading the Poems of Scholar Shih An-jen) and "*Shih Man-ch'ing shih-chi* hsü" 石曼卿詩集序 (Preface to the *Poetry Collection of Shih Man-ch'ing*), he praised the heroic and forceful language in the poems of Shih Yen-nien 石延年 (*tzu,* Man-ch'ing, 994–1041), and also expressed his disdain for the decadent style of a contemporary circle of poets. In fighting against florid language, he advocated a style which is simple, vigorous, and without ornamentation. His "Pi hsien li" 彼縣吏 (The Officials of That County) and "Tu Chao-shu" 讀詔書 (Written on Reading an Imperial Edict) both expressed indignation at greedy officials, whom he compared to tigers and wolves. "Ho chüeh" 河決 (The Yellow River Burst) described the disastrous scenes of a floods from antiquity to the present, urging the ruler to emphasize control of the river. ""Pien Ch'ü" 汴渠 (The Pien Canal) points out that a single man (the emperor) has profited from the flesh and blood of the commoners who built this canal centuries before and have maintained it since that time. "Hsi-pei" 西北 (The Northwest) showed his concern about the conditions of the Western frontier and criticized the generals who were supposed to be maintaining a defense there. In all these poems, he used straightforward language to recount and comment on important current events and showed his concern for his state and its people.

Like his predecessor Liu K'ai, Shih Chieh in his emphasis on the ancient Way did not pay enough attention to the niceties of prose style. Under Shih's influence, a laconic but lackluster style replaced the current-prose style and became dominant in the world of letters. It was not until Ou-yang Hsiu became chief examiner in 1059 that Ou-yang's more elegant *ku-wen* took its place and ancient-prose movement entered a new stage.

Editions and References

Shih Shou-tao Hsien-sheng chi 石守道先生集. In *Cheng-i T'ang ch'üan-shu* 正誼堂全書. *Pai-pu* edition.

Ts'u-lai Shih Hsien-sheng wen-chi 徂徠石先生文集. Ch'en Chih-o 陳植鍔, ed. Peking: Chung-hua, 1984.

Studies

Bol, *This Culture of Ours,* pp. 181-83.

Chin, Chung-shu 金中樞. "Sung-tai ku-wen yün-tung chih fa-chan yen-chiu" 宋代古文運動之發展研究, *Hsin-ya hsüeh-pao* 5.2 (1963): 97-102.

Chu, Shang-shu 祝尚樞. *Pei Sung ku-wen yün-tung fa-chan-shih* 北宋古文運動發展史. Chengtu: Pa-Shu Shu-she, 1995, pp. 129-51.

Egan, Ronald C. *The Literary Works of Ou-yang Hsiu (1007–72).* Cambridge: Cambridge University Press, 1984, pp. 17-21.

P'an, Fu-en 潘富恩 and Hsü Yü-ch'ing 徐餘慶."Lun Shih Chieh" 論石介, *Wen shih che* 1989.1: 84-91.

Tung, Chin-yü 董金裕. "Sung ju chung te k'uang-che: Shih Chieh" 宋儒中的狂者石介, in *Sung ju feng-fan* 宋儒風範. Taipei: Tung-ta, 1979, pp. 10-13.

Weiguo Cao
University of Wisconsin

Sun Ch'o 孫綽 (*tzu,* Hsing-kung 興公, *ca.* 314–*ca.* 371) was the grandson of Sun Ch'u 孫楚 (*ca.* 218–293), a well-known author of *hsüan-yen shih* 玄言詩 ("mysterious-word" poetry, i.e., a type of verse written on philosophical topics) in the Western Chin, and Sun Tsuan 孫纂, who apparently held no official posts. Although originally from Chung-tu 中都 (modern P'ing-yao 平遙, Shansi), Sun Tsuan moved the family to K'uai-chi 會稽 (modern Chekiang) around 309.

His father having died early, Sun was bought up by his uncle in a family no longer prosperous. After a decade of reclusive life in K'uai-chi during which he wrote the "Sui-ch'u fu" 遂初賦 (Rhapsody on Fulfilling My Original Resolve), which testified to his satisfaction with the eremitic life, he was finally led to seek patronage among the elite to support himself and his family. He first joined the staff of Yü Liang 庾亮 (289–340) as military adjutant. Later, he was assigned to different posts in the provinces and at court. He served under powerful men such as Yin Hao 殷浩 (305–356), Wang Hsi-chih 王羲之 (321–

379), and even Huan Wen 桓溫 (312–373), the famous generalissimo and king-maker of the Eastern Chin, as attendant or aide, before reaching his highest position, T'ing-wei ch'ing 廷尉卿 (Chief Minister for Law Enforcement); he was also ennobled as Marquis of Ch'ang-lo 長樂, and both titles, that of the high office and his noble rank, were commonly used to designate Sun and his subsequent collections of writings.

Although Sun achieved considerable literary renown, the information about his life is sparse and anecdotal. The *Shih-shuo-hsin-yü* 世説新語 (New Account of Tales of the World)* depicts him as quick-witted and capable of clever repartee, but sometimes coarse in speech and vulgar in conduct. Possibly because by nature he spurned official life, he was prone to sarcasm in dealing with officials, openly satirizing influential men like Hsi Tso-ch'ih 習鑿齒 (d. 384). He even risked his life to present a memorial opposing Huan Wen's proposal to move the capital back to Lo-yang.

Of his oeuvre of thirty-seven poems and thirty-six pieces of prose, Sun is best known for his *hsüan-yen* verse (following his grandfather). This type of poetry flourished in the mid-fourth century; it usually expounded Taoist philosophical texts and ideas in diction common to these texts and four-syllable lines. Although Sun's success made him one of the major literary figures of his time, for many later readers these poems seemed arcane, even apoetic. Thus Chung Jung's 鍾嶸 (*ca.* 465–518) classification of Sun as a "third-rank poet" in the *Shih-p'in* 詩品 (An Evaluation of Poetry)* represents not only Sun Cho's literary reputation, but Chung's assessment of this kind of verse in general.

Sun's prose includes a series of *tsan* 贊 (encomiums) on men of wisdom, such as Lao-tzu, Yüan Hsien 原憲, and several eminent Buddhist monks. Given his contemporary repute, he undoubtedly had little choice but to author several epitaphs and grave inscriptions for distinguished figures such as Wang Tao 王導 (276–339), Hsi Chien 郗鑒, and Yü Liang, his first patron. In his *Wen-hsin tiao-lung* 文心雕龍* Liu Hsieh 劉勰 (*ca.* 465–*ca.* 520) praises Sun's work in these two genres and considers him a successor to Ts'ai Yung 蔡邕 (133– 192),* doyen of early funerary writings. Sun's best-known work, nevertheless, is the "Yu Tien-t'ai-shan fu" 遊天台山賦 (Rhapsody on Roaming the Celestial Terrace Mountains), a piece that recounts his mystical ascent of Mount Tien-t'ai (in the eastern part of modern Chekiang). He reputedly showed this piece to his friend Fan Ch'i 范啟 (*fl.* mid-fourth century) and said, "Try to throw it on the ground! It will surely resound like metal bells and stone chimes!" This work, the only *fu* from the Eastern Chin collected in the *Wen-hsüan,* * is the earliest *fu* on mountains. The rhapsody begins with a preface introducing the great mountain where immortals dwell. In the first half of the piece, the author is an explorer who reports what he sees during the journey to the peak. In the second half, he begins to philosophize about the mystical experience of this climb. Sun skillfully synthesizes images and phrases from both Buddhism and Taoism: with a monk's metal staff he follows the trails Lao-tzu and Lao Lai-tzu 老萊子 trod to reach the Numinous Stream, where he was able to cleanse the "five hindrances" (Buddhist vices), before reaching the peak of T'ien-t'ai where there was the "city of immortals." Thus, his physical journey is gradually transformed into a mystical experience. In a concluding moment of enlightenment, Sun equates the removal of the Buddhist "three banners" (form, emptiness, contemplation) with the Taoist idea of *wu-wei* 無為 (non-existence).

Sun also authored some apologetic essays. For example, the "Yü-tao lun" 喻道論 (Discourse Elucidating the Way), collected in the *Hung-ming chi* 弘明集, is a straightforward manifesto arguing that Buddhism and Confucianism are not irreconcilably opposed. Sun shows that the teachings of the Duke of Chou, Confucius, and the Buddha are nearly identical, differing only in their terminology. He also tries to resolve the main question dividing Buddhists and Taoists: the Buddhist rejection of filial piety. After an account of Buddha's life and his noble destiny, Sun argues that a monk's seeking to become a Buddha parallels closely the ideal of glorifying one's parents. In the partially lost "Tao-hsien-lun" 道賢論 (Discourse on Monks and Worthies, surviving only in the *Kao-seng chuan* 高僧傳 [Biographies of Eminent Monks]*) Sun similarly compares the seven contemporary Buddhist monks with the Seven Worthies of the Bamboo Grove (*Chu-lin ch'i-hsien* 竹林七賢).

Editions and References

Sun T'ing-wei chi 孫廷尉集. *Han Wei Liu-ch'ao pai-san-chia chi* 漢魏六朝百三家集. Ming edition.

Translations

Chang, *Six Dynasties Poetry*, pp. 5-6.
Frodsham, John D. "The Origins of Chinese Nature Poetry," *AM, N.S.* 8 (1960): 79.
Knechtges, *Wen xuan*, 2:243-53.
Mather, Richard. "The Mystical Ascent of the T'ien-t'ai Mountains: Sun Ch'o's Yu T'ien-t'ai-shan fu," *MS* 20 (1961): 226-45.
Watson, *Chinese Rhyme-Prose*, pp. 162-71.
von Zach, *Anthologie*, 1:159-62.

Studies

Fukunaga, Mitsuji 福永光司. "Son Shaku no shisô—Tôshin ni okeru sankyô kôshô no ikkeitai" 孫綽の思想—東晋における三教交渉の一形態, *Aichi Gakugei Daigaku kenkyû hôkô* 愛知学芸大学研究報告 20 (1961).
Hachiya, Kunio 蜂屋邦夫. "Son Shaku no shôgai to shisô" 孫綽の生涯と思想, *Tôyô bunka* 57 (1977): 65-100.
Hung, Shun-lung 洪順隆. "Hsüan-yen shih-lun" 玄言詩論. In his *Yu Yin-i tao Kung-t'i* 由隱逸到宮體. Taipei: Wen-shih-che,

1984, pp. 97-122.
Knechtges, David R. "Sun Chuo." In Knechtges' *Wen xuan*, v. 2, pp. 361-362. The only concise biography of Sun Ch'o in English.
Li, Wen-ch'u 李文初. "Tung-Chin shih-jen Sun Ch'o k'ao-i" 東晉詩人孫綽考議, *Wen-shih* 28 (1987): 207-20.
Link, Arthur E. and Tim Lee. "Sun Ch'o's 'Yü-tao-lun': A Clarification of the Way," *MS* 25 (1966): 169-196.
Ts'ao, Tao-heng 曹道衡, "Chin-tai tso-chia liu-k'ao" 晉代作家六考, *Wen-shih* 20 (1983), pp. 185-94.
Wilhelm, Helmut. "Sun Ch'o's Yü-tao-lun," *Sino-Indian Studies* 5 (1957): 261-71.

Jui-lung Su
The National University of Singapore

Sung Ch'i 宋祁 (*tzu*, Tzu-ching 子京, posthumous name, Ching-wen 景文, 998-1062) was a renowned historian who, with Ou-yang Hsiu 歐陽修 (1007-1072),* co-authored the *Hsin T'ang shu* 新唐書 [New T'ang History] and a noted poet of the early Sung. Born into a provincial official's family at An-lu 安陸 (modern Hupei), Sung Ch'i moved with his family to Yung-ch'iu 雍邱, in the vicinity of the capital Pien-liang 汴梁 (modern Kai-feng 開封, Honan). When Sung Ch'i and his elder brother, Sung Hsiang 宋庠 (996-1066) grew up, the family had fallen on hard times. In 1023, the Sung brothers took the civil-service examinations together. Sung Ch'i was initially named the top graduate. Then the Empress Dowager Chang-hsien 章獻 (969-1033) insisted that the younger brother should give way to the elder. Sung Hsiang was therefore named top graduate and Sung Ch'i ranked tenth. But the Sung brothers thereby earned their fame as the "Two Sungs."

Sung Ch'i was first appointed Chün-shih T'ui-kuan 軍事推官 (Military Judge) of Fu-chou 復州 (modern Foo-chow). He was later recommended by Sun Shih 孫奭 (962-1033) to be Ta-li-ssu Ch'eng 大

151

理寺丞 (Assistant Minister of Court of Judicial Review), and Kuo-tzu-chien Chih-chiang 國子監直講 (Lecturer in Directorate of Education). After court-administered examination, he joined the Shih-kuan 史官 (Office of History), and shortly after was promoted to T'ai-ch'ang Po-shih 太常博士 (Erudite of the Chamberlain for Ceremonial) and then T'ung-chih Li-i-yüan 同知禮儀院 (Associate Administrator of Ritual Academy). Together with Li Chao 李照 (*fl.* 1034) and Hu Yüan 胡瑗 (993-1059), he renovated instruments and musical works, and compiled the *Kuang-yeh chi* 廣業記 (A Record of Enlarging the Foundation). In 1045, he was promoted to be Shang-shu Kung-pu Yüan-wai-lang 尚書工部員外郎 (Vice Director of the Ministry of Works), then T'ung-hsiu Ch'i-chü-chu 同修起居注 (Associated Editor of Imperial Diary), and finally Ch'üan San-ssu Tu-chih P'an-kuan 權三司度支判官 (Probationary Administrative Assistant of the Revenue Section of the State Finance Commission). According to convention, he should be further promoted to the post of Chih Chih-kao 知制誥 (Imperial Edict Drafter), equivalent to the modern position of Vice Prime Minister. However, since his brother Sung Hsiang was *Ts'an-chih Cheng-shih* 參知政事 (Participant in Determining Governmental Matters) at that time, to avoid the younger brother again overtaking the elder, Sung Ch'i was transferred to several alternate positions, finally becoming *P'an T'ai-ch'ang Li-yüan* 判太常禮院 (Administrative Assistant of Ritual Academy of Imperial Sacrifices Court). When Sung Hsiang was deprived of his post in 1047, Sung Ch'i was also demoted to a series of provincial posts. In a short time, however, Sung Ch'i was called back to the capital to become Academician of Lung-t'u Ko Hsüeh-shih 龍圖閣學士 (Dragon Diagram Hall), and Shih-kuan Hsiu-chuan 史館修撰 (Senior Compiler of Office of History). These were positions related to the project of compiling a new history of the T'ang dynasty (see below) and held no real political power. When Sung Hsiang regained his position as Prime Minister, Sung Ch'i had mixed emotions, since he had hoped to hold high office himself, but must have realized that his inability to work within official circles as well as his brother's prominence would thwart his hopes.

Thus he applied himself earnestly to the task of compiling a new history to replace the *Chiu T'ang shu* 舊唐書 [Old T'ang History], a task that had originally been given him in an edict from Emperor Jen 仁 (r. 1022-1063) in 1044. The *Old T'ang History* had been put together rather haphazardly during the Five Dynasties under the supervision of Chao Ying 趙瑩 (d. 943) and Liu Hsü 劉昫 (887-946) and had been criticized for a number of shortcomings. The Sung, of course, also wanted its own history of the dynasty which preceded it. Sung Ch'i proved an excellent choice for compiler. He spent the next dozen years working especially on the *lieh-chuan* 列傳 (memoirs or biographies), discarding 61 lives from the *Old T'ang History* and adding 331 new biographical accounts. Although these replacements reflected somewhat the philosophy of Sung times, they also helped present a more balanced picture of the T'ang dynasty—the *Old T'ang History* had generally slighted the post-An Lu-shan eras because there was much less official documentation for the later periods to draw upon. Sung Ch'i's solution was to seek other sources—epitaphs, eulogies, *hsing-chuang* 行狀 (accounts of conduct), genealogies, even unofficial histories and anecdotal works. He also added chapters on non-Chinese regimes such as those of Po-ssu 波斯 (Persia) and the Sha-t'o 沙陀 Turks. Joined in his work by Ou-yang Hsiu, Fan Chen 范鎮 (1007-1087), and Lü Hsia-ch'ing 呂夏卿 (b. *ca.* 990), the *New T'ang History* has generally had a good

152

reputation with critics and scholars.

Aside from his work on the *New T'ang History,* Sung Ch'i left a prodigious legacy of prose writings (nearly 2000 pieces). This corpus includes 45 *fu* 賦, hundreds of official rescripts and other documents, several dozen biographical works, a postface to Liu Tsung-yüan's 柳宗元 (773-819)* collected works, and other writings suggesting an interest in the *Ku-wen* Movement.* Other works suggest interest in both Buddhism and Taoism.

Sung Ch'i was also know as a poet. Three-hundred *shih** and only eight *tz'u** are extant, however. In another anecdote related to the civil-service examinations, Sung Ch'i acquired the sobriquet "Sung Ts'ai-hou" 宋采侯 "Colorful Target" Sung) for his success in writing a poem during the examination on the topic "Colorful Target," an archery ritual first practiced in the Chou dynasty to establish prestige among the neighboring countries and peoples, a goal shared by the Sung rulers.

His *shih* were written in the ornate, allusive style of the late T'ang. He and his brother, Sung Hsiang, were considered the leading Hsi-k'un 西崑 style poets of the second generation (following the deaths of the founders of this style, Yang I 楊億 (974-1020/1), Ch'ien Wei-yen 錢惟演 (977-1034), and Liu Yün 劉筠 (970-1030). His poetry reveals Li Shang-yin's 李商隱 (*ca.* 813-858) influence as the following "Lo hua" 落花 (Fallen Flowers) shows:

> The falling whites and reeling reds each
> grieve for themselves,
> Unforgettable the mist and rain by the
> azure tower.
> About to fly, once more they do the
> Whirlwind Dance,
> Once fallen, their faces still only half
> made-up.
> As the travelers return from the vast sea,
> pearls shed tears,
> Long after men depart the Chang
> Terrace, the fragrance of their lovers'
> bones remains.

> Unconsciously might they have
> conveyed their feelings to a pair of
> butterflies
> To bestow completely their fragrant
> hearts to the honeycomb.

墜素翻紅各自傷, 青樓煙雨忍相忘.
將飛更作迴風舞, 已落猶成半面妝.
滄海客歸珠迸淚, 章臺人去骨遺香.
可能無意傳雙蝶, 盡委芳心與蜜房.

This poem is an elegy for all the exquisitely beautiful women (i.e., flowers) of the world who fall victim to the crassness of their lovers and the world. It embodies the proverbial idea of *hung-yen po-ming* 紅顏博命, "fate is never kind to those born with a beautiful face." Yet there is in the final couplet a wistfulness as if the poet was vowing to treat such a beauty better than the travelers and gadabouts of the previous couplet (the Chang Terrace was a conventional reference to a house of assignment). Both these emotions and the syntactic features of the poem evoke associations with two celebrated pieces by Li Shang-yin, "Lo hua" and "Chin se" 錦瑟 (The Ornamented Zither), as well as Tu Mu's 杜牧 (803-852)* "Chin-ku yüan" 金谷園 (Golden Valley Park).

Sung Ch'i's *tz'u* also won him renown, although he wrote *hsiao-ling* much in the style and conventions of the time. His best known poem is "Yü-lou ch'un" 玉樓春 (Springtime in the Jade Loft), in which the line "On red apricot branches the vernal air vitalizes" 紅杏枝頭春意鬧 was supposedly considered so exceptional that Sung was given the nickname "Hung-hsing Shang-shu" 紅杏尚書 (Prime Minister of the Red Apricot), perhaps suggesting that although he had political ambitions, his greatest success was achieved in the world of literature.

Editions and References

Chin-wen chi 景文集. 62 *chüan. Supple-ments* 22 *chüan.* Mien-yang 沔陽: Lu-shih Shen-shih-chi Chai 盧氏慎始基齋,1923. Photolithographically repro-duced from the edition of *Hu-pei hsien-cheng i-shu* 湖北先正遺書, in the Wu-ying-Tien Chü-chen 武英殿聚珍 collection.

Ch'üan Sung tz'u, 1:116-117.

Ch'üan Sung shih, 4:1-12.2330-2621.

Ch'üan Sung wen, 12:482-520:72-739 and 13:521-531.1-190.

I-pu fang-wu lüeh-chi 益部方物略記. 1 *chüan.* In *I-ts'un ts'ung-shu. TSCCCP* edition. Shanghai: Shang-wu Yin-shu-kuan, 1923.

I-pu fang-wu lüeh-chi 益部方物略記. 1 *chüan.* In *Ssu-k'u.*

Sung Chin-wen kung chi 宋景文公集. 32 *chüan.* In *I-ts'un ts'ung-shu* 佚存叢書. Shanghai: Han-fen Lou 涵芬樓, 1924. Photolithographically reproduced from a Japanese edition first published between 1789-1818.

Sung Ching-wen tsa-shuo 宋景文雜説. 1 *chüan.* In *Shuo-fu ts'un ts'ung-shu. Ts'ung-shu chi-ch'eng ch'u-pien* 叢書集成初編 edition. Shanghai: Shang-wu Yin-shu-kuan, 1923.

Translations

Ch'u Ta-kao. *Chinese Love Poems from Ancient to Modern Times.* New York: Peter Pauper Press, 1942, p. 57.

Imbault-Huart, C. *La Poésie chinoise du xive au xixe siècle extraits des poètes chinois.* Paris: E. Leroux, 1886, pp. 23-32.

Studies

Chang, Chia-fan 張家璠. "Sung Ch'i" 宋祁. In Chang Shun-hui 張舜徽, ed *Chung-kuo shih-hsüeh-chia chuan* 中國史學家傳. Shenyang: Liao-ning Chiao-yü, 1984.

Ch'en, Hsüeh-kuang 陳學廣. "Tzu-jan chih-ching yü hsin-ling hsin-hsi, shuo Sung Ch'i 'Yü-lou-ch'un'" 自然之景與心靈信息—説宋祁玉樓春, *Wen-shih chih-shih* 1992.5: 61-63.

Chou, Tsung-sheng 周宗盛. "Sung Tzu-ching, 'Hung-hsin Shang-shu'" 宋子京, 紅杏尚書, *Ta-hua wan-pao* 15 June 1975.

Lo, K'ang-lieh 羅慷烈. "Sung Ch'i Lien-tzu" 宋祁煉字. In *Tz'u-hsüeh tsa-tsu* 辭學雜俎, Chengtu: Pa-Shu Shu-she, 1990, pp. 54-5.

Tseng, Tsao-chuang 曾棗莊. *Lun Hsi-k'un t'i* 論西崑體. Kaohsiung: Li-wen Wen-hua, 1993, pp. 355-67.

Chen Zhi
The National University of Singapore

T'ao Hung-ching 陶弘景 (*tzu,* T'ung-ming 通明, *hao,* Yin-chü 隱居, posthumous name Chen-po 貞白, also known as Master Hua-yang 華陽先生, 456–536) is primarily remembered as the systematizer of the Shang-ch'ing scriptural tradition 上清經 of medieval Taoism (see essay on "Taoist Literature"). T'ao's efforts as textual critic, conservator, and commentator are in large measure responsible for the elevated place the Shang-ch'ing corpus occupies both in the Taoist canon and in the aesthetic and literary appreciation of Chinese literati beyond the movement's esoteric following.

A native of Mo-ling 秣陵 in Tan-yang Commandery 丹陽郡 (modern Chiang-ning 江寧 county on the outskirts of Nanking), T'ao Hung-ching was descended from a line of distinguished officials, military men, and scholars that originally hailed from Shantung. After emigrating to the South and settling in the area of Chien-k'ang 建康 (Nanking) at the end of the Han dynasty, T'ao's ancestors regularly served in high office. His grandfather T'ao Lung 陶隆, Marquis of Chin-an 晉安, and his father T'ao Chen-pao 陶貞寶 were both men of learning whose interests in book collecting, calligraphy, and pharmacology are cited by T'ao Hung-ching's biographers as early influences on his intellectual development. The Buddhist faith of his mother Chih-chan 智湛 likely also left its mark. Hagiographic accounts attribute to him a supernatural birth, the looks of an immortal, and profound learning in Confucianism, Taoism, and Buddhism as well as a wide range of technical subjects, including medicine, pharmacology, alchemy, metallurgy, astronomy, and geography.

T'ao lived under three successive southern dynasties with capitals in Chien-k'ang: the Liu Sung (420–479), under whose protection Heavenly Master Taoism (*T'ien-shih tao* 天師道) flourished in Southern China, the Ch'i

(479–502), whose princely establishments patronized Shen Yüeh 沈約 (441–513),* Jen Fang 任昉 (460–508),* Hsieh T'iao 謝朓 (464–499)* and other leading literary figures of the age, and finally the Liang (502–557). He began his temporal career at the age of seventeen as a clerk in the entourage of the Governor of Tan-yang Commandery, Liu Ping 劉秉. At the end of the Sung and beginning of the Ch'i, T'ao served briefly in tutorial and secretarial posts as attendant gentleman (*shih-lang* 侍郎) and reader-in-waiting (*shih-tu* 侍讀) in the households of several imperial princes.

Despite T'ao's adherence to the Sung loyalist cause after the seizure of power by the Ch'i, he continued in the employment of the new court until the death of his father in 481. At the end of the mourning period, in 483, T'ao was appointed palace general of the left guard (*tso-wei tien-chung chiang-chün* 左衛殿中將軍), a unit of the heir apparent's guard troops. This post, however, he was to resign the following year when he entered mourning for his mother. T'ao Hung-ching's Taoist instruction under the abbot Sun Yu-yüeh 孫遊嶽 (399–489) in Chien-k'ang, a disciple of the Liu Sung master Lu Hsiu-ching 陸修靜 (406–477), fell into this period (484–486). His initiation into the textual traditions of Ling-pao 靈寶經, codified by Lu Hsiu-ching, and the Shang-ch'ing revelations of nearby Mao-shan 茅山 was complemented by a journey in search of Shang-ch'ing scriptures in Chekiang, the native region of Sun Yu-yüeh, in 490. The works assembled during this period laid the foundation for T'ao's subsequent text-critical studies and the compilation of the *Chen-kao*. At the same time, his literary talents were noted and his poetry praised by Shen Yüeh. T'ao's early scholarship found expression in a series of commentaries on Confucian and Taoist classics and the compilation of an extensive anthology, the Florilegium of Learning (*Hsüeh-yüan* 學苑). Conceived as comprising 100 *chüan*, the unfinished manuscript was eventually lost.

In 486 T'ao had resumed official duties as general of the Chen-wu Army 振武將軍, a post he seems to have occupied, with some reluctance, until his definitive retirement from court life in 492. The remaining forty-four years of T'ao's life were spent, mostly at Mao-shan, in the pursuit of Taoist scholarship and the esoteric practices advocated by the Shang-ch'ing revelations. His main interests and activities during this period can be subsumed under the headings (1) collection, authentication, and annotation of dispersed fragments from the original corpus of Shang-ch'ing autographs; (2) pharmacological and medical studies; and (3) alchemical and metallurgical experiments.

T'ao's earliest major work, *Teng-chen yin-chüeh* 登真隱訣 (The Esoteric Instructions for Ascent to Perfection), was mostly completed during 492–499, but he continued and supplemented it until about 514. Only a fragment of three out of an original twenty-five *chüan* survives. *Ascent to Perfection* was an annotated manual for initiates of methods of visualization and meditation, ritual procedures, drug recipes and other techniques for attaining immortality. These were drawn from separate instructions and the biographies of the Perfected revealed to the Mao-shan visionary Yang Hsi 楊羲 during 363–370 and recorded in the autographs of Yang and his patrons Hsü Mi 許謐 (303–373) and Hsü Hui 許翽 (341–*ca.* 370), father and son. *The Organization Chart of the Perfected and Spirits,* an inventory of the pantheon including the names, ranks and official functions of the deities grouped in seven hierarchical levels, which circulated separately since T'ang times as *Tung-hsüan ling-pao chen-ling wei-yeh t'u* 洞玄靈寶真靈位業圖 probably formed part of the original *Teng-chen yin-chüeh*.

If *Ascent to Perfection* addressed the practitioners of esoteric Mao-shan Taoism, T'ao Hung-ching's celebrated *Chen-kao* 真誥 (Proclamations of the Perfected, 499), became a major vehicle for the broad dissemination of Shang-ch'ing writings and ensured their lasting literary influence. The *Proclamations* were based on the same source materials as the *Ascent,* i.e. miscellaneous fragments of the revelation experienced by Yang Hsi considered as accessory to the Shang-ch'ing scriptures. These were meticulously authenticated by T'ao on the basis of their distinctive calligraphy as well as text-critical criteria defined in the final section of the *Proclamations* (*chüan* 19-20). Interspersed with T'ao's commentary, the *Chen-kao* presents accounts, including hymns and poems, of the descent and pronouncements of the Shang-ch'ing Perfected, alchemical recipes, insights into underworld proceedings conducted against Hsü family ancestors, methods and techniques deemed fit for public divulgation, descriptions of Mao-shan and of Feng-tu 豐都, the capital of the underworld, and personal documents relating to Yang Hsi and the Hsü family.

Shortly after the completion of the *Chen-kao,* T'ao Hung-ching assembled his pharmacological writings into the *Pen-ts'ao ching chi-chu* 本草經集諸 (Collected Commentaries to the Pharmacopoeia).

The succession of the Liang dynasty and reign of Emperor Wu (r. 502–550), a fervent patron of Buddhism, brought a period of repressive measures against Taoism to Southern China. T'ao Hung-ching and his religious establishment at Mao-shan, however, were exempt from Wu-ti's anti-Taoist policies. T'ao indeed enjoyed the emperor's personal protection and favors motivated no doubt in part by Wu-ti's interest in T'ao Hung-ching's technological skills.

T'ao's experiments in elixir alchemy began in 504 at imperial command. In 505 he was ordered to supervise the forging of swords for the Liang dynasty. His interest in metal foundry and the fabrication of Taoist magical swords can be traced to the year 497, under the Ch'i. A commentary by T'ao on the lost *Chien-ching* 劍經 (Sword Scripture), is preserved in *T'ai-p'ing yü-lan* 太平御覽, *chüan* 665. The *Ku-chin tao-chien lu* 古今刀劍錄 (Register of Ancient and Recent Swords) is a list of dynastic swords from the Hsia down to the Liang, with those of lesser kingdoms appended. It ends with an entry regarding thirteen "divine swords" (*shen-chien* 神劍) made by T'ao Hung-ching at the behest of Liang Wu-ti in 520.

Extended travels in the southeast (modern Chekiang and Fukien) between 508–512 led T'ao to the sacred mountain Huo-shan 霍山 located in Chin-an, the fief of his grandfather T'ao Lung in modern Nan-an 南安 (Fukien). In the course of this journey, terminated in 512 by an imperial recall, T'ao Hung-ching met the visionary Chou Tzu-liang 周子良 (497–516) who became his disciple. The revelations of the Perfected to Chou and the latter's ritual suicide in answer to a supernatural summons are the subject of the *Chou-shih ming-t'ung chi* 周氏冥通記 (Record of Master Chou's Communications with the Beyond), edited, annotated, and introduced by T'ao Hung-ching. The work was presented to the emperor in 517; subsequent editions contain both the presentation memorial and Wu-ti's missive of acceptance.

After 520, when T'ao was aged 65 *sui,* his main preoccupation seems to have been the quest for alchemical elixirs. A Sui-dynasty catalogue credits T'ao Hung-ching with several alchemical compilations (*Sui shu* 隋書 34:1048). Although no authentic writings by T'ao can be reliably dated after this period, the great prestige he already enjoyed in his lifetime invited many spurious attributions, including a commentary on the *Kuei-ku tzu* 鬼谷子 dating to the T'ang period (TT 671, no. 1025); the *Yang-hsing yen-ming lu* 養性延命錄 (TT 572, no. 838), a later compilation, probably also of T'ang date, of techniques for nourishing vitality, extensively based on the writings of the seventh-century physician Sun Ssu-mo 孫思邈; the *Shang-ch'ing wo-chung chüeh* 上清握中訣 (TT 60, no. 140), a T'ang compilation of extracts from the *Teng-chen yin-chüeh* and other writings by T'ao; the *T'ai-shang ch'ih-wen tung-shen san-lu* 太上赤文洞神三籙 (TT 324, no. 589), a Sung compilation of divination methods, falsely attributed to T'ao Hung-ching; the *Shang-ch'ing ming-t'ang yüan-chen* [i.e., *Hsüan-chen*] *ching-chüeh* 上清明堂元[玄]真經訣 (TT 194, no. 424), a collection of meditational techniques drawn from Mao-shan hagiography and the writings of T'ao.

Collections of T'ao's literary works were first compiled in the sixth century. In Sui times two versions circulated, comprising fifteen and thirty *chüan* respectively (cf. *Sui shu* 隋書 35.1077), but their contents were largely lost by the Sung. The *Hua-yang T'ao yin-chü chi* (containing samples of T'ao's poetry, official correspondence, prefaces, and inscriptions) and other editions in one or two *chüan* (see below) are later reconstructions. For detailed bibliographies of the works attributed to T'ao, see Mugitani, "Tô Kôkei" (2), pp. 67-83, and Chung Lai-yin, *Ch'ang-sheng pu-ssu*, pp. 25-28 under "Studies" below.

Biographical sources on T'ao Hung-ching are relatively abundant. The most important is the *Hua-yang T'ao Yin-chü nei-chuan* 華陽陶隱居內傳, probably of late Tang date, by Chia Sung 賈嵩 (TT 151, no. 300), which is based on the *Hua-yang Yin-chü Hsien-sheng pen-ch'i lu* 華陽隱居先生本起錄 by T'ao's nephew T'ao I 陶翊 (cf. *Yün-chi ch'i-ch'ien* 雲笈七籤) and a continuation, now lost, by P'an Ch'üan-wen 番泉文. The *nei-chuan* also reproduces a number of important primary documents, including funerary and commemorative inscriptions, a

statue inscription, and the canonization edict of 1124 by the Sung emperor Hui-tsung (cf. Ishii Masako, *Dôkyô gaku*, pp. 41-119).

The life of T'ao Hung-ching is also documented in the dynastic histories (*Liang shu* 梁書 51:742-43; *Nan shih* 南史 76:1897-1901) and Taoist hagiography, notably the "*Liang Mao-shan Chen-po hsien-sheng chuan* 梁茅山貞白先生傳 in the *Chen-hsi* 真系 (805) of Li Po 李渤 (*Yün-chi ch'i-ch'ien chüan* 5), the *Li-shih chen-hsien t'i-tao t'ung-chien* 歷世真仙體道通鑑 (pref. 1294; TT 139-48, no. 296), and the *Mao-shan chih* 茅山志 (pref. 1328, TT 153-58, no. 304).

Editions and References

Chen-kao 真誥 (499). Compiled and annotated by T'ao Hung-ching. TT 637-40, no. 1016. See also Ishii Masako 石井昌子, *Shinkô* 真誥, Tokyo: Meitoku Shuppansha, 1991, and Mugitani Kunio 麥谷邦夫, *Shinkô sakuin* 真誥索引, Kyoto: Kyôto Daigaku Jimbun Kagaku Kenkyûjo, 1991.

Chou-shih ming-t'ung chi 周氏冥通記 (presented in 517). By Chou Tzu-liang 周子良 (497–516). T'ao Hung-ching, ed. and annot. TT 152, no. 302.

Hua-yang T'ao yin-chü chi 華陽陶隱居集. Collection of writings by T'ao Hung-ching, edited by Fu Hsiao 傅霄 (d. 1159). TT 726, no. 1050. See also *Liang Chen-po hsien-sheng T'ao yin-chü chi* 梁貞白先生陶隱居集 (Taipei: Hsüeh-sheng, 1973 reproduction of 1552 printed edition.) and collectanea editions listed in *Chung-kuo ts'ung-shu tsung-lu* 中國叢書綜錄 2:1210 (Shanghai: Shang-hai Ku-chi, 1982).

Ko Hsien-weng Chou-hou pei-chi fang 葛仙翁肘後備急方 (TT 1013-15, no. 1306). Vade-mecum of medicinal prescriptions and procedures by Ko Hung 葛洪 (283–343). Revised edition and preface by T'ao Hung-ching.

Ku-chin tao-chien lu 古今力劍錄 (after 520). Compiled by T'ao Hung-ching. In *Han Wei ts'ung-shu* 漢魏叢書.

Pen-ts'ao ching chi-chu 本草經集諸. Compiled by T'ao Hung-ching. Edited by Mori Risshi 森立之 (1807-1885), *Honzôkyô shûchû* 本草經集諸. Osaka 1972 edition.

157

Teng-chen yin-chüeh 登真隱訣. Compiled and annotated by T'ao Hung-ching. TT 193, no. 421.

Tung-hsüan ling-pao chen-ling wei-yeh t'u 洞玄靈寶真靈位業圖 (*ca.* 500). Compiled by T'ao Hung-ching, edited by Lü-ch'iu Fang-yüan 閭丘方遠 (d. 902). TT 73, no. 167.

Translations

Bokenkamp, Stephen R. "Answering a Summons." In *Religions of China in Practice.* Donald S. Lopez, ed. Princeton: Princeton University Press, 1996, pp. 188-202 [partial translations of *Chou-shih ming-t'ung chi* and T'ao's preface].

Cedzich, Ursula-Angelika. "Das Ritual der Himmelsmeister im Spiegel früher Quellen: Übersetzung und Untersuchung des liturgischen Materials im 3. *chüan* des *Teng-chen yin-chüeh*" Unpublished Ph. D. dissertation, Würzburg University, 1987.

Strickmann, Michel. "The Mao Shan Revelations; Taoism and the Chinese Aristocracy." *TP* 63 (1977): 1-64 [includes a translation of *Chen-kao* 19.9b-20.4b]

Studies

Chung, Lai-yin 鍾來因. *Ch'ang-sheng pu-ssu ti t'an-ch'iu: Tao-ching* Chen-kao *chih mi* 長生不死的探求一道經〔真誥〕之謎 Shanghai: Wen-hui, 1992.

Ishii, Masako 石井昌子. *Dôkyô gaku no kenkyû: Tô Kôkei o chûshin ni* 道教學の研究一陶弘景中心に. Tokyo: Kokusho Kankokai, 1980.

Mugitani, Kunio 麥谷邦夫. "Tô Kôkei nempu kôryaku 陶弘景年譜考略 (1-2)." *Tôhô shûkyô* 47 (1976): 30-61 and 48 (1976): 56-83.

Strickmann, Michel. "On the alchemy of T'ao Hung-ching." In *Facets of Taoism.* Holmes Welch and Anna Seidel, eds. New Haven: Yale University Press, 1979, pp. 123-92.

Franciscus Verellen
Member of EFEO

Tou-p'eng hsien-hua 豆棚閒話 (Idle Talk Under the Bean Arbor) is the only bona fide frame-story in the history of Chinese fiction. Written by a Hangchow 杭州 writer under the pseudonym Ai-na Chü-shih 艾衲居士 (Buddhist Layman Artemisia-Cassock), it was probably published during the late 1660s. Ai-na chü-shih has been identified as the obscure writer Wang Meng-chi 王夢吉, who also wrote the novel *Chi-tien chüan-chuan* 濟顛全傳 (The Complete Biography of Master Crazy Chi; published in 1668). Little else is known about the author.

The collapse of the Ming provides the immediate historical and political context for understanding *Tou-p'eng hsien-hua.* Although entitled *Idle Talk,* the work actually expresses the author's serious concerns and frustrations about his times; it reminds the reader that only when there is no warfare can one have the luxury of leisure (*hsien* 閒, "being idle"), and only when one feels at leisure can one recover one's original conscience and childlike heart, observe the world calmly, contemplate life, reflect inwardly, and cultivate the self.

Tou-p'eng hsien-hua exemplifies the experimentation with new subject matter and writing techniques evidenced by such seventeenth-century authors as Tung Yüeh 董説 (1620–1686) and Li Yü 李漁 (1610/11–1680).* The book has twelve chapters or sections (*tse* 則), each containing one or two stories. The author invented some stories and also drew on diverse sources—official and unofficial histories, anecdotes, drama, fiction, and hearsay. Although generally viewed as a collection of vernacular short stories, it reads like a novel complete with author's preface, in which he states his motivation for writing, a foreword, the text itself, and end-of-chapter commentaries written by a friend of the author under the pseudonym Tzu-jan K'uang-k'o 紫髯狂客 (Purple-Bearded Crazy Man). The stories are woven into a coherent whole through a unique thematic framework—the bean arbor. It is a fiction of ideas. The creation of a bean-arbor framework provides an open forum for multiple narrators and members of the fictional audience to converse about pragmatic virtues, debate current issues, and express differing opinions on moral, philosophical, and religious matters.

The primary story tells of the construction and eventual destruction of a bean arbor under which villagers exchange yarns. Each chapter records a session of storytelling, and these sessions are interconnected through markers of seasonal change as well as references to the beans' growth, flowering, podding and final withering—all of which also provide topics for the embedded stories and discussion. The cultivation of beans is a simile for the nurturing and education of youth. A type of good-looking but actually hollow and unsavory bean stands for the idler-charlatans of Soochow, for example, and the cooking of beans reminds one storyteller of a tale about fraternal rivalry.

Tou-p'eng hsien-hua blends vernacular and classical in its diction and style. The language varies from one story to another, ranging from heavily colloquial (use of the Soochow dialect in the dialogues in Chapter 10) to rather classical (as in the narration of the historical events concerning Chieh Chih-t'ui 介之推 in Chapter 1). In terms of narrative style, the conventional storytellers' rhetoric common in vernacular fiction is used sparingly. Occasionally the novel resembles classical fiction in its presentation of a natural setting on a mimetic level with little mediation by an intrusive narrator.

While the narrator of traditional vernacular fiction assumes the persona of a storyteller, *Tou-p'eng hsien-hua* reenacts a literal storytelling situation among the lower classes with some of the characters serving as narrators. This allows inclusion of the audience's response to the storyteller, as well as their questions and their psychological reactions to the stories.

The author employs wit, humor, and irony in his parody of philosophical ideas, in a manner that recalls *Chuang Tzu* 莊子.** His portrayal of characters and historical figures is reminiscent of the biographies in the *Shih chi* 史記 (Records of the Grand Historian).* In a few stories on more polemical issues, he deliberately suspends judgment and creates moral ambivalence. His satire is so subtle that the commentator strongly urges the reader to read between the lines. Chapter 7, "Shu-ch'i Changes His Loyalty on Mt. Shou-yang," for example, while ostensibly reducing the historically exalted stature of Po-i, actually exposes Shu-ch'i as a hypocrite.

The author enjoys revising or overthrowing established ideas. He reconfigures Confucian morality, upholding chivalry and selflessness, reinterpreting filial piety, and casting doubt on loyalty to the state. Supplementing Confucian teaching with Buddhist and Taoist philosophies, he also advocates a return-to-basics pragmatism. Satirizing abstract, high-minded, and often empty talk, he lauds the useful and constructive approach to life.

The major story in Chapter 1 demythologizes Chieh Chih-t'ui, a model of Confucian eremitism and filiality in *Tso chuan* 左傳* and *Shih chi*, portraying him as a fearful husband. After following his prince into exile, Chih-t'ui refuses to serve him upon their return nineteen years later. Instead, Chih-t'ui hurries to Mount Mien-chu 綿竹 to look for his wife, Shih Yu 石尤, a figure invented by the author. Shih Yu, meanwhile, has been so consumed by jealous fury that she beats Chih-t'ui and ties him up. An impatient officer, dispatched by the prince to find Chih-t'ui, sets fire to the mountain in order to smoke him out. Chih-t'ui, feeling mortified, decides to allow himself and his wife to burn alive.

Chapter 2, which also concerns

women and marital relationships, retells the story of Hsi-shih 西施, the legendary patriotic beauty. Presented to the King of Wu 吳 as a political ruse, Hsi-shih helped destroy Wu and restore the State of Yüeh 越, and was happily reunited with her Yüeh lover. According to the author's new version, Hsi-shih possessed merely ordinary looks, and in place of the happy ending, she was drowned by her former Yüeh lover. The author blames her for betraying her husband and benefactor, the King of Wu, instead of making peace between Wu and Yüeh.

The story in Chapter 3 relates the unexpected success of an ostensibly idiotic young man from a wealthy family. Failing in business himself, he assists a penniless man out of chivalry and generosity and ends up playing a major role in the founding of the T'ang dynasty. The importance of acquiring virtue for one's descendants is illustrated in Chapter 4, which tells of a "wastrel" who deliberately squanders all of his ancestral property upon discovering that it was ill-gotten, but eventually restores his property with the help of a former recipient of his munificence.

Chapter 5 praises a beggar who, though impecunious, is honest, chivalrous, and filial, serving his mother with devotion until she dies. In a conversation with a distinguished official, he argues persuasively that keeping his mother company and making her happy is superior to the official's Confucian notions of filial piety, i.e., seeking high rank and emolument in order to honor one's parents. Chapter 6 criticizes abuses in Buddhist religious practices, attacking in particular the so-called *ta-ho-shang* 大和尚 (eminent monks) who swindle money by claiming to possess spiritual powers. In this story a resourceful general talks one charlatan "eminent monk" into staging a scene of ascending to heaven in the midst of fire, but then locks the escape door. The monk burns to death, allowing the general to collect the large sum of money donated by the masses for this occasion.

Chapters 7 and 8 reflect the great anxiety, confusion, and disillusionment caused by the Manchu conquest of China. Chapter 7 debunks the legend of the loyalist brothers Po-i 伯夷 and Shu-ch'i 叔齊 who, when the Chou dynasty overthrew the Shang in 1112 B.C., refused to eat the grain of the Chou. According to the legend, they retreated to a mountain and gathered ferns for food until they starved to death. In the author's revised story, Po-i stubbornly stays on the mountain, while Shu-ch'i, unable to withstand his hunger, secretly leaves to seek employment with the Chou. Both Shu-ch'i's disloyalty and Po-i's rigid patriotism are ridiculed, thus calling for a re-examination of the Confucian dictum of eternal loyalty to a ruler.

The parable in Chapter 8 tells of Tien-kuang Tsun-che's 電光尊者 (Arhat Lightning) descent to earth during the period of dynastic change and his destruction of a part of the world. Tzu-tsai Tsun-che 自在尊者 (Arhat Free-and-Easy) tries to help the people, but is told not to interfere with heaven's design. Two blind men seek help from Free-and-Easy. Regaining their eyesight, however, they become so saddened at the sight of the bustling world that they plead to remain blind. Eventually Free-and-Easy lets them crawl into a wine jar where they find paradise.

Contemporary problems are the focus of Chapters 9 through 11. Chapter 9 exposes the shocking malpractices of the late Ming police force, showing how the police colluded with veteran thieves to deliberately lead ignorant youths astray and then frame them for the serious crimes committed by the thieves. The story warns against the temptations of crime even in times of adversity, using the example of a young wastrel who is talked into committing robbery when he is poor, later reforms, but is caught and punished for his crime a few years later.

Chapter 10 presents a lively caricature of some impoverished, sycophantic charlatans in Soochow who compete with one another to ingratiate themselves with wealthy patrons. Failing at their various attempts to swindle money, they end up giving their own sons and daughters to their patrons as compensation.

Chapter 11 urges people to cherish peaceful times by relating the bandit-rebels' ruthless killing in the late Ming and other wartime horror stories. In one gruesome anecdote, a man is beheaded by the bandits, but continues to live for another four years. In the main story, Captain Tang 黨, a hero of righteous vigor, avenges his sister's death. Having been kidnapped by the lustful Captain Nan 南, the sister commits suicide to preserve her chastity. Captain Nan then joins forces with the bandits to defeat Captain Tang. Before dying of rage, Tang bites his tongue into pieces and spits them out into Nan's face to disgrace him. But when Nan approaches Tang's corpse to retaliate, Tang suddenly revives, seizes a sword and beheads Nan, then falls back again on the ground, dead.

Chapter 12 clearly depicts contemporary reactions to the syncretic movement that became very popular in the late Ming. The trend of combining Three Teachings—Confucianism, Taoism, and Buddhism—drew heated objections from staunch defenders of orthodox Confucianism. In this chapter, Proctor Ch'en 陳, an arrogant pedant from town, delivers a Neo-Confucian lecture criticizing Taoism and ruthlessly attacking Buddhism. He attempts to expose Buddhist doctrines as worthless superstition and Buddhist clergy as hypocrites and crooks, but his listeners argue with him, for they have been trying to spread the pacifist teachings of Buddhist thought. After Proctor Ch'en has left, some people worry that under the government's strict bans, their idle talk might be taken as dangerous heterodoxy. At that moment, someone leans against one of the bean arbor's poles, accidentally bringing about the entire structure's collapse and thereby also bringing to an end the structure's use as a narrative device.

The author's political concerns must have motivated—at least in part—his use of such a narrative frame. Throughout all the stories, the background narrator remains detached, abstaining from any direct comment. In contrast, the foreground narrators—at least seven of them can be identified—sometimes express strong opinions. By delegating the narratorial and argumentative function to some of his characters, the author manages to reduce some of his own responsibility and even partially obscure his socio-political satire in order to avoid censorship.

Tou-p'eng hsien-hua has received little critical attention to date. However, as an original narrative exploring philosophical, historical, and religious issues, it has much to contribute to socio-cultural studies of seventeenth-century China. Its language and narrative techniques deserve further literary study. As a frame-story, it could be compared with similar Sanskrit stories, the famous oriental collection *The One Thousand and One Nights*, Boccaccio's *Decameron* (1353), and Chaucer's *Canterbury Tales* (ca. 1385).

Editions and References

Tou-p'eng hsien-hua 豆棚閒話. Shanghai: Shang-hai Ku-chi, 1990. *Ku-pen hsiao-shuo chi-ch'eng* 古本小説集成 facsimile edition of the Han-hai Lou 翰海樓 blockprint edition (K'ang-hsi period, 1662-1722).

Tou-p'eng hsien-hua. Shanghai: Shang-hai Tsa-chih Kung-ssu, 1935. Modern typeset edition.

Tou-p'eng hsien-hua. Shanghai: Shang-hai Ku-chi, 1983. Modern typeset edition in simplified characters and without the end-of-chapter comments.

Tou-p'eng hsien-hua. Peking: Jen-min Wen-hsüeh, 1984. Modern typeset edition in simplified characters.

Translations

Wu, Yenna. "Jie Zhitui Traps His Jealous Wife In An Inferno." In *Renditions* 44 (Autumn 1995), pp. 17-32. Translation of chapter one of *Tou-p'eng hsien-hua*. A slightly different version appears in Yenna Wu, *The Lioness Roars: Shrew Stories from Late Imperial China*. Ithaca, New York: Cornell University, East Asia Series, 1995, pp. 57-71.

Studies

Hanan, Patrick. *The Chinese Vernacular Story.* Cambridge, Massachusetts: Harvard University Press, 1981, pp. 191-207.

Hu, Shih 胡適. *"Tou-p'eng hsien-hua."* In *Tou-p'eng hsien-hua*. Shanghai: Shang-hai Tsa-chih Kung-ssu, 1935, pp. 1-3.

Hu, Shih-ying 胡士瑩. *Hua-pen hsiao-shuo kai-lun* 話本小説概論合. 2v. Peking: Chung-hua, 1980, v. 2, pp. 649-650.

Lévy, André. "Études sur trois recueils anciens de contes chinois," *TP* 52.1-3 (1965): 110-137.

Wu, Yenna. "The Debunking of Historical Heroes in *Idle Talk Under the Bean Arbor*," *Selected Papers in Asian Studies* (Western Conference of the Association for Asian Studies), new series, 43 (1992): 1-27.

___. "The Bean Arbor Frame: Actual and Figural," *JCLTA* 30.2 (1995): 1-32.

Yenna Wu
University of California, Riverside

Ts'ao Ts'ao 曹操 (*tzu*, Meng-te 孟德, 155–220), became the most powerful political and military leader of his time and also gained fame for his literary achievement. According to *San-kuo chih* 三國志,** Ts'ao was a descendent of Ts'ao Shen 曹參 (d. 190 B.C.), a famous minister in the early years of the Han dynasty. But reliable information on his background really goes back only as far as Ts'ao Ts'ao's grandfather Ts'ao T'eng 曹騰. Ts'ao T'eng was castrated in childhood so that he might become a palace eunuch. While serving in a minor eunuch office, he was selected to be a companion to the heir apparent, and from then on he advanced in office, serving four emperors during a period of over thirty years.

Ts'ao T'eng's adopted son was Ts'ao Sung 曹嵩, whose origins are obscure. Works antagonistic to Ts'ao Ts'ao claim that Ts'ao Sung was a member of the Hsia-hou 夏侯 clan of Ch'iao 譙, the Ts'aos' home area. Were that true, Ts'ao Ts'ao would have broken a taboo by marrying women from his family into the Hsia-hou clan. But it is extremely unlikely that Ts'ao Sung was a Hsia-hou. When Ts'ao T'eng died, Ts'ao Sung was left in favorable circumstances. He occupied high posts in the central government under Emperor Ling 靈 (r. 168–189), apparently obtained through bribes and purchase, common practice at the time.

Ts'ao Ts'ao's own entry into officialdom was assured by his family's position. In 174, he was recommended for government service and then appointed to a succession of offices. But in 178, when Empress Sung was divorced by Emperor Ling, Ts'ao was dismissed for having a cousin who was the wife of a brother of the empress. He seems to have returned to Ch'iao. Two events of the next dozen years speeded Ts'ao Ts'ao's rise to prominence: the Taoist millenarian Yellow Turban Rebellion and the breakdown of the central government and seizure of power by Tung Cho 董卓 (d. 192).

The Yellow Turbans were defeated by early 185, though related outbreaks continued for years. The uprising weakened Han control of the country and enhanced the power of those who had a hand in suppressing it, including Ts'ao Ts'ao. Emperor Ling's death in 189 precipitated yet another crisis—a rift between the eunuchs and officials that cost many lives and brought chaos to Lo-yang, the capital. Almost immediately the military leader Tung Cho took control of the capital. Before long he had Emperor Ling's young successor deposed—and ultimately killed—and replaced him with Liu Hsieh 劉協 (Emperor Hsien 獻, r. 189–220), who was himself but a boy at the time. An alliance against Tung Cho was formed but did not last long, and the would-be allies soon began to fight each other. There ensued a period of nearly continuous military campaigns, during which Ts'ao Ts'ao emerged *primus inter pares*. The fighting resulted in a temporary partitioning of the country into the three states of Wei 魏 (220–265) in the North, founded by Ts'ao Ts'ao's son Ts'ao P'i 曹丕 (187–226)*; Wu 吳 (222–280) in the Southeast; and Shu 蜀 (or Shu Han 蜀漢, 221–263) in the Southwest.

Ts'ao Ts'ao is also famous as a leading poet and literary patron of the influential Chien-an 建安 period (196–220). As a literary period, Chien-an may be viewed as encompassing the lives of Ts'ao Ts'ao and his son Ts'ao Chih 曹植 (192–232).* Besides Ts'ao Ts'ao and Ts'ao Chih, the figures most closely associated with Chien-an literature are Ts'ao P'i and the Seven Masters of the Chien-an Period: K'ung Jung 孔融 (153–208),* Ch'en Lin 陳琳 (d. 217),* Wang Ts'an 王粲 (177–217),* Hsü Kan 徐幹 (171–218), Juan Yü 阮瑀 (*ca.* 165–212),* Ying Yang 應瑒 (d. 217), and Liu Chen 劉楨 (d. 217). The relationships between the Ts'aos and these writers were close—all of them were familiar with and influenced by the works of the others. In fact, they frequently wrote in one another's company or in response to one another's works. Ts'ao Ts'ao's role in attracting these men to his seat in Yeh 鄴 (near modern Yeh-chen 鄴鎮, Hopei) cannot be ignored, and while not all of them were accomplished poets, important developments and innovations in poetry characterize Chien-an times. These developments include relatively greater lyricalness and topical particu-

larity, the growth of poetic themes such as the quest for immortality and the plight of abandoned women, and the gradual emergence of pentasyllabic-line poetry.

Both poetry and prose by Ts'ao Ts'ao exist today. Twenty-one or twenty-two poems are extant, all of them *yüeh-fu*. The most famous is a tetrasyllabic-line *yüeh-fu* entitled "Tuan-ko hsing" 短歌行 (Short Song) that begins "Tui chiu tang ko" 對酒當歌 ("Facing wine one should sing") and comprises ambiguously connected sections. Another important poem in this meter is "Pu-ch'u Hsia-men hsing" 不出夏門行 (Striding out the Hsia Gate), which is composed of four stanzas (or separate poems) and a preface. The descriptive passages in parts of the poem presage the slightly later development of Chinese landscape poetry. Events of the day are a powerful presence in Ts'ao Ts'ao's works, and he often chose to write about them using the pentasyllabic line that began to gain popularity among literati poets from Chien-an times: one of his poems entitled "Shan tsai hsing" 善哉行 (Excellent Oh!) is a pentasyllabic-line piece that begins "I deplore my unhappy lot" 自惜身薄祜 and refers indirectly to the murder of his father and the escape to Lo-yang of Emperor Hsien; "Hsieh lu hsing" 薤露行 (Dew on the Shallot) is a poetic treatment of events surrounding the fall of the Han; "Hao li hsing" 蒿里行 (Artemesia Village), similarly, is a lament over the devastation that resulted from the fragmenting of the alliance against Tung Cho; and "K'u han hsing" 苦寒行 (Bitter Cold), a soldier's lament possibly written in 206, is about the hardships of a northern campaign. Another soldier's lament—one that cannot readily be tied to a specific campaign—is "Ch'üeh tung hsi men hsing" 卻東西門行 (Variation on the East and West Gates), an excellent poem in which images from the natural world stand in a metaphorical relationship to the endless soldiering of the speaker.

Among the most notable of Ts'ao's prose works are an edict that has come to be called "Jang hsien tzu ming pen chih ling" 讓縣自明本志令 (Edict Relinquishing Prefectures and Explaining My Aims; 210 or 211) and his three famous pieces on seeking men of talent, sometimes referred to as "Ch'iu hsien ling" 求仙令 (Edict Seeking Worthies; 210), "Ch'ih yu-ssu ch'ü shih wu fei p'ien-tuan ling" 敕有司取士勿廢偏短令 (Edict Directing the Relevant Officials Not to Reject Those with Partial Failings; 215), and "Chü hsien wu chü pin hsing ling" 舉賢勿拘品行令 (Edict on Not Being Bound by Moral Qualities or Behavior in Recommending Worthies; 217). "Edict Relinquishing Prefectures and Explaining My Aims" is important as an example of early Chinese autobiography and for what it tells us about Ts'ao's thoughts on current affairs; the other three are indicative of the strong emphasis on innate talent that marks the age.

Ts'ao's poetry was not considered very important by critics until perhaps the seventeenth century. There are at least two possible reasons for this: first, the literary tastes of the Six Dynasties were very different from the rough immediacy that characterizes Ts'ao's verse; second, the negative image of Ts'ao that prevailed for much of history, partly due to the writings of the Eastern Chin historian Hsi Tso-ch'ih 習鑿齒 (d. 384), may have influenced literary scholars and critics' opinions of his works. In Ch'ing and modern times, more attention has been paid to Ts'ao and his poetry, and during the late 1950s and the Cultural Revolution efforts to rehabilitate his reputation led to the publication of hundreds of books and articles —most concerned with the political Ts'ao and many of negligible value.

Editions and References

Anhwei Po-hsien *Ts'ao Ts'ao chi i-chu* hsiao-tsu 安徽亳縣曹操集譯注小組. *Ts'ao Ts'ao chi i-chu* 曹操集譯注. Peking: Chung-hua, 1979.

Chao, Fu-t'an 趙福壇, ed. *Ts'ao Wei fu-tzu shih-hsüan* 曹魏父子詩選. Hong Kong: San-lien, 1982. Chengtu: Pa-Shu Shu-she, 1989.

Ch'iu, Ying-sheng 邱英生 and Kao Shuang 高爽 , trans. and comm. *San Ts'ao shih i-shih* 三曹詩譯釋. Harbin: Hei-lung-chiang Jen-min Wen-hsüeh, 1982.

Huang, Chieh 黃節 (1875–1935), ed. *Wei Wu-ti Wei Wen-ti shih-chu* 魏武帝魏文帝詩註. Rpt. Hong Kong: Shang-wu Yin-shu-kuan, 1976.

Ts'ao Ts'ao chi 曹操集. Peking: Chung-hua, 1959.

Yin, I-hsiang 殷義祥. *San Ts'ao shih hsüan-i* 三曹詩選譯. Chengtu: Pa-Shu Shu-she, 1989.

Yü, Kuan-ying 余冠英, ed. and comm. *San Ts'ao shih-hsüan* 三曹詩選. Peking: Jen-min Wen-hsüeh, 1956.

___. *Ts'ao Ts'ao Ts'ao P'i Ts'ao Chih shih-hsüan* 曹操曹丕曹植詩選. Hong Kong: Ta-kuang, 1960.

Translations

Demiéville, *Anthologie,* pp. 111-114.

Kroll, Paul William. "Portraits of Ts'ao Ts'ao: Literary Studies on the Man and the Myth." Unpublished Ph.D. dissertation, University of Michigan, 1976.

Steinen, Diether von den. "Poems of Ts'ao Ts'ao." *MS* 4 (1939–1940): 125–181.

Studies

Chang, Hsiao-hu 張嘯虎. "Ts'ao Ts'ao wen-chang yü Chien-an feng-ku" 曹操文章與建安風骨. *She-hui ko-hsüeh chi-k'an* 4 (July 1981): 126–131.

Chang, K'o-li 張可禮. *Chien-an wen-hsüeh lun-kao* 建安文學論稿. Chi-nan: Shantung chiao-yü, 1986.

___. *San Ts'ao nien-p'u* 三曹年譜. Tsinan: Ch'i-Lu Shu-she, 1983.

Chang, Sung-sheng Yvonne. "Generic Transformation from 'Yuefu' to 'Gushi': Poetry of Cao Cao, Cao Pi, and Cao Zhi." Unpublished Ph.D. dissertation, Stanford University, 1985.

Chang, Wen-chu 張文珠. "Lun Ts'ao shih fu-tzu te wen-hsüeh" 論曹氏父子的文學. *Hua-kuo,* no. 3 (June 1960): 78–92.

Chang, Ya-hsin 張亞新. *Ts'ao Ts'ao ta chuan*

曹操大傳. Peking: Chung-kuo Wen-hsüeh, 1994.

Chang, Ying-ko 章映閣. *Ts'ao Ts'ao hsin chuan* 曹操新傳. Shanghai: Shang-hai Jen-min, 1989.

Chien-an wen-hsüeh yen-chiu wen-chi 建安文學研究文集. Hofei: Huang-shan Shu-she, 1984.

Ch'iu, Chen-ching 邱鎮京. *Ts'ao shih fu-tzu shih lun* 曹氏父子詩論. Taipei: Wen-chin, 1973.

de Crespigny, Rafe. "Man from the Margin: Cao Cao and the Three Kingdoms." The Fifty-first George Ernest Morrison Lecture in Ethnology. Canberra: Australian National University, 1990.

Ho-pei Shih-fan Hsüeh-yüan, Chung-wen Hsi, Ku-tien Wen-hsüeh Chiao-yen Tsu 河北師範學院中文系古典文學教研組. *San Ts'ao tzu-liao hui-pien* 三曹資料彙編. Peking: Chung-hua, 1980.

Inami, Ritsuko 井波律子. "Sô So ron" 曹操論. *Chûgoku bungaku hô* 23 (October 1972): 1–27.

Kroll, "Portraits of Ts'ao Ts'ao" (see "Translations" above).

Leban, Carl. "Ts'ao Ts'ao and the Rise of Wei: The Early Years." Unpublished Ph.D. dissertation, Columbia Univ., 1971.

Li, Ching-hua 李景華, ed. *San Ts'ao shih-wen shang-hsi chi* 三曹詩文賞析集. Chengtu: Pa-Shu Shu-she, 1988.

Li, Pao-chün 李寶均. *Ts'ao shih fu-tzu ho Chien-an wen-hsüeh* 曹氏父子和建安文學. Peking: Chung-hua, 1962. New ed., Shanghai: Shang-hai Ku-chi, 1978.

Liu, Chi-hua 劉紀華. *Han Wei chih chi wen-hsüeh te hsing-shih yü nei-jung* 漢魏之際文學的形式與內容. Taipei: Shih-chi, 1978.

Suzuki, Shûji 鈴木修次. *Kan Shin shi no kenkyû* 漢晉詩の研究. Tokyo: Daishukan, 1967.

Syrokomla-Stefanowska, Agnieszka Dorota. "The Development of Chinese Poetry from the Chien-an Period to the End of the Western Chin." Unpublished Ph.D. dissertation, University of Sydney, 1977.

Ts'ao Ts'ao lun chi 曹操論集. Peking: San-lien, 1960.

Ueki, Hisayuki 植木久行. "Sô So gafushi ronkô" 曹操楽府詩論考. In *Mekada Makoto Hakushi koki kinen: Chûgoku bungaku ronshû* 目加田誠博士古稀記念中国文学論集. Tokyo: Ryûkei Shosha, 1974, pp. 99-120.

Wang, Li-chung 王立中 and T'ang Ling-i 唐凌譯. *Ts'ao Ts'ao* 曹操. Peking: Chung-hua, 1985.

Wang, Chung-lo 王仲犖. *Ts'ao Ts'ao* 曹操. Shanghai: Shang-hai Jen-min, 1956.

Yü, Kuan-ying. "Lun Chien-an Ts'ao shih fu-tzu te shih" 論建安曹氏父子的詩, *Wen-hsüeh i-ch'an tseng-k'an* 1 (1955):139–158.

Robert Joe Cutter
University of Wisconsin, Madison

Tzu-shu 字書 or ***tzu-tien*** 字典 (dictionaries), according to the traditional Chinese bibliographical scheme, were classified as belonging to *hsiao-hsüeh* 小學 (minor learning—the functional equivalent of "linguistics" in pre-modern times), which was contrasted with *ta-hsüeh* 大學 (major learning—i.e., learning that had moral implications). *Hsiao-hsüeh* was divided into texts dealing with *wen-tzu* 文字 (script—analogous to grammatology), *hsün-ku* 訓詁 (exegesis—similar to philology), and *yin-yün* 音韻 ("sounds and rhymes," comparable to phonology). Starting from the Han period, numerous dictionaries which focused on one or another of these three areas of language study were compiled.

In terms of their arrangement, traditional Chinese dictionaries fall into three different types: 1. those which are arranged according to categories of knowledge, 2. those which are arranged according to classifiers (often called "radicals"), and 3. those which are arranged according to the tones and final sounds of the characters. The first principle of arrangement has been followed in a great number of works, including encyclopedias and other kinds of books that are not properly dictionaries. It was also generally adopted in the compilation of pre-modern Chinese dictionaries of foreign languages (Mongolian, Manchu, Tibetan, Uighur, etc.), since there was no practicable transcriptional scheme by means of which the words of such languages could

165

be arranged according to their sounds.

As examples of the various kinds of Chinese dictionaries used by traditional scholars, about a dozen of the best-known ones will be briefly surveyed, in roughly chronological order of their appearance, together with pertinent commentaries and revisions. Specialized dictionaries useful to students of literature will also be introduced in a section near the end. Several ancient dictionaries mentioned in the biblio-graphical treatise ("I-wen chih" 藝文志**) of the *Han-shu* 漢書 (History of the Han)* which are no longer extant will not be discussed because there is no way of knowing what they were like or even whether they ever actually existed.

In the twentieth century, there has been a vast proliferation of all sorts of dictionaries, many of which are increasingly arranged according to the alphabetical order of the romanized graphs or words. (Dozens of other finding systems are also in use [four corners, total stroke count, sequence of types of strokes, etc.) There are now hundreds of dictionaries dealing with *ch'eng-yü* 成語 ("set phrases," usually misleadingly rendered as "idioms"), proverbs, maxims, sayings, quotations, allusions, dialects and topolects, vernacularisms and colloquialisms from different times and places, each of the major novels, poetry of the various dynasties, and so forth. Adequate treat-ment of the lexicographical resources available to modern scholars of tradi-tional literature would require lengthy treatment in a separate article and frequent updating.

The anonymously authored *Erh-ya* 爾雅 (Approaching Elegance), one of the Confucian classics, is generally recognized as the first Chinese dictionary. In a sense, it is not really a dictionary *per se*, since it is essentially a list of glosses explaining terms in pre-Han classical works. As such, the *Erh-ya*

is a *hsün-ku* (exegetical) work. The glosses, which appear originally to have been annotations for early texts, are very important for identifying ancient plants, animals, and so forth. The *Erh-ya* may be divided into two main parts, the first consisting of three sections concentrat-ing on verbs and grammatical particles, the last made up of sixteen sections focusing on kinship, architectural, geographical, calendrical, and other types of specific terms, mostly nouns. Altogether, it includes approximately 4,300 terms in over 2,000 entries. The earliest references to the *Erh-ya* are from Later Han times, and it is evidently by diverse hands, but the first part may date from as early as the third century B.C., while the dating of the second part is uncertain. The earliest and most important commentary is that by Kuo P'u 郭璞 (276–324)**; to this was added a subcommentary completed in 994 by Hsing Ping 邢昺 (932–1010). The *Erh-ya* spawned a vast number of supplements and annotations, beginning with the *Hsiao Erh-ya* 小爾雅 (Abbreviated Approaching Elegance) by an unknown author at the end of the Han period and the *Kuang-ya* 廣雅 (Expanded Elegance) by Chang I (or Chang Chi) 張揖/楫 (*fl.* 227), and culminating in the meticulous research of Shao Chin-han 邵晉涵 (1743–1796), which was com-pleted in 1775, and the very thorough and detailed *Erh-ya i-shu* 爾雅義疏 of Hao I-hsing 郝懿邢 (1757–1825).

Fang-yen 方言 (Topolecticisms) is also a *hsün-ku* text. It is attributed to Yang Hsiung 揚雄 (53 B.C.–A. D. 18)* who is said to have devoted 27 years to its compilation. Nonetheless, it seems to have remained unfinished. The format is modeled after the *Erh-ya*, although instead of collecting items from classical sources, Yang Hsiung gathered his lexical entries from local sources, including some that were non-Sinitic. A rough idea of the distribution of languages during the Han may be gained from the *Fang-yen* and it is important for the study of ancient vocabulary, but its comparative approach is insufficiently rigorous to enable modern researchers to employ data from it directly and uncritically. Originally consisting of over 9,000 items, current editions of the *Fang-yen* include more than 11,900 terms. Kuo P'u also wrote a valuable commentary on the *Fang-yen* and Tai Chen 戴震 (1723–1777) added a major subcommentary. Dozens of dictionaries dealing with localisms in the tradition of the *Fang-yen* appeared during the Ming and Ch'ing periods.

By far the most important dictionary for the conceptualization and systematization of the Chinese script is the *Shuo wen chieh tzu* 説文解字 (Explanations of Simple and Compound Graphs) by Hsü Shen 許慎 (*ca.* 58–*ca.* 147). Completed in the year 100 and presented to the throne in 121, the *Shuo wen* was the first dictionary to establish the paradigm of *hsing* 形 (shape, i.e., structure), *yin* 音 (sound), and *i* 義 (meaning) for the analysis of Chinese characters. It was also the first dictionary to devise a system of graphic classifiers (the *pu-shou* 部首 ["radicals"], 540 in number) under which to group its 9,353 graphs, and it was the first work to present the scheme of *liu-shu* 六書 (six categories of script) for dividing up all characters. Hsü Shen mainly based his discussions of the characters on their *hsiao-chuan* 小篆 (small seal) forms that were standardized during the Ch'in period at the end of the third century B.C., but he also sometimes mentioned large seal and other presumably earlier forms. Hsü Shen was a proponent of the so-called Old Text School rather than the officially sanctioned New Text School. One of his principal aims in compiling the *Shuo wen* was to remove doubts concerning the ancient classics so that their wisdom could be utilized by the Han dynasty for the programmatic purpose of ordering society. In his "Postface," Hsü Shen

maintained that the script constitutes the foundation of all texts and that these are the basis for effecting government. It is through ancient writings that men of the present know the truths of the past.

During the T'ang period, the *Shuo wen* was poorly edited by Li Yang-ning (*sic*) 李陽冰 (*fl.* 758–780). Hsü K'ai 徐鍇 (920–974) and his brother Hsü Hsüan 徐鉉 (917–992) attempted to undo the damage of Li Yang-ning by collating all available quotations, fragments, and recensions that were extant at the time. In the following centuries, scores of other scholars pored over the *Shuo wen* and its annotations, with the result that massive collections were compiled to cope with the flood of scholarship on the subject. Among the more notable of these works are Tuan Yü-ts'ai's 段玉裁 (1735–1815) *Shuo wen (chieh tzu) chu* 説文(解字)注, written over a period of thirty years from 1776-1807, which relies on pre-Sung commentaries to explain the origin of multiple meanings of graphs and makes significant contributions to the study of ancient phonology, and Ting Fu-pao's 丁福保 (1874–1952) *Shuo wen chieh tzu ku-lin* 説文解字詁林 (1928; 1932) which likewise required thirty years to compile and drew from 182 earlier works.

An interesting variant on the *Shuo wen* model was the *Tzu-shuo* 字説 (Explanations of Graphs) by the famous Sung statesman, Wang An-shih 王安石 (1021–1086).* Although it is lost, the preface and 23 entries survive, and there are references to it in other works. The *Tzu-shuo* often departs radically from conventional *Shuo wen* explanations. Arranged by 240 classifiers and four tones, it is a highly imaginative approach to the Chinese characters but not very reliable. Chang Yu 張有 (b. 1054) wrote his *Fu-ku pien* 復古編 (Compilation for Returning to Antiquity) between 1111–1117 in an attempt to refute Wang An-shih's idiosyncratic theories, but his own formulations are so muddled and archaistic as to be well-nigh worthless.

Still another *hsün-ku* dictionary, but one of a very different nature from those fashioned on the *Shuo wen*, was the *Shih ming* 釋名 (Explanations of Terms) by Liu Hsi 劉熙/熹 which was completed around the year 200. It was based primarily on his native language of the state of Ch'i, but also took into account other local varieties and the language used by the officials of the central government. The layout of the *Shih ming* follows that of the *Erh-ya*, but it uses the novel method of employing homophones or near-homophones to explain words. Most noteworthy are its conjectures on the reasons why things have the names they do. Liu Hsi treats 1,502 lexical items under 27 semantic categories (heaven, earth, body parts, kinship terms, etc.), relying primarily on paronomastic (punning) glosses to elucidate them. That is to say, one graph is held to be more or less equivalent to another graph in both sound and sense, but the sound values of the two characters remain phonologically indeterminate and any authentic, convincing etymological connections between the two characters are usually totally nonexistent. Although many of Liu Hsi's explanations are thus highly forced and sometimes even mystical, the data he records is nevertheless useful for investigating phonology and semantics during the first couple of centuries of our era. The *Shih ming*, furthermore, provides evidence for theories of language near the end of the Han, according to which words were thought to be immutable cosmological entities possessing ethical and moral properties.

Hsün-ku studies reached a new level of sophistication in the *Ching-tien shih-wen* 經典釋文 (Explanations of Terms in the Classics), compiled in 583 by Lu Te-ming 陸德明 (556–630). Based on the works of 230 scholars writing during the Han, Wei, and Six Dynasties periods,

the *Ching-tien shih-wen* analyzes the meanings and sounds of terms in the 14 Confucian classics as well as in the *Lao Tzu* and the *Chuang Tzu*. Lu Te-ming provides detailed explanations which are extremely important for the close reading of ancient texts.

A new type of dictionary appeared with the *Ch'ieh-yün* 切韻 (Tomic Rhymes) of Lu Fa-yen 陸法言 (b. 562), issued in 601. Although this work no longer survives, fragments from Tun-huang and descriptions in other sources enable us to know that it included around 11,500 characters divided into 193 rhyme groups in four tones. The *Ch'ieh-yün* reflected the enhanced phonological awareness that developed in China after the advent of Buddhism and the elaborate Indian linguistic science that came in its wake. The *Ch'ieh-yün* was succeeded by the *T'ang yün* 唐韻 (T'ang Rhymes), which was compiled sometime after 732 by Sun Mien 孫愐, and the *Kuang-yün* 廣韻 (Expanded Rhymes), completed in 1008 by Ch'en P'eng-nien 陳彭年 (961–1017) *et al.* The *Kuang-yün* contains 26,194 entries divided into 206 rhyme groups in four tones. It was followed in short order by the *Chi yün* 集韻 (Collected Rhymes), edited by Ting Tu 丁度 (990–1053) *et al.* Consisting of 53,525 entries, it was completed in 1039 but was fraught with errors.

There were also dictionaries intended exclusively for reading Buddhist texts. Two of the most remarkable were both entitled *I-ch'ieh ching yin i* 一切經音義 (The Sounds and Meanings of All the Scriptures). The first, originally called *Chung-ching yin i* 眾經音義, written by the T'ang monk Hsüan-ying 玄應 before 664, followed the layout of *Ching-tien shih-wen* and concentrated on terms with multiple pronunciations, although not exclusively so. Its explanations of occasional vernacular expressions are particularly valuable. The second, compiled between 783–807 by the monk Hui-lin 慧琳 (737–820), who hailed from

Kashgar, added coverage of texts translated after the mid-seventh century and earlier ones that had been overlooked by Hsüan-ying. Whereas the two *I-ch'ieh ching yin-i* dealt with the sound and meaning of Buddhist texts, the *Lung-k'an shou-chien* 龍龕手鑑 (Hand-mirror for the Dragon Niche; preface 997) by the Liao monk Hsing-chün 形均, who worked five years to compile it, is dedicated to the grammatological aspects of Buddhist texts. It is especially important for identifying rare characters and characters used exclusively in Buddhist texts. Altogether it includes 26,430 graphs grouped under 242 classifiers.

After the *Kuang-yün*, the most important phonologically oriented dictionary was the *Chung-yüan yin-yün* 中原音韻 (Sounds and Rhymes [i.e., Initials and Finals] of the Central Plains) * issued in 1324 by Chou Te-ch'ing 周德清 (1277–1365). With 5,866 characters arranged according to 19 rhyme groups (finals) and various *ch'ü* 曲 (aria) patterns, the *Chung-yüan yin-yün* is vital for the study of early Mandarin and Yüan period arias.

A specialized work for the study of *tz'u* rhymes is the *Tz'u lin cheng yün* 詞林正韻 (Correct Rhymes from the Grove of Lyric Meters). Authored by Ko Tsai 戈載 (*fl.* 1807), it included over 11,400 characters divided into 19 rhyme groups.

Arguably the best-known and most influential traditional Chinese dictionary in the West is the *K'ang-hsi tzu-tien* 康熙字典 (Character Dictionary of the K'ang-hsi Reign Period). Despite the fact that it is actually quite sloppy and full of mistakes, this imperially commissioned tome, begun in 1710 by Chang Yü-shu 張玉書 (1642–1711) *et al.* and completed in 1716, set the parameters for many later dictionaries in terms of its arrangement by 214 radicals (still the standard except recently in mainland China with the promulgation of simplified characters) and its compre-

hensiveness (a total of 47,035 characters plus 1,995 ancient forms). The *K'ang-hsi tzu-tien* is fundamentally an outgrowth of the *Shuo wen chieh tzu*, with numerous evolving incarnations during the intervening centuries. Among the more noteworthy of these were the *Yü p'ien* 玉篇 (Jade Leaves), completed in 543 by Ku Yeh-wang 顧野王 (519–581), which offered more characters (originally 16,917 but later increased to 22,561) with more citations and annotations all arranged under 542 classifiers, the *Lei p'ien* 類篇 (Classified Leaves) of Ssu-ma Kuang 司馬光 (1019–1086) *et al.*, issued in 1066 and conceived as a complement to the *Chi yün*, which presented 31,319 characters plus 21,846 variants arranged under 544 classifiers, the widely used *Tzu-hui* 字彙 (Lexicon) issued by Mei Ying-tso 梅膺作 in 1615, which sensibly reduced the number of classifiers to 214 while still offering coverage of 33,179 graphs, and Chang Tzu-lieh's 張字烈 (1564–1650) *Cheng-tzu t'ung* 正字通 whose size and arrangement were similar.

Also following one branch of the path forged by the *Shuo wen* were a series of works centering on the *liu-shu*. This trend was initiated by the great encyclopedist, Cheng Ch'iao 鄭樵 (1104–1162), whose *Liu-shu lüeh* 六書略 (Outline of the Six Categories of Graphs) was the first to apply the concept thoroughly and systematically, and continued by Tai T'ung 戴侗 (*fl.* 1241–1277), author of the *Liu-shu ku* 六書故 (Instantiations of the Six Categories of Graphs), who believed that the *liu-shu* were the key to comprehending the classifiers and, through them, the script as a whole.

Probably the single most valuable premodern dictionary for students of Chinese literature is the *P'ei-wen yün-fu* 佩文韻府 (Rhyme Treasury from the Studio of Pendant Literature), compiled at the command and under the supervision of the K'ang-hsi emperor. Completed in 1711 under the nominal editorship of Chang Yü-shu, this enormous work in 212 *chüan* brought together over 480,000 quotations under 10,000 some head characters arranged according to 106 finals distributed among five tones. As regards lexicographical advancement, while not yet realizing that the basic unit of language was the word rather than the graph, the *P'ei-wen yün-fu* clearly recognized the importance of the polysyllabic unit in literary expression. The *P'ei-wen yün-fu* was heavily relied upon by the landmark twentieth-century *Dai Kan-Wa jiten* 大漢和辭典 (Great Sino-Japanese Dictionary) of Morohashi Tetsuji 諸橋轍次 (1883-1982) and, in turn, by the *Chung-wen ta tz'u-tien* 中文大辭典 (Great Dictionary of Written Chinese). The *Han-yü ta tz'u-tien* 漢語大詞典 (Great Dictionary of Sinitic), in contrast, represents the first decisive departure by a modern encyclopedic dictionary from the repackaging of the contents of traditional reference works.

Designed as a one-volume abridgement of the *P'ei-wen yün-fu* was the *P'ei-wen shih-yün* 佩文詩韻 (Poetic Rhymes from the Studio of Pendant Literature) with 10,235 characters. Similarly under the editorship of Chang Yü-shu, this was the authoritative standard for writing poetry on the civil-service examinations. As such, it played a role similar to the *Li-pu yün-lüeh* 禮部韻略 (An Outline of Rhymes from the Bureau of Rites) of the Sung period, completed in 1037 by Ting Tu, *et al.* With 9,590 characters arranged under 106 rhymes in four main tonal divisions, it was designed for use by examination candidates and had official status.

Another complement to the *P'ei-wen yün-fu* was the *P'ien-tzu lei-pien* 駢字類編 (Classified Compilation of Yoked Graphs), compiled between 1719 and 1726. Containing 1,604 head graphs arranged under 12 categories, it is a rich fund of bisyllabic expressions illustrated by appropriate quotations. Together, the *P'ei-wen yün-fu* and the *P'ien-tzu lei-pien*

constitute a huge repository for locating the occurrence of specific expressions in citations from works of poetry and prose.

An excellent *hsün-ku* dictionary which follows the *P'ei-wen yün-fu* arrangement is the *Ching-chi tsuan-ku* 經籍纂詁 (Assembled Exegeses of Classical Texts) by Juan Yüan 阮元 (1764–1849). With a total of 13,349 head characters, this is a very useful reference tool for reading early literature. Its explanations were culled from over 100 sources, including many important literary works (e.g., *Ch'u-tz'u** and *Wen hsüan**).

Not falling under any of the above types of dictionaries are several innovative works from the Ch'ing period. Liu Ch'i's 劉淇 *Chu-tzu pien lüeh* 助字辨略 (Differentiating Outline of Auxiliary Graphs), published in 1711, sets as its task the elucidation of particle usage in ancient texts. With 1,140 entries in 30 categories under 476 head characters, examples are drawn from pre-Ch'in texts to T'ang poetry and Sung lyric meters, and include some T'ang and Sung vernacular expressions. It would appear that the *Chu-tzu pien lüeh* was anticipated by the *Yü chu* 語助 (Language Auxiliaries) of Lu I-wei 盧以緯 before 1324 with over 100 entries. Perhaps the most remarkable volume devoted to the meaning and usage of particles is the *Ching chuan shih tz'u* 經傳釋詞 (Explanations of Words in the Classics and Chronicles) by Wang Yin-chih 王引之 (1766–1834). Although he only includes 160 characters and his citations stop with the Western Han period, Wang's scholarship is very careful and he surprisingly acknowledges a number of bisyllabic particles.

The *T'ung-su pien* 通俗編 (Compilation of Popularisms), published in 1751 by Chai Hao 翟灝 (1736-1788) is full of vernacularisms, idioms, dialecticisms, phrases, and clauses divided by different types of objects, social affairs, art, theater, and narratives into 38 categories.

Citations include an unusually wide variety of sources (history, classics, *pi-chi*,* poetry, and even colloquial speech). The *T'ung-su pien* is extremely important for understanding popular customs and common language. Other similar works from around the same time are the *Chih-yü pu-cheng* 直語補正 (Supplements and Corrections of Plain Language) by Liang T'ung-shu 梁同書 (1723–1815), with over 400 entries and the *Heng-yen lu* 恆言錄 (Record of Common Speech) with more than 800 entries by Ch'ien Ta-hsin 錢大昕 (1728–1804).

The most revolutionary work in pre-twentieth-century Chinese lexicography was Nicolas Trigault's (1577–1628) *Hsi-ju erh-mu tzu* 西儒耳目資 (An Aid to the Eyes and Ears of Western Literati). Completed in 1625 and published the following year in Hangchow, this was the first Chinese dictionary which used the Roman alphabet to indicate the sounds of the characters as pronounced in Mandarin (at that time based on the language of Nanking). It consisted of three parts: a general discussion of Chinese phonology, a glossary of graphs arranged according to sound, and a glossary for looking up the sounds of graphs. Around the same time, a number of foreign scholars began to compile dictionaries of various varieties of Mandarin and other Sinitic languages, but these were written in Western languages and did not have as great an impact upon the development of Chinese lexicography and linguistics as *Hsi-ju erh-mu tzu* which was written in Chinese. By the end of the Ch'ing dynasty, native Chinese scholars would be devising their own alphabetical systems for indicating the sounds of their languages.

It is clear from the above survey that the Chinese lexicographical tradition is both long and possessed of abundant resources for the study of pre-modern language and literature. Nonetheless, it displayed a number of adverse features that persisted right up to the present century and, for the most part, have still not been overcome to this day. Among these deficiencies of traditional Chinese lexicography are the following: (1) a pervasive confusion of spoken word with written graph; (2) lack of etymological science as opposed to the analysis of script; (3) absence of the concept of word (this drawback was only to be partially obviated in such twentieth-century works as Chu Ch'i-feng's 朱起鳳 splendid *Tz'u-t'ung* 辭通 (Interchangeable Orthographies) and, to a lesser extent, Fu Ting-i's 符定一 *Lien-mien tzu-tien* 聯綿字典 (Dictionary of Bisyllabic Terms); (4) ignorance of the origins of the script in the oracle bones and lack of familiarity with its development in the bronze inscriptions; (5) no accurate, unambiguous, and convenient means for specifying the pronunciations of graphs and words; (6) no standardized, user-friendly means for looking up words and graphs; (7) failure to distinguish grammatically, syntactically, phonologically, and lexically between vernacular and literary registers of language, between usages peculiar to different places and different times, and between Sinitic and non-Sinitic languages; and (8) open-endedness of the writing system (whereas it is natural and even desirable for a lexicon to expand–providing obsolete words are pruned from time to time and preserved in specialized dictionaries of archaic terms–it is a tremendous disadvantage for the elements of a script to grow without constraint: current unabridged character dictionaries contain 60,000 to 85,000 graphs and dictionaries with over 100,000 graphs are planned.

The primary strengths of traditional Chinese lexicography lies in the three areas with which we began: *wen-tzu* (the construction and analysis of the graphs), *hsün-ku* (the exegesis of graphs and terms in the context of specific quoted passages), and *yin-yün* (the classification of initials and finals). It is to be expected that, in the next century, the drawbacks of Chinese lexicography will be, for the most part, eliminated, while the strengths will be further enhanced and refined.

Studies

Bodman, Nicholas Cleaveland. *A Linguistic Study of the "Shih ming": Initials and Consonant Clusters.* Harvard-Yenching Institutes Studies, 11. Cambridge: Harvard University Press, 1954.

Boltz, William G. *"Shuo wen chieh tzu."* In *Early Chinese Texts.* Pp. 429-442.

Carr, Michael E. "A Linguistic Study of the Flora and Fauna Sections of the *Erh ya.*" Unpublished Ph.D. dissertation, University of Arizona, 1972.

Chao, Chen-to 趙振鐸. *Ku-tai tz'u-shu shih-hua* 古代辭書史話 (A Historical Account of Ancient Dictionaries). Chengtu: Ssu-ch'uan Jen-min, 1986.

Ch'ien, Chien-fu 錢劍夫. *Chung-kuo ku-tai tzu-tien tz'u-tien kai-lun* 中國古代字典辭典概論 (A Summary Discussion of Ancient Chinese Character and Word Dictionaries). Peking: Shang-wu Yin-shu-kuan, 1986.

Chûgoku Gogaku Kenkyûkai 中国語学研究会 (Society for Chinese Language Studies), ed. *Chûgoku gogaku shin jiten* 中国語学新辞典 (A New Dictionary for Chinese Language Studies). Tokyo: Kôseikan, 1969; 4th printing, 1977.

Chung-kuo ta pai-k'o ch'üan-shu 中國大百科全書 (Great Chinese Encyclopedia). Volume on *Yü-yen wen-tzu* 語言文字 (Language and Script). Peking: Chung-kuo Ta Pai-k'o Ch'üan-shu Ch'u-pan-she, 1988.

Coblin, W. South. "An Introductory Study of Textual and Linguistic Problems in *Erh ya.*" Unpublished Ph.D. dissertation, University of Washington, 1972.

____. *"Erh ya."* In *Early Chinese Texts.* Pp. 94-99.

Lin, Yü-shan 林玉山. *Chung-kuo tz'u-shu pien-tsuan shih-lüeh* 中國辭書編纂史略 (A Historical Sketch of the Compilation of Chinese Dictionaries). Chengchow: Chung-chou Ku-chi, 1992.

Liu, Yeh-ch'iu 劉葉秋. *Chung-kuo tzu-tien shih-lüeh* 中國字典史略 (A Historical Sketch of Chinese Dictionaries). Peking: Chung-hua, 1983.

Loewe, Michael, ed. *Early Chinese Texts: A Bibliographical Guide.* Early China Special Monograph Series, No. 2. Berkeley: The Society for the Study of Early China and The Institute of East Asian Studies, 1993.

Miller, Roy Andrew. "Problems in the Study of *Shuo wen chieh tzu.*" Unpublished Ph.D. dissertation, Columbia University, 1953.

____. *"Shih ming."* In *Early Chinese Texts*, pp. 424-428.

von Rosthron, A. "The *Erh-ya* and Other Synonymicons," *JCLTA* 10.2 (1975): 137-145.

Serruys, Paul. *The Chinese Dialects of Han Time According to the "Fang Yen."* Berkeley and Los Angeles: University of California Press, 1959. *University of California Publications in East Asiatic Philology,* 2.

Stimson, Hugh M. *The Jongyuan In Yunn: A Guide to Old Mandarin Pronunciation.* Sinological Series, No. 12. New Haven: Yale University, Far Eastern Publications, 1966.

Ts'ao Hsien-cho 曹先擢 and Yang Jun-lu 楊潤陸. *Ku-tai tz'u-shu chiang-hua* 古代辭書講話 (Lectures on Ancient Diction-aries). Shanghai: Shang-hai Chiao-yü, 1990.

Yang, Paul Fu-mien, comp. *Chinese Dialectology: A Selected and Classified Bibliography.* Hong Kong: Chinese University Press, 1981. See especially sections 4.3.2 and 4.3.3.

____, comp. *Chinese Lexicology and Lexicography: A Selected and Classified Bibliography.* Hong Kong: The Chinese University Press, 1985.

____, comp. *Chinese Linguistics: A Selected and Classified Bibliography.* Hong Kong: The Chinese University Press, 1974. See especially sections 5.1, 7.1.3, and 12.3.4.

Victor H. Mair
University of Pennsylvania

Wan-ko 挽歌 (dirges) were originally songs sung by pall-bearers or coffin-pullers to distract them from their hard work and/or to lament the dead; in the hands of the literati the term later came to designate any sort of poem which dealt with the hardship and transience of life.

*Chuang-tzu*** explains that the function of *wan-ko* was to relieve the hard work involved. In the *Tso-chuan** Kung-sun Hsia 公孫夏 ordered his soldiers to sing the "Yü-pin" 虞殯 (*yü* refers to the post-burial ceremony in the memorial hall, *pin* to the burial itself), a dirge predicting their inevitable and immediate death, before a battle to show their decisiveness to fight to the death. However, in the Confucian classics it is clear that the early Confucians disapproved of this practice. According to the *Li-chi* 禮記, when Confucius went to visit his friend Yüan Jang 原壤, whose mother had just passed away, to help him ready the coffin, Yüan tapped on it and began to sing. Confucius was greatly displeased and took leave immediately.

During the Three Kingdoms period, the erudite historian, Ch'iao Chou 譙周 (199–270), argued that *wan-ko* originated when T'ien Heng 田橫, the King of Ch'i 齊, refused to surrender to Liu Pang 劉邦 (256–195 B.C.) and committed suicide *ca.* 200 B.C. T'ien's retainers dared not cry out in grief and thus composed the "Hsieh-lu" 薤露 (Dew on the Shallots) and the "Hao-li" 蒿里 to bemoan their master. The dew in the first title expresses the fleeting quality of human life and Hao-li refers to a place located beneath Mount T'ai 泰 to which human souls allegedly return. Both Ts'ui Pao 崔豹 (*fl.* 300) in his *Ku-chin chu* 古今注 and Kan Pao 干寶 (*fl.* 320) in his *Sou-shen chi* 搜神記 (In Search of the Supernatural)* endorse Ch'iao Chou's view. Tsui further argues that the Han-dynasty musician, Li Yen-nien 李延年, wrote the melody for the two famous *wan-ko* and prescribed that the "Hsieh-lu" was for the nobles, while the "Hao-li" was for the officials and commoners. These two songs were probably funeral songs of the Ch'i area (modern Shantung). Thus, it is natural to assume that T'ien Heng's retainers would have sung these local dirges to express their sorrow.

The "Monograph on Ritual" of the *Chin-shu* 晉書 claims that *wan-ko* originated from the songs sung by conscript laborers mourning for their hard life under of Emperor Wu 武 of the Han (r. 141-87 B.C.). However, the modern consensus is that singing *wan-ko* was already popular in the pre-Ch'in era. The fact that the Confucian classics proscribe singing at a funeral supports this view. Furthermore, as early as the Eastern Han, the *wan-ko* was performed at the funeral of Empress Yin 陰 (d. A.D. 64). It seems certain that *wan-ko* became part of the funeral ritual and that the term began to be used in Han times at the latest, to refer to songs that existed much earlier.

During the Eastern Han dynasty, the *wan-ko* became a popular artistic form that penetrated all levels of society. In his *Feng-su t'ung-i* 風俗通義, Ying Shao 應劭 (*ca.* 140–*ca.* 206) censured the singing of the *wan-ko* as one of the corrupt customs of the capital because the songs were regularly performed after wedding ceremonies in Lo-yang. Thus it is clear the dirges had become a form of entertainment for the Han people. The popularity of the *wan-ko* did not wane in the Six Dynasties. According to Chin-dynasty laws, sixty young men from a family who held positions of the sixth rank should be selected to become *wan-lang* 挽郎 (pallbearers) to perform at the funeral of the nobles and princes. The *Shih-shuo hsin-yü* 世説新語 also records that some literati were fond of singing *wan-ko* at various times and places. The famous poet Yen Yen-chih 顏延之 (384–456)* was found half naked singing dirges in a wineshop. The literati interest in *wan-ko* was part of a tendency in the Eastern Han to appreciate literary works that displayed melancholy and sorrow.

The best-known *wan-ko* pieces are the "Hsieh-lu" and the "Hao-li," which were probably written in the Han. They consist of some three- and five-syllable lines, but the major rhythm is seven-syllables. They sing of the ephemerality of human life and the inevitability of death. Many scholars have attempted to identify *wan-ko* among extant pre-Ch'in poems by arguing that the "Erh-tzu ch'eng-chou" 二子乘舟 (Mao #44), "Ko-sheng" 葛生 (Mao #124), and "Huang-niao" 黃鳥 (Mao #131) in the *Shih-ching* 詩經 were dirges. The "Ku-shih shih-chiu shou" 古詩十九首 (Nineteen Ancient Poems)* in the Eastern Han contain themes similar to *wan-ko,* though they are not so titled, lamenting the brevity of human life and sorrowing over death. Yet the earliest extant literati composition that uses *wan-ko* as a title is Miao Hsi's 繆襲 (186–245) "Wan-ko shih" 挽歌詩. In the Wei dynasty, Ts'ao Ts'ao 曹操 (155-220)** and his son Ts'ao Chih 曹植 (192–232)* wrote several dirges titled "Hsieh-lu" and "Hao-li." However, these works lament the chaos and destruction of the state, rather than personal loss. Famous *wan-ko* poets of the Chin dynasty include Fu Hsüan 傅玄 (217–278),* Lu Chi 陸機 (261–303),* and T'ao Ch'ien 陶潛 (365–427).* P'an Yüeh 潘岳 (247–300),* although he wrote no verses titled *wan-ko,* is famous for his poems anguishing over the deaths of his wife and his children. Moreover, among his "Tao-wang shih" 悼亡詩 (Poems Lamenting the Departed) are three poems that resemble in structure the dirges-sequences of the Chin poets, which sang of three points in time in three verses—the pre-funeral rites, the funeral ceremony, and finally the burial.

Not only in P'an Yüeh's corpus, but in general the *wan-ko* should be identified by theme rather than title. Poems with titles such as "Ch'ang ko" 長歌 (Long Songs), "Tuan-ko" 短歌 (Short Songs), "T'ai-shan Liang-fu ko" 泰山梁甫歌 (Chants of Liang-fu at Mount T'ai), "T'ai-shan yin" 泰山吟 (Mount T'ai Chants), "Tung-wu yin" 東武吟 (Tung-wu Chants), and "Hsing-lu nan" 行路難 (The Hardships of Travelling) should all be considered part of this ancient genre.

Thus in the Southern Dynasties, the most famous *wan-ko* pieces are Pao Chao's 鮑照 (*ca.* 414-466)* "Hardships of Travelling." This title was originally affixed to popular songs sung by shepherds from North China during the Chin dynasty. These poems conventionally open with the line "Chün pu-chien" 君不見 "Don't you see. . ." followed by seven-syllable lines bemoaning the hardships of travel or the sadness of separation. Although the original folksongs to this title are no longer extant, Pao Chao's imitations retain the seven-syllable meter of the originals and in that sense resemble early dirges such as "Hsieh-lu" and "Hao-li" (most other literati *wan-ko* were written in five-syllable lines). Pao's poems were composed at different times and treat a variety of subjects which can be grouped into three general categories: poems that express indignation about Pao's lack of status; laments on the transience of life; and expressions of the sorrows of the boudoir sung through a female persona. The broader range of topics Pao Chao introduced to the *wan-ko* continued the expansion of its parameters. From a ancient song-type related to the funerary profession, *wan-ko* had become a dirge that could be applied to numerous situations and occasions.

The genre continued to evolve during the T'ang and Sung dynasties, adopting itself to the popularity of *chin-t'i shih* 今體詩 (recent-style verse). The protagonist of a well-known *ch'uan-ch'i* tale,* "Li Wa chuan" 李娃傳 (An Account of Li Wa), became famous in Ch'ang-an through his skill in singing dirges. Even in modern Taiwan it is still common to hear descendants of the *wan-ko* sung at funerals.

Editions and References
Ku-chin t'u-shu chi-ch'eng 古今圖書集成: "Ching-chi hui-pien–Li-i tien, San-tsang pu" 經濟彙編—禮儀典，喪葬部, *chüan* 98, "I-wen" 藝文, 6.

Studies

Chi, T'ien-chü 齊天舉. "Wan-ko k'ao" 挽歌考, *Wen shih* 29 (1988): 277-85. Ch'i argues that the *wan-ko* began after the Ch'in.

Gotô, Akinobu 後藤秋正 and Yoshikawa Masaki 吉川雅樹. "Tôdai bankashi kenkyû" 唐代挽歌詩研究, *Hokkaido Kyôiku Daigaku kiyô–Jinbun kagaku hen,* 45 (1995): 17-31.

Huang, Ching-chin 黃景進. "Wan-ko chi ch'i ying-hsiang–Hsien-Ch'in chih Nan-pei ch'ao" 挽歌及其影響—先秦至南北朝, *Chung-hua hsüeh-yüan* 34 (1986): 31-82.

Jen, Pan-t'ang 任半塘. *T'ang sheng-shih* 唐聲詩. Shanghai: Shang-hai Ku-chi, 1982, pp. 419-430.

Ikkai, Tomoyoshi 一海知義. *"Mo zen 'bankashi' kô"* 文選挽歌詩考, *Chûgoku bungaku hô* 12 (1960): 19-48.

Nishioka, Hiroshi 西岡弘. *Chûgoku kodai no sôrei to bungaku* 中国古代の葬礼と文学. Tokyo: Sankosha, 1970, pp. 641-679.

Russell, T. C. "Coffin-Pullers' Songs: The Macabre in Medieval China," *Papers on Far Eastern History* 27 (1983): 99-130.

Ts'ai, Mao-t'ang 蔡懋棠, trans. "Wan-ko k'ao" 挽歌考, by Nishioka Hiroshi, *T'ai-wan feng-wu* 29.4 (1979): 17-33.

Jui-lung Su
The National Singapore University

Wan-yüeh p'ai 婉約派 (School of Delicate Restraint) is to a certain extent a misnomer, since it actually depicts poets who wrote in the normative style of the *tz'u* 詞 (lyric)* since the genre began. Although the term was used as early as pre-Ch'in times, Chang Yen 張綎 (*fl.* 1513) first applied *wan-yüeh* to designate one of the two "schools" of lyrics (the other being the *Hao-fang p'ai* 豪放派 [School of the Heroic and Unrestricted])** in the Sung dynasty.

Wan 婉 (delicate) may be seen as referring to the rise of the *tz'u* in the T'ang,, when it developed from a popular form into a professional one practiced by female singers at court (in the Chiao-fang 教坊) and in the demimonde (in the Ch'i-t'ing 旗亭 [Entertainment Houses]). The feminine aura was maintained by the literati who joined the mix in the 9th and 10th centuries. Poets like Wen T'ing-yün 溫庭筠 (*ca.* 812-870)* and Wei Chuang 韋莊 (*ca.* 836-910)*–indeed most of the lyricists whose works can be found in the *Hua-chien chi* 花間集 (Anthology Midst the Flowers)*–put many of their poetic statements in the mouths of female persona. Theirs was the world of the boudoir, the roomscape, and the *table de toilette.* The extravagance of their life-style in this elegant, but fragile world, enhanced the "delicacy" of their work. *Yüeh* 約 (restraint) can be read as a reference to the limited diction of the lyric, to restrictions imposed by its tune patterns, and to the relatively small world of settings and themes available to the lyricist. The compound *wan-yüeh* also suggests a terse, implicit style, which fits well the world of women's communication at the turn of the last millennium.

The necessity for this designation arose when Su Shih 蘇軾 (1037–1101)* began to write in a style that differed from the accepted, writing about subjects which had previously not been treated in this genre. Indeed, other than his *tz'u* and those of Hsin Ch'i-chi 辛棄疾 (1140–1207),* most Sung lyrics and lyricists can be considered part of the School of Delicate Restraint. Su and Hsin's School of the Heroic and Unrestricted can be considered an entity created to define their deviations, and those of a few followers, from the norm.

The literary influence and reputation of the School of Delicate Restraint remained dominant. Aside from a few Hao-fang poets of the early Southern Sung and a number of their followers in the Ch'ing, almost all of the *tz'u* poets in the Sung and subsequent dynasties were Wan-yüeh adherents. Twentieth century critics reflect this development: Wang Kuo-wei 王國維 (1877–1927),* while acknowledging the talent of the Hao-fang lyricists, recognized the Wan-yüeh School and its style as normative.

Editions and References

Hui, Ch'i-yüan 惠淇源, ed. *Wan-yüeh tz'u* 婉約詞. Hofei: An-hui Wen-i, 1989.

Li, Ch'in-yin 李勤印, ed. *Wan-yüeh tz'u-p'ai hsüan-chi* 婉約詞派選集. Peking: Pei-ching Shih-fan Hsüeh-yüan, 1993.

Sun, Ju-jung 孫如容. *Wan-yüeh tz'u shang-hsi* 婉約詞賞析. Nanning: Kuang-hsi Jen-min, 1986.

Studies

Ku, I-sheng 顧易生. "Pei-Sung Wan-yüeh tz'u te ch'uang-tso ssu-hsiang ho Li Ch'ing-chao te tz'u-lun" 北宋婉約詞的創作思想和李清照的詞論, *Wen-i li-lun yen-chiu* 1982.2.

Ts'ao, Chi-p'ing 曹濟平. "Ts'ung Wan-yüeh tz'u t'an i-shu feng-ko te to-yang-hua" 從婉約詞壇藝術風格的多樣化, *Kuang-ming jih-pao* 24 October 1979.

Wan, Yün-chün 萬雲駿. "Shih-lun Sung-tz'u te hao-fang yü Wan-yüeh p'ai te p'ing-chia wen-t'i: chien-p'ing Hu Yün-i te *Sung-tz'u hsüan*" 試論宋詞的豪放與婉約派的評價問題—兼評胡雲翼的宋詞選, *Hsüeh-shu yüeh-k'an* 1979.4.

Wu, Wen-chih 吳文治. "Wan-yüeh tz'u-p'ai yen-chiu chung te chi-ko wen-t'i" 婉約詞派研究中的幾個問題. In *Tz'u-hsüeh yen-chiu lun-wen chi* 詞學研究論文集. Shang-hai: Shang-hai Ku-chi, 1982, pp. 44-54.

Chen Bingmei
University of Wisconsin

Wang Ch'ung 王充 (*tzu*, Chung-jen 仲任, 27–*ca.* 97) was a critical Confucian philosopher, whose *Lun-heng* 論衡 (Balanced Treatise) represents an immense repertorium of knowledge. Although from a ruined family in Kuei-chi 會稽 (modern Shang-yü 上虞 County in Chekiang), he came to Lo-yang to study in 54 at the Imperial Academy under the guidance of the historian Pan Piao 班彪 (3–54), the father of Pan Ku 班固 (32–92)*; all three were adherents of the Old Text School. Being poor, he studied at the book-stalls in the streets. He had a photographic memory which enabled him after his return to Ch'ang-an in 59 to compose writings full of allusions to numerous books. Still at Lo-yang, probably in 58, he wrote for Emperor Ming 明 (r. 57–75 A.D.) his *Ta-ju lun* 大儒論 (On the Great Confucian[s]); the variant *Liu* 六 *ju lun* is less probable).

His official career was mediocre and short. He was very critical, even to his colleagues and this might have been one of the reasons why he left his posts, living as a teacher and alone. The titles of his writings—*Chi-su* 譏俗 (Critique of the Vulgar) and *Chieh-i* 節義 (Chaste and Righteous) in twelve chapters (possibly one book only: *Chi-su chieh-i*)—show that "he wished to rouse the vulgar people." He wrote a book on politics *Cheng-wu* 政務 (The Duties of Government). In 77, a year with a bad harvest, Wang Ch'ung wrote memorials to the Grand Administrator of his commandery entitled "Pei-fa" 備乏 (Provisions in the Time of Want) and "Chin-chiu" 禁酒 (Prohibition of Spirits) to prevent grain from being used for the production of alcohol. Wang Ch'ung described his gnoseology in "Shih-lun" 實論 (Treatise on the Truth). Near the end of his life Wang wrote the *Yang-hsing shu* 養性書 (The Nourishment of the Inner Nature) in sixteen chapters.

The present text of *Lun-heng*, existing already at the end of the second century, has eighty-five chapters, of which the forty-fourth, "Chao-chih" 招致 (Attracting and Accepting), has been lost while the last, an autobiographical essay, might have been written by somebody else. The titles of at least four other lost chapters are known and the book might have had some one-hundred chapters originally. With the exception of a small fragment of "Kuo fu" 果賦 (*Fu* on Fruit) all his mentioned writings could well be part of the present *Lun-heng*, although this title probably originally represented only a part of the entire book and was written between 70–80.

The original *Lun-heng* might have contained only the nine chapters on falsities (*hsü* 虛) and three on exaggerations (*tseng* 增) which, together with the chapters on Han-fei, Mencius and Confucius, undoubtedly present the philosophical basis of Wang Ch'ung's ideas. Other chapters now in the *Lun-heng* were probably originally in other works by Wang. For example, the *Cheng-wu* must originally have included sections such as the present *Lun-heng* chapters "Ch'ien-kao" 譴告 (On Reprimands) and "Shih-ying" 是應 (Auguries Verified); the *Chi-su* contained chapters like "Pu-shih" 卜筮 (On Divination) and "Chieh-ch'u" 解除 (On Exorcism). Two chapters, 78 and 79, "Shih-chih" 實知 (Real Nature) and "Chih-shih" 知實 (Knowledge of the Truth) belong surely to what was originally the *Shih-lun*. The *Lun-heng* in its present form may thus represent a kind of collected works of Wang Ch'ung, reflecting also the development of his ideas.

Wang's brilliant essay on death, which uses philosophical Taoist ideas concerning spontaneity, demonstrates his principle of opposing the will of Heaven, but it does not impose any restraints upon his consequent fatalism. His criticism of many unfounded accounts of the past, like those of the Taoists on the Yellow Emperor, and his coherent gnoseological method enabled him to oppose the *ch'an-wei* 讖緯 prognostication texts. He did not hesitate to claim that many utterings of Confucius were rather ambiguous; Wang Ch'ung's wish was to differentiate between real (*shih* 實) and false, void (*hsü* 虛). However, he sometimes criticized ideas because of the meaning he personally imputed to them.

He was not only much learned but also bookish. Living for a long time alone with his texts, he was evidently inexperienced in practical, non-official activities. Otherwise he would have been unable to assert in fifteen arguments and four analogies that not only the "real" dragon,

but also an earthen one, were able to attract rain from heaven. He was right when stating that for the solution of present problems the Classics were less useful than contemporary, practical attitudes. However, he supported his actual theses with hundreds of examples taken from history, his supreme authority; moreover, he wrote eulogies on present rulers.

The ideas of Wang Ch'ung were forgotten for centuries and rediscovered, even for the Chinese, by A. Forke. After 1919 he became one of the representatives of the materialist trend in philosophy started by Huan T'an 桓譚 (*ca.* 43 B.C.–*ca.* A.D. 28),** Wang Ch'ung, Pan Ku and others in the first century A.D., and of the Old Text School, representing a more realistic trend in Confucianism.

Editions and References

Ch'eng Hsiang-ch'ing 程湘清 *et al.*, eds. *Lun-heng so-yin* 論衡索引. Peking: Chung-hua, 1994. Includes the original text and name indexes for persons and places.

Huang, Hui 黃暉. *Lun-heng chiao-shih* 論衡校釋. Changsha, 1938; 2v. Taipei: T'ai-wan Shang-wu Yin-shu-kuan, 1964.

Liu, P'an-sui 劉盼遂. *Lun-heng chi-chieh* 論衡集解. Peking, 1957; rpt. Taipei, 1964.

Pokora, Timoetus. "Two Recent Commented Editions of the *Lun-heng*," *AO* 34 (1966): 593–601.

Wu, Cheng-shih 吳承仕. *Lun-heng chiao-shih* 論衡校釋. Peking: Pei-ching Ta-hsüeh, 1986.

Translations

Forke, A. *Lun-heng. Part I. Philosophical Essays of Wang Ch'ung. Part II. Miscellaneous Essays of Wang Ch'ung.* Leipzig, 1907; Berlin, 1911; rpt. New York, 1962. For a partial translation of 44 chapters from these volumes, see: "*Lun-Heng,* Selected Essays of the Philosopher Wang Ch'ung," *MSOS* IX (1906): 181–400; X (1907): 1–172; XI (1908): 1–88.

Leslie, D. "Contributions to a New Translations of the *Lun-heng*," *TP* XLIV (1956), 100-149.

Otaki, Kazuo 大滝一雄. *Ronkoo: Kandai no itanteki shisoo* 論衡の異端的思想. Tokyo, 1965. Annotated transl. of 14 chapters.

Studies

Ch'en, Cheng-hsiung 陳正雄. *Wang Ch'ung hsüeh-shu ssu-hsiang shu-p'ing* 王充學術思想述評. Taipei: Wen-chin, 1987.

Ch'en, Yü-sen 陳玉森. "Shih lun Wang Ch'ung ti ssu-hsiang yüan-yüan" 試論王充的思想淵源, *Che-hsüeh yen-chiu* 8–9 (1958): 75–84.

Cheng, Wen 鄭文. *Wang Ch'ung che-hsüeh ch'u-t'an* 王充哲學初探 Peking, 1958.

Chiang, Tsu-i 蔣祖怡. *Wang Ch'ung ti wen-hsüeh li-lun* 王充的文學理論. Shanghai, 1963.

Hsü, Tao-lin 徐道鄰. "Wang Ch'ung lun" 王充論, *Tung-hai hsüeh-pao* 3 (1960): 1–19.

Lanciotti, L. *Considerazioni sull' estetica letteraria nella Cina antica: Wang Ch'ung ed il sorgere dell' autonomia delle lettere.* Roma, 1965.

Li, Shih-yi, "Wang Ch'ung." *T'ien Hsia Monthly* 5 (1937): 162–184.

Liu, P'an-sui. "Wang Ch'ung *Lun-heng* p'ien-shu ts'an-i k'ao" 王充論衡篇數殘儀考, *Hsüeh-wen tsa-chih* 1 (1932): 23–25; rpt. in *Ku-shih pien* 古史辨 4 (1935): 691–693 and in *Lun-heng chi-chieh*, pp. 642–643.

Liu, Yü-ch'ang 劉禹昌. "Wang Ch'ung te wen-lun" 王充的文論, *Chi-lin Ta-hsüeh She-hui K'o-hsüeh hsüeh-pao* 2 (1963): 43–60.

Pokora, Timoetus. "The Works of Wang Ch'ung," *AO* 36 (1968): 122–134.

T'ien, Ch'ang-wu 田昌五. *Lun-heng tao-hsü* 論衡導續. Chengtu: Pa-Shu Shu-she, 1989.

T'ien, Ch'ang-wu 田昌五. *Wang Ch'ung chi ch'i Lun-heng* 王充及其論衡. Peking, 1962.

___. "Wang Ch'ung: An Ancient Chinese Militant Materialist," *Chinese Studies in Philosophy* 7 (1975–1976): 4–197.

Wang, Chin-kuang 王錦光 and Wen Jen-chün 聞人軍. "Lun-heng ssu-nan hsin k'ao yü fu yüan fang-an 論衡司南新考與復原方案." *Wen-shih* 31 (1988): 25-32.

Zufferey, Nicolas. "Pourquoi Wong Chong critique-t-il Confucius?" *Études chinoises* 14.1 (Spring 1995): 25-54.

Timoteus Pokora
Prague

Wang Jung 王融 (*tzu*, Yüan-ch'ang 元長, 468–493) was a descendant of two of the most powerful aristocratic families of South China: his father was from the Wang 王 clan of Lang-yeh 瑯琊 (modern Lin-i 臨沂, Shantung) and his mother was a daughter of the Hsieh 謝 clan of Yang-hsia 陽夏 (modern T'ai-k'ang 太康, Honan). He passed the *hsiu-ts'ai* 秀才 (cultivated talent) examination before he reached the age of twenty. At sixteen he began to compose poetry and caught the attention of his uncle, Wang Chien 王儉 (452–489). Wang especially excelled in writing essays and poetry extempore.

In 485 he joined the staff of Hsiao Ch'ang-mao 蕭長懋 (458-493), the Prince of Chin-an 晉安, as military adjutant. Two years later he held a similar position under Hsiao Tzu-liang 蕭子良 (460-494), the Prince of Ching-ling 竟陵. Despite his prestigious background, Wang's father had not achieved high office, making Wang all the more ambitious; he vowed to gain a powerful post before age thirty. Towards this end, he presented several daring memorials urging Emperor Wu 武 (r. 482–493) to attack and attempt to recover the North, this is an era when the North-South division had long been accepted as fact.

As the Emperor lay dying in 493, Wang Jung became involved in the struggle for power. The heir apparent and Wang's former superior, the Prince of Chin-an, had passed away six months earlier and no new successor had been named. The court was divided, one group supporting Hsiao Chao-yeh 蕭昭業 (473–494), the eldest son of the Prince of Chin-an, and the other supporting Hsiao Tzu-liang. As rumors began to circulate that the Emperor had already died, Wang, having just been appointed Ning-shuo Chiang-chün 寧朔將軍 (General to Pacify the North) by Hsiao Tzu-liang, gathered several hundred Northerners on his own initiative and rushed to the quarters of

178

the heir apparent to prevent Hsiao Chao-yeh from entering. However, Hsiao Tzu-liang failed to follow Wang's lead and lost his opportunity to rule. When Hsiao Chao-yeh eventually ascended the throne, one of his first acts was to have Wang June arrested and to order him to commit suicide in prison.

Even in the twenty-five years he was alive, however, Wang Jung left a mark on the history of Chinese poetry. The last decade of his life coincided with the ˙ Yung-ming 永明 era (483–493), when literature flourished in the salon of Hsiao Tzu-liang around a circle of the "Ching-ling pa-yu" 竟陵八友 (Eight Friends of Pa-ling): Shen Yüeh 沈約 (441–513),* Hsieh T'iao 謝朓 (464– 499),* Hsiao Ch'en 蕭琛 (478–529), Fan Yün 范雲 (451–503), Jen Fang 任昉 (460–508),* Lu Ch'ui 陸倕 (470–526), and Wang Jung.

Despite his earlier appointment under the Prince of Chin-an, Wang's career revolved around the Prince of Ching-ling. He first came to be associated with the Prince through participating in a literary project, the compilation of an encyclopedia entitled *Ssu-pu yao-lüeh* 四部要略 (The Essential Compendium of the Four Categories). It was the style of the Ch'i and Liang dynasties to utilize numerous allusions in writing and Wang, with his erudition, was certainly among the most qualified to compile such a literary handbook.

Wang Jung shared Hsiao Tzu-liang's commitment to Buddhism. Under the patronage of the Prince, chanting masters and monks who mastered Sanskrit and Buddhist psalmody gather in Chien-k'ang 建康 (modern Nanking). The famous Western Villa of the Prince became a center for both Buddhism and literature. Hsiao not only summoned experts in Buddhist doctrines to the Villa, but gave lectures himself on Buddhist theology. Like his patron, Wang had a deep understanding of Buddhism and its psalmody. It was the Sanskrit theory of poetic defects that led the Yung-ming

poets to construct the basis for a tonal prosody which shaped the poetry of the golden age of verse, the T'ang dynasty. Most scholars credit the formation of the Yung-ming Style and the concept of the *Ssu-sheng pa-ping* 四聲八病 (Four Tones and Eight Maladies) to Shen Yüeh, but it is also possible that Wang Jung, who must have been familiar with the chanting of Buddhist sutras, could at least have contributed to Shen's ideas. Chung Jung 鍾嶸 (*ca.* 465–518) in his *Shih-p'in* 詩品 (An Evaluation of Poetry)* goes further to argue that it was Wang Jung himself who originated the movement to examine how tones could influence *shih* prosody, while Shen Yüeh and Hsieh T'iao merely "stirred up its waves." Chung also mentions that Wang Jung intended to write a "Chih-yin lun" 知音論 (Essay on Understanding Music), but he never completed the work.

Whether an innovator of poetic form or not, Wang was a versatile poet who excelled in writing many types of verse. His extant poetic corpus contains 107 poems and comprises a wide range of types and titles, including religious works, *yüeh-fu,** *yu-hsien shih* 遊仙詩 (poems on roaming as a transcendent), *yung-wu shih* 詠物詩 (poetry on objects), and various kinds of poetic games. Religious poems abound. The two major sets of poems on Buddhist topics are his "Fa-lo tz'u" 法樂辭 (Songs of Religious Joy) and "Ching-chu tzu ching-hsing fa-men sung" 淨住子靜行法門頌 (Hymns on the Devotee's Entrance into the Pure Life). The first set, composed around 487, consists of twelve poems in five-syllable lines. The first eight pieces recount the life cycle of Gautama Buddha: his nativity on earth, his life in the palace, the process of how he relinquishes his kingdom to attain the Bodhimanda, and his final enlightenment. The remaining four poems are devoted to Buddhist activities of both clergy and laity.

The second set containing thirty-one hymns in four-syllable lines was inspired by Hsiao Tzu-liang's "Ching-chu tzu ching-hsing fa-men" 淨住子靜行法門 (A Devotee's Entrance in the Pure Life). Although Wang's hymns were composed to match Hsiao's treatise which contains thirty-one sections, Wang does not follow the original work that closely. Rather he selects and elaborates on important issues that demonstrate his profound knowledge of Buddhism, both in general terms and in more technical issues such as self-cultivation and various doctrines. Through these pieces, he ponders his own life and shows a reflective aspect of his personality.

In addition to religious poetry, Wang also has a substantial *yüeh-fu* corpus, primarily five-syllable quatrains, that includes many new *yüeh-fu* titles such as "Shao-nien tzu" 少年子 (The Rowdy Youth), "Chiang-kao ch'ü" 江皋曲 (Melody of the River-bank), and "Ssu Kung-tzu" 思公子 (Thinking of My Lord). These poems treat a variety of topics; their style, characteristic of the Southern dynasties, is simple and refreshing, with few allusions or difficult phrases. The other category of Wang's poetry was personal pieces written to his friends and colleagues on different occasions. Works such as "Ku-i shih" 古意詩 (Poem with Ancient Intent) and "Chien Hsieh Wen-hsüeh li-yeh shih" 餞謝文學離夜詩 (Poem Given to Hsieh Wen-hsüeh [Hsieh T'iao 謝朓 (464-499)*] On Parting At Night) Wang also wrote such poetic exercises *hui-wen* 迴文 (palindromes), *shuang-sheng shih* 雙聲詩 (alliterative poems), and *li-ho* 離合 (recombination verse [literally "dividing and bringing together again"]). These exercises were popular at court under the Southern Dynasties and reflect Wang's life as a courtier.

Despite his talent, Wang Jung is not well-known for his poetry. His most famous piece is the "San-yüeh san-jih Ch'ü-shui shih hsü" 三月三日曲水詩序 (Preface to the Poems Composed at the Winding Waterway Gathering on the Third Day of the Third Month). It was written in the spring of 491 when Emperor Wu 武 of Ch'i 齊 arrived in Fang-lin 芳林 Garden to celebrate the Lustration Festival. Famed for its highly embellished and allusive language, the Preface begins by glorifying the founding of the dynasty and then launches into praise for Emperor Wu, his officials and ministers as well as the auspicious signs that had made their appearance to signal Heaven's approval of the new regime. Finally, it focuses on the activities related to the Lustration Festival, the preparations for the celebration, and the imperial banquet. Wang's piece serves not only to introduce the poems by the other literati present, but also is the ultimate eulogy of the Ch'i dynasty and its ruler. To be given the task of composing the Preface, there is little doubt that Wang Jung was considered the best prose writer at court. The Preface became so famous in Wang's time that even diplomats from the Northern Wei inquired about it when they came South. Critics have compared it favorably to a work of the same title by Yen Yen-chih 顏延之 (384–456)*– these two works alone represent the genre in the *Wen-hsüan.*

Editions and References

Chang, P'u 張溥, ed. *Wang Ni-shuo chi* 王寧朔集. In *Han Wei Liu-ch'ao pai-san chia.*

Studies

Fujii, Mamoru 藤井守. "Rikuchô bunjin den–Ô Yû (*Nanseijo*) 六朝文人伝一王融 (南齊書), *Chûgoku chûsei bungaku kenkyû* 14 (1980).

___. "Ô Yû no 'Saku shûsei ron' ni tsuite" 王融の策秀才論について. *Obi [Kôichi] Hakasei taikyû kinen Chûgoku bungaku ronbunshû* 小尾「郊一」博士退休記念中国文学論文集, Tokyo: Daiichi, 1976.

Mather, Richard B. "Wang Jung's 'Hymns on the Devotee's Entrance into the Pure Life," *JAOS* 106.1 (1986): 79-98.

___. "The Life of the Buddha and the Buddhist Life: Wang Jung's (468-93)

'Songs of Religious Joy' (*Fa-le tz'u*)," *JAOS* 107.1 (1987): 31-38. These two articles by Richard Mather are the most authoritative studies of Wang Jung's religious poetry.

Morino, Shigeo 森野繁夫. "Ô Yû 'Sangatsu mika kyokusui shisho'" 王融「三月三日曲水詩序. In *Obi [Kôichi] Hakasei koki kinen Chûgoku bungaku ronbunshû* 小尾「郊一」博士古稀記念中国文学論文, Tokyo: Kyûko Shoin, 1983, pp. 257-74.

Toppata, Shigenao 鳥羽田重直. "Ô Yû ron" 王融論, *Wayô kokubun kenkyû* 18 (1983).

Yüan, Shih-shuo 袁世碩, ed. "Wang Jung" 王融. In Yüan's *Shan-tung ku-tai wen-hsüeh chia p'ing-chuan* 山東古代文學家評傳. Shantung: Shan-tung Jen-min, 1983, pp. 361-385.

Jui-lung Su
The National University of Singapore

Wang Ling 王令 (*tzu*, Feng-yüan 逢原, original *tzu*, Chung-mei 鍾美, 1032–1059), of Kuang-ling 廣陵, north of Yangchow, was orphaned at five *sui*, taught school from seventeen *sui*, was discovered by Wang An-shih 王安石 (1021–1086)* at 23 *sui* and died at 28 *sui*, leaving almost 500 poems and some prose works. Compiled by a careful grandson, their first complete printing did not occur until 1922. Wang's writing is of interest because it shows facets of the thinking of a bright young man in the intellectually fertile Lower Yangtze and Huai River region during the Northern Sung. In at least four ways, his work is less "layered" than what one finds in many better-known collections: (1) it has been largely unavailable for posterity to interpret and categorize; (2) Wang had no chance to re-edit later in life; (3) his conscious literary antecedents seem fewer and easier to identify than those of wealthier or more-travelled writers who had easier access to books; (4) one assumes that he exhibits a fairly consistent regional consciousness, as he spent his whole life in the Yangchow orbit except for a trip to Kiangsi the year before he died.

He grew up in the home of a great-uncle, the minor official Wang I 王乙. Wang Ling claims to have been a wild youth who terrorized the neighborhood by day and studied all night. By seventeen *sui* he had left Wang I's house and was teaching at a clan school to support a widowed elder sister, her children, and himself. He was not a recluse. If he had the means, he would probably have sat for the 1052 and 1057 *chin-shih* examinations. He circulated among local scholars, managing to meet Sun Chüeh 孫覺 (1028–1090), the brilliant student of Hu Yüan 胡瑗 (993–1059), and also Shao Pi 邵必, prefect of Kao-yu 高郵 and friend of Mei Yao-ch'en 梅堯臣 (1002–1060).* But when the painfully incorruptible Shao Pi offered the staunchly principled Wang Ling a post in his administration, having unsuccessfully recommended him to the imperial court, Wang refused the position on grounds of the moral impasse that the offer created: "My aspiration (*chih* 志) lies in being poor and humble," wrote Wang to Shao, ". . . please do not try to bend it. Remember also, that if I did not have this kind of aspiration, you would find no use for me on your staff to begin with." One doubts that Wang actually aspired to remain poor; more likely, "poverty" should be taken to mean the kind of life he preferred over one of public service wrongly attained. His friendship with Wang An-shih, then a prefectural official in his mid-thirties, showed promise of opening a route into public life which Wang Ling would have accepted. He introduced himself to Wang An-shih in 1054, aided by the numerous academic and social connections that Wang An-shih had with Wang Ling's friends and family. Wang An-shih, eleven years older, admired the younger man so much that he arranged a marriage with a woman from the same Kiangsi Wu clan that Wang An-shih's wife and mother belonged to. Seven months into the marriage, Wang Ling died, apparently of beriberi; a daughter was born soon after. Eventually she also married a Wu, again with Wang An-shih's help.

Although posterity has placed him into Wang An-shih's school of political thought, it is likely that Wang Ling, while interested in creative statecraft, was ideologically more traditional than his cousin-in-law. Occasional hints do indicate that he might have evolved into an interesting reformist thinker, as when he challenged his students to explain "how higher taxes can make the people prosper" (in a mock examination question, *Wang Ling chi, chüan* 21.) Both Wangs seem to have shared a stiff sense of propriety, of the kind which kept the elder Wang busy serving the court as a constantly rotating replacement for incompetent or dishonest officials, and which prevented the younger Wang from entering politics at all. Both men despised "mediocrity" (Wang An-shih's "common crowd" or *liu-su* 流俗), although Wang Ling seems to have tempered his dislike of "commonness" with a recognition that for many people not blessed with wealth or large families, "excellence" in terms of career was not an option. Even while he was building a name as an expert on Confucius and Mencius, he admitted, late one night, "In my vanity I expound upon the study of sagehood / While in fact I'm headed straight to where the middlebrows live. . ." 虛云聖賢學，實從庸俗歸 ("Chung yeh" 中夜, *chüan* 4).

His strongest poetry shows considerable flair, although like many young poets he wore his influences earnestly and obviously, Han Yü 韓愈 (768–824)* and his mid-T'ang circle being especially prominent. Reading Han Yü seems to have nourished a taste for gnarled textures, belligerent awkwardness and gritty similes. Wang was equally smitten by Meng Chiao 孟郊 (751–814)* and it is interesting to compare his delighted poem written after discovering that poet with the bemused half-satires of Su Shih 蘇軾 (1037–1101)*–who nevertheless also imitated Meng on occasion. Wang Ling's work confirms a few common impres-sions about Northern Sung literary taste: a love for Tu Mu 杜牧 (803–852)* (surely intensified in Wang's case by the Yang-chow connection); admiration for Lu T'ung 盧仝 (*ca.* 775–835) and his wild, outraged "Yüeh-shih shih" 月蝕詩 (Eclipse of the Moon); the tendency for young poets to imitate the *Shih-ching*,* (or its glosses) and the *Ch'u-tz'u*,* with fond use of archaic diction that goes beyond school exercises; and finally the sense of being somewhat more at ease following Tu Fu 杜甫 (712–770)* than Li Po 李白 (701–762).* Wang's era also valued searing ballads about social evils: a highlight of his collection is the 130-line "Meng huang" 夢蝗 (I Dreamed of Locusts, *Wang Ling chi, chüan* 3), in which locusts lecture him in a nightmare about how human beings are the real pests to humanity. He may also be studied as one of the Sung poets who did not write *tz'u* 詞 (lyrics)*–in his case, partly because he did not circulate in the milieu where *tz'u* flourished, but also perhaps for temperamental reasons. In writing few or no *tz'u*, he is in company with Mei Yao-ch'en, Tseng Kung 曾鞏 (1019–1083),* Lin Pu 林逋 (967–1028), Su Ch'e 蘇轍 (1039–1112),* and Wang An-shih, and stands in contrast to Mei Yao-ch'en's friend Ou-yang Hsiu 歐陽修 (1007–1072),* Wang Ling's fellow Kao-yu resident Ch'in Kuan 秦觀 (1049–1100),** Su Ch'e's elder brother Su Shih, and Wang An-shih's younger brother Wang An-kuo 王安國 (1028–1074). Instead of *tz'u*, Wang Ling does have a few rather old-fashioned substitutes: five-line poems about sitting by the river; delicate conceits in deflected rhymes about butterflies blurring one's vision or peach blossoms setting the wind on fire. A heptasyllabic piece of wistful reproach seems to be his only love poem ("Lou-shang ch'ü" 樓上曲, *Wang Ling chi* addenda, p. 379.) In rare cases he echoes Li Yü 李煜 (937–978).*

If one looks beyond his sources of inspiration and reads his collection, like a novel, from beginning to end as Ch'ien Mu recommends for collected works, one does find a distinct poetic voice. It is a youthful voice, as seen in the way Wang careens toward breakneck closures, and it abounds with masculine phrases such as "lofty tune" 高歌, "man-child" 男兒, or epithets for "keen blade," "tiger claws," etc. Some poems detail his life, such as "Pu chü" 卜居 (Divining a Place to Live) about his struggles with a dilapidated rental house where pigs wandered through the rooms, with the workmen hired to fix it who were only interested in drinking his liquor, and with a neighbor who said Wang was making himself a slave to limitations and should just go get a government job (*Wang Ling chi, chüan* 5). Modern readers may be drawn toward the personal perspective of such pieces; Wang's contemporaries, however, praised him more often for writings that conveyed noble sentiments, such as the following regulated verse in which he rebukes cruel nature with the type of gusto that was considered worthy of a statesman (*Wang Ling chi chüan* 10):

> Longing for a Wind in Summer Heat
> Now as we sit, letting red heat plague the
>   earth,
> Where shall we gain a loan of breezes
>   clear?
> Winds! Flex your might! Coil rain upon
>   us, end these arid years–
> Blast every cloud aloft, unleash them to
>   the sky!
> Why do you dally at the Tiger's mouth
>   and make him growl so lightly?
> Better you helped the Swan's pinions
>   ease her far-flung toil.
> You could delight in Sea and River, with
>   no boundary or beach:
> Borrow them in your lazy times, make on
>   them waves and wash.

暑熱思風
坐將赤熱憂天下　安得清風借我曹
力卷雨來無歲旱　盡吹雲去放天高
豈隨虎口令輕嘯　願助鴻毛絕遠勞
江海可憐無際岸　等閑假借坐波濤

Although his strengths show best in his longest poems, some of his quatrains contain the kind of subtlety beneath an obvious surface that is usually seen more often in older poets (*Wang Ling chi, chüan* 10):

> Night Moon
> you can grieve at a set sun, gone so far
>   away
> but then come throngs of stars
>   displaying themselves to Heaven
> night moon shines just so
>   people love the moon just so
> but it does not stop them closing their
>   doors, to sleep

夜月
可嗟落日去悠然　便有群星出見天
夜月自明人自愛　不妨人亦閉門眠

Editions and References
Ch'üan Sung shih, 12:690-707.8067-8192.
Ch'üan Sung wen, 40:1741-1748.438-557.
Kuang-ling Hsien-sheng wen-chi 廣陵先生文集, 20 *chüan* plus 3 *chüan.* Chia-yeh T'ang ts'ung-shu 嘉業棠叢書 edition, 1922.
Wang Ling chi 王令集. 21 *chüan* plus 1 *chüan* addenda, also appendices including chronology. Shen Wen-cho 沈文倬, ed. Shanghai: Shang-hai Ku-chi, 1980. Punctuated, definitive version based on 1922 edition.

Translations
Demiéville, *Anthologie,* p. 345.
Pease, Jonathan, translation and introduction. "I Dreamed of Locusts," *Comparative Criticism* 15 (1993): 215-222.

Studies
Hu, Shou-jen 胡守仁. "Shen Wen-cho chiao-tien-pen *Wang Ling chi* san-wen piao-tien shang-ch'üeh" 沈文倬校點本（王令集）散文標點尚榷, *Chiang-hsi Shih-yüan hsüeh-pao (Che-hsüeh she-hui k'o-hsüeh-pan)* 1982.2: 55-58.
Pease, Jonathan. "Pei-Sung Wang Ling te

183

'Chu fu' ho 'Ts'ang-chih fu'" 北宋王令的竹賦和藏芝賦, *Wen-shih-che* 200 (1990.5): 76-80.

Shen, Wen-cho, ed. *Wang Ling chi* (see above).

Jonathan Pease
Portland State University

Wang Tuan 汪端 (1793–1839) was born into an exceptionally prominent lineage in Hangchow. Her father was not as distinguished as her two grandfathers, but she still belonged to the highest level of society. She learned to read and write at an early age. Her mother died young, and she was brought up by her aunt, Liang Te-sheng 梁德繩, (1771-1845), who took great pride in her niece's talent and saw to its development, as did Liang's husband, the historian Hsü Tsung-yen 許宗彥 (1768-1819). Her husband Ch'en P'ei-chih 陳裴之 (1794-1826) and her father-in-law Ch'en Wen-shu 陳文述 (1775-1845) likewise furthered her literary career. Wang Tuan's writing was never perceived to be in conflict with her family responsibilities, despite the fact that she was somewhat deficient in domestic skills. She had a reputation for filial piety, and one of her most celebrated pieces was a eulogy to a Ch'en P'ei-chih's concubine Wang Tzu-lan 王子蘭 (1803-1824).

Wang Tuan's later years were marred by the early death of her husband in about 1825 and the consequent deterioration of her son's state of mind. These two developments led her to turn to Taoism during the thirteen years between her husband's death and her own, at age 46. Over her later years, she edited a collection of her husband's writings and continued writing poetry of her own. Her collected poems were published just after her death in 1839 under the title *Tzu-jan Hao-hsüeh Chai chi* 自然好學齋集. This second publication was paid for by her father-in-law Ch'en Wen-shu, who prefaced them with a long and admiring biography.

Perhaps her most famous and innovative project was an edited collection of writings by thirty male writers of the Ming dynasty. Entitled *Ming San-shih chia shih-hsüan* 明三十家詩選 (Selected Poems of Thirty Ming Poets), it was published in sixteen *chüan* in 1822, three years before the death of her husband. Publication was paid for by her family, and the collection, in its original edition, carried prefaces by her aunt, Liang Te-sheng, among others. Each *chüan* was proofread by a female friend or family member of the editor, including some names already famous for their association with Yüan Mei 袁牧 (1716–1798).* Wang Tuan's work on this editing project is said to have taken her five or six years; she had spent ten years reading before she took up her editorial pen.

More than any other work, *Ming san-shih chia shih-hsüan* enhanced Wang Tuan's literary celebrity, for it displayed her fine taste, as well as the iconoclastic spirit which led her to question the literary judgment of such notables as Ch'ien Ch'ien-i 錢謙益 (1582–1664)* and Shen Te-ch'ien 沈德潛 (1673–1769).* It was also unusual in that she broke away from the stereotypical woman anthologist, whose normal subjects were other women writers.

Wang Tuan's motivation for this project is generally traced to her wide reading in poetry, in particular, to her high valuation of the late-Yüan and early-Ming poet Kao Ch'i 高啟 (1336– 1374).* In fact, she regarded herself as a latter day incarnation of one of Kao's disciples. Kao had been put to death during the early Ming, and his poetry was not as highly valued as Wang Tuan thought it ought to be. One aim of *Ming san-shih chia shih-hsüan* was to set the historical record straight on Kao; another was to reassess the canon, whose partiality

Wang Tuan saw revealed in its undervaluation of Kao.

Wang Tuan's sense of outrage at the vagaries of Yüan and Ming historical accounting motivated her to undertake a second project, a revisionist retelling of the story of Chang Shih-ch'eng 張士誠 (1321-1367), who had been a rival of the first Ming emperor as successor to the Yüan. This work was entitled *Yüan Ming i-shih* 元明佚史 (Lost History of the Yüan and Ming). Wang Tuan's interest in Chang developed out of her interest in Kao Ch'i to whom Chang was sympathetic. Wang Tuan burned this work before it was completed, but she included some remnants of it in *Tzu-jan Hao-hsüeh Chai chi*.

According to the modern scholar Sun K'ai-ti 孫楷第, *Yüan Ming i-shih* may have been either a *tan-tz'u** or a novel. The former possibility is intriguing in view of Wang Tuan's close intellectual connection to her aunt Liang Te-sheng. More than for her poetry, Liang is known today for her work on the leading *tan-tz'u* 彈詞,* *Tsai-sheng yüan* 再生緣, whose author was Ch'en Tuan-sheng 陳端生 (1751–1796?), a relative of Wang's husband's family. After Tuan-sheng's premature death, Liang supplemented the text with three chapters (out of a total of twenty), which in most critics' estimation, markedly dilute its original feminist tone. However, Wang Tuan's own literary responses to Liang say nothing about *Tsai-sheng yüan*. Unlike Sun K'ai-ti, T'an Cheng-pi 譚正璧 unhesitatingly assumes that *Yüan Ming i-shih* was a novel, most likely a historical novel or *p'ing-hua* 評話.* Were *Yüan Ming i-shih* indeed a novel, it would be another mark of Wang Tuan's iconoclasm, for until her time, women writers had not published in this genre. Ch'en Wen-shu's preface to *Tzu-jan Hao-hsüeh Chai chi* states that when Wang Tuan burned her work, it was a substantial text, at least eighteen-*chüan* in length. Wang Tuan's decision to burn it is attributed to her husband's death, which subdued the contentious spirit that lay behind her interest in Chang Shih-ch'eng.

Editions and References

Wang, Tuan 汪端. *Tzu-jan Hao-hsüeh Chai chi* 自然好學齋集, 1839. Preface by Ch'en Wen-shu 陳文述, in Ch'en K'un 陳坤, ed., *Ju-pu-chi Chai hui-ch'ao* 如不及齋彙鈔. Hangchow, 1864-1884.
——, ed. *Ming San-shih chia shih-hsüan* 明三十家詩選 (Selected Poems of Thirty Ming Poets), 2 *chi* 集, 16 *chüan*, 1822. Prefaces by Liang Te-sheng 梁德繩 and others.

Studies

Chang, Kang-i Sun. "Ming and Qing Anthologies of Women's Poetry and Their Selection Strategies." In *Writing Women in Late Imperial China*. Ellen Widmer and Kang-i Sun Chang, eds. Stanford: Stanford University Press, 1997, pp. 168-69.
Chung, Hui-ling 鍾慧玲. "Ch'ing-tai nü-shih-jen yen-chiu" 清代女詩人研究. Unpublished doctoral dissertation, Chengchih Ta-hsüeh (Taiwan), 1981, pp. 363-389.
Hu, Wen-k'ai 胡溫楷. *Li-tai fu-nü chu-tso k'ao* 歷代婦女著作考. Rev. ed. Shanghai: Kuchi, 1985, p. 357.
Hummel, Arthur. *Eminent Chinese of the Ch'ing Period.* Rpt. Taipei: Ch'eng-wen, 1967 (1943), pp. 839-40.
Sun, K'ai-ti 孫楷第. *Chung-kuo hsiao-shuo shu-mu* 中國通俗小說書目. Rpt. Taipei: Feng-huang, 1974 (1957), pp. 216-17.
T'an, Cheng-pi 譚正璧. *Chung-kuo nü-hsing wen-hsüeh shih-hua* 中國女性文學詩話. Tientsin: Pai-hua Wen-i Ch'u-pan-she, 1984, pp. 373-78.

Ellen Widmer
Wesleyan University

Wang Tuan-shu 王端淑 (1621–after 1701) was the second daughter of Wang Ssu-jen 王思任 (1575–1646) of Shaohsing. She was said to be a better reader than any of his eight sons. Her elder sister Wang Ching-shu 王靜淑 was also known as a poet. Wang Tuan-shu married Ting Sheng-chao 丁聖肇 who was from the Peking area. Her husband's family, like her own, had ties in both the Peking and the Shao-hsing areas. Before the fall of the Ming and perhaps again thereafter, Tuan-shu lived in or near Peking, but in the years just after 1644, she returned to Shao-hsing with her husband. The two of them then kept company with a group of Ming loyalists which included Chang Tai 張岱 (1599–1684)* and the painter Tseng I 曾益 (*fl.* 1650). Perhaps it was during this sojourn in Shao-hsing that she rented a house which had once belonged to the dramatist Hsü Wei 徐渭 (1521–1593).* Later, she lived in Hangchow, where she became acquainted with celebrities from various places She was a very sociable and engaging person who did not hesitate to enter into poetical competitions with all who came to see her. Her acquaintance with Li Yü 李漁 (1610–1680)* and with two well known female loyalist-poets, Huang Yüan-chieh 黃媛介 and Wu Shan 吳山, almost certainly date from her stay in Hangchow.

Her best known collection of writings, *Yin-hung chi* 吟紅集, (Collected Female Chantings) was published between 1651 and 1655, probably in Shao-hsing. Its publication was financed by her husband, Tseng I, Tai Chen, and the other members of their poetry group. This collection made a sensation and established Wang Tuan-shu's reputation. It claimed to be uncharacteristic of other writings by women in its emphasis on loyalism rather than love. Despite her loyalty to the Ming, Wang was summoned at around the same time to become a tutor of women in the Ch'ing court, an assignment she vigorously refused.

Wang Tuan-shu's next datable publication is her preface to Li Yü's drama *Pi-mu yü* 比目魚 (Soul-mates) of 1661. This short preface is interesting in its attempt to link Li's drama with the dramas of Hsü Wei, an author whom her father admired. A much more substantial piece of work is her *Ming-yüan shih-wei* 名媛詩緯 (Classics of Poetry by Famous Women) of 1667. Like *Yin-hung chi, Ming-yüan shih-wei* was privately financed—this time mainly by her family. Copies were hard to come by not long after its publication, but the collection attracted considerable interest among male and female writers. She is also the author of a number of writings which no longer survive.

In addition to her writings, Wang Tuan-shu was widely known and praised for her artistic talent. She was accomplished at both painting and calligraphy. One of her landscape screens bears the date 1664. A second work, a painted fan, is listed in a recent Christie's catalogue. Another accomplishment was her extraordinarily wide-ranging readings, which included classics and history as well as popular fiction.

Wang Tuan-shu received considerable encouragement from her husband Ting Sheng-chao throughout much of her career as writer and publisher. Ting thought of her as a literary companion and seemed not to mind her total indifference to housework, though he mentions it in his preface to *Yin-hung chi*. Without his strong support, it is unlikely that *Yin-hung chi* would ever have been published. Ting was also behind the publication of *Ming-yüan shih-wei,* for which he wrote one of the prefaces, another being by Ch'ien Ch'ien-i 錢謙益 (1582–1664).* He may have encouraged his wife in other ways to turn her talent at history to the chronicling and collecting of work by women writers, a field previously dominated by male editors. *Ming-yüan shih-wei* is one of the earliest anthologies of women's writings to be edited by a woman, and in 38 *chüan,* one of the most substantial. It is widely cited in premodern and modern writings on traditional women, and it is the chief reason Wang Tuan-shu is known today.

Editions and References

Teng, Han-i 鄧漢儀. *Shih kuan* 詩觀, 12. Preface 1680, in the Naikaku Bunko.

Wang, Tuan-shu 王端淑. *Ming-yüan shih-wei* 名媛詩緯 (Classic of Poetry by Famous Women). 42 *chüan*. Hangchow: Ch'ing-yin T'ang 清音堂,1667. Copies in Beijing Library and Central Library (Taipei). Includes works by almost 1000 women poets.

___. "Preface" to Li Yü's *Pi-mu yü* 比目魚 (Soul-mates), *Li Li-weng shih-chung tien* 李笠翁十種典, Pu-yüeh Lou k'o-pen 步月樓刻本, 1661.

___. *Yin-hung chi* 吟紅集 (Collected Female Chantings). 1651–55. Hangchow? Prefaces by Ting Sheng-chao 丁聖肇 and Ch'ien Ch'ien-i 錢謙益. In Naikaku Bunko.

Studies

Chang, Kang-i Sun. "Ming and Qing Anthologies of Women's Poetry and Their Selection Strategies." In *Writing Women in Late Imperial China*. Ellen Widmer and Kang-i Sun Chang, eds. Stanford: Stanford University Press, 1997, pp. 157-59.

Chung, Hui-ling 鍾慧玲. "Ch'ing-tai nü-shih-jen yen-chiu" 清代女詩人研究. Unpublished doctoral dissertation, Cheng-chih Ta-hsüeh (Taiwan), 1981.

Hanan, Patrick. *The Invention of Li Yü.* Cambridge, Massachusetts: Harvard University Press, 1988.

Hu, Wen-k'ai 胡文楷. *Li-tai fu-nü chu-tso k'ao* 歷代婦女著作考. Rev. ed. Shanghai: Shang-hai Ku-chi, 1985.

Weidner, Marsha, *et al. Views from Jade Terrace.* Indianapolis and New York: Rizzoli, 1988.

Yü, Chien-hua 俞劍華. *Chung-kuo mei-shu-chia jen-ming tz'u-tien* 中國美術家人名詞典. Shanghai: Jen-min Mei-shu, 1981.

Ellen Widmer
Wesleyan University

Wang Yen-shou 王延壽 (*tzu*, Wen-k'ao 文考; alternative *tzu*, Tzu-shan 子山, *ca.* 124–148) was a native of I-ch'eng 宜城 in Nan Commandery 南郡 (modern Hupei). The son of *Ch'u-tz'u* commentator Wang I 王逸 (*ca.* 89–158), his brief biography is appended to his father's memoir in the *Hou Han-shu* 後漢書 (80A:2618). Additional biographical information is found in anecdotes in Chang Hua's 張華 (232-300)* *Po-wu chih* 博物志 and Li Tao-yüan's 李道元 (d. 527) *Shui-ching chu* 水經注 (A Commentary to the Classic of Water-ways).* These accounts tell that Wang Yen-shou was possessed of extraordinary talent, and as a youth, he accompanied his father to Lu to study the Classics and calculations with a certain Pao Tzu-chen 鮑子真 of Mount T'ai. While in Lu, Wang composed the "Lu Ling-kuang Tien fu" 魯靈光殿賦 (Rhapsody on the Hall of Numinous Brilliance in Lu). When Ts'ai Yung 蔡邕 (133-192)* set out to compose a rhapsody on this same topic, he encountered Wang Yen-shou's piece and was so impressed that he put down his writing brush and never completed his own treatment of the hall. Wang's biography reports that at the age of twenty, he encountered misfortune, and had a strange dream. In an effort to encourage himself, he composed the "Meng fu" 夢賦 (Rhapsody on a Nightmare [literally "On a Dream]). Returning home from Lu, Wang Yen-shou drowned while crossing the Hsiang 湘 River. He was just over twenty years of age.

Wang Yen-shou is noted exclusively for his rhapsodies. The *Sui shu* bibliographic treatise records a *Wang Yen-shou ch'üan-chi* 王延壽全集 (Collected Works of Wang Yen-shou) in three fascicles as being no longer extant. Only three pieces of Wang's writings survive today: the two important rhapsodies mentioned above, and a shorter "Wang-sun fu" 王孫賦 (Rhapsody on an Ape). Wang Yen-shou's "Rhapsody on the Hall of Numinous Brilliance in Lu," contained in *Wen-hsüan** *chüan* 11, describes in great detail the palace built by the Han King Kung 恭 of Lu (r. 154–*ca.* 129 B.C.)

near Ch'ü-fu 曲阜 in Lu. Wang's rhapsody begins with praises of the early Han rulers and the builder of the palace. He then enumerates every nook and hall of the structure, drawing out the cosmological significance of its design and the minutiae of its construction. It concludes with yet another praise for the "great genius in tune with the gods who accomplished this great achievement." The piece resonates with previous descriptions of palaces and halls by earlier Han rhapsodes. Its language is lavish and ornate, and its intent is to glorify the palace and praise its creator.

Wang's most famous rhapsody, "Rhapsody on a Nightmare" was written after experiencing a dream in which he was menaced by demons. The preface claims his demons were exorcised by demon-cursing writings from Tung-fang Shuo 東方朔 (154-93 B.C.) and by the efforts of composing the rhapsody. Wang Yen-shou further urges readers to chant his rhapsody in order to expel their own demons. The rhapsody itself describes the battle between the poet and the hoard of demons encountered in the dream. It shifts between narrative and descriptive modes, and concludes with the demons fleeing the cock's crowing of the dawn. The epilogue relates stories of other persons who experienced bad dreams yet attained success and was apparently designed to bolster the obviously disturbed Wang Yen-shou's confidence. Modern scholars classify this rhapsody as a type of "dream incantation" or "exorcism" text.

Wang's remaining work, "Rhapsody on an Ape" describes a small tailless ape known as the *wang-sun*. Wang enumerates the creature's physical characteristics, then describes the playful ape in its natural environment. After this rather light-hearted account, Wang Yen-shou compares the desires of the ape with those of man, in particular his fondness for sweets and alcohol. The tone of the rhapsody turns dark as Wang then tells how trappers place wine in the path of the ape. After it drinks, like a human it becomes drunk, staggers, and loses consciousness. Then, the creature is captured and tied to a ribbon or string, and kept as a pet. The piece ends on a tragic note, with the pitiful ape tethered in a courtyard, with faces staring at it interminably.

Editions and References
"Rhapsody on the Hall of Numinous Brilliance in Lu," *Wen-hsüan*, 11:168-172.
"Rhapsody on a Nightmare," *I-wen lei-chü* 藝文類聚. Peking: Chung-hua, 1965, 79: 1356-1357; *Ku-wen yüan* 古文苑, 6:9a-11b (*SPTK* edition)
"Rhapsody on an Ape," *I-wen lei-chü*, 95:1653-1654; *Ku-wen yüan*, 6:11b-13b (*SPTK* edition).

Translations
Of "Rhapsody on the Hall of Numinous Brilliance in Lu:"
Knechtges, *Wen xuan*, 2:262-277.
von Zach, *Anthologie*, pp. 164-169.
Waley, *The Temple*, pp. 95-97.
Of "Rhapsody on a Nightmare:"
Harper, Donald. "Wang Yen-shou's Nightmare Poem." *HJAS* 47:1 (1987): 239-283.
Waley, *The Temple*, pp. 91-94.
Of "Rhapsody on an Ape:"
Waley, *The Temple*, pp. 88-91.

Studies
Harper, Donald. "Wang Yen-shou's Nightmare Poem." *HJAS* 47:1 (1987): 239-283.
Knechtges, *Wen xuan*, 2:262-277.
von Zach, Erwin. "Das Lu-ling-kwang-tien-fu des Wang Wen-kao," *AM* 3 (1926): 467-476.

J. Michael Farmer
University of Wisconsin-Madison

Wu-hsia hsiao-shuo 武俠小説 is a term which has been variously translated into English as "gallant fiction," "martial arts novels," "chivalric fiction," etc. Literally it refers to "fiction" (*hsiao-shuo* 小) which takes for its themes and settings the world of Chinese martial arts (*wu* 武) and that complex of altruism, gallantry, and sometimes anarchy associated with the figure of the *hsia* 俠. As the designation for a genre of popular fiction, the term gained currency in the early decades of this century, when aficionados and May Fourth detractors alike used it to refer both to the martial adventures prominent in the popular urban press of the 1920s–1940s (the so-called *Yüan-yang hu-tieh p'ai* 鴛鴦蝴蝶派 or "Mandarin Ducks and Butterflies School"), and to the many martial novels of the late-Ch'ing period (also often referred to as *hsia-i hsiao-shuo* 俠義小説 "novels of chivalry and righteousness"). As currently used, the term includes the *Hsin-p'ai* 新派 (New School) *Wu-hsia hsiao-shuo* produced since the 1950s in Hong Kong and Taiwan, and also encompasses the genre's thematic predecessors in earlier literature.

Martial exploits and the deeds of chivalric or free-spirited *hsia* can be found in some of the earliest monuments of Chinese literature, and accounts of *Wu-hsia hsiao-shuo* commonly trace the genre from its roots in Ssu-ma Ch'ien's 司馬遷 (*ca.* 145–*ca.* 86 B.C.)* *Shih-chi* 史記* through Six Dynasties *chih-kuai,* T'ang *ch'uan-chi,* *hua-pen* stories* supposedly dating from the Sung and Yüan periods, and the Ming novel *Shui-hu chuan* 水滸傳.* While the influence of such works and of the popular traditions they adumbrate is inarguable, it is not until the late-Ch'ing period that *Wu-hsia hsiao-shuo* can be said to achieve an identity as a distinct genre. From the fusion of popular adventure tales and the above-noted literary precedents with the general narrative and formal developments of late-Ch'ing vernacular fiction, there emerged a sizable body of novels with recognizable thematic and narrative conventions.

The best-known of the Ch'ing novels are the *kung-an hsiao-shuo* 公案小説 (court-case novels), in which the judicial investigations of a righteous official serve as the sometimes tenuous context for acts of derring-do by warriors and champions in his service. The best-known of these works, *San-hsia wu-i* 三俠五義 (Three Heroes and Five Gallants;* first edition 1879), together with its revision *Ch'i-hsia wu-i* 七俠五義 (Seven Heroes and Five Gallants; 1889) and its many sequels, draw on the long tradition of tales about Judge Pao 包 of the Sung. Novels such as *Shih-kung an* 施公案 (Cases of Lord Shih; preface dated 1798) and *P'eng-kung an* 彭公案 (Cases of Lord P'eng; 1892) similarly employ a judicial framework, while other works erect analogous structural and thematic patterns around figures of other sorts. *Yung-ch'ing sheng-p'ing ch'üan-chuan* 永慶升平全傳 (The Complete Tale of the Everlasting Blessings of Peace; 1892) narrates the adventures of bravos who gather around the K'ang-hsi 康熙 emperor during his incognito wanderings, and their suppression of sectarian uprisings. *P'ing-yen Chi-kung chuan* 平演齊公傳 (The Storyteller's Tale of Lord Chi; 1898) links its heroes with the Southern-Sung monk "Crazy Chi" 濟顛; its accounts of magical warfare suggest both popular religious beliefs and the literary tradition of *Feng-shen yen-i* 封神演義 (The Investiture of the Gods)* and *Hsi-yu chi* 西游記 (Journey to the West).* Still other novels eschew the above works' episodic, endlessly extensible story lines for more closed plots; in *Lü mu-tan ch'üan-chuan* 綠牧丹全傳 (The Complete Tale of the Green Peony; 1800), for instance, the protagonist encounters heroic outlaws who aid in the overthrow of the empress Wu Tse-t'ien 武則天 and the restoration of the T'ang dynasty.

Some twentieth-century critics have discerned glimmerings of revolutionary consciousness in these novels' presentation of heroes willing to serve as champions of the common folk against corrupt and oppressive officials. Generally, though, these works are profoundly conservative in their ideology, combining a delight in violence and a fascination with *chiang-hu* 江湖, the "rivers and lakes" of society's geographic and social margins, with a heavy-handed allegiance to orthodox social hierarchies and sexual morality. The novels themselves are but one manifestation of material widely current in late-Ch'ing popular culture. Many of the works above were adapted from oral narratives, and their plots and characters also featured prominently in the various regional operas of the period. The limited language and formulaic plotting of some of the novels, as well as the poor physical quality of many of the editions, suggest that their readership included some of the less educated and privileged strata of society. But *wu-hsia* material was popular among the literate elite as well. Martial anecdotes abound in late Ch'ing classical *pi-chi* 筆記* fiction; and one of the most polished of the period's *pai-hua* 白話 (vernacular-language) novels, Wen K'ang's 文康 (*fl.* mid-nineteenth century) *Erh-nü ying-hsiung chuan* 兒女英雄傳 (A Tale of Tender-hearted Heroes, 1878),** cunningly works a swordswoman and other typical *chiang-hu* types into a novel of manners in the tradition of *Hung-lou meng* 紅樓夢 (Dream of the Red Chamber).*

While traditional fiction continued to circulate during the first decades of this century, by the 1920s new patterns of authorship, publication, and readership had emerged in Shanghai and other urban centers. *Wu-hsia* fiction (later designated *Chiu-p'ai* 舊派, "Old School" *Wu-hsia hsiao-shuo*) was one of the most prominent genres in this new popular literature. The trend was set by P'ing-chiang Pu-hsiao-sheng 平江不肖生 (nom de plume of Hsiang K'ai-jan 向愷然, 1890–1957) with his *Chiang-hu ch'i-hsia chuan* 江湖奇俠傳 (Strange Knights of the Rivers and Lakes), serialized beginning in 1922. Pu-hsiao-sheng combined traditional themes and narrative structures with an interest in local lore, a

personal familiarity with the martial arts, and a fantastic imagination. His *Chin-tai hsia-i ying-hsiung chuan* 近代俠義英雄傳 (A Tale of Righteous Heroes of Our Age; 1923–1924) further wedded *Wu-hsia* fiction to modern nationalist pride. His phenomenally popular work not only inspired a flood of *Wu-hsia* fiction, but was adapted into opera and film as well; China's first martial arts film, *Huo-shao Hung-lien Ssu* 火燒紅蓮寺 (The Burning of Red Lotus Monastery; 1928), was based on an episode from "Strange Knights." A "Northern School" of *Wu-hsia* fiction flourished a decade or so later than the Shanghai authors. Its best-known proponent, Huan-chu-lou-chu 還珠樓主 (Li Shou-min 李壽民, 1902-1961), began serialization of *Shu-shan chien-hsia chuan* 蜀山劍俠傳 (Swordsmen of the Mountains of Shu) in Tientsin in 1932; the last installment of the still unfinished work appeared in 1949. Huan-chu-lou-chu's amazing tales of flying swordsmen, monsters, and magical combat carry on the more fantastic side of the *wu-hsia* tradition.

After 1949, the production and circulation of *Wu-hsia hsiao-shuo* dwindled and ceased on the Chinese mainland, but continued in Hong Kong, Taiwan, and overseas Chinese communities. The emergence of a *Hsin-p'ai* 新派 "New School" of *Wu-hsia hsiao-shuo* is credited to Liang Yü-sheng 梁羽生 (Ch'en Wen-t'ung 陳文統, b. 1922), whose *Lung hu tou ching-hua* 龍虎鬥京華 (Dragon and Tiger Vie in the Capital) began serialization in Hong Kong in 1954, soon after a much-publicized match between two local martial arts schools. Among his numerous subsequent novels are *Pai-fa mo-nü chuan* 白髮魔女傳 (The White-haired Demoness, 1957–1958) and *Yün-hai yü-kung yüan* 雲海玉弓緣 (The Jade Bow from the Sea of Clouds; 1961–1963). The "newness" of these and other "new school" works lies in their use of modern novelistic techniques of plotting, description, and psychological focalization. They can be considered "traditional" in two respects: on the one hand, they inherit certain of their predecessors' linguistic, structural, and thematic characteristics; on the other, they are among the most widespread vehicles for the representation of the Chinese past and traditional arts in the popular imagination.

Chin Yung 金庸 (Cha Liang-yung 查良鏞 or Louis Cha, b. 1924), founder of Hong Kong's *Ming-pao* 明報 publishing empire, is the most highly regarded modern author of *Wu-hsia hsiao-shuo* and possibly the most widely read of all twentieth-century Chinese writers. His novels, densely plotted and of epic length, employ elegant classicizing *pai-hua* prose and a romantic evocation of traditional Chinese culture, and devote as much attention to the characters' relationships and emotional trials as to their martial prowess. While the short and intricate *Hsüeh-shan fei-hu* 雪山飛狐 (Flying Fox on Snowy Mountain; 1959, rev. 1974) has received some attention in the west, among Chinese readers his best-known works include the romantic *Shen-tiao hsia-lü* 神鵰俠侶 (The Giant Eagle and its Companion; 1959, rev. 1967), set against the Mongol conquest of the Southern Sung, and the satiric "anti-*Wu-hsia hsiao-shuo*" *Lu-ting chi* 鹿鼎記 (The Deer and the Cauldron; 1969–72, rev. 1981), whose rascally protagonist becomes involved in skull-duggery at the K'ang-hsi emperor's court.

The above two authors' plots generally center on some crux or puzzle of Chinese dynastic history. The most successful of their many contemporaries and successors, the Taiwan author Ku Lung 古龍 (Hsiung Yao-hua 熊耀華, 1936–1985), represents another strong current in modern *Wu-hsia* fiction: his rakes, gallants, idealists and lost souls move through the *wu-lin* 武林 (world of the martial arts) and *chiang-hu* of a mythicized Chinese past whose referents are less historical than cultural and existentialist. His brisk prose, melodramatic epigrams, and cinematic plotting are featured in over sixty novels, including *Liu-hsing, hu-tieh, chien* 流星、蝴蝶、劍 (Falling Star, Butterfly, Sword; 1973) and the *Ch'u Liu-hsiang ch'uan-ch'i* 楚留香傳奇 series (The Legend of Ch'u Liu-hsiang: 1968-1978).

Editions and References
Late Ch'ing

Dates of the earliest known editions are given above. For complete bibliographic information see *Chung-kuo t'ung-su hsiao-shuo tsung-mu t'i-yao* 中國通俗小説總目提要. Peking: Chung-kuo Wen-lien, 1990. Listed below are reliable and accessible modern editions.

Anonymous. *Lü mu-tan ch'üan-chuan* 綠牡丹全傳. Shanghai: Shang-hai Ku-chi, 1986.

Anonymous. *Shih-kung ch'üan an* 施公全案. 2v. Nanking: Chiang-su Ku-chi, 1994.

Kuo, Hsiao-t'ing 郭小亭, ed. *Chi-kung chuan* 齊公傳 [=*P'ing-yen Chi-kung chuan* 平演齊公傳]. 2v. Hangchow: Che-chiang Ku-chi, 1991.

Kuo, Kuang-jui 郭廣瑞, ed. *Yung-ch'ing sheng-p'ing ch'üan-chuan* 永慶升平全傳. Peking: Pei-ching Shih-fan Ta-hsüeh, 1993.

Shih, Yü-k'un 石玉昆 and Yü Yüeh 俞樾. *Ch'i-hsia wu-i* 七俠五義. 2v. Peking: Pao-wen T'ang, 1980.

Wen, K'ang 文康. *Erh-nü ying-hsiung chuan* 兒女英雄傳. Commentary by Tung Hsün 董恂. Tsinan: Ch'i-Lu Shu-she, 1989.

Yang, I-tien 楊挹殿. *P'eng-kung an* 彭公案. 3v. Peking: Chung-kuo Hsi-chü, 1991.

"Old School"

Huan-chu-lou-chu 環珠樓主. *Shu-shan chien-hsia chuan* 蜀山劍俠傳. 26v. Series *Chin-tai Chung-kuo Wu-hsia hsiao-shuo ming-chu ta-hsi* 近代中國武俠小説名著大系. Yeh Hung-sheng 葉洪生, ed. Taipei: Lien-ching, 1984.

P'ing-chiang Pu-hsiao-sheng 平江不肖生. *Chiang-hu ch'i-hsia chuan* 江湖奇俠傳. 7v. Series *Chin-tai Chung-kuo Wu-hsia hsiao-shuo ming-chu ta-hsi*. Yeh Hung-sheng, ed. Taipei: Lien-ching, 1984.

"New School"

Authorized and unauthorized editions of the "new school" authors abound in Hong Kong, Taiwan, and the mainland; listed below are recent authorized editions of these authors' complete works.

Chin, Yung 金庸. *Chin Yung tso-p'in chi* 金庸作品集. 36v. Peking: San-lien, 1994.

Ku, Lung 古龍. *Ku Lung tso-p'in chi* 古龍作品集. 59v. Chu-hai: Chu-hai, 1995.

Liang Yü-sheng 梁羽生. *Liang Yü-sheng hsiao-shuo ch'üan-chi* 梁羽生小説全集. 78v. Canton: Kuang-tung Lü-you, 1996.

Translations

Cha, Louis [Chin Yung]. *The Deer and the Cauldron: The Adventures of a Chinese Trickster. Two Chapters from a Novel by Louis Cha.* John Minford, trans. Canberra: Institute of Advanced Studies, Australian National University, 1994.

Huanzhulouzhu [Huan-chu-lou-chu]. *Blades from the Willows.* Robert Chard, trans. London: Wellsweep Press, 1991.

Jin Yong [Chin Yung]. *Fox Volant of the Snowy Mountain.* Olivia Mak, trans. Hong Kong: Chinese University Press, 1993.

Studies

There is a vast amount of recent secondary literature in Chinese; most of it is more appreciative than scholarly. Ch'en's study offers the most perceptive analysis of the genre. The dictionaries by Hu and Ning contain useful bibliographies.

Blader, Susan. "A Critical Study of *San-hsia wu-yi* and Its Relationship to the *Lung-tu kung-an Ch'ang-pen.*" Unpublished Ph.D. dissertation, University of Pennsylvania, 1977.

Cao, Zhengwen. "Chinese Gallant Fiction." In *Handbook of Chinese Popular Culture.* Wu Dingbo and Patrick D. Murphy, ed. Westport: Greenwood, 1994, pp. 237-55.

Ch'en, P'ing-yüan 陳平原. *Ch'ien-ku wen-jen hsia-k'o meng: Wu-hsia hsiao-shuo lei-hsing yen-chiu* 千古文人俠客夢：武俠小説類型研究 (The Scholar's Age-old Dream of the Knight-Errant: Genre Studies of *Wu-hsia hsiao-shuo*). Peking: Jen-min Wen-hsüeh, 1992.

Hu, Wen-pin 胡文彬 *et al.*, eds. *Chung-kuo Wu-hsia hsiao-shuo tz'u-tien* 中國武俠小説辭典 (A Dictionary of Chinese *wu-hsia hsiao-shuo*). Shih-chia-chuang: Hua-shan Wen-i, 1992.

Link, Perry. *Mandarin Ducks and Butterflies: Popular Fiction in Early Twentieth-Century Chinese Cities.* Berkeley: University of California Press, 1981.

Liu, James J. Y. *The Chinese Knight-errant.* London: Routledge and Kegan Paul, 1967.

Lo, Li-ch'ün 羅立群. *Chung-kuo Wu-hsia hsiao-shuo shih* 中國武俠小説史 (A History of Chinese *Wu-hsia hsiao-shuo*). Shenyang: Liao-ning Jen-min, 1990.

Ma, Y. W. "The Knight-errant in *Hua-pen* Stories," *TP* 61.4-5 (1975): 266-300.

____. "Kung-an Fiction: A Historical and Critical Introduction," *TP* 65 (1979): 200-259.

Ning, Tsung-i 寧宗一 *et al.*, eds. *Chung-kuo Wu-hsia hsiao-shuo chien-shang tz'u-tien* 中國武俠小説鑑賞辭典 (A Connoisseur's Dictionary of Chinese *Wu-hsia hsiao-shuo*). Peking: Kuo-chi Wen-hua, 1992.

Wang, Hai-lin 王海林. *Chung-kuo Wu-hsia hsiao-shuo shih lüeh* 中國武俠小説史略 (A General History of Chinese *Wu-hsia hsiao-shuo*). Taiyuan: Pei-yüeh Wen-i, 1988.

John Christopher Hamm
University of California, Berkeley

Yüeh chi 樂記 (Record of Music) stands at the head of China's long tradition of aesthetics and literary criticism. No other single text has exerted as profound an influence upon the way the Chinese have traditionally understood the nature and value of their own works of art, music, and literature.

According to the "I-wen chih" 藝文志 of the *Han-shu* 漢書 (History of the Han Dynasty), there were at least two different early editions of the *Yüeh chi*, one in twenty-four *chüan* 卷, and one in twenty-three *p'ien* 篇. Of this latter, eleven of the twenty-three *p'ien* were incorporated into the *Li-chi* 禮記 sometime before the time of Liu Hsiang 劉向 (77-6 B.C.)*; this is the version of the *Yüeh chi* available to us today, forming the nineteenth part of that work. Nothing now remains of the other twelve *p'ien* except their titles, recorded by Liu Hsiang into his *Pieh-lu* 別錄 and transmitted to us by K'ung Ying-ta 孔穎達 (574–648).

The question of the authorship and time of composition of the *Yüeh chi* has been the subject of considerable dispute in recent decades. The "I-wen chih" of the *Han-shu* states that "in the time of Emperor Wu 武 (r. 141–87 B.C.), King Hsien 獻 of Ho-chien 河間 (Liu Te 劉德, r. 155–130 B.C.) held fondness for Juist (i.e., Confucianist) thought, and, along with Mao Ch'ang 毛萇 and other scholars, took material from the *Chou kuan* 周官 and those works of the various philosophers that spoke of musical affairs, to make the *Yüeh chi.. .*" In seeming conflict with this account, however, is a quote attributed to the noted Six Dynasties musicologist Shen Yüeh 沈約 (441–513)* in the "Yin-Yüeh chih" 音樂志 of the *Sui-shu* 隋書 (History of the Sui), which states, "the *Yüeh chi* takes from Kung-sun Ni-tzu 公孫尼子" –a figure identified as a second-generation disciple of Confucius. The attribution of the *Yüeh chi* to Kung-sun Ni-tzu has been argued for by a number of Chinese scholars over the past fifty years, ever since Kuo Mo-jo 郭沫若 (1892–1978) first championed the cause in an article in 1944. However, a careful reading of Shen Yüeh's *Sui-shu* quotation in its full context reveals that Shen himself actually cites the *Han-shu* account as a given fact, and thus the only way to reasonably account for Shen's statement that "the *Yüeh chi* took from the Kung-sun Ni-tzu" is to assume that he was simply trying to suggest one of the "various philosophers" (*chu-tzu pai-chia*) from whom Liu Te had taken his material.

It may thus be asserted with some confidence that the *Yüeh chi* was compiled by Liu Te *et al.* during the decade of 140–130 B.C. on the basis of passages on music from various pre-Ch'in texts, among which may have been the work of a certain Kung-sun Ni-tzu. Though the pre-Ch'in texts of Kung-sun's philosophy are no longer available, there is sufficient overlap between the *Yüeh chi* and other pre-Ch'in philoso-

phical texts to reveal a number of those sources upon which the compilers drew. Much of the work's material can be found, often nearly verbatim, in such texts as Hsün-tzu's 荀子 "Yüeh lun" 樂論 (Essay on Music), the *Hsi-tzu chuan* 繫辭傳 commentary to the *I ching* 易經, and various chapters of the *Lü-shih ch'un-ch'iu* 呂氏春秋, not to mention sections of such later works as the *Shuo-yüan* 說苑 and the "Ta hsü" 大序 (Great Preface) to the *Shih-ching* 詩經.*

To be sure, the *Yüeh chi* reveals, to some extent, traces of having derived from such disparate philosophical sources. Overall, however, it exhibits an integral coherence of thought all its own. Indeed, its greatest contribution is that it was able to weave all of these scattered, disparate bits of former musical wisdom together into a single, unified, philosophical vision that incorporated all the best features of its individual precursors.

The *Yüeh chi* opens with a description of the origins and development of musical expression. It portrays a path along which man develops from being initially little more than a medium though which external things touch off different forms of emotion and musical expression, to the point where man himself becomes a *creative* being, conscious of himself, his nature, and his emotions, and strives to *effect* influence in others through music. Throughout this journey, music itself is seen in a continual process of growth: from mere *sheng* 聲 (sound), on to *yin* 音 (ordered sound), and final on to the supreme type of *yüeh* 樂 (music) which exemplifies nothing less than all the order of the natural world and man's place within it. In the words of the text, "Those who know *sheng* but do not know *yin*–these are the birds and beasts. Those who know *yin* but do not know *yüeh*–these are the common masses. Only the gentleman can know *yüeh.*"

Throughout much of the remainder of the work, music, *yüeh* 樂, is then discussed in connection with its complimentary opposite, *li* 禮, or "ritual." The close pairing of these two concepts was first introduced by Hsün-tzu (whose "Yüeh lun" chapter follows directly upon his "Li lun"), but the *Yüeh chi* is the first text in which the relationship between the two is spelled out systematically. Ritual is that through which the hierarchical differentiation required for society to function properly is imposed, while music is the source of harmonizing power that brings society's members together toward unified ends. Each of these two great tools of enlightened rulership serves as a check upon the other; a proper balance of the two ensures that ritual will not lead toward social estrangement, or music toward reckless dissoluteness. Ultimately, however, "the natures of ritual and music are the same"—true ritual produces within its participants feelings of social solidarity, while true music exemplifies a hierarchical structure: a well-balanced society functions like a well-balanced piece of music, in which each instrumental member maintains its position in such a way as to allow for the harmonious operation of the whole.

In keeping with the correlative spirit of the early Han, the ritual/music pair is then mapped onto correspondence within the natural and social orders. The pair is given philosophical justification through its derivation from the fundamental paradigm of all such complimentary pairs: Heaven and Earth. "Music is the harmony of Heaven and Earth. Ritual is the order of Heaven and Earth. Harmony, thus the hundred things all transform; order, thus the myriad things are all differentiated. Music is created from Heaven, Ritual is instituted through Earth. . . . Only after having a clear understanding of Heaven and Earth can one give rise to Ritual and Music." The mapping is extended to encompass human virtues: music is creative, internal, transformative, and akin to *jen*

仁 (humanity); ritual is passive, external, structive, and akin to *i* 儀 (propriety).

Of particular importance to later aesthetic tradition is the idea that music invariably expresses, in an unalterable way, the true sentiments of its creator-performer: "only music is unable to create falsehood." As such, collected folk music was thought to serve as a reliable barometer through which the ruling class could accurately judge the degree of success achieved by its rule: "the music of a well-governed age is peaceful, so as to express happiness in the harmony of the administration." Related to this is the work's unique theory of human nature: neither intrinsically good nor bad, man's nature is "still" in the sense that his heart/mind is set into motion only after being "touched off by external things," and musical expression thus invariably follows as a direct reaction to the external stimuli. The notion that outward form follows (or should follow) as a spontaneous and natural outgrowth of inner substance is one that would be carried over to other theories of artistic expression as well, as, for example, Liu Hsieh's 劉勰 (*ca.* 465–*ca.* 520) theory of literature in his *Wen-hsin tiao-lung* 文心雕龍.*

The *Yüeh chi* has also had important influence in other areas. The great neo-Confucian philosopher Chu Hsi 朱熹 (1130–1200) was a strong admirer of the work, in particular for its statement that man's *t'ien-li* 天理 (heavenly principles) would be destroy-ed were he to be enticed by external things and "unable to return to himself"—which to Chu provided man with a fundamentally good nature after all, and one with a normative basis in Heaven. More significantly, even a cursory glance at the musical treatises of the later dynastic histories attests to the fact that the ideas and injunctions put forth in the *Yüeh chi* were given serious attention in the imperial courts of subsequent dynasties, where such issues as the naming of imperial compositions, the implementation of musical sumptuary regulations, etc., continued to be the sources of hotly contested debates.

Editions and References

K'ung, Ying-ta 孔穎達 *et al. Li-chi chu-shu* 禮記注疏. *Chüan* 37-39. *SPPY.*

Sun, Hsi-tan 孫希旦. *Li-chi chi-chieh* 禮記集解. *Chüan* 37-39. Shen Hsiao-huan and Wang Hsing-hsien, eds. Taipei: Wen-shih-che, 1990, pp. 975-1039.

Translations

Cook, Scott. *"Yue Ji:* Record of Music" (see below under "Studies").

Kaufmann, Walter. *Musical References in the Chinese Classics.* Detroit: Information Coordinators, 1967.

Legge, James. *Li Chi, The Book of Rites.* V. 2. Oxford, 1885; rpt. New York: University Books, 1967.

Studies

Chao, Feng 趙渢, ed. *Yüeh-chi lun-pien* 樂記論辯. Peking: Jen-min Yin-yüeh, 1983. A collection of articles on the *Yüeh chi* dating from 1944–1981.

Cook, Scott. *"Yue Ji* 樂記–Record of Music: Introduction, Translation, Notes, and Commentary," *Asian Music,* XXVI.2 (Spring/Summer 1995): 1-96.

Kuo, Mo-jo 郭沫若. "Kung-sun Ni-tzu yü ch'i yin-yüeh li-lun" 公孫尼子與其音樂理論. In *Ch'ing-t'ung shih-tai,* 1944. Rpt. in Chao Feng, ed., *Yüeh-chi lun-pien* (see above).

Ts'ai, Chung-te 蔡仲德. *"Yüeh chi* tso-che pien-cheng" 樂記作者辨證, in *Chung-kuo Yin-yüeh Hsüeh-yüan hsüeh-pao, ch'uan-k'an hao* 創刊號 1980.12.

___. *Chung-kuo yin-yüeh mei-hsüeh-shih* 中國音樂美學史. Taipei: Lan-teng, 1993, Chapter 16, pp. 341-396.

Scott Cook
Grinnell College

Yün Shou-p'ing 惲壽平 (*tzu,* Cheng-shu 正叔; *hao,* Nan-t'ien 南田, Tung-yüan Ts'ao-i Sheng 東園草衣生, Pai-yün Wai-shih 白雲外史, etc., 1633–90), whose original name was Yün Ko 惲格, had the rare distinction of excelling in all three classical fields–painting, poetry, and calligraphy. He was best known as an artist and because of his multi-faceted talent his contemporaries labeled a painting by him "the three perfections of Nan-t'ien" (南田三絕). A native of Yang-hu 陽湖 (Ch'ang-chou prefecture, Kiangsu), he was born into a family known for its scholarship and its loyalty to the Ming court. His great-grandfather was a high official in Fukien. His father, Yün Jih-ch'u 惲日初, was a member of the patriotic Fu-she 復社 (Restoration Society) founded by Chang P'u 張溥 (1602–41). But owing to the turmoil of the Ming-Ch'ing succession, Yün Shou-p'ing's genius was allowed to blossom only after he had endured enormous hardships. The story of his survival became a legend in his own time and the subject of an opera.

Actually, two strong intellectual forces can be said to have shaped and nourished Yün Shou-p'ing's life, and one of these was loyalty. As a degree candidate in Peking, his father had submitted memorials to the throne advocating various defense policies, but, sensing the hopelessness of his cause, he decided to retire to Mount T'ien-t'ai with his library of three-thousand volumes. In 1644, he aided the loyalist courts in Fukien and Kwangtung, but soon after the Lung-wu 隆武 emperor's defeat at T'ing-chou 汀州 in the autumn of 1646, he became a Buddhist priest and took the name of Abbot Ming-t'an 明曇 (The Night-blooming Cereus of the Ming). In 1648, after the restoration efforts of princes Lu 魯王 and T'ang 唐王 had failed, he yielded to the plea of his patriot-friends to come out of the monastery and join in the defence of Chien-ning 建寧 in northern Fukien. When the fighting ended, Yün Jih-ch'u was taken prisoner and separated from his two sons. Yün Shou-p'ing's elder brother was killed, while he, barely fifteen years old, was lost and presumed dead.

Fleeing the melee, Yün Shou-p'ing was fortunate to be taken into the service of the Manchu governor of Fukien, Ch'en Chin 陳錦. It was also said that the governor's wife took a particular interest in Yün's artistic ability in drawing intricate jewelry designs and treated him as an adopted son. One day, however, while Yün Shou-p'ing was still in the governor's employ, his father chanced to encounter him at the Ling-yin Monastery 靈隱寺 in Hangchow. Father and son had a joyful reunion. However, because of the power and prestige of the governor, the father was unable to claim the boy as his lost son. Finally, with the connivance of the abbot, the governor's wife was told that they boy would die an early death unless tonsured as a monk and kept at the monastery. Thus father and son were reunited. From this time until his father's death Yün Shou-p'ing supported him by selling his paintings.

As a result of these events, Yün inherited a deep sense of loyalty to the Ming and throughout his life never took the Ch'ing civil-service examination. The fame of this story also led Wang Pien 王抃, son of the artist Wang Shih-min 王時敏 (1590–1680) and one of the "Four Wangs" whose painting dominated the orthodox school of painting in the early Ch'ing, to turn the events of Yün's youth into a *ch'uan-ch'i* romance* entitled *Ch'iu-feng yüan* 鶩峰緣 (Predestiny at Condor Peak; 1679).

The second force that molded Yün's life and won him further fame was the artistic milieu of his day: a belief in the supremacy of all artistic endeavors, particularly painting and calligraphy, above even political considerations. The K'ang-hsi 康熙 emperor (r. 1662-1722), though surely aware of the artist's family background and anti-Manchu sentiment, valued so highly his own collection of Yün Shou-p'ing's paintings that he wrote a preface for it. Art, it would

appear, had its own legitimacy and Yün Shou-p'ing's work was respected by members of society, high and low.

Yün Shou-p'ing began the study of Chinese painting after the age of twenty, first under his uncle Yün Hsiang 惲向 (1586–1655), a painter whose reputation was especially strong during the Ch'ung-chen 崇禎 reign period (1628–1643). Although his uncle was said to have been schooled in the painting styles of the tenth-century landscape painters, Yün Shou-ming also studied and absorbed techniques from later masters such as Wang Meng 王蒙 (1301–1385), Huang Kung-wang 黃公望 (1269-1355), Ni Tsan 倪瓚 (1301–1374), and T'ang Yin 唐寅 (1470–1523). He studied not just the artists of the past, but also his contemporaries. Wang Hui 王翬 (1632–1717), another of the Four Wangs of the early Ch'ing, was a close friend for four decades. Other well-known collectors and artists in his circle of friends included T'ang Yü-chao 唐宇昭, Cha Shih-piao 查士標, Ta Ch'ung-kuang 笪重光, and Wang Shih-min. They met sometimes over wine or a game of chess, sometimes to view and discuss ancient scrolls, sometimes to write and exchange impromptu poems. Other poems were written for each other's paintings. Many of these are preserved in Yün Shou-p'ing's collected works, the best of them underscoring the intimate relationship between these artists' painting and poetry.

While today Wang Hui is widely admired as a master painter, Yün Shou-p'ing is best known as an artist who revitalized the subgenre of flowers, birds and insects. Yün also perfected a technique of achieving special effects through the use of ink wash and by working without preliminary outlines, allowing him to render flowers in more natural, softer tones.

Though less famous as a poet, Yün's poems deserve further notice. Though most are occasional poems written at outings, addressed to friends, or inscribed on paintings, they reveal a spontaneity and freshness, and sometimes an originality, not often found in this kind of verse. Perhaps if one accepts the truth of the dictum that art is an imitation of nature, what is found in Yün Shou-p'ing's works might also be considered a kind of "nature poetry," though it is nature one step removed.

Yün Shou-p'ing reveals in his poetry a strong predilection for verbal puns combined with a degree of unconventionality. In several instances, his poems show little regard for formal distinctions. For example, he experiments with the number of words in a line. In "A Song of Falling Blossoms and Sporting Fish" 落花戲魚曲, he combines lines of three words with those of four, five, seven or even eight words. Similarly, a poem entitled "Wu Mountain Is High: A Song" 吳山高曲 contains lines of three, four, five, six and seven words.

Yün Shou-p'ing was also fond of making puns on names. For example, a Yüan painter he respected named Huang Kung-wang 黃公望 (1269–1355) had the courtesy-name (*tzu*) Tzu-chiu 子久. The first character has two common meanings—"son" (which was the intended meaning in the original name) and the common pronoun "you." *Chiu* 久 means of long duration. In a poem entitled "After the Artistic Style of Tzu-chiu" 仿子久畫, Yün Shou-p'ing repeats the earlier painter's name in six successive lines, as follows "The ancients had Tzu-chiu;/ Our contemporaries have no Tzu-chiu./ Tzu-chiu is not here;/ Who can know Tzu-chiu?/ This one cannot be Tzu-chiu,/But he strongly resembles Tzu-chiu." 古人有子久/今人無子久/子久不在茲/誰能知子久/此不作子久/而甚似子久。 These lines can also be read, alternately, as "Long were you with the ancients;/ Our contem-poraries have long missed you./ Long have you not been here,/ But who can be said to have known you for a long time?/ This one

cannot act like you for long,/ And yet he has long much resembled you."

Such verbal acts of levity aside, the spontaneity in Yün's verse also stems from another source, a preponderance of natural imagery derived from synesthesia. Often sights are combined with sounds, as in the following couplet:

From the ancient woods half of the leaves
    have fallen:
Autumn wine is just beginning to swell
    the forest.
古木半落葉，秋風初滿林。

Or the following couplet in which appeal is made simultaneously to four senses —the visual, olfactory, auditory, and tactile:

Wind among the duckweeds about to
    disperse the green,
Fragrant air on the verge of turning into
    mist.
萍風將散綠，香氣欲成霧。

The abundance of such imagery is a testimony to the poet's keen observation of nature, nature recreated in painting and poetry.

At its best, Yün's verse contained the simplicity and pictorial power which is almost evocative of Wang Wei 王維 (701–761),* as this final example , "After the Style of Chü-jan's Painting 'The Sound of a Mountain Stream', illustrates:

The rock hangs so steep, clouds and
    birds find themselves alone;
The mountain empty, the sun and moon
    are unattended;
Across the stream I summon the gibbons
in the night,
Together to spend the night on top of the
    cliff.

石峭雲鳥孤，山空日月獨，
隔溪招夜猿，同向巖頭宿。

Editions and References
Yün, Shou-p'ing. *Ou-hsiang kuan chi* 甌香館集. In *Ts'ung-shu chi-ch'eng* (with a Supplement).

Translations

Chaves, *Later Chinese Poetry,* pp. 388-403.
Waiting for the Unicorn, pp. 122-6.

Studies

Chang, Lin-sheng 張臨生. "Ch'ing-ch'u hua-chia Yün Shou-p'ing" 清初畫家惲壽平. In *Ku-kung chi-k'an* 故宮季刊, 10.2 (1976): 45-80 and 27-31 (English summary).
Ch'eng, Ming-shih 承名世. "Yün Nan-t'ien yen-chiu" 惲南田研究. In *Shang-hai Po-wu Kuan chi-k'an,* 1982: 159-78.
ECCP, pp. 960-1.

Irving Yucheng Lo

Updated Bibliographies for *The Indiana Companion to Traditional Chinese Literature,* Volume 1

General Bibliography

This bibliography and those which follow are intended to update the General Bibliography and those for the Essays and Entries that appeared in the *Indiana Companion to Traditional Chinese Literature,* volume 1. In most cases they include items published between 1984 (when the volume 1 bibliographies were finalized) and 1996, with some items from 1997 and 1998 added. These lists are not intended as a complete bibliographic updates of these items. Like this project from the beginning, it has reflected the needs and results of an introductory course in Chinese literature for graduate students at the University of Wisconsin, Madison. The following entries are also determined by the interests and limitations of the compiler and the editors. Readers are expected to expand these entries through use of bibliographic items cited below (often annotated). For example, in the entry on "*Ching* 京 (classics)" below, although a few Japanese items are listed (especially for the period 1992-1996), the reference to Lin Ch'ing-chang 林慶彰, ed. *Jih-pen yen-chiu ching-hsüeh lun-chu mu-lu* (1900-1992) 日本研究經學論箸目錄 (Nankang: Wen-che So, Chung-yang Yen-chiu Yüan, 1993) seems sufficient to guide further exploration of Japanese scholarship in this area.

These bibliographies include primarily items in Chinese, English, French, German and Japanese, although a small number of items in other languages have been added. Some of these items are incomplete; the most common problem is the lack of page numbers for journal articles. The editor decided to retain all entries for items not seen as long as enough information was provided for the reader to locate the work on his own.

A monumental debt of thanks is owed the students who worked on these bibliographies over the years, in particular those who helped bring it to its final shape: Weiguo Cao and Bruce Knickerbocker. Any errors or omissions are the responsibility of the compiler alone.

N.B. Chinese and Japanese characters for journal titles and publishers can be found in the "List of Chinese and Japanese Journals" and "List of Chinese and Japanese Publishers" in the front-matter. Chinese publishers are abbreviated by omitting "Ch'u-pan-she, Shu-tien, etc." whenever possible. For many useful related bibliographies, see the "Asian Resources on the World Wide Web" published regularly in *Asian Studies Newsletter.*

Arai, Ken 荒井健, ed. *Chûka bunjin no seikatsu* 中華文人の生活. Tokyo: Heibonsha, 1994. A book of essays on subjects such as literati and eremitism, painting, love for writing tools, hygiene, eating and drinking, family relations, and publishing.

Bauer, Wolfgang. *Das Antlitz Chinas, die autobiographische Selbstdarstellung in der chinesischen Literatur von ihren Anfängen bis heute.* Munich, Vienna: Hanser, 1990.

Birrell, Anne. "Studies in Chinese Myth Since 1970: An Appraisal, Parts I and II," *History of Religions* 33 (1994): 380-393 and 34 (1994): 70-94.

_____. *Chinese Mythology--An Introduction.* Baltimore: Johns Hopkins University Press, 1993.

Bol, Peter K. *"This Culture of Ours:" Intellectual Transitions in T'ang and Sung China.* Stanford: Stanford University Press, 1992.

_____. *Research Tools for the Study of Sung History. Sung-Yuan Research Aids, II.* Binghamton: Journal of Sung-Yuan Studies, 1990.

Brooks, E. Bruce. "Review Article: The Present State and Future Prospects of Pre-Han Text Studies, a Review of Michael Loewe, ed. *Early Chinese Texts: A Bibliographic Guide,*" *Sino-Platonic Papers* 46 (July 1994): 1-74.

Chan, Hok-lam. "Ming T'ai-tsu's Manipulation of Letters: Myth and Reality of Literary Persecution," *Journal of Asian History* 29 (1995): 1-60.

Chan, Sin-wai and David Pollard, eds. *An Encyclopaedic Dictionary fo Chinese-English/English-Chinese Translation.* Hong Kong: Chinese University Press, 1994.

Chang, Chih-yüeh 張志岳. *Hsien-Ch'in wen-hsüeh chien-shih* 先秦文學簡史. Harbin: Hei-lung-chiang Jen-min, 1986.

Chang, Lin-ch'uan 張林川. *Chung-kuo ku-chi shu-ming k'ao-shih tz'u-tien* 中國古籍書名考釋辭典. Tientsin: Ho-nan Jen-min, 1993.

Chang, P'ei-heng 章培恆 and Lo Yü-ming 駱玉明, eds. *Chung-kuo wen-hsüeh shih* 中國文學史. 3v. Shanghai: Fu-tan Ta-hsüeh, 1996.

Chaves, Jonathan, trans. and ed. *The Columbia Book of Later Chinese Poetry--Yüan, Ming and Ch'ing Dynasties.* New York: Columbia University Press, 1986.

Ch'en, Chu-min 陳鉄民. *T'ang-tai wen-hsüeh shih* 唐代文學史. V. 1. Peking: Jen-min Wen-hsüeh, 1995.

Ch'en, Hsiang-chung 陳象鍾 *et al.*, eds. *T'ang-tai wen-hsüeh shih* 唐代文學史. 2v. Peking: Jen-min, 1995.

Ch'en, Po-hai 陳伯海 and Chu I-an 朱易安. *T'ang-shih shu-lu* 唐詩書錄. Tsinan: Ch'i-Lu Shu-she, 1988. Excellent bibliography to supplement Wan Man 萬曼, *T'ang-chi hsü-lu* 唐集敍錄 (Peking: Chung-hua, 1980).

Ch'en, Yü-kang 陳玉剛. *Chung-kuo wen-hsüeh t'ung-shih chien-pien* 中國文學通史簡編. 2v. Peking: Ta-chung Wen-i 大眾文藝, 1992.

_____. *Chung-kuo wen-hsüeh t'ung-shih.* 2v. Peking: Hsi-yüan 西苑, 1996.

Cheng, Anne. *Histoire de la pensée chinoise.* Paris: Seuil, 1997.

Ch'ien, Ch'i-po 錢其博. *Chung-kuo wen-hsüeh shih* 中國文學史. 3v. Peking: Chung-hua, 1993.

Ch'ien Chung-lien 錢仲聯 and Ch'ien Hsüeh-tseng 錢學增, ed. *Ch'ing-shih ching-hua lu* 清詩精華錄. Tsinan: Chi-Lu Shu-she, 1987.

Ch'ien Chung-lien 錢仲聯 and Fu Hsüan-ts'ung 傅璇琮, eds. *Chung-kuo wen-hsüeh ta tz'u-tien* 中國文學大辭典. Shanghai: Shang-hai Tz'u-shu, 1997.

Ch'ien, Nien-sun 錢念孫. *Chung-kuo wen-hsüeh yen-i* 中國文學演義. Shanghai: Shang-hai Wen-i, 1994.

Ch'ien Po-ch'eng 錢伯城, Wei T'ung-hsien 魏同賢 and Mao Chang-ken 毛樟根, eds. *Ch'üan Ming wen* 全明文. V. 1-2. Shanghai: Ku-chi, 1993-.

Ch'in-ting Ssu-k'u ch'üan-shu k'ao-cheng 欽定四庫全書考證. 3v. Peking: Shu-mu Wen-hsien, 1991.

Ch'in-ting Ssu-k'u ch'üan-shu tsung-mu 欽定四庫全書總目. 2v. Peking: Chung-hua, 1997.

Chinese Academy of Social Sciences, Institute of History, ed. *Chung-kuo shih-hsüeh lun-wen so-yin* 中國史學論文索引. 3v. Peking: Chung-hua, 1995.

Chou, Hsing-chien 周行建 *et al*, eds. *Chung-kuo wen-hsüeh jen-wu hsing-hsiang tz'u-tien* 中國文學人物形象辭典. Chungking: Ch'ung-ch'ing, 1994.

Chou, Shan. "Literary Reputations in Context," *TS* 10-11 (1992-3): 41-66.

Chou, Tsu-hsüan 周祖譔, ed. *Chung-kuo wen-hsüeh chia ta tz'u-tien, T'ang Wu-tai chüan* 中國文學家大辭典唐五代卷. Peking: Chung-hua, 1992. Excellent entries; the best such dictionary encountered.

Chou, Tu-wen 周篤文. *Ch'üan Sung tz'u p'ing chu* 全宋詞評注. 10v. Peking?: Wen-hsüeh 文 學, 1994.

Chou, Ying-hsiung, ed. *The Chinese Text, Studies in Comparative Literature.* Hong Kong: The Chinese University Press, 1986.

Chow, Tse-tsung. *Wen-lin II: Studies in the Chinese Humanities.* Hong Kong: The Chinese University Press, 1989.

Ch'üan Ming shih 全明詩. Shanghai: Shang-hai Ku-chi, 1990-. V. 1-. Through 1992 only 3 volumes had appreared.

Chûgoku kankei ronsetsu shiryô 中国関係論説資料 (Collected Articles on China). Annual. Part 2, Literature, Langauge; Part 3, History and Social Sciences. Annual (v. 35, 1995).

Chûgoku Shibun Kenkyûkai 中国詩文研究会, ed. *Roku Kinritsu shûkô SenShin Kan Gi Shin Nanboku chô shi kakusha sakuin* 逯欽立輯校先秦漢魏晉南北朝詩作者索引. Tokyo: Tôhô Shoten, 1984

Chûgoku tosho 中國圖書. Tokyo: Uchiyama Shoten 內山書店,1989. V. 1-. This monthly guide to new and recent books on Chinese literature (especially PRC works) is extremely useful.

Chung-kuo ch'u-pan jen-ming tz'u-tien 中國出版人名詞典. Chung-kuo Ch'u-pan K'o-hsüeh Yen-chiu-so and Ho-pei-sheng Hsin-wen Ch'u-pan-chü, eds. Peking: Chung-kuo Shu-chi, 1984.

Chung-kuo ku-tien wen-hsüeh yen-chiu lun-wen so-yin 1949-1980 中國古典文學研究論文索引. Nanning, 1984.

Chung-kuo ku-tien wen-hsüeh yen-chiu lun-wen so-yin 1980.1-1981.12 中國古典文學研究論文索 引. Peking, 1985.

Chung-kuo ta pai-k'o ch'üan-shu 中國大百科全書. *Chung-kuo wen-hsüeh chüan* 中國文學卷. 2v. Peking: Chung-kuo Ta- Pai-k'o Ch'üan-shu, 1986.

Chung-kuo wen-hsüeh ta tz'u-tien 中國文學大辭典. T'ien-chin Jen-min Ch'u-pan-she and Pai-ch'uan Shu-chü Ch'u-pan-pu, eds. 10v. Taipei: Pai-ch'uan Shu-chü, 1994.

Cutter, Robert Joe. *The Brush and the Spur: Chinese Culture and the Cockfight.* Hong Kong: Chinese University of Hong Kong Press, 1989.

De Bary, William Theodore and Irene Bloom, eds. *Eastern Canons: Approaches to the Asian Classics.* New York: Columbia University Press, 1990.

Debon, Günther. *Chinesische Dichtung, Geschichte, Struktur, Theorie.* Leiden: E. J. Brill, 1989. This important volume contains three sections: (1) a brief historical overview with references to section 2, (2) a list of 370 terms integral to traditional Chinese poetry, and (3) 100 translations as examples.

Deeney, John J. "Historical Sketch of Chinese Comparative Literature Studies," *TkR,* 17.3(1987):197-220.

Diény, Jean-Pierre. *Hommage à Kwong Hing Foon: Études d'histoire culturelle de la Chine.* Paris: Collège de France, Institut des Hautes Études Chinoises, 1995.

Drége, Jean Pierre. *Les bibliothèques en Chine au temps des manuscrits (jusq'au Xe siècle).* Paris: École Française d'Extrême Orient, 1991.

___. *La Commercial Press de Shanghai, 1897-1949.* Paris: Collège de France, Institut des Hautes Études Chinoises, 1978.

Durand, Pierre-Henri. *Lettres et pouvoirs un proces littéraire dans la Chine imperiale.* Paris: École Hautes Études en Sciences Sociales, 1991.

Egan, Ronald, trans. *Limited Views: Essays on Ideas and Letters by Qian Zhongshu.* Cambridge, Mass.: Council on East Asian Studies, Harvard University, 1998. Harvard-Yenching Institute Monographs, 44.

Eggert, Marion. *Rede von Traum: Traumauffassungen der Literatenschicht im späten kaiserlichen*

China. Stuttgart: F. Steiner, 1993.

Eoyang, Eugene and Lin Yaofu, ed. *Translating Chinese Literature*. Bloomington: Indiana University Press, 1995.

Eoyang, Eugene Chen. *The Transparent Eye, Reflections on Translation, Chinese Literature, and Comparative Poetics*. Honolulu: University of Hawaii Press, 1993.

Ess, Hans von. *Politik und Gelehrsamkeit in der Zeit der Han (202 v. Chr.-220 n. Chr.): die Alttext/Neutext Kontroverse*. Wiesbaden: Harrassowitz, 1993.

Europe Studies China: Papers from an International Conference on the History of European Sinology. Ming Wilson and John Cayley, eds. London: Han-shan Tang Books, 1995.

Fang, Ming 方銘. *Chan-kuo wen-hsüeh shih* 戰國文學史. Wuhan: Wu-han Ch'u-pan-she, 1996.

Feifel, Eugen. *Bibliographie zur Geschichte der chinesischen Literatur*. Hildesheim, Zurich, New York: Georg Olms, 1992.

Gescher, Christa. *Literatur, Sprache und Politik: Helmut Martin, Schriften über China (1965-1991)*. Bockum: Brockmeyer, 1991. *Chinathemen*, 62.

Gumbrecht, Cordula. *Die Monumenta Serica--eine sinologische Zeitschrift und ihre Redaktionsbibliothek in ihrer Pekinger Zeit (1935-1945)*. Cologne: Greven, 1994. See the review by Hartmut Walravens in *OLZ* 90 (1995): 491-94.

Guy, R. Kent. *The Emperor's Four Treasuries--Scholars and the State in the Late Ch'ien-lung Era*. Cambridge, Mass.: Harvard University Press, 1987.

Hegel, Robert E. and Richard C. Hessney, eds. *Expressions of Self in Chinese Literature*. New York: Columbia University Press, 1985.

Henderson, John B. *Scripture, Canon, and Commentary, A Comparison of Chinese and Western Exegeses*. Princeton: Princeton University Press, 1988.

Henry, Eric. "The Motif of Recognition in Early China," *HJAS* 47(1987): 5-30.

Hsieh, Wei 謝巍, ed. *Chung-kuo li-tai jen-wu nien-p'u k'ao-lu* 中國歷代人物年譜考錄. Peking: Chung-hua, 1992.

Hsü, I-min 許逸民 and Ch'ang Chen-kuo 常振國, eds. *Chung-kuo li-tai shu-mu ts'ung-k'an (Ti-i chi)* 中國歷代書目叢刊 (第一集). Peking: Hsien-tai, 1987. Contains eight bibliographies (all but one of Sung dynasty provenance) including *Ch'ung-wen tsung-mu* 崇文總目 and *Chih-chai shu-lu chieh-t'i* 直齋書錄解題.

Huang, Ch'i-fang 黃起方. *Liang Sung wen-hsüeh lun-ts'ung* 兩宋文史論叢. Taipei: Hsüeh-hai, 1985.

Huang, Hsiu-wen 黃秀文, ed. *Chung-kuo nien-p'u tz'u-tien* 中國年譜辭典. Shanghai: Pai-chia, 1997.

Huang, Li-chen 黃立振, ed. *Pa-pai-chung ku-tien wen-hsüeh chu-tso chieh-shao hsü-pien* 800 種古典文學著祚介紹續編. Chengchow: Chung-chou Ku-chi, 1987. This sequel, like the original volume, introduces traditional works with a focus on modern critical editions done in the PRC.

Huang, Wen-hsing 黃文興 *et al.*, eds. *Tz'u-shu lei-tien* 辭書類典. Peking: Chung-kuo Kuang-po Tien-shih, 1993. A huge, annotated listing of dictionaries in all fields.

Hung, Eva, ed. *Paradoxes of Traditional Chinese Literature*. Hong Kong: The Chinese University Press, 1994.

Idema, W. L. and Lloyd Haft. *A Guide to Chinese Literature*. Ann Arbor: Center for Chinese Studies, University of Michigan, 1997. A translation of the Dutch original (1985).

Itô, Seiji 伊藤清司. *Mukashibanashi Densetsu no keifu–Higashi Ajia no hikaku setsuwa gaku* 昔話伝説の系譜–東アジアの比較説話学. Tokyo: Daiichi Shobô, 1991.

Iwaki, Hideo 岩城秀夫. *Chûgoku bungaku gairon* 中国文学概論. Kyoto: Hôyû Shoten, 1995.

Jachontov, Konstantin S. *Kitajskie rukopisi i ksiligrafy publichnoj biblioteki; Sistematiches kij katalog*. St. Petersberg, 1993. Catalogue of the Russian State Library in St. Petersburg, see the review by Hartmut Walravens in *OLZ* 90 (1995): 325-30.

Jens, Walter, ed. *Kindlers Neues Literaturelexikon*. 20v. Munich: Kindler, 1988-1992.

Kaji, Nobuyuki 加地伸行. *Kôshi gaden–seisekizu ni miru Kôshi rurô no shôgai to oshie* 孔子画伝–聖蹟図にみる孔子流浪の生涯と教え Tokyo: Shûeisha, 1991.

Kampen, Th. "Die Entwicklung der Ostasienforschung in der DDR: Diplomarbeiten und Dissertationen über China, Japan und Korea (1949-1990)," *Bochumer Jahrbuch zur Ostasienforschung* 20 (1996).

Kao, Kuo-kan 高國淦, ed. *Chung-kuo ch'u-pan fa-hsing chi-kou ho pao-k'an ming-lu* 中郭出版發行機構和報刊名錄. Peking: Hsien-ta, 1985.

Kent, Guy. *The Emperor's Four Treasuries: Scholars and the State in the Late Ch'ien-lung Era.* Cambridge, Mass.: Harvard University Press, 1987.

Ko, Susan Schor. "Literary Politics in the Han." Unpublished Ph. D. dissertation, Yale University, 1991.

Köster, Hermann. *Symbolik des chinesichen Universismus.* Stuttgart: Anton Hiersemann, 1958.

Kondô, Mitsuo 近藤光男. *Shiko zensho sômoku teiyô Tô shishû no kenkyû* 四庫全書総目提要唐詩集の研究. Tokyo: Kenbun Shuppan, 1984.

___. *Shinchô kôshô gaku no kenkyû* 清朝考証学の研究. Tokyo: Kenbun Shuppan, 1987.

Kubin,Wolfgang, ed. Bonner Geschichte der chinesischen Literatur. 8v. Frankfurt: Surkamp, 1999-. Although forthcoming works are generally not listed herein, this important series seems to merit an except. Expected volumes include Wolfgang Kubin's *Die chinesische Dichtkunst der Zhou-Zeit bis 1911;* Monika Motsch, *Die klassische chinesische Erzählung von den Anfängen bis zur Qing-Zeit;* Kubin, Rolf Trauzettel and Marion Eggert, *Die chinesische Prosa von den Anfängen bis zur Gegenwart;* Thomas Zimmer, *Der chinesische Roman der Ming- und Qing-Zeit;* Karl-Heinz Pohl, *Die chinesische Literaturtheorie und Literaturkritik von den Anfängen bis zur Qing-Zeit;* and Lutz Bieg, Bibliographies zur chinesische Literatur in deutscher Sprache.

Kuo-wu Yüan Ku-chi cheng-li Chu-pan she 國務院古籍整理出版社, ed. *Ku-chi cheng-li tu-chu mu-lu (1949–1991)* 古籍整理圖書目錄. Peking: Chung-hua, 1992.

Kuo, Ying-te 郭英德, *et al.,* eds. *Chung-kuo ku-tien wen-hsüeh yen-chiu shih* 中國古典文學史研究史. Peking: Chung-hua, 1995.

Kuo, Yü-heng 郭預衡, ed. *Chung-kuo ku-tai wen-hsüeh shih ch'ang-pien* 中國古代文學史長編研究. *Sui T'ang Wu-tai chüan* 隋唐五代卷. Peking: Pei-ching Shih-fan Ta-hsüeh, 1993. *Sung Liao Chin chüan* 宋遼金卷. Peking: Pei-ching Shih-fan Ta-hsüeh, 1993. *Ch'in Han Wei Chin Nan-pei ch'ao chüan* 秦漢魏晉南北朝卷. Peking: Shou-tu Shih-fan Ta-hsüeh, 1995.

Lang-tan, Goatkoei. *Der unauffindbare Einsiedler: eine Untersuchung zu einem Topos der Tang-Lyrik, (618-906).* Frankfurt: Haag und Herchen, 1985. *Heidelberger Schriften zu Ostasienkunde,* 7. Revision of Lang-tan's dissertation; interesting introduction on types of hermits prior to T'ang, followed by a study of the topos of "seeking a hermit but not finding him" in T'ang verse.

Lau, Joseph S. M. "The Courage to Die: Suicide as Self-Fulfillment in Chinese History and Literature," *Asian Culture Quarterly,* 16.3(1988): 33-48.

Lévy, André. *La littérature chinoise ancienne et classique.* Paris: Presses Universitaires de France, 1991. A concise, significant survey by a leading scholar in traditional fiction; chapters on antiquity, prose, poetry, and the novel and theater.

Li, Chih-chung 李致忠. *Ku-shu pan-pen chien-ting* 古書版本鑒定. Peking: Wen-wu, 1997.

___. *Sung-pan shu hsü-lu* 宋版書敍錄. Peking: Shu-mu Wen-hsien, 1994.

Li, Meng-sheng 李夢生. *Chung-kuo chin-hui hsiao-shuo pai-hua* 中國禁毀小説百話. Shanghai: Shang-hai Ku-chi, 1994.

Li, Ts'ung-chün 李從軍. *T'ang-tai wen-hsüeh yen-pien shih* 唐代文學演變史. Peking: Jen-min Wen-hsüeh,1993.

Li, Yü-an 李玉安 and Ch'en Ch'uan-i 陳傳藝, eds. *Chung-kuo tsang-shu-chia tz'u-tien* 中國藏書家辭典. Wuhan: Hu-pei Chiao-yü, 1989. Lists 1155 men and women who held private collections of books, worked in libraries, or were bibliographers.

Liao, K'o-bin 廖可斌. *Ming-tai wen-hsüeh fu-ku yün-tung yen-chiu* 明代文學復骨運動研究. Shanghai: Shang-hai Ku-chi, 1994.

Lin, Ch'ing-chang 林慶彰, *et al.,* ed. *Jih-pen yen-chiu ching-hsüeh lun-chu mu-lu (1900-1992)* 日本研究經學論箸目錄. Taipei: Chung-yang Yen-chiu Yüan, Wen-che So, 1993.

Liu, Guojun. *Die Geschichte des chinesischen Buches.* Zhou Yicheng, trans. (from Chinese); Hans-Wolfgang Gartmann, trans. (from English). Peking: Foreign Languages Press, 1988.

Liu, K'an-ju 劉侃如. *Chung-kuo wen-hsüeh hsi-nien* 中國文學系年. Peking: Jen-min Wen-hsüeh, 1985.

Liu, Yung-chi 劉永濟. *Shih-ssu ch'ao wen-hsüeh yao-lüeh* 十四朝文學要略. Harbin: Hei-lung-chiang Jen-min, 1984.

Lo, Lien-t'ien 羅聯添, ed. in chief. *Chung-kuo wen-hsüeh lun-chu chi-mu cheng-pien* 中國文學論箸集目正編. 7v. Taipei: Wu-nan, 1996.

Lo, Lin 羅琳. *"Hsü-hsiu Ssu-k'u ch'üan-shu tsung-mu t'i-yao kao-pen* tsuan-hsiu shih-mo" 續修四庫全書總目提要稿本纂修始末, *Shu-mu chi-k'an* 30.3 (December 1996): 3-10. An important bibliography of studies and translations from 1912-1990.

Lo, Tsung-ch'iang 羅宗強. *Sui T'ang Wu-tai wen-hsüeh shih—Chung chüan* 隋唐五代文學史—中卷. Peking: Kao-teng Chiao-yü, 1994.

Lo, Wei-kuo 羅偉國 and Hu P'ing 胡平. *Ku-chi pan-pen t'i-chi so-yin* 古籍版本題記索引. Shanghai: Shang-hai Shu-tien, 1991.

Loewe, Michael, ed. *Early Chinese Texts, A Bibliographic Guide.* Berkeley: The Society for the Study of Early China and The Institute of East Asian Studies, U. of California, 1993.

Lu, Ch'in-li 逯欽立. *Han Wei Liu-ch'ao wen-hsüeh lun-chi* 漢魏六朝文學論集. Wu Yün 吳雲, ed. Sian: Shan-hsi Jen-min, 1984.

Lung, Ch'ien-an 龍潛庵. *Sung Yüan yü-yen tz'u-tien* 宋元語言詞典. Shanghai: Shang-hai Tz'u-shu, 1985.

Ma, Liang-ch'un 馬良春 and Li Fu-t'ien 李福田. *Chung-kuo wen-hsüeh ta-tz'u-tien* 中國文學大辭典. 8v. Tientsin: T'ien-chin Jen-min, 1991.

McMullen, David. *State and Scholars in T'ang China.* Cambridge: Cambridge University Press, 1988.

Mair, Victor H. *The Columbia Anthology of Traditional Chinese Literature.* New York: Columbia University Press, 1994. An outstanding collection of translations which emphasizes popular genres.

Mathieu, Rémi. *Anthologie des mythes et légendes de la Chine ancienne.* Paris: Gallimard, 1993.

Matsuura, Tomohisa 松浦友久, ed. *Tôshi kaishaku jiten* 唐詩解釈辞典. Tokyo: Taishûkan Shoten, 1987.

Monschein, Ylva. *Der Zauber der Fuchsfee, Entstehung und Wandel eines "Femme-fatale"--Motivs in der chinesischen Literatur.* Frankfurt: Haag and Herchen, 1988. *Heidelberger Schriften zur Ostasienkunde,* Volume 10. Treats the development of the fox-fairy and its cultural as well as literary contexts.

Murakami, Tetsumi 村上哲見. *Chûgoku bunjin ron* 中国文人論. Tokyo: Kyûko Shoin, 1994.

Nienhauser, William H., Jr., ed. *Bibliography of Selected Western Works on T'ang Dynasty Literature.* Taipei: Center for Chinese Studies, 1988.

Nieh, Shih-ch'iao 聶石樵. *Hsien Ch'in Liang-Han wen-hsüeh shih kao* 先秦兩漢文學史稿. 2v. Peking: Pei-ching Shih-fan Ta-hsüeh, 1994.

Owen, Stephen. *The End of the Chinese 'Middle Ages'; Essays in Mid-Tang Literary Culture.* Stanford: Stanford University Press, 1996.

___. *Mi-Lou, Poetry and the Labyrinth of Desire*. Cambridge: Harvard University Press, 1989. *Harvard Studies in Comparative Literature*, 39.

___. *Remembrances. The Experience of the Past in Classical Chinese Literature*. Cambridge and London: Harvard University Press, 1986.

___. *The Reading of Imagery in the Chinese Poetic Tradition*. Madison: University of Wisconsin Press, 1985.

Palumbo-Liu, David. "The Utopias of Discourse: On the Impossibility of Chinese Comparative Literature," *CLEAR* 14(1992): 165-83.

P'ei, Fei 裴斐. *Chung-kuo ku-tai wen-hsüeh shih* 中國古代文學史. 2v. Peking: Chung-yang Min-tsu Ta-hsüeh, 1996.

P'eng, Ch'ing-sheng 彭慶生 and Yen Ch'un-te 閻純德, eds. *Chung-kuo wen-hsüeh chia tz'u-tien* 辭典.

Pimpaneau, Jacques. *Histoire de la littérature chinoise*. Arles: Editions Philippe Picquier, 1989.

Plaks, Andrew H. *The Four Masterworks of the Ming Novel*. Princeton: Princeton University Press, 1987.

Schmidt-Glintzer, Helwig. *Geschichte der chinesischen Litratur. Die 3000 jährige Entwicklung der poetischen, erzählenden und philosophisch-religiösen Literatur Chinas von den Anfängen bis zur Gegenwart*. Bern, Munich, Vienna: Scherz Verlag, 1990.

Shang-hai Ku-chi, eds. *Wei-shu chi-ch'eng* 緯書集成. Shanghai: Shang-hai Ku-chi, 1995.

Shaughnessy, Edward L. "On the Authenticity of the *Bamboo Annals*," *HJAS* 46 (1986): 149-180.

Ssu-ch'uan Ta-hsüeh, Ku-chi So 四川大學古籍所, ed. *Hsien-ts'un Sung-jen pieh-chi pan-pen mu-lu* 現存宋人別集版本目錄. Chengtu: Pa Shu, 1990.

Ssu-k'u ching-chi t'i-yao so-yin 四庫經籍提要索引. 2v. National Central Library, ed. Taipei: Chung-yang T'u-shu-kuan, 1994.

Stackmann, Ulrich. *Die Geschichte der chinesischen Bibliothek Tian Yi Ge vom 16. Jahrhundert bis in die Gegenwart*. Stuttgart: Steiner, 1990. *Münchener Ostasiatische Studies*, 54. Based on his Ph. D. dissertation (Göttingen University, 1989?).

Suh, Kyung Ho. "A Study of *Shan-hai ching*: Ancient Worldviews under Transformation." Ph.D. Harvard University, 1993. Concludes that this multiple-author text emphasized a gradual weakening and final severance of what was once a close and harmonious relationship between the heavenly and terrestial realms.

T'ang, Fu-ling 唐富齡. *Ming Ch'ing wen-hsüeh shih, Ming-tai chüan* 明清文學史，明代卷. Wuhan: Wu-han Ta-hsüeh, 1991.

Teng, Shao-chi 鄧紹基, ed. *Yüan-tai wen-hsüeh shih* 元代文學史. Peking: Jen-min Wen-hsüeh, 1991.

Ts'ao, I-ping 曹亦冰, ed. *Chung-kuo tang-tai ku-chi cheng-li yen-chiu hsüeh-che ming-lu* 中國當代古籍整理研究學者名錄. Peking: Pei-ching T'u-shu-kuan, 1997. Biographical sketches of 1500 modern scholars working on ancient texts (each entry about 400 Chinese characters w/ a photo).

Ts'ao, Tao-heng 曹道衡. *Chung-ku wen-hsüeh shih lun-wen ch'i* 中古文學史論文集. Peking: Chung-hua, 1986.

___ and Shen Yü-ch'eng 沈玉成. *Nan-pei ch'ao wen-hsüeh shih* 南北朝文學史. Peking: Jen-min Wen-hsüeh, 1991.

Tsuan-hsiu Ssu-k'u ch'üan-shu tang-an 纂修四庫全書當案. 2v. Li-shih Tan-an Kuan 歷史當案 館, ed. Shanghai: Shang-hai Ku-chi, 1997.

Ueki, Hisayuki 植木久行. "Tôdai sakka shin ginen roku (3)" 唐代作家新疑年錄 (三), *Bunkei ronsô*, 25.3 (1990): 147-207 (this installment includes a study of the dates of 14 T'ang literati, including Meng Chiao and Liu Tsung-yüan); (四), 26.3 (1991): 89-135 (Li Hua, Hsiao Ying-shih and 9 others); (五), 27.3 (1992): 323-363 (another 11 literati including Po Chü-i, Po Hsing-chien, and Liu Yü-hsi).

Wang, Wei 王巍 *et al.*, eds. *Chien-an shih-wen chien-shang tz'u-tien* 建安詩文鑒賞辭典. Shenyang: Tung-pei Shih-ta, 1994.

Vandermeersch, Léon. *Études sinologiques*. Paris: Presses Universitaires de France, 1994.

Vervoorn, Aat. *The Development of the Chinese Eremitic Tradition to the End of the Han Dynasty*. Hong Kong: The Chinese University Press, 1990.

Wang, Ch'eng-chi 王成驥. *Chung-kuo wen-hsüeh-shih ming-tz'u chieh-shih* 中國文學史明詞解釋. Peking: Chung-kuo Chan-wang, 1983.

Watson, Burton. *The Columbia Book of Chinese Poetry from Early Times to the Thirteenth Century*. New York: Columbia University Press, 1984.

Wills, John E., Jr. *Mountain of Fame: Portraits in Chinese History*. Princeton: Princeton University Press, 1994.

Wixted, John Timothy. *Japanese Scholars of China, A Bibliographic Handbook*. Lewiston, N.Y.: Edwin Mellen Press, 1992.

Wu, Chih-ta 吳志達. *Ming Ch'ing wen-hsüeh shih, Ch'ing-tai chüan* 明清文學史，清代卷. Wuhan: Wu-han Ta-hsüeh, 1991.

Wu, Ju-yü 吳汝煜 and Hu K'o-hsien 胡可先. *Ch'üan T'ang shih jen-ming k'ao* 全唐詩人名考. Nanking: Chiang-su Chiao-yü, 1990.

Yang, Na 楊訥 and Li Hsiao-ming 李曉明, eds. *Wen-yüan Ko Ssu-k'u ch'üan-shu pu-i* 文淵閣四庫全書補遺. 15v. Peking: Pei-ching T'u-shu-kuan, 1997.

Yen, Shao-hsi 嚴紹璗. *Han-chi tsai Jih-pen te liu-pu yen-chiu* 漢籍在日本的流布研究. Nanking: Chiang-su Ku-chi, 1992.

Yen, Tso-chih 嚴佐之. *Chin San-pai-nien ku-chi mu-lu chü-yao* 近三百年古籍目錄舉要. Shanghai: Hua-tung Shih-fan Ta-hsüeh, 1994.

Yin, Meng-lun 殷孟倫, ed. *Han Wei Liu-ch'ao pai-san chia chi t'i tz'u-chu* 漢魏六朝百三家集題辭注. Rpt. Peking: Jen-min Wen-hsüeh, 1981 (1960).

Yoshikawa, Kôjiro 吉川幸次郎. Wixted, John Timothy, trans. *Five Hundred Years of Chinese Poetry, 1150-1650*. Princeton: Princeton University Press, 1992.

Yu, Pauline. *The Reading of Imagery in the Chinese Poetic Tradition*. Princeton: Princeton University Press, 1987.

Yüan, Hsing-yün 袁行雲. *Ch'ing-jen shih-chi hsü-lu* 清人詩集敍錄. 3v. Peking: Wen-hua Y-shu, 1994.

Yuan, Ke. *Dragons and Dynasties–An Introduction to Chinese Mythology*. Selected and translated by Echlin Kim and Zhixiong Nieh. Harmondsworth: Penguin, 1993.

Zurndorfer, Harriet T. *China Bibliography, A Research Guide to Reference Works about China Past and Present*. Leiden: E. J. Brill, 1995.

Essays

These updated bibliographies for the essays which appeared in the *Indiana Companion to Traditional Chinese Literature,* volume 1 have been expanded dramatically through the assistance fo the following colleagues: Buddhist literature–Stephen F. Teiser and Neil Schmid, Drama–W. L. Idema, Fiction–Robert E. Hegel and Y. W. Ma, Literary Criticism–Haun Saussy and Pauline Yu, Popular Literature–W. L. Idema and Victor H. Mair, Rhetoric–Karl S. Y. Kao, Taoist Literature–Thomas Hahn and Franciscus Verellen, and Women's Literature–Kang-i Sun Chang, Grace Fong, and Ellen Widmer. The compiler is extremely grateful for the contributions of these experts, but retains responsibility for any and all errors in these updates.

Buddhist Literature

App, Urs Erwin. "Facets of the Life and Teaching of Chan Master Yünmen Wenyan 864-949." Unpublished Ph. D. dissertation, Temple University, 1989.

___. *"Treatise on No-Mind,* A Chan Text from Dunhuang," *The Eastern Buddhist,* N.S. 28(1996): 70-107.

Bantly, Francisca Cho. "Buddhist Allegory in the *Journey to the West,*" *JAS* 48.3 (1989): 512-524.

Barnes, Nancy Schuster. "Buddhism," in Arvind Sharma, ed. *Women in World Religions.* Albany: State University of New York Press, 1987, pp. 105-159.

Barrett, T.H. "Religious Traditions in Chinese Civilization: Buddhism and Taoism," in Paul S. Ropp, ed., *Heritage of China.* Berkeley: University of California Press, 1990, pp. 138-163.

Berling, Judith A. "Bringing the Buddha Down to Earth: Notes on the Emergence of *Yü-lu* as a Buddhist genre," *History of Religion* 27 (1987): 56-88.

Birnbaum, Raoul. "The Manifestations of a Monastery: Shen-ying's Experiences on Mount Wu-t'ai in T'ang Context," *JAOS* 106, 99-119. Translations and comments on a number of T'ang Buddhist texts.

___. "Seeking Longevity in Chinese Buddhism: Long Life Deities and Their Symbolism," *JCR* 13-14(1985-6): 127-142.

Bokenkamp, Stephen R. "Stages of Transcendence," in *Chinese Buddhist Apocrypha.* Robert Buswell, ed. Honolulu: University of Hawaii Press, 1990.

Boucher, Daniel. "Buddhist Translation Procedures in Third-Century China: A Study of Dharmaraksa and His Translation Idiom." Unpublished Ph. D. dissertation, University of Pennsylvania, 1996.

"Buddhism in China," in *Books and Articles on Oriental Subjects Published in Japan. Tokyo: The Tôhô Gakkai. Annual Bibliography.*

Buswell, Robert E. Jr., ed. *Chinese Buddhist Apocrypha.* Honolulu: University of Hawaii Press, 1990.

___. *The Formation of Ch'an Ideology in China and Korean: The Vajrasamaadhi-Sûtra, A Buddhist Apocryphon.* Princeton: Princeton University Press, 1989.

Campany, Robert Ford. "Buddhist Revelation and Taoist Translation in Early Medieval China," *TkR* 4.1 (1993): 1-29.

____. *Strange Writing: Anomaly Accounts in Early Medieval China.* Albany: SUNY Press, 1996.

Includes discussions of Buddhist *chih-kuai.*

Chang, Hsi-k'un 張錫坤. *Fo-chiao yü tung-fang i-shu* 佛教與東方藝術. Changchun: Chi-lin Chiao-yü, 1989. A collection of previously published articles (all translated into Chinese) from Europe, the United States, Australia, China, Taiwan, and Japan on various topics regarding the arts and Buddhism. The majority of articles in Section Three ("Buddhism and Chinese Arts," pp. 385-372) concern literature.

Chang, Po-wei 張伯偉. "Lüeh lun fo-hsüeh tui wan T'ang Wu-tai shih-ko te ying-hsiang" 略論佛學對晚唐五代詩格的影響. In *T'ang-tai wen-hsüeh yen-chiu* 唐代文學研究, v. 3. Kweilin: Kuang-hsi Shih-fan Ta-hsüeh, 1992, pp. 393-412.

Chappell, David W., ed. *Buddhist and Taoist Practice in Medieval Chinese Society; Buddhist and Taoist Studies II.* Honolulu: University of Hawaii Press, 1987.

Ch'en, Yün-chi 陳允吉 and Ch'en Yin-ch'ih 陳引馳. *Fo-chiao wen-hsüeh ching-pien* 佛教文學精編. Shanghai: Shang-hai Wen-i, 1997.

____. *T'ang-yin Fo-chiao pien-ssu lu* 唐音佛教辨思錄. Shanghai: Shang-hai Ku-chi, 1988.

Chiang, Hung 江洪 *et al.,* eds. *Chung-kuo Ch'an-shih chien-shang tz'u-tien* 中國禪詩鑑賞詞典. Peking: Jen-min Ta-hsüeh, 1992.

Cheung, Samuel Hung-nin. "The Use of Verse in the Dun-huang *Bian-wen,*" *Journal of Chinese Linguistics* 8 (1980): 149-162.

Ch'ü, Chin-liang 曲金良. *Tun-huang Fo-chiao wen-hsüeh yen-chiu* 敦煌佛教文學研究. Taipei: Wen-chin, 1995.

Cleary, J. C. Zen Dawn: Early Zen Texts from Tun Huang. Boston: Shambala, 1986.

De Jong, J.W. "Buddhist Studies, 1984-1990," *Chung-yang Hsüeh-shu Yen-chiu-so chi-yao* 中央學術研究所紀要, 1991: 1-60.

Demiéville, Paul. "The Mirror of the Mind," in *Sudden and Gradual Approaches to Enlightenment in Chinese Thought,* edited by Peter N. Gregory. *Studies in East Asian Buddhism,* 5. Honolulu: University of Hawaii Press, 1987, pp. 13-40. A comparative study of earlier uses of the metaphor (made famous in poems by Shen-hui and Hui-neng) in earlier Chinese sources and non-Chinese works.

____. *Poèmes chinois d'avant la mort.* Jean-Pierre Diény, ed. Paris: L'Asiatheque, 1984. Translations of poems written on facing death; about a dozen are by T'ang poets, most of them Buddhists.

Döhrn, Gerhard A. *Kurzgedichte chinesischer Chan-Meister: Übersetzung, Kommentierung, und Interpretation.* Frankfurt: Peter Lang, 1993. *Frankfurter China-Studien,* 4. Based on Döhrn's Ph. D. dissertation (Frankfurt University, 1992).

Donner, Neal and Daniel B. Stevenson. *The Great Calming and Contemplation: A Study and Annotated Translation of the First Chapter of Chih-i's Mo-ho chih-kuan.* Kuroda Institute Classics in East Asian Buddhism Series. Honolulu: University of Hawaii Press, 1993.

Dumoulin, Heinrich. *Zen Buddhism: A History–Volume 1, India and China.* James W. Heisig and Paul Knitter, trans. New York: Macmillan, 1988. A translation of the German original (*Zen-Buddhismus* [Bern and Munich: Francke, 1985]).

Durt, Hubert, ed. *Hôbôgirin* 法寶義林, *dictionnaire encyclopédique du Bouddhisme d'après les sources chinoises et japonaises.* V. 7. *Daijô-Daishi.* Paris and Kyoto: École Française d'Extrême-Orient, 1994.

Ermakova, M.E., trans. *Zhizneopisania dostojnyh monahov (Gaoseng zhuan).* Moscow: Nauka, 1991. V. 1.

Faure, Bernard. "Bodhidharma as Textual and Religious Paradigm," *History of Religions* 25 (1986): 187-198.

____. *Le Bouddhisme Ch'an en mal d'histoire: gen d'une tradition religieuse dans la Chine des T'ang.* Paris: École Française d'Extrême-Orient, 1989.

___. *Chan Insights and Oversights, An Epistemological Critique of the Chan Tradition.* Princeton: Princeton University Press, 1993.

___. *The Rhetoric of Immediacy: A Cultural Critique of Chan/Zen Buddhism.* Princeton: Princeton University Press, 1991.

___. "Tsung-mi's Perfect Enlightenment Retreat: Ch'an Ritual during the T'ang Dynasty," *Cahiers d'Extrême-Asie* 7 (1993-1994): 115-147.

___, trans. and comm. *Le Traité de Bodhidharma.* Paris: Editions le Mail, 1986.

Forte, Antonio. "Activities in China of the Tantric Master Manicintana (Pao-ssu-wei:? -721 A.D.) from Kashmir and of his Northern Indian Collaborators," *East and West,* 34.1-3 (September 1984): 301-347. Gives biographical background for Manicintana and a discussion of the works he translated (Part I); also discusses his collaborators, Chinese and non-Chinese.

___. "Brevi note sul testo kashmito del Dharnisutra di Avalokitesvara dall'infallibile Laccio introdotto in Cina da Minicintana," in *Oreintalia Iosephi Tucci Memoriae Dicata* (Rome, 1985), v. 1, pp. 371-393.

___. "Divakara (613-688), un monaco indiano nella Cina dei T'ang," *Annali di Ca'Foscari,* XIII (Ser. Or. 5): 1974, 135-164.

___. "Hui-chih, a Brahmin Born in China (*fl.* 676-703 A.D.)," *AION, NS* XXXV (1985): 105-134.

___. "Il persiano Aluohan (616-710) nella capitale cinese Luoyang, sede del Cakravartin," in Lionello Lanciotti, ed., *Incontro di religioni in Asia tra il III e il X secolo d. C.,* Florence, 1984, pp. 169-198.

Gardner, Daniel K. "Modes of Thinking and Modes of Discourse in the Sung: Some Thoughts on the Yü-lu ("Recorded Conversations") Texts," *JAS* 50.3 (1991): 574-603.

Gjertson, Donald. *Miraculous Retribution: A Study and Translation of T'ang Ling's Ming Pao chi. Buddhist Studies Series,* v. 8. Berkeley: Center for South and Southeast Asia Studies, 1989.

___. "A Study and Translation of the *Ming-pao chi:* A T'ang Dynasty Collection of Buddhist Tales." Unpublished Ph. D. dissertation, Stanford University, 1975. Contains a completed translation of the text (pp. 199-450), a discussion of Buddhism and karmic retribution, and a survey of the Buddhist miracle-tale tradition.

Gómez, Luis O. "Purifying Gold: The Metaphor of Effort and Intuition in Buddhist Thought and Practice," in *Sudden and Gradual, Approaches to Enlightenment in Chinese Thought,* edited by Peter N. Gregory. *Studies in East Asian Buddhism,* 5. Honolulu: University of Hawaii Press, 1987, pp. 67-168. Modeled on Demiéville's "The Mirror of the Mind" (see supra) this study begins with considerations of Shen-hui and Shen-hsiu.

Granoff, Phyllis and Koichi Shinohara. *Speaking of Monks: Religious Biography in India and China.* Oakville, Ontario: Mosaic Press, 1992.

Gregory, Peter N., ed. *Sudden and Gradual, Approaches to Enlightenment in Chinese Thought. Studies in East Asian Buddhism,* 5. Honolulu: University of Hawaii Press, 1987. Studies examining the historical basis of the Northern and Southern schools of Ch'an in the eighth century.

___. "Sudden Enlightenment followed by Gradual Cultivation: Tsung-mi's Analysis of Mind," in *Sudden and Gradual Approaches to Enlightenment in Chinese Thought.* Peter N. Gregory. ed. *Studies in East Asian Buddhism,* 5. Honolulu: University of Hawaii Press, 1987, pp. 279-320.

___, ed. *Traditions of Meditation in Chinese Buddhism.* Honolulu: University of Hawaii Press, 1986. *Studies in East Asian Buddhism,* 4.

Halvor, Eifring. *A Concordance to Pai yü ching* [百喻經]. Introduction by L. N. Menshikov. Oslo: Solum Forlag, 1992.

Höke, Holger. "Das *P'u-sa Pen-yüan Ching* (Frühere Leben des Bodhisattva): Eline Sammlung buddhistischer Geschichten," *Bochumer Jahrbuch zur Ostasienforschung* 7 (1984): 113-213.

Hou, Chung-i 侯忠義. "Fo-chiao tui chih-kuai hsiao-shuo te ying-hsiang" 佛教對志怪小説的影響. In *Han Wei Liu-ch'ao hsiao-shuo-shih* 漢魏六朝小説史. Shenyang: Ch'un-feng Wen-i, 1989.

Howard, Diane. "A Survey of Some Western Works on Chinese Buddhism from the Han to the Sui Dynasty Written since 1960," *Newsletter for Research in Chinese Studies* 6.1 (March 1987): 8-15.

Hsiang, Ch'u 項楚. *Tun-huang wen-hsüeh ts'ung-k'ao* 敦煌文學叢考. Shanghai: Shang-hai Ku-chi, 1991.

___. *Tun-huang shih-ko tao-lun* 敦煌詩歌導論. Taipei: Hsin-wen-feng, 1993.

Hsüeh, Hui-ch'i 薛惠琪. *Liu-ch'ao Fo-chiao chih-kuai hsiao-shuo yen-chiu* 六朝佛教志怪小説研究. Taipei: T'ien-chin, 1995.

Hsüeh, K'o-ch'iao 薛克翹. *Fo-chiao yü Chung-kuo wen-hua* 佛教與中國文化. Peking: Chung-kuo Hua-ch'iao, 1994, pp. 7-53 on Buddhism and fiction; pp. 54-124 on Buddhism and poetry; pp. 178-200 on Buddhist dance and drama.

Huang, San and Jean Blasse, trad. *Moines et nonnes dans l'océan des péchés*. Arles: Editons Picquier, 1992.

Hubbard, James B. "Salvation in the Final Period of the Dharma: The Inexhaustible Storehouse of the *San-chieh-chiao*." Unpublished Ph. D. dissertation, University of Wisconsin, 1986.

Jacob, Paul, trans. *Poètes bouddhistes des Tang*. Paris: Gallimard, 1987.

Jan, Yün-hua 冉雲華. "A Study of *Ta-ch'eng ch'an-men yao-lu*: Its Significance and Problems," *Han-hsüeh yen-chiu* 4.2 (December 1986): 533-47.

___. *Ts'ung Yin-tu Fo-chiao tao Chung-kuo Fo-chiao* 從印度佛教到中國佛教. Taipei: Tung-ta T'u-shu Kung-ssu, 1995.

Johnson, David. "Mu-lien in *Pao-chüan*: The Performance Context and Religious Meaning of the *Yu-ming Pao-ch'uan*." In *Ritual and Scripture in Chinese Popular Religion: Five Studies*. David Johnson, ed. Berkeley: Publications of the Chinese Popular Culture Project: 3, 1995.

Jorgensen, John. "The `Imperial' Lineage of Ch'an Buddhism: The Role of Confucian Ritual and Ancestor Worship in Ch'an's Search for Legitimation in the Mid-T'ang Dynasty," *Papers on Far Eastern History* 35 (March 1987): 89-134.

Kaji, Tetsujo 加地哲定. *Chung-kuo Fo-chiao wen-hsüeh* 中國佛教文學. Liu Wei-hsing 劉韋星, trans. Peking: Chin-jih Chung-kuo, 1990. A translation of Kaji's work, published in a revised edition in Kyoto (Hôyu 朋友) in 1979.

Kamata, Shigeo 鎌田茂雄. *Chûgoku bukkyô shi* 中国仏教史. V. 3. Nanboku chô no bukkyô jô 南北朝の仏教(上). Tokyo: Tokyo Daigaku Shuppankai, 1984.

Kanaoka Shôkô 金岡照光. *Tonkô no emonogatari* 敦煌の絵物語. Tokyo: Tôhô shoten, 1981.

Kanno, Hiroshi 菅野博史. *Chûgoku Hôka shisô no kenkyû* 中国法華思想の研究. Tokyo: Shunjûsha, 1994.

___, annot. *Shin Kokuyaku Daizôkyô* 新国訳太蔵經. Tokyo: Daizô, ongoing.

Kao, Kuo-fan 高國藩. *Tun-huang min-chien wen-hsüeh* 敦煌民間文學. Taipei: Lien-ching, 1994.

Kawaguchi Hisao 川口久雄. *Etoki no sekai—Tonkô kara no kage* 絵解きの世界—敦煌からの影. Tokyo: Meiji Shoin, 1981.

___. "Tonkô shutsudo no 'zokkô gishiki' to ryakushutsu innen shohon--waga kuni setsuwa bungaku no sozai" 敦煌出土の俗講儀式と略出因縁諸本—我が国説話文学の素材. In *A Festschrift in Honour of Professor Jao Tsung-i on the Occasion of His Seventy-fifth Anniversary*. Editiorial Boards, eds. The Institute of Chinese Studies, The Chinese

University of Hong Kong, 1993, pp. 181-194.

Kieschnick, John Henry. "The Idea of the Monk in Medieval China: Asceticism, Thaumaturgy, and Scholarship in the 'Biographies of Eminent Monks.'" Unpublished Ph. D. dissertation, Stanford University, 1995.

___. *The Eminent Monk: Buddhist Ideals in Medieval Chinese Hagiography.* Honolulu: University of Hawaii, 1997.

Kim, Young-ho. *Tao-sheng's Commentary on the Lotus Sûtra: A Study and Translation.* Albany: SUNY Press, 1990.

Ko, Ch'ao-kuang 葛兆光. "'Shen-shou t'ien-shu' yü 'pu-li wen-tzu'—Fu-chiao yü Tao-chiao te yü-yen ch'uan-t'ung chi ch'i tui Chung-kuo ku-tien shih-ko te ying-hsiang" 神授天書與不立文字—佛教與道教的語言傳統及其對中國古典詩歌的影響, *Wen-hsüeh i-ch'an* 1998.1: 37-49.

Kohn, Livia. *Laughing at the Tao, Debates among Buddhist and Taoists in Medieval China.* Princeton: Princeton University Press, 1995.

Kolmas, Josef. *Buddhisticka svata pisma, Sestnact arhatu.* Prague: Prah, 1995. A slim volume which provides a good survey of the history of the Buddhist Canon.

Komazawa Daigaku *Zengaku Daijiten* Hensanjo, ed. *Zengaku daijiten* 禅学大辞典. 3v. Tokyo: Taishûkan Shoten, 1978.

Kuo, Shao-lin 郭紹林. *T'ang-tai shih-ta-fu yü Fo-chiao* 唐代士大夫與佛教. Rpt. Taipei: Wen-shih-che, 1993.

Kuo, Tsai-i 郭在貽 *et al. Tun-huang pien-wen chi chiao-i* 敦煌變文集校譯. Changsha: Yüeh-lu Shu-she, 1990.

Lai, Whalen. "The Transmission Verses of the Ch'an Patriarchs: An Analysis of the Genre's Evolution," *Han-hsüeh yen-chiu* 1.2 (December 1983): 593-623.

Lan, Chi-fu 藍吉富. *Tang-tai Chung-kuo-jen de Fo-chiao yen-chiu* 當代中國人的佛教研究. Taipei: Shang-ting Wen-hua, 1993. Includes brief biographies of 162 Buddhist scholars arranged by their home country (Taiwan, China, U.S., etc.).

Lancaster, Lewis R. "Buddhist Literature: Its Canons, Scribes, and Editors." In Wendy Doniger O'Flaherty, ed. *The Critical Study of Sacred Texts.* Berkeley: Berkeley Religious Studies Series, 1979, pp. 215-229.

Lau, Chor-Wah. "La pensée du maitre de Dhyana Shenxiu (606-706)." Unpublished Ph. D. dissertation, Paris VII, 1981.

Lievens, Bavo. *The Recorded Sayings of Ma-tsu.* Translated from the Dutch by Julian Pas. Lewiston., N.Y.: Edwin Mellen Press, 1987.

Lin, Ts'ung-ming 林聰明. *Tung-huang su-wen-hsüeh yen-chiu* 敦煌俗文學研究. Taipei: Tung-wu Ta-hsüeh, 1984.

Liu, Ming-Wood. *Madhyamika Thought in China.* Leiden: E. J. Brill, 1994.

Lo, Tsung-t'ao 羅宗濤. "Hsien-yü-ching yü Chih-yüan yin-yu-chi, Hsiang-mo pien-wen chih pi-chiao yen-chiu:" 賢愚經與祇園因由記, 降魔變文之比較研究. In *Chung-kuo ku-tien hsiao-shuo yen-chiu chuan-chi* 中國古典小說研究專輯, no. 2. Taipei: Lien-ching, 1980, pp. 109-188.

Lopez, Donald S., Jr., ed. *Religions of China in Practice.* Princeton: Princeton University Press, 1996.

Lu, Sheldon Hsiao-peng. "The Fictional Discourse of *Pien-wen*: The Relation of Chinese Fiction to Historiography," *CLEAR* 9 (1987): 49-70.

____. *From Historicity to Fictionality: The Chinese Poetics of Narrative.* Stanford: Stanford University Press, 1994.

Ma, Ta-ch'ang 馬大昌, *et al.,* ed. *Chung-kuo Fo-Tao shih-ko tsung-hui* 中國佛道詩歌總匯. Shih-chia-chuang: Chung-kuo Shu-tien, 1993.

McRae, John R. "Buddhism" in "Chinese Religions: The State of the Field (Part II)," *JAS*

54.2 (May 1995): 354-371.

___. *The Northern School and the Formation of Early Ch'an Buddhism.* Honolulu: University of Hawaii Press, 1986. *Studies in East Asian Buddhism, 3.*

___. "Shen-hui and the Teaching of Sudden Enlightenment in Early Ch'an Buddhism," in *Sudden and Gradual Approaches to Enlightenment in Chinese Thought.* Peter N. Gregory, ed. *Studies in East Asian Buddhism, 5.* Honolulu: University of Hawaii Press, 1987, pp. 227-78.

___. "Ch'an Commentaries on the *Heart Sûtra," Journal of the International Association of Buddhist Studies* 11.2 (1988): 87-115.

___. "Report: The *Platform Sûtra* in religious and cultural perspective," *The Eastern Buddhist* 22.2 (1989): 130-35.

___. "The Legend of Hui-neng and the Mandate of Heaven," *Fo Kuang Shan Report of International Conference on Ch'an Buddhism,* Kaohsiung: Fo Kuang Publisher, 1990, pp. 69-82.

___. "Encounter Dialogue and Transformation of the Spiritual Path in Chinese Ch'an." In Robert E. Buswell, Jr. and Robert M. Gimello, eds., *Path to Liberation: The Mârga and its Transformations in Buddhist Thought.* Honolulu: University of Hawaii Press, 1992, pp. 339-369.

Mair, Victor H. "Buddhist and the Rise of the Written Vernacular in East Asian: The Making of National Languages," *JAS* 53(1994): 707-750.

___. "Notes on the Maudgalyayana Legend in East Asia," *MS* 37(1986-87):83-93.

___. "Oral and Written Aspects of Chinese Sutra Lectures (*Chiang-ching-wen* [講經文])," *Han-hsüeh yen-chiu* 4.2 (December 1986), 311-34. Distinguishes two genres of Tun-huang popular literature that are commonly treated as one.

___. "The Buddhist Tradition of Prosimetric Oral Narrative in Chinese Literature," *Oral Tradition* 3.1-2 (1988): 106-121.

___ and Tsu-lin Mei. "The Sanskrit Origins of Recent Style Prosody," *HJAS* 51.2 (1991): 375-470.

___. *Painting and Performance: Chinese Picture Recitation and its Indian Genesis.* Honolulu: University of Hawaii, 1988.

___. *T'ang Transformation Texts.* Cambridge, Mass.: Harvard University, 1989.

Mair, Victor H. and Tsu-Lin Mei. "The Sanskrit Origins of Recent Style Prosody," *HJAS* 51 (1991): 375-470.

Mather, Richard B. "The Life of the Buddha and the Buddhist Life: Wang Jung's (468-493) 'Songs of Religious Joy' *(Fa-le tz'u)," JAOS* 107(1987):31-38.

___. "Wang Jung's Hymns on the Devotee's Entrance into the Pure Life," *JAOS* 106 (1986): 79-98.

Meisig, Konrad. *Das Sutra von den vier Ständen: das Aggañña-sutra im Licht seiner chinesischen Parallen.* Wiesbaden: Harrassowitz, 1988. *Freiburger Beiträge zur Indologie,* 20.

Nattier, Jan. "The *Heart Sûtra*: A Chinese Apocryphal Text?" *Journal of the International Association of Buddhist Studies* 15.2 (1992): 153-223.

Orlando, Raffaello. "Buddhism in the T'ang Hui-yao," *Annali di Ca'Foscari Serie Orientale,* 6, XIV.3 (1975): 265-276.

Orzech, Charles D. *Politics and Transcendent Wisdom: the Scripture for Humane Kings in the Creation of Chinese Buddhism.* University Park, Pa.: Pennsylvania State University Press, 1998. Interpretation of the Jen wang po je ching...

___. "Seeing Chen-yen Buddhism: Traditional Scholarship and the Vajrayâna in China," *History of Religions* 29.2 (1989): 87-114.

Ôtsuka, Hidetaka 大塚秀高. "Rekishi gogen kenkyû shozô no kyokuhon ni tsuite" 歴史語言研究所所蔵の曲本について, *Chûgoku koten shôsetsu kenkyû dôtai* 6 (1994): 51-61.

Overmyer, Daniel L. "Buddhism in the Trenches: Attitudes toward Popular Religion in Chinese Scriptures Found at Tun-huang," *HJAS* 50.1 (1990): 197-222.

Pai, Wen-hua 白化文 and Sun Hsi 孫欣. *Ku-tai hsiao-shuo yü tsung-chiao* 古代小説與宗教. Shenyang: Liao-ning Chiao-yü, 1992.

Pang, Bingjun, trans. "Fifteen Parables from *The Sutra of One Hundred Parables,*" *Renditions,* 37(1992): 69-76.

Pas, Julian F. *Visions of Sukhavati, Shan-tao's Commentary on the Kuan Wu-Liang-Shou-Fo Ching.* Albany: SUNY Press, 1995.

Peterman, Scott Dennis. "The Legend of Huihai." Unpublished Ph. D. dissertation, Stanford University, 1986. Focuses on Dazhu Huihai whose major works hold a special place in Chan history.

Powell, William F. *The Record of Tung-shan.* Honolulu: University of Hawaii Press, 1986. *Classics in East Asian Buddhism*, No. 1. Translation of the works of Tung-shan Liang-chieh (807-869), one of the few early Ch'an masters to have committed his teachings to writing.

Robert, Yves, trans. *L'Ivresse d'éveil, Faits et gests de Ji Gong, le moine fou, roman bouddhique.* Paris: Les Deux Océans, 1989.

Rummel, Stefan. *Der Mönche und Nonnen Sündenmeer; Der buddhistische Klerus in der chinesichen Roman–und Erzählliteratur des 16. und 17. Jahrhunderts mit einer vollständigne Übersetzung der Sammlung Sengni Niehai.* Bochum: Brockmeyer, 1992.

Ryûkoku Daigaku Bukkyô Bunka Kenkyûjo 竜谷大学仏教文化研究所, ed. *Kambun Daizôkyô tensekihin daimei sakuin*漢文太蔵經典籍品題名索引. Kyoto: Ryûkoku Daigaku Bukkyô Bunka Kenkyûjo, 1994.

Saso, Michael R., trans. and ed. *Buddhist studies in the People's Republic of China, 1990-1991.* Honolulu: Tendai Education Foundation, 1992.

Satô, Kazuyoshi 佐藤一好. "'Hyakuyu kyô' no dentô–Chin Shieki 'Ezu shin hyakuyu' ni tsuite" 『百喩経』の伝統--陳四益『絵図新百喩』について, *Nihon Ajia gengo bunka kenkyû* 2 (1995): 88-112

Satô, Tatsugen 佐藤龍源. *Chûgoku Bukkyô ni okeru kairitsu no kenkyû* 中国仏教における戒律 の研究. Tokyo: Mokujisha, 1986.

Schmidt, Gerhard and Thomas Thilo, eds. *Katalog chinesischer Buddhistischer Textfragmente.* Berlin: Akademischer Verlag, 1985.

Schmidt-Glintzer, Helwig. "Der Buddhismus der Tang-Zeit," *minima sinica, Zeitschrift zum chinesichen Geist,* 2(1993): 98-116.

___. "Buddhistische Erzählungen und Berichte von übernaturlichen Ereignissen (ca. 200-900 p. Chr. n.)." In Kurt Ranke and Hermann Bausinger, eds. *Enzyklopaedie des Märchens, Handwörterbuch zur historischen und vergleichenden Erzählforschung* Berlin: Walter de Gruyter, 1979, v. 2, pp. 1294-1310.

___. "Eine Ehrenrettung für den Süden, Pao-chih (418/25-514) und Fu Hsi (497-569)–Zwei Heilige aus dem unteren Yangtse-Tal." In *Religion und Philosophie in Ostasien, Festschrift für Hans Steininger.* Gert Naudorf, Karl-Heinz Pohl, and Hans-Hermann Schmidt, eds. Würzburg: Königshausen and Neumann, 1985, pp. 247-265.

Schmid, D. Neil. "*Yuanqi* 緣起: Medieval Chinese Buddhist Narratives." Unpublished Ph.D. dissertation, University of Pennsylvania, 1988.

Shahar, Meir. "Fiction and Religion in the Early History of the Chinese God Jigong." Unpublished Ph.D. dissertation, Harvard University, 1992. Analyzes, among other topics, works of fiction on Daoji (d. 1209).

Sharf, Robert H. "The 'Treasure Store Treatise' (*Pao-tsang lun*) and the Sinification of Buddhism in Eighth Century China." Unpublished Ph. D. dissertation, University of Michigan,

215

1991. Includes a translation of the *Pao-tsang lun*).

Shibata, M. and M. Shibata. *Les maîtres du Tch'an (Zen) en China*. Paris: Editions Maisonneuve & Larose, 1985. *Collection Lumiere d'Asie*, 2. Chapters 5-10 (pp. 101-212) treat various T'ang monks and schools.

Shih, Heng-ching. "The Ch'an-Pure Land Syncretism in China: With Special Reference to Yung-ming Yen-shou." Unpublished Ph. D. dissertation, 1984, University of Wisconsin.

Shina, Kôyû 椎名宏雄. *Sô Gen han Zenseki no kenkyû* 宋元版禅籍の研究. Tokyo: Daitô Shuppansha, 1993.

Shinohara, Koichi. "Two Sources of Chinese Buddhist Biographies: Stupa Inscriptions and Miracle Stories." In Phyllis Granoff and Koichi Shinohara, eds., *Monks and Magicians: Religious Biographies in India and China*. Oakville: Mosaic Press, 1988, pp. 119-228.

_____. "Daoxuan's Collection of Miracle Stories about Supernatural Monks (*Shenseng gantong lu*): An Analysis of Its Sources," *Chung-hua Buddhist Journal* 3 (1990): 319-379.

_____. "'Biographies of Eminent Monks' in a comparative perspective: The function of the holy in medieval Chinese Buddhism," *Chung-hua Buddhist Journal* 5 (1994).

Shinohara, Koichi and Gregory Schopen, eds. *From Benares to Beijing: Essays on Buddhism and Chinese Religion in Honour of Professor Jan Yun-Hua*. Oakville [Ont.]: Mosaic Press, 1991.

Sommer, Deborah, ed. *Chinese Religion, An Anthology of Sources*. New York and Oxford: Oxford University Press, 1995.

Sponberg, Alan. "The Vijnaptimatrata Buddhism of the Chinese monk K'uei-chi (A.D. 632-682)." Unpublished Ph. D. dissertation, University of British Columbia, 1979.

Stevenson, Daniel Bruce. "The T'ien-t'ai Forms of Samadhi and Late North South Dynasties, Sui and Early T'ang Buddhist Devotionalism." Unpublished Ph. D. dissertation, Columbia University, 1987. Includes discussions of Buddhist liturgical/devotional manuals and annotated translations of two of Chih-i's samadhi manuals.

Swanson, Paul Loren. "The Two Truths Controversy in China and Chih-i's Threefold Truth Concept." Unpublished Ph. D. dissertation, University of Wisconsin (Madison), 1985.

Storch, Tany G. "Chinese Buddhist Bibliography (Scriptural Catalogues)." Unpublished Ph.D. dissertation, University of Pennsylvania, 1995.

Sugimoto, Takushû 杉本卓洲, comm. *Shin kokuyaku Daizôkyô–Hon'en bu 2* 新国訳大蔵経–本縁部 2. Tokyo: Daizô Shuppan, 1994.

Sun, Ch'ang-wu 孫昌武. *Fo-chiao yü Chung-kuo wen-hsüeh* 佛教與中國文學. Shanghai: Shang-hai Jen-min, 1988.

_____. *T'ang-tai wen-hsüeh yü Fo-chiao* 唐代文學與佛教. Sian, 1985.

_____. "Chung wan T'ang te Ch'an wen-hsüeh" 中晚唐的禪文學. In *T'ang-tai wen-hsüeh yen-chiu* 唐代文學研究, vol. 3. Kueilin: Kuang-hsi Shih-fan Ta-hsüeh, 1992, pp. 268-286.

_____. *Chung-kuo wen-hsüeh chung te Wei-mo yü Kuan-yin* 中國文學中的維摩與觀因. Peking: Kao-teng Chiao-yü, 1996.

Sundararajan, Kuen-wei Lu. "Chinese Stories of Karma and Transmigration." Unpublished Ph. D. dissertation, Harvard University, 1979.

Suzuki, Tetsuo 鈴木哲雄. "Tô–Godai no Zen kankei bunron bonrai tekiyô" 唐五代の禪関係文論分類摘要," *Aichi Gakuin Daigaku Bungakubu kiyô* 23 (1994): 183-222.

Swanson, Paul Loren. *Foundations of Tien-Tai philosophy: The Flowering of the Two Truths Theory in Chinese Buddhism*. Berkeley: Asian Humanities Press, 1989.

Takasaki, Jikidô 高崎直道. "A History of East Asian Buddhist Thought: The Formation of a Sphere of Chinese-canon-based Buddhism," *Acta Asiatica* 66 (1994): 1-32.

Tanaka Kenji Hakushi shôju kinen ronshû kankôkai 田中謙二博士頌寿記念論集刊行会, ed. *Chûgoku koten gikyoku ronshû* 中国古典戯曲論集 Tokyo: Kyûko Shoin, 1991.

Teiser, Stephen F. "Ghosts and Ancestors in Medieval Chinese Religion: The *Yu-lan-p'en* Festival as Mortuary Ritual," *History of Religions,* forthcoming.

___. *The Scripture on the Ten Kings and the Making of Purgatory in Medieval Chinese Buddhism.* Honolulu: University of Hawaii Press, 1994. *Studies in East Asian Buddhism,* 9.

___. "T'ang Buddhist Encyclopedias: An Introduction to *Fa-yüan chu-lin* and *Chu-ching yao-chi,*" *TS* 3 (1985): 109-128.

___. "The Yu-lan-p'en Festival in Medieval Chinese Religion." Unpublished Ph. D. dissertation, Princeton University, 1986. Uses T'ang poetry and prose, including Tun-huang mss., to discuss this festival founded on the myth of Mu-lien.

Tsai, Kathryn Ann, trans. *Lives of the Nuns, Biographies of Chinese Buddhist Nuns from the Fourth to Sixth Centuries.* Honolulu: University of Hawaii Press, 1994. A translation of *Pi-ch'iu ni chuan* 比丘妮傳.

Ts'ao, Shih-pang 曹仕邦. *Chung-kuo Fo-chiao i-ching shih lun-chi* 中國佛教譯經史論集. Taipei: Tung-ch'u, 1990.

Tsukamoto, Zenryu. *A History of Early Chinese Buddhism: From Its Introduction to the Death of Hui-yuan.* Leon Hurvitz, trans. 2v. Tokyo and New York: Kodansha International, 1985. Translation of *Chûgoku Bukkyo tsushi.*

Tuan, Yü-ming 段玉明. *Chung-kuo ssu-miao wen-hua* 中國寺廟文化. Shanghai: Shang-hai Ch'u-pan-she, 1995.

Tun-huang pi-hua chung te fo-ching ku-shih 敦煌壁畫中的佛經故事. Tun-huang Wen-wu Yen-chiu-so 敦煌文物研究所, ed. Lanchow: Kan-su Jen-min, 1981.

Verellen, Franciscus. "Evidential Miracles in Support of Taoism," *TP* 78 (1992): 217-63. Adoption of Buddhist motifs in Taoist miracle tales.

Wagner, Robin B. "Buddhist Biography, A Study of Dao Xuan's 'Continued Lives of Eminent Monks.'" Unpublished Ph. D. dissertation, Harvard, 1995

Wang, Ch'ing-shu 王慶菽. *Tun-huang wen-hsüeh lun-wen-chi* 敦煌文學論文集. Changchun: Chi-lin Ta-hsüeh, 1987.

Wang, Ch'ung-min 王重民. *Tun-huang ku-chi hsü-lu* 敦煌古籍敍錄. Shanghai: Shang-wu, 1958.

Wang, Hung 王洪 *et al.,* eds. *Chung-kuo Ch'an-shih chien-shang tz'u-tien* 中國禪詩鑒賞辭典. Peking: Jen-min Ta-hsüeh, 1996.

Wang, Wen-yen 王文顏. *Fo-tien han-i chih yen-chiu* 佛典漢譯之研究. Taipei: T'ien-hua, 1984.

Wang, Yu-san 王有三. *Tun-huang i-shu lun-wen-chi* 敦煌遺書論文集. Taipei: Ming-wen Shu-chü, 1985.

Watson, Burton "Buddhism in the Poetry of Po Chü-i," *East Buddhist* 21.1 (Spring 1988): 1-22.

___, translator. *The Lotus Sutra.* New York: Columbia University Press, 1993.

Weinstein, Stanley. "Biographical Study of Tz'u-en, Fa-hsiang School Patriarch]," *Monumenta Nipponica,* 15(1959), 119-49.

___. *Buddhism Under the T'ang.* Cambridge: Cambridge University Press, 1987.

Willemen, Charles. "Vinaya in Two Early collections of Parables." In Charles Wei-hsün Fu and Sandra A. Wawrytko, eds. *Buddhist Behavioral Codes and the Modern World: An International Symposium.* Contributions to the Study of Religion, number 38. Westport, Conn.: Greenwood Press, 1994, pp. 95-99.

___, trans. *The Storehouse of Sundry Valuables* (Bukkyô Dendô Kyôkai English Tripitaka 10-I). Berkeley: Numata Center for Buddhist Translation and Research, 1994.

Yanagida, Seizan. "The 'Recorded Sayings' Texts of Chinese Ch'an Buddhism" John R. McRae, trans. In Whalen Lai and Lewis R. Lancaster, eds. *Early Ch'an in China and*

Tibet Berkeley: Asian Humanities Press, 1983, pp. 186-205.

Yang, Hsiung 楊雄. *Tun-huang yen-chiu wen-chi: Tun-huang lun-kao* 敦煌研究文集：敦煌論稿. Lanchow: Kan-su Wen-hua, 1995.

Yen, T'ing-liang 顏廷亮. *Tun-huang wen-hsüeh kai-shuo* 敦煌文學概説. Taipei: Hsin-wen-feng, 1995.

___. *Tun-huang wen-hsüeh* 敦煌文學. Lanchow: Kan-su Jen-min, 1989.

Yoshizu, Yoshihide 吉津宜英. *Kegon Zen no shisô shiteki kenkyû* 華嚴禪の思想史的研究. Tokyo, 1985.

Zacchetti, Stefano. "Dharmagupta's Unfinished Translation of the *Diamond-cleaver*," *TP* 82 (1996): 137-152.

Zürcher, Erik. "A New Look at the Earliest Buddhist Texts." In *From Benares to Beijing: Essays on Buddhism and Chinese Religion in Honour of Professor Jan Yün-hua.* Koichi Shinohara and Gregory Schopen, eds. Oakville, Ontario: Mosaic Press, 1991, pp. 277-304.

Drama

Birch, Cyril. *Scenes for Mandarins, The Elite Theater of the Ming.* New York: Columbia University Press, 1995.

Chang, Ching 張敬. *Ch'ing-hui hsüeh-shu lun-wen-chi* 清徽學術論文集. Taipei: Hua-cheng, 1993.

Chang, Yen-chin 張燕瑾. *Chung-kuo hsi-ch'ü shih lun-chi* 中國戲曲史論集. Peking: Yen-shan, 1996.

Chang, Yüeh-chung 張月中. *Chung-kuo ku-tai hsi-chü tz'u-tien* 中國古代戲劇辭典. Harbin: Hei-lung-chiang Jen-min, 1993. Has an excellent section of previous studies of drama (pp. 1094-1220) which includes traditional works as well as those of Western scholars (see the entry on W. L. Idema, p. 1094, for example).

Chao, Ching-shen 趙景深 and Chang Tseng-yüan 張增元, comps. *Fang-chih chu-lu Yüan Ming Ch'ing ch'ü-chia chuan-lüeh* 方志著錄元明清曲家傳略. Peking: Chung-hua, 1987.

Chao, Jung-ching 趙榮靜 and Ch'en Yün-fa 陳雲發. *Li-tai ming-yu ch'uan-ch'i* 歷代名優傳奇. Peking: Chung-kuo Wen-lien, 1989. A study of more than a dozen traditional actors of note.

Chao, Shan-lin 趙山林. *Chung-kuo hsi-ch'ü kuan-chung-hsüeh* 中國戲曲觀眾學. Shanghai: Hua-tung Shih-fan Ta-hsüeh, 1990.

___, comp. *Li-tai yung-chü shih-ko hsüan-chu* 歷代詠劇詩歌選注. Peking: Shu-mu Wen-hsien, 1988.

Ch'en, Fang 陳芳. *Ch'ing-ch'u tsa-chü yen-chi* 清初雜劇研究. Taipei: Hsüeh-hai, 1991.

___. *Wan-Ch'ing ku-tien hsi-chü te li-shih i-i* 晚清古典戲劇的歷史意義. Taipei: Hsüeh-sheng, 1988.

Ch'en, Pao-ch'eng 陳抱成. *Chung-kuo te hsi-ch'ü wen-hua* 中國的戲曲文化. Peking: Chung-kuo Hsi-chü, 1995.

Ch'en, To 陳多. *Chü-shih hsin-shuo* 劇史新説. Taipei: Hsüeh-hai, 1994.

___ and Yeh Ch'ang-hai 葉長海, comps. *Chung-kuo li-tai chü-lun hsüan-chu* 中國歷代劇論選注. Changsha: Hu-nan Wen-i, 1987.

Ch'en, Wei-yü 陳為瑀. *K'un-chü che-tzu-hsi ch'u-t'an* 昆戲折子戲初探. Chengchow: Chung-chou Ku-chi, 1991.

Cheng, Ch'uan-yin 鄭傳寅. *Ch'uan-t'ung wen-hua yü ku-tien hsi-ch'ü* 傳統文化與古典戲曲. Wuhan: Hu-pei Chiao-yü, 1990.

Chi, Kuo-p'ing 季國平. *Yüan tsa-chü fa-chan-shih* 元雜劇發展史. Taipei: Wen-chin, 1993.

Ch'i, Sen-hua 齊森華. *Ch'ü-lun t'an-sheng* 渠論探勝. Shanghai: Hua-tung Shih-fan Ta-hsüeh,

1987.

Chien-ming hsi-chü tz'u-tien 簡明戲劇詞典. Shanghai: Shang-hai Tz'u-shu, 1990.

Chin, I 金毅, ed. *Hsi-chü ch'uan-t'ung chü-mu k'ao-lüeh* 戲曲傳統劇目考略. Shanghai: Shang-hai Wen-i, 1989.

Chin, Ning-fen 金寧芬. *Nan-hsi yen-chiu pien-ch'ien* 南戲研究變遷. Tientsin: T'ien-chin Chiao-yü, 1992.

Ching, Hai 荊海. *Chung-kuo hsi-ch'ü yen-chiu shu-mu t'i-yao* 中國戲劇研究書目提要. Peking: Chung-kuo Hsi-chü, 1992. Excellent bibliography with extensive annotation; 1600 entries cover music, actors, plays, playwrights and stagecraft.

Ch'iu, K'un-liang. *Les aspects rituels du theatre chinoise.* Paris: Collège de France, Institut des Hautes Études Chinoises, 1991.

Chou, Ch'uan-chia 周傳家. *Chung-kuo ku-tai hsi-ch'ü* 中國古代戲曲. Peking: Shang-wu, 1997.

Chou, Hua-pin 周華斌. *Ching-tu ku-hsi-lou* 京都古戲樓. Peking: Hai-yang, 1993.

Chou, Miao-chung 周妙中. *Ch'ing-tai hsi-ch'ü shih* 清代戲曲史. Chengchow: Chung-chou Ku-chi, 1987.

Chou, Yü-te 周育德. *Chung-kuo hsi-ch'ü yü Chung-kuo tsung-chiao* 中國戲曲與中國宗教. Peking: Chung-kuo Hsi-chü, 1990.

Chu, Heng-fu 朱恆夫. *Mu-lien-hsi yen-chiu* 目連戲研究. Nanking: Nan-ching Ta-hsüeh, 1993.

Chu, I-hsüan 朱一玄, Hsiao Tse-yün 蕭澤雲, and Liu Chien-tai 劉建岱, comps. *Ku-tien hsiao-shuo hsi-chü shu-mu 1949-85* 古典小説戲劇書目. Changchun: Chi-lin Wen-shih, 1991.

Chu, Kun-liang. *Les aspects rituels du théâtre chinois.* Paris: Collège de France, 1991.

Ch'ü, Liu-i 曲六乙 and Li Hsiao-ping 李肖冰, comps. *Hsi-yü hsi-chü yü hsi-chü te fa-sheng* 西域戲劇與戲劇的發生. Urumchi: Hsin-chiang Jen-min, 1992.

Chuang, I-fu 莊一拂. *Ku-tien hsi-ch'ü ts'ung-mu hui-k'ao* 古典戲曲存目彙考. 3v. Shanghai: Shang-hai Ku-chi, 1982. Annotated list of nearly 2000 existing *tsa-chü* and 2600 *ch'uan-ch'i* providing information on authorship, plots, texts, etc.; several indexes.

Chung, Ssu-ch'eng 鐘嗣城 (1279–1360). Wang Kang 王綱, coll. *Chiao-ting Lu-kuei-pu san-chung* 校訂錄鬼簿三種. Chengchow: Chung-chou Ku-chi, 1991.

___ and Chia Chung-ming 賈仲明 (*ca.* 1343–*ca.* 1422). P'u Han-ming 浦漢明, annot. *Hsin-chiao Lu-kuei-pu cheng-hsü pien* 新校錄鬼簿正續編. Chengtu: Pa-Shu Shu-she, 1996.

Chung-kuo hsi-ch'ü chih 中國戲曲志. Peking: Chung-kuo ISBN Ch'u-pan-she, 199?-. A multi-volume encyclopedic survey of traditional drama in all its variety; each province is covered by a separate volume. In the meantime, each province has started to publish its own *hsi-ch'ü chih.*

Chung-kuo hsi-ch'ü nien-chien 中國戲曲年鑑. Peking: Chung-kuo Wen-lien. An annual survey of activities in the field of traditional Chinese drama; includes a bibliography of publications concerning traditional drama.

Chung-kuo hsi-ch'ü chü-chung ta-tz'u-tien 中國戲曲劇種大辭典. Shanghai: Shang-hai Tz'u-chu, 1995.

Chung-kuo hsi-ch'ü yin-yüeh chi-ch'eng 中國戲曲音樂集成. Peking: Chung-kuo ISBN, 199?-. A multi-volume survey; one or two volumes are devoted to each province.

Chung-kuo hsi-ch'ü yen-chiu shu-mu t'i-yao 中國戲曲研究書目提要. Peking: Chung-kuo Hsi-chü, 1992.

Chung-kuo ku-tien hsi-ch'ü yen-chiu tzu-liao so-yin 中國古典戲曲研究資料索引. Hong Kong: Kuang-chiao-ching, 1989.

Chung-kuo ku-tien hsi-ch'ü lun-chu chi-ch'eng 中國古典戲曲論箸集成. V. 1. Peking: Chung-kuo Hsi-chü, 1993.

Chung-kuo I-shu Yen-chiu So, Hsi-ch'ü Yen-chiu So. *Wu-t'ai mei-i wen-chi* 舞台美藝文集. Peking: Chung-kuo Hsi-chü, 1982. A collection of 60 articles (written 1949-1966) on

219

the aesthetics and role of the stage.

Chung-kuo pang-tzu hsi-chü mu ta-tz'u-tien 中國梆子戲劇目大辭點. Taiyuan: Shan-hsi Jen-min, 1991. These 4000 entries were edited and compiled by the provincial I-shu (Hsi-chü) Yen-chiu So of Honan, Hopei, Shansi, Shantung, and Shensi.

Chung-kuo Ta-pai-k'o Ch'üan-shu Tsung-pien-chi Wei-yüan-hui, Hsi-ch'ü, Ch'ü-i Pien-chi Wei-yüan-hui 中國大百科全書總編輯委員會，戲曲，曲藝編輯委員會, ed. *Chung-kuo ta pai-k'o ch'üan-shu, Hsi-ch'ü, Ch'ü-i* 中國大百科全書，戲曲，曲藝. Peking: Chung-kuo Ta-pai-k'o Ch'üan-shu, 1983.

Corniot, Christine, trans. *L'Orphelin de Zhao–Drame chinois en cinq actes et un prologue par Ji Junxiang.* Paris: Christine Corniot/Tigre Noir, 1993.

Coyaud, Maurice, trans. *Les operas des bords de l'eau (theatre Yuan).* Paris: Pour l'Analyse du Folklore, 1983.

Darrobers, Roger. *Le théatre chinois. Que sais-je.* Paris: Universitaires de France, 1995.

Dolby, William. *Eight Chinese Plays from the 13th Century to the Present.* New York: Columbia University Press, 198*?

Dolezelová-Verlingerová. "Traditional Chinese Theories of Drama and the Novel," *AO* 59 (1992): 83-91.

Feng, Guozhong. "'Tragedies' in Yuan Drama." Unpublished Ph. D. dissertation, Washington University, 1992.

Fu, Hsiao-hang 傅曉航 and Chang Hsiu-lien 張休蓮, comps. *Chung-kuo chin-tai hsi-ch'ü lun-chu tsung-mu* 中國近代戲曲論著總目. Peking: Wen-huo I-shu, 1994.

Fu, Jen-chieh 傅仁傑 and Hsing Lo-hsien 行樂賢, comps. *Ho-tung hsi-ch'ü wen-wu yen-chiu* 河東戲曲文物研究. Peking: Chung-kuo Hsi-chü, 1992.

Ho, Hsin-hui 賀新輝, ed. *Yüan-ch'ü chien-sheng tz'u-tien* 元曲鑑賞辭典. Peking: Chung-kuo Fu-nü, 1988.

Ho, Kuei-ch'u 何貴初, comp. *Yüan-ch'ü ssu-ta-chia lun-chu so-yin* 元曲四大家論著索引. Hong Kong: Yü-ching Shu-hui, 1996.

___. *Yüan-tai hsi-chü lun-chu so-yin (1912-1982)* 元代戲劇論著索引 (1912-1982). Hong Kong, 1983.

Ho, Wei 何為 and Wang Ch'in 王琴, comps. *Chien-ming hsi-ch'ü yin-yüeh tz'u-tien* 簡明戲曲音樂辭典. Peking: Chung-kuo Hsi-chü, 1990.

Hou, Hsi-san 候希三. *Pei-ching lao hsi-yüan-tzu* 北京老戲園子. Peking: Chung-kuo Cheng-chih, 1996.

Hsia, Hsieh-shih 夏寫時. *Lun Chung-kuo hsi-chü p'i-p'ing* 論中國戲劇批評. Tsinan: Ch'i-Lu, 1988.

Hsieh, Po-liang 謝柏梁. *Chung-kuo pei-chü shih-kang* 中國悲劇史綱. Shanghai: Hsüeh-lin, 1993.

Hsü, Chin-pang 許金榜. *Chung-kuo hsi-ch'ü wen-hsüeh-shih* 中國戲曲文學史. Peking: Chung-kuo Wen-hsüeh, 1994. A survey from the Ch'in to the Ch'ing dynasties.

___. *Yüan tsa-chü kai-lun* 元雜劇概論. Tsinan: Ch'i-Lu, 1986.

Hsü, Fu-ming 徐扶名. *Yüan Ming Ch'ing hsi-ch'ü t'an-so* 明元明清戲曲探索. Shanghai: Shang-hai Ku-chi, 1986.

Hsü, P'ei-chün 徐培均 and Fan Min-sheng 范民聲, comps. *Chung-kuo ku-tien ming-hsi chien-shang tz'u-tien* 中國古典名戲鑑賞辭典. Shanghai: Shang-hai Ku-chi, 1990. Treats 318 plays by 199 authors; appends a glossary of dramatic terms and a bibliography.

Hsü, Shuo-fang 徐朔方. *Wan-Ming ch'ü-chia nien-p'u* 晚明曲家年譜. 3v. Hangchow: Che-chiang Ku-chi, 1996.

Hsu, Tau Ching. *The Chinese Conception of the Theatre.* Seattle: University of Washington Press, 1985.

Hsü, Wei 徐渭 (1521–1593). Li Fu-po 李覆波 and Hsiung Ch'eng-yü 熊澄宇, annot. Peking: Chung-kuo Hsi-chü, 1989.

Hsüeh, Pao-k'un 薛寶琨. *Chung-kuo te ch'ü-i* 中國的曲藝. Peking: Jen-min Wen-hsüeh, 1987.

Hu, Chi 胡忌 and Liu Chih-chung 劉致中. *K'un-chü fa-chan-shih* 昆劇發展史. Peking: Chung-kuo Hsi-chü, 1989.

Hu, Miao-sheng 胡妙勝. *Ch'ung-man fu-hao te hsi-chü k'ung-chien: Wu-t'ai she-chi lun-wen* 充滿符號的戲劇空間：舞台設計論集. Peking: Chih-shih, 1985. 18 studies of Western and Chinese stages and their role in drama (with plates).

Hu, Shih-hou 胡世厚 and Teng Shao-chi 鄧紹基, comps. *Chung-kuo ku-tai hsi-ch'ü-chia p'ing-chuan* 中國古代戲曲家評傳. Chengchow: Chung-chou Ku-chi, 1992.

Huang, Pen 黃奔. *Yüan-tai hsi-ch'ü shih-kao* 元代戲曲史稿. Tientsin: T'ien-chin Ku-chi, 1995.

Huo, Sung-lin 霍松林 and Shen Shih-yao 申士堯, comps. *Chung-kuo ku-tai hsi-ch'ü ming-chu chien-shang tz'u-tien* 中國古代戲曲名著鑑賞辭典. Peking: Chung-kuo Kuang-po Tien-shih, 1992.

I, Sheng 藝生 ed. *Yü-chü ch'uan-t'ung chü-mu hui-shih* 豫劇傳統劇目彙釋. Chengchow: Huang-ho Wen-i, 1986.

Idema, Wilt L. "The Pilgrimage to Taishan in the Dramatic Literature of the Thirteenth and Fourteenth Centuries," *CLEAR* 19 (1997): 23-58.

Johnson, David, ed. *Ritual and Scripture in Chinese Popular Religion, Five Studies*. Berkeley: Chinese Popular Culture Project, 1995. Publications of the Chinese Popular Culture Project, 3.

___. *Ritual Opera, Operatic Ritual—'Mulien Rescues his Mother' in Chinese Popular Culture*. Berkeley: IEAS, 1989.

Jung, Shih-ch'eng 容世成. *Hsi-ch'ü jen-lei-hsüeh ch'u-t'an* 戲曲人類學初探. Taipei: Mai-t'ien, 1997.

Kanamaru, Kunizô 金丸邦三. *Chûgoku koten gikyoku jisho sôgô sakuin* 中国古典戲曲辭書總合索引. Tokyo: Tôkyô Gaikokugo Daigaku Gogaku Kyôiku Kenkyû Shingikai, 1984.

Kao, Yü 高宇. *Ku-tien hsi-ch'ü tao-yen-hsüeh lun-chi* 古典戲曲導演學論集. Peking: Chung-kuo Hsi-chü, 1985. Seven articles, based on traditional accounts, of direction, acting, singing and stagecraft in traditional plays.

Kersting, Theo. "Der Barbar auf der Bühne, eine Untersuchung zum Bild des Fremden im frühen chinesischen Theater (Yüan- und Ming-Zeit)." Ph. D. dissertation, Göttingen University, 1986.

Ku, Ling-kuang 古苓光. *Chou Te-ch'ing chi ch'i ch'ü-hsüeh yen-chiu* 周德清及其曲學研究. Taipei: Wen-shih-che, 1992.

Kuo, Ching-jui 郭精銳, *et al.*, comps. *Ch'e-wang-fu ch'ü-pen t'i-yao* 車王府曲本提要. Canton: Chung-shan Ta-hsüeh, 1989.

Kuo, Ying-te 郭英德. *Ming Ch'ing wen-jen ch'uan-ch'i yen-chiu* 明清文人傳奇研究. Peking: Pei-ching Shih-fan Ta-hsüeh, 1992.

Li, Ch'un-hsiang 李春祥. *Yüan tsa-chü lun-kao* 元雜劇論稿. Kaifeng: Ho-nan Ta-hsüeh, 1988.

___. *Yüan tsa-chü shih-kao* 元雜劇史稿. Kaifeng: Ho-nan Ta-hsüeh, 1989.

Li, Han-fei 李漢飛, ed. *Chung-kuo hsi-ch'ü chü-chung shou-ts'e* 中國戲曲劇種手冊. Peking: Chung-kuo Hsi-chü, 1987.

Li, Hsiao-ping 李肖冰, *et al.*, comps. *Chung-kuo hsi-chü ch'i-yüan* 中國戲劇起源. Shanghai: Chih-shih, 1990.

Li, Hsiu-sheng 李修生. *Yüan tsa-chü shih* 元雜劇史. Nanking: Chiang-su Ku-chi, 1996.

___, ed. *Yüan-ch'ü ta-tz'u-tien* 元曲大辭典. Nanking: Chiang-su Chiao-yü, 1995.

Liang, Shu-an 梁淑安 and Yao K'o-fu 姚柯夫. *Chung-kuo chin-tai ch'uan-ch'i tsa-chü ching-yen-lu* 中國近代傳奇雜劇經眼錄. Peking: Shu-mu Wen-hsien, 1996.

Liao, Pen 廖奔. *Chung-kuo hsi-ch'ü sheng-ch'iang yüan-liu shih* 中國戲曲聲腔源流史. Taipei: Kuan-ya Wen-hua, 1992.

___, comp. *Chung-kuo hsi-ch'ü t'u-shih* 中國戲曲圖史. Chengchow: Ho-nan Chiao-yü, 1997.

An exhaustive collection of the archaeological and visual materials concerning traditional Chinese drama from its earliest beginnings up to the end of the Ch'ing dynasty.

___. *Sung Yüan hsi-ch'ü wen-wu yü min-su* 宋元戲曲文物與民俗. Peking: Wen-hua I-shu, 1989.

Leung, Pui-chee. *Wooden-Fish Books. Critical Essays and an Annotated Catalogue Based on the Collections in the University of Hong Kong.* Hong Kong: University of Hong Kong Center of Asian Studies, 1978. The text is mostly in Chinese.

Lin, Feng-hsiung 林鋒雄. *Chung-kuo hsi-chü shih lun-kao* 鍾國戲劇史論稿. Taipei: Kuo-chia, 1995.

Lin, Ho-i 林鶴宜. *Wan-Ming hsi-ch'ü-chung chi sheng-ch'iang yen-chiu* 晚明戲曲種及聲腔研究. Taipei: Hsüeh-hai, 1994.

Liu, Ching-chih 劉靖之. *Yüan-jen Shui-hu tsa-chü yen-chiu* 元人水滸雜劇研究. Hong Kong: San-lien, 1990.

Li, Hsiu-sheng 李修生 and Li Chen-yü 李真瑜. *Ku-tai hsiao-shuo yü hsi-ch'ü* 古代小説與戲曲. Shenyang: Liao-ning Chiao-yü, 1992.

Liu, Lieh-mao 劉烈茂, *et al.*, eds. *Ch'e-wang-fu ch'ü-pen ching-hua* 車王府曲本菁華. 6v. Canton: Chung-shan Ta-hsüeh, 1993. An extensive selection of plays from the voluminous manuscript holdings of prosimetric and dramatic literature of the 18th and the 19th centuries originally kept at the princely mansion of the Mongol Princes of Ch'e in Peking; the complete collection has also been reproduced in facsimile.

Liu, Jilin. *Chinese Shadow Puppet Plays.* Peking: Morning Glory Publishers, 1988.

Liu, Nien-tzu 劉念茲. *Hsi-ch'ü wen-wu ts'ung-k'ao* 戲曲文物叢考. Peking: Chung-kuo Hsi-chü, 1986.

___. *Nan hsi hsin-cheng* 南戲新證. Peking: Chung-hua, 1986.

Liu, Wu-chi. "Some Additions to Our Knowledge of the Sung-Yüan Drama—A Bibliographic Study," *Wen-lin*, v. 2, pp. 175-203.

Liu, Yen-chün 劉彥君 and Liao Pen 廖奔. *Chung-kuo hsi-chü te ch'an-t'ui* 中國戲劇的蟬蛻. Peking: Wen-hua I-shu, 1989.

Lopez, Manual D. *Chinese Drama: An Annotated Bibliography of Commentary, Criticism and Plays in English Translation.* Metuchen, N.J.: The Scarecrow Press, 1991.

Lu, O-t'ing 陸萼庭. *Ch'ing-tai hsi-ch'ü chia ts'ung-k'ao* 清代戲曲家叢考. Peking: Hsüeh-lin, 1995.

Lu, Tan-an 陸澹安, ed. *Hsi-ch'ü tz'u-yü hui-shih* 戲曲詞語匯釋. Shanghai: Shang-hai Ku-chi, 1981. Entries are drawn primarily from *Yüan-pen* and *Tsa-chü* with some from *Chu-kung-tiao;* no material from later drama is included.

Lü, T'ien-ch'eng 呂天成 (ca. 1575–ca. 1619). Wu Shu-yin 吳書陰, coll. and annot. *Ch'ü-p'in chiao-chu* 曲品校注. Peking: Chung-hua, 1990.

Lu, Ying-k'un 路應昆. *Chung-kuo hsi-ch'ü yü she-hui chu-se* 中國戲曲與社會諸色. Changchun: Chi-lin Chiao-yü, 1992.

Luk, Yun-tong, ed. *Studies in Chinese-Western Comparative Drama.* Hong Kong: The Chinese University Press, 1990.

Mair, Victor H. *T'ang Transformation Texts—A Study of the Buddhist Contribution to the Rise of Vernacular Fiction and Drama in China.* Cambridge, Mass.: Harvard University Press, 1989.

Mackerras, Colin. *Chinese Drama—A Historical Survey.* Peking: New World Press, 1990.

___. *Chinese Theater, from Its Origin to the Present Day.* Honolulu: University of Hawaii Press, 1983.

Meng, Fan-shu 孟繁樹. *Chung-kuo pan-shih pien-hua-t'i hsi-ch'ü yen-chiu* 中國板式變化體戲曲研究. Taipei: Wen-chin, 1991.

Ni, Chung-chih 倪鍾之. *Chung-kuo ch'ü-i shih* 中國曲藝史. Shenyang: Ch'un-feng Wen-i, 1991.

Ning, Tsung-i 寧宗一, *et al. Yüan tsa-chü yen-chiu kai-shu* 元雜劇研究概述. Tientsin: T'ien-chin Chiao-yü, 1987.

P'eng Fei 彭飛.. *Chung-kuo te hsi-chü* 中國的戲劇. Peking: Chung-kuo Ch'ing-nien, 1986.

Pimpaneau, Jacques. *Promenade au Jardin des Poiriers–L'opéra chinois classique.* Paris: Musée Kwok On, 1983.

P'u, Chien 卜鍵, ed. *Yüan-ch'ü pai-k'o ta-tz'u-tien* 元曲百科大辭典. Peking: Hsüeh-yüan, 1991.

Riley, Jo. *Chinese Theatre and the Actor in Performance.* Cambridge: Cambridge University Press, 1997. Cambridge Studies in Modern Theatre.

Rudelsberger, Hans. *Altchinesiche Liebeskomödien.* Zürich: Manesse-Verlag, 1988.

Schaab-Hanke, Dorothee. "Die Entwicklung des höfischen Theaters in China zwischen dem 7. und 10. Jahrhundert." Unpublished Ph. D. dissertation, University of Hamburg, 1993.

Shang, T'ao 商韜. *Lun Yüan-tai tsa-chü* 論元代雜劇. Tsinan: Ch'i-Lu Shu-she, 1986.

Shou-chieh Yüan-ch'ü kuo-chi yen-t'ao-hui lun-wen chi 首屆元曲國際研討會論文集. 2v. Shih-chia-chuang: Ho-pei Chiao-yü, 1994.

Silber, Cathy. "From Daughter to Daughter-in-Law in the Women's Script of Southern Hunan." In Christina Gilmarten, *et al.,* eds. *Engendering China: Women, Culture and the State.* Cambridge, Mass.: Harvard University Press, 1994, pp. 47–68.

Ssu-nan no-t'ang-hsi 思南儺堂戲. Kweiyang: Kuei-chou Min-tsu, 1993.

Sun, Ch'ung-t'ao 孫崇濤 and Hsü Hung-t'u 徐宏圖. *Hsi-ch'ü yu-ling shih* 戲曲優伶史. Peking: Wen-hua I-shu, 1995.

Sun, K'ai-ti 孫楷第. *Hsi-ch'ü hsiao-shuo shu-lu chieh-t'i* 戲曲小說書錄解題. Peking: Jen-min Wen-hsüeh, 1990.

Sung Chin Yüan hsi-ch'ü wen-wu t'u-lun 宋金元戲曲文物圖論. T'aiyüan: Shan-hsi Jen-min, 1987.

Tanaka Kenji Hakushi Shôju kinen ronshû kankô kai 田中謙二博士松寿記念論集刊行会. *Chûgoku koten gikyoku ronshû* 中国古典戲曲論集. Tokyo: Kyûko, 1991.

T'an, Fan 譚帆 and Lu Wei 陸煒. *Chung-kuo ku-tien hsi-chü li-lun shih* 中國古典戲劇理論史. Peking: Chung-kuo She-hui, 1993.

T'ang, Shih 唐湜. *Min-tsu hsi-ch'ü san-lun* 民族戲曲散論. Shanghai: Shang-hai Ku-chi, 1987.

Te-chiang no-t'ang-hsi 德江儺堂戲. Kweiyang: Kuei-chou Min-tsu, 1993.

Teng, Ch'ang-feng 鄧長風. *Ming Ch'ing hsi-ch'ü-chia k'ao-lüeh* 明清戲曲家考略. Shanghai: Shang-hai Ku-chi, 1994.

Teng, Chiao-pin 鄧喬彬. *Wu Mei yen-chiu* 吳梅研究. Shanghai: Hua-tung Shih-fan Ta-hsüeh, 1990.

Ts'ai, Chung-hsiang 蔡鍾翔. *Chung-kuo ku-tien chü-lun kai-yao* 鍾國古典劇論概要. Peking: Chung-kuo Jen-min Ta-hsüeh, 1988.

Ts'ai, I 蔡毅, ed. *Chung-kuo ku-tien hsi-ch'ü hsü-pa hui-pien* 中國古典戲曲序跋彙編. 4v. Tsinan: Ch'i-Lu Shu-she, 1989.

___. *Ming Ch'ing hsi-ch'ü-chia k'ao-lüeh hsü-pien* 明清戲曲家考略續編. Shanghai: Shang-hai Ku-chi, 1997.

Ts'ai, Meng-chen 蔡孟珍. *Chin-tai ch'ü-hsüeh erh-chia yen-chiu (Wu Mei, Wang Chi-lieh)* 近代曲學二家研究（吳梅，王季烈）. Taipei: Hsüeh-sheng, 1992.

Tseng, Pai-jung 曾白融, comp. *Ching-chü chü-mu tz'u-tien* 京劇劇目辭典. Peking: Chung-kuo Hsi-chü, 1989.

Tseng, Yung-i 曾永義. *Chung-kuo ku-tien hsi-chü te jen-shih yü hsin-shang* 中國古典戲劇的認識與欣賞. Taipei: Cheng-chung, 1991. Appends a 102-page annotated bibliography of over 100 ancient and modern works related to traditional Chinese drama.

___. *Lun-shuo hsi-ch'ü* 論説戲曲. Taipei: Lien-ching, 1997.

___. *Ts'an-chün-hsi yü Yüan tsa-chü* 參軍戲與元雜劇. Taipei: Lien-ching, 1992.

Wang, An-ch'i 王安祈. *Ming-tai ch'uan-ch'i chih chü-ch'ang chi ch'i i-shu* 明代傳奇之劇場及其藝術. Taipei: Hsüeh-sheng, 1986.

___. *Ming-tai hsi-ch'ü wu-lun* 明代戲曲五論. Taipei: Ta-an, 1990.

Wang, Chih-wu 王志武, ed. *Ku-tai hsi-ch'ü shang-hsi tz'u-tien (Yüan-ch'ü chüan)* 古代戲曲賞析辭典（元曲卷）. Sian: Shan-hsi Jen-min, 1988. Literary close readings of 117 dramas by 51 Yüan authors, 5 from later periods, and 45 anonymous Yüan plays.

Wang, Chih-yung 汪志勇. *T'an su shuo hsi* 談俗説戲. Taipei: Wen-shih-che, 1991.

Wang, Ch'iu-kuei 王秋桂, ed. *Min-su ch'ü-i ts'ung-shu* 民俗曲藝叢書. Taipei: Shih Ho Cheng Min-su Wen-hua Chi-chin Hui, 1993–. A multi-volume series devoted to the documentation of the various forms of ritual drama in Mainland China; 60 volumes have been published so far.

Wang, Hsiao-chia 王曉家. *Shui-hu-hsi k'ao-lun* 水滸戲考論. Tsinan: Chi-nan, 1989.

Wang Li-ch'i 王利器. *Yüan Ming Ch'ing san-tai chin-hui hsiao-shuo hsi-ch'ü shih-liao* 元明清三代禁毀小説戲曲史料. Rev. ed. Shanghai: Shang-hai Ku-chi, 1989.

Wang, Wei-min 王衛民. *Wu Mei p'ing-chuan* 吳梅評傳. Peking: She-hui K'o-hsüeh Wen-hsien, 1995.

Wang, Yung-k'uan 王永寬. *Chung-kuo hsi-ch'ü shih pien-nien (Yüan-ming chüan)* 中國戲曲史編年（元明卷）. Chengchow: Chung-chou Ku-chi, 1996.

___. *Ch'ing-tai tsa-chü hsüan* 清代雜劇選. Chengchow: Chung-chou Ku-chi, 1991.

Wei, Fei 隗芾 and Wu Yü-hua 吳毓華, comps. *Ku-tien hsi-ch'ü mei-hsüeh tzu-liao chi* 古典戲曲美學資料集. Peking: Wen-hua I-shu, 1992.

Wei, Jen 韋人 and Wei Ming-hua 韋明鏵. *Yang-chou ch'ü-i shih-hua* 楊州曲藝史話. Peking: Chung-kuo Ch'ü-i, 1985.

___ and Wei Ming-hua 韋明鏵, comps. *Yang-chou ch'ing-ch'ü* 楊州清曲. Shanghai: Shang-hai Wen-i, 1985.

Woodbury, Lael J. "Chinese Theatre before the Emergence of Beijing Opera." Ph.D. Brigham Young University, 1994.

Wu, Hua 吳華, comp. *Chung-kuo ku-tai hsi-ch'ü hsü-pa chi* 鍾國古代戲曲序跋集. Peking: Chung-kuo Hsi-chü, 1990.

Wu, Hsin-lei 吳新雷. *Chung-kuo hsi-ch'ü shih-lun* 中國戲曲史論. Nanking: Chiang-su Chiao-yü, 1996.

Wu, T'ung-pin 吳同賓 and Chou Ya-hsün 周亞勳, comps. *Ching-chü chih-shih tz'u-tien* 京劇知識詞典. Tientsin: T'ien-chin Jen-min, 1990.

Yang, Chen-liang 楊振良. *Wang Chi-te lun-ch'ü chen-i* 王驥德論曲斟疑. Taipei: Li-jen, 1994.

Yang, Shih-hsiang 楊世祥. *Chung-kuo hsi-ch'ü chien-shih* 中國戲曲簡史. Peking: Wen-hua I-shu, 1989.

Yeh, Ch'ang-hai 葉長海. *Chung-kuo hsi-chü-hsüeh shih-kao* 中國戲劇學史稿. Shanghai: Shang-hai Wen-i, 1986; Rpt. Panchiao, Taiwan: Lo-t'o Ch'u-pan-she, 1987.

___. *Ch'ü-lü yü ch'ü-hsüeh* 曲律與曲學. Taipei: Hsüeh-hai, 1993.

Yeh, Hung-hung 葉紅紅. *Hua-chuang chi-pen chih-chih* 化妝基本知智. Hangchow: Che-chiang Wen-i, 1983. A study of traditional and modern dramatic makeup.

Yen, Shao-k'uei 顏少奎. *Ching-chü lien-p'u* 京劇臉譜. Nanking: Chiang-su Jen-min, 1987.

Yen, T'ien-yu 嚴天佑. *Yüan tsa-chü pa lun* 元雜劇八論. Taipei: Wen-shih-che, 1996.

Yü, Ch'iu-yü 余秋雨. *Chung-kuo hsi-chü wen-hua shih-shu* 中國戲劇文化史述. Changsha: Hu-nan Jen-min, 1985.

Yü, Man-ling 于曼玲, comp. *Chung-kuo ku-tien hsi-ch'ü hsiao-shuo yen-chiu so-yin* 中國古典戲曲小説研究索引. 2v. Canton: Kuang-tung Chiao-yü, 1992.

Yu, Qiuyu. "Some Observations on the Aesthetics of Primitive Chinese Theatre." Hu Dongsheng, Elizabeth Wichmann and Gregg Richardson, trans. *Asian Theatre Journal* 6.1 (1989):12-30.

Yü, Wei-min 俞為民. *Sung Yüan nan-hsi k'ao-lun* 宋元南戲考論. Taipei: T'ai-wan Shang-wu, 1994.

Yüan, Shih-shih 袁世碩. *Yüan-ch'ü pai-k'o tz'u-tien* 元曲百科辭典. Tsinan: Shan-tung Chiao-yü, 1989.

Yung, Bell. *Cantonese Opera—Performance as Creative Process*. Cambridge: Cambridge University Press, 1989.

Fiction

An, P'ing-ch'iu 安平秋 and Chang P'ei-heng 章培恆, comp. *Chung-kuo chin-shu ta-kuan* 中國禁書大觀. Shanghai: Shang-hai Wen-hua, 1990.

Aying 阿英. *Hsiao-shuo hsien-t'an ssu-chung* 小説閒彈四種. Shanghai: Shang-hai Ku-chi, 1985.

Bauer, Wolfgang, trans. *Die Laiche im Strom—Die seltsame Kriminalfälle des Meisters Bao*. Freiburg: Herder, 1992.

Berry, Margaret. *The Chinese Classical Novels. An Annotated Bibliography of Chiefly English-language Studies*. New York: Garland, 1988.

Breuer, Rüdiger. *Vorbilder für die Welt: zwei Novellen aus der Sammlung Xing shi yan (um 1632)*. Dortmund: projekt, 1997.

Campany, Rob. "Cosmogony and Self-cultivation: The Demonic and the Ethical in Two Chinese Novels," *Journal of Religious Ethics* 14(1986): 81-112.

Chang, Chi-kao 張季鷯, ed. *Ming-Ch'ing hsiao-shuo tz'u-tien* 明清小説辭典. Shih-chia-chuang: Hua-shan Wen-i 花山文藝, 1992. Over 1000 pages of this 1300-page book are devoted to glosses for words encountered in Ming-Ch'ing fiction; the remaining pages have entries on fictional works.

Chang, Chin-ch'ih 張錦池. *Chung-kuo ssu-ta ku-tien hsiao-shuo lun-kao* 中國四大古典小説論稿. Peking: Hua-i, 1993.

Chang, Chün 張俊. *Ch'ing-tai hsiao-shuo shih* 清代小説史. Hangchow: Che-chiang Ku-chi, 1997.

Chang, Ping 張兵. *Hua-pen hsiao-shuo shih-hua* 話本小説史話. Shenyang: Liao-ning Chiao-yü, 1992.

Chang, Shelley Hsueh-lun. *History and Legend—Ideas and Images in the Ming Historical Novels*. Ann Arbor: University of Michigan Press, 1990.

Chao, Hsing-ch'in 趙興勤. *Ku-tai hsiao-shuo yü lun-li* 古代小説與倫理. Shenyang: Liao-ning Chiao-yü, 1992.

Chen, Jianing, ed. *The Core of Chinese Classical Fiction*. Peking: New World Press, 1990.

Ch'en, Ch'ien-yü 陳謙豫. *Chung-kuo ku-tien hsiao-shuo li-lun p'i-p'ing shih* 中國小説理論批評史. Shanghai: Hua-tung Shih-fan Ta-hsüeh, 1989.

Ch'eng, I-chung 程毅中. *Ku hsiao-shuo chien-mu* 古小説書目. Peking: Chung-hua, 1981. Entries cite traditional bibliographies and editions; see also the review of this volume and that immediately below (*Chung-kuo wen-yen hsiao-shuo shih-kao*) by John B. Brennan in *CLEAR* 7 (1985): 179-185.

___. *Ku-tai hsiao-shuo shih-liao man-hua* 古代小説史料漫話. Shenyang: Liao-ning Chiao-yü, 1992.

___. *T'ang-tai hsiao-shuo shih-hua* 唐代小説史話. Peking: Wen-hua I-shu, 1990.

Ch'i, Yü-k'un 齊裕焜. *Ming-tai hsiao-shuo shih* 明代小説史. Hangchow: Che-chiang Ku-chi, 1997.

Ch'in, Ho-ming 秦和鳴, ed. *Min-kuo chang-hui hsiao-shuo ta-kuan* 民國章回小説大觀. Peking: Chung-kuo Wen-lien, 1995.

Ch'in, K'ang-tsung 秦亢宗, ed. *Chung-kuo hsiao-shuo tz'u-tien* 中國小説辭典. Peking: Pei-ching Chu-pan-she, 1990.

Chu, I-hsüan 朱一玄, Hsiao Tse-yün 蕭澤雲, and Liu Chien-tai 劉建岱, comp. *Ku-tien hsiao-shuo hsi-chü shu-mu 1949-85* 古典小説戲劇書目. Changchun: Chi-lin Wen-shih, 1991.

Chu, I-hsüan, comp. *Ku-tien hsiao-shuo pan-pen tzu-liao hsüan-pien* 中國小説版本資料選編. 2v. Taiyuan: Shan-hsi Jen-min, 1986.

___. *Ming Ch'ing hsiao-shuo tzu-liao hsüan-pien* 明清小説資料選編. 2v. Tsinan: Ch'i Lu, 1989.

Chung-kuo ku-tai hsiao-shuo pai-k'o ch'üan-shu 中國古代小説百科全書. Peking: Chung-kuo Ta-pai-k'o Ch'üan-shu, 1993..

Chung-kuo ku-tai pai-chia hsiao-shuo ts'ung-shu 中國古代百家小説叢書. 4v. Peking: Pei-ching T'u-shu-kuan, 1998. Photolithic reprint of *Wu-ch'ao hsiao-shuo ta-kuan* 五朝小説大觀 and three other works.

Chung-kuo ku-tai t'ung-su hsiao-shuo hsü-pen ts'ung-chu 中國古代通俗小説續本叢書. Collection 1. Nanking: Chiang-su Ku-chi, 1998. Punctuated versions of 20 works of fiction including most of the major novels.

Chung-kuo ku-tien hsiao-shuo yen-chiu 中國古典小説研究, 1– (1995–).

Chung-kuo ku-tien hsiao-shuo yung-yü tz'u-tien 中國古典小説用語辭典. Taipei: Lien-ching, 1985.

Chung-kuo li-tai hsiao-shuo tz'u-tien 中國歷代小説辭典. 4v. Wang Chi-ch'üan 王繼權, *et al.*, ed. Kunming: Yün-nan Jen-min, 1993.

Chung-kuo t'ung-su hsiao-shuo tsung-mu t'i-yao 中國通俗小説總目提要. Peking: Chung-kuo Wen-lien, 1990.

Cutter, Robert Joe. "The Death of Empress Zhen: Fiction and Historiography in Early Medieval China," *JAOS* 112(1992): 577-583.

Dars, Jacques. *En mouchant la chandelle: nouvelles chinoises des Ming.* Paris: Gallimard, 1986.

DeWoskin, Kenneth J. "On Narrative Revolutions," *CLEAR* 5 (1983): 29-45.

Dolezelová-Verlingerová. "Traditional Chinese Theories of Drama and the Novel," *AO* 59 (1992): 83-91.

Dudbridge, Glen. "A Pilgrimage in Seventeenth-century Fiction: T'ai-shan and the *Hsing-shih yin-yüan chuan,*" *TP* 77 (1991): 226-252.

Epstein, Maram. "Beauty is the Beast: The Dual Face of Woman in Four Ch'ing Novels." Unpublished Ph.D. dissertation, Princeton University, 1992.

Franz, Rainer von. "Fiktionalität in der klassischen chinesischen Literatur." In *Der Abbruch des Turmbaus, Studien zum Geist in China und im Abendland.* Wolfgang Kubin *et al.*, eds. Sankt Augustin: Institute Monumenta Serica/Nettetal: Steyler Verlag, 1995, pp. 199-210.

Fu, Hui-sheng 傅惠生. *Sung Ming chih chi te she-hui hsin-li yü hsiao-shuo* 宋明之際的社會心理與小説. Peking: Tung-fang, 1997.

Han, Hsi-to 韓錫鐸 and Wang Ch'ing-yüan 王清原, comp. *Hsiao-shuo shu-fang lu* 小説書坊錄. Shenyang: Ch'un-feng Wen-i, 1987.

Hanan, Patrick. "The Fiction of Moral Duty: The Vernacular Story in the 1640s." In Robert E. Hegel and Richard C. Hessney, eds. *Expressions of Self in Chinese Literature.* New York: Columbia University Press, 1985, pp. 189-213.

___. *The Invention of Li Yu.* Cambridge: Harvard University Press, 1988.

___, trans. *The Sea of Regret: Two Turn-of-the-Century Chinese Romantic Novels.* Honolulu: University of Hawaii Press, 1995. Translations of *Ch'in hai shih* (Stones in the Sea) by Fu Lin and *Hen-hai* (The Sea of Regret) by Wu Chien-jen.

Hegel, Robert E. "Distinguishing Levels of Audiences for Ming-Ch'ing Vernacular Literature," in David Johnson et al., eds. *Popular Culture in Late Imperial China.* Berkeley: University of California Press, 1985, pp. 112-43.

___. *Reading Illustrated Fiction in Late Imperial China*. Stanford: Stanford University Press, 1998.

___. "Traditional Chinese Fiction—The State of the Field," *JAS* 53.2 (May 1994): 394-426. The most up-to-date and most thorough bibliographic introduction to the field.

Ho, Man-tzu 何滿子. *Ku-tai hsiao-shuo i-shu man-hua* 古代小説藝術漫話. Shenyang: Liao-ning Chiao-yü, 1992.

Ho, Man-tzu 何滿子 and Li Shih-jen 李時人, eds. *Ming Ch'ing hsiao-shuo chien-shang tz'u-tien* 明清小説鑒賞辭典. Hangchow: Che-chiang Ku-chi, 1992. Lengthy essays (10-20 paragraphs) on the majors works of fiction from these two dynasties.

Hou, Chung-i 侯忠義. *Chung-kuo li-tai hsiao-shuo tz'u-tien* 中國歷代小説辭典; 先秦至唐五代; V. 1: Hsien Ch'in chih T'ang—Wu-tai. Kunming: Yün-nan Jen-min, 1986.

___.(w/ Liu Shih-lin 劉世林 for volume 2). *Chung-kuo wen-yen hsiao-shuo shih-kao* 中國文言小説史稿. 2v. Peking: Pei-ching Ta-hsüeh, 1990 and 1993. The first volume is dedicated to pre-Sung classical-language fiction; see also comments under Ch'eng I-chung above.

___, ed. *Chung-kuo wen-yen hsiao-shuo ts'an-k'ao tzu-liao* 中國文言小説參考資料. Peking: Pei-ching Ta-hsüeh, 1985. Excerpts from prefaces, bibliographies, etc. similar to Huang Ling and Han T'ung-wen's works supplemented by a more catholic selection of comparative materials from dynastic histories and related works.

___. *Han Wei Liu-ch'ao hsiao-shuo shih* 漢魏六朝小説史. Shenyang: Ch'un-feng, 1989.

___, ed. *Ming Ch'ing hsiao-shuo chi-k'an* 明清小説輯刊. 2v. Chengtu: Pa Shu Shu-she, 1993, 1996.

___. *Sui T'ang Wu-tai hsiao-shuo shih* 隋唐五代小説史. Hangchow: Che-chiang Ku-chi, 1997.

Hou, Chung-i 侯忠義 and Li Ch'in-hsüeh 李勤學. *Chung-kuo ku-tai chen-hsi pen hsiao-shuo hsü* 中國古代珍稀小説續. 20v. Peking: Ch'un-feng Wen-i, 1997.

Hsiao, Hsiang-ch'i 蕭相愷. *Shih-ch'ing hsiao-shuo shih-hua* 世情小説史話. Shenyang: Liao-ning Chiao-yü, 1992.

___. *Sung Yüan hsiao-shuo shih* 宋元小説史. Hangchow: Che-chiang Ku-chi, 1997.

Hsiao, Ping 蕭兵. *Ku-tai hsiao-shuo yü shen-hua* 古代小説與神話. Shenyang: Liao-ning Chiao-yü, 1992.

"Hsien-Ch'in chih Sui-T'ang te hsiao-shuo" 先秦至隋唐的小説, in *Chung-kuo hsiao-shuo shih* 中國小説史. Chinese Department, Peking University, compilers. Peking: Jen-min Wen-hsüeh, 1978. A standard, sixty-page account of pre-Sung fiction; bibliography, although outdated, lists modern editions.

Hsü, Chüeh-min 許覺民 *et al.*, eds. *Chung-kuo ch'ang-p'ien hsiao-shuo tz'u-tien* 中國長篇小説辭典. Lanchow: Tun-huang Wen-i, 1991.

Hsü, Shuo-fang 徐朔方. "Chung-kuo ku-tai ko-jen ch'uang-tso te ch'ang-p'ien hsiao-shuo te hsing-ch'i" 中國古代個人創作的長篇小説的興起, *Chung-wai wen-hsüeh* 25.1 (June 1996): 125-45.

Hsü, Shuo-fang 徐朔方. *Hsiao-shuo k'ao hsin-pien* 小説考信編. Shanghai: Shang-hai Ku-chi, 1997.

Hu, Pang-wei 胡邦煒 and Wu Hung 吳紅. *Chung-kuo ku-tien hsiao-shuo i-shu te ssu-k'ao* 中國古典小説藝術思考. Chungking: Hua-hsia, 1986.

Hu, Ta-lei 胡大雷 and Huang Li-piao 黃理彪. *Hung-kou yü ch'ao-yüeh hung-kou te li-ch'eng: Chung-kuo ku-tai wen-yen tuan-p'ien hsiao-shuo shih* 鴻溝與超越鴻溝的歷程：中國古代文言短篇小説史. Sian: Shan-hsi Shih-fan Ta-hsüeh, 1995.

Huang, Ch'ing-huang 黃清泉 *et al*. *Ming Ch'ing hsiao-shuo te i-shu shih-chieh* 明清小説的藝術世界. Taipei: Hung-yeh, 1995.

Huang, Lin 黃霖 and Han T'ung-wen 韓同文, ed. *Chung-kuo li-tai hsiao-shuo hsü-pa hsüan* 中

國歷代小説序跋選. 2v. Nanchang: Chiang-hsi Chiao-yü, 1982-1985.

___. *Chung-kuo li-tai hsiao-shuo lun-chu hsüan* 中國歷代小説論著選. Nanchang: Chiang-hsi Jen-min, 1990.

___. *Chung-kuo li-tai hsiao-shuo tz'u-tien* 中國歷代小説辭典. Kunming: Yün-nan Jen-min, 1993.

Huang, Lin 黃霖 and Wan Chün-pao 萬君寶. *Ku-tai hsiao-shuo p'ing-tien man-hua* 古代小説評點漫話. Shenyang: Liao-ning Chiao-yü, 1992.

Huang, Martin W. "Author(ity) and Reader in Traditional Chinese *Xiaoshuo* Commentary," *CLEAR* 16 (1994): 41-67.

___. "Dehistorization and Intertextualization: The Anxiety of Precedents in the Evolution of the Traditional Chinese Novel," *CLEAR* 12(1990), 45-68.

___. *Literati and Self-Re/Presentation, Autobiographical Sensibility in the Eighteenth-Century Chinese Novel.* Stanford: Stanford University Press, 1994.

Huang, San and Lionel Epstein, trans. *Histoire hétéroxe d'un lit brodé, Roman libre des Ming (1597 de Lü Tiancheng.* Paris: Phillipe Picquier, 1997.

Huang, Tse-hsin 黃澤新 and Sung An-na 宋安娜. *Chen-t'an hsiao-shuo hsüan* 偵探小説選. Tientsin: Pai-hua Wen-i, 1996.

Huang, Yen-po 黃嚴柏. *Kung-an hsiao-shuo shih-hua* 公案小説史話. Shenyang: Liao-ning Chiao-yü, 1992.

___. *Chung-kuo kung-an hsiao-shuo shih* 中國公案小説史. Shenyang: Liao-ning Jen-min, 1991.

Kao, Karl S. Y. "Bao and Baoying: Narrative Causality and External Motivations in Chinese Fiction," *CLEAR* 11 (1989): 115-38.

___. *Classical Chinese Tales of the Supernatural and Fantastic--Selections from the Third to the Tenth Century.* Bloomington: Indiana University Press, 1986.

Ku-pen hsiao-shuo chi-ch'eng 古本小説集成. 693v. Shanghai: Shang-hai Ku-chi, 1994. Contains over 400 traditional works of fiction.

Ku-tai hsiao-shuo chien-shang tz'u-tien pien-chi wei-yüan hui 古代小説鑑賞詞典編輯委員會. *Ku-tai hsiao-shuo chien-shang tz'u-tien* 古代小説鑑賞詞典. Peking: Hsüeh-yüan, 1989.

Kuan, Yung-li 關永禮 *et al.*, comp. *Chung-kuo ku-tien hsiao-shuo chien-shang tz'u-tien* 中國古典小説鑑賞辭典. Peking: Chung-kuo Chan-wang, 1989.

Kuriyama, Joanna Ching-yüan Wu. "Confucianism in Fiction: A Study of Hsia Ching-ch'ü's 'Yeh-sou p'u-yen.'" Unpublished Ph. D. dissertation, Harvard University, 1993.

Lanselle, Rainier. *Le cheval de jade: 4 contes chinoises du XVII° siècle.* Paris: Picquier, 1987.

Levi, Jean. *La Chine romanesque; Fictions d'Orient et d'Occident.* Paris: Seuil, 1995.

Lévy, André. "On the Question of Authorship in Chinese Traditional Fiction," *Han-hsüeh yen-chiu* 6 (1988): 249-268.

Li, Ch'en 林辰. *Chung-kuo hsiao-shuo te fa-chan yüan-liu* 中國小説的發展源流. Shenyang: Liao-ning Chiao-yü, 1992.

Li, Chih-t'ien 李稚田. *Ku-tai hsiao-shuo yü min-su* 古代小説與民俗. Shenyang: Liao-ning Chiao-yü, 1992.

Li, Chung-ch'ang 李忠昌. *Ku-tai hsiao-shuo hsü-shu man-hua* 古代小説續書漫話. Shenyang: Liao-ning Chiao-yü, 1992.

Li, Hsiu-sheng 李修生 and Li Chen-yü 李真瑜. *Ku-tai hsiao-shuo yü hsi-ch'ü* 古代小説與戲曲. Shenyang: Liao-ning Chiao-yü, 1992.

Li, Ko-fei 李格非 and Wu Chih-ta 吳志達, ed. *Wen-yen hsiao-shuo, Hsien Ch'in--Nan-pai Ch'ao chüan* 文言小説, 先秦--南北朝卷. Chengchow: Chung-chou Ku-chi, 1987.

Li, Meng-sheng 李夢生. *Chung-kuo chin-hui hsiao-shuo pai-hua* 中國禁毀小説百話. Shanghai: Shang-hai Ku-chi, 1995.

Li, Pao-chün 李保均. *Ming Ch'ing hsiao-shuo pi-chiao yen-chiu* 明清小説比較研究. Chengtu: Ssu-ch'uan Ta-hsüeh, 1996.

Li, Shih-jen 李時人. *Chung-kuo chin-hui hsiao-shuo ta-ch'üan* 中國禁毀小説大全. Hofei: Huang-shan Shu-she, 1992.

Li, Te-fang 李德芳 and Yü T'ien-ch'ih 于天池. *Ku-tai hsiao-shuo yü min-chien wen-hsüeh* 古代小説與民間文學. Shenyang: Liao-ning Chiao-yü, 1992.

Li, Wai-yee. *Enchantment and Disenchantment: Love and Illusion in Chinese Literature.* Princeton: Princeton University Press, 1993.

Lin, Ch'en 林辰. *Ku-tai hsiao-shuo yü shih-tz'u* 古代小説與詩詞. Shenyang: Liao-ning Chiao-yü, 1992.

___. *Shen-kuai hsiao-shuo shih-hua* 神怪小説史話. Shenyang: Liao-ning Chiao-yü, 1992.

Liu, I-p'ing 劉一平, ed. *Pei-ching T'u-shu-kuan tsang-chen-pen hsiao-shuo ts'ung-k'an* 北京圖書館藏珍本小説叢刊. Ti-i chi 第一輯. 15v. Peking: Shu-mu Wen-hsien, 1996.

Liu, Liang-ming 劉良明. *Chung-kuo hsiao-shuo li-lun p'i-p'ing shih* 中國小説理論批評史. Taipei: Hung-yeh, 1997.

Liu, Shih-te 劉世德 *et al.*, eds. *Chung-kuo ku-tai hsiao-shuo pai-k'o ch'üan-shu* 中國古代小説百科全書. Peking: Chung-kuo Ta Pai-ko Ch'üan-shu, 1993.

Liu, Yen-p'ing 劉燕萍. *Ai-ch'ing yü meng-huan: T'ang-ch'ao ch'uan-ch'i chung te pei-chü i-shih* 愛情與夢幻：唐朝傳奇中的悲劇意識. Hong Kong: Shang-wu Yin-shu-kuan, 1996.

Lu, Sheldon Hsiao-peng. *From Historicity to Fictionality, The Chinese Poetics of Narrative.* Stanford: Stanford University Press, 1994.

___. "The Order of Narrative Discourse: Problems of Chinese Histories and Fiction." Unpublished Ph. D. dissertation, Indiana University, 1990.

Ma, Yu-yüan 馬幼垣. *Chung-kuo hsiao-shuo shih chi-kao* 中國小説史集稿. Rpt. Taipei: Shih-pao Wen-hua, 1987.

Mair, Victor H. *T'ang Transformation Texts–A Study of the Buddhist Contribution to the Rise of Vernacular Fiction and Drama in China.* Cambridge, Mass.: Harvard University Press, 1989.

Maurey, Martin, trans. *Du Rouge au Gynécée–Roman érotique de la dynastie Ming.* Arles: Philippe Picquier, 1989.

McLaren, Anne. *The Chinese Femme Fatale, Stories from the Ming Period.* Broadway: Wild Peony, 1994. *University of Sydney, East Asian Series,* No. 8.

McMahon, Keith. "A Case for Confucian Sexuality: The Eighteenth Century Novel *Yesou Puyan,*" *Late Imperial China* 9.2(1988):32-55.

___. *Causality and Containment in Seventeenth Century Fiction.* Leiden: E. J. Brill,1988.

___. "Eroticism in Late Ming, Early Qing Fiction: The Beauteous Realm and the Sexual Battlefield," *TP* 73 (1987): 217-64.

___. *Misers, Shrews, and Polygamists: Sexuality and Male-female Relations in Eighteenth-century Chinese Fiction.* Durham, N.C.: Duke University Press, 1995.

Meng, Li-yeh 孟犁野. *Chung-kuo kung-an hsiao-shu i-shu liu-pien* 中國公案小説藝術發展史. Peking: Ching-kuan Chiao-yü, 1996.

Miao, Chuang 苗壯, ed. *Chung-kuo ku-tai hsiao-shuo jen-wu tz'u-tien* 中國古代小説人物辭典. Tsinan: Ch'i-Lu Shu-she, 1991. Lists 1700 literary characters from classical tales, vernacular stories, and novels.

___. *Ts'ai-tzu chia-jen hsiao-shuo shih-hua* 才子佳人小説史話. Shenyang: Liao-ning Chiao-yü, 1992.

Miao, Shen 苗深 *et al. Ming Ch'ing hsi-chien hsiao-shuo ts'ung-k'an* 明清稀見小説叢刊. Tsinan: Ch'i-Lu Shu-she, 1996. Contains *Shan-shui ch'ing* 山水情 and nine other works.

Ming Ch'ing hsiao-shuo hsü-pa hsüan 明清小説序跋選. Dalien Library, comp. Shenyang: Ch'un-feng Wen-i, 1983.

Ming Ch'ing hsiao-shuo yen-chiu 明清小説研究. V. 1-. 1984-.

Ming Ch'ing shan-pen hsiao-shuo ts'ung-k'an 明清善本小説叢刊. Taipei: T'ien-i, 1985-.

Ming-mo Ch'ing-ch'u hsiao-shuo 明末清初小説. Shenyang: Ch'un-feng, 1985-.

Nakajima, Osafumi 中島長文. "Chûgoku shôsetsu shiryaku kôshô (#8)" 中国小説史略考証, *Kobe Gaidai ronsô* XL.4 (1990): 23-48. Commentaries on Lu Hsün's *Chung-kuo hsiao-shuo shih-lüeh.*

Nienhauser, William H., Jr. *Chuan-chi yü hsiao-shuo: T'ang-tai wen-hsüeh lun-wen chi* 傳紀與小說：唐代文學論文集. Taipei: Southern Materials, 1995. Contain articles on early fiction and its relation with history.

___. "The Origins of Chinese Fiction," *MS* 38(1988-89): 191-219.

___. "A Reading of the Poetic Captions in an Illustrated Version of the *Sui Yang-ti yen-shih,*" *Han-hsüeh yen-chiu* 6.1(1988): 17-36.

Ning, Tsung-i 寧宗一. *Chung-kuo hsiao-shuo t'ung-lun* 中國小說通論. Hofei: An-hui Chiao-yü, 1995.

Ôtsuka, Hidetaka 大塚秀高. *Zôho Chûgoku tsûzoku shôsetsu shomoku* 增補中国通俗小説書目. Tokyo: Iwanami, 1987.

Ou-yang, Chien 歐陽健. *Chung-kuo t'ung-su hsiao-shuo tsung-mu t'i-yao* 中國通俗小説總目提要. Peking: Wen-lien, 1990.

___. *Ku-tai hsiao-shuo pan-pen man-hua* 古代小説版本漫話. Shenyang: Liao-ning Chiao-yü, 1992.

___. *Ku-tai hsiao-shuo ts'ung-shu man-hua* 古代小説禁書漫話. Shenyang: Liao-ning Chiao-yü, 1992.

___. *Ku-tai hsiao-shuo tso-chia man-hua* 古代小説作家漫話. Shenyang: Liao-ning Chiao-yü, 1992.

___. *Chung-kuo shen-kuai hsiao-shuo t'ung-shih* 中國神怪小説通史. Nanking: Chiang-su Chiao-yü, 1997.

___. *Ku hsiao-shuo yen-chiu lun* 古小説研究論. Chengtu: Pa-Shu Shu-she, 1997.

___. *Ku-tai hsiao-shuo yü li-shih* 古代小説與歷史. Shenyang: Liao-ning Chiao-yü, 1992.

___. *Wan-Ch'ing hsiao-shuo shih* 晚清小説史. Hangchow: Che-chiang Ku-chi, 1997.

Pai, Wei-kuo 白維國. *Ku-tai hsiao-shuo pai-k'o ta tz'u-tien* 古代小説百科大辭典. Peking: Hsüeh-yüan, 1992.

Pai, Wen-hua 白化文 and Sun Hsi 孫欣. *Ku-tai hsiao-shuo yü tsung-chiao* 古代小説與宗教. Shenyang: Liao-ning Chiao-yü, 1992.

Pimpaneau, Jacques, trans. *Royaumes en proie à la perdition.* Paris: Flammarion, 1985. A translation of *Tung-Chou lieh-kuo chih* 東周列國志.

Poon, Mingsun 潘銘燊, ed. *Chung-kuo ku-tien hsiao-shuo lun-wen mu, 1912-1980* 中國古典小説論文目. Hong Kong: The Chinese University Press, 1984.

Plaks, Andrew H. *The Four Masterworks of the Ming Novel, Ssu ta ch'i shu.* Princeton: Princeton University Press, 1987.

Rolston, David, ed. *How to Read the Chinese Novel.* Princeton: Princeton University Press, 1990. A study of traditional commentaries on the novel.

___. "Point of View in the Writings of Traditional Chinese Fiction Critics," *CLEAR* 15 (1993): 113-142.

___. *Traditional Chinese Fiction and Fiction Commentary.* Stanford: Stanford University Press, 1997.

Ropp, Paul S. "The Distinctive Art of Chinese Fiction," in Paul S. Ropp, ed., *Heritage of China.* Berkeley: University of California Press, 1990, pp. 309-334.

Rummel, Stefan. *Der Mönche und Nonnen Sündenmeer; Der buddhistische Klerus in der chinesischen Roman- und Erzählliteraturdes 16. und 17. Jahrhunderts, mid einer vollständigen Übersetzungder Sammlung Sengni niehai.* Bochum: Brockmeyer, 1992.

Salmon, Claudine, ed. *Literary Migrations: Traditional Chinese Fiction in Asia (17-20th Centuries).* Peking: International Culture Publishing Corporation, 1987.

Seaman, Gary. *Journey to the North—An Ethnohistorical Analysis and Annotated Translation of the*

Chinese Folk Novel Pei-yu chi. Berkeley: University of California Press, 1987.

Shih, Ch'ang-yü 石昌渝. *Chung-kuo hsiao-shuo yüan-liu lun* 中國小說源流論. Peking: San-lien Shu-tien, 1993.

Shôji, Kakuitsu 庄司格一. *Chûgoku chûsei no setsuwa–ko shôsetsu no sekai* 中国中世の説話–古小説の世界. Tokyo: Hakuteisha, 1992.

Smith, Thomas Eric. "Ritual and the Shaping of Narrative: The Legend of the Han Emperor Wu (Volumes I and II)." Ph.D. dissertation, University of Michigan, 1992.

Sun, Hsün 孫遜. *Ming Ch'ing hsiao-shuo lun-kao* 明清小說論稿. Shanghai: Shang-hai Ku-chi, 1986.

Sun, I-chen 孫一珍. *Ming-tai hsiao-shuo te i-shu liu-pien* 明代小說的藝術流變. Chengtu: Ssu-ch'uan Wen-lien, 1996.

Sun, K'ai-ti 孫楷第. *Hsi-ch'ü hsiao-shuo shu-lu chieh-t'i* 戲曲小說書錄解題. Peking: Jen-min Wen-hsüeh, 1990.

Sung, K'o-fu 宋克夫. *Sung Ming li-hsüeh yü chang-hui hsiao-shuo* 宋明理學與章回小說. Wuhan: Wu-han Ch'u-pan-she, 1995.

Takeda, Akira 竹田晃. *Chûgoku no setsuwa to koshôsetsu.* 中国の説話と古小説. Tokyo: Daizô, 1992.

Tan, Feng-liang 淡風梁. *Ku hsiao-shuo lun-kao* 古小說論稿. Hangchow: Che-chiang Ku-chi, 1989. An interesting collection of essays and reviews on both classical-language and vernacular fiction.

T'an, Cheng-pi 譚正璧 and T'an Hsün 譚尋. *Ku-pen hsi-chien hsiao-shuo hui-k'ao* 古本稀見小說匯考. Hangchow: Che-chiang Wen-i, 1984.

Ting, Hsi-ken 丁錫根, ed. *Chung-kuo li-tai hsiao-shuo hsü-pa* 中國歷代小說序跋. 3v. Peking: Men-min, 1990. The fullest collection currently available.

Ts'ai, Kuo-liang 蔡國梁. *Feng-yü hsiao-shuo shih-hua* 諷喻小說史話. Shenyang: Liao-ning Chiao-yü, 1992.

____. *Ming Ch'ing hsiao-shuo t'an-yu* 明清小說探幽. Hangchow: Che-chiang Wen-i, 1985.

Ts'ao, I-ping 曹亦冰. *Hsia-i hsiao-shuo shih-hua* 俠義小說史話. Shenyang: Liao-ning Chiao-yü, 1992.Tseng, Tsu-yin 曾祖隱 and Huang Ch'ing-ch'üan 黃清泉, comp. *Chung-kuo li-tai hsiao-shuo hsü-pa hsüan-chu* 中國歷代小說序跋選注. N.p.: Ch'ang-chiang Wen-i, 1982.

Tschanz, Dieter. "Ein illegitimes Genre: Zu den Auseinandersetzungen um die fiktionale Literatur in niederer Literatursprache im vormodernen China, 1550-1750: Ein Dokumentation." Ph. D. dissertation, University of Zurich, 1990.

Tu, Yün 杜雲, ed. *Ming Ch'ing hsiao-shuo hsü-pa hsüan* 明清小說序跋選. Nanning: Kuang-hsi Jen-min, 1983.

Tuan, Ch'i-ming 段啟明. *Chung-kuo ku-tien hsiao-shuo i-shu chien-shang tz'u-tien* 中國古典小說藝術鑒賞辭典. Peking: Pei-ching Shih-fan Ta-hsüeh, 1991. More than 300 analyses of works and selections from works from *Shan-hai ching* to late Ch'ing novels.

Tung, Nai-pin 董乃斌. *Chung-kuo ku-tien hsiao-shuo te wen-t'i tu-li* 中國古典小說的文體獨立. Peking: Chung-kuo She-hui K'o-hsüeh, 1994.

Waltner, Ann. "From Casebook to Fiction: *Kung-an* in Late Imperial China," *JAOS* 110.2 (1990): 281-89.

Wang, Ch'i-chou 王齊嗖. *Ssu ta ch'i shu yü Chung-kuo ta-ch'ung wen-hua* 四大奇書與中國大眾文化. Wuhan: Hu-pei Chiao-yü, 1991.

Wang Chih-chung 王枝忠. *Han Wei Liu-ch'ao hsiao-shuo shih* 漢魏六朝小說史. Hangchow: Che-chiang Ku-chi, 1997.

Wang, Hai-ming 王海明 and P'eng Wei-kuo 彭衛國. *Ku-tai hsiao-shuo shu-mu man-hua* 古代小說書目漫話. Shenyang: Liao-ning Chiao-yü, 1992.

Wang, Heng-chan 吳淳邦. *Chung-kuo hsiao-shuo fa-chan shih kai-lun* 中國小說發展史概論.

Shenyang: Liao-ning Chiao-yü, 1992.

Wang, Hsien-p'ei 王先霈. *Ku-tai hsiao-shuo hsü-pa man-hua* 古代小説序跋漫話. Shenyang: Liao-ning Chiao-yü, 1992.

Wang, Hsien-p'ei 王先霈 and Chou Wei-min 周偉民. *Ming-Ch'ing hsiao-shuo li-lun p'i-p'ing shih* 明清小説理論批評史. Kwangchow: Hua-ch'eng, 1988.

Wang, Hsing-ch'i 王星琦. *Chiang-shih hsiao-shuo shih-hua* 講史小説史話. Shenyang: Liao-ning Chiao-yü, 1992.

Wang, Jing. "The Poetics of Chinese Narrative: An Analysis of Andrew Plaks' *Archetype and Allegory in the Dream of the Red Chamber,*" *Comparative Literature Studies* 26.3 (1989): 252-270.

Wang, John C. Y. "Lu Xun as a Scholar of Traditional Chinese Literature." In Leo Ou-fan Lee, ed. *Lu Xun and His Legacy*. Berkeley: University of California Press, 1985, pp. 90-103.

Wen Tzu-chien 溫子建, ed. *Wu-hsia hsiao-shuo chien-shang ta-tien* 武俠小説鑑賞大典. Kweilin: Li-chiang 漓江, 1994.

Wormit, Helga, trans. and comm. *Zwei Novellen des "Ugetsu-monogatari" und ihre chinesischen Vorlagen.* Berlin: Reimer, 1985.

Wu, Ch'un-pang 王恆展. *Wan-Ch'ing feng-tz'u hsiao-shuo te feng-tz'u i-shu* 晚清諷刺小説的諷刺藝術. Shanghai: Fu-tan Ta-hsüeh, 1994.

Wu, Hua Laura. "Jin Shengtan (1608-1661): Founder of a Chinese Theory of the Novel." Unpublished Ph. D. dissertation, University of Toronto, 1993.

Wu, Jian-hsin. "Distinguishing Characteristics of Domestic Novels in the Ming and Qing Dynasties." Ph.D. University of Wisconsin, 1994.

Wu, Shih-hsün 吳士勘 and Wang Tung-ming 王東明, eds. *Sung Yüan Ming Ch'ing pai-pu hsiao-shuo yü-tz'u ta-tz'u-tien* 宋元明清百部小説語詞大辭典. Sian: Shan-hsi Jen-ming, 1992. Glosses which give meanings and sources of 30,000 words and terms.

Wu, Yuantai. *Pérégrination vers l'Est.* Nadine Perront, trans. Paris: Gallimard, 1993.

Yang, I 楊義. *Chung-kuo hsiao-shuo shih lun* 中國小説史論. Peking: Chung-kuo She-hui K'o-hsüeh, 1995.

___. *Chung-kuo ku-tien pai-hua hsiao-shuo shih lun* 中國古典白話小説史論. Taipei: Yu-shih, 1995.

Yen, Ching-ch'ang 顏景常. *Ku-tai hsiao-shuo yü fang-yen* 古代小説與方言. Shenyang: Liao-ning Chiao-yü, 1992.

Yin, Lung-yüan 尹龍元, *et al. Chung-kuo t'ung-su hsiao-shuo tsung-mu t'i-yao* 中國通俗小説總目提要. Peking: Chung-kuo Wen-hsüeh, 1994.

Yu, Anthony. *Rereading the Stone: Desire and the Making of Fiction in* Dream of the Red Chamber. Princeton: Princeton University Press, 1997.

___. "Rest, Rest, Perturbed Spirit! Ghosts in Traditional Chinese Prose Fiction," *HJAS* 47.2(December 1987): 397-434.

Yü, Chia-yü 宇稼雨. *Chung-kuo wen-yen hsiao-shuo tsung-mu t'i-yao* 中國文言小説總目提要. Tsinan: Ch'i-Lu Shu-she, 1996.

Yüan, Hang-p'ei 袁行霈 and Hou Chung-i 侯忠義, eds. *Chung-kuo wen-yen hsiao-shuo shu-mu* 中國文言小説書目. Peking: Pei-ching Ta-hsüeh, 1981. Contains a long section on *chih-kuai* and another on *ch'uan-ch'i* (T'ang); each entry cites traditional bibliographies, lists important editions, and occasionally mentions a modern study. Modern critical editions are not listed.

Zhao, Henry Y. H. *The Uneasy Narrator: Chinese Fiction from the Traditional to the Modern.* Oxford: Oxford University Press, 1995. *London Oriental Series,* 40.

Literary Criticism

Allen, Joseph R. "Macropoetic Structures: The Chinese Solution," *Comparative Literature* 45 (1993): 305-329.

Bailey, C. D. Alison. "The Mediating Eye: Mao Lun, Mao Zonggang and the Reading of the *Sanguo zhi yanyi.*" Unpublished Ph. D. dissertation, University of Toronto, 1990.

___ and Hua L. Wu. *Seventeenth-century Chinese Theories of the Novel.* Forthcoming.

Bokenkamp, Stephen R. "Chinese Metaphor Again: Reading–and Understanding–Imagery in the Chinese Poetic Tradition," *JAOS* 109 (1989): 211-221.

Bush, Susan and Christian Murck, eds. *Theories of the Arts in China.* Princeton: Princeton University Press, 1983.

Chang, Lien-ti 張連第, Wang Ju-mei 王汝梅, and Ch'eng T'ien-hu 程天祜, eds. *Chung-kuo ku-tai wen-lun chia shou-ts'e* 中國古代文論家手冊. Changchun: Chi-lin Jen-min, 1985.

Chang, Kang-i Sun and Haun Saussy, eds. *Chinese Women Poets: An Anthology of Poetry and Criticism from Early Times to 1911.* Stanford: Stanford University Press, 1998. Contains an extensive section of criticism on and by women writers.

Chang, Peng. *Modernisierung und Europäsierung der klassischen chinesischen Prosadichtung; Untersuchungen zum Überzetzungswerk von Franz Kuhn (1884-1961).* Frankfurt: Peter Lang, 1991.

Chang, Shao-k'ang 張少康 and Liu San-fu 劉三富. *Chung-kuo wen-hsüeh li-lun p'i-p'ing fa-chan shih* 中國文學理論批評發展史. V. 1. Peking: Pei-ching Ta-hsüeh, 1995.

Chang, Shao-k'ang 張少康 and Lu Yung-lin 廬永琳, eds. *Hsien-Ch'in Liang-Han wen-lun hsüan* 先秦兩漢文論選. Peking: Jen-min Wen-hsüeh, 1996.

Chang, Wen-hsün 張文勛. *Chung-kuo ku-tai wen-hsüeh li-lun lun-kao* 中國古代文學理論論稿. Shanghai: Shang-hai Ku-chi, 1984.

Ch'ang, Chen-kuo 常振國. *Li-tai shih-hua lun tso-chia* 歷代詩話作家. 2v. Changsha: Hu-nan Wen-i, 1986. Volume 1 through the end of the Sung dynasty; v. 2 is post-Sung.

Chao, Sheng-te 趙盛德, ed. *Chung-kuo ku-tai wen-hsüeh li-lun ming-chu t'an-so* 中國古代文學理論探索. Kweilin: Kuang-hsi Shih-fan Ta-hsüeh, 1980.

Chao, Tse-ch'eng 趙則誠 *et al.,* eds. *Chung-kuo ku-tai wen-hsüeh li-lun tz'u-tien* 中國古代文學理論辭典. Changchun: Chi-lin Wen-shih, 1985.

Ch'en, Liang-yüan 陳良遠. *Chung-kuo shih-hsüeh p'i-p'ing shih* 中國詩學批評史. Nanking: Chiang-hsi Ch'u-pan-she, 1996.

Ch'eng, Fu-wang 成復旺 *et al. Chung-kuo wen-hsüeh li-lun hsiao-shih* 中國文學理論小史. Peking: Pei-ching Ch'u-pan-she, 1987.

Chiang Fan 蔣凡 and Ku I-sheng 顧易生, ed. *Hsien Ch'in Liang Han wen-hsüeh p'i-p'ing shih* 先秦兩漢文學批評史. Shanghai: Shang-hai Ku-chi, 1990.

Chien, Chin-sung 簡錦松. *Ming-tai wen-hsüeh p'i-p'ing yen-chiu: Ch'eng-hua, Chia-ching chung ch'i p'ien (1465-1544)* 明代文學批評研究：成化，嘉靖中期篇 (1465-1544). Taipei: T'ai-wan Hsüeh-sheng, 1989.

Ch'ien Chung-shu 錢鍾書. *Kuan chui pien* 管錐編. 4v. Peking: Chung-hua, 1979.

Chiu, Kuei-fen. "Writing and Rewriting in the Chinese Long Vernacular *Hsiao-shuo,*" *TkR* 21(1990): 49-61.

Chou, Hsün-ch'u 周勛初. *Chung-kuo wen-hsüeh p'i-p'ing hsiao-shih* 中國文學批評小史. Shenyang: Liao-ning Ku-chi, 1996. An interesting history by a major scholar.

Chu, Yiu Wei. "Reading Traditional Chinese Poetics from the West: Three Exemplary Positions," *THHP, NS* 23.3 (1993): 287-339.

Chung-kuo ku-tai wen-i li-lun tzu-liao mu-lu hui-pien 中國古代文藝理論學資料目錄彙編. Chinese Department, Shantung University. Tsinan: Ch'i Lu, 1983.

Chung-kuo li-tai shih-hua hsüan 中國歷代詩話選. Study Committee on the Theory of the Arts of the Chinese Social Science Research Council. 2v. Changsha: Yüeh -lu, 1985. Through the Yüan dynasty.

Chung-kuo wen-hsüeh p'i-p'ing shih 中國文學批評史. Chinese Department, Fu-tan University. 3v. Shanghai: Shang-hai Ku-chi, 1964, 1981, 1985.

Chung-kuo wen-hsüeh p'i-p'ing tzu-liao hui-pien 中國文學批評資料彙編. 11v. Taipei: Ch'eng-wen, 1978-9. A major source for critical materials drawn from prefaces, letters, colophons as well as formal literary critical works; materials are arranged in volumes devoted to particular periods.

Deeney, John J., ed. *A Prolegomena to an Encyclopedic Dictionary of Classical Chinese Literary Terms in English, TkR* 24.3-4 (1994).

Dolezelová-Velingerová, Milena, ed. *Poetics, East and West.* Toronto: Toronto Semiotic Circle, University of Toronto, 1989.

___. "Traditional Chinese Theories of Drama and the Novel," *AO* 59 (1992): 83-91.

Durand, Pierre-Henri. *Lettrés et pouvoirs—Un procès littéraire dans la Chine imperiale.* Paris: École des Hautes Études en Sciences Sociales, 1992.

Eggert, Marion. *Nur wir Dichter; Yuan Mei: Eine Dichtungstheorie des 18. Jahrhunderts zwischen Selbstbehauptung und Konvention.* Bochum: Brockmeyer, 1989.

Eoyang, Eugene. *The Transparent Eye: Reflections on Translation, Chinese Literature, and Comparative Poetics.* Honolulu: University of Hawaii Press, 1993.

Fan, Te-san 樊德三. *Chung-kuo ku-tai wen-hsüeh yüan-li* 中國古代文學原理. Peking: Kuang-ming Jih-pao, 1991.

Gottheiner, Klaus. *Licht und Dunkel in der Dichtung der T'ang-Zeit; Eine Untersuchung zur Bildlichkeit chinesischer Lyrik.* Frankfurt: Hagg & Herchen, 1990. *Heidelberger Schriften zur Ostasienkunde,* 13.

Hanan, Patrick. *The Invention of Li Yu.* Cambridge: Harvard University Press, 1988.

Hsia, Ch'uan-ts'ai 夏傳才. *Chung-kuo ku-tai wen-hsüeh li-lun ming-p'ien chin-i* 中國古代文學理論名篇今譯. Tientsin: Nan-k'ai Ta-hsüeh, 1985.

Hsiao, Hua-jung 蕭華蓉. *Chung-kuo shih-hsüeh ssu-hsiang shih* 中國詩學思想史. Shanghai: Hua-tung Shih-fan Ta-hsüeh, 1996.

Hsu, Hsiao-ching. "'Talks on Poetry' (*Shih hua*) as a form of Sung Literary Criticism." Unpublished Ph. D. dissertation, University of Wisconsin, 1991.

Hsü Chung-yü 徐中玉 and Wang Yün-hsi 王運熙 *et al.,* eds. *Ku-tai wen-hsüeh li-lun yen-chiu* 古代文學理論研究. Shanghai: Shang-hai Ku-chi, 1997.

Hsu, Pi-ching. "Celebrating the Emotional Self: Feng Meng-lung and Late Ming Ethics and Aesthetics." Unpublished Ph. D. dissertation, University of Minnesota, 1994.

Huang, Lin 黃霖 and Han T'ung-wen 韓同文, eds. *Chung-kuo li-tai hsiao-shuo hsü-pa hsüan* 中國歷代小説序跋選. 2v. Nanchang: Chiang-hsi Jen-min, 1982-1985.

Huang, Martin W. "Author(ity) and Reader in Traditional Chinese *Xiaoshuo* Commentary," *CLEAR* 16 (1994): 69-92.

Huang, Pao-chen 黃保真, Ts'ai Chung-hsiang 蔡鐘翔, and Ch'eng Fu-wang 成復旺. *Chung-kuo wen-hsüeh li-lun shih* 中國文學理論史. 5v. Peking: Pei-ching Ch'u-pan-she, 1987. Reprinted in Taipei by Hung-yeh Wen-hua 洪葉文化, 1994.

Huters, Theodore. "From Writing to Literature: The Development of Late Qing Theories of Prose," *HJAS* 47.1 (June 1987): 51-96.

Idema, W. L. "Some Recent Studies of Chinese Poetics, A Review Article," *TP* 75(1989): 277-88. Review of James J. Y. Liu's *Language, Paradox, Poetics* (Princeton: Princeton University Press, 1988), François Jullien, *La valeur allusive* (Paris: École Française d'Extrême-Orient, 1985), Günther Debon, *Chinesische Dichtung* (Leiden: E. J. Brill, 1989), and Debon's *Mein Weg verliert sich fern in weissen Wolken* (Heidelberg: Lambert Schneider, 1988).

Jullien, François. *Le Détour et l'accès: stratégies du sens en Chine.* Paris: Grasset, 1995.

___. *Procès ou création: une introduction a la pensée des lettrés chinois: essai de problématique interculturelle.* Paris: Editions du Seuil, 1989.

___. *La Propension des choses: Pour une histoire de l'efficacité en Chine.* Paris: Editions du Seuil, 1992; translated by Janet Lloyd as *The Propensity of Things: Toward a History of Efficacity in China.* New York: Zone Books, 1995.

___. *La valeur allusive–des catégories originales de l'interprétation poétique dans la tradition chinoise (Contribution à une réflexion sur l'altérité interculturelle).* Paris: École Française d'Extrême-Orient, 1985.

Kao, Karl. "Recent Studies of Chinese Rhetoric," *CLEAR* 15 (1993): 143-154.

Klöpsch, Volker. *Die Jadesplitter der Dichter, Die Welt der Dichtung in der Sicht eines Klassikers der chinesichen Literaturkritik.* Bochum: Brockmeyer, 1983. Introduction to and annotated translation of selections from the Southern Sung work, *Shih-jen yü-hsieh* 詩人玉屑.

___. *Die seidene Faden: Gedichte der Tang.* Frankfurt am Main: Insel, 1991. A complete translation of the *T'ang-shih san-pai-shou.**

Kôzen, Hiroshi 興膳宏. *Chûgoku no bungaku riron* 中国の文学理論. Tokyo: Chikuma Shobô, 1988.

Ku, I-sheng 顧易生 and Chiang Fan 蔣凡. *Hsien Ch'in liang Han wen-hsüeh p'i-p'ing shih* 先秦兩漢文學批評史. Shanghai: Shang-hai Ku-chi, 1990.

Ku-tai wen-hsüeh li-lun yen-chiu 古代文學理論研究. 1979-. A journal which appears irregularly.

Kuo, Shao-yü 郭紹虞, ed. *Ch'ing shih-hua hsü-pien* 清詩話續編. 4v. Shanghai: Shang-hai Ku-chi, 1983.

Li, Tse-hou 李則厚 and Liu Kang-chi 劉綱記. *Chung-kuo mei-hsüeh shih* 中國美學史. 2v. Peking: Jen-min, 1984 and 1987.

Li-tai shih-hua tz'u-hua hsüan 歷代詩話詞話選. Chinese Department, Wu-han University, comp. Wuhan: Wu-han Ta-hsüeh, 1994.

Liang, Shi. "The Leopardskin of Dao and the Icon of Truth: Natural Birth versus Mimesis in Chinese and Western Literary Theories," *Comparative Literature Studies,*31(1994): 148-164.

Liu, James J.Y. *Language–Paradox–Poetics: A Chinese Perspective.* Richard John Lynn, ed. Princeton: Princeton University Press, 1988.

Liu, Liang-ming 劉良明. *Chung-kuo hsiao-shuo li-lun p'i-p'ing shih* 中國小説理論批評史. Taipei: Hung-yeh, 1997.

Liu, Wei-lin 劉偉林. *Chung-kuo wen-i hsin-li hsüeh-shih* 中國文藝心理學史. Peking: San-huan 三環, 1989.

Lu, K'an-ju 陸侃如. *Lu K'an-ju ku-tien wen-hsüeh lun-wen chi* 陸侃如古典文學論文集. Shanghai: Shang-hai Ku-chi, 1987.

Lu, Sheldon Hsiao-peng. *From Historicity to Fictionality, The Chinese Poetics of Narrative.* Stanford: Stanford University Press, 1994.

Lu, Xing. "Recovering the Past: Identification of Chinese Senses of *Pien* [辯] and A Comparison of *Pien* to Greek Senses of Rhetoric in the Fifth and Third Centuries BCE." Unpublished Ph. D. dissertation, University of Oregon, 1991.

Min, Tse 敏澤. *Chung-kuo wen-hsüeh li-lun p'i-p'ing shih* 中國文學理論批評史. Tsilin: Chi-lin Chiao-yü, 1993.

Murath, Clemens. "Literaturtheorie und Rhetorik in der Weijin Nanbeichao Zeit (220-589 A.D.)." M.A. thesis. Freie Universität, Berlin, 1990.

Owen, Stephen. *Mi-Lou, Poetry and the Labyrinth of Desire.* Cambridge, Mass.: Harvard University Press, 1989.

___. "Ruined Estates: Literary History and the Poetry of Eden," *CLEAR* 10(1988): 21-42.

___. *Readings in Chinese Literary Thought.* Cambridge, Mass.: Council on East Asian Studies, Harvard University, 1992.

___. *Remembrances: The Experience of the Past in Classical Chinese Literature.* Cambridge: Harvard University Press, 1986.

___. *Traditional Chinese Poetry and Poetics: Omen of the World.* Madison: University of Wisconsin Press, 1985.

Plaks, Andrew H. "Where the Lines Meet: Parallelism in Chinese and Western Literatures," *CLEAR* 10(1988): 21-42.

Rolston, David. *Traditional Chinese Fiction and Fiction Commentary.* Stanford: Stanford University Press, 1996.

Saussy, Haun. *The Problem of a Chinese Aesthetic.* Stanford: Stanford University Press, 1993.

Tang, Yanfang. "Mind and Manifestation: The Intuitive Art (*Miaowu*) of Traditional Chinese Poetry and Poetics." Unpublished Ph. D. dissertation, Ohio State University, 1993.

Tschanz, Dieter. "Ein illegitimes Genre: Zu den Auseinandersetzungen um die fiktionale Literatur in niederer Literatursprache im vormodernen China, 1550-1750: Ein Dokumentation." Ph. D. dissertation, University of Zurich, 1990.

Wang, Chin-ling 王金淩. *Chung-kuo wen-hsüeh li-lun shih* 中國文學理論史. V. 1. *Shang-ku p'ien* 上古篇. Taipei: Hua-cheng 花城, 1987.

Wang, Hsien-p'ei 王先霈 and Chou Wei-min 周偉民. *Ming-Ch'ing hsiao-shuo li-lun p'i-p'ing shih* 明清小說理論批評史. Kwangchow: Hua-ch'eng, 1988.

Wang, Jing. "The Poetics of Chinese Narrative: An Analysis of Andrew Plaks' *Archetype and Allegory in the Dream of the Red Chamber*," *Comparative Literature Studies* 26.3 (1989): 252-270.

Wang, John C. Y., ed. *Chinese Literary Criticism of the Ch'ing Period.* Hong Kong: Hong Kong University Press, 1993.

Wang, Meng-ou 王夢鷗. *Ku-tien wen-hsüeh lun t'an-so* 古代文學論探索. Taipei: Cheng-chung, 1984.

Wang, Peter B. "Classicism in Aristotle's 'Poetics' and Liu Xie's 'Wenxin diaolong." Unpublished Ph. D. dissertation, University of Washington, 1990.

Wang, Ta-chin 王達津. *Ku-tai wen-hsüeh li-lun yen-chiu lun-wen chi* 古代文學理論研究論文集. Tientsin: Nan-k'ai Ta-hsüeh, 1985.

Wang, Yün-hsi 王運熙 and Ku I-sheng 顧易生. *Chung-kuo wen-hsüeh p'i-p'ing shih* 中國文學批評史. 3v. Shanghai: Shang-hai Ku-chi, 1995.

Wang, Yün-hsi 王運熙 and Yang Ming 楊明. *Wei Chin Nan-pei ch'ao wen-hsüeh p'i-p'ing shih* 魏晉南北朝文學批評史. Shanghai: Shang-hai Ku-chi, 1989. *Chung-kuo wen-hsüeh p'i-p'ing t'ung-shih*, 2.

Wixted, John Timothy. "Some Chin Dynasty Issues in Literary Criticism," *TkR* 21.1 (Autumn 1990): 63-73.

Wong, Siu-kit, ed. and trans. *Early Chinese Literary Criticism.* Hong Kong: Joint Publishing Co., 1983.

Wu, Chuan-cheng. "A Comparative Study of the Poetic Sequence: Tu Fu and W. B. Yeats." Unpublished Ph. D. dissertation, University of Washington, 1989.

Wu, Hua Laura. "Jin Shengtan (1608-1661); Founder of a Chinese Theory of the Novel." Unpublished Ph. D. dissertation, University of Toronto, 1993.

Yang, Sung-nien 楊松年. *Chung-kuo ku-tien wen-hsüeh p'i-p'ing lun-chi* 中國古典文學批評論集. Hong Kong: San-lien, 1987.

Ye, Yang. "Beyond the Cast Image: Poetic Endings in Chinese Tradition." Unpublished Ph. D. dissertation, Harvard University, 1989.

Yip, Wai-lim. *Diffusion of Distances, Dialogues between Chinese and Western Poetics.* Berkeley: University of California Press, 1993.

Yu, Pauline. "The Chinese Poetic Canon and Its Boundaries," in John Hay, ed. *Boundaries in China.* London: Reaktion Books, 1994,pp. 105-23.

___. "Poems in Their Place: Collections and Canons in Early Chinese Literature," *HJAS* 50(1990): 163-96.

___. *The Reading of Imagery in the Chinese Poetic Tradition.* Princeton: Princeton University Press, 1987.

Yüan, Chen-yü 袁震宇 and Liu Ming-chin 劉明今. *Ming-tai wen-hsüeh p'i-p'ing shih* 明代文學批評史. Wang Yün-hsi 王運熙 and Ku I-sheng 顧易生, eds. Shanghai: Shang-hai Ku-chi, 1991. *Chung-kuo wen-hsüeh p'i-p'ing t'ung-shih,* 5.

Yü, Ying-ch'un 于迎春. *Han-tai wen-jen yü wen-hsüeh kuan-nien te yen-chin* 漢代文人與文學觀念的演進. Peking: Tung-fang, 1997.

Zhang, Longxi 張隆溪. *The Tao and the Logos, Literary Hermeneutics East and West.* Durham: Duke University Press, 1993.

van Zoeren, Steven. *Poetry and Personality–Reading, Exegesis, and Hermeneutics in Traditional China.* Stanford: Stanford University Press, 1991.

Poetry

Bokenkamp, Stephen R. "Chinese Metaphor Again: Reading–and Understanding–Imagery in the Chinese Poetic Tradition," *JAOS* 109(1989): 211-221.

Chai, Jen-nien. "Time in pre-T'ang Poetry." Unpublished Ph. D. dissertation, University of Wisconsin, 1992.

Chang, Kang-i Sun. *Six Dynasties Poetry.* Princeton: Princeton University Press, 1986.

Chang, Sung-ju 張松如, ed. *Hsien Ch'in shih-ko shih-lun* 先秦詩歌史論. Changchun: Chi-lin Chiao-yü, 1995.

Chaves, Jonathan, trans. and ed. *The Columbia Book of Later Chinese Poetry–Yüan, Ming and Ch'ing Dynasties.* New York: Columbia University Press, 1986.

Ch'en Po-hai 陳伯海 and Chu I-an 朱易安. *T'ang shih shu-lu* 唐詩書錄. Tsinan: Ch'i Lu Shu-she, 1988.

Cheng, Meng-t'ung 鄭孟彤. *Chung-kuo shih-ko fa-chan shih-lüeh* 中國詩歌發展史略. Harbin: Hei-lung-chiang Jen-min, 1984.

Ch'ing shih hsüan 清詩選. Ting Li 丁力 and Ch'iao Ssu 喬斯, comm. Peking: Jen-min Wen-hsüeh, 1984.

Ch'ing-shih chi-shih 清詩紀事. Ch'ien Chung-lien 錢仲聯, ed. Nanking: Chiang-su Ku-chi, 1987.

Chou, Hsün-ch'u 周勛初, ed. *T'ang-shih ta tz'u-tien* 唐詩大辭典. Nanking: Chiang-su Chiao-yü, 1990.

Ch'üan Chin shih 全金詩. Hsüeh Tuan-chao 薛端兆 and Kuo Ming-chih 郭明志, eds. 4v. Tientsin: Nan-k'ai Ta-hsüeh, 1995.

Ch'üan Sung tz'u jen-ming tz'u-tien 全宋詞人名詞典. Peking: Hua-ling, 1996.

Debon, Günther. *Chinesische Dichtung, Geschichte, Struktur, Theorie.* Leiden: E. J. Brill, 1989. This important volume contains three sections: (1) a brief historical overview with references to section 2, (2) a list of 370 terms integral to traditional Chinese poetry, and (3) 100 translations as examples.

___. *Mein Haus liegt menschenfern doch nah den Dingen, Dreitausend Jahre chinesischer Poesie.* Munich: Diederichs, 1988.

Diény, Jean-Pierre. "La vitalité de la poésie chinoise médiévale," *JAOS* 109 (1988): 449-455.

Field, Stephen. "Ruralism in Chinese Poetry: Some Versions of Chinese Pastoral," *Comparative Literature Studies* 28 (1991):1-35.

Frankel, Hans H. "English Translations of Classical Chinese Poetry Since the 1930s: Problems and Achievements," *TkR* 15 (1984-85), 307-28.

Fu, Hsüan-ts'ung 傅璇琮, ed. *Chung-kuo ku-tien shih-ko chi-ch'u wen-k'u* 中國古典詩歌基礎文庫. 8v. Hangchow: Che-chiang Wen-i, 1994.

___, ed. *Ch'üan Sung shih* 全宋詩. 25v. Peking: Pei-ching Ta-hsüeh, 1991.

Fung, Sydney S. K. and S. T. Lai, compilers. *25 T'ang Poets, Index to English Translations*. Hong Kong: The Chinese University Press, 1984.

Gimm, Martin. *Kaiser Qianlong (1711-1799) as Poet: Anmerkungen zu seinem schriftstellerischen Werk*. Stuttgart: Steiner, 1993. *Sinologica Coloniensia*, 15.

Gottheiner, Klaus. *Licht und Dunkel in der Dichtung der Tang-Zeit, eine Untersuchung zur Bildlichkeit chinesischer Lyrik*. Frankfurt: Haag und Herchen, 1990.

Holzman, Donald. "Immortality-Seeking in Early Chinese Poetry," Willard J. Peterson, *et al.*, eds. *The Power of Culture, Studies in Chinese Cultural History*. Hong Kong: Chinese University Press, 1994, pp. 103-18.

Hou, Chien 侯健. *Hsin-pien shih tz'u ch'ü fu tz'u-tien* 新編詩詞曲賦辭典. Nanchang: Chiang-hsi Jen-min, 1989.

Hu-Sterk, Florence. "'Les poèmes de lamentations du palais' sous les Tang, La vie recluse des dames de la Cour," *Études chinoises,* 11.2 (1992):7-33.

Ko, Hsiao-yin 葛曉音. *Pa-tai shih-shih* 八代詩史. Sian: Shan-hsi Jen-min, 1989.

Kern, Martin. "Die Hymnen der chinesischen Staatsopfer: Von der Westlichen Han-Zeit bis zu den Sechs Dynastien (206/2 v. Chr.–589 n. Chr.)." Unpublished Ph. D. dissertation, University of Cologne, 1996.

Kondô, Haruo 近藤春雄. *Shikei kara Tô Enmei made* 詩経から陶陶淵明まで. Tokyo: Masashino Shoin, 1989.

Lee, Haewon. "The Transformation of Landscape Poetry," *JOSA* 20/21 (1988-89):80-101.

Levy, Dore J. "Constructing Sequences: Another Look at the Principles of *Fu* 'Enumeration,'" *HJAS* 46 (1986): 471-93.

Lin, Shao-te 林紹德. *Shih tz'u ch'ü yü tsa-shih* 詩詞曲語雜釋. Chengtu: Ssu-ch'uan Jen-min, 1986.

Lin, Shuen-fu and Stephen Owen, ed. *The Vitality of the Lyric Voice–Shih Poetry from the Late Han to the T'ang*. Princeton: Princeton University Press, 1986.

Liu, Ch'ung-te 劉崇德, ed. *Hsin-ting chiu-kung ta-ch'eng nan-pei tz'u-kung p'u chiao-i* 新定九宮大成南北詞宮譜校譯. 8v. Tientsin: T'ien-chin Ku-chi, 1997. Contains translations of 4500 *tz'u* and *ch'ü* from the Sung through Ch'ing dynasties included in this compilation of poetry made in 1746.

Lo, Irving Yucheng and William Schultz, ed. *Waiting for the Unicorn–Poems and Lyrics of China's Last Dynasty, 1644-1911*. Bloomington: Indiana University Press, 1986.

Lu, Ch'in-li 逯欽立, ed. *Hsien-Ch'in Han Wei Chin Nan-pei ch'ao shih* 先秦漢魏晉南北朝詩. 3v. Peking: Chung-hua, 1983.

Ma, Hsing-jung 馬興榮, ed. *Chung-kuo ku-tai shih tz'u ch'ü tz'u-tien* 中國古代詩詞曲詞典. Nanchang: Chiang-hsi Chiao-yü, 1987.

Nienhauser, William H., Jr. "Studies of Traditional Chinese Poetry in the U.S., 1962-1996 (Parts I and II)," *Chûgoku bungakuhô* 55 and 56 (October 1997 and April 1998).

Owen, Stephen. "The Formation of the T'ang Estate Poem," *HJAS* 55 (1995): 39-59.

___. "Place: Meditation on the Past at Ching-ling," *HJAS* 50 (1990), 417-457.

___. *Mi-Lou, Poetry and the Labyrinth of Desire*. Cambridge: Harvard University Press, 1989. *Harvard Studies in Comparative Literature,* 39.

___. "Poetry and Its Historical Ground," *CLEAR* 12 (1990), 417-57.

___. "Poetry in the Chinese Tradition," in Paul S. Ropp, ed., *Heritage of China*. Berkeley: University of California Press, 1990, pp. 294-308.

___. *Remembrances. The Experience of the Past in Classical Chinese Literature.* Cambridge and London: Harvard University Press, 1986.

___. *The Reading of Imagery in the Chinese Poetic Tradition.* Madison: University of Wisconsin Press, 1985.

Radtke, Kurt W. *Poetry of the Yuan Dynasty.* Canberra: Faculty of Asian Studies, Australian National University, 1984.

Riegel, Jeffrey K. "Poetry and the Legend of Confucius' Exile," *JAOS* 106 (1986): 13-22.

Russell, T. C. "Coffin-Pullers' Songs: The Macabre in Medieval China," *Papers on Far Eastern History* 27 (1983): 99-130.

Satô, Tamotsu 佐藤保. *Kanshi no imêji* 漢詩のイメージ. Tokyo: Yaishûkan Shoten, 1992.

Saussy, Haun. *The Problem of a Chinese Aesthetic.* Stanford: Stanford University Press, 1993.

Shimizu, Shigeru 清水茂. *Chûgoku shibun ronsô* 中国詩文論薮. Tokyo: Sôbunsha, 1989.

Sun, Cecile C. C. *Pearls from the Dragon's Mouth: Evocation of Feeling and Scene in Chinese Poetry.* Ann Arbor: Center for Chinese Studies, The University of Michigan, 1996.

Wang, C. H. *From Ritual to Allegory–Seven Essays in Early Chinese Poetry.* Hong Kong: The Chinese University Press, 1988.

Wang, Pu-kao 王步高, ed. *Chin Yüan Ming Ch'ing tz'u chien-shang tz'u-tien* 金元明青辭鑒賞辭典. Nanking: Nan-ching University, 1989.

Watson, Burton. *The Columbia Book of Chinese Poetry from Early Times to the Thirteenth Century.* New York: Columbia University Press, 1984.

Wawrytko, Sandra A. and Catherine Yi-Yu Cho. *Crystal: Spectrums of Chinese Culture through Poetry.* Frankfurt am Main: P. Lang, 1995. *Asian Thought and Culture,* 14.

Wu, Fusheng. *The Poetics of Decadence, Chinese Poetry of the Southern Dynasties and Late Tang Periods.* Albany: SUNY Press, 1998.

Yang, Xiaoshan. *To Perceive and to Represent: A Comparative Study of Chinese and English Poetics of Nature Imagery.* Frankfurt am Main: P. Lang, 1996. *Asian Thought and Culture,* 24.

Yang, Ye. *Chinese Poetic Closure.* Peter Lang, 1996. *Asian Thought and Culture,* v. 10.

Yoshikawa, Kôjirô. *Five Hundred Years of Chinese Poetry, 1150-1650; The Chin, Yüan and Ming Dynasties.* Translated with a Preface by John Timothy Wixted. Princeton: Princeton University Press, 1989.

Yu, Pauline. *The Reading of Imagery in the Chinese Poetic Tradition.* Princeton: Princeton University Press, 1987.

van Zoeren, Steven. *Poetry and Personality–Reading, Exegesis, and Hermeneutics in Traditional China.* Stanford: Stanford University Press, 1991.

Popular Literature

Berthier, Brigitte. *La Dame-du-bord-de-l'eau.* Nanterre: Société d'Ethnologie, 1988

Bordahl, Vibeke. *The Oral Tradition of Yangzhou Storytelling.* Richmond: Curzon, 1996.

Chang, Li-ching and Victor H. Mair, trans. "The Wall, A Folk Opera," *Chinoperl Papers* 14 (1986): 97-152.

Chang, Tzu-ch'en 張紫晨. *Chang Tzu-ch'en min-chien wen-i-hsüeh min-su-hsüeh lun-wen-chi.* 張紫晨民間文藝學民俗學論文集. Peking: Pei-ching Shih-fan Ta-hsüeh, 1993.

___. *Chung-kuo min-chien hsiao-hsi* 中國民間小戲. Hangchow: Che-chiang Chiao-yü, 1989.

Chung-kuo min-chien ko-ch'ü chi-ch'eng 中國民間歌曲集成. Peking: Chung-kuo ISBN, 199?-. A massive multi-volume collection of folktales, devoting one volume to each of China's provinces.

Ch'i, Lien-hsiu 祁連休 and Hsiao Li 肖莉, eds. *Chung-kuo ch'uan-shuo ku-shih ta-tz'u-tien* 中國傳説故事大辭典. Peking: Chung-kuo Wen-lien, 1992.

Chiang, Pin 姜彬, ed. *Chiang-nan shih-ta min-chien hsü-shih shih: ch'ang-p'ien Wu-ko chi* 江南十大民間敍事詩：長篇吳歌集. Shanghai: Shang-hai Wen-i, 1989. Includes explanations and examples of commonly-used expressions in the Wu dialect.

___, ed. *Chung-kuo min-chien wen-hsüeh ta tz'u-tien* 中國民間文學大辭典. Shanghai: Shang-hai Wen-i, 1992.

Chiang, William W. *"We Two Know the Script, We Have Become Good Friends." Linguistic and Social Aspects of the Women's Script Literature in Southern Hunan, China.* Lanham: University Press of America, 1995.

Chien-ming hsi-chü tz'u-tien 簡明戲劇詞典. Shanghai: Shang-hai Tz'u-shu, 1990.

Chin, Ming-bien, Yetta S. Cernter, and Mildred Ross. *Traditional Chinese Folktales.* Armonk, New York: East Gate/M. E. Sharpe, 1989.

Chin-Bing, Noreen Mei-lan. "Back to the Future: Prophecy and the Worlds of the T'ui-pei-t'u." Unpublished Ph. D. dissertation, Harvard University, 1990.

Chûbachi, Masakasu 中鉢雅量. "Yô Kashô setsuwa to *Suikoden*" 楊家将説話と水, *Aichi Kyôiku Daigaku kenkyû hôkoku–Jinbun kagaku* 41 (1992): 65-77.

Chung, Ching-wen 鍾敬文 *et al*, eds. *Chung-kuo min-chien wen-hsüeh ta tz'u-tien* 中國民間文學大辭典. 2v. Harbin: Hei-lung-chiang Jen-min, 1997.

Hartman, Charles. "Stomping Songs: Word and Image," *CLEAR* 17 (1995): 1-49.

Idema, W. L. "Some Notes on a Clown with a Clapper and Foot-stomping Songs (T'a-ko)," *Han-hsüeh yen-chiu /Chinese Studies* 8.1 (June 1990): 655-664.

Idema, W. L. *Vrouwenschrift. Vriendschap, huwelijk en wanhoop van Chinese vrouwen, opgetekend in een eigen schrift.* Amsterdam: Meulenhoff, 1996. An extensive anthology of popular songs and ballads which were noted down in the "women's script" of the Chiang-yung district in southern Hunan.

Itô, Takamaro 伊藤貴麿. *Chûgoku minwa sen* 中国民話選. Tokyo: Kôdansha, 1973.

Jen, Chia-ho 任嘉禾, *et al.*, comps. *K'u-sang ko* 哭喪歌. Shanghai: Shang-hai Wen-i, 1988.

Johnson, David, Andrew J. Nathan, and Evelyn S. Rawski, eds. *Popular Culture in Late Imperial China.* Berkeley: University of California Press, 1985.

Johnson, David, ed. *Ritual and Scripture in Chinese Popular Religion.* Berkeley: Chinese Popular Culture Project, 1995.

___, ed. *Ritual Opera, Operatic Ritual–'Mulien Rescues his Mother' in Chinese Popular Culture.* Berkeley: IEAS, 1989.

Kanaoka, Shoko. "Tun-huang Popular Narratives," *Asian Folklore Studies* XLVI.2 (1987): 273-300. [A review article.]

Kerr, Janet MacGregor Lynn. "Precious Scrolls in Chinese Popular Relgious Culture." Ph.D. University of Chicago, 1995.

Kim, Bunkyû 金文京, *et al.*, comps. *Mokugyosho mokuroku* 木魚書目録. Tokyo: Kôbun Shuppansha, 1995.

Kwong, Hing Foon. "L'évolution de théâtre populaire depuis les Ming jusqu'à nos jours: le cas de Wang Zhaojun," *TP* 77 (1991): 179-225.

___. *Wang Zhaojun. Une héroïne chinoise de l'histoire à la légende.* Mémoires de l'Institut des Hautes Études Chinoises, 1986.

Lévy, André. "La ballade de la heroine française; Notes pour servir à l'histoire de Madame Roland en Chine," *Revue de littérature comparée* 67.7 (1973): 177-192. A discussion of the *Fa-kuo nü-hsing t'an-tz'u* 法國女性彈詞.

Li, Fu-ch'ing 李福清 (Boris Riftin) and Ma Ch'ang-i 馬昌儀, comps. *Chung-kuo shen-hua ku-shih lun-chi* 中國神話故事論集. Taipei: Hsüeh-sheng, 1991.

Li, Te-fang 李德芳 and Yü T'ien-ch'ih 于天池. *Ku-tai hsiao-shuo yü min-chien wen-hsüeh* 古代小説與民間文學. Shenyang: Liao-ning Chiao-yü, 1992.

Liu, Kuang-min 劉光民, ed. *Ku-tai shuo-ch'ang pien-t'i hsi-p'ien* 古代説唱辨體析篇. Peking:

Shou-tu Shih-ta, 1996.

Liu, Mau-tsai. *Der Tiger mit dem Rosenkrantz, Rätsel aus China.* Berlin, 1986.

Liu, Shouhau and Hu Xiaoshan. "Folk Narrative in Chinese Nüshu: An Amazing New Discovery." *Asian Folklore Studies* 53 (1994): 307–18.

Lu [Lü], Zongli 呂宗力 and Luan Pao-ch'ün 欒保群, eds. *Chih-nan ch'üan-chi* 智囊全集. Shih-chia-chuang: Ho-pei Jen-min, 1988.

___. *Ku-chin hsiao* 古今笑. Shih-chia-chuang: Ho-pei Jen-min, 1985.

___. *Tzu pu yü ch'üan-chi* 子不語全集. Shih-chia-chuang: Ho-pei Jen-min, 1987.

___. *Yü-ch'u hsin-chih* 虞初新志. Shih-chia-chuang: Ho-pei Jen-min, 1985.

McLaren, Anne. "Women's Voices and Textuality. Chastity and Abduction in Chinese *Nüshu* Writing." *Modern China* 22.4 (1996): 382–416.

Mair, Victor H. "Anthologizing and Anthropologizing: The Place of Nonelite and Nonstandard Culture in the Chinese Literary Tradition." In Eugene Eoyang and Lin Yao-fu, eds. *Translating Chinese Literature.* Bloomington and Indianapolis: Indiana University, 1995, pp. 231-261.

___. "Chinese Popular Literature from Tun-huang: The State of the Field (1980-1990)," in Alfredo Cadonna, ed. *Turfan and the Tun-huang Texts, Encounter of Civilizations on the Silk Route* (Florence: Leo S. Olschki, 1992), pp. 171-240.

___. "The Contributions of T'ang and Five Dynasties Transformations Texts *(pien-wen)* to Later Chinese Popular Literature," *Sino-Platonic Papers,* 12(1989).

___. *Painting and Performance–Chinese Picture Recitation and Its Indian Genesis.* Honolulu: University of Hawaii Press, 1988.

___. "A Partial Bibliography for the Study of Indian Influence on Chinese Popular Literature," *Sino-Platonic Papers* 3 (1987).

___. "The Prosimetric Form in the Chinese Literary Tradition." In Joseph Harris and Karl Reichl, eds. *Prosimetrum: Crosscultural Perspectives on narrative in Prose and Verse.* Cambridge: D. S. Brewer, 1997, pp. 365-385.

___. "Sâriputra Defeats the Six Heterodox Masters: Oral-Visual Aspects of an Illustrated Transformation Scroll (P4524)," *AM, 3ᵈ Ser.* 8 (1995): 1-52.

Men, K'uei 門巋 and Chang Yen-chin 張燕瑾. *Chung-kuo su-wen-hsüeh shih* 中國俗文學史. Taipei: Wen-chin, 1995.

Meng, Fan-shu 孟繁樹. *Chung-kuo pan-shih pien-hua-t'i hsi-ch'ü yen-chiu* 中國板式變化體戲曲研究. Taipei: Wen-chin, 1991.

Mochizuki, Akira 望月彰. *Chûgoku minyô shû* 中国民謡集. Tokyo: Tôyô Shobô 1988.

Ni, Chung-chih 倪鍾之. *Chung-kuo ch'ü-i shih* 中國曲藝史. Shenyang: Ch'un-feng Wen-i, 1991.

Miller, Alan L. "The Woman Who Married a Horse–Five Ways of Looking at a Chinese Folktale," *Asian Folklore Studies* 54(1996): 275-305.

Min-chien wen-i chi-k'an 民間文藝集刊. Shanghai: Shang-hai Wen-i, 1979-.

Rolston, David. "Oral Performing Literature in Traditional Chinese Fiction: Nonrealistic Usages in the *Jin Ping Mei cihua* and Their Influence," *Chinoperl Papers* 17 (1995): 1-110.

Sawada, Mizuho 沢田瑞穂. *Shôrin kanwa* 笑林閑話. Tokyo: Tôhô Shoten, 1985.

Sawayama, Seizaburô 沢山晴三郎. *Chûgoku no minwa* 中国の民話. Shakai Shisôsha, 1976.

Schaffrath, Helmut. *Einhundert chinesische Volkslieder: eine Anthologie.* Frankfurt: P. Lang, 1993. *Studien zur Volksliedforschung,* 14.

Schimmelpenninck, Antoinet. *Chinese Folk Songs and Folk Singers. Shan'ge Traditions in Southern Jiangsu.* Leiden: Chime Foundation, 1997.

Shibuya, Yoichirô 渋谷誉一郎. "Tôdai no 'kôshô bungaku–'setsuwa' to 'hyakugi' no kankei o chûshin ni shite" 唐代の講唱文学–「説話」と「百戯」の関係を中心にして,

Geibun kenkyû 61 (1992).

Shiomi, Kunihiko 塩見邦彦. *Tôshi kôgo no kenkyû* 唐詩口語の研究. Fukuoka: Chûgoku Shoten, 1995.

Shuo-ch'ang i-shu chien-shih 説唱藝術簡史. Chung-kuo I-shu Yen-chiu Yüan, Ch'ü-i Yen-chiu So 中國藝術研究院, 曲藝研究所. Peking: Wen-hua I-shu, 1988.

T'an, Cheng-pi 譚正璧 and T'an Hsün 譚尋, comps. *Mu-yü-ko Ch'ao-chou-ko hsü-lu* 木魚歌潮州歌敍錄. Peking: Shu-mu Wen-hsien, 1982.

T'u, Yüan-chi 涂元濟 and T'u Shih 涂石. *Shen-hua, min-su yü wen-hsüeh* 神話民俗與文學. Foochow: Hai-hsia Wen-i, 1993.

Tuan, Pao-lin 段寶林. *Chung-kuo min-chien wen-hsüeh kai-yao* 中國民間文學概要. Peking: Peiching Ta-hsüeh, 1985.

___ and Ch'i Lien-hsiu 祁連休, eds. *Min-chien wen-hsüeh tz'u-tien* 民間文學詞典. Shih-chiachuang: Ho-pei Chiao-yü, 1988.

Tuan, Yü-ming 段玉明. *Chung-kuo shih-ching wen-hua yü ch'uan-t'ung ch'ü-i* 中國市井文化與傳統曲藝. Changchun: Chi-lin Chiao-yü, 1992.

Uchida, Tomoo 內田智雄. *Chûgoku kodai no sairei to kayô [gurane]* 中国古代の祭礼と歌謡 ［グラネ］. Tokyo: Heibonsha, 1989.

Wang, Chih-chien 王志健. *Shuo-ch'ang i-shu* 説唱藝術. Taipei: Wen-shih-che, 1994.

Wang, Fang 王仿 and Cheng Shuo-jen 鄭碩人. *Min-chien hsü-shih-shih te ch'uang-tso* 民間敍事詩的創作. Shanghai: Shang-hai Wen-i, 1993.

Watson, Rubie S. "Chinese Bridal Laments: The Claims of a Dutiful Daughter." In Bell Yung, *et al.*, eds. *Harmony and Counterpoint. Ritual Music in a Chinese Context*. Stanford: Stanford University Press, 1996, 107-129.

Wei, Jen 韋人 and Wei Ming-hua 韋明鏵. *Yang-chou ch'ü-i shih-hua* 楊州曲藝史話. Peking: Chung-kuo Ch'ü-i, 1985.

___ and Wei Ming-hua 韋明鏵, comps. *Yang-chou ch'ing-ch'ü* 楊州清曲. Shanghai: Shang-hai Wen-i, 1985.

Wöbking, Annette. *Scherz und tiefere Bedeutung, Literarische Beispiele im Ming- und Qing-zeitlichen China*. Koblenz: Dietmar Fölbach, 1994.

Wong, Eva, trans. *Seven taoist Masters—A Folk Novel of China*. Boston: Shambhala, 1990.

Wu, T'ung-jui 吳同瑞, Wang Wen-pao 王文寶 and Tuan Pao-lin 段寶林, comps. *Chung-kuo su-wen-hsüeh ch'i-shih-nien* 中國俗文學七十年. Peking: Pei-ching Ta-hsüeh, 1994.

___, comps. *Chung-kuo su-wen-hsüeh kai-lun* 中國俗文學概論. Peking: Pei-ching Ta-hsüeh, 1997.

Wu, Wen 武文. *Kan-su min-chien wen-hsüeh kai-lun* 甘肅民間文學概論. Lanchow: Kan-su Jen-min, 1996.

Yang, Liang-ts'ai 楊亮才 *et al.*, eds. *Chung-kuo min-chien wen-i tz'u-tien* 中國民間文藝辭典. Lanchow: Kan-su Jen-min, 1989.

Yao-Weyrauch, Wan-Hsuan. *Die Rolle der Frau im deutschen und chinesischen Sprichwort*. Bochum: Brockmeyer, 1990. *Chinathemen*, 55. Based on Yao-Weyrauch's Ph. D. dissertation, Giessen University, 1989.

Yung, Shui-shing. "*Mu-yü shu* and the Cantonese Popular Singing Arts," *Gest Library Journal*, 2.1(1987):16-30.

Prose

Bol, Peter K. *'This Culture of Ours': Intellectual Transitions in T'ang and Sung China*. Stanford: Stanford University Press, 1992. Much discussion of the relationship between thought and writing.

Chen, Yu-shih. *Images and Ideas in Chinese Classical Prose, Studies of Four Masters.* Stanford: Stanford University Press, 1988.

Chou, Shao-liang 周紹良, ed. *T'ang-tai mu-chih hui-pien* 昂代墓誌彙編. 2v. Shanghai: Shang-hai Ku-chi, 1992.

Chu, Shih-ying 朱世英 *et al. Chung-kuo san-wen hsüeh t'ung-lun* 中國散文學通論. Hofei: An-hui Chiao-yü, 1995.

Ch'üan Ming wen 全明文. Ch'ien Po-ch'eng 錢伯城, *et al.,* eds. 2v. to date. Shanghai: Shang-hai Ku-chi, 1993-.

Ch'üan Sung wen 全宋文. Ho Chih-hua 何志華, *et al.,* ed. V. 1- Chengtu: Pa Shu Shu-she, 1988-.

Franz, Rainer von. *Die chinesische Innengrabinscrhift für Beamte un Privatiers des 7. Jahrhunderts.* Stuttgart: Steiner, 1996. *Münchener Ostasiatische Studien, 74.*

Gardner, Daniel. "Modes of Thinking and Modes of Discourses in the Sung: Some Thoughts on the *Yü-lu* (Recorded Conversations) Texts," *JAS* 50(1991): 574-603.

Han, Chao-ch'i 韓兆琦 and Lü Po-t'ao 呂伯濤. *Han-tai san-wen shih-kao* 漢代散文史稿. Taiyuan: Shan-hsi Jen-min, 1986.

Huters, Theodore. "From Writing to Literature: The Development of Late Qing Theories of Prose," *HJAS* 47.1 (June 1987): 51-96.

Ikeda, On 池田温. *T'ang-tai chao-ch'ih mu-lu* 唐代詔敕目錄. Sian: San Ch'in, 1991.

Kakehi, Fumio 筧文生. *Kanshô Chûgoku no koten* 鑑賞中国の古典. V. 20 *Tô Sô hakka bun* 唐宋八家文. Tokyo: Kawokawa Shoten, 1989.

Kamatani, Takeshi 釜谷武志. "Kan Gi Rikuchô ni okeru "Mei" 銘, *Chûgoku bungakuhô* 40(1989): 16-46.

Kinney, Anne Behnke. *The Art of the Han Essay: Wang Fu's Ch'ien-fu lun.* Tempe: Center for Asian Studies, Arizona State University, 1990.

Knechtges, David R. *Wen xuan or Selections of Refined Literature. Volume 2: Rhapsodies on Sacrifices, Hunting, Travel, Sightseeing, Palaces and Halls, Rivers and Seas.* Princeton: Princeton University Press, 1987. *Volume 3: Rhapsodies on Natural Phenomena, Birds and Animals, Aspirations and Feelings, Sorrowful Laments, Literature, Music and Passions.* Princeton: Princeton University Press, 1996.

Kuo, Yü-heng 郭預衡. *Chung-kuo san-wen chien-shih* 中國散文簡史. Peking: Pei-ching Shih-fan Ta-hsüeh, 1994.

Liu, Ta-chieh 劉大杰, comp. *Ming-jen hsiao-p'in hsüan* 明人小品選. Ch'ih Chao-o 遲超俄, ed. Peking: Chung-hua, 1995.

Liu, Yen 劉衍, ed. *Chung-kuo san-wen shih-kang, Ku-tai chüan* 中國散文史綱. Changsha: Hu-nan Chiao-yü, 1994.

McMullen, David. *State and Scholars in T'ang China.* Cambridge: Cambridge University Press, 1988. See especially "Attitudes to Literary Composition," pp. 206-249.

Nienhauser, William H., Jr. *Chuan-chi yü hsiao-shuo: T'ang-tai wen-hsüeh lun-wen chi* 傳紀與小説：唐代文學論文集. Taipei: Southern Materials, 1995. Contains several articles on the relationship between fiction and *ku-wen* prose.

Shao, Ch'uan-lieh 邵傳烈. *Chung-kuo tsa-wen shih* 中國雜文史. Shanghai: Shang-hai Wen-i, 1991.

Spring, Madeline. *Animal Allegories in T'ang China.* New Haven: American Oriental Society, 1993.

Strassberg, Richard E. *Inscribed Landscapes, Travel Writing from Imperial China.* Berkeley: University of California Press, 1994.

Sun, Wang 孫望 and Yü Hsien-hao 郁賢皓, eds. *T'ang-tai san-wen* 唐代文學. 3v. Nanking: Chiang-su Ku-chi, 1994. Excellent annotations; selection is mainly standard works, but does include a number of not often seen texts.

243

T'ang, Kuei-jen 湯貴仁. "Chien-kuo i-lai T'ang-tai san-wen yen-chiu" 建國以來唐代散文研究,*T'ang-tai wen-hsüeh yen-chiu nien-chien* 唐代文學研究年鑒, 1985: 405-419.

T'an Tsung-chien 譚宗健. *Hsien Ch'in san-wen i-shu hsin-t'an* 先秦散文藝術新探. Peking: Shou-tu Shih-ta, 1996.

Wang, Chin-kuei 王錦貴. *Chung-kuo chi-chuan-t'i wen-hsien yen-chiu* 中國紀傳體文獻研究. Peking: Pei-ching Ta-hsüeh, 1996.

Rhetoric

Alt, Wayne. "The Eight-Legged Essay: Its Reputation, Structure, and Limitations," *TkR* 17.2 (1986): 155–174.

Broschat, Michael Robert. "*Guiguzi*: A Textual Study and Translation," Unpublished Ph. D. dissertation., University of Washington, 1985.

Ch'eng, Wei-chün 成偉鈞, ed. *Hsiu-tz'u t'ung-chien* 修辭通鑒. Peking: Chung-kuo Ch'ing-nien, 1991.

Chang, Hsiao-mang 張曉芒. *Hsien Ch'in pien-hsüeh fa-tse shih-lun* 先秦辯學法則史論. Peking: Jen-min Wen-hsüeh, 1996.

Chang, Yen 張嚴. *Hsiu-tz'u lun-shuo yü fang-fa* 修辭論說語方法. Taipei: Shang-wu, 1978.

Chao, K'o 趙克. *Ku Han-yü hsiu-tz'u chien-lun* 古漢語修辭簡論. Peking: Shang-wu, 1983.

Cheng, Tien 鄭奠 and T'an Ch'üan-chi 譚全基, eds. Ku Han-yü hsiu-tz'u-hsüeh tzu-liao hui-pien 古代漢語修辭學資料彙編. Peking: Shang-wu, 1980.

Cheng, Tzu-yü 鄭子瑜 and Tsung T'ing-hu 宗廷虎, eds. *Chung-kuo hsiu-tz'u hsüeh t'ung-shih* 中國修辭學通史. 5v. Chi-lin chiao-yü ch'u-pan-she 吉林教育, 1997.

Cheng, Yüan-han 鄭遠漢. *Tz'u ko pien-i* 辭格辨異. Wuhan: Hu-pei Jen-min, 1982.

Chiang, Chien-she 姜建設. "Yu-shih pin-k'o tsai Ch'in Han shih hsing-shuai yen-pien" 游士賓客在秦漢時興衰演變, *Shih-hsüeh yüeh-k'an wu* 史學月刊物 (Chengchow 鄭州) 5 (1986): 16–21.

Chmielewski, Janusz. "Concerning the Problem of Analogic Reasoning in Ancient China (Review Article)," *Rocznik Orientalistcyzny* 40 (1979): 65–78.

Chou, Chen-fu 周振甫. *Chung-kuo hsiu-tz'u hsüeh-shih* 中國修辭學史. Peking: Shang-wu, 1991.

Cikoski, John. "On Standards of Analogic Reasoning in the Late Chou," *JCP* 2 (June 1975): 325–357.

Crump, James I., trans. and annot. *Chan-kuo Ts'e.* Ann Arbor: Center for Chinese Studies, University of Michigan, 1996.

___. *Intrigues: Studies of the Chan-kuo Ts'e.* Ann Arbor: University of Michigan Press, 1964.

Cua, Anthony. *Ethical Argumentation: A Study in Hsün Tzu's Moral Epistemology.* Honolulu: University of Hawaii Press, 1985.

___. "Hsün Tzu's Theory of Argumentation: A Reconstruction," *Review of Metaphysics* 36 (June 1983): 867–94.

Garrett, Mary. "The *Mo-tzu* and the *Lü-shih ch'un-ch'iu*: A Case Study of Classical Chinese Theory and Practice of Arguments." Unpublished Ph. D. dissertation., University of California, Berkeley, 1983.

___. "Pathos Reconsidered from the Perspective of Classical Chinese Rhetorical Theories," *The Quarterly Journal of Speech* 79 (Feb. 1993): 19–39.

___. "Asian Challenge [to the Rhetorical Tradition]." In *Contemporary Perspectives on Rhetoric.* Sonja K. Foss, Karen A. Foss and Robert Trapp, eds. Second edition, Prospect Heights, Il.: Waveland Press, 1991, pp. 295–314.

Gunn, Edward. *Rewriting Chinese: Style and Innovation in Twentieth Century Chinese Prose.* Stanford: Stanford University Press, 1991.

Harbsmeier, C. *Towards a Philosophical Ethnography of Early Chinese Literary Communication: Comparative Studies in Latin and Classical Chinese Grammar and Rhetoric.* Oslo: Department of East European and Oriental Studies, 1993.

Heidbüchel, Ursula. "Rhetorik im antiken China, eine Untersuchung der Ausdrucksformen höfischer Rede im *Zuozhuan.*" Unpublished Ph. D. dissertation, University of Münster, 1993.

Hsiao, Hua-jung 蕭華榮. "Hsiung pien-shu yü ku wen-hua: ku Hsi-la yü hsien-Ch'in te pi-chiao" 雄辯術與古文化：古希臘與先秦的比較, *Wen i li-lun yen-chiu* 文藝理論研究 5 (October 1987): 16–21.

Hsiu-tz'u hsüeh lun-wen chi 修辭學論文集. Foochow: Fu-chien Jen-min, 1984.

Hsiu-tz'u hsüeh yen-chiu 修辭學研究. Chung-kuo Hsiu-tz'u-hsüeh Hui, Hua-tung Fen-hui, ed. V. 1-. 1983-.

Hsü, Hsing-hai 徐興海 and Li Ch'ün-pao 李群寶. *Chung-kuo ku-tai lun-pien i-shu* 中國古代論 辯藝術. Sian: Shan-hsi Jen-min Chiao-yü, 1992.

I, P'u 易蒲 (Tsung T'ing-hu 宗廷虎) and Li Chin-ling 李金苓. *Han-yü hsiu-tz'u hsüeh shih -kang* 漢語修辭學史鋼. Changchun: Chi-lin Chiao-yü,1989.

Jensen, J. Vernon. "Rhetorical Emphases of Taoism," *Rhetorica* 5.3 (Summer 1987): 219–229.

___. "Rhetoric of East Asia—A Bibliography," *Rhetoric Society Quarterly* 17 (Spring 1987): 213–231.

Kao, Karl. "Recent Studies of Chinese Rhetoric," *CLEAR* 15(1993): 143-154.

Kern, Martin. *Zum Topos "Zimtbaum" in der chinesischen Literatur: rhetorische Funktion und poetischer Eigenwert des Naturbildes kuei.* Stuttgart: Steiner, 1994. *Sinologica Coloniensia,* 18. Based on Kern's M.A. thesis (Cologne University, 1992).

Kirkpatrick, Andy. "Chinese Rhetoric: Methods of Argument," *Multilingua* 14.3 (1995): 271–295.

Knechtges, David. *The Han Rhapsody: A Study of the* Fu *of Yang Hsiung (53 B.C.– A.D. 18).* Cambridge: Cambridge University Press, 1976.

Kroll, J.L. "Disputation in Ancient Chinese Culture," *EC* 11–12 (1985–87): 118–145.

Lau, D.C. "On Mencius' Use of the Methods of Analogy in Argument," *AM, NS* 10 (1963): 173–194.

Li, Wei-ch'i 李維琦. *Hsiu-tz'u hsüeh* 修辭學. Changsha: Hu-nan Jen-min, 1986.

Li, Wai-yee. "Rhetoric and Fantasy and Rhetoric of Irony: Studies in *Liao-chai chih-i* and *Hung-lou Meng.*" Unpublished Ph. D. dissertation, Princeton University, 1988.

Lu, Xing. "Recovering the Past: Identification of Chinese Sense of *Pien* and a Comparison of *Pien* to Greek Sense of Rhetoric in the Fifth and Third Centuries BCE." Unpublished Ph. D. dissertation, University of Oregon, 1991.

Lu, Xing. "Recovering the Past: Identification of Chinese Senses of *Pien* and a Comparison of *Pien* to Greek Senses of Rhetoric in the Fifth and Third Centuries BCE." Unpublished University of Oregon dissertation, 1991.

Oliver, Robert T. *Communication and Culture in Ancient India and China.* Syracuse: Syracuse University Press, 1971.

Plaks, Andrew H. "Where the Lines Meet: Parallelism in Chinese and Western Literatures," *CLEAR* 10 (1988): 43–60.

___. "The Prose of Our Time." In *The Power of Culture: Studies in Chinese Cultural History.* Willard J. Peterson, ed. Hong Kong: Chinese University Press, 1994, pp. 206–217.

Pokora, Timoteus. "Ironic Critics at Ancient Chinese Courts (*Shih chi* 126)," *OE* 20 (1973): 49–64.

Raphals, Lisa. *Knowing Words: Wisdom and Cunning in the Classical Traditions of China and Greece.* Ithaca and London: Cornell University Press, 1992.

Redding, Jean-Paul. "Analogical Reasoning in Early Chinese Philosophy," *Etudes Asiatiques*

(1986): 40–57.

___. *Les fondements philosophiques de la rhétorique chez les sophistes grecs et chez les sophistes chinois.* Bern, Frankfurt, and New York: Peter Lang, 1985.

Reynolds, Beatrice. "Lao Tzu: Persuasion Through Inaction and Non-Speaking," *Today's Speech* 17 (February 1969): 23–25.

Saussy, Haun. *The Problem of a Chinese Aesthetic.* Stanford: Stanford University Press, 1993.

T'an, Yung-hsiang 譚永祥. *Han-yü hsiu-tz'u mei-hsüeh* 漢語修辭美學. Peking: Pei-ching Yü-yen Hsüeh-yüan, 1992.

T'ao, Hsi-sheng 陶希聖. *Pien shih yü yu-hsia* 辯士與游俠. Shanghai: Shang-wu, 1931.

Tsao, Ding-ren. "The Persuasion of *Kuei Ku Tzu*." Unpublished Ph. D. dissertation, University of Minnesota, 1985.

Tsung, T'ing-hu 宗廷虎 and Yüan Hui 袁暉, eds. *Han-yü hsiu-tz'u hsüeh-shih* 漢語修辭學史. Hofei: An-hui Ch'u-pan-she, 1990.

Tsung, T'ing-hu 宗廷虎 *et al. Hsiu-tz'u hsin-lun* 修辭新論. Shanghai: Chiao-yü, 1988.

Tu, Ching-I. "The Chinese Examination Essay: Some Literary Considerations," *MS* 31 (1974–75): 393–406.

Unger, Ulrich. *Rhetorik des klassischen Chinesisch.* Wiesbaden: Harrassowitz, 1995.

Wang, Te-ch'un 王德春. *Hsiu-tz'u hsüeh t'an-so* 修辭學探索. Peking: Pei-ching Ch'u-pan-she, 1983.

Williams, Jay C. "On Reading a Confucian Classic: The Rhetoric of the *Lunyu*," *JCR*, 19(1992): 105-111.

Wu, Shih-wen 吳士文. *Hsiu-tz'u ko-lun hsi* 修辭格論析. Shanghai: Chiao-yü, 1986.

Yang, Shu-ta 楊樹達 (1885-1956). *Chung-kuo hsiu-hsüeh* 中國修辭. Shanghai: Shang-hai Ku-chi, 1983.

Yeh, Michelle. "Metaphor and Bi: Western and Chinese Poetics," *Comparative Literature* 39.3 (Summer 1987): 237–254.

Yu, Pauline. *The Reading of Imagery in the Chinese Poetic Tradition.* Princeton: Princeton University Press, 1987.

Yü, Ying-shih 余英時. "Ku-tai chih-shih chieh-ts'eng te hsing-ch'i yü fa-chan" 古代知識階層的興起與發展. In *Shih yü Chung-kuo wen-hua* 士與中國文化. Yü Ying-shih, ed. Shanghai: Jen-min, 1987, pp. 1–83.

Yüan, Hui 袁暉. *Han-yü hsiu-tz'u hsüeh shih* 漢語修辭學史. Hofei: An-huei Chiao-yü, 1990.

Zhang, Zhenhua. *Chinesische und europäische Rhetorik: ein Vergleich in Grundzügen.* Frankfurt am Main: P. Lang, 1991. Based on Zhang's dissertation (Trier University, 1990).

Taoist Literature

Akizuki Kan'ei 秋月観暎, ed. *Dôkyô no susume–sono genjô to mondaiten o kangaeru* 道教研究のすすめ–その現状と問題点を考える. Tokyo: Hirakawa Shuppansha, 1986.

"Books and Articles on Taoist Religion" [Annual Bibliography] in *Tôhô shûkyô* 東方宗教.

Baldrian-Hussein, Farzeen. "Lü Tung-pin in Northern Sung Literature," *Cahiers d'Extrême-Asie* 2 (1986): 133-169.

___. "Yüeh-yang and Lü Tung-bin's Ch'in-yüan ch'un: A Sung Alchemical Poem." In Gerd Naundorf *et al.*, eds. *Religion und Philosophie in Ostasien–Festschrift für Hans Steininger.* Würzburg: Königshausen und Neumann 1985, pp. 19-32.

Barrett, Timothy Hugh. "Religious Traditions in Chinese Civilization: Buddhism and Taoism," in Paul S. Ropp, ed., *Heritage of China.* Berkeley: University of California Press, 1990, pp. 138-163.

___. "The Taoist Canon in Japan: Some Implications of the Research of Ho Peng Yoke," *Taoist Resources* 5.2 (December 1994):71-8.

___. *Taoism under the T'ang: Religion and Empire During the Golden Age of Chinese History.* London: Wellsweep, 1996.

Bell, Catherine M. "The Ritualization of Texts and the Textualization of Ritual in the Codification of Taoist Ritual," *History of Religions* 27 (1988): 366-392.

Berkowitz, Alan. "Reclusion and the Chinese Eremetic Tradition," *JAOS* 113(1993):575-584.

Bokenkamp, Steven. *Early Daoist Scriptures.* Berkeley: University of California Press, 1997.

Bokenkamp, Stephen R. "The Peach Flower Font and the Grotto Passage," *JAOS* 106(1986):65-77.

Boltz, Judith M. *A Survey of Taoist Literature, Tenth to Seventeenth Centuries.* Berkeley: Institute of East Asian Studies, 1987. *China Research Monographs,* 32.

Boltz, William G. "The Religious and Philosophical Significance of the 'Hsiang erh' *Lao tzu* in the Light of the Ma wang tui Silk Manuscripts," *BSOAS* 45 (1982): 95-117.

___. "The *Lao tzu* Text that Wang Pi and Ho-shang Kung Never Saw," *BSOAS* 48 (1985): 493-501.

Brashier, K. E. "A Poetic Exposition on Heaven and Earth by Chenggong Sui (231-273)," *JCR* 24 (1996): 1-36.

Cadonna, Alfredo. "Astronauti taoisti da Chang-an alla Luna: note sul manoscritto di Dunhuang S 6836 alla luce di alcuni lavori di Edward H. Schafer," *Orientalia Venetiana* 1 (1985): 69-132.

Cahill, Suzanne E. "Sex and the Supernatural in Medieval China: Cantos on the Transcendent Who Presides over the River," *JAOS* 105 (1985): 197-220.

___. *Transcendence and Divine Passion–The Queen Mother of the West in Mediaeval China.* Stanford: Stanford University Press, 1993.

Campany, Robert Ford. "Buddhist Revelation and Taoist Translation in Early Medieval China," *TkR,* 4.1(1993):1-29.

___. *Strange Writing: Anomaly Accounts in Early Medieval China.* Albany: SUNY Press 1996.

Cedzich, Ursula-Angelika. "Das Ritual der Himmelsmeister im Spiegel früher Quellen: Übersetzung und Untersuchung des liturgischen Materials im 3. ch. des *Teng-chen yin-yüeh.*" Ph. D. dissertation, Würzburg University.

___. "Wu-t'ung: Zur bewegten Geschichte eines Kultes." In Gerd Naundorf *et al.,* eds. *Religion und Philosophie in Ostasien–Festschrift für Hans Steininger.* Würzburg: Königshausen und Neumann 1985, pp. 33-60.

Chan, Alan K. L. *Two Visions of the Way, A Study of the Wang Pi and the Ho-shang Kung Commentaries on the* Lao Tzu. Albany: SUNY Press, 1995.

Chan, Shih-ch'uang 詹石窗 *et al.* "Tao-chiao hsiao-shuo lüeh-lun" 道教小説略論, *Tao-chiao wen-hua yen-chiu* 4 (1994): 252-276.

___. "Lun Yüan-tai Tao-chiao hsi-chü te liang-ko i-shu t'e-cheng" 論元代道教戲劇的兩個藝術特徵, *Tao-chiao wen-hua yen-chiu* 7 (1995): 352-372.

___. *Tao-chiao wen-hsüeh shih* 道教文學史. Shanghai: Shang-hai Wen-i, 1992.

Chang, Chih-che 張志哲, ed. *Tao-chiao wen-hua tz'u-tien* 道教文化辭典. Nanking: Chiang-su Ku-chi, 1994.

Chang, Sung-hui 張宋輝. "Tao-chiao yü hsüan-yen shih" 道教與懸言詩, *Tao-chiao wen-hua yen-chiu* 7 (1995): 338-351.

Chappell, David W., ed. *Buddhist and Taoist Practice in Medieval Chinese Society; Buddhist and Taoist Studies II.* Honolulu: University of Hawaii Press, 1987.

Ch'en Yüan 陳垣, comp. *Tao-chia chin-shih lüeh* 道家金石略. Peking" Wen-wu, 1988.

Cheng, Chih-ming 鄭志明. *Chung-kuo shan-pen yu tsung-chiao* 中國善本與宗教. Taipei: Hsüeh-sheng, 1990.

與明清文藝啟蒙, *Tao-chiao wen-hua yen-chiu* 5 (1994): 20-35.

Chiang, Chien-yüan 蔣見元. "Li Pai yü Tao-chiao" 李白與道教, *Tao-chiao wen-hua yen-chiu* 4 (1994): 318-325.

Ch'ing, Hsi-t'ai 卿希泰. *Tao-chiao wen-hua hsin-t'an* 道教文化新探. Chengtu: Ssu-ch'uan Jen-min, 1988.

Chu, Yüeh-li 朱越利. *Tao-tsang fen-lei chieh-t'i* 道藏分類解題. Peking: Hua-hsia, 1995.

Chung, Lai-yin 重來因. *Su Shih yü Tao-chia Tao-chiao* 蘇軾與道家道教. Taipei: Hsüeh-sheng, 1990.

Csikszentmihalyi, Mark. "Emulating the Yellow Emperor: The Theory and Practice of HuangLao, 180-141 B.C." Unpublished Ph.D. dissertation, Stanford University, 1994.

Dai, Fang. "Drinking, Thinking, and Writing: Ruan Ji and the Culture of His Era." Ph.D. Harvard University, 1994.

Despeux, Catherine. "L'ordination des femmes taoistes sous les Tang," *Études chinoises* 5 (1987): 53-100.

DeWoskin, Kenneth. "Xian Descended–Narrating Xian Among Mortals," *Taoist Resources* 2.2 (1990): 70-86.

Dooling, Amy D. "Feminist Narrative Strategies in Modern Chinese Women's Writing." Unpublished Ph. D. dissertation, Columbia University, 1998. The first chapter treats Ch'iu Chin 秋瑾)1875-1907) and other pre-modern writers.

Drexler, Monika. *Daoistische Schriftmagie: Interpretation zu den Scriftamuletten–Fu–in Daozang.* Stuttgart: Franz Steiner Verlag, 1994.

Dudbridge, Glen "Women Pilgrims to T'ai Shan: Some Pages from a Seventeenth-Century Novel." In Susan Naquin and Chün-fang Yü, eds. Pilgrims and Sacred Sites in China; Berkeley: University of California Press 1992, pp. 39-64.

Eichhorn, Werner "Das Tung-Ming Chi des Kuo Hsien." In Gerd Naundorf *et al.,* eds. *Religion und Philosophie in Ostasien–Festschrift für Hans Steininger.* Würzburg: Königshausen und Neumann 1985, pp. 291-300.

Emmerich, Reinhard. "Bemerkungen zu Huang und Lao in der Frühen Han-Zeit: Erkenntnisse aus *Shiji* und *Hanshu," MS* 43 (1995): 53-140.

Engelhardt, Ute. *Die klassische Tradition der Qi-Übungen (Qigong), eine Darstellung anhand des Tang-zeitlichen Textes 'Fuqi jingyi lun' von Sima Chengzhen. Münchener ostasiatische Studien,* v. 44. Stuttgart: Franz Steiner Verlag, 1987. Translation and study of a Taoist text, prefaced by a study of Ssu-ma Ch'eng-chen.

Endress, Günther. *Die sieben Meister der Vollkommenen Verwirkliehung; Der Taoistische Lehrroman Ch'i-chen chuan in Übersetzung und im Spiegel seiner Quellen.* Frankfurt: Peter Lang, 1985.

___. *Die sieben Meister des wunderbaren Tao–Taoistische Geschichten aus der Schule der Volkommenen Verwirklichung, von Werdegang der sieben Schüler des Grossmeisters Wang im China des 12. Jarhunderts.* Bern: Schern, 1990.

Fu, Hongchu. "The Feminist Issues in Yüan *Tsa-chü:* Rereading Kuan Han-ch'ing's *Chiu Feng Ch'en."* In Tseng Yong-yih [Tseng Yung-i], *Proceedings of International Conference on Kuan Han-ch'ing.* Taipei: Faculty of Arts, National Taiwan University, 1994, pp. 303-25.

Fukui, Fumimasa 福井文雅. "Le fonction des *song* [頌]ou 'strophes' dan la littérature taoïste." In *Bouddhisme et cultures locales.* Fumimasa Fukui and Gérard Fussman, eds. Paris: École Française d'Extrême-Orient, 1994, pp. 173-177.

___. "The History of Taoist Studies in Japan and Some Related Issues," *Acta Asiatica* 68 (1995): 1-18.

Fukui, Fumimasa *et al.* "The Bibliography for the Study of Chinese Religion in Japanese, 1985–1995–Buddhism and Taoism," Typescript distributed at the 35th ICANAS,

Budapest, Hungary, July 6-12, 1997, pp. 100-144.

Fukui, Kojun *et al.* *Tao-chiao* 道教," Shanghai: Shang-hai Ku-chi, 1992.

Franke, Herbert. "The Taoist Elements in the Buddhist *Great Bear Sutra* (*Pei-tou ching*)," *AM,* *3rd Series* 3 (1990): 75-112.

Goosesaert, Vincent. "L'image variée du Taoîsme dans quatre nouveaux dictionnaires," *RBS* 1996: 461-68.

Güntsch, Gertrud. *Das Shen-hsien chuan und das Erscheinungsbild eines Hsien: Vollständige annotierte Übersetzung des Berichtes über die göttlichen Unsterblichen und Beschreibung des Hsien in einigen typischen Bildern.* Frankfurt/Main: Lang, 1988.

Henricks, Robert G., trans. *Lao Tzu, Te-Tao Ching.* New York: Ballantine Books, 1990.

Hendrischke, Barbara. "Der Taoismus in der Tang-Zeit," *mimima sinica, Zeitschrift zum chinesichen Geist* 2(1993):110-143.

Holzman, Donald. "Immortality–Seeking in Early Chinese Poetry." In W. J. Peterson *et al.,* eds. *The Power of Culture: Studies in Chinese Cultural History.* Hong Kong: The Chinese University Press, 1994, pp. 103-118.

Hu, Fu-ch'eng 胡孚琛. *Chung-kuo Tao-chiao ta tz'u-tien* 中國道教大辭典. Peking: Chung-kuo She-hui K'o-hsüeh, 1995.

Hu, Tao-ching 胡道靜, *et al,* eds. *Tsang-wai tao-shu* 藏外道書. 36v. Chengtu: Pa Shu, 1994.

Huang, Shih-chung 黃世中. *T'ang shih yü Tao-chiao* 唐詩與道教. Kweilin: Li-chiang, 1996.

Ishii, Masako 石井昌子. "Daidô shinkyô to gyokokyô rai kyôten to no kankei" 太洞真經と玉經類經典との関係, *Tôhô shûkyô* 66 (1986): 22-44.

Jen, Chi-yü 任繼愈, ed. *Tao-tsang t'i-yao* 道藏提要. Peking: Chung-kuo She-hui K'o-hsüeh-yüan, 1991.

Johnson, David, ed. *Ritual and Scripture in Chinese Popular Religion.* Berkeley: Chinese Popular Culture Project, 1995.

Kalinowski, Marc. "La littérature divinatoire dans le *Daozang,*" *Cahiers d'Extrême-Asie* 5 (1989/1990): 85-114.

___. "La transmission du dispositif des Neuf palais sous les Six dynasties." In M. Strickmann, ed. *Tantric and Taoist Studies in Honour of R. A. Stein.* Brussels: Institut Belge des Hautes Études Chinoises, 1985, v. 3, pp. 773-811.

Kandel, Barbara. *Wen tzu: ein Beitrag zur Problematik und zum Verständnis eines taoistischen Textes.* Bern: Frankfurt: Lang, 1974.

Kao, Cheng 高正. "Liu E shou-chi k'ao-shih" 劉鶚手記考試, *Tao-chiao wen-hua yen-chiu* 5 (1994): 477-491.

Katz, P. R. "Temple Inscriptions and the Study of Taoist Cults: A Case Study of Inscriptions at the Palace of Eternal Joy," *Taoist Resources* 7.1 (April 1997): 1-22.

Kirkland, Russell J. "The Historical Contours of Taoism in China: Thoughts on Issues of Classification and Terminology," *JCR* 25 (Fall 1997): 57-82.

___. "Taoists of the High T'ang: An Inquiry into the Perceived Significance of Eminent Taoists in Medieval Chinese Society." Unpublished Ph. D. dissertation, Indiana University, 1986. Biographies of seven Taoists of the High T'ang, including the poet Wu Yün 吳筠.

Kleeman, Terry F. *A God's own Tale: The Book of Transformations' of Wenchang, the Divine Lord of Zitong.* Albany: SUNY Press, 1994.

Knaul, Livia (see also Kohn, Livia). "Kuo Hsiang and the *Chuang Tzu,*" *JCP* 12 (1985): 429-47.

___. "The Teaching of T'ien-yin-tzu," *JCR* 15 (Fall 1987), 1-28.

Ko, Chao-kuang 葛兆光. *Tao-chiao yü Chung-kuo wen-hua* 道教與中國文化. Shanghai: Shang-hai Jen-min, 1987.

___. "'Shen-shou t'ien-shu' yü 'pu-li wen-tzu'–Fu-chiao yü Tao-chiao te yü-yen ch'uan-t'ung chi ch'i tui Chung-kuo ku-tien shih-ko te ying-hsiang" 神授天書與不立文字—佛教與道教的語言傳統及其對中國古典詩歌的影響, *Wen-hsüeh i-ch'an* 1998.1: 37-49.

Kobayashi, Masayoshi 小林正義. *Rikuchô Dôkyôshi kenkyû* 六朝道教史研究. Tokyo: Sôbunsha, 1990.

Kohn, Livia (see also Knaul, Livia). *Laughing at the Tao, Debates among Buddhist and Taoists in Medieval China.* Princeton: Princeton University Press, 1995.

___. *Seven Steps to the Tao: Sima Chengzhen's Zuowanglun.* St. Augustin/Nettetal: *Monumenta Serica,* 1987. *Monumenta Serica Monograph* 20.

___. *Taoist Mystical Philosophy: The Scripture of Western Ascension.* Albany: SUNY Press, 1991.

___. ussell J. "Yin Xi: The Master at the Beginning of the Scripture," *JCR* 25 (Fall 1997): 83-139.

___ and Michael LaFargue, eds. *Lao-tzu and the Tao-te-ching.* Albany: SUNY Press, 1997.

Kominami, Ichirô 小南一郎. *Chûgoku no shinwa to monogatari: Koshôsetsushi no tenkai* 中国の神話と物語：古小説の展開. Tokyo: Iwanami, 1984.

Kroll, Paul W. "In the Halls of the Azure Lad," *JAOS* 105 (1985): 75-94. Study of the paradise realm of the Taoist divinity Ch'ing-t'ung 青童, as revealed in canonical sources.

___. "Li Po's Transcendent Diction," *JAOS* 106 (1986): 99-117.

___. "Notes on Three Taoist Figures of the T'ang Dynasty," *Society for the Study of Chinese Religions Bulletin* 9 (1981): 19-41. On the Taoist patriarch Ssu-ma Ch'eng-chen 司馬承禎, the eighth-century priestess Chiao *lien-shih* 焦煉師, and the goddess Shang-yüan fu-jen 上元夫人.

___. "Spreading Open the Barrier of Heaven," *Asiatische Studien/ Études Asiatiques* 40.1 (1986): 22-39. An annotated translation of the *Ch'ing-yao tzu-shu* 青要紫書 (HY 1304).

___. "Ssu-ma Ch'eng-chen in T'ang Verse," *Society for the Study of Chinese Religions Bulletin* 6 (1978): 16-30. A study and translations of poems about the great prelate by writers of the eighth century.

LaFargue, Michael. *Tao and Method: A Reasoned Approach to the "Tao Te Ching."* Albany: SUNY Press, 1994.

___. *The Tao of the "Tao Te Ching," A Translation and Commentary.* Albany: SUNY Press, 1992.

Li, Feng-mao 李豐楙. *Liu-ch'ao Sui T'ang hsien-tao lei hsiao-shuo yen-chiu* 六朝隋唐仙道類小説研究. Taipei: Hsüeh-sheng, 1986.

___. *Wu-ju yü che-chiang: Liu-ch'ao Sui T'ang Tao-chiao wen-hsüeh lun-chi* 誤入與謫降: 六朝隋唐道教文學論集. Taipei: Hsüeh-sheng, 1996.

Li, Pin-ch'eng 李斌城. "Chin shih-nien lai te Tao-chiao yen-chiu" 近時年來的道教研究, *Shih-chieh tsung-chiao yen-chiu* 1994.1.

Li, Yang-cheng 李養正. *Tao-chiao ching shih lun-kao* 道教經史論稿. Chang Chi-yü 張驥禹, ed. Peking: Hua-hsia, 1995.

Liu, Shou-hua 劉守華. *Tao-chiao yü Chung-kuo min-chien wen-hsüeh* 道教與中國民間文學. Taipei: Wen-chin, 1991.

Lo, Tsung-ch'iang 羅宗強. *Tao-chia Tao-chiao ku-wen lun t'an-p'ien* 道家道教古文論談片. Taipei: Wen-chin, 1995.

Lopez, Donald S., Jr., ed. *Religions of China in Practice.* Princeton: Princeton University Press, 1996.

Lynn, Richard John. "Annotated Bibliography and Glossary to Kristofer Schipper's *The Taoist Body,*" *Taoist Resources* 6.1 (December 1995): 1-30.

Ma, Ta-ch'ang 馬大昌, *et al.,* ed. *Chung-kuo Fo-Tao shih-ko tsung-hui* 中國佛道詩歌總匯. Shih-chia-chuang: Chung-kuo Shu-tien, 1993.

Mair, Victor H. *Lao Tzu, Tao Te Ching, The Classic Book of Integrity and the Way. An Entirely New Translation Based on the Recently Discovered Ma-wang-tui Manuscripts.* New York:

Bantam Books, 1990.

Min, Chih-t'ing 閔智亭 and Li Yang-cheng 李養正, eds. *Tao-chiao ta tz'u-tien* 道教大辭典. Peking: Hua-hsia, 1994.

Mitsuda, Masato. "Taoist Philosophy and Its Influence on T'ang Naturalist Poetry," *JCP* 15.2 (June 1988): 199-216.

Mollier, Christine. *Une Apocalypse Taoïste du vième siècle: Le livre des incantations divines des grottes abyssales.* Paris: Collège de France, Institut des Hautes Études Chinoises, 1990.

Möller, Hans-Georg. *Laotse Tao Te King, nach den Seidentexten aus Mawangdui.* Frankfurt: Fischer, 1995. The first German translation based on the manuscripts discovered at Ma-wang-tui.

Mugitani, Kunio 麦谷邦夫, ed. *Shinkô sakuin* 真誥索引 Kyoto: Kyoto Daigaku Jinbun Kagaku Kenkyûjo, 1991.

Noguchi, Tetsurô 野口鉄郎, ed. *Dôkyô jiten* 道教事典. Tokyo: Hirakawa, 1994.

Nylan, Michael, trans. Yang Hsiung. *The Canon of Supreme Mystery, a Translation with Commentary of the T'ai Hsüan Ching.* Albany: State University of New York, 1993.

Ôfuchi, Ninji 大淵忍爾. *Shoki no Dôkyôshi–Dôkyôshi no kenkyû, #1* 初期の道教史—道教史の研究. Tokyo: Sôbunsha, 1991.

Ozaki, Masaharu. "The History of the Evolution of Taoist Scriptures," *Acta Asiatica* 68 (1996): 37-53.

Pai, Wen-hua 白化文 and Sun Hsi 孫欣. *Ku-tai hsiao-shuo yü tsung-chiao* 古代小說與宗教. Shenyang: Liao-ning Chiao-yü, 1992.

Palmer, Martin, ed. *T'ung Shu–The Ancient Chinese Almanac.* London: Rider & Co. 1986.

Pas, Julian F. *Historical Dictionary of Taoism.* Lanham, Maryland: Scarecrow, 1998.

___, comp. *A Select Bibliography on Taoism.* New York: Institute for Advanced Studies in World Religion, 1988.

Peerenboom, R. P. *Law and Morality in Ancient China: The Silk Manuscripts of Huang-Lao.* Albany: SUNY Press, 1993.

Petersen, J. Ø. "The Early Traditions Relating to the Han Dynasty Transmission of the *Taiping jing,*" *AO,* 50(1989):133-71; 51(1990):173-216.

Raphals, Lisa. "Poetry and Argument in the *Zhuangzi,*" *JCR* 22 (1994): 103-116.

Reiter, Florian C. "Fan Tsu-yü's (1041-1098) Lectures on T'ang Emperors and their Taoist Inclinations," *Oriens* 31 (1988): 290-313.

___. *Grundelemente und Tendenzen des religiösen Taoismus: das Spannungsverhältnis von Intergration und Individualität in seiner Geschichte zur Chin-, Yüan- und frühen Ming-Zeit.* Wiesbaden: Steiner, 1988.

___. "The 'Investigation Commissioner of the Nine Heavens' and the Beginning of His Cult in Northern Chiang-hsi in 731 A.D.," *Oriens* 31 (1988): 266-289. Uses late T'ang and Sung texts from the *Tao-tsang* to examine this cult.

___. "Kategorien und Realien im Shang-ch'ing Taoismus," in *Arbeitsmaterialien zum Taoismus der frühen T'ang Zeit.* Wiesbaden: Harrassowitz, 1992.

___. *Der Perlenbeutel aus den Drei Höhlen (San-tung chu-nang); Arbeitsmaterial zum Taoismus der fruehen T'ang-Zeit.* Wiesbaden: Harrassowitz, 1990.

___. "Das Selbstverständnis des Taoismus zur frühen T'ang Zeit in der Darstellung Wang Hsüan-ho's," *Saeculum* 33 (1982): 240-245.

Reed, Barbara E. "Taoism," in Arvind Sharma, ed. *Women in World Religions.* Albany: State University of New York Press, 1987, pp. 174-180.

Robinet, Isabelle. *Histoire du taoïsme des origines au XIVe siècle.* Paris: Cerf, 1991.

___. "The Place and the Meaning of the Notion of *Taiji* in Taoist Sources Prior to the Ming Dynasty," *History of Religions* 29 (1990): 373-411.

___. *Taoist Meditation: The Mao-shan Tradition of Great Purity.* Julian Pas and Norman Girardot, trans. Albany: SUNY Press, 1993 (original 1979).

Roth, Harold D. *The Textual History of the 'Huai-nan Tzu.'* Ann Arbor: Association for Asian Studies, 1992.

Russell, Terrence Craig. "Songs of the Immortals: The Poetry of the *Chen Kao.*" Unpublished Ph. D. dissertation, Australian National University, 1985.

Sakade, Yoshinobu 坂出祥伸 *et al.,* eds. *Dôkyô no daijiten–Dôkyôkai o yomu* 道教の大事典一道教を読む. Tokyo: Shin Jinbutsu Ôraisha, 1994.

Schafer, Edward H. "The Dance of the Purple Culmen," *TS* 5(1987): 45-68. Includes translations of two T'ang *fu* on this dance.

___. "Empyreal Powers and Chthonian Edens: Two Notes on T'ang Taoist Literature," *JAOS* 106(1986): 667-677. Two Taoist themes as illustrated primarily in the poetry of Wu Yün and Ts'ao T'ang.

___. *Mirages on the Sea of Time, The Taoist Poetry of Ts'ao T'ang.* Berkeley: University of California Press, 1985.

___. Notes on Lord Lao in T'ang Times," *Schafer Sinological Papers* 27(1985).

___. "The Snow of Mao Shan: A Cluster of Taoist Images," *JCR,* 13/14(198?): 107-126.

___. "Transcendent Elder Mao," *Cahiers d'Extrême-Asie* 2(1986): 111-122.

___. "Wu Yün's Stanzas on Sylphdom," *MS* 35(1981-3):309-45.

Schipper, Kristofer M. *The Taoist Body.* Karen C. Duval, trans. Berkeley: University of California Press, 1993.

___. "Taoist Ritual and Local Cults of the T'ang Dynasty," in *Tantric and Taoist Studies in Honour of R. A. Stein.* Michel Strickman, ed. V. 3. Bruxelles: Institut Belge des Hautes Études Chinoises, 1987.

Schmidt, Hans-Hermann. "Die Hundertachtzig Vorschriften von Lao-chün." In *Religion und Philosophie in Ostasien, Festschfift für Hans Steininger.* Gert Naudorf, Karl-Heinz Pohl, and Hans-Hermann Schmidt, eds. Würzburg: Königshausen and Neumann, 1985, pp. 149-160.

Seidel, Anna. "Chronicle of Taoist Studies in the West 1950-1990," *Cahiers d'Extrême-Asie,* 5(1989-1990): 233-347. This survey, and that by Franciscus Verellen (below), should be the basic point of departure for those interested in Taoist literature.

___. *La divinisation de Lao Tseu dans le Taoïsme des Han.* Paris: École Française d'Extrême-Orient, 1992.

Shi, Mingfei. "Li Po's Ascent of Mount O-mei: A Taoist Vision of the Mythology of a Sacred Mountain," *Taoist Resources,* 4.2(1993):31-46.

Smith, Thomas E. "Record of the Ten Continents," *Taoist Resources* 2.2 (1990): 87-119. Translation of the *Shih-chou chi* 十洲記.

___. "Ritual and the Shaping of Narrative: The Legend of the Han Emperor Wu (Volumes I and II)." Ph.D. dissertation, University of Michigan, 1992.

Sommer, Deborah, ed. *Chinese Religion, An Anthology of Sources.* New York and Oxford: Oxford University Press, 1995.

Su, Chin-jen 蘇晉仁. *Tun-huang Tao-chia i-ching* 敦煌道家遺經. Chengtu: Pa-Shu Shu-she, 1995.

Tao-chia ta tz'u-tien 道教大辭典. Chung-kuo Tao-chiao Hsieh-hui, ed. Peking: Hua Hsia 華夏, 1993.

Tao-chiao chin-shih lüeh 道教金石略. Peking: Wen-wu, 1988.

Taoist Resources. Bloomington, Indiana, v. 1- (1988-). The only Western-language journal devoted to Taoist literature.

Tao-tsang t'i-yao 道藏提要. Jen Chi-yü 任繼愈 and Chung Chao-p'eng 鍾肇鵬, ed. Peking: Chung-kuo She-hui K'o-hsüeh Ch'u-pan-she, 1991.

Tuan, Yü-ming 段玉明. *Chung-kuo ssu-miao wen-hua* 中國寺廟文化. Shanghai: Shang-hai

Ch'u-pan-she, 1995.

van der Loon, Piet. *Taoist Books in the Libraries of the Sung Period—a Critical Study and Index...* London: Ithaca Press 1984.

Verellen, Franciscus. "'Evidential Miracles in Support of Taoism': The Inversion of a Buddhist Apologetic Tradition in Late T'ang China," *TP* 78 (1992): 217-263.

___. "Luo Gongyuan, Legende et culte d'un Saint Taoïste," *JA* CCLXXV.3/4 (1987): 283-332.

___. "Mythologie des Taoismus." In E. Schmalzriedt and H. W. Haussig, eds. *Wörterbuch de Mythologie.* Stuttgart: Klett-Cotta, 1994, v. 6, pp. 743-863.

___. "Taoism" in "Chinese Religions: The State of the Field (Part II)," *JAS* 54.2 (May 1995): 322-346. This bibliography, and that by Anna Seidel (supra), should be the basic point of departure for those interested in Taoist literature.

Wagner, Rudolf. "Wang Bi's Recension of the *Laozi*," *EC* 14 (1989): 27-54.

Walters, Derek, trans. Yang Hsiung. *The T'ai Hsüan Ching, the Hidden Classic.* Wellington: The Aquarian Press, 1993.

Wang, Mei 王玫. "Chin Sung shan-shui shih yü Tao-chiao ching-shen" 晉宋山水詩與道精神, *Tao-chiao wen-hua yen-chiu* 8 (1995): 299-309.

Wang, Yao 王堯. "*Chin P'ing Mei* yü Ming-tai Tao-chiao huo-tung" 金瓶梅與明代道教活動, *Tao-chiao wen-hua yen-chiu* 7 (1995): 373-398.

Wong, Eva, trans. *Seven taoist Masters—A Folk Novel of China.* Boston: Shambhala, 1990.

Wong, Shiu Hon. *Investigations into the Authenticity of the "Chang San-Feng Ch'uan-Chi"—The Complete Works of Chang San-feng.* Canberra: Australian National University Press, 1982.

Wu, Feng 吳楓 and Sung I-fu 宋一夫. *Chung-hua Tao-hsüeh t'ung-tien* 中華道學通典. Haikou.: Nan-hai 南海, 1994.

Wu, Wei-min 伍偉民. *Tao-chiao wen-hsüeh san-shih t'an* 道教文學三十談. Shanghai: Shang-hai She-hui K'o-hsüeh-yüan, 1993.

Yu, Shiao-ling. "Taoist Themes in Yüan Drama (with Emphasis on the Plays of Ma Chih-yüan)," *JCP* 15.2 (1988):123-49.

Women's Literature

Armstrong, Nancy. "Chinese Women in a Comparative Perspective: A Response." In Widmer and Chang, *Writing Women,* pp. 397-422.

Carlitz, Katherine. "Desire and Writing in the Late Ming Play *Parrot Island.*" In Widmer and Chang, *Writing Women,* pp. 147-170.

___. "The Social Uses of Female Virtue in Late Ming Editions of the *Lienü zhuan,*" *Late Imperial China* 12.2 (December 1991): 117-148.

Chang, Hsiu-jung 張修蓉. *Han-T'ang kuei-tsu yü ts'ai-nü shih-ko yen-chiu* 漢唐貴族與才女詩歌研究. Taipei: Wen-shih-che, 1985.

Chang, Kang-i Sun 孫康宜 and Haun Saussy, eds. *Chinese Women Poets: An Anthology of Poetry and Criticism.* Stanford: Stanford University Press, 1998.

___. "A Guide to Ming-Ch'ing—Anthologies of Female Poetry and Their Selection Strategies," *Gest Library Journal,* 5.2(1992):119-60.

___. "Hsing-pieh te k'un-huo—ts'ung 'nan-nü chün-ch'en tao 'nü pan nan chuang'" 性別的困惑—從男女君臣到女扮男裝, *Chin-tai Chung-kuo fu-nü shih yen-chiu* 6 (June 1998).

___. *Ku-tien yü hsien-tai te nü-hsing ch'an-shih* 古典與現代的女性闡釋. Taipei: Lien-ho Wen-hsüeh, 1998. Several studies on traditional women, including women as poets and the canonization of women's poetry.

___. "Liu Shih and Hsü Ts'an, Feminine or Feminist?" in Yu, *Voices,* pp. 169-187.

___. "Ming-Qing Women Poets and the Notions of 'Talent' and 'Morality.'" In *Culture and State in Chinese History: Conventions, Conflicts, and Accommodations*. Bing Wong, Ted Huters, and Pauline Yu, eds. Stanford: Stanford University Press, 1998.

___. "Ming and Qing Anthologies of Women's Poetry and Their Selection Strategies," in Widmer and Chang, *Writing Women,* pp. 147-170.

Ch'en, Hsin 陳新, Chou Wei-te 周維德 and Yü Wan-p'ing 俞浣萍, ed. *Li-tai fu-nü shih-tz'u hsüan-chu* 歷代婦女詩詞選注. Peking: Chung-kuo Fu-nü, 1985.

Ch'en, Li-tung 沈立東 and Ko Ju-t'ung 葛汝桐, eds. *Li-tai fu-nü shih-tz'u chien-shang tz'u-tien* 歷代婦女詩詞鑒賞辭典. Peking: Chung-kuo Fu-nü, 1992. This 1878-page volume surpasses an earlier collection by Ch'en Li-tung.

Chiang, William W. *"We Two Know the Script, We Have Become Good Friends." Linguistic and Social Aspects of the Women's Script Literature in Southern Hunan, China.* Lanham: University Press of America, 1995.

Ch'iao, I-kang 喬以鋼. *Chung-kuo nü-hsing te wen-hsüeh shih-chieh* 中國女性的文學世界. Wuhan: Hu-pei Chiao-yü, 1993.

___. "Chung-kuo ku-tai fu-nü wen-hsüeh te kan-shang ch'uan-t'ung" 中國古代婦女文學的捍傷傳統, *Wen-hsüeh i-ch'an* 1991.4: 16-23.

Chiu-Duke, Josephine. "The Role of Confucian Revival in the Confucianization of T'ang Women," *AM, TS* 8.1 (1995): 51-93.

Chou, Tao-jung 周道榮 *et al.,* eds. *Chung-kuo li-tai nü-tzu shih-tz'u hsüan* 中國歷代女子詩詞選. Peking: Hsin-hua, 1983.

Choy, Elsie. *Leaves of Prayer, the Life and Poetry of He Shuangqing, a Farmwife in Eighteenth-century China. Selected Translations from Shi Zhenlin's West Green Random Notes.* Hong Kong: The Chinese University Press, 1993.

Chung, Hui-ling 鍾慧玲. "Ch'ing-tai nü shih-jen yen-chiu" 清代女詩人研究. Unpublished Ph. D. dissertation, Cheng-chih University (Taipei), 1981.

Chung-kuo li-tai ts'ai-nü shih-ko chien-shang tz'u-tien 中國歷代才女詩歌鑒賞辭典. Cheng Kuang-i 鄭光儀, ed. Peking: Chung-kung Kung-jen, 1991, p. 1656.

Cutter, Robert Joe and William Gordon Crowell, trans. *Empresses and Consorts, Translations from Chen Shou's* Records of the Three States *with Pei Songzhi's Commentary.* Honolulu: University of Hawaii Press, 1998.

Deweerdy, Hilde. "Grief for Departed Women in *Shi* from Jin to Sui: Pan Yue's 'Daowang shi," *Papers on Chinese Literature,* 1 (Spring 1993): 21-39.

Edwards, Louise P. *Men and Women in Qing China: Gender in the Red Chamber Dream.* Leiden: E. J. Brill, 1994.

___. *Recreating the Literary Canon: Communist Critiques of Women in the Red Chamber Dream.* Dortmund: projekt, 1995. *Edition Cathay,* 12.

___. "Women Warriors and Amazons of the Mid Qing Texts *Jinghuayuan* and *Hongloumeng,"* *Modern Asian Studies* 29(1996): 225-55.

Epstein, Maram. "Beauty is the Beast: The Dual Face of Woman in Four Ch'ing Novels." Ph.D. dissertation. Princeton University, 1992.

___. "Engendering Order: Structure, Gender and Meaning in the Qing Novel *Jinghua yuan,"* *CLEAR* 18 (1996): 101-129.

Fong, Grace S. "De/Constructing a Feminine Ideal in the Eighteenth Century: *Random Records of West-Green* and the Story of Shuangqing." In Widmer and Chang, *Writing Women,* pp. 264-281.

___. "Engendering the Lyric: Her Image and Voice in Song," in Yu, *Voices,* pp. 107-144.

Frost, Molly Spitzer. "Chinese Matriarchy: Clues from Legends and Characters." Unpublished Ph. D. dissertation, Georgetown University, 1982.

Freudenberg, Michael. *Dei Frauenbewegung in China am Ende der Qingdynastie.* Bochum:

Brockmeyer, 1985. *Chinathemen,* 20.

Furth, Charlotte. "The Patriarch's Legacy: Household Instructions and the Transmission of Orthodox Values." In *Orthodoxy in Late Imperial China.* Liu Kuang-ching, ed. Berkeley: University of California Press, 1990.

___, ed. *Symposium on Poetry and Women's Culture in Late Imperial China. Late Imperial China* 13.1(1992).

Gerstlacher, Anna *et al. Women and Literature in China.* Bochum: Brockmeyer, 1985.

Gilmartin, Christina K. *et al.,* ed. *Engendering China–Women, Culture and the State.* Cambridge, Massachusetts and London, England: Harvard University Press, 1994.

Grant, Beata. "Patterns of Female Religious Experience in Qing Dynasty Popular Literature," *JCR,* 23 (1995): 29-58.

___. "Who Is This I? Who Is That Other? The Poetry of an Eighteenth Century Buddhist Laywoman," *Late Imperial China* 15.1(1994):47-86.

Hinsch, Bret. "Women in Early Imperial China." Unpublished Ph. D. dissertation, Harvard University, 1994.

___. "Women, Kinship, and Property as Seen in a Han Dyansty Will," *TP* 84 (1998): 1-20.

Ho, Clara Wing-chung. "Conventionality versus Dissent: Designation of the Titles of Women's Collected Works in Qing China," *Ming Qing yanjiu,* 3(1994):47-90.

Holgrem, Jennifer. "Myth, Fantasy or Scholarship: Images of the Status of Women in Traditional China," *Australian Journal of Chinese Affairs,* 6(1981): 147-70.

___. "Widow Chastity in the Northern Dynasties: The *Lieh-nü* Biographies in the *Wei-shu,*" *PFEH* 23 (1981): 165-186.

Hsiung, Hsien-kuan Ann-Marie. "Seeking Women in Pre-modern Chinese Texts: A Feminist Re-vision of Ming Drama (1368-1644)." Unpublished Ph. D. dissertation, University of Hawaii, 1995.

Hu, Hsiao-chen 胡曉真. "Literary *Tanci:* A Woman's Tradition of Narrative in Verse." Unpublished Ph. D. dissertation, Harvard University, 1994.

___. "Tsui-chin Hsi-fang Han-hsüeh-chieh fu-nü wen-hsüeh-shih yen-chiu chih p'ing-chieh" 最近西方漢學界婦女文學史研究之評介, *Chin-tai Chung-kuo fu-nü shih yen-chiu* 2 (June 1994): 271-295.

Hu, Wen-kai 胡文楷. *Li-tai fu-nü chu-tso k'ao* 歷代婦女箸作考. Shanghai: Shang-hai Ku-chi, 1985.

___. "Yüeh-tu fan-ying yü t'an-tz'u hsiao-shuo te ch'uang-tso–Ch'ing-tai nü-hsing hsü-shih wen-hsüeh ch'uan-t'ung chien-li chih i-yü," 閱讀反應與彈詞曉説的創作—清代女性敍事文學傳統建立之一隅, *Chung-kuo wen-che yen-chiu chi-k'an* 8 (March 1996): 305-362.

Hu, Ying. "Angling with Beauty: Two Stories of Women as Narrative Bait in *Sanguozhi yanyi,*" *CLEAR* 15 (1993): 99-112.

Hua, Wei 華瑋. "Hsi-lun Liu Ch'ing-yün 'Hsiao P'eng-lai hsien-kuan ch'uan-ch'i' chih nei-jung ssu-hsiang" 析論劉清韻〔小蓬萊仙館傳奇〕之內容思想, *Chung-kuo wen-che yen-chiu chi-k'an* 7 (September 1995): 183-243.

___. "The Lament of Frustrated Talents: An Analysis of Three Women's Plays in Late Imperial China," *Ming Studies* 32 (April 1994): 28-42.

Idema, W. L. *Vrouwenschrift. Vriendschap, huwelijk en wanhoop van Chinese vrouwen, opgetekend in een eigen schrift.* Amsterdam: Meulenhoff, 1996. An extensive anthology of popular songs and ballads which were noted down in the "women's script" of the Chiang-yung district in southern Hunan.

K'ang, Cheng-kuo 康正果. *Feng-sao yü yen-ch'ing* 風騷與艷情. Tientsin: Ho-nan Jen-min, 1988; rpt. Taipei: Yün-lung, 1991.

Knechtges, David R. "The Poetry of an Imperial Concubine, The Favorite Beauty Ban," *OE,*

36 (1993):127-144.

Ko, Dorothy. "Lady-Scholars at the Door: The Practice of Gender Relations in Eighteenth-century Suzhou," in John Hay, ed. *Boundaries in China*. London: reaktion books, 1994, pp. 198-216.

___. *Teachers of the Inner Chambers, Women and Culture in Seventeenth-Century China*. Stanford: Stanford University Press, 1994.

___. "The Written Word and the Bound Foot: A History of the Courtesan's Aura." In Widmer and Chang, *Writing Women*, pp. 74-100.

Kwong, Hing Foo. *Wang Zhaojun, une héroïne chinoise—de l'histoire à la légende. Mémoires de l'Institut des Hautes Études Chinoises,* v. 27. Paris: Collège de France, Institut des Hautes Études Chinoises, 1986.

Lee, Lily Xiao Hong. *The Virtue of Yin, Studies on Chinese Women*. Broadway, Australia: Wild Peony, 1994. Several studies on traditional women, including Pan Chao.

Li, Wai-yee. "The Late Ming Courtesan: Invention of a Cultural Ideal." In Widmer and Chang, *Writing Women,* pp. 46-73.

Liang, I-chen 梁乙真. *Chung-kuo fu-nü wen-hsüeh shih-kang* 中國婦女文學史綱. Rpt. Shanghai: Shang-hai Shu-tien, 1990 (1932).

Liu, Shouhau and Hu Xiaoshan. "Folk Narrative in Chinese Nüshu: An Amazing New Discovery." *Asian Folklore Studies* 53 (1994): 307–18.

Liu, Yong-ts'ung 劉詠聰. "Ch'ing-tai ch'ien-ch'i kuan-yü nü-hsing fo-yu 'ts'ai' chih t'ao-lun" 清代前期關於女性否有才之討論, *Chung-hua wen-shih lun-ts'ung* 45 (1989): 315-343.

Lu, Tonglin. *Rose and Lotus: Narrative of Desire in France and China*. Albany: State University of New York, 1991.

McLaren, Anne. *The Chinese Femme Fatale, Stories from the Ming Period*. Broadway, Australia:: Wild Peony, 1995? *University of Sydney, East Asian Series,* No. 8.

___. "Women's Voices and Textuality. Chastity and Abduction in Chinese *Nüshu* Writing." *Modern China* 22.4 (1996): 382–416.

McMahon, Keith R. *Misers, Shrews and Polygamists; Sexuality and Male-Female Relations in Eighteenth-Century China Fiction*. Durham: Duke University Press, 1995.

Mann, Susan. "Historical Change in Female Biography from Song to Qing Times: The Case of Early Qing Jiangnan," *Transactions of the International Conference of Orientalists in Japan* 30 (1985): 65-77.

___. *Precious Records: Women in China's Long Eighteenth Century*. Stanford: Stanford University Press, 1997.

Martin-Liao, Tienchi. *Frauenerziehung im Alten China, Eine Analyse der Frauenbücher*. Bochum: Brockmeyer, 1984.

Mou, Sherry Jenq-yunn. "Gentlemen's Prescriptions for Women's Lives: Liu Hsiang's 'The Biographies of Women' and Its Influence on the 'Biographies of Women' Chapters in Early Chinese Dynastic Histories." Ph.D. Ohio State University, 1994.

Nan Nü. 1998?-. A new journal devoted to women and gender issues, edited by Harriet T. Zurndorfer.

Nienhauser, William H., Jr. "Female Sexuality and Standards of Virtue in T'ang Narratives," in Eva Hung, ed., *Paradoxes of Traditional Chinese Literature*. Hong Kong: The Chinese University Press, 1994, pp. 1-20.

Ôki, Hasushi. "Women in Feng Menglong's *Mountain Songs.*" In Widmer and Chang, *Writing Women,* pp. 131-143.

Palm, Christoph. "Yang Guifei in der chinesischen Literatur: Rezeptionsgeschichte eines tragischen Frauenschicksals von der Tangzei bis zur Gegenwart." Unpublished Ph. D. dissertation, Free University, Berlin, 1993.

Pan, Yu-shu 班友書, ed. *Chung-kuo nü-hsing shih-ko ts'ui-pien* 中國女性詩歌粹編. Peking:

Chung-kuo Wen-lien, 1996.

Pao, Chia-lin 鮑家麟. *Chung-kuo fu-nü shih lun-chi* 中國婦女史論集. 4v. Taipei: Tao-hsiang, 1986–1994.

Robertson, Maureen. "Changing the Subject: Gender and Self-inscription in Authors' Prefaces and *Shi* Poetry." In Widmer and Chang, *Writing Women,* pp. 171-217.

___. "Voicing the Feminine: Construction of the Gendered Subject in Lyric Poetry by Women of Medieval and Late Imperial China," *Late Imperial China* 13.1 (June 1992): 82-84.

Ropp, Paul S. "Ambiguous Images of Courtesan Culture in Late Imperial China." In Widmer and Chang, *Writing Women,* pp. 17-45.

___. "Love, Literacy and Laments: Themes of Women Writers in Late Imperial China," *Women's History Review,* 2.1(1993):107-41.

Saussy, Haun and Kang-i Sun Chang 孫康宜, eds. *Chinese Women Poets: An Anthology of Poetry and Criticism.* Stanford: Stanford University Press, 1998.

Saussy, Haun. "Women's Writing Before and Within the *Hong lou meng.*" In Widmer and Chang, *Writing Women,* pp. 285-305.

Sharma, Arvind, ed. *Women in World Religions.* Albany: State University of New York Press, 1987.

Shen, Li-tung 沈立東, ed. *Li-tai hou-fei shih-tz'u chi-chu* 歷代后妃詩詞集註. Peking: Chung-kuo Fu-nü, 1985.

Su, Che-ts'ung 蘇者聰. *Sung-tai nü-hsing wen-hsüeh* 宋代女性文學. Wuhan: Wu-han Ta-hsüeh, 1997.

Sung, Marina H. "The Chinese *Lieh-nü* Tradition," *History of Religions* 8.3 (Fall 1981): 63-74.

T'an, Cheng-pi 譚正璧. *Chung-kuo nü-hsing wen-hsüeh shih-hua* 中國女性文學詩話. Tientsin: Pai-hua Wen-i, 1984.

T'ao, Mu-ning 陶慕寧. *Ch'ing-lou wen-hsüeh yü Chung-kuo wen-hua* 青樓文學與中國文化. Peking: Tung-fang, 1993.

Tsai, Kathryn Ann, trans. *Lives of the Nuns, Biographies of Chinese Buddhist Nuns from the Fourth to Sixth Centuries.* Honolulu: University of Hawaii Press, 1994. A translation of *Pi-ch'iu ni chuan* 比丘妮傳.

Waltner, Ann. "Tan-yang-tzu and Wang Shih-chen: Visionary and Bureaucrat in the Late Ming," *Late Imperial China* 8.1 (June 1987): 105-133.

___. "Writing Her Way Out of Trouble: Li Yuying in History and Fiction." In Widmer and Chang, *Writing Women,* pp. 221-241.

Watson, Rubie S. "Chinese Bridal Laments: The Claims of a Dutiful Daughter." In Bell Yung, *et al.,* eds. *Harmony and Counterpoint. Ritual Music in a Chinese Context.* Stanford: Stanford University Press, 1996, 107-129.

Widmer, Ellen. "The Epistolary World of Female Talent in Seventeenth-Century China," *Late Imperial China* 10.2 (December 1989): 1-43.

___. "Hou Zhi 侯芝 (1764-1829), Poet and *Tanci* Writer," *Chin-tai Chung-kuo fu-nü shih yen-chiu* 5 (August 1997): 155-173.

___. "Ming Loyalism and the Women's Voice in Fiction after *Hong lou meng.*" In Widmer and Chang, *Writing Women,* pp. 366-396.

___ and Kang-i Sun Chang, eds. *Writing Women in Late Imperial China.* Stanford: Stanford University Press, 1997.

___. "Xiaoqing's Literary Legacy and the Place of the Woman Writer," *Late Imperial China* 13.1 (June 1992): 126-135.

Wu, Hung. "Beyond Stereotypes: The Twelve Beauties in Qing Court Art and the *Dream of the Red Chamber.*" In Widmer and Chang, *Writing Women,* pp. 306-365.

Wu, Yenna. *The Chinese Virago, A Literary Theme.* Cambridge, Mass.: Harvard University

Press, 1996.

___, trans. *The Lioness Roars: Shrew Stories from Late Imperial China*. Ithaca, N.Y.: Cornell University Press, 1995.

Wu, Qingyun. *Female Rule in Chinese and English Literary Utopias*. Liverpool: Liverpool University Press, 1995.

Yao-Weyrauch, Wan-Hsuan. *Die Rolle der Frau im deutschen und chinesischen Sprichwort*. Bochum: Brockmeyer, 1990. *Chinathemen*, 55. Based on Yao-Weyrauch's Ph. D. dissertation, Giessen University, 1989.

Zeitlin, Judith T. "Embodying the Disembodied: Representations of Ghosts and the Feminine." In Widmer and Chang, *Writing Women*, pp. 242-263.

___. "Shared Dreams: The Story of the Three Wives' Commentary on *The Peony Pavilion*," *HJAS* 54(1994): 127-179.

Zhu, Hong. "China," in *Bloomsbury Guide to Women's Literature*. Claire Buck, ed. London: Bloomsbury, 1992.

Zurndorfer, Harriet T. "Han-hsüeh, 'Evidential Research', and Female Chastity: A Re-examination of Intellectual Attitudes and Social Ideals in 18th Century China." In *Thought and Law in Qin and Han China*. Leiden: E. J. Brill, 1990, pp. 208-224.

Entries

Dates for individuals and translations of titles for the most part follow those given in volume one of the *Indiana Companion*. For some individuals (Ch'en Shih-tao 陳師道, for example) new dates have been proposed recently. They are included in the following format: Ch'en Shih-tao (1052-1102 or 1053-1101), where "1052-1102" are the dates that appeared in the "Ch'en Shih-tao" entry in volume one and "1053-1101" those recently proposed by scholars.

Bunkyô hifuron 文鏡秘府論

Editions and References
Kôzen, Hiroshi 興膳宏. *Bunkyô hifuron, Bunpitsu ganshin shô* 文鏡秘府論、文筆眼心抄. In *Kôbô Daishi Kûkai zenshû* 弘法大詩空海全集, v. 5. Tokyo: Chikuma Shobô, 1986.
Wang, Li-ch'i 王力器. *Wen-ching mi-fu lun chiao-chu* 文鏡秘府論校注. Peking: Chung-kuo She-hui K'o-hsüeh, 1983. Appends a selection of Kûkai's verse and a list of his writings.

Studies
Furukawa, Sueki 古川末喜. *"Bunkyô hifuron* ni miru shishôritsu to hyôsokuritsu" 文鏡秘府論にみる四聲律と平仄律, *Saga Daigaku Kyôyôbu kenkyû kiyô* 27 (1995): 13-28.

Cha Shen-hsing 查慎行 (1650–1727)

Editions and References
Cha, Shen-hsing. *Cha Hui-yü wen-chi* 查悔余文集. 3v. Tientsin: T'ien-chin Ku-chi, 1987. Reprint of a manuscript compiled by Hsüeh Ch'uan 薛傳 held in the Peking University Library.
___. *Jen-hai chi* 人海記. Taipei: Hsin-hsing, 1990. *Pi-chi hsiao-shuo ta-kuan,* 7.
___, comm. *Su shih pu-chu* 蘇詩補註. Taipei: T'ai-wan Shang-wu, 1983.
Chou, Shao-piao 周邵標, ed. *Ching-yeh T'ang shih-chi* 敬業堂詩集. Shanghai: Shang-hai Ku-chi, 1986. Chung-kuo Ku-tien Wen-hsüeh Ts'ung-shu. The standard modern critical edition; appends prefaces by various traditional scholars.

Chan-kuo ts'e 戰國策 (Intrigues of the Warring States)

Editions and References
Chan-kuo ts'e tsung-heng chia shu 戰國策縱橫家書. Peking: Wen-wu, 1976.
Chang, Ch'ing-ch'ang 張清常 and Wang Yen-tung 王延棟, ed. *Chan-kuo ts'e chien-chu* 戰國策箋注. Tientsin: Nan-k'ai Ta-hsüeh, 1993.
Ch'ien, Chao-ch'en 錢趙塵. *Chan-kuo ts'e i-chu* 戰國策釋注. Peking: Yen-shan, 1993.
Chu, Tsu-keng 諸祖耿. *Chan-kuo ts'e chi chu hui-k'ao* 戰國策集注彙考. 3v. Yangchow: Chiang-su Ku-chi, 1985.

Ho, Chien-chang 何見章. *Chan-kuo ts'e chu shih* 戰國策注釋. 4v. Peking: Chung-hua, 1990.

Ku, Chieh-kang 顧頡剛. *Ch'un-ch'iu chih chuan chi Kuo-yü chih tsung-ho yen-chiu* 春秋之傳及國語之綜合研究. Liu Ch'i-yü 劉起紆, recorder. Chengtu: Shu-Pa Shu-she, 1988.

Lau, D. C. and Chen Fong Ching. *A Concordance to the Zhanguoce* 戰國策逐字索引. *ICS Series*. Hong Kong: Commercial Press, 1992.

Miao, Wen-yüan 繆文遠. *Chan-kuo ts'e hsin chiao-chu* 戰國策新校注. 2v. Chengtu: Shu-Pa Shu-she, 1987. Appends personal- and place-name indexes.

___. *Chan-kuo ts'e k'ao-pien* 戰國策考辨. Peking: Chung-hua, 1984.

Kudô, Motoo 工藤元男, Sanae Yoshio 早苗良雄 and Fujita Katsuhisa 藤田勝久, trans. and comm. *Sengoku Jûô kasho-Ma ô tai hakusho* 戦国縱横家書–馬王堆帛書. Kyoto: Hôyû Shoten, 1994.

Translations

Fukuda, Jônosuke 福田襄之介 and Mori Kumao 森熊男. *Shinshaku kanbun taikei 49–Sengoku saku (ge)* 新釈漢文体系４９–戦国策　（下）. Tokyo: Meiji Shoin, 1987.

Kondô, Mitsuo 近藤光男. *Sengoku saku* 戦国策. Tokyo: Kôdansha, 1987.

Studies

Blanford, Yumiko Fukushima. "Studies of the 'Zhanguo zonghengjia shu' Silk Manuscript." 2v. Unpublished Ph. D. dissertation, University of Washington, 1989.

___. "Discovery of Lost Eloquence: New Insight from the Mawangdui 'Zhanguo zonghengjia shu,'" *JAOS* 114 (1994), 77-93.

___. "A Textual Approach to 'Zhanguo Zonghengjia Shu': Methods of Determining the Proximate Original Word among Variants," *EC*, 16 (1991): 187-207.

Chan-kuo ts'e chiao-shih erh-chung 戰國策校釋二種. Chao Li-sheng 趙立聲 *et al.*, eds. Peking: Shou-tu Shih-fan Ta-hsüeh, 1994. Contains Wang Nien-sun 王念孫, "Chan-kuo ts'e" 戰國策, in his *Tu-shu tsa-chih* 讀書雜志, and Chin Cheng-wei 金正煒, *Chan-kuo ts'e pu-shih* 戰國策補釋.

Hsiung, Hsien-kuang 熊憲光. *Chan-kuo ts'e yen-chiu yü hsüan-i* 戰國策研究與選譯. Chungking: Hsin-hua, 1988. Study (pp. 1-111) followed by selected translations (pp. 113-320).

Tsien, Tsuen-hsuin. *"Chan kuo ts'e* 戰國策," in Loewe, *Early Chinese Texts,* pp. 1-11.

Ch'an yü-lu 禪語錄

Editions and References

Ch'an-tsung yü-lu chi-yao 禪宗語錄輯要. Shang-hai Ku-chi, ed. Shanghai: Shang-hai Ku-chi, 1992.

Studies

Iriya, Yoshitaka 入矢義高. "Goroku no kotoba to buntai" 語録の言葉と文体, *Zengaku kenkyû* 68 (1990): 1-19.

Chang Chi 張繼 (mid-eighth century)

Studies

Chou, Ming 周銘. "Chien-lun 'Feng-ch'iao yeh po' te chung-sheng" 簡論楓橋夜泊的鍾聲, *Chiang-su Chiao-yü Hsüeh-yüan hsüeh-pao* 1991.4.

Ch'u, Chung-chün 儲仲君. "Chang Chi te hsing-chi chi ch'i-t'a" 張繼的行跡及其他, *Wen-hsüeh i-ch'an* 1991.3.

Yang, Ming 楊明. "Chang Chi shih chung Han-shan-ssu pien" 張繼詩中寒山寺辨, *Chung-hua wen-shih lun-ts'ung* 1987.2/3: 297-304.

Chang Chi 張籍 (*ca.* 776–*ca.* 829)

Editions and References
Chang Chi chüan 張籍卷. In *Ch'üan T'ang shih so-yin,* 1994.
Li, Shu-cheng 李樹政, ed. *Chang Chi, Wang Chien shih-hsüan* 張籍，王建詩選. Canton: Kuang-tung Jen-min, 1984.
Li, Tung-sheng 李冬生, comm. *Chang Chi chi-chu* 張籍集注. Hofei: Huang-shan Shu-she, 1988.
Luan, Kuei-ming 欒貴明 ed. *Ch'uan T'ang Shih so-yin: Chang Chi chüan* 全唐詩索引：張籍卷. Ch'in-huang-tao: Hsien-tai, 1994.

Studies
Chang, Kuo-kuang 張國光. "T'ang Yüeh-fu shih-jen Chang Chi sheng-p'ing k'ao-cheng: Chien-lun Chang Chi shih te fen-ch'i" 唐樂府詩人張籍生平考證：簡論張籍詩的分期. In *Ch'uan-kuo T'ang-shih T'ao-lun-hui Lun-wen Hsüan* 全國唐詩討論會論文選, Ho Sung-lin 霍松林, ed. Sian: Shan-hsi Jen-min, 1984, pp. 230-80.
Chi, Chen-huai 季鎮淮. "Chang Chi erh t'i" 張籍二題. *Wen-hsüeh i-ch'an* 1996.1: 49-51.
Chi, Tso-liang 紀作亮. *Chang Chi yen-chiu* 張籍研究. Hofei: Huang-shan Shu-she, 1986.
Li, I-fei 李一飛. "Chang Chi, Wang Chien chiao-yu k'ao-shu" 張籍，王建交游考述. *Wen-hsüeh i-ts'an* 1993.2: 54-63.
T'ung, P'ei-chi c培基. "Chang Chi Shih Ch'ung-ch'u Chen-pien" 張籍詩重出甄辨. *Ho-nan Ta-hsüeh hsüeh-pao* 98 (1987): 80-84.

Chang Chiu-ling 張九齡 (678–740)

Editions and References
Chang, Chiu-ling. *Chang Chiu-ling chi* 張九齡集. Shanghai: Shang-hai Ku-chi, 1981. Photolithic reprint of Ming-dynasty edition of the *T'ang wu-shih chia shih-chi* 唐五十家詩集.

Studies
Ch'en, Hsin-chang 陳新璋. "Chi Chang Chiu-ling shih-ko te chu-t'i hsing-hsiang yü i-shu feng-ko" 記張九齡詩歌的主體形象與藝述風格, *Hsüeh-shu yen-chiu,* 1989.4.

Chang Cho 張鷟 (657–730)

Editions and References
Yü, T'ien-ch'ih 于天池. "Ying-yin 'Yu-hsien k'u ch'ao' t'i-chi" 影印游仙窟鈔題記, *Pei-ching Shih-ta hsüeh-pao* 1992.6.

Translations
Imamura, Yoshio 今村与志雄. *Yûsenkutsu* 遊仙窟. Tokyo: Iwanami Shoten, 1990.

Studies
Kinugawa, Kenji 衣川賢次. "'Yu-hsien k'u' chiu-chu chiao-tu chi (shang)" 遊仙窟舊注校讀記，上 [in Chinese], *Hanazono Daigaku Bungakubu kenkyû kiyô* 27 (1995): 97-144.

Chang, Shih-t'ung 張世同. "Ts'ung 'Yu-hsien k'u' k'an hsiao-shuo yu chih-kuai erh ch'uan-ch'i te yen-chin chih chi" 叢游仙窟看小説由志怪而傳奇的演進之跡, *Ku-tien wen-hsüeh chih-shih* 1991.4.

K'ang, Shu-hsin 康樹欣. "Chang Cho" 張鷟, *Ho-pei hsüeh-k'an,* 1983.4.

Liu, Chen-lun 劉真倫. "Chang Cho shih-chi hsi-nien k'ao" 張鷟事跡系年考, *Chung-ch'ing Shih-yüan hsüeh-pao,* 1987.4.

Chang Feng-i 張鳳翼 (1527-1613)

Editions and References

Hung-fu chi 紅拂記. Nanking?: Chiang-su Kuang-lin Ku-chi, 1982. Reprints the Kuei-ch'ih Liu-shih Yüan-hung Shih 貴池劉事爰紅室 edition.

Sui, Shu-sen 隋樹森 *et al.*, eds. *Chang Feng-i hsi-ch'ü hsüan* 張鳳翼戲曲選. Peking: Chung-hua, 1994.

Chang Heng 張衡 (78–139)

Editions and References

Chang, Heng 張衡. *Chang Heng shih-wen chi-chiao-chu* 張衡詩文集校注. Chang Chen-tse 張震澤, ed. and comm. Shanghai: Shang-hai Ku-chi, 1986.

Chang, Tsai-i 張在義 *et al.*, eds. *Chang Heng wen hsüan-i* 張衡文選譯. Chengtu: Pa-Shu Shu-she, 1990. *Ku-tai wen-shih ming-chu hsüan-i ts'ung-shu.*

Studies

Arai, Shinji 新井普司. "Chô Kô: Kongi shu Konggito shu saikô" 張衡：渾儀注渾儀圖注再考 . *Chûgoku kodai kagakushiron* (1989): 317-336.

Chang Hsien 張先 (990–1078)

Editions and References
Ch'üan Sung shih, 3:170.1934-1939.

Translations
Landau, *Beyond Spring,* pp. 54-60.

Studies
Liu, Wen-chu 劉文注. *Chang Hsien chi ch'i An-lu shih* 張先及其安陸詩. Peking: Pei-ching Ta-hsüeh, 1990.

Miao, Yüeh 繆鉞. "Lun Chang Hsien tz'u" 論張先詞, *Wen-hsüeh i-ch'an* 1986.3.

Chang Hua 張華 (232–300)

Editions and References

Chang, Hua. *Ch'in ching* 禽經. Taipei: Hsin-hsing, 1985. *Pi-chi hsiao-shuo ta-kuan,* 38.

___. *Po-wu chih* 博物志. Shanghai: Shang-hai Ku-chi, 1990. Bound with *Mu T'ien-tzu chuan* 穆天子傳* *Shen-i ching* 神異經, and *Shih-chou chi* 十洲記.*

Chu, Hung-chieh 祝鴻杰, comm. and trans. *Po-wu chih ch'üan-i* 博物志全譯. Kweiyang:

Kuei-chou Jen-min, 1992. *Chung-kuo Li-tai Ming-chu Ch'üan-i Ts'ung-shu.*
Fan, Ning 范寧, ed. *Po-wu chih chiao-cheng* 博物志校證. Peking: Chung-hua, 1980; rpt. Taipei: Ming-wen, 1981.

Translations
Geatrex, Roger. *The Bowu Zhi: An Annotated Translation.* Stockholm: Föreningen för Orientaliska Studier, 1987.

Studies
Satô, Rikô 佐藤利行. "Rikuchô bunjinden Chô Ka–*Shinsho* 'Chô Ka den'" 六朝文人伝張華–晋書張華伝, *Chûgoku Chûsei bungaku kenkyû* 21 (1991): 55-69.

Chang Hui-yen 張惠言 (1761–1802)

Editions and References
Chang, Hui-yen and Tung Tzu-yüan 董子遠, compilers. *Tz'u-hsüan chien-chu* 詞選箋註. Chiang Liang-fu 姜亮夫, ed. and comm. Taipei: Kuang-wen, 1980.
Huang, Li-hsin 黃力新, ed. *Ming-k'o wen pien* 茗柯文編. Shanghai: Shang-hai Ku-chi, 1984. *Chung-kuo Ku-tien Wen-hsüeh Ts'ung-shu.* The standard modern critical edition.

Chang Jo-hsü 張若虛 (660–720)

Editions and References
Wang, Ch'i-hsing 王啟興 and Chang Hung 張虹, comm. *Chang Jo-hsü shih-chu* 張若虛詩注. Shanghai: Shang-hai Ku-chi, 1985.

Studies
Nakamori, Kenji 中森健二. "Chô Jakuki 'Shunkô kagetsuya'" 張若虛「春江花月夜」について, *Gakurin* 22 (1995): 31-55.

Chang K'o-chiu 張可久 (1270-1348)

Studies
Lü, Wei-fen 呂薇芬. "Chiang K'o-chiu san-ch'ü chien-lun" 張可久散曲簡論, *Wen-hsüeh p'ing-lun* 1985.2.

Chang Ping-lin 章炳麟 (1868–1936 or 1869-1936)

Editions and References
Chang T'ai-yen ch'üan-chi 章太炎全集. Shanghai: Shang-hai Jen-min, 1984-86.
Hu, Wei-hsi 胡偉希, ed. *Ch'iu shu* 訄書. Shenyang: Liao-ning Jen-min, 1994.
T'ang, Kuo-li 湯國梨, ed. *Chang T'ai-yen Hsien-sheng chia-shu* 章太炎先生家書. Shanghai: Shang-hai Ku-chi, 1985.

Studies
Chang, Nien-ch'ih 章念馳, ed. *Chang T'ai-yen sheng-p'ing yü ssu-hsiang yen-chiu wen-hsüan* 章太炎生平與思想研究文選. Hangchow: Che-chiang Jen-min, 1986.
____. *Chang T'ai-yen sheng-p'ing yü hsüeh-shu* 章太炎生平與學術. Peking: San-lien, 1988.

263

Chiang, I-hua 姜義華. *Chang T'ai-yen p'ing-chuan* 章太炎評傳. Peking?: Pai-hua-chou 百花洲 Wen-i, 1995.

Hsieh, Ying-ning 謝櫻寧. *Chang T'ai-yen nien-p'u shih-i* 章太炎年譜摭遺. Peking: Chung-kuo She-hui K'o-hsüeh, 1987.

Hsü, Li-t'ing 徐立亭. *Chang T'ai-yen* 章太炎. Harbin: Ha-erh-pin Ch'u-pan-she, 1996.

Kaluznaâ, N. M. "Czan Binlin' koncepciâ samoubijsstva," *Obsestvo i gosudarstvo v Kitae* 1995: 228-35.

Weber, Jürgen. "Chang Ping-lin und der Su-pao Vorfall," *Nachrichten der Gesellschaft für Natur- und Völkerkunde Ostasiens* 135 (1986): 5-19.

Chang Ta-fu 張大復 (1554-1630)

Editions and References

Chang, Ta-fu 張大復. *Mei-hua-ts'ao T'ang chi* 梅花草堂集. Taipei: Hsin-hsing, 1988. *Pi-chi hsiao-shuo ta-kuan, 29 pien.*

___. *Mei-hua-ts'ao T'ang pi-t'an* 梅花草堂筆談. Changsha: Yüeh-lu Shu-she, 1991.

___. *Mei-hua-ts'ao T'ang pi-t'an.* 3v. Shanghai: Shang-hai Ku-chi, 1986.

___. *Wu-chün jen-wu chih* 吳郡人物志. Taipei: Ming-wen, 1991.

___. *Wu-chün Chang Ta-fu Hsien-sheng Ming-jen lieh-chuan kao* 吳郡張大復明人列傳稿. Fang Wei-i 方惟一 (Ch'ing dynasty), ed. Taipei: Hsüeh-sheng, 1987.

Chou, Kung-p'ing 周鞏平, ed. *Tsui P'u-t'i* 醉菩提. Peking: Chung-hua, 1996.

Chang Tai 張戴 (1599–1684? or 1597-1685?)

Editions and References

Chang, Tai 張戴. *Shih-kuei shu hou-chi lieh-chuan* 十匱書後集列傳. 56 *chüan.* Taipei: Ming-wen, 1991. *Ming-tai chuan-chi ts'ung-k'an,* 104.

___. *Hsi-hu meng-hsün* 西湖夢尋. Sun Chia-sui 孫家遂, ed. Hangchow: Che-chiang Wen-i, 1984.

___. *Hsi-hu meng-hsün.* Ma Hsing-jung 馬興榮, ed. Shanghai: Shang-hai Ku-chi, 1982.

___. *T'ao-an meng-i* 陶庵夢憶. Ma Hsing-jung 馬興榮, ed. and comm. Shanghai: Shang-hai Ku-chi, 1982. *Ming Ch'ing pi-chi ts'ung-shu.* Printed together with the above in 1 vol.

Hsia, Hsien-ch'un 夏咸淳, ed. *Chang Tai shih-wen chi* 張戴詩文集. Shanghai: Shang-hai Ku-chi, 1991.

Translations

Teboul-Wang, Brigitte. *Souvenirs rêvés de Tao'an.* Gallimard: 1995. An annotated translation of *T'ao-an meng-i* 陶庵夢憶.

Studies

Kafalas, Philip Alexander. "Nostalgia and the Reading of the Late Ming Essay: Zhang Dai's 'Tao'an mengyi.'" Unpublished Ph.D. dissertation, Stanford University, 1995.

Strassberg, *Inscribed Landscapes*, pp. 335-352.

Chang Tsai 張載 (*fl.* 289)

Studies

Kung, Chieh 龔杰. *Chang Tsai p'ing-chuan* 傅玄評傳. Nanking: Nan-ching Ta-hsüeh, 1997.

Miyazaki, Junko宮崎順子. "Chô Sai no "kyoshin" ni tsuite" 張載の「虚心」について, *Chûgoku gakushi* 5 (1990): 53-76.

Chang Wen-t'ao 張問陶 (1764–1814)

Editions and References
Chang, Wen-t'ao 張問陶. *Ch'uan-shan shih-ts'ao* 船山詩草. 2v. Peking: Chung-hua, 1986. *Chung-kuo ku-tien wen-hsüeh chi-pen ts'ung-shu.* Based on a printed edition of 1541; appends a list of materials for the study of Chang Wen-t'ao.
Chou, Yü-cheng 周宇征, ed. *Ch'uan-shan shih-hsüan* 船山詩選. Peking: Shu-mu Wen-hsien, 1986.

Chang Yüeh 張説 (667–731)

Editions and References
Luan, Kuei-ming 欒貴明 *et al.,* eds. *Ch'üan T'ang shih so-yin: Ch'en Tzu-ang, Chang Yüeh chüan* 全唐詩索引：陳子昂，張説卷. Ch'in-huang-tao: Hsien-tai, 1994.

Studies
Chang, Pu-yün 張步云. "Lun Ts'ung Ch'u-T'ang tao Sheng T'ang te Kuo-tu Shih-jen Chang Yüeh" 論從初唐到盛唐的過渡詩人張説. *Shanghai Shih-fan Ta-hsüeh hsüeh-pao* 41 (1989): 15-19.
Chen, Zu-yan [Ch'en Tsu-yen] 陳祖言. "Chang Yüeh: First Poet of the High T'ang,." *TS 12* (1994): 1-10.
___. *Chang Yüeh Nieh-p'u* 張説年譜. Hong Kong: Chung-wen Ta-hsüeh, 1984.
___. "Impregnable Phalanx and Splendid Chamber: Chang Yüeh's Contributions to the Poetry of the High T'ang." Unpublished Ph.D. dissertation, University of Wisconsin, 1989.
___. "Impregnable Phalanx and Splendid Chamber: Chang Yüeh and the Aesthetics of High T'ang Poetry." *CLEAR* 17 (1995): 69-88.
Li, Chien-kuo 李劍國. "Chang Yüeh te ch'uan-ch'i k'ao-lun" 張説的傳奇考論. *Liao-ning Chiao-yü Hsüeh-yüan hsüeh-pao* 遼寧教育學院學報 1985.4 (1985): 38-44.
Tsou, Chin-hsien 鄒進先 and Chang An-tsu 張安祖. "Chang Yüeh tui T'ang-shih Fa-chan te Kung-hsien" 張説對唐詩發展的貢獻, *Ch'iu Shih* 1991.3 (1991): 57-61.

Ch'ang Chien 常建 (*fl.* 749)

Studies
Chang, Hsüeh-chung 張學忠. "Ch'ang Chien wan-nien yin yü Ch'in-chung pien" 常建晚年隱於秦中辨, *Wen-hsüeh i-ch'an*, 1989.5.

Chao I 趙翼 (1727–1814)

Editions and References
Chao, I 趙翼. *Ou-pei chi* 甌北集. 2v. Shang-hai: Shang-hai Ku-chi, 1997.
___. *Ou-pei shih-hua* 甌北詩話. Fu Shou-sun 富壽蓀, ed. Shang-hai: Shang-hai Ku-chi, 1983. *Ch'ing shih-hua hsü-pien,* 1.

___. *Ou-pei shih-hua*. Huo Sung-lin 霍松林 and Hu Chiu-yu 胡主佑, eds. Shang-hai: Shang-hai Ku-chi, 1983. *Chung-kuo ku-tien wen-hsüeh li-lun p'i-p'ing chuan-chu hsüan-chi.*

___. *P'ing-ting T'ai-wan shu-lüeh* 平定臺灣述略. Chengtu: Pa-Shu Shu-she, 1993. *Chung-kuo yeh-shih chi-ch'eng,* 40. Reprinted from the Hsiao-fang-hu Chai 小方壺齋 mss. ed.

___. *Sui-yü ts'ung-k'ao* 陔余叢考. Luan Pao-ch'ün 樂寶群 and Lü Tsung-li 呂宗力, eds. Shih-chia-chuang: Ho-pei Jen-min, 1990.

Hu, I-hsiao 胡憶肖, ed. *Chao I shih-hsüan* 趙翼詩選. Chengchow: Chung-chou Ku-chi, 1985.

Chao Ping-wen 趙秉文 (1159-1232)

Editions and References

Chao, Ping-wen. *Fu shui chi* 滏水集. 20 *chüan* + 1 *chüan*. 8v. Taipei: Shih-chieh, 1988.

Che-hsi tz'u-p'ai 浙西詞派

Editions and Reference

Chu, I-tsun 朱彝尊 (1629-1709), ed. *Tz'u tsung* 詞綜. Chengchow: Chung-chou Ku-chi, 1990.

Ch'en Liang 陳亮 (1143–1194)

Editions and References

Ch'en, Liang 陳亮. *Ch'en Liang chi tseng-ting pen* 陳亮集增訂本. Teng Kuang-ming 鄧廣銘, ed. 2v. Peking: Chung-hua, 1987. Appends traditional prefaces.

___. *Ch'en Liang Lung-ch'uan tz'u chien-chu* 陳亮龍川詞箋注. Chiang Shu-ko 姜書閣 (1907-), ed. and comm. Peking: Jen-min Wen-hsüeh, 1980. Appends biographical material.

___. *Lung-ch'uan tz'u chiao-chien* 龍川詞校箋. Hsia Ch'eng-t'ao 夏承燾 (1900-1986), ed. Mou Chia-k'uan 牟家寬, comm. Hong Kong: Chung-hua, 1977.

Studies

Chao, Min 趙敏 and Hu Kuo-chün 胡國鈞, eds. *Ch'en Liang yen-chiu lun-wen chi* 陳亮研究論文集. Hangchow: Hang-chou Ta-hsüeh, 1994. Appends a bibliography.

Ch'en Lin 陳琳 (157-217)

Editions and References

Ch'en, Lin 陳琳. *Ch'en Lin chi* 陳琳集. Yü Shao-ch'u 俞紹初, ed. In *Chien-an Ch'i-tzu chi* 建安七子集. Peking: Chung-hua, 1989. *Chung-kuo ku-tien wen-hsüeh chi-pen ts'ung-shu.*

Han, Ko-p'ing 韓格平, ed. *Chien-an ch'i tzu shih-wen chi chiao-chu hsiang-hsi* 建安七子詩文集校注詳析. Changchun: Chi-lin Wen-shih, 1991.

Yü, Hsien-hao 郁賢皓, ed. *Chien-an ch'i tzu shih chien-chu* 建安七子詩箋注. Chengtu: Pa-Shu Shu-she, 1990.

Ch'en Shih-tao 陳師道 (1052–1102 or 1053-1101)

Editions and References

Ch'üan Sung shih, 19:1114-1120.12631-12752.

266

Studies

Cheng, Ch'ien 鄭騫. *Ch'en Hou-shan nien-p'u* 陳后山年譜. Taipei: Lien-ching, 1984.

Hou-shan shih-chu pu-chien 後山詩注補箋. Annotated by Jen Yüan 任淵 (Sung Dynasty) and others. Peking: Chung-hua, 1995.

Ch'en To 陳鐸 (*fl.* 1506)

Editions and References

Yang, Ch'üan-ch'ang 楊權長, ed. *Ch'en To san-ch'ü* 陳鐸散曲. Shanghai: Shang-hai Ku-chi, 1985.

Ch'en Tuan-sheng 陳端生 (1751–1796)

Editions and References

Ch'en Tuan-sheng 陳端生. *Tsai-sheng yüan* 再生緣. Liu Ch'ung-i 劉崇義, ed. 3v. Chengchow: Chung-chou Shu-hua-she, 1982. *Chung-kuo ku-tien chiang-ch'ang wen-hsüeh ts'ung-shu.*

___. *Tsai sheng yüan.* Sun Chü-yüan 孫菊園, ed. Changsha: Hu-nan Wen-i, 1986.

Studies

Sung, Marina H. *The Narrative Art of Tsai-sheng Yüan: A Feminist Vision in Traditional Chinese Society.* Taipei: CMC, 1994.

Ch'en Tzu-ang 陳子昂 (661–702)

Editions and References

Hsü, P'eng 徐鵬. *Ch'en Tzu-ang chi* 陳子昂集. Peking: Chung-hua, 1980. Standard modern critical edition.

Luan, Kuei-ming 欒貴明 *et al.,* eds. *Ch'üan T'ang Shih so-yin: Ch'en Tzu-ang, Chang Yüeh chüan* 全唐詩索引：陳子昂張説卷. Ch'in-huang-tao: Hsien-tai, 1994.

P'eng, Ch'ing-sheng 彭慶生. *Ch'en Tzu-ang shih-chu* 陳子昂詩注. Hsi-ning: Ch'ing-hai Jen-min, 1980; Chengtu: Ssu-ch'uan Jen-min, 1981. Appends various biographies.

Studies

Chang, Pu-yün 張步云. "Shih P'ing Ch'u-T'ang Shih-jen Ch'en Tzu-ang" 試評初唐詩人陳子昂. *Shanghai Shih-fan Ta-hsüeh hsüeh-pao* 1988.3: 51-56.

Ch'en Tzu-ang yen-chiu lun-chi 陳子昂研究論集. Peking: Chung-kuo Wen-lien, 1989.

Chou, Hsiao-t'ien 周嘯天. "Wu-hou shih-tai yü Ch'en Tzu-ang te cheng-chih feng-tz'u shih" 武后時代與陳子昂的政治諷刺詩. *Cheng-tu Shih-chuan hsüeh-pao* 成都師專學報 1986.1 (1986): 22-26.

Han, Li-chou 韓理洲. *Ch'en Tzu-ang p'ing-chuan* 陳子昂評傳. Sian: Hsi-pei Ta-hsüeh, 1987.

___. *Ch'en Tzu-ang yen-chiu* 陳子昂研究. Shanghai: Shang-hai Ku-chi, 1988.

Ho, Richard M. W. *Ch'en Tzu-ang, Innovator in T'ang Poetry.* London and Hong Kong: School of Oriental and African Studies, University of London and the Chinese University Press, 1993.

Liu, Shih 劉石. "Ch'en Tzu-ang Hsin-lun" 陳子昂新論. *Wen-hsüeh P'ing-lun* 1988.2 (1988): 131-37.

Liu, Yüan-chih 劉遠智. *Ch'en Tzu-ang chi-ch'i "Kan-yü Shih" yen-chiu* 陳子昂及其感遇詩研究. Taipei: Wen-chin, 1987.

Lo, K'ang 羅庸. *T'ang Ch'en Tzu-ang Hsien-sheng Po-yü nien-p'u* 陳唐陳子昂先生佰玉年譜. Taipei: T'ai-wan Shang-wu Yin-shu-kuan, 1986.

Mair, Victor H. *Four Introspective Poets: A Concordance to Selected Poems by Roan Jyi, Chern Tzyy-arng, Jang Jeouling, and Lii Bor.* V. 2. *Center for Asian Studies, Monograph,* Tempe: Center for Asian Studies, Arizona State University, 1987.

Morino, Shigeo 森博行. "Chin Shigô 'Kangûshi' sanjûhachi shu no sekai" 陳子昂三十八首の世界. *Chûgoku bungakuhô* 36 (1985): 15-46.

Pi, Wan-ch'en 畢萬忱. "Lun Ch'en Tzu-ang shih-ko li-lun te ch'uan-t'ung t'e-chih" 論陳子昂詩歌理論的傳統特質. *Wen-hsüeh i-ch'an* (1990): 42-49.

Shen, Hui-yüeh 沈惠樂 and Ch'ien, Hui-k'ang 錢惠康. *Ch'u-T'ang Ssu-chieh ho Ch'en Tzu-ang* 初唐四杰和陳子昂. Shanghai: Shang-hai Ku-chi, 1987.

Ssu-ch'uan She-hung Hsien Ch'en Tzu-ang Yen-chiu Lien-lo-tsu 四川射洪縣陳子昂研究聯絡組, ed. *Ch'en Tzu-ang yen-chiu lun-chi* 陳子昂研究論集. Peking: Chung-kuo Wen-lien Ch'u-pan Kung-ssu, 1989.

Wang, Kuo-an 王國安 and Wang Yu-min 王幼敏, ed. *Ch'u-T'ang Ssu-chieh yü Ch'en Tzu-ang shih-wen hsüan-chu. Chung-kuo Ku-tien Wen-hsüeh Tso-p'in Hsüan-tu Ts'ung-shu.* Shanghai: Shang-hai Ku-chi, 1995.

Wang, Yün-hsi 王運熙 and Wu Ch'eng-hsüeh 吳承學. "Lun Ch'en Tzu-ang te li-shih kung-hsien" 論陳子昂的歷史貢獻. *Hsü-ch'ang Shih-chuan hsüeh-pao* 1989.3: 33-38.

Wu, Ming-hsien 吳明賢. *Ch'en Tzu-an lun-k'ao* 陳子昂論考. Chengtu: Pa-Shu Shu-she, 1995.

Ch'en Tzu-lung 陳子龍 (1608–1647)

Editions and References

Shih, Chih-ts'un 施蟄存 and Ma Tzu-hsi 馬祖熙, eds. *Ch'en Tzu-lung shih-chi* 陳子龍詩集. Shanghai: Shang-hai Ku-chi, 1983. The standard, modern critical edition of the poetry.

Shang-hai Wen-hsien Ts'ung-shu Pien-wei-hui 上海文獻叢書編委會, eds. *Ch'en Tzu-lung wen-chi* 陳子龍文集. Shanghai: Hua-tung Shih-fan Ta-hsüeh, 1988.

Translations

Chang, *The Late Ming Poet Ch'en Tzu-lung* (see "Studies" below).

Studies

Atwell, William S. "Chen Tzu-lung: 1608-1647." Unpublished Ph. D. dissertation, Princeton University, 1975.

Chang, Kang-i Sun. *The Late Ming Poet Ch'en Tzu-lung, Crises of Love and Loyalism.* New Haven-London: Yale University Press, 1990.

Chu, Tung-jun 朱東潤. *Ch'en Tzu-lung chi ch'i shih-tai* 陳子龍及其時代. Shanghai: Shang-hai Ku-chi, 1984.

McCraw, *Chinese Lyricists,* pp. 10-24.

Ch'en Wei-sung 陳維崧 (1626-1682 or 1625-1682)

Editions and References

Chou, Shao-chiu 周韶九, comm. *Ch'en Wei-sung hsüan-chi* 陳維崧選注. Shanghai: Shang-hai Ku-chi, 1994.

Liang, Chien-chiang 梁鑒江, ed. and comp. *Ch'en Wei-sung tz'u hsüan-chu* 陳維崧詞選注. Shanghai: Shang-hai Ku-chi, 1990.

Studies

McCraw, *Chinese Lyricists*, pp. 63-86.

Ch'en Yü-i 陳與義 (1090-1139 or 1090-1138)

Editions and References

Ch'en, Yü-i 陳與義. *Ch'en Yü-i chi* 陳與義集. 2v. Wu Shu-yin 吳書蔭 and Chin Te-hou 金德
    厚, eds. Peking: Chung-hua, 1982. Critical edition based on the Tseng-kuang edition
    with excellent notes, finding list of titles, traditional prefaces, and a bibliography.
___. *Ch'en Yü-i chi chien-chiao* 陳與義集箋校. 2v. Pai Tun-jen 白敦仁, ed. and comm. Shanghai:
    Shang-hai Ku-chi, 1990. Appends 7 works which had been lost from the collection.

Studies

Hargett, James M. "Sung Biographies, Supplementary Biography No. 1 [Ch'en Yü-i]," *JSYS*
    23 (1993): 110-122.
___. "Tensions of Tang and Song Influence in the Poetry of Chen Yuyi (1090-1139)." In
    *Collected Studies on Song History Dedicated to Professor James T. C. Liu in Celebration of
    His Seventieth Birthday*. Kinugawa Tsuyoshi, ed. Kyoto: Dohôsha, 1989, pp. 429-451.
McCraw, David R. "The Poetry of Chen Yuyi." Ph. D. dissertation, Stanford Univ., 1986.
___. "Chen Yuyi's Place in Tang and Song Poetry," *CLEAR* 9 (1987): 1-21.
Pai, Tun-jen 白敦仁. *Ch'en Yü-i nien-p'u* 陳與義年譜. Peking: Chung-hua, 1983.

Cheng Chen 鄭珍 (1806–1864)

Editions and References

Cheng, Chen 鄭珍. *Ch'ao-ching-ch'ao shih-ch'ao chien-chu* 巢經巢詩鈔箋注. Pai Tun-jen 白敦
    仁, ed. 2v. Chengtu: Pa-Shu Shu-she, 1996. Liberally annotated, useful biographical
    data..
___. *Ch'ao-ching-ch'ao shih-ch'ao teng san-chung* 巢經巢詩鈔等三種. Taipei: Shih-chieh, 1966.
    SPPY.
___. *Cheng Chen chi, Ching-hsüeh* 鄭珍集，經學. Wang Ying 王鍈 *et al.,* eds. Kweiyang:
    Kuei-chou Jen-min, 1991. *Kuei-chou ku-chi chi-ts'ui.*
___ and Liang Chang-chü 梁章鉅. *Ch'eng-wei lu Ch'in-shu chi* 稱謂錄親屬記. Peking: Chung-
    hua, 1996.

Studies

Huang, Wan-chi 黃萬機. *Cheng Chen p'ing-chuan* 鄭珍評傳. Chengtu: Pa-Shu Shu-she, 1988.
    Appends a chronological biography of Cheng.
Ling, T'i-an 凌惕安. *Cheng Tzu-yin (Chen) Hsien-sheng nien-p'u* 鄭子尹（珍）先生年譜. Hong
    Kong: Ch'ung-wen, 1975.
___. *Cheng Tzu-yin nien-p'u* 鄭子尹年譜. Rpt. Taipei: Shang-wu Yin-shu-kuan, 1975 (1937).
Wei, Chung-yu 魏仲佑. *Wan Ch'ing shih yen-chiu* 晚清詩研究. *Wen-shih-che Ta-hsi* 98. Taipei:
    Wen-chin, 1995. Chapter six treats the verse of Cheng Chen.

Cheng Hsieh 鄭燮 (1693–1765)

Editions and References

Ch'eng, Hsieh 鄭燮. *Cheng Pan-ch'iao chi* 鄭板橋集. Shang-hai Ku-chi Ch'u-pan-she, ed.

Shanghai: Shang-hai Ku-chi, 1979. Appended biographical and other materials.

___. *Cheng Pan-ch'iao chi hsiang-chu* 鄭板橋集詳注. Wang Hsi-jung 王錫榮, comm. Changchun: Chi-lin Wen-shih, 1986.

___. *Cheng Pan-ch'iao wai chi* 鄭板橋外集. Cheng, Ping-ch'un 鄭炳純, ed. Taiyuan: Shan-hsi Jen-min, 1987.

___. *Pan-ch'iao chia-shu i-chu* 板橋家書譯注. Hua, Yao-hsiang 華耀祥 and Ku, Huang-ch'u 顧 黃初, eds. Peking: Jen-min Wen-hsüeh, 1994.

Tiao, Chün 刁駿, ed. *Cheng Pan-ch'iao tui-lien chi-chu* 鄭板橋對聯輯注. Shanghai: Shang-hai Wen-hua I-shu, 1991.

Ying-yin chen-chi Cheng Pan-ch'iao ch'üan-chi 影印真跡鄭板橋全集. Collated by Wang Tzu-ch'en 王緇塵. Chengchow: Chung-chou Ku-chi, 1992.

Studies

Ch'en, Shu-liang 陳書良. *Cheng Pan-ch'iao p'ing-chuan* 鄭板橋評傳. Chengtu: Pa-Shu Shu-she, 1989.

Chou, Chi-yin 周積寅. *Cheng Pan-ch'iao* 鄭板橋. Shenyang: Chi-lin Mei-shu, 1996.

Fukumoto, Masakazu 福本雅一. *Tei Hankyô shishô* 鄭板橋詩抄. Kyoto: Dôhô Shuppansha, 1994.

Pohl, Karl-Heinz. *Cheng Pan-ch'iao: Poet, Painter and Calligrapher*. Nettetal: Steyler Verlag, 1990. *Monumenta Serica Monograph Series*, 21.

Studies

Huang, Chu-ch'eng 黃俶程. "Cheng Hsieh shih-wen chi pan-pen yüan-liu k'ao" 鄭燮詩文集 版呋源流考, *She-hui k'o-hsüeh chan-hsien*, 1994.5: 267-274.

Yang, Shih-lin 楊士林. *Cheng Pan-ch'iao p'ing-chuan* 鄭板橋評傳. Hofei: An-huei Jen-min, 1992.

Cheng Jo-yung 鄭若庸 (*ca.* 1480-*ca.* 1565)

Editions and References
Cheng, Jo-yung. *Lei chüan* 類雋. Shanghai: Shang-hai Tz'u-shu, 1991.

Cheng Kuang-tsu 鄭光祖 (*ca.* 1260 or earlier–*ca.* 1320)

Editions and References
Cheng, Kuang-tsu 鄭光祖. *Cheng Kuang-tsu chi* 鄭光祖集. Feng Chün-chieh 馮俊杰, ed. Taiyuan: Shan-hsi Jen-min, 1992. Appends a bibliography.

Chi Yün 紀昀 (1724–1805)

Editions and References
Chi, Yün 紀昀. Chi Hsiao-lan wen-chi 紀曉嵐文集. Sun Chih-chung 孫致中 *et al.*, eds Shih-chia-chuang: Ho-pei Chiao-yü, 1991. Appends a chronological biography.

___. *Ho-yüan chi-lüeh* 河源紀略. Tientsin: T'ien-chin Ku-chi, 1987. Hsi-pei k'ai-fa shih-liao ts'ung-pien. Study of the origins of the Yellow River.

___. *Wu-lu-mu Chai tsa-shih* 烏魯木齋雜詩. Lanchow: Lan-chou Ku-chi, 1990. *Chung-kuo Hsi-pei wen-hsien ts'ung-shu*. Photocopy of an 1815 woodblock edition edited by Chang Hai-peng 張海鵬.

____. *Wu-ying Tien pen Ssu-k'u ch'üan-shu tsung-mu t'i-yao* 武英殿本四庫全書總目提要. 5v. Taipei: T'ai-wan Shang-wu, 1983. Accompanied the republication of the entire *Ssu-k'u* by T'ai-wan Shang-wu.

____. *Yüeh-wei Ts'ao-tang pi-chi chu-i* 閱微草堂筆記注譯. Pei Yüan 北原 *et al.,* comm. Peking: Chung-kuo Hua-ch'iao, 1994. *Ku-tien pi-chi ming-chu ts'ung-shu.* An extensive commentary in 1306 pages.

____. *Yüeh-wei Ts'ao-tang pi-chi hsüan-i* 閱微草堂筆記選譯. Chou Hsü-* 周續賡 and Chang Ming-kao 張明高 trans. and comm. Peking: Jen-min Wen-hsüeh, 1991. *Chung-kuo ku-tien wen-hsüeh chin-i ts'ung-shu.*

Translations

Chou, Hsü-keng 周續賡 and Chang Ming-kao 張明高, trans. and comm. *Yüeh-wei Ts'ao-t'ang pi-chi hsüan-i* 閱微草棠筆記選譯. Peking: Jen-min Wen-hsüeh, 1991. Chung-kuo ku-tien wen-hsüeh chin-i ts'ung-shu.

Hermann, Konrad. *Pinselnotizen aus der Strohhutte der Betrachtung des Grossen im Kleinen, Kurzgeschichten und Anekdoten.* Bremen: Carl Schüremann Verlag, 1983.

Huang, Kuo-sheng 黃國聲, trans. and comm. *Yüeh-wei Ts'ao-t'ang pi-chi hsüan-i* 閱微草棠筆記選譯. Chengtu: Pa-Shu Shu-she, 1990. Ku-tien wen-shih ming-chu hsüan-i ts'ung-shu.

Keenan, David. *Shadows in a Chinese Landscape, Chi Yun's Notes from a Hut for Examining the Subtle.* Armonk, N.Y.: M. E. Sharpe, 1997. *New Studies in Asian Culture.*

Maeno, Naoaki 前也直彬. *Etsubi Sôdô hikki* 閱微草堂筆記. Tokyo: Heibonsha, 1994. *Chûgoku koten bungaku taikei,* 42. A selected translation (250 pp.) with maps and a critical introduction appended.

Pei, Yüan 北原, *et al.,* trans and comm. *Yüeh-wei Ts'ao-t'ang pi-chi chu-i* 閱微草棠筆記注譯. 5v. Peking: Chung-kuo Hua-ch'iao, 1994.

Pimpaneau, Jacques. *Notes de la chaumière des observations subtiles, Recueil de courts récits ou anecdotes du 18ᵉ siècle.* Paris: Kwok On, 1995. Translation of *Yüeh-wei Ts'ao-t'ang pi-chi.*

Studies

Chan, Leo Tak-Hung. *The Discourse on Foxes and Ghosts: Ji Yun and Eighteenth-Century Literati Storytelling.* Hong Kong: Chinese University Press, 1997.

____. "Narrative as Argument: The *Yuewei caotang biji* and the Late Eighteenth-century Elite Discourse on the Supernatural." *HJAS* 53 (1993): 25-62.

Chang, Hui 張輝. *Chi Yün yü Yüeh-wei Ts'ao-t'ang pi-chi* 紀昀與閱微草堂筆記. Shenyang: Liao-ning Chiao-yü, 1993.

Chou, Chi-ming 周積銘. *Chi Yün p'ing-chuan* 紀昀評傳, *A Critical Biography of Jiyun.* Nanking: Nan-ching Ta-hsüeh, 1994. *Chung-kuo ssu-hsiang-chia p'ing-chuan ts'ung-shu* (Critical Biography Series of Chinese Thinkers), 170. Appends a name index.

Dars, Jacques. "Ji Yun et son *Yunwei caotang biji,* Les *Notes la chaumière de la subtile perception,*" *Études chinoises* 13 (1994): 361-75.

Ho, Chih-ch'i 賀治起 *et al. Chi Hsiao-lan nien-p'u* 紀曉嵐年譜. Peking: Shu-mu Wen-hsien, 1993.

Keenan, David Laurence. "The Forms and Uses of the Ghost Story in Late Eighteenth China as Recorded in the 'Yüeh wei ts'ao t'ang pi-chi' of Chi Yün." Unpublished Ph. D. dissertation, Harvard University, 1987.

Kent, Guy. *The Emperor's Four Treasuries: Scholars and the State in the Late Ch'ien-lung Era.* Cambridge, Mass.: Harvard University Press, 1987.

Wang, Tz'u-ch'eng 王次澄. "*Ssu-k'u ch'üan-shu tsung-mu t'i-yao* cheng-pu erh-shih wu tse" 四庫全書總目提要正補二十五則, *Chung-kuo ku-chi yen-chiu* 中國古籍研究. V. 1.

Shanghai: Shang-hai Ku-chi, 1996, pp. 391-403.

Yang, Chin-lung 楊晉龍. "'Ssu-k'u hsüeh' yen-chiu te fan-ssu" 四庫學研究的反思, *Chung-kuo wen-che yen-chiu chi-k'an* 1994.4: 349-394.

Ch'i-chi 齊己 (*ca.* 863-*ca.* 937)

Studies

Ho, Lin-t'ien 何林天. "Ch'i-chi ch'u-t'an" 齊己初探, *Shan-hsi Shih-ta hsüeh-pao* 1992.2.

Hsia, Lien 夏蓮. "Shih-seng Ch'i-chi" 詩僧齊己, *Wen-shih chih-shih* 1992.2.

Ts'ao, Hsün 曹汛. "Ch'i-chi sheng-tsu nien k'ao-cheng" 齊己生卒年考證, *Chung-hua wen-shih lun-ts'ung* 1983.3.

Ch'i-lu teng 歧路燈 (A Lamp at the Fork)

Studies

Borotová, Lucie. *A Confucian Story of the Prodigal Son—Li Lü-yüan's Novel "Lantern at the Crossroads," Qiludeng; Structure, Thought and Ethics.* Bochum: Brockmeyer, 1991. *Chinathemen,* 63.

Ch'i-wu Ch'ien 綦毋潛 (692–749)

Studies

Fu, Ju-i 傅如一. "Ch'i-wu Ch'ien sheng-p'ing shih-chi k'ao-p'ien" 綦毋潛生平事跡考辨, *Chung-kuo she-hui k'o-hsüeh* 1984.4.

Chia I 賈誼 (200–168 B.C.)

Editions and References

Chia, I 賈誼. *Chia I chi chiao-chu* 賈誼集校注. Wu Yün 吳雲 and Li Ch'un-t'ai 李春臺, ed. and comm. Chengchow: Chung-chou Ku-chi, 1989. *Chung-kuo wen-hsien ts'ung-shu.* Contains both *Chia I Hsin-shu* 賈誼新書 and his *fu* and appends a chronology of Chia's life.

___. *Chia I chi chiao-chu* 賈誼集校注. Wang Chou-ming 王洲明 and Hsü Ch'ao 徐超, ed. and comm. Peking: Jen-min Wen-hsüeh, 1996.

Studies

Ts'ai, T'ing-chi 蔡廷吉, ed. *Chia I yen-chiu* 賈誼研究. Taipei: Wen-shih-che, 1984. A study of the life and works.

Wang, Chou-ming 王洲明. "Chia I san-wen te t'e-tien chi tsai wen-hsüeh shih shang te ti-wei" 賈誼散文的特店及在文學上的地位. *Wen-shih-che* 1982.3: 63-67.

Wang, Hsing-kuo 王興國. *Chia I p'ing-chuan (fu Lu Chia, Ch'ao Ts'o p'ing-chuan)* 賈誼評傳（附陸賈晁錯評傳）. Nanking: Nan-ching Ta-hsüeh, 1993. *Chung-kuo ssu-hsiang-chia p'ing-chuan ts'ung-shu.*

Wen, Ssu 聞思. "Chia-shih so tsou 'Pieh lü' pien" 賈氏所奏別錄辨, *Wen-shih* 33 (1991): 200-228.

Chia-ku-wen tzu 甲骨文字 (oracle-bone inscriptions)

Editions and References

Chang, Yü-chin 張玉金, ed. *Chia-ku-wen hsü-tz'u tz'u-tien* 甲骨文虛詞詞典. Peking: Chung-hua, 1994.

Chao, Ch'eng 趙誠, ed. *Chia-ku-wen chien-ming tz'u-tien: pu-tz'u fen-lei tu-pen* 甲骨文簡明詞典：卜辭分類讀本. Peking: Chung-hua, 1988.

Fang, Shu-hsin 方述鑫. *Chia-ku chin-wen tzu-tien* 甲骨金文字典. Chengtu: Pa-Shu Shu-she, 1993.

Kobayashi, Sekiju 小林石寿, ed. *Kôkotsu monji jiten–Takuei tendai* 甲骨文字字典–拓影展大. Tokyo: Mokujisha, 1987.

Liu, Hsing-lung 劉興隆, ed. *Hsin-pien chia-ku-wen tzu-tien* 新編甲骨文字典. Peking: Kuo-chi Wen-hua, 1993.

Meng, Shih-k'ai 孟世凱, ed. *Chia-ku-hsüeh hsiao tz'u-tien* 甲骨學小辭典. Shanghai: Tz'u-shu, 1987.

Studies

Chang, Ping-ch'uan 張秉權. *Chia-ku-wen yü chia-ku-hsüeh* 甲骨文與甲骨學. Taipei: Kuo-li Pien-i-kuan, 1988.

Ch'en, Wei-chan 陳煒湛. *Chia-ku t'ien-lieh k'o-tz'u yen-chiu* 甲骨田獵刻辭研究. Nanning: Kuang-hsi Chiao-yü, 1995.

Fang, Shu-hsin 方述鑫. *Yin-hsü pu-tz'u tuan-tai yen-chiu* 殷虛卜辭斷代研究. Taipei: Wen-chin, 1992.

Hu, Hou-hsüan 胡厚宣, ed. *Chia-ku-wen yü Yin-Shang shih* 甲骨文與殷商史. Shanghai: Shang-hai Ku-chi, 1983. *Chia-ku-wen yü Yin-Shang shih, ti erh chi* 甲骨文與殷商史, 第二集. Shanghai: Shang-hai Ku-chi, 1986.

Hsü, Hsi-t'ai 徐錫台. *Chou-yüan chia-ku-wen tsung-shu* 周原甲骨文綜述. Sian: San-Ch'in, 1987.

Lefeuvre, Jean A. *Ollecrions d' inscriptions oraculaires en France.* Taipei: Kuang-ch'i, 1985.

Li, Hsüeh-ch'in 李學勤 and P'eng, Yü-shang 彭裕商. *Yin-hsü chia-ku fen-ch'i yen-chiu* 殷虛甲骨分期研究. Shanghai: Shang-hai Ku-chi, 1996.

Li, Hsüeh-ch'in 李學勤 *et al.*, eds. *Ying-kuo so ts'ang chia-ku chi* 英國所藏甲骨集. Peking: Chung-hua, 1985.

Liu, Heng 劉恆. *Yin-ch'i ts'un-kao* 殷契存稿. Harbin: Hei-lung-chiang Chiao-yü, 1990.

Lo, Chen-yü 羅振玉, Wang Kuo-wei 王國維, Tung Tso-pin 董作賓, and Chu Ch'i-hsiang 朱岐祥. *Chia-ku ssu-t'ang lun-wen hsüan-chi* 甲骨四堂論文選集. Taipei: Hsüeh-sheng, 1990.

Ma, Ju-sen 馬如森. *Yin-hsü chia-ku-wen yin-lun* 殷虛甲骨文引論. Shanghai: Hua-tung Shih-ta, 1993.

Shaughnessy, Edward L., ed. *New Sources of Early Chinese History: An Introduction to the Reading of Inscriptions and Manuscripts.* Berkeley: The Society for the Study of Early China and The Institute of East Asian Studies, University of California, 1997. The only monograph in a Western language on this subject; basic reference which appends an excellent bibliography.

Shirakawa, Shizuka 白川青爭. *Kôkotsu kimbungaku ronshû* 甲骨金文學論集. Kyoto: Hôyû, 1996.

Wang, Yü-hsin 王宇信, ed. *Chia-ku-wen yü Yin-Shang shih* 甲骨文與殷商史. v. 3. Shanghai: Shang-hai Ku-chi, 1991.

Wu, Hao-k'un 吳浩坤 and P'an Yu 潘悠. *Chung-kuo chia-ku-hsüeh shih* 中國甲骨學史. Taipei: Kuan-ya Wen-hua, 1990.

Yang, Shu-ta 楊樹達. *Chi-wei-chü chia-wen shuo* 積微居甲文説. Shanghai: Shang-hai Ku-chi, 1986.

Yü, Sheng-wu 于省吾 and Yao Hsiao-sui 姚孝遂. *Chia-ku wen-tzu ku-lin* 甲骨文字詁林. Peking: Chung-hua, 1996.

Chia Tao 賈島 (779-843)

Editions and References

Chia Tao chüan 賈島卷. In *Ch'üan T'ang shih so-yin,* 1994.

Li, Chia-yen 李嘉言. *Ch'ang-chiang Chi hsin-chiao* 長江集新校. Shanghai: Shang-hai Ku-chi, 1983. Appends chronological biographies and a study of Chia's friends.

Liu, Ssu-han 劉斯翰. *Meng Chiao, Chia Tao shih hsüan* 孟郊賈島詩選. Hong Kong: San-lien, 1986.

Luan, Kuei-ming 欒貴明. *Ch'uan T'ang Shih so-yin: Chia Tao chüan* 全唐詩索引：賈島卷. Ch'in-huang-tao: Hsien-tai, 1994.

Studies

Ashidate, Ichirô 芦立一郎. "Ka Tô shi shitan" 賈島詩試探, *Yamagata Daigaku kiyô–Jinbun kagaku* XIII.1 (1996): 147-162.

Ching, K'ai-hsüan 景凱旋. "Chia Tao shih-chi k'ao-pien" 賈島事跡考辨. *Wen shih* 37 (1993): 213-29.

Fang, Jih-hsi 房日晰. "Chia Tao k'ao-cheng erh-tse" 賈島考證二則. *Wen-hsüeh i-ch'an* 1992.6: 106-8.

Li, Chih-wen 李知文. "Lun Chia Tao tsai T'ang-shih fa-chan-shih te ti-wei" 論賈島在唐詩發展史的地位. *Wen-hsüeh i-ts'an* 1989.5: 79-86.

T'ung, P'ei-chi 童培基. "Chia Tao shih ch'ung-ch'u chen-pien" 賈島詩重出甄辨. *Ho-nan Ta-hsüeh hsüeh-pao* 60 (1985): 44-49.

Wu, Ju-yü 吳汝煜 and Hsieh Jung-fu 謝榮福. "Li Chia-yen *Chia Tao Nien-p'u* Ting-pu" 李嘉言賈島年譜訂補, *Liao-ning Kuang-po Tien-shih Ta-hsüeh hsüeh-pao* 1987.3: 1-6.

Chiang Chieh 蔣捷 (1245–1310)

Editions and References

Chiang, Chieh 蔣捷. *Chu-shan tz'u* 竹山詞. *Ssu-k'u,* 1983, v. 1488.

Chu, Hsiao-tsang 朱孝藏 (1857-1931), comp. *Chiang-ts'un ts'ung-shu* 疆村叢書. Hsia Chin-kuan 夏敬觀, ed. Rpt. Shanghai: Shang-hai Ku-chi, 1989 (1922).

Studies

Liu, Ch'ing-yün 劉慶雲. "Chiang Chieh jen-p'in tz'u-p'in tzu-feng ch'u-t'an" 蔣捷人品詞品詞風初探, *Wen-hsüeh i-ch'an* 1984.1: 74-83.

Yang, Hai-ming 楊海明. "Kuan-yü Chiang Chieh te chia-shih ho shih-chi" 關於蔣捷的家試和試跡唐宋詞論稿. In *T'ang Sung tz'u lun-kao.* Hangchow: Che-chiang Ku-chi, 1988, pp. 311-313.

Ye, Yang 葉揚. "Chiang Chieh and His *Tz'u* Poetry," *JSYS* 24 (1994): 21-41.

Chiang Ch'un-lin 蔣春霖 (1818–1868)

Editions and References

Chiang, Ch'un-lin 蔣春霖. *Shui-yün Lou shih-tz'u kao-ho pen* 水雲樓詩詞稿合本. Taipei: Wen-hai, 1969.

Studies

Feng, Ch'i-yung 馮其庸, ed. *Chiang Lu-t'an nien-p'u k'ao-lüeh; Shui-yün-lou shih tz'u chi-ciao* 蔣鹿潭年譜考略，水雲樓詩詞輯校. Tsinan: Ch'i-Lu Shu-she, 1986.

Chiang-hsi shih-p'ai 江西詩派

Studies

Mo, Li-feng 莫礪鋒. *Chiang-hsi shih-p'ai yen-chiu* 江西詩派研究. Tsinan: Ch'i-Lu Shu-she, 1986. *Nan-ching Ta-hsüeh Ku-tien Wen-hsien Yen-chiu So chuan-k'an.* Appends essays on the politics of the school members and Huang T'ing-chien's* literary theories.

Chiang K'uei 姜夔 (1155–1221) 1163-1203

Editions and References

Chiang, K'uei 姜夔. *Chiang Pai-shih shih-chi chien-chu* 姜白石詩集箋注. Sun Hsüan-ch'ang 孫玄常, comm. Li An-kang 李安綱, coll. Taiyuan: Shan-hsi Jen-min, 1986.

___. *Hsü Shu p'u* 續書譜. 1 *chüan.* Taipei: Hsin-hsing, 1988. *Pi-chi hsiao-shuo ta-kuan, 9 pien.*

___. *Po-shih Tao-jen shih-chi* 白石道人詩集. Shanghai: Shang-hai Shu-tien, 1987.

Yin, Kuang-hsi 殷光熹. *Chiang K'uei shih tz'u shang-hsi chi* 姜夔詩詞賞析集. Chengtu: Pa-Shu Shu-she, 1994.

Translations

Landau, *Beyond Spring,* pp. 202-214.

Studies

Liu, Wan. "Allusion and Vision: Chiang K'uei's Twin Poems on Plum Blossoms in the Yung-wu (Poetry on Objects) Tradition," *AM, TS* 8.1 (1995): 94-121.

Chiang Shih-ch'üan 蔣士銓 (1725–1784) 1785?

Editions and References

Chiang, Shih-ch'üan 蔣士銓. *Chiang Shih-ch'üan hsi-ch'ü chi* 蔣士銓戲曲集. Chou Miao-chung 周妙中, ed. Peking: Chung-hua, 1993. Modern critical edition.

___. *Chung-ya T'ang chi chiao-chien* 忠雅堂集校箋. Shao Hai-ch'ing 邵海清, coll. Li Meng-sheng 李夢生, comm. 5v. Shanghai: Shang-hai Ku-chi, 1993. *Chung-kuo ku-tien wen-hsüeh ts'ung-shu.* Appends biographical material.

___. *Chung-ya T'ang shih-ch'ao* 忠雅堂詩鈔. Hirai Taka 平井翰. ed. Tokyo: Iwanami, 1978. Reprint of an 1815 edition printed in Kyoto by Kinkudô 金翹堂.

___. *Lin-ch'uan meng* 臨川夢. 2 *chüan.* Shao Hai-ch'ing 邵海清, ed. and comm. Shanghai: Shang-hai Ku-chi, 1989. *Ku-tai hsi-ch'ü ts'ung-shu.* Modern critical edition which appends material relevant to Chiang's life.

___. *Tung-ch'ing shu* 冬青樹. Shao Hai-ch'ing 邵海清, ed. and comm. Shanghai: Shang-hai Ku-chi, 1988. *Ku-tai hsi-ch'ü ts'ung-shu.*

Translations

Forke, Alfred and Martin Gimm. *Zwei chinesische Singsspiele der Qing-Dynastie (Li Yu und Jiang Shiquan) übersetzt von Alred Forke.* Stuttgart: Steiner, 1993. *Übersetzungen chinesischer Dramentexte,* 2; *Sinologica Coloniensia* 16. Appends a translation of an anonymous

"Singspiel" from the Yüan dynasty by John Hefter.

Chiang Yen 江淹 (444–505)

Studies

Chang, Ya-hsin 張亞新. "Yung Chiang Yen "hsiao-juan-kung shih shih-wu shou" 詠江淹〔效阮公詩十五首〕. *Kuei-chou wen-shih ts'ung-k'an* 27 (1987): 107–113.

Chou, Feng 周風. "Chiang Yen ts'ai-chin yü Yung-ming wen-feng de kuan-hsi" 江淹才盡與永明文風的關係. *Hsüeh-shu yen-chiu* 100 (1990): 89–93.

Ts'ao, Tao-heng 曹道衡. "Chiang Yen, Shen Yüeh he Nan-Ch'i shih-feng" 江淹，沈約和南齊詩風. *Ho-pei Shih-yüan hsüeh-pao* (1986): 21–33.

___. "Chiang Yen tso-p'in hsieh-tso nien-tai k'ao" 江淹作品寫作年代考. *I-wen chih* 1985: 55–97.

___. "Pao Chao yü Chiang Yen" 鮑照與江淹. *Ch'i-Lu hsüeh-k'an* 91.6 (1991).

Yü, Shao-ch'u 俞紹初. "Chiang Yen nien-p'u" 江淹年譜, *Chung-kuo ku-chi yen-chiu* 中國古籍研究. V. 1. Shanghai: Shang-hai Ku-chi, 1996, pp. 405-441.

Chiao-fang chi 教坊記 (Record of the Court Entertainment Bureau)

Editions and References

Jen, Pan-t'ang 任半塘, ed. and comm. *Chiao-fang chi* 教坊記. Peking: Chung-hua, 1962. Appends a useful study of the chiao-fang in Lo-yang and Ch'ang-an.

Translations

Saitô, Shigeru 斎藤茂. *Kyôbô ki, Hokuri shi* 教坊記・北里志. Tokyo: Heibonsha, 1992.

Chiao-Hung chi 嬌紅記

Editions

Meng, Ch'eng-shu 孟稱舜. *Chiao-Hung chi* 嬌紅記. Ou-yang Kuang 歐陽光, ed. and comm. Shanghai: Shang-hai Ku-chi, 1988. *Ku-tai hsi-ch'ü tsung-shu.*

Translations

Ito, Sôhei 伊藤漱平. *Kyô Kô ki* 嬌紅記. Tokyo: Heibonsha, 1994.

Chiao-jan 皎然 (730–799)

Editions and References

Hsü, Ch'ing-yün 許清云. *Chiao-jan 'Shih shih' chi-chiao hsin-pien* 皎然詩式輯校新編. Taipei: Wen-shih-che, 1984.

Li, Chuang-ying 李壯鷹, annot. *'Shih shih' chiao-chu* 詩式校註. Tsinan: Ch'i-Lu Shu-she, 1986.

Studies

Ch'en, Hsi-chung 陳曦鍾. "Chiao-jan shih-lun pan-pen hsiao-lun" 皎然詩論版本小論. *Chûgoku bungaku ronshû* 16 (1988): 1-10.

Ch'i, Hsü-pang 漆緒邦. "Chiao-jan chiao-yu sheng-p'ing k'ao" 皎然交游生平考. *Pei-ching*

276

She-hui K'o-hsüeh 1991.3: 106-17.

Chia, Chin-hua 賈晉華. "Chiao-jan lun Ta-li Chiang-nan shih-jen pien-hsi" 皎然論大歷江南詩人辨析. In *T'ang-tai wen-hsüeh yen-chiu nien-chien, 1986* 唐代文學研究年鑑, *1986*. Sian: Shan-hsi Jen-min, 1987, pp. 147-151.

___. *Chiao-jan nien-p'u* 皎然年譜. Amoy: Hsia-men Ta-hsüeh, 1992.

Hsü, Ch'ing-yün 許清云. *Chiao-jan shih shih yen-chiu* 皎然詩式研究. Taipei: Wen-shih-che, 1988.

Kawachi, Shôen 河内昭圓. "Shisô Kôzen no bukkyô" 詩僧皎然の仏教, *Bungei Ronshû* 42 (1994): 84-107.

Kôzen, Hiroshi 興膳宏. "Kôzen *Shishiki* no kôzô to riron" 皎然詩式の構造と理論, *Chûgoku bungakuhô,* 50 (1995): 68-80.

Sun, Ch'ang-wu 孫昌武. "Lun Chiao-jan *Shih shih*" 論皎然詩式. *Wen-hsüeh p'ing-lun* 1986.1: 102-11.

Wang, Meng-ou 王夢鷗. "Lun Chiao-jan *Shih shih*" 論皎然詩式. *Chung-hua wen-hua fu-hsing yüeh-kan* 14.3 (1981): 8-14.

Wang, Yün-hsi 王運熙. "Chiao-jan shih-hsüeh shu-p'ing" 皎然詩學述評, *Kuei-chou Ta-hsüeh hsüeh-pao* 1991.1: 7-16.

Chiao-se 腳色 or 角色

Studies

Liao, T'eng-yeh 廖藤葉. "Yüan Ming hsi-ch'ü 'hun' chiao-se yen-chiu" 元明戲曲魂腳色研究, *T'ai-chung Shang-chuan hsüeh-pao* 29 (1997.6): 193-223.

Wang, Kuo-wei 王國維 (1877-1927). *Ku-chü Chiao-se k'ao* 古劇腳色考. 1 *chüan. Hai-ning Wang Chung-ch'üeh Kung i-shu* 海甯王忠愨公遺書, Ssu chi 四集. 1927.

Chien-teng hsin-hua 剪燈新話 (New Stories Written While Trimming the Wick)

Editions and References

Akiyoshi, Kukio 秋吉久紀夫. *Sentô shinwa kôtei* 剪燈新話校訂. Kyoto: Chûgoku Bungaku Hyôronsha, 1985.

Ch'ü, Yu 瞿佑. *Chien-teng hsin-hua wai erh-chung* 剪燈新話外二種. Shanghai: Ku-tien Wen-hsüeh, 1957. Standard modern critical edition. Also contains *Chien-teng yü-hua* 剪燈餘話 and *Mi-teng yin-hua* 覓燈因話.

___. *Kuei-t'ien shih-hua* 歸田詩話. 2 *chüan.* Taipei: Hsin-hsing, 1989. *Pi-chi hsiao-shuo ta-kuan, 6 pien,* 6.

___. *Ssu-shih i-chi* 四時宜忌. Peking: Chung-hua, 1985. *TSCC* edition.

___. *Le-ch'üan shih chi* 樂全詩集. Tokyo: Takahashi Seihô 高橋情報, 1991. Based on a mss. held in the Naikaku Bunko.

Translations

Dars, Jacques. *En mouchant la chandelle, nouvelles chinoises des Ming.* Paris: Gallimard, 1986.

Iizuka, Akira 飯塚朗. *Zentô shinwa* 前燈新話. Tokyo: Heibonsha, 1994. *Chûgoku koten bungaku taikei,* 39.

Studies

Ch'en, I-yüan 陳益源. Chien-teng hsin-hua *yü* Ch'uan-ch'i man-lu *chih pi-chiao yen-chiu* 剪燈新話與傳奇漫錄之比較研究. Taipei: Hsüeh-sheng, 1990. *Chung-kuo hsiao-shuo yen-chiu*

277

ts'ung-k'an, 11.

Ishimi, Kenji 石見憲治. "Shōnen jidai no Ku Ya to *Sentō shinwa*" 少年時代の瞿佑と剪燈新話, *Gakurin* 13 (1989): 15-29.

Hsüeh, K'o-ch'üeh 薛克翹. *Chien-teng hsin-hua yü ch'i-t'a* 剪燈新話與其他. Liaoyang: Liao-ning Chiao-yü, 1993.

Ch'ien Ch'i 錢起 (722–780)

Editions and References

Tabei, Fumio 田部井文雄, ed. *Sen Ki shi sakuin* 錢起詩索引. Tokyo: Kyūin Shoin, 1986

Wang, Ting-chang 王定璋, ed. *Ch'ien Ch'i shih-chi chiao-chu* 錢起詩集校注. Hangchow: Che-chiang Ku-chi, 1992.

Studies

Ashidate, Ichirô 芦立一郎. "Sen Ki no shisaku–taireki shi e no apurôchi" 錢起の詩作一大歷詩へのアプローチ, *Yamagata Daigaku kiyô* 山形大学紀要, 13.3 (1994): 404-418.

Lo, Yüan-lieh 羅元烈. "Kuan-yü Ch'ien Ch'i 'Hsiang-ling ku-se' shih te i-hsieh wen-t'i" 關於錢起湘靈鼓瑟詩的一些問題, *Kuang-chou jih-pao,* 14 August 1991.

Ma, Chih-chin 馬汁金. "Kuan-yü Ch'ien Ch'i te teng-ti shih-chien yü tso-chu" 關於錢起的登第時間與座主, *Chiang-hai hsüeh-k'an* 1991.5.

Ch'ien Ch'ien-i 錢謙益 (1582-1664)

Editions and References

Ch'ien, Ch'ien-i 錢謙益. *Lieh-ch'ao shih-chi* 列昭詩集. Shanghai: San-lien, 1989. Photolithic reprint of the 1652 Chi-ku Ko 汲古閣 edition.

___. *Mu-chai ch'u-hsüeh chi* 牧齋初學集. Ch'ien Tseng 錢曾 (1629-1701), comm. Ch'ien Chung-lien 錢仲聯 (1908-), ed. 3v. Shanghai: Shang-hai Ku-chi, 1985. *Chung-kuo ku-tien wen-hsüeh ts'ung-shu.* Modern critical edition.

___. *Mu-chai yu-hsüeh chi* 牧齋有學集. Ch'ien Chung-lien 錢仲聯 (1908-), ed. 3v. Shanghai: Shang-hai Ku-chi, 1996. Modern critical edition.

Translations

Strassberg, *Inscribed Landscapes,* pp. 313-316.

Studies

Chaves, Jonathan. "The Yellow Mountain Poems of Ch'ien Ch'ien-i (1582-1664): Poetry as *Yu-chi,*" *HJAS* 48(1988), 465-92.

Chien, Hsiu-chüan 簡秀娟. *Ch'ien Ch'ien-i tsang-shu yen-chiu* 錢謙益藏書研究. Taipei: Han-mei, 1991. *T'u-shu-kuan hsüeh yü tzu-hsün k'o-hsüeh lun-wen ts'ung-k'an,* Series 2, #6.

Ch'ien Wei-yen 錢惟演 (977–1034 or 962-1034)

Editions and References

Ch'ien, Wei-yen 錢惟演. *Chia-wang ku-shih* 家王故事. Taipei: Hsin-hsing, 1985. *Pi-chi hsiao-shuo ta-kuan, 38 pien.*

Ch'üan Sung shih, 2:94-95.1056-1072.

chih-kuai 志怪 (records of anomalies)

Editions and References

Ch'eng, I-chung 程毅中. *Ku hsiao-shuo chien-mu* 古小説書目. Peking: Chung-hua, 1981. Entries cite traditional bibliographies and editions; see also the review of this volume and that immediately below (*Chung-kuo wen-yen hsiao-shuo shih-kao*) by John B. Brennan in *CLEAR* 7 (1985): 179-185.

Chou, T'ien-ch'ing 周田青, ed. *Liu-ch'ao chih-kuai hsiao-shuo hsüan-i* 六朝志怪小説選譯. *Ku-tai wen-shih ming-chu hsüan-i ts'ung-shu* 古代文史明箸選譯叢書. Chengtu: Pa-Shu Shu-she, 1990.

Hou, Chung-i 侯忠毅 (w/ Liu Shih-lin 劉世林 for volume 2). *Chung-kuo wen-yen hsiao-shuo shih-kao* 中國文言小説史稿. 2v. Peking: Pei-ching Ta-hsüeh, 1990 and 1993. The first volume is dedicated to pre-Sung classical-language fiction; see also comments under Ch'eng I-chung above.

____. *Chung-kuo wen-yen hsiao-shuo ts'an-k'ao tzu-liao* 中國文言小説參考資料. Peking: Pei-ching Ta-hsüeh, 1985. Excerpts from prefaces, bibliographies, etc. similar to Huang Ling and Han T'ung-wen's works supplemented by a more catholic selection of comparative materials from dynastic histories and related works.

"Hsien-Ch'in chih Sui-T'ang te hsiao-shuo" 先秦至隋唐的小説, in *Chung-kuo hsiao-shuo shih* 中國小説史. Chinese Department, Peking University, compilers. Peking: Jen-min Wen-hsüeh, 1978. A standard, sixty-page account of pre-Sung fiction; bibliography, although outdated, lists modern editions.

Liu, Chien-kuo 李劍國. *Sung-tai chih-kuai ch'uan-ch'i hsü-lu* 宋代志怪傳奇敍錄. Tientsin: Nan-k'ai Ta-hsüeh, 1997.

____, ed. *T'ang-ch'ien chih-kuai hsiao-shuo chi-shih* 唐前志怪小説輯釋. Shanghai: Shang-hai Ku-chi, 1986.

Li, Ko-fei 李格非 and Wu Chih-ta 吳志達, ed. *Wen-yen hsiao-shuo, Hsien Ch'in–Nan-pai Ch'ao chüan* 文言小説, 先秦–南北朝卷. Chengchow: Chung-chou Ku-chi, 1987.

Liu, Shih-te 劉世德, ed. *Wei Chin Nan-pei ch'ao hsiao-shuo hsüan-chu*. Shanghai: Shang-hai Ku-chi, 1984.

Liu, Yung-lien 劉永濂, ed. *Chung-kuo chih-kuai hsiao-shuo hsüan-i* 中國志怪小説璇譯. Peking: Chung-kuo Hsi-chü, 1996.

Lu, Jun-hsiang 盧潤祥 and Shen Wei-lin 沈偉麟, eds. *Li-tai chih-kuai ta-kuan* 歷代志怪大觀. Shanghai: San-lien, 1996.

Morino, Shigeo 森野繁夫. *Rikuchô koshôsetsu goi shû* 六朝古小説語彙集. Kyoto: Hôyû Shoten, 1989.

Tominaga, Kazuto 富永一登. "Ro Jin shû *Ko shôsetsu kôshin* kôshaku–*Retsui den*" 魯迅集『古小説鉤沈』校釈–『列異伝』, *Hiroshima Daigaku Bungakubu kiyô* 54.2 (1994): 1-90.

Tominaga, Kazuto 富永一登. "Ro Jin shû *Ko shôsetsu kôshin* kôshaku–Shikai 魯迅集『古小説鉤沈』校釈–志怪, *Hiroshima Daigaku Bungakubu kiyô* 53 (1993): 80-92.

Wang, Ju-t'ao 王汝濤, ed. *Ch'üan T'ang hsiao-shuo* 全唐小説. Tsinan: Shan-tung Wen-i, 1993. A collection of 49 *ch'uan-ch'i* and 138 collections of *"hsiao-shuo;"* most useful for an overview of T'ang "fiction" but should be used in tandem with scholarly editions.

____, ed. *T'ang-tai chih-kuai hsiao-shuo hsüan-i* 唐代志怪小説選譯. Tsinan: Ch'i Lu Shu-she, 1985. Selections primarily from *Hsüan kuai-lu* and its sequel.

Yüan, Hang-p'ei 袁行霈 and Hou Chung-i 侯忠義, eds. *Chung-kuo wen-yen hsiao-shuo shu-mu* 中國文言小説書目. Peking: Pei-ching Ta-hsüeh, 1981. Contains a long section on *chih-kuai* and another on *ch'uan-ch'i* (T'ang); each entry cites traditional bibliographies, lists important editions, and occasionally mentions a modern study. Modern critical editions are not listed.

Translations

Kao, Karl S. *Classical Chinese Tales of the Supernatural and Fantastic–Selections from the Third to the Tenth Century.* Bloomington: Indiana University Press, 1986. The most extensive collection of *chih-kuai* and *ch'uan-ch'i* in English; interesting theoretical preface.

Yüan, Mei. *Censored by Confucius, Ghost Stories by Yuan Mei.* Translated by Kam Louie and Louise Edwards. Armonk, N.Y.: M.E. Sharpe, 1996.

Studies

Campany, Robert F. "Ghosts Matter: The Culture of Ghosts in Six Dynasties *Zhiguai.*" *CLEAR* 13 (1991): 15-34.

Campany, Robert Ford. *Strange Writing, Anomaly Accounts in Early Medieval China.* Ithaca, N.Y.: SUNY Press, 1996. Standard study of the genre in English.

Chan, Tak-hung Leo. "'To Admonish and Exhort': The Didactics of the *Zhiguai* Tale in Ji Yun's 'Yuewei caotang biji.'" Unpublished Ph. D. dissertation, Indiana Univ., 1991.

Chiang, Lan-sheng 江藍生. *Wei Chin Nan-pei ch'ao hsiao-shuo tz'u-yü hui-shih* 詞語匯釋. Peking: Yü-wen, 1988.

Chou, Tz'u-chi 周次吉. *Liu-ch'ao chih-kuai hsiao-shuo yen-chiu* 六朝志怪小説研究. Taipei: Wen-chin, 1986. Short study revised from an M.A. thesis.

Dudbridge, Glen. *Religious Experience and Lay Society in T'ang China, A Reading of Tai Fu's Kuang-i chi.* Cambridge and New York: Cambridge University Press, 1996. Careful, meticulous study which suggests *chih-kuai* were not conceived as fiction.

Eichhorn, Werner. "Das *Tung-ming chi* des Kuo Hsien." In *Religion und Philosophie in Ostasien: Festschrift für Hans Steininger,* ed. G. Naundort. 291-300. Würzburg: Könighausen und Neumann, 1985.

Fyler, Jennifer Lynn. "Social Criticism in Traditional Legends: Supernatural Women in Chinese *Zhiguai* and German *Sagen.*" Unpublished Ph.D. dissertation, University of Massachusetts, 1993.

Hsüeh, Hui-ch'i 薛惠琪. *Liu-ch'ao Fo-chiao chih-kuai hsiao-shuo yen-chiu.* Taipei: Wen-chin, 1995.

Kondô, Haruo 近藤春雄. *Chûgoku no kaiki to bijo–shikai, denki no sekai* 中国の怪奇と美女–志怪・伝奇の世界. Tokyo: Musashino Shoin 1992.

Liu, Chien-kuo 李劍國. *T'ang-ch'ien chih-kuai hsiao-shuo shih* 唐前志怪小説史. Tientsin: Nan-k'ai Ta-hsüeh, 1984.

Liu, Yeh-ch'iu 劉葉秋. *Ku-tien hsiao-shuo pi-chi lun-ts'ung.* Tientsin: Nan-k'ai Ta-hsüeh, 1985.

Liu, Yüan-ju 劉苑如. "Tsa-chuan-t'i chih-kuai yü shih-chuan te kuan-hsi–ts'ung wen-lei kuan-nien so-tso te kao-ch'a" 雜傳體志怪與史傳的關係—從文類觀念所作的考察, *Chung-kuo wen-che yen-chiu chi-k'an,* 8 (March 1996): 365-400.

Wang Chih-chung 王枝忠. *Han Wei Liu-ch'ao hsiao-shuo shih* 漢魏六朝小説史. Hangchow: Che-chiang Ku-chi, 1997.

Wang, Kuo-liang 王國良. *Liu-ch'ao chih-kuai hsiao-shuo k'ao-lun* 六朝志怪小説考論. Taipei: Wen-shih-che, 1988.

Yen, Hui-ch'i 顏慧琪. *Liu-ch'ao chih-kuai hsiao-shuo i-lei yin-yüan ku-shih yen-chiu* 異類姻緣故事研究. Taipei: Wen-chin, 1994.

Yuan, Mei. *Censored by Confucius, Ghost Stories by Yuan Mei.* Kam Louie and Louise Edwards, eds. and trans. Armonk, New York: M.E. Sharpe, 1996.

Chih Yü 摯虞 (d. 311)

Editions and References

Chih, Yü 摯虞. *Chih T'ai-ch'ang i-shu* 摯太常遺書. Chang P'eng-i 張鵬一 (1867-1944), ed.

Lanchow: Lan-chou Ku-chi, 1990. Photolithic copy of 1935 Shan-hsi T'ung-chih-kuan 山西通志館 edition. *Kuan-chung ts'ung-shu.*

___, annot. *San-fu chüeh-lu* 三輔決錄. Peking: Chung-hua, 1991.

Chin Ho 金和 (1819–1885)

Studies
Ma, Ch'ün 馬群. "Lüeh-lun Chin Ho te feng-tz'u shih chi ch'i 'Lan-ling nü-erh hsing'." *Jen-wen tsa-chih* 11 (1981): 60-4.

Chin-ku ch'i-kuan 今古奇觀 (Wonders of the Present and Past)

Editions and References
Chin-ku ch'i-kuan 今古奇觀. 40 *chüan*. 4v. Shanghai: Shang-hai Ku-chi, 1990. *Ku-pen hsiao-shuo chi-ch'eng.* Photolithic reprint of the Ta-hsing 大型 edition held in the Shanghai Library.

___. Feng Shang 馮裳, ed. and comm. Shanghai: Shang-hai Ku-chi, 1992. *Shih-ta ku-tien pai-hua tuan-p'ien hsiao-shuo ts'ung-shu.*

Translations
Chida, Kyûichi 千田九一 and Komada Shinji 駒田信二. *Kinko kikan* 今古奇観. 2v. Tokyo: Heibonsha, 1994. *Chûgoku koten bungaku taikei,* 37-38.

Kanaoka, Makoto 金岡璞. *Hokukei kanwa Kinko kikan* 北京官話今古奇観. Tokyo: Fuji, 1985.

Chin P'ing Mei 金瓶梅 (The Plum in the Golden Vase)

Editions and References
Chang, Hui-ying 張惠英. *Chin P'ing Mei li-su nan-tz'u chieh* 金瓶梅俚俗難詞解. Peking: She-hui K'o-hsüeh Wen-hsien, 1992.

Ch'i-yen 齊煙 and [Wang] Ju-mei [王] 汝梅, eds. *Hsin-k'o hsiu-hsiang p'i-p'ing Chin P'ing Mei* 新刻繡像批評金瓶梅. 2v. Hong Kong: San-lien and Tsinan: Ch'i-Lu Shu-she, 1990.

Chin P'ing Mei chien-shang tz'u-tien 金瓶梅鑒賞辭典. Shang-hai-shih *Hung-lou meng* Hsüeh-hui and Shang-hai Shih-fan Ta-hsüeh Wen-hsüeh Yen-chiu-so, eds. Shanghai: Shang-hai Ku-chi, 1990. Appends a chart (inserted page) of the characters in the novel and essays on the author, period of completion, and editions.

Chu, I-hsüan 朱一玄, ed. *Chin P'ing Mei tzu-liao hui-pien* 金瓶梅資料匯編. Tientsin: Nan-k'ai Ta-hsüeh, 1985. Appends a list of characters in the novel and a chronological list of events.

Fang, Ming 方銘, ed. *Chin P'ing Mei tzu-liao hui-lu* 金瓶梅資料匯錄. Hofei: Huang-shan Shu-she, 1986.

Hou, Chung-i 侯忠義 and Wang Ju-mei 王汝梅, eds. *Chin P'ing Mei tzu-liao hui-pien (Tseng-ting pen)* 金瓶梅資料匯編 (增訂本). Peking: Pei-ching Ta-hsüeh, 1995. *Chung-kuo ku-tien hsiao-shuo hsi-ch'ü yen-chiu tzu-liao ts'ung-shu.* Appends a bibliography.

Hu, Wen-pin 胡文彬. *Chin P'ing Mei ta tz'u-tien* 金瓶梅書錄. Shenyang: Liao-ning Jen-min, 1986. Appends an index.

Huang, Lin 黃琳, ed. *Chin P'ing Mei ta tz'u-tien* 金瓶梅大辭典. Chengtu: Pa-Shu Shu-she, 1991. Appends an index of entries.

___, ed. *Chin P'ing Mei tzu-liao hui-pien* 金瓶梅資料匯編. Peking: Chung-hua, 1987. *Ku-tien wen-hsüeh yen-chiu tzu-liao hui-pien.*

Li, Pu-ch'ing 李布青. *Chin P'ing Mei li-yü su-yen* 金瓶梅俚語俗諺. Peking: Pao-wen T'ang Shu-tien, 1988.

Li, Shen 李申. *Chin P'ing Mei jen-wu pei-chü lun* 金瓶梅方言俗語匯釋. Peking: Pei-ching Shih-fan Hsüeh-yüan, 1992. Appends a Pinyin index.

Li, Yü 李漁 (1611-1680). *Hsin-k'o hsiu-hsiang p'i-p'ing Chin P'ing Mei* 新刻繡像批評金瓶梅. Huang Lin 黃琳, Chang Ping 張兵, and Ku Yüeh 顧越, comm. Hangchow: Che-chiang Ku-chi, 1992.

Liu, Pen-tung 劉本棟 and Liao T'ien-hua 繆天華, eds. *Chin P'ing Mei* 金瓶梅. Taipei: San-min, 1990. Appends a glossary.

Pai, Wei-kuo 白維國. *Chin P'ing Mei tz'u-tien* 金瓶梅詞典. Peking: Chung-hua, 1991. Appends a list of *hsieh-hou yü* 歇後語 found in the novel.

Pao, Yen-i 鮑延毅, ed. *Chin Ping Mei yü-tz'u su-yüan* 金瓶梅語詞溯源. Peking: Hua-hsia, 1997.

Shih, Ch'ang-yü 石昌渝. *Chin P'ing Mei chien-shang tz'u-tien* 金瓶梅鑒賞辭典. Peking: Pei-ching Shih-fan Ta-hsüeh, 1989.

Wang, Ju-mei 王汝梅 and Li Chao-hsün 李昭恂, eds. Chang Chu-p'o p'i-p'ing Chin P'ing Mei 張竹坡批瓶金瓶梅. 2v. Tsinan: Ch'i-Lu Shu-she, 1991. This 100-chapter version appends a bibliography.

Wang, Li-ch'i 王力器, ed. *Chin P'ing Mei tz'u-tien* 金瓶梅詞典. Changchun: Chi-lin Wen-shih, 1988. Appends essays on problems in explicating the language of the *Chin P'ing Mei* as well as an index.

Translations

Hatano, Tarô 波多野太郎, ed. and annot. *Chûgoku bungaku gogaku shiryô shûsei dai 1 pen dai 1 kan* 中国文学語学資料集成, 第 1 篇第 1 卷. Okanami Kankyô 岡南閑喬. *Kinpeibai yakubun* 金瓶梅訳文. Tokyo: Fuji Shuppan, 1988.

Kibat, Artur. *Djin-ping-meh: Sittenroman aus der Ming-Zeit–Schlehenblüten in goldener Vases.* Herbert Franke, ed. Frankfurt: Uttstein, 1987.

Murakami, Tomoyuki 村上知行. *Kin Pei Bai* 金瓶梅, 1-4. Tokyo: Shakai Shisôsha, 1984?.

Ono, Shinobu 小野忍 and Chida, Kyûichi 千田九一. *Kon Hei Bai* 金瓶梅. 3v. Tokyo: Heibonsha, 1994. *Chûgoku koten bungaku taikei,* 33-35.

Okanami Kankyô 岡南閑喬. *Kon Hei Bai yakubun* 金瓶梅訳文. Tokyo: Fuji, 1989. *Chûgoku bungaku gogaku shiryô shusei* 中国文学語学資料集成, First Series, #1.

Roy, David. *The Plum in the Golden Vase, or, Chin P'ing Mei. Volume 1: The Gathering.* Princeton: Princeton University Press, 1993.

Studies

Bieg, Lutz. "Das kommentierte *Jin Ping Mei*," *Hefte* 8 (May 1995): 140-145.

___. "Marginalien zum gegenwärtigen Stand der *Jin Ping Mei-Forschung*," *Hefte* 2 (April 1984): 94-105.

Bischoff, Friedrich Alexander. *Djin Ping Meh: Epitome und analytischer Namenindex gemäss der Überstezung der Bruder Kibat.* Vienna: Verlag der Österrichischen Akademie der Wissenschaften, 1997.

Brömmelhoerster, Jörn. *Chinesische Romanliteratur im Western: Eine Überstezungskritik des mingzeitlichen Romans Jin Ping Mei.* Bochum: Brockmeyer, 1990. *Chinathemen* 50.

Carlitz, Katherine. *The Rhetoric of the Chin p'ing mei.* Bloomington: Indiana University Press, 1985.

Chang, Chin-ch'ih 張錦池. *Chung-kuo ssu-ta ku-tien hsiao-shuo lun-kao* 中國四大古典小説論稿. Peking: Hua-i, 1993.

Chang, Kuo-feng 張國風. *Chin P'ing Mei miao-hui te shih-su jen-chien* 金瓶梅描繪的世俗人間. Peking: Shu-mu Wen-hsien, 1992.

Chang, Lin 張琳. *Chin P'ing Mei tsung-heng t'an* 金瓶梅縱衡談. Nanning: Kuang-hsi Jen-min, 1990.

Chang, Yeh-min 張業敏. *Chin P'ing Mei te i-shu mei* 金瓶梅的藝術美. Peking: Chiao-yü K'o-hsüeh, 1992.

Chang, Yüan-fen 張還芬. *Chin P'ing Mei hsin-cheng* 金瓶梅新證. Tsinan: Ch'i-Lu Shu-she, 1984. Appends biographical materials on Chia San-chin 賈三近.

Cheng, Jun 鄭閏. *Chin P'ing Mei ho T'u Lung* 金瓶梅和屠隆. Shanghai: Hsüeh-lin, 1994. Appends a chronological biography of T'u Lung (1543-1605).

Chin P'ing Mei lun-chi 金瓶梅論集. Hsü Shuo-fang 徐朔方 and Liu Hui 劉輝, eds. Peking: Jen-min Wen-hsüeh, 1986.

Chin P'ing Mei yen-chiu 金瓶梅研究. Chung-kuo *Chin P'ing Mei* Hsüeh-hui 中國金瓶梅學會, eds. Nanking: Chiang-su Ku-chi, 1990.

Chin P'ing Mei yen-chiu 金瓶梅研究. *Fu-tan hsüeh-pao* 復旦學報 and She-hui k'o-hsüeh-pan 社會科學版, eds. Shanghai: Fu-tan Ta-hsüeh, 1984. Appends a history of *Chin P'ing Mei* studies and a bibliography.

Chou, Chung-ming 周中明. *Chin P'ing Mei i-shu lun* 金瓶梅藝術論. Nanning: Kuang-hsi Chiao-yü, 1992.

Chou, Chün-t'ao 周鈞韜. *Chin P'ing Mei su-ts'ai lai-yüan* 金瓶梅素材來源. Chengchow: Chung-chou Ku-chi, 1991.

Chou, Hui-fan 舟揮帆. *Chin P'ing Mei shih-hsüan* 金瓶梅詩選. Changsha: Hu-nan Wen-i, 1992.

Cheng, Ch'ing-shan 鄭慶山. *Chin P'ing Mei lun kao* 金瓶梅論稿. Shenyang: Liao-ning Jen-min, 1987.

Chin P'ing Mei i-shu shih-chieh 金瓶梅藝術世界. Chi-lin Ta-hsüeh Chung-kuo Wen-hua Yen-chiu-so, eds. Changchun: Chi-lin Ta-hsüeh, 1991. *Chung-kuo hsiao-shuo yü ch'uan-t'ung wen-hua yen-chiu ts'ung-shu*.

Chu, Hsing 朱星 (1912-1982) *Chin P'ing Mei k'ao-cheng* 金瓶梅考證. Tientsin: Pai-hua Wen-i, 1989.

Fu, Tseng-heng 傅憎亨. *Chin P'ing Mei yin-yü chieh-mi* 金瓶梅隱語揭祕. Tientsin: Pai-hua Wen-i, 1993. A study of the colloquial expressions in the novel.

Hayata, Teruhiro 早田輝洋. "Manbun 'Kon Hei Bai jo' yakuchû" 満文金瓶梅序訳注, *Ajia Afurika bunpô kenkyû* 23 (1995): 27-38.

Hsiao, Meng 蕭夢 and Ch'ü Jen 屈仁. *Chin P'ing Mei feng-su t'an* 金瓶梅風俗談. Chengchow: Chung-yüan Nung-min, 1993.

Hsieh, Ch'ing-lan 解慶蘭. *Chin P'ing Mei yü Fo-tao* 金瓶梅與佛道. Peking: Pei-ching Yen-shan, 1994.

Hu, Wen-pin 胡文彬. *Chin P'ing Mei te shih-chieh* 金瓶梅的世介. Harbin: Pei-fang Wen-i, 1987. Appends a bibliography.

Huang, Lin 黃琳. *Chin P'ing Mei man-hua* 金瓶梅漫話. Shanghai: Hsüeh-lin, 1986.

___ and Wang Kuo-an 王國安, trans. *Jih-pen yen-chiu Chin P'ing Mei lun-wen chi* 日本研究金瓶梅論文集. Tsinan: Ch'i-Lu Shu-she, 1989.

Huang, Martin Weizong. "The Dilemma of Chinese Lyricism and the Qing Literati Novel." Unpublished Ph. D. dissertation, Washington University, 1991. Studies how basic assumptions of lyricism are expressed in this novel and in *Hung-lou meng*.

Kao, Yüeh-feng 高越峰. *Chin P'ing Mei jen-wu pei-chü lun* 金瓶梅人物藝術論. Tsinan: Ch'i-Lu Shu-she, 1988.

Kusaka, Midori 日下翠. "Kon Hei Bai sakuhinkô" 金瓶梅作品考. *Chûbun kenkyû shûkan*, 2 (1990): 13-40.

Li, Shih-jen 李時人. *Chin P'ing Mei hsin-lun* 金瓶梅新論. Shanghai: Hsüeh-lin, 1991.

Liu, Hui 劉輝 and Yang Yang 揚揚, eds. *Chin P'ing Mei chih mi* 金瓶梅之謎. Peking: Shu-mu Wen-hsien, 1989.

___. *Chin P'ing Mei ch'eng-shu yü pan-pen yen-chiu* 金瓶梅成書與版本研究. Shenyang: Liao-ning Jen-min,1986.

Lo, Te-jung 羅德榮. *Chin P'ing Mei san nü-hsing t'ou-shih* 金瓶梅三女性透視. Tientsin: T'ien-chin Ta-hsüeh, 1992. Contains three studies of the major female characters.

Ning, Tsung-i 寧宗一 and Lo Te-jung 羅德榮, eds. *Chin P'ing Mei tui hsiao-shuo mei-hsüeh te kung-hsien* 金瓶梅對小説美學的貢獻. Tientsin: T'ien-chin She-hui K'o-hsüeh-yüan, 1992.

Pao, Chen-nan 包振南, K'ou Hsiao-wei 寇曉偉 and Chang Hsiao-ying 張曉影, eds. *Chin P'ing Mei chi chi-t'a* 金瓶梅及其他. Changchun: Chi-lin Wen-shih, 1991.

Pu, Chien 卜鍵. *Chin P'ing Mei tso-che Li K'ai-hsien k'ao* 金瓶梅作者李開先考. Lanchow: Kan-su Jen-min, 1988. Appends a bibliography and a chronological biography of Li K'ai-hsien.

Rushton, Peter Halliday. *The Jin Ping Mei and the Non-linear Dimensions of the Traditional Chinese Novel.* San Francisco: Mellen Research University Press, 1994. Revised version of Rushton's Ph. D. dissertation.

Satyendra, Indira Suh. "Toward a Poetics of the Chinese Novel: A Study of the Prefatory Poems in the *Chin P'ing Mei tz'u-hua.*" Unpublished Ph. D. dissertation, University of Chicago, 1989.

Scott, Mary Elizabeth. "Azure from Indigo: *Hong lou meng*'s Debt to *Jin Ping Mei.*" Unpublished Ph. D. dissertation, Princeton University, 1989.

Shen, T'ien-yu 沈天佑. *Chin P'ing Mei yü Hung-lou meng tsung-heng t'an* 金瓶梅與紅樓夢縱衡談. Peking: Pei-ching Ta-hsüeh, 1990.

Shih, Ch'ang-yü 石昌渝 and Yin Kung-hung 尹恭弘. *Chin P'ing Mei jen-wu pei-chü lun* 金瓶梅人物譜. Nanking: Chiang-su Ku-chi, 1988.

Sun, Chin-hua 孫緊華. *Chin P'ing Mei te nü-hsing shih-chieh* 金瓶梅的女性世介. Chengchow: Chung-chou Ku-chi, 1991.

Sun, Sun 孫遜 and Chan Tan 詹丹. *Chin P'ing Mei kai-shuo* 金瓶梅概説. Shanghai: Shang-hai Ku-chi, 1994. *Chung-kuo ku-tien wen-hsüeh chi-pen chih-shih ts'ung-shu.*

Ting, Yao-k'ang 丁耀亢 (1599-1669). *Chin P'ing Mei hsü-shu san-chung* 金瓶梅續書三種. Lu-ho 陸合 and Hsing-yüeh 星月, eds. Tsinan: Ch'i-Lu Shu-she, 1988. Contains *Hsü Chin P'ing Mei* 續金瓶梅, *Ko-lien hua-ying* 隔帘花影, and *Chin-wu meng* 金屋夢.

Ts'ai, Kuo-liang 蔡國梁. *Chin P'ing Mei k'ao-cheng yü yen-chiu* 金瓶梅考證與研究. Sian: Shan-hsi Jen-min, 1984.

Ts'ai, Tun-yung 蔡敦勇. *Chin P'ing Mei tz'u-hua chü-ch'ü p'in-t'an* 金瓶梅辭話劇曲品探. Nanking: Chiang-su Wen-i, 1989.

Tu, Wei-mo 杜維沫 and Liu Hui 劉輝, eds. *Chin P'ing Mei yen-chiu* 金瓶梅研究集. Tsinan: Ch'i-Lu Shu-she, 1988.

Wang, Chih-wu 王志武. *Chin P'ing Mei jen-wu pei-chü lun* 金瓶梅人物悲劇論. Sian: Shan-hsi Jen-min Chiao-yü, 1992.

Wang, Ching-lin 王景琳 and Hsü T'ao 徐陶. *Chin P'ing Mei chung te Fo-tsung Tao-ying* 金瓶梅中佛蹤道影. Peking: Wen-hua I-shu, 1991.

Wang, Ju-mei 王汝梅. *Chin P'ing Mei t'an-so* 金瓶梅探索. Changchun: Chi-lin Ta-hsüeh, 1990.

Wei, Tzu-yün 魏子雲. *Chin P'ing Mei te yu-yin tan-chao* 金瓶梅的幽隱探照. Taipei: Hsüeh-sheng, 1988. *Chung-kuo hsiao-shuo yen-chiu ts'ung-k'an,* 9.

___. *Chin P'ing Mei yen-chiu erh-shih nien* 金瓶梅研究二十年. Taipei: T'ai-wan Shang-wu Yin-shu-kuan, 1993. *Hsin-jen jen-wen k'u,* 35.

___, ed. *Chin P'ing Mei yen-chiu tzu-liao hui-pien* 金瓶梅研究資料彙編. 2v. Taipei: T'ien-i, 1987-89. The first volume contains essays, prefaces, and illustrations; the second

Wei's analysis of chapters 52-58.

___. *Chin P'ing Mei yüan-mao t'an-so* 金瓶梅原貌探索. Taipei: Hsüeh-sheng, 1985. Various useful appendixes.

___. *Hsiao-shuo Chin P'ing Mei* 小説金瓶梅. Taipei: Hsüeh-sheng, 1988.

Wu, Hung 吳紅 and Hu Pang-wei 胡邦煒. *Ch'in P'ing Mei te ssu-hsiang ho i-shu* 金瓶梅的思想和藝術. Chengtu: Pa-Shu Shu-she, 1987.

Yeh, Kuei-t'ung 葉桂桐 and Sung P'ei-hsien 宋培憲, eds. *Chin P'ing Mei jen-wu cheng-chuan* 金瓶梅人物正傳. Peking: Nan-hai, 1991.

Yü, Ch'eng-wu 于承武. *Chin P'ing Mei p'ing-i* 金瓶梅平議. Peking: Wen-chin, 1992.

Chin Sheng-t'an 金聖嘆 (1608/10–1661) 1607-1661

Editions and References

Chin, Sheng-t'an 金聖嘆. *Chin Sheng-t'an chüan-chi* 金聖嘆全集. Ts'ao Fang-jen 曹方人 and Chou Hsi-shan 周錫山, ed. 4v. Nanking: Chiang-su Ku-chi, 1985.

___. *Chin Sheng-t'an hsüan-p'i T'ang-shih* 金聖嘆選批唐詩. Che-chiang Ku-chi Chu-pan-she, ed. Hangchow: Che-chiang Ku-chi, 1985.

___. *Chin Sheng-t'an hsüan-p'i T'ang-shih liu-pai shou* 金聖嘆選批唐詩六百首. Shih Chien-chung 施建中 and Sui Shu-fen 隋淑芬, eds. Peking: Pei-ching, 1989. Appends a biography of Chin.

___. *Chin Sheng-t'an p'i-p'ing Shui-hu chuan* 金聖嘆批評水滸傳. Liu I-chou 劉一舟, ed. Tsinan: Ch'i-Lu Shu-she, 1991. Based on the 120-chapter version.

___. *Chin Sheng-t'an p'i ts'ai-tzu ku-wen* 金聖嘆批才子古文. Chang Kuo-kuang 張國光, ed. Wuhan: Hu-pei Jen-min, 1986.

___. *Ti-liu ts'ai-tzu shu 'Hsi-hsiang chi'* 第六才子書西廂記. 8 *chüan*. Tsinan: Shan-tung Wen-i, 1987.

___. *Ti-wu ts'ai-tzu shu 'Hsi-hsiang chi'* 第五才子書施耐庵水滸傳. Wen Tzu-sheng 文子生, ed. Chengchow: Chung-chou Ku-chi, 1985.

Studies

Chang Kuo-kuang 張國光. *Shui-hu yü Chin Sheng-t'an yen-chiu* 水滸與金聖嘆研究. Chengchow: Chung-chou Shu-hua-she, 1981. Appends correspondence between Chin Sheng-t'an and Hsi Yung-jen 嵇永仁 and a study of reactions to Chin's revision of *Shui-hu*.

Church, Sally Kathryn. "Jin Shengtan's Commentary on the 'Xixiang ji' (The Romance of the Western Chamber)." Unpublished Ph. D. dissertation, Harvard University, 1993.

Hsü, Li 徐立 and Ch'en Yü 陳瑜. *Wen-t'an Kuai-chieh Chin Sheng-t'an* 文壇怪杰金聖嘆. Changsha: Hu-nan Chiao-yü, 1987. Appends a chronological biography.

Kuo, Tuan 郭端. *Chin Sheng-t'an de hsiao-shuo li-lun yü hsi-chü li-lun* 金聖嘆的小説理論與戲劇理論. Peking: Chung-kuo Wen-lien, 1993.

Liu, Hsin-chung 劉欣中. *Chin Sheng-t'an te hsiao-shuo li-lun* 金聖嘆的小説理論. Shih-chia-chuang: Ho-pei Jen-min, 1986.

Liu, Yüan-jung 劉元蓉 and Lin Ti 林棣. *Chin Sheng-t'an ch'uan-ch'i* 金聖嘆傳奇. Hofei: Huang-shan Shu-she, 1991.

T'an, Fan 譚帆. *Chin Sheng-t'an yü Chung-kuo hsi-ch'ü p'i-p'ing* 金聖嘆與中國戲曲批評. Shanghai: Hua-tung Shih-fan Ta-hsüeh, 1992.

Wang, Yao 王堯. "*Chin P'ing Mei* yü Ming-tai Tao-chiao huo-tung" 金瓶梅與明代道教活動, *Tao-chiao wen-hua yen-chiu* 7 (1995): 373-398.

Wu, Hua Laura. "Jin Shengtan (1608-1661); Founder of a Chinese Theory of the Novel." Unpublished Ph. D. dissertation, University of Toronto, 1993.

Chin-wen 金文 (bronze inscriptions)

Editions and References

Chao, Ming-ch'eng 趙明誠 (Sung dynasty). *Chin-shih lu chiao-cheng* 金石錄校證. Chin Wen-ming 金文名, ed. Shanghai: Shang-hai Shu-hua 上海書畫, 1985.

Ch'en, Ch'u-sheng 陳初生, ed. *Chin-wen ch'ang-yung tzu-tien* 金文常用字典. Sian: Shan-hsi Jen-min, 1987.

Chin-wen ku-lin pu 金文詁林補. Chou Fa-kao 周法高, *et al.*, eds. 8v. Nankang: Academia Sinica, 1982.

Fang, Shu-hsin 方述鑫. *Chia-ku chin-wen tzu-tien* 甲骨金文字典. Chengtu: Pa-Shu Shu-she, 1993.

Hsü, Chung-shu 徐中舒. *Yin Chou chin-wen chi-lu* 殷周金文集錄. Yipin: Ssu-ch'uan Tz'u-shu, 1986.

Ma, Ch'eng-yüan 馬承源 *et al.*, ed. *Shang Chou ch'ing-chin-t'ung ch'i ming-wen hsüan* 商周青金銅器銘文選. 4v. Peking: Wen-wu, 1988. Originally compiled by Chao Ming-ch'eng 趙明誠 of the Sung dynasty.

Ma, Ch'eng-yüan. *Chung-kuo ch'ing-t'ung ch'i* 中國青銅器. Shanghai: Shang-hai Ku-chi, 1988.

Shirakawa, Shizuka 白川青爭, ed. *Kimbun tsûshaku* 金文通釋. 7v. Kobe: Hakutsuru Bijutsukan, 1964-84.

Sun, Wei-tsu 孫慰祖 *et al.*, eds. *Ch'in Han chin-wen hui-pien* 秦漢金文匯編. Shanghai: Shang-hai Shu-tien, 1996.

Yeh, Ch'eng-i 葉程義. *Han Wei shih-k'o wen-hsüeh k'ao-shih* 漢魏石刻文學考釋. 3v. + 1v. addenda. Taipei: Hsin-wen-feng, 1997.

Studies

Behr, Wolfgang. "Reimende Bronzeinschriften und die Entstehung der chinesischen Endreimdichtung." Unpublished Ph. D. dissertation, University of Frankfurt, 1996.

Schaberg, David. "Literary Form in Bronze Inscriptions," in Schaberg, "Foundations of Chinese Historiography: Literary Representation in *Zuo zhuan* and *Guoyu.*" Unpublished Ph. D. dissertation, Harvard University, 1996, pp. 46-60.

Shaughnessy, Edward L., ed. *New Sources of Early Chinese History: An Introduction to the Reading of Inscriptions and Manuscripts.* Berkeley: The Society for the Study of Early China and The Institute of East Asian Studies, University of California, 1997. Especially the "Western Zhou Bronze Inscriptions" by Shaughnessy and "Eastern Zhou Bronze Inscriptions" by Gilbert L. Mattos; appends an excellent bibliography.

____. *Sources of Western Zhou History: Inscribed Bronze Vessels.* Berkeley: University of California Press, 1991.

Shirakawa, Shizuka 白川青爭. *Kôkotsu kimbungaku ronshû* 甲骨金文學論集. Kyoto: Hôyû, 1996.

Tsai, Yen-zen. *"Ching* and *Chuan:* Towards Defining the Confucian Scriptures in Han China (206 BCE–220 CE)." Unpublished Ph. D. dissertation, Harvard University, 1993.

Zhao, Chao. "Some Inscriptions of the Wei-Jin Nanbei Chao Period," *Early Medieval China* 1(1995):84-96.

Chinese as a Literary Language-Vietnam

Editions and References

Marr, David G. *Vietnam.* Oxford: Clio Press, 1992. World Bibliographical Series, 147. A thorough and extensive annotated bibliographical guide; the Vietnamese literature bibliography can be found on pages 290-307.

Ngô, Sî Liên (15th c.). *Dai Viêt Sú Kỳ Toân Thu.* 4v. Hà Nôi: Khoa Hoc Xâ Hôi, 1993. Includes bibliographical references.

Ngô, Thê Long and Nguyên Kim Hung. *Dai Viêt Sú Kỳ Tuc Biên (1676-1789).* Hà Nôi: Khoa Hoc Xâ Hôi, 1991. Includes bibliographical references.

Nguyên, Dình Thâm. *Studies on Vietnamese Language and Literature: A Preliminary Bibliography.* Ithaca: Cornell University Press, 1992. A valuable bibliographical tool which contains about 2500 entries; lacks Vietnamese-language publications.

Nguyên, Tài (1380-1442). *Môt Sô Vân Dê Vê Chû Nôm.* Hà Nôi: Dai Hoc Và Trung Hoc Chuyên Nghiêp, 1985. Includes bibliographical references.

Singleton, Carl. *Vietnam Studies: An Annotated Bibliography.* Pasedena and Englewood Cliffs: Scarecrow Press, 1997.

Translations

Bui, Quang Tung, *et al*, trans. and comms. *Le Dai Viêt et ses voisins: d'apres le Dai Viêt Sú Kỳ Toân Thu.* Paris: L'Harmatton, 1990. An annotated translation into French of the standard work on the history of pre-modern Vietnam.

Dong, Trân Con and Phan Huy Ich. Huynh Sanh Thông, trans. and annot. *Chinh Phu Ngam* [The Song of a Soldier's Wife]. New Haven: Yale University Press, 1986. Translation of the eighteenth-century verse narrative originally written in classical Chinese; texts in English, Vietnamese and Chinese.

Duong, Dinh Khue. *Les chefs d'oeuvre de la littérature vietnamienne.* Saigon: Kim Lai An-Quan, 1966. Includes historical sketches, poems and prose pieces written in Chinese.

Giang, Hà Vy, *et al.* *Tuóng Quân Lỳ Thuòng Kiêt: Truyên Lich Sù.* Hà Nôi: Quan Doi Nhân Dan, 1991. Translation and discussion of the Lỳ dynasty fiction of Lỳ Thuòng Kiêt. Includes bibliographical references.

Huynh, Sanh Thông, ed. and trans. *An Anthology of Vietnamese Poetry: From the Eleventh through the Twentieth Centuries.* New Haven: Yale University Press, 1996. Contains 322 poems by some 150 poets, many of whom wrote in classical Chinese; valuable introduction.

Trân, Trong San. *Tho Duòng.* Hô Chí Minh: Tu Sách Dai Hoc Tông Hóp, 1990. Translations of T'ang dynasty Chinese poetry into Vietnamese and English with Sino-Vietnamese readings; includes bibliographical references.

Studies

Davidson, J.H.C.S. "A New Version of the Chinese-Vietnamese Vocabulary of the Ming Dynasty." *BSOAS* 38 (1975): 296-315.

DeFrancis, John. "Vietnamese Writing Reform in Asian Perspective." In Truong Buu Lâm, ed. *Borrowings and Adaptations in Vietnamese Culture.* Honolulu: University of Hawaii Press, Southeast Asian Studies Center for Asian and Pacific Studies, 1987, pp. 41-51.

Durand, Maurice. Nguyên Trân Huân, ed. and D. M. Hawke, trans. *Introduction to Vietnamese Literature.* New York: Columbia University Press, 1985. An English translation of the survey of Vietnamese literary history written by one of the most respected scholars in the field; originally in French and published in Paris in 1969. See the review by Stephen O'Harrow in *JAS* 46 (1987): 209-11.

Lam, Giang and Nguyên Quang Hông. *Vân Khâc Hán Nôm Viêt-Nam: Tuyên Chon-luoc Thuât.* Hà Nôi: Nhà Xuât Ban Khoa Hoc Xâ Hôi, 1992. A study of 2000 Chinese inscriptions engraved on stalae, bells and gongs from various historical periods and locations in Vietnam; contains translations into modern Vietnamese. Appends bibliographical references and an index.

Nguyên, Dình Hoa. *Vietnamese Literature: A Brief Survey.* San Diego: San Diego State University, 1994. Includes bibliographical references and an index.

Nguyên, Ngoc Bích. *The State of Chû Nôm Studies: The Demotic Script of Vietnam.* Fairfax, Virginia: George Mason University, 1984.

Trân, Qrôc Voung. "Popular Culture and High Culture in Vietnamese History." *Crossroads* 7 (1992): 5-38.

Wolters, Oliver W. "A Stranger in His Own Land: Nguyên Trai's Sino-Vietnamese Poems Written during the Ming Occupation." *Vietnam Forum* 4 (1986): 60-90.

Chinese Literature in Japanese Translation

Editions and References

Chûgoku bungaku gogaku bunken annai 中国文学語学文献案内. 3rd rev. ed. Tokyo: Waseda University, 1988.

Kambun kenkyû no tebiki 漢文研究の手びき. 3rd rev. ed. Tokyo: Waseda University, 1994. Edited by the Chûgoku Shibun Kenkyûkai 中国詩文研究会, this is a most useful list of Japanese studies and translations of traditional Chinese works.

Lin, Ch'ing-chang 林慶彰, ed. *Jih-pen yen-chiu ching-hsüeh lun-chu mu-lu (1900-1992)* 日本研究經學論箸目錄. Nankang: Wen-che So, Chung-yang Yen-chiu Yüan, 1993. Extensive coverage (900 pages) of Japanese scholarship on and translations of the Chinese classics.

See also Japanese bibliographies devoted to individual works or authors listed here or the annuals, *Tôhôgaku kankei chosho rombun mokuroku* 東方学関係著書論文目録, *Books and Articles on Oriental Subjects* (Tokyo: The Tôhô Gakkai) and *Tôyôshi kenkyû bunken ruimoku* 東洋史研究文献類木, *Annual Bibliography of Oriental Studies* (Kyoto: Institute for Research in Humanities, Kyoto University).

Translations

Rimer, J. Thomas and Jonathan Chaves. *Japanese and Chinese Poems to Sing: The Wakan roei shu.* New York: Columbia University Press, 1997.

Studies

Machida, Saburô 町田三郎. "Jih-pen chih *Lun-yü* yen-chiu" 日本之論語研究, *Chung-kuo wen-che yen-chiu t'ung-hsün* 7.3 (September 1997): 1-16.

Mizuno, Heiji 水野平次. *Haku Rakuten to Nihon bungaku* 白楽天と日本文学. Tokyo: Daigakudô Shoten, 1982.

Nakanishi, Susumu 中西進 and Yen Shao-tang 嚴紹璗, eds. *Nichi-Chû bunka kôryûshi sôsho, Dairokukan—Bungaku* 日中文化交流史宗書, 第六巻—文学. Tokyo: Taishûkan Shoten 大修館書店, 1995.

Ng, W. M. "The History of *I-ching* in Medieval Japan," *Journal of Asian History* 31 (1997): 25-46.

Chinese Literature in Korean Translation

Editions and References

Hang-chou Ta-hsüeh 杭州大學, ed. *Han-kuo yen-chiu Chung-wen wen-hsien mu-lu* 韓國研究中文文獻目錄. Hangchow: Hang-chou Ta-hsüeh, 1994. Useful bibliography.

Yi, Chang-u 李章佑. "Kangoku no Tôdai bungaku kenkyû gaikyô" 韓国の唐代文学研究概況, *Chûgoku—Shakai to bunka* 5 (1991): 288-293.

Translations

An, Ui-un. *Tang-Songsa paeksu* 唐宋詞一百首. Simyang: Yonyong Inmin Chulpansa, 1985. Translation of the collection compiled and annotated by Hu Yün-i 胡雲翼; original Chinese text published in Peking by Chung-hua in 1961.

Cho, Hyun-suk. *Noja Todokkyong* 老子道德經. Seoul: Sogwangsa, 1991.

Cho, Yong-man 趙容萬. *Tu Si sonyok* 杜詩選譯. Seoul: Koryo Taehakkyo Chulpabu, 1986.

Choe, Sung-il, *et al. Yirim oesa* 儒林外史. 3v. Seoul: Yogang Chulpansa, 1991.

Chong, Chae-so. *Sanhaeyong* 山海經. Seoul: Minumsa, 1985; 1993.

Chong, Ku-bok. *Haedong akpu chipsong* 3v. Seoul: Yogang Chulpansa, 1988. Translations of *yüeh-fu* poetry.

Chunchu Chwassi chon 春秋左傳. Seoul: Pogynag Munhwasa, 1983.

Kim, Chi-yong 金知泳. *Hanguk ui yoryu Hansi* 韓國〔之〕女流漢詩. Seoul: Yogang Chulpansa, 1991. A collection of poetry by female poets.

Kim, Chung-nyol 金忠烈. *Chachi tonggam* 資治通鑑. Seoul: Samsong Chulpahsa, 1987.

Kim, Jong-gil. *Slow Chrysanthemums: Classical Korean Poems in Chinese.* London; Dover, NH: Anvil Press, 1987. Chinese and Korean poetry introduced and translated into English.

Kim, Pyong-chong 金並總. *Sama Chon ui wanyok Sagi* 司馬遷與完譯史記. 10v. Seoul: Chimmundang, 1994.

Kim, Sang-hun 金相鉉. *Hansijip* 漢詩集. 3v. Pyongyang: Munye Chulpansa, 1985. A wealth of Chinese poetry translated into Korean.

Kim, Tal-chin 金達鎮. *Hanguk hansi* 韓國漢詩. 3v. Seoul: Minumsa, 1989. A collection of translations of Chinese poems.

___. *Tangsi chonso* 唐詩全書. Seoul: Minumsa, 1987.

Pak, Chong-hwa 朴鍾和. *Samgukchi* 三國志. 8v. Seoul: Omungak, 1984. Translation of the *San-kuo chih yen-i* 三國志演義.

Pak, Su-jin. *Wanyok Kum Pyong Mae* 全譯金瓶梅. 6v. Seoul: Chongnyosa, 1991-93.

Sin, Nae-am? *Suhoji* 水滸傳. 10v. Seoul: Minumsa, 1996.

Song, Tae-gyong. *Sogyong* 書經. 22v. Seoul: Songgyungwan Taehakkyo Chulpanbu, 1993.

To, Kwang-sun. *Sigyong* 詩經. Seoul: Samjungdang, 1983.

U, Hyon-min 禹玄民. *To Yonmyong si chonjip* 陶淵明詩全集. 2v. Seoul: Somundang, 1976.

Yi, Chu-hu and Yu Mun-dong. *Sama Chon Sagi* 司馬遷史記. 3v. Seoul: Paejon Sogwan, 1985.

Chinese Literature in Manchu Translation

Studies

Gimm, Martin. *Historische und bibliographische Studien zur Mandschuforschung.* Wiesbaden: Harrassowitz, 1992.

___, Giovanni Stari and Michael Weiers, eds. *Klassische, moderne und bibliographische Studien zur Mandschuforschung.* Wiesbaden: Harrassowitz, 1991.

_____. "Manchu Translations of Chinese Novels and Short Stories: An Attempt at an Inventory," *AM, NS* 1 (1988): 77-114.

Hayata, Teruhiro 早田輝洋. "Manbun '*Kon Hei Bai* jo' yakuchû" 満文金瓶梅序訳注, *Ajia Afurika bunpô kenkyû* 23 (1995): 27-38.

Manchu Studies Newsletter 1- (1977-).

Stary, Giovanni, ed. *Ars poetic Manjurica: 7 sibe-mandschurische Lieder und Gedichtsammunglen in Umschrift.* Wiesbaden: Harrassowitz, 1986.

___. *Epengesängen der Sibe-Mandschuren.* Wiesbaden: Harrassowitz, 1988.

Wadley, Stephen A. *The Mixed Language Verse from the Manchu Dynasty in China.* Bloomington: Research Institute for Inner Asian Studies, Indiana University, 1991.

Zibet, U. L. G. "Laterna stimulans, tsuipa, Kung Fu und Ritsch-ratsch; Anmerkungen zu einer wirklichen frühen *Jin Ping* Mei-Übersetzung der zwanziger Jahre und einer angeblichen Übersetzung der mandjurischen *Jin Ping* Mei-Fassung ins Deutsche." In *Erotische Literatur, Mitteilungen zur Erforschung und Bibliographie/Newsletter for the Study and Bibliography of Erotic Literature* 3 (1996): 63-89.

Chinese Literature in Mongol Translation

Studies

Cleaves, Francis Woodman. "The First Chapter of an Early Mongolian Version of the *Hsiao ching*" *Acta Orientalia Academiae Scientiarum Hungaricae* 36 (1982): 69-88.

___. "The Fourth Chapter of an Early Mongolian Version of the *Hsiao ching*," *Mongolian Studies* 15 (1992): 137-150.

Ligeti, Louis. "A propos de la traduction mongole préclassique du *Hsiao-king*" *Acta Orientalia Academiae Scientiarum Hungaricae* 38 (1984): 303-349.

Rachewiltz, Igor de. "The Preclassical Mongolian Version of the *Hsiao-ching*," *Zentralasiatischen Studien,* 16 (1982): 7-109.

Ching 京 (classics)

Editions and References

Huang, Chih-ming 黃智明. "Tun-huang ching-chi chüan-tzu yen-chiu kai-k'uang (hsia)" 敦煌經籍卷子研究概況 (上，下), *Chung-kuo wen-che yen-chiu t'ung-hsün* 6.3 (September 1996): 89-125; 6.4 (December 1996): 51-74.

Huang, K'ai-hui 黃開回, ed. *Ching-hsüeh tz'u-tien* 經學辭典. Chengtu: Ssu-ch'uan Jen-min, 1994.

Hung, Liang-chi 洪亮吉 (1746–1809). *Ch'un-ch'iu, Tso-chuan ku* 春秋左傳詁. Li Chieh-min 李解民, ed. Peking: Chung-hua, 1987.

The ICS Ancient Chinese Text Concordances Series: Hsien Ch'in, Liang Han, ku-chi chu tzu so-yin ts'ung-k'an 先秦兩漢古籍逐字索引叢刊. D. C. Lau 劉殿爵 and Chen Fong Ching 陳方正, eds. Hong Kong: The Commercial Press, 1992-. New concordances of the classics with textual notes by D. C. Lau.

Li, Po 理波 *et al.*, eds. *Shih-san ching hsin so-yin* 十三經新索引. Peking: Kuang-po Tien-shih, 1997. Keyed to the 1979 Chung-hua edition of the thirteen classics.

Lin, Ch'ing-chang 林慶彰, ed. *Jih-pen yen-chiu ching-hsüeh lun-chu mu-lu* (1900-1992) 日本研究經學論箸目錄. Nankang: Wen-che So, Chung-yang Yen-chiu Yüan, 1993. The first source to consult for information on Japanese studies of the Chinese classics.

Wu, Shu-p'ing 吳樹平, ed. *Shih-san ching piao-tien pen.* Taipei: Hsiao-yüan 曉園, 1995*?

Yang, Po-chün 楊伯峻 and Hsü T'i 徐提. *Ch'un-ch'iu Tso-chuan tz'u-tien* 春秋左傳詞典. Peking: Chung-hua, 1985.

Yang, T'ien-yü 楊天宇. *Li chi i-chu* 禮記譯注. Shanghai: Shang-hai Ku-chi, 1997.

Translations

Brooks, E. Bruce, with A. Taeko Brooks. *The Original Analects, Sayings of Confucius and His Successors.* New York: Columbia University Press, 1998.

Cheng, Anne. *Entretiens de Confucius.* Paris: Éditions du Seuil, 1981.

Hasse, Martine. *Tseng-tseu, La grande étude, avec le commentaire traditionnel de Tchou Hi.* Paris: Editions du Cerf, 1984.

Huang, Chichung. *The Analects of Confucius, A Literal Translation with and Introduction and*

Notes. Oxford: Oxford University Press, 1997.

Kôyô Chûso Kenkyûkai 公羊注疏研究会, ed. *Kôyô chûso yakuchû kô* 4 公羊注疏訳注稿 4. Urawa: Kôyô Chûso Kenkyûkai, 1987.

Kunst, Richard. "The Original 'Yijing:' A Text, Phonetic Transcription, Translation and Indexes; with Sample Glosses, Parts I and II." Ph.D., University of California, Berkeley, 1985.

Lynn, Richard John. *The Classic of Changes, A New Translation of the I Ching as Interpreted by Wang Bi*. New York: Columbia University Press, 1994. An important new translation.

Ogura, Yoshihiko 小倉芳彦. *Shunjû Sashi den (Jô, chû, ge)* 春秋左氏伝(上・中・下). 3v. Tokyo: Iwanami Shoten, 1988-89.

Yasumoto, Hiroshi 安本博. Shunjû Sashi den 春秋左氏伝. *Kanshô chûgoku no koten* 鑑賞中国 の古典, 6. Tokyo: Kadokawa Shoten, 1989.

Ryckmans, Pierre. *Les Entretiens de Confucius*. Paris: Gallimard, 1987.

Studies

Ch'ang, Pi-te 昌彼得. *"Lun-yü* pan-pen yüan-liu k'ao-hsi" 論語版本源流考析, *Ku-kung hsüeh-shu chi-k'an*, 12.1 (1994): 141-152.

Ch'en, Meng-chia 陳夢家. *Shang-shu t'ung-lun* 尚書通論. Peking: Chung-hua, 1985.

Cheng, Anne. *Étude sur le Confucianism Han: l'elaboration d'une tradition exegetique sur les classiques*. Paris: Collège France, Institut des Hautes Études Chinoises,, 1985.

Chou, Yü-t'ung 周予同 (1898-1981). *Chou Yü-t'ung ching-hsüeh shih lun-chu hsüan-chi* 周予同經 學史論著選集. Chu Wei-cheng 鉄維錚, ed. Rpt. Shanghai: Jen-min, 1996 (1983).

Gentz, Joachim. "Die *Chunqiu*-Auslegung in der *Gongyang*-Tradition bis zum *Chunqiu fanlu*." Unpublished Ph. D. dissertation, University of Heidelberg, 1996.

Goodman, Howard L. "Exegetes and Exegeses of the *Book of Changes* in the Third Century A.D.: Historical and Scholastic Contexts for Wang Pi." Unpublished Ph. D. dissertation, Princeton University, 1985.

Heidbüchel, Ursula. "Rhetorik im antiken China, eine Untersuchung der Ausdrucksformen höfischer Rede im *Zuozhuan*."Unpublished Ph. D. dissertation, University of Münster, 1993.

Jullien, François. "Ni Ecriture sainte ni œuvre classique: du statut du Texte confucéen comme texte fondateur vis-à-vis de la civilisation chinoises," *Extrême-Orient Extrême-Occident* 6 (1985): 23-81.

Kaji, Nobuyuki 加地伸行. *Rongo no sekai* 論語の世界. Tokyo: Chûô Kôronsha, 1992.

Kano, Naoki 狩野直樹. *Shunshû kenkyû* 春秋研究. Tokyo: Misuzu Shobô みすず書房, 1994.

Ku, Chieh-kang 顧頡剛. *Ch'un-ch'iu san-chuan chi Kuo-yü chih tsung-ho yen-chiu* 春秋三傳及國 語之總合研究. Chengtu: Pa Shu, 1988.

Kunst, Richard (see *Translations* above).

Liu, Ch'i-yü 劉起釪. *Shang-shu hsüeh-shih* 尚書學史. Peking: Chung-hua, 1989.

___. *Shang-shu yüan-liu chi ch'uan-pen k'ao* 尚書源流及傳本考. Shenyang: Liao-ning Ta-hsüeh, 1997.

Loewe, *Early Chinese Texts*. See the excellent articles on early of the Chinese classics in this important volume.

Lu, Te-ming 陸德明. *Ching-tien shih-wen* 經典釋文. Shanghai: Shang-hai Ku-chi, 1985.

Makeham, John. "The Formation of *Lunyu* as a Book," *MS* 44 (1996): 1-24.

___. The Earliest Extant Commentary on *Lunyu: Lunyu Zheng shi zhu*," *TP* LXXXIII (1997):260-299.

Matsukawa, Kenji 松川健二, ed. *Rongo no shisô shi* 論語の思想史. Tikyo: Kyûko Shoin, 1994.

Matsumoto, Masaaki 松本雅明. *Shunjû, Sengoku ni okeru Shôso no tenkai* 春秋戦国における尚 書の展開. Tokyo: Kazama, 1988.

Mizuno, Kôgen 水野弘元. *Keiten-sono seiritsu to tenkai* 経典ーその成立と展開. Tokyo: Kôsei Shuppansha, 1990.

Mollgard, Eske Janus. "Aspects of Early Confucian Ethics." Unpublished Ph.D. dissertation, Harvard University, 1993. Focuses on *Meng Tzu* and *Lun-yü.*

Noma, Fumichika 野間文史. "Gokyô seigi shoin teihonkô" 五経正義所引定本考, *Nippon Chûgoku gakkaihô* 37 (1986): 89-102.

Seo, Kunio 瀬尾邦雄, ed. *Kôji, Môji ni kansuru bunken mokuroku* 孔子孟子に関する文献目録. Tokyo: Hakuteisha 白帝社, 1994.

Shaughnessy, Edward L. *Before Confucius, Studies in the Creation of the Chinese Classics.* Albany: State University of New York Press, 1997. Although six of the eight articles collected here have been previously published elsewhere, this brings them together in a handy form.

___. "The Composition of the *Zhouyi.*" Unpublished Ph. D. dissertation, Stanford University, 1983.

Shen, Yü-ch'eng 沈玉成 and Liu Ning 劉寧. *Ch'un-ch'iu Tso-chuan hsüeh shih-kao* 學史稿. Nanking: Chiang-su Ku-chi, 1992.

Tsai, Yen-zen. "*Ching* and *Chuan:* Towards Defining the Confucian Scriptures in Han China (206 BCE-220 CE)." Unpublished Ph. D. dissertation, Harvard University, 1993.

Wang, Pao-hsüan 王葆玹. *Hsi Han ching-hsüeh yüan-liu* 西漢經學源流. Taipei: Tung-ta, 1994.

Wu, Ch'eng-shih 吳承仕. *Ching-tien shih-wen hsü-lu shu-cheng* 經典釋文序錄疏證. Peking: Chung-hua, 1984.

Ching-chü 京劇 (Peking Opera)

Editions and References

Hsü, Ch'eng-pei 徐城北. *Ching-chü i-pai t'i* 京劇一百題. Peking: Jen-min Erh-pao, 1988.

Tseng, Po-jung 曾白融, ed. *Ching-chü chü-mu tz'u-tien* 京劇劇目辭典. Peking: Chung-kuo Hsi-chü, 1989. Entries on 5300 related subjects, titles and persons followed by Pinyin and stroke-order indexes.

Wu, T'ung-pao 吳同寶 *et al.,* eds. *Ching-chü chih-shih tz'u-tien* 京劇知識辭典. Tientsin: T'ien-chin Jen-min, 1990.

Studies

Chang, Meng-keng 張夢庚 *et al. Ching-chü man-hua* 京劇漫話. Peking: Pei-ching, 1982.

Hsü, Ch'eng-pei 徐城北. *Chung-kuo ching-chü* 中國京劇. Canton: Kuang-tung Lu-yu, 1996.

Kaulbach, Barbara. *Ch'i Ju-shan (1871-1961), Die Erforschung und Systematisierung der Praxis des chinesischen Dramas.* Frankfurt: Peter Lang, 1977.

Ma, Shao-po 馬少波 *et al,* ed. *Chung-kuo ching-chü shih* 中國京劇史. Peking: Chung-kuo Hsi-chü, 1990.

Pan, Xiafeng. *The Stagecraft of Peking Opera, From Its Origins to the Present Day.* Peking: New World Press, 1995.

Su, I 蘇移. *Ching-chü erh-pai-nien kai-kuan* 京劇二百年概觀. Peking: Pei-ching Yen-shan, 1989.

"Symposium: What More Do We Need to Know about Chinese Theatre?" *Asian Theatre Journal* 11 (1994): 81-118. Contributions by William Dolby on *tsa-chü*, Elizabeth Wichmann on *ching-chü*, and Colin Mackerras on theater of the minority peoples.}

Wichman, Elizabeth. *Listening to Theatre: The Aural Dimension of Beijing Opera.* Honolulu University of Hawaii, 1991.

Wu, T'ung-pin 吳同賓. *Ching-chü chih-shih shou-ts'e* 京劇知識手冊. Tientsin: T'ien-chin Chiao-yü, 1995.

Ching-hua yüan 鏡花緣 (**Romance of the Mirrored Flowers**)

Editions and References

Liu, Ju-chen 李汝珍. *Ching-hua yüan* 鏡花緣. Yu Hsin-hsiung 尤信雄 and Miao T'ien-hua 繆天華, eds. Taipei: San-min, 1989. *Chung-kuo ku-tien ming-chu.* Appends a glossary of words and terms from the novel.

___. *Ching-hua yüan.* 20 *chüan.* 4v. Shanghai: Shang-hai Ku-chi, 1990. *Ku-pen hsiao-shuo chi-ch'eng.* Photolithic copy of an 1832 reprint by the Chieh-tzu Yüan 芥子園 now held in Fu-tan University Library.

Studies

Chan, Leo Tak-hung. "Religion and Structure in the *Ching-hua yüan.*" *TkR* 20.1 (1989): 45-66.

Elvin, Mark. "The Spectrum of Accessibility, Types of Humour in *The Destinies of the Flowers in the Mirror.*" In *Interpreting Culture through Translation.* Roger T. Ames *et al.,* eds. Hong Kong: The Chinese University Press, 1991, pp. 101-117.

Epstein, Maram. "Beauty is the Beast: The Dual Face of Woman in Four Ch'ing Novels." Unpublished Ph.D. dissertation, Princeton University, 1992.

Ching-pen t'ung-su hsiao-shuo 京本通俗小説 (**Popular Stories from Capital Editions**)

Editions and References

Ching-pen t'ung-su hsiao-shuo 京本通俗小説. Ch'eng Yu-ch'ing 程有慶, ed. Nanking: Chiang-su Ku-chi, 1991. *Chung-kuo hua-pen ta-hsi.*

Yen, Ch'ung-ch'ü 閻崇璩. *Ching-pen t'ung-su hsiao-shuo tz'u-yü hui-shih* 京本通俗小説詞語匯釋. Tokyo: Dai Tôbunwa Daigaku 大東文話大學, 1983.

Ch'ing-lou chi 青樓集 (**Green Lofts Collection**)

Editions and References

Hsia, T'ing-chih 夏庭芝 (Huang, Hsüeh-so 黃雪簑, Yüan dynasty), ed. *Ch'ing-lou chi* 青樓集. Peking: Chung-kuo Hsi-chü, 1959. *Chung-kuo ku-tien hsi-ch'ü lun-chu chi-ch'eng,* 2.

___. *Ch'ing-lou chi.* Peking: Chung-hua, 1985. *TSCC* edition. A reprint of the *Ku-chin shuo-hai* 古今説海 edition.

Ch'ing-pai lei-ch'ao 清稗類鈔 (**A Classified Collection of Ch'ing Fiction**)

Editions and Reference

Liu, Cho-ying 劉卓英, ed. *Ch'ing-pai lei-ch'ao* 清稗類鈔. Peking: Chung-hua, 1986.

Ch'ing-p'ing shan-t'ang hua-pen, see *Liu-shih chiao hsiao-shuo.*

Ch'ing shih-hua 青詩話 (**Poetry Talks of the Ch'ing Dynasty**)

Editions and References

Shang, Jung 尚鎔 (Ch'ing dynasty). *Ch'ing shih-hua hsü-pien* 青詩話續編. Shanghai: Shang-hai

Ku-chi, 1983. Various editors for the different volumes.

Kuo, Shao-yü 郭紹虞 *et al.*, eds. *Ch'ing shih-hua hsü-pien* 清詩話續編. Shanghai: Shang-hai Ku-chi, 1983.

Wang, Shih-chen 王室禎 (1634-1711). *Ch'ing shih-hua* 青詩話. Peking: Chung-hua, 1963.

Ch'iu Yüan 邱園 (1616–1689)

Editions and References

Ch'iu, Yüan 邱園. *Tang-jen pei* 黨人碑. Chang Shu-ying 張樹英, ed. Peking: Chung-hua, 1988. *Ming Ch'ing ch'uan-chi hsüan-k'an.*

Chou Chi 周濟 (1781–1839)

Editions and References

Chou, Chi 周濟. *Sung Ssu-chia tz'u-hsüan* 宋四家詞選. Peking: Chung-hua, 1985. TSCC edition.

___. *T'an-p'ing tz'u pien* 譚評詞辨. Taipei: Kuang-wen, 1962.

Chou Mi 周密 (1232–1299 or 1232-1298)

Editions and References

Chou, Mi 周密. *Ch'i-tung yeh-yü* 齊東埜語. Taipei: Hsin-hsing, 1985. *Pi-chi hsiao-shuo ta-kuan.*

___. *Ch'i-tung yeh-yü* 齊東野語. Chang Mao-p'eng 張茂鵬, ed. Peking: Chung-hua, 1983. *T'ang Sung shih-liao pi-chi ts'ung-k'an.*

___. *Ch'i-tung yeh-yü.* Shanghai: Shang-hai Shu-tien, 1990. Photolithic reprint of Han-fen Lou 涵芬樓 edition (n.d.).

___. *Chih-ya T'ang tsa-ch'ao* 志雅堂雜抄. 1 *chüan*. Shanghai: Shang-hai Wen-i, 1991. *Ku-chin shuo-pu ts'ung-shu.* Reprint of Chung-kuo T'u-shu Kung-ssu 1915 edition.

___, ed. *Chüeh miao-hao tz'u chien* 絕妙好詞箋. Chengchow: Chung-chou Ku-chi, 1990. Photolithic reprint of Kuo-hsüeh Cheng-li-she 1935 edition. Includes commentaries by Cha Wei-jen 查為仁 (1693-1749) and Li E 厲鶚 (1692-1752).**

___. *P'ing-chou yü-ti p'u* 蘋洲漁笛譜. 2 chüan. Nanking: Chiang-su Ku-chi, 1988.

___. *Ts'ao-ch'uang Tz'u chiao-chu* 草窗詞較注. Shih K'o-chen 史克振, ed. Tsinan: Ch'i-Lu Shu-she, 1993.

Translations

Strassberg, *Inscribed Landscapes*, pp. 251-256.

Studies

Hu, Le-p'ing 胡樂平. "Chou Mi tz'u hsi-lun" 周密詞析論, *Wen-hsüeh i-ch'an* 1987.3: 77-88.

Chou Pang-yen 周邦彥 (1056–1121)

Editions and References

Chou, Pang-yen 周邦彥. *Chou Pang-yen chi* 周邦彥集. Chiang Che-lun 蔣哲倫, ed. Nanchang: Chiang-hsi Jen-min, 1983. *Pai-hua-chou wen-k'u,* 2nd Series. Standard modern critical edition which appends a critique of the collection and a number of poems previously "lost."

____. *Chou Pang-yen tz'u-hsüan* 周邦彥詞選. Liu Ssu-fen 劉斯奮, ed. Hong Kong: San-lien, 1981.

____. *Hsiang-chu Chou Mei-ch'eng P'ien-yü chi* 詳註周美成片玉集. 10 *chüan*. Nanking: Chiang-su Ku-chi, 1988.

Ch'üan Sung shih, 20:1188:13421-13432.

Translations

Landau, *Beyond Spring,* pp. 138-152.
Watson, *Early Chinese Verse,* p. 369.

Studies

Huang, Ch'ing-shih 黃清士. "P'ing Chou Pang-yen tz'u 評周邦彥詞," *Shang-hai Chiao-yü Hsüeh-yüan hsüeh-pao* 1984.1.
Ku, Wei-lieh 顧偉列. "Lun Ch'ing-chen tz'u te shu-huai chieh-kou" 論清真詞的抒懷結構, *Wen-hsüeh i-ch'an* 1987.1.
Lo, Kang-lieh 羅慷烈. "Man-t'an Pei-Sung tz'u-jen Chou Pang-yen" 漫談北宋詞人周邦彥, *Wen-hsüeh i-ch'an* 1983.2.
Smitheram, Robert Hale. "The Lyrics of Zhou Bangyan, 1056-1121." Unpublished Ph. D. dissertation, Stanford University, 1987.
Yüan, Hsing-*p'ei* 袁行霈. "I fu wei tz'u: Shih-lun Ch'ing-chen tz'u te i-shu t'e-se" 以賦為詞: 試論清真詞的藝術特色. *Pei-ching Ta-hsüeh hsüeh-pao* 1985.5

Chu Ch'üan 朱權 (1378–1448)

Editions and References

Ch'u, Ch'üan 朱權 *et al. Ming kung-tz'u* 明宮詞. Peking: Pei-ching Ku-chi, 1987.

Chu Hao 朱㬒 (*fl.* 1644)

Editions and References

Chu, Hao 朱㬒. *Ssu ta ch'ing* 四大慶. 3v. Shanghai: Shang-hai Ku-chi, 1986. *Ku-pen hsi-ch'ü ts'ung-k'an,* 5th Series, #16. Photolithic reprint of a mss. in the Bibliothèque Nationale.
____. *Wen-hsing hsien* 文星現. 2 *chüan*. Shanghai: Shang-hai Ku-chi, 1986. *Ku-pen hsi-ch'ü ts'ung-k'an,* 5th Series, #15. Photolithic reprint of a mss. in the Bibliothèque Nationale.

Chu I-tsun 朱彝尊 (1629–1709)

Editions and References

Chu, I-tsun 朱彝尊. *Ching-chih Chü shih-hua* 靜志居詩話. Peking: Jen-min Wen-hsüeh, 1990.
____, ed. *Ming shih tsung* 明詩綜. 2v. Shanghai: Shang-hai Ku-chi, 1993.

Translations

Strassberg, *Inscribed Landscapes,* pp. 361-366.

Studies

Fong, Grace S. "Inscribing Desire: Zhu Yizun's Love Lyrics in *Jingzhiju qinqu.*" *HJAS* 54 (1994): 437-60.
McCraw, *Chinese Lyricists,* pp. 87-116.

Su, Shu-fen 蘇淑芬. *Chu I-tsun chih tz'u yü tz'u-hsüeh yen-chiu* 朱彝尊之詞與詞學研究. Taipei: Wen-shih-che, 1986.

Tseng, Ch'un-ch'un 曾純純. "Chu I-tsun tz'u-chi te pan-pen liu-ch'uan" 朱彝尊詞集的版本流傳, *Chung-kuo wen-che yen-chiu t'ung-hsün,* 4.2 June 1994): 124-138.

Chu-kung-tiao 諸宮調 (all keys and modes)

Editions and References

Ling, Ching-yen 凌景埏 and Hsieh Po-yang 謝伯陽. *Chu-kung-tiao liang-chung* 諸宮調兩種. Tsinan: Ch'i-Lu Shu-she, 1988.

Studies

Akamatsu, Norihiko 赤松紀彦. *Tô Kaigen Seishôki shôkyûchô kenkyû* 董解元西廂記諸宮調研究. Tokyo: Kyûko Shobo, 1998.

Chen, Fan Pen. "Yang Kuei-fei" in *Tales from the T'ien-pao Era: A Chu-kung-tiao.*" *JSYS* 22 (1990-92): 1-22.

Chu, P'ing-fan 朱平梵 and Chu Hung 朱鴻. *Chu-kung-tiao kai-shuo* 概説. Sian: Shan-hsi Jen-min, 1994.

Idema, Wilt. "Satire and Allegory in All Keys and Modes." In *China under Jurchen Rule.* Hoyt C. Tillman and Stephen H. West, eds. Albany: SUNY Press, 1995, pp. 238-80.

___. "Data on the *Chu-kung-tiao:* A Reassessment of Conflicting Opinions." *TP* 79 (1993): 69-112.

Chu Shu-chen 朱淑真 (*fl.* late 11th c.)

Editions and References

Cheng, Yüan-tso, 鄭元佐 (Sung dynasty), comm. *Tuan-ch'ang shih tz'u* 斷腸詩詞. Changchun: Ch'ang-ch'un Ku-chi, 1983.

Chu, Shu-chen 朱淑真. *Chu Shu-chen chi* 朱淑貞集. Chang Chang 張璋 and Huang Yü 黃畬, eds. Shanghai: Shang-hai Ku-chi, 1986. Various useful appendixes.

___. *Chu Shu-chen chi-chu* 朱淑貞集注. Chi Ch'in 冀勤, ed. Hangchow: Che-chiang Ku-chi, 1985. Contains the commentary by Cheng Yüan-tso 鄭元佐 of the Sung and appends traditional prefaces.

___. *Tuan-ch'ang tz'u* 斷腸詞. Peking: Chung-hua, 1985. *TSCC* edition. Photolithic reprint of the *Shih-tz'u tsa-tsu* 詩詞雜俎 edition.

Studies

Huang, Ai-hua 黃愛華. "Chu Shu-chen chi-kuan hsin-k'ao" 籍貫新考, *Chung-hua wen-shih lun-ts'ung* 1985.1.

Huang, Yen-li 黃嫣梨. *Chu Shu-chen chi ch'i tso-p'in.* Hong Kong: San-lien, 1991.

Jen, Te-k'uei 任德魁. "Chu Shu-chen 'Tuan-ch'ang tz'u' pan-pen k'ao-shu yü tso-p'ing pien-wei" 朱淑真斷腸詞版本考述與祚品辨偽, *Wen-hsüeh i-ch'an* 1998.1: 84-93.

Chu Tun-ju 朱敦儒 (1080/1–*ca.* 1175)

Editions and References

Chu, Tun-ju 朱敦儒. *Ch'iao ko* 樵歌注. Sha Ling-na 沙靈娜, comm. Ch'en Chen-huan 陳振寰, ed. Kweiyang: Kuei-chou Jen-min, 1985.

____. *Ch'iao ko.* Nanking: Chiang-su Ku-chi, 1988.
Ch'üan Sung shih, 25:1478.16880-16882.

Studies

Chang, Hsi-ch'ing 張希清. "Chu Tun-ju sheng-tsu nien ch'üeh-k'ao" 朱敦儒生卒年確考. *Pei-ching Ta-hsüeh hsüeh-pao* 1986.6.
Ko, Chao-kuang 葛兆光. "Lun Chu Tun-ju chi ch'i tz'u" 論朱敦儒及其詞, *Wen-hsüeh i-ch'an* 1983.3.
Liu, Yang-chung 劉楊忠. "Kuan-yü Chu Tun-ju te sheng-tsu nien" 關於朱敦儒的生卒年. *Wen-hsüeh i-ch'an* 1984.3: 157-163.
Yang, Hai-ming 楊海明. "Lun Chu Tun-ju te tz'u" 論朱敦儒的詞, *Hang-chou Shih-yüan hsüeh-pao* 1985.3.

Chu-tzu pai-chia 諸子百家 (Various Masters and the Hundred Schools)

Editions and References

Chu-tzu chi-ch'eng pu-pien 諸子集成補編. 10v. Ssu-ch'uan Ta-hsüeh Ku-chi So 四川大學古籍所, ed. Chengtu: Ssu-ch'uan Ch'u-pan-she, 1997. Includes 150 texts in supplementation of the *Chu-tzu chi-ch'eng.*
Liu, Liu-ch'iao 柳柳橋. *Hsün-tzu ku-i* 荀子詁譯. Tsinan: Ch'i-Lu Shu-she, 1985.

Translations

Ames, Roger. *Sun-tzu: The Art of Warfare, The First English Translation Incorporating the Recently Discovered Yin-ch'üeh-shan Texts.* New York: Ballantine Books, 1993.
Cook, Scott. "Xun Zi on Ritual and Music," *MS* 45 (1997): 1-38.
Henricks, Robert G., trans. *Lao Tzu, Te-Tao China.* New York: Ballantine Books, 1990.
Holzer, Rainer. *Yen-tzu und das Yen-tzu ch'un-ch'iu.* Frankfurt: Peter Lang, 1983.
Kamenarovic, Ivan T. *Xun Zi (Siun Tseu).* Paris: Les Editions du Cerf, 1987.
Kao, Cheng 高正. *Chu-tzu pai-chia yen-chiu* 諸子百家研究. Peking: She-hui K'o-hsüeh, 1997.
Knoblock, John. *Xunzi–A Translation and Study of the Complete Works.* V. 1, 2, 3. Stanford: Stanford University Press, 1988, 1990, 1994.
Larre, Claude, Isabelle Robinet and Elisabeth Rochat de Vallée. *Les Grants Traités du Huainanzi.* Paris: Édition du Cerf, 1993. An annotated translation of chapters 1, 7, 11, 13 and 18.
LeBlanc, Charles. *Huai-Nan Tzu, Philosophical Synthesis in Early Han Thought–the Idea of Resonance, with a Translation and Analysis of Chapter Six.* Hong Kong: Hong Kong University Press, 1985.
Mair, Victor H., trans. *Lao Tzu, Tao Te Ching–The Classic Book of Integrity and the Way. An Entirely New Translation Based on the Recently Discovered Ma-wang-tui Manuscripts.* New York: Bantam Books, 1990.
Major, John S. *Heaven and Earth in Early Han Thought; Chapters Three, Four, and Five of the Huainanzi.* Albany: SUNY Press, 1993.
Neugebauer, Klaus Karl. *Ho-kuan Tsi, Eine Untersuchung der dialogischen Kapitel (mit Übersetzung und Annotationen).* Frankfurt: Peter Lang, 1986.
Rickett, W. Allyn. *Guanzi–Political, Economic and Philosophical Essays from Early China, A Study and Translation.* 2v. Princeton: Princeton University Press, 1985 and 1997.
Schmidt-Glintzer, Helwig, ed. and trans. *Mo Ti, von der Liebe des Himmels zu den Menschen.* Munich: Diedrichs, 1992. Diedrichs Gelbe Reihe, 94.
Yoav, Ariel. *K'ung-ts'ung-tz'u, The K'ung Family Masters' Anthology, Study and Translation of Chapters 1-10, 12-14.* Princeton: Princeton University Press, 1989.

_____. *K'ung-ts'ung-tz'u, The K'ung Family Masters' Anthology, Study and Translation of Chapters 15-23 with a Reconstruction of the Hsiao Erh-ya Dictionary.* Leiden: E. J. Brill, 1996.

Studies

Ames, *Sun-tzu: The Art of Warfare* (see "Translations" above).

Chen, David Tse-yen. "The Nine Songs: A Re-examination of Shamanism in Ancient China." Unpublished Ph. D. dissertation, University of Southern California, 1986.

Defoort, Cathrine. *The Pheasant Cap Master (He Guan Zi), A Rhetorical Reading.* Albany: SUNY Press, 1997.

Fujikawa, Masakazu 藤川正数. *Junshi chûshaku shi jô ni okeru Hôju no katsudô zokuhen* 荀子注釈史上における邦儒の活動(続篇). Tokyo: Kazama Shobô, 1990.

Lafargue, Michael. *Tao and Method, A Reasoned Approach to the Tao Te Ching.* Albany: SUNY Press, 1994.

LeBlanc, *Huai-Nan Tzu, Philosophical Synthesis in Early Han Thought* (see "Translations" above).

Lundahl, Bertil. *Han Fei Zi, The Man and the Work.* V. 4. Stockholm East Asian Monographs, Stockholm: Institute of Oriental Languages, 1992.

Machle, Edward J. *Nature and Heaven in the Xunzi, A Study of the Tian Lun.* Albany: SUNY, 1995.

Major, *Heaven and Earth in Early Han Thought* (see "Translations" above).

Neugebauer, *Ho-kuan Tsi* (see "Translations" above).

Paper, Jordan. *The Fu-tzu, A Post-Han Confucian Text.* Leiden: E. J. Brill, 1987.

Rickett, *Guanzi–Political, Economic and Philosophical Essays from Early China* (see "Translations" above).

Roth, Harold David. *The Textual History of the Huai-nan Tzu.* Ann Arbor: Association for Asian Studies, 1992. *AAS Monograph Series*, 46.

Yen, Ling-feng 嚴靈峰. *Chou Ch'in Han Wei chu-tzu chih-chien shu-mu* 周秦漢魏諸子知見書目. Peking: Chung-hua, 1993.

Yoav, *K'ung-ts'ung-tz'u, The K'ung Family Masters' Anthology* (see "Translations" above).

Chu Yu-tun 朱有燉 (1379-1439)

Studies

Idema, W. L. *The Dramatic Oeuvre of Chu Yu-tun, 1370-1439.* Leiden: E. J. Brill, 1985.

Ch'u Kuang-hsi 儲光羲 (*fl.* 742)

Editions and References

Ch'u, Kuang-hsi 儲光羲. *Ch'u Kuang-hsi chi* 儲光羲集. Shanghai: Shang-hai Ku-chi, 1981. *T'ang Wu-shih-chia shih-chi,* 4. Based on a Ming printed edition.

Studies

Ch'eng, Yu-chui 程郁綴. "Ch'u Kuang-hsi chi-kuan k'ao-pien" 儲光羲藉貫考辨, *T'ang-tai wen-hsüeh lun-ts'ung* 1982.2.

Ch'u tz'u 楚辭 (Songs of Ch'u–see also Ch'ü Yüan)

Editions and References

Chiang, Liang-fu 姜亮夫, ed. *Ch'ung-ting Ch'ü Yüan fu chiao-chu* 重訂屈原賦校注. Tientsin:

T'ien-chin Jen-min, 1987. Contains "Li-sao," "Chiu-ko," "T'ien-wen," "Chiu-chang," "Yüan-yu," "Pu-chü," and "Yü-fu."

Chiang, T'ien-shu 蔣天樞, ed. and trans. *Ch'u tz'u chiao i* 楚辭校譯. Shanghai: Shang-hai Ku-chi, 1989.

Chu, Hsi 朱熹 (1130-1200). *Ch'u tz'u chi-chu* 楚辭集注. *Kuo-li T'u-shu Kuan shan-pen ts'ung-k'an* 國立圖書館善本叢刊, 6. Taipei: National Central Library, 1991. Copy of the Yüan edition produced by Ch'en Chung-fu 陳忠甫 in 1330.

___. *Ch'u tz'u pien-cheng* 楚辭辯證. *2 chüan*. Li Ch'ing-chia 李慶甲, ed. Rpt. Shanghai: Shang-hai Ku-chi, 1987 (1979).

Chu, Pi-lien 朱碧蓮, ed. *Sung Yü tz'u-fu i-chieh* 宋玉辭賦譯解. Peking: Chung-kuo She-hui K'o-hsüeh, 1987. Appends works attributed to Sung Yü as well as biographical and bibliographical materials.

Ch'u tz'u chien-shang chi 楚辭鑑賞集. Chinese Department, Liao-ning University, ed. Shenyang: Liao-ning Ta-hsüeh, Chung-wen Hsi, 1984.

A Concordance to the Chu ci 楚辭一逐索引. D. C. Lau and Chen Fong Ching, ed. ICS Series. Hong Kong: Commercial Press, 1996.

Ho, Chien-hsün 何劍熏 (1911-1988). *Ch'u tz'u hsin ku* 楚辭新詁. Wu Hsien-che 吳賢哲, ed. Chengtu: Pa-Shu Shu-she, 1993.

Huang, Shou-ch'i 黃壽祺 and Mei T'ung-sheng 梅桐生, trans. and eds. *Ch'u tz'u ch'üan-i* 楚辭全譯. Kweiyang: Kuei-chou Jen-min, 1984. *Chung-kuo li-tai ming-chu ch'üan-i ts'ung-shu*.

Kominami, Ichirô 小南一郎. *Ô En: Soji kaishû* 汪瑗：楚辞集解. 2v. Kyoto: Dôhôsha Shuppan,1984.

Li, Chung-hua 李中華 and Chu Ping-hsiang 朱炳祥. *Ch'u-tz'u hsüeh shih* 楚辭學史. Wuhan: Wu-han Ch'u-pan-she, 1997.

Ma, Mao-yüan 馬茂原, ed. *Ch'u tz'u yen-chiu chi-ch'eng* 楚辭研究集成. Wuhan: Hu-pei Jen-min, 1985. Contains *Ch'u tz'u chu-shih* 楚辭注釋, *Ch'u tz'u yao-chi chieh-t'i* 楚辭要籍解題, *Ch'u tz'u yen-chiu lun-wen chi* 楚辭研究論文集, and *Ch'u tz'u p'ing-lun tzu-liao hsüan* 楚辭評論資料選.

Ts'ui, Fu-chang 崔富章, ed. *Ch'u tz'u shu-mu wu-chung hsü-pien* 楚辭書目五種續編. Shanghai: Shang-hai Ku-chi, 1993.

Wang, Ssu-yüan 王泗原, ed. and trans. *Ch'u tz'u chiao-i* 楚辭校譯. Peking: Jen-min Chiao-yü, 1990.

Wu, Hsiao-ming 鄔雪鳴. *Ch'ü fu ch'üan-i* 屈賦全譯. Shenyang: Liao-ning Chiao-yü, 1986.

Translations

Hawkes, David. *The Songs of the South: An Anthology of Ancient Chinese Poems by Qu Yuan and Other Poets.* Harmondsworth: Penguin Books Ltd., 1985. Second revised edition of Hawkes' *Ch'u tz'u: The Songs of the South, An Ancient Chinese Anthology.* Oxford: Clarendon Press, 1959. Contains some important changes especially in the front-matter.

Makizumi, Etsuko 牧角悦子 *et al*... *Shikyô Soji* 詩経・楚辞. *Kanshô Chûgoku no koten* 鑑賞中国の古典, 11. Tokyo: Kadokawa Shoten, 1989.

Mekada, Makoto 目加田誠. *Soji yakuchû* 楚辞訳注. *Mekada Makoto shosaku shû* 目加田誠著作集, 3. Tokyo: Ryûkei Shosha 1983.

Rollin, Jean-François. *Li sao, précédé de Jiu ge.* Paris: La Différence, 1990.

Studies

Akatsuka, Kiyoshi 赤塚忠, ed. *Akatsuka Tadashi shosaku shû* 赤塚忠著作集. V. 6. *Soji kenkyû* 楚辞研究. Tokyo: Kenbunsha, 1986

Chang Ch'ung-ch'en 章崇琛. *Ch'u tz'u wen-hua t'an-wei* 楚辭文化探微. Peking: Hsin-hua, 1993.

Chao, Hui 趙輝. *Ch'u tz'u wen-hua pei-ching yen-chiu* 楚辭文話背景研究. Wuhan: Hu-pei Chiao-yü, 1995.

Chao, Hun 趙琿. "Chien-lun *Ch'u tz'u* t'e-chih te hsing-ch'eng yüan-yin" 簡論楚辭特質的形成原因, *Chung-nan Min-tsu Hsüeh-yüan hsüeh-pao,* 5(1990), 100-108.

Ch'en, I-liang 陳怡良. *Ch'ü Yüan wen-hsüeh lun-chi* 屈原文學論集. Taipei: Wen-chin, 1992.

Ch'en, Tzu-chan 陳子展 *et al. Ch'u tz'u chi-chieh* 楚辭直解. Nanking: Chiang-su Ku-chi, 1988.

Cheng, Tsai-ying 鄭再瀛. *Ch'u tz'u t'an-ch'i* 楚辭探奇. Hong Kong: Hsiang-kang Cheng-chih, 1992.

Chiang, Liang-fu 姜亮夫. *Ch'u tz'u lun-wen chi* 楚辭論文集. Shanghai: Shang-hai Ku-chi, 1984.

___. *Ch'u tz'u t'ung-ku* 楚辭通故. Tientsin: Ch'i-Lu Shu-she, 1986.

Ch'ien, Sung-kan 錢誦甘. *Chiu-ko hsi-lun* 九歌析論. Taipei: T'ai-wan Shang-wu, 1994.

Chin, K'ai-ch'eng 金開誠. *Ch'ü Yüan tz'u yen-chiu* 屈原辭研究. Nanking: Chiang-su Ku-chi, 1992.

Chou, Hsün-ch'u 周勛初. *Chiu-ko hsin-k'ao* 九歌新考. Shanghai: Shang-hai Ku-chi, 1986. An interesting exploration of the relationship between the "Nine Songs" and Ch'u religion.

Chu, Pi-lien 朱碧蓮. *Ch'u tz'u lun-kao* 楚辭論稿. Shanghai: San-lien, 1993.

___. *Sung Yü tz'u-fu i-chieh* 宋玉辭賦譯解. Peking: Chung-kuo She-hui K'o-hsüeh, 1987.

Ch'u tz'u yen-chiu 楚辭研究. Chinese Department, Liao-ning University, ed. Shenyang: Liao-ning Ta-hsüeh, Chung-wen Hsi, 1984.

Gallagher, Martha Liwen. "A Study of Reduplications in the 'Ch'u Ci.'" Unpublished Ph. D. dissertation, Yale University, 1993.

Hawkes, David. "*Ch'u tz'u* 楚辭," in *Early Chinese Texts,* pp. 48-55.

Hsiao, Ping 蕭兵. *Ch'u tz'u hsin-t'an* 楚辭新探. Tientsin: T'ien-chin Ku-chi, 1988.

___. *Ch'u tz'u wen-hua* 楚辭文化. Chin-chou 錦州: Chung-kuo She-hui,1990.

___. *Ch'u tz'u yü shen-hua* 楚辭與神話. Nanking: Chiang-su Ku-chi, 1986.

Hsü, Chih-hsiao 徐志嘯. *Ch'u tz'u tsung-lun* 楚辭綜論. Taipei: Tung-ta, 1994.

Hsü, I-chih 許逸之. *"Chiu ko" chin i* 九歌今譯. Taipei: Cheng-chung, 1993.

Huang, Chung-mo 黃中模. *Yü Jih-pen hsüeh-che t'ao-lun Ch'ü Yüan wen-t'i* 與日本學者討論屈原問題. Wuhan: Hua-chung Li-kung Ta-hsüeh, 1990.

Hung, Chan-hou 洪湛侯, ed. *Ch'u tz'u yao-chi chieh-t'i* 楚辭要籍解題. Wuhan: Hu-pei Jen-min, 1985. In *Ch'u tz'u yen-chiu chi-ch'eng* (see Ma Mao-yüan under "Editions and References" above).

I, Chung-lien 易重廉. *Chung-kuo "Ch'u tz'u" hsüeh-shih* 中國楚辭學史. Changsha: Hu-nan, 1991. Surveys studies of the *Ch'u tz'u* through the end of the Ch'ing dynasty.

Ishikawa, Misarô 石川三佐郎. *"Soji* ni okeru 'Kyûta' to 'Kyûshô' no kankei ni tsuite–sono meishô to hensu to heishô no imi surumono" 楚辞における九歌と九章の関係について–その名称と篇数と併称の意味するもの, *Tôyôgaku* 70 (1993): 1-22.

___. *'Soji* no 'Kyûka' no imi suru mono ni tsuite–'Risôhen' no kôzô awasete 'shôsen zu' to no hikaku ni oyobu 『楚辞』の「九歌」の意味するものについて–離騒篇の構造併せて「昇仙図」との比較に及ぶ. Saitama: Private publication, 1987.

Li, Ta-ming 李大明. *Ch'u tz'u wen-hsien hsüeh shih lun k'ao* 楚辭文獻學史論考. Chengtu: Pa-Shu Shu-she, 1997.

Lü, Ch'ing-fei 呂晴飛. *Ch'ü Yüan shih-ko p'ing-shang* 屈原詩歌評賞. Peking: Chung-kuo Fu-nü, 1991. Appends "Ch'ü Yüan wai-chuan" from the T'ang.

Ma, Mao-yüan 馬茂原. *Ch'u tz'u yen-chiu lun-wen hsüan* 楚辭研究論文選. Wuhan: Hu-pei Jen-min, 1985.

Mei, T'ung-sheng 梅桐生. *Ch'u tz'u ju-men* 楚辭入門. Kweiyang: Kuei-chou Jen-min, 1991.

Chung-kuo ch'uan-t'ung wen-hua ju-men ts'ung-shu.

Miyano, Naoya 宮野直也. *"Soji shôku* insho kô" 『楚辞章句』引書考, *Kagoshima Joshi Daigaku kenkyû kiyô* XI (1990).

Schimmelpfennig, Michael. "Der Kommentar von Wang Yi zu den *Liedern von Chu (Chu-ci)."* Unpublished Ph. D. dissertation, University of Heidelberg, 1995.

Shih, Mo-ch'ing 史墨卿. *Ch'u tz'u wen-i kuan* 楚辭文藝觀. Taipei: Hua-cheng, 1989.

Su, Hsüeh-lin 蘇雪林. *Ch'ü fu lun-ts'ung* 屈賦論叢. Taipei: Kuo-li Pien-i-kuan, 1980.

___. *Ch'ü Yüan yü" Chiu-ko"* 屈原與九歌. Taipei: Wen-chin, 1992.

___. *"T'ien wen" cheng-chien* 天問正簡. Taipei: Wen-chin, 1992.

Tai. Chih-chün 戴志鈞. *Tu "Sao" shih-lun* 讀騷十論. Harbin: Hei-lung-chiang Jen-min, 1986.

T'ang, Ping-cheng 湯炳正. *Ch'u tz'u lei-kao* 楚辭類稿. Tientsin: Ch'i-Lu Shu-she, 1986; Pa-Shu Shu-she, 1988.

___. *Ch'u tz'u hsin-t'an* 楚辭新探. Tientsin: Ch'i-Lu Shu-she, 1984.

Tung, Ch'u-p'ing 董楚平. *Ch'u tz'u i-chu* 楚辭藝注. Shanghai: Shang-hai Ku-chi, 1986.

Wu, Meng-fu 吳孟復. *"Chiu chang" hsin-chien* 九章新箋. Hofei: Huang-shan Shu-she, 1987.

Yang, Chin-ting 楊金鼎, ed. *Ch'u tz'u p'ing-lun tzu-liao hsüan* 楚辭評論資料選. Wuhan: Hu-pei Jen-min, 1985. In *Ch'u tz'u yen-chiu chi-ch'eng* (see Ma Mao-yüan under "Editions and References" above).

___, ed. *Ch'u tz'u yen-chiu lun-wen hsüan* 楚辭研究論文選. Wuhan: Hu-pei Jen-min, 1985. In *Ch'u tz'u yen-chiu chi-ch'eng* (see Ma Mao-yüan under "Editions and References" above).

Yao, P'ing 姚平. *"Li sao" yen-chiu* 離騷研究. Taipei: Chung-kuo Wen-hua Ta-hsüeh, 1992.

Yu, Kuo-en 游國恩. *"T'ien-wen" tsuan-i* 天問纂義. Peking: Chung-hua, 1982. The second volume of Yu's studies of *Ch'u tz'u* texts.

Ch'ü 曲 (arias)

Editions and References

Chang, Wen-ch'ien 張文潛. *Yüan-tai san-ch'ü hsüan* 元代散曲選. Foochow: Fu-chien Chiao-yü, 1985.

Chang Yüeh-chung 張月中, ed. *Yüan-ch'ü yen-chiu tzu-liao so-yin* 元曲研究資料索引. Tientsin: Ho-pei Ta-hsüeh, 1993.

Ho, Hsin-hui 賀新輝, ed. *Yüan-ch'ü chien-shang tz'u-tien* 元曲鑒賞辭典. Peking: Chung-kuo Fu-nü, 1988.

Hsieh, Po-yang 謝伯陽, ed. *Ch'üan Ming san-ch'ü* 全明散曲. 5v. Tsinan: Ch'i-Lu Shu-she, 1994.

Hsü, Cheng 徐征 and Liu Ch'ing-kuo 劉慶國, ed. *Yüan-ch'ü shang-hsi* 元曲賞析. Shih-chia-chuang: Huan-shan Wen-i, 1985.

Lü, T'ien-ch'eng 呂天成. *Ch'ü-p'in chiao-chu* 曲品校註. Wu Shu-yin 吳書陰, ed. Peking: Chung-hua, 1990.

Sung, Hao-ch'ing 宋浩慶. *Yüan Ming san-ch'ü* 元明散曲. Shanghai: Shang-hai Ku-chi, 1987.

Wang, Hsüeh-ch'i 王學奇 *et al*, eds. *Yüan-ch'ü hsüan chiao-chu* 元曲選校注. 8v. Tientsin: Ho-pei Chiao-yü, 1996. Over 4000 pages of text and annotation.

Wang, Wen-ts'ai 王文才, ed. *Yüan-ch'u chi-shih* 元曲紀事. Peking: Jen-min Wen-hsüeh, 1985. Contains material on 83 authors.

Translations

Crump, James Irving. *Songs from Xanadu: Studies in Mongol-dynasty Song-poetry (san-ch'ü)*. Ann Arbor: Center for Chinese Studies, University of Michigan, 1983.

Studies

Akamatsu, Norihiko 赤松紀彦. "'Genkyokusen' ga mezashitan mono" 『元曲選』がめざしたもの, *Chûgoku koten gikyoku ronshû,* 1991: 161-186.

Li, Ch'ang-chi 李昌集. *Chung-kuo ku-tai san-ch'ü shih* 中國古代散曲史. Shanghai: Hua-tung Shih-fan Ta-hsüeh, 1991.

Li, Hsiu-sheng 李修生 and Chao I-shan 趙義山. "Chin-nien-lai Yüan san-ch'ü yen-chiu kai-shu" 近年來元曲散曲研究概述, *Wen-hsüeh i-ch'an,* 1992.4: 121-126.

Sui, Shu-sen 隋樹森. *Yüan-jen san-ch'ü lun-ts'ung* 元人散曲論叢. Tsinan: Ch'i-Lu Shu-she, 1986.

Ch'ü Yüan 屈原 (340?–278 B.C.–see also *Ch'u-tz'u*)

Editions and References

Chin, K'ai-ch'eng 金開誠 *et al,* eds. *Ch'ü Yüan chi chiao-chu* 屈原集校注. 2v. Peking: Chung-hua, 1997.

Studies

Chiang, Liang-fu 姜亮夫 and Chiang K'un-wu 姜昆武. *Ch'ü Yüan yü Ch'u tz'u* 屈原與楚辭. Hofei: An-hui Chiao-yü, 1991. *Chung-kuo ku-tai wen-hsüeh chih-chih ts'ung-shu.* Appends a chronology of Ch'ü Yüan's life and a bibliography.

Ch'ü Yüan yen-chiu lun-chi 屈原研究論集. Wuhan: Ch'ang-chiang Wen-i, 1983.

Hawkes, David. "The Heirs of Gao-yang," *TP* LXIX (1983): 1-21.

___. *The Songs of the South: An Anthology of Ancient Chinese Poems by Qu Yuan and Other Poets.* Harmondsworth: Penguin Books Ltd., 1985. Second revised edition of Hawkes' *Ch'u tz'u: The Songs of the South, An Ancient Chinese Anthology.* Oxford: Clarendon Press, 1959. Contains some important changes especially in the front-matter.

Hu, Nien-i 胡念貽. "Ch'ü Yüan sheng-nien hsin-k'ao 屈原生年新考," *Wen-shih* 5 (1978).

Huang, Chung-mo 黃中模. *Ch'ü Yüan wen-t'i lun-cheng shih kao* 屈原問題論爭史稿. Peking: Shih-yüeh Wen-i, 1987.

Kadowaki, Hirobumi 門脇広文. "Bunshin choryô kô–Ryû Shô no Kutsu Gen, *Soji* ninshiki ni tsuite 認識 ni tsuite" 文心彫龍考–劉勰の屈原, 楚辞認識について, *Daitô Bunka Daigaku kiyô–Jimbun Kagaku* 27 (1989): 89-112.

Kuo, Wei-sen 郭維森. *Ch'ü Yüan* 屈原. Shanghai: Shang-hai Ku-chi, 1979.

Pohl, Karl-Heinz. "Dichtung, Philosophie, Politik–Qu Yuan in den 80er Jahren." In *Chinesische Intellektuelle im 20 Jahrhundert: Zwischen Tradition und Moderne.* Karl-Heinz Pohl *et al.,* eds. Hamburg: Institut für Asienkunde, 1993, pp. 405-425.

Takeji, Sadao 竹治貞夫. *Kutsu Gen–Yûkoku shijin* 屈原–憂国詩人. *Chûgoku no shijin* 中国の詩人, 1. Tokyo: Shûeisha, 1983.

T'ang, Ping-cheng 湯炳正. *Ch'u tz'u lei-kao* 楚辭類稿. Tientsin: Ch'i-Lu Shu-she, 1986.

___. *Ch'u tz'u hsin-t'an* 楚辭新探. Tientsin: Ch'i-Lu Shu-she, 1986.

Ting, Ping 丁冰. *Ch'ü Yüan* 屈原. Harbin: Hei-lung-chiang Jen-min, 1982.

Tseng, Cheng-chen. "Mythopoesis Historicized: Qu Yuan's Poetry and Its Legacy." Unpublished Ph. D. dissertation, University of Washington, 1992. Studies Ch'ü Yüan's influence on T'ao Ch'ien, Li Po and Hsieh Ling-yün.

ch'uan-ch'i 傳奇 (romance)

Editions and References

Ch'i, T'ien-fa 戚天法. *Ssu-ming ch'uan-ch'i* 四明傳奇. Shanghai: Shang-hai Wen-i, 1983.

Li, Fu-ch'ing 李福清 (Boris Riftin) and Li P'ing 李平, eds. *Hai-wai ku-pen Wan-Ming hsi-chü hsüan-chi san-chung* 海外孤本晚明戲劇選集三種. Shanghai: Shang-hai Ku-chi, 1993. *Hai-wai chen-ts'ang shan-pen ts'ung-shu.*

Ming Ch'ing chao-pen ku-pen ch'ai-ch'ü ts'ung-k'an 明清抄本孤本戈曲叢刊. Shou-tu T'u-shu-kuan, eds. Peking: Shou-tu T'u-shu-kuan, 1995.

Translations
Birch, Cyril. *Scenes for Mandarins, The Elite Theater of the Ming.* New York: Columbia University Press, 1995. Contains annotated translations of plays by five playwrights, including T'ang Hsien-tsu, Liang Chen-yü, Shan Pen, Wu Ping, Juan Ta-ch'eng.

Studies
Chu, Ch'eng-p'u 朱承樸 and Tseng Ch'ing-ch'üan 曾慶全. *Ming Ch'ing ch'uan-ch'i kai-shuo* 明清傳奇概說. Hong Kong: San-lien; Canton: Kuang-tung Jen-min, 1985.

Kuo, Ying-te 郭英德. *Ming Ch'ing wen-jen ch'uan-ch'i yen-chiu* 明清文人傳奇研究. Taipei: Wen-chin, 1991. *Ta-lu ti-ch'ü Po-shih lun-wen ts'ung-k'an,* 1. Revised version of Kuo's dissertation at Pei-ching Shih-fan Ta-hsüeh (1988) and was subsequently (1992) published by that university's press.

Wang, An-ch'i 王安祈. *Ming-tai ch'uan-ch'i chih chü-ch'ang chi ch'i i-shu* 明代傳奇之劇場及奇藝術. Taipei: T'ai-wan Hsüeh-sheng, 1986. *Chung-kuo wen-hsüeh yen-chiu ts'ung-k'an.* Appends a bibliography.

Yü, Wei-min 俞為民. *Ming Ch'ing ch'uan-ch'i k'ao-lun* 明清傳奇考論. Taipei: Hua-cheng, 1993.

ch'uan-ch'i 傳奇 (tale)

Editions and References
Ch'en, Yin-k'o 陳寅恪. "*T'ang-jen hsiao-shuo,* Wang Pi-ch'iang chiao-lu p'i-chu" 唐人小說汪辟疆校錄批注, *Chung-kuo ku-chi yen-chiu* 中國古籍研究. V. 1. Shanghai: Shang-hai Ku-chi, 1996, pp. 1-37. Posthumous publication edited by Pao Ching-ti 包敬第.

Ch'eng, I-chung 程毅中. *Ku hsiao-shuo chien-mu* 古小說書目. Peking: Chung-hua, 1981. Entries cite traditional bibliographies and editions; see also the review of this volume and that immediately below (*Chung-kuo wen-yen hsiao-shuo shih-kao*) by John B. Brennan in *CLEAR* 7 (1985): 179-185.

Ch'eng, Yao 程遙. *T'ang-tai ch'uan-ch'i hsüan-i* 唐人傳奇選譯. Chengtu: Pa-Shu Shu-she, 1990.

___ and Ch'ien-li 千里. *T'ang-tai ch'uan-ch'i i-chu* 唐人傳奇譯註. Changchun: Chi-lin Chiao-yü, 1986. Contains original text, light annotation, and translations of about 40 tales.

Chiang, I-fang 蔣宜芳. "T'ang-jen hsiao-shuo yen-chiu lun-chu chien-mu" 唐人小說研究論著簡目, *Chung-kuo wen-che yen-chiu t'ung-hsün* 6.1 (March 1996): 79-126. An important bibliography of works on T'ang fiction done in China, Taiwan, Japan and Korea from 1912-1995; divided into two sections, one general works, and the second separate listings for 47 of the major *ch'uan-ch'i* titles and collections.

Chou, Ch'en 周晨 and Ch'ien-li 千里. *T'ang-jen ch'uan-ch'i i-chu* 唐人傳奇譯注. Changchun: Chi-lin Chiao-yü, 1986.

Fang, Chi-liu 方積六 and Wu Tung-hsiu 吳冬秀, eds. *T'ang Wu-tai wu-shih-erh chung pi-chi hsiao-shuo jen-ming so-yin* 唐五代五十二種筆記小說人名索引. Peking: Chung-hua, 1992.

Hou, Chung-i 侯忠毅 (w/ Liu Shih-lin 劉世林 for volume 2). *Chung-kuo wen-yen hsiao-shuo shih-kao* 中國文言小說史稿. 2v. Peking: Pei-ching Ta-hsüeh, 1990 and 1993. The first volume is dedicated to pre-Sung classical-language fiction.

___. *Chung-kuo wen-yen hsiao-shuo ts'an-k'ao tzu-liao* 中國文言小説參考資料. Peking: Pei-ching Ta-hsüeh, 1985. Excerpts from prefaces, bibliographies, etc. similar to Huang Ling and Han T'ung-wen's works supplemented by a more catholic selection of comparative materials from dynastic histories and related works.

"Hsien-Ch'in chih Sui-T'ang te hsiao-shuo" 先秦至隋唐的小説, in *Chung-kuo hsiao-shuo shih* 中國小説史. Chinese Department, Peking University, compilers. Peking: Jen-min Wen-hsüeh, 1978. A standard, sixty-page account of pre-Sung fiction; bibliography, although outdated, lists modern editions.

Hu, Kuang-chou 胡光舟. *T'ang ch'uan-ch'i shang-hsi* 唐傳奇賞析. Nanning: Kuang-hsi Chiao-yü, 1993.

Liu, Chien-kuo 李劍國, ed. *Sung-tai chih-kuai ch'uan-ch'i hsü-lu* 宋代志怪傳奇敍録. Tientsin: Nan-k'ai Ta-hsüeh, 1997.

___. *T'ang Wu-tai chih-kuai ch'uan-ch'i hsü-lu* 唐五代志怪傳奇敍録. Tientsin: Nan-k'ai Ta-hsüeh, 1993. Appends a bibliography and a listing of Sung and Yüan notices on this literature.

Wang, Ju-t'ao 王汝濤, ed. *Ch'üan T'ang hsiao-shuo* 全唐小説. Tsinan: Shan-tung Wen-i, 1993. A collection of 49 *ch'uan-ch'i* and 138 collections of *"hsiao-shuo;"* these versions are most useful for an overview of T'ang "fiction" but should be used only in tandem with scholarly editions.

___, ed. *T'ang-tai chih-kuai hsiao-shuo hsüan-i* 唐代志怪小説選譯. Tsinan: Ch'i Lu Shu-she, 1985. Selections primarily from *Hsüan kuai-lu* and its sequel.

Yao, Sung 姚松. *Sung-tai ch'uan-ch'i hsüan-i* 宋代傳奇選譯. Chengtu: Pa-Shu Shu-she, 1990.

Yüan, Hang-p'ei 袁行霈 and Hou Chung-i 侯忠義, eds. *Chung-kuo wen-yen hsiao-shuo shu-mu* 中國文言小説書目. Peking: Pei-ching Ta-hsüeh, 1981. Contains a long section on *chih-kuai* and another on *ch'uan-ch'i* (T'ang); each entry cites traditional bibliographies, lists important editions, and occasionally mentions a modern study. Modern critical editions are not listed.

Translations

Imamura, Yoshio 今村与志雄. *Tôdai denki shû* 唐代伝奇集. 2v. Tokyo: Iwanami Shoten, 1988.

Kao, Karl S. *Classical Chinese Tales of the Supernatural and Fantastic—Selections from the Third to the Tenth Century.* Bloomington: Indiana University Press, 1986. The most extensive collection of *chih-kuai* and *ch'uan-ch'i* available in a Western language; interesting theoretical preface.

Lévy, André. *Histoires d'amour et de mort de la Chine ancienne, Chefs-d'oeuvre de la nouvelle (Dynastie des Tang. 618-907).* Paris: Aubier, 1992.

___. *Histoires extraordinaires et récits fantastiques de la Chine ancienne.* Paris: Aubier, 1993.

Masi, Eduarda. *Chuanqi, storie fantastiche Tang.* Parma: Nuove Pratiche Editrice, 1994.

Pimpaneau, Jacques. *Biographie des regrets éternels.* Paris: Philippe Picquier, 1989.

Studies

Chang, Shirley. "Stories of the 'Others': The Presentation of the Unconventional Characters in Tang (618-907) *chuanqi.*" Unpublished Ph. D. dissertation, University of Wisconsin, 1993.

Ch'eng, I-chung 程毅中. *T'ang-tai hsiao-shuo shih-hua* 唐代小説史話. Peking: Wen-hua I-shu, 1990.

Cutter, Robert Joe. "History and 'The Old Man of the Eastern Wall,'" *JAOS* 106.3 (July-September 1986): 503-28.

Golygina, Karina Ivanovna. "Genezis i formirovanie novellisti-cheskoi prozy v Kitae (III-XIV vv.) [The Genesis and Formation of Short-story Prose in China from the Third to the Fourteenth Century]." Unpublished Ph. D. dissertation, Institut Vos-tokovedeniia Akademii Nauk SSSR, 1983.

Hou, Chung-i 侯忠義. *Sui T'ang Wu-tai hsiao-shuo shih* 隋唐五代小説史. Hangchow: Che-chiang Ku-chi, 1997.

Kominami, Ichirô 小南一郎. "Gen Haku bungaku shûdan no shôsetsu–'Ôôden' o chûshin ni shite" 元白文学集団の小説ー「鶯鶯伝」を中心にして, *Nippon Chûgoku Gakkaihô* 47 (1995): 63-74.

Lau, Joseph S. M. "Love and Friendship in T'ang *Ch'uan-ch'i*," *MS* 37 (1986-87). Interesting study of relationships in these tales and on why they have been little studied in traditional criticism.

Levi, Jean. "Les Fonctionnaires et le divin: Luttes de pouvoirs entre divinites et administrateurs dans les contes des Six Dynasties et des Tang," *Cahiers d'Extreme-Asie,* 2(1986): 81-110.

Li, Tsung-wei 李宗為. *T'ang-jen ch'uan-ch'i* 唐人傳奇. Peking: Chung-hua, 1985. *Chung-kuo wen-hsüeh-shih chih-chih ts'ung-shu*. Appends a list of the most important works and a chart of their inclusion in collectanea of the Ming and Ch'ing periods.

Liu, Yen-p'ing 劉燕萍. *Ai-ch'ing yü meng-huan: T'ang-ch'ao ch'uan-ch'i chung te pei-chü i-shih* 愛情與夢幻：唐朝傳奇中的悲劇意識. Hong Kong: Shang-wu Yin-shu-kuan, 1996.

Nienhauser, William H., Jr. *Chuan-chi yü hsiao-shuo: T'ang-tai wen-hsüeh lun-wen chi* 傳紀與小説：唐代文學論文集. Taipei: Southern Materials, 1995. Contain articles on early fiction and its relation with history.

___. "Female Sexuality and Standards of Virtue in T'ang Narratives." In Eva Hung, ed., *Paradoxes of Traditional Chinese Literature.* Hong Kong: The Chinese University Press, 1994, pp. 1-20.

___. "Literature as a Source for Traditional History: The Case of Ou-yang Chan," *CLEAR* 12 (1990): 1-14.

___. "The Origins of Chinese Fiction," *MS* 38 (1988-89): 191-219.

Park, Ming Woong. "Niu Seng-ju (780-848) and His *Hsüan-kuai lu.* Unpublished Ph. D. dissertation, University of Wisconsin, 1993.

Thilo, Thomas. "Ausländer und Kostbarkeiten: zu einem Motiv in der Erzälhungsliteratur der Tang-Zeit," *AO* 11(1985): 149-73.

___. "Erzählungen der Tang-Zeit als sozialgeschichtliche Quellen," *AO* 9(1985), 237-255.

___. "Historische Persönlichkeiten als Gestalten in Tang-Erzählungen: Wei Gao und Wei Dan," *AO* 12 (1986): 150-61. Compares T'ang stories (from the *T'ai-p'ing kuang-chi*) about these two figures with their official biographies in the dynastic histories.

Wang, Chih-chung 王枝忠. *Han Wei Liu-ch'ao hsiao-shuo shih* 漢魏六朝小説史. Hangchow: Che-chiang Ku-chi, 1997.

Wu, Hung. "The Earliest Pictorial Representations of Ape Tales, An Interdisciplinary Study of Early Chinese Narrative Art and Literature," *TP* LXXIII (1987): 87-113. Includes discussion of the "Pai-yüan chuan" 白猿傳.

Wu, Keng-shun 吳庚舜. "T'ang-tai Ch'uan-ch'i yen-chiu" 唐代傳奇研究. In *T'ang-tai wen-hsüeh yen-chiu nien-chien, 1985* 唐代文學研究年鑑, *1985.* Sian: Shan-hsi Jen-min, 1987, pp. 420-429.

Ch'üan Chin-shih 全金詩 (**Complete Chin Poetry**)

Editions and References

Hsüeh, Jui-chao 薛瑞兆, ed. *Chüan Chin shih* 全金詩. Tientsin: Nan-k'ai Ta-hsüeh, 1995.

Yü-ting Ch'üan Chin shih tseng-pu Chung-chou chi 玉御訂全金詩增補中州集. 72 chüan.

Kuo Yüan-yü 郭元紆, ed. Taipei: T'ai-wan Shang-wu Yin-shu-kuan, 1983. *Ssu-k'u.*

Ch'üan Sung Tz'u 全宋詞 (**Complete Lyrics of the Sung**)

Editions and References
Chin, Ch'i-hua 金啟華. *Ch'üan Sung Tz'u tien-ku k'ao-shih tz'u-tien* 全宋詞典故考釋辭典. Changchun: Chi-lin Wen-shih, 1991.

Chin, Ch'ien-ch'iu 金千秋. *Ch'üan Sung Tz'u chung te yüeh-wu tzu-liao* 全宋詞中的樂舞資料. Peking: Jen-min Yin-yüeh, 1990.

Ch'üan Sung Tz'u pu-chi 全宋詞補輯. K'ung Fan-li 孔凡禮, ed. Peking: Chung-hua, 1981. Appends an index to authors.

Ch'üan Sung Tz'u 全宋詞. 5v. Rpt. Shih-chieh Shu-chü Pien-chi-pu, eds. Taipei: Shih-chieh, 1984. *Chung-kuo hsüeh-shu ming-chu,* 7. Appends a bibliography.

Kao, Hsi-t'ien 高喜田 and K'ou Ch'i 寇琪, eds. *Ch'üan Sung Tz'u tso-che tz'u-tiao so-yin* 全宋詞作者詞調索引. Peking: Chung-hua, 1992.

Shen, Pai-ch'i 瀋百齊, ed. *Ch'üan Sung Tz'u ching-hua feng-lei chien-shang chi-ch'eng* 全宋詞精華分類鑒賞集成. Peking: Chung-hua, 1992. Appends biographies of authors and an index of titles.

Ch'üan T'ang shih 全唐詩 (**Complete Poetry of the T'ang**)

Editions and References
Chang, Ti-hua 張滌華, ed. *Ch'üan T'ang shih jen-ming k'ao* 全唐詩大辭典. Taiyuan: Shan-hsi Jen-min, 1992.

Ch'en, Shang-chün 陳尚君. *Ch'üan T'ang shih pu-pien* 全唐詩補編. 3v. Rev. ed. Peking: Chung-hua, 1992. A revised edition of the 1982 collection (here in nearly 1800 pages) of four supplements to the *Ch'üan T'ang shih.*

Ch'üan T'ang shih ch'ung-p'ien so-yin 全唐詩重篇索引. Ho-nan Ta-hsüeh T'ang-shih Yen-chiu-shih, eds. Kaifeng: Ho-nan Ta-hsüeh, 1985.

Ch'üan T'ang shih so-yin 全唐詩索引. 10v. Peking: Chung-hua, 1991-. Beginning with v. 11 (1992), published by Hsien-tai. Individual indexes are listed under the bibliography of the appropriate poets.

Fan, Chih-lin 范之麟 and Wu Keng-shun 吳庚舜, ed. *Ch'üan T'ang shih tien-ku tz'u-tien* 全唐詩典故辭典. Wuhan: Hu-pei Jen-min, 1989.

Lin, Te-pao 林德保 *et al.,* eds. *Hsiang-chu Ch'üan T'ang shih* 詳注全唐詩. 2v. Talien, 1997.

Shen, Pai-ch'i 瀋百齊, ed. *Ch'üan T'ang shih ching-hua fen-lei chien-shang chi-ch'eng* 全唐詩精華分類鑒賞集成. Nanking: Ho-hai Ta-hsüeh, 1989. Appends biographies of authors and an index of titles.

Wang, Chung-min 王重民 *et al.,* eds. *Ch'üan T'ang shih wai-pien* 全唐詩外編. Rpt. Peking: Chung-hua, 1992 (1982). A revision of the original 1982-edition copy-edited by Ch'en Shang-chün 陳尚君. Appends an index.

Wu, Ju-mei 吳汝煜 and Hu K'o-hsien 胡可先. *Ch'üan T'ang shih jen-ming k'ao* 全唐詩人明考 (An Appraisal of the Names Concerned in T'ang Poetry). Nanking: Chiang-su Chiao-yü, 1990.

Studies
Chi, Shao-fu 吉少甫. "Ts'ao Yin k'o-shu k'ao" 曹寅刻書考, *Chung-hua wen-shih lun-ts'ung* 1985.2: 291-304.

Ch'üan T'ang shih-hua 全唐詩 (**Complete Poetry Talks on the T'ang**)

Editions and References

Yu, Mou 尤袤 (1127-1194). *Ch'üan T'ang shih-hua* 全唐詩話. Peking: Chung-hua, 1985. *TSCC* edition.

Ch'üan T'ang wen 全唐文 (**Complete Prose of the T'ang**)

Editions and References

Li, Chih-p'ing 禮季平, ed. *Ch'üan T'ang wen cheng-chih, ching-chi tzu-liao hui-pien* 全唐文政治經濟資料匯編. Sian: San Ch'in, 1992.

Ma, Hsü-ch'uan 馬緒傳, ed. *Ch'üan T'ang wen pien-ming mu-lu chi tso-che so-yin* 全唐文編名目錄及作者索引. Peking: Chung-hua, 1985. Appends an index.

Tung, Kao 董誥 (1740-1818), ed. *Ch'üan T'ang wen* 全唐文. 11v. Peking: Chung-hua, 1983. Photolithic reprint of a printed edition of Chi-ch'ien Yüan 及潛園 printed in 1814. With minimal punctuation.

Wu, Kang 吳鋼 *et al.*, eds. *Ch'üan T'ang wen pu-i* 全唐文補遺. Sian: San-Ch'in, 1997. Appends author and title indexes.

Studies

Yeh, Shu-jen 葉樹仁. "*Ch'üan T'ang wen* yen-chiu" 全唐文研究, *Ku-chi cheng-li yen-chiu hsüeh-k'an* 1993.1.

___. "Tu *Ch'üan T'ang wen* cha-chi pu" 讀全唐文扎記補, *Pei-ching Shih-fan Hsüeh-yüan hsüeh-pao* 1991.5.

chüeh-chü 絕句

Studies

Egan, Charles H. "A Critical Study of the Origins of *Chüeh-chü* Poetry," *AM, NS III,* 6.1(1993), 83-125.

Hsieh, Daniel. "The Origin and Development of Jueju Verse." Unpublished Ph. D. dissertation, University of Washington, 1991.

Chui pai-ch'iu 綴白裘 (**Piecing Together a White Fur Coat**)

Editions and References

Chui pai-ch'iu 綴白裘. 15v. Taipei: Hsüeh-sheng, 1984. *Shan-pen hsi-ch'ü ts'ung-k'an,* 5th Series, #58-72.

Chung Hsing 鍾惺 (1574–1624)

Editions and References

Chung, Hsing 鍾惺, comm. *Chung p'i Shui-hu chuan* 鍾批水滸傳. 5v. Peking: Chung-hua, 1990. *Ku-pen hsiao-shuo ts'ung-k'an,* 24th Series, #1-5.

___. *Yin-hsiu hsüan chi* 隱秀軒集. 8v. Tokyo: Takahashi Jôhô 情報, 1990. Reprint of a 1622 edition held in the Naikaku Bunko.

___. *Yin-hsiu hsüan chi* 隱秀軒集. Li Hsien-keng 李先耕 and Ts'ui Chung-ch'ing 崔重慶, eds.

Shanghai: Shang-hai Ku-chi, 1992. *Chung-kuo ku-tien wen-hsüeh ts'ung-shu.* Appends traditional prefaces, a chronological biography, and a study of Chung's *shih* poetry and prose.

Studies

Tomasko, Nancy Morton. "Chung Hsing (1574-1625), A Literary Name in the Wan-li Era (1573-1620) of Ming China." Unpublished Ph. D. dissertation, Princeton University, 1995. Argues that Chung Hsing deliberately imbedded a wealth of detail in his writing in order to record and thereby preserve his own name.

Chung-yüan yin-yün 中原音韻 (Central Plain Songs and Rhymes)

Studies

Endô, Mitsuaki 遠藤光曉. *"Chûgen on'in* no seisho katai" 「中原音韻」の成書過程, *Tôyô gakuhô* 76 (1995): 1-25.
Chung-yüan yin-yün hsin-lun 中原音韻新論. Peking: Pei-ching Ta-hsüeh, 1991.
Li, Hsin-k'uei 李新魁. *Chung-yüan yin-yün yin-hsi yen-chiu* 中原音韻音系研究. Chengchow: Chung-chou Shu-hua-she, 1983.
Ning, Chi-fu 寧繼福. *Chung-yüan yin-yün piao-kao* 中原音韻表稿. Changchun: Chi-lin Wen-shih, 1985. Appends traditional prefaces, an index and a discussion of editions.

Fa-yüan chu-lin 法苑珠林 (A Grove of Pearls in the Dharma Garden)

Editions and References

Tao Shih 道世. *Fa-yüan chu-lin* 法苑珠林. Taipei: Hsin-wen-feng, 1983. In *Ta-cheng hsin-hsiu Ta-tsang-ching* 大正新修大藏經 (v. 53).
___. *Fa-yüan chu-lin.* 1 *chüan.* Shanghai: Shang-hai Wen-i, 1991. Reprint of *Ku-chin shuo-pu ts'ung-shu* 古今說部叢書 (1915 Chung-kuo T'u-shu Kung-ssu edition).
___. *Fa-yüan chu-lin.* Kuang-ling?: Chiang-su Kuang-ling Ku-chi, 1990.

Translations

Konan, Ichirô 小南一郎. *Hô'on shurin* 法苑珠林. Tokyo: Chung-yang Kung-lun-she, 1993.

Studies

Teiser, Stephen F. "T'ang Buddhist Encyclopedias: An Introduction to *Fa-yüan chu-lin* and *Chu-ching yao-chi.*" *TS* 3 (1985): 109-28.

Fan Ch'eng-ta 范成大 (1126–1191)

Editions and References

Fan, Ch'eng-ta 范成大. *Shih-hu tz'u* 石湖詞. Peking: Chung-hua, 1985. *TSCC* (based on the *Chih-pu-tsu Chai ts'ung-shu* edition).
Ku, Chih-hsing 顧志興, ed. *Fan Ch'eng-ta shih-ko shang-hsi chi* 范成大詩歌賞析集. Chengtu: Shu Pa Shu-she, 1991. Appends a chronological biography. *Chung-kuo ku-tien wen-hsüeh shang-hsi ts'ung-shu.*
K'ung, Fan-li 孔凡禮, ed. *Fan Ch'eng-ta i-chu chi-ts'un* 范成大佚著輯存. Peking: Chung-hua, 1983. Adds 135 works of prose, 9 *shih,* and 8 *tz'u* to what is included in standard collections.

Translations
Strassberg, *Inscribed Landscapes*, pp. 213-218.

Studies
K'ung, Fan-li 孔凡禮. *Fan Ch'eng-ta nien-p'u* 范成大年譜. Tsinan: Ch'i-Lu Shu-she,1985.
    Appends a bibliography.
Schmidt, J. D. *Stone Lake: The Poetry of Fan Chengda (1126-1193)*. Cambridge and New York:
    Cambridge University Press, 1992.
Yü, Pei-shan 于北山. *Fan Ch'eng-ta nien-p'u* 范成大年譜. Shanghai: Shang-hai Ku-chi, 1987.
    Traditional biographical materials and a bibliography are appended.

Fan Chung-yen 范仲淹 (989–1052)

Editions and References
Ch'üan Sung shih, 3:164-169:1857-1919.
Ch'üan Sung wen, 9:367-386, 392-779 and 10:387-391.1-88.

Translations
Landau, *Beyond Spring,* pp. 50-52.
Strassberg, *Inscribed Landscapes*, pp. 157-160.

Studies
Chikusa, Masaaki 竺沙雅章. *Han Chû'en* 范仲淹. Tokyo: Hakuteisha, 1995.
Fan Chung-yen I-ch'ien-nien Tan-ch'en Kuo-chi Hsüeh-shu Yen-t'ao-hui lun-wen chi 范仲淹一千年
    誕辰國際學術研討會論文集. Taipei: College of Literature, National Taiwan
    University, 1989.
Yü, Ta-nien. "Lüeh-lun Fan Chung-yen te tz'u." *Ch'eng-te Shih-chuan hsüeh-pao* 承德師專學報
    1985.1.

Fang Hsiao-ju 方孝孺 (1357–1402)

Studies
Chi, Hsiu-chu 姬秀珠. i 明初大儒方孝孺研究. Taipei: Wen-shih-che, 1991. *Wen-shih-che hsüeh-*
    shu ts'ung-k'an, 4. Appends a chronological biography and a bibliography.
Hu, Meng-ch'i 胡夢琪. *Fang Hsiao-ju nien-p'u* 方孝孺年譜. Sian: Shan-hsi Jen-min, 1988.

Fang Pao 方苞 (1668–1749)

Editions and References
Fang, Pao 方苞. *Fang Wang-hsi i-chi* 方望溪遺集. Hsü T'ien-hsiang 徐天祥 and Ch'en Lei 陳
    蕾, eds. Hofei: Huang-shan Shu-she, 1990. *An-hui ku-chi ts'ung-shu.*
Yang, Jung-hsiang 楊榮祥, ed. and trans. *Fang Pao, Yao Nai wen hsüan-i* 方苞姚鼐文選譯.
    Chengtu: Pa-Shu Shu-she, 1991. *Ku-tai wen-shih ming-chu hsüan-i ts'ung-shu.*

Translations
Strassberg, *Inscribed Landscapes*, pp. 399-402.

Fang-shih 方士

Studies

Lü, Hsi-ch'en 呂錫琛. *Tao-chia, fang-shih yü wang-ch'ao cheng-chih* 道家，方士與王朝政治. Changsha: Hu-nan Ch'u-pan-she, 1991.

Feng Meng-lung 憑夢龍 (1574–1646)

Editions and References

Two sets of collected works of Feng Meng-lung have been published in recent years: (1) Li Chi-ning 李際寧 and Li Hsiao-ming 李曉明, eds. *Feng Meng-lung ch'üan-chi* 憑夢龍全集 (Nanking: Chiang-su Ku-chi, 1993); and (2) Wei, T'ung-hsien 魏同賢, ed. *Feng Meng-lung ch'üan-chi* 憑夢龍全集. 43v. (Shanghai: Shang-hai Ku-chi, 1993). Works individually noted below can be identified as belonging to one or the other by the place and date of publication.

Ch'ien, Po-ch'eng 錢伯城, ed. *Hsin-p'ing Ching-shih t'ung-yen.* Shanghai: Shang-hai Ku-chi, 1992.

Feng, Meng-lung 憑夢龍, ed. *Che-mei chien* 折梅箋. Wei T'ung-hsien 魏同賢, ed. Nanking: Chiang-su Ku-chi, 1993. In *Feng Meng-lung ch'üan-chi.*

___. *Ch'ing shih* 情史. Chou Fang 周方 and Hu Hui-pin 胡慧斌, eds. Nanking: Chiang-su Ku-chi, 1993. In *Feng Meng-lung ch'üan-chi.*

___. *Hsin-chu Hsing-shih heng-yen* 新注醒世恆言. Peking: Pei-ching Shih-yüeh Wen-i, 1994.

___. *Hsing-shih heng-yen* 醒世恆言. Chung Jen 鍾仁, ed. Sian: Shan-hsi Jen-min, 1985.

___. *Hsin-chu Hsing-shih t'ung-yen* 新注醒世通言. Peking: Pei-ching Shih-yüeh Wen-i, 1994.

___. *Hsin Lieh-kuo chih* 新列國志. Huang Hsi-chien 黃希監, ed. Nanking: Chiang-su Ku-chi, 1993. In *Feng Meng-lung ch'üan-chi.*

___. *Hsin-p'ing Ching-shih t'ung-yen* 新評警世通言. Ch'ien Po-ch'eng 錢伯誠, ed. Shanghai: Shang-hai Ku-chi, 1992.

___. *Ku-chin t'an-kai* 古今譚概. Liu Te-ch'üan 劉德權, ed. Foochow: Hai-hsia Wen-i, 1985.

___. *Kua-chih erh* 掛枝兒. Lu Kuo-pin 陸國斌, ed. Nanking: Chiang-su Ku-chi, 1993. In *Feng Meng-lung ch'üan-chi.*

___. *Shan-ko* 山歌. Lu Kuo-pin 陸國斌, ed. Nanking: Chiang-su Ku-chi, 1993. In *Feng Meng-lung ch'üan-chi.*

___. *T'ai-p'ing kuang-chi ch'ao* 太平廣記鈔. 2v. Hsüeh Cheng-hsing 薛正興, ed. Nanking: Chiang-su Ku-chi, 1993. In *Feng Meng-lung ch'üan-chi.*

Hua, Kuang-sheng 華廣生, ed. *Ming Ch'ing min-ko shih-t'iao chi* 明清民歌時調集. Shanghai: Shang-hai Ku-chi, 1987. Collected by Feng Meng-lung.

Poon, Ming-sun 潘明燊, ed. *San-yen Erh-p'ai t'i-yao.* Hong Kong: Chung-kuo Hsüeh-she, 1988.

Shih, Ju-chieh 石汝傑 and Ch'en Liu-ching 陳榴兢, comp. *Sanka sakuin* 山歌索引. Tokyo: Kôbun Shuppan, 1989.

T'an, Cheng-pi 譚正璧, ed. *San-yen Liang-p'ai tzu-liao* 三言兩拍資料. Shanghai: Shang-hai Ku-chi, 1980.

Translations

Pimpaneau, Jacques. *Royaumes en proie à la perdition.* Paris, 1985. Partial translation of *Tung Chou Lieh-kuo chih* 東周列國志.

Porkert, Manfred, trans. *Der Aufstand der Zauberer—Ein Roman aus der Ming Zeit in der Fassung von Feng Menglong.* Frankfurt: Insel, 1986.

Studies

Hsu, Pi-ching. "Celebrating the Emotional Self: Feng Meng-lung and Late Ming Ethics and Aesthetics." Unpublished Ph. D. dissertation, Univerity of Minnesota, 1994.

Lowry, Kathryn. "Feng Menglong's Prefaces on Currently Popular Songs," Papers in Chinese History 2 (Spring 1993): 91-119.

Lu, Shu-lun 陸樹侖. *Feng Meng-lun yen-chiu* 馮夢龍研究. Shanghai: Fu-tan Ta-hsüeh, 1987.

Lu, Yi-lu. *Feng Meng-lung so-chi min-ko yen-chiu* 馮夢龍所集民歌研究. Taipei: Hsüeh-hai, 1988.

Ôki, Yasushi 大木康. "Fû Muryû 'Jo sanka' kô: *Shikyô* gaku to minkan kayô" 馮夢龍叙山歌考：詩経学と民間歌謡, *Tôyô bunka* 71 (1990): 121-145.

___. *Min matsu no hagure chishiki jin–Fû Bôryô to Soshû bunka* 明末のはぐれ知識人–馮夢竜と蘇州文化. Tokyo: Kôdansha, 1995.

Rummel, Stefan. *Die traditionelle chinesische Novelle, Analyse und Übersetzung der Erzählung von der Kurtisane Du Shiniang aus dem Sanyan Zyklus.* Bochum: Brockmeyer, 1992. *Chinathemen,* 66.

Swatek, Catherine Crutchfield. "Feng Menglong's *Romantic Dream:* Strategies of Containment in His Revisions of *The Peony Pavilion.*" Ph. D., Columbia University, 1990.

___. "Plum and Portrait: Feng Meng-lung's Revision of *The Peony Pavilion.*" *AM, TS* 6 (1993): 127-60.

Yang, Shuhui. "Storytelling and Ventriloquism: The Voice of a Literatus in the 'Sanyan' Collections." Unpublished Ph. D. dissertation, Washington University, 1994.

Feng-shen yen-i 封神演義 (**Investiture of the Gods**)

Editions

Kao, Yang 高陽, ed. *Feng-shen yen-i* 封神演義. Taipei: Feng-yün Shih-tai, 1987.

Translations

Anô, Tsutomu 安能務. *Hôjin engi (jô, chû, ge)* 封神演義 (上・中・下). Tokyo: Kôdansha, 1988-1989.

Gu, Zhizhong. *Creation of the Gods.* Peking: New World Press, 1992.

Studies

Brewster, Paul G., "Some Parallels between the 'Feng-shen Yen-i' and the 'Shahnamen' and the Possible Influences of the Former upon the Persian Epic," *Asian Folklore Studies* (Nagoya, Japan) 31.1 (1972): 115-22.

Chang, Ying 張穎 and Ch'en Su 陳速, "*Feng-shen yen-i* te shen-ch'üan" 封神演義的神權 (The Divine Power in *Feng-shen yen-i*), *Ming Ch'ing hsiao-shuo yen-chiu* 15 (1990): 131-41.

Ch'ien, Ching-fang 錢靜方. *Feng-shen yen-i tsa-k'ao* 封神演義雜考. Taipei: T'ien-i, 1991.

Hsiao, Ping 蕭兵, "*Feng-shen yen-i* de ni shih-shih-hsing chi ch'i sheng-ch'eng" 封神演義的擬史詩性集其生成 (The Pseudo-epic Style of *Feng-shen yen-i* and Its Formation), *Ming Ch'ing hsiao-shuo yen-chiu* 12 (1989): 112-25.

Liang, Kuei-chih 梁歸智. *Shen-hsien i-ching: Feng-shen yen-i–Tao-chiao wen-hua de i-shu mo-t'e-erh* 神仙意境–封神演義：道教文話的藝術模特兒 (The Realm of the Gods and Immortals: *Feng-shen yen-i,* the Artistic Model of Taoist Culture). Taiyuan: Shan-hsi Chiao-yü, 1994.

___. "Tsai-lun *Feng-shen yen-i* yü ni shih-shih: chien-lun Chung-kuo-shih shih-shih fa-yü pu-ch'üan de yüan-yin"再論封神演義與擬史詩–兼論中國式史詩發育不全的原因 (The Question of the Pseudo-epic Style of *Feng-shen yen-i* Revisited–With an Extended Discussion of the Reasons of the Underdevelopment of Chinese Epic), *Ming Ch'ing hsiao-shuo yen-chiu* 14 (1989): 26-44.

Nikaidō, Yoshihiro 二階堂善弘. "'Hôshin engi' no seiritsu ni tsuite" 『封神演義』の成立について, *Tôyô Bunka (Mukyûkai)* 68(1992): 13-21.

Wan, Pin-pin, "Investiture of the Gods ('Fengshen yanyi'): Sources, Narrative Structure, and Mythical Significance." Unpublished Ph. D. dissertation, University of Washington, 1987.

Wei, Chü-hsien 衛聚賢. *Feng-shen yen-i ku-shih t'an-yüan* 封神演義故事探源. Taipei: T'ien-i, 1991.

Feng Wei-min 馮惟敏 (1511–1578)

Editions and References

Wang, Hsien-tu 汪賢度, ed. *Hai-fu shan-t'ang shih-kao* 海浮山堂詩稿. Shanghai: Shang-hai Ku-chi, 1991.

Feng Yen-ssu (903–960)

Editions and References

Tseng, Chao-min 曾昭岷, ed. *Wen, Wei, Feng tz'u hsin-chiao* 溫韋馮詞新校. Shanghai: Shang-hai Ku-chi, 1988.

Studies

Chang, Tzu-wen 張自文. "Feng Yen-ssu tz'u te shen-mei chieh-chih" 審美价值. *Wen-hsüeh i-ch'an* 1989.5.

Yang, Hai-ming 楊海明. "Lun Feng Yen-ssu tz'u." *Wen-shih-che* 1985.2.

Yeh, Chia-ying 葉嘉瑩. *Wen T'ing-yün, Wei Chuang, Feng Yen-ssu, Li Yü* 溫庭筠韋莊馮延巳李煜. Taipei: Ta-an, 1992. *T'ang Sung ming-chia tz'u shang-hsi*, 1.

fu 賦

Editions, References

Ch'en Yüan-lung 陳元龍 (1652-1736), ed. *Li-tai fu-hui* 歷代賦匯. Rpt. Nanking: Chiang-su Ku-chi, 1987.
The most extensive collection of *fu*, this reprint is based on Yang-chou Shih-chü 揚州詩局 (1886) edition.

Ch'i, Wen-chün 遲文浚, Hsü Chih-kang 許志剛, and Shen Hsü-lien 沈緒連, eds. *Li-tai fu tz'u-tien* 歷代賦辭典. Shenyang: Liao-ning Jen-min, 1992.

Fang, Po-jung 方伯榮. *Li-tai ming-fu shang-hsi* 歷代名賦賞析. Chungking: Ch'ung-ch'ing Chu-pan-she, 1988.

Fei, Chen-kang 費振剛 *et al.*, eds. *Ch'üan Han fu* 全漢賦. Peking: Pei-ching Ta-hsüeh, 1993.
Mostly textual notes in this lightly annotated, but useful collection.

Huang, Jui-yün 黃瑞雲. *Li-tai shu-ch'ing hsiao-fu hsüan* 歷代抒情小賦選. Shanghai: Shang-hai Ku-chi, 1986.

Huo, Hsü-tung 霍旭東 *et al. Li-tai tz'u-fu chien-shang tz'u-tien* 歷代辭賦鑒賞辭典. Hofei: An-hui Wen-i, 1992.

Huo, Sung-lin 霍松林, ed. *Tz'u-fu ta tz'u-tien* 辭賦大辭典. Nanking: Chiang-su Ku-chi, 1996.

Liu, Chen-hsiang 劉禎祥 and Li Fang-ch'en 李方晨, ed. and comm. *Li-tai tz'u-fu hsüan* 歷代辭賦選. Changsha: Hu-nan Jen-min, 1984; 2nd printing, 1991.

Pi, Wan-ch'en 畢萬忱, Ho P'ei-hsiung 何沛雄, and Lo K'ang-lieh 羅慷烈, eds. and comm. *Chung-kuo li-tai fu-hsüan, Hsien Ch'in Liang Han chüan* 中國歷代賦選先秦兩漢卷. Nanking: Chiang-su Chiao-yü, 1990.

Tominaga, Kazutaka 富永一登, ed. *Sen Shin, Ryô Kan, Saingoku jifu sakuin (jô ge kan)* 先秦・両漢・三国辞賦索引（上下卷）. 2v. Tokyo: Kenbun Shuppan, 1996. This 1118-page set is one of very few concordances to *fu*.

Ts'ao, Tao-heng 曹道衡. *Han Wei Liu-ch'ao tz'u-fu* 漢魏六朝辭賦. Shanghai: Shang-hai Ku-chi, 1989.

Wang, Ch'en-kuang 王晨廣, ed. *Wei Chin Nan-pei ch'ao tz'u-fu hsüan-ts'ui* 魏晉南北朝辭賦選粹. Tientsin: T'ien-chin Chiao-yü, 1987.

Translations

Knechtges, David R. *Wenxuan or Selections of Refined Literature. Volume Two: Rhapsodies on Sacrifices, Hunting, Travel, Sightseeing, Palaces and Halls, Rivers and Seas.* Princeton: Princeton University Press, 1987; *Volume Three: Rhapsodies on Natural Phenomena, Birds and Animals, Aspirations and Feelings, Sorrowful Laments, Literature, Music, and Passions.* Princeton: Princeton University Press, 1996.
Contains closely annotated translations of the *fu* in *chüan* 7-12 and 13-19 respectively of the *Wen-hsüan* along with excellent Introduction, Biographical Sketches, and Bibliography.

Li, Hui 李暉 and Yü Fei 于非, ed. and comm. *Li-tai fu i-shih* 歷代賦譯釋. Harbin: Hei-lung-chiang Jen-min, 1984.

Studies

Bokenkamp, Stephen. "The "Ledger on the Rhapsody:" Studies in the Art of the T'ang 'Fu.'" Ph.D., University of California, Berkeley, 1986.

Chang, Hsiao-hu 張嘯虎. "T'ang fu lüeh-lun" 唐賦略論, *Kuei-chou she-hui k'o-hsüeh* 1986.8.

Chang, Lun-shou 章論授. "Shih-nien Han fu yen-chiu tsung-shu" 十年漢賦研究綜述. *Wen-hsüeh i-ch'an* 3 (1992): 118-127.

Ch'eng, Chang-ts'an 程章燦. *Wei Chin Nan-pei ch'ao fu-shih* 魏晉南北朝賦史. *Chung-kuo fen-t'i tuan-tai wen-hsüeh shih* 中國分體段代文學史. Nanking: Chiang-su Ku-chi, 1992. Appends list of lines attributed to pre-T'ang *fu* from *lei-shu* and archaeological finds as well as a useful bibliography.

Chiang, Shu-ko 姜書閣. *Han-fu t'ung-i* 漢賦通義. Tientsin: Ch'i-Lu Shu-she, 1988.

Fang, Kuang-chih 方廣治. *Han-fu t'ung-lun* 漢賦通論. Chengtu: Pa-Shu Shu-she, 1988.

Fang, Po-jung 方伯榮, ed. *Li-tai ming fu shang-hsi* 歷代名賦賞析. Chungking: Ch'ung-ch'ing Ch'u-pan she, 1988.

Fu, Chün-lien 伏俊連. *Tun-huang fu chu* 敦煌賦注. Lanchow: Kan-su Jen-min, 1994.

Harbsmeier, Christoph. "Fu in the Mawangdui manuscripts of the *Laozi* and in the *Remnants of Qin law*." In *From Classical Fu to 'Three Inches High:' Studies on Chinese in Honor of Erik Zürcher*, eds. J.C.P. Liang and R.P.E. Sybesma. Leuven/Apeldoorn: Garant, 1993.

Ho, Chung-jung 何忠榮. "T'ang-tai lü-fu chien-lun" 唐代律賦簡論, *Ch'ing-hai Shih-ta hsüeh-pao* 1995.1.

Ho, Hsin-wen 何新文. *Chung-kuo fu-lun shih-kao* 中國賦論史稿. Peking: K'ai-ming, 1993.

Ho, P'ei-hsiung 何沛雄. *Han Wei Liu-ch'ao fu-chia lun-lüeh* 漢魏六朝賦家論略. Taipei: Hsüeh-sheng, 1986.

Hsin-Ya hsüeh-shu chi-k'an, 13 (1994). Includes 34 studies of the *fu* presented the 2nd International Conference on the *Fu* held at The Chinese University in 1992.

Hsü, Chih-hsiao 徐志嘯, ed. *Li-tai fu lun chi-yao* 歷代賦論輯要. Shang-hai: Fu-tan Ta-hsüeh, 1991.

K'ang, Chin-sheng 康金聲. *Han-fu tsung-heng* 漢賦縱橫. Taiyuan: Shan-hsi Jen-min, 1992.

Kao, Kuang-fu 高光復. *Fu-shih shu-lüeh* 賦史述略. Harbin?: Tung-pei Shih-fan Ta-hsüeh, 1987.

___. *Han Wei Liu-ch'ao ssu-shih-chia fu shu-lun* 漢魏六朝四十家賦述論. Harbin: Hei-lung-chiang Chiao-yü, 1988.

Knechtges, David R. "The Emperor and Literature: Emperor Wu of the Han." In *Imperial Rulership and Cultural Change in Traditional China* Frederick P. Brandauer and Chun-chieh Huang, eds. Seattle: Washington University Press, 1989, pp. 51-76.

___. "Pao Chao's "Rhapsody on a Ruined City:" Date and Circumstances of Composition." In *A Festschrift in Honour of Professor Jao Tsung-i on the Occasion of His Seventy-Fifth Anniversary.* Hong Kong: Chinese University Press, 1993, pp. 319-330.

___. "Riddles as Poetry: The 'Fu Chapter' of the Hsun-tzu," *Wen-lin,* V. 2, pp. 1-32

Kung, K'o-ch'ang 龔克昌. *Han fu yen-chiu* 漢賦研究. Rev. ed.; Tsinan: Shang-tung Wen-i, 1990. (Published by various presses from 1984 on.) Chapters on Chia I, Mei Sheng, Ssu-ma Hsiang-ju, Yang Hsiung, Pan Ku, Chang Heng, and Chao T'ai; appends an essay on Liu Hsieh's discussion of Han *fu* in *Wen-hsin tiao-lung.*

Kuo, Wei-sen 郭維森 and Hsü Chieh 許結. *Chung-kuo tz'u-fu fa-chan shih* 中國辭賦發展史. Nanking: Chiang-su Chiao-yü, 1996.

Levy, Dore. "Constructing Sequences: Another Look at the Principle of *Fu* 'Enumeration,'" *HJAS* 46 (1986): 471-493.

Li, Ssu-han 李斯翰. "Fu te su-yüan" 賦的溯源. *Hua-nan Shih-fan Ta-hsüeh hsüeh-pao* 1988.1.

Liao, Kuo-tung 廖國棟. *Wei Chin yung-wu fu yen-chiu* 魏晉詠物賦研究. Taipei: Wen-shih-che, 1990.

Ma, Chi-kao 馬積高. *Fu shih* 賦史. Shang-hai: Shang-hai Ku-chi, 1987. An extensive history of *fu* from earliest times through the Ch'ing dynasty; interesting review by Ch'eng Ta-tsan 程章燦 in *Nan-ching Ta-hsüeh hsüeh-pao,* 1988.3.

___. "Lun T'ang fu te hsin fa-chan" 論唐賦的新發展. In *T'ang-tai wen-hsüeh yen-chiu nien-chien, 1987* 唐代文學研究年鑑, 1987. Sian: Shan-hsi Jen-min, 1988, pp. 218-221.

T'ao, Ch'iu-ying 陶秋英. *Han fu yen-chiu.* Nanking: Chiang-su Ku-chi, 1986.

Ts'ao, Ming-kang 曹明剛. "Hsi Han shu-ch'ing fu kai-lun" 西漢抒情復概論. *Wen-hsüeh i-ch'an* 1987.1: 29-36.

___. "Sung Yü fu chen-wei pien" 宋玉賦真偽辨. *Shang-hai Shih-fan Hsüeh-yüan hsüeh-pao* 1984.2.

Ts'ao, Tao-heng 曹道衡. *Han Wei Liu-ch'ao tz'u-fu* 漢魏六朝辭賦. Shang-hai: Shang-hai Ku-chi, 1989.

Wan, Kuang-chih 萬光治. *Han fu t'ung-lun* 漢賦通論. Chengtu: Pa-Shu Shu-she, 1988.

Yeh, Yu-ming 葉幼明. *Tz'u-fu t'ung-lun.* Changsha: Hu-nan Chiao-yü, 1991.

Zhang, Cangshou 章滄授 and Jonathan Pease. "The Roots of Han Rhapsody in Philosophical Prose." *Monumenta Serica* 41 (1993): 1-27.

Fu Hsüan 傅玄 (217–278)

Studies

Paper, Jordan. "Fu Hsüan as Poet: A Man of His Season," *Wen-lin,* V. 2, pp. 45-60.

Matsuka, Yûko 松家裕子. "Fu Gen gafu shotan" 傅玄樂府初探, *Tôyô bunka gakka nenpô* 東洋文化学科年報 9 (November 1994).

Wei, Ming-an 魏明安 and Chao I-wu 趙以武. *Fu Hsüan p'ing-chuan* 傅玄評傳. Nanking: Nan-ching Ta-hsüeh, 1997.

Fu-sheng liu-chi 浮生六記 (**Six Chapters of a Floating Life**)

Editions and References
Li-jen 立人, ed. *Fu-sheng liu-chi* 浮生六記. Peking: Tso-chia, 1995.
Shen, Fu 沈復. *Fu-sheng liu-chi chu* 浮生六記注. 6 *chüan*. Fu Ch'ang-tse 傅昌澤, comm. Yü
    P'ing-po 俞平伯, ed. Peking: Pei-ching Shih-fan Hsüeh-yüan, 1992.
___. *Fu-sheng liu-chi* 浮生六記. Changsha: Yüeh-li Shu-she, 1991.
Yü, P'ing-po 俞平伯 *et al*, eds. *Fu-sheng liu-chih chu* 浮生六記注. Peking: Pei-ching Shih-fan
    Ta-hsüeh, 1992.

Translations
Teng, Shaoquan and Zhang Zhaoji. *Sechs Aufzeichnungen über ein unstetes Leben.* Leipzig: Reclam,
    1989. Rainer von Franz provides a postface and notes and front-matter from Feng
    Ch'i-yung, Yü P'ing-po and others is also translated.

Han-shan 寒山 (**Cold Mountain**)

Editions and References
Han-shan 寒山. *Han-shan shih chiao-chu* 寒山詩校注. Ch'ien Hsüeh-lieh 錢學烈, ed. Canton:
    Kuang-tung Kao-teng Chiao-yü, 1991.
___. *Han-shan shih chiao-chu* 寒山詩校注. Hsü, Kuang-ta 張學烈, ed. Canton: Kuang-tung
    Kao-teng Chiao-yü, 1991.

Translations
Carré, Patrick. *Le mangeur de brumes, l'oeuvre de Han-shan* poète *et vagabond.* Paris: Editions
    Phoebus, 1985.
Henricks, Robert G. *The Poetry of Han-shan, A Complete Annotated Translation of Cold Mountain.*
    Albany: SUNY, 1990.
Nishitani, Keiji 西谷啓治. *Kanzan shi* 寒山詩. Tokyo: Chikuma Shobô, 1986.

Studies
Borgen, Robert. "The Legend of Hanshan: A Neglected Source." *JAOS* 111 (1991): 575-579.
Ch'ien, Hsüeh-lieh 張學烈, ed. *Han-shan-tzu shih chiao-chu (fu Shih-te shih)* 寒山子詩校注附拾
    得詩. Canton: Kuang-tung Kao-teng Chiao-yü, 1991.
Hsiang, Ch'u. 項楚 "Han Shan shih chou-tu cha-chi" 寒山詩籀讀扎記, *Chung-kuo ku-chi
    yen-chiu* 中國古籍研究. V. 1. Shanghai: Shang-hai Ku-chi, 1996, pp. 113-149.
Mair, Victor H. "Script and Word in Medieval Vernacular Sinitic." *JAOS* 112 (1992): 269-78.
    Review of Robert G. Henricks' *The Poetry of Han-shan; A Complete, Annotated Translation
    of Cold Mountain.*

Han shu 漢書 (**History of the Han Dynasty**)

Editions and References
Chang, Lieh 張烈, ed. *Han shu chu-shih* 漢書注釋. 4v. Haikow: Hai-nan Kuo-chi Hsin-wen
    Ch'u-pan Chung-hsin, 1997.
Chang, Shun-hui 張舜徽. *Han shu "I-wen chih" t'ung-shih* 漢書藝文志通釋. Wuhan: Hu-pei
    Chiao-yü, 1990.
Ch'en, Chia-lin 陳家麟 and Wang Jen-k'ang 王仁康, eds. *Han shu ti-ming so-yin* 漢書地名索
    引. Peking: Chung-hua, 1990.

Ch'in, T'ung-p'ei 秦同培, comm. *Liang Han shu ching-hua* 兩漢書精華. Sung Ching-ju 宋晶如, ed. Chengchow: Chung-chou, 1991.

Kano, Naoki 狩野直喜. "*Hansho* hochū ho" 漢書補注補. In Kano, *Ryô Han gakujutsu kô* 両漢学術考. Rpt. Tokyo: Chikuma Shobô, 1989 (1962), pp. 257-342.

Li, K'ung-huai 李孔懷 and Shen Chung 瀋重. *Han shu chi-chuan hsüan-i* 漢書紀傳選譯. Shanghai: Shang-hai Ku-chi, 1994.

Li, Pu-chia 李步嘉, ed. *Wei Chao "Han shu yin-i" chi-shih* 韋昭漢書音義集釋. Wuhan: Wuhan Ta-hsüeh, 1990.

Shih, Ting 施丁, ed. *Han shu hsin chu* 漢書新注. Sian: San-Ch'in, 1994. Useful critical edition with copious notes; appendixes on place and personal names and prefaces to important editions.

Ts'ang, Hsiu-liang 倉修良, ed. *Han shu tz'u-tien* 漢書辭典. Tsinan: Shang-tung Chiao-yü, 1994.

Wu, Hsün 吳恂. *Han shu chu-shang* 漢書注尚. Shanghai: Shang-hai Ku-chi, 1983.

Translations

Fukushima, Tadashi 福島正. *Shiki, Kanjo* 史記・漢書. *Kanshô Chûgoku no koten* 鑑賞中国の古典, 7. Tokyo: Kadokawa Shoten, 1989.

Honda, Wataru 本田済. *Kanjo, Go Kanjo, Sangokushi retsuden sen* 漢書・後漢書・三国志列伝選. Tokyo: Heibonsha, 1994.

Kano, Naosada 狩野直禎 and Nishiwaki Tsuneki 西脇常記, trans. and annot. *Han Ko: Kanjo "Kôshi shi"* 班固：漢書郊祀志. Tokyo: Heibonsha, 1987.

Nagata, Hidemasa 永田英正 and Umehara Kaoru 梅原郁, tran. and annot. Han Ko 班固. *Kanjo shokka, chiri, kôkyoku shi* 漢書食貨・地理・溝血志. Tokyo: Heibonsha, 1988.

Tomiya, Itaru 冨谷至 and Yoshikawa Tadao 吉川忠夫. *Kanjo "Gogyôshi"* 漢書五行志. Tokyo: Heibonsha, 1986.

Wagner, Donald B. *A Classical Chinese Reader: The Han shu Biography of Huo Guang* 漢書霍光傳. London: Curzon, 1997.

Studies

Ch'en, Kuo-ch'ing 陳國慶, ed. *Han shu "I-wen chih" chu-shih hui-pien* 漢書藝文志注釋彙編. Peking: Chung-hua, 1983. Twelves articles on the first bibliographic treatise; appends a bibliography.

Hsü, Shuo-fang 徐朔方. *Shih Han lun-kao* 史漢論稿. Nanking: Chiang-shu Ku-chi, 1984.

Hulsewé, A. F. P. "*Han shu* 漢書," in Loewe, *Early Chinese Texts*, pp. 129-136.

Wang, I-min 王依民. "*Hou Han shu* so chi "Ch'i yen" hsiao-k'ao" 後漢書所記七言小考. *Wen-shih* 31 (1988): 158-171.

Wang, Li-ch'i 王利器. "*Han-shu* ts'ai-liao lai-yüan k'ao" 書材料來源考. *Wen shih* 21 (1983): 1-20.

Yang, Shu-ta 楊樹達 (1885-1956). *Han shu k'uei-kuan* 漢書窺管. Shanghai: Shang-hai Ku-chi, 1984.

Yoshikawa, Tadao 吉川忠夫. "Gan Shiko no *Kanjo* chû" 顏師古の漢書注. In Yoshikawa, *Rikuchô seishinshi kenkyû* 六朝精神史研究. Kyoto: Hôyû, 1984, pp. 303-421.

Han Wo 韓偓 (844–923 or 843-923)

Editions and References

Han, Wo 韓偓. *Chin luan mi chi* 金鑾密記. 1 *chüan*. Chengtu: Pa-Shu Shu-she, 1993. A reproduction of the *T'ang-tai ts'ung-shu ch'u-chi* 唐代叢書初集 edition.

___. *Han Han-lin chi* 韓翰林集. Wu Ju-lun 吳汝綸 (1840-1903), comm. Lanchow: Lan-chou Ku-chi, 1990. Based on a 1936 edition published by Shan-hsi T'ung-chih Kuan 陝西 通志館. *Chung-kuo Hsi-pei wen-hsien ts'ung-shu.*

___. *Hsiang-lien chi* 香奩集. 3 *chüan.* Tokyo: Kyûko Shoin, 1978. Based on a Ch'ing edition from 1810.

Luan, Kuei-ming 欒貴明 *et al.*, ed. *Ch'üan T'ang shih so-yin, Han Wo chüan* 全唐詩索引，韓偓 卷. Peking: Hsien-tai, 1995.

Studies

Huo, Sung-lin 霍松林 and Teng Hsiao-chün 鄧小軍. "Han Wo nien-p'u (hsia) 韓偓年譜， 下," *Shan-hsi Shih-ta hsüeh-pao (Che-hsüeh she-hui k'o-hsüeh)* 1989.1 (#66): 83-86.

Han Wu-ti nei-chuan 漢武帝內傳 (Intimate Biography of Emperor Wu of the Han)

Editions and References

Pan Ku 班固. *Han Wu-ti nei-chuan* 漢武帝內傳. Ch'ien Hsi-tso 錢熙祚 (1801-1844), coll. Peking: Chung-hua, 1985. Based on the *Shou-shan Ko ts'ung-shu* 守山閣叢書 edition of 1844.

Studies

Kominami, Ichirô 小南一郎. *"Kan Mutei naiden* no seiritsu" 漢武帝内伝の成立. In Kominami, *Chûgoku no shinwa to monogratri—Koshsetsushi no tenkai* 中国の神話と物語ー古小説史 の展開. Tokyo: Iwanami, 1984, pp. 237-433.

Smith, Thomas Eric. "Ritual and the Shaping of Narrative: The Legend of the Han Emperor Wu." 2v. Unpublished Ph. D. dissertation, University of Michigan, 1992. A massive, important study of various aspects of the text; the most important since Schipper's work.

Han Yü 韓愈 (768–824)

Editions and References

Chang, Ch'ing-hua 張清華. *Han Yü shih-wen p'ing-chu* 韓愈詩文評注. Chengchow: Chung-chou Ku-chi, 1991. Extensive annotations of seventy prose pieces and over one-hundred poems.

Ch'en, Êrh-tung 陳邇冬, comm. *Han Yü shih hsüan* 韓愈詩選. Peking: Jen-min Wen-hsüeh, 1984.

Ch'en, K'ang 陳抗 *et al.*, eds. *Ch'uan T'ang Shih So-yin: Han Yü Chüan* 全唐詩索引：韓愈卷. Peking: Chung-hua, 1992.

Ch'ien, Chung-lien 錢仲聯, ed. *Han Ch'ang-li shih hsi-nien chi-shih* 韓昌黎詩析年集釋. 2v. Shanghai: Shang-hai Ku-chi, 1984. *Chung-kuo ku-tien wen-hsüeh ts'ung-shu.* Excellent annotation, especially useful for identification of allusions.

Ch'ü, Shou-yüan 屈守元 and Ch'ang Ssu-ch'un 常思春, eds. *Han Yü ch'üan-chi chiao-chu* 韓 愈全集校注. 4v. Chengtu: Ssu-ch'uan Ta-hsüeh, 1996. A important modern critical editions with useful notes.

Han Yü 韓愈. *Ching-yin Sung-pen Ch'ang-li Hsien-sheng chi* 景印宋本昌黎先生集. 40 *chüan. Wai chi* 外集. 10 *chüan. Fu-lu* 付錄, 1 *chüan.* Taipei: Kuo-li Ku-kung Po-wu-kuan, 1982. *Shan-pen ts'ung-shu.*

Huang, Yung-nien 黃永年, comm. *Han Yü shih-wen hsüan-i* 韓愈詩文選譯. Chengtu: Pa-Shu

Shu-she, 1990.

Hung, Po 洪波 and Kuan Chien 關鍵, eds. *Han Yü hsiao-p'in* 韓昌黎小品. Peking: Wen-hua
I-shu, 1997.

Ku, I-sheng 顧易聲 and Hsü Ts'ui-yü 徐粹育, eds. *Han Yü san-wen hsüan-chi* 韓愈散文選集.
Shanghai: Shang-hai Ku-chi, 1997.

Sun, Ch'ang-wu 孫昌武, ed. *Han Yü hsüan-chi* 韓愈選集. Shanghai: Shang-hai Ku-chi, 1996.

T'ang, Kuei-jen 湯貴仁. *Han Yü Shih Hsüan-chu* 韓愈詩選註. Shanghai: Shang-hai Ku-chi,
1984.

T'ung, Ti-te 童第德. *Han Chi Chiao Ch'uan* 韓集校詮. Peking: Chung-hua Shu-chü, 1986.

T'ung, Ti-te 童第德. *Han Yü Wen-hsüan* 韓愈文選. Peking: Jen-min Wen-hsüeh, 1985.

Wu, Wen-chih 吳文治, ed. *Han Yü tzu-liao hui-pien* 韓愈資料匯編. Peking: Chung-hua, 1983.

Yin, Meng-lun 殷孟倫 and Yang, Hui-wen 楊彗文. *Han Yü San-wen Hsüan-chu* 韓愈散文選註
. Shanghai: Shang-hai Ku-chi, 1986.

Translations

Shimizu, Shigeru 清水茂. *Kan Yu* 韓愈. 2v. Tokyo: Chikuma Shobô, 1990. A translation of
the prose works in *Ch'ang-li Hsien-sheng chi* 昌黎先生集 (Tung-ya T'ang 東雅堂
edition).

Strassberg, *Inscribed Landscapes*, pp. 121-126.

Studies

Chang, Ch'ing-hua 張清華. *Han Yü shih-wen p'ing-chu* 韓愈詩文評註. Chengchow: Chung-chou
Ku-chi, 1991. Extensive annotations of seventy prose pieces and over one hundred
poems.

Ch'en, K'o-ming 陳克明. *Han Yü shu p'ing* 韓愈年譜及詩文系年. Chengtu: Pa-Shu Shu-she,
1996.

___. *Han Yü shu p'ing* 韓愈述評. Peking: Chung-kuo She-hui K'o-hsüeh, 1985.

Cheng, T'ao-chou. *Han Yü yen-chiu.* Changsha: Hu-nan Chiao-yü, 1991.

Ch'ien, Po-ch'eng 錢伯誠. *Han Yü wen-chi tao-tu* 韓愈文集導讀. Chengtu: Pa-shu Shu-she,
1993.

Han, T'ing-i 韓廷一. *Han Ch'ang-li ssu-hsiang yen-chiu* 韓昌黎思想研究. Taipei: T'ai-wan
Shang-wu Yin-shu-kuan, 1982.

Hartman, Charles. *Han Yü and the T'ang Search for Unity*. Princeton: Princeton University
Press, 1986.

Hightower, James R. "Han Yü as Humorist." *HJAS* 44.1 (1984): 5-27.

Ho, Fa-chou 何法周. *Han Yü Hsin-lun* 韓愈新論. Kaifeng: Ho-nan Ta-hsüeh, 1988.

Hsü, C.Y. "The Stone Drums." *Asian Culture Quarterly* 13.1 (1985): 87-109. A study of the
poems on ancient drum-shaped stelae and Wei Ying-wu, Han Yü and later poets'
verses on them.

Fang, Sung-ch'ing 方崧卿 (Sung dynasty). *Han Yü nien-p'u* 韓愈年譜. Hsü, Min-hsia 徐敏霞,
ed. Peking: Chung-hua Shu-chü, 1991.

Hu-sterk, Florence. "Semantique Musicale et Tradition Chinoise: Une Controverse Millénaire
Autour d'un Poème de Han Yu." *TP* 76(1-3) (1990): 1-15.

Knechtges, David R. "The Old-Style *Fu* of Han Yu," *TS* 13 (1995): 51-80.

Liu, Kuo-ying 劉國盈. *Han Yü p'ing-chuan* 韓愈評傳. Peking: Pei-ching Shih-fan Hsüeh-yüan,
1991.

Lü, Ta-fang.呂大防 (1027-1097). *Han Yü nien-p'u* 韓愈年譜. Hsü Min-hsia 徐敏霞. Peking:
Chung-hua, 1991.

Manley, Victor Eugene. "A Conservative Reformer in T'ang China: The Life and Thought
of Han Yü (768-824)." Unpublished Ph.D. dissertation, University of Arizona, 1986.

McMullen, David. "Han Yü: An Alternative Picture." *HJAS* 49.2 (1989): 603-57. Review article on Charles Hartman's book.

Monahan, Mark Chang. "Han Yü and His Literary Contribution." Ph.D., Georgetown University, 1987.

Nienhauser, William H., Jr. "The Reception of Han Yü in America, 1936-1992," *Asian Culture* 21.1 (1993): 18-48.

Nishigami, Masaru 西上勝. "Kan Yu no boshimei ni tsuite" 韓愈の墓志銘について, *Nippon-Chûgoku-gakkai-hô* 39 (1987): 132-145.

Ono, Shihei 小野四平. *Kan Yu to Ryû Sôgen: Tôdai kokubun kenkyû shôsetsu* 韓愈と柳宗元：唐代古文研究序説. Tokyo: Iwanami, 1995.

Ôta, Tsugio 太田次男. *Chû Tô bunjin kô–Kan Yu, Ryû Sôgen, Haku Kyoi* 中唐文人考–韓愈・柳宗元、白居易 Tokyo: Kenbun Shuppan, 1993.

Schmidt, J. D. "Disorder and the Irrational in the Poetry of Han Yü," *TS* 7 (1989): 137-167.

Shang, Wei. "Prisoner and Creator: The Self-Image of the Poet in Han Yu and Meng Jiao." *CLEAR* 16 (1994): 19-40.

Shang, Yung-liang 尚永亮. *Yüan-ho wu ta shih-jen yü pien-che wen-hsüeh k'ao-lun* 元和五大詩人與貶謫文學考論. *Ta-lu ti-ch'ü po-shih lun-wen ts'ung-k'an*, Taipei: Wen-chin, 1993.

Sun, Ch'ang-wu 孫昌武. *Han Yü San-wen I-shu Lun* 韓愈散文藝術論. Tientsin: Nan-k'ai Ta-hsüeh, 1986.

Teng, T'an-chou 鄧潭洲. *Han Yü yen-chiu* 韓愈研究. Changsha: Hu-nan Chiao-yü, 1991.

Wang, Ch'un 汪淳. *Han, Ou shih-wen pi-chiao yen-chiu* 韓歐詩文比較研究. Taipei: Wen-shih-che, 1989.

Wei, Fu 隗芾, ed. *Han Yu yen-chiu lun-wen Chi* 韓愈研究論文集. Kuangchow: Kuang-tung Jen-min, 1988.

Yen, Ch'i 閻琦. *Han shih lun-kao* 韓詩論稿. Sian: Shan-hsi Jen-min, 1984.

Hao-ch'iu chuan 好逑傳 (**The Fortunate Union**)

Editions and References

Hao-ch'iu chuan 好逑傳. Canton: Kuang-tung Jen-min, 1980.

Hao-ch'iu chuan 好逑傳. Li Shu 李書, coll. Peking: Pei-ching, Shih-fan Ta-hsüeh, 1993. A punctuated and collated edition based on a *Kuei-hai* 癸亥 year ed. held in Pei-ching Shih-fan Ta-hsüeh Library.

Hao-ch'iu chuan 好逑傳 = *The Happy Couple*. Taipei: Shuang-t'i, 1995. *Chung-kuo li-tai chin-hui hsiao-shuo hai-nei-wai chen tsang mi-pen chi-ts'ui* 中國歷代禁毀小說海內外珍藏秘本集粹.

Ho Ching-ming 何景明 (**1483–1521**)

Editions and References

Li, Shu-i 李叔毅 *et al.*, eds. *Ho Ta-fu chi* 何大復集. Chengchow: Chung-chou Ku-chi, 1989.

Studies

Ch'ien, Chin-sung 簡錦松 *Ming-tai wen-hsüeh p'i-p'ing yen-chiu* 明代文學批評研究. Taipei: Hsüeh-sheng, 1989.

Fu, K'ai-p'ei 傅開沛. "Ho Ta-fu nien-p'u" 何大復年譜, *Hsin-yan Shih-fan Hsüeh-yüan hsüeh-pao (Che-hsüeh, She-hui k'o-hsüeh pan)* 1982.2: 115-118 and 1982.3: 34-57.

Li, Shu-i 李叔毅 *et al.*, eds. *Ho Ching-ming yen-chiu* 何景明研究. Chengchow: Chung-chou Ku-chi, 1987.

Pai, Jun-te 白潤德 (Daniel Bryant). *Ho Ching-ming ts'ung-k'ao* 何景明叢考. Taipei: Hsüeh-sheng,

1997. Dates Ho's works, before presenting a detailed biography, studies of his works and editions, and a bibliography.

Ts'ao, Mu 草木. "Kuan-yü 'Ho Ta-fu nien-p'u' jo-kan wen-t'i te k'ao-cheng" 關於何大復年譜若干問題的考證," *Hsin-yang Shih-fan Hsüeh-yüan hsüeh-pao,* 1991.3: 58-61.

Yao, Hsüeh-hsien 姚學賢. *Ho Ching-ming p'ing-chuan* 何景明評傳. Chengchow: Ho-nan Ta-hsüeh, 1985?.

Ho Chu 賀鑄 (1052–1125)

Editions and References

Ho, Chu 賀鑄. *Tung-shan tz'u* 東山詞. Chung Chen-chen 鍾振振, ed. Shanghai: Shang-hai Ku-chi, 1989.

____. *Ch'ing-hu i-lao shih-chi* 慶湖遺老詩集. Taipei: T'ai-wan Shang-wu, 1983. *Ssu-k'u* edition. *Ch'üan Sung shih,* 19:1102-1112.12497-12614.

Ho Liang-chün 何良俊 (1506-1573)

Editions and References

Ho, Liang-chün 何良俊. *Ho-shih yü-lin* 何氏語林. Taipei: Hsin-hsing, 1984. *Pi-chi hsiao-shuo ta-kuan* edition.

____. *Ssu-yu Chai ts'ung-shuo* 四友齋叢説. Taipei: Hsin-hsing, 1988. *Pi-chi hsiao-shuo ta-kuan* edition.

____. *Ssu-yu Chai ts'ung-shu shuo t'i-ch'ao* 四友齋叢書説摘抄. Peking: Chung-hua, 1985. *TSCC* edition.

Hsi-ching tsa-chi 西京雜記 (Miscellanies of the Western Capital)

Editions and References

Ch'eng, Lin 成林 and Ch'eng Chang-tsan 程章燦, eds. *Hsi-ching tsa-chi ch'üan-i* 西京雜記全譯. Kweiyang: Kuei-chou Jen-min, 1993. *Chung-kuo li-tai ming-chu ch'üan-i ts'ung-shu.*

Hsiang, Hsin-yang 向新陽 and Liu K'o-jen 劉克任, eds. *Hsi-ching tsa-chi chiao-chu* 西京雜記校注. Shanghai: Shang-hai Ku-chi, 1991.

Translations

Seikei zakki Kenkyû Zeminaru 西京雜記研究ゼミナル, ed. "*Seikei zakki* yakushû (3)" 西京雜記訳注 (三), *Shiteki* 12 (1991): 90-113. To date translations (in at least 7 segments) have been published in *Shiteki.*

Studies

Kominami, Ichirô 小南一郎. "*Seikei zakki* no denshôsha tachi" 西京雜記の伝承者たち. In Kominami, *Chûgoku no shinwa to monogratri–Koshsetsushi no tenkai* 中国の神話と物語－古小説史の展開. Tokyo: Iwanami, 1984, pp. 95-144.

Hsi-hsiang chi 西廂記

Editions and References

Chang, Yen-chin 張燕瑾, ed. *Hsi-hsiang chi* 西廂記. *Chung-kuo ku-tien wen-hsüeh tu-pen ts'ung-shu.*

Peking: Jen-min Wen-hsüeh, 1995.

Chiang, Hsing-yü 蔣星煜. *Hsi-hsiang chi han-chien pan-pen k'ao* 西廂記罕見版本考. Tokyo: Fuji 不二, 1984.

Fu, Hsi-hua 傅惜華 (1907-1970), ed. *Hsi-hsiang shuo-ch'ang chi* 西廂記説唱集. Shanghai: Shang-hai Ku-chi, 1986.

Fu, Hsiao-hang 傅曉航, ed. *Hsi-hsiang chi chi-chieh* 西廂記集解. Lanchow: Kan-su Jen-min, 1989. Based on Ling Meng-ch'u's *Hsi-hsiang chi wu-pen chieh-cheng,* this text compares 7 texts and brings together their commentaries and explanations.

Fu, K'ai-p'ei 傅開沛 and Yüan Yü-ch'i 袁玉琦, ed. *Ti-ch'i ts'ai-tzu-shu, Hsi-hsiang chi.* Chengchow: Chung-chou Ku-chi, 1987. Collates several Ch'ing editions and notes differences.

Wang, Chi-ssu 王季思 and Chang Jen-ho 張仁和, ed. *Chi-p'ing chiao-chu Hsi-hsiang chi.* Shanghai: Shang-hai Ku-chi, 1987. Brings together most traditional commentaries; appends related (source) texts and bibliography.

Editions, References

Wang Shih-fu 王實甫. *Chi-p'ing chiao-chu Hsi-hsiang chi* 集評校註西廂記. Wang Chi-ssu 王季思, annotator. Chang Jen-ho 張人和, compiler. Shanghai: Shang-hai Ku-chi, 1987.

Translations

Idema, Wilt L. and Stephen H. West. *The Moon and the Zither: The Story of the West Wing by Wang Shifu.* Berkeley: University of California Press, 1991.

Studies

Chang, Kuo-kuang 張國光, ed. *Chin Sheng-t'an p'i-pen Hsi-hsiang chi.* Shanghai: Shang-hai Ku-chi, 1986. Traces the development of *Hsi-hsiang chi* and compares several editions.

Chiang, Hsing-yü 蔣星煜. "Lun Chu Su-ch'en chiao-ting pen 'Hsi-hsiang chi yen-chü'" 論朱素臣校訂本西廂記演劇, *Wen-hsüeh i-ch'an* 1983.4: 132-141.

Chiang, Hsing-yü 蔣星煜, ed. *Hsi-hsiang chi k'ao-cheng* 西廂記考證. Shanghai: Shang-hai Ku-chi, 1988. Collects 20 studies divided into 3 categories: Ming and Ch'ing editions, date of composition and authorship, and the interrelationship with fictional accounts.

Chiang, Hsing-yü 蔣星煜. *Hsi-hsiang chi te wen-hsien hsüeh yen-chiu* 西廂記的文獻學研究. Shanghai: Shang-hai Ku-chi, 1997.

Church, Sally Kathryn. "Jin Shengt'an's Commentary on the 'Xixiang ji' (The Romance of the Western Chamber)." Unpublished Ph. D. dissertation, Harvard University, 1993.

Dolby, William. "Wang Shifu's Influence and Reputation." *Ming Qing yanjiu* 3 (1994): 19-45.

Huo, Sung-lin 霍松林, ed. *Hsi-hsiang hui-pien* 西廂匯編. Tsinan: Shang-tung Wen-i, 1987. Collection of various works in the "West Chamber" story complex beginning with Yüan Chen's 元稹 "Ying-ying chuan" 鶯鶯傳.

Ye, Tan. "The Presentation of Love Idols: A Comparison between 'The Romance of the Western Chamber' and 'Romeo and Juliet.'" Unpublished Ph. D. dissertation, Washington University, 1991.

Hsi K'ang 嵇康 (223–262 or 224-263)

Editions and References

Wu, Hsiu-ch'eng 武秀成, ed. *Hsi K'ang shih-wen hsüan-i* 嵇康詩文選譯. Chengtu: Pa-Shu Shu-she, 1991.

Studies

Chuang, Wan-shou 莊萬壽. *Hsi K'ang yen-chiu chi nien-p'u* 嵇康研究及年譜. Taipei: Hsüeh-sheng, 1990.

Egan, Ronald. "The Controversy over Music and 'Sadness' and Changing Conceptions of the Qin in Middle Period China," *HJAS* 57 (1997): 5-66.

Hsi-k'ung ch'ou-ch'ang chi 西崑酬唱集 (**Anthology of Poems Exchanged in the Hsi-k'un Archives**)

Editions and References

Cheng, Tsai-shih 鄭再時, ed. *Hsi-k'ung ch'ou-ch'ang chi chien-chu* 西崑酬唱集箋注. 2v. Tsinan: Ch'i-Lu Shu-she, 1986.

Hsi-yu chi 西遊記 (**Journey to the West**)

Editions and References

Chen-fu Chü-shih 貞复居士. *Hsü Hsi-yu chi* 續西遊記. Nanking: Chiang-su Wen-i, 1986.

Ch'en, Hsien-hsing 陳先行 and Pao Yü-fei 包于飛, eds. *Hsi-yu chi—Li Cho-wu p'ing-pen (shang, hsia)* 西遊記—李卓吾評本（上，下）. 2v. Shanghai: Shang-hai Ku-chi, 1994.

Chiang, Shih-tung 姜世棟 *et al.*, eds. *"San-kuo yen-i," "Shui-hu chuan," "Hsi-yu chi" shih-tz'u chu-hsi* 三國演義水滸傳西遊記詩詞注析. Harbin: Ha-erh-pin Ch'u-pan-she, 1993.

Chu, I-hsüan 朱一玄 and Liu Yü-ch'en 劉毓忱, ed. *Hsi-yu chi tzu-liao hui-pien* 西遊記資料彙編. Chengchow: Chung-chou, 1983.

Chu, T'ung 朱彤 and Chou Chung-ming 周中明, ed. *Hsi-yu chi* 西遊記. Chengtu: Ssu-ch'uan Wen-i, 1987.

Ch'ü, Hsiao-ch'iang 屈小強. *Hsi-yu chi chung te hsüan-an* 西遊記中的懸案. Chengtu: Ssu-ch'uan Jen-min, 1994.

Liu, Hsiu-yeh 劉修業, ed. *Wu Ch'eng-en shih-wen chi* 吳承恩詩文集. Shanghai: Ku-tien Wen-hsüeh, 1958.

Liu, Yin-po 劉陰柏, ed. *Hsi-yu chi yen-chiu tzu-liao* 西遊記研究資料. Shanghai: Shang-hai Ku-chi, 1990; rpt. Taipei: Wen-chin, 1995.

Shun, Haruo 荀春夫. *Saiyûki shigo kaishaku* 西遊記詞語准譯. Tokyo: Daitô Bunka Daigaku Chûgokugo Daijiten Hensanshitsu, 1983.

Tseng, Shang-yen 曾上炎. *Hsi-yu chi tz'u-tien* 西遊記辭典. Chengchow: Ho-nan Jen-min, 1994.

Translations

Jenner, W. J. F. *Journey to the West.* V. I. Peking: Foreign Languages Press, 1990.

Jenner, W. J. F. *Journey to the West.* Peking: Foreign Languages Press, 1982-86.

Lévy, André. *Le pérégrination vers l'ouest = Xiyouji.* 10v. Paris: Gallimard, 1991. A reliable, scholarly rendition by one of the leading scholars of vernacular fiction.

Lin, Shuen-fu. *The Tower of Myriad Mirrors: A Supplement to "Journey to the West" by Yüeh Tung (1620-1686).* Berkeley: Asian Humanities Press, 1988.

Nakano, Miyoko 中野美代子. *Saiyûki* 西遊記. V. 1-8. Tokyo: Iwanami Shoten, 1985-1995.

Ono, Shinobu 小野忍 *et al.* Saiyûki 西遊記, 1-10. Tokyo: Iwanami Shoten Iwanami Bunko 1977-.

Ôta, Tatsuo 太田辰夫 and Torii Hisayasu 鳥居久靖. *Saiyûki* 西遊記. Tokyo: Heibonsha, 1994.

Perront, Nadine. *Pérégrinations vers d'est de Wu Yuantai.* Paris: Gallimard, 1993.

Seaman, Gary. *Journey to the North, An Ethnohistorical Analysis and Annotated Translation of the Chinese Folk Novel Pei-yu-chi.* Berkeley: University of California Press, 1987.

Comparison of *Pei-yu chi* and *Hsi-yu chi*.

Wu, Yuantai. *Pérégrination vers l'Est*. Paris: Gallimard, 1993.

Studies

Andres, Mark F. "Ch'an Symbolism in *Hsi-yu pu:* The Enlightenment of Monkey." *TkR* 20 (1989): 23-44.

Bantly, Francisca Cho. "Buddhist Allegory in the *Journey to the West*." *JAS* 49 (1989): 512-24.

Brandauer, Frederick P. "The Significance of a Dog's Tail: Comments on the *Xu Xihou ji*" *JAOS* 113 (1993): 418-22.

Campany, Robert F. "Demons, Gods and Pilgrims: The Demonology of the *Hsi-yu chi*." *CLEAR* 7 (1985): 95-115.

Chang, Chin-ch'ih 張錦池. *Chung-kuo ssu-ta ku-tien hsiao-shuo lun-kao* 中國四大古典小説論稿. Peking: Hua-i, 1993.

Chang, Ching-erh 張敬二. *Hsi-yu chi jen-wu yen-chiu* 西游記人物研究. Taipei: Hsüeh-sheng, 1984.

Chiang-su She-hui K'o-hsüeh Yüan, ed. *Hsi-yu chi yen-chiu* 西游記研究. Nanking: Chiang-su Ku-chi, 1984.

Despeux, Catherine. "Les lectures alchimiques du *Hsi-yu chi*." In *Religion und Philosophie in Ostasien, Festschrift für Hans Steininger*. Gert Naudorf, Karl-Heinz Pohl, and Hans-Hermann Schmidt, eds. Würzburg: Königshausen and Neumann, 1985, pp. 61-76.

Dudbridge, Glen. "The *Hsi-yu Chi* Monkey and the Fruits of the Last Ten Years." *Han-hsüeh yen-chiu* 6 (1988): 463-86.

Isobe, Akira 磯部彰. *'Saiyûki' juyô shi no kenkyû* 『西遊記』受容史の研究. Tokyo: Taga Shuppan, 1995.

___. *Seiyuki keiseishi no kenkyû* 西遊記形成史の研究. Tokyo: Sôbunsha 創文社, 1993.

Li, Shih-jen 李時人. *Hsi-yu chi k'ao-lun* 西游記考論. Hangchow: Che-chiang Ku-chi, 1991.

Li, Wai-yee. *The Story of Stone: Intertextuality, Ancient Chinese Stone Lore, and the Stone Symbolism in Dream of the Red Chamber, Water Margin, and the Journey to the West*. Durham, N.C.: Duke University Press, 1992.

Lin, Pao-ch'un 林保淳. "Hou Hsi-yu chi lüeh-lun." *Chung-wai wen-hsüeh* 14 (1985): 49-67.

Liu, Xiaolian. "A Journey of the Mind: The Basic Allegory in the *Hou Xiyou ji*," *CLEAR* 13 (1991): 35-56.

___. *The Odyssey of the Buddhist Mind, The Allegory of the Later Journey to the West*. Lanham, Maryland: University Press of America, 1994. A study of allegory in *Hou Hsi-yu chi* 後西游記 with an appended synopsis of the novel and a study of its authorship.

Liu, Yung-ch'iang 劉勇強. *Hsi-yu chi lun-yao* 西游記論要. Taipei: Wen-chin, 1991. A revised version of his dissertation, Peking University, 1988.

Mair, Victor H... "Suen Wu-kung=Hanumat? The Progress of a Scholarly Debate." In *Chung-yang Yen-chiu Yüan, Ti-erh-chieh Kuo-chi Han-hsüeh Hui-i lun-wen-chi*. Taipei: Academia Sinica, 1989, pp. 659-752.

___. "Parallels between Some Tun-huang Manuscripts and the 17th Chapter of the Kôzanji Journey to the West," *Cahiers d'Extrême-Asie* 3 (1987): 41-54.

Nakano, Miyoko 中野美代子. *Son Gokû no tanjô–Saru no minwa gaku to 'Saiyûki'* 孫悟空の誕生–サルの民話学と「西遊記」. Tokyo: Fukutake Shoten, 1987.

Ôta, Tatsuo 太田辰夫. *Saiyûki no kenkyû* 西遊記の研究. Tokyo: Kenbun Shuppan, 1984.

Plaks, Andrew H. *The Four Masterworks of the Ming Novel: Ssu ta ch'i-shu*. Princeton: Princeton University Press, 1987.

Ptak, Roderich. "*Hsi-yang chi*–An Interpretation and Some Comparisons with *Hsi-yu chi*," *CLEAR* 7 (1985): 117-41.

Seaman, Gary. "The Divine Authorship of *Pei-yu chi*," *JAS* 45 (1986): 483-97.

___. *Journey to the North, An Ethnohistorical Analysis and Annotated Translation of the Chinese Folk*

Novel Pei-yu-chi. Berkeley: University of California Press, 1987. Comparison of *Pei-yu chi* and *Hsi-yu chi.*

Shahar, Meir. "The Lingyin Si Monkey Disciples and the Origins of Sun Wukong." *HJAS* 52 (1992): 192-224.

Wang, Jing. *The Story of Stone—Intertextuality, Ancient Chinese Stone Lore and the Stone Symbolism of Dream of the Red Chamber, Water Margin, and the Journey to the West.* Durham, N.C.: Duke University Press, 1992.

Widmer, Ellen. "*Hsi-yu Cheng-tao Shu* in the Context of Wang Ch'i's Publishing Enterprise," *Han-hsüeh yen-chiu* 6 (1988): 37-64.

Wu, Kuai-hsi 吳怪昔. "*Hsi-yu chi* Shih-pen san-t'i" 西遊記世本三題, *Ku-chi cheng-li yen-chiu hsüeh-k'an* 57 (1995): 18-21.

Yu, Anthony C. "Religion and Literature in China: The 'Obscure Way' of *The Journey to the West*" In *Tradition and Creativity: Essays on East Asian Civilization.* Ching-I Tu, ed. New Brunswick: Transaction, 1987.

Zhou, Zuyan. "Carnivalization in *The Journey to the West:* Cultural Dialogism in Fictional Festivity," *CLEAR* 16 (1994): 69-92.

Hsi-yu pu 西遊補 (Supplement to Journey to the West)

Editions and References

Tung, Yüeh 董説. *Hsi-yu pu* 西遊補. Shanghai: Shang-hai Ku-chi, 1983.

Studies

Fu, Shih-i 傅世怡. *Hsi-yu pu ch'u-t'an* 西遊補初探. *Chung-kuo hsiao-shuo yen-chiu ts'ung-k'an,* Taipei: Hsüeh-sheng, 1986.

Andres, Mark Francis, "New Perspectives on Two Late Ming Novels: 'Hsi-yu pu' and 'Jou p'u t'uan.'" MA thesis, U of Arizona, 1988.

___. "Ch'an Symbolism in Hsi-yu Pu: The Enlightenment of Monkey," *TkR* 20.1 (Autumn 1989): 23-44.

Ch'en, Tung-chi 陳冬季. "Pien-hsing, huang-tan, yü hsiang-cheng: lun 'huang-tan' hsiao-shuo *Hsi-yu pu* de mei-hsüeh t'e-cheng" 變形，荒誕與象征—論荒誕小説西游補的美學特征 (Metamorphoses, Absurdity, and Symbolism: in the Esthetic Characteristics of the 'Absurd' Novel, *Supplement to Journey to the West*), *Ming Ch'ing hsiao-shuo yen-chiu* 12 (1989): 144-55.

Chu, Madeline. "Journey into Desire: Monkey's Secular Experience in the *Xiyoubu*," *JAOS* 117 (1997): 654-64.

Kao, Hung-chün 高洪鈞, "*Hsi-yu pu* tso-che shih-shei chih tsai-pien" 析遊補作者是誰之再辨 (A Re-discerning of the authorship of *Hsi-yu pu*), *Ming Ch'ing hsiao-shuo yen-chiu* 11 (1989): 238-245.

Kao, Karl S. Y., "A Tower of Myriad Mirrors: Theory and Practice of Narrative in the *Hsi-yu Pu.*" In *Wen-lin,* V. 2, pp. 205-242.

Hsi Yung-jen 嵇永仁 (1637–1676)

Editions and References

Hsi, Yung-jen 嵇永仁. *Yang-chou yün* 揚州雲. Shanghai: Shang-hai Ku-chi, 1986. *Ku-pen hsi-ch'ü ts'ung-k'an, Wu-chi,* 25. Based on a printed edition from the K'ang-hsi era (1662-1723) held in the Shanghai Library.

hsiao-shuo 小説

Editions and References

Chin, Hui 金輝, ed. *Chin Yung hsiao-shuo tz'u-tien* 金庸小説詞典. Peking?: Hua-ling 華齡, 1996.

Chung-kuo ku-tai hsiao-shuo pai-k'o chüan-shu 中國古代小説百科全書. Peking: Chung-kuo Ta Pai-k'o Ch'üan-shu, 1993.

Ku-pen hsiao-shuo ts'ung-k'an 古本小説叢刊. Peking: Chung-hua, 1987-.

Li, Min-fa 李民發 and Hou Jun-chang 侯潤章, ed. *Chung-kuo chang-p'ien hsiao-shuo tz'u-tien* 中國長篇小説辭典. Lanchow: Tun-huang Wen-i, 1991.

Ou-yang, Chien 歐陽健, ed. *Chung-kuo t'ung-su hsiao-shuo tsung-mu t'i-yao* 中國通俗小説總目提要. Peking: Wen-lien, 1990. Useful and important reference.

Translations

Bauer, Wolfgang, trans. *Die Laiche im Strom—Die seltsame Kriminalfälle des Meisters Bao.* Freiburg: Herder, 1992.

Faithweather, Ian. *The Drunken Buddha.* Brisbane: University of Queensland Press, 1965.

Roberts, Yves. *L'Ivresse d'éveil—Faits et gestes de Ji Gong, le monie fou; Roman bouddhique.* Paris: Les deux Océans, 1989.

Studies

Chan, Tak-hung Leo. "'To Admonish and Exhort': The Didactics of the *Zhiguai* Tale in Ji Yun's 'Yuewei caotang biji.'" Unpublished Ph. D. dissertation, Indiana Univ., 1991.

Inoue, Gengo 井上源吾. *Chûgoku kodai no setsuwa* 中国古代の説話. Fukuoka: Ashi Shobô 葦書房, 1993.

Kominami, Ichirô 小南一郎. "Go kara setsu e—Chûgoku ni okeru 'shôsetsu' no kigen o megutte" 語から説へ—中国における小説の起源をめぐって, *Chûgoku bungakuhô,* 50 (1995): 1-9.

Liu, Yin-po 劉蔭柏. *Chung-kuo wu-hsia hsiao-shuo shih, Ku-tai pu-fen* 中國武俠小説史，古代部分. Shih-chia-chuang: Hua-shan Wen-i, 1992.

Lo, Li-ch'un 羅立群. *Chung-kuo wu-hsia hsiao-shuo* 中國武俠小説. Shenyang: Liao-ning Jen-min, 1990.

Nienhauser, William H., Jr. *Chuan-chi yü hsiao-shuo: T'ang-tai wen-hsüeh lun-wen chi* 傳紀與小説：唐代文學論文集. Taipei: Southern Materials, 1995. Contain articles on early fiction and its relation with history.

___. "The Origins of Chinese Fiction," *MS* 38 (1988-89): 191-219.

Shih, Ch'ang-yü 石昌渝. *Chung-kuo hsiao-shuo yüan-liu lun* 中國小説源流論. *Ha-fo Yen-ching hsüeh-shu ts'ung-shu,* ed. Lü Hsiang ßf≤ª. Hong Kong: Joint Publications, 1994.

Wu, Laura Hua. "From *Xiaoshuo* to Fiction: Hu Yinglin's Genre Study of *Xiaoshuo,*" *HJAS* 55 (1995): 339-371.

Yüan, Hsing-p'ei 袁行霈. *"Han shu* "I-wen chih" hsiao-shuo k'ao-pien" 漢書藝文志小説考辨, *Wen-shih* 7 (1979): 179-189.

Zißler-Gürtler, Dagmar. *Nicht erzählte Welt noch Welterklärung, der Begriff "Hsiao-shuo" in der Han-Zeit.* Bad Honnef: Bock and Herchen, 1994. Review by R. Emmerich in *OLZ* 90 (1995): 585-90.

Hsiao Ying-shih 蕭穎士 (717–758 or 708?–759)

Studies

Ch'en, T'ieh-min 陳鐵民. "Hsiao Ying-shih hsi-nien k'ao-cheng" 蕭穎士繫年考證, *Wen-shih*

37 (1993): 187-212.

Yüeh, Chi-tung 俞紀東. "Hsiao Ying-shih shih-chi k'ao" 蕭穎士事跡考, *Chung-hua wen-shih lun-ts'ung*, 1983.2.

Hsieh Hui-lien 謝惠連 (379–433)

Editions and References

T'ang, Keng 唐庚 (1071-1121), ed. *San Hsieh shih* 三謝詩. Shanghai: Shang-hai Ku-chi, 1983. Collected works of Hsieh Hui-lien, Hsieh Ling-yün, and Hsieh T'iao. Based on a Sung edition.

Studies

Yamamoto, Seiji 山本誠司. "Sha Keiren no shifu ni tsuite" 謝惠連の詩風について. *Chûgoku shibun ronsô* 7(1988): 102-115.

Hsieh Ling-yün 謝靈運 (385–433)

Editions and References

Ku, Shao-po 顧紹柏. *Hsieh Ling-yün chi chiao-chu* 謝靈運集校注. Chengchow: Chung-chou Ku-chi, 1987. Several useful appendixes including a bibliography.

T'ang, Keng 唐庚 (1071-1121), ed. *San Hsieh shih* 三謝詩. Shanghai: Shang-hai Ku-chi, 1983. Collected works of Hsieh Hui-lien, Hsieh Ling-yün, and Hsieh T'iao. Based on a Sung edition.

Wang, Shao-tseng 王紹曾 and Liu Hsin-ming 劉心明, comm. *Hsieh Ling-yün, Pao Chao shih hsüan-i* 謝靈運, 鮑照詩選譯. Chengtu: Pa-Shu Shu-she, 1991.

Translation

Morino, Shigeo, trans. 森野繁夫. *Sha Senjô shishû* 謝宣城詩集. 2v. Tokyo: Hakuteisha, 1991 and 1994.

Ono, Shigeo 小野茂夫. *Sha Kôraku shishû* 謝康楽詩集. Tokyo: Hakuteisha, 1995.

Studies

Ch'en, Mei-tzu 陳美足. *Nan-chao Yen-Hsieh shih yen-chiu* 南朝顏謝詩研究. Taipei: Wen-chin, 1989.

Ch'ien, Chih-hsi 錢志熙. "Hsieh Ling-yün pien-tsung lun he shan-shui shih" 謝靈運辨宗論和山水詩. *Pei-ching Ta-hsüeh hsüeh-pao 135* (1989): 39-46.

Chang, Kuo-hsing 張國星. "Fo-hsüeh yü Hsieh Ling-yün te shan-shui shih" 佛學與謝靈運的山水詩. *Hsüeh-shu Yüeh-k'an 210* (1986): 60–67.

Chang, Kang-i Sun 長孫康宜. "Hsieh Ling-yün: The Making of a New Descriptive Code." In *Six Dynasties Poetry*, 47–78. Princeton: Princeton University Press, 1986, pp. 47-78.

Chao, Ch'ang-p'ing 趙昌平. "Hsieh Ling-yün yü shan-shui shih ch'i-yüan" 謝靈運與山水詩起源. *Chung-kuo She-hui k'o-hsüeh 64* (1990): 79–94.

Chou, Hsün-ch'u 周勛初. "Lun Hsieh Ling-yün shan-shui wen-hsüeh te chuang-tso ching-yen." *Wen-hsüeh i-ch'an* 1989.5.

Kan, Genshu 乾源俊. "Sha Reiun to Sha Cho 謝靈運と謝朓." *Shukan Tôyôgaku 59* (1988): 20-37.

Li, Hai-yüan 李海元. "Hsieh Ling-yün yü Pao Chao shan-shui shih yen-chiu" 謝靈運與鮑照山水詩研究. M.A. thesis, Cheng-chih Ta-hsüeh, 1987.

Li, Kuang-che 李光哲. "Hsieh Ling-yün shih yung-tien k'ao-lun" 謝靈運詩用典考論.

Unpublished Ph. D. dissertation, National Taiwan University, 1987.

Li, Sen-nan 李森南. *Shan-shui shih-jen Hsieh Ling-yün* 山水詩人謝靈運. Taipei: Wen-shih-che, 1989.

Lin, Wen-yung 林文用. "Hsieh Ling-yün lin-chung shih k'ao-lun" 謝靈運臨終詩考論. In *Chung-yang Yen-chiu-yüan Kuo-chi Han-hsüeh hui-i* 中央研究院國際漢學會議 *in Academia Sinica, Taipei,*, 839–854, 1989.

Makikado, Etsuko 牧角悦子. "Sha Reiun shi kô" 謝靈運詩考, *Bungaku kenkyû 84* (1987): 99-131.

Morino, Shigeo 森野繁夫. "Sha Reiun 'Sankyo fu' ni tsuite (jô)" 謝霊運『山居賦』について (上), *Hiroshima Daigaku Bungakubu kiyô* 52 (1992): 22-45.

Shen, Chen-ch'i 沈振奇. *T'ao-Hsieh shih chih pi-chiao* 陶謝詩之比較. Taipei: Hsüeh-sheng Shu-chü, 1986.

Shen, Yü-ch'eng 沈玉成. "Hsieh Ling-yün te cheng-chih t'ai-tu he ssu-hsiang hsing-ko" 謝靈運的政治態度和思想□格. *She-hui k'o-hsüeh chan-hsien 38* (1987): 259–270.

Tsang, Ch'ing 臧清. "Shih-lun Hsieh Ling-yün ch'uang-tso shan-shui shih te she-hui t'iao-chien he shen mei shin-li" 試論謝靈運創作山水詩的社會條件和審美心理. *Pei-ching Ta-hsüeh hsüeh-pao 141* (1990): 28–34.

Wang, Kuo-ying 王國瓔. "Hsieh Ling-yün shan-shui shih chung te you he you" 謝靈運山水詩的憂和遊. *Han-hsüeh yen-chiu 5: 1* (1987): 161–181.

Wang, Tz'u-teng 王次澄. "Hsieh Ling-yün chi ch'i shih" 謝靈運及其詩. *Tung-wu Wen-shih hsüeh-pao 6* (1988): 45–74.

Yin, Hai-kuo 殷海國. *Hsieh Ling-yün, Hsieh Tiao shih hsüan-chu: shan shui shih chi pa* 謝靈運謝朓詩選注：山水詩之跋. Chengchow: Chung-chou Ku-chi, 1989.

Hsieh T'iao 謝朓 (464–499)

Editions and References

Hsieh, T'iao 謝朓. *Hsieh Hsüan-ch'eng chi chiao-chu* 謝宣城集校注. Shanghai: Shang-hai Ku-chi, 1991. *Chung-kuo ku-tien wen-hsüeh ts'ung-shu.*

T'ang, Keng 唐庚 (1071-1121), ed. *San Hsieh shih* 三謝詩. Shanghai: Shang-hai Ku-chi, 1983. Collected works of Hsieh Hui-lien, Hsieh Ling-yün, and Hsieh T'iao. Based on a Sung edition.

Translations

Morino, Shigeo 森野繁夫. *Sha Senjô shishû* 謝宣城詩集. Tokyo: Hakuteisha 1991.

Studies

Chang, Kang-i Sun 長孫康宜. "Hsieh T'iao: The Inward Turn of Landscape," in *Six Dynasties Poetry,* pp. 112-144.

Chou, Chao-ming. "Hsieh T'iao and the Transformation of Five-Character Poetry." Unpublished Ph. D. dissertation, Princeton University, 1986.

Morino, Shigeo 森野繁夫. "Sha Chô kenkyû– Senjôgun ni okeru Sha Chô" 謝朓研究–宣城郡における謝朓, *Chûgoku Chûsei Bungaku kenkyû* 22 (1992): 39-57.

Hsin Ch'i-chi 辛棄疾 (1140–1207)

Editions and References

Hsin, Ch'i-chi 辛棄疾. *A-chi-t'i chuan* 阿計替傳. 1 *chüan*. Chengtu: Pa-Shu Shu-she, 1993. *Chung-kuo yeh-shih chi-ch'eng* 中國野史集成, 6. This reprint of the *Hsüeh-hai lei-pien*

學海類編 edition also includes other similar works by Hsin such as *Nan-tu lu* 南渡錄.

___. *Hsin Ch'i-chi ch'üan-chi* 辛棄疾全集. Hsü Han-ming 徐漢明, ed. Chengtu: Ssu-ch'uan Wen-i, 1997. Modern critical edition of Hsin's collected works.

___. *Mei ch'in shih lun* 美芹十論. Peking: Chieh-fang-chün, 1992.

Hsü, Han-ming 徐漢明, ed. *Chia-hsüan chi* 稼軒集. Wuhan: Ch'ang-chiang Wen-i, 1990. Appends a biography of Hsin Ch'i-chi, traditional prefaces to this collection, and comments on his lyrics by important traditional critics.

Liu, Yang-chung 劉揚忠. *Chia-hsüan tz'u pai-shou i-hsi* 稼軒詞百首譯析. Shih-chia-chuang: Hua-shan Wen-i, 1983.

Teng, Kuang-ming 鄧廣銘. *Chia-hsüan chi pien-nien chien-chu* 稼軒集編年箋注. Shanghai: Shang-hai Ku-chi, 1993.

Yang, Chung 楊忠, comm. *Hsin Ch'i-chi tz'u hsüan-i* 辛棄疾詞選譯. Chengtu: Pa-Shu Shu-she, 1991.

Studies

Landau, *Beyond Spring,* pp. 184-199.

Hsü Fu-tso 徐復祚 (1560–after 1630)

Editions and References

Chiang, Chih 姜智 and Li Fu-po 李復波, eds. *Hung-li chi, Hsi-lou chi* 紅梨記，西樓記. Peking: Chung-hua, 1988. *Ming Ch'ing ch'uan-ch'i hsüan-k'an* 明清傳奇選刊. Collated versions of these two plays by Hsü and Yüan Yü-ling 袁于令 (1592-1674) respectively.

Hsü, Fu-tso 徐復祚. *Ch'ü lun* 曲論. 1 *chüan.* Peking: Chung-kuo Hsi-chü, 1959.

Hsü Wei 徐渭 (1521–1593)

Editions and References

Chou, Chung-ming 周中明, ed. *Ssu-sheng yüan, Ko-tai hsiao (fu)* 四聲猿，歌代嘯（附）. Shanghai: Shang-hai Ku-chi, 1984. After some useful introductory matter, provides careful annotation.

Hsü, Wei 徐渭. *Hsü Wei chi* 徐渭集. 4v. *Chung-kuo ku-tien wen-hsüeh chi-pen ts'ung-shu* 中國古典文學基本叢書. Peking: Chung-hua, 1983.

___. *I-chih T'ang kao* 一枝堂稿. Tokyo: Takahashi Seihô 高橋情報, 1990. Based on a Ming Wan-li era (1573-1619) edition held in the Naikaku Bunkô.

___. *Ming Hsü Wei ts'ao-shu shih-chüan* 明徐渭草書詩卷. Peking: Wen-wu, 1982.

___. *Ying-lieh ch'üan-chuan* 英烈全傳. Peking?: Hua-hsia, 1995.

Li, Fu-po 李復波 and Hsiung Ch'eng-yü 熊澄宇, comm. *Nan-tz'u hsü-lu chu-shih* 南詞敍錄注釋. Peking: Chung-kuo Hsi-chü, 1989.

Translations

Leung, K.C. *Hsu Wei as Drama Critic—An Annotated Translation of the Nan-tz'u hsü-lu.* Eugene: University of Oregon, 1988.

Studies

Ch'eng, I-chung 程毅中. "Hsü Wei chi ch'i 'Ssu-sheng yüan'" 徐渭及其四聲猿. *Wen-hsüeh i-ch'an* 1984.1: 120-5.

Lo, Yü-ming 羅玉明 and Ho Sheng-sui 賀聖遂. *Hsü Wen-chang/ch'ang p'ing-chuan* 徐文長評

傳. Hangchow: Che-chiang Ku-chi, 1987.

Hsüan-ho i-shih 宣和遺事 (Past Events of the Hsüan-ho Period)

Editions and References
Ts'ao, Chi-p'ing 曹濟平, ed. *Hsüan-ho i-shih teng liang-chung* 宣和遺事等兩種. Nanking: Chiang-su Ku-chi, 1993. Contains *Hsüan-ho i-shih* and *Hsin-pien Wu-tai shih p'ing-hua* 新編五代史平話.

Studies
Hennessey, William O. "Classical Sources and Vernacular Resources in *Xuanhe yishi:* The Presence of Priority and the Priority of Presence," *CLEAR* 6 (1984): 33-52.

Hsüeh T'ao 薛濤 (768–831 or 770-832)

Editions and References
Ch'en, Wen-hua 陳文華, ed. *T'ang nü shih-jen chi san-chung* 唐女詩人集三種. Shanghai: Shang-hai Ku-chi, 1984. Collects poems by Hsüeh T'ao, Li Yeh 李冶, and Yü Hsüan-chi 魚玄機.
Hsüeh T'ao, Li Yeh shih-chi 薛濤, 李冶. Taipei: T'ai-wan Shang-wu, 1983. *Ssu-k'u.*

Translations
Lorain, Pierre. *Hsüeh T'ao, un torrent de montagne.* Paris: Editions Orphée/La différence, 1992.

Studies
Chang, P'eng-chou 張篷舟. "Hsüeh T'ao sheng-tsu chiu ho nien" 薛濤生卒究何年, *Tu-shu* 1982.9. Concludes she was born in 770 and died in 832.

Hu Ying-lin 胡應麟 (1551–1602)

Editions and References
Hu, Ying-lin 胡應麟. *Chia-i sheng yen* 甲乙剩言. 1 *chüan.* Taipei: Hsin-hsing, 1989. *Pi-chi hsiao-shuo ta-kuan,* 4 pien 編, 6.

Studies
Ch'en, Kuo-ch'iu 陳國球. *Hu Ying-lin shih-lun yen-chiu* 胡應麟詩論研究. Hong Kong: Hua-feng Shu-chü, 1986.
Tschanz, Dieter. "Ein illegitimes Genre: Zu den Auseinandersetzungen um die fictionale Literatur in niederer Literatursprache im vormodernen China, 1550-1750; Eine Dokumention." Unpublished M. A. thesis, Zurich University, 1990.
Wu, Laura Hua. "From *Xiaoshuo* to Fiction: Hu Yinglin's Genre Study of *Xiaoshuo,*" *HJAS* 55 (1995): 339-371.

Hua-chien chi 花間集 (Among the Flowers Collection)

Editions and References
Hua-chien chi 花間集. Chengchow: Chung-chou Ku-chi, 1990. Also includes the *tz'u* collection

329

Chüeh miao-hao tz'u chien 絕妙好詞箋; reprint of the Kuo-hsüeh Cheng-li She 國學整理社 edition of 1935.

Hua-chien chi chu-shih 花間集全譯. Kweiyang: Kuei-chou Jen-min, 1990.

Hua-chien tz'u-p'ai hsüan-chi 花間詞派選集. Wang Hsin-hsia 王新霞, ed. Peking: Pei-ching Shih-yüan, 1993.

Li, I 李誼, ed. *Hua-chien chi chu-shih* 花間集注釋. Chengtu: Ssu-ch'uan Wen-i, 1986. Appends traditional comments on *Hua-chien chi* and a bibliography.

Li, Ping-jo 李冰若, comm. *Hua-chien chi p'ing-chu* 花間集評注. Peking: Jen-min Wen-hsüeh, 1993.

Studies

Chang, I-jen 張以仁. "*Hua-chien* tz'u chiu-shuo shang-chüeh" 花間詞舊說商榷. *Han-hsüeh yen-chiu* 13 (1995): 207-22.

___, ed. *Hua-chien tz'u lun-chi* 花間詞論集. Nankang: Wen-che So, Academia Sinica, 1997.

Chang, Shih-ming 張式　"Lun 'Hua-chien tz'u' te ch'uang-tso ch'ing-hsiang" 論花間詞的創作傾向. *Wen-hsüeh i-ch'an* 1984.1.

Hua-pen 話本 (vernacular short story)

Editions and References

Hsiao, Hsiang-k'ai 蕭相愷 and Ou-yang Chien 歐陽健, eds. *Sung Yüan hua-pen tsung-chi; Sung Yüan shuo-ching hua-pen chi* 宋元話本總集宋元說經話本集. Chengchow: Chung-chou Ku-chi, 1990.

Translations

Huang, San and Jean Blasse. *Moines et nonnes dan l'océan des péchés*. Arles: Editions Picquier, 1992.

Lanselle, Rainer. *Le cheval de jade, quatre contes chinois du XVIIe siècle*. Paris: Editions Picquier, 1987.

___. *Le poisson de jade et l'épingle au phénix, Douze contes chinoise du XVIIe siècle*. Paris: Gallimard, 1987. Preface by André Lévy.

Rummel, Stefan. *Der Mönche und Nonnen Sündenmeer; Der buddhistische Klerus in der chinesichen Roman–und Erzählliteratur des 16. und 17. Jahrhunderts mit einer vollständigne Übersetzung der Sammlung Sengni Niehai* Bochum: Brockmeyer, 1992.

Studies

Chang, Ping 張兵. *Hua-pen hsiao-shuo shih-hua* 話本小說史話. Shenyang: Liao-ning Chiao-yü, 1992.

Dars, Jacques. *Contes de la Montagne Sereine*. Paris: Gallimard, 1987. Preface by Jeannine Kohn-Etiemble.

Hsia, Yün 夏耘. *Hua-pen hsiao-shuo* 話本小說. Peking: Chung-kuo Wen-i Lien-ho, 1984.

Hu, Wan-ch'uan 胡萬川. *Sung Ming hua-pen* 宋明話本. Taipei: Shih-pao Ch'u-pan Kung-ssu, 1987.

Hu, Shih-ying 胡士瑩. *Hua-pen hsiao-shuo kai-lun* 話本小說概論. Peking: Chung-hua, 1980.

Hu, Wan-ch'uan 胡萬川. *Hua-pen yü Ts'ai-tzu chia-jen hsiao-shuo chih yen-chiu* 話本與才子佳人小說言究. Taipei: Ta-an, 1994.

Lauwaert, Francoise. "Comptes des dieux, calculs des hommes: essai sur la rétribution dans les contes en langue vulgaire de 17e siècle." *TP* 76 (1990): 62-94.

___. "La mauvaise graine: Le gendre adopté dans le conte d'imitation de la fin des Ming," *Études chinoises* 12 (1993): 51-94.

Lévy, André and Michel Cartier. *Inventaire analytique et critique du conte chinois en langue vulgaire, Tome quatrième.* Paris: Collège de France, 1991. Selections from *Hsi-hu erh-chi* and other collections with the collaboration of Rainier Lanselle.

Ou-Yang, Tai-fa 歐陽代發. *Hua-pen hsiao-shuo shih* 話本小説史. Wuhan: Wu-han Ch'u-pan-she, 1994.

Satô, Haruhiko 佐藤晴彦. *"Seisei kôgen to Seki ten tô–Hanan Shi setsu no kentô"* 「醒世恒言」と「石点頭」–Hanan 氏説の検討, *Chûgokugo-shi no shiryô to hôhô*, 1994: 225-253.

T'an, Cheng-pi 譚正璧 and T'an Hsün 譚尋. *Hua-pen yü ku-chü (Ch'ung-ting pen)* 話本與古劇 (重訂本). Shanghai: Shang-hai Ku-chi, 1985.

Teng, Shao-chi 鄧紹基, ed. *Ming Ch'ing hsiao-shuo ching-p'in* 明清小説精品. Peking: Shih-tai Wen-i, 1995.

Wu, Yenna. "The Bean Arbor Frame: Actual and Figural." *JCLTA* 30 (1995): 1-32.

Yeh, Kuei-kang 葉桂剛 *et al.*, eds. *Chung-kuo ku-tai chu-ming hua-pen hsiao-shuo shang-hsi* 中國古代著名話本小説賞析. Peking: Pei-ching Kuang-po Hsüan-yüan, 1992.

Huang Ching-jen 黃景仁 (1749–1783)

Editions and References

Huang, Ch'ing-jen 黃景仁. *Liang-tang Hsüan chi* 兩當軒集. 22 *chüan; k'ao-i* 考異, 2 *chüan; fu-lu* 附錄, 6 *chüan*. Li, Kuo-chang 李國章, ed. Shanghai: Shang-hai Ku-chi, 1983.

Huang T'ing-chien 黃庭堅 (1045–1105)

Editions and References

Chu, An-ch'ün 朱安群 *et al.*, comm. *Huang T'ing-chien shih-wen hsüan-i* 黃庭堅詩文選譯. Chengtu: Pa-Shu Shu-she, 1991.

Ch'üan Sung shih, 17:979-1027.11330-11745.

Studies

Cheng, Yung-hsiao 鄭永曉. *Huang T'ing-chien nien-p'u hsin-pien* 黃庭堅年譜新編. Peking: K'o-hsüeh Wen-hsien, 1997.

Fu, Hsüan-ts'ung 傅璇琮. *Huang T'ing-chien ho Chiang-hsi Shih-p'ai chüan* 黃庭堅和江西詩派卷. 2v. Rpt. Peking: Chung-hua, 1993 (1978).

Palumbo-Liu, David. *The Poetics of Appropriation: The Theory and Practice of Huang Tingjian.* Stanford: Stanford University Press, 1993.

Huang Tsun-hsien 黃遵憲 (1848–1905)

Editions and References

Ch'ien, Chung-lien 錢仲聯, comm. *Jen-ching Lu shih-ts'ao chien-chu* 人境廬詩草箋注. Shanghai: Ku-tien Wen-hsüeh, 1957.

Chung, Hsien-p'ei 鍾賢培 *et al.*, ed. *Huang Tsun-hsien shih-hsüan* 黃遵憲詩選. Rpt. Canton: Kuang-tung Jen-min, 1994 (1985).

Chung, Shu-ho 鍾叔河, ed. *Jih-pen tsa-shih shih kuang-chu* 日本雜事詩廣注. Changsha: Hu-nan Jen-min, 1981.

Ts'ao, Hsü 曹旭, ed. *Huang Tsun-hsien shih-hsüan* 黃遵憲詩選. Shanghai: Shang-hai Ku-chi, 1990.

Translations

Schmidt, J. D. *Within the Human Realm, The Poetry of Huang Zunxian, 1848-1905*. Cambridge: Cambridge University Press, 1994. A number of translations preceded by a 200-page biographical and critical introduction. See also Richard John Lynn's review, *China Review International* 3.2 (Fall 1996): 305-332.

Studies

Chang, T'ang-ch'i 張堂錡. *Huang Tsun-hsien chi ch'i shih yen-chiu* 黃遵憲及其詩研究. Taipei: Wen-shih-che, 1991.

Cheng, Hai-lin 鄭海麟 and Cheng Wei-hsiung 鄭偉雄, eds. *Huang Tsun-hsien wen-chi* 黃遵憲文集. Kyoto: Chûbun, 1991.

Cheng, Wu 鄭蕪, ed. *Huang Tsun-hsien yen-chiu* 黃遵憲研究. Canton, 1982.

Lynn, Richard John. "'This Culture of Ours' and Huang Zunxian's Literary Experiences in Japan (1877-82)." *CLEAR* 19 (1997): 113-138.

Schmidt, J. D. *Within the Human Realm* (see Translations above).

Wei, Chung-yu 魏仲佑. *Huang Tsun-hsien yü Ch'ing-mo 'Shih-chieh ko-ming'* 黃遵憲與清末世界革命. Taipei: Kuo-li Pien-i-kuan, 1994.

____. *Wan Ch'ing shih yen-chiu* 晚清詩研究. *Wen-shih-che Ta-hsi* 98, Taipei: Wen-chin, 1994. Chapters three and five treat the verse of Huang Tsun-hsien, chapter six that of Cheng Chen.

Hung Liang-chi 洪亮吉 (1746–1809)

Editions and References

Hung, Liang-chi 洪亮吉. *Ch'un-ch'iu, Tso-chuan ku* 春秋左傳詁. Li Chieh-min 李解民, ed. Peking: Chung-hua, 1987.

____. *Pei-chiang shih-hua* 北江詩話. Ch'en Erh-tung 陳邇冬, ed. Peking: Jen-min Wen-hsüeh, 1983.

Studies

Kataoka, Kazutada 片岡一忠. *Kô Ryôkichi den (shokô) (3)* 洪亮吉伝（初稿）（三）, *Rekishi jinrui* 22 (1994): 59-83.

Satô, Haruhiko 佐藤晴彦. *"Seisei kôgen to Seki ten tô*–Hanan Shi setsu no kentô" 「醒世恒言」と「石点頭」–Hanan 氏説の検討, *Chûgokugo-shi no shiryô to hôhô* 1994: 225-253.

Yen, Ming 嚴明. *Hung Liang-chi p'ing-chuan* 洪亮吉評傳. Taipei: Wen-chin, 1993.

Hung-lou meng 紅樓夢 (Dream of the Red Chamber)

Editions and References

Chang, Chün 張俊 *et al.,* comm. *Hung-lou meng* 紅樓夢. 4v. Kung Shu-to 龔書鐸, coll. Peking: Pei-ching Shih-fan Ta-hsüeh, 1987.

Chou, Ju-ch'ang 周汝昌, ed. *Hung-lou meng tz'u-tien* 紅樓夢辭典. Canton: Kuang-tung Jen-min, 1987.

Chou, Ting-i 周定一. *Hung-lou meng yü-yen tz'u-tien* 紅樓夢語言詞典. Peking: Shang-wu, 1995.

Chou, Yü-ch'ing 周玉清. *"Ts'ao-Chou pen" Hung-lou meng* 曹周本紅樓夢. Chengtu: Ssu-ch'uan Wen-i, 1997.

Chih-yen Chai ch'uan-pen Ts'ao Hsüeh-ch'in Shih-t'ou chi 脂硯齋傳本曹雪芹石頭記. 2v. Lao K'uei 老葵 (Chu Yung-k'uei 朱詠葵), ed. Peking: Wen-chin, 1988.

Chih-yen Chai ch'ung-p'ing Shih-t'ou chi 脂硯齋重評石頭記. Peking: Chung-hua, 1990. Based on a Ch'ien-lung era (1736-1796) mss. preserved by Hu Shih 胡適; contains chapters 1-8, 13-16 and 25-28.

Chu, I-hsüan 朱一玄, ed. *Hung-lou meng chih-p'ing chiao-lu* 紅樓夢脂評校錄. Tientsin: Ch'i-Lu Shu-she, 1986.

___, ed. *Hung-lou meng tzu-liao hui-pien* 紅樓夢資料會編. Tientsin: Nan-k'ai Ta-hsüeh, 1985.

Feng, Ch'i-yung 馮其庸, ed. *Chih-yen Chai ch'ung-p'ing Shih-t'ou chi hui-chiao* 脂硯齋重評石頭記彙校. Peking: Wen-hua I-shu, 1987-89.

Feng, Ch'i-yung 馮其庸 and Li Hsi-fan 李希凡, ed. *Hung-lou meng ta tz'u-tien* 紅樓夢大辭典. Peking: Wen-hua I-shu, 1990. Consists of two sections—the first arranged according to topic such as clothing, food, medicines, buildings, the second dealing with the author, editions, commentaries etc.; several useful appendixes including a list of characters in the novel.

Ho, Hsin-hui 賀新輝, ed. *Hung-lou meng shih-tz'u chien-shang tz'u-tien* 紅樓夢詩詞鑒賞詞典. Peking: Tzu-chin-ch'eng, 1990.

Hu, Wen-pin 胡文彬, ed. *Hung-lou meng shu-lu* 紅樓夢書錄. Changchun: Chi-lin Jen-min, 1980.

Hung-lou meng (San-chia p'ing pen) 紅樓夢（三家評本）. Shanghai: Shang-hai Ku-chi, 1988.

Hung-lou meng san-chia-p'ing pen 紅樓夢三家評本. Shanghai: Shang-hai Ku-chi, 1988.

Hung-lou meng tsui-hsin yen-chiu lun-chu mu-lu 紅樓夢最新研究論著目錄, *1982-1987*. Peking: Pei-ching Shih-fan Ta-hsüeh, 1988.

Jao, Pin 饒彬, ed. *Hung-lou meng* 紅樓夢. Rpt. Taipei: San-min, 1990 (1976). Appends an annotated glossary of terms in the novel.

Kao, Ko-tung 高歌東 and Chang Chih-ch'ing 張志清, eds. *Hung-lou meng ch'eng-yü tz'u-tien* 紅樓夢成語辭典. Tientsin: T'ien-chin She-hui K'o-hsüeh Yüan, 1997.

Ku, P'ing-tan 顧平旦, ed. *Hung-lou meng yen-chiu lun-wen tzu-liao so-yin* 紅樓夢研究論文資料索引, *1874-1982*. Peking: Shu-mu Wen-hsien, 1983.

Liu, Keng-lu 劉耕路, ed. *Hung-lou meng shih-tz'u chieh-hsi* 紅樓夢詩詞解析. Changchun: Chi-lin Wen-shih, 1986.

Mao, Te-piao 毛德彪, Chu Chün-t'ing 朱俊亭 *et al.*, eds. *Hung-lou meng chu-p'ing* 紅樓夢注評. Nanning: Kuang-hsi Chiao-yü, 1992.

Roku, Sôsei 鹿琮世 *et al.*, eds. *Kôrômu shigo kaushaku* ＜紅樓夢＞詞語匯譯. Tokyo: Daitô Bunka Daigaku Chûgokugo Daijiten Hensanshitsu, 1985,

Shang-hai Shih-fan Ta-hsüeh Wen-hsüeh Yen-chiu So, ed. *Hung-lou meng chien-shang tz'u-tien* 紅樓夢鑒賞辭典. Shanghai: Shang-hai Ku-chi, 1988.

Shen, P'ing-an 沈瓶庵 and Wang Meng-juan 王夢阮, eds. *Hung-lou meng so-yin* 紅樓夢索引. Peking: Pei-ching Ta-hsüeh, 1989.

Shih, Pao-i 施寶義 *et al.*, eds. *Hung-lou meng jen-wu tz'u-tien* 紅樓夢人物辭典. Nanning: Kuang-hsi Jen-min, 1989.

Shih-t'ou chi wei-yen 石頭記微言. 8v. Peking: Shu-mu Wen-hsien, 1996.

Ts'ai, I-chiang 蔡義江. *Hung-lou meng shih tz'u fu p'ing-chu* 紅樓夢詩詞賦評注. Peking: T'uan-chieh, 1991.

Wang, Meng-juan 王夢阮, ed. *Hung-lou meng so-yin* 紅樓夢索引. Peking: Pei-ching Ta-hsüeh, 1989.

Yang, Wei-chen 楊為珍 and Kuo Jung-kuang 郭榮光, ed. *Hung-lou meng tz'u-tien* 紅樓夢辭典. Tsinan: Shan-tung Wen-i, 1986.

Translations

Itô, Sôhei 伊藤漱平. *Kôrômu* 紅楼夢. 3v. Tokyo: Heibonsha, 1994.

Matsueda, Shigeo 松枝茂夫. *Kôrômu* 紅楼夢, 1-12. Tokyo: Iwanami Shoten, 1972-85.

Wong, Laurence Kwok Pun. "*A Study of the Literary Translations of the Honglou meng* with

Special Reference to David Hawkes' English Version." Ph.D., University of Toronto, 1992.

Studies

Chan, Hing-ho [Ch'en Ch'ing-hao] 陳慶浩. "Pa-shih-hui pen *Shih-t'ou chi* ch'eng-shu tsai-k'ao 八十回本石頭記成書再考," *THHP* 24.2 (June 1994): 241-62. Ch'en sees the creation of the novel in three stages: the original entitled *Feng-yüeh pao-chien* 風月寶鑑, a revised *Hung-lou meng*, and the final, but still incomplete, *Shih-t'ou chi*.

____. *Le Hongloumeng et les commentaires de Zhiyanzhai.* Paris: Collège de France, Institut des Hautes Études Chinoises,1982.

____. "Pa-shih-hui pen *Shih-t'ou chi* ch'eng-shu ch'u-k'ao" 八十回本石頭記成書初考, *Wen-hsüeh i-ch'an*, 1992.2: 80-92.

____. "Pa-shih-hui pen *Shih-t'ou chi* ch'eng-shu tsai-k'ao" 八十回本石頭記成書再考, *THHP* 24.2 (1994): 241-262.

Chang, Chih 張之. *Hung-lou meng hsin-p'u* 紅樓夢新補. Taiyuan: Shan-hsi Jen-min, 1984.

Chang, Chin-ch'ih 張錦池. *Chung-kuo ssu-ta ku-tien hsiao-shuo lun-kao* 中國四大古典小說論稿. Peking: Hua-i, 1993.

Chao, Kang 趙岡 and Ch'en Chung-i 陳鍾毅. *Hung-lou meng hsin-t'an* 紅樓夢新探. Peking: Wen-hua I-shu, 1991.

Ch'i, Tung-p'ing 齊東平. *Hung-lou meng: Shih-t'ou te chen-han* 紅樓夢: 石頭的震憾. Shenyang: Ch'un-feng Wen-i, 1992.

Ch'ing-shan shan-nung 青山山農. *Hung-lou meng kuang-i* 紅樓夢廣義. Peking: Jen-min Chung-kuo, 1992.

Chou, Chung-ming 周中明. *Hung-lou meng te yü-yen i-shu* 紅樓夢的語言藝術. Nanning: Li-chiang, 1982.

Chu, Tan-wen 朱淡汶. *Hung-lou meng lun-yüan* 紅樓夢論源. Nanking: Chiang-su Ku-chi, 1992. Appends a useful chart of editions.

____. *Hung-lou meng yen-chiu* 紅樓夢研究. Taipei: Kuang-wen, 1991.

Chu, T'ung 朱彤. *Hung-lou meng san-lun* 紅樓夢散論. Nanking: Nan-ching Ta-hsüeh, 1992.

Edwards, Louise P. "Gender Imperatives in *Honglou meng:* Baoyu's Bisexuality." *CLEAR* 12 (1990): 69-81.

____. *Men and Women in Qing China, Gender in The Red Chamber Dream.* Leiden: E. J. Brill, 1994.

____. *Recreating the Literary Canon: Communist Critiques of Women in the Red Chamber Dream.* Dortmund: projekt, 1995. *Edition Cathay,* 12.

Epstein, Maram. "Beauty is the Beast: The Dual Face of Woman in Four Ch'ing Novels." Unpublished Ph.D. dissertation, Princeton University, 1992.

Han, Chin-lien 韓進廉. *Hung-hsüeh shih-kao* 紅學史稿. Shih-chia-chuang: Ho-pei Jen-min, 1987.

Han, Po 韓勃, ed. *Hung-lou meng k'ao-p'ing liu-chung* 紅樓夢考評六種. Peking: Jen-min Chung-kuo, 1992.

Hsü, Chün-hui 徐君慧. *Ts'ung Chin-p'ing mei tao Hung-lou meng* 從金瓶梅到紅樓夢. Nanning: Kuang-hsi Jen-min, 1987.

Hu, Hsiao-ming 胡曉明. *Hung-lou meng yü Chung-kuo ch'uan-t'ung wen-hua* 紅樓夢與中國傳統文化. Peking: Ts'e-hui K'o-ta 測繪科大, 1996.

Hu, Pang-wei 胡邦煒. *Hung-lou meng chung te hsüan-an* 紅樓夢中的懸案. Chengtu: Ssu-ch'uan Jen-min, 1994.

Huang, Martin Weizong. "The Dilemma of Chinese Lyricism and the Qing Literati Novel." Unpublished Ph. D. dissertation, Washington University, 1991. Studies how basic assumptions of lyricism, which encompassed the tensions of attempting to imbue the increasingly chaotic reality into the desire for harmony, find their expression in the context of this novel and in *Chin P'ing Mei.*

Itô, Sôhei 伊藤漱平. 'Kôrômu' seiritsu she okusetsu–nanajikkai kôhon sonsei no kanôsei o megutte" 『紅楼夢』成立史憶説–七十回稿本存在の可能性をめぐって, *Tôhôgaku* 83 (1992): 1-19. Itô claims that Ts'ao Hsüeh-ch'in, imitating Chin Sheng-t'an, rewrote a 70-chapter version to avoid offending the Manchu court.

Kuo, Yü-shih 郭豫適, ed. *Hung-lou meng yen-chiu wen-hsüan* 紅樓夢研究文選. Shanghai: Hua-tung Shih-fan Ta-hsüeh, 1988.

Kuo, Yü-wen 郭玉雯. *Hung-lou meng jen-wu yen-chiu* 紅樓夢人物研究. Taipei: Ta-an, 1994.

Li, Wai-yee. *Enchantment and Disenchantment–Love and Illusion in Chinese Literature.* Princeton: Princeton University Press, 1993.

___. "Rhetoric and Fantasy and Rhetoric of Irony: Studies in *Liao-chai chih-i* and *Hung-lou Meng.*" Unpublished Ph. D. dissertation, Princeton University, 1988.

Li, Yü-ching 李玉敬. *<Kôrômu> shigo taishô reishaku* 「紅楼夢」詞語対象例釈. Tokyo: Ryôgen Shoten 1987.

Lin, Kuan-fu 林冠夫. *Hung-lou meng ts'ung-heng t'an* 紅樓夢縱橫談. Nanning: Kuang-hsi Jen-min, 1985.

Lin, Shuen-fu. "Chia Pao-yü's First Visit to the Land of Illusion: An Analysis of a Literary Dream in an Interdisciplinary Perspective." *CLEAR* 14 (1992): 77-106.

Lu, Hsing-chi 盧興基 and Kao Ming-i 高鳴*鷿*, eds. *Hung-lou meng te yü-yen i-shu* 紅樓夢的語言藝術. Peking: Yü-wen, 1985.

Lun Hung-lou meng i-kao 論紅樓夢遺稿. Hangchow: Che-chiang Ku-chi, 1989.

Mo Jen 墨人. *Hung-lou meng te hsieh-tso chi-ch'iao* 紅樓夢的寫作技巧. Peking: Chung-kuo Wen-lien, 1993.

Saussy, Haun. "Reading and Folly in *Dream of the Red Chamber.*" *CLEAR* 9 (1987): 23-47.

Saussy, Haun. "Women's Writing Before and Within the *Hong lou meng.*" In Widmer and Chang, *Writing Women,* pp. 285-305.

Scott, Mary Elizabeth. "Azure from Indigo: *Hung lou meng's* Debt to *Jin Ping Mei.*" Unpublished Ph. D. dissertation, Princeton University, 1989.

Tseng, Yang-hua 曾揚華. *Hung-lou meng hsin-t'an* 紅樓夢新探. Canton: Kuang-tung Jen-min, 1987.

Tu, Shih-chieh 杜世杰. *Hung-lou meng k'ao-shih* 紅樓夢考釋. Peking: Chung-kuo Wen-hsüeh, 1998.

Tuan, Ch'i-ming 段啟明. *Hung-lou meng i-shu lun* 紅樓夢藝術論. Peking: Pei-ching Shih-fan Hsüeh-yüan, 1990.

Wang, Jing. "The Poetics of Chinese Narrative: An Analysis of Andrew Plaks' *Archetype and Allegory in the Dream of the Red Chamber.*" *Comparative Literature Studies* 26 (1989): 252-270.

___. *The Story of Stone: Intertextuality, Ancient Chinese Stone Lore, and the Stone Symbolism in Dream of the Red Chamber, Water Margin, and the Journey to the West.* Durham, N.C.: Duke University Press, 1992.

Wong, Laurence Kwok Pun. "A Study of the Literary Translations of the "Hong lou meng:" With Special Reference to David Hawkes's English Version." Unpublished Ph.D. dissertation, University of Toronto, 1992.

Wu, Hung. "Beyond Stereotypes: The Twelve Beauties in Qing Court Art and the *Dream of the Red Chamber.*" In Widmer and Chang, *Writing Women,* pp. 306-365.

Xiao, Chi. "The Garden as Lyric Enclave: A Generic Study of 'The Dream of the Red Chamber'." Unpublished Ph.D. dissertation, Washington University, 1993.

Yee, Angelina C. "Counterpoise in *Honglou meng,*" *HJAS* 50.2 (December 1990): 613-50.

___. "Self, Sexuality, and Writing in *Honglou meng,*" *HJAS* 55(1995), 373-407.

Yi, Jinsheng. "The Allegory of Love: 'The Dream of the Red Chamber' and Selected Western European Allegories." Unpublished Ph. D. dissertation, Washington

University, 1993.

Yu, Anthony C. "The Quest of Brother Amor: Buddhist Intimations in *The Story of the Stone.*" *HJAS* 49 (1989): 55-92.

___. *Rereading the Stone: Desire and the Making of Fiction in a Dream of the Red Chamber.* Princeton: Princeton University Press, 1997. An important study by a major scholar of traditional fiction.

Yü, Chen-chu 余珍珠 (Angelina C. Yee). *"Hung-lou meng te to-yüan i-chih yü ch'ing-kan"* 紅樓夢的多元意旨與情感, *THHP* 23.2 (June 1993): 193-211.

Yün-ch'a Wai-shih 雲槎外史 (Ku Ch'un 顧春, 1799-1876). *Hung-lou meng ying* 紅樓夢影. Wei Yang-ch'ieh 尉仰茄, ed. Peking: Pei-ching Ta-hsüeh, 1988.

Hung Mai 洪邁 (1123-1202)

Editions and References

Hung, Mai 洪邁. *I-chien chih* 夷堅志. 6v. Li Hung 李洪, ed. Peking: Pei-ching Yen-shan, 1997. Juxtaposes original and a vernacular translation.

___. *I-chien chih hsüan-chu* 夷堅志選注. Hsü I-min 徐逸民, ed. Peking: Wen-hua I-shu, 1988. *Li-tai pi-chi hsiao-shuo ts'ung-shu.*

___. *Nan-ch'ao shih ching-yü* 南朝史精語. Shanghai: Shang-hai Shu-tien, 1994. *TSCC* ed. Appended notes by Miao Ch'üan-sun 繆荃孫 (1844-1919).

___. *Wen-pai tui-chao ch'üan-i I-chien chih* 文白對照全譯夷堅志. Chengchow: Chung-chou Ku-chi, 1994.

Studies

Kerr, Katherine L. *"Yijian zhi:* A Didactic Diversion." *Papers on Far Eastern History* 35 (1987): 79-88.

Suzuki, Kiyoshi 鈴木清. Kô Kô to Kô Mai" 洪晧と洪邁, *Hôsei Daigaku Kyôyôbu kiyô jimbun-kagakuhen* 74 (1990): 1-17.

Ter Haar, B. J. "Newly Recovered Anecdotes from Hong Mai's (1123-1202) *Yijian zhi,*" *JSYS* 23 (1993): 19-42.

Wang, Hsiu-huei. "Vingt-sept récits retrouvés du *Yijian zhi,*" *TP* 75 (1989): 191-208

Wang, Nien-shuang 王年雙. "Hung Mai sheng-p'ing chi ch'i *I-chien chih* chih yen-chiu" 洪邁生平及其夷堅志之研究. Unpublished Ph. D. dissertation, Cheng-chih Ta-hsüeh (Taiwan), 1988.

Hung Sheng 洪升 (1645-1704)

Editions and References

Hung, Sheng 洪升. *Chang-sheng Tien* 長生殿. Shanghai: Shang-hai Ku-chi, 1986. *Ku-pen hsi-ch'ü ts'ung-k'an, Wu chi* 古本戲曲叢刊, 五集, 32. Reproduction of a K'ang-hsi era (1662-1723) edition preserved in Peking Library.

Liu, Hui 劉輝, ed. *Hung Sheng chi* 洪升集. Hangchow: Che-chiang Ku-chi, 1992. *Liang-Che tso-chia wen-ts'ung.*

Ts'ai, Yün-chang 蔡運長, ed. *Chang-sheng Tien t'ung-su chu-shih* 長生殿通俗注釋. Kunming: Yün-nan Jen-min, 1987.

Studies

Chang, P'ei-yüan 章培垣. *Hung Sheng nien-p'u* 洪升年譜. Shanghai: Shang-hai Ku-chi, 1979. Preface includes a discussion of Hung's life and works.

Chung-wen Hsi, Chung-shan Ta-hsüeh, ed. *Chang-sheng Tien t'ao-lun chi* 長生殿討論集. Canton: Wen-hua I-shu, 1989. Collected papers from a 1987 conference on this play; appends a description of trends in study of *Ch'ang-sheng Tien* since 1949, a collection of traditional colophons, and a bibliography.

Meng, Chin-shu 孟緊樹. *Hung Sheng chi Chang-sheng Tien yen-chiu* 洪升及長生殿研究. Peking: Chung-kuo Hsi-chü, 1985. *Hsi-chü chia chuan-lun ts'ung-shu* 戲劇家傳論叢書.

Wang, Ay-ling. "The Artistry of Hong Sheng's 'Changshengdian.'" Unpublished Ph.D. dissertation, Yale University, 1992.

Wang, Yung-chien 王永健. *Hung Sheng ho Ch'ang-sheng Tien* 洪升和長生殿. Shanghai: Shang-hai Ku-chi, 1982.

Jou p'u-t'uan 肉蒲團 (**Prayer Mat of Flesh**)

Editions and References

Jou p'u-t'uan 肉蒲團. Taipei: T'ai-wan Ta-ying Pai-k'o, 1994.

____. *Chung-kuo li-tai ching-hui hsiao-shuo hai-nei-wai cheng-ts'ang mi-pen chi-ts'ui.* Taipei: Shuang-ti, 1994.

Translations

Hanan, Patrick. *The Carnal Prayer Mat.* Reprint ed. Honolulu: University of Hawaii Press, 1996. The standard translation, scholarly and readable.

Ju-lin wai-shih 儒林外史 (**Unoffical History of the Literati**)

Editions and References

Ch'en, Mei-lin 陳美林, ed. *Ju-lin wai-shih tz'u-tien* 儒林外史辭典. Nanking: Nan-ching Ta-hsüeh, 1994.

Li, Han-ch'iu 李漢秋, ed.*Ju-lin wai-shih hui-chiao hui-p'ing pen* 儒林外史會校會評本. Shanghai: Shang-hai Ku-chi, 1984.

____, ed. *Ju-lin wai-shih yen-chiu tzu-liao* 儒林外史研究資料. Shanghai: Shang-hai Ku-chi, 1985.

____, ed.*Ju-lin wai-shih chien-shang tz'u-tien* 儒林外史鑒賞辭典. Peking: Fu-nü, 1991.

Translations

Inada, Takashi 稻田孝.*Jurin gaishi* 儒林外史. Rpt. Tokyo: Heibonsha, 1994 (1968).

Yang, Enlin and Gerhard Schmitt, ed. *Der Weg zu den weisen Wolken, Geschichten aus dem Gelehrten Wald.* Munich: C. H. Beck, 1990.

Studies

Altenburger, Roland. *Eremitische Konzepte und Figuren im Roman Rulin Waishi: Eine intertextuelle Studie, mid einem Vorwort von Robert H. Gassmann.* Bochum: Brockmeyer, 1994.

Brandauer, F. R. "Realism, Satire and the *Ju-lin wai-shih.*" *TkR* 20 (1989): 1-22.

Chang, Kuo-feng 張國風.*Ju-lin wai-shih chi-ch'i shih-tai* 儒林外史及其時代. Taipei: Wen-chin, 1993.

Ch'en, Mei-lin 陳美林. *Hsin p'i Ju-lin wai-shih* 新批儒林外史. Nanking: Chiang-su Ku-chi, 1989.

Ju-lin wai-shih hsüeh-k'an 儒林外史學刊. Chung-kuo Ju-lin wai-shih hsüeh-hui 中國儒林外史學會, ed. Hofei: Huang-shan Shu-she, 1988-

Li, Han-ch'iu 李漢秋, ed.*Ju-lin wai-shih yen-chiu lun-wen chi* 儒林外史研究論文集. Peking:

Chung-hua, 1987. A selection of essays chosen from post-1949 scholarship on this novel and its author followed by an extensive bibliography.

_____. *Ju-lin wai-shih yen-chiu tsung-lan* 儒林外史研究縱覽. *Hsüeh-shu yen-chiu chih-nan ts'ung-shu*. Tientsin: T'ien-chin Chiao-yü, 1992.

Rolston, David L. "Theory and Practice: Fiction, Fiction Criticism, and the Writing of *Julin wai-shih.*" Unpublished Ph. D. dissertation, University of Chicago, 1988.

Shang, Wei. "The Collapse of the Taibo Temple: A Study of 'The Unofficial History of the Scholarship'." Unpublished Ph.D. dissertation, Harvard University, 1995.

Slupski, Zbigniew. "On the Authenticity of Some Fragments of the *Rulin waishih.*" *AO* 59 (1992): 194-207.

_____. "Three Levels of Composition of the *Rulin Waishi.*" *HJAS* 49 (1980): 5-53.

Juan Chi 阮籍(210-263)

Editions and References

Ch'en, Po-chün 陳伯君, ed. and comm. *Juan Chi chi chiao-chu* 阮藉集校注. Peking: Chung-hua, 1987. See also Han Ko-p'ing's 韓格平 supplements in *Ku-chi cheng-li yen-chiu hsüeh-k'an*, 54(1995.1/2):45-47.

Ch'i, Hsin 祁欣, ed. *Juan Chi shih-wen hsüan-i* 阮藉詩文選譯. Chengtu: Pa-shu Shu-tien 巴蜀書店, 1990.

Fujii, Yoshio 藤井良雄, ed. *Gen Seki shû sakuin* 阮籍集索引. Fukuoka: Chukoku Shoten, 1984.

Han, Ko-p'ing 韓格平, ed. *Chien-an ch'i tzu shih-wen chi chiao-chu hsiang-hsi* 建安七子詩文集校注詳析. Changchun: Chi-lin Wen-shih, 1991.

Ni, Ch'i-hsing 倪其心, ed. *Juan Chi shih wen hsüan i* 阮籍詩文選譯. *Ku-tai wen-shih ming-chu hsüan i ts'ung-shu*. Chengtu: Pa-Shu Shu-she, 1990.

Yü, Hsien-hao 郁賢皓, ed. *Chien-an ch'i tzu shih chien-chu* 建安七子詩箋注. Chengtu: Pa-Shu Shu-she, 1990.

Translations

Mair, Victor H. "Roan Jyi." In *Four Introspective Poets: A Concordance to Selected Poems by Roan Jyi, Chern Tzyy-arng, Jang Jeou-ling and Lii Bor*, ed. Victor H. Mair. 15–60. Tempe, Arizona: Arizona State University, 1987.

Studies

Cai, Zong-qi. "The Symbolic Mode of Presentation in the Poetry of Juan Chi." *CLEAR* 15 (1993): 37-56.

Dai, Fang. "Drinking, Thinking, and Writing: Ruan Ji and the Culture of His Era." Unpublished Ph.D. dissertation, University of Michigan, 1994.

Han, Ch'uan-ta 韓傳達. *Juan Chi p'ing chuan* 阮藉評傳. Peking: Pei-ching Ta-hsüeh, 1997.

Holzman, Donald. "On the Authenticity of the Tetrameter Poetry Attributed to Ruan Ji." In *Chung-yang Yen-chiu-yüan Ti-erh-chieh Kuo-chi Han-hsüeh hui-i* 中央研究院第二屆國際漢學會議. Taipei: Academia Sinica,1989, v. 6, pp. 173-200.

Hsia, Wen-yü 夏文郁, comm. *Juan Chi shih chieh-i* 阮藉詩解譯. Hsining: Ch'ing-hai Jen-min, 1989.

Hsü, Pao-pei 余寶貝. "Juan Chi yen-chiu" 阮藉研究. M.A. thesis, Wen-hua Ta-hsüeh, 1986.

Kao, Ch'en-yang 高晨陽. *Juan Chi p'ing-chuan* 阮藉評傳. Nanking: Nan-ching Ta-hsüeh, 1994. An interesting study with a good, useful index.

Lin, Ming-te 林明德. "Juan Chi te sheng-ming t'ai-tu" 阮藉的生命態度. *Fu-jen kuo-wen hsüeh-pao* 1 (1985): 123–139.

Lo, Tsung-ch'iang 羅宗強. "Lun Juan Chi te hsin-t'ai" 論阮籍的心態. *She-hui k'o-hsüeh chan-hsien* 52 (1990): 266–272.

Mair, Victor H. *Four Introspective Poets: A Concordance to Selected Poems by Roan Jyi, Chern Tzyy-arng, Jang Jeouling, and Lii Bor.* V. 2. Center for Asian Studies, *Monograph*, Tempe: Center for Asian Studies, Arizona State University, 1987.

Maliavin, Vladimir Viacheslavovich. *Zhuan Tszi.* Moscow: Nauka, 1978.

Morita, Koiichi 森田浩一. "Haikai to shoyo–Gen Seki eikaishi no kôsatzu 徘徊と逍遥–阮籍詠懷詩の考查, *Chugoku bungaku hô 41* (1990): 40-65.

Numaguchi, Masaru 沼口勝. "Gen Seki no shigen 'Eikaishi' ni tsuite" 阮籍の四言「詠懷詩」 について, *Nippon Chûgoku Gakkaihô,* 38 (1986): 103-119.

Tanaka, Junko 田中順子. "Gen Seki bikô fu shiron" 阮籍獼猴賦試論, *Nippon Chûgoku Gakkaihô* 38 (1986): 88-102.

T'ien, Li 田笠. "Juan Chi shih-li te hsiang yü *I-ching* kua-tz'u" 阮籍詩裡的象與易經卦辭. *Ssu-chuan Ta-hsüeh hsüeh-pao 65* (1990): 71–78.

Wei, Chün-ying 衛軍英. "Lun Juan Chi Yung-huai shih te ch'ing-kan chi ssu-wei lo-chi" 論阮籍詠懷詩的情感及思維邏輯. *Hang-chou Ta-hsüeh pao* (1990): 92–98.

Yü, Te-mao 虞德懋. "Ts'ao Chih yü Juan Chi shih-ko i-yün pi-chiao" 曹植與阮籍詩歌意蘊比較. *Yang-chou Shih-yüan hsüeh-pao 81* (1990): 23–28.

Juan Ta-ch'eng 阮大鋮 (1587-1646)

Editions and References

Hsü, Ling-yün 徐凌雲 and Hu, Chin-wang 胡金望, eds. *Juan Ta-ch'eng hsi-chü ssu chung* 阮大鋮戲曲四種. Hofei: Huang-shan Shu-she, 1993.

Ts'ai, I 蔡毅, ed. *Yen-tzu chien* 燕子箋. Peking: Chung-hua, 1988.

Ei kai dô shishû 詠懷堂詩集. Tokyo: Takahashi Jôhô, 1990.

Juan Yü 阮瑀 (d. 212)

Editions and References

Han, Ko-p'ing 韓格平, ed. *Chien-an ch'i tzu shih-wen chi chiao-chu hsiang-hsi* 建安七子詩文集校注詳析. Changchun: Chi-lin Wen-shih, 1991.

Yü, Hsien-hao 郁賢皓, ed. *Chien-an ch'i tzu shih chien-chu* 建安七子詩箋注. Chengtu: Pa-Shu Shu-she, 1990.

Yü, Shao-ch'u 俞紹初, ed. *Juan Yü chi* 阮瑀集. in *Chien-an ch'i tzu chi* 建安七子集. Peking: Chung-hua, 1989.

K'ang Yu-wei 康有為 (1858-1927)

Editions

Chiang, I-hua 姜義華 and Wu, Keng-liang 吳根樑, eds. *K'ang Yu-wei chüan chi* 康有為全集. Shanghai: Shang-hai Ku-chi, 1987.

Chiang, Kuei-lin 蔣貴麟, ed. *Wan-mu ts'ao-t'ang i-kao wai-pien hsü-chi* 萬木草堂遺稿外編續集. Taipei: Ch'eng-wen, 1983.

Chung, Shu-ho 鍾書河, ed. *Ou-chou shih-i kuo yu-chi* 歐洲十一國游記. Changsha: Hu-nan Jen-min, 1980.

K'ang, Yu-wei. *Ta-t'ung shu* 大同書. Shenyang: Liao-ning Jen-min, 1994.

Lou, Yü-lieh 樓宇烈, ed. *K'ang Yu-wei hsüeh-shu chu-tso hsüan* 康有為學術著作選. Peking:

Chung-hua, 1988. Multi-volume collection with many important works by K'ang.

Ma, Tzu-i 馬自毅, ed. *K'ang Yu-wei shih-wen hsüan* 康有為詩文選. Shanghai: Hua-tung Shih-ta, 1993.

Studies

Takeuchi, Hiroyuki 竹内弘行. *Kô ki Kô Yûi ron: bômei, shingai, fukuheki, goshi* 後期康有為論： 亡命、辛亥、復辟、五四. Kyoto: Dôhôsha, 1987.

Sakade, Yoshinobu 坂出祥伸. *Kô Yûi: yûtopia no kaika* 康有為： ヨートピアの開花. Tokyo: Shueisha, 1985.

Chang, Po-chen 張伯楨. *Nan-hai K'ang hsien-sheng chuan* 南海康先生傳. *Ts'ung-shu chi-ch'eng hsü-pien.* Shanghai: Shang-hai Shu-tien, 1994.

Lin, K'o-kuang 林克光. *Ko-hsin-p'ai chü-jen K'ang Yu-wei* 革新派巨人康有為. *Ch'ing-shih yen-chiu ts'ung-shu* Peking: Chung-kuo Jen-min Ta-hsüeh, 1990.

Ma, Hung-lin 馬洪林. *K'ang Yu-wei ta chuan* 康有為大傳. Shenyang: Liao-ning Jen-min, 1988.

Tung, Shih-wei 董士偉. *K'ang Yu-wei p'ing-chuan* 康有為評傳. *Kuo-hsüeh ta-shih ts'ung-shu.* Nanchang: Pai-hua-chou Wen-i, 1994.

Kao Ch'i 高啟 (1336-1374)

Editions and References

Chin, T'an 金檀 *et al*, eds. *Kao Ch'ing-ch'iu chi* 高青丘集. *Chung-kuo ku-tien wen-hsüeh ts'ung-shu.* Shanghai: Shang-hai Ku-chi, 1985.

Translations

Strassberg, *Inscribed Landscapes,* pp. 283-288.

Kao Lien 高濂 (fl. 1573-1581)

Editions and References

T'ao, Wen-t'ai 陶文台, ed. *Yin chuan fu shih chien* 飲饌服食牋. *Chung-kuo P'eng-jen ku-chi ts'ung-shu* Peking: Chung-kuo Shang-yeh, 1985.

Tsun sheng pa chien 遵生八箋. *Chung-kuo i-hsüeh ta-ch'eng san pien.* Changsha: Yüeh-lu Shu-she, 1994.

Kao Ming 高明(*ca.* 1305-*ca.* 1370)

Editions and References

Chang, Hsien-wen 張憲文 and Hu, Hsüeh-kang 胡雪岡, eds. *Kao Tse-ch'eng chi* 高則誠集. Hangchow: Che-chiang Ku-chi, 1992.

Hou, Pai-p'eng 侯百朋,ed. *P'i-'pa chi tzu-liao hui-pien* 琵琶記資料匯編. Peking: Shu-mu Wen-hsien, 1989.

Kao-seng chuan 高僧傳 (Lives of Eminent Monks)

Editions and References

Kao-seng chuan 高僧傳. Annotated and collated by T'ang Yung-t'ung 湯用彤. Peking: Chung-hua, 1992.

Kao-seng chuan ho-chi 高僧傳合集. *Fo-hsüeh ming-chu ts'ung-k'an.* Shanghai: Shang-hai Ku-chi, 1991.

Liang Kao-seng chuan so-yin 梁高僧傳索引. Shanghai: Shang-hai Shu-tien, 1989.

Translation

Hasegawa, Shigenari 長谷川滋成." Shi Ton den yakuchû jô ("Kôso den" kan 4) 支遁伝訳注 上（『高僧伝』巻四）, *Hiroshima Daigaku Kyôikubu kiyô* 42 (1994).

Zhizneopisaniia dostoinykh monakov: v 3-x tomakh / Khuei-tsziao; perevod s kitaiskogo, issledovanie, kommentarii i ukazateli M.E. Ermakova. Moscow: Nauka," Glav. red. vostochnoi lit-ry, 1991-

Studies

Cheng, Yü-ch'ing 鄭郁卿. *Kao-seng chuan yen-chiu* 高僧傳研究. Taipei: Wen-chin, 1990.

Hirai, Shun'ei 平井俊榮. "Kôsôden no chûshaku teki kenkyû" 高僧伝の注釈的研究 (IV), *Kumazawa Daigaku Bukkyô Gakubu ronshû* 25 (1994).

Kao Shih 高適 (716-765)

Editions and References

Hsieh, Ch'u-fa 謝楚發, ed. *Kao Shih Ts'en Shen shih* 高適岑參詩. Taipei: Chin-hsiu, 1993.

Kao, Kuang-fu 高光復, ed. *Kao Shih, Ts'en Shen shih i-shih* 高適岑參詩譯釋. Harbin: Hei-lung-chiang Jen-min, 1984.

Liu, K'ai-yang 劉開揚, ed. *Kao Shih shih-chi pien-nien chien-chu* 高適詩集編年箋注. Taipei: Han-ching wen-hua shih-yeh, 1983.

Sun, Ch'in-shan 孫欽善, annot. *Kao Shih chi chiao chu* 高適集校註. Shanghai: Shang-hai Ku-chi, 1984.

Studies

Allen, Joseph Roe III. "From Saint to Singing Girl: The Rewriting of the Lo-fu Narrative in Chinese Literati Poetry," *HJAS* 48.2 (December 1988), 321-341. Contains a translation and discussion of a Lo-fu poem by Kao Shih.

Chou, Hsün-ch'u 周勛初 and Yao Sung 姚松. *Kao Shih ho Ts'en Shen* 高適和岑參. Shanghai: Shang-hai Ku-chi, 1991.

Kawaguchi, Yoshiharu 川口喜治. "Kô Teki kenkyû no genjô to tenbô" 高適研究の現状と展望, *Chûgoku gakushi* 3 (1988): 15-28.

Pien, Hsiao-hsüan 卞孝萱. "Kao Ts'en i t'ung lun" 高岑異同論, *Wen-shih chi-lin* 1985.4 (1985): 151-73.

Sun, Ch'in-shan 孫欽善. "*Kao Shih chi* chiao Tun-huang ts'an-chüan chi" 高適集校敦煌殘卷記, *Wen Hsien* 17 (1983): 35-55.

Tso, Yün-lin 左云霖. *Kao Shih chuan lun* 高適傳論. Peking: Jen-min Wen-hsüeh, 1985.

Yü, Cheng-sung 余正松. *Kao Shih yen-chiu* 高適研究. Chengtu: Pa-Shu Shu-she, 1992.

Ko Ch'ao-fu 葛巢甫 (*fl.* 400)

Studies

Bokenkamp, Stephen R. *Early Daoist Scriptures.* Berkeley: University of California Press, 1997.

Ko Hung 葛洪 (283-343)

Editions and References

Yang, Ming-chao 楊明照, ed. *Pao-p'u tzu wai-p'ien chiao-chien* 抱朴子外篇校箋. Peking: Chung-hua, 1991.

Translation

Fukui, Kôjun 福井康順. *Shinsen den* 神仙伝. Tokyo: Meitoku Shuppansha, 1983.

Honda, Wataru 本田済. *Hô Bokushi zen 3 satsu* 抱朴子全 3 冊. Tokyo: Heibonsha, 1990

Kôma, Miyoshi 高馬三良. *Hô Bokushi Retsusen den Sengai kyô* 抱朴子・列仙伝・山海経. Tokyo: Heibonsha, 1969

Kominami, Ichirô 小南一郎. *"Shinsen den*–atarashii shinsen shisô" 神仙伝–新しい神仙思想. In Kominami, *Chûgoku no shinwa to monogratri–Koshsetsushi no tenkai* 中国の神話と物語–古小説史の展開. Tokyo: Iwanami, 1984, pp. 145-236.

Ozaki, Masaji 尾崎正治 *et al. Hô Bokushi, Retsusen den* 抱朴子・列仙伝. *Kanshô Chûgoku no koten 9* 鑑賞中国の古典 9 . Tokyo: Kadokawa Shoten 1988.

Sawada, Mizuho 沢田瑞穂. *Retsusen den, Shinsen den* 列仙伝, 神仙伝. Rpt. Tokyo: Heibonsha, 1993 (1969).

Studies

Feng, Han-yung 馮漢鏞. "Ko Hung ts'eng-chü Yin-chih k'ao" 葛洪曾去印支考. *Wen-shih 39* (1994): 59–70.

Fukui, Kôjun 福井康順. *"Shinsen den* kô" 神仙伝考. *Tôhô sôkyô, Sôkangô*, 1951.

___. *"Shinsen den* saikô" 神仙伝再考. *Sôkyô kenkyû* 137 (1953).

Hu, Fu-ch'en 胡孚琛. *Wei Chin shen-hsien tao-chiao: Pao p'u-tzu nei-p'ien yen-chiu* 魏晉神仙道教：抱朴子內篇研究. Peking: Jen-min, 1989.

Kominami, Ichirô 小南一朗. "Shinsen den no fukugen" 神仙伝の復元. In *Iriya Kyôju Ogawa Kyôju taikyû kinen Chûgoku Bungaku Gogaku ronshû* 入矢教授小川教授退休記念中国文学語学論集. Kyoto: Kyoto University, 1974, pp: 301-313.

Lai, Chi Tim. "The Taoist Vision of Physical Immortality: A Study of Ko Hung's *Pao-p'u tzu*" Unpublished Ph.D. dissertation, University of Chicago, 1995.

Liu, Chung-yü 劉仲宇. "Ko Hung 'chen-chung shu' ch'u-t'an" 葛洪枕中書初探. *Chung-kuo tao-chiao 16* (1990): 23–27.

Liu, Hsiang-fei, 劉翔飛. "Ko Hung te wen-lun" 葛洪的文論. *Chung-wai wen-hsüeh* 11:8 (1983): 165–188.

Sailey, Jay. *The Master Who Embraces Simplicity: A Study of the Philosopher Ko Hung, A.D. 283–343*. San Francisco: CMC, 1978. Trans. of 21 chaps. of the *Pao-p'u tzu Wai-p'ien.*

Schmidt, Franz-Rudolph. *Die magische Rüstung–Naturbilder aus dem Pao-pu tzu Nei-p'ien des Ko Hung (283-343)*. Frankfurt and New York: Lang, 1996.

Wang, Li-ch'i 王利器. "Ko Hung chu-shu k'ao-lüeh" 葛洪著述考略. *Wen-shih* 37 (1993): 33–54.

Ku-chi 滑稽

Editions and References

Chieh-i 解頤, ed. *Li-tai hsiao-hua lei-pien* 歷代笑話類編. Shih-chia-chuang: Ho-pei Jen-min, 1986.

Wang, Li-ch'i 王利器, ed. *Li-tai hsiao-hua chi hsü-pien* 歷代笑話集續編. Shenyang: Ch'un-feng Wen-i, 1985.

Studies

Ômuro, Mikio 大室幹雄. *(Shinpen) Kokkei–Kodai Chûgoku no ijin tachi* （新編）滑稽−古代中国の異人たち.Tokyo: Serika Shobô, 1986

Sawada, Mizuho 沢田瑞穂. *Shôrin kanwa* 笑林閑話. Tokyo: Tôhô Shoten,1985.

Ku-chin chu 古今注 *(fl.* 300)

Editions and References

Ku-chin chu. Ts'ung-shu chi-ch'eng ch'u-pien. Peking: Chung-hua, 1985.

Ku K'uang 顧況 *(ca.* 725-814)

Editions and References

Ku K'uang chi 顧況集. *T'ang wu-shih chia shih chi.* Shanghai: Shang-hai Ku-chi, 1981.

Wang, Ch'i-hsing 王啟興 and Chang, Hung 張虹, eds. *Ku K'uang shih chu* 顧況詩注. *T'ang shih hsiao-chi* 唐詩小集. Shanghai: Shang-hai Ku-chi, 1994.

Studies

Dudbridge, Glen. *The Tale of Li Wa.* London: Ithaca Press,1983, pp. 61-64.

Russell, Terence. "The Taoist Elegies of Ku K'uang." *T'ang Studies* 7 (1990): 169-195.

Ku-shih hsüan 古詩選

Translations

Iritani, Sensuke 入谷仙介. *Ko shi sen (Jô, ge)* 古詩選　上・下. *Chûgoku koten sen* 23, 24 中国古典選 23, 24. Tokyo: Asahi Shinbunsha, 1978

Studies

Kuo, Cheng-i 郭正宜. "Chü-yu ch'uang-i te pei-p'an: ts'ung Fang Tung-shu tui Wang Shih-chen 'Ku-shih hsüan' te k'an-fa t'an-ch'i" 具有創意的背叛：從方東樹對王士禎古詩選的看法談起, *Kao-yüan hsüeh-pao* 5.2 (1996): 413-23.

Ku-shih shih-chiu shou 古詩十九首 (Nineteen Old Poems)

Studies

Chang, Ch'ing-chung 張清鍾. *Ku-shih shih-chiu shou hui-shuo shang hsi yü yen-chiu* 古詩十九首彙說賞析與研究. Taipei: T'ai-wan Shang-wu, 1988.

Ma, Mao-yüan 馬茂元. *Ku-shih shih-chiu shou t'an-so* 古詩十九首探索. Kaohsiung: Kao-hsiung Fu-wen Shu-chü, 1988.

Ku-tzu-tz'u 鼓子詞 (drum lyric)

Studies

Abe, Yasuki 阿部泰記. "Koshi ＜Ryû Kôan zenden＞ sanbu saku no hensan" 鼓詞＜劉公案全伝＞三部作の編纂, *Chûgoku Bungaku Ronshû* 21(1992).

Ku-wen 古文 (ancient-style prose)

Editions and References

Ch'in, K'ang-tsung 秦亢宗, ed. *Chung-kuo san-wen tz'u-tien* 中國散文辭典. Peking: Pei-ching Ch'u-pan-she, 1993.

Liu, Lan-ying 劉蘭英, ed. *Ku-wen chih-shih tz'u-tien* 古文知識辭典. Nanning: Kuang-hsi, 1992.

Lü, Ch'ing-fei 呂晴飛, ed. *T'ang-Sung pa-ta-chia san-wen chien-shang tz'u-tien* 唐宋八大家散文鑒賞辭典. Peking: Chung-kuo Fu-nü, 1991.

Mao, K'un 茅坤 (1512-1601). *T'ang Sung pa-ta chia wen-ch'ao* 唐宋八大家文鈔. Ch'en Chia 陳加 *et al.*, eds. Shenyang: Shen-yang Ch'u-pan-she, 1997.

T'ang-Sung pa-ta-chia san-wen chüan-chi 唐宋八大家散文全集. Peking: Chin-jih Chung-kuo, 1996.

Wu, Kung-cheng 吳功正, ed. *Ku-wen chien-shang tz'u-tien* 古文鑒賞辭典. Nanking: Chiang-su Wen-i, 1987.

Yü, Ch'eng 余誠 (Ch'ing dynasty). *Ku-wen shih-i* 古文釋義. Lü Ying 呂鶯 *et al.*, eds. Peking: Pei-ching Ku-chi, 1998.

Yü, Kuan-ying 余冠英 *et al.*, eds. *T'ang-Sung pa-ta-chia ch'üan-chi* 唐宋八大家全集. Peking: Kuo-chi Wen-hua, 1997.

Translation

Kakei, Fumio 筧文生. *Tô Sô hakka bun* 唐宋八家文. *Kanshô Chûgoku no koten 20* 鑑賞中国の古典２０. Tokyo: Kadokawa Shoten 1989

Studies

Chu, Shang-shu 祝尚書. *Pei-Sung ku-wen-yün-tung fa-chan-shih* 北宋古文運動發展史. Chengtu: Pa-Shu Shu-she, 1995.

Jen, Fang-ch'iu 任訪秋. "Yün Ching te ku-wen wen-lun chi ch'i yü T'ung-ch'eng-p'ai te kuan-hsi" 惲敬的古文文論及其與桐城派的關係. *Wen-hsüeh i-ch'an* 1984.3: 87-93.

Kuo, Yü-heng 郭豫衡. *Chung-kuo san-wen shih* 中國散文史. Shanghai: Shang-hai Ku-chi, 1993.

Liu, Kuo-ying 劉國盈. *T'ang-tai ku-wen-yün-tung lun-kao* 唐代古文運動論稿. Sian: Shan-hsi Jen-min, 1984. '

Ono, Shihei 小野四平. "Ryô Shoku kara Ryû Sôgen e–'Tôdai kobun no genryû' hosetsu" 梁蕭から柳宗元へ—「唐代古文の源流」補説, *Shûkan Tôyôgaku* 66 (1992): 83-101.

___. "Tôdai kobun no genryû–Kaigen, Tenbô ki o chûshin ni" 唐代古文源流–開元天宝期を中心に, *Miyagi Kyôiku Daigaku kiyô,* 25 (1991): 31-66.

Sun, Ch'ang-wu 孫昌武. *T'ang-tai ku-wen-yün-tung t'ung-lun* 唐代古文運動通論. Tientsin: Pai-hua Wen-i, 1984.

Wang, Chou-ming 王洲明. *Ku-wen yü p'ien-wen* 古文與駢文. Tsinan: Shang-tung Wen-i, 1992.

Wu, Hsiao-lin 吳小林. *Chung-kuo san-wen mei-hsüeh shih* 中國散文美學史. Harbin: Hei-lung-chiang Jen-min, 1993.

Ku-wen kuan-chih 古文觀止 (The Finest of Ancient Prose)

Editions and References

Liu, Hsüeh-lin 劉學林 and Ch'ih-to 遲鐸, eds. *Ku-wen kuan-chih tz'u-tien* 古文觀止辭典. Sian: Shan-hsi Jen-min, 1994.

Kuan, Yung-li 關永禮, ed. *Ku-wen kuan-chih Hsü ku-wen kuan-chih chien-shang tz'u-tien* 古文觀止續古文觀止鑑賞辭典. Shanghai: Shang-hai T'ung-chi Ta-hsüeh, 1990.

Ming-chia ching-i Ku-wen kuan-chih 名家精譯古文觀止. Peking: Chung-hua, 1993.

Yang, Chin-ting 楊金鼎, ed. *Ku-wen kuan-chih ch'üan i* 古文觀止全譯. Hofei: An-hui Chiao-yü, 1990.

Yin, Fa-lu 陰法魯, ed. *Ku-wen kuan-chih i-chu* 古文觀止譯注. Rev. ed. Peking: Pei-ching Wen-hsüeh, 1997.

Yüan Mei 袁梅 *et al.*, eds. *Ku-wen kuan-chih chin i* 古文觀止今譯. Tsinan: Ch'i-Lu Shu-she, 1983.

Ku-wen-tz'u lei-tsuan 古文辭類纂(A Classified Compendium of Ancient-style Prose and Verse)

Editions

Mu-jung, Chen 慕容真, ed. *Lin Shu hsüan p'ing Ku-wen-tz'u lei tsuan* 林紓選評古文辭類纂. Hangchow: Che-chiang Ku-chi, 1986.

Sung, Ching-ju 宋晶如 and Chang, Jung 章榮 eds. *Ku-wen-tz'u lei tsuan* 古文辭類纂. Peking: Chung-kuo Shu-tien, 1986.

Yao, Nai 姚鼐 (1732-1815), ed. *Hsi-pao-hsüan ch'üan-chi* 惜抱軒全集. Peking: Chung-kuo Shu-tien, 1991.

Studies

Wang, Chen-yüan 王鎮遠. *T'ung-ch'eng-p'ai* 桐城派. Shanghai: Shang-hai Ku-chi, 1990.

Wang, Hsien-yung 王獻永. *T'ung-ch'eng wen-p'ai* 桐城文派. Peking: Chung-hua, 1984.

Ku Yen-wu 顧炎武 (1613-1682)

Editions and References

Huang, Ju-ch'eng 黃汝誠 (1799-1837), comm., ed. *Jih-chih lu chi-shih* 日知錄集釋. Changsha: Yüeh-Lu, 1994. Punctuated and edited by Ch'in K'o-ch'eng 秦克誠.

Ku, Yen-wu. *Tsa lu* 雜錄. *Pi-chi hsiao-shuo ta-kuan san pien*. Taipei: Hsin-hsing Shu-chü, 1988.

____. *Sheng-an pen-chi* 聖安本紀. *Chung-kuo yeh-shih chi-ch'eng*. Chengtu: Pa-Shu Shu-she, 1993.

Li, Yung-yu 李永祐 and Kuo, Ch'eng-t'ao 郭成韜, eds. *Ku Yen-wu shih wen hsüan i* 顧炎武詩文選譯. Chengtu: Pa-Shu Shu-she, 1991.

Wang, Ch'ü-ch'ang 王蘧常 *et al*, eds. *Ku T'ing-lin shih-chi hui-chu* 顧亭林詩集彙注. *Chung-kuo ku-tien wen-hsüeh ts'ung-shu*. Shanghai: Shang-hai Ku-chi, 1983.

Translations

Strassberg, *Inscribed Landscapes,* pp. 353-360.

Studies

Chen, Tsu-wu 陳祖武. *Ku Yen-wu* 顧炎武. *Chung-kuo li-shih hsiao ts'ung-shu*. Peking: Chung-hua, 1984.

Fukumoto, Masakazu 福本雅一. "Ko Enbu to Konzan Yôshi" 顧炎武と崑山葉氏, *Bungei ronsô* 42 (1994): 235-55.

Lu, Hsing-chi 盧興基. *Ku Yen-wu* 顧炎武. Taipei: Wan-chüan-lou, 1993. (Rpt. of Shang-hai Ku-chi, 1978.)

Kuan Han-ch'ing 關漢卿 (*ca.* 1240-*ca.* 1320)

Editions and References

Hsü, Ch'in-chün 徐沁君, ed. *Yüan ch'ü ssu ta-chia ming-chü hsüan* 元曲四大家名劇選. Tsinan: Ch'i-Lu Shu-she, 1987. Annotation versions of 16 plays by 4 of the best Yüan playwrights.

Huang, Shih-chung 黃仕忠, ed. *Kuan Han-ch'ing tsa-chü hsüan-i* 關漢卿雜劇選譯. Chengtu: Pa-Shu Shu-she, 1991.

Lan, Li-ming 藍立蓂. *Kuan Han-ch'ing hsi-ch'ü tz'u-tien* 關漢卿戲曲辭典. Chengtu: Ssu-ch'uan, 1997.

Li, Han-ch'iu 李漢秋 and Yüan Yu-fen 袁有芬, eds. *Kuan Han-ch'ing yen-chiu tzu-liao* 關漢卿研究資料. Shanghai: Shang-hai Ku-chi, 1988.

Li, Han-chiu 李漢秋 and Chou, Wei-p'ei 周維培, eds. *Kuan Han-ch'ing san-chü chi* 關漢卿散曲集. Shanghai: Shang-hai Ku-chi, 1990.

Ma, Hsin-lai 馬欣來, ed. *Kuan Han-ch'ing chi* 關漢卿集. Taiyuan: Shan-hsi, 1997.

Wang, Hsüeh-ch'i 王學琪, Wu Chen-ch'ing 吳振清, and Wang Ching-chu 王靜竹, eds. *Kuan Han-ch'ing ch'üan-chi chiao-chu* 關漢卿全集校注. Shih-chia-chuang: Ho-pei Chiao-yü, 1988. Annotated versions of 18 plays, 3 fragments, and 76 *san-ch'ü* followed by a bibliography.

Wang, Kang 王鋼, ed. *Kuan Han-ch'ing yen-chiu tzu-liao hui-k'ao* 關漢卿研究資料會考. Peking: Chung-kuo Hsi-chü, 1988.

Wu, Kuo-ch'in 吳國欽, ed. *Kuan Han-ch'ing ch'üan-chi* 關漢卿全集. Canton: Kuang-tung Kao-teng Chiao-yü, 1988. Includes all of Kuan's *san-ch'ü* and his 18 plays; appends a discussion of materials on Kuan's life and works.

Studies

Chang, Yüeh-chung 張月中 and Lu Pin 盧彬, eds. *Kuan Han-ch'ing yen-chiu hsin-lun* 關漢卿研究新論. Shih-chia-chuang: Hua-shan Wen-i, 1989. Contains 30 papers from a conference held in 1988 in Hopei.

Chang, Yün-sheng 張雲生. *Kuan Han-ch'ing chuan lun* 關漢卿傳論. Peking: K'ai-ming 開明, 1990.

Chung, Lin-pin 鍾林斌. *Kuan Han-ch'ing hsi-chü lun-kao* 關漢卿戲劇論稿. *Chung-kuo ku-tai tso-chia yen-chiu ts'ung-shu,* Sian: Shan-hsi Jen-min, 1986.

Fu, Hongchu. "The Feminist Issues in Yüan *Tsa-chü;* Rereading Kuan Han-ch'ing's *Chiu Feng Ch'en.*" In *Proceedings of International Conference on Kuan Han-ch'ing,* ed. Tseng Yong-yih [Tseng Yung-i]. 303-25. Taipei: Faculty of Arts, National Taiwan University, 1994.

Hsü, Tzu-fang 徐子方. *Kuan Han-ch'ing yen-chiu* 關漢卿研究. Taipei: Wen-chin, 1994.

Idema, W. L. "Some Aspects of *Pai-yüeh-t'ing:* Script and Performance." In *Proceedings of International Conference on Kuan Han-ch'ing,* ed. Tseng Yong-yih [Tseng Yung-i]. 55-77. Taipei: Faculty of Arts, National Taiwan University, 1994.

Kuan Han-ch'ing Kuo-chi Hsüeh-shu Yen-t'ao-hui 關漢卿國際學術討論會, ed. *Kuan Han-ch'ing kuo-chi hsüeh-shu yen-t'ao-hui lun-wen chi* 關漢卿國際學術研討會論文集. Taipei: Wen-chien Hui, 1994.

Li, Han-ch'iu 李漢秋. *Kuan Han-ch'ing ming-chü hsin-shang* 關漢卿名劇欣賞. Hofei: An-huei Wen-i, 1986.

Liu, Wu-chi. "Kuan Han-ch'ing: The Man and His Life," *JSYS* 22 (1990-92): 63-87.

Oberstenfeld, Werner. *China's bedeutendster Dramatiker der Mongolenzeit (1280-1368), Kuan Han-ch'ing; Kuan Han-ch'ings Rezeption in der Volksrepublik China der Jahre 1954-65 mit einer kommentierten Übersetzung des Singspiels vom Goldfadenteich (Chin-chien ch'ih) sowie einer ausführlichen bibliographischen Übersicht zu Kuan Han-ch'ing als Theaterschriftsteller.* Frankfurt: Peter Lang, 1983.

Shih, Chung-wen. "The Images of Women in Kuan Han-ch'ing's Plays." In *Proceedings of International Conference on Kuan Han-ch'ing* Tseng Yong-yih [Tseng Yung-i], ed... Taipei: Faculty of Arts, National Taiwan University, 1994, pp. 291-301.

Sieber, Patricia Angela. "Rhetoric, Romance, and Intertextuality: The Making and Remaking of Guan Hanqing in Yuan and Ming China." Ph.D., University of California, Berkeley, 1994. Argues that Yüan *tsa-chü* and *san-ch'ü* were authored in colloboration with Yüan authors and Ming imperial, commercial and literati editors.

West, Stephen H. "A Study in Appropriation: Zang Maoxun's Injustice to Dou E." *JAOS* 111 (1991): 283-302.

West, Stephen H. "Law and Ethics, Appearance and Actuality in *Rescriptor in Waiting; Pao Thrice Investigates the Butterfly Dream*" In *Proceedings of International Conference on Kuan Han-ch'ing*. Tseng Yong-yih [Tseng Yung-i], ed. Taipei: Faculty of Arts, National Taiwan University, 1994, pp. 93-112.

Kuan-hsiu 貫休 (832-912)

Studies
Liu, Fang-ching 劉芳璟. "Kuan-hsiu shih-ko ting-pu" 貫休詩歌訂補, *Wen-hsien* 1991.3.

Nienhauser, William H., Jr. "The Development of Two *Yueh-fu*:Themes in the Eighth and Ninth Centuries–Implications for T'ang Literary History," *TkR* 10(1984-5): 118-9. Translations of and commentary on three *yueh-fu* by Kuan-hsiu.

Kuan Yün-shih 貫雲石 (1286-1324)

Editions and References
Ch'en Chia-ho 陳稼禾, ed. *Suan t'ien yüeh-fu* 酸甜樂府. Shanghai: Shang-hai Ku-chi, 1989.

Kuei Fu 桂馥 (1736-1805)

Editions and References
Chao, Chih-hai 趙智海, ed. *Cha-p'u* 札樸. Peking: Chung-hua, 1992.

Wan-hsüeh chi 晚學集. Peking: Chung-hua, 1985.

Kuei Yu-kuang 歸有光 (1507-1517)

Editions
Chang, Chia-ying 張家英 and Hsü, Chih-hsien 徐治嫻, eds. *Kuei Yu-kuang san-wen hsüan-chi* 歸有光散文選集. Tientsin: Pai-hua Wen-i, 1995.

Hsieh, Chen 謝榛, ed. *Chen-ch'uan chi* 震川集. Shanghai: Shang-hai Ku-chi, 1993.

K'un-ch'ü 崑曲

Editions
I-an 怡庵, ed. *Hui-t'u ching-hsüan k'un-ch'ü ta-ch'üan* 繪圖精選崑曲大全. Tokyo: Fuji Shuppan, 1991. (Rpt. of Shang-hai Shih-chieh Shu-chü, 1925.)

K'un-ch'ü ch'ü-p'ai chi t'ao-shu fan-li chi–Nan-t'ao 崑曲曲牌及套數範例集—南套. 2v. Shanghai:

Shang-hai Wen-i, 1994.

Studies

Hu, Chi 胡忌 and Liu Chih-chung 劉致忠. *K'un-chü fa-chan shih* 崑劇發展史. *Chung-kuo hsi-chü chü-chung shih ts'ung-shu* Peking: Chung-kuo Hsi-ch'ü, 1989.

K'un-shan Kuo-yüeh Pao-ts'un-hui 崑山國樂保存會, ed. *K'un-ch'ü ts'ui-ts'un ch'u-chi* 崑曲粹存初集. Tokyo: Fuji Shuppan, 1990. (Rpt. of Shang-hai Ch'ao-chi Shu-chuang, 1919.)

Leung, K. C. "Balance and Symmetry in the *Huan-sha chi.*" *THHP, NS* 16 (1984): 179-201.

Mackerras, Colin. "Regional Theatre in South China during the Ming." *Han-hsüeh yen-chiu* 6 (1988): 645-72.

Mark, Lindi Li. "*Kunju* and Theatre in the Transvestite Novel *Pinhua Baojian* (Mirror of Flowered Ranks)." *Chinoperl* 14 (1986): 37-59.

Wang, Shou-t'ai 王守泰. *K'un-ch'ü ko-lü* 昆曲格律. Nanking: Chiang-su Jen-min, 1982.

Kung-t'i shih 宮體詩 (palace-style poetry)

Studies

Itô, Masafumi 伊藤正文. "Kyû tai shi no seiritsu ni tsuite" 宮体詩の成立について, *Kansai Daigaku Chûgoku Bungakkai kiyô* 10 (1989): 25-49.

Nakasuji, Kenkichi 中筋健吉. "Kyû tai shi to 'Gyokudai shinei'" 宮体詩と玉台新詠, *Nippon-Chûgoku-gakkai-hô* 41 (1989): 92-106.

Rouzer, Paul. "Watching the Voyeurs: Palace Poetry and *Yuefu.*" *CLEAR* 11 (1989): 13-34.

Sakagushi, Miki 坂口三樹. "Kyûtaishi kenkyû josetsu–sono seikaku o megutte" 宮体詩研究序説–その性格をめぐって, *Chûgoku koten kenkyû,* 36 (1991): 14-27.

Kung Tzu-chen 龔自珍 (1792-1841)

Editions

Kung Ting-an ch'üan-chi lei-pien 龔定庵全集類編. Peking: Chung-kuo Shu-tien, 1994.

Kuo, Yen-li 郭延禮, ed. *Kung Tzu-chen shih hsüan* 龔自珍詩選. Tsinan: Ch'i-Lu Shu-she, 1981.

Sun, Ch'in-shan 孫欽善, ed. *Kung Tzu-chen shih wen hsüan* 龔自珍詩文選. Peking: Jen-min Wen-hsüeh, 1991.

Sun, Wen-kuang 孫文光 and Wang, Shih-yün 王世芸, eds. *Kung Tzu-chen yen-chiu tzu-liao chi* 龔自珍研究資料集. Hofei: Huang-shan Shu-she, 1984.

Translations

Strassberg, *Inscribed Landscapes,* pp. 416-472.

Studies

Ch'en, Ming 陳銘. *Kung Tzu-chen tsung lun* 龔自珍綜論. Kueilin: Li-chiang, 1991.

Fan, K'o-cheng 樊克政. *Kung Tzu-chen sheng-p'ing yü shih-wen hsin-t'an* 龔自珍生平與詩文新探. Tientsin: T'ien-chin Jen-min, 1992.

Hama, Hisao 濱久雄. "Kyô Jichin no kaigaku shisô" 龔自珍の経学思想, *Tôhôgaku* 71 (1986): 106-120.

Kuan, Lin 管林. *Kung Tzu-chen yen-chiu* 龔自珍研究. Peking: Jen-min Wen-hsüeh, 1984.

Sun, Wen-kuang 孫文光 and Wang, Shih-yün 王世芸, eds. *Kung Tzu-chen yen-chiu lun-wen chi* 龔自珍研究論文集. Shanghai: Shang-hai Shu-tien, 1992.

K'ung Jung 孔融 (153-208)

Editions

Han, Ko-p'ing 韓格平, ed. *Chien-an ch'i tzu shih-wen chi chiao-chu hsiang-hsi* 建安七子詩文集校注詳析. Changchun: Chi-lin Wen-shih, 1991.

Yü, Hsien-hao 郁賢皓, ed. *Chien-an ch'i tzu shih chien-chu* 建安七子詩箋注. Chengtu: Pa-Shu Shu-she, 1990.

Yü, Shao-ch'u 俞紹初, ed. *K'ung Jung chi* 孔融集, in *Chien-an ch'i tzu chi* 建安七子集. Peking: Chung-hua, 1989.

K'ung Shang-jen 孔尚任 (1648-1718)

Editions and References

Tai, Sheng-lan 戴勝蘭, ed. *Hsiao hu-lei ch'uan-ch'i* 小呼雷傳奇. Tsinan: Ch'i-Lu Shu-she, 1988. An annotated, collated version of this play with an introduction which introduces its authors and analyses its dramaturgy.

Wang I 王毅, ed. *Hsiao hu-lei ch'uan-ch'i* 小忽雷傳奇. Chengchow: Chung-chou Ku-chi, 1986. Contains a collated edition–by Wang I 王毅–of this play by K'ung Shang-jen and Ku Ts'ai 顧彩 (Ch'ing Dynasty) along with a discussion of its authors, origins, and artistry.

Translations

Strassberg, *Inscribed Landscapes,* pp. 373-388.

Studies

Hu, Hsüeh-kang 胡雪岡. *K'ung Shang-jen ho 'T'ao-hua shan'* 孔尚任和桃花扇. Taipei: Wan-chüan-lou, 1993.

Hsü, Chen-kuei 徐振貴. *K'ung Shang-jen p'ing-chuan* 孔尚任評傳. Tsinan: Shan-tung Ta-hsüeh, 1991.

Hung, Po-chao 洪柏昭. *K'ung Shang-jen yü 'T'ao-hua shan'* 孔尚任與桃花扇. *Ku-tien wen-hsüeh yen-chiu ts'ung-shu,* Canton: Kuang-tung Jen-min, 1988. A study of the thought and artistry of this masterpiece.

Li, Wai-yee. "The Representation of History in *The Peach Blossom Fan.*" *JAOS* 115 (1995): 421-433.

Wang, C. H. "The Double Plot of *T'ao-hua shan.*" *JAOS* 110 (1990): 9-18.

Yüan, Shih-shuo 袁世碩. *K'ung Shang-jen nien-p'u* 孔尚任年譜. Tsinan: Ch'i-Lu Shu-she, 1987.

Kuo yü 國語

Editions and References

Chang, I-jen 張以仁. *Kuo yü chiao-cheng* 國語斠證. Taipei: Tai-wan Shang-wu, 1969.

Cheng, Liang-shu 鄭良樹. "*Kuo yü* chiao-cheng"國語校證(上中下), *Yu-shih hsüeh-chih,* 8.1/2(1968/9).

Li, Wei-ch'i 李維奇. *Pai-hua Kuo-yü* 白話國語. Changsha: Yüeh-lu Shu-she, 1994. Popular version with light annotation and brief postface.

Kuo yü 國語. Shanghai: Shang-hai Ku-chi, 1995.

Kuo yü chüan i 國語全譯. Kweiyang: Kuei-chou Jen-min, 1990.

Tung, Tseng-ling 董增齡(Ch'ing dynasty), annot. *Kuo yü cheng-i* 國語正義. Chengtu: Pa-Shu

Shu-she, 1985.

Wu, Kuo-i 鄔國義 *et al.*, eds. *Kuo-yü i-chu* 國語譯注. Shanghai: Shang-hai Ku-chi, 1994. Short preface and more extensive annotation than the Li Wei-ch'i translation.

Translations

d'Harmon, André. *Guoyu* 國語, *Propos sur les principaute;s, Tome I–Zhouyu* 周語. Paris: Collège France, Institut des Hautes Études Chinoises, 1985. Translation with extensive annotation.

Ôno, Takashi 大野峻. *Kokugo* 国語. 2v. Rpt. (1993); Tokyo Meiji Shoten, 1975. Long critical introduction (pp. 1-56), collation notes, Japanese translation, glosses for difficult terms, translator's comments.

Studies

Bissell, Jeff. "Literary Studies of Historical Texts: Early Narrative Accounts of Chong'er, Duke Wen of Jin." Unpublished Ph. D. dissertation, University of Wisconsin, 1996.

Chang, I-jen 張以仁. *Kuo yü Tso-chuan lun-chi* 國語左傳論集. Taipei: Tung-sheng 東升, 1980.

Huang, Mo 黃模. *Kuo yü pu Wei* 國語補韋 Peking: Chung-hua, 1959.

Imber, Alan. *Kuo yü: An Early Chinese Text and Its Relationship with the Tso Chuan.* 2v. Stockholm: Stockholm University Press, 1975.

P'eng, I-lin 彭益林. "*Kuo yü* 'Chin-yü' chiao-tu chi" 國語晉語校讀記, *Hua-chung Shih-fan Ta-hsüeh hsüeh-pao,* 1986.9.

Shen, Yü-ch'eng 沈玉成 and Liu Ning 劉寧. *Ch'un-ch'iu Tso-chuan hsüeh shih-kao* 春秋左傳學史稿. Nanking: Chiang-su Ku-chi, 1992.

Tung, Li-chang 董立章. *Kuo-yü i-chu pien-hsi* 國語譯注辨析. Canton: Chi-nan Ta- hsüeh, 1993. Nine page introduction, selected analyses of about 50 passages; translations and notes for all passages.

Wang, Ching-yü 王靖宇. "Tsai-lun *Tso-chuan* yü *Kuo-yü* te kuan-hsi" 再論左傳與國語的關係, *Chung-kuo wen-che yen-chiu t'ung-hsün* 6.4 (December 1996): 95-101.

Lan Ts'ai-ho 藍采和 (Yüan dynasty comedy)

Studies

Idema, W. L. "Some Notes on a Clown with a Clapper and Foot-stomping Songs (*T'a-ko*)," *Han-hsüeh yen-chiu* 8.1 (June 1990): 655-664. Contains a translation of the biography of Lan in *Hsü Hsien chuan* 續仙傳 and a discussion of the immortal as a foot-stomping singer.

Lei-shu 類書 (classified book)

Studies

Chang, Ti-hua 張滌華. *Lei-shu liu-pieh* 類書流別. Peking: Shang-wu, 1985.

Fang, Shih-to 方師鐸. *Ch'uan-t'ung wen-hsüeh yü lei-shu chih kuan-hsi* 傳統文學與類書之關係. Tientsin: T'ien-chin Ku-chi, 1986.

Loewe, Michael. *The Origins and Development of Chinese Encyclopedias.* London: The China Society, 1987.

Shaw, Shiow-jyu Lu. *The Imperial Printing of Early Ch'ing China.* San Francisco: Chinese Materials Center, 1983.

Li Ao 李翱 (774-836)

Editions and References
Li Wen-kung chi 李文公集. Shanghai: Shang-hai Ku-chi, 1993.

Translations
Strassberg, *Inscribed Landscapes*, pp. 127-132.

Studies
Barrett, T. H. *Li Ao: Buddhist, Taoist, or Neo-Confucian?* Oxford: Oxford University Press, 1992.
Emmerich, Reinhard. *Li Ao (ca. 772-ca. 841): Ein chinesisches Gelehrtenleben.* Wiesbaden: Harrassowitz, 1987. An interesting biography based on a number of original sources, but sometimes too speculative.
Kunugi, Tadashi 功刀正. *Ri Kô no kenkyû, shiryôhen* 李翱の研究, 資料編. Tokyo: Hakuteisha 白帝社, 1987.. Japanese translation (unannotated) of the 18 *chüan* of *Li Wen-kung chi* 李文公集.
Spring, Madeline. "Roosters, Horses, and Phoenixes: A Look at Three Fables by Li Ao." *MS* 39 (1990-91): 199-208.

Li Ch'i 李頎 (690-754?)

Studies
Liu, Pao-ho 劉寶和. "Li Ch'i shih-chi k'ao" 李頎事跡考, *Chung-chou hsüeh-k'an* 1982.5.
____. "Chien-lun Li Ch'i chi-ch'i shih" 簡論李頎及其詩, *Cheng-chou Ta-hsüeh hsüeh-pao* 1989.2.
Yao, Tien-chung 姚奠中. "Li Ch'i li-chü sheng-p'ing k'ao-pien ho shih-ko ch'eng-chiu" 李頎里居生平考辨和詩歌成就, *Shan-hsi Ta-hsüeh hsüeh-pao (Che-hsüeh)* 1983.1.

Li Chiao 李嶠 (644-713)

Editions and References
Hsü, Pao-hsiang 徐寶祥, ed. *Li Chiao shih-chu, Su Wei-tao shih-chu* 李嶠詩注，蘇味道詩注. Shanghai: Shang-hai Ku-chi, 1995.
Yanase, Kiyoshi. 柳瀨喜代志. *Ri Kyô hyaku nijû ei sakuin* 李嶠百二十詠索引. Tokyo: Tôhô Shoten, 1991.

Li Chien 黎簡 (1747-1799)

Editions and References
Chou, Hsi-fu 周錫馥, ed. *Li Chien shih hsüan* 黎簡詩選. Canton: Kuang-tung Jen-min, 1983.

Li Chih 李贄 (1527-1602)

Editions and References
Chang, Fan 張凡, ed. *Li Chih san-wen hsüan-chu* 李贄散文選注. Peking: Pei-ching Shih-fan Hsüeh-yüan, 1991.

Ku, Chung 古眾, coll. *Li Cho-wu p'i-p'ing Hsi-yu-chi, i-pai hui* 李卓吾批評西遊記 一百回. Tsinan: Ch'i-Lu Shu-she, 1991.

Li Cho-wu p'i-p'ing Chung-i shui-hu-chuan i-pai chüan 李卓吾批評忠義水滸傳 一百卷. *Ku-pen hsiao-shuo chi-ch'eng* 古本小説集成. Shanghai: Shang-hai Ku-chi, 1990.

Studies

Lin, Hai-ch'üeh 林海榷. *Li Chih nien-p'u k'ao-lüeh* 李贄年譜考略. Fuchow: Fu-chien Jen-min, 1992.

Mizoguchi, Yûzo. 溝口雄三. *Ri Takugo* 李卓吾. Tokyo: Shûeisha,1985.

Tso, Tung-ling 左東岭. *Li Chih yü wan-Ming wen-hsüeh ssu-hsiang* 李贄與晚明文學思想. Tientsin: T'ien-chin Jen-min, 1997.

Li Ch'ing-chao 李清照 (1084-1151)

Editions and References

Ch'u, Pin-chieh 褚斌杰 *et al.*, eds. *Li Ch'ing-chao tzu-liao hui-pien* 李清照資料匯編. Peking: Chung-hua, 1984.

Hou, Chien 侯健 and Lü, Chih-min 呂智敏, eds. *Li Ch'ing-chao shih tz'u p'ing-chu* 李清照詩詞評註. T'aiyüan: Shan-hsi Jen-min, 1985.

Hsü, Pei-wen 徐北文,ed. *Li Ch'ing-chao ch'uan-chi p'ing-chu* 李清照全集評註. Tsinan: Chi-nan Ch'u-pan-she, 1990.

Liu, I-sheng 劉逸生 and Ch'en Chin-jung 陳錦榮, eds. *Li Yü Li Ch'ing-chao tz'u chu* 李煜李清照詞注. Hong Kong: San-lien, 1986.

P'ing, Hui-shan 平彗善, ed. *Li Ch'ing-chao shih wen tz'u hsüan-i* 李清照詩文詞選譯. Chengtu: Pa-Shu Shu-she, 1988.

Sun, Ch'ung-en 孫崇恩, ed. *Li Ch'ing-chao shih tz'u hsüan* 李清照詩詞選. Peking: Jen-min Wen-Hsüeh, 1988.

Ts'ao, Shu-ming 曹樹銘, ed. *Li Ch'ing-chao shih tz'u wen ts'un* 李清照詩詞文存. Taipei: Tai-wan Shang-wu, 1992.

Wang, Yen-t'i 王延梯,ed. *Shu-yü-chi chu* 漱玉集註. Tsinan: Shan-tung Wen-i, 1984.

Translations

Cryer, James, trans. *Plum Blossom, Poems of Li Ch'ing-chao.* Chapel Hill: Carolina Wren Press, 1984.

Idema, W. L. *Liederen van Li Qingzhao.* Amsterdam: Meulenhoff, 1990.

Landau, *Beyond Spring,* pp. 160-174.

Wang, Chiao-sheng, trans. *The Complete Ci-poems of Li Qingzhao: A New English Translation...* Philadelphia: *Sino-Platonic Papers,* No.13, 1989.

Studies

Ch'en, Tsu-mei 陳祖美. *LI Ch'ing-chao p'ing-chuan* 李清照評傳. Nanking: Nan-ching Ta-hsüeh, 1995.

_____. "Kuan-yü I-an cha-chi erh tse" 關於易安札記二則. *Chung-hua wen-shih lun-ts'ung* 36 (1985): 87-97.

Cheng, Meng-t'ung 鄭孟彤, ed. *Li Ch'ing-chao tz'u shang-hsi* 李清照詞賞析. Harbin: Hei-lung-chiang Jen-min, 1984.

Chi-nan Shih She-k'o Yen-chiu-so 濟南市社科研究所, ed. *Li Ch'ing-chao yen-chiu lun-wen chi* 李清照研究論文集. Peking: Chung-hua, 1984.

_____ ed. *Li Ch'ing-chao yen-chiu lun-wen hsüan* 李清照研究論文選. Shanghai: Shang-hai Ku-chi, 1986.

Ch'ien, Kuang-p'ei 錢光培 *et al.*, eds. *Li Ch'ing-chao ming-p'ien shang-hsi* 李清照名篇賞析. Peking: Shih-yüeh Wen-i, 1987.

Chin, Chi-ts'ang 靳极蒼. *Li Yü, Li Ch'ing-chao tz'u hsiang-chieh* 李煜李清照詞詳解. Chengtu: Ssu-ch'uan Jen-min, 1985.

Chou, Chen-fu 周振甫, *et al. Li Ch'ing-chao tz'u chien-shang* 李清照詞鑒賞. Tsinan: Ch'i-Lu Shu-she, 1986.

Chung, Ling 鍾玲. "Li Ch'ing-chao jen-ko chih hsing-ch'eng" 李清照人格之形成, *Chung-wai wen-hsüeh* 13.5 (1984): 38-68.

Li, Han-ch'ao 李漢超, ed. *Li Ch'ing-chao tz'u shang-hsi* 李清照詞賞析. Peking: Chung-kuo Fu-nü, 1988.

Liu, Jui-lien 劉瑞蓮. *Li Ch'ing-chao hsin lun* 李清照新論. *Chung-kuo wen-hsüeh shih chin-hsiu ts'ung-shu* T'aiyüan: Shan-hsi Jen-min, 1990.

P'ing, Hui-shan 平彗善. *Li Ch'ing-chao chi ch'i tso-p'in* 李清照及其作品. Changchun: Shih-tai Wen-i, 1985.

Shih, I-tui 施議對. "LI Ch'ing-chao te tz'u-lun chi-ch'i 'I-an-t'i'" 李清照的詞論及其易安體, *Chung-kuo ku-tien wen-hsüeh lun-ts'ung* 4 (1986): 172-91.

Sun, Ch'ung-en 孫崇恩 and Fu, Shu-fang 傅淑芳, eds. *Li Ch'ing-chao yen-chiu lun-wen-chi* 李清照研究論文集. Tsinan: Ch'i-Lu Shu-she, 1991.

T'ang, Kuei-chang 唐圭璋 and P'an, Chün-chao 潘君昭. *T'ang Sung tz'u-hsüeh lun-chi* 唐宋詞學論集. Tsinan: Ch'i-Lu Shu-she, 1985. Especially "Li Ch'ing-chao P'ing-chuan" 李清照評傳, pp. 115-32.

Wang, Fan 王璠. *Li Ch'ing-chao yen-chiu ts'ung-kao* 李清照研究叢稿. Huhehaote: Nei-meng-ku Jen-min, 1987.

Wixted, Timothy. "The Poetry of Li Ch'ing-chao: A Woman Author and Women's Authorship," in Yu, *Voices,* pp. 145-168.

Li Ho 李賀 (791-817)

Editions and References

Feng, Hao-fei 馮浩菲 and Hsü, Ch'uan-wu 徐傳武, eds. *Li Ho shih hsüan-i* 李賀詩選譯. Chengtu: Pa-Shu Shu-she, 1991.

Liu, Ssu-han 劉斯翰, ed. *Li Ho shih hsüan* 李賀詩選. Canton: Kuang-tung Jen-min, 1984.

Liu, Yen 劉衍. *Li Ho shih chiao chien cheng-i* 李賀詩校箋証異. Changsha: Hu-nan Ch'u-pan-she, 1990.

Luan, Kuei-ming 欒貴明 ed. *Ch'üan T'ang shih so-yin: Li Ho chüan* 全唐詩索引：李賀卷. Peking: Chung-hua, 1992.

Sung, Hsü-lien 宋緒連 and Ch'u, Hsü 初旭, eds. *San Li shih chien-shang tz'u-tien* 三李詩鑑賞辭典. Changchun: Chi-lin Wen-shih, 1992. Contains numerous close readings of poems by Li Ho, Li Po and Li Shang-yin as well as short biographies and useful bibliographies for these three important poets.

T'ang, Wen 唐文 *et al.*, eds. *Li Ho shih so-yin* 李賀詩索引. Tsinan: Ch'i-Lu Shu-she, 1984.

Wu, Ch'i-ming 吳啟明 ed. *Li Ho tzu-liao hui-pien* 李賀資料匯編. Peking: Chung-hua, 1994.

Yeh, Ts'ung-ch'i 葉蔥奇, ed. *Li Ho shih-chi* 李賀詩集. Peking: Jen-min Wen-hsüeh, 1984.

Translations

Frodsham, J. D. *Goddess, Ghost and Demons: The Collected Poems of Li He (790-816).* London: Anvil Press Poetry Ltd., 1983.

Kurokawa, Yôichi 黒川洋一, ed. *Riga shisen* 李賀詩選. Tokyo: Iwanami Shoten, 1993.

Lambert, Marie-Thérèse and Guy Degen. *Li He, Les visions et les jours.* Paris: La Différence, 1994.

Studies

Ch'en, Yün-chi 陳允吉. "Li Ho: Shih-ko t'ien-ts'ai yü ping-t'ai chi-ling-erh te chieh-ho" 李賀：詩歌天才與病態畸零兒的結合. *Fu-tan hsüeh-pao* 1988.6 (1988): 1-9.

Fu, Ching-shun 傅經順. *Li Ho shih-ko shang-hsi chi* 李賀詩歌賞析集. Chengtu: Pa-Shu Shu-she, 1988.

Hsu, C. Y." The Queen Mother of the West: Historical or Legendary? (Part I)," *Asian Culture Quarterly* XVI.2 (Summer 1988):29-42. Includes a translation and discussion of a poem by Li.

LaFleur, Frances Ann. "The Evolution of a Symbolist Aesthetic in Classical Chinese Verse: The Role of Li Ho Compared with That of Charles Baudelaire in Nineteenth-century French Poetry." Unpublished Ph.D. dissertation, Princeton University, 1993.

Lambert, Marie-Thérèse and Guy Degen. *Li He, Les visions et les jours.* Paris: La Différence, 1994.

Lang-tan, Goat Koei. "Traditionelles und Individuelles in der Bild und Versgestaltung des T'ang-Dichters Li Ho (791-817)," In *Ganz Allmaehlich, Festschrift fur Gunther Debon,* Heidelberg: Heidelberger Verlagsanstalt und Druckerei, 1986, pp. 132-45.

Li, Cho-fan 李卓藩. *Li Ho shih hsin-t'an* 李賀詩新探. Taipei: Wen-shih-che, 1997.

Li, Wen-pin 李文彬. "Li Ho's Poetry through Transformational-Generative Grammar," *Cheng-ta hsüeh-pao* 56 (1987): 1-19.

____. "The Imagery in Li Ho's Poetry," *Cheng-ta hsüeh-pao* 60 (1989): 1-18.

Liu, Jui-lien 劉瑞蓮. *Li Ho* 李賀. Peking: Chung-hua, 1981.

Liu, Yen 劉衍. *Li Ho shih chuan* 李賀詩傳. T'aiyüan: Shan-hsi Jen-min, 1984.

T'ao, Erh-fu 陶爾夫. "Li Ho shih-ko te t'ung-hua shih-chieh" 李賀詩歌的童話世界, *Wen-hsüeh p'ing-lun* 1991.3 (1991): 36-47.

Wu, Ch'i-ming 吳啟明. *Li Ho* 李賀. Shanghai: Shang-hai Ku-chi, 1986.

Yang, Ch'i-ch'ün 楊其群. *Li Ho yen-chiu lun-chi* 李賀研究論集. T'aiyüan: Pei-yüeh Wen-i, 1989.

Yang, Wen-hsiung 楊文雄. *Li Ho shih yen-chiu* 李賀詩研究. Taipei: Wen-shih-che, 1983.

Li Hua 李華 (d. *ca.* 769)

Studies

Yang, Ch'eng-tsu 楊承祖. "Li Hua hsi-nien k'ao-cheng" 李華系年考証, *Tung-hai hsüeh-pao* 33 (1992.6) 53-66.

Li I 李益 (748-827)

Editions and References

Chang, Shu 張澍, ed. *Li shang-shu shih-chi* 李尚書詩集. Lanchow: Lan-chou Ku-chi Shu-tien, 1990.

Luan, Kuei-ming 欒貴明, ed. *Chüan T'ang shih so-yin: Li I Lu Lun chüan* 全唐詩索引：李益盧倫卷. Peking: Tso-chia, 1997.

Wang, I-chün 王亦君 and P'ei, Yü-min 裴豫敏, eds. *Li I chi chu* 李益集註. Lanchow: Kan-su Jen-min, 1989.

Studies

Chan, Marie. "The Life of Li Yi (748?-827)," *MS* 38 (1988-89): 173-89.

Li K'ai-hsien 李開先 (1502-1568)

Editions and References

Li, K'ai-hsien. *I hsiao san* 一笑散. Peking: Wen-hsüeh Ku-chi K'an-hsing-she, 1955.

Studies

Iwaki, Hideo 岩城秀夫. *Ri Kaisen nenpu* 李開先年譜, *Mimei* 8 (1989): 63-106.

Pu, Chien 卜健. *Li K'ai-hsien chuan lüeh* 李開先傳略. *Hsi-chü-chia chuan-lun ts'ung-shu*, Peking: Chung-kuo Hsi-chü, 1989.

Li Kung-tso 李公佐 (*ca.* 770-*ca.* 848)

Studies

Ch'en, Cheng-chiang 陳正江. "T'ang-tai tsui chieh-ch'u te hsiao-shuo-chia chih i: Li Kung-tso" 唐代最杰出的小說家之一：李公佐. *Wen-shih chih-shih* 1988.3 (1988): 89-92.

Liu, Ying 劉瑛. *T'ang-tai ch'uan-ch'i yen-chiu* 唐代傳奇研究. Taipei: Lien-ching Ch'u-pan Kung-ssu, 1994. Studies of "Nan-k'o-t'ai-shou chuan" 南柯太守傳 and "Hsieh-hsiao-o chuan" 謝小娥傳 in pp. 237-41; 313-24.

Lu, Kung 路工. "Nan-k'o yü 'Nan-k'o-t'ai-shou chuan'" 南柯與南柯太守傳. *Wen-hsüeh i-ch'an* 1984.1 (1984): 41-45.

Nienhauser, William H., Jr. "'Nan-k'o-t'ai-shou chuan' te yü-yen yung-tien ho wai-yen i-i" 南柯太守傳的語言用典和外延意義. *Chung-wai wen-hsüeh* 17.6 (1988): 54-79.

Shen, Hui-ju 沈惠如. "Hsieh Hsiao-o yü Ni-miao-chi ku-shih ch'u-t'an" 謝小娥與尼妙寂故事初探. *Chung-hua wen-hua fu-hsing yüeh-k'an* 19.9 (1986): 65-70.

Wang, Meng-ou 王夢鷗. "'Nan-k'o-t'ai-shou chuan' chi-ch'i tso-che" 南柯太守傳及其作者. *Fu-jen hsüeh chih* 13 (1984): 17-24.

Wu, Yü-lien 吳玉蓮. "Tu 'Nan-k'o-t'ai-shou chuan'" 讀南柯太守傳. *Chung-hua wen-hua fu-hsing yüeh-k'an* 15.10 (1982): 46-51.

Li Meng-yang 李夢陽 (1475-1529 or 1531)

Editions and References
K'ung-t'ung chi 空同集. Shanghai: Shang-hai Ku-chi, 1991.

Studies
Ch'ien, Chin-sung 簡錦松 *Ming-tai wen-hsüeh p'i-p'ing yen-chiu* 明代文學批評研究. Taipei: Hsüeh-sheng, 1989. Argues that Li Tung-yang was the culmination of the *t'ai-ko-t'i* rather than its executioner.

Li P'an-lung 李攀龍 (1514-1570)

Editions and References

Li, Po-ch'i 李伯齊 *et al.*, eds. *Li P'an-lung shih-wen hsüan* 李攀龍詩文選. Tsinan: Chi-nan Ch'u-pan-she, 1993.

Pao, Ching-ti 包敬第, ed. *Ts'ang-ming hsien-sheng chi* 滄溟先生集. Shanghai: Shang-hai Ku-chi, 1992.

Studies

Hsü, Chien-k'un 許建崑. *Li P'an-lung wen-hsüeh yen-chiu* 李攀龍文學研究. Taipei: Wen-shih-che, 1987.

Wang, Shih-ch'ing 汪世清. "Ming Hou-ch'i-tzu chi-ch'i chiao-yu sheng-tsu pei-k'ao" 明後七子及其交游生卒備考, *Hsiang-kang Chung-wen Ta-hsüeh Chung-kuo Wen-hua Yen-chiu-so hsüeh-pao* 22 (1991): 31-51.

Li Pao-chia 李寶嘉 (1867-1906)

Editions and References

Huo ti-yü 活地獄. Shanghai: Shang-hai Ku-chi, 1987.

Kuan-ch'ang hsien-hsing chi 官場現形記. Leng Shih-chün 冷時峻, ed. Shanghai: Shang-hai Ku-chi, 1997. Annotated modern edition.

Translations

Lancashire, Douglas. *Modern Times, A Brief History of Enlightenment* Hong Kong: The Research Centre for Translation, The Chinese University of Hong Kong, 1996.

Iriya, Yoshitaka 入矢義高 and Ishikawa, Kensuku 石川賢作. *Kanjô genkeiki* 官場現形記. Tokyo: Heibonsha, 1969.

Li Po 李白 (701-762)

Editions and References

Chan, Ying 詹鍈. "*Li Po chi* hsi-chien pan-pen k'ao-lüeh" 李白集稀見版本考略, *Chung-kuo ku-chi yen-chiu* 中國古籍研究. V. 1. Shanghai: Shang-hai Ku-chi, 1996, pp. 339-369..

___, ed. *Li Po ch'üan-chi chiao-chu hui-shih chi-p'ing* 李白全集校注彙釋集評. 8v. Tientsin: Pai-hua Wen-i 百花文藝, 1997.

___ *et al.,* eds. *Li Po shih hsüan-i* 李白詩選譯. *Ku-tai wen-shih ming-chu hsüan-i ts'ung-shu.* Chengtu: Pa-Shu Shu-she, 1991.

Ying Sung Hsien-ch'un-pen Li Han-lin chi 景宋咸淳本李翰林集. Yangchow: Chiang-su Kuang-ling Ku-chi, 1980.

Chu, Chin-ch'eng 朱金城 and Ch'ü Shui-yüan 瞿蛻園, eds. *Li Po chi chiao-chu* 李白集校注. Shanghai: Shang-hai Ku-chi, 1980. Most extensively annotated edition. See also Yin Ch'u-pin's 尹楚彬 article pointing out errors in this collection in *Ku-chi cheng-li yen-chiu hsüeh-k'an,* 58(1995), 38-46.

Li Po hsüeh-k'an 李白學刊. Li Po Hsüeh-k'an Pien-chi-pu 李白學刊編輯部, ed. V. 1-. Shanghai: San-lien, 1989-.

Li Po shih-hsüan 李白詩選. Fu-tan Ta-hsüeh Ku-tien Wen-hsüeh Chiao-yen-tsu 復旦大學古典文學教研組, eds. Peking: Jen-min Wen-hsüeh, 1997.

Li Po yen-chiu lun-ts'ung 李白研究論叢. Li Po Yen-chiu Hsüeh-hui 李白研究學會, ed. V. 1-. Chengtu: Pa-Shu Shu-she, 1987-.

Li T'ai-po ch'üan-chi 李太白全集. 3v. Wang Ch'i 王琦 (1696-1744), commentator. Peking: Chung-hua, 1977. Annotated edition of Wang Ch'i commentary.

Li T'ai-po wen-chi 李太白文集. *Sung Shu-k'o-pen T'ang-jen chi ts'ung-k'an* 宋蜀刻本唐人集叢刊. Shanghai: Shang-hai Ku-chi, 1994.

Liu, I-sheng 劉逸生, ed. *Li Po shih hsüan* 李白詩選. Ma Li-ch'ien 馬里千, annot. Hong Kong: San-lien, 1982.

Luan, Kuei-ming 欒貴明 *et al,* ed. *Ch'üan T'ang shih so-yin, Li Po chüan* 全唐詩索引李白卷. Peking: Hsien-tai, 1995.

Mair, Victor H. *Four Introspective Poets, A Concordance to Selected Poems by Roan Jyi, Chern Tzyy-arng, Jang Jeouling, and Lii Bor.* Tempe: Center for Asian Studies, Arizona State University, Monograph No. 20, 1987. Translates all 49 of Li's "Ku-feng;" however, these translations are only designed to "serve as points of reference for those who consult the concordance"–a concordance to words, themes, and topics (under 247 English headings such as "flowers, blossoms, fruit," "luxuriance," and "fragrance") in these poems and those of Chang Chiu-ling and Li Po).

Niu, Pao-t'ung 牛寶彤, ed. *Li Po wen-hsüan* 李白文選. Peking: Hsüeh-yüan, 1989. Closely annotated versions of most of Li Po's prose.

P'ei, Fei 裴斐 and Liu, Shan-liang 劉善良, ed. *Li Po tzu-liao hui-pien*李白資料匯編. Peking: Chung-hua, 1994.

Shen, Feng 申風. "Li chi shu-lu" 李集書錄, *Li Po hsüeh-k'an* 李白學刊 1(1989): 210-233. Excellent discussion of the traditional editions.

Sung, Hsü-lien 宋緒連 and Ch'u, Hsü 初旭, eds. *San Li shih chien-shang tz'u-tien* 三李詩鑒賞辭典. Changchun: Chi-lin Wen-shih, 1992. Contains numerous close readings of poems by Li Ho, Li Po and Li Shang-yin as well as short biographies and useful bibliographies for these three important poets.

Terao, Takeshi 寺尾剛. "Nihon teki Ri Haku kenkyû kan kai" 日本的李白研究簡介, *Chung-kuo Li Po yen-chiu shang* 中國李白研究上 (1990), pp. 245-84.

Yü Hsien-hao 郁賢皓, ed. *Li Po shih hsüan chi* 李白詩選集. Shanghai: Shang-hai Ku-chi, 1990. Extremely useful; good preface, extensive annotation of about 150 poems and 20 prose works.

____ ed. *Li Po ta-tz'u-tien* 李白大辭典. Nanning: Kuang-hsi Chiao-yü, 1995. Entries arranged under topics like "life," "friends," "editions," "scholars and works on Li Po," etc.; appends an extensive bibliography of studies through 1991.

Translations

Almberg, S. P. E. "Li Bai: Two Prose Pieces," *Renditions* 33-34 (1990): 116-19.

Cheng, Wing fun and Hervé Collet. *Li Po, ermite du lotus bleu, immortel banni.* 2nd corrected ed. Millemont, France: Moundarren, 1985.

Hoizey, Dominique. *Li Bai: Sur notre terre exilé.* Paris: La Différence, 1990.

Jacob, Paul. *Florilège.* Paris: Gallimard, 1985.

Mair, Victor H. *Four Introspective Poets,* see Editions, References above.

Ôno, Jitsunosuke 大野実之助. *Ri Taihaku shika zenkai* 李太白詩歌全解. Tokyo: Waseda Daigaku, 1981.

Studies

Allen, Joseph R. "R/endings: The Disruptive Poetics of Li Bo," in Allen, *In the Voice of Others, Chinese Music Bureau Poetry. Michigan Monographs in Chinese Studies,* 63. Ann Arbor: Center for Chinese Studies, University of Michigan, 1992, pp. 165-206.

An, Ch'i 安旗. *Li Po ch'üan-chi pien-nien chu shih* 李白全集編年注釋. 3v. Chengtu: Pa-Shu Shu-she, 1990. A very useful book with a long, important preface.

____. *Li Po yen-chiu* 李白研究. Rpt. Taipei: Shui-niu, 1992.

____ and Hsüeh, T'ien-wei 薛天緯. *Li Po nien-p'u* 李白年譜. Tsinan: Ch'i-Lu Shu-she, 1982.

Baus, Wolf Lutz Bieg. "Ein Gedicht und seine Metamorphosen–22 Übersetzungen von Li Bais Jing ye-si–(Dauz: 2 weitere Übersetzungen des Gedichts von Hugo Dittberner und Manfred Hausmann)," in *Hefter für ostasiatische Literatur* 9 (December 1989): 98-109 and 122.

Belivanova, B. "On the Work and Personality of Li Tai-Bo," in Marian Galik, *Proceedings of the Fourth International Conference on the Theoretical Problems of Asian and African Literatures.* Bratislava: Literary Institute of Slovak Academy of Sciences, 1983.

357

Bryant, Daniel. "On the Authenticity of the *Tz'u* Attributed to Li Po." *T'ang Studies* 7 (1989):105-136.

Chan, Shelley W. "How the Story is Told and Who is Telling: Reading Li Bai's 'Ballad of Changan' and 'Ballad of Jiangxia,'" *T'ang Studies* 12 (1994), 39-55.

Chang, Shu-ch'eng 張書誠. *Li Po chia-shih chih mi* 李白家室之謎. Lanchow: Lan-chou Ta-hsüeh, 1994.

Cheng, Hsiu-p'ing 鄭修平. *Li Po tsai Shan-tung lun-ts'ung* 李白在山東論叢. Tsinan: Shan-tung Yu-i Shu-she, 1991.

Cheng, Wen 鄭文. *Li Tu lun chi* 李杜論集. Lanchow: Kan-su Min-tsu, 1994.

Chu, Chin-ch'eng 朱金城. *Chung-kuo Li Po yen-chiu (shang)* 中國李白研究 (上). Nanking: Chiang-su Ku-chi, 1990.

Dolby, William. "Song Qi: Biography of Li Bai," *Renditions* 33/34 (1990): 111-115.

Frankel, Hans H. "The Problem of the Authenticity of the Eleven *Tz'u* Attributed to Li Po," *Proceedings of the Second International Conference on Sinology, Academia Sinica (Taipei)*. Taipei: Academia Sinica, 1989, pp. 319-34.

Fu, Shao-liang 傅紹良. *Hsiao ao jen-sheng: Li Po te jen-ko yü feng-ko.* 笑傲人生：李白的人格与風格. T'aiyüan: Shan-hsi Chiao-yü, 1993.

Giraud, Daniel. *Ivre de Tao: Li Po, voyageur, poète et philosophe en Chine au VIIIᵉ siècle.* Paris: Michel, 1989.

Huang, Kuo-pin. "Li Po and Tu Fu: A Comparative Study," *Renditions* 21 & 22 (Spring and Autumn 1984): 99-126.

Kakehi, Kumiko 筧久美子 *Kanshô Chûgoku no koten dai 16 kan–Ri Haku* 鑑賞中国の古典　第１６巻–李白. Tokyo: Kadokawa Shoten, 1988

Ko, Ching-ch'un 葛景春. *Li Po ssu-hsiang i-shu t'an-li* 李白思想藝術探驪. Chengchow: Cheng-chou Ku-chi, 1991.

Kroll, Paul W. "Bibliography of Li Po." Unpublished manuscript.

_____. "Li Po's Rhapsody on the Great P'eng-bird," *Journal of Chinese Religions* 12(1984), 1-17. Annotated translation of the "Ta-p'eng fu" 大鵬賦.

_____. "Li Po's Transcendent Diction," *JAOS* 106.1-2 (January-June 1986), 99-118. Study, with translations, of Taoist influence and imagery in some of Li Po's poems.

_____. "Verses from on High: The Ascent of T'ai-shan," *TP,* 69(1983), 223-260. Study, with translations, of poems about Mount T'ai from the third through the eighth centuries, with particular attention to Li Po's set of six poems on "Yu T'ai shan." Revised version in *Lyric Voice,* pp. 167-216.

_____. "Li Po's Inscription for the Great Bell of the Hua-ch'eng Monastery," *TS* 13 (1995): 33-50

Li Po shih hsüan-chiang 李白詩選講. Liu I-hsüan 劉憶萱, Wang Yü-chang 王玉璋, commentators. Shenyang: Liao-ning Jen-min, 1985.

Li, Ts'ung-chün 李從軍. *Li Po k'ao-i lu* 李白考異錄. Tsinan: Ch'i-Lu Shu-she, 1986.

Lo Lien-t'ien 羅聯添. "Li Po shih-chi san-ko wen-t'i t'an-t'ao" 李白事蹟三個問題探討. In Lo, *T'ang-tai ssu-chia shih-wen lun-chi* 唐代四家詩文論集. Taipei: Hsüeh-hai, 1996, pp. 1-42.

Ma-an-shan shih Li Po yen-chiu-hui 馬鞍山市李白研究會, ed. *Chung Jih Li Po yen-chiu lun-wen-chi* 中日李白研究論文集. Peking: Chung-kuo Chan-wang, 1986.

Mair, Victor H. "Li Po's Letters in Pursuit of Political Patronage," *HJAS* 44.1 (June 1984):123-53. The only English-language study of Li Po's prose.

Matsuura, Tomohisa 松浦友久. *Ri Haku denki ron–kakugû no shisô* 李白伝記論一客寓の詩想. Tokyo: Kenkyû Shuppan, 1994.

Shi, Mingfei. "Li Po's Ascent of Mount O-mei," *Taoist Resources* 4 (1993): 31-46.

Shih, Feng-yu. "Li Po: A Biographical Study." Unpublished Ph. D. dissertation, University of British Columbia, 1983. Treats controversy about Li Po's background, chronology of his life, his political ambitions, and his life as a Taoist recluse.

Shih, Feng-yü 施逢雨. "Li Po sheng-p'ing k'ao-so" 李白生平考索, *THHP* 23.4, 24.1 (Dec. 1993, March 1994): 361-369; 45-84.

Tseng, Chen-chen. "Mythopoesis Historicized: Qu Yuan's Poetry and Its Legacy." Unpublished Ph.D. dissertation, University of Washington, 1992.

Varsano, Paula M. "Immediacy and Allusion in the Poetry of Li Po," *HJAS* 52.1 (June 1992): 225-261.

_____. "Transformation and Imitation: The Poetry of Li Pai." Unpublished Ph. D. dissertation, Princeton University, 1988.

Wang, Françoise. "La quête de l'immotalité chez Li Taibo (701-762)." Unpublished Ph. D. dissertation, Paris VII, 1994.

Yang Hai-po 楊海波. *Li Po ssu-hsiang yen-chiu* 李白思想研究. Peking: Hsüeh-lin, 1997.

Li Shang-yin 李商隱 (813?-858)

Editions and References

Chou, Chen-fu 周振甫, ed. *Li Shang-yin hsüan-chi*. 李商隱選集. Shanghai: Shang-hai Ku-chi, 1986.

Fan-nan wen-chi 樊南文集. 2v. Including *Fan nan wen-chi hsiang-chu* 樊南文集詳注 Feng Hao 馮浩 (1719-1801), annot. and *Fan nan wen-chi pu-pien* 樊南文集補編 Ch'ien Chen-lun 錢振倫 (1816-1879) and Ch'ien Chen-ch'ang 錢振常 (1825-1898), annot... Shanghai: Shang-hai Ku-chi, 1988.

Li Shang-yin shih-chi shu-chu 李商隱詩集疏注. Yeh Ts'ung-ch'i 葉蔥奇, annot. Peking: Jen-min Wen-hsüeh, 1985.

Li Shang-yin shih hsüan-i 李商隱詩選譯. Ch'en Yung-cheng 陳永正, annot. Chengtu: Pa-Shu Shu-she, 1991.

Liu, Hsüeh-k'ai 劉學鍇 and Yü, Shu-ch'eng 余恕誠, eds. *Li Shang-yin shih-ko chi-chieh* 李商隱詩歌集解. *Chung-kuo ku-tien wen-hsüeh chi-pen ts'ung-shu* 中國古典文學基本叢書. Peking: Chung-hua, 1988.

Luan, Kuei-ming 欒貴明 *et al.*, eds. *Ch'üan T'ang shih so-yin: Li Shang-yin chüan* 全唐詩索引：李商隱卷. Peking: Chung-hua, 1991.

San Li shih chien-shang tz'u-tien 三李詩鑑賞辭典. Sung Hsü-lien 宋緒連 and Ch'u Hsü 初旭, eds. Changchun: Chi-lin Wen-shih, 1992. Contains numerous close readings of poems by Li Ho, Li Po and Li Shang-yin as well as short biographies and useful bibliographies for these three important poets.

Wang, Ju-pi 王汝弼 and Nieh, Shih-ch'iao 聶石樵. *Yü-hsi-sheng shih ch'un* 玉谿生詩醇. Tsinan: Ch'i-Lu Shu-she, 1987.

Translations

Bonmarchand, Georges. *Li Yi-chan*. Notes and preface by Pascal Quignard. Paris: Gallimard, 1992 (rpt. of Tokyo: Maison Franco-Japonaise, 1955).

Hervouet, Yves. *Amour et politique dans la Chine ancienne, Cent poèmes de Li Shangyin (812-858)*. Paris: De Bocard, 1995.

Yeh, Chia-ying. "Li Shang-yin's "Four Yen-t'ai Poems," *Renditions* 21/22 (1984): 41-92. Translated into English by James R. Hightower.

Studies

Chang, Shu-hsiang 張淑香. *Li Shang-yin shih hsi-lun* 李商隱詩析論. Taipei: I-wen, 1985.

Huang, Sheng-ch'eng 黃盛雄. *Li I-shan shih yen-chiu* 李義山詩研究. Taipei: Wen-shih-che, 1987.

Hervouet, Yves. "Short Titles in the Poetry of Li Shang-yin." In *Chung-yang Yen-chiu Yüan Kuo-chi Han-hsüeh Hui-i lun-wen chi* 中央研究院國際漢學會議論文集, Taipei: Academia Sinica, 1981, pp. 289-317.

Ko, Chao-kuang 葛兆光 and Tai, Yen 戴燕. *Wan T'ang feng-yün–Tu Mu yü Li Shang-yin* 晚唐風韻一杜牧與李商隱. Nanking: Chiang-su Ku-chi, 1991.

Li, Ch'ang-ch'ing 李長慶, Chang, Fu-lin 張輔麟 and Mi, Chih-kuo 米治國. *Li Shang-yin chi ch'i tso-pin* 李商隱及其作品. Changchun: Shih-tai wen-i, 1989.

Li, Miao 李淼. *Li Shang-yin shih san-pai shou i-shang* 李商隱詩三百首譯賞. Taipei: Li-wen Wen-hua, 1988.

Li Shang-yin shih yen-chiu lun-wen chi 李商隱詩研究論文集. Chinese Department, National Chung-shan University, Taiwan, ed. Taipei: T'ien-t'u Shu-chü, 1986.

Liu, Wan. "Poetics of Allusion: Tu Fu, Li Shang-yin, Ezra Pound, and T. S. Eliot." Unpublished Ph.D. dissertation, Princeton University, 1992.

Owen, Stephen. "What Did Liuzhi Hear? The 'Yan Terrace Poems' and the Culture of Romance," *TS* 13 (1995): 81-118.

Pai, Kuan-yün 白冠雲. *Li Shang-yin yen-ch'ing shih chih mi* 李商隱艷情詩之謎. Taipei: Ming-wen, 1991.

Rigisan, Shichiritsu Chûshakuhan 李義山七律注釈班. "*Rigisan shichiritsu shûkô.*" 李義山七律集釈稿, *Tôhô Gakuhô* 66 (1994): 381-424.

Tung, Nai-pin 董乃斌. *Li Shang-yin chuan* 李商隱傳. Sian: Shan-hsi Jen-min, 1981.

Yen, K'un-yang 顏崑陽. *Li Shang-yin shih chien-shih fang-fa lun* 李商隱詩箋釋方法論. Taipei: Hsüeh-sheng, 1991.

Yu, Teresa Yee-Wah. "Li Shang-yin: The Poetry of Allusion." Unpublished Ph. D. dissertation, University of British Columbia, 1990.

Li T'iao-yüan 李調元 (1734-1803)

Editions and References

Lo, Huan-chang 羅煥章, ed. *Li T'iao-yüan shih chu* 李調元詩注. Chengtu: Pa-Shu Shu-she, 1993.

Yüeh-tung huang-hua chi 粵東皇華集. Peking: Chung-hua, 1991.

Li Tung-yang 李東陽 (1447-1516)

Editions and References

Chou Yin-pin 周寅賓, ed. *Li Tung-yang chi* 李東陽集. Changsha: Yüeh-lu Shu-she, 1984–85.

Huai lu t'ang chi 懷麓堂集. Shanghai: Shang-hai Ku-chi, 1991.

Studies

Ch'ien, Chin-sung 簡錦松 *Ming-tai wen-hsüeh p'i-p'ing yen-chiu* 明代文學批評研究. Taipei: Hsüeh-sheng, 1989. Argues that Li Tung-yang was the culmination of the *t'ai-ko-t'i* rather than its executioner.

Li Yü 李煜 (937-978)

Editions and References

Liu I-sheng 劉逸生, ed. Ch'en Chin-jung 陳錦榮, annot. *Li Yü Li Ch'ing-chao tz'u-chu* 李煜李清照詞注. Hong Kong: San-lien, 1986.

Translations

Landau, *Beyond Spring,* pp. 31-43.

Studies

Bryant, Daniel. "The 'Hsieh Hsia En' Fragments by Li Yü and His Lyric to the Melody 'Lin Chiang Hsien,'" *CLEAR* 7 (1985): 37-66.

Chiang, Hai-feng 姜海峰. "Kuan-yü Li Yü chi ch'i tz'u p'ing-chieh chung te wen-t'i" 關於李煜及其詞評价中的問題. *Ho-nan Ta-hsüeh hsüeh-pao* 1988.5.

Chin, Chi-ts'ang 靳极蒼. *Li Yü, Li Ch'ing-chao tz'u hsiang-chieh* 李煜李清照詞詳解. Chengtu: Ssu-ch'uan Jen-min, 1985.

Fan, Wei-kang 樊維綱. "Li Yü tz'u i-shu mei-li t'an-wei" 李煜詞藝術魅力探微. *Wen-hsüeh i-ch'an* 1989.2: 79-85.

Hsieh, Shih-yai 謝世涯. *Nan T'ang Li Hou-chu tz'u yen-chiu* 南唐李后主詞研究. Shanghai: Hsüeh-lin, 1994.

Liu Hsiao-yen 劉孝嚴, ed. *Nan-T'ang Erh-chu tz'u shih wen chi i-chu* 南唐二主詞詩文集譯注. Changchun: Chi-lin Wen-shih, 1997.

T'ien, Chü-chien 田居儉. *Li Yü chuan* 李煜傳. Peking: Tang-tai Chung-kuo, 1995.

Ts'ai, Hou-shih 蔡厚示, ed. *Li Ching, Li Yü tz'u shang-hsi chi* 李璟李煜詞賞析集. Chengtu: Pa-Shu Shu-she, 1987.

Yeh, Chia-ying 葉嘉瑩. *Wen T'ing-yün, Wei Chuang, Feng Yen-ssu, Li Yü* 溫庭筠韋莊馮延巳李煜. Taipei: Ta-an, 1992. *T'ang Sung ming-chia tz'u shang-hsi,* 1.

Li Yü 李玉 (*ca.* 1591-*ca.* 1671)

Editions and References

Pei tz'u kuang cheng p'u 北詞廣正譜. Taipei: T'ai-wan hsüeh-sheng shu-chü, 1984.

Ou-yang, Tai-fa 歐陽代發, ed. *I-p'eng hsüeh* 一捧雪. *Ku-tai hsi-chü ts'ung-shu.* Shanghai: Shang-hai Ku-chi, 1989. Also contains an introduction to the author and his accomplishments.

Studies

Yen, Ch'ang-k'o 顏長珂. *Li Yü p'ing-chuan* 李玉評傳. Peking: Chung-kuo hsi-chü, 1985.

Li Yü 李漁 (1611-1680 or1611–1676/1679)

Editions and References

Ai, Yin-fan 艾蔭范 and Hsieh, Pao-ch'in 解保勤, annot. *Li-weng tui yün hsin chu* 笠翁對韻新注. Peking: Shu-mu Wen-hsien, 1985.

Chan, Wei-en 湛偉恩, ed. *Feng-cheng wu* 風箏誤. Shanghai: Shang-hai Ku-chi, 1985. Following a critical introduction, provides an annotated, collated version.

Chang, K'o-fu 張克夫 and Shu, Ch'ih 舒弛, eds. *Ku chin shih lüeh* 古今史略. Hangchow: Che-chiang ku-chi, 1992.

Chao, Wen-ch'ing 趙文卿, Chiang Yü-hsiu 蔣聿修 and Chang Shou-mei 章壽眉, eds. *Li-weng mi shu* 笠翁秘書. Chungking: Ch'ung-ch'ing Ch'u-pan-she, 1990.

Hsiao, Jung 蕭容, ed. *Shih-erh lou* 十二樓. Shanghai: Shang-hai Ku-chi, 1986.

Huang, Hsi-nien 黃熙年, ed. *Li-weng tui-yün* 笠翁對韻. Changsha: Yüeh-lu Shu-she, 1987.

Huang, T'ien-chi 黃天驥 and Ou-yang Kuang 歐楊光, eds. *Li Li-weng hsi-chü hsüan* 李笠翁喜劇選. Changsha: Yüeh-lu Shu-she, 1984. Collated and annotated versions of three plays: "Feng-cheng wu" 風箏誤, "Shen-chung Lou" 蜃中樓, and "Nai-ho t'ien" 奈何天.

Li, Chung-shih 李忠實, ed. *Wen pai tui-chao chüan-i Hsien-ch'ing ou-chi* 文白對照全譯閑情偶寄. Tientsin: T'ien-chin Ku-chi, 1996.

Li, Jui-shan 李瑞山 *et al* eds. *Pai-hua Hsien-ch'ing ou-chi* 白話閑情偶寄. Tientsin: T'ien-chin Ku-chi, 1993.

Li Yü sui-pi ch'üan-chi 李漁隨筆全集. Chengtu: Pa-Shu Shu-she, 1997.

Li Yü ch'üan-chi 李漁全集. Hangchow: Che-chiang Ku-chi, 1992. This is a multi-volume work, with different editors undertaking punctuation and collation for the different titles within the collection.

Wu sheng hsi 無聲戲. Chengchow: Chung-chou Ku-chi, 1994.

Yü, Wen-tsao 于文藻 ed. *Li Li-weng hsiao-shuo shih-wu chung* 李笠翁小説十五種. Hangchow: Che-chiang Jen-min, 1983.

Translations

Corniot, Christine. *De la chair à l'extase.* Paris; Arles: Philippe Picquier, 1994.

Forke, Alfred. *Zwei chinesische Singspiele der Qing-Dynastie (Li Yu und Jiang Shiquan.* Martin Gimm, ed. Stuttgart: Franz Steiner, 1993.

Gimm, Martin and Helmut Martin. *Der schönste Knabe aus Peking, Vier Novellen aus der frühen Qing-Zeit* Vol. 7. Arcus Chinatexte, Dortmund: Projekt Verlag, 1995.

Hanan, Patrick. *The Carnal Prayer Mat (Rou Putuan).* Reprint ed. Honolulu: University of Hawaii Press, 1996. A translation of *Jou-p'u t'uan* 肉蒲團. The standard translation, scholarly and readable.

_____. *Silent Operas.* Hong Kong: The Chinese University Press, 1990. Translation of *Wu-sheng hsi* 無聲戲.

_____. *A Tower for the Summer Heat.* New York: Ballantine Books, 1992. Stories selected from the collections *Chueh-shih ming-yen* 覺世名言 and *Shih-erh lou* 十二樓.

Itô, Sôhei 伊藤漱平. ed. *Ri Gyo: Renjôheki* 李漁 : 連城璧. Tokyo: Kyûko Shoin, 1988.

Kaser, Pierre. *A mari jaloux femme fidèle, récits de 17e siècle.* Paris; Arles: Philippe Picquier, 1990.

Klossowski, P. *Jeou-p'ou-t'ouan ou la chair comme tapis de prière.* Paris: Pauvert, 1989.

Studies

Chang, Chun-shu and Shelley Hsueh-lun Chang. *Crisis and Transformation in Seventeenth-Century China: Society, Culture, and Modernity in Li Yü's World.* Ann Arbor: University of Michigan Press, 1992.

Hanan, Patrick. *The Invention of Li Yu.* Cambridge, Mass.: Harvard University Press, 1988.

Hegel, Robert E. "Inventing Li Yu," *CLEAR* 13 (1991): 95-100.

Hsiao, Jung 蕭榮. *Li Yü p'ing-chuan* 李漁評傳. Hangchow: Che-chiang Wen-i, 1985.

Itô, Sôhei 伊藤漱平. "Ri Gyo no gikyoku shôsetsu no seititsu to sono kankokuho ni" 李漁の戲曲小説の成立とその刊刻補二, *Nishô* 3 (1989): 311-49.

___. "Ri Gyo no shôsetsu *Museigeki* no hampon ki ni tsuite" 李漁之小説無声戯の版本記について, *Chû tetsubun gakkaihô* 9 (1984): 126-33.

Kaser, Pierre. "L'œuvre romanesque de Li Yu (1611-1680), parcours d'un novateur." Unpublished Ph.D. dissertation, Paris VII, 1994.

Ôtsuka, Hidetaka 大塚秀高. "*Jûni shô* to Ri Gyo 十二笑と李漁." In *Itô Sôhei Kyôju taikan kinen Chûgokugaku ronshû* 伊藤漱平教授退官記念中国学論集 Tokyo: Kyûko Shoin, 1986, pp. 649-76.

Pohl, Stephan. *Das Lautlose Theater des Li Yu (um 1655); eine Novellensammlung der frühen Qing-Zeit* Walldorft-Hessen: Verlag für Orientkunde Dr. H. Vorndran, 1994.

Shan, Chin-heng 單錦珩. *Li Yü chuan* 李漁傳. Chengtu: Ssu-ch'uan Wen-i, 1986.

Ts'ui, Tzu-en 崔子恩. *Li Yü hsiao-shuo lun-kao* 李漁小説論稿. Peking: Chung-kuo She-hui

K'o-hsüeh-yüan, 1989.

Tu, Shu-ying 杜書瀛. *Lun Li Yü te hsi-chü mei-hsüeh* 論李漁的戲劇美學. Peking: Chung-kuo
She-hui K'o-hsüeh, 1982. A study of Li's plays and his critical writings on drama.

Yü, Wei-min 俞為民. *Li Yü "Hsien-ch'ing ou-chi" ch'ü-lun yen-chiu* 李漁閑情偶寄曲論研究.
Nanchang: Chiang-hsi Chiao-yü, 1994.

Yüan, I-chih 袁益之. "Li Yü sheng-tsu nien k'ao-pien" 李漁生卒年考辨. *Wen-hsüeh p'ing-lun
ts'ung-k'an* 13 (1982): 200-205.

Liang Ch'en-yü 梁辰魚 (*ca.* 1520-*ca.* 1593)

Editions and References

Chang, Ch'en-shih 張忱石, ed. *Huan-sha chi chiao-chu* 浣紗記校注. Peking: Chung-hua, 1994.

Studies

Leung, K. C. "Balance and Symmetry in the *Huan-sha chi.*" *THHP, NS* 16 (1984): 179-201.

Liang Ch'i-ch'ao 梁啟超 (1873-1929)

Editions and References

Chu, Wei-cheng 朱維錚, ed. *Liang Ch'i-ch'ao lun Ch'ing hsüeh shih erh-chung* 梁啟超論清學史
二種. *Chunk-kuo chin-hsien-tai ssu-hsiang wen-hua shih shih-liao ts'ung-shu* 中國近現代
思想文化史史料叢書. Shanghai: Fu-tan ta-hsüeh, 1985.

___, ed. *Ch'ing-tai hsüeh-shu kai-lun* 清代學術概論. Shanghai: Hsia-tan ta-hsüeh, 1985.

Huang, Shen 黃珅. *Liang Ch'i-ch'ao shih wen hsüan* 梁啟超詩文選. *Chung-kuo chin-tai wen-hsüeh
ts'ung-shu.* Shanghai: Hua-tung Shih-fan Ta-hsüeh, 1990.

Liang Ch'i-ch'ao cheng-lun hsüan 梁啟超政論選. *Chung-kuo chi-che ts'ung-shu* 中國記者叢書.
Peking: Hsin-hua, 1994.

Liang, Ch'i-ch'ao. *Lun Chung-kuo hsüeh-shu ssu-hsiang pien-ch'ien chih ta-shih* 論中國學術思想
變遷之大勢. Yangchow: Chiang-su Kuang-ling Ku-chi K'o-yin-she, 1990. Based on
the 1936 Chung-hua edition.

Studies

Ko, Mao-ch'un 葛懋春 and Chiang, Chün 蔣俊, eds. *Liang Ch'i-ch'ao che-hsüeh ssu-hsiang
lun-wen hsüan* 梁啟超哲學思想論文選. *Chung-kuo hsien-tai che-hsüeh shih tzu-liao hsüan-
pien* 中國現代哲學史資料選編. Peking: Pei-ching Ta-hsüeh, 1984.

Tang, Xiaobing. "Writing a History of Modernity: A Study of the Historical Consciousness
of Liang Ch'i-ch'ao." Unpublished Ph.D. Dissertation, Duke University, 1991.

___. *Global Space and the Nationalist Discourse of Modernity: The Historical Thinking of Liang
Qichao.* Stanford: Stanford University. Press, 1996.

Liang Su 梁肅 (753-793)

Studies

Ono, Shihei 小野四平. "Ryô Shoku kara Ryû Sôgen e–'Tôdai kobun no genryû' hosetsu" 梁
肅から柳宗元へ–「唐代古文の源流」補説, *Shûkan Tôyôgaku* 66 (1992): 83-101.

Liao-chai chih-i 聊齋志異 (Strange Stories from the Leisure Studio, early Ch'ing dynasty)

Editions and References

Chang, Shih-ming 張式銘, ed. *Liao-chai chih-i* 聊齋志異. Changsha: Yüeh-lu Shu-she, 1988.

Chu, I-hsüan 朱一玄, Keng, Lien-feng 耿廉楓 and Sheng, Wei 盛偉, eds. *Liao-chai chih-i tz'u-tien* 聊齋志異辭典. Tientsin: T'ien-chin Ku-chi, 1991.

Fujita, Hiroyoshi 藤田祐賢 and Yagi, Akiyoshi 八木章好. *Ryôsai kenkyû bunken yôran* 聊斎研究文献要覧. Tokyo: Tôhô Shoten, 1985

Hsiao, Ai 蕭艾, *et al.* trans. *Pai-hua Liao-chai* 白話聊齋. 20 *chüan. Ku-tien ming-chu chin-i tu-pen.* Changsha: Yüeh-lu Shu-she, 1990.

Liao-chai chih-i i-kao 聊齋志異遺稿. *Pi-chi hsiao-shuo ta-kuan.* Taipei: Hsin-hsing Shu-chü, 1986.

Pai, Lan-ling 白嵐玲, ed. *Liao-chai chih-i* 聊齋志異. Peking: Shih-yüeh Wen-i, 1997.

Sheng, Wei 盛偉, ed. *Liao-chai i-wen chi chu* 聊齋佚文輯注. Tsinan: Ch'i-Lu Shu-she, 1986.

_____.*I shih* 異史. Hofei: An-huei Wen-i, 1993.

Translations

Roy, Claude. *Histoires et légendes de la Chine mystérieuse.* Paris: Sand, 1987.

Chang, Ch'ing-nien, Chang Tz'u-yün, and Yang Yi. *Strange Tales from the Liaozhai Studio.* 3v. Peking: People's China Publishing House, 1997.

Chatelain, Hélène. *Le Studio des Loisirs.* Paris: U. G. E., 1993.

Laloy, Louis. *Contes étranges du cabinet Leao.* Paris: Philippe Picquier, 1994.

Lu, Yün-cheng *et al. Strange Tales of Liaozhai.* Hong Kong: Commericial Press, 1988.

Mair, Denis C. and Victor H. Mair. *Strange Tales from Make-Do Studio.* Peking: Foreign Languages Press, 1989.

Masuda, Wataru 增田涉 *et al. Ryôsai shii* 聊斎志異. Rpt. Tokyo: Heibonsha, 1994 (1970-71).

Rösel, Gottfried. *Umgang mit Chrysanthemen—81 Erzählungen der ersten vier Bücher aus der Sammlung Liao-dschai-dschi-yi.* Zurich: Die Waage, 1987.

_____. *Zwei Leben im Traum—67 Erzählungen der Bände fünf bis acht aud der Sammlung Liao-dschai-dschi-yi.* Zurich: Die Waage, 1987.

_____. *Besuch bei den Seligen—86 Erzählungen der Bände neun bis zwölf aus der Sammlung Liao-dschai-dschi-yi.* Zurich: Die Waage, 1991.

_____. *Kontakte mit Legenden—109 Erzählungen der letzten beiden Bücher sechzehn und siebzehn Gesamtwerks.* Zurich: Die Waage, 1992.

_____. *Schmetterlinge fliegen lassen—158 Erzählungen der Bände dreizehen bis fünfzehn aus der Sammlung Liao-dschai dschi-yi.* Zurich: Die Waage, 1992.

Wu, Fatima. "Foxes in Chinese Supernatural Tales, I and II." *TkR* 17 (2 and 3 1987): 121-154; 263-294.

Yagi, Akiyoshi 八木章好. "Ryôsai shii no 'chi' ni tsuite" 聊斎志異のちについて, *Geibun kenkyû* 48 (1986): 81-98.

Zeitlin, Judith T. *Historian of the Strange—Pu Songlin and the Chinese Classical Tale.* Stanford: Stanford University Press, 1993.

Studies

Barr, Alan. "Pu Songling and *Liaozhai zhiyi:* A Study of Textual Transmission, Biographical Background, and Literary Antecedents." Unpublished Ph. D. dissertation, Oxford University, 1983.

_____. "The Textual Transmission of *Liaozhai zhiyi.*" *HJAS* 44 (1984): 515-562.

_____. "A Comparative Study of the Early and Late Tales in *Liaozhai zhiyi.*" *HJAS* 45 (1985): 157-202.

____. "Pu Songling and the Qin Examination System." *Late Imperial China* 7 (1986): 87-111.

____. "Disarming Intruders: Alien Women in *Liaozhai zhiyi*." *HJAS* 49 (1989): 501-18.

Inada, Takashi 稲田孝 *Ryôsai Shii–Gansei to kaii no nozoki karakuri* 聊斎志異–玩世と怪異の覗きからくり. Tokyo: Kôdansha, 1994

Lanciotti, L. "An Introduction to the Work of Pu Songling." *Ming Qing yen-chiu* (1993): 67-80.

Lei, Chün-ming 雷群明. *P'u Sung-ling yü Liao-chai chih-i* 蒲松齡與聊齋志異. Shanghai: Shanghai Ku-chi, 1993.

Li, Ling-nien 李靈年. *P'u Sung-ling yü Liao-chai chih-i* 蒲松齡與聊齋志異. Shengyang: Liao-ning Chiao-yü, 1993.

Li Wai-yee. "Rhetoric and Fantasy and Rhetoric of Irony: Studies in *Liao-chai chih-i* and *Hung-lou Meng*." Unpublished Ph. D. dissertation, Princeton University, 1988.

Liao-chai chih-i chien-shang chi 聊齋志異鑒賞集. Peking: Jen-min Wen-hsüeh, 1983.

Lo, Ching-chih 羅敬之. *P'u Sung-ling chi ch'i Liao-chai chih-i* 蒲松齡及其聊齋志異. *Chung-hua ts'ung-shu. Taipei*: Kuo-li Pien-i-kuan, 1986.

Ma, Chen-fang 馬振方, ed. *Liao-chai chih-i p'ing-shang ta-ch'eng* 聊齋志異評賞大成. Kweilin: Li-chiang, 1992.

Nakano, Miyoko 中野美代子. *Ho Shôrei–Ryôsai shii* 蒲松齡–聊斎志異. Tokyo: Kokusho Kankôkai 1988. 國書刊行會, 1988.

Pak, Chûng-do 朴增道. *Liao-chai chih-i yen-chiu* 聊齋志異研究. Ph.D dissertation. Taipei: Kuo-li T'ai-wan Shih-fan Ta-hsüeh Kuo-wen Yen-chiu-so, 1988.

P'u Sung-ling yen-chiu 蒲松齡研究. P'u Sung-ling Yen-chiu-so 蒲松齡研究所, ed. Established in 1993 in Tzu-po 淄博, this journal is devoted to studies of P'u Sung-ling.

P'u Sung-ling yen-chiu chuan-k'an 蒲松齡研究專刊. Shan-tung Ta-hsüeh P'u Sung-ling Yen-chiu-shih 山東大學蒲松齡研究室, ed. Tsinan: Ch'i-Lu Shu-she, 1980-

Wang, Chih-chung 王枝忠. *P'u Sung-ling lun-chi* 蒲松齡論集. Peking: Wen-hua I-shu, 1990.

Yang, Liu 楊柳. *Liao-chai chih-i yen-chiu* 聊齋志異研究. Nanking: Chiang-su Jen-min, 1985.

Yüan, Shih-shuo 袁世碩. *P'u Sung-ling shih-chi chu-shu hsin-k'ao* 蒲松齡事跡著述新考. Tsinan: Ch'i-Lu Shu-she, 1988.

Zeitlin, Judith T. *Historian of the Strange, Pu Songling and the Chinese Classical Tale*. Stanford: Stanford University Press, 1993.

____. "Pu Songling's (1654-1715) *Liaozhai zhiyi* and the Chinese Discourse on the Strange." Unpublished Ph. D. dissertation, Harvard University, 1988.

Lieh-hsien chuan 列仙傳 (Biographies of Immortals)

Editions and References

Lieh-hsien chuan chiao-cheng-pen 列仙傳校正本. Collated by Wang, Chao-yüan 王照圓 (Ch'ing Dynasty). In *Tao-tsang ching-hua lu*. Hangchow: Che-chiang Ku-chi, 1989.

Lieh-hsien chuan, Shen-hsien chuan. 列仙傳，神仙傳. Shanghai: Shang-hai Ku-chi, 1990.

Wang, Shu-min 王叔岷, ed. *Lieh-hsien chuan chiao-chien* 列仙傳校箋. Taipei: Chung-yang Yen-chiu-yüan Wen-che-so, 1995.

Translations

Kôma, Miyoshi 高馬三良. *Hô Bokushi Retsusen den Sengai kyô* 抱朴子, 列仙伝, 山海経. Tokyo: Heibonsha, 1969

Maeno, Naoaki 前野直彬. *Sengaikyô Retsusen den* 山海経・列仙伝. *Zenshaku kanbun taikei* 33 全釈漢文大系３３. Tokyo: Shûeisha, 1975.

Ozaki, Masaharu 尾崎正治, Hiraki, Kôhei 平木康平 and Ôgata, Tôru 大形徹. *Kanshô Chûgoku no koten dai 9 kan–Hô Bokushi, Retsusen den* 鑑賞中国の古典, 第９巻–抱朴子, 列仙伝.

Tokyo: Kadokawa Shoten, 1988

Sawada, Mizuho 沢田瑞穂. *Retsusen den Shinsen den.* 列仙伝, 神仙伝. Tokyo: Heibonsha, 1993.

Studies

Fukui, Kôjun 福井康順. *"Retsusen den kô"* 列仙伝考, in *Tôyô shisô no shi kenkyû* 東洋思想の史研究. Tokyo: Shoseki Bunbutsu Ryûtsukai, 1960.

Lin Hung 林鴻 (*ca.* 1340-*ca.* 1400)

Editions and References

Ming-sheng chi 鳴盛集. Shanghai: Shang-hai Ku-chi, 1991.

Lin Shu 林紓 (1852-1924)

Editions and References

Hsüeh, Sui-chih 薛綏之 and Chang Chün-ts'ai 張俊才, eds. *Lin Shu yen-chiu tzu-liao* 林紓研究資料. *Chung-kuo hsien-tai tso-chia tso-p'in yen-chiu tzu-liao ts'ung-shu.* Fuchow: Fu-chien Jen-min, 1983.

Lin Shu fan-i hsiao-shuo wei-k'an chiu chung 林紓翻譯小説未刊九種. Fuchow: Fu-chien Jen-min, 1994.

Lin, Wei 林薇, ed. *Lin Shu hsüan chi* 林紓選集. Chengtu: Ssu-ch'uan Jen-min, 1985.

Studies

Chang, Chün-ts'ai 張俊才. *Lin Shu p'ing chuan* 林紓評傳. Tientsin: Nan-k'ai Ta-hsüeh, 1993.

Hu, Ying. "The Translator Transfigured: Lin Shu and the Cultural Logic of the Late Qing." *Positions* 3 (1995): 159-93.

Tseng, Hsien-hui 曾憲輝. *Lin Shu* 林紓. *Fu-chien chin-tai ming-jen chuan-chi ts'ung-shu.* Fuchow: Fu-chien Chiao-yü, 1993.

Ling Meng-ch'u 凌濛初 (1580-1644)

Editions and References

Ch'en, Erh-tung 陳邇冬 and Kuo, Chün-chieh 郭雋杰, eds. *Erh-k'o P'o-an ching-ch'i* 二刻拍案驚奇. 2v. Peking: Wen-hsüeh, 1997. Based on a manuscript held in the Naikaku Bunkô.

Ch'in, Hsü-ch'ing 秦旭卿, ed. *Ch'u-k'o, Erh-k'o P'o-an ching-ch'i* 初刻二刻拍案驚奇. *Ku-tien ming-chu p'u-chi wen-k'u* 古典名著普及文庫. Changsha: Yüeh-lu Shu-she, 1988.

Katsuyama, Minoru 勝山稔. "'Sangen nihaku' 'Keihon tsûzoku shôsetsu' 'Seihei sandô wahon' kankei ronbun mokuroku (chûbun hen)" 『三言二拍』『京本通俗小説』『清平山堂話本』関係論文目録（中文篇） *Chûô daigaku Daigakuin Ronkyû–Bungaku Kenkyûsha-hen* 26, 1994

Shih, Ch'ang-yü 石昌渝, ed. *P'o-an ching-ch'i* 拍案驚奇. *Chung-kuo hua-pen ta-hsi.* Nanking: Chiang-su Ku-chi, 1990.

Translations

Lévy, André. *L'amour de la renarde: marchands et lettrés de la vieille Chine (douze contes du XVII siècle par Ling Mong-ts'chou).* Paris: Gallimard, 1988. An excellent annotated translation.

Studies

Chang, Ping 張兵. *Ling Meng-ch'u yü Liang p'o* 凌濛初與兩拍. *Ku-tai hsiao-shuo p'ing-chia ts'ung-shu* Shenyang: Liao-ning Chiao-yü, 1992.

Lauwaert, Francoise. "Comptes des dieux, calculs des hommes: essai sur la rétribution dans les contes en langue vulgaire de 17e siècle." *TP* 76 (1990): 62-94.

_____."La mauvaise graine: Le gendre adopté dans le conte d'imitation de la fin des Ming." *Études chinoises* 12 (1993): 51-94.

Ma, Mei-hsin 馬美信. *Ling Meng-ch'u ho Erh p'o* 凌濛初和二拍. *Chung-kuo wen-hsüeh chi-pen chih-shih ts'ung-shu.* Shanghai: Shang-hai Ku-chi, 1994.

Liu Ch'ang-ch'ing 劉長卿 (*ca.* 710-*ca.* 787)

Editions and References

Ch'u, Chung-chün 儲仲君. *Liu Chang-ch'ing shih pien-nien chien-chu* 劉長卿詩編年箋注. Peking: Chung-hua, 1996.

Luan, Kuei-ming 欒貴明, ed. *Chüan T'ang-shih so-yin: Liu Ch'ang-ch'ing chüan* 全唐詩索引：劉長卿卷. Peking: Hsien-tai, 1995.

Studies

Liu, Ch'ien 劉乾. "Liu Ch'ang-ch'ing shih tsa-k'ao" 劉長卿詩雜考, *Wen-hsien* 1989.1.

Liu Ch'en-weng 劉辰翁 (1232-1297 or 1231-1294)

Editions and References

Hsü-hsi chi 須溪集. *Ts'ung-shu chi-ch'eng hsü-pien.*Shanghai: Shang-hai Ku-chi, 1994.

Tuan, Ta-lin 段大林, ed. *Liu Ch'en-weng chi* 劉辰翁集. Nanchang: Chiang-hsi Jen-min, 1987.

Liu Chi 劉基 (1311-1375)

Editions and References

Liu, Yün-hsing 劉運興, ed. *Tuan-meng mi-shu chu-shih* 斷夢秘書注釋. *Chung-kuo ch'i wen-hua ts'ung-shu* Taipei: Ming-wen Shu-chü, 1994.

Translations

Strassberg, *Inscribed Landscapes,* pp. 279-282.

Studies

Chou, Ch'ün 周群. *Liu Chi p'ing-chuan* 劉基評傳. Nanking: Nan-ching Ta-hsüeh, 1995.

Hao, Chao-chü 郝兆矩 and Liu, Wen-feng 劉文峰. *Liu Po-wen ch'üan-chuan* 劉伯溫全傳. Dairen: Ta-lien Ch'u-pan-she, 1994.

Wang, Li-ch'ün 王立群. *Hsün-chao li-hsiang-kuo: Liu Po-wen cheng-chih yü-yen chi* 尋找理想國：劉伯溫政治寓言集. *Shih-yung li-shih ts'ung-shu* Taipei: Yüan-liu, 1994.

Liu Chih-chi 劉知幾 (661-721)

Editions and References

Chang, Chen-p'ei 張振珮, ed. *Shih t'ung chien-chu* 史通箋注. Kweiyang: Kuei-chou Jen-min, 1985.

Chao, Lü-fu 趙呂甫, ed. *Shih t'ung hsin chiao-chu* 史通新校注. Chungking: Ch'ung-ch'ing Ch'u-pan-she, 1990.

Hou, Ch'ang-chi 侯昌吉, *ed. Shih t'ung hsüan i* 史通選譯. Chengtu: Pa-Shu Shu-she, 1990.

Wu, Ch'i 吳琦 *et al.*, eds. *Shih-t'ung* 史通. Changsha: Yüeh-lu Shu-she, 1993.

Translation

Nishiwaki, Tsuneki 西脇常記. *Shi tsû nai hen* 史通內篇. Tokyo: Keisô Shobô, 1990.

Studies

Chang, San-hsi 張三夕. *P'i-p'an shih-hsüeh te p'i-p'an* 批判史學的批判. Taipei: Wen-chin, 1992.

Lao, Ch'ung-hsing 勞充興. "Kuan-yü Shih-t'ung chiao-tien chih-i" 關於史通校點質疑, *Pei-ching she-hui k'o-hsüeh* 1987.1.

P'eng, Ya-ling 彭雅玲. *Shih t'ung te li-shih hsü-shu li-lun* 史通的歷史敘述理論. *Wen shih che-hsüeh chi-ch'eng* Taipei: Wen-shih-che, 1993.

Ôhama, Hiroshi 大濱浩皓. *Shiki shitsû no sekai–Chûgoku no rekishi kan* 史記史通の世界–中國の歷史観. Tokyo: Tôhô Shoten, 1993

Sun, Ch'ing-shan 孫慶善. "Liu Chih-chi tsai ku wen-hsien-hsüeh shang te ch'eng-chiu" 劉知幾在古文獻學上的成就, *Wen-hsien* 1988.4.

Liu Chih-yüan chu-kuang-tiao 劉知遠諸宮調 (**All Keys and Notes about Liu Chih-yuan**)

Editions and References

Liao, Hsün-ying 廖珣英, ed. *Liu Chih-yüan chu-kung-tiao chiao-chu* 劉知遠諸宮調校注. Peking: Chung-hua, 1993.

Liu E 劉鶚 (**1857-1907 or 1909**)

Editions and References

Liu, Hui-sun 劉蕙孫, ed. *T'ieh-yün shih-ts'un* 鐵雲詩存. Tsinan: Ch'i-Lu Shu-she, 1980.

Liu, Te-lung 劉德隆, Chu, Hsi 朱禧, and Liu, Te-p'ing 劉德平, eds. *Liu E chi Lao-ts'an yu-chi tzu-liao* 劉鶚及老殘遊記資料. Chengtu: Ssu-ch'uan Jen-min, 1985.

Tarumoto, Teruo 樽本照雄. "*Rôsan yûki* jimmei sakuhin" 老殘遊記人名作品, *Osaka Keidai ronshû,* 193 (1990): 101-170.

Translations

Okazaki, Toshio 岡崎俊夫. *Rôzan yûki* 老殘遊記. Tokyo: Heibonsha, 1965

Iizuka, Akira 飯塚朗. *Rôzan yûki, zokushû* 老殘遊記, 続集. *Chûgoku koten bungaku taikei* 51 中国古典文学大系 5 1. Tokyo: Heibonsha 1969

Kühner, H. *Die Reisen des Lao Can*. Frankfurt: Insel, 1989.

Reclus, Jacques and Sheng Cheng. *L'Odyssee de Lao Ts'an*. Rpt. Paris: Gallimard, 1990 (1964).

Studies

Ch'en, Liao 陳遼. *Liu E yü* Lao-ts'an yu-chi 劉鶚與老殘遊記. Chengchow: Chung-chou Ku-chi, 1989.

Kao, Cheng 高正. "Liu E shou-chi k'ao-shih" 劉鶚手記考釋, *Tao-chia wen-hua yen-chiu* 5 (1994): 477-491.

Liu Hsiang 劉向 (*ca.* 79-*ca.* 6 B.C.)

Editons and References

Chao, Shan-i 趙善詒, ed. *Shuo-yüan shu-cheng* 説苑疏證. Shanghai: Hua-tung Shih-fan Ta-hsüeh, 1985.

Hsiang, Tsung-lu 向宗魯 (1895-1941), ed. *Shuo-yüan chiao-cheng* 説苑校證. *Chung-kuo ku-tien wen-hsüeh chi-pen ts'ung-shu*. Peking: Chung-hua, 1987. Carefully edited edition with useful cross-references in the notes.

Li, Hua-nien. *Hsin-hsü ch'üan i* 新序全譯. Kweiyang: Kuei-chou Jen-min, 1994. *Chung-kuo li-tai ming-chu ch'üan i ts'ung-shu*

Liu Tien-chüeh 劉殿爵, ed. *Hsin-hsü chu tzu so-yin* 新序逐字索引. Hong Kong: Shang-wu, 1992.

____, ed. *Shuo-yüan chu tzu so-yin* 説苑逐字索引. Hong Kong: Shang-wu, 1992.

____, ed. *Ku lieh-nü chuan chu tzu so-yin* 古列女傳逐字索引. Hong Kong: Shang-wu Yin-shu-kuan, 1993. Chinese University of Hong Kong Institute of Chinese Studies the ICS ancient Chinese texts concordance series. Historical works; no. 3

Lu, Yüan-chün 盧元駿, ed. *Hsin-hsü chin-chu chin-i* 新序今注今譯. Taipei: T'ai-wan Shang-wu, 1975.

____, ed. *Shuo-yüan chin-chu chin-i* 説苑今注今譯. Taipei: T'ai-wan Shang-wu, 1981.

Tso, Sung-ch'ao 左松超, ed. *Hsin-i Shuo-yüan tu-pen* 新譯説苑讀本. Taipei: San-min, 1997.

Wang, Ying 王鍈 and Wang, T'ien-hai 王天海, eds. *Shuo-yüan ch'üan i* 説苑全譯. *Chung-kuo li-tai ming-chu ch'üan i ts'ung-shu* Kweiyang: Kuei-chou Jen-min, 1992.

Studies

Hsü, Fu-kuan, 3:49-115.

Ikeda, Shûzô 池田秀三. *Setsuen–Chie no hanazono* 説苑–知恵の花園. Tokyo: Kôdansha, 1991.

Katô, Minoru 加藤実. "Ryû Kô no *Shikyôgaku*–yûrei jidai o megutte 劉向の詩經學—幽厲時代をめぐつて, *Tôyô no shisô to shûkyô* 11 (1994): 1-16.

Mou, Sherry Jenq-yunn. "Gentlemen's Prescriptions for Women's Lives: Liu Hsiang's 'The Biographies of Women' and Its Influence on the 'Biographies of Women' Chapters in Early Chinese Dynastic Histories." Ph.D. dissertation, Ohio State Univ., 1994.

Shimomi, Takao 下見隆雄. *Ryû Kô 'Retsujo den' no kenkyû* 劉向『列女伝』の研究. Tokyo: Tôkai Daigaku Shuppankai 1989

Yamazaki, Junichi 山崎純一. *Retsujo den–Rekishi o kaeta onna tachi* 列女伝–歴史を変えた女たち. Tokyo: Satsuki Shobô 1991.

Wen, Ssu 聞思. "Liu Hsiang sheng tsu nien pien" 劉向生卒年辨. *Wen-shih* 32 (1990): 172-195.

Wu, Min-hsia 吳玟霞. "*Lieh-nü chuan* te pien-tsuan ho liu-ch'uan" 列女傳的編纂和流傳. *Jen-wen tsa-chih* 1988.3: 121-124.

Liu Hsin 劉歆 (*ca.* 50 B.C.-A.D. 23)

Studies

Chien, Fu-hsing 簡福興. "Liu Hsin ko-lieh *Tso chuan* chieh-ching shuo te shang-ch'üeh" 劉歆

割裂左傳解經説的商榷, *K'ung Meng yüeh-k'an* 32.4 (1993): 2-10.

Liu K'o-chuang 劉克莊 (1187-1269)

Editions and References

Chao, Chi 趙季 and Yeh Yen-ts'ai 葉言材, eds. *Liu Hou-ts'un hsiao-p'in* 劉後村小品. Peking: Wen-hua I-shu, 1997.

Chiang-hsi shih-p'ai hsiao-hsü 江西詩派小序. *Ts'ung-shu chi-ch'eng ch'u-pien*. Peking: Chung-hua, 1985.

Ch'ien Chung-lien 錢仲聯, ed. *Hou-ts'un tz'u chien-chu* 後村詞箋注. Shanghai: Shang-hai Ku-chi, 1989.

Hou-ts'un shih-hua 後村詩話. Punctuated and Collated by Wang, Hsiu-mei 王秀梅. Peking: Chung-hua, 1983.

Hu, Wen-nung 胡問儂 and Wang, Hao-sou 王皓叟, eds. *Hou-ts'un Ch'ien-chia-shih chiao-chu* 後村千家詩校注. Kweiyang: Kuei-chou Jen-min, 1986.

Studies

Ch'eng, Chang-ts'an 程章燦. *Liu K'o-chuang nien-p'u* 劉克莊年譜. *Nan-ching Ta-hsüeh Ku-tien Wen-hsien Yen-chiu-so chuan-k'an* Kweiyang: Kuei-chou Jen-min, 1993.

Fuller, Michael. "Liu Kezhuang on Tang Poetry," *TS* 13 (1995): 119-141.

Liu-shih chia hsiao-shuo 六十家小説 (Sixty Stories)

Editions and References

Katsuyama, Minoru 勝山稔. "'Sangen nihaku' 'Keihon tsûzoku shôsetsu' 'Seihei sandô wahon' kankei ronbun mokuroku (chûbun hen)" 『三言二拍』『京本通俗小説』『清平山堂話本』関係論文目録（中文篇）　*Chûô daigaku Daigakuin Ronkyû–Bungaku Kenkyûsha-hen* 26, 1994

T'an, Cheng-pi 譚正璧, ed. *Ch'ing-p'ing-shan T'ang hua-pen* 清平山堂話本. Shanghai: Shang-hai Ku-chi, 1987.

Wang, I-kung 王一工, ed. *Ch'ing-p'ing-shan T'ang hua-pen* 清平山堂話本. Shanghai: Shang-hai Ku-chi, 1992.

Studies

Dar, Jacques. *Contes de Montag ne screine…* Paris: Gallimand, 1987.

Nakazatomi, Satoshi 中里見敬. "Seihei sendô *Rokujûka shôsetsu* o megutte–*Hôbundô shomoku choroku wahon shôsetsu no saikentô*" 清平山堂「六十家小説」をめぐって–「宝文堂書木」著録話本小説の再検討, *Tôhôgaku* 85 (1993): 100-115.

Liu Tsung-yüan 柳宗元 (773-819)

Editions and References

Kao, Wen 高文 and Chü Kuang 屈光, eds. *Liu Tsung-yüan hsüan-chi* 柳宗元選集. Shanghai: Shang-hai Ku-chi, 1992.

Liu Tsung-yüan san-wen ch'üan-chi 柳宗元散文全集. Peking: Chin-jih Chung-kuo, 1996.

Luan, Kuei-ming 欒貴明 *et al.,* eds. *Ch'üan T'ang shih so-yin, Liu Tsung-yüan chüan* 全唐詩索引：柳宗元卷. Peking: Hsien-tai, 1995.

Nienhauser, William H., Jr. "A Selected Bibliography of Liu Tsung-yüan," *Shu-much'i-k'an* 20.1(June 1986): 204-243. Covers works in Chinese, Japanese, English, French and German written through 1985 other than those from the Cultural Revolution treating Liu as a "Legalist."

Wang, Hsien-tu 汪賢度, ed. *Liu Tsung-yüan san-wen hsüan-chi* 柳宗元散文選集. Shanghai: Shang-hai Ku-chi, 1997.

Wang, Pin 王彬. *T'ang-Sung pa-ta-chia ming-p'ien shang-hsi yü i-chu: Liu Tsung-yüan chüan* 唐宋 八大家名篇賞析與譯注：柳宗元卷. Peking: Ching-chi Jih-pao, 1997.

Wang, Kuo-an 王國安, ed. *Liu Tsung-yüan shih-chi chien-shih* 柳宗元詩集箋釋. Shanghai: Shang-hai Ku-chi, 1993.

Wang, Sung-ling 王松齡 and Yang, Li-yang 楊立揚, eds. *Liu Tsung-yüan shi wen hsüan i* 柳宗 元詩文選譯. *Ku-tai wen-shih ming-chu hsüan-i ts'ung-shu.* Chengtu: Pa Shu Shu-she, 1991.

Translations

Strassberg, *Inscribed Landscapes*, pp. 139-150.

Studies

Ch'ang, Chi-ch'eng 常輯成. *Liu Tsung-yüan chi-hsü wen-chang fa yen-chiu* 柳宗元記敍文章法研 究. Taipei: Wen-sheng 文笙, 1980.

Ch'en, Jo-shui. *Liu Tsung-yüan and Intellectual Change in T'ang China, 773-819.* Cambridge: Cambridge University Press, 1992. A very solid study of the intellectual stage as Liu found it in the late eighth century and his role as political philosophical and literary thinker upon it.

Chen, Yu-shih. "Liu Tsung-yüan: The Individual in History." In Chen Yu-shih, *Images and Ideas in Chinese Classical Prose: Studies of Four Masters.* Stanford: Stanford University Press, 1988, 71-107. A number of translations from Liu's prose grace the argument; also contains chapters on the *ku-wen* movement of the T'ang and Han Yü.

Chin, Hsing-yao 金性堯. *Yeh-lan hua Han, Liu* 夜闌話韓柳. Hong Kong: Chung-hua, 1991.

Chin, T'ao 金濤, ed. *Liu Tsung-yüan shih-wen shang-hsi chi* 柳宗元詩文賞析集. Chengtu: Pa-Shu Shu-she, 1989.

Chou, Kuei-hsi and Kuo Shao-ming. "Liu Zongyuan's Concept of Heaven," Zhao Qinghua, trans. *SSC* 6.2(1986).

Ho, Shu-chih 何書置. *Liu Tsung-yüan yen-chiu* 柳宗元研究. Changsha: Yüeh-lu Shu-she, 1994.

Liang, Ch'ao-jan 梁超然 and Hsieh, Han-ch'iang 謝漢強, eds. *Kuo-chi Liu Tsung-yüan yen-chiu chieh-ying* 國際柳宗元研究擷英. Nanning: Kuang-hsi Jen-min, 1994. A collection of papers from the 1993 conference held in Liuchow.

McMullen, D. L."Views of the State in Du You and Liu Zongyuan," in Stuart R. Schram, ed. *Foundations of State Power in China.* London:School of Oriental and African Studies, 1987.

Nienhauser, William H., Jr. "Floating Clouds and Dreams in Liu Tsung-yüan's Yung-chou Exile Writings." *JAOS* 106 (1986):169-181. A study of two dominant motifs in Liu's Yung-chou corpus.

Ono, Shihei 小野四平. *Kan Ko to Ryû Sôgen: Tôdai kokubun kenkyû shôsetsu* 韓愈と柳宗元：唐 代古文研究序説. Tokyo: Iwanami, 1995.

Ôta, Tsugio 太田次男. *Chû Tô bunjin kô–Kan Yu, Ryû Sôgen, Haku Kyoi* 中唐文人考–韓愈・柳 宗元、白居易 Tokyo: Kenbun Shuppan, 1993.

Shang, Yung-liang 尚永亮. *Yüan-ho wu ta shih-jen yü pien-che wen-hsüeh k'ao-lun* 元和五大詩人 與貶謫文學考論. *Ta-lu ti-ch'ü po-shih lun-wen ts'ung-k'an*, Taipei: Wen-chin, 1993.

Shinkai, Hajime 新海一. *Ryû bun kenkyû shosetsu* 柳文研究序説. Tokyo: Iwanami, 1987.

Soejima, Ichirô 副島一郎. "Sôjin no mieta Ryû Sôgen" 宋人の見えた柳宗元, *Chûgoku bungakuhô,* 47 (1993): 103-145.

Tai, I-k'ai 戴義開. *Liu Tsung-yüan, Liu-chou* 柳宗元, 柳州. Nanning: Kuang-hsi Chiao-yü, 1989.

Tozaki, Tetsuhiko 戸崎哲彦. *Tô dai chûki no bungaku to shisô* 唐代中期の文学と思想. Hikone: Shiga Daigaku Keizai Gakubu, 1990.

___. "Ryû Sôgen 'Tsui ni Eishû no tami ni naru ni amanzu'" 柳宗元「終に永州の民になる甘んず, *Tôhôgaku* 86 (1995).

___. "'Bun'en eika' no chûki no kaisôsei–shoshû no Ryû Sôgen no sakuhin o chûshin ni shite"『文苑英華』の注記の階層性–所収の柳宗元の作品を中心にして, *Hikone Ronsô,* 1994

___. "'Bun'en eika' izen no 'Ryûshû' no shurui, tokuchô oyobi sono kankei, keitô o rei ni shite"『文苑英華』以前の『柳集』の種類・特徴およびその関係・系統を例にして, *Hikone Ronsô,* 1994

Wang, Keng-sheng 王更生. *Liu Tsung-yüan san-wen yen-tu* 柳宗元散文研讀. Taipei: Wen-shih-che, 1994.

Wang, Kuo-an 王國安, ed. *Liu Tsung-yüan shih chien-shih* 柳宗元詩箋釋. Shanghai: Shang-hai Ku-chi, 1993. *Chung-kuo ku-tien wen-hsüeh ts'ung-k'an.*

Wen, Shao-k'un 溫紹坤. *Liu Tsung-yüan shih-ko chien-shih chi-p'ing* 柳宗元詩歌箋釋集評. Peking: Chung-kuo Kuo-chi Kuang-po, 1994.

Whitfield, Susan. "Politics against the Pen: History, Politics and Liu Zongyuan's (773-819) Literary Reputation." Unpublished Ph. D. dissertation, University of London, 1995.

Wu, Hsiao-lin 吳小林. *Liu Tsung-yüan san-wen i-shu* 柳宗元散文藝術. Taiyüan: Shan-hsi Jen-min, 1989.

Liu Yü-hsi 劉禹錫 (772-842)

Editions and References

Ch'ü, Shui-yüan 瞿蜕園, ed. *Liu Yü-hsi chi chien-cheng* 劉禹錫集箋証. Shanghai: Shang-hai Ku-chi, 1989.

Luan, Kuei-ming 欒貴明 *et al*, eds. *Ch'üan T'ang shih so-yin: Liu Yü-hsi chüan* 全唐詩索引：劉禹錫卷. Peking: Chung-hua, 1992.

Pien, Hsiao-hsüan 卞孝萱, ed. *Liu Yü-hsi chi* 劉禹錫集. Peking: Chung-hua, 1990.

Spaar, Wilfried. "Liu Yuxi (772-842), An Annotated Bibliography of Editions, Translations, and Studies," *Bochumer Jahrbuch zur Ostasienforschung,* 1986, 1-81.

Wu, Ju-yü 吳汝煜. *Liu Yü-hsi hsüan-chi* 劉禹錫選集. Tsinan: Ch'i-Lu Shu-she, 1989.

Wu, Kang 吳鋼, Chang, T'ien-ch'ih 張天池 and Liu, Kuang-han 劉光漢, eds. *Liu Yü-hsi shih wen hsüan chu* 劉禹錫詩文選注. Sian: San-Ch'in, 1987.

Studies

Ch'en Hsin-huan 陳昕環 and T'an Li-hsing 譚力行, eds. *Liu Yü-hsi Lien-chou shih wen chien chu* 劉禹錫連州詩文箋注. Canton: Kuang-tung Kao-teng Chiao-yü, 1993.

Holzman, Donald. "The Image of the Merchant in Medieval Chinese Poetry," in *Ganz allmählich, Aufsätze zur ostasiatischen Literatur, insbesondere zur chinesischen Lyrik.* Roderich Ptak and Siegfried Englert, eds.Heidelberg: Heidelberger Verlagsanstalt, 1986, pp. 92-108.Contains translations and discussions of 2 poems by Liu Chia in addition to works by Li Po, Po Chü-i, Yüan Chen, and Liu Yü-hsi on the theme.

Hsiao, Jui-feng 蕭瑞峰. *Liu Yü-hsi shih-lun* 劉禹錫詩論. Changchun: Chi-lin Chiao-yü, 1995.

Kao, Chih-chung 高志忠. *Liu Yü-hsi shih-wen hsi-nien* 劉禹錫詩文繫年. Nanning: Kuang-hsi Jen-min, 1988.

Kubin, Wolfgang. "Der Empfindsame und der Leidvolle, Bemerkungen zu Liu Yü-hsi's

Bambuszweigliedern (822)." In *Ganz allmählich, Festschrift fur Günther Debon*, ed. Roderich Ptak and Englert Siegfried. 120-31. Heidelberg: Heidelberg Verlagsanstalt und Druckerei, 1986.

Lim, Chooi Kua [Lin Shui-kao] 林水檺. "A Biography of Liu Yuxi," *Chinese Culture* 36.2, 37.1 (1994, 1996): 115-50, 111-141. A useful study based on original sources with a chronology and a map of Liu's posts appended.

Liu Yü-hsi shih wen shang-hsi chi 柳禹錫詩文賞析集. Chengtu: Pa-Shu Shu-she, 1989.

Lu, Ti 蘆荻 and Chu, Fan 朱帆. *Liu Yü-hsi chi ch'i tso-p'in* 劉禹錫及其作品. *Ku-tien wen-hsüeh ts'ung-shu* Changchun: Shih-tai Wen-i, 1985.

Miyauchi, Katsuhiro 宮內克浩. "Ryû Ushaku no ron shôkô" 劉禹錫の論小考, *Kokugakuin zasshi* XCV.3 (1994): 34-45.

Pien, Hsiao-hsüan 卞孝萱. *Liu Yü-hsi ts'ung-k'ao* 劉禹錫叢考. Cheng-tu: Pa-Shu Shu-she, 1988.

___. *Liu Yü-hsi p'ing-chuan* 劉禹錫評傳. Nanking; Nan-ching Ta-hsüeh, 1996.

Richardson, Tori Cliffon Anthony. "*Liu Pin-k'o chia-hua lu* ('A Record of Adviser to the Heir Apparent Liu (Yü-hsi's) Fine Discourses'): A Study and Translation. Unpublished Ph. D. dissertation, University of Wisconsin, 1994.

Shang, Yung-liang 尚永亮. *Yüan-ho wu ta shih-jen yü pien-che wen-hsüeh k'ao-lun* 元和五大詩人與貶謫文學考論. *Ta-lu ti-ch'ü po-shih lun-wen ts'ung-k'an*, Taipei: Wen-chin, 1993.

Spring, Madeline K. "Equine Allegory in the Writings of Liu Yü-hsi." In *Ti-i chieh Kuo-chi T'ang-tai wen-hsüeh hui-i lun-wen chi* 第一結屆國際唐代文學會議論文集. Taipei: Student Book Company, 1989, pp. 1-35.

Wang, Yün-hsi 王運熙. "Liu Yü-hsi te wen-hsüeh p'i-p'ing" 劉禹錫的文學批評, *Yin-tu Hsüeh-k'an* 殷都學刊 1992.2 (1992): 39-43.

Wu, Ju-yü 吳汝煜. *Liu Yü-hsi chuan lun* 劉禹錫傳論. Sian: Shan-hsi Jen-min, 1988.

Wu, Tsai-ch'ing 吳在慶. "Pien chu *Liu Yü-hsi nien-p'u* pien-pu" 卞著劉禹錫年譜辨補. *T'ang-tai Wen-hsüeh Lun-ts'ung* 8 (1986): 225-45.

Ueki, Hisayuki, "Tôdai kakka shin ginen roku (5)–Gi Chô, Gu Seinan, Jôkan Shôyô, Tei Ryôshi, Haku Kyoi, Haku Gyôkan, Gô Hô, Ra In, Ri Riran, Raku Shi, Ryû Ushaku" 植木久行　唐代作家新疑年録（５）–魏徵, 虞世南, 上官昭容, 鄭良士, 白居易, 白行簡, 鮑防, 羅隱, 李李蘭, 陸贄 and 劉禹錫, *Bunkei Ronsô* XXXVII, 3, 1992.

Liu Yung 柳永 (987-1053)

Editions

Chou, Tzu-yü 周子瑜, ed. *Liu Yung Chou Pang-yen tz'u hsüan chu* 柳永周邦彦詞選注. *Chung-kuo ku-tien wen-hsüeh tso-pin hsüan-tu.* Shanghai: Shang-hai Ku-chi, 1990.

Hsüeh, Jui-sheng 薛瑞生, ed. *Yüeh-chang chi chiao-chu* 樂章集校注. *Chung-kuo ku-tien wen-hsüeh chi-pen ts'ung-shu.* Peking: Chung-hua, 1994.

Liang, Hsüeh-yün 梁雪雲. *Liu Yung tz'u-hsüan* 柳永詞選. Hong Kong: Joint Publishing, 1989.

Translations

Landau, *Beyond Spring,* pp. 76-90.

Studies

Chou, Tzu-lai 周子來. "Liu Yung sheng-nien hsin-cheng" 柳永生年新証, *Wen-hsüeh i-ch'an* 1987.4: 128-32.

Hagiwara, Masaki 萩原正樹. "Ryû Eei no kôhansei to sono shi" 柳永の后半生とその詞, *Gakurin* 12 (1989): 34-48.

Hsieh, T'ao-fang 謝桃坊. *Liu Yung* 柳永. *Chung-kuo ku-tien wen-hsüeh chi-pen chih-shih ts'ung-shu,*

Shanghai: Shang-hai Ku-chi, 1986.

____, ed. *Liu Yung tz'u shang-hsi chi* 柳永詞賞析集. *Chung-kuo ku-tien wen-hsüeh shang-hsi ts'ung-shu* Chengtu: Pa-Shu Shu-she, 1987.

Lai, Ch'iao-pen 賴橋本. *Liu Yung tz'u chiao-chu* 柳永詞校注. Taipei: Li-ming 黎明, 1995.

Li, Ssu-yung 李思永. "Liu Yung chia-shih sheng-p'ing hsin-k'ao" 柳永家世生平新考. *Wen-hsüeh i-ch'an* 1986.1: 22-32.

Liang, Li-fang 梁麗芳. *Liu Yung chi ch'i tz'u chih yen-chiu* 柳永及其詞之研究. Hong Kong: San-lien Shu-tien, 1985.

Tseng, Ta-hsing 曾大興. *Liu Yung ho t'a te tz'u* 柳永和他的詞. Canton: Chung-shan Ta-hsüeh, 1990.

Uno, Naoto 宇野直人 *Chûgoku koten shiika no shuhô to gengo–Ryû Ei o chûshin to shite* 中国古典詩歌の手法と言語-柳永を中心として. Tokyo: Kenbun Shuppan, 1991

Yao, Hsüeh-hsien 姚學賢 and Lung, Chien-kuo 龍建國, eds. *Liu Yung tz'u hsiang-chu chi chi-p'ing* 柳永詞詳注及集評. Chengchow: Chung-chou Ku-chi, 1991.

Lo Kuan-chung 羅貫中

Editions and References

Li Hsing-tao, K'ung Wen-Ch'ing, Lo Kuan-chung chi 李行道，孔文卿，羅貫中集. Annotated and Collated by T'ing, Pao-ch'üan 廷保全. Taiyuan: Shan-hsi Jen-min, 1993.

Studies

Yao, Chung-chieh 姚仲傑. *Lo Kuan-chung hsin-t'an* 羅貫中新探. Chengchow: Chung-chou Ku-chi, 1992.

Lo Pin-wang 駱賓王 (before 640-684 or 619-687)

Editions and References

Ch'en, Chin-hsi 陳晉熙, ed. *Lo Lin-hai chi chien-chu* 駱臨海集箋注. Shanghai: Shang-hai Ku-chi, 1985.

Lo, Hsiang-fa 駱祥發. *Lo Ping-wang shih p'ing-chu* 駱賓王詩評注. Peking: Pei-ching Ch'u-pan-she, 1989.

Luan, Kuei-ming 欒貴明 *et al*, eds. *Ch'üan-T'ang shih so-yin. Wang Po, Yang Chiung, Lu Chao-lin, Lo Pin-wang chüan* 全唐詩索引。王勃，楊炯，盧照鄰，駱賓王卷. Peking: Chung-hua, 1992.

Wang, Kuo-an 王國安 and Wang, Yu-min 王幼敏, eds. *Ch'u-T'ang Ssu-chieh yü Ch'en Tzu-ang shih-wen hsüan-chu* 初唐四傑與陳子昂詩文選注. *Chung-kuo Ku-tien Wen-hsüeh tso-p'ing hsüan-tu ts'ung-shu* Shanghai: Shang-hai Ku-chi, 1995.

Studies

Chang, Chih-lieh 張志烈. *Ch'u T'ang Ssu-chieh nien-p'u* 初唐四傑年譜. Chengtu: Pa-Shu Shu-she, 1992.

Che-chiang-sheng ku-tai wen-hsüeh hsüeh-hui 浙江省古代文學學會, ed. *Lo Pin-wang yen-chiu lun-wen-chi* 駱賓王研究論文集. Hangchow: Hang-chou Ta-hsüeh, 1993.

Klöpsch, Volker. "Lo Pin-wang's Survival: Traces of A Legend." *TS* 6 (1988): 77-97.

Lo, Hsiang-fa 駱祥發. *Ch'u T'ang ssu-chieh yen-chiu* 初唐四傑研究. Peking: Tung-fang, 1993.

____ and Yang, Liu 楊柳. *Lo Pin-wang p'ing-chuan* 駱賓王評傳. Peking: Pei-ching Ch'u-pan-she, 1987.

Lo-yang ch'ieh-lan chi 洛陽伽藍記 (**Record of the Monasteries of Lo-yang**)

Editions and References

Chang, Tsung-hsiang 張宗祥, ed. *Lo-yang ch'ieh-lan chi ho-chiao-pen*洛陽伽藍記合校本. *Chung-kuo fo-shih shih-chih hui-k'an.* Taipei: Ming-wen Shu-chü, 1980.

Translations

Wang, Yi-t'ung. *Yang Hsüan-chih–A Record of Buddhist Monasteries in Lo-yang.* Princeton: Princeton University Press, 1984. Includes an index and a good bibliography.

Iriya, Yoshitaka 入矢義高, trans. and annot. *Yô Genshi: Rakuyô garan ki* 楊衒之：洛陽伽藍記. Tokyo: Heibonsha, 1990

Studies

Fang, Chung-mien 房眾棉. "Lun *Lo-yang ch'ieh-lan chi*" 論洛陽伽藍記. *Lo-yang Shih-fan Hsüeh-yüan hsüeh-pao 42* (1987): 86-90.

Lin, Chin-shih 林晉士. "Lo-yang ch'ieh-lan chi chih pan-pen k'ao-shu" 洛陽伽藍記之版本考述. *Shu-mu chi-k'an*, 29.3 (1995): 41-54.

Lin, Wen-yüeh 林文月. "*Lo-yang ch'ieh-lan chi* te leng-pi yü je-pi" 洛陽伽藍記的冷筆與熱筆. *T'ai-ta chung-wen hsüeh-pao* 1 (1985): 105–137.

_____. "*Lo-yang ch'ieh-lan chi* te wen-hsüeh chia-chih" 洛陽伽藍記的文學價值. In *Mao Tzu-shui hsien-sheng chiu-wu shou-ch'ing lun-wen-chi*毛子水先生九五壽慶論文集. Taipei: Yu-shih Wen-hua, 1987, pp. 147–173.

Lo Yin 羅隱 (833-909)

Editions and References

Ch'an shu 讒書. Collated by Wu Ch'ien 吳騫 (1733-1813). *Ts'ung-shu chi-ch'eng ch'u-pien.* Peking: Chung-hua, 1985.

Chao, Chi 趙季 and Yeh Yen-ts'ai 葉言材, ed. *P'i Shao-chien hsiao-p'in* 羅邵諫小品. Peking: Wen-hua I-shu, 1997. *T'ang Sung hsiao-p'ing shih-chia.*

*Lo Yin chi*羅隱集. Yung Wen-hua 雍文華, ed. *Chung-kuo ku-tien wen-hsüeh chi-pen ts'ung-shu.* Peking: Chung-hua, 1983.

Wang, Hsiao-ning 王小寧, ed. *Lo Chao-chien hsiao-p'in* 羅昭諫小品. Peking: Wen-hua I-shu, 1997.

Studies

De Meyer, Jan. "Confucianism and Daoism in the Political Thought of Lo Yin," *T'ang Studies* 8 (1990): 67-80.

_____. "'Listing the Past to Disparage the Present': Luo Yin and his *Slanderous Writings.*" *Chinese Culture* 37 (1996): 69-85.

P'an, Hui-hui 潘慧惠. "Lun Lo Yin chi ch'i shih-wen" 論羅隱及其詩文 *Wen-shih-che* 226 (1995): 76-80.

Ueki, Hisayuki, Tôdai kakka shin ginen roku (5)–Gi Chô, Gu Seinan, Jôkan Shôyô, Tei Ryôshi, Haku Kyoi, Haku Gyôkan, Gô Hô, Ra In, Ri Riran, Raku Shi, Ryû Ushaku" 植木久行, 唐代作家新疑年録 （5）–魏徵, 虞世南, 上官昭容, 鄭良士, 白居易, 白行簡, 鮑防, 羅隱, 李李蘭, 陸贄 and 劉禹錫, *Bunkei Ronsô* XXXVII, 3, 1992.

Lu Chao-lin 盧照鄰 (*ca.* 634-*ca.* 684)

Editions

Chu, Shang-shu 祝尚書, ed. *Lu Chao-lin chi chiao-chu* 盧照鄰集校注. Shanghai: Shang-hai Ku-chi, 1994.

Jen, Kuo-hsü 任國緒. *Lu Chao-lin chi pien-nien chien-chu* 盧照鄰集編年箋註. Harbin: Hei-lung-chiang Jen-min, 1989.

Li, Yün-i 李雲逸, ed. *Lu Chao-lin chi chiao-chu* 盧照鄰集校注. Peking: Chung-hua, 1998.

Studies

Chang, Chih-lieh 張志烈. *Ch'u T'ang ssu-chieh nien-p'u* 初唐四傑年譜. Chengtu: Pa-Shu Shu-she, 1992.

Jen Kuo-hsü 任國緒. *Lu Chao-lin nien-p'u* 盧照鄰年譜: Harbin: Hei-lung-chiang Jen-min, 1991.

___. "Lu Chao-lin sheng-p'ing shih-chi hsin-k'ao" 盧照鄰生平事跡新考, *Wen-hsüeh i-ch'an* 1985.2: 51-56.

___. "Lüeh lun Lu Chao-lin Lo Pin-wang te ch'i-yen ko-hsing" 略論盧照鄰駱賓王的七言歌行. *Pei-fang lun-ts'ung* 1985.3 (1985): 38-43.

___. "Lu Chao-lin ssu-hsiang shu-p'ing" 盧照鄰思想述評. *Pei-fang lun-ts'ung* 1993.6 (1993): 66-72.

Ko, Hsiao-yin 葛曉音. "Kuan-yü Lu Chao-lin sheng-p'ing te jo-kan wen-t'i" 關于盧照鄰生平的若干問題. *Wen-hsüeh i-ch'an* 1989.6 (1989): 68-73.

Kôzen, Hiroshi 興膳宏. "Shoki no shijin to shûkyô–Ro Shôrin no baai" 初期の詩人と宗教-盧照隣の場合, *Chûgoku ko-Dôkyô-shi kenkyû*,1992: 417-70.

Kroll, Paul W. "The Memories of Lu Chao-lin." *JAOS* 109.4 (1989): 581-92.

Liu, Ch'eng-chi 劉成紀. "Lu Chao-lin te ping-pien yü wen-pien" 盧照鄰的病變與文變. *Wen-hsüeh i-ch'an* 1994.5 (1994): 43-49.

Lo, Hsiang-fa 駱祥發. *Ch'u T'ang ssu-chieh yen-chiu* 初唐四傑研究. Peking: Tung-fang, 1993.

Shang, Ting 尚定. "Lu Lo ko-hsing te chieh-kou mo-shih yü i-shu yüan-yüan" 盧駱歌行的結構模式與藝術淵源. *Wen-hsüeh p'ing-lun* 1993.6 (1993): 94-104.

Lu Chi 陸機 (261-303)

Editions and References

Chang, Huai-chin 張懷瑾, ed. *"Wen-fu" i-chu* 文賦譯注. Peking: Pei-ching Ch'u-pan-she, 1984. *Chung-kuo ku-tien wen-i li-lun ts'ung-shu.* Appends the biography of Lu Chi in the *Chin shu* among other biographical materials.

Chang, Shao-k'ang 張少康, ed. *Wen-fu" chi-shih* 文賦集釋. Shanghai: Shang-hai Ku-chi, 1984.

Chin, T'ao-sheng 金濤聲, ed. and comm. *Lu Chi chi* 陸機集. Peking: Chung-hua, 1982.

Translations

Hamill, Sam, trans. *The Art of Writing: Lu Chi's Wen Fu.* Minneapolis: Milkweed Editions, 1991.

Studies

Ch'en, Chuang 陳莊. "Lu Chi yüan-ch'ing shuo hsin-lun" 陸機緣情説新論. *Ssu-ch'uan Ta-hsüeh hsüeh-pao ts'ung-k'an* 28 (1985): 67–74.

Ch'en, Yü-hui 陳玉惠. "Lu Chi shih yen-chiu" 陸機詩研究. M. A. Thesis, Cheng-chih Ta-hsüeh, 1987.

Fan, T'ien-ch'eng 范天成. "Lu Chi 'wen-fu' te i-shu pien-cheng i-shih" 陸機文賦的藝術辯證

376

意識, *Hsi-pei Ta-hsüeh hsüeh-pao* 67 (1990): 41–47.

Hsü, Fu-kuan 徐復觀. "Lu Chi 'Wen fu' shu-shih ch'u-kao" 陸機文賦疏釋初稿, *Chung-wai wen-hsüeh* 97 (1980).

Kôzen, Hiroshi 興膳宏. "Bungaku Riron-shi jyo kara mita *Bunfu* 文学理論史上から見た文賦, *Mimei* 7(1988): 23-38.

Lai, Chiu-mi. "River and Ocean: The Third Century Verse of Pan Yue and Lu Ji." Unpublished Ph. D. dissertation, University of Washington, 1990.

Lin, Wen-yüeh 林文月. "Lu Chi te ni-ku shih" 陸機的擬古詩, *Yu-shih hsüeh-chih* 20:3 (1989): 60–86.

Satô, Toshiyuki 佐藤利行. *Sei Shin bungaku kenkyû–Riku Ki o chûsin to shite* 西晉文学研究陸機を中心として. Tokyo: Hakuteisha 白帝社, 1995.

Wang, Ching-hsien 王靖獻. "Lu Chi 'Wen fu' chiao-shih" 陸機文賦校釋, *Wen shih che* 32 (1983).

Wang, I 王毅. "Lu Chi chien-lun" 陸機簡論, *Chung-kuo ku-tien wen-hsüeh lun-ts'ung* 2 (1985): 55–72.

Yanagawa, Junko 柳川順子. "Riku Ki rakufu shi shiron" 陸機樂府詩私論, *Bungaku Kenkyu* 86(1989): 47-74.

Yang, Mu 楊牧. *Lu Chi wen-fu chiao-shih* 陸機文賦校釋. Taipei: Hung-fan Shu-tien 洪範書店, 1985.

Lu Chih 陸贄 (754-805)

Studies

Chiang, Yin 蔣寅. "Lu Chih ho t'a te cheng-chih-wen" 陸贄和他的政治文. *Ku-tien wen-hsüeh chih-shih* 1990.2 (1990): 71-75.

Liu, Hsüeh-p'ei 劉學沛. "Lu Chih lun chih-kuo-chih-tao" 陸贄論治國之道. *Fu-chien lun-t'an* 24 (1985): 56-60.

Shen, Shih-jung 沈時蓉. "Shih lun Lu Chih tui Han Yü chi T'ang Ku-wen-yün-tung te ying-hsiang" 試論陸贄對韓愈及唐古文運動的影響. *Ssu-chüan Shih-fan Ta-hsüeh hsüeh-pao* 1991.1 (1991): 22-27.

Ueki, Hisayuki, Tôdai kakka shin ginen roku (5)–Gi Chô, Gu Seinan, Jôkan Shôyô, Tei Ryôshi, Haku Kyoi, Haku Gyôkan, Gô Hô, Ra In, Ri Riran, Raku Shi, Ryû Ushaku" 植木久行, 唐代作家新疑年録（5）–魏徴, 虞世南, 上官昭容, 鄭良士, 白居易, 白行簡, 鮑防, 羅隠, 李李蘭, 陸贄 and 劉禹錫, *Bunkei Ronsô* XXXVII, 3, 1992.

Lu Kuei-meng 陸龜蒙 (d. *ca.* 881)

Editions

Po, Chün-ts'ai 柏俊才, ed. *Lu Fu-li hsiao-p'in* 陸甫里小品. Peking: Wen-hua I-shu, 1997. *T'ang Sung hsiao-p'ing shih-chia.*

Studies

Cahill, Suzanne. "Night-Shining White:Traces of a T'ang Dynasty Horse in Two Media," *TS* 4(1986): 91-94.

Chung, Te-heng 鍾德恆. "Kuan-yü Lu Kuei-meng te k'ao-pien" 關於陸龜蒙的考辨, *Kuei-chou Min-yüan hsüeh-pao*, 1983.2.

Li, Feng 李鋒. "Lu Kuei-meng sheng-tsu nien k'ao" 陸龜蒙生卒年考, *Ku-chi cheng-li yen-chiu hsüeh-k'an* 1989.3.

Maegawa, Yukio 前川幸雄. "Hi, Riku shôwa shi no tokushitsu ni tsuite" 皮・陸唱和詩の特

質について, *Kokugakuin Chûgoku Gakkaihô* 40 (1994).

Marney, John. *Chinese Anagrams and Anagram Verse.* Asian Library Series, Taipei: Chinese Materials Center, 1993. Traces the history of anagrams in literature; three chapters devoted to exchanges between Lu Kuei-meng and P'i Jih-hsiu.

Miller, David Charles. "Self-presentations in the Poetry of Lu Kuei-meng (d. 881?)." Ph.D., Stanford University, 1990.

Wada, Hidenobu 和田英信. "Riku Kimô ni tsuite" 陸亀蒙について, *Shûkan Tôyôgaku* 64 (1990).

Lu kuei pu 錄鬼簿 (A Register of Ghosts)

Editions and References

P'u, Han-ming 浦漢明, ed. *Hsin-chiao Lu-kuei p'u cheng-hsü pien* 新校錄鬼簿正續編. Chengtu: Pa-Shu Shu-she, 1997.

Wang, Kang 王鋼, ed. *Chiao-ting Lu kuei pu san chung* 校訂錄鬼簿三種. *Chung-chou wen-hsien ts'ung-shu* Chengchow: Chung-chou Ku-chi, 1991.

Studies

Chang, Jen-ho 張人和. "Tien-kuei pu yü Lu kuei pu" 點鬼簿與錄鬼簿. *Hsi-ch'ü yen-chiu* 111 (1984): 188-96.

Li, Ch'un-hsiang 李春祥. "Chung Ssu-ch'eng sheng-tsu nien pien-hsi" 鍾嗣城生卒年辨析, *Ho-nan Ta-hsüeh hsüeh-pao* 1984.5: 87-91.

Liu, Hsin-wen 劉新文. *Lu kuei pu chung li-shih-chü t'an-yüan* 錄鬼簿中歷史劇探源. Tientsin: Nan-k'ai Ta-hsüeh, 1989.

Yao, Shu-i 么書儀. "'Lu kuei pu' Chia Chung-ming tiao-tz'u san shih" 錄鬼簿賈仲明吊詞三釋, *Chung-hua wen-shih lun-ts'ung* 37 (1986): 227-33.

Lu Lun 盧綸 (737?-798? or 738-798)

Editions and References

Chang, Teng-ti 張登第, Chiao, Wen-pin 焦文彬 and Lu, An-shu 魯安澍. *Ta-li shih-ts'ai tzu shih-hsüan* 大曆十才子詩選. Sian: Shan-hsi Jen-min, 1988.

Liu, Ch'u-t'ang 劉初棠, ed. *Lu Lun shih-chi chiao-chu* 盧綸詩集校注. Shanghai: Shang-hai Ku-chi, 1989.

Luan, Kuei-ming 欒貴明, ed. *Chüan T'ang shih so-yin: Li I Lu Lun chüan* 全唐詩索引：李益盧倫卷. Peking: Tso-chia, 1997.

Studies

Ashidate, Ichirô 芦立一郎. "Ro Ron shi shotan–Tairekishi e no apurôchi" 盧綸詩初探–大歷詩へのアプローチ, *Yamagata Daigaku kiyô–Jimbun kagaku* 12.4 (1993): 189-206.

Chiang, Yin 蔣寅. *Ta-li shih-jen yen-chiu* 大歷詩人研究. Peking: Chung-hua, 1995.

Wang, Ta-chin 王大津. "Lu Lun, Jung Yü sheng-p'ing hsi-shih" 盧綸戎昱生平系詩, *Nan-k'ai Ta-hsüeh hsüeh-pao,* 1979.4

Lu Ts'ai 陸采 (1497-1537)

Editions and References

Huai-hsiang chi 懷香記. Taipei: T'ien-i, 1983.

Lu T'ien-ch'ih Hsi-hsiang chi 陸天池西廂記. Taipei: T'ien-i, 1983.

Lu Yu 陸游 (1125-1210)

Editions and References

Ch'en, Hsin 陳新, ed. *Sung-jen Ch'ang-chiang yu-chi* 宋人長江遊記. Shanghai: Hua-tung Shih-fan Ta-hsüeh, 1987. Contains Lu Yu's "Ju Shu chi" 入蜀記 and Fan Ch'eng-ta's 范成大 "Wu-ch'uan lu" 吳船錄.

Ch'ien, Chung-lien 錢仲聯, ed. *Chien-nan shih kao chiao-chu* 劍南詩稿校注. *Chung-kuo ku-tien wen-hsüeh ts'ung-shu.* Shanghai: Shang-hai Ku-chi, 1985.

Chi-feng 疾風. *Lu Fang-weng shih tz'u hsüan* 陸放翁詩詞選. Hangchow: Che-chiang Jen-min, 1984.

Chu, Te-ts'ai 朱德才 and Yang, Yen 楊燕. *Lu Yu shih-ko hsüan-i* 陸游詩歌選譯. Tsinan: Shan-tung Ta-hsüeh, 1991.

Hsia, Ch'eng-t'ao 夏承燾 and Wu, Hsiung-ho 吳熊和, annotators. *Fang-weng tz'u pien-nien chien-chu* 放翁詞編年箋注. Shanghai: Shang-hai Ku-chi, 1981.

K'ung, Ching-ch'ing 孔鏡清, ed. *Lu Yu shih wen hsüan-chu* 陸游詩文選註. Shanghai: Shang-hai Ku-chi, 1987.

Lu, Chien 陸堅, ed. *Lu Yu shih-tz'u shang-hsi chi* 陸游詩詞賞析集. Chengtu: Pa-Shu Shu-she, 1990.

Lu, Yu. *Lu Fang-weng ch'üan-chi* 陸放翁全集. Peking: Pei-ching-shih Chung-kuo Shu-tien, 1986.

Miao, Hung 苗洪, ed. *Lu Fang-weng hsiao-p'in* 陸放翁小品. Peking: Wen-hua I-shu, 1997.

Nohara, Yasuhiro 野原康宏. "Riku Yû kenkyû shoshi (1) (2)" 陸游研究書誌 (一) (二), *Mimei* 10, 1994.

Sun, Ch'i-hsiang 孫啟祥, ed. *Lu Yu Han-chung shih tz'u hsüan* 陸游漢中詩詞選. Sian: Shan-hsi Jen-min, 1993.

Wang, Hsiao-hsiang 王曉祥, ed. *Lu Yu shih-erh shih-hsüan* 陸游示兒詩選. Nanking: Nan-ching Ta-hsüeh, 1988.

Yü, Min-hsiung 于民雄, ed. *Lu Yu shih-tz'u ching-hua* 陸游詩詞精華. Kweiyang: Kuei-chou Jen-min, 1993.

Translations

Gordon, David M. *The Wild Old Man: Poems of Lu Yu.* San Francisco: North Point Press, 1984.

Iwaki, Hideo 岩城秀夫. *Nyû Shoku ki* 入蜀記. Tokyo: Heibonsha 1987

Landau, *Beyond Spring,* pp. 176-182.

Strassberg, *Inscribed Landscapes,* pp. 205-212.

Studies

Backstrom, Martin Gerald. "The Castles of Shu: Dream Motives in the Poetry of Lu You (1125-1210)." Unpublished Ph.D. dissertation, University of California, Berkeley, 1989.

Ch'i, Chih-p'ing 齊治平. *Lu Yu chuan lun* 陸游傳論. Changsha: Yüeh-lu Shu-she, 1984.

Chang, Fu-hsün 張福勛. *Lu Yu san-lun* 陸游散論. Huhehaote: Nei-meng-ku Jen-min, 1993.

Chou, Chih-wen 周志文. "Lu Yu te shih-lun" 陸游的詩論. *Tan-chiang hsüeh-pao* 22 (1985): 67-78.

Chu, Tung-jun 朱東潤. *Lu Yu chuan* 陸游傳. Peking: Chung-hua, 1993.

Chu, Fu-yü 朱傳譽, ed. *Lu Yu chuan-chi tzu-liao* 陸游傳記資料. Taipei: T'ien-i, 1985.

K'ung, Fan-li 孔凡禮. "Lu Yu chia-shih hsü-lu" 陸游家世敍錄. *Wen shih* 31 (1988): 263-82.

Li, Chih-chu 李致洙. *Lu Yu shih yen-chiu* 陸游詩研究. Taipei: Wen-shih-che, 1991.

Lu, Chien 陸堅. *Lu Yu shih tz'u shang-hsi chi* 陸游詩詞賞析集. Chengtu: Pa-Shu Shu-she, 1990.

Murakami, Tetsumi 村上哲見 *et al. So Shoku, Riku Yû Kanshô, Chûgoku no koten 21* 蘇軾陸游, 鑑賞中国の古典２１. Tokyo: Kadokawa Shoten 1989

Mo, Li-feng 莫礪鋒. "Lu Yu 'Shih-chia san-mei' pien" 陸游詩家三昧辨. *Nan-ching Ta-hsüeh hsüeh-pao* 1992.1 (1992): 120-28.

Nishioka, Atsushi 西岡淳. "Kyô no shijin Riku Hôô" 狂の詩人陸放翁, *Chugoku Bungakuhô* 40 (1989): 47-75.

Ou, Hsiao-wu 歐小物. *Lu Yu chuan* 陸游傳. Chengtu: Ch'eng-tu, 1994.

Tiao, Pao-shih 刁抱石. *Sung Lu Fang-weng hsien-sheng Yu nien-p'u* 宋陸放翁先生游年譜. *Hsin-pien Chung-kuo ming-jen nien-p'u chi-ch'eng* 新編中國名人年譜集成. Taipei: Shang-wu, 1990.

Wang, Chung-hou 王仲厚. "Lu Yu tz'u-hua" 陸游詞話 *Liao-ning Ta-hsüeh hsüeh-pao* 1987.5.

Yeh, Chia-ying 葉嘉瑩. "Lun Lu Yu tz'u" 論陸游詞, *Ssu-ch'üan Ta-hsüeh hsüeh-pao* 47 (1985): 53-61.

Yü, Ch'ao-kang 喻朝剛. "Fang-weng tz'u lun" 放翁詞論, *She-hui k'o-hsüeh chan-hsien* 39 (1987): 287-95.

Yü, Pei-shan 于北山. *Lu Yu nien-p'u* 陸游年譜. Shanghai: Shang-hai Ku-chi, 1985.

Yüan, Hsing-p'ei 袁行霈. "Lu Yu shih-ko i-shu t'an-yüan" 陸游詩歌藝術探源, *Wen-shih chih-shih* 1987.2: 80-85.

Ma Chih-yüan 馬致遠 (1260-1325)

Editions and References

Chü, Chün 瞿鈞, ed. and annot. *Tung-li yüeh-fu ch'üan-chi* 東籬樂府全集. Tientsin: T'ien-chin Ku-chi, 1990.

Hsiao, Shan-yin 蕭善因, *et al.*, eds. *Ma Chih-yüan chi* 馬致遠集. T'aiyüan: Shan-hsi Ku-chi, 1993. Includes Ma's *tsa-chü* and *san-ch'ü*.

Hsü, Ch'in-chün 徐沁君, ed. *Yüan-ch'ü ssu ta-chia ming-chü hsüan* 元曲四大家名劇選. Tsinan: Ch'i-Lu Shu-she, 1987. Annotated versions of 16 plays.

Studies

Wang, Linda Greenhouse. "A Study of Ma Chih-yüan's *San-ch'ü* and *Tsa-chü* Lyrics." Unpublished Ph. D. dissertation, University of California, Berkeley, 1992.

Yü, Ta-p'ing 余大平. *Ma Chih-yüan tsa-chü yen-chiu* 馬致遠雜劇研究. Wuhan: Wu-han Ch'u-pan-she, 1994.

Ma Jung 馬融 (79-166)

Editions and References

Ku-wen Shang-shu 古文尚書. Peking: Chung-hua, 1991. Contains Ma's commentary and that of Wang, Ying-lin 王應麟 (1223-1296).

Ma-wang tui 馬王堆

Editions and References

Ch'un-ch'iu shih-yü 春秋事語. Peking: Wen-wu Ch'u-pan-she, 1987. *Ma-wang tui Han-mu po-shu*, 3.1

Li, Cheng-kuang 李正光, ed. *Ma-wang tui Han-mu po-shu chu-chien* 馬王堆漢慕帛書竹簡. Changsha: Hu-nan Mei-shu, 1988.

Li, Mei-li 李梅麗. *Ma-wang-tui Han-mu yen-chiu mu-lu (1972-1992)* 馬王堆漢墓研究目錄. Changsha: Hu-nan Sheng Po-wu Kuan, 1992.

Tso, Sung-ch'ao 左松超. "Ma-wang-tui Han-mu yen-chiu tzu-liao mu-lu so-yin," 馬王堆漢墓研究資料目錄索引 *Chung-kuo shu-mu chi-k'an* 23 (1989): 95-115.

Studies

Blanford, Yumiko F. "Discovery of Lost Eloquence: New Insight from the Mawangdui 'Zhanguo zonghengjia shu.'" *JAOS* 114 (1994): 77-82. Argues that the Ma-wang tui *Chan-kuo tsung-heng shu* manuscript displays highly schematic rhetorical techniques which the *Chan-kuo ts'e* lacks.

___. "A Textual Approach to 'Zhanguo Zonghengjia Shu': Methods of Determining the Proximate Original Word among Variants." *EC* 16 (1991): 187-207.

Boltz, William G. "Textual Criticism and the 'Ma-wang tui *Lao-tzu*.'" *HJAS* 44 (1984): 185–224.

Chou, Shih-ying 周世瑩. *Ch'ang-sha Ma Wang-tui san-hao Han-mu chu-chien yang-sheng-fang shih-wen* 長沙馬王堆三號漢慕竹簡養生方釋文. Chengtu: Pa-Shu Shu-she, 1992. *Tsang-wai Tao-shu*, 1.

Harbsmeier, Christoph. "*Fú* [弗] in the Mawangdui Manuscripts of the *Laozi* and in the *Remnants of Qin Law*." In *From Classical Fú to Three Inches High, Studies on Chinese in Honor of Erik Zürcher*. J C. P. Liang and R. P. E. Sybesma, eds. Leuven/Apeldoorn: Garant, 1993, pp. 1-59.

Ikeda, Tomohisa 池田知久. *Maôtai Kanbo hakusho gogyôhen kenkyû* 馬王堆漢慕帛書五行篇研究. Tokyo: Kyûko Shoin, 1993. *Tôkyô Daigaku Bungakubu fuse kikin gakujitsu sosho*.

Li, Ling 李零. "Ma-wang tui fang-chung shu yen-chiu" 馬王堆房中書研究. *Wen shih* 35 (1992): 21-48.

Liao, Ming-ch'un 廖名春. *Ma-wang tui po-shu Chou I-ching-chuan shih-wen* 馬王堆帛書周易經傳釋文. Shanghai: Shang-hai Ku-chi, 1995.

Suzuki, Kiichi 鈴木喜一. *Maôtai Rôshi* 馬王堆老子. Tokyo: Meitoku Shuppansha, 1987. *Chûgoku koten shinsho, zokuhen*, 6.

Tamura, Masataka 田村正敬. *Maôtai no subete* 馬王堆のすべて. Fukuoka: Chûgoku Shoten, 1994.

Satô, Taketoshi 佐藤武敏, ed. and Kudô Motoo 工藤元男, *et al.*, trans. and comms. *Maôtai Hakusho Sengoku jûô kasho* 馬王堆帛書戦国縦横家書. Kyoto: Hôyû Shoten, 1993.

Wei, Ch'i-p'eng 魏啟鵬. *Te-hsing chiao-shih* 德行校釋. Chengtu: Pa-Shu Shu-she, 1991.

Yen, Ling-feng 嚴靈峰. *Ma-wang tui po-shu I-ching ch'u-pu yen-chiu* 馬王堆帛書易經初步研究. Taipei: Ch'eng-wen, 1980.

Mao Tsung-kang 毛宗崗 *(fl.* 1660)

Editions and References

Ch'i, Yen 齊煙, ed. *Mao Tsung-kang p'i-p'ing San-kuo yen-i* 毛宗崗批評三國演義. 2v. Tsinan: Ch'i-Lu Shu-she, 1991.

Studies

Bailey, Catherine Diana Alison. "The Mediating Eye: Mao Lun, Mao Zonggang and the Reading of 'Sanguo zhi yanyi'." Ph.D. dissertation, Univ. of Toronto, 1991.

Campbell, Duncan M. "The Techniques of Narrative: Mao Tsung-kang *(fl.* 1661) and *The Romance of the Three Kingdoms*" *TkR* 16 (1985): 139-61.

Mei Sheng 枚乘 (d. 141 B.C.)

Translations

Mair, Victor H. *Mei Cherng's "Seven Stimuli" and Wang Bai's "Pavilion of King Terng," Chinese Poems for Princes.* Lewiston: Edwin Mellen, 1988.

Studies

Kung, K'o-ch'ang 龔克昌. "San-fu tso-chia Mei Sheng" 散賦作家枚乘. *Wen-shih-che* 1984.1 (1984): 67-72.

Mei Ting-tso 梅鼎祚 (1549-1615)

Editions and References

Mei Yü-chin shih-ts'ao 梅禹金詩草. 3v. Tokyo: Kôkyû Shûhô, 1991. Based on the 1623 edition held in the Naikoku Bunkô.

T'ien, P'u 田璞 and Ch'a Hung-te 查洪德, eds. and comms. *Ch'ing-ni lien-hua chi* 青泥蓮花記. Chengchow: Chung-chou Ku-chi, 1988.

___ and Ch'a Hung-te 查洪德, eds. and comms. *Ts'ai-kui chi* 才鬼記. Chengchow: Chung-chou Ku-chi, 1989.

Mei Yao-ch'en 梅堯臣 (1002-1060)

Editions and References

Chu, Tung-jun 朱東潤, ed. amd comm. *Mei Yao-ch'en chi pien-nien chiao-chu* 梅堯臣集編年校注. 3v. Shanghai: Shang-hai Ku-chi, 1980.

Wan-ling chi 宛陵集. 18v. Taipei: Shih-chieh Shu-chü, 1988.

Meng Chiao 孟郊 (751-814)

Editions and References

Hua, Ch'en-chih 華忱之 and Yü Hsüeh-ts'ai 喻學才, eds. *Meng Chiao shih-chi* 孟郊詩集. Peking: Jen-min, 1995.

Liu, Ssu-han 劉斯翰. *Meng Chiao chia-tao shih-hsüan* 孟郊賈島詩選. Hongkong: San-lien Shu-tien, 1986.

Luan, Kuei-ming 欒貴明 *et al.*, eds. *Ch'üan T'ang shih so-yin, Meng Chiao chüan* 全唐詩索引：孟郊卷. Peking: Hsien-tai, 1995.

Noguchi, Kazuo 野口一雄. *Mô Kô shi sakuin* 孟郊詩索引. Tokyo: Tôkyô Daigaku Tôyô Bunka jo Fuzoku Tôyôgaku Bunken Sentâ, 1984.

Translations

Hinton, David. *The Late Poems of Meng Chiao.* Princeton: Princeton University Press, 1997.

Studies

Hsieh, Chien-chung 謝建忠. "Tao-chiao yü Meng Chiao shih-ko" 道教與孟郊詩歌. *Wen-hsüeh i-ch'an* 1992.2 (1992): 42-50.

Hung, Ch'a 鴻槎. "Tu Meng Chiao shih cha-chi" 讀孟郊詩札記. *T'ang-tai wen-hsüeh Lun-ts'ung* 6 (1985): 187-95.

Shang, Wei. "Prisoner and Creator: The Self-Image of the Poet in Han Yu and Meng Jiao."

CLEAR 16 (1994): 19-40.

Shih, Che-ts'un 施蟄存. "Shuo Meng Chiao shih" 說孟郊詩. *Ming-tso hsin-shang* 1986.2 (1986): 14-17.

Wada, Hidenobu 和田英信. "Mô Kô kankei kyûshu shiron 孟郊寒渓九首試論." *Shukan Toyogaku* 58 (1987): 1-20.

Yu, Hsin-hsiung 尤信雄. *Meng Chiao yen-chiu* 孟郊研究. Taipei: Wen-chin, 1984.

Meng Hao-jan 孟浩然 (689-740)

Editions and References

Chao, Kuei-fan 趙桂藩, comm. *Meng Hao-jan chi-chu* 孟浩然集注. Peking: Lü-yu Chiao-yü, 1991.

Ch'en, I-hsin 陳貽焮, ed. and comm. *Meng Hao-jan shih-hsüan* 孟浩然詩選. Peking: Jen-min Wen-hsüeh, 1983.

Hsü, P'eng 徐鵬, comm. *Meng Hao-jan chi chiao-chu* 孟浩然集校注. Peking: Jen-min Wen-hsüeh, 1989.

Li, Ching-pai 李景白, ed. and comm. *Meng Hao-jan shih-chi chien-chu* 孟浩然詩集箋注. Chengtu: Pa-Shu Shu-she, 1988. Contains biographical and critical materials, and Meng's preface.

Li, Hua 李華, ed. and comm. *Meng Hao-jan shih pai shou* 孟浩然詩百首. Chengchow: Chung-chou Ku-chi, 1990.

Wang, P'ei-lin 王沛霖, ed. and Ts'ao Yung-tung 曹永東, comm. *Meng Hao-jan shih-chi chiao-chu* 孟浩然詩集校注. Tientsin: T'ien-chin Ku-chi, 1989. Appends Meng's preface, critical materials, and a *nien-p'u.*

Wang, Ta-chin 王達津, ed. and comm. *Wang Wei Meng Hao-jan hsüan-chi* 王維孟浩然選集. Shanghai: Shang-hai Ku-chi, 1990. Includes biographical material.

Studies

Liu, Wen-kang 劉文剛. *Meng Hao-jan nien-p'u* 孟浩然年譜. Peking: Jen-min Wen-hsüeh, 1995. Contains the official biographies of Meng Hao-jan as well as T'ang dynasty prose pieces and poems concerning Meng.

Ting, Hsi-hsien 丁錫賢. "Meng Hao-jan 'Yu-t'ien t'ai-shan' k'ao" 孟浩然游天台山考. *Tung-nan wen-hua* 1990.6.

Wang, Ts'ung-jen 王從仁. *Wang Wei ho Meng Hao-jan* 王維和孟浩然. Shanghai: Shang-hai Ku-chi, 1984.

Min-ko 民歌 (folksongs)

Editions and References

Chiang, Pin 姜彬, ed. *Chiang-nan shih-ta min-chien hsü-shih shih: ch'ang-p'ien Wu-ko chi* 江南十大民間敘事詩：長篇吳歌集. Shanghai: Shang-hai Wen-i, 1989.

___, ed. *Chung-kuo min-chien wen-hsüeh ta tz'u-tien* 中國民間文學大辭典. Shanghai: Shang-hai Wen-i, 1992.

Ch'ien, Hsiao-pai 錢小柏, ed. *Chiang-pei min-chien ch'ing-ko* 江北民間情歌. Taipei: Tung-fang Wen-hua Shu-chü.

Chou, Chung-ming 周中明, *et al.*, eds. *Chung-kuo li-tai min-ko chien-shang tz'u-tien* 中國歷代民歌鑒賞辭典. Nanning: Kuang-hsi Chiao-Yü, 1993.

Chou, Pao-chung 周保中, ed. *Feng Meng-lung min-ko chi* 馮夢龍民歌集. Shih-chia-chuang: Ho-pei Jen-min, 1992.

383

Chung, Ching-wen 鍾敬文, ed. *Ko-yao lun-chi* 歌謠論集. Shanghai: Shang-hai Shu-tien, 1992.

Ho, Hung-i 何紅一, ed. *Ch'ang-chih shan-ko tso mei-jen* 唱支山歌做媒人. Wuhan: Hu-pei Jen-min, 1994. Collects an assortment of folksongs from various ethic groups in China. Appends a bibliography.

Hsia-men Ta-hsüeh 廈門大學, ed. *Li-tai min-ko hsüan-hsi* 歷代民歌選析. Foochow: Fu-chien Jen-min, 1981.

Hua, Kuang-sheng 華廣生, ed. *Ming Ch'ing min-ko shih-t'iao chi* 明清民歌時調集. 2v. Shanghai: Shang-hai Ku-chi, 1987. Collected by Feng Meng-lung.

Itô, Takamaro 伊藤貴麿. *Chûgoku minwa sen* 中国民話選 Tokyo: Kôdansha, 1973.

Jen-min Wen-hsüeh 人民文學出版社, ed. *Han Wei Liu-ch'ao shih-ko chien-shang chi* 漢魏六朝詩歌鑑賞集. Peking: Jen-min Wen-hsüeh, 1985.

Tuan, Pao-lin 段寶林, *et al.,* eds. *Min-chien wen-hsüeh tz'u-tien* 民間文學詞典. Shih-chia-chuang: Ho-pei Chiao-yü, 1988.

Ku, Tun-jo 顧敦鍒, ed. and comm. *Nan-pei liang-ta min-ko chien-chiao* 南北兩大民歌箋校. Taipei: Shih-chieh Shu-chü, 1961.

Wei, Chia-lin 蔚家麟, *et al.,* eds. *Ko-yao yen-chiu tzu-liao hsüan* 歌謠研究資料選. Wuchang: Chung-kuo Min-chien Wen-i Yen-chiu Hui Hu-pei Fen-hui, 1989.

Studies

Chang, Tzu-ch'en 張紫晨. *Ko-yao hsiao-shih* 歌謠小史. Foochow: Fu-chien Jen-min, 1981.

Chin, Hsien-chu 金賢珠. *T'ang Wu-tai Tun-huang min-ko* 唐五代敦煌民歌. Taipei: Wen-shih-che, 1994.

Lu, I-lu 鹿憶鹿. *Feng Meng-lung so-chi min-ko yen-chiu* 馮夢龍所輯民歌研究. Taipei: Hsüeh-hai, 1986. Appends a bibliography.

Kuo, Pai-kung 郭伯恭. *Wei Chin shih-ko kai-lun* 魏晉詩歌概論. Shanghai: Shang-hai Shu-tien, 1992. Reprint of the 1936 text. Discussion centers around *yüeh-fu* 樂府 and Han dynasty Chien-an 建安 era literature.

Mochizuki, Akira 望月彰. *Chûgoku minyô shû* 中国民謠集. Tokyo: Tôyô Shobô, 1988.

Sawayama, Seizaburô 沢山晴三郎. *Chûgoku no minwa* 中国の民話. Tokyo: Shakai Shisôsha, 1976.

Schaffrath, Helmut. *Einhundert chinesische Volkslieder: eine Anthologie.* Frankfurt: P. Lang, 1993. Studien zur Volksliedforschung, 14.

T'an, Ta-hsien 譚達先. *Chung-kuo min-chien hsi-chü yen-chiu* 中國民間戲劇研究. Taipei: T'ai-wan Shang-wu, 1987.

Wang, Lan-ying 王蘭英. *Han yüeh-fu min-ko shang-hsi* 漢樂府民歌賞析. Huhehot: Nei Meng-ku Jen-min, 1987.

Ming-pao chi 冥報記 (**Records of Miraculous Retribution, T'ang dynasty**)

Editions and References

Fang, Shih-ming 方詩銘, ed. *Ming-pao chi* 冥報記. Peking: Chung-hua, 1992. Appends a bibliography.

Studies

Gjertson, Donald E. *Miraculous Retribution: A Study and Translation of T'ang Lin's Ming-pao chi.* Berkeley: Berkeley Buddhist Studies Series, 1989.

P'ien-ku Ching-tzu 片谷景子. "Ming-pao chi yen-chiu" 冥報記研究. Unpublished Master's thesis, Tai-wan Ta-hsüeh, 1981.

Ming-shih chi-shih 明時紀事 (**Recorded Occasions in Ming Poetry**)

Editions and References

Ch'en T'ien 陳田, ed. *Ming-shih chi-shih* 明時紀事. 6v. Shanghai: Shang-hai Ku-chi, 1993.
     Appends an index.
Ming-shih chi-shih 明時紀事. Taipei: Shih-chieh Shu-chü, 1988.

Ming-shih tsung 明時綜

Editions and References
Ming-shih tsung 明時綜. Taipei: Shih-chieh Shu-chü, 1988.

Ming-wen heng 明文衡 (**1445-1499**)

Editions and References
Ming-wen heng 明文衡. Taipei: Shih-chieh, 1988.

Mu T'ien-tzu chuan 穆天子傳 (**An Account of the Travels of Emperor Mu**)

Editions and References

Lau, D. C. 劉殿爵 and Liu Fang-cheng 劉方正, eds. *Mu T'ien-tzu chuan chu-tzu so-yin* 穆天子
     傳逐字索引. Taipei: Shang-wu Yin-shu-kuan, 1994. ICS ancient Chinese text
     concordance series.

Studies

Cheng, Chieh-wen 鄭杰文. "*Mu T'ien-tzu chuan* chih-chien pan-pen shu-yao" 穆天子傳知見
     版本述要," *Wen-hsien* 1994.2: 170-196.
___. *Mu T'ien-tzu chuan t'ung-chieh* 穆天子傳通解. Tsinan: Chi-nan Shan-tung Wen-i, 1992.
___, Wang, I-liang 王貽梁, *et al.*, comms. *Mu T'ien-tzu chuan hui-chiao chi-shih* 穆天子傳匯校
     集釋. Shanghai: Hua-tung Shih-fan Ta-hsüeh, 1994.
Porter, Deborah Lynn. *From Deluge to Discourse—Myth, History and the Generation of Chinese
     Fiction.* Albany: SUNY, 1996.

Na-lan Hsing-te 納蘭性德 (**1655-1685**)

Editions and References

Chang, Ts'ao-jen 張草紉, ed. *Na-lan tz'u chien-chu* 納蘭詞箋注. Shanghai: Shang-hai Ku-chi,
     1995. Chung-kuo ku-tien wen-hsüeh ts'ung-shu.
Ma, Nai-liu 馬酒驑 and K'o Tsung-chi 寇宗基, eds. and comm. *Na-lan Ch'eng-te shih-chi
     shih-lun chien-chu* 納蘭成德詩集詩論箋注. Taiyuan: Shan-hsi Jen-min, 1988.

Studies

Chang, Jen-cheng 張任政. *Ch'ing Na-lan Jung-jo hsien-sheng Hsing-te nien-p'u* 清納蘭容若先生
     性德年譜. Taipei: T'ai-wan Shang-wu Yin-shu-kuan, 1981.
McCraw, David R. *Chinese Lyricists,* pp. 117-143.

Nan Hsi 南戲

Editions and References

Lung, Pi-te 龍彼得, ed. *Ming-k'an Min-nan hsi-ch'ü hsien-kuan hsüan-pen san-chung* 明刊閩南戲曲絃管選本三種. Taipei: Nan-t'ien Shu-chü, 1992. Collects dramatic pieces from southern Fukien.

Wang, Ch'iu-kuei 王秋桂, ed. *Shan-pen hsi-ch'ü ts'ung-k'an* 善本戲曲叢刊. Taipei: T'ai-wan Hsüeh-sheng, 1984.

Studies

Chin, Yü-fen 金宇芬. *Nan hsi yen-chiu pien-ch'ien* 南戲研究變遷. Tientsin: T'ien-chin Chiao-yü, 1992. Appends an index.

Fu-chien Sheng Hsi-ch'ü yen-chiu So 福建省戲曲研究所, ed. *Nan hsi lun-chi* 南戲論集. Peking: Chung-kuo Hsi-ch'ü, 1988.

Hsü, Wei 徐渭 (1521–1593). Li Fu-p'o 李复波 and Hsiung Teng-yü 熊澄宇, comm. *Nan tz'u hsü lu chu-shih* 南詞敘錄注釋. Peking: Chung-kuo Hsi-chü, 1989.

Liu, Nien-tzu 劉念茲. *Nan hsi hsin-cheng* 南戲新證. Peking: Chung-hua, 1986.

Sun, Ch'ung-tao 孫崇濤. "Chung-kuo nan-hsi yen-chiu shih-nien—-hsü Chung-kuo nan-hsi yen-chiu chih chien-t'ao" 中國南戲研究十年—續中國南戲研究之檢討. *Chung-kuo wen-che yen-chiu t'ung-hsün* 6.3 (September 1996): 3-23.

Sun, M. "Reconsidering *Nanxi*'s Position in the History of *Xiqu*." *American Journal of Chinese Studies* 3.1 (April 1996): 22-30.

Tanaka, Issei 田仲一成. Ch'ien Hang 錢杭 and Jen Yü-pai 任余白, trans. *Chung-kuo te tsung-tsu yü hsi-chü* 中國的宗族與戲劇. Shanghai: Shang-hai Ku-chi, 1992. Japanese edition originally published by Tokyo University in 1985 under the title *Chûgoku no sôzoku to engeki* 中国の宗族と演劇.

Yü, Tsung-i 宇宗一, *et al.* *Ming-tai nan hsi yen-chiu kai-shu* 明代南戲研究概述. Tientsin: T'ien-chin Chiao-yü, 1992.

Yü, Wei-min 俞為民. *Sung Yüan nan-hsi k'ao-lun* 宋元南戲考論. Taipei: T'ai-wan Shang-wu, 1994.

Ou-yang Chiung 歐陽炯 (896-971)

Editions and References

Chao, Ch'ung-tso 趙崇祚, ed. *Hua-chien chi hsin-chu* 花間集新注. Nanchang: Chiang-hsi Jen-min, 1987.

Hua-chien chi 花間集. Peking: Wen-hua I-shu, 1985.

Ou-yang Hsiu 歐陽修 (1007-1072)

Editions and References

An, Yüeh 安越, ed. *Ou-yang Hsiu hsiao-p'in* 歐陽修小品. Peking: Wen-hua I-shu, 1997.

Ch'en, Pi-hsiang 陳必詳, ed. *Ou-yang Hsiu san-wen hsüan-chi* 歐陽修散文選集. Shanghai: Shang-hai Ku-chi, 1997.

Higashi, Hidetoshi 東英寿. "Ô-yô Shû kenkyû ronsha mokuroku kô (1945-1986)" 欧陽修研究論著目録稿. *Kyûshû Daigaku Chûgoku bungaku ronshû* 16 (1987).

Hokari, Yoshiaki 保苅佳昭. "Ô-yô Shû shi yakuchû kô 欧陽修詩訳注稿 *Kanran* 3-4 (1990).

Hsü, Shih-cheng 徐世琤, ed. *Kuei-t'ien lu, Sheng-shui yen-t'an lu* 歸田錄，澠水燕談錄. Hangchow: Che-chiang Ku-chi, 1984. In this volume, Ou-yang Hsiu's *Kuei-t'ien lu* is bound together with Wang P'i-chih's 王闢之 (*fl.* 1067) *Sheng-shui yen-t'an lu.*

Huang, Yü 黃畬. *Ou-yang Hsiu tz'u chien-chu* 歐陽修詞箋注. Peking: Chung-hua, 1986. Includes biographical and critical information.

Hung, Pen-chien 洪本健, ed. *Ou-yang Hsiu tzu-liao hui-pien* 歐陽修資料彙編. 3v. Peking: Chung-hua, 1995.

Li, Wei-kuo 李偉國, ed. *Kuei-t'ien lu erh-chüan, i-wen i-chüan* 歸田錄二卷，佚文一卷. Peking: Chung-hua, 1981. Appends the *SKCS* notice and a bibliography.

Lin, Kuan-ch'ün 林冠群 and Chou Chi-fu 周濟夫, comms. *Ou-yang Hsiu shih-wen hsüan-i* 歐陽修詩文選譯. Chengtu: Pa-Shu Shu-she, 1990.

Liu, I-sheng 劉逸生, *et al.*, eds. and comms. *Ou-yang Hsiu Ch'in Kuan tzu-hsüan* 歐陽修秦觀詞選. Hong Kong: San-lien, 1987.

Translations

Landau, *Beyond Spring,* pp. 94-106.

Strassberg, *Inscribed Landscapes,* pp. 161-168.

Studies

Bourgon, Jérome. "Between Signs and Precedents—Notes on the Historical Writings of Ouyang Xiu (1007-1072)." *Extrême-Orient* 19 (1996).

Chen, Yu-shih. "Ou-yang Hsiu: The Return to Universality." In Chen's *Images and Ideas in Chinese Classical Prose, Studies of Four Masters.* Stanford: Stanford University Press, 1988, pp. 109-132.

Egan, Ronald C. "Ou-yang Hsiu and Su Shih on Calligraphy," *HJAS* 49.2 (December 1989): 365-419.

Hawes, Colin Seamus. "Competing with Creative Transformation: The Poetry of Ouyang Xiu (1007-1072)." Unpublished Ph. D. dissertation, University of British Columbia, 1996.

Hsieh, T'ao-fang 謝桃坊. "Ou-yang Hsiu tz'u-chi k'ao" 歐陽修. *Wen-hsien* 文獻 1986.2 (1986).

Hung, Pen-chien 洪本健, ed. *Tsui-weng te shih-chieh: Ou-yang Hsiu p'ing-chuan* 醉翁的世界：歐陽修評傳. Chengchow: Chung-chou Ku-chi, 1990. Appends a *nien-piao* and bibliography.

Kuo, Cheng-chung 郭正忠. *Ou-yang Hsiu* 歐陽修. Shanghai: Shang-hai Ku-chi, 1982.

Liu, Te-ch'ing 劉德清. *Ou-yang Hsiu lun-kao* 歐陽修論稿. Peking: Pei-ching Shih-fan Ta-hsüeh, 1991.

Sung, Pai-nien 宋柏年. *Ou-yang Hsiu yen-chiu* 歐陽修研究. Chengtu: Pa-Shu Shu-she, 1995.

Tietze, Klaus. "Erzählung im *Hsin wu-tai shih* des Ou-yang Hsius" In *XXIII. Deutscher Orientalistentag vom 16. bis 20. September 1985 in Würzburg, Ausgewählte Vortraege.* Einar von Schuler, ed. *ZDMG,* Supplement VII. Stuttgart: Franz Steiner Verlag, 1989, pp. 482-7.

Van Zoeren, Steven. *Poetry and Personality—Reading, Exegesis, and Hermeneutics in Traditional China.* Stanford: Stanford University Press, 1991, pp. 159-89. (On Ou-yang Hsiu's interpretation of the Odes.)

Yen, Chieh 嚴杰. *Ou-yang Hsiu nien-p'u* 歐陽修年譜. Nanking: Nan-ching Ch'u-pan-she, 1993. *Nan-ching Ta-hsüeh ku-tien wen-hsien yen-chiu chuan-k'an.*

Pa-ku wen 八股文 (eight legged essay or composition in eight limbs)

Editions and References

Li-tai chuang yüan pa-ku wen ching-p'in 歷代壯元八股文精品. Peking: Ching-kuan Chiao-yü,

1990?.

Translations

Lo, Andrew. "Four Examination Essays of the Ming Dynasty." *Renditions; Special Issue: Classical Prose* 33/34 (1990): 167-181.

Studies

Ch'i, Kung 啟功 and Chang Chung-hsing 張中行. *Chin K'o-mu kung-che Shuo pa-ku* 金克木共著說八股. Peking: Chung-hua, 1994.

Teng, Yün-hsiang 鄧雲鄉. *Ch'ing-tai pa-ku wen* 清逮八股文. Peking: Chung-kuo Jen-min Ta-hsüeh, 1993.

Pai P'u 白朴 (1226-1306)

Editions and References

Hsü, Ch'in-chün 徐沁君, ed. *Yüan ch'ü ssu ta-chia ming-chü hsüan* 元曲四大家名劇選. Tsinan: Ch'i-Lu Shu-she, 1987. Annotated versions of 16 plays by 4 of the best Yüan playwrights.

Wang, Chi-ssu 王季思, *et al.*, eds. *Hsi-hsiang chi* 西廂記. In *Chung-kuo shih-ta ku-tien hsi-chü chih* 中國十大古典喜劇集. Shanghai: Shang-hai Wen-i, 1982.

Wang, Wen-ts'ai 王文才, ed and comm. *Pai P'u hsi-ch'ü chi chiao-chu* 白朴戲劇集校注. Peking: Jen-min Wen-hsüeh, 1984. Contains 5 plays and most of the *san-ch'ü;* bibliographies and a chronological biography make up the back-matter.

Studies

Ho, Hsin-hui 賀新輝, *et al.*, eds. *Pai P'u* 白朴. Taipei: Ti-ch'iu, 1992.

Hu, Shih-hou 胡世厚. "Lun Pai P'u te san-ch'ü" 論白朴的散曲. *Wen-hsüeh ts'ung-k'an* 2 (1984).

Wu, Ch'ien-hao 吳乾浩. *Pai P'u p'ing-chuan* 白朴評傳. Peking: Chung-kuo Hsi-chü, 1987. Hsi-chü-chia chuan-lun ts'ung-shu. This biography contains readings of many of Pai's plays and poems.

Pan Ku 班固 (32-92)

Editions and References

Ch'ien Han shu i-wen chih 前漢書藝文志. Shanghai: Shang-wu Yin-shu-kuan, 1936. Contains the commentary of Yen Shih-ku 顏師古 (581–645) and Ch'ien Ta-chao 錢大昭 (1744–1813).

Li, Ch'ing-shan 李慶善, ed. and Chin Shao-ying 金少英 (1899–1979), comm. *Han shu shih-huo chih chi shih* 漢書食貨志集釋. Peking: Chung-hua, 1986. Based on the Wu-ying tien 武英殿 edition; includes the commentary of Wang Hsien-ch'ien 王先謙 (*fl.* 1900).

Li, Wei 李維, *et al. Han shu shih-huo chih chi ch'i-ta erh-chung* 漢書食貨志及其他二種. Shanghai: Shang-wu Yin-shu-kuan, 1936. Also includes Hao I-hsing's 郝懿行 (1757–1825) *Pu Sung shu shih-huo chih* 補宋書食貨志 and *Pang chi hui-pien* 邦計彙編 written by Li Wei.

Shih, Ting 施丁, ed. *Han shu hsin-chu* 漢書新注. Sian: San-Ch'in, 1994.

Sun, Hsing-hua 孫星華 (Ch'ing dynasty), ed. *Po-hu t'ung ssu-chüan, chiao-k'an chi ssu-chüan* 白虎通四卷，校勘記四卷. Lanchow: Lan-chou Ku-chi, 1990.

Yang, Chia-lo 揚家駱, ed. *Hsin-chiao pen Han shu pin-fu pien erh-chung* 新校本漢書并附編二

種. 5v. Taipei: Ting-wen Shu-chü, 1986. Contains the commentary of Yen Shih-ku 顏師古 (581–645); appends indexes.

Translations

Honda, Wataru 本田济, trans. and comm. *Kanjo, Gokanjo, Sangokushi retsuden sen* 漢書・後漢書・三国志列伝選. Tokyo: Heibonsha, 1994.

Kano, Naosada 狩野直禎 and Nishiaki Tsuneki 西脇常記, trans. and comms. *Kanjo Koshishi* 漢書郊祀志. Tokyo: Heibonsha, 1987.

Otake, Takeo 小竹武夫. *Kanjo* 漢書. 3v. Tokyo: Chikuma Shobo, 1977–81.

Tomiya, Itaru 富谷至 and Yoshikawa Tadao 吉川忠夫, trans. and comms. *Kanjo Gogyôshi* 漢書五行志. Tokyo: Heibonsha, 1986. Includes maps and charts.

Studies

An, Tso-chang 安作璋. *Pan Ku yü Han shu* 班固與漢書. Tsinan: Shan-tung Jen-min, 1979. Includes various biographical materials.

Cheng, Ho-sheng 鄭鶴聲, ed. *Han Pan Meng-chien hsien-sheng Ku nien-p'u* 漢班孟堅先生固年譜. Taipei: T'ai-wan Shang-wu Yin-shu-kuan, 1980.

Fukushima, Tadashi 福島正. *Shiki, Kanjo* 史記・漢書. Tokyo: Kadokawa Shoten, 1989. Kanshô Chûgoku no koten, 7.

Ku, Shih 顧實. *Han shu i-wen chih chiang-shu* 漢書藝文志講疏. Shanghai: Shang-hai Ku-chi, 1987.

P'an Yüeh 潘岳 (247-300)

Editions and References

Kuan-chung chi 關中記. Lanchow: Lan-chou Ku-chi Shu-tien, 1990.

Studies

Lai, Chiu-Mi. "River and Ocean: The Third Century Verse of Pan Yue and Lu Ji." Unpublished Ph. D. dissertation, University of Washington, 1990.

Pao Chao 鮑照 (414-466)

Editions and References

Huang, Chieh-pu 黃節補 and Ch'ien Chung-lien 錢仲聯, eds. *Pao Ts'an-chün chi-chu* 鮑參軍集注. Shanghai: Shang-hai Ku-chi, 1980. Contains the commentary by Ch'ien Chen-lun 錢振倫 (1816–1879).

Yamada, Hideo 山田英雄. *Hô Sangun shû sakuin* 鮑参軍集索引. Nagoya: Konron Shobô, 1988.

Translations

Chen, Robert Shanmu. "A Study of Bao Zhao and His Poetry: With A Complete English Translation of His Poems." Unpublished Ph.D. dissertation, University of British Columbia, 1989.

Strassberg, *Inscribed Landscapes*, pp. 73-76.

Wang, Shao-tseng 王紹曾 and Liu Hsin-ming 劉心明, trans. and comms. *Hsieh Ling-yün Pao Chao shih* 謝靈運鮑照詩. Chengtu: Pa-Shu Shu-she, 1991. *Ku-tai wen-shih ming-chu hsüan-i ts'ung-shu.* Taiwan reprint by Chin-hsiu in 1993.

Studies

Chang, Kang-i Sun 長孫康宜. "Pao Chao: In Search of Expression." In *Six Dynasties Poetry*. Princeton: Princeton University Press, 1986, pp. 79–111.

Chen, Robert Shanmu. "A Biographical Study of Bao Zhao." *THHP* 21.1; 21.2 (1991): 125–200; 377–404.

____. "A Study of Bao Zhao and His Poetry: With a Complete English Translation of His Poems." Unpublished Ph. D. dissertation, University of British Columbia, 1989.

____. "An Examination of Allegorical Interpretations of the Poems of Bao Zhao." *B.C. Asian Review* 3/4 (1990): 88-105.

Ch'en, Ch'ing-he 陳慶和. "Pao Chao yüeh-fu shih yen-chiu" 鮑照樂府詩研究. M.A. thesis, Tung-hai Ta-hsüeh, 1990.

Chung, Yu-min 鐘優民. "Chien-lun Pao Chao te wen-hsüeh ch'eng-chiu" 簡論鮑照的文學成就. *Pei-fang lun-ts'ung* 78 (1986): 49-56.

____. "Pao Chao te san-wen" 鮑照的散文. *Hsüeh-shu yen-chiu ts'ung-k'an* (1985)

____. *She-hui shih-jen Pao Chao* 社會詩人鮑照. Taipei: Wen-chin, 1994. Appends a bibliography.

Hsü, Hsüeh-fang 余學芳. *Pao Chao sheng-p'ing chi ch'i shih-wen yen-chiu* 鮑照生平及其詩文研究. Taipei: Ching-sheng Wen-wu Kung-ying Kung-ssu, 1983.

Knechtges, David R. "Pao Chao's 'Rhapsody on a Ruined City': Date and Circumstances of Composition." In *A Festschrift in Honour of Professor Jao Tsung-i on the Occasion of His Seventy-Fifth Anniversary*. Hong Kong: Chinese University Press, 1993, pp. 319-330.

Kuttler, Michel. "Le poète Bao Zhao." Unpublished Ph. D. dissertation, École des Haute Études en Sciences Sociales, 1988.

Li, Hai-yüan 李海元. "Hsieh Ling-yün yü Pao Chao shan-shui shih yen-chiu" 謝靈運與鮑照山水詩研究. M.A. thesis, Cheng-chih Ta-hsüeh, 1987.

Liu, Hsiang-fei 劉翔飛. "Pao Chao shih yen-chiu" 鮑照詩研究. *Wen-shih-che hsüeh-pao* 37 (1989): 59–98.

Liu, Wen-chung 劉文忠. *Pao Chao ho Yü Hsin* 鮑照和庾信. Shanghai: Shang-hai Ku-chi, 1986. Taiwan reprint by Kuo-wen T'ien-ti Tsa-chih in 1991.

Su, Jui-lung. "Versatility Within Tradition: A Study of the Literary Works of Bao Zhao (414?-466)." Unpublished Ph.D., University of Washington, 1994.

T'ang, Hai-t'ao 唐海濤. "Pao Chao mo-ni shih te ch'eng-chiu" 鮑照模擬詩的成究. *Chung-yang t'u-shu-kuan kuan-k'an* 20:2 (1987): 51–62.

____. "Pao Chao shih chung chih ch'an-lien-chü" 鮑照詩中之禪聯句. *Chung-wai wen-hsüeh* (1985): 134–142.

____. "Pao Chao te ni-hsing-lu-nan" 鮑照的擬行路難. *Chung-yang t'u-shu-kuan kuan-k'an* 19:2; 20:1 (1986; 1987): 1–20; 95–111.

____. "Pao Chao yü Tu Fu" 鮑照與杜甫. *Yu-shih hsüeh-chih* 19:4 (1987): 75–84.

Ts'ao, Tao-heng 曹道衡. "Pao Chao yü Chiang Yen" 鮑照與江淹. *Ch'i-Lu Shu-she hsüeh-k'an* 91:6 (1991).

Wu, P'i-chi 吳丕績, ed. *Nan Ch'ao Sung Pao Ming-yüan hsien-sheng Chao nien-p'u* 南朝宋鮑明遠先生照年譜. Taipei: T'ai-wan Shang-wu Yin-shu-kuan, 1982.

Pei-li chih 北里志 **(Records of the Northern Sectors)**

Editions and References

Pei-li chih 北里志. Taipei: Hsin-hsing Shu-tien, 1985.

Ch'i, T'eng-mao 齊藤茂. "*Pei-li chih* cha-chi" 北里志札記. *Jimbun kenkyū*, 1991.

Translations

Saitô, Shigeru 斎藤茂. *Kyôbô ki, Hokuri shi* 教坊記, 北里志. Tokyo: Heibonsha, 1992.

Studies

Ch'i, T'eng-mao 齊藤茂. "Kuan-yü *Pei-li chih–T'ang-tai wen-hsüeh yü chi-kuan*" 關於北里志一
唐代文學與妓館. In *T'ang-tai wen-hsüeh yen-chiu* 唐代文學研究, 3. Kwangsi: Kuang-hsi
Shih-fan Ta-hsüeh, 1992.

Saitô, Shigeru 斎藤茂. "*Hokurishi* no bungaku sokumen–shi o chûshin ni" 北里志の文学側面
–詩の中心に, *Higashi Ajia bunka ronsô*, 1991: 299-316.

___. *Hokurishi* satsuki" 北里志札記, *Osaka Shiritsu Daigaku Bungakubu kiyô–Jinbun kenkyû*,
43.11 (1991): 1-16.

Pi-chi 筆記 (note-form literature)

Editions and References

Fang, Chi-liu 方積六 and Wu Tung-hsiu 吳冬秀, eds. *T'ang Wu-tai wu-shih-erh chung pi-chi
hsiao-shuo jen-ming so-yin* 唐五代五十二種筆記小説人名索引. Peking: Chung-hua,
1992.

Hsü, Ling-yün 徐凌雲 and Hsü Shan-shu 許善述, eds. *T'ang Sung pi-chi hsiao-shuo san-chung*
唐宋筆記小説三種. Hofei: Huang-shan Shu-she, 1991.

Tseng, Tsu-yin 曾祖蔭, ed. *Chung-kuo li-tai hsiao-shuo hsü-pa chi-lu: wen-yen pi-chi hsiao-shuo
hsü-pa pu-fen* 中國歷代小説序跋輯錄：文言筆記小説序跋部分. Changsha: Hua-
chung Shih-fan Ta-hsüeh, 1989.

Yeh, Kuei-kang 葉桂剛 and Wang Kuei-yüan 王貴元, eds. *Chung-kuo ku-tai shih-ta i-shih
hsiao-shuo shang-hsi* 中國古代十大軼事小説賞析. 2v. Peking: Pei-ching Kuang-po
Hsüeh-yüan, 1992.

Translations

Chu, Jui-hsi 朱瑞熙 and Ch'eng Chün-chien 程君建, trans. and comms. *Sung-tai pi-chi
hsiao-shuo hsüan-i* 宋代筆記小説選譯. Chengtu: Pa-Shu Shu-she, 1991. *Ku-tai wen-shih
ming-chu hsüan-i ts'ung-shu.*

Yen, Chieh 嚴杰, trans and comm. *Tang Wu-tai pi-chi hsiao-shuo hsüan-i* 唐五代筆記小説選
譯. Chengtu: Pa-Shu Shu-she, 1990. *Ku-tai wen-shih ming-chu hsüan-i ts'ung-shu.* Rpt.
Taipei: Chin-hsiu, 1993.

Studies

Campany, Robert F. "Chinese Accounts of the Strange: A Study in the History of Religions."
Unpublished Ph. D. dissertation, University of Chicago, 1988.

Chang, Shun-hui 張舜徽. *Ch'ing-jen pi-chi t'iao-pien* 清人筆記條辨. Peking: Chung-hua, 1986.

Ch'en, Chi-ju 陳繼儒 (1558–1639). *Pi-chi* 筆記. Peking: Chung-hua, 1985.

Chou, Kuang-p'ei 周光培. *Yüan-tai pi-chi hsiao-shuo* 元代筆記小説. 4v. Shih-chia-chuang:
Ho-pei Chiao-yü, 1994. *Li-tai pi-chi hsiao-shuo chi-ch'eng.*

Liu, Yeh-ch'iu 劉葉秋. *Ku-tien hsiao-shuo pi-chi lun-ts'ung* 古典小説筆記論叢. Tientsin: Nan-k'ai
Ta-hsüeh, 1985.

Wu, Li-ch'üan 吳禮權. *Chung-kuo pi-chi hsiao-shuo shih* 中國筆記小説史. Taipei: T'ai-wan
Shang-wu Yin-shu-kuan, 1993; 1996.

Pi-chi man-chih 碧雞漫志 (Random Notes from Pi-chi)

Editions and References

Pi-chi man-chih 碧雞漫志. Peking: Chung-hua, 1991.

Pi-chi man-chih 碧雞漫志. Taipei: T'ai-wan Shang-wu Yin-shu-kuan, 1983. Reprint of the edition held in the National Palace Museum in Taiwan.

P'i Jih-hsiu 皮日休 (*ca.* 833-*ca.* 883)

Editions and References

Kuan, Chien 關鍵, ed. *P'i Lu-men hsiao-p'in* 皮鹿門小品. Peking: Wen-hua I-shu, 1997. T'ang Sung hsiao-p'ing shih-chia.

Mo, Tao-ts'ai 莫道才 and Shen Wei-tung 沈偉東, eds. *P'i Lu-men hsiao-p'in* 皮鹿門小品. Peking: Wen-hua I-shu, 1997.

P'i Jih-hsiu wen-chi 皮日休文集. Shanghai: Shang-hai Shu-tien, 1989. *SPTK* edition.

Shen Pao-k'un 申寶昆, ed. *P'i Jih-hsiu shih-wen hsüan-chu* 皮日休詩文選注. Shanghai: Shang-hai Ku-chi, 1991.

Studies

Huang Pao-chen 黃保真. "Lun P'i Jih-hsiu te wen-hsüeh ssu-hsiang" 論皮日休的文學思想. In *T'ang-tai wen-hsüeh yen-chiu nien-chien* 唐代文學研究年鑒. Sian: Shensi Jen-min, 1984, pp. 197-8.

P'ien-wen 駢文 or *p'ien-ti wen* 駢體文 (**parallel prose**)

Editions and References

Hsü, I-min 許逸民, ed. and comm. *Ku-tai p'ien-wen ching-hua* 古代駢文精華. Taipei: Chin-hsiu, 1993. *Chung-kuo wen-hsüeh tsung hsin-shang.*

I, Ming 逸名, ed. and comm. *Kuang-chu Sung Yüan Ming Ch'ing p'ien-t'i wen* 廣注宋元明清駢體文. Taipei: Kuang-wen, 1982.

Lu, Ch'ang-ch'un 陸長春 (*fl.* 1900). *Meng-hua t'ing p'ien-t'i wen chi* 夢花亭駢體文集. 4 *chüan.* Shanghai: Shang-hai Shu-tien, 1994.

T'an, Chia-chien 譚家健, ed. *Li-tai p'ien-wen ming-p'ien chu-hsi* 歷代駢文名篇注析. Hofei: Huang-shan Shu-she, 1988.

Studies

Chiang, Shu-ko 姜書閣. *P'ien-wen shih-lun* 駢文史論. Peking: Jen-min Wen-hsüeh, 1986. Covers from pre-Ch'in times through the end of the Ch'ing.

Chung, T'ao 鍾濤. *Liu-ch'ao p'ien-wen hsing-shih chi ch'i wen-hua i-yün* 六朝駢文形式及其文化意蘊. Peking: Tung-fang, 1998.

Fukui, Yoshio 福井佳夫. "Rikuchô henbun no taigû ni kansuru ichi kôsatsu–settoku teki kôka o megutte" 六朝駢文の待遇に関する一考察–説得的効果をめぐって, *Tôhôgaku* 85 (1993): 68-82.

Hsu, Winnifred Wang-hua W. Tung. "A Study of Four Historical *Pien-wen* Stories." Unpublished Ph. D. dissertation, Ohio State University, 1984.

Wang, Ch'eng-chih 王承之. *P'ien-t'i wen tso-fa* 駢體文作法. Taipei: Kuang-wen, 1989.

Yü, Ching-hsiang 于景祥. *T'ang Sung p'ien-wen shih* 唐宋駢文史. Shenyang: Liao-ning Jen-min, 1991. With a preface by Pien Hsiao-hsüan 卞孝萱.

P'ing-hua 平話

Editions and References

Ch'eng, Yu-Ch'in 程有慶 and Ch'eng I-chung 程毅中, eds. *Hsin-pien Wu-tai shih p'ing-hua*

新編五代史平話. Kiangsu: Chiang-su Ku-chi, 1993. Chung-kuo hua-pen ta-hsi.

Chung, Chao-hua 種兆華, ed. and comm. *Yüan-k'an Ch'üan-hsiang p'ing-hua wu-chung chiao-chu* 元刊全相平話五種校注. Chengtu: Pa-Shu Shu-she, 1990.

Hsüan-ho i-shih teng liang-chung 宣和遺事等兩種. Nanking: Chiang-su Ku-chi, 1993. Contains *Hsüan-ho i-shih* and *Hsin-pien Wu-tai shih p'ing-hua* 新編五代史平話.

Lu, Kung 路工 and T'an T'ien 譚天, eds. *Ku-pen p'ing-hua hsiao-shuo chi* 古本平話小説集. 2v. Peking: Jen-min Wen-hsüeh, 1984. Chung-kuo hsiao-shuo shih liao ts'ung-shu.

Ting, Hsi-ken 丁錫根, ed. *Sung Yüan p'ing-hua chi* 宋元平話集. 2v. Shanghai: Shang-hai Ku-chi, 1990. Chung-kuo ku-tien hsiao-shuo yen-chiu tzu-liao ts'ung-shu.

Yen, Tsung-ch'ü 閻宗璩. *Zensô heiwa goshu shigo kaishaku* 全相平話五種詞語匯釋. Tokyo: Daitô Bunka Daigaku, 1983.

P'ing-yao chuan 平妖傳

Editions and References

Chang, Jung-ch'i 張榮起, ed. *San Sui P'ing-yao chuan* 三遂平妖傳. 20 chapters. Peking: Pei-ching Ta-hsüeh, 1983. Pei-ching Ta-hsüeh T'u-shu-kuan kuan-tsang shan-pen ts'ung-shu. Based on the Peking University Library copy of the late sixteenth-century edition. Includes original prefatory material.

Feng, Meng-lung 馮夢龍 (1574–1646), revised and expanded and Chang Wu-chiu 張無咎 (Ming dynasty), ed. *T'ien-hsü chai p'i-tien P'ing-yao chuan* 天許齋批點平妖傳. 40 chapters. 3v. Peking: Chung-hua, 1990. Ku-pen hsiao-shuo ts'ung-k'an, 33.2-4. Based on the 1620 edition preserved in the Naikaku Bunkô in Japan.

San Sui P'ing-yao chuan 三遂平妖傳. 20 chapters. Peking: Chung-hua, 1990. Ku-pen hsiao-shuo ts'ung-k'an, 33.1. Based on the copy of the late sixteenth-century edition which is preserved in the Tenri Library in Japan.

Wei, T'ung-hsien 魏同賢, ed. *Hsin P'ing-yao chuan* 新平妖傳. In *Feng-meng lung ch'üan chi* 馮夢龍全集. 22v. Nanking: Chiang-su Ku-chi, 1993, v. 1.

Translations

Porkert, Manfred, trans. *Der Aufstand der Zauberer–Ein Roman aus der Ming Zeit in der Fassung von Feng Menglong.* Frankfurt: Insel, 1986.

Ôda, Tatsuo 太田辰夫? *Heiyô den* 平妖傳 Tokyo: Heibonsha, 1994. *Chûgoku koten bungaku taikei*, 36.

Satô, Haruo 佐藤春夫. *Heiyô den* 平妖伝. Tokyo: Chikuma Shobô Chikuma Bunko, 1993.

Studies

Hu, Wan-ch'uan 胡萬川. *P'ing-yao chuan yen-chiu* 平妖傳研究. Taipei: Hua-cheng Shu-chü, 1984.

Po Chü-i 白居易 (772-846)

Editions and References

Chou, Lü-ching 周履靖 (*fl.* 16th-17th c.), ed. *Hsiang-shan chiu-sung* 香山酒頌. Peking: Chung-hua, 1985.

Chu, Chin-ch'eng 朱金城, ed. and comm. *Po Chü-i chi chien-chiao* 白居易集箋校. 6v. Shanghai: Shang-hai Ku-chi, 1988. Contains prefaces, biographical and bibliographical information, and an index.

Fu, Tung-hua 傅東華, ed. and comm. *Po Chü-i shih* 白居易詩. Taipei: T'ai-wan Shang-wu

Yin-shu-kuan, 1990.

Hiraoka, Takeo 平岡武夫 and Imai Kiyoshi 今井清, eds. *Hakushi bunshû kashi sakuin* 白氏文集歌詩索引. 3v. Tokyo: Dôhôsha, 1989.

Ku, Hsüeh-chieh 顧學頡, ed. *Po Chü-i chi* 白居易集. 4v. Peking: Chung-hua, 1979. Appends a *nien-p'u.*

Luan, Kuei-ming 欒貴明 *et al.,* eds. *Ch'üan T'ang shih so-yin: Po Chü-i chüan* 全唐詩索引：白居易卷. Ch'in-huang tao: Hsien-tai, 1994.

Po-shih Ch'ang-ch'ing chi 白氏長慶集. 3v. Shanghai: Shang-hai Shu-tien, 1989. *SPTK* edition.

Takagi, Hiroshi 高木博. *Chôkonka zakki* 長恨歌襍記. Tokyo: Sôbunsha Shuppan, 1988.

Translations

Alley, Rewi, trans. *Bai Juyi, 200 Selected Poems.* Peking: New World Press, 1983. Lightly annotated translations.

Costantini, Vilma, ed. *Coppe di giada.* Turin, 1985. Contains translations of about forty poems each by Li Po, Tu Fu and Po Chu-i.

Hoizey, Dominique. *Bai Juyi, poèmes.* Paris: Albédo, 1985. An "artistic" quartet with woodblock prints.

Idema, W.L. *Gans, papegaii en kraanvogel–Gedichten uit het oude China.* Amsterdam: Meulenhoff, 1986. Translations of 100 poems, chronologically arranged, with short explanatory notes.

Jaeger, Georgette. *Bai Juyi, Chant des regrets éternels et autre poèmes.* Paris: Editions Orphé e La différence, 1992.

Okamura, Shigeru 岡村繁. *Hakushi bunshû* 白氏文集. 13v. Tokyo: Meiji Shoin, 1988-93. *Shinshaku kanbun taikei,* 97-109.

Strassberg, *Inscribed Landscapes,* pp. 133-138.

Studies

Chan, Chiu Ming. "Between the World and the Self–Orientations of Pai Chü-i's (772-846) Life and Writings." Unpublished Ph. D. dissertation, University of Wisconsin, 1991.

Dagdanov, G. B. "Vliianie chan'buddizma na tvorchestvo tanskikh poetov. Na primere Van Veia (701-761) i Bo TSziu-ii (772-846) [The Influence of Ch'an Buddhism on the Writings of the T'ang Poets: The Cases of Wang Wei (701-761) and Po Chü-i (772-846)]." Unpublished Ph. D. dissertation, Institut vostokovedeniia Akademii nauk SSSR, 1980.

Field, Stephen Lee. "Taking Up the Plow: Real and Ideal Versions of the Farmer in Chinese Literature." Unpublished Ph. D. dissertation, University of Texas, 1985. Ch. 6-7 (pp. 106-148) deal with Po Chü-i and other T'ang poets.

Goldin, Paul Rakita. "Reading Po Chü-i." *TS* 12 (1994): 57-96.

Hanabusa, Hideki 花房英樹. *Haku Rakuten* 白楽天. Tokyo: Shimizu Shoin, 1990. *Hito to shisô shirîzu,* 87.

Hirakawa, Sukehiro. "Chinese Culture and Japanese Identity: Po Chu-i in a Peripheral Country." *TkR* 16.1-4 (Autumn 1984-Summer 1985): 201-20.

Hsieh, Ssu-wei 謝思煒. "Jih-pen ku-ch'ao-pen *Po-shih wen-chi* te yüan-liu chi chiao-k'an chia-chih" 日本古抄本白氏文集的源流及校勘價值, *Chung-kuo ku-chi yen-chiu* 中國古籍研究. V. 1. Shanghai: Shang-hai Ku-chi, 1996, pp. 371-389.

___. *Po Chü-i chi tsung-lun* 白居易集總論. Peking: She-hui K'o-hsüeh, 1997.

Kominami, Ichirô 小南一郎. "Gen Haku bungaku shûdan no shôsetsu–'Ôôden' o chûshin ni shite" 元白文学集団の小説ー「鶯鶯伝」を中心にして. *Nippon Chûgoku Gakkaihô* 47 (1995): 63-74.

Kondô, Haruo 近藤春雄. *Chôkonka to Yô Kihi* 長恨歌と楊貴妃. Tokyo: Meiji Shoin, 1993.

___. *Hakushi bonshû to kokubun gaku* 白氏文集と国文学. Tokyo: Meiji Shoin, 1990. *Shin gafu shin chûgin no kenkyû.*

Mizuno, Heiji 水野平次. *Haku Rakuten to Nihon bungaku* 白楽天と日本文学. Tokyo: Daigakudô Shoten 1982.

Nienhauser, William H., Jr. "Po Chü-i Studies in English, 1916-1992." *Asian Culture Quarterly* XXII.3 (Autumn 1994): 37-50.

Nishimura, Tomiko 西村富美子. *Haku Rakuten* 白楽天. Tokyo: Kadokawa Shoten, 1988. Kanshô Chûgoku no koten, 18.

Ôta, Tsugio 太田次男. *Chû Tô bunjin kô–Kan Yu, Ryû Sôgen, Haku Kyoi* 中唐文人考–韓愈・柳宗元、白居易. Tokyo: Kenbun Shuppan, 1993.

___, et al., eds. *Haku Kyoi kenkyû kôza* 白居易研究講座. 7v. Tokyo: Benseisha, 1994. Treats Po's life and works, Japanese and foreign studies, editions and his reputation in Japan. Excellent bibliography.

Shang, Yung-liang 尚永亮. *Yüan-ho wu ta shih-jen yü pien-che wen-hsüeh k'ao-lun* 元和五大詩人與貶謫文學考論. Taipei: Wen-chin, 1993. *Ta-lu ti-ch'ü po-shih lun-wen ts'ung-k'an.*

Spring, Madeline K. "The Celebrated Cranes of Po Chü-i." *JAOS* 111 (1991): 8-18.

Thilo, Thomas. "Aspekte der arbeitenden Volkes in den spaeteren Werken des Dichters Bo Juyi." *AF* 16 (1989): 153-181.

Twitchett, Denis. "Po Chü-i's 'Government Ox'." *T'ang Studies* 7 (1989): 23-38.

Ueki, Hisayuki 植木久行. "Tôdai kakka shin ginen roku (5)–Gi Chô, Gu Seinan, Jôkan Shôyô, Tei Ryôshi, Haku Kyoi, Haku Gyôkan, Gô Hô, Ra In, Ri Riran, Raku Shi, Ryû Ushaku" 唐代作家新疑年録（５）–魏徴, 虞世南, 上官昭容, 鄭良士, 白居易, 白行簡, 鮑防, 羅隠, 李李蘭, 陸贄 and 劉禹錫. *Bunkei Ronsô* 37.3 (1992).

Wang, Ernestine H. "Po Chü-i: The Man and His Influence in Chinese Poetry." Unpublished Ph.D. dissertation, Georgetown University, 1987.

Yamada, Yûhei. 山田侑平. *Haku Kyoi* 白居易. Tokyo: Nicchû Shuppan, 1985.

Po Hsing-chien 白行簡 (775-826)

Editions and References

San-meng chi 三夢記. Peking: Chung-hua, 1985.

San-meng chi 三夢記. Taipei: Hsin-hsing Shu-chü, 1985.

Translations

Iida, Yoshirô 飯田吉郎. *Haku Kôkan Tairaku fu* 白行簡太楽賦. Tokyo: Kyûko, 1995.

Studies

Cheng, Ch'iao-fang 鄭喬方. "Li Wa ku-shih te yen-pien" 李娃故事的演變. *Fu-ta Chung-yen-suo hsüeh-k'an* 輔大中研所學刊 4 (1995): 307-19.

Ch'eng, Kuo-fu 程國賦. "'Li Wa chuan' yen-chiu tsung-shu" 李娃傳研究綜述. *Chiang-han lun-t'an* 1993.4 (1993): 73-75.

Fang, Shih-ming 方詩銘. "T'ang Po Hsing-chien 'San-meng-chi' k'ao-pien" 唐白行簡三夢記考辨. *Chung-hua wen-shih lun-ts'ung* 53 (1994): 168-84.

Fu, Hsi-jen 傅錫壬. "Shih t'an 'Li Wa chuan' te hsieh-tso tung-chi chi shih-tai" 試探李娃傳的寫作動機及時代. *Tan-chiang hsüeh-pao* 20 (1983): 211-20.

Kominami, Ichirô 小南一郎. "'Ri Ai den' no kôzô" 李娃伝の構造. *Toho gakuho* 62 (1990): 271-309.

Lee, Yu-hwa. *Fantasy and Realism in Chinese Fiction: Tang Love Themes in Contrast.* San Francisco: Chinese Material Center, 1984.

Li, Wang-chang 李王章. "Chung-T'ang ch'uan-ch'i-chia Po Hsing-chien" 中唐傳奇家白行簡. *Wei-nan Shih-chuan hsüeh-pao* 1988.1.

Liu, Ying 劉瑛. *T'ang-tai ch'uan-ch'i yen-chiu* 唐代傳奇研究. Taipei: Lien-ching, 1994. A study of "Li Wa chuan" is found on pp.336-44.

Matsuzaki, Haruyuki 松崎治之. "Tôdai denki 'Ri Ai den' ronkô" 唐代伝奇李娃伝論考. *Chikushi Jogakuen Tanki Daigaku kiyô* 21 (1986): 55-86.

Pien, Hsiao-hsüan 卞孝萱. "'Li Wa chuan' hsin-t'an" 李娃傳新探. *Yen-t'ai Shih-fan Hsüeh-yüan hsüeh-pao* 1991.4 (1991): 12-19.

Ueki, Hisayuki 植木久行. "Tôdai kakka shin ginen roku (5)–Gi Chô, Gu Seinan, Jôkan Shôyô, Tei Ryôshi, Haku Kyoi, Haku Gyôkan, Gô Hô, Ra In, Ri Riran, Raku Shi, Ryû Ushaku" 唐代作家新疑年録（5）—魏徵, 虞世南, 上官昭容, 鄭良士, 白居易, 白行簡, 鮑防, 羅隱, 李李蘭, 陸贄 and 劉禹錫. *Bunkei Ronsô* 37.3 (1992).

Wang, Meng-ou 王夢鷗. "Tu 'Li Wa chuan' ou-chi" 讀李娃傳偶記. In *Ch'uan-t'ung wen-hsüeh lun-heng* 傳統文學論衡. Taipei: Shih-pao, 1987, pp. 241-46.

___. *T'ang-jen hsiao-shuo chiao-shih* 唐人小説校釋. Taipei: Cheng-chung, 1983. A study of "Li Wa chuan" is found on pp.165-91.

San-hsia wu-i 三俠五義 (Three heroes and Five Gallants, late nineteenth century)

Editions and References

Chung-lieh hsia-i chuan 忠烈俠義傳. 120 chapters. 6v. Shanghai: Shang-hai Ku-chi, 1990. *Ku-pen hsiao-shuo chi-ch'eng*, 3.135–40.

Ch'en, K'o-sen 陳可森, ed. *Sankyô gogi shigo ishaku* 三俠五義詞語彙釈. Tokyo: Tôkyô Daigaku Tôyô Bunka Daigaku, 1984.

Wang, Chün 王軍, ed. *San-hsia wu-i* 三俠五義. 2v. Peking Chung-hua, 1996. *Ku-pen hsiao-shuo tu-pen ts'ung-k'an.*

Translations

Torii, Hisayasu 鳥居久靖, trans. *Sankyô gogi* 三俠五義. Tokyo: Heibonsha, 1994.

Studies

Blader, Susan. "'Yen Ch'a-san Thrice Tested': Printed Novel to Oral Tale." In *Chinese Ideas about Nature and Society, Studies in Honour of Derk Bodde.* Charles le Blanc and Susan Blader, ed. Hong Kong: Hong Kong University Press, 1987, pp. 153-74.

Hou, Chung-i 侯忠義, comm. *San-hsia wu-i hsi-lieh hsiao-shuo* 三俠五義系列小説. Shenyang: Liao-ning Chiao-yü, 1992. *Ku-tai hsiao-shuo p'ing-chieh ts'ung-shu,* 8.5.

San-kuo chih yen-i 三國志演義

Editions and References

Cheng, T'ieh-sheng 鄭鐵生. *San-kuo yen-i shih-tz'u chien-shang* 三國演義詩詞鑑賞. Peking: Pei-ching, 1995.

Ch'en, Hsi-chung 陳曦鍾, *et al* eds. *San-kuo yen-i* 三國演義. 120 *chüan.* 2v. Peking: Pei-ching Ta-hsüeh, 1986. Chung-kuo ku-tien hsiao-shuo hsi-ch'ü yen-chiu tzu-liao ts'ung-shu.

Ch'i, Yen 齊煙, ed. *Mao Tsung-kang p'i-p'ing San-kuo yen-i* 毛宗崗批評三國演義。120 *chüan.* 2v. Tsinan: Ch'i-Lu Shu-she, 1991.

Murakami, Tetsumi 村上哲見 and Nakagawa Satoshi 中川諭, eds. *Sangoku shi engi jinmei sakuin* 三国志演義人名索引. Kyoto: Hôyû Shoten, 1987.

San-kuo chih chuan 三國志傳. 3v. Peking: Chung-hua, 1990. *Ku-pen hsiao-shuo ts'ung-k'an*, 3.1–3.

San-kuo chih t'ung-su yen-i 三國志通俗演義. 6v. Shanghai: Shang-hai Ku-chi, 1990.

San-kuo yen-i hsüeh-k'an 三國演義刊. V. 1-. Chengtu: Ssu-ch'uan Sheng She-hui K'o-hsüeh Yüan, 1985-.

Shen, Po-chün 沈伯俊 and T'an Liang-hsiao 譚良嘯, eds. *San-kuo yen-i tz'u-tien* 三國演義辭典. Chengtu: Pa-Shu Shu-she, 1989. Contains chronological tables and indexes.

Translations

Levi, Jean, Louis Ricaud, *et al. Les Trois Royaumes*. 7v. Paris: Flammarion, 1987-1991.

Nghiêm, Toan. *Luo Guanzhong: Les trois royaumes*. Paris: Flammarion, 1987.

Roberts, Moss, trans. *Three Kingdoms: A Historical Novel, Attributed to Luo Guanzhong*. Berkeley: University of California Press, 1992.

Tatsuma, Shôsuke 立間祥介. *Sangoku shi engi* 三国志演義. 8v. Tokyo: Tokuma Shoten, 1983.

Studies

Bailey, Catherine Diana Alison. "The Mediating Eye: Mao Lun, Mao Zonggang and the Reading of *Sanguo zhi yanyi.*" Unpublished Ph.D. dissertation, University of Toronto, 1991.

Besio, Kimberly. "Zhang Fei in Yuan Vernacular Literature: Legend, Heroism, and History in the Reproduction of the Three Kingdoms Story Cycle." *JSYS* 27 (1997): 63-98.

Cheng, T'ieh-sheng 鄭鐵生. *San-kuo yen-i i-shu hsin-shang* 三國演義藝術欣賞. Peking: Chung-kuo Kuo-chi Kuang-po, 1992.

Chin, Cheng-ch'i 金正起. "*San-kuo yen-i* hsiu-tz'u i-shu t'an-chiu" 三國演義修辭藝術探究. Unpublished M. A. thesis, Tung-wu Ta-hsüeh, 1992.

Ch'iu, Chen-sheng 邱振聲. *San-kuo yen-i tsung-heng t'an* 三國演義縱橫談. Nanning: Li-chiang, 1983.

Chou, Chao-hsin 周兆新, ed. *San-kuo yen-i ts'ung-k'ao* 三國演義叢考. Peking: Pei-ching Ta-hsüeh, 1994. A collection of 16 essays by various Chinese, Japanese and Australian scholars.

Ho-nan Sheng She-hui K'o-hsüeh Yüan Wen-hsüeh Yen-chiu So 河南省社會科學院文學研究所, ed. *San-kuo yen-i yen-chiu wen-chi* 三國演義研究文集. Peking: Chung-hua, 1991.

Kao, Ming-ko 高明閣. *San-kuo yen-i lun-kao* 三國演義論稿. Shenyang: Liao-ning Ta-hsüeh, 1986.

Kin, Bunkei 金文京. "*Sangoku engi* hanbon shitan-Ken'an shohon o chûshin ni" 『三国演義』版本試探-建安諸本を中心に. *Shûkan Tôyôgaku* 1989.

___. *Sangokushi engi no sekai* 三国志演義の世界. Tokyo: Tôhô Shoten, 1983.

Li, Fu-ch'ing 李福清 [Boris Riftin]. *San-kuo yen-i yü min-chien wen-hsüeh ch'uan-t'ung* 三國演義與民間文學傳統. Shanghai: Shang-hai Ku-chi, 1996. *Hai-wai Han-hsüeh ts'ung-shu.*

___, Nakagawa Satoshi 中川諭 and Ueda Nozomu 上田望之. "*Sangoku shi engi* kenkyû bunken mokuroku kô hoi" 『三国志演義』研究文献目録稿補遺. *Chûgoku Koten Shôsetsu Kenkyû Dôtai* 1994.

Li, Hou-chi 李厚基 and Lin Hua 林驊. *San-kuo yen-i chien-shuo* 三國演義簡説. Taipei: San-min, 1993.

Li, Tien-yüan 李殿元 and Li Shao-hsien 李紹先. *San-kuo yen-i chung te hsüan-an* 三國演義中的案. Chengtu: Ssu-ch'uan Jen-min, 1994. *Chung-kuo ku-tien wen-hsüeh ming-chu hsüan-an hsi-lieh ts'ung-shu.*

McLaren, Anne E. "Chantefables and the Textual Evolution of the *San-kuo-chih yen-i.*" *TP* 61 (1985): 159-227.

___. "Ming Audiences and Vernacular Hermeneutics: The Uses of The Romance of the Three Kingdoms." *TP* 81 (1995): 51-80.

Plaks, Andrew H. *The Four Masterworks of the Ming Novel: Ssu ta ch'i-shu.* Princeton: Princeton University Press, 1987.

Ssu-ch'uan Sheng She-hui K'o-hsüeh Yüan Wen-hsüeh Yen-chiu So 四川省社會科學院文學研究所, ed. *San-kuo yen-i yen-chiu chi* 三國演義研究集. Chengtu: Ssu-ch'uan Sheng She-hui K'o-hsüeh Yüan, 1983.

T'an, Lo-fei 譚洛非, *et al.*, eds. *San-kuo yen-i yü Chung-kuo wen-hua* 三國演義與中國文化. Chengtu: Pa-Shu Shu-she, 1992.

West, Andrew Christopher. "Quest of the Urtext: The Textual Archaeology of 'The Three Kingdoms' (Volumes I and II)." Unpublished Ph.D. dissertation, Princeton University, 1993.

Yao, Yao. "A Literary Analysis: The Interlace Structure in the *Romance of the Three Kingdoms.*" Unpublished Ph. D. dissertation, University of California, Berkeley, 1990.

Yeh, Wei-ssu 葉維四 and Mao Hsin 冒炘. *San-kuo yen-i ch'uang-tso lun* 三國演義創作論. Nanking: Chiang-su Jen-min Wen-hsüeh, 1984.

Shan-hai ching 山海經 (The Classic of Mountains and Seas)

Editions and References

Hao, I-hsing 郝懿行 (1757-1825), comm. *Shan-hai ching chien-shu* 山海經箋疏. Chengtu: Pa-Shu Shu-she, 1985.

Lau, D. C. 劉殿爵 and Liu Fang-cheng 劉方正, eds. *Shan-hai ching chu-tzu so-yin* 山海經逐字索引. Taipei: Shang-wu Yin-shu-kuan, 1994. ICS ancient Chinese text concordance series.

Wu, Jen-ch'en 吳任臣 (1628?–1689?), comm. *Shan-hai ching kuang-chu* 山海經廣注. Taipei: Shang-wu Yin-shu-kuan, 1985.

Translations

Cheng, Hsiao-chieh, *et al.*, trans. *Shan-hai ching: Legendary Geography and Wonders of Ancient China.* Taipei: Committee for Compilation and Examination of the Series of Chinese Classics, National Institute for Compilation and Translation, 1985.

Koma, Miyoshi 高馬三良, trans. *Sengai kyô: Chûgoku kodai no shinwa sekai* 山海経-中国古代の神話世界. Tokyo: Heibonsha, 1994.

___. *Hô Bokushi Retsusen den Sengai kyô* 抱朴子, 列仙伝, 山海経. Tokyo: Heibonsha, 1969.

Studies

Chung-kuo *Shan-hai ching* Hsüeh-shu T'ao-lun Hui 中國山海經學述討論會, ed. *Shan-hai ching hsin-t'an* 山海經新探. Chengtu: Ssu-ch'uan Sheng She-hui K'o-hsüeh Hsüeh-yüan, 1986.

Hsü, Hsien-chih 徐顯之. *Shan-hai ching t'an-yüan* 山海經探原. Wuhan: Wu-han Ch'u-pan-she, 1991.

Itô, Seiji 伊藤清司. Liu Yeh-yüan 劉曄原, trans. *Shan-hai ching chung te Kuei-shen shih-chieh* 山海經中的鬼神世界. Peking: Chung-kuo Min-chien Wen-i, 1990. Appends a bibliography and an index; Itô's original published as *Chûgoku no shinjû akuki tachi–Sengai kyô no sekai* 中国の神獣・悪鬼たち–山海経の世界. Tokyo: Tôhô Shoten, 1986.

Golygina, K.I. "Obrâdobyj kalendar: 'Samanskaâ kniga'v literature." *Obsetsvo i gosudarstvo v Kitae*, 1994.

Kyung, Ho Suh. "A Study of *Shan-hai Ching*: Ancient Worldviews under Transformation." Unpublished Ph.D. dissertation, Harvard University, 1993.

Matsuda, Minoru 松田稔. *Sengaikyô no kisoteki kenkyû* 山海経の基礎的研究. Tokyo: Kazama

Shoin, 1995.

Shan-hai ching hsin-t'an 山海經新探. Chengtu: Ssu-ch'uan Sheng She-hui K'o-hsüeh, 1986. Contains 27 pieces presented at a conference in 1983.

Yüan, K'o 袁珂, trans. and comm. *Shan-hai ching chiao-i* 山海經校譯. Shanghai: Shang-hai Ku-chi, 1985.

___. *Shan-hai ching ch'üan-i* 山海經全譯. Kueiyang: Kuei-chou Jen-min, 1991. *Chung-kuo li-tai ming-chu ch'üan-i ts'ung-shu.* Appends a bibliography.

Shan-ko 山歌 (rustic songs)

Editions and References

Chiang, Pin 姜彬, ed. *Chiang-nan shih-ta min-chien hsü-shih shih: ch'ang-p'ien Wu-ko chi* 江南十大民間敍事詩：長篇吳歌集. Shanghai: Shang-hai Wen-i, 1989. Includes explanations and examples of commonly-used expressions in the Wu dialect.

Feng, Meng-lung 馮夢龍 (1574–1646). *Shan-ko* 山歌. Lu Kuo-pin 陸國斌, ed. In *Feng Meng-lung ch'üan-chi* 馮夢龍全集. Nanking: Chiang-su Ku-chi, 1993.

Tu, Shan-hsiung 杜山雄. *T'ai-wan yüan-wan min-ko-wu chiao-ts'ai* 臺灣原民歌舞教材. Vol. 1. Taipei: Chiao-yü-pu, 1991.

Shen Chi-chi 沈既濟 (c.a 740-ca. 800)

Studies

Ho, Man-tzu 何滿子. "Shen Chi-chi 'Jen-shih chuan' tu-te" 沈既濟任氏傳讀得. *Ming-tso hsin-shang* 1987.2 (1987).

Lin, Po-ch'ien 林伯謙. "T'ang-jen hsiao-shuo 'Jen-shih chuan' hsin-t'an" 唐人小說任氏傳新探. *Chung-hua wen-hua fu-hsing yüeh-k'an* 20.4 (1987): 65-72.

Liu, Ying 劉瑛. *T'ang-tai ch'uan-ch'i yen-chiu* 唐代傳奇研究. Taipei: Lien-ching, 1994. Studies of "Jen-shih chuan" and "Chen-chung chi" 枕中記 are found on pp. 299-313 and pp. 350-56.

Mei, Chia-ling 梅家玲. "Lun 'Tu Tzu-ch'un' yü 'Chen-chung chi' te jen-sheng t'ai-tu" 論杜子春與枕中記的人生態度. *Chung-wai wen-hsüeh* 15.12 (1987): 122-33.

Pien, Hsiao-hsüan 卞孝萱. "'Chen-chung chi' chu-chiao yüan-hsing san-shuo chih-i" 枕中記主角原型三説質疑. *Hsi-pei Shih-ta hsüeh-pao* 1993.6 (1993): 49-55.

Wang, Meng-ou 王夢鷗. *T'ang-jen hsiao-shuo chiao-shih* 唐人小説校釋. Taipei: Cheng-chung Shu-chü, 1983. A study of "Chen-chung chi" is found on pp. 23-57.

___. "Tu Shen Chi-chi 'Chen-chung chi' pu-k'ao" 讀沈既濟枕中記補考. *Chung-kuo wen-che yen-chiu chi-k'an* 1 (1991): 1-10.

Shen Ching 沈璟 (1553-1610)

Editions and References

Hsü, Shuo-fang 徐朔方, ed. *Shen Ching chi* 沈璟集. 2v. Shanghai: Shang-hai Ku-chi, 1991. Chung-kuo ku-tien wen-hsüeh ts'ung-shu.

Studies

Li, Chen-yü 李真瑜. "Shen Ching hsi-ch'ü ch'uang-tso te tsai jen-shih" 沈璟戲曲創作的再認識. *Wen-hsüeh i-ch'an* 1985.4 (1985): 104-112.

Shen Ch'üan-chi 沈佺期 (*ca.* 650-713)

Editions and References

Matsuoka, Eiji 松岡栄治, ed. *Shin Senki shi sakuin* 沈期佺詩索引. Tokyo: Tôkyô Daigaku Tôyô Bunka Kenkyû Sho, 1987.

Studies

Ch'a, Hung-te 查洪德. "Ch'u-T'ang shih-t'an te i-tai tsung-shih: Shen Ch'üan-ch'i hsin-lun" 初唐詩壇的一代宗師：沈佺期新論. *T'ang-tu hsüeh-k'an* 1991.3.

T'ao, Min 陶敏. "*T'ang ts'ai-tzu chuan chiao-chien* 'Shen Ch'üan-ch'i chuan' pu-chien" 唐才子傳校箋沈佺期傳補箋. *Hsien-ning Shih-chuan hsüeh-pao* 1992.2.

Shen-hsien chuan 神仙傳 (**Biographies of Divine Immortals**)

Editions and References

Lieh-hsien chuan Shen-hsien chuan 列仙傳神仙傳. Shanghai: Shang-hai Ku-chi, 1990.

Shen-hsien chuan 神仙傳. Hangchow: Che-chiang Ku-chi, 1989. *Tao-tsang ching-hua, 2.*

Wang, Chao-hsiang 王兆祥, ed. *Chung-kuo Shen-hsien chuan* 中國神仙傳. Taiyuan: Shan-hsi Jen-min, 1992. Not seen, appends an index.

Translations

Fukui, Kôjun 福井康順. *Shinsen den* 神仙伝. Tokyo: Meitoku Shuppansha, 1983.

Güntsch, Gertrud. *Das Shen-hsien chuan un das Erscheinungsbild eines Hsien.* Frankfurt am Main: Verlag Peter Lang, 1988.

Sawada, Mizuho 沢田瑞穂. *Retsusen den, Shinsen den* 列仙伝, 神仙伝. Tokyo: Heibonsha, 1993.

Studies

Fukui, Kôjun 福井康順. "*Shinsen den kô*" 神仙伝考. *Tôhô sôkyô, Sôkangô* 東方宗教, 創刊号, 1951.

___. "*Shinsen den* saikô" 神仙伝再考. *Sôkyô kenkyû* 137 (1953).

Kan, Ch'un-sung 干春松. *Shen-hsien hsin-yang yü ch'uan-shuo* 神仙信仰與傳説. Peking: Chung-kuo Jen-min Ta-hsüeh, 1991.

Kominami, Ichirô 小南一朗. "Shinsen den no fukugen" 神仙伝の復元. In *Iriya Kyôju Ogawa Kyôju taikyû kinen Chûgoku Bungaku Gogaku ronshû* 入矢教授小川教授退休記念中国文学語学論集 (Studies on Chinese Literature and Linguistics Dedicated to Professors Iriya Yoshitaka and Ogawa Tamaki on Their Retirement from Kyoto University). Kyoto: Kyoto University, 1974, pp: 301-313.

___. "*Shinsen den*–atarashii shinsen shisô" 神仙伝–新しい神仙思想. In Kominami, *Chûgoku no shinwa to monogratri–Koshsetsushi no tenkai* 中国の神話と物語—古小說史の展開. Tokyo: Iwanami, 1984, pp. 145-236.

Shen Te-ch'ien 沈德潛 (1673-1769)

Editions and References

Shen, Te-ch'ien 沈德潛, ed. and Sung Ching-ju 宋晶如, comm. *T'ang Sung pa-ta chia ku-wen* 唐宋八大家古文. 30 *chüan*. 2v. Peking: Chung-kuo Shu-tien, 1987.

Studies

Hu, Yu-feng. *Shen Te-chien shih-lun t'an-yen* 沈德潛詩論探研. Taipei: Hsüeh-hai, 1986.

Shen Yüeh 沈約 (441-513)

Editions and References

Ch'en, Ch'ing-yüan 陳慶元, ed. *Shen Yüeh chi chiao-chien* 沈約集校箋. Hangchow: Che-chiang Ku-chi, 1996.

Translations

Mather, *The Poet Shen Yüeh* (see "Studies" below).

Studies

Kawai, Yasushi 川合安. "Shin Yaku *Sôsho* no kai ishiki" 沈約「宋書」の華夷意識. *Tôhoku Daigaku Bungakubu kiyô* 6 (1995): 125-145.

___. "Shin Yaku *Sôsho* no shiron (4)" 沈約「宋書」の史論（四）. *Hokkaido Daigaku Bungakubu kiyô* 64.1 (1995): 1-65.

Kôzen, Hiroshi 興膳宏. "Enshi no keishi to Shin Yaku" 豊詩の形成と沈約. *Nihon Chûgoku gakkaiho* 24 (1972): 114–134.

Lai, Whalen. "Beyond the Debate on 'The Immortality of the Soul': Recovering an Essay by Shen Yüeh." *JOAS* (1981): 138–157.

Liang, Ch'eng-teh 梁承德. "Shen Yüeh chi ch'i tso-p'in yen-chiu" 沈約及其作品研究. M. A. Thesis, Wen-hua Ta-hsüeh, 1991.

Mather, Richard B. *The Poet Shen Yüeh (441–513), The Reticent Marquis*. Princeton: Princeton University Press, 1987.

Sung, Hsiao-yung 宋效永. "Shen Yüeh te hsin-pien wen-hsüeh ssu-hsiang" 沈約的新變文學思想. *Wen-hsüeh p'ing-lun ts'ung-k'an* 31 (1989): 134–145.

Suzuki, Torao 鈴木虎雄. *Sung Shen Hsiu-wen hsien-sheng Yüeh nien-p'u* 宋沈休文先生約年譜. Ma Tao-yüan 馬導源, trans. Taipei: T'ai-wan Shang-wu Yin-shu-kuan, 1980.

Ts'ao, Tao-heng 曹道衡. "Chiang Yen, Shen Yüeh ho Nan Ch'i shih-feng" 江淹沈約和南齊詩風. *Ho-pei Shih-yüan hsüeh-pao* (1986): 21–33.

Yao, Chen-li 姚振黎. *Shen Yüeh chi ch'i hsüeh-shu chih t'an-so* 沈約及其學術之探索. Taipei: Wen-shih Che-hsüeh, 1989.

___. "Shen Yüeh shih chih nei-han hsi-lun" 沈約詩之內涵析論. *Kuo-li Chung-yang Ta-hsüeh Wen-hsüeh-yüan yüan-k'an* 4 (1986): 93-117.

Yen, K'un-yang 諺崑陽. "Lun Shen Yüeh te wen-hsüeh kuan-nien: *Sung shu* Hsieh Ling-yün chuan lun wei chu-chü" 論沈約的文學觀念—以宋書謝靈運傳論為主據. In *Wen-hsüeh yü mei-hsüeh* 文學與美學 Taipei: Wen-shih-che, 1990, pp. 85–108.

Yoshikawa, Tadao 吉川忠夫. "Shin Yaku kenkyû" 沈約研究. In Yoshikawa, *Rikuchô seishinshi kenkyû* 六朝精神史研究. Kyoto: Hôyû, 1984, pp. 199-259.

Shih 詩 (poetry or classical poetry)

Editions and References

Chou, Hsün-ch'u 周勛初, ed. *T'ang-shih ta-tz'u-tien* 唐詩大辭典. Nanking: Chiang-su Ku-chi, 1990.

Iritani, Sensuke 入谷仙介. *Ko shi sen jô* 古詩選. 2v. 中国古典選. Tokyo: Asahi Shinbunsha, 1978. Chûgoku koten sen 23-24.

Studies

Hsieh, Daniel. "The Origin and Development of Jueju Verse." Unpublished Ph.D. dissertation, University of Washington, 1991.

Lin, Shuen-fu and Stephen Owen, eds. *The Vitality of the Lyric Voice: Shih Poetry from the Late Han to the T'ang.* Princeton: Princeton University Press, 1986.

Mair, Victor H. "The Sanskrit Origins of Recent Style Prosody." *HJAS* 51 (1991): 345-470.

Marney, John. *Chinese Anagrams and Anagram Verse.* Taipei: Chinese Materials Center, 1993. *Asian Library Series.* Traces the history of anagrams in prose fiction from the earliest times; three chapters are devoted to exchanges between Lu Kuei-meng 陸龜蒙 and P'i Jih-hsiu 皮日休.

Satô, Tamotsu 佐藤保. *Kanshi no imêji* 漢詩のイメージ. Tokyo: Yaishûkan Shoten, 1992.

Shih, I-tui 施議對 and Chiang Yin 蔣寅. *Chung-kuo shih-hsüeh* 中國詩學. Nanking: Nan-ching Ta-hsüeh, 1997. This first volume of a projected mutli-volume history covers the poetry of the *ta-li* period.

Wilkerson, Douglas Keith. "*Shih* and Historical Consciousness in Ming Drama." Unpublished Ph.D. dissertation, Yale University, 1992.

Shih-chi 史記 (Records of the Grand Historian)

Editions and References

An, P'ing-ch'iu 安平秋. "*Shih-chi* pan-pen shu-yao" 史記版本述要. *Ku-chi cheng-li yü yen-chiu* 古籍整理與研究 1987.1 (reprinted in Chang Kao-p'ing 張高評, ed. *Shih-chi yen-chiu ts'ui-pen* 史記研究粹本 [Taipei: Fu-wen T'u-shu, 1992], pp. 837-889). The most detailed study available.

Chang, K'o 張克, *et al. Shih-chi jen-wu tz'u-tien* 史記人物辭典. Nanning: Kuang-hsi Jen-min, 1991.

Chang, Yüan-chi 張元濟. *Po-na pen Erh-shih-ssu shih chiao-k'an chi–Shih-chi chiao-k'an chi* 百衲本二十四史校勘濟—史記校勘記. Shanghai: Shang-wu, 1998.

Ch'eng, Chin-tsao 程金造, ed. *Shih-chi So-yin yin-shu k'ao-shih* 史記索隱引書考實. Peking: Chung-hua, 1994.

Chi, Ch'ao 稽超, *et al. Shih-chi ti-ming so-yin* 史記地名索引. Peking: Chung-hua, 1990.

Ch'ien, Mu 錢穆. *Shih-chi ti-ming k'ao* 史記地名考. Hong Kong: T'ai-p'ing Shu-chü, 1962. Rpt. Taipei: San-min Shu-chü, 1984.

Chou, Hsiao-t'ien 周嘯天 and Yu Ch'i 尤其, eds. *Shih chi ch'uan-pen tao-tu tz'u-tien* 史記全本導讀辭典. 2v. Chengtu: Ssu-ch'uan Tz'u-shu, 1997. Despite the title, this is merely a *pai-hua* rendition of the text.

Fujita, Katsuhisa 藤田勝久. Sun Wen-ko 孫文閣, trans. "Chin-nien lai Jih-pen te Shih-chi yen-chiu" 近年來日本的史記研究. *Ku-chi cheng-li yen-chiu hsüeh-k'an* 57 (1995): 45-48.

Han, Chao-ch'i 韓兆琦, ed. *Shih-chi hsüan-chu chi-p'ing* 史記選注集評. Kweilin: Kuang-hsi Shih-fan Ta-hsüeh, 1995. {A similar volume to those published under various titles by various presses by Han Chao-ch'i in recent years.}

Ho, Tz'u-chun. *Shih-chi shu-lu* 史記書錄. Shanghai: Shang-wu Yin-shu-kuan, 1958.

Hsü, Hsing-hai 徐興海, ed. *Ssu-ma Ch'ien yü Shih-chi lun-chi* 司馬遷與史記論集. Sian: Shan-hsi Jen-min Chiao-yü, 1995.

___, ed. *Ssu-ma Ch'ien yü Shih-chi yen-chiu lun-chu chuan-t'i so-yin* 司馬遷與史記研究論著專題索引. Sian: Shan-hsi Jen-min Chiao-yü, 1995.

Ikeda, Hideo 池田英雄. *Shikigaku 50 nen–Ni-Chû Shiki kenkyû no dôkô (1945-1995 nen)* 史記学50年一日中史記研究の動向 (1945-1995年). Tokyo: Meitoku, 1996.

Ikeda, Shirôjirô 池田四郎次郎 and Ikeda Eiyû 池田英雄. *Shiki kenkyû shomuku kaidai (kôhon)* 史記研究書目解提, 稿本. Tokyo: Meitoku Shuppansha, 1978.

Kuo, I 郭逸 and Kuo Man 郭曼, comm. *Shih chi* 史記. 2v. Shanghai: Shang-hai Ku-chi, 1997.

Li, Hsiao-kuang 李曉光 and Li Po 李啵, eds. *Shih-chi so-yin* 史記索引. Peking: Chung-kuo Kuang-po Tien-t'ai Ch'u-pan-she, 1989. The only comprehensive index.

Li, Mien 李勉, ed. *Shih-chi ch'i-shih p'ien lieh-chuan p'ing-chu* 史記七十篇列傳評注. Taipei: Kuo-li Pien-i Kuan, 1996.

Ling, Chih-lung 淩稚隆 (*fl.* 1576-1587), ed. *Shih-chi p'ing-lin* 史記評林. Changsha: Wei-shih Yang-ho Shu-wu, 1874. Rpt. Tokyo: Kyûko Shoin, 1989.

Ozaki, Yasushi' 尾崎康. *Seishi Sô Gen ban no kenkyû* 正史宋元版の研究. Tokyo: Kyûko Shoin, 1989, pp. 161-231. Discussion of Sung editions of the *Shih-chi*.

Takigawa, Kametarô 瀧川亀太郎 (1865-1946). *Shiki kaichû kôshô fu kôho* 史記会注考証附校補 Rpt. of Tokyo: Tôhô Bunka Gakuin, 1934 ed. with supplementary collation notes by Mizusawa Toshitada 水澤利忠. Shanghai: Shang-hai Ku-chi, 1986.

Ts'ang, Hsiu-liang 倉修良, ed. *Shih-chi tz'u-tien* 史記辭典. Tsinan: Shan-tung Chiao-yü, 1991.

Tuan, Shu-an 段書安. *Shih-chi San-chia chu yin-shu so-yin* 史記三家注引書索引. Peking: Chung-hua, 1982.

Wang, Hui 王恢. *Shih-chi pen-chi ti-li t'u-k'ao* 史記本紀地理圖考. Taipei: Kuo-li Pien-i-kuan, 1990.

Wu, Shu-p'ing 吳樹平, Liu Ch'i-yü 劉起釪, *et al. Ch'üan-chu ch'üan-i Shih-chi* 全注全譯史記. 3v. Tientsin: T'ien-chin Ku-chi, 1996. These huge tomes provide a useful commentary.

Wu, Shu-p'ing 吳樹平. *Shih-chi jen-ming so-yin* 史紀人名索引. Peking: Chung-hua, 1977.

Yang, Yen-ch'i 楊燕起 and Yü Chang-hua 俞樟華, eds. *Shih-chi yen-chiu tzu-liao so-yin ho lun-wen, chuan-chu t'i-yao* 史紀研究資料索引和論文，專著提要. Lanchow: Lan-chou Ta-hsüeh Ch'u-pan-she, 1989.

Yoshiwara, Hideo 吉原英夫. *Shiki ni kansuru bunken mokuroku* 史記に関する文献目録. Hokkaido: Hokkaidô Kyoiku Daigaku, 1997. A fifty-page bibliography of editions (since 1911) and studies.

Translations

Dawson, Raymond. *Historical Records* Oxford, New York and Toronto: Oxford University Press, 1994.

Dolby, William and John Scott, trans. *Sima Qian, War-lords, Translated with Twelve Other Stories from His Historical Records.* Edinburgh: Southside, 1974.

Fukushima, Chûrô 福島中郎. *Shiki* 史記. 11v. Tokyo: Gakushû Kenkyûsha, 1981–1991. Chûgoku no koten.

Kurosu, Shigehiko 黒須重彦, trans. *Shiki* 史記. Tokyo: Gakushû Kenkyûsha, 1984. Chûgoku no koten, 14.4.

Nienhauser, William H. Jr., ed. Cheng Tsai-fa, Lu Zongli, William H. Nienhauser, Jr. and Robert Reynolds, trans. *The Grand Scribe's Records.* Volume 1, *The Basic Annals of Pre-Han China.* Volume 7, *The Memoirs of Pre-Han China.* Bloomington and Indianapolis: Indiana University Press, 1994.

Page, John. *Los adversarios: Dos biografías de Las memorias históricas de Sima Qian.* Mexico City: El Colegio de México, 1979. Centro de Estudios de Asia y Africa del Norte. Ensayos, 6. Lightly annotated translations of Chapters 7 and 8.

Pokora, Timoteus. "Shih chi 127, the Symbiosis of Two Historians." In *Chinese Ideas about Nature and Society, Studies in Honour of Derk Bodde.* Charles Le Blanc and Susan Blader, eds. Hong Kong: Hong Kong University Press, 1987, pp. 215-234.

Wang, Li-ch'i 王利器, ed. *Shih-chi chu-i* 史記注譯. 4v. Sian: San Ch'in, 1988.

Watson, Burton. *Records of the Grand Historian: Han Dynasty I and II* (Revised Edition). 2v. Hong Kong and New York: Renditions-Columbia University Press, 1993.

___. *Records of the Grand Historian: Qin Dynasty.* V. 3. Rev. ed. Hong Kong and New York: The Research Centre for Translation, The Chinese University of Hong Kong and

Columbia University Press, 1993.

Viatkin, R. V. *Istoricheskie zapiski ("Shi tszi")*. 5v. Moscow: Nauka, 1972-.

Yang, Chung-hsien 楊鐘賢 and Hao Chih-ta 郝志達. *Wen-pai tui-chao ch'üan-i Shih-chi* 文白對照全譯史記. 5v. Peking: Kuo-chi Wen-hua, 1992.

Yoshida, Kenko 吉田賢抗 (v. 1-2 and 4-6) and Mizusawa Toshitada 水澤利忠 (v. 7-9). *Shiki* 史記. Volumes 1-2 and 4-9. Tokyo: Meiji Shoin, 1973–1993.

Studies

Bissell, Jeff. "Literary Studies of Historical Texts: Early Narrative Accounts of Chong'er, Duke Wen of Jin." Unpublished Ph. D. dissertation, University of Wisconsin, 1996.

Chang, Chia-ying 張家英. *Shih chi shih-erh pen-chi i-ku* 史記十二本紀疑詁. Harbin: Hei-lung-chiang Chiao-yü, 1997.

Chang, Hsin-k'o 張新科. *Shih-chi yü Chung-kuo wen-hsüeh* 史記與中國文學. Sian: Shan-hsi Jen-min Chiao-yü, 1995. *Ssu-ma Ch'ien yü hua-hsia wen-hua ts'ung-shu.*

___ and Yü Chang-hua 俞樟華. *Shih-chi yen-chiu shih-lüeh* 史記研究史略. Sian: San-Ch'in Ch'u-pan-she, 1990.

Chang, Ta-k'o 張大可. *Shih-chi ch'üan-pen hsin-chu* 史記全本新注. 4v. Sian: San Ch'in Ch'u-pan-she, 1990.

___. *Shih-chi lun-tsan chi-shih* 史記論贊輯釋. Sian: Shan-hsi Jen-min Ch'u-pan-she, 1986.

___. *Shih-chi yen-chiu* 史記研究. Lanchow: Kan-su Jen-min, 1985.

___. *Ssu-ma Ch'ien i-chia yen* 司馬遷一家言. Sian: Shan-hsi Jen-min Chiao-yü, 1995. *Ssu-ma Ch'ien yü hua-hsia wen-hua ts'ung-shu.*

___. *Ssu-ma Ch'ien p'ing-chuan* 司馬遷評傳. Nanking: Nan-ching Ta-hsüeh, 1994.

Chang, Wei-yüeh 張維嶽. *Ssu-ma Ch'ien yü Shih-chi hsin-t'an* 司馬遷與史記新探. Taipei: Sung-kao Shu-she, 1985.

Chang, Yen-t'ien 張衍田, ed. *Shih-chi "Cheng-i" i-wen chi-chiao* 記紀正義佚文輯校. Peking: Pei-ching Ta-hsüeh Ch'u-pan-she, 1985.

Chang, Yu-ming 張友銘. "Tu Shih-chi 'Hsiang Yü pen-chi' cha-chi" 讀史記項羽本紀札記. *Kuo-wen yüeh-k'an* 20 (March 1943). Not seen.

Chao, Sheng-ch'ün 趙生群. "*Shih-chi* ch'ü-ts'ai yü chu-hou Shih-chi" 史記取材於諸侯史記. *Jen-wen tsa-chih* 1984.2: 92-94.

Ch'en, Ch'i 陳琪. "'Yao tien' yü 'Wu-ti pen-chi' tzu-chü chih pi-chiao yen-chiu" 堯典與五帝本紀字句之比較研究 *Shu-mu chi-k'an* 17.3 (December 1983): 50-72.

Ch'en, Chih 陳直. "Han Chin jen tui Shih-chi te ch'uan-po chi ch'i p'ing-chia" 漢晉人對史記的傳播及其評價. In *Ssu-ma Ch'ien yü Shih-chi lun-chi* 司馬遷與史記論集. Sian: Shan-hsi Jen-min Ch'u-pan-she, 1982, pp. 215-42.

Ch'en, Ts'ang-chieh 陳蒼杰. "Liu Pang nien-piao" 劉邦年表. In *Liu Pang chuan* 劉邦傳. Peking: I-ch'ün, 1985.

Ch'en, T'ung-sheng 陳桐生. *Chung-kuo shih-kuan wen-hua yü Shih-chi* 中國史官文化與史記. Shantou: Shan-t'ou Ta-hsüeh, 1993. Explores various aspects of Ssu-ma Ch'ien's historiography; useful bibliography.

___. *Shih-chi yü chin-ku-wen ching-hsüeh* 史記與今古文經學. Sian: Shan-hsi Jen-min Chiao-yü, 1995. *Ssu-ma Ch'ien yü hua-hsia wen-hua ts'ung-shu.*

Ch'eng, Chin-tsao 程金造. *Shih-chi kuan-k'uei* 史記管窺. Sian: Shan-hsi Jen-min, 1985.

Chou, Ching 周經. *Ssu-ma Ch'ien Shih-chi yü tang-an* 司馬遷史記與檔案. Peking: Tang-an Ch'u-pan-she, 1986.

Chou, Hsiao-t'ien 周嘯天 and Yu Ch'i 尤其, eds. *Shih-chi ch'üan-pen tao-tu* 史記全本導讀. Chengtu: Ssu-ch'uan Tz'u-shu, 1997.

Chou, Hsien-min 周先民. *Ssu-ma Ch'ien te shih-chuan wen-hsüeh shih-chieh* 司馬遷的史傳文學世界. Taipei: Wen-chin, 1995. Wen-shih-che ta-hsi, 93.

Di Cosmo, Nicola. "Inner Asia in Chinese History: An Analysis of the Hsiung-nu in the

'Shih chi.'" Unpublished Ph. D. dissertation, Indiana University, 1991.

Durrant, Stephen. *The Cloudy Mirror: Tension and Conflict in the Writings of Sima Qian*. Albany: State University of New York Press, 1995.

___. "Redeeming Sima Qian." *CRI* 4.2 (Fall 1997): 307-313.

___. "Self as the Intersection of Traditions: The Autobiographical Writings of Ssu-ma Ch'ien." *JAOS* 106 (1986): 33-40.

___. "Ssu-ma Ch'ien's Conception of *Tso chuan*." *JAOS* 112 (1992): 295-301.

___. "Takigawa Kametaro's Commentary on Chapter 47 of *Shih-chi*." In *Proceedings of the Second Annual International Conference on Chinese Language Works Outside of China*. Taipei: Lien-ching, 1989, pp. 995-1007.

Fan, Wen-fang 范文芳. *Ssu-ma Ch'ien te ch'uang-tso i-chih yü hsieh-tso chi-ch'iao* 司馬遷的創作意識與寫作技巧. Taipei: Wen-shih-che Ch'u-pan-she, 1987.

Fujita, Katsuhisa 藤田勝久. *Shiki Sengoku shiryô no kenkyû* 史記戦国史料の研究. Tokyo: Tokyo University, 1997. An thoughtful study of Ssu-ma Ch'ien's use of sources.

Fukushima, Tadashi 福島正. *Shiki, Kanjo* 史記・漢書. Tokyo: Kadokawa Shoten, 1989. *Kanshô Chûgoku no koten*, 7.

Han, Chao-ch'i 韓兆琦, ed. *Shih-chi hsüan-chu chi-p'ing* 史記選注集評. Kweilin: Kuang-hsi Shih-fan Ta-hsüeh, 1995.

___. *Shih-chi hsüan-chu chi-shuo* 史記選注集説. Nanchang: Chiang-hsi Jen-min Ch'u-pan-she, 1982.

___. *Shih-chi hsüan-chu hui-p'ing* 史記選注匯評. Chungchow: Chung-chou Ku-chi Ch'u-pan-she, 1990.

___. *Shih-chi shang-hsi chi* 史記賞析集. Chengtu: Pa-Shu Shu-she, 1988.

___, *et al. Shih-chi t'ung-lun* 史記通論. Peking: Pei-ching Shih-fan Ta-hsüeh, 1990.

___ and Lü Po-t'ao 呂伯濤. "Ssu-ma Ch'ien yü Shih-chi" 司馬遷與史記. In Han and Lü, *Han-tai san-wen shih-kao* 漢代散文史稿. Taiyuan: Shan-hsi Jen-min Ch'u-pan-she, 1986, pp. 95-167.

Hardy, Grant Ricardo. "Form and Narrative in Ssu-ma Ch'ien's *Shih-chi*." *CLEAR* 1 (1992): 1-23.

___. "Objectivity and Interpretation in the 'Shih-chi.'" Unpublished Ph. D. dissertation, Yale University, 1988.

___. "The Interpretive Function of *Shih-chi* 14, 'The Table by Years of the Twelve Feudal Lords." *JAOS* 113 (1993): 14-24.

Hirase, Takao 平勢隆郎. *Shinpen Shiki tôshû nenpyô—Chûgoku kodai nenki no kenkyû joshô* 新編史記東周年表–中国古代紀年の研究序章. Tokyo: Tôkyô Daigaku Shuppankai, 1995.

Hsiang, Li-ling 項立嶺 and Lo Yi-chün 羅義俊. "Liu Pang nien-piao" 劉邦年表. In *Liu Pang*. Peking: Jen-min, 1976.

Hsiao, Li 肖黎. *Ssu-ma Ch'ien p'ing-chuan* 司馬遷評傳. Changchun: Chi-lin Wen-shih Ch'u-pan-she, 1986.

Hsü, Shuo-fang 徐朔方. *Shih Han lun-kao* 史漢論稿. Nanking: Chiang-shu Ku-chi, 1984.

Huang, Hsin-yeh 黃新業. *Ssu-ma Ch'ien p'ing-chuan* 司馬遷評傳. Peking: Kuang-ming Jih-pao Ch'u-pan-she, 1991.

Huang, P'ei-jung 黃沛榮, ed. *Shih-chi lun-wen hsüan-chi* 史記論文選集. Taipei: Ch'ang-an, 1982.

Ishikawa, Misao 石川三佐男. "*Shiki* no Kutsu Gen den ni tsuite" 史記の屈原伝について *Shibun* 97 (1989): 68-101.

Itô, Tokuo 伊藤徳男. *Shiki jippyô ni miru Shiba Sen no rekishikan* 史記十表に見る司馬遷の歴史観. Tokyo: Hirakawa Shuppansha, 1994.

Jian, Xiaobin. "Spatialization in the 'Shiji.'" Unpublished Ph. D. dissertation, Ohio State University, 1992.

Juan, Chih-sheng 阮芝生. "*Shih-chi* 'Ho-cho shu' hsin-lun" 史記河渠書新論. *Kuo-li T'ai-wan Ta-hsüeh Li-shih Hsüeh-hsi hsüeh-pao* 15 (1990): 65-80.

Kao, Chen-to 高振鐸. "Li-tai tui *Shih-chi* t'i-ch'u te i-nan wen-t'i pien-hsi" 歷代對史記提出的疑難問題辨析, *Ku-chi cheng-li yen-chiu hsüeh-k'an* 古籍整理研究學刊 1986.4.

Kobayashi, Haruki 小林春樹. "Shiba Sen ni okeru *Shiki* chojutsu no dôki no tsuite-*Shiki* kenkyû josetsu" 司馬遷における『史記』著述の動機について-『史記』研究序説. *Shikan* 127 (1992).

Ku, Kuo-shun 古國順. *Shih-chi shu Shang shu yen-chiu* 史記述尚書研究. Taipei: Wen-shih-che Ch'u-pan-she, 1985.

Kuo, Shuang-ch'eng 郭雙成. *Shih-chi jen-wu chuan-chi lun-kao* 史記人物傳記論稿. Chungchow: Chung-chou Ku-chi, 1985.

Li, Shao-yung 李少雍. *Ssu-ma Ch'ien chuan-chi wen-hsüeh lun-kao* 司馬遷傳記文學論稿. Chungking: Ch'ung-Ch'ing Ch'u-pan-she, 1987.

Li, Te-yüan 李德元. "T'ang-tai tien-ting *Shih-chi* yen-chiu te chien-shih chi-ch'u" 唐代奠定史記研究的堅實基礎, *T'ung-hua Shih-yüan hsüeh-pao* 通化師院學報 1991.1.

Li, Wai-yee. "The Idea of Authority in the *Shih chi* (Records of the Historian)." *HJAS* 54 (2 1994): 345-405.

Liu, Nai-ho 劉乃和, ed. *Ssu-ma Ch'ien ho Shih-chi* 司馬遷和史記. Peking: Pei-ching Ch'u-pan-she, 1987.

Liu, Ts'ao-nan 劉操南. *Shih-chi Ch'un-ch'iu Shih-erh Chu-hou shih shi chi-cheng* 史記春秋十二諸侯史事輯證. Tientsin: T'ien-chin Ku-chi, 1992; 1995.

Lu, Yung-p'in 陸永品. *Ssu-ma Ch'ien yen-chiu* 司馬遷研究. Nanking: Chiang-su Jen-min, 1983.

Lu, Zongli. "Problems Concerning the Authenticity of *Shih chi* 123 Reconsidered," *CLEAR* 15 (1993): 51-68.

Makizumi Etsuko 牧角悦子. *Shikyô, Soji* 詩経, 楚辞. Tokyo: Kadokawa Shoten 1989. *Kanshô Chûgoku no koten*, 11.

Miyazaki, Ichisada 宮崎市定. *Shiki to kataru* 史記と語る. Tokyo: Iwanami, 1996. Essays on how to read the *Shih-chi*, its various genres, and a brief piece on women who appear in it; originally published in the early 1990s as part of Miyazaki's collected works.

Mizusawa, Toshitada 水澤利忠. *Shiki 'Seigi' no kenkyû* 史記正義の研究. Tokyo: Kyûko Shoyin, 1993.

Murayama, Makoto 村山孚. *Shiba Sen Shiki rekishi kikô* 司馬遷史記歷史紀行. Tokyo: Shôbunsha, 1995.

Nieh, Shih-ch'iao 聶石樵. *Ssu-ma Ch'ien lun-kao* 司馬遷論稿. Peking: Pei-ching Shih-fan Ta-hsüeh Ch'u-pan-she, 1987.

Nienhauser, William H., Jr. "A Century (1895-1995) of *Shih chi* 史記 Studies in the West." *Asian Culture Quarterly* 24.1 (Spring 1996): 1-51.

___. "A Reexamination of 'The Biographies of the Reasonable Officials' in the *Records of the Grand Historian.*" *Early China* 16 (1991): 209-233.

___. "The Study of the *Shih chi* 史記 (The Grand Scribe's Records) in the People's Republic of China," *Das andere China*. Wiesbaden: Harrassowitz, 1995, pp. 381-403.

P'an, Yin-ko 潘吟閣. *Shih-chi "Huo-chih chuan" hsin ch'üan* 史記貨殖傳新詮. Shanghai: Shang-wu Yin-shu-kuan, 1931.

Pankenier, David. "'The Scholar's Frustration' Reconsidered: Melancholia or Credo?" *JAOS* 110 (1990): 434-459.

Park, Jae-Woo 朴宰雨. "Han-kuo *Shih-chi* wen-hsüeh yen-chiu te hui-ku yü ch'ien-chan" 韓國史記文學研究的回顧與前瞻, *Wen-hsüeh i-ch'an* 1998.1: 20-28.

___. *Shih chi, Han shu pi-chiao yen-chiu* 史記漢書比較研究. Peking: Chung-kuo Wen-hsüeh, 1994.

Satô, Taketoshi 佐藤武敏. *Shiba Sen no kenkyû* 司馬遷の研究. Tokyo: Kyûko, 1997.

Sung, Yün-pin 宋雲彬. "Liu Pang nien-piao" 劉邦年表. In *Liu Pang* 劉邦. Peking: Chung-hua, 1964.

Takahashi, Minoru 高橋稔. "*Shiki* to rekishikatari ni tsuite" 史記と歴史語りについて. *Higashi Ajia bunka ronsô* (1991): 33-48.

Wang, Nien-sun 王念孫 (1744-1832). "Shih-chi tsa-chih" 史記雜志. In Wang's *Tu-shu tsa-chih* 讀書雜志. Originally printed from 1812-1831; 2v; Rpt. Taipei: Shih-chieh, 1963, v. 1, pp. 71-173.

Wang, Shu-min 王叔岷. *Shih-chi chiao-cheng* 史記斠證. 10v. Taipei: Chung-yang Yen-chiu Yüan, Li-shih Yü-yen Yen-chiu So, 1982, No. 87.

Watson, Burton. "The *Shih chi* and I." *CLEAR* 17 (1995): 199-206. Watson's reminiscences on his study of the *Shih-chi.*

Wu, Ju-yü 吳如煜. *Shih-chi lun-kao* 史記論稿. Nanking: Chiang-su Chiao-yü, 1986.

___. "Ssu-ma Chen Shih-chi So-yin yü Chu-shu chi-nien" 司馬貞史記索隱與竹書紀年. *Wen-hsien* 16 (1983): 73-81.

Wu, Kuo-t'ai 吳國泰. *Shih-chi chieh-ku* 史記解詁. Tientsin: T'ien-chin She-hui K'o-hsüeh-yüan Ch'u-pan-she, 1993.

Wu, Shu-p'ing 吳樹平, ed. *Shih-chi Han shu chu-piao ting-pu shih-chung* 史記漢書諸表訂補十種. 2v. Peking: Chung-hua, 1982. Includes Liang Yü-sheng's "Jen-piao k'ao" 人表考 (pp. 465-943) and Wang Yüeh's 汪越 (*fl* 1720) "Tu Shih-chi shih-piao" 讀史記十表 (pp. 1-81).

Yang, Hsü-min 楊緒敏. "Shih-t'ung tsun Pan i Ma pien" 史通尊班抑馬辨. *Hsü-chou Shih-yüan hsüeh-pao* 徐州師院學報 1983.3.

Yang, Yen-ch'i 楊燕起. *Shih-chi te hsüeh-shu ch'eng-chiu* 史記的學術成就. Peking: Pei-ching Shih-fan Ta-hsüeh, 1996.

___. "Shih-chi yen-chiu shih shu-lüeh" 史記研究史述略. In *Shih-hsüeh lun-heng* 史學論衡. Pei-ching Shih-fan Ta-hsu/ehLi-shih Hsi, ed. Peking: Pei-ching Shih-fan Ta-hsüeh Ch'u-pan-she, pp. 103-116.

___, Ch'en K'o-ch'ing 陳可青, Lai Chang-yang 賴長揚, eds. *Li-tai ming-chia p'ing Shih-chi* 歷代名家評史記. Peking: Pei-ching Shih-fan Ta-hsueh, 1986.

Yoshihara, Hideo 吉原英夫. "*Shiki* ni mieru 'chôja' ni tsuite" 『史記』に見える「長者」について. *Kanbungaku ronshû* (1991).

Shih-ching 詩經 (Classic of Poetry)

Editions and References

Ch'en, Hung-ta 陳宏天 and Lü Lan 呂嵐, eds. *Shih-ching so-yin* 詩經索引. Peking: Shu-mu Wen-hsien, 1984. Concordance and original text.

Ch'en, Tzu-chan 陳子展. *Kuo-feng hsüan-i* 國風選譯. Shanghai: Ch'un-ming, 1956.

___ *Ya Sung hsüan-i* 雅頌選譯. Shanghai: Shang-hai Ku-chi, 1986 (rev. ed.). One of the best modern commentaries on the last two sections of the *Shih-ching.* Ch'en's *Kuo-feng hsüan-i* and *Ya Sung hsüan-i* have been published together in a single volume entitled *Kuo-feng Ya Sung hsüan-i* in Hsin-chu, Taiwan by Yang-che Ch'u-pan-she in 1987.

Ch'eng, Chün-ying 程俊英, comm. *Shih-ching i-chu* 詩經譯註. Shanghai: Shang-hai Ku-chi, 1985.

Chiang, Yin-hsiang 江陰香, comm. *Shih-ching i-chu* 詩經譯注. Peking: Chung-kuo Shu-tien, 1982.

Chou, Hsiao-t'ien 周嘯天, ed. *Shih-ching chien-shang chi-ch'eng* 詩經鑑賞集成. 2v. Taipei: Wu-nan, 1994. Contains various indexes, maps and bibliograhical information.

___ ed. *Shih-ching Ch'u-tz'u chien-shang tz'u-tien* 詩經楚辭鑑賞辭典. Chengtu: Ssu-ch'uan Tz'u-shu, 1990. Useful bibliography.

Chu, Min-ch'e 祝敏徹, *et al.*, comms. *Shih-ching i-chu* 詩經譯注. Lanchow: Kan-su Jen-min, 1984.

Chung, Fu 鐘夫 and T'ao Chün 陶鈞, eds. *Tu-shih wu-chung so-yin* 杜詩五種索引. Shanghai: Shang-hai Ku-chi, 1992.

Chung-kuo *Shih-ching* Hsüeh-hui Ch'ou-ch'ou Lüeh-hui 中國詩經學會愁籌略會, ed. *Shih-ching yao-chi chi-ch'eng* 史經要籍集成. Tientsin: Nan-k'ai Ta-hsüeh,1994.

Hsiang, Hsi 向熹. *Shih-ching tz'u-tien* 詩經辭典. Chengtu: Ssu-ch'uan Jen-min, 1986. Contains various phonological charts, bibliographical materials and an index.

Jen, Tzu-pin 任自斌 and Ho Chin-chien 和近健, eds. *Shih-ching chian-shang tz'u-tien* 辭典. Peking: Ho-hai Ta-hsüeh, 1989. Appends a very useful bibliography.

Lan, Chü-sun 藍菊蓀. *Shih-ching Kuo-feng chin-i* 詩經國風今譯. Chengtu: Ssu-ch'uan Jen-min, 1982. Appends a bibliography.

Lau, D. C. and Fong Ching, eds. *Shih-ching chu-tzu so-yin* 詩經逐字索引. Hong Kong: Shang-wu Yin-shu-kuan, 1994. ICS ancient Chinese text concordance series.

Li, Tzu-wei 李子偉, comm. *Shih-ching i-chu kuo-feng pu-fen* 詩經譯注國風部分. Lanchow: Lan-chou Ta-hsüeh, 1992.

Lin, Ch'ing-chang 林慶彰, *et al.*, eds. "*Shih-ching* 史經." In *Ching-hsüeh yen-chiu lun-chu mu-lu* 經學研究論著目錄 (Bibliography of Research on the Classics). 2v. Taipei: Han-hsüeh Yen-chiu Chung-hsin (Center for Chinese Studies): 1989, pp. 272-496.

Loewe, Michael. "Shih-ching" 史經. In *Early Chinese Texts*, pp. 415–423.

Murayama, Yoshihiro 村山吉広 and Eguchi Naozumi 江口尚純, eds. *Shikyô kenkyû bunken mokuroku* 史紀研究文献目録. Tokyo: Kyûko Shoin, 1992.

Shikyô kenkyû 史紀研究. v. 1- (1974-). Tokyo: Waseda Daigaku. Publishes an annual bibliography of studies in Japan on the *Shih-ching*.

Tung, Chih-an 董治安, ed. *Shih-ching tz'u-tien* 詞典. Tsinan: Shan-tung Chiao-yü, 1989.

Wang, Hsien-ch'ien 王先謙, comm. *Shih San-chia i-chi shu* 詩三家義集疏. 2v. Peking: Chung-hua, 1987.

Translations

Hsü, Yüan-ch'ung 許淵沖, trans. and Chiang Hsing-chang 姜胜章, ed. *Book of Poetry*. Changsha: Hu-nan Ch'u-pan-she, 1993.

Koeser, Heide, trans. *Das Liederbuch der Chinesen: Guofeng. Lieder aus den einzelnen Landesteilen*. Frankfurt: Insel Verlag, 1990.

Mekada, Makoto 目加田誠. *Shikyô* 詩経. Tokyo: Kôdansha, 1991.

Okamura, Shigeru 岡村繁. *Mô shi seigi yakuchû, vol. 1* 毛詩正義訳注第 1 冊. Fukuoka: Chûgoku Shoten, 1986.

Shirakawa, Shizuka 白川静. *Shikyô kokufû* 詩経国風. Tokyo: Heibonsha, 1990.

Stukina, A. *Siczin.* Moscow: Chudôzestv. Literatura, 1987.

Wang, Shou-min 王守民. *Shih-ching erh-ya hsüan-p'ing* 詩經二雅選評. Sian: Shan-hsi Shih-fan Ta-hsüeh, 1989.

Wu, Hung-i 吳宏一. *Pai-hua Shih-ching* 白話詩經. 2v. Taipei: Lien-ching, 1993.

Studies

Akatsuka, Kiyoshi 赤塚忠, ed. *Shikyô kenkyû* 詩経研究. Tokyo: Kenbunsha, 1986. *Akatsuka Kiyoshi chosaku shû*, 5.

Asselin, Mark Laurent. "The Lu-School Reading of 'Guanju' as Preserved in an Eastern Han *fu.*" *JAOS* 117 (1997): 427-443.

Baxter, William H. III. "Zhou and Han Phonology in the *Shijing.*" In *Studies in the Historical*

Phonology of Asian Languages. William G. Boltz and Michael G. Shapiro, eds. Amsterdam and Philadelphia: Benjamins, 1991, pp. 1-34.

Chang, Christopher Shang-kuan. "The Lost Horizon: A Study of English Translations of the 'Shijing'." Unpublished Ph.D. dissertation, University of Texas, Austin, 1992.

Chang, Yün-chung 張允中. *Shih-ching ku-yün chin-chu* 詩經古韻今注. Taipei: T'ai-wan Shang-wu, 1987.

Chao, Chih-yang 趙制陽. *Shih-ching ming-chu p'ing-chieh* 詩經明著評介. Taipei: Hsüeh-sheng, 1983.

Chao, P'ei-lin 趙沛霖. *Shih-ching yen-chiu fan-ssu* 詩經研究反思. Tientsin: T'ien-chin Chiao-yü, 1989. Appends a variety of bibliographical information and an index.

Ch'en, T'ieh-pin 陳鐵鑌. *Shih-ching chieh-shuo* 詩經解説. Peking: Shu-mu Wen-hsien, 1985.

Ch'en, Tzu-chan 陳子展. *Shih-ching chih-chieh* 詩經直解. 2v. Shanghai: Fu-tan Ta-hsüeh, 1983.

___ and Tu Yüeh-ts'un 杜月村. *Shih-ching tao-tu* 詩經導讀. Chengtu: Pa-Shu Shu-she, 199?*.

Ch'eng, Chün-ying 程俊英. *Shih-ching man-hua* 詩經漫話. Shanghai: Shang-hai Wen-i, 1983.

___, ed. *Shih-ching shang-hsi chi* 詩經賞析集. Chengtu: Pa-Shu Shu-she, 1989.

___ and Chiang Chien-yüan 蔣見元. *Shih-ching chu-hsi* 詩經注析. Peking: Chung-hua, 1991. Chung-kuo ku-tien wen-hsüeh chi-pen ts'ung-shu. Useful explications and notes.

Chi, Hsü-sheng 季旭昇. *Shih-ching ku-i hsin-cheng* 詩經古義新證. Taipei: Wen-shih-che, 1994.

Chiang, Chien-t'ien 蔣見天 and Chu Chieh-jen 朱杰人. *Shih-ching yao-chi chieh-t'i* 史經要籍解題. Shanghai: Shang-hai Ku-chi, 1997.

Chin, Ch'i-hua 金啟華, comm. *Shih-ching ch'üan-shih* 詩經全釋. Nanking: Chiang-su Ku-chi, 1984. Appends a bibliography.

Dai, Wei-qun. "*Xing* Again: A Formal Re-investigation." *CLEAR* 13 (1991): 1-14.

Dobson, W.A.C.H. "On Translating the *Book of Songs,*" *Wen-lin,* v. 2, pp. 33-44.

Fang, Yü-jun 方玉潤 (1811–1883). *Shih-ching yüan-shih* 詩經原始. Peking: Chung-hua, 1986.

Fowler, Verson. "Popular Improvised Poetry of Ancient China: The Origins of the *Shijing*" *British Columbia Asian Review* 3-4 (1990): 192-226.

Fu, Li-p'u 傅隸樸. *Shih-ching Mao-chuan i-chieh* 譯解. V. 1. Taipei: T'ai-wan Shang-wu, 1985.

Han, Ming-an 韓明安 and Lin Hsiang-cheng 林祥征. *Shih-ching mo-i* 詩經末議. Harbin: Hei-lung-chiang Jen-min, 1991.

___. *Shih-ching yen-chiu kai-kuan* 詩經研究概觀. Harbin: Hei-lung-chiang Chiao-yü, 1988.

Harbsmeier, Christoph. "Eroticism in Early Chinese Poetry, Sundry Comparative Notes." In *Das andere China, Festschrift für Wolfgang Bauer zum 65. Geburtstag.* Helwig Schmidt-Glintzer, ed. Wiesbaden: Harrassowitz, 1995, pp. 323-380.

Hsia, Ch'uan-ts'ai 夏傳才. "*Shih-ching* hsüeh ssu ta kung-an te hsien-tai chin-chan" 詩經學四大公案的閒代進展, *Chung-kuo wen-che yen-chiu t'ung-hsün* 7.3 (September 1997): 17-34.

___. *Shih-ching yen-chiu shih kai-yao* 詩經研究史概要. Rpt. Taipei: Hsüeh-sheng, 1993 (1982).

___. *Shih-ching yü-yen i-shu* 詩經語言藝術. Chengchow: Chung-chou Shu-hua She, 1982. Rpt. Taipei: Lung-yün, 1990 (1985).

___. *Shih-ching yü-yen i-shu hsin-pien* 詩經語言藝術新編. Peking: Yü-wen, 1998.

Hsiang, Hsi 向熹. *Shih-ching yü-yen yen-chiu* 詩經語言研究. Chengtu: Ssu-ch'uan Jen-min, 1987.

___. *Shih-ching ku-chin yin shou-ts'e* 詩經古今音手冊. Tientsin: Nan-k'ai Ta-hsüeh, 1988.

Hsieh, Ch'ien-i 謝謙議. "*Chung yü ku*"–*Shih-ching te t'ao-yü chi ch'i chuang-tso fang-shih* 鍾與鼓—詩經的套語及其創作方式. Chengtu: Ssu-ch'uan Jen-min, 1990.

Huang, Cho 黃焯. *Mao-shih Cheng-chien p'ing-i* 毛詩鄭箋評譯. Shanghai: Shang-hai Ku-chi, 1985.

Huang, Chung-shen 黃忠慎. *Nan Sung san-chia Shih-ching hsüeh* 南宋三家詩經學. Taipei: Shang-wu, 1988. Discusses theories of Cheng Ch'iao 鄭樵, Ch'eng Ta-ch'ang 程大昌, and Chu Hsi 朱熹.

Huang, Tien-ch'eng 黃典誠. *Shih-ching t'ung-i hsin-ch'üan* 詩經通譯新銓. Shanghai: Hua-tung Shih-fan Ta-hsüeh, 1992.

Ko, Susan Schor. "Literary Politics in the Han." Unpublished Ph. D. dissertation, Yale University, 1991. Focuses on the *Shih-ching*.

Kung, Yü-hai 宮玉海. *Shih-ching hsin-lun* 詩經新論. Changsha: Chi-lin Jen-min, 1985.

Kuo, Chin-hsi 郭晉稀. *Shih-ching li-ts'e* 詩經蠡測. Lanchow: Kan-su Jen-min, 1993.

Li, Chia-shu 李家樹. *Shih ching te li-shih kung-an* 詩經的歷史公案. Taipei: Ta-an, 1990.

Li, Hsiang 李湘. *Shih-ching yen-chiu hsin-pien* 詩經研究新編. Kaifeng: Ho-nan Ta-hsüeh,1990.

Lin, Ch'ing-chang 林慶彰, ed. *Shih-ching yen-chiu lun-chi* 詩經研究論集. Taipei: Hsüeh-sheng, 1987. Lin himself has appended a bibliography of basic works on the *Shih-ching* (Volume 1, pp. 503-514).

Lin, Yeh-lien 林. *Chung-kuo li-tai Shih-ching hsüeh* 中國歷代詩經學. Taipei: Hsüeh-sheng Shu-chü, 1993.

Liu, David Jason. "Parallel Structures in the Canon of Chinese Poetry: the *Shih Ching*." *Poetics Today* 4 (1983): 639-53.

Lo. Pin-chi 羅賓基. *Shih-ching hsin-chieh yü ku-shih hsin-lun* 詩經新解與古史新論. Taiyuan: Shan-hsi Jen-min, 1985.

Lo, Wen-tsung 羅文宗. *Shih-ching shih-cheng* 詩經釋証. Sian: Shan-hsi Jen-min, 1995.

Ma, Tuan-ch'en 馬端辰 and Hung Wen-t'ing 洪文婷. *Mao-shih chuan chien t'ung-shih hsi-lun* 毛詩傳箋通釋析論. Taipei: Wen-chin, 1995?.

Makizumi, Etsuko 牧角悦子 and Fukushima Yoshihiko 福島吉彦. *Shikyô Soji* 詩経楚辞. Tokyo: Kadokawa Shoten, 1989.

Matsmoto, Masaaki 松本雅明. *Shikyô kokufû hen no kenkyû* 詩経国風篇の研究. In Matsumoto Masaaki Chosakushû Henshû Iinkai 松本雅明著作集編集委員会, ed. *Matsmoto Masaaki chosaku shû*, vol. 1 松本雅明著作集, 1. Tokyo: Kôsei Shorin, 1987.

___. *Shikyô shohen no seiritsu ni kansuru kenkyû* 詩経諸篇の成立に関する研究. In Matsumoto Masaaki Chosakushû Henshû Iinkai 松本雅明著作集編集委員会, ed. *Matsmoto Masaaki chosaku shû*, vols. 5-6 松本雅明著作集, 5-6. Tokyo: Kôsei Shorin, 1987.

Mekada, Makoto 目加田誠. *Shikyô kenkyû* 詩経研究. Tokyo: Ryûkei Shosha, 1985.

Miao, Ronald C. Review of *The Reading of Imagery in the Chinese Poetic Tradition* by Pauline Yu. *HJAS,* 51 (1991): 726-756.

Nieh, Shih-ch'iao 聶石樵, *et al. Shih-ching chien-shang chi* 詩經鑒賞集. Peking: Jen-min Wen-hsüeh, 1986

Ôhama, Hiroshi 大濱浩皓. *Shiki shitsû no sekai–Chûgoku no rekishi kan* 史記史通の世界–中国の歴史観. Tokyo: Tôhô Shoten, 1993.

Okamura, Shigeru 岡村繁. *Mô Shi seigi gakuchû* 毛詩正義訳注. Fukuoka: Chûgoku Shoten, 1986.

Owen, Stephen. "The Great Preface." In *Readings in Chinese Literary Thought*. Cambridge: Council on East Asian Studies, Harvard University, 1992, pp. 37-56.

Pfister, Lauren. "James Legge's Metrical *Book of Poetry*." *BSOAS* 60.1 (1997): 64-85. Points out Legge translated the *Shih-ching* into three distinct versions.

Ren, Y. "Traditional Chinese Critics' Response to the Confucian Exegesis of the *Classic of Poetry:* A Counter Tradition." *American Journal of Chinese Studies* 3 (1996): 40-53.

Riegel, Jeffrey. "Eros, Introversion, and the Beginnings of *Shijing* Commentary." *HJAS* 57 (1997): 143-177. Important study of the *Wu-hsing p'ien* 五行篇 commentary (found at Ma-wang Tui) on several poems in the *Shih-ching.*

Röllicke, Hermann-Josef. *Die Fährte des Herzens: die Lehre vom Herzenbestreben (zhi) im groseen Vorwort zum Shijing.* Berlin: Reimer, 1992.

Saussy, Haun. *The Problem of a Chinese Aesthetic.* Stanford: Stanford University Press, 1993.

___. "Repetition, Rhyme, and Exchange in the *Book of Odes.*" *HJAS* 57.2 (December 1997):

519-542.

Schaberg, David. "Calming the Heart: The Use of *Shijing* in *Zuozhuan* Narrative." *Papers on Chinese Literature* 1 (1993): 1-20.

Schmölz, Andrea. *Vom Lied in der Gemeinschaft zur Liedzitat im text: Liedzitate in den Texten der Gelehrtentradition der späten Chou-Zeit* Egelsbach: Hänsel-Hohenhausen, 1993. Published version of a dissertation (Munich University, 1991).

Shaughnessy, Edward L. "From Liturgy to Literature, the Ritual Contexts of the Earliest Poems in the *Book of Poetry*." *Han-hsüeh yen-chiu* 13.1 (June 1995): 133-164.

Shih-ching yao-chi chi-ch'eng 史經要籍集成. Chung-kuo *Shih ching* Hsüeh-hui Ch'ou-ch'ou Lüeh-hui 中國詩經學會愁籌略會, ed. Tientsin: Nan-k'ai Ta-hsüeh,1994.

Su, Tung-t'ien 蘇東天. *Shih-ching pien-i* 辨義. Hangchow: Che-chiang Ku-chi, 1992.

Sun, Cecile Chu-chin. "Two Modes of Stanzaic Interaction in *Shih-Ching* and Their Implications for a Comparative Poetics." *TkR* 19 (1988/89): 803-33.

Sun, Chien-yüan 孫見元 and Chu Chieh-jen 朱杰人. *Shih-ching yao-chi chieh-t'i* 要籍解題. Shanghai: Shang-hai Ku-chi, 1997.

Ti, Hsiang-chün 翟相君. *Shih-ching hsin-chieh* 詩經新解. Chengchow: Chung-chou Ku-chi, 1993.

Van Zoeren, Steven. *Poetry and Personality: Reading, Exegesis, and Hermeneutics in Traditional China.* Stanford: Stanford University Press, 1991. A study of the history of the *Shih-ching.* Haun Saussy review in *HJAS* 53 (1993): 272-280.

Wang, Chan-wei 王占威. *Shih-ching ming-p'ien chi-shih chi-p'ing* 詩經名篇集釋集評. Huhehot: Nei Meng-ku Chiao-yü, 1992.

Wang, Changhong. "'Have no twisty thoughts': Ezra Pound's Translation of the 'Shih ching.'" Unpublished Ph.D. dissertation, University of Pennsylvania, 1991.

Wang, Ching-chih 王靜芝. *Shih-ching t'ung-shih* 詩經通釋. Taipei: Fu-jen Ta-hsüeh, 1985.

Wang, Fu-chih 王夫之 (1619–1692). *Shih-ching pai-shu* 詩經稗疏. Ch'uan-shan Ch'üan-shu Pien-chi Wei-yüan Hui 船山全書編輯委員會, ed. Changsha: Yüeh-lu Shu-she, 1992. Ch'uan-shan Ch'üan-shu, 3.

Wang, Li 王力 (1900–1986). *Shih-ching yün-tu* 詩經韻讀. Shanghai: Shang-hai Ku-chi, 1980.

Wang, Shou-ch'ien 王守謙 and Chin Shu-chen 金淑珍. *Shih-ching p'ing-chu* 詩經評注. Changchun: Tung-pei Shih-fan Ta-hsüeh, 1989.

Wang, Tsung-shih 王宗石. *Shih-ching fen-lei ch'üan-shih* 詩經分類詮釋. Changsha: Hu-nan Chiao-yü, 1993.

Wei, Chiung-jo 魏炯若. *Tu Feng chih hsin-chi* 讀風知新記. Sian: Shan-hsi Jen-min, 1987.

Wen, Hsing-fu 文幸福. *Shih-ching Mao-chuan Cheng-chien pien-i* 鄭箋辨異. Taipei: Wen-shih-che, 1989.

Wong, Siu-kit and Lee Kar-shui. "Poems of Depravity: A Twelfth Century Dispute on the Moral Character of the *Book of Songs*." *TP* 75 (1989): 209-225.

___. "Three English Translations of the *Shijing*." *Renditions* 25 (1986): 113-139.

Wu, Ko 吳格, ed. *Shih San-chia i-chi shu* 詩三家義集疏. Wang Hsien-ch'ien 王先謙 (1842-1918), comm. 2v. Taipei: Ming-wen, 1988.

Yang, Ho-ming 楊合鳴. *Shih-ching chü-fa yen-chiu* 詩敬句法研究. Wuchang: Wu-han Ta-hsüeh, 1993. Appends a bibliography and an index.

___ and Li Chung-hua 李中華. *Shih-ching chu-t'i pien-hsi* 詩經主題辨析. 2v. Nanning: Kuang-hsi Chiao-yü, 1989.

Yao, Chi-heng 姚際恆. *Shih-ching t'ung-lun* 詩經通論. Taipei: Kuang-wen, 1988.

Yeh, Shu-hsien 葉舒憲. *Shih-ching te wen-hua ch'an-shih—Chung-kuo shih-ko te fa-sheng yen-chiu* 詩經的文化闡釋—中國詩歌的發生研究 *(The Book of Songs—A Cultural Hermeneutics).* Wuhan: Hu-pei Jen-min, 1994.

Yin, Chien-chang 尹建章 and Hsiao Yüeh-hsien 蕭月賢. *Shih-ching ming-p'ien hsiang-hsi* 詩經名篇詳析. Chengchow: Chung-chou Ku-chi, 1993.

Yip, Wai-lim. "Vestiges of the Oral Dimension: Examples from the *Shih-ching*." *Tamkang Review* 16.1 (1985): 17-49.

Yu, Pauline R. "Imagery in the *Classic of Poetry*." In *The Reading of Imagery in the Chinese Poetic Tradition*. Princeton: Princeton University Press, 1987, pp. 44-83. See also the important reviews by David R. McCraw in *CLEAR* 9 (July 1987): 129–39, and by Donald Holzman in *JAS* 47 (May 1988): 365–7.

Yü, P'ei-lin 余培林. *Shih-ching cheng-ku* 詩經正詁. 2v. Taipei: San-min, 1993.

Yüan, Pao-ch'üan 袁寶泉 and Ch'en Chih-hsien 陳智賢. *Shih-ching t'an-wei* 詩經探微. Canton: Hua-ch'eng, 1987.

Zhang, Longxi. "The Letter or the Spirit: The Song of Songs, Allegoresis, and the Book of Poetry." *Comparative Literature* 39 (1987): 193-217.

Shih-chou chi 十洲記 (Record of Ten Islands, fourth or fifth century)

Editions and References
Shih-chou chi 十洲記. Shanghai: Shang-hai Ku-chi, 1990

Shih-hua 詩話 (talks on poetry)

Editions and References
Chiang, Tsu-i 蔣祖怡 and Ch'en Chih-ch'un 陳志椿, eds. *Chung-kuo shih-hua tz'u-tien* 中國詩話辭典. Peking: Pei-ching Ch'u-pan-she, 1997.

Li-tai shih-hua tz'u-hua hsüan 歷代詩話詞話選. Wuhan: Wu-han Ta-hsüeh, 1984. Compiled by the Chinese Department of Wu-han University.

Wang, Hsiu-mei 王秀梅 and Wang Ching-t'ung, *et al.*, 王景桐, eds. *Sung-jen shih-hua wai-pien* 宋人詩話外編. Peking: Kuo-chi Wen-hua, 1997.

Translations
Wong, Siu-kit, trans. *Notes on Poetry from the Ginger Studio*. Hong Kong: The Chinese University Press, 1987. Translation of Wu Fu-chih's 王夫之 *Chiang-chai shih-hua* 薑齋詩話.

Studies
Hsü, Hsiao-ching. "'Talks on Poetry' (*Shih hua*) as a Form of Sung Literary Criticism." Unpublished Ph.D. dissertation, University of Wisconsin, 1991.

Kôzen, Hiroshi 興膳宏. "*Shihin* kara shiwa e" 詩品から詩話へ. *Chûgoku bungakuhô* 47 (1993): 31-63.

Shih Nai-an 施耐庵

Studies
Yü, Ta-p'ing 余大平. *Shih Nai-an hua Shui-hu: Ts'ao-mang lung-she* 施耐庵話水滸—草莽龍蛇. Taipei: Ya-t'ai T'u-shu, 1995.

Shih-p'in 詩品 (An Evaluation of Poetry)

Editions and References
Chao, Fu-t'an 趙福壇. *Shih-p'in hsin-shih* 新釋. Canton: Hua-ch'eng, 1986.

Hsiang, Ch'ang-ch'ing 向長清, ed. and comm. *Shih-p'in chu-shih* 詩品注釋. Tsinan: Ch'i-Lu Shu-she, 1986.

Hsü, Ta 許達, comm. *Shih-p'in ch'üan-i* 詩品全譯. Kweiyang: Kuei-chou Jen-min, 1990. Chung-kuo li-tai ming-chu ch'üan-i ts'ung-shu.

Lü, Te-shen 呂德申, ed. *Chung Jung Shih-p'in chiao-shih* 鍾嶸詩品校釋. Peking: Pei-ching Ta-hsüeh, 1986.

Ts'ao, Hsü 曹旭. *Shih-p'in chi-chu* 詩品集注. Shanghai: Shang-hai Ku-chi, 1994. Excellent front-matter on the text and its history.

Wang, Shu-min 王叔岷. *Chung Jung Shih-p'in chien-cheng kao* 鍾嶸詩品箋證稿. Taipei: Chung-yang Yen-chiu Yüan, Chung-kuo Wen-che Yen-chiu So, 1992.

Yüeh, Chung-i 越仲邑, ed. *Chung Jung Shih-p'in chiao-shih* 鍾嶸詩品校釋. Nanning: Kuang-hsi Chiao-yü, 1990.

Studies

Chang, Pai-wei 張伯偉. "Chung Jung *Shih-p'in* te p'i-p'ing fang-fa lun" 鍾嶸詩品的批評方法論. *Chung-kuo She-hui k'o-hsüeh* 39 (1986): 159–170.

___. *Chung Jung Shih-p'in yen-chiu* 鍾嶸詩品研究. Nanking: Nan-ching Ta-hsüeh, 1993. Tang-tai wen-hsüeh ts'ung-k'an.

Ch'en, Yüan-hsing 陳元胜. *Shih-p'in pien-tu* 詩品辨讀. Hofei: An-hui Chiao-yü, 1994.

Ch'iao, Li 喬力. *Erh-shih-ssu Shih-p'in t'an-wei* 探微. Tsinan: Ch'i-Lu Shu-she, 1983.

Führer, Bernhard. *Chinas erste Poetik: das Shipin (Kriterion Poietikon) des Zhong Hong (467?-518)*. Dortmund: Projekt-Verl., 1995.

___. "Zur Biographies des Zhong Hong (467-518)." *Acta Orientalia* 46 (1-3 1992-3): 163-188.

Hsü, Wen-yü 許文雨, ed. *Chung Jung Shih-p'in chiang-shu* 鍾嶸詩品講疏. Chengtu: Ch'eng-tu Ku-chi Shu-tien, 1983.

Kôzen, Hiroshi 興膳宏." *Shihin* kara shiwa e" 詩品から詩話へ, *Chûgoku bungakuhô* 47 (1993): 31–63.

Mei, Yün-sheng 梅運生. *Chung Jung ho Shih-p'in* 鍾嶸和詩品. Shanghai: Shang-hai Ku-chi, 1982

Li, Hui-chiao 李徽教 (1938–1982). *Shih-p'in hui-chu* 詩品彙註. Han-kuo Ch'ing-pei: Ling-nan Ta-hsüeh-hsiao Ch'u-pan-pu, 1983. Portions of the study are written in Korean; appends a bibiliography and an index.

Liao, Tung-liang 廖棟樑. "Lun Chung Jung te hsing-hsiang p'i-p'ing" 論鍾嶸的形象批評. In *Ku-tien wen-hsüeh; Ti-pa chi* 古典文學，第八集. Hsüeh-sheng Shu-chü, ed. Taipei: Hsüeh-sheng Shu-chü, 1986, 51–78.

Shimizu, Yoshio 清水凱夫. "Chûgoku ni okeru 1980 nen ikô no Shô Kô *Shihin* kenkyû gaikan (2)-*Shihin* to *Bunshin chôryô* no bungakukan no idô ronsô o chûshin to shite" 中国における一九八〇年以降の鍾嶸「詩品」研究概観（二）-『詩品』と『文心雕龍』の文学観の異同論争を中心として. *Chûgoku bungakuhô* 45 (1992).

Wang, Fa-kuo 王發國. *Shih-p'in k'ao-so* 詩品考索. Chengtu: Ch'eng-tu K'o-chih Ta-hsüeh, 1993.

Wang, Shu-min 王叔岷. "Chung Jung *Shih-p'in* kai-lun" 鍾嶸詩品概論. *Chung-kuo wen-che yen-chiu chi-k'an* 1 (1991): 11–24.

Wang, Yün-hsi 王運熙. "Chung Jung *Shih-p'in* lun li-tai wu-yen shih" 鍾嶸詩品論歷代五言詩. *Chung-hua wen-shih lun-ts'ung* 41 (1987): 223–251.

Wixted, John Timothy. "The Nature of Evaluation in the *Shih-p'in* by Chung Jung (A.D. 469–518)." In *Theories of Arts in China*. Susan Bush and Christopher Murck, eds. Princeton: Princeton University Press, 1983, pp. 225–264.

Yeh, Ch'ing-ping 葉慶炳. "*Shih-p'in* yü jen-p'in" 詩品與人品. *Chung-wai wen-hsüeh* 14:12 (1986): 6-13.

Yü, K'o-k'un 禹克坤. *Wen-hsin tiao-lung yü Shih-p'in*. Peking: Jen-min, 1989.

Shih-shuo hsin-yü 世說新語 (New Account of Tales of the World)

Editions and References

Chang, Hui-chih 張撝之, *et al.*, eds. and comms. *Shih-shuo hsin-yü hsüan-chu* 世說新語選注. Shanghai: Shang-hai Ku-chi, 1987.

___, *et al.*, comms. *Shih-shuo hsin-yü i-chu* 世說新語譯注. Shanghai: Shang-hai Ku-chi, 1997. Chung-hua ku-chi i-chu ts'ung-shu.

Chang, Yung-yen 張永言, *et al.*, eds. *Shih-shuo hsin-yü tz'u-tien* 世說新語辭典. Chengtu: Ssu-ch'uan Jen-min, 1992. Contains chronological tables and a bibliography.

Ch'en, T'ao 陳濤, comm. *Shih-shuo hsin-yü hsüan-ts'ui* 世說新語選粹. Tientsin: T'ien-chin Chiao-yü, 1987.

Hsü, Chen-e 徐震堮, ed. *Shih-shuo hsin-yü chiao-chien* 世說新語校箋. Peking: Chung-hua, 1984 and 1998. Chung-kuo ku-tien wen-hsüeh chi-pen tsung-shu. Yang Yung's 陽勇 1973 edition, Yü Chia-hsi's 余嘉錫 text (1983), and this book are the most useful modern commentaries; see also Chiang Tsung-hsü's 蔣宗許 notes on Hsü's work in *Ku-chi cheng-li yen-chiu hsüeh-k'an* 56 (1995): 15-22.

Hsü, Shao-tsao 許紹早, ed. *Shih-shuo hsin-yü i-chu* 譯注. Changchun: Chi-lin Chiao-yü, 1980; 1991.

Liu, Shih-chen 柳士鎮, ed. *Shih-shuo hsin-yü hsüan-i* 世說新語選譯. Chengtu: Pa-Shu Shu-she, 1990. *Ku-tai wen-shih ming-chu hsüan-i ts'ung-shu.*

Lo, Kuo-wei 羅國威, ed. *Liu Hsiao-piao chi chiao-chu* 劉孝標集校注. Shanghai: Shang-hai Ku-chi, 1988.

Yang, Mu-chih 楊牧之 and Hu Yu-ming 胡友鳴, eds. *Shih-shuo hsin-yü* 世說新語. Hangchow: Che-chiang Ku-chi, 1986.

Yü, Chia-hsi 余嘉錫, ed. *Shih-shuo hsin-yü chien-shu* 箋疏. 2v. Peking: Chung-hua, 1984. Rpt. Taipei: Hua-cheng Shu-chü, 1984; Shanghai: Shang-hai Ku-chi, 1993. Yang Yung's 陽勇 1973 edition, Hsü Chen-e's 徐震堮 text (1984), and this book are the most useful modern commentaries.

Translations

Inami, Ritsuko 井波律子. *Seisetsu shingo* 世說新語. Tokyo: Kadokawa Shoten, 1988. *Kanshô Chûgoku no koten,* 14.

Takeda, Akira 竹田晃. *Seisetsu shingo* 世說新語. Tokyo: Gakushû Kenkyûsha, 1983-84. *Chûgoku no koten,* 21-2.

Studies

Chang, Chen-te 張振德, *et al. Shih-shuo hsin-yü yü-yen yen-chiu* 世說新語語言研究. Chengtu: Pa-Shu Shu-she, 1995.

Chang, Pei-pei 張蓓蓓. "*Shih-shuo hsin-yü* pieh-chieh—jung-chih p'ien" 世說新語別解一容止篇. *Wen-shih-che hsüeh-pao* 37 (1989): 99-122.

___. "*Shih-shuo hsin-yü* pieh-chieh—jen-tan p'ien" 世說新語別解一任誕篇. *Wen-shih-che hsüeh-pao* 38 (1990): 17–45.

Chang, Yung-hao 張永昊. "*Shih-shuo hsin-yü* te shen mei-kuan" 世說新語的審美觀. *Wen-shih-che* 195 (1989): 78-85.

Ch'en, Hui-ling 陳慧玲. "Yu *Shih-shuo hsin-yü* t'an-t'ao: Wei Chin ch'ing-t'an yü chün-yü chih kuan-hsi" 由世說新語探討一魏晉清談與雋語之關係. M.A. thesis, Tung-wu Ta-hsüeh, 1987.

Chiang, Hsing-yu 江興祐. "Lun *Shih-shuo hsin-yü* tui jen te shen-shih chi ch'i i-chü" 論世說新語對人的審視及其依據. *Hang-chou Ta-hsüeh hsüeh-pao* (1990): 12–18.

Chou, Fa-kao 周法高. "Tu *Shih-shuo hsin-yü* hsiao-chi" 讀世說新語小記. *Shu-mu chi-k'an* 24:2 (1990): 3–13.

Chou, I-liang 周一良 and Wang I-t'ung 王伊同. "Ma-i *Shih-shuo hsin-yü* shang-tui" 馬譯世説新語商兑. *THHP* 20:2 (1990): 197–256.

Diény, Jean-Pierre. *Portrait anecdotique d'un gentilhomme chinois: Xie An, 320–385; d'après le Shishuo xinyu.* Paris: Collège de France, Institut des Hautes Études Chinoises, 1993.

___. "Portraits de femmes, Le chapitre XIX du *Shishuo xinyu*." In *Hommage à Kowng Hing Foon, Études d'histoire culturelle de la Chine.* Jean-Pierre Diény, ed. Paris: Collège de France, Institut des Hautes Études Chinoises, 1995, pp. 77-113.

Fang, I-hsin 方一新. "*Shih-shuo hsin-yü* yü-tz'u yen-chiu" 語詞研究. Unpublished Ph.D. dissertation, Hang-chou Ta-hsüeh, 1989.

Ho, Lo-shih 何樂士. "Tun-huang pien-wen yü *Shih-shuo hsin-yü* jo-kan yü-fa t'e-tien te pi-chiao" 煌變文與世説新語若干語法特點的比較. In *Sui T'ang Wu-tai Han-yü yen-chiu* 隋唐五代漢語研究. Ch'eng Hsiang-ch'ing 程湘清, ed. Tsinan: Shan-tung Chiao-yü, 1992.

K'ang, Yün-mei 康韻梅. "Shih-lun Wei Chin ch'ing-t'an te hsing-shih ho yü-yen–chu-i *Shih-shuo hsin-yü* wei k'ao-ch'a fan-wei" 試論魏晉清談的形式和語研—主以世説新語為考察範圍. *Chung-kuo wen-hsüeh yen-chiu* 4 (1990): 177–199.

Kominami, Ichirô 小南一郎. "*Sesetsu shingo* no bigaku–Gi Shin no sai to jô o megutte" 世説新語」の美学—魏晋の才と情をめぐって. *Chûgoku chûseishi kenkyû* (1995): 434-472.

Lee, Lily Hsiao Hung. "The Historical Significance of the *Shih-shuo hsin-yü*." *PFEH* 34 (September 1986): 121-148.

___. "Yü lin and Kuo-tzu: Two Predecessors of *Shih-shuo hsin-yü*." In *A Festschrift in Honour of Professor Jao Tsung-i on the Occasion of his Seventy-fifth Anniversary.* Hong Kong: Chinese University Press, 1993, pp. 357-87.

Liao, Li-feng 廖麗鳳. "*Shih-shuo hsin-yü* chih jen-wu chün-hsiang chi miao-hsieh chi-ch'iao yen-chiu" 世説新語之人物群像及描寫技巧研究. M.A. thesis, Shih-fan Ta-hsüeh, 1990.

Mei, Chia-ling 梅家玲. "*Shih-shuo hsin-yü* ming-shih yen-t'an chung te yung-tien chi-ch'iao" 世説新語名士言談中的用典技巧. *T'ai-ta chung-wen hsüeh-pao* 2 (1988): 341–376.

___. "*Shih-shuo hsin-yü* te yü-yen i-shu" 世説新語的語言藝術. Unpublished Ph.D. dissertation, National Taiwan University, 1991.

Ôyane, Bunjirô 大矢根文次郎. *Sesetsu shingo to Rikuchô bungaku* 世説新語と六朝文学. Tokyo: Waseda Daigaku Shuppanbu, 1983.

Qian, Nanxiu. "Being One's Self: Narrative Art and Taxonomy of Human Nature in the 'Shih-shuo Hsin-yü'." Unpublished Ph.D. dissertation, Yale University, 1994.

T'ung, Chin-ch'ien 董晉騫. "Lun *Shih-shuo hsin-yü* te jen-wu mei ssu-hsiang" 論世説新語的人物美思想. *She-hui k'o-hsüeh chi-k'an* 68 (1990): 134–140.

Wang, Neng-hsien 王能憲. *Shih-shuo hsin-yü yen-chiu* 世説新語研究. Nanking: Chiang-su Ku-chi, 1992.

Wu, Chin-hua 吳金華. *Shih-shuo hsin-yü k'ao-shih* 世説新考釋. Hofei: An-hui Chiao-yü, 1994.

___. "*Shih-shuo hsin-yü* tz'u-yü k'ao-shih" 世説新語詞語考釋. *Nan-ching Shih-ta hsüeh-pao* 66 (1990): 57–64.

Yu, Ya-tzu 尤雅姿. "*Shih-shuo hsin-yü* hsiu-tz'u i-ch'iao t'an-wei" 世説新語修辭藝巧探微. *Hsing-ta chung-wen hsüeh-pao* 3 (1990): 225–238.

___. "*Shih-shuo hsin-yü* san-wen chih ch'eng-chiu" 世説新語散文之成就. *Hsing-ta chung-wen hsüeh-pao* 2 (1989): 157–165.

Shih Ta-tsu 史達祖 (*c.* 1200)

Editions and References

Lei, Lü-p'ing 雷履平 and Lo Huan-chang 羅煥章, comms. *Mei-hsi tz'u* 梅溪詞. Shanghai: Shang-hai Ku-chi, 1988. Contains materials for the study of Shih's life. Sung-tz'u pieh-chi ts'ung-k'an.

Mei-hsi tz'u 梅溪詞 1 *chüan*. Taipei: T'ai-wan Shang-wu Yin-shu-kuan, 1983. Based on the edition preserved in the National Palace Museum in Taiwan.

Shih Yün-yü 石韞玉 (1756-1837)

Editions and References

Hung-lou meng 紅樓夢. Peking: Chung-hua, 1978. Hung-lou meng hsi-ch'ü, 2.

Shui-ching chu 水經注 (A Commentary to the Classic of Waterways)

Editions and References

Ch'en, Ch'iao-i 陳橋驛, ed. and comm. *Shui-ching chu* 水經注. Shanghai: Shang-hai Ku-chi, 1990.

Shui-ching chu ch'üan-i 水經注全譯. Kweiyang: Kuei-chou Jen-min, 1990. *Chung-kuo li-tai ming-chu ch'üan-i ts'ung-shu.*

Wang, Hsien-ch'ien 王先謙 (1842–1918), ed. *Shui-ching chu* 水經注. Chengtu: Pa-Shu Shu-she, 1985.

Wang Kuo-wei 王國維 (1877–1927), ed. Yüan Ying-kuang 袁英光 and Liu Yin-sheng 劉寅生, revised. *Shui-ching chu chiao* 水經注校. Shanghai: Shang-hai Jen-min, 1984.

Yang, Shou-ching 楊守敬 (1839–1914), annot. Hsiung Hui-chen 熊會貞 *et al.*, eds. *Shui-ching chu shu* 水經注疏. 40 *chüan*. 3v. Nanking: Chiang-su Ku-chi, 1989. Contains various studies of editions.

Yüeh, Yung-hsia 越永夏, ed. *Shui-ching chu tung-chien chin-shih* 水經注通檢今釋. Fu-tan Ta-hsüeh, 1985. Appends an index.

Translations

Strassberg, *Inscribed Landscapes*, pp. 77-90.

Yüeh, Wang-ch'in 越望秦, *et al.* trans. and comms. *Shui-ching chu hsüan-i* 水經注選譯. Chengtu: Pa-Shu Shu-she, 1990. *Ku-tai wen-shih ming-chu hsüan-i ts'ung-shu.*

Studies

Ch'en, Ch'iao-i 陳橋驛. "Min-kuo i-lai yen-chiu *Shui-ching chu* chih tsung ch'eng-chi" 民國以來研究水經注之總成績. In *Chung-hua wen-shih lun-ts'ung* 中華文史論叢, 53. Ch'ien Po-ch'eng 錢伯城, ed. Shanghai: Shang-hai Ku-chi, 1994, pp. 52-74.

___. *Shui-ching chu yen-chiu* 水經注研究. Tientsin: T'ien-chin Ku-chi, 1985. Contains maps, charts and a bibliography.

___. *Shui-ching chu yen-chiu erh-chi* 水經注研究二集. Taiyuan: Shan-hsi Jen-min, 1987.

Fang, Li-na 方麗娜. "*Shui-ching chu* chih hsieh-ching-wen yen-chiu" 水經注之寫景文研究. *T'ai-nan Shih-yüan hsüeh-pao* 23 (1990): 239–263.

Su, Li-feng 蘇麗峰. "*Shui-ching chu* chih wen-hsüeh ch'eng-chiu lun-hsi" 水經注之文學成就論析. M.A. Thesis, Wen-hua Ta-hsüeh, 1987.

Shui-hu chuan 水滸傳 (Water Margin)

Editions and References

Chang, Kuo-kuang 張國光, ed. *Shui-hu chuan (Hsin cheng-li pen)* 水滸傳（新整理本）. Peking: Hua-i, 1998.

Chiang, Shih-tung 姜世棟, Wang Hui-min 王惠民 and I Tien-ch'en 衣殿臣, eds. *San-kuo yen-i Shui-hu chuan Hsi-yu chi shih-tz'u chu-hsi* 三國演義水滸傳西遊記詩詞注析. Harbin: Ha-erh-pin, 1993.

Chih, Heng 遲恆. *Shui-hu hou-chuan* 水滸後傳. Shanghai: Shang-hai Ku-chi, 1993.

Ho, Shih-lung, ed. 何士龍. *Shui-hu chuan shang-hsi* 水滸傳賞析. Nanning: Kuang-hsi Chiao-yü, 1991. Chung-kuo ku-tien wen-hsüeh tso-p'in hsüan-hsi ts'ung-shu.

Hu, Chu-an 胡竹安, ed. *Shui-hu tz'u-tien* 水滸詞典. Shanghai: Han-yü Ta-tz'u-tien, 1989. Glosses include parts of speech, meanings and examples.

Komada, Shinji 駒田信二. *Suiko den* 水滸伝. 8v. Tokyo: Kôdansha, 1984-85.

Li, Ch'üan 李泉 and Chang Yung-hsin 張永鑫, eds. *Ts'ai-hua pen Shui-hu ch'üan-chuan chiao-chu* 彩畫本水滸全傳校注. Taipei: Li-jen, 1994.

Li, Fa-pai 李法白 and Liu Ching-fu 劉鏡芙, eds. *Shui-hu yü-tz'u tz'u-tien* 語詞詞典. Shanghai: Shang-hai Tz'u-shu, 1989.

Li, Yung-hu 李永祜, ed. *Shui-hu chuan* 水滸傳. Peking: Chung-hua, 1997. Based on the Jung-yü T'ang 容與堂 edition (Peking Library).

Liu, I-chou 劉一舟, ed. *Chin Sheng-t'an p'i-p'ing Shui-hu chuan* 金聖嘆批評水滸傳. Tsinan: Ch'i Lu Shu-she, 1991. Based on the 120-chapter version.

Ma, Ti-chi 馬蹄疾, ed. *Shui-hu tzu-liao hui-pien* 資料匯編. Peking: Chung-hua, 1980.

___. *Shui-hu shu-lu* 水滸書錄. Shanghai: Shang-hai Ku-chi, 1986.

Miao, T'ien-hua 繆天華, ed. *Shui-hu chuan* 水滸傳. Taipei: San-min, 1990

Ts'ai, Chung-min, ed. *Shui-hu ch'üan-chuan (Hsin chiao-chu pen)* 全傳 （新校注本）. Chengtu: Ssu-ch'uan Wen-i, 1986.

Ts'ao, Fang-jen 曹方人 and Chou Hsi-shan 周錫山, eds. *Kuan-hua t'ang Ti-wu ts'ai-tzu shu Shui-hu chuan* 貫華堂第五才子書水滸傳. 2v. Nanking: Chiang-su Ku-chi, 1985.

Wang, Li-ch'i 王利器, ed., Li Ch'üan 李泉 and Chang Yung-hsin 張永鑫, comms. *Shui-hu ch'üan-chuan: hsin chiao-chu pen* 水滸全傳：新較注本. 3v. Chengtu: Ssu-ch'uan Wen-i, 1986. Contains different versions of the novel, along with various prefaces.

Wen, Tzu-sheng 文子生, ed. *Ti-wu ts'ai-tzu shu Shih Nai-an Shui-hu chuan* 第五才子書施耐庵水滸傳. 2v. Chengchow: Chung-chou Ku-chi, 1985.

Yoshikawa, Kôjirô 吉川幸次郎, *et al* *Suiko den* 水滸伝. Tokyo: Taishûkan Shoten, 1987.

Translations

Au bord de l'eau coffret. 2v. Paris: Gallimard, 1983.

Dent-Young, John and Alex Dent-Young. *The Broken Seals: Part One of The Marshes of Mount Liang.* Ann Arbor: University of Michigan Press, 1996; Hong Kong: The Chinese University Press, 1994.

___. *The Tiger Killers: Part Two of The Marshes of Mount Liang.* Ann Arbor: University of Michigan Press, 1997.

Nakamura, Yukihiko 中村幸彦, trans. *Tsûzoku chûgi Suiko den* 通俗忠義水滸伝. Tokyo: Kyûko Shoin, 1987. *Kinsei hakuwa shôsetsu hon'yaku shû,* 1-6.

Yoshikawa, Kôjirô 吉川幸次郎 and Shimizu Shigeru 清水茂, trans. *Zenyaku Suikoden* 全訳水滸伝. Tokyo: Iwanami, 1996.

Studies

Brandauer, Frederick P. "The Emperor and the Star Spirits: A Mythological Reading of the *Shui-hu chuan.*" In *Imperial Rulership and Cultural Change in Traditional China.* Frederick P. Brandauer and Chun-chieh Huang, eds. Seattle: University of Washington Press, 1994, pp. 206-29.

Chang, Chin-ch'ih 張錦池. *Chung-kuo ssu-ta ku-tien hsiao-shuo lun-kao* 中國四大古典小說論稿. Peking: Hua-i, 1993.

Ch'en, Hsi-chung 陳曦鐘, *et al.*, eds. *Shui-hu chuan hui-p'ing pen* 水滸傳會評本. 2v. Peking:

417

Pei-ching Ta-hsüeh, 1981, 1987.

Chûbachi, Masakazu. 'The Role of Hangchow in the Formation of *Shui-hu chuan.*" *Tôhôgaku* 85 (1993) 83-99.

Kao, Ming-ko 高明閣. *Shui-hu chuan lun-kao* 水滸傳論稿. Shenyang: Liao-ning Ta-hsüeh, 1987.

Kôsaka, Jun'ichi 香坂順一. *Suiko goi no kenkyû* 水滸語彙の研究. Tokyo: Kôseikan, 1987.

Li, Tien-yü 李殿元 *et al. Shui-hu ta-kuan* 水滸大觀. Chengtu: Ssu-ch'uan Jen-min, 1995.

Lo, Erh-kang 羅爾綱, ed "*Shui-hu chuan* k'ao-cheng" 水滸傳考證. In *Shui-hu chuan yüan-pen* 水滸傳原本. Kweiyang: Kuei-chou Jen-min, 1989, pp. 1-73.

_____. *Shui-hu chuan yüan-pen ho chu-che yen-chiu* 水滸傳原本和著者研究. Nanking: Chiang-su Ku-chi, 1992.

Ma, Yu-yüan 馬幼垣. *Shui-hu lun-heng* 水滸論衡. Taipei: Lien-ching, 1992.

Mühlhahn, Klaus. *Geschichte, Frauenbild und kulturelles Gedächtnis, Die ming-zeitliche Roman Shuihu zhuan.* Munich: Minerva, 1994.

Plaks, Andrew H. *The Four Masterworks of the Ming Novel: Ssu ta ch'i-shu.* Princeton: Princeton University Press, 1987.

Porter, Deborah L. "The Formation of an Image: An Analysis of Linguistic Patterns that Form the Character of Song Jiang." *JAOS* 112 (2 1992): 233-53.

___. "Setting the Tone: Aesthetic Implications of Linguistic Patterns in the Opening Section of the *Shui-hu chuan*" *CLEAR* 14 (1992): 51-75.

___. "The Style of 'Shui-hu chuan.'" Unpublished Ph. D. dissertation, Princeton University, 1989.

___. "Toward an Aesthetic of Chinese Vernacular Fiction: Style and the Colloquial Medium of *Shui-hu chuan*" *TP* 79 (1993): 113-53.

Satake, Yasuhiko 佐竹靖彦. *Ryô Sanpaku–Suiko den hyakuhachi nin no gôketsu tachi* 梁山泊-水滸伝１０８人の豪傑たち. Tokyo: Chûô Kôronsha, 1992.

Shen, Po-chün 沈伯俊. *Shui-hu yen-chiu lun-wen chi* 水滸研究論文集. Peking: Chung-hua, 1994.

Sheng, Jui-yü 盛瑞裕, ed. *Shui-hu–Jih-pen Lun-wang Ssu mi-tsang* 水滸—日本輪王寺秘藏. Wuhan: Wu-han Ch'u-pan-she, 1994.

Takashima, Toshio 高島俊男. *Suikoden no sekai* 水滸伝の世界. Tokyo: Taishûkan Shoten, 1987.

___. *Suikoden to Nihonjin–Edo kara Shôwa made* 水滸伝と日本人–江戸から昭和まで. Tokyo: Taishûkan Shoten, 1991.

Wang, Hsiao-chia 王曉家. *Shui-hu so-i* 瑣議. Tsinan: Shan-tung Wen-i, 1990.

Wang, Jing. *The Story of Stone: Intertextuality, Ancient Chinese Stone Lore, and the Stone Symbolism in Dream of the Red Chamber, Water Margin, and the Journey to the West.* Durham, N.C.: Duke University Press, 1992.

Widmer, Ellen. *The Margins of Utopia: "Shui-hu hou-chuan" and the Literature of Ming Loyalism.* Cambridge: Harvard University, Council on East Asian Studies, 1987.

Yü, Ta-p'ing 余大平. *Shih Nai-an hua Shui-hu: Ts'ao-mang lung-she* 草莽龍蛇. Taipei: Ya-t'ai T'u-shu, 1995.

Sou-shen chi 搜神記 (**In Search of the Supernatural**)

Editions and References

Chang, Su 張甦, ed. and comm. *Chüan-pen Sou-shen chi p'ing-i* 全本搜神記評譯. Shanghai: Hsüeh-lin, 1994.

Hu, Huai-ch'en 胡懷琛, ed. *Sou-shen chi* 搜神記. 20 *chüan.* Shanghai: Shang-wu Yin-shu-kuan, 1957.

Huang, Ti-ming 黃滌明. *Sou-shen chi ch'üan-i* 搜神記全譯. Kueiyang: Kuei-chou Jen-min, 1991. This work was praised by Crump and DeWoskin (see Translations).

Ku, Hsi-chia 顧希佳, ed. *Sou-shen chi* 搜神記. Hangchow: Che-chiang Ku-chi, 1985.

T'ang, Fu-ch'un 唐富春 (Ming dynasty), ed. *Hsin-k'o ch'u-hsiang tseng-pu Sou-shen chi ta-ch'üan* 新刻出像增補搜神記大全. Taipei: T'ai-wan Hsüeh-sheng, 1989.

Wang, Ch'iu-kuei 王秋桂. *Hui-t'u san-chiuao yüan-liu Sou-shen chi ta-ch'üan* 繪圖三教源流搜神記大全. Taipei: Lien-ching, 1980.

Yang, Chen-chiang 楊振江, ed. *Sou-shen chi* 搜神記. Hofei: Hua-shan Wen-i, 1986.

Translations

DeWoskin, Kenneth J. and J. I. Crump, Jr. *In Search of the Supernatural: The Written Record* Stanford: Stanford University Press, 1996. A complete translation preceded by a brief introduction (pp. xxiii-xxxvi) and followed by observations on editions and other passages attributed to this text.

Mathieu, Remi, ed. *Gan Bao: À la recherche des esprits* Paris: Gallimard, 1992.

Studies

Ch'in, Ch'u 項楚. "Tun-huang pen chü-tao yü *Sou-shen chi* pen-shih k'ao" 敦煌本句道與搜神記本事考. *Tun-huang-hsüeh chi-k'an* 18 (1990): 43–59.

Chung, Yün-ying 種雲鶯. "*Sou-shen chi* chung pien-t'ai hun-yin ch'u-t'an" 搜神記中變態婚姻初探. *K'ung Meng yüeh-k'an* 30:4 (1991): 28–42.

Hsieh, Ming-hsün 謝明勳. "Ts'ung Kan Pao chu-tso t'an *Sou-shen chi* chih chu-shu lü-yu" 從干寶著作談搜神記之著述緣由. *Shu-mu chi-k'an* 25:1 (1991): 85–87.

Kominami, Ichirô 小南一郎. "Kan Hô *Sôshin ki* no hensan (jô)" 干寶「搜神記」の編纂 (上), *Tôhô Gappô* 1997.

Li, Wei-kuo 李偉國. "Yüan Ming i-pen *Sou-shen chi* san-chung yüan-yüan i-t'ung lun" 元明異本搜神記三種淵源異同論. In *Chung-hua wen-shih lun-ts'ung* 中華文史論叢, 48. Ch'ien Po-ch'eng 錢伯城, ed. Shanghai: Shang-hai Ku-chi, 1991, pp. 243-258.

Liu, Yüan-ju 劉苑如. "*Sou-shen chi* chi *Sou-shen hou-chi* yen-chiu–ts'ung kuan-nien shih-chieh yü hsü-shih chieh-kou k'ao-ch'a" 搜神記暨搜神後記研究—從觀念世界與敍事結構考察. M.A. thesis, Cheng-chih Ta-hsüeh, 1990.

Taga, Namisa 多賀浪砂. *Kan Hô Sôshinki no kenkyû* 干宝『搜神記』の研究. Tokyo: Kindai Bungeisha 近代文藝社, 1994. Study of the contexts (cultural and literary) of this text with an appended essay on Chinese mirrors.

Ssu-k'ung T'u 司空圖 (837-908)

Editions and References

Kao, Chung-chang 高仲章, *et al.*, eds. *Ssu-k'ung T'u hsüan-chi chu* 司空圖選集注. Taiyuan: Shan-hsi Jen-min, 1989.

Ts'ai, Nai-chung 蔡乃中, Wu Tsung-hai 吳宗海 and Lo Chung-ting 羅仲鼎, eds. *Shih-p'in chin-hsi* 詩品今析. Nanking: Chiang-su Jen-min, 1983.

Translations

Wong, Y. W. *Sikong Tu's Shih-p'in.* Singapore: Department of Chinese Studies, 1994. Includes an introduction.

Studies

Chao, Fu-t'an 趙福壇. *Shih-p'in hsin-shih* 詩品新釋. Canton: Hua-ch'eng, 1986.

Ch'en, Kuo-ch'iu 陳國球. "Ssu-k'ung T'u yen-chiu lun-chu mu-lu" 司空圖研究論著目錄.

Shu-mu chi-k'an 21.3 (1987): 93-100.

Ch'en, Shang-chün 陳尚君 and Wang Yung-hao 汪涌豪. "Ssu-k'ung T'u *Erh-shih-ssu shih-p'in pien-wei*" 司空圖二十四詩品辨偽, *Chung-kuo ku-chi yen-chiu* 中國古籍研究. V. 1. Shanghai: Shang-hai Ku-chi, 1996, pp. 39-73.

Chiang, Kuo-chen 江國貞. *Ssu-k'ung piao-sheng yen-chiu* 司空表聖研究. Taipei: Wen-chin, 1985.

Ch'iao, Li 喬力. *Erh-shih-ssu Shih-p'in t'an-wei* 二十四詩品探微. Tsinan: Ch'i-Lu Shu-she, 1984.

Hung, Cheng 弘征. *Ssu-k'ung T'u Shih-p'in chin-i chien-hsi fu-li* 司空圖詩品今譯簡析附例. Yinchuan: Ning-hsia Jen-min, 1984. Rpt. Nanchang: Chiang-hsi Jen-min, 1993.

Lu, Yüan-ch'ih 陸元熾. *Shih te che-hsüeh, che-hsüeh te shih* 詩的哲學哲學的詩. Peking: Pei-ching Ch'u-pan-she, 1984.

Owen, Stephen. "The Twenty-four Categories of Poetry." In *Readings in Chinese Literary Thought* Cambridge: Harvard University Press, 1992, pp. 299-357.

Tsu, Pao-ch'üan 祖保泉. *Ssu-k'ung T'u te shih-ko li-lun* 詩歌理論. Shanghai: Shang-hai Ku-chi, 1984. Rpt. Taipei: Kuo-wen T'ien-ti Tsa-chih, 1992.

Ts'ao, Leng-ch'üan 曹冷泉, comm. *Shih-p'in t'ung-shih* 詩品通釋. Sian: Shan-hsi Shih-fan Ta-hsüeh, 1990?.

Tu, Li-chün 杜黎均. *Erh-shih-ssu Shih-p'in i-chu p'ing-hsi* 二十四詩品譯註評析. Peking: Pei-ching Ch'u-pan-she, 1988.

Wang, Hung 汪泓. "Ssu-k'ung T'u *Erh-shih-ssu Shih-p'in* chen-wei pien tsung-shu" 司空圖二十四詩品真偽辨綜述. *Fu-tan hsüeh-pao* 1996.2 (1996): 32-37.

Wang, Jun-hua 王潤華. *Ssu-k'ung T'u hsin-lun* 司空圖新論. Taipei: Tung-ta T'u-shu Kung-ssu, 1989.

Ssu-ma Ch'eng-chen 司馬承禎 (647–735)

Studies

Engelhardt, Ute. *Die klassisches Tradition der Qi-Übungen (Qigong), eine Darstellung anhangend des Tang-zeitlichen Textes 'Fuqi jingyi lun' von Sima Chengzhen.* Stuttgart: Franz Steiner Verlag, 1987. Münchener ostasiatische Studien, v. 44. Translation and study of a Taoist text, prefaced by a study of Ssu-ma Ch'eng-chen's life and the sources.

Kohn, Livia. "Seven Steps to the Tao: Ssu-ma Ch'eng-chen's *Tso-wang-lun*," *MS* 36 (1985). Translation and study on a specific process of meditation explained in the *Tso-wang-lun*.

___. *Seven Steps to the Tao: Sima Chengzhen's Zuowanglun.* St. Augustin/Nettetal: Monumenta Serica, 1987. Monumenta Serica Monograph, 20.

Ssu-ma Ch'ien 司馬遷 (*ca.* 145-*ca.* 85 B.C.)

Studies

Chang, Ch'iang 張強. *Ssu-ma Ch'ien yü tsung-chiao shen-hua* 司馬遷與宗教神化. Sian: Shan-hsi Jen-min Chiao-yü, 1995. *Ssu-ma Ch'ien yü hua-hsia wen-hua ts'ung-shu.*

Chang, Ta-k'o 張大可. *Ssu-ma Ch'ien i-chia yen* 司馬遷一家言. Sian: Shan-hsi Jen-min Chiao-yü, 1995. *Ssu-ma Ch'ien yü hua-hsia wen-hua ts'ung-shu.*

___. *Ssu-ma Ch'ien p'ing-chuan* 司馬遷評傳. Nanking: Nan-ching Ta-hsüeh, 1994.

Chang, Wei-yüeh 張維嶽. *Ssu-ma Ch'ien yü Shih-chi hsin-t'an* 司馬遷與史記新探. Taipei: Sung-kao Shu-she, 1985.

Ch'en, K'o-ch'ing 陳可青 and Shih Ting 施丁, eds. *Ssu-ma Ch'ien yen-chiu hsin-lun* 司馬謙研究新論. Chengchow: Ho-nan Jen-min, 1982.

Chi, Ch'un 吉春. *Ssu-ma Ch'ien nien-p'u hsin-pien* 司馬遷年譜新編. Sian: San-Ch'in, 1992.

Chou, Ching 周經. *Ssu-ma Ch'ien Shih-chi yü tang-an* 司馬遷史記與檔案. Peking: Tang-an, 1986.

Chou, Hsien-min 周先民. *Ssu-ma Ch'ien te shih-chuan wen-hsüeh shih-chieh* 司馬遷的史傳文學世界. Taipei: Wen-chin, 1995. *Wen-shih-che ta-hsi,* 93.

Chou, Hu-lin 周虎林. *Ssu-ma Ch'ien yü ch'i shih-hsüeh* 司馬遷與其史學. Taipei: Wen-shih-che, 1987. Appends a lengthy bibliography.

Chou, I-p'ing 周一平. *Ssu-ma Ch'ien shih-hsüeh p'i-p'ing chi ch'i li-lun* 思馬遷史學批評及其理論. Shanghai: Hua-tung Shih-fan Ta-hsüeh, 1989.

Durrant, Stephen. *The Cloudy Mirror: Tension and Conflict in the Writings of Sima Qian.* Albany: State University of New York Press, 1995.

___. "Redeeming Sima Qian." *CRI* 4.2 (Fall 1997): 307-313.

___. "Self as the Intersection of Traditions: The Autobiographical Writings of Ssu-ma Ch'ien." *JAOS* 106 (1986): 33-40.

___. "Ssu-ma Ch'ien's Conception of *Tso chuan.*" *JAOS* 112 (1992): 295-301.

Fan, Wen-fang 范文芳. *Ssu-ma Ch'ien te ch'uang-tso i-chih yü hsieh-tso chi-ch'iao* 司馬遷的創作意識與寫作技巧. Taipei: Wen-shih-che Ch'u-pan-she, 1987.

Hayashida, Shinnosuke 林田慎之助. *Shiba Sen: kishi kaisei o kisu* 司馬遷：起死回生を期す. Tokyo: Shûeisha, 1984; 1991. *Chûgoku no hito to shisô,* 6.

Hsiao, Li 蕭黎. *Ssu-ma Ch'ien p'ing-chuan* 司馬謙評傳. Changchun: Chi-lin Wen-shih, 1986.

Hsü, Ch'ien-fu 徐謙夫, ed. *Ssu-ma Ch'ien ch'uan-shuo* 司馬謙傳説. Peking: Wen-hua I-shu, 1987.

Hsü, Ling-yün 許淩雲. *Ssu-ma Ch'ien p'ing-chuan* 司馬遷評傳. Nanning: Kuang-hsi Chiao-yü, 1994.

Hsü, Hsing-hai 徐興海, ed. *Ssu-ma Ch'ien yü Shih-chi lun-chi* 司馬遷與史記論集. Sian: Shan-hsi Jen-min Chiao-yü, 1995.

___, ed. *Ssu-ma Ch'ien yü Shih-chi yen-chiu lun-chu chuan-t'i so-yin* 司馬遷與史記研究論著專題索引. Sian: Shan-hsi Jen-min Chiao-yü, 1995.

Huang, Hsin-ya 黃新亞. *Ssu-ma Ch'ien p'ing-chuan* 司馬遷評傳. Peking: Kuang-ming Jih-pao Ch'u-pan-she, 1991.

Itô, Tokuo 伊藤德男. *Shiki jippyô ni miru Shiba Sen no rekishikan* 史記十表に見る司馬遷の歷史観. Tokyo: Hirakawa Shuppansha, 1994.

Kobayashi, Haruki 小林春樹. "Shiba Sen ni okeru *Shiki* chojutsu no dôki no tsuite-*Shiki* kenkyû josetsu" 司馬遷における『史記』著述の動機について-『史記』研究序説. *Shikan* 127 (1992).

Li, Shao-yung 李少雍. *Ssu-ma Ch'ien chuan-chi wen-hsüeh lun-kao* 司馬遷傳記文學論稿. Chungking: Ch'ung-Ch'ing Ch'u-pan-she, 1987.

Liu, Kuang-i 劉光義. *Ssu-ma Chien yü Lao-Chuang ssu-hsiang* 司馬遷與老莊思想. Taipei: T'ai-wan Shang-wu, 1992.

Liu, Nai-ho 劉乃和, ed. *Ssu-ma Ch'ien ho Shih-chi* 司馬遷和史記. Peking: Pei-ching Ch'u-pan-she, 1987.

Lu, Yung-p'in 陸永品. *Ssu-ma Ch'ien yen-chiu* 司馬遷研究. Kiangsu: Jen-min, 1983.

Murayama, Makoto 村山孚. *Shiba Sen Shiki rekishi kikô* 司馬遷史記歷史紀行. Tokyo: Shôbunsha, 1995.

Nieh, Shih-ch'iao 聶石樵. *Ssu-ma Ch'ien lun-kao* 司馬遷論稿. Peking: Pei-ching Shih-fan Ta-hsüeh, 1987.

Pankenier, David. "'The Scholar's Frustration' Reconsidered: Melancholia or Credo?" *JAOS* 110 (1990): 434-459.

Shih, Ting 施丁. *Ssu-ma Ch'ien hsing-nien hsin-k'ao* 司馬遷行年新考. Sian: Shan-hsi Jen-min Chiao-yü, 1995. *Ssu-ma Ch'ien yü hua-hsia wen-hua ts'ung-shu.*

Ssu-ma Hsiang-ju 司馬相如 (179-117 B.C.)

Editions and References

Chin, Kuo-yung 金國永, comm. and ed. *Ssu-ma Hsiang-ju chi chiao-chu* 司馬相如集校注. Shanghai: Shang-hai Ku-chi, 1993. Useful preface (1986) followed by annotated versions of six *fu* and eight other writings attributed to Ssu-ma Hsiang-ju; lines from *lei-shu* cited from lost works and some biographical material are appended.

Hsü, Ch'ao 徐超, *et al.*, comms. *Chia I Ssu-ma Hsiang-ju wen* 賈誼司馬相如文. Taipei: Chin-hsiu, 1993.

Translations

Fei, Chen-kang 費振剛 and Ch'iu Chung-ch'ien 仇仲謙, trans. and comms. *Ssu-ma Hsiang-ju wen hsüan-i* 司馬相如文選譯. Chengtu: Pa-Shu Shu-she, 1991.

Studies

Idema, W. L. "The Story of Ssu-ma Hsiang-ju and Cho Wen-chün in Vernacular Literature of the Yüan and Early Ming Dynasties." *TP* 70 (1984): 60-109.

Shu, Ching-nan 束景南. "Kuan-yü Ssu-ma Hsiang-ju yu Liang nien-tai yü sheng-nien" 關於司馬相如游梁年代與生年. *Wen-hsüeh i-ch'an* 1984.3: 105-107.

Su Ch'e 蘇轍 (1039-1112)

Editions and References

Ch'en, Hung-t'ien 陳宏天 and Kao Hsiu-fang 高秀芳, eds. *Su Ch'e chi* 蘇轍集. 4v. Peking: Chung-hua, 1990. Chung-kuo ku-tien wen-hsüeh chi-pen ts'ung-shu. Contains chronological tables, prefaces, a bibliography and an index.

Ch'üan Sung shih, 15:849-873.9814-10164.

Ch'üan Sung wen, 46:2037-2060.357-768 and 47:2061-2106.1-684.

Koten Kenkyūkai 古典研究会, ed. *So Shoku Tōba shū* 蘇轍東坡集. Tokyo: Kyūko Shoin, 1991.

Shen, Hui-yüeh 沈惠樂, ed. *Su Hsün, Su Ch'e san-wen hsüan-chi* 蘇洵蘇轍散文選集. Shanghai: Shang-hai Ku-chi, 1997.

Tseng, Tsao-chuang 曾棗莊 and Ma Te-fu 馬德富, eds. *Luan-ch'eng chi wu-shih chüan, Hou chi erh-ssu chüan, San-chi shih chüan, Ying-chao chi shih-erh chüan* 欒城集五十卷，後集二四卷，三集十卷，應詔集十二卷. 3v. Shanghai: Shang-hai Ku-chi, 1987. Appends prefaces, a *nien-piao*, and other useful information.

Wang, Pin 王彬, ed. "Su Ch'e chüan" 蘇轍卷. In *T'ang Sung pa-ta-chia ming-pien shang-hsi yü i-chu* 唐宋八大家名篇賞析與譯注. *Ching-chi jih-pao* 1997.

Yü, Tsung-hsien 俞宗憲, ed. *Lung-ch'uan lüeh-chih* 龍川略志. 10 *chüan*. Bound together with *Lung-ch'uan pieh-chih* 龍川別志. 2 *chüan*. Peking: Chung-hua, 1982.

Translations

Strassberg, *Inscribed Landscapes*, pp. 195-198.

Studies

Liu, Shang-jung 劉尚榮. "Su Ch'e i-chu chi-k'ao" 蘇轍佚著輯考. *Wen-hsüeh i-ch'an* 1984.3 (1984): 111-5.

Tseng, Tsao-chuang 曾棗莊. *Su Ch'e nien-p'u* 蘇轍年譜. Sian: Shan-hsi Jen-min, 1986. Chung-kuo ku-tai tso-chia yen-chiu ts'ung-shu.

Su Hsün 蘇洵 (1009-1066)

Editions and References

Chia-yu chi chien-chu 嘉祐集箋注. Shanghai: Shang-hai Ku-chi, 1993. Chung-kuo ku-tien wen-hsüeh ts'ung-shu.

Ch'üan Sung shih, 7:351-352.4358-4374.

Ch'üan Sung wen, 22:918-927.2-183.

Shen, Hui-yüeh 沈惠樂, ed. *Su Hsün, Su Ch'e san-wen hsüan-chi* 蘇洵蘇轍散文選集. Shanghai: Shang-hai Ku-chi, 1997.

Wang, Pin 王彬, ed. "Su Hsün chüan" 蘇洵卷. In *T'ang Sung pa-ta-chia ming-pien shang-hsi yü i-chu* 唐宋八大家名篇賞析與譯注. *Ching-chi jih-pao* 1997.

Studies

Chin, Kuo-yung 金國永. *Su Hsün* 蘇洵. Peking: Chung-hua, 1984. Chung-kuo wen-hsüeh shih chih-shih ts'ung-shu.

Hatch, George. "Su Hsün's Pragmatic Statecraft." In *Ordering the World*. Conrad Schirokauer and Robert P. Hymes, eds. Berkeley: University of California Press, 1993, pp. 59-75.

Hsieh, Wu-hsiung 謝武雄. *Su Hsün yen-lun chi ch'i wen-hsüeh chih yen-chiu* 蘇洵言論及其文學之研究. Taipei: Wen-shih-che, 1981. Wen-shih-che-hsüeh chi-ch'eng, 55.

Kondô, Kazunari 近藤一成. "Chô Hôhei 'Bun An sensei bohyô' to benkan ron" 張方平「文安先生墓表」と弁姦論. *Waseda Daigaku Daigakuin Bungaku Kenkyûka kiyô–Tetsugaku Shigaku-hen* 39 (1994): 137-150.

Tseng, Tsao-chuang 曾棗莊. *Su Hsün p'ing-chuan* 蘇洵評傳. Chengtu: Ssu-ch'uan Jen-min, 1983.

Su Shih 穌軾 (1037-1101)

Editions and References

Ch'eng, Po-an 程伯安. *Su Tung-p'o min-su shih chieh* 蘇東坡民俗詩解. Peking: Chung-kuo Shu-chi, 1997.

Chinese Department, Szechwan University, ed. *Su Shih tzu-liao hui-pien* 穌軾資料匯編. 5v. Peking: Chung-hua, 1994.

Chiu, Yung-ming 仇永明 *et al*, eds. *Tung-p'o tz'u so-yin* 東坡詞索引. Shanghai: Hua-tung Shih-fan Ta-hsüeh, 1994.

Chou, Hui-chen 周慧珍. *Su Shih wen-hsüan chu* 蘇軾文選注. Taiyuan: Shan-hsi Chiao-yü, 1990.

Chu, Ch'uan-yü 朱傳譽, ed. *Su Shih chuan-chi tzu-liao* 蘇軾傳記資料. 22v. Taipei: T'ien-i, 1985.

Ch'üan Sung shih, 14:784-832.9084-9661.

Ch'üan Sung wen, 42:1849-1873.458-1042; 43:1874-1922.1-971; 44:1923-1971.1-938; and 45:1972-2004.1-712.

Fan, Hui-chün 范會俊 and Chu I-hui 朱逸輝, eds. *Su Shih Hai-nan shih-wen hsüan-chu* 蘇軾海南詩文選注. Shanghai: Shang-hai Ku-chi, 1990.

Hua-tung Shih-fan Ta-hsüeh Ku-chi Yen-chiu So 華東師範大學古籍研究所, ed. and comm. *Tung-p'o chih-lin* 東坡志林. 5 *chüan*. Shanghai: Hua-tung Shih-fan Ta-hsüeh, 1983. Bound together with *Ch'iu-chih pi-chi* 仇池筆記.

Hsiao, P'ing-tung 蕭屏東, ed. *Su Tung-p'o pi-chi* 蘇東坡筆記. Changsha: Hu-nan Wen-i, 1991.

Koten Kenkyûkai 古典研究会, ed. *So Shoku Tôba shû* 蘇軾東坡集. Tokyo: Kyûko Shoin,

1991.

Kuan, San 貫三, ed. *Tung-p'o shih* 東坡詩. Changsha: Yüeh-lu, 1992.

K'ung, Fan-li 孔凡禮, ed. *Su Shih wen-chi* 蘇軾文集. 6v. Peking: Chung-hua, 1986.

Li, Fu-shun 李福順, ed. *Su Shih lun shu-hua shih-liao* 蘇軾論書畫史料. Shanghai: Shang-hai Jen-min Mei-shu, 1988.

Ling-nan Hsüeh-yüan 嶺南學院, ed. *Su tz'u so-yin* 蘇詞索引. Canton: Ling-nan Hsüeh-yüan, 1992.

Liu, Nai-ch'ang 劉乃昌 and Kao Hung-k'uei 高洪奎, eds. *Su Shih san-wen hsüan-chi* 蘇軾散文選集. Shanghai: Shang-hai Ku-chi, 1997.

___ and Ts'ui Hai-cheng 崔海正, eds. and comms. *Tung-p'o tz'u* 東坡詞. Hangchow: Che-chiang Ku-chi, 1992.

Lung, Mu-shun 龍沐勛 and Chu Tsu-mou 朱祖謀, comms. *Tung-p'o yüeh-fu chien-chiang shu* 東坡樂府箋講疏. Taipei: Kuang-wen Shu-chü, 1972.

Shih, Sheng-huai 石聲淮 and T'ang Ling-ling 唐玲玲, eds. *Su Shih wen-hsüan* 蘇軾文選. Shanghai: Shang-hai Ku-chi, 1989.

___. *Tung-p'o yüeh-fu pien-nien chien-chu* 東坡樂府編年箋注. Wuchang: Hua-chung Shih-fan Ta-hsüeh, 1990.

Su Tung-p'o ch'üan-chi 蘇東坡全集. 10v. Peking: Pei-ching Yen-shan, 1997.

Ts'ao, Mu-fan 曹慕樊 and Hsü Yung-nien 徐永年, eds. *Tung-p'o hsüan-chi* 東坡選集. Chengtu: Ssu-ch'uan Jen-min, 1987.

Tseng, Tsao-chuang 曾棗莊, *et al.*, eds. and comms. *Su Shih shih-wen-tz'u hsüan-i* 蘇軾詩文詞選譯. Chengtu: Pa-Shu Shu-she, 1990. Rpt. Taipei: Chin-hsiu, 1993.

Wang, Shui-chao 王水照. *Su Shih hsüan-chi* 蘇軾選集. Shanghai: Shang-hai Ku-chi, 1984. Excellent preface, commentary to about 200 poems and 20 prose pieces; *nien-p'u* appended.

___. *Su Shih lun-kao* 蘇軾論稿. Taipei: Wan-chüan-lou T'u-shu Kung-ssu, 1994.

___ and Wang I-yüan 王宜瑗, comms. *Su Shih shih-tz'u hsüan-chu* 蘇軾詩詞選注. Shanghai: Shang-hai Ku-chi, 1990.

Wang, Sung-ling 王松齡, ed. *Tung-p'o chih-lin* 東坡志林. 5 *chüan*. Peking: Chung-hua, 1981.

Wang, Wen-kao 王文誥, (1764–?) comp. and K'ung Fan-li 孔凡禮, coll. *Su Shih shih-chi* 蘇軾詩集. 8v. Peking: Chung-hua, 1982, 1987.

Wu, Lu-shan 吳鷺山, *et al.*, eds. *Su Shih shih-hsüan chu* 蘇軾詩選注. Tientsin: Pai-hua Wen-i, 1982.

Yen, Chung-ch'i 顏中其. *Su Tung-p'o i-shih hui-pien* 遺事匯編. Changsha: Yüeh-lu Shu-she, 1984.

Translations

Landau, *Beyond Spring*, pp. 108-135.

Ôgawa, Tamaki 小川環樹 and Yamamoto Kazuyoshi 山本和義. *So Tôba shû* 蘇東坡集. Tokyo: Asahi Shinbunsha, 1972.

___ and Yamamoto Kazuyoshi 山本和義. *So Tôba shishû* 蘇東坡詩集. 5v. Tokyo: Chikuma Shobô, 1984-1990. Only firve of the thirteen planned volumes of this careful translation were completed before Professor Ôgawa passed away.

Roy, Claude. *L'ami qui venait de l'an mil: Su Dongpo 1037-1101*. Paris: Gallimard, 1994.

Simon, Rainald, trans. *Die frühen Lieder des Su Dong-po*. Frankfurt am Main: Peter Lang, 1985. An extended introduction followed by translations of about 75 poems from the years 1071-1077.

Strassberg, *Inscribed Landscapes*, pp. 183-194.

Toyofuku, Kenji 豊福健二. *So Tôba shiwa shû* 蘇東坡詩話集. Tokyo: Hôyû Shoten, 1994.

Watson, Burton. *Selected Poems of Su Tung-p'o*. Port Townsend, Washington: Copper Canyon Press, 1994. Translations of 112 poems and a 12-page Introduction. Obverse of the title page reads "Many of these poems originally appeared in *Sung Tung-p'o: Selections from a Sung Dynasty Poet*, Columbia University Press, 1965.

Studies

Chang, Fu-ch'ing 張福慶. *Su Shih shih-tz'u ming-p'ien hsiang-hsi* 蘇軾詩詞名篇詳析. Peking: Pei-ching Shih-fan Ta-hsüeh, 1992.

Cheang, Alice Wen-chuen. "Poetry, Politics, Philosophy: Su Shih as the Man of the Eastern Slope." *HJAS* 53 (1993): 325-87.

___. "The Way and the Self in the Poetry of Su Shih (1037-1101)." Unpublished Ph. D. dissertation, Harvard University, 1991.

Chen, Yu-shih. "Su Shih: A Theory of Perception in Art." In Chen's *Images and Ideas in Chinese Classical Prose: Studies of Four Masters*. Stanford: Stanford University Press, 1988, pp. 133-53.

Ch'en, Ying-chi 陳英姬. "Su Tung-po te cheng-chih sheng-ya yü wen-hsüeh te kuan-hsi" 政治生涯與文學的關係. Unpublished Ph.D. dissertation, National Taiwan Normal University, 1989.

Chu, Ching-hua 朱靖華. *Su Shih hsin-lun* 蘇軾新論. Tsinan: Ch'i-Lu Shu-she, 1983.

___. *Su Shih hsin-p'ing* 蘇軾新評. Peking: Chung-kuo Wen-hsüeh, 1993.

___. *Su Shih lun* 蘇軾論. Peking: Ching-hua, 1997.

Chung, Lai-yin 鐘來因. *Su Shih yü Tao-chia Tao-chiao* 蘇軾與道家道教. Taipei: T'ai-wan Hsüeh-sheng Shu-chü, 1990.

Egan, Ronald C. "Ou-yang Hsiu and Su Shih on Calligraphy." *HJAS* 49.2 (December 1989): 365-419.

___. "Poems on Paintings: Su Shih and Huang T'ing-chien." *HJAS* 43 (1983):* 413-451.

___. "Su Shih's 'Notes' as a Historical and Literary Source." *HJAS* 50.2 (December 1990): 561-588.

___. *Word, Image and Deed in the Life of Su Shi*. Cambridge: Council on East Asian Studies and the Harvard-Yenching Institute, 1994. Harvard Yenching-Institute Monograph Series, 39. Includes texts of Su Shi's poems in Chinese with translations in English; appends bibliographical references and an index.

Fuller, Michael Anthony. *The Road to East Slope: The Development of Su Shi's Poetic Voice*. Stanford: Stanford University Press, 1990.

Grant, Beata. "Buddhism and Taoism in the Poetry of Su Shi (1036-1101)." Unpublished Ph. D. dissertation, Stanford University, 1987.

___. *Mount Lu Revisited: Buddhism in the Life and Writings of Su Shih*. Honolulu: University of Hawaii Press, 1994.

Hawes, Colin. "Su Shi (1037-1101) as Mystical Poet." *British Columbia Asian Review* 8 (1994-5): 105-116.

Hokari, Yoshiaki 保苅佳昭. "So Tôba no shi ni mirareru 'yume' no go ni tsuite" 蘇東坡の詞に見られる「夢」の語について. *Kangaku kenkyû* 29 (1991): 17-35.

Hsieh, T'ao-fang 謝桃坊. *Su Shih shih yen-chiu* 蘇軾詩研究. Chengtu: Pa-Shu Shu-she, 1987.

Huang, Ming-fen 黃鳴奮. *Lun Su Shih te wen-i hsin-li kuan* 論蘇軾的文藝心理觀. Foochow: Hai-hsia Wen-i, 1987.

I, Jo-fen 衣若芬. "Su Shih t'i-hua wen-hsüeh yen-chiu" 蘇軾題畫文學研究. Unpublished Ph. D. dissertation, National Taiwan University, 1995.

Idema, W. L. "Poet versus Minister and Monk: Su Shih on Stage in the Period 1250-1550," *TP* 73 (1987): 190-216.

Jikusa, Masaaki 竺沙雅章. *Tôba shû* 東坡集. Tokyo: Kyûko Shoin, 1991. *Koten kenkyûkai sôsho Kanseki no bu*, 16.

Li, I-ping 李一冰. *Su Tung-p'o hsin-chuan* 蘇東坡新傳. 2v. Taipei: Lien-ching, 1983.

Liu, Nai-ch'ang 劉乃昌. *Su Shih wen-hsüeh lun-chi* 蘇軾文學論集. Tsinan: Ch'i-Lu Shu-she,

1982.

Liu, Shang-jung 劉尚榮. *Su Shih chu-tso pan-pen lun-ts'ung* 蘇軾著作版本論叢. Chengtu: Pa-Shu Shu-she, 1988.

Liu, Shih 劉石. *Su Shih tz'u yen-chiu* 蘇軾詞研究. Taipei: Wen-chin, 1992. *Ta-lu ti-ch'ü po-shih lun-wen ts'ung-k'an,* 22.

Murakami, Tetsumi 村上哲見, *et al. So Shoku, Riku Yû* 蘇軾・陸游. Tokyo: Kadokawa Shoten 1989. *Kanshô Chûgoku no koten,* 21.

Ôgawa, Tamaki 小川環樹. *So Shoku* 蘇軾. 2v. Tokyo: Iwanami, 1962.

Pease, Jonathan. "Contour Plowing on East Slope: A New Reading of Su Shi," *JAOS* 112 (1992): 470-7.

P'u, Yung-huan 朴永煥. *Su Shih ch'an-shih yen-chiu* 蘇軾禪詩研究. Peking: Chung-kuo She-hui K'o-hsüeh, 1995.

Reubi, Francois C. "Astronomie et poésie chinoise, a propos de la Première Ode de la Falaise Rouge de Su Dongpo," *AS* 46 (1992): 640-52.

Roy, Claude. *L'ami qui venait d l'an mil: Su Dongpo 1037-1101.* Paris: Gallimard, 1994.

Sargent, Stuart H. "City of Lotuses," *JSYS* 24 (1994): 165-204. An extensive close reading of Su's "Fu-jung cheng shih" 芙蓉城詩.

____. "Colophons in Countermotion: Poems by Su Shih and Huang T'ing-chien on Painting," *HJAS* 52.1 (June 1992): 263-302.

Shen, K'uo 沈括 (1029–1093) and Ch'eng Yung-p'ei 程永培, ed. *Su Shih yang-sheng liang-fang* 蘇軾養生良方. Peking: T'uan-chieh, 1994.

Su Shih Yen-chiu Hsüeh-hui 蘇軾研究學會, ed. *Chi-nien Su Shih pien-tan pa-pai chiu-shih chou-nien hsüeh-shu t'ao-lun chi* 紀念蘇軾貶儋八百九十周年學術討論集. Chengtu: Ssu-ch'uan Ta-hsüeh, 1991.

____. *Ch'üan-kuo ti-pa-tz'u Su Shih yen-t'ao hui lun-wen chi* 全國第八次蘇軾研討會論文集. Chengtu: Ssu-ch'uan Ta-hsüeh, 1997.

____. *Tung-p'o shih lun-ts'ung* 東坡詩論叢. Chengtu: Ssu-ch'uan Jen-min, 1983.

____. *Tung-p'o tz'u lun-ts'ung* 東坡詞論叢. Chengtu: Ssu-ch'uan Jen-min, 1982.

____. *Tung-p'o wen lun-ts'ung* 東坡文論叢. 2v. Chengtu: Ssu-ch'uan Wen-i, 1986.

____. *Tung-p'o yen-chiu lun-ts'ung* 東坡研究論叢. Chengtu: Ssu-ch'uan Wen-i, 1986.

Takahata, Tsunenobu 高畑常信. *Tôb daibatsu–shogei hen* 東坡題跋-書芸篇. Tokyo: Mokujisha, 1989.

Tomlonovic, Kathleen M. "Poetry of Exile and Return: A Study of Su Shi (1037-1101)." Unpublished Ph. D. dissertation, University of Washington, 1989.

Toyofuku, Kenji 豊福健二. *So Tôba bungei hyôronshû* 蘇東坡文芸評論集. Tokyo: Mokujisha, 1989.

Tseng, Tsao-chuang 曾棗莊. *Su Shih p'ing-chuan* 蘇軾評傳. Rev. ed. Chengtu: Ssu-ch'uan Jen-min, 1984.

Ts'ung, Chien 叢鑒 and K'o Ta-k'o 柯大課. *Su Shih chi ch'i tso-p'in* 蘇軾及其作品. Changchun: Chi-lin Jen-min, 1984.

Wang, Hung 王洪. *Su Shih shih-ko yen-chiu* 蘇軾詩歌研究. Peking: Ch'ao-hua, 1993.

____. *Su Tung-p'o yen-chiu* 蘇東坡研究. Kweilin: Kuang-hsi Shih-fan Ta-hsüeh, 1997.

Wang, Ssu-yü 王思宇, ed. *Su Shih tz'u shang-hsi chi* 蘇軾詞賞析集. Chengtu: Pa-Shu Shu-she, 1987.

Wu, Hsüeh-t'ao 吳雪濤. *Su Shih k'ao lun-kao* 蘇軾考論稿. Huhehot: Nei Meng-ku Chiao-yü, 1994.

____. "Su tz'u pien-nien pien-cheng–*Tung-p'o yüeh-fu pien-nien chien-chu* hsien-i chih i" 蘇詞編年辨證–東坡樂府編年箋注獻疑之一. *Wen shih* 40 (1994): 195-204.

Yang, Vincent. *Nature and Self: A Study of the Poetry of Su Dongpo with Comparisons to the Poetry of William Wordsworth.* Frankfurt am Main and New York: Peter Lang, 1989.

Yen, Chung-ch'i 顏中其. *Su Shih lun wen-i* 蘇軾論文譯. Peking: Pei-ching Ch'u-pan-she,

426

1985.

___. *Su Tung-p'o i-shih hui-pien* 軼事匯編. Changsha: Yüeh-lu Shu-she, 1984.

Yü, Feng 于風. *Wen-t'ung Su Shih* 文同蘇軾. Shanghai: Shang-hai Jen-min Mei-shu, 1988.

Su Shun-ch'in 蘇舜欽 (1008-1048)

Editions and References

Fu, P'ing-hsiang 傅平驤 and Hu Wen-t'ao 胡問濤, eds. *Su Shun-ch'in chi pien-nien chiao-chu* 蘇舜欽集編年校注. Chengtu: Pa-Shu Shu-she, 1991.

Shen, Wen-cho 沈文倬, ed. *Su Shun-ch'in chi* 蘇舜欽集. 16 *chüan*. Peking: Chung-hua, 1961.

Translations

Strassberg, *Inscribed Landscapes*, pp. 169-172.

Su T'ing 蘇頲 (670-727)

Studies

Ch'en, Chün 陳鈞. "Su T'ing nien-p'u (i-liu)" 蘇頲年譜（一–六）. *Yen-ch'eng Shih-chuan hsüeh-pao* 1991.1, 4; 1992.4; 1993.2, 4; 1994.1.

___. "Su T'ing nien-p'u ting-pu (i, erh)" 蘇頲年譜訂補（一，二）. *Yen-ch'eng Shih-chuan hsüeh-pao* 1994.2, 3.

Sui T'ang yen-i 隨唐演義 (Romance of the Sui and the T'ang)

Editions and References

Hsü, Wen-ch'ang 徐文長, comm. *Sui T'ang yen-i* 隨唐演義. 3v. Shanghai:. Shang-hai Ku-chi, 1990.

Su, Pi 蘇碧, *et al.*, eds. *Sui T'ang yen-i* 隨唐演義. 10 *chüan*. Chengtu: Pa-Shu Shu-she, 1993.

Sung Chih-wen 宋之問 (d. 712)

Editions and References

Luan, Kuei-ming 欒貴明 *et al.*, eds. *Ch'üan T'ang shih so-yin: Shen Ch'üan-ch'i/Sung Chih-wen chüan* 全唐詩索引：沈佺期宋之問卷. Peking: Hsien-tai, 1995.

Matsuoka, Eiji 松岡栄志. *Sô Shimon shi sakuin* 宋之問詩索引. Tokyo: Tôkyô Daigaku, 1985.

Studies

Chao, Min 昭民. "Sung Chih-wen 'tzu-ssu' Ch'in-chou k'ao" 宋之問賜死欽州考. *Hsüeh-shu lun-t'an* 1982.6.

Takagi, Shigetoshi 高木重俊. "Sô Shimon ron" 宋之問論. *Hokkaidô Kyôiku Daigaku kiyô, Jimbun kagaku* 37 (1-2 1988).

Sung Lien 宋濂 (1310-1381)

Studies

Cleaves, Francis Woodman. "Additional Data on Sung Lien, Wang Wei, and Chao Hsün."

Appended to "The 'Postscript to the Table of Contents of the *Yüan shih*.'" *JSYS* 23 (1993): 13-18 (1-18).

Translations
Strassberg, *Inscribed Landscapes*, pp. 269-278.

Sung-shih ch'ao 宋詩鈔 (Jottings from Sung Dynasty Poetry)

Editions and References
Li, Hsüan-kung 李宣龔, ed. *Sung-shih ch'ao ch'u-chi* 宋詩鈔初集. 3v. Peking: Chung-hua, 1986.

Sung-shih chi-shih 宋詩紀事 (Recorded Occasions in Sung Poetry)

Editions and References
K'ung, Fan-li 孔凡禮. *Sung-shih chi-shih hsü-pu* 宋詩紀事續補. 2v. Peking: Pei-ching Ta-hsüeh, 1987. *Ch'üan Sung-shih yen-chiu tzu-liao ts'ung-k'an*.

Ta-ku 大鼓 (drum ballad)

Editions and References
Hu, Meng-hsiang 胡孟祥 and Wang Chung-i 王中一, eds. *Sun Shu-yün ching-yün ta-ku yen-ch'ang chi* 孫書筠京韻大鼓演唱集. Peking: Chung-kuo Min-chien Wen-i, 1989. *Tung-fang shuo-ch'ang i-shu hsi-lieh ts'ung-shu*.

Studies
Chao, Ching-shen 趙景深. *Ta-ku yen-chiu* 大鼓研究. Changsha: Shang-wu Yin-shu-kuan, 1936. Pai-k'o hsiao ts'ung-shu. Rev. ed. Shanghai: Shang-hai Shu-tien, 1991. *Min-kuo ts'ung-shu*.

Ta-li shih-ts'ai tzu 大曆十才子 (Ten Talents of the Ta-li Period)

Editions and References
Chiao, Wen-pin 焦文彬, *et al.*, eds. *Ta-li shih-ts'ai tsu shih-hsüan* 大曆十才子詩選. Sian: Shan-shi Jen-min, 1988.

Studies
Chu, Chung-chün 儲仲君. "Ta-li shih-ts'ai-tzu te ch'uang-tso huo-tung t'an-so" 大曆十才子的創作活動探索. *Wen-hsüeh i-ch'an* 4 (1983): 58-63.
Shih, I-tui 施議對 and Chiang Yin 蔣寅. *Chung-kuo shih-hsüeh* 中國詩學. Nanking: Nan-ching Ta-hsüeh, 1997. First volume of a projected history covers the *Ta-li* period.

T'ai-ko-t'i 臺閣體 (cabinet style)

Studies
Ch'ien, Chin-sung 簡錦松 *Ming-tai wen-hsüeh p'i-p'ing yen-chiu* 明代文學批評研究. Taipei:

Hsüeh-sheng, 1989. Argues that Li Tung-yang was the culmination of the *t'ai-ko-t'i* rather than its executioner.

T'ai-p'ing kuang-chi 太平廣記 (**Extensive Gleanings of the Reign of Great Tranquility**)

Editions and References

Wang, Hsiu-mei 王秀梅 *et al.*, eds. *T'ai-p'ing kuang-chi so-yin* 太平廣記索引. Peking: Chung-hua, 1997. Keyed to the 1986 Chung-hua edition.

Wang, San-yüan 王三元, *et al,* eds. *T'ai-p'ing kuang-chi (chin-chu pen)* 太平廣記（今注本）. Peking: Chung-kuo Kuang-po, 1997.

Studies

Baluth, Birthe. *Altchinesische Geschichten über Fuchsdämonen, Kommentierte bersetzung der Kapitel 447 bis 455 des Taiping Guangji.* Frankfurt and New York: Lang, 1996.

Chang, Kuo-feng 張國風. "Shih-lun *T'ai-p'ing kuang-chi* te pan-pen yen-pien" 試論太平廣記的版本演變, *Wen-hsien* 1994.4: 3-17.

Hammond, Charles Edward. "T'ang Stories in the *T'ai-p'ing kuang-chi.*" Unpublished Ph. D. dissertation, Columbia University, 1987.

Kirkland, Russell. "A World in Balance: Holistic Synthesis in the T'ai-p'ing Kuang-Chi." *JSYS* 23 (1993): 43-70. A good survey of scholarship which concludes the work was designed to promote the wholeness of life, the strange as well as the mundane.

T'ai-ping yü-lan 太平御覽 (**Imperial Digest of the T'ai-ping Reign Period**)

Editions and References

T'ai-p'ing yü-lan 太平御覽. Taipei: T'uan-chieh, 1994. *Mi-shu chi-ch'ung.*

T'an-tz'u 彈詞 (**plucking rhymes**)

Studies

Bender, Mark. "Tan-ci, Wen-ci, Chang-ci." *CLEAR* 6 (1984): 121-124.

Hu, Hsiao-chen 胡曉真. "Yüeh-tu fan-ying yü t'an-tz'u hsiao-shuo te chuang-tso—Ch'ing-tai nü-hsing hsü-shih wen-hsüeh ch'uan-t'ung chien-li chih i yü" 閱獨反應與彈詞小説的創作—清代女性敘事文學傳統建立之一隅. *Chung-kuo wen-che yen-chiu chi-k'an* 8 (March 1996): 305-364.

Lien, P'o 連波. *T'an-tzu yin-yüeh ch'u-t'an* 彈詞音樂初探. Shanghai: Shang-hai Wen-i, 1979.

Sung, Marina H. "*T'an-tz'u* and *t'an-tz'u* Narratives." *TP* 79 (1993): 1-22.

Tsao, Pen-yeh. *The Music of Su-chou T'an-tz'u.*' Hong Kong: The Chinese University Press, 1988.

T'an Yüan-ch'un 譚元春 (**1585-1637**)

Editions and References

Ching-ling p'ai chung-hsing T'an Yüan-ch'un hsüan-chi 竟陵派鍾惺譚元春選集. Wu T'iao-kung 吳調公, *et al*, comms. and eds. Wuhan: Hu-pei Jen-min, 1993.

Tanshi shiki 譚子詩歸. 4v. Tokyo: Kôkyû Shûhô, 1990. Photolithographic reproduction of an edition held in Japan.

T'ang chih-yen 唐摭言 (Picked-up Words of T'ang)

Studies

Moore, Oliver. "The Literary Arena: Social and Ceremonial Aspects of Chinese State Examination in the *T'ang chih-yen* by Wang Ting-pao (AD 870-940)." Unpublished Ph. D. dissertation, Pembroke College, Cambridge University, 1992.

T'ang Hsien-tsu 湯顯祖 (1550-1617)

Editions and References

Ch'ien Nan-yang 錢南揚, ed. *T'ang Hsien-tsu hsi-ch'ü chi* 湯顯祖戲曲集. 2v. Shanghai: Shang-hai Ku-chi, 1982. Chung-kuo ku-tien wen-hsüeh ts'ung-shu.

Hsü, Fu-ming 徐扶明. *Mu-tan T'ing yen-chiu tzu-liao k'ao-shih* 牡丹亭研究資料考釋. Shanghai: Shang-hai Ku-chi, 1987.

Hsü, Shuo-fang 徐朔方 and Yang Hsiao-mei 楊笑梅, comms. and eds. *Mu-tan T'ing* 牡丹亭. Peking: Jen-min Wen-hsüeh, 1978. Chung-kuo ku-tien wen-hsüeh ts'ung-shu.

Mao, Hsiao-t'ung 毛效同, ed. *T'ang Hsien-tsu yen-chiu tzu-liao hui-pien* 湯顯祖研究資料匯編. Shanghai: Shang-hai Ku-chi, 1986. Includes records of lost works, biographical information, comments on 159 pieces of prose and verse and 400 dramas.

Studies

Birch, Cyril. "A Comparative View of Dramatic Romance: *The Winter's Tale* and *The Peony Pavilion*." In Roger T. Ames, *et al.* eds. *Interpreting Culture through Translation.* Hong Kong: The Chinese University Press, 1991, pp. 59-77.

Cheng, P'ei-k'ai 鄭培凱. *T'ang Hsien-tsu yü Wan-Ming wen-hua* 湯顯祖與晚明文化. Taipei: Yün-ch'en Wen-hua, 1995. Yün-ch'en ts'ung-k'an, 61.

Chiang-hsi Sheng Wen-hsüeh I-shu Yen-chiu So 江西省文學藝術研究所, ed. *T'ang Hsien-tsu yen-chiu lun-wen chi* 湯顯祖研究論文集. Peking: Chung-kuo Hsi-chü, 1984. More than 30 papers from a 1982 conference; appends a "T'ang Hsien-tsu yen-chiu tzu-liao so-yin" 湯顯祖研究資料索引.

Chou, Yü-te 周育德. *T'ang Hsien-tsu lun-kao* 湯顯祖論稿. Peking: Wen-hua I-shu, 1991.

Chu, Hsüeh-hui 朱學輝 and Chi Hsiao-yen 季曉燕. *Tung-fang hsi-chü i-shu chü-chiang T'ang Hsien-tsu* 東方戲劇藝術巨匠湯顯祖. Nanchang: Chiang-hsi Jen-min, 1986. Appends a bibliography and chronological biography.

Hsü, Fu-ming 徐扶明. *T'ang Hsien-tsu yü Mu-tan T'ing* 湯顯與牡丹亭. Shanghai: Shang-hai Ku-chi, 1993. Chung-kuo ku-tien wen-hsüeh chi-pen chih-shih ts'ung-shu.

Hsü, Shuo-fang 徐朔方. *Lun T'ang Hsien-tsu chi ch'i-t'a* 論湯顯祖及其他. Shanghai: Shang-hai Ku-chi, 1983. A collection of 28 articles by Hsü published between 1954 and 1981.

___. *T'ang Hsien-tsu p'ing-chuan* 湯顯祖評傳. Nanking: Nan-ching Ta-hsüeh, 1993. Chung-kuo ssu-hsiang chia p'ing-chuan ts'ung-shu, 131. Appends a *nien-piao*, an index and a bibliography.

Huang, Chih-kang 黃芝岡. *T'ang Hsien-tsu pien-nien p'ing-chuan* 湯顯祖編年評傳. Peking: Chung-kuo Hsi-chü, 1992.

Huang, Wen-hsi 黃文錫 and Wu Feng-ch'u 吳風雛. *T'ang Hsien-tsu* 湯顯祖. Peking: Chung-kuo Hsi-chü, 1986. Hsi-chü chia chuan lun ts'ung-shu.

Kung, Chung-mo 龔重謨, *et al. T'ang Hsien-tsu chuan* 湯顯祖傳. Nanchang: Chiang-hsi Jen-min, 1986. A biography organized according to units in T'ang's hometown.

Swatek, Catherine. "Plum and Portrait: Feng Meng-lung's Revision of *The Peony Pavilion*." *AM, TS* 6.1 (1993): 127-60.

Wei, Hua. "Dreams in Tang Xianzu's Plays." *Chinoperl* 16 (1992-93): 145-64.

___. "The Search for Great Harmony: A Study of Tang Xianzu's Dramatic Art." Unpublished Ph. D. dissertation, University of California, Berkeley, 1991.

Yung, Sai-shing. "A Critical Study of 'Han-tan chi." Unpublished Ph. D. dissertation, Princeton University, 1992.

Zeitlin, Judith T. "Shared Dreams: The Story of the Three Wives' Commentary on *The Peony Pavilion.*" *HJAS* 54 (1994): 127-179.

T'ang-shih chi-shih 唐詩紀事 (Recorded Occasions in T'ang Poetry)

Editions and References

Wang, Chung-yung 王仲鏞, ed. *T'ang-shih chi-shih chiao-chien* 唐詩紀事校箋. 81 *chüan.* 2 v. Chengtu: Pa-Shu Shu-she, 1989. The text is the 1234 edition from Wang Hsi 王禧; includes an index.

T'ang-shih san-pai-shou 唐詩三百首 (Three Hundred Poems of the T'ang dynasty)

Editions and References

Fukazawa, Kazuyuki 深沢一幸. *Tôshi sanbyakushu* 唐詩三百首. Tokyo: Kadokawa Shoten 1989. *Kanshô Chûgoku no koten,* 19.

T'ang-shih san-pai-shou chu-shu 唐詩三百首注疏. Chang Hsieh 章燮, ed. Hofei: An-hui Wen-i, 1983. Reprint of Chang Hsieh's 1834 edition, further edited by Wu Shao-lieh 吳紹烈 and Chou I 周藝.

T'ang-shih san-pai-shou hsin-pien 唐詩三百首新編. Ma Mao-yüan 馬茂元 and Chao Ch'ang-p'ing 趙昌平, comms. Changsha: Yüeh-lu Shu-she, 1992.

T'ang-shih san-pai-shou p'ing-chu 唐詩三百首評注. Wang Ch'i-hsing 王啟興 and Mao Chih-chung 毛治中, eds. Hupei: Hu-pei Jen-min, 1984. Contains the original preface by Sun Chu 孫洙 (1711-1778).

Translations

T'ang-shih san-pai-shou ch'üan-i 唐詩三百首全譯. Sha Ling-na 沙靈娜, trans., Ho Nien 何年, comm. and Ch'en Ching-jung 陳敬容, ed. Kweiyang: Kuei-chou Jen-min, 1989. *Chung-kuo li-tai ming-chu ch'üan-i ts'ung-shu.* Contains the original preface by Sun Chu 孫洙.

Studies

Tabei, Fumio 田部井文雄. *Tôshi sanbyaku shu shôkai* 唐詩三百首詳解. 2v. Tokyo: Taishûkan Shoten, 1980; 1988.

T'ang ts'ai-tzu chuan 唐才子傳 (Biographies of T'ang Geniuses)

Editions and References

Chou, Pen-ch'un 周本淳, ed. *T'ang ts'ai-tzu chuan chiao-cheng* 唐才子傳校正. Nanking: Chiang-su Ku-chi, 1987. Includes an index.

Fu, Hsüan-ts'ung 傅璇琮, ed. *T'ang ts'ai-tzu chuan chiao-chien* 唐才子傳校箋. V. 5. Peking: Chung-hua, 1995. The fifth volume continues the superb annotation of the first four.

Sun, Yang-lu 孫映逵, ed. *T'ang ts'ai-tzu chuan chiao-chu* 唐才子傳校注. Peking: Chung-kuo She-hui K'o-hsüeh, 1991.

Translations

Li, Li-p'u 李立樸, ed. *T'ang ts'ai-tzu chuan ch'üan-i* 唐才子傳全譯. Kweiyang: Kuei-chou Jen-min, 1990, 1997. Chung-kuo li-tai ming-chu ch'üan-i ts'ung-shu.

T'ang-wen ts'ui 唐文粹 (*ca.* 1011)

Translations

T'ang-wen ts'ui hsüan-i 唐文粹選譯. Chang Hung-sheng 張宏生, trans. and comm. Chengtu: Pa-Shu Shu-she, 1991. Reprinted in Taiwan as *T'ang-wen ts'ui* 唐文粹. Taipei: Chin-hsiu, 1993. *Chung-kuo ming-chu hsüan-i ts'ung-shu,* 65.

T'ang Yin 唐寅 (1470-1524)

Editions and References

Tô Hakuko shû 唐伯虎集. 3v. Tokyo: Kôkyû Shûhô, 1993. Reproduction of a 1612 edition compiled by Shen Ssu 沈思 and which is held in Japan.

T'ang Po-hu shu-fa hsüan 唐伯虎書法選. Hsiao Lan 肖嵐, *et al.*, eds. Shenchün: Hai-t'ien, 1992. *Chung-kuo li-tai shu-fa ming-tso hsi-lieh ts'ung-shu.*

T'ang Ying 唐英 (1682-1755)

Editions and References

T'ang Ying chi 唐英集. 2v. Shenyang: Liao-Shen Shu-she, 1991.

Studies

Chou, Yü-te 周育德, ed. *Ku-pai-t'ang hsi-ch'ü chi* 古柏堂戲曲集. Shanghai: Shang-hai Ku-chi, 1987. A punctuated version of this collection followed by a number of materials for the study of T'ang Ying's life and writings.

Tao-tsang 道藏 (Taoist Canon)

Editions and References

Ch'in-ting Tao-tsang ch'üan-shu tsung-mu 欽定道藏全書總目. Ho Lung-hsiang 賀龍驤, recorder and P'eng Han-jan 彭瀚然, ed. Chengtu: Pa-Shu Shu-she, 1992. *Tsang-wai tao-shu,* 24.

San-tung feng-tao liao-chieh i-fan 三洞奉道料戒儀範. Chengtu: Pa-Shu Shu-she, 1992. *Tsang-wai tao-shu,* 21.

Tao-tsang ch'i-kung yao-chi 道藏氣功要集. Hung P'i-mo 洪丕謨, ed. 2v. Shanghai: Shang-hai Shu-tien, 1995.

Tao-tsang chi-yao 道藏輯要. P'eng Wen-jui 彭文瑞 (1731–1803), ed. 25v. Taipei: K'ao-cheng, 1971.

Tao-tsang chi-yao mu-lu 道藏輯要目錄. Chiang Yüan-t'ing 蔣元庭 (Ch'ing dynasty), ed. Hangchow: Che-chiang Ku-chi, 1989.

Tao-tsang chi-yao shu-mu tsung-lu 道藏輯要書目總錄. Hu Tao-ching 胡道靜, *et al.*, eds. Chengtu: Pa-Shu Shu-she, 1992. Tsang-wai tao-shu, 36.

Tao-tsang ching-hua 道藏精華. Hu Tao-ching 胡道靜, *et al.*, eds. 4v. Changsha: Yüeh-lu Shu-she, 1993.

Tao-tsang ching-hua lu 道藏精華錄. Shou I-tzu 守一子, ed. 2v. Hangchow: Che-chiang Ku-chi, 1989

Tao-tsang mu-lu hsiang-chu 道藏目錄詳註. Pai Yün-chi 白雲霽 (Ming dynasty), comm. 4 *chüan.* Taipei: Hsin-wen-feng, 1988.

Tao-tsang tan-yao i-ming so-yin 道藏丹藥異名索引. Huang Chao-han黃兆漢, ed. Taipei: Tai-wan Hsüeh-sheng Shu-chü, 1989. *Tao-chiao yen-chiu ts'ung-shu.*

*Tao-tsang t'i-yao*道藏提要. Jen Chi-yü 任繼愈, *et al.*, eds. Peking: Chung-kuo She-hui K'o-hsüeh, 1991. Based on the 1926 edition.

Tao-tsang tzu-mu yin-te, Fo-tsang tzu-mu yin-te 道藏子目引得，佛藏子目引得. Hung Yeh 洪業, *et al.*, eds. Shanghai: Shang-hai Ku-chi 1986. The *Tao-tsang* indexes were published in Peking in 1935 and in 1966 in Taipei by Ch'eng-wen Ch'u-pan-she as index no. 25 in the *Harvard-Yenching Institute Sinological Index Series.*

Tao-tsang yao-chi hsüan-k'an 道藏要籍選刊. Hu Tao-ching 胡道靜, *et al.*, eds. 10v. Shanghai: Shang-hai Ku-chi, 1989. Based on the 1926 edition.

Yin Wen-tzu 尹文子. In 2 *chüan.* Shanghai: Shang-hai Ku-chi, 1989. *Tao-tsang yao-chi hsüan-k'an,* 5. Based on the 1926 edition.

Yün-chi ch'i-ch'ien 雲笈七籤. In 122 *chüan.* Shanghai: Shang-hai Ku-chi, 1989. *Tao-tsang yao-chi hsüan-k'an,* 1. Based on the 1926 edition.

Translations
Sugimoto, Takushû 杉本卓洲, trans. and annot. *Shin kokuyaku Daizôkyô–Hon'en bu 2* 新国訳 大蔵経–本縁部 2. Tokyo: Daizô Shuppan, 1994.

Studies
Chu, Yüeh-li. *Tao-tsang fen-lei chieh-t'i* 道藏分類解題. Peking: Hua-hsia, 1995.

Ch'ü, Chi-kao 曲繼皋. *Tao-tsang k'ao-lüeh* 道藏考略. Shanghai: Shang-hai Ku-chi, 1989. *Tao-tsang yao-chi hsüan-k'an,* 10.4.

Hu, Fu-ch'en 胡孚琛 and Fang Kuang-ch'ang 方廣錩. *Tao-tsang yü Fo-tsang* 道藏與佛藏. Taipei: Hsin-hua, 1993. *Shen-chou wen-hua chi-ch'eng ts'ung-shu.*

T'ao Ch'ien 陶潛 (365-427)

Editions and References
Kung, Pin 龔斌, comm. *T'ao Yüan-ming chi chiao-chien* 陶淵明集校箋. Shanghai: Shang-hai Ku-chi, 1997. Excellent annotation.

Li, Kung-huan 李公煥. *Chien-chu T'ao Yüan-ming chi* 箋注陶淵明集. Taipei: Kuo-li Chung-yang T'u-shu-kuan, 1991.

Lu, Ch'in-li 逯欽立. *T'ao Yüan-ming chi* 陶淵明集. Peking: Chung-hua, 1979. Remains the standard critical edition.

Meng, Erh-tung 孟二冬, ed. *T'ao Yüan-ming chi shih-chu*陶淵明集譯注. Tsilin: Chi-lin Wen-shih, 1997.

Wei, Cheng-chung 魏正中, ed. *T'ao Yüan-ming chi chiao-chu* 陶淵明集校注. Peking: Wen-chin, 1994.

Base editions include *Ching-chieh Hsien-sheng chi* 靖節先生集. T'ao Shu 陶澍 (1779-1839), commentator. Wei Huan-hsün 威煥塤, editor. Peking: Wen-hsüeh Ku-chi K'an-hang-she 文學古藉刊行涉, 1956. This is similar to the *SPPY* edition. *SPTK* has Li Kung-huan 李公煥 as commentator. Wang Yao 王瑤 is another important commentator (of *T'ao Yüan-ming chi* 陶淵明集). There is also a recent reprint, *Chien-chu T'ao Yüan-ming chi*箋注陶淵明集. Taipei: Chung-yang T'u-shu-kuan, 1991. This is a reprint of a Southern Sung edition.

Translations

Davis and Hightower remain the standards (see *Companion* v. 1 entry).

Jacob, Paul. *Œuvres complètes de Tao Yuan-ming.* Paris: Gallimard, 1990. Carefully annotated versions–arranged in chronological order–following an extensive, interesting introduction.

Kuo, Wei-sen 郭維森, *et al. T'ao Yüan-ming chi ch'üan-i* 陶淵明集全譯. Kweiyang: Kuei-chou Jen-min, 1992.

Matsueda, Shigeo 松枝茂夫, *et al. Tô Emmei zenshû* 陶淵明全集. 2v. Tokyo: Iwanami Shoten, 1990.

Pohl, Karl-Heinz. *Der Pfirsichblütenquell, Gesammelte Gedichte.* Cologne: Diederichs, 1985. *Deiderichs Gelbe Reihe,* 58. A complete, lightly annotated translation of the *shih* and *fu* following a general introduction.

Suzuki, Toraô 鈴木虎雄. *Tô Emmei shikai* 陶淵明詩解. Tokyo: Heibonsha, 1991.

Tan, Shilin [T'an, Shih-lin] 譚時霖. *The Complete Works of Tao Yuanming.* Hong Kong: Joint Publishing, 1992; Taipei: Shu-lin, 1993. A bilingual edition with annotation by a professor at Jinan University. Quality to be probed.

Wei, Cheng-shen 魏正申. *T'ao Yüan-ming chi i-chu* 陶淵明集譯注. Taipei: Wen-chin, 1994.

Studies

Bokenkamp, Stephen R. "The Peach Flower Font and the Grotto Passage." *JAOS* 106 (1986): 65-77.

Chan, Wing-ming. "T'ao Ch'ien on Life and Death: The Concept of *Tzu-jan* in His Poetry." Unpublished Ph. D. dissertation, University of Wisconsin, 1981.

Chang, Kang-i Sun. "T'ao Ch'ien: Defining the Lyric Voice." In *Six Dynasties Poetry.* Princeton: Princeton University Press, 1986, pp. 3–46. See also the important review by Donald Holzman in *HJAS* 48 (1988): 244–49.

Ch'en, Chün-shan 陳俊山. *T'ao Yüan-ming* 陶淵明. Hanchang: Pai-hua-chou Wen-i, 1994.

Ch'en, I-liang 陳怡良. *T'ao Yüan-ming chih jen-p'in yü shih-pin* 陶淵明之人品與詩品. Taipei: Wen-chin, 1993.

Ching, Shu-hui 景蜀慧. *Wei Chin shih-jen yü cheng-chih* 魏晉詩人與政治. Taipei: Wen-chin, 1991. *Ta-lu ti-ch'ü po-shih lun-wen ts'ung-k'an,* 12. This dissertation, done at Szechwan University under Miao Yüeh 繆鉞, focuses on Ts'ao Chih, Juan Chi, Hsi K'ang and T'ao Ch'ien.

Chung, Yu-min 鍾优民. *T'ao Yüan-ming lun-chi* 陶淵明論集. Changsha: Hu-nan Jen-min, 1982.

Frankel, Hans H. Review of *The Poetry of T'ao Ch'ien* by James R. Hightower. *HJAS* 31 (1971): 313-19.

Hasegawa, Shigenari 長谷川滋成. *Tô Emmei no seishin seikatsu* 陶淵明の精神生活. Tokyo: Kyûko Shoin, 1995.

Ho, P'ei-hsiung 何沛雄. "Ying-i T'ao Yüan-ming chi p'ing-chieh" 英譯陶淵明集評介. *Shu-mu chi-k'an* 19.4 (1986): 176-184.

Hsieh, Hsien-chün 謝先俊, *et al. T'ao Yüan-ming shih-wen hsüan-i* 陶淵明詩文選譯. Chengtu: Pa-Shu Shu-she, 1990.

Hsü, I-min 許逸民, ed. *T'ao Yüan-min nien-p'u* 陶淵明年譜. Originally compiled by Wang Chih 王質, *et al.* (1127–1189). Peking: Chung-hua, 1986.

Ikkai, Tomoyoshi 一海知義 and Iriya Yoshitaka 入谷義高. *Tô Emmei, Kanzan* 陶淵明・寒山. Tokyo: Iwanami Shoten, 1984. *Shinshû Chûgoku shijin senshû,* 1.

Inoue, Kazuyuki 井上一之. "Tô Emmei shigenshi kô-Tôshi no gikoshû ni soku shite" 陶淵明四言詩考一陶詩の擬古性に即して. *Chûgoku shibun ronsô* 8 (1989): 25-47.

Ishikawa, Tadahisa 石川忠久. *Tô Emmei to sono jidai* 陶淵明とその時代. Tokyo: Kembon

Shuppan, 1994.

Itô, Naoya 伊藤直哉. "Goryû sensei den shiron–Kôshi no keishô shisô Yô Yû no ei" 五柳先生伝試論―高士の形象思想楊雄の影. *Shibun* 98 (1989): 95-105.

Ku, Yün-i 谷雲義. *T'ao Yüan-ming* 陶淵明. Harbin: Hei-lung-chiang Jen-min, 1983.

Kurz, Elisabeth. "Spurensuche–Tao Yuanmings 'Aufzeichnung vom Pfirsichblütenquell' als Klage des skeptischen Visionärs." *AS* 47.3 (1993): 453-488.

Kwong, Charles Yim-tze. "The Rural World of Chinese 'Farmstead Poetry' (*Tianyuan Shi*): How Far Is It Pastoral?" *CLEAR* 15 (1993): 57-84.

___. *Tao Qian and the Chinese Poetic Tradition, The Quest for Cultural Identity*. Ann Arbor: Center for Chinese Studies, University of Michigan, 1994. *Michigan Monographs in Chinese Studies,* 66. Chapters on the backgrounds to T'ao's age and Tao's poetic art.

Li, Chen-tung 李震冬. *T'ao Yüan-ming p'ing-lun* 陶淵明評論. Taipei: Tung-ta T'u-shu, 1984. Contains a chronology of T'ao's works; but the reliability of some of Li's work has been called into question.

Li, Hua 李華. *T'ao Yüan-ming hsin-lun* 陶淵明新論. Peking: Pei-ching Shih-fan Hsüeh-yüan, 1992.

___, ed. *T'ao Yüan-ming shih-wen shang-hsi chi* 陶淵明詩文賞析集. Chengtu: Pa-Shu Shu-she, 1988.

Li, Wen-ch'u 李文初. *T'ao Yüan-ming lun-lüeh* 陶淵明論略. Canton: Kuang-tung Jen-min, 1986.

Liu, Chi-ts'ai 劉繼才 and Min Chen-kuei 閔振貴, eds. *T'ao Yüan-ming shih-wen i-shih* 陶淵明詩文譯釋. Harbin: Hei-lung-chiang Jen-min, 1986.

Liu, I-sheng 劉逸生, ed. and Hsü Wei 余巍, annot. *T'ao Yüan-ming shih-hsüan* 陶淵明詩選. Canton: Kuang-tung Jen-min, 1984.

Lu, Ch'in-li 逯欽立. Han Wei Liu-ch'ao wen-hsüeh lun-chi 漢魏六朝文學論集. Wu Yün 吳雲, ed. Sian: Shan-hsi Jen-min, 1984. The second section of this posthumously edited and published work is devoted to T'ao Ch'ien and his poetry.

Matsuoka, Eiji 松岡栄志. "'Tô Enmei shû' hanpon shôshiki–Sô hon sanshu" 『陶淵明集』版本小識―宋本三種. *Kanbun Kyôshitsu* 173, 1992.

___. "Zoku 'Tô Enmei shû' hanpon shôshiki–Sô, Gen ban nishu" 続 『陶淵明集』版本小識―宋・元版二種. *Kanbun Kyôshitsu* 173, 1992.

Meng, Mong. "Configuration of a Lyrical World: A Study of T'ao Yüan-ming's Poetics from a Cultural Perspective." Unpublished Ph.D. dissertation, Rutgers University, 1990.

Mori, Hiroyuki 森博行. "Tô Emmei 'Tôkagen shi heiki' sono go" 陶淵明 「桃花源詩并記」 その後, *Osaka Geijutsu Daigaku Kiyô–Geijutsu* 13, 1990.

Minami, Fumikazu 南史一. *Shiden Tô Emmei–Kaerinan iza* 詩伝陶淵明―帰りなんいざ. Osaka: Sôgensha, 1984.

Obi, Kôichi 小尾郊一. *Chûgoku no inton shisô–Tô Emmei no kokoro no kiseki* 中国の隠遁思想―陶淵明の心の軌跡. Tokyo: Chûô Kôronsha, 1988.

Owen, Stephen. "The Self's Perfect Mirror: Poetry as Autobiography." In Shuen-fu Lin and Stephen Owen, eds. *The Vitality of the Lyric Voice*. Princeton: Princeton University Press, 1986, pp. 71-102.

Rohrer, Maria. *Das Motiv der Wolke in der Dichtung Tao Yuanmings.* V. 2. Freiburger Fernöstliche Forschungen, Wiesbaden: Harrassowitz, 1992.

Shen, Chen-ch'i 沈振奇. *T'ao Hsieh shih chih pi-chiao* 陶謝詩之比較. Taipei: Hsüeh-sheng, 1985. An introduction followed by chapters comparing their lives and then their works.

Sun, Chün-hsi 孫鈞錫. *T'ao Yüan-ming chi chiao-chu* 陶淵明集校注. Chengchow: Chung-chou Ku-chi, 1986.

T'ang, Man-hsien 唐滿先, ed. *T'ao Yüan-ming chi ch'ien-chu* 陶淵明集淺注. Nanchang: Chiang-hsi Jen-min, 1985.

Teng, An-sheng 鄧安生. *T'ao Yüan-ming hsin-t'an* 陶淵明新探. Taipei: Wen-chin, 1995.

___. *T'ao Yüan-ming nien-p'u* 陶淵明年譜. Tientsin: T'ien-chin Ku-chi, 1991.

Tseng, Chen-chen. "Mythopoesis Historicized: Qu Yuan's Poetry and Its Legacy." Unpublished Ph.D. dissertation, University of Washington, 1992.

Tsuru, Haruo 都留春雄, *et al*... *Tô Emmei* 陶淵明. Tokyo: Kadokawa Shoten, 1988. *Kanshô Chûgoku no koten,* 13.

Ueda, Takeshi 上田武. *Ryô Chûan: Tô Emmei den–Chûgoku ni okeru sono ningenzô no keisei katei* 廖仲安：陶淵明伝–中国におけるその人間像の形成過程. Tokyo: Kyûko Shoin, 1987.

___. "Tô Enmei ni okeru hinkyû no imi" 陶淵明における貧窮の意味. *Chûgoku bunka* 中国文化 50 (1995). Argues that T'ao Ch'ien's "poverty" was spiritual (caused by his isolation), not economic.

Wang, Meng-po 王孟白, ed. *T'ao Yüan-ming shih-wen chiao-chien* 陶淵明詩文校箋. Harbin: Hei-lung-chiang Jen-min, 1985.

Wang, Shu-min 王叔岷, comm. *T'ao Yüan-ming shih-chien cheng-kao* 陶淵明詩箋證稿. Taipei: I-wen Yin-shu-kuan, 1975. An interesting and important commentary.

Wei, Cheng-shen 魏正申. *T'ao Yüan-ming p'ing-chuan* 陶淵明評傳. Peking: Wen-chin, 1996.

Yüan, Hsing-p'ei 袁行霈. *T'ao Yüan-ming yen-chiu* 陶淵明研究. Peking: Pei-ching Ta-hsüeh, 1997.

Yoshikawa, Kojirô 吉川古次郎. *Tô Emmei den* 陶淵明伝. Tokyo: Shinchôsha, 1974. An important study.

Ti-fang hsi 地方戲 (regional drama)

Studies

Kwong, H. F. "L'évolution du théâtre populaire depuis les Ming jusqu'à nos jours: le cas de Wang Zhaojun." *TP* 77 (1991): 179-225.

Tanaka, Issei. "The Social and Historical Context for Ming-Ch'ing Local Drama." In Andrew J. Nathan, David Johnson and Evelyn S. Rawski, eds. *Popular Culture in Late Imperial China.* Berkeley: University of California Press, 1985, pp. 143-160.

Yung, Bell. *Cantonese Opera, Performance as Creative Process.* Cambridge: Cambridge University Press, 1989.

Tsa-chü 雜劇

Editions and References

Chao, Ching-shen 趙景深 and Shao Tseng-ch'i 邵曾祺, eds. *Yüan Ming pei tsa-chü tsung-mu k'ao-lüeh* 元明北雜劇總目考略. Chengchow: Chung-chou Ku-chi, 1985. Introductions to 112 Yüan and early Ming authors and all anonymous *tsa-chü* prior to the *Chia-ching* era.

Chuang, I-fu 莊一拂. *Ku-tien hsi-ch'ü ts'ung-mu hui-k'ao* 古典戲曲存目彙考. 3v. Shanghai: Shang-hai Ku-chi, 1982. Annotated list of nearly 2000 existing *tsa-chü* and 2600 *ch'uan-ch'i* providing information on authorship, plots, texts, etc.; several indexes.

Ho, Hsin-hui 賀新輝, ed. *Yüan-ch'ü chien-shang tz'u-tien* 元曲鑑賞辭典. Peking: Chung-kuo Fu-nü, 1988. Close readings of 800 *tsa-chü* and *san-ch'ü* of the Yüan.

Ho, Kuei-ch'u 何貴初, comp. *Yüan-ch'ü ssu-ta-chia lun-chu so-yin* 元曲四大家論著索引. Hong Kong: Yü-ching Shu-hui, 1996.

Hsü, Ch'in-chün 徐沁君, ed. and comm. *Hsin-chiao Yüan-k'an tsa-chü san-shih chung* 新校元刊

雜劇三十種. Peking: Chung-hua, 1980.

Jen-min Wen-hsüeh Ch'u-pan she, 人民文學出版社 ed. *Yüan tsa-chü chien-shang chi* 元雜劇鑑賞集. Peking: Jen-min wen-hsüeh, 1983. Chung-kuo ku-tien wen-hsüeh chien-shang ts'ung-k'an, 6.

Li, Hsiu-sheng 李修生, ed. *Yüan-ch'ü ta-tz'u-tien* 元曲大辭典. Nanking: Chiang-su Chiao-yü, 1995.

Li, Wen-ch'i 黎文琦, ed. *Yüan tsa-chü shang-hsi* 元雜劇賞析. Lanchow: Kan-su Jen-min, 1988. Readings of 12 plays or scenes from plays by 10 dramatists.

Ning, Hsi-yüan 寧希元, ed. *Yüan-k'an tsa-chü san-shih-chung hsin-chiao* 元刊雜劇三十種新校. Lanchow: Lan-chou Ta-hsüeh, 1988. Based on the *Yüan-k'an tsa-chü san-shih-chung* edition, plot summaries and reference materials are provided for each of these classical dramas.

P'u, Chien 卜鍵, ed. *Yüan-ch'ü pai-k'o ta-tz'u-tien* 元曲百科大辭典. Peking: Hsüeh-yüan, 1991.

Wang, Chih-wu 王志武, ed. *Ku-tai hsi-ch'ü shang-hsi tz'u-tien (Yüan-ch'ü chüan)* 古代戲曲賞析辭典（元曲卷）. Sian: Shan-hsi Jen-min, 1988. Literary close readings of 117 dramas by 51 Yüan authors, 5 from later periods, and 45 anonymous Yüan plays.

Wang, Yung-k'uan 王永寬. *Ch'ing-tai tsa-chü hsüan* 清代雜劇選. Chengchow: Chung-chou Ku-chi, 1991.

Yüan, Shih-shuo 袁世碩, ed. *Yüan-ch'ü pai-ko tz'u-tien.* 元曲百歌辭典 Tsinan: Shan-tung Chiao-yü, 1989. Over 2100 entries on various aspects of Yüan *tsa-chü* and *san-ch'ü*.

Translations

Coyaud, Maurice. *Les operas des bords de l'eau (theatre Yuan).* Paris: Pour l'Analyse du Folklore, 1983.

Studies

Abe, Yasuki 阿部泰記." Koshi *Ryû Kôan zenden* sanbu saku no hensan" 鼓詞＜劉公案全伝＞三部作の編纂. *Chûgoku Bungaku Ronshû* 21, 1992.

Akamatsu, Norihiko 赤松紀彦. "'Genkyokusen' ga mezashitan mono" 『元曲選』がめざしたもの. *Chûgoku Koten gikyoku ronshû*, 1991.

Besio, Kimberly Ann. "The Disposition of Defiance: Zhang Fei as a Comic Hero of Yuan *Zaju.* "Unpublished Ph.D. dissertation, University of California, Berkeley, 1992.

Chang, Shu-hsiang 張淑香. *Yüan tsa-chü chung te ai-ch'ing yü she-hui* 元雜劇中的愛情與社會. Taipei: Ch'ang-an, 1980.

Chang, Yen-chin 張燕瑾. *Chung-kuo hsi-ch'ü shih lun-chi* 中國戲曲史論集. Peking: Yen-shan, 1996.

Ch'ang, Chen-kuo 常振國 and Chiang Yün 降雲, eds. *Yüan tsa-chü fa-chan shih* 元雜劇發展史. Taipei: Li-ming, 1995.

Ch'en, Fang 陳芳. *Ch'ing-ch'u tsa-chü yen-chi* 清初雜劇研究. Taipei: Hsüeh-hai, 1991.

Chi Kuo-p'ing 季國平. *Yüan tsa-chü fa-chan shih* 元雜劇發展史. Taipei: Wen-chin, 1993. Ta-lu ti-ch'u po-shih lun-wen ts'ung-k'an, 37. Reprint of a Ph.D dissertation done at Yang-chou Shih-fan Hsüeh-yüan in 1991.

Dolby, William. "Some Mysteries and Mootings about the Yuan Variety Play." *Asian Theatre Journal* 11 1994.1: 81-89.

Hsü, Chin-pang 許金榜. *Chung-kuo hsi-ch'ü wen-hsüeh-shih* 中國戲曲文學史. Peking: Chung-kuo Wen-hsüeh, 1994. A survey from the Ch'in to the Ch'ing dynasties.

___. *Yüan tsa-chü kai-lun* 元雜劇概論. Tsinan: Ch'i-Lu Shu-she, 1986. Emphasizing the thought and artistry of the genre.

Huang, Hui 黃卉. *Yüan-tai hsi-ch'ü shih-kao* 元代戲劇史稿. Tientsin: T'ien-chin Ku-chi, 1995.

Huang, Shih-chi 黃士吉. *Yüan tsa-chü tso-fa lun* 元雜劇作法論. Hsining: Ch'ing-hai Jen-min,

1983. Diverse studies (14) of the genre; bibliography appended.

Idema, W. L. "Emulation through Readaptation in Yüan and Early Ming *Tsa-chü*." *AM, TS* 3 (1990): 113-28.

___. "*Yüan-pen* as a Minor Form of Dramatic Literature in the Fifteenth and Sixteenth Centuries." *CLEAR* 6 (1984): 20-42.

___. "The Tsa-jiu of Yang Tz: An International Tycoon in Defense of Collaboration." In *Proceedings of the Second International Conference on Sinology.* Taipei: Academia Sinica, 1989, pp. 523-48.

___. "Why You Never Have Read a Yuan Drama: The Transformation of *Zaju* at the Ming Court." In *Studi in onore di Lanciello Lanciotti.* S. M. Carletti, M. Sacchetti and P. Santangelo, eds. Naples: Instituo Universiatorio Orientale, Dipartimento di Studi Asiatici, 1996, pp. 765-91.

Inoue, Taizan 井上泰山. "Genkyoku kankei gosho goshaku sakuin" 元曲関係五書語釈索引 *Kansai Daigaku chûgoku bungakkai kiyô* 10 (1989): 60-117.

Li, Ch'un-hsiang 李春祥. *Yüan tsa-chü lun-kao* 元雜劇論稿. Kaifeng: Ho-nan Ta-hsüeh, 1988.

___. *Yüan tsa-chü shih-kao* 元雜劇史稿. Kaifeng: Ho-nan Ta-hsüeh, 1989

Li, Hsiu-sheng 李修生. *Yüan tsa-chü shih* 元雜劇史. Nanking: Chiang-su Ku-chi, 1997.

___, Li Chen-yü 李真渝 and Hou Kuang-fu 侯光復, eds. *Yüan tsa-chü lun-chi* 元雜劇論集. 2v. Tientsin: Pai-hua Wen-i, 1985. About 40 articles equally divided between general studies of the genre, Kuan Han-ch'ing, Wang Shih-fu, and other dramatists; bibliographies appended.

Liang, Shu-an 梁淑安 and Yao K'o-fu 姚柯夫. *Chung-kuo chin-tai ch'uan-ch'i tsa-chü ching-yen-lu* 中國近代傳奇雜劇經眼錄. Peking: Shu-mu Wen-hsien, 1996.

Ling, Chia-wei 凌嘉爵. *Yüan tsa-chü ku-shih chi* 元雜劇故事集. Nanking: Chiang-su Jen-min, 1983.

Liu, Yin-pai 劉蔭柏. *Yüan-tai tsa-chü shih* 元代雜劇史. Shih-chia-chuang: Hua-shan Wen-i, 1990.

Lo, Wai Luk. "The Tragic Dimensons of Traditional Chinese Drama: A Study of the Yuan *zaju.*" Unpublished Ph.D. dissertation, City University of New York, 1994.

Lu, Tan-an 陸澹安, ed. *Hsi-ch'ü tz'u-yü hui-shih* 戲曲詞語匯釋. Shanghai: Shang-hai Ku-chi, 1981. Entries are drawn primarily from *Yüan-pen* and *Tsa-chü* with some from *Chu-kung-tiao;* no material from later drama is included.

Men, K'uei 門巋. "Yüan-ch'ü chia erh-shih-jen tzu-liao tien-ti" 元曲家二十人資料點滴. *Wen-hsüeh i-ch'an* 1985.1 (1985): 144–48.

Ning, Tsung-i 寧宗一, *et al*, eds. *Yüan tsa-chü yen-chiu kai-shu* 元雜劇研究概述. Tientsin: T'ien-chin Chiao-yü, 1987.

Pien-chi-pu, Jen-min Wen-hsüeh Ch'u-pan-she, ed. *Yüan tsa-chü chien-shang chi* 元雜劇鑑賞集. Peking: Jen-min Wen-hsüeh, 1983. Close readings of 20 *tsa-chü.*

Shang, T'ao 商韜. *Lun Yüan-tai tsa-chü* 論元代雜劇. Tsinan: Ch'i-Lu Shu-she, 1986.

Shih, Kuang-sheng. "Ritualistic Aspects of Yüan *Tsa-chü* Theater." Unpublished Ph.D. dissertation, University of California, Los Angeles, 1992.

"Symposium: What More Do We Need to Know about Chinese Theatre?" *Asian Theatre Journal* 11 (1994): 81-118. Contributions by William Dolby on *tsa-chü,* Elizabeth Wichmann on *ching-chü,* and Colin Mackerras on theater of the minority peoples.

Ts'ung, Ching-wen 叢靜文. *Yüan tsa-chü hsi-lun* 元雜劇析論. 2v. Taipei: Tai-wan Shang-wu Yin-shu-kuan, 1987.

Wang, Kuo-wei 王國維. "Yüan-k'an tsa-chü san-shih-chung hsü-lu" 元刊雜劇三十種敘錄." In *Wang Kuo-wei hsi-ch'ü lun-wen chi* 王國維戲曲論文集. Peking: Chung-kuo Hsi-chü, 1984.

Wang, Linda Greenhouse. "A Study of Ma Chih-yüan's San-ch'ü and Tsa-chü Lyrics." Unpublished Ph. D. dissertation, University of California, Berkeley, 1992.

Wang, Shou-chih 王壽之. *Yüan tsa-chü hsi-chü i-shu* 元雜喜劇藝術. Hofei: An-hui Wen-i, 1985. An-hui hsi-chü li-lun ts'ung-shu.

Yen, T'ien-yu 嚴天佑. *Yüan tsa-chü pa lun* 元雜劇八論. Taipei: Wen-shih-che, 1996.

___. *Yüan tsa-chü so fan-yang chih Yüan-tai she-hui* 元雜劇所反映之元代社會. Taipei: Hua-cheng Shu-chü, 1984.

Ts'ai-tzu chia-jen hsiao-shuo 才子佳人小説 (scholar and beauty novels)

Editions and References

Ching-hu I-sou 鏡湖逸叟. *Li I-hsüeh yüeh-mei chuan* 李義雪月梅傳. Peking: Pei-ching Shih-fan Ta-hsüeh, 1993. Pei-ching Shih-fan Ta-hsüeh t'u-shu-kuan kuan-tsang ts'ai-tzu chia-jen hsiao-shuo hsüan-k'an.

Hsi-yang t'ang chu-jen 惜陽堂主人. *Erh-tu mei* 二度梅. Peking: Pei-ching Shih-fan Ta-hsüeh, 1993. Pei-ching Shih-fan Ta-hsüeh t'u-shu-kuan kuan-tsang ts'ai-tzu chia-jen hsiao-shuo hsüan-k'an.

Li-weng Hsien-sheng 笠翁先生. *Ho chin hui-wen chuan* 合錦回文傳. Peking: Pei-ching Shih-fan Ta-hsüeh, 1993. Pei-ching Shih-fan Ta-hsüeh t'u-shu-kuan kuan-tsang ts'ai-tzu chia-jen hsiao-shuo hsüan-k'an.

Lin, Ch'en 林辰 *et al.,* eds. *Ts'ai-tzu chia-jen hsiao-shuo chi-ch'eng* 才子佳人小説集成. 5v. Shenyang: Liao-ning Ku-chi, 1997. Contains 26 works in this genre.

Ming-chiao Chung-jen 名教中人. *Hao-ch'iu chuan* 好逑傳. Peking: Pei-ching Shih-fan Ta-hsüeh, 1993. Pei-ching Shih-fan Ta-hsüeh t'u-shu-kuan kuan-tsang ts'ai-tzu chia-jen hsiao-shuo hsüan-k'an.

Ti-an San-jen 荻岸散人, ed. *P'ing-shan leng-yen* 平山冷燕. Peking: Pei-ching Shih-fan Ta-hsüeh, 1993. Pei-ching Shih-fan Ta-hsüeh t'u-shu-kuan kuan-tsang ts'ai-tzu chia-jen hsiao-shuo hsüan-k'an.

Studies

Hu Wan-ch'uan 胡萬川. *Hua-pen yü ts'ai-tzu chia-jen hsiao-shuo chih yen-chiu* 話本與才子佳人小説之研究. Taipei: Ta-an, 1994.

Ts'ai Yen 蔡琰 (b. *ca.* 178)

Studies

Levy, Dore J. "Transforming Archetypes in Chinese Poetry and Painting: The Case of Ts'ai Yen." *AM, TS* 6 (2 1993): 147-68.

Ts'ang-lang shih-hua 滄浪詩話 (Poetry Talks)

Editions and References

Ch'en, Ting-yü 陳定玉. *Yen Yü chi* 嚴羽集. Chengchow: Chung-chou Ku-chi, 1997.

Kuo, Shao-yü 郭紹虞, ed. *Ts'ang-lang shih-hua chiao-shih* 滄浪詩話校釋. Peking: Jen-min Wen-hsüeh, 1983.

Studies

Chang, Chien 張健. "Ts'ang-lang shih-hua yen-chiu" 滄浪詩話研究. Unpublished M.A. thesis, National Taiwan University, 1965.

Chen, Ruey-shan Sandy. "An Annotated Translation of Yan Yu's 'Canglang shihua': An

Early Thirteenth Century Chinese Poetry Manual." Unpublished Ph.D. dissertation, University of Texas-Austin, 1996.

Ch'en, Pai-hai 陳伯海. *Yen Yü ho Ts'ang-lang shih-hua* 嚴羽和滄浪詩話. Taipei: San-min, 1993. Chung-kuo ku-tien wen-hsüeh chi-pen chih-shih ts'ung-shu, 52.

Hsü, Chih-kang 許志剛. *Yen Yü p'ing-chuan* 嚴羽評傳. Nanking: Nan-ching Ta-hsüeh, 1997.

Lynn, Richard John. "The Talent Learning Polarity in Chinese Poetics: Yan Yu and the Later Tradition." *CLEAR* 5 (1983): 157-84.

Wang, Shih-po 王士博. "Yen Yü te sheng-p'ing" 嚴羽的生平. *Wen-hsüeh i-ch'an* 1985.4 (1985): 82-86.

Ts'ao Chih 曹植 (192-232)

Editions and References

Chao, Yu-wen 趙幼文, comm. and ed. *Ts'ao Chih chi chiao-chu* 曹植集校注. Peking: Jen-min Wen-hsüeh, 1984.

Studies

Chang, K'o-li 張可禮. *San Ts'ao nien-p'u* 三曹年譜. Tsinan: Ch'i-Lu Shu-she, 1983.

Cheng, Yung-k'ang 鄭永康. *Wei Ts'ao Tzu-chien hsien-sheng Chih nien-p'u* 魏曹子建先生植年譜. Taipei: Tai-wan Shang-wu Yin-shu-kuan, 1981. Hsin-pien Chung-kuo ming-jen nien-p'u chi-ch'eng, 16.

Ching, Shu-hui 景蜀慧. *Wei Chin shih-jen yü cheng-chih* 魏晉詩人與政治. Taipei: Wen-chin, 1991. Ta-lu ti-ch'ü po-shih lun-wen ts'ung-k'an, 12. A reprint of a Ph.D. dissertation done under the guidance of Miao Yüeh 繆鉞 at Ssu-chuan Ta-hsüeh in 1991. Includes a section devoted to Ts'ao Chih.

Chung, Yu-min 種優民. *Ts'ao Chih hsin-t'an* 曹植新探. Hofei: Huang-shan Shu-she, 1984.

Connery, Christopher Leigh. "Jian'an Poetic Discourse." Unpublished Ph.D. dissertation, Princeton University, 1991.

Cutter, Robert Joe. "The Incident at the Gate: Cao Zhi, The Succession, and Literary Fame." *TP* 71 (1985): 228-62.

___. "On Reading Cao Zhi's 'Three Good Men': *Yongshi shi* or *Deng lin shi*." *CLEAR* 11 (1989): 1-11.

Holzman, Donald. "Ts'ao Chih and the Immortals." *AM, TS* 1 (1988): 15-57.

Nieh, Wen-yü 聶文郁. *Ts'ao Chih shih chieh-i* 曹植詩解譯. Hsining: Ching-hai Jen-min, 1985.

Yü, Te-mao 虞德懋. "Ts'ao Chih yü Juan Chi shih-ko i-yün pi-chiao" 曹植與阮藉詩歌意藴比較. *Yang-chou shih-yüan hsüeh-pao 81* (1990): 23–28.

Ts'ao Hsüeh-ch'in 曹雪芹 (*ca.* 1715-1763)

Editions and References

Cheng Chen-to tsang-ts'an pen Hung-lou meng 鄭振鐸藏殘本紅樓夢. Peking: Shu-mu Wen-hsien, 1991.

Chih-yen chai chuan pen Ts'ao Hsüeh-ch'in Shih-t'ou chi 脂硯齋傳本曹雪芹石頭記. Chu Yung-k'uei 朱詠葵, ed. 2v. Peking: Wen-chin, 1988.

Hung-lou meng 紅樓夢. Chang Chün 張俊, *et al.*, comms. 4v. Peking: Pei-ching Shih-fan Ta-hsüeh, 1987. Includes the notes by Ch'i-kung 啟功.

___. Jao Pin 饒彬, ed. Taipei: San-min, 1990.

Shu Yüan-wei hsü pen Hung-lou meng 舒元煒序本紅樓夢. 2v. Peking: Chung-hua, 1987. Based on *Ch'ien-lung chien ch'ao Shu Yüan-wei hsü pen* 乾隆間鈔舒元煒序本 (Ch'ing) edition.

440

Studies

Chou, Ju-ch'ang 周汝昌. *Ts'ao Hsüeh-ch'in hsin-chuan* 曹雪芹新傳. Peking: Wai-wen, 1995.

Feng, Ch'i-yung 馮其庸. *Ts'ao Hsüeh-ch'in mu-shih lun-cheng chi* 曹雪芹墓石論爭集. Peking: Wen-hua I-shu, 1997.

Ts'ao P'i 曹丕 (187-226)

Editions and References

Chang, K'o-li 張可禮. *San Ts'ao nien-p'u* 三曹年譜. Tsinan: Ch'i-Lu Shu-she, 1983.

Cheng, Hsüeh-t'ao 鄭學弢, ed. *Lieh-i chuan teng wu-chung* 列異傳等五種. Peking: Wen-hua I-shu, 1988. *Li-tai pi-chi hsiao-shuo ts'ung-shu.*

Hsia, Ch'uan-ts'ai 夏傳才 and T'ang Shao-chung 唐紹忠, eds and comms. *Ts'ao P'i chi chiao-chu* 曹丕集校注. Chengchow: Chung-chou Ku-chi, 1997. A *nien-p'u* is appended.

Ts'en Shen 岑參 (715-770)

Editions and References

Ch'en, K'ang 陳抗 *et al.*, eds. *Ch'üan T'ang shih so-yin: Ts'en Shen ch'üan* 全唐詩索引：岑參卷. Peking: Chung-hua, 1992.

Kao, Kuang-fu 高光復, ed. *Kao Shih, Ts'en Shen shih i-shih* 高適岑參詩譯釋. Harbin: Hei-lung-chiang Jen-min, 1984.

Liu, K'ai-yang 劉開揚, ed. *Ts'en Shen shih hsüan* 岑參詩選. Chengtu: Ssu-ch'uan Jen-min, 1986.

Morino, Shigeo 森野繁夫 and Shinmen Keiko 新免惠子. *Shin Shin kashi sakuin* 參歌詩索引. Tyoto: Hôyû Shoten, 1987.

Studies

Ch'ai, Ying-hung 柴映虹. "Ts'en Shen pien-sai shih te i-shu feng-ko" 岑參邊塞詩的藝術風格. *Wen-hsüeh p'ing-lun ts'ung-k'an* 22 (1984): 103-20. Also in *T'ang-tai wen-hsüeh yen-chiu nien-chien, 1986* 唐代文學研究年鑑, 1986. Sian: Shan-hsi Jen-min, 1987, pp. 137-140.

Chou, Hsün-ch'u 周勛初 and Yao Sung 姚松. *Kao Shih ho Ts'en Shen* 高適和岑參. Shanghai: Shang-hai Ku-chi, 1991.

Ichikawa, Kiyoshi 市川清志. "Kennan jidai no Shin Shin" 劍南時代の岑參. *Nisho* 3 (1989): 245-79.

Liao, Li 廖立. "Ts'en shih hsi-cheng tui-hsiang chi ch'u-shih ti-tien tsai-t'an" 岑詩西征對象及出師地點再探. *Chung-chou hsüeh-k'an* 1992.2: 104-8.

Pien, Hsiao-hsüan 卞孝萱. "Kao Ts'en i-t'ung lun" 高岑異同論. *Wen-shih chi-lin* 1985.4 (1985): 151-73.

Sun, Ying-ta 孫映達. *Ts'en Shen shih chuan* 岑參詩傳. Chengchow: Chung-chou Ku-chi, 1989.

T'ao, Erh-fu 陶爾夫. "Ts'en Shen pien-sai-shih hsin-t'an" 岑參邊塞詩新探. *Wen-hsüeh p'ing-lun* 1987.3: 130-40.

Wang, Hsün-ch'eng 王勛成. "Ts'en Shen wan-ko k'ao" 岑參挽歌考. *Wen-hsüeh i-ch'an* 1990.2 (1990): 54-60.

Tseng Kung 曾鞏 (1019-1083)

Editions and References

Ch'üan Sung shih, 8:454-462.5513-5613.

Ch'üan Sung wen, 29:1231-1274.2-689.

Pao, Ching-ti 包敬第 and Ch'en Wen-hua 陳文華, eds. *Tseng Kung san-wen hsüan-chi* 曾鞏散文選集. Shanghai: Shang-hai Ku-chi, 1997.

Tseng Kung chi 曾鞏集. Ch'en Hsin-chen 陳杏珍 and Ch'ao Chi-chou 晁繼周, eds. Peking: Chung-hua, 1984. *Chung-kuo ku-tien wen-hsüeh chi-pen ts'ung-shu.*

Studies

Chiang-hsi Sheng Wen-hsüeh I-shu Yen-chiu So 江西省文學藝術研究所, ed. *Tseng Kung yen-chiu lun-wen chi* 曾鞏研究論文集. Nanchang: Chiang-hsi Jen-min, 1986. A collection of essays from a conference held in Chiang-hsi in December of 1983 commemorating the 900th anniversary of Tseng Kung's death.

Chou, Ming-ch'in 周明秦. *Sung Tseng Wen-ting kung Kung nien-p'u* 宋曾文定公鞏年表. Taipei: Tai-wan Shang-wu Yin-shu-kuan, 1981. *Hsin-pien Chung-kuo ming-jen nien-p'u chi-ch'eng,* 15.

Chu, Shang-shu 祝尚書 and Tseng Tsao-chuang 曾棗莊. *Tseng Kung shi-wen* 曾鞏詩文. Taipei: Chin-hsiu, 1993. *Chung-kuo ming-chu hsüan-i ts'ung-shu.*

Hsia, Han-ning 夏漢寧. *Tseng Kung* 曾鞏. Peking: Chung-hua, 1993. *Chung-kuo wen-hsüeh-shih chih-shih ts'ung-shu.*

Ma, Hsing-ying 馬興榮. "Lun Tseng Kung tz'u" 論曾鞏詞. *Fu-chou Shih-chuan hsüeh-pao* 1988.4 (1988).

Translations

Chu, Shang-shu 祝尚書. *Tseng Kung shih-wen hsüan-i* 曾鞏詩文選譯. Chengtu: Pa-Shu Shu-she, 1990. *Ku-tai wen-shih ming-chu hsüan-i ts'ung-shu.*

Tseng Kuo-fan 曾國藩 (1811-1872)

Editions and References

Chiang, Shih-jung 江世榮, ed. and comm. *Tseng Kuo-fan wei-k'an hsin-kao* 曾國藩未刊信稿. Peking: Chung-hua, 1959.

Tseng, Kuo-fan 曾國藩. *Shih-pa chia shih-ch'ao* 十八家詩鈔. Ch'en Ts'un-hui 陳存悔, *et al,* comms. Taipei: Kuang-wen Shu-chü, 1981.

___. *Tseng Kuo-fan chia-shu* 曾國藩家書. Chengchow: Chung-chou Ku-chi, 1994. Li-tai ming-jen chia-shu.

___. *Tseng Kuo-fan chiao-tzu shu* 曾國藩教子書. Hainan, 1994.

___. *Tseng Kuo-fan ch'üan-chi* 曾國藩全集. Changsha: Yüeh-lu Shu-she, 1985-1994. 30v. Ch'uan-chung Shu-chü 傳忠書局 edition.

___. *Tseng Kuo-fan ch'üan-chi: chia-shu* 曾國藩全集：家書. 2v. Teng Yün-sheng 鄧雲生, ed. and comm. Changsha: Yüeh-lu Shu-she, 1985.

___. *Tseng Kuo-fan ch'üan-chi: jih-chi* 曾國藩全集：日記. 3v. Hsiao Shou-ying 蕭守英 *et al,* comps. Changsha: Yüeh-lu Shu-she, 1987–89. Appends name and subject indexes.

___. *Tseng Kuo-fan ch'üan-chi: p'i-tu* 曾國藩全集：批牘. Li Lung-ju 李龍如, comp. Changsha: Yüeh-lu Shu-she, 1994.

___. *Tseng Kuo-fan ch'üan-chi:shih-wen* 曾國藩全集：詩文. P'eng Ching 彭靖, comp. Changsha: Yüeh-lu Shu-she, 1986.

___. *Tseng Kuo-fan ch'üan-chi: shu-hsin* 曾國藩全集：書信. 10v. Yin Shao-chi 殷紹基, comp. Changsha: Yüeh-lu Shu-she, 1990–94.

___. *Tseng Kuo-fan jih-chi* 曾國藩日記. 3v. Tientsin: T'ien-chin Jen-min, 1995.

___. *Tseng Kuo-fan wei-k'an wang-lai han-kao* 曾國藩未刊往來函稿. Chung-kuo she-hui k'o-hsüeh-yüan chin-tai shih yen-chiu-so tzu-liao shih 中國社會科學院近代史研究所資

料室, ed. Changsha: Yüeh-lu Shu-she, 1986. Hsiang-chün shih-liao ts'ung-shu.

Tseng Ku-fan sheng-p'ing chi chia-tsu ts'ung-shu 曾國藩生平及家族叢書. 5v. Shenyang: Liao-ning Ku-chi, 1997. Collects an assortment of Tseng's writings as well as critical studies of his life and works.

Translations

Mei, Chi 梅季. *Ching-shih pai-chia chien-pien* 經史百家簡編. Tseng Kuo-fan 曾國藩, ed. Nan-chou: Kuang-hsi Jen-min, 1988.

Tseng, Kuo-fan 曾國藩. *Tseng Kuo-fan chia-shu wen pai tui-chao ch'üan-i* 曾國藩家書文白對照全譯. 3v. Peking: Chung-kuo Hua-ch'iao, 1994.

Wang, Shu-lin 王樹林. *Ch'iu ch'üeh-chai sui-pi* 求闕齋隨筆. Chengchow: Chung-chou Ku-chi, 1994.

Studies

Ch'eng, Hsiao-chün 成曉軍. *Tseng Kuo-fan yü Chung-kuo chin-tai wen-hua* 曾國藩與中國近代文化. Changsha: Ho-nan Wen-i, 1991.

Chu, Ch'uan-yü 朱傳譽. *Tseng Kuo-fan chuan-chi tzu-liao* 曾國藩傳記資料. 11v. Taipei: T'ien-i, 1979-85.

Chu, Tung-an 朱東安. *Tseng Kuo-fan chuan* 曾國藩傳. Chengtu: Ssu-ch'uan Jen-min, 1985. Chung-kuo chin-tai shih chuan-t'i yen-chiu ts'ung-shu. Appends a bibliography and a *nien-piao*.

T'ang, Hao-ming 唐浩明. *Tseng Kuo-fan* 曾國藩. 3v. Changsha: Ho-nan Wen-i, 1994. Ch'ang-p'ien li-shih hsiao-shuo.

Wang, Chen-yüan 王鎮遠. "Lun Tseng Kuo-fan te wen-hsüeh ti-wei" 論曾國藩的文學地位. In *Chung-hua wen-shih lun-ts'ung* 中華文史論叢. Shanghai: Shang-hai Ku-chi, 1986.3, pp. 65-84.

Tseng P'u 曾樸 (1872-1935)

Translations

Bijou, Isabelle. *Fleur sur l'océan des péchés*. Paris, 1983.

Studies

Ch'eng, I-chi 成宜濟. *Nieh-hai hua yen-chiu* 孽海花研究. Taipei: Chia-hsin Shui-ni Kung-ssu Wen-hua Chi-chin Hui, 1969.

Hinz, Blanka. *Der Roman Eine Blume im Sündenmeer ("Nieh-hai hua") und sein Platz in der chinesischen Literatur*. Bochum: Brockmeyer, 1995.

Shih, Meng 時萌. *Tseng P'u yen-chiu* 曾樸研究. Shanghai: Shang-hai Ku-chi, 1982.

Tso chuan 左傳

Editions and References

Fang, Hsüan-ch'en 方炫琛. "*Tso chuan* jen-wu ming-hao yen-chiu" 左傳人物名號研究. Ph.D. dissertation, Cheng-chih University Taiwan, 1983.

Li, Tsung-t'ung 李宗侗, comm. *Ch'un-ch'iu Tso chuan chin-chu chin-i* 春秋左傳今註今譯. 3v. Taipei: Tai-wan Shang-wu Yin-shu-kuan, 1987.

Ogura, Yoshihiko 小倉芳彦. *Shunjû sashi den* 春秋左氏伝. 3v. Tokyo: Iwanami Shoten, 1988-89.

Shigezawa, Toshio, ed. *Tso chuan jen-ming ti-ming so-yin* 左傳人名地名索引. Taipei: Kuang-wen

Shu-chü, 1980.

Takezoe, Kôkô 竹添光鴻, comm. *Tso chuan hui-chien* 左傳會箋. Taipei: Ming-ta, 1986. Also includes the commentary of Tu Yü 杜預 (222–284).

Shen, Ch'in-han 沈欽韓 (1755–1831), comm. *Ch'un-ch'iu Tso-shih chuan ti-ming pu-chu* 春秋左氏傳地名補注. 2v. Peking: Chung-hua, 1985. *TSCC.*

Yang, Po-chün 楊伯峻, ed and comm. *Ch'un-ch'iu Tso chuan chu* 春秋左傳注. 4v. Peking: Chung-hua, 1982.

___ and Hsü T'i 徐提, eds. *Ch'un-ch'iu Tso chuan tz'u-tien* 春秋左傳詞典. Peking: Chung-hua, 1985.

Translations

Ch'ü, Hsüan-ying 瞿宣穎 trans. *Tso chuan hsüan-i* 左傳選譯. Shanghai: Shang-hai Ku-chi, 1982.

Feng, Tso-min 馮作民. *Pai-hua Tso chuan* 白話左傳. Changsha: Yüeh-lu Shu-she, 1989.

Shen, Yü-ch'eng 沈玉成, trans. *Tso chuan i-wen* 左傳譯文. Peking: Chung-hua, 1981. *Chung-kuo ku-tien ming-shu chu i chu ts'ung-shu.* Translation by the noted scholar and former student of Yang Po-chün who worked with Yang on his annotation and dictionary.

Wang, Shou-lien 王守謙, trans. and comm. *Tso chuan hsüan i-chu* 左傳選譯注. Kweiyang: Kuei-chou Jen-min, 1974.

___, *et al*, trans. and comms. *Tso chuan ch'üan-i* 左傳全譯. Kweiyang: Kuei-chou Jen-min, 1990. *Chung-kuo li-tai ming-chu ch'üan-i ts'ung-shu.*

Watson, Burton. *Selections from the Tso Chuan, China's Oldest Narrative History.* New York: Columbia University Press, 1989.

Studies

Bissell, Jeff. "Literary Studies of Historical Texts: Early Narrative Accounts of Chong'er, Duke Wen of Jin." Unpublished Ph. D. dissertation, University of Wisconsin, 1996.

Blakeley, Barry B. "Notes on the Reliability and Objectivity of the Tu Yü Commentary on the *Tso Chuan.*" *JAOS* 101 (1981): 207-212.

Boltz, William G. "Notes on the Textual Relation Between the *Kuo yü* and the *Tso chuan.*" *BSOAS* 53 (1990): 491-502.

Chang, I-jen 張以仁. *Kuo yü Tso chuan lun-chi* 國語左傳論集. Taipei: Tung-sheng, 1980.

Chang, Kao-p'ing 張高評. *Tso chuan chih wen-hsüeh chia-chih* 左傳之文學價值. Taipei: Wen-shih-che, 1982. *Wen-shih-che-hsüeh chi-ch'eng,* 69. Appends bibliographical references.

___. *Tso chuan chih wen-t'ao* 左傳之文韜. Kaoshiung: Li-wen Wen-hua, 1994. *Liang-an ts'ung-shu,* 10.

Chang, Su-ch'ing 張素卿. *Tso chuan ch'eng shih yen-chiu* 左傳稱詩研究. Taipei: Kuo-li T'ai-wan Ta-hsüeh, 1991. *Kuo-li T'ai-wan Ta-hsüeh wen-shih ts'ung-k'an,* 89.

Cheng, Chün-hua 鄭君華. "*Tso chuan-ch'ang-p'ien hsü-shih wen-hsüeh te ch'u-hsing*" 左傳—長篇敍事文學的雛形. *Wen-hsüeh p'ing-lun ts'ung-k'an* 18 (1983).

Chou, Tz'u-chi 周次吉. *Tso chuan tsa-k'ao* 左傳雜考. Taipei: Wen-chin, 1986.

Durrant, Stephen. "Smoothing Edges and Filling Gaps: *Tso chuan* and the 'General Reader'." *JAOS* 112 (1992): 36-41.

___. "Ssu-ma Ch'ien's Conception of the *Tso chuan.*" *JAOS* 112 (1992): 295-301.

Heidbüchel, Ursula. "Rhetorik im antiken China, eine Untersuchung der Ausdrucksformen höfischer Rede im *Zuozhuan.*" Ph. D. dissertation, University of Münster, 1993.

Ho, Le-shih 何樂士. *Tso chuan fan-wei fu-tz'u* 左傳範圍副詞. Changsha: Yüeh-lu Shu-she, 1994. *Tso chuan yü-yen yen-chiu wen-chi,* 1.

Hsü, Jen-fu 徐仁甫. *Tso chuan shu-cheng* 左傳疏証. Chengtu: Ssu-ch'uan Jen-min, 1981.

Hung, Liang-chi 洪亮吉 (1746-1809). *Ch'un ch'iu Tso chuan ku* 春秋左傳詁. Li Chieh-min 李解民, ed. 2v. Peking: Chung-hua, 1987.

Imber, Alan. *Kuo yü: An Early Chinese Text and Its Relationship with the Tso Chuan.* 2v. Stockholm: Stockholm University Press, 1975.

Kamata, Tadashi 鎌田正. *Saden no seiritsu to sono tenkai* 左伝の成立と其の展開. Tokyo: Taishûkan Shoten. First published in 1963. Appends an index.

Kao, Shih-ch'i 高士奇 (1645-1703). *Tso chuan chi-shih pen-mo*左傳紀事本末. Peking: Chung-hua, 1979.

Kuan, Hsieh-ch'u 管燮初. *Tso chuan chü-fa yen-chiu* 左傳句法研究. Hofei: An-hui Chiao-yü, 1994.

*Tso chuan chan-tz'u chi-chieh*左傳占辭集解. Hong Kong: Wan-ch'ing Shu-wu, 1965.

Sailey, Jay. "T'ung Shu-yüeh, the *Tso chuan,* and Early Chinese History." *JAOS* 104 (1984): 529-536.

Shen, Yü-ch'eng 沈玉成 and Liu Ning 劉寧. *Ch'un-ch'iu Tso chuan hsüeh shih-kao* 春秋左傳學史稿. Nanking: Chiang-su Ku-chi, 1992. *Chung-kuo ku wen-hsien yen-chiu ts'ung-shu.*

Sun, Lu-i 孫綠怡. *Tso chuan yü Chung-kuo ku-tien hsiao-shuo* 左傳與中國古典小説. Peking: Pei-ching Ta-hsüeh, 1992.

Tai, Chün-jen 戴君仁, *et al. Ch'un ch'iu San-chuan yen-chiu lun-chi* 春秋三傳研究論集. Taipei: Li-ming, 1981.

Tseng, Ch'in-liang 曾勤良. *Tso chuan yin shih-fu shih chih shih chiao yen-chiu* 左傳引詩賦詩之詩教研究. Taipei Wen-chin, 1993. *Wen-shih-che ta-hsi,* 61.

T'ung, She-yeh 童書業 (1908–1968). *Ch'un-ch'iu Tso chuan yen-chiu* 春秋左傳研究. Shanghai: Shang-hai Jen-min, 1980.

Wang, Ching-yü 王靖宇. "Tsai-lun *Tso chuan* yü *Kuo-yü* te kuan-hsi" 再論左傳與國語的關係. *Chung-kuo wen-che yen-chiu t'ung-hsün* 6.4 (December 1996): 95-101.

___. *Tso chuan yü ch'uan-t'ung hsiao-shuo lun-chi* 左傳與傳統小説論集. Peking: Pei-ching Ta-hsüeh, 1989.

Yang, Po-chün 楊伯峻. "*Tso chuan* ch'eng-shu nien-tai lun-shu" 左傳成書年代論述. *Wen-shih* 6 (1979).

Yasamoto, Hiroshi 安本博. *Shunjû Sashiden* 春秋左氏伝. Tokyo: Kadokawa Shoten, 1989. *Kanshû Chûgoku no koten,* 6. Includes maps, charts, references and an index.

Tso Ssu 左思 (*ca. 253-ca.* 307)

Studies

Hsü, Ch'uan-wu 徐傳武. "Tso Ssu, Tso Fen hsing-nien k'ao-pien" 左思左棻行年考辨. *Chung-kuo wen-che yen-chiu t'ung-hsün* 5.3 (September 1995): 159-172.

Wei, Feng-chüan 韋鳳娟. "Lun Tso Ssu chi ch'i wen-hsüeh ch'uang-tso" 論左思及其文學創作. *Chung-kuo ku-tien wen-hsüeh lun-ts'ung* 2 (1985): 37–54.

Ts'ui Hao 崔顥 (d. 754)

Editions and References

Wan, Ching-chün 萬竟君, comm. *Ts'ui Hao shih-chu* 崔顥詩注. Shanghai: Shang-hai Ku-chi, 1985. *T'ang-shih hsiao-chi,* 1:4.

Tsun-ch'ien chi 尊前集

Studies

Bryant, Daniel. "Messages of Uncertain Origin: The Textual Tradition of the *Nan-T'ang erh-chu tz'u.*" in Yu, *Voices,* pp. 298-348. Important study with implications for all textual filiations.

Ts'ung-shu 叢書 (collectanea)

Studies
Shaw, Shiow-jyu Lu. *The Imperial Printing of Early Ch'ing China.* San Francisco: Chinese Materials Center, 1983.

Tu Fu 杜甫 (712-770)

Editions and References
Chao, Tz'u-kung 趙次公 (Ch'ing dynasty), comm. and Lin Hsü-chung 林繼中, ed. *Tu shih Chao Tz'u-kung hsien-hou chieh chi-chiao* 杜詩趙次公先後解輯校. Shanghai: Shang-hai Ku-chi, 1994.

Cheng, Ch'ing-tu 鄭慶篤, *et al.*, eds. *Tu chi shu-mu t'i-yao* 杜詩書目提要. Tsinan: Ch'i Lu Shu-she, 1986. A thorough study of editions with a 120-page bibliography of modern studies appended.

Chou, Ts'ai-ch'üan 周采泉, ed. *Tu chi shu-lu* 杜集書錄. 2v. Shanghai: Shang-hai Ku-chi, 1986. The most extensive bibliography of editions, commentaries, studies, etc.; with indexes.

Chung, Fu 鍾夫 and T'ao Chün 陶鈞, eds. *Tu Fu wu-chung so-yin* 杜甫五種索引. Shanghai: Shang-hai Ku-chi, 1992.

Luan, Kuei-ming 欒貴明, ed. *Ch'uan T'ang-shih so-yin: Tu Fu chüan* 全唐詩索引：杜牧卷. 2v. Peking: Chung-hua, 1997.

Ts'ao, Shu-ming 曹樹銘. *Tu Fu ts'ung-chiao* 杜甫叢校. Peking: Chung-hua, 1978. Critical studies of various traditional editions.

Tu Fu ts'ao-t'ang li-shih wen-hua ts'ung-shu 杜甫草堂歷史文化叢書. Chengtu: Ssu-ch'uan Wen-i, 1997.

Tu Fu yen-chiu hsüeh-k'an 杜甫研究學刊. Chengtu: Tu Fu Yen-chiu Hsüeh-k'an Pien-chi-pu, 1981, V. 1-.

Tu shih hsiang-chu 杜詩詳注. Ch'iu Chao-ao 仇兆鰲 (1638-1713), commentator. 5v. Peking: Chung-hua, 1979. Best modern critical edition.

Translations
Cheng, Wing-fun and Hervé Collet, trans. *Tu Fu, dieux det diables pleurent.* Millemont, France: Moundarren, 1987. Free, unannotated versions of about 70 poems preceded by a 14-pp. introduction.

Ch'eng, Ch'ien-fan. "One Sober and Eight Drunk; Du Fu's 'Song of the Eight Drunken Immortals.'" Song Zianchun, trans. *SSC* 6.1 (1986).

Costantini, Vilma, ed. *Coppe di giada.* Turin, 1985. Contains translations of about forty poems each by Li Po, Tu Fu and Po Chu-i.

Idema, W. L. *De verweesde boot—klassieke Chinese gedichten.* Amsterdam: Meulenhoff, 1989. Translations of 144 poems with explanatory notes.

Studies
Bezin, Leonid E. *Du Fu.* Moscow: Molodaja Gvardija, 1987.

Ch'en, I-hsin 陳貽焮. *Tu Fu p'ing-chuan* 杜甫評傳. 3v. Shanghai: Shang-hai Ku-chi, 1982 and 1988. A careful biography of over 1300 pages.

446

Ch'en, Wei 陳偉. *Tu Fu shih-hsüeh t'an-wei* 杜甫詩學探微. Taipei: Wen-shih-che, 1985.

Ch'en, Wen-hua 陳文華. *Tu Fu chuan-chi T'ang-Sung tzu-liao k'ao-pien* 杜甫傳記唐宋資料考辨. Taipei: Wen-shih-che, 1987.

Cherniack, Susan. "Three Great Poems by Du Fu: 'Five Hundred Words: A Song of My Thoughts on Traveling from the Capital to Fengxian,' 'Journey North,' and 'One Hundred Rhymes: A Song of My Thoughts on an Autumn Day in Kuifu, Respectfully Sent to Director Zheng and Adviser to the Heir Apparent Li.'" Unpublished Ph. D. dissertation, Yale University, 1988.

Chiang, Jui-ts'ao 蔣瑞藻. *Hsü Tu Kung-pu shih-hua* 續杜公部詩話. Chang Chung-wang 張忠綱, ed. Peking: Shu-mu Wen-hsien, 1994.

Chin, Ch'i-hua 金啟華. *Tu Fu shih lun-ts'ung* 杜甫詩論叢. Shanghai: Shang-hai Ku-chi, 1985.

___ and Hu Wen-t'ao 胡問濤. *Tu Fu p'ing-chuan* 杜甫評傳. Sian: Shan-hsi Jen-min, 1984.

Chin, Sheng-t'an 金聖嘆 (1610-1661). *Tu shih chieh* 杜詩解. Chung Lai-en 鍾來恩, ed. Shanghai: Shang-hai Ku-chi, 1984.

Chou, Eva Shan. "Allusion and Periphrasis as Modes of Poetry in Tu Fu's Eight Laments." *HJAS* 45 (1985): 77-128.

___. *Reconsidering Tu Fu, Literary Greatness and Cultural Context.* New York and Cambridge: Cambridge University Press, 1996.

___. "Tu Fu's 'Eight Laments': Allusion and Imagery as Modes of Poetry." Unpublished Ph. D. dissertation, Harvard University, 1984.

___. "Tu Fu's Social Conscience: Compassion and Topicality in His Poetry." *HJAS* 51 (1991): 5-53.

Chung, Ling. "This Ancient Man Is I: Kenneth Rexroth's Versions of Tu Fu." *Renditions* 21 and 22 (Spring and Autumn 1984), pp. 307-30. A study of Rexroth's (1905-1982) critically regarded renditions of Tu Fu.

Davis, A. R. "'The Good Lines of the World Are a Common Possession': A Study of the Effect of Tu Fu upon Su Shih." In *Chung-yang Yen-chiu Yuan Kuo-chi Han-hsüeh hui-i lun-wen chi* Taipei: Chung-yang Yen-chiu Yüan, 1981, pp. 471-504. Although the focus is on Su Shih, a number of poems by Tu Fu and Li Po are discussed.

Fang, Shen-tao 方深道 (Sung dynasty). *Chu-chia Lao Tu shih-p'ing* 諸家老杜詩評. Chang Chung-wang 張忠綱, ed. Peking: Shu-mu Wen-hsien, 1994.

Fu, Keng-sheng 傅庚生. *Tu Fu shih-lun* 杜甫詩論. Shanghai: Shang-hai Ku-chi, 1985.

Hsia, Sung-liang 夏松涼. *Tu Shih chien-shang* 杜詩鑑賞. Shenyang: Liao-ning Chiao-yü, 1986. Interesting close readings of nearly forty poems.

Hsieh, Daniel. "Du Fu's 'Gazing at the Mountain.'" *CLEAR* 16 (1994): 1-18.

Hsü, Yung-chang 許永璋. *Tu shih ming-p'ien hsin-hsi* 杜詩名篇新析. Nanking: Nan-ching Ta-hsüeh, 1989.

Jaeger, Georgette. *Du Fu: Il y a homme errant.* Paris: La Différence, 1989.

Kan, Mitsu 韓美津, *et al. To Ho-shi to shôgai* 杜甫-詩と生涯. Tokyo: Tokuma Shoten, 1992.

Kurokawa, Yôichi 黒川洋一. *To Ho* 杜甫. Tokyo: Kadokawa Shoten, 1987. *Kanshô Chûgoku no toten,* 17.

___. *To Ho shisen* 杜甫詩選. Tokyo: Iwanami Shoten, 1991.

Ko, Chao-kuang 葛兆光 and Tai Yen 戴燕. *Wan T'ang Feng-yün—Tu Mu yü Li Shang-yin* 晚唐風韻—杜牧與李商隱. Nanking: Chiang-su Ku-chi, 1991.

Li, I 李誼. *Tu Fu Ts'ao-tang shih-chu* 杜甫草堂詩注. Chengtu: Ssu-ch'uan Jen-min, 1982.

Lin, Ming-hua. *Tu Fu hsiu-tz'u i-shu* 杜甫修辭藝術. Chengchow: Chung-chou Ku-chi, 1991.

Liu, Chien-hui 劉健輝 *et al.*, eds. *Tu Fu tsai K'uei-chou* 杜甫在夔州. Chungking: Ch'ung-ch'ing Chu-pan-she, 1992.

Liu, Feng-kao 劉鳳誥 (1761-1830). *Tu Kung-pu shih-hua* 杜公部詩話. Chang Chung-wang 張忠網, ed. Peking: Shu-mu Wen-hsien, 1994.

Liu, Wan. "Poetics of Allusion: Tu Fu, Li Shang-yin, Ezra Pound, and T. S. Eliot." Unpublished

447

Ph.D. dissertation, Princeton University, 1992.

Ma, Ch'ung-ch'i 馬重奇. *Tu Fu ku-shih yün-tu* 杜甫古詩韻讀. Peking: Chung-kuo Chan-wang, 1985.

McCraw, David R. *Du Fu's Laments from the South.* Honolulu: University of Hawaii Press, 1992.

Mekada, Makoto 目加田誠. *To Ho no shi to shôgai* 杜甫の詩と生涯. Tokyo: Ryûkei Shosha, 1983.

Mo, Li-feng 莫礪鋒. *Tu Fu p'ing-chuan* 杜甫評傳. Nanking: Nan-ching Ta-hsüeh, 1993. *Chung-kuo ssu-hsiang chia p'ing-chuan ts'ung-shu,* 66.

Mori, Kainan 森槐南. *To shi kôgi* 杜甫講義. 4v. Tokyo: Heibonsha, 1993.

Morino, Shigeo 森野繁夫. *Chinutsu shijin To Ho* 沈鬱詩人杜甫. Tokyo: Shûeisha, 1982.

Motsch, Monika. *Mit Bambusrohr und Ahle, von Qian Zhongshus Guanzhuibian zu einer Neubetrachtung Du Fus.* Frankfurt: Peter Lang, 1994.

Nieh, Shih-ch'iao 聶石樵 and Teng K'uei-ying 鄧魁英. *Tu Fu hsüan-chii* 杜甫選集. Shanghai: Shang-hai Ku-chi, 1983. Carefully annotated versions of about 200 poems following a fine introduction to Tu Fu. May be seen as a companion volume to that on Li Po by Yü Hsien-hao 郁賢浩 (also published by Shang-hai Ku-chi in 1990).

Nienhauser, William H., Jr. "You Had to Be There: A Call for an Uncommon Poetics." *Asian Cultural Quarterly* 14.3 (Autumn 1986): 41-62. Contains a lengthy analysis of Tu Fu's "Tu cho" 獨酌.

Owen, Stephen. *Traditional Chinese Poetry and Poetics: Omen of the World.* Madison: University of Wisconsin Press, 1985. Much of the discussion is based on poems by Tu Fu.

P'an, Te-yü 潘德輿 (1785-1839). *Yang-i Chai Li, Tu shih-hua* 養一齋李杜詩話. Chang Chung-wang 張忠網, ed. Peking: Shu-mu Wen-hsien, 1994.

Tagawa, Junzô 田川純三. *To Ho no tabi* 杜甫の旅. Tokyo: Shinchôsha, 1991.

T'ao, Tao-shu 陶道恕. *Tu Fu shih-ko shang-hsi chi* 杜甫詩歌賞析集. Chengtu: Pa-Shu Shu-she, 1993.

Ts'ao, Mu-fan 曹慕樊. *Tu shih tsa-shuo* 杜詩雜説. Chengtu: Ssu-ch'uan Jen-min, 1984. A collection of essays and notes by a traditional-style scholar.

Wang, Shih-ching 王士菁. Tu shih pien lan 杜詩便覽. Chengtu: Ssu-ch'uan Wen-i, 1986.

Wu, Chuan-cheng. "A Comparative Study of the Poetic Sequence: Tu Fu and W. B. Yeats." Unpublished Ph.D. dissertation, University of Washington, 1989.

Tu Hsün-ho 杜旬鶴 (846-907)

Editions and References
Yeh, Sen-huai 葉森槐. *Tu Hsün-ho shih hsüan* 杜旬鶴詩選. Hofei: Huang-shan Shu-she, 1988.

Studies
Ku, Ch'ien 顧黔. "Tu Hsün-ho shih yung-yün k'ao" 杜旬鶴詩用韻考. *T'ien-chin Shih-ta hsüeh-pao* 1990.3: 76-79.

Sung, Erh-k'ang 宋爾康. "Chien lun Tu Hsün-ho te shih-ko chi-ch'i t'e-tien" 簡論杜旬鶴的詩歌及其特點. *Ho-nan Ta-hsüeh hsüeh-pao* 1991.5: 39-42.

T'ang, Hua-ch'üan 湯華泉. "Tu Hsün-ho sheng-p'ing shih-chi k'ao-cheng" 杜旬鶴生平事跡考証. *Fu-yang Shih-yüan hsüeh-pao* 1986.1: 40-48.

Wen, Kung-i 溫公翊. "Tu Hsün-ho hsing-shih k'ao-lüeh" 杜旬鶴行實考略. *Yin-shan hsüeh-k'an* 1988.1: 18-23.

Yang, Wei-chung 楊維中. "Tu Hsün-ho ho t'a-te shih-ko feng-mang" 杜旬鶴和他的詩歌鋒芒. *Pei-fang lun-ts'ung* 1992.2: 67-69.

Tu Kuang-t'ing 杜光庭 (850-933)

Editions and References

Wang, Meng-ou 王夢鷗. *T'ang-jen hsiao-shuo chiao-shih* 唐人小説校釋. Taipei: Cheng-chung Shu-chü, 1983, pp. 319-38. Excellent annotated version of "Ch'iu-jan-k'o chuan."

Studies

Ling, Tzu 凌子. "T'an 'Ch'iu-jan-k'o chuan' te i-shu shih-chiao" 談虬髯客傳的藝術視角. *Wen-shih chih-shih* 1992.1 (1992): 56-60.

Liu, Ying 劉瑛. *T'ang-tai ch'uan-ch'i yen-chiu* 唐代傳奇研究. Taipei: Lien-ching Ch'u-pan Kung-ssu, 1994. Study of "Ch'iu-jan-k'o chuan," pp. 376-83.

Swatek, Catherine. "The Self in Conflict: Paradigms of Change in a T'ang Legend." In *Expressions of Self in Chinese Literature*, Robert E. Hegel and Richard C. Hessney, eds. New York: Columbia University Press, 1985, 153-88. A comparison between "Ch'iu-jan-k'o chuan" and "Hung-fu-chi" 紅拂記.

Verellen, Franciscus. *Du Guangting (850-933): Taoïst de cour à la fin de la Chine médiévale.* Paris: Collège de France, Institut des Hautes Études Chinoises, 1989. *Mémoires de l'Institut des Hautes Études Chinoises,* 30.

Wang, Yün-hsi 王運熙. "Tu 'Ch'iu-jan-k'o chuan' cha-chi" 讀虬髯客傳札記. *Hsüeh-lin man-lu* 11 (1985): 130-36.

Tu Mu 杜牧 (803-852)

Editions and References

Luan, Kuei-ming 欒貴明, ed. *Ch'uan T'ang-shih so-yin: Tu Mu chüan* 全唐詩索引：杜牧卷. Peking: Chung-hua, 1992.

Yamauchi, Haruo 山内春夫, ed. *To Boku shi sakuin* 杜牧詩索引. Kyoto: Ibundô Shoten, 1972 and 1986.

Translations

Burton, R.F., trans. *Plantains in the Rain: Selected Chinese Poems of Du Mu.* London: Wellsweep, 1990.

Wu, Ou-i 吳鷗譯, trans. and comm. *Tu Mu shih-wen hsüan-i* 杜牧詩文選譯. Chengtu-Pa-Shu Shu-she, 1991. *Ku-tai wen-shih ming-chu hsüan-i ts'ung-shu.*

___, trans. and comm. *Tu Mu shih-wen* 杜牧詩文. Taipei: Chin-hsiu Ch'u-pan Shih-yeh Ku-fen Yu-hsien Kung-ssu, 1993. *Chung-kuo ming-chu hs'üan-i ts'ung-shu,* 60.

Studies

Chu, Pi-lien 朱碧蓮. "Lun Tu Mu yü niu-li tang-cheng" 論杜牧與牛李黨爭. *Wen-hsüeh i-ch'an* 1989.2: 69-78.

Fishlen, Michael. "Wine, Poetry and History: Du Mu's Pouring Alone in the Prefectual Residence." *TP* 80 (1994): 260-97.

Hsiao, Ching-song Gene. "Semiotic Interpretation of Chinese Poetry: Tu Mu's Poetry as Example." Unpublished Ph. D. dissertation, University of Arizona, 1985.

Hu, K'o-hsien 胡可先. *Tu Mu yen-chiu ts'ung-k'ao* 杜牧研究叢考. Peking: Jen-min Wen-hsüeh, 1993. *Chung-kuo ku-tien wen-hsüeh yen-chiu ts'ung-shu.* An important collection of basic scholarly studies on the dating and reliability of Tu Mu's works, his biographies, and his influence.

K'ou, Yang-hou 寇養厚. "Tu Mu te wen-hsüeh ssu-hsiang" 杜牧的文學思想. *Wen-shih-che* 1993.6: 64-73.

Kung, Wen-k'ai. "The Official Biography of Tu Mu (803-852) in the Old T'ang History." *Chinese Culture* 29 (1987): 87-99.

___. *Tu Mu (805-852)–His Life and Poetry*. San Francisco: Chinese Materials Center, 1990. Asian Library Series, 38.

___. "Tu Mu's Poetry of Social Criticism and the Historical Past." *Chinese Culture* 26.1 (March 1985): 47-77.

Lü, Wu-chih 呂武志. *Tu Mu san-wen yen-chiu* 杜牧散文研究. Taipei: Tai-wan Hsüeh-sheng Shu-chü, 1994. Chung-kuo wen-hsüeh yen-chiu ts'ung-k'an.

Miao, Yüeh 繆鉞. "Lüeh-t'an Tu Mu yung-shih-shih" 略談杜牧詠史詩. *Wen-shih chih-shih* 1985.7: 8-13.

___. "Tu Mu tsu-nien tsai-k'ao pien" 杜牧卒年再考辨. *Wen shih* (1992): 183-6.

Pilière, Marie-Christine Verniau. "Du Mu: Comment rendre justice à la homme et à l'oeuvre?." *Études Chinoises* 6 (1987): 47-71.

Teng, Young-sheng. "Tu Mu as a Literary Critic: Gleanings from the Villa on Fan Stream." Unpublished Ph.D dissertation, Indiana University, 1987.

Tsao, Chung-fu 曹中孚. *Wan T'ang shih-jen Tu Mu* 晚唐詩人杜牧. Sian: Shan-hsi Jen-min, 1985.

Verniau Pilière, Marie-Christine. "Du Mu: comment rendre justice à l'homme et à l'oeuvre?" *Études chinoises* VI (1987): 47-72.

Wang, Hsi-p'ing 王西平 and Chang T'ien 張田. *Tu Mu p'ing-chuan* 杜牧評傳. Sian: Shan-hsi Jen-min, 1993.

___ and Kao Yün-kuang 高雲光. *Tu Mu shih-mei t'an-so* 杜牧詩美探索. Sian: Shan-hsi Jen-min, 1993. Chung-kuo ku-tai tso-chia yen-chiu ts'ung-shu. Appends an index to scholarly works on Tu Mu published between 1985 and 1990.

Wu, Tsai-ch'ing 吳在慶. *Tu Mu lun-kao* 杜牧論稿. Amoy: Hsia-men Ta-hsüeh, 1991.

Yamauchi, Haruo 山內春夫. *To Boku no kenkyû* 杜牧の研究. Kyoto: Ibundô Shoten, 1985.

Tu Shen-yen 杜審言 (d. *ca.* 705)

Editions and References

Hsü, Ting-hsiang 徐定詳, comm. *Tu Shen-yen shih-chu* 杜審言詩注. Shanghai: Shang-hai Ku-chi, 1982. *T'ang shih hsiao-chi*, 1:2.

Fujisawa, Takaharu 藤沢隆治. *To Shin genshi sakuin* 杜審言詩索引. Nagoya: Konron Shobô, 1986.

Tun-huang wen-hsüeh 敦煌文學 (Tun-huang Literature)

Editions and References

Ch'ai, Chien-hung 柴劍虹, *et al* "Tun-huang tz'u chi-chiao ssu-t'an" 敦煌詞輯校四談. *Tun-huang hsüeh chi-k'an* 1988.2.

Chang, Hsi-hou 張錫厚. *Tun-huang fu-hui* 賦匯. Nanking: Chiang-su Ku-chi, 1997.

___, ed. and annot. *Wang Fan-chih shih chiao-chi* 王梵志詩校輯. Peking: Chuang-hua, 1983. Appends a concordance to some of the words used by Wang.

Chang, Hung-hsün 張鴻勳, ed. and comm. *Tun-huang chiang-ch'ang wen-hsüeh tso-p'in hsüan-chu* 敦煌講唱文學作品選注. Langchow: Kan-su Jen-min, 1987; 1993.

Cheng, Ah-ts'ai 鄭阿財 and Chu Feng-yü 朱鳳玉, eds. *Tun-huang hsüeh yen-chiu lun-chu mu-lu* 敦煌學研究論著目錄. Taipei: Center for Chinese Studies, 1987. Han-hsüeh yen-chiu tzu-liao chi fu-wu chung-hsin ts'ung-k'an, 4.

Chiang, Li-hung 蔣禮鴻, ed. *Tun-huang wen-hsien yü-yen tz'u-tien* 敦煌文獻語言詞典. Hangchow:

Hang-chou Ta-hsüeh, 1994.

Chou, Shao-liang 周紹良, ed. *Tun-huang wen-hsüeh tso-p'in hsüan* 敦煌文學作品選. Peking: Chung-hua, 1987. Hsin-wen Feng published a reprint in Taipei in 1988.

___, *et al.* eds. *Ying-tsang Tun-huang wen-hsien: Han-wen fo-ching i-wai pu-fen* 英藏敦煌文獻：漢文佛經以外部份. 15v. Chengtu: Ssu-ch'uan Jen-min, 1990. Photographic reproductions of the Chinese texts exclusive of Buddhist scriptures from Tun-huang held in British collections. Chinese and English indexes are appended.

___ and Pai Wen-hua, eds. *Tun-huang pien-wen lun-wen lu* 敦煌變文論文錄. 2v. Shanghai: Shang-hai Ku-chi, 1982.

Chung-kuo Wen-hua Ta-hsüeh 中國文化大學, ed. *Lun-tun tsang Tun-huang Han-wen chüan-tzu mu-lu t'i-yao* 倫敦藏敦煌漢文卷子目錄提要. 3v. Taipei: Fu-chi, 1993.

Fu, Chün-lien 伏俊連. *Tun-huang fu chiao-chu* 敦煌賦校注. Lanchow: Kan-su Jen-min, 1994. Tun-huang wen-hsien ts'ung-shu.

Fukui, Fumimasa 福井文雅 and Makita Tairyô 牧田諦亮, eds. *Daijô butten (Chûgoku, Nihon hen)* 大乗仏典「中国日本篇」. Vol. 10. Tokyo: Chûô Kôronsha, 1992. Tonkô, 1.

Hsiang, Ch'u 項楚. "*Tun-huang ko-tz'u tsung-pien* k'uang-pu (liu)" 敦煌歌辭總編匡補（六）. *Wen shih* 40 (1994): 185-93.

___, ed. *Tun-huang pien-wen hsüan-chu* 敦煌變文選注. Chengtu: Pa-Shu Shu-she, 1989.

Huang, Hui 黃徵 *et al.*, eds. *Tun-huang pien-wen chiao-chu* 敦煌變文校注. Peking: Yen-shan, 1997. Edited and annotated version of 84 transformation texts.

Kanaoka, Shôkô 金岡照光, ed. *Tonkô no bungaku bunken* 敦煌の文学文献. Tokyo: Daitô, 1991. Kôza Tonkô, 9.

Kuo, Tsai-i 郭在貽 (1939-1989), Chang Yung-ch'üan 張涌泉 and Huang Hui 黃徵, eds. *Tun-huang pien-wen chi chiao-i* 敦煌變文集校議. Changsha: Yüeh-lu, 1990. In manuscript form left by Kuo on his death; reviewed by Ch'eng Tung-yui 陳東輝 in *Tun-huang yen-chiu* 29 (November 1991): 115-7.

Lin, Ch'i-t'an 林其錟 and Ch'en Feng-chin 陳鳳金, eds. *Tun-huang i-shu Wen-hsin tiao-lung ts'an-chüan chi-chiao* 敦煌遺書文心彫龍殘卷集校. Shanghai: Shang-hai Shu-tien, 1991.

Kuo-li Chung-yang T'u-shu-kuan 國立圖書館, ed. *Kuo-li Chung-yang T'u-shu-kuan tsang Tun-huang chüan-tzu* 國立圖書館藏敦煌卷子. 6v. Lanchow: Lan-chou Ku-chi Shu-tien, 1990.

Mair, Victor H. "Chinese Popular Literature from Tun-huang: The State of the Field (1980-1990)." In *Turfan and Tun-huang—The Texts, Encounter of Civilizations on the Silk Route.* Alfredi Cadonna, ed. Florence: Leo S. Olschki, 1992, pp. 171-240.

Pei-ching Ta-hsüeh 北京大學, ed. *Pei-ching Ta-hsüeh tsang Tun-huang wen-hsien* 北京大學藏敦煌文獻. 2v. Shanghai: Shang-hai Ku-chi, 1996. Tun-huang Tu-lu-fan wen-hsien chi-ch'eng.

Tun-huang hsüeh chi-k'an 敦煌學輯刊. V. 31 appeared in 1997. Published by Lan-chou Ta-hsüeh.

Tun-huang hsüeh-tao lun ts'ung-k'an 敦煌學導論叢刊. 10v. Taipei: Hsin Wen-feng, 1993.

Translations

Johnstone, Simon. "Dunhuang Lyrics." *Chinese Literature* (Spring 1988): 116-120.

Mair, Victor H. *Tun-huang Popular Narratives.* Cambridge: Cambridge University Press, 1983.

Studies

Barrett, T. M. "The Origin of the Term *pien-wen*: An Alternative Hypothesis." *JRAS, TS* 2 (1992): 241-6.

Chang, Hsi-hou 張錫厚, ed. *Wang Fan-chih shih yen-chiu hui-lu* 王梵志 詩研究 彙錄. Shanghai: Shang-hai Ku-chi, 1990. Rpt. Taipei: Hsin Wen-feng, 1993. Contains useful bibliography.

Chang, Hung-hsün 張鴻勳. *Tun-huang hua-pen tz'u-wen su-fu tao-lun* 敦煌話本詞文俗賦導論

Taipei: Hsin-wen-feng, 1993. *Tun-huang-hsüeh tao-lun ts'ung-k'an,* 7.

Chiang, Liang-fu 姜亮夫. *Tun-huang-hsüeh lun-wen chi* 敦煌學論文集. Shanghai: Shang-hai Ku-chi, 1987.

Chin, Hsien-chu 金賢珠. *T'ang Wu-tai Tun-huang min-ko* 唐五代敦煌民歌. Taipei: Wen-shih-che, 1994. *Wen-shih-che-hsüeh chi-ch'eng,* 327.

Chow, Tse-tsung and Wayne Schlepp. "Ten *P'u-sa-ma* Poems from Tunhuang." In *Interpreting Culture Through Translation.* Roger Ames *et al,* eds. Hong Kong: The Chinese University Press, 1991, pp. 87-100.

Ch'ü, Chin-liang 曲金良. *Tun-huang fo-chiao wen-hsüeh yen-chiu* 敦煌佛教文學研究. Taipei: Wen-chin, 1995. *Wen-shih-che ta-hsi,* 94.

___. "Tun-huang 'pien-wen' yen-chiu shih shu-lun" 敦煌變文研究史述論. In *T'ang-tai wen-hsüeh yen-chiu nien-chien, 1992* 唐代文學研究年鑑, 1992. Kweilin: Kuang-hsi Shih-fan Ta-hsüeh, 1993, pp. 233-245.

Chung-cheng Ta-hsüeh 中正大學, ed. *Ch'üan-kuo Tun-huang-hsüeh yen-t'ao hui lun-wen chi* 全國敦煌學研討會論文集. Kaohsiung: Chung-cheng Ta-hsüeh, 1995.

Chung-kuo Tun-huang T'u-lu-fan-hsüeh Hui 中國敦煌吐魯番學會, ed. *Tun-huang yü-yen wen-hsüeh yen-chiu* 敦煌語言文學研究. Peking: Pei-ching Ta-hsüeh, 1988.

Drège, Jean-Pierre. "Étude formelle des manuscrits de Dunhuang conserves à Taipei: datation et authenticité." *BEFEO* 74 (1985).

___. "Quelques collections "nouvelles" de manuscrits du Dunhuang." *Cahiers d'Extrême-Asie* 3 (1987): 113-129. Discusses three collections in China: those of Peking National Library, the Provincial Museum of Gansu, and Northwest Normal Academy in Lanchow.

Han-hsüeh Yen-chiu Chung-hsin 漢學研究中心, ed. *Ti-erh chi Tun-huang-hsüeh kuo-chi yen-t'ao hui lun-wen chi* 第二屆敦煌學國際研討會論文集. Taipei: Han-hsüeh Yen-chiu Chung-hsin, 1991.

Hangchow Ta-hsüeh 杭州大學, ed. *Tun-huang yü-yen wen-hsüeh lun-wen chi* 敦煌語言文學論文集. Hangchow: Che-chiang Ku-chi, 1988.

Ho, Lo-shih 何樂士. "Tun-huang pien-wen yü *Shih-shuo hsin-yü* jo-kan yü-fa t'e-tien te pi-chiao" 敦煌變文與世說新語若干語法特點的比較. In *Sui T'ang Wu-tai Han-yü yen-chiu* 隋唐五代漢語研究. Ch'eng Hsiang-ch'ing 程湘清, ed. Tsinan: Shan-tung Chiao-yü, 1992.

Hrdlicková, Vera. "The Significance of the Dunhuang *Jiangjing Wen* for Chinese Literary History." *AO* 59 (1992): 173-180.

Hsiang, Ch'u 項楚. *Tun-huang wen-hsüeh ts'ung-k'ao* 敦煌文學叢考. Shanghai: Shang-hai Ku-chi, 1991. *Chung-hua hsüeh-shu ts'ung-shu.*

___. *Tun-huang shih-ko tao-lun* 敦煌詩歌導論. Taipei: Hsin Wen-feng, 1993.

Hsiao, Teng-fu 蕭登福. *Tun-huang su-wen-hsüeh lun-ts'ung* 敦煌俗文學論叢. Taipei: Tai-wan Shang-wu Yin-shu-kuan, 1988.

Huang, Chih-ming 黃智明. "Tun-huang ching-chi chüan-tzu yen-chiu kai-k'uang (hsia)" 敦煌經藉卷子研究概況(下). *Chung-kuo wen-che yen-chiu t'ung-hsün* 6.4 (December 1996): 51-74.

Huang, Yung-wu 黃永武. *Tun-huang te T'ang shih* 敦煌的唐詩. Taipei: Hung-fan Shu-tien, 1987. *Hung-fan wen-hsüeh ts'ung-shu,* 172.

Huntington, John C. "A Note on Dunhuang Cave 17, 'The Library,' or Hong Bian's Reliquary Chamber." *Ars Orientalis* 16(1986): 93-101.

Idema, W. L. "Chasing Shadows, A Review Article." *TP* 76 (1990): 299-310.

Jen, Pan-t'ang 任半塘, ed. *Tun-huang ko-tz'u tsung-pien* 敦煌歌辭總編. Shanghai: Shang-hai Ku-chi, 1987.

Kanaoka, Shôkô. "Tun-huang Popular Narratives." *Asian Folklore Studies* 46.2 (1987): 273-300. A review article.

Kansu Sheng She-hui K'o-hsüeh Yüan 甘肅省社會科學院, ed. *Tun-huang-hsüeh lun chi* 敦煌

452

學論集. Lanchow: Kan-su Jen-min, 1985.

Kao, Kuo-fan 高國藩. "T'an Tun-huang ch'ü-tzu tz'u" 談敦煌曲子詞. *Wen-hsüeh i-ch'an* 1984.3: 28-35.

___. *Tun-huang min-chien wen-hsüeh* 敦煌民間文學. Taipei: Lien-ching, 1994.

Kotzenberg, Heike. "Das Motiv des Hunnenbraut Wang Chao-chün in der Dichtung und Malerei Chinas." In *Ganz allmählich, Aufsätze zur ostasiatischen Literatur, insbesondere zur chinesischen Lyrik.* Roderich Ptak and Siegfried Englert, eds. *Heidelberg:* Heidelberger Verlagsanstalt, 1986, pp. 109-119. Contains a discussion of the "Wang Chao-chün pien-wen" in support of the author's contention that the story was used primarily to criticize the imperial government during the T'ang.

Kuo, Feng 郭鋒, *et al.,* eds. *Chung-wai chu-ming Tun-huang-hsüeh-chia p'ing-chuan* 中外著名敦煌學家評傳. Lanchow: Kan-su Jen-min, 1997.

Lanciotti, Lionello. "Some Terminological Observations about Tun-huang Pien-wen." *Tôhôgaku* (1986): 148-151.

Liu, Chin-ting. *Tun-huang hsüeh shu-lun* 敦煌學書論. Lanchow: Kan-su Chiao-yü, 1991.

Liu, Ts'un-yan. "Some Lyrics from Tun-huang." In *Interpreting Culture Through Translation.* Roger Ames *et al,* eds. Hong Kong: Chinese University Press, 1991, pp. 155-66.

Mair, Victor H. "The Contributions of T'ang and Five Dynasties transformation texts (pien-wen) to later Chinese popular literature." Philadelphia: University of Pennsylvania Press, 1989. *Sino-Platonic papers,* 12.

___. "Lay Students and the Making of Written Vernacular Narrative: An Inventory of Tun-huang Manuscripts." *Chinoperl Papers* 10 (1981): 5-96. A close study of 599 items extracted from the entire corpus of Tun-huang mss. that shows many popular literary works were copied by students.

___. "The Narrative Revolution in Chinese Literature: Ontological Presuppositions." *CLEAR* 5.1 (January 1983): 1-27. Seeks to demonstrate the influence of Indian philosophical concepts on the development of Chinese fiction.

___. "A Newly Identified Fragment of the 'Transformation on Wang Ling.'" *Chinoperl Papers* 12 (1983): 130-42.

___. "The Origins of an Iconographical Form of the Pilgrim Hsüan-tsang." *TS* 4 (1986): 29-41 plus 7 plates. Traces the common representation of the famous pilgrim back to pictures of foreign itinerants that were found at Tun-huang.

___. *Painting and Performance: Chinese Picture Recitation, its Indian Genesis, and Analogues Elsewhere.* Honolulu: University of Hawaii Press, 1987. Essentially a world history of illustrated storytelling. Has chapters on China, Ancient and Modern India, Indonesia, Central Asia, Japan, Iran, and Europe.

___. "Parallels between Some Tun-huang Manuscripts and the Seventeenth Chapter of the Kozanji *Journey to the West." Cahiers d'Extrême-Asie* 3 (1987): 41-53.

___. "A Partial Bibliography for the Study of Indian Influence on Chinese Popular Literature." *Sino-Platonic Papers* 3 (March 1987): 1-214.

___. "The Prosimetric Form in the Chinese Literary Tradition." In Karl Reichl and Joseph Harris, eds. *Prosimetrum: Crosscultural Perspectives on Narrative in Prose and Verse.* Woodbridge, Suffolk: Boydell and Brewer, 1997.

___. "Records of Transformation Tableaux (*pien-hsiang*)." *TP* 72 (1986): 3-43. Discusses the relationships between *pien-wen* and *pien-hsiang.*

___. *T'ang Transformation Texts: A Study of the Buddhist Contribution to the Rise of Vernacular Fiction and Drama in China.* Cambridge, Mass.: Harvard Council on East Asian Studies, 1989. Chapters on (1) the historical background, (2) the corpus, (3) the meaning of the term *pien,* (4) the form and features of the genre, (5) the performers and scribes, (6) contemporary references.

___. *Tun-huang Popular Narratives.* Cambridge: Cambridge University Press, 1983.

Makita, Tairyô 牧田諦亮 and Fukui, Fumimasa 福井文雅. *Tonkô to Chûgoku Bukkyô* 敦煌と中国仏教. Tokyo: Daitô Shuppansha, 1984. *Kôza Tonkô*, 7.

Meng, Ch'u 夢初. "Ch'ien-t'an Tun-huang ch'ü-tzu-tz'u te i-shu" 淺談敦煌曲子詞的藝術. *She-hui k'o-hsüeh* 1985.2.

Schneider, Richard. "Un moine Indien au Wou-t'ai Chan." *Cahiers d'Extrême-Asie* 3 (1987): 27-39. A study of Tun-huang mss. Pelliot 3931 which tells the story of an Indian monk's pilgrimage to Wu-t'ai shan and its antecedents (hagiographies and hymns).

Tanaka, Ryôshô 田中良昭. *Tonkô Zenshû bunken no kenkyû* 敦煌禅宗文献の研究. Tokyo: Daitô Shuppansha, 1984.

Tun-huang Wen-wu Yen-chiu So 敦煌文物研究所, ed. *1983-nien ch'üan-kuo Tun-huang hsüeh-shu t'ao-lun hui* 1983年全國敦煌學術討論會. 5v. Lanchow: Kan-su Jen-min, 1985. Collected works on various aspects of Tun-huang studies presented at the 1983 National Academic Symposium of literature and history.

Vetch, Hélène. "En marge de l'oeuvre de Wang le Zélaeur: deux manuscrits inédits (P. 3724 et S. 6032) du volume sans titre." In *Contributions aux études de Touen-houang*, 3.

Wang, Chung-min 王重民 (1903–1975). *Pa-li Tun-huang ts'an-chüan hsü-lu* 巴黎敦煌殘卷敍錄. Lanchow: Lan-chou Ku-chi Shu-tien, 1990.

Wang, Fan-chou 汪泛舟. "Tun-huang ch'ü-tzu-tz'u te ti-wei t'e-tien ho ying-hsiang" 敦煌曲子詞的體味特點和影響. *Lan-chou hsüeh-k'an* 1985.1.

Wang, Yü-kung 王禹功, ed. *Tun-huang yü-yen wen-hsüeh yen-chiu* 敦煌語言文學研究. Peking: Pei-ching Ta-hsüeh, 1988.

Wu, Hung. "What is *Bianxiang*–On the Relationship between Dunhuang Art and Dunhuang Literature." *HJAS* 5 (1992): 111-92.

Yang, Hsiung 楊雄, ed. *1994 nien Tun-huang-hsüeh kuo-chi hsüeh-shu yen-t'ao hui lun-wen t'i-yao* 1994年敦煌學國際學術研討會論文提要. N.P.: Tun-huang Yen-chiu Yüan, 1994. Abstracts of papers presented at the 1994 conference on Tun-huang Studies in commemoration of the 50th anniversary of the Tun-huang Academy.

Yen, T'ing-liang 顏廷亮, *et al.*, eds. *Tun-huang wen-hsüeh kai-lun* 敦煌語文學概論. Lanchow: Kan-su Jen-min, 1993.

___. *Tun-huang wen-hsüeh kai-shuo* 敦煌文學概説. Taipei: Hsin-wen-feng, 1997. Appends a useful bibliography.

***Tung-ching meng Hua lu* 東京夢華錄 (The Eastern Capital: A Dream of Splendors Past)**

Editions and References

Umehara, Kaoru 梅原郁. *Tôkei makaroku Muryôroku tô goi sakuin* 東京夢華録夢梁録等語彙索引. Taipei: Tsung-ch'ing T'u-shu Ch'u-pan Kung-ssu, 1986. *Han-hsüeh so-yin chi-ch'eng*. Reprint of the 1979 Japanese publication.

Studies

Kan, Han-ch'üan 甘漢銓. *Tung-ching meng Hua lu chung te yin-shih wen-t'i chi ch'i tz'u-hui* 東京夢華錄中的飲食問題及其詞彙. Taichung: Tung-hai Ta-hsüeh chung-wen yen-chiu so, 1990.

Tung Chung-shu 董仲舒 (*ca.* 179-*ca.* 104 B.C.)

Editions and References

Ch'un-ch'iu fan-lu chiao-shih 春秋繁露校釋. Chung Chao-p'eng 鍾肇鵬, *et al.*, comms. Tsinan:

454

Shan-tung Yu-i Shu-she, 1994

Translations

Gassmann, Robert H. *Tung Chung-shu, Ch'un-ch'iu fanf-lu, Üppiger Tau des Frühling-und-Herbst-Klassikers. Übersetzung und Annotation der Kapitel Eins bis Sechs.* Bern: Peter Lang, 1988. *Schweizer Asiatische Studien, Études asiatiques suisses,* 8.

Studies

Arbuckle, Gary. "A Note on the Authenticity of the *Chunqiu Fanlu*." *TP* 75 (1989): 226-34.
___. "Restoring Dong Zhongshu (*c.* 195-115 BCE)." Unpublished Ph. D. dissertation, University of British Columbia, 1991.
Chou, Kuei-t'ien 周桂鈿. *Tung Chung-shu p'ing-chuan* 董仲舒評傳. Nanning: Kuang-hsi Chiao-yü, 1995.
Hua, Yu-ken 華有根. *Tung Chung-shu ssu-hsiang yen-chiu* 董仲舒思想研究. Shanghai: Shang-hai She-hui K'o-hsüeh, 1992.
Queen, Sarah A. *From Chronicle to Canon: The Hermeneutics of the* Spring and Autumn Annals *According to Tung Chung-shu.* New York and Cambridge: Cambridge University Press, 1996. Publication of her Ph.D. dissertation which bears the same title and was completed at Harvard University in 1991.
Teng, Hung 鄧紅. *Kô Chûjo shisô no kenkyû* 薫仲舒思想の研究. Tokyo: Hito to Bunkasha, 1995.
Wei, Cheng-t'ung 韋政通. *Tung Chung-shu* 董仲舒. Taipei: Tung-ta T'u-shu Kung-ssu, 1986. Shih-chieh che-hsüeh-chia ts'ung-shu. Appends bibliographical references, an index and a *nien-piao.*

T'ung-ch'eng P'ai 桐城派

Studies

Wang, Chen-yüan 王鎮遠. *T'ung-ch'eng P'ai* 桐城派. Shanghai: Shang-hai Ku-chi, 1990. Chung-kuo ku-tien wen-hsüeh chi-pen chih-shih ts'ung-shu. There is a Taiwan reprint published in Taipei by Chün-yü-t'ang Ch'u-pan Kung-ssu, 1990.
Wang, Hsien-yung 王獻永. *T'ung-ch'eng wen p'ai* 桐城文派. Peking: Chung-hua, 1992. Chung-kuo wen-hsüeh-shih chih-shih ts'ung-shu.
Wu, Meng-fu 吳孟复. *T'ung-ch'eng wen p'ai shu-lun* 桐城文派述論. Hofei: An-wei Chiao-yü, 1992.

tzu-chuan 自傳 (autobiography)

Studies

Bauer, Wolfgang. *Das Antlitz Chinas–Die autobiographische Selbstdarstellung in der chinesischen Literatur von irhen Anfängen bis Heute.* Munich: Carl Hanser, 1990.
___. "Selbst und Selbstdarstellung in der T'ang-Zeit." *Minima Sinica* 1 (1993): 85-109.
Frühauf, Manfred W. *Frühformen der chinesischen Autobiographie.* Frankfurt am Main: Lang, 1987.
Huang, Martin W. *Literati and Self-Re/Presentation, Autobiographical Sensibility in the Eighteenth-Century Chinese Novel.* Stanford: Stanford University Press, 1994.
Kawai, Kôzô 川合康三. *Chûgoku no jiden bungaku* 中国の自伝文学. Tokyo: Sôbunsha, 1996.
Wu, Pei-yi. *The Confucian's Progress: Autobiographical Writings in Traditional China.* Princeton: Princeton University Press, 1990.

Tzu-ti shu 子弟書

Studies

Ch'en, Chin-chao 陳錦釗. "Tzu-ti shu chih t'i-ts'ai lai-yüan chi ch'i tsung-ho yen-chiu" 子弟書之題材來源及其綜合研究. Unpublished Ph.D. dissertation, Cheng-chih University (Taiwan), 1977.

Hu, Wen-pin 胡文彬, ed. *Hung-lou meng tzu-ti shu* 紅樓夢子弟書. Peking: Ch'un-feng Wen-i, 1983. Collects 27 texts, 5 by known authors.

Wadley, Stephen A. *The Mixed Language Verses from the Manchu Dynasty in China.* Bloomington, Indiana: Research Institute for Inner Asian Studies, Indiana University, 1991. Papers on Inner Asia, 16.

_tz'u_ 詞 (lyric)

Editions and References

Chang, Hui-min 張惠民. *Sung-tai tz'u-hsüeh tzu-liao hui-pien* 宋代詞學資料匯編. Shantou: Shan-t'ou Ta-hsüeh, 1993.

Chang, Kao-k'uan 張高寬, *et al.*, eds. *Sung-tz'u ta-tz'u-tien* 宋詞大辭典. Shenyang: Liao-ning Jen-min, 1990.

Chao, Tsun-yüeh 趙尊嶽, ed. *Ming tz'u hui-k'an* 明辭彙刊. Shanghai: Shang-hai Ku-chi, 1996?.

Chin, Ch'i-hua 金啟華, *et al.*, eds. *Ch'üan Sung-tz'u tien-ku k'ao-shih tz'u-tien* 全宋詞典故考釋辭典. Changchun: Chi-lin Wen-shih, 1991.

___, *et al.*, eds. *T'ang Sung tz'u-chi hsü-pa hui-pien* 唐宋詞集序跋匯編. Kiangsu: Chiang-su Chiao-yü, 1990.

Hu, Chao 胡昭 *et al.*, eds. *T'ang Wu-tai tz'u so-yin* 唐五代詞索引. Peking: Tang-tai Chung-kuo, 1997.

Huang, Pa-ching 黃拔荊. *Tz'u shih (Shang chuan)* 詞史（上卷）. V. 1. Foochow: Fu-chien Jen-min, 1989. Covers from the inception of the genre through the Yüan dynasty.

Huang, Wen-chi 黃文吉, ed. *Tz'u-hsüeh yen-chiu shu-mu* 詞學研究書目 *(1912-1992)*. 2v. Taipei: Wen-chin, 1993. A 1202-pp. listing including Japanese and some Western works.

Kung, Chao-chi 龔趙吉, ed. *Li-tai tz'u-lun hsin-pien* 歷代詞論新編. Peking: Pei-ching Shih-fan Ta-hsüeh, 1984.

Shih, Chih-ts'un 施蟄存, ed. *Tz'u-chi hsü-pa ts'ui-pien* 詞籍序跋萃編. Peking: Chung-kuo She-hui K'o-hsüeh, 1994.

Sheng, P'ei 盛配. *Tz'u-tiao tz'u-lü ta-tien* 詞調詞律大典. Peking: Chung-kuo Hua-ch'iao, 1998.

T'ang, Kuei-chang 唐圭璋, ed. *T'ang Sung tz'u chien-shang tz'u-tien* 唐宋詞鑑賞辭典. Nanking: Chiang-su Ku-chi, 1986. Contains five useful appendixes: an annotated bibliography, basic facts necessary to read tz'u, etc.

Tominaga, Kazutaka 富永一登, ed. *Sen Shin Ryô Kan Saingoku jifu sakuin* 先秦, 両漢, 三国 辭賦索引. Tokyo: Kenbun Shuppan, 1996.

Tuan, Pao-lin 譚寶林. *Min-chien wen-hsüeh tz'u-tien* 民間文學詞典. Shih-chia-chuang: Ho-pei Chiao-yü, 1988.

Wang, Hung 王洪, ed. *T'ang-tai tz'u pai-k'o ta tz'u-tien* 唐代詞辭典. *Chung-kuo wen-hsüeh pai-k'o tz'u-tien hsi-lieh* Peking: Hsüeh-yüan, 1990, 1993. Appends an extensive bibliography of Chinese editions and studies (pp. 1342-1412).

Yeh, Kung-ch'o 葉恭綽, ed. *Ch'üan Ch'ing tz'u-ch'ao* 全清詞鈔. Peking: Chung-hua, 1982.

Yen, Ti-ch'ang 嚴迪昌. *Ch'ing tz'u shih* 清詞史. Soochow: Chiang-su Ku-chi, 1990.

456

Translations

Landau, Julie. *Beyond Spring, Tz'u Poems of the Sung Dynasty.* New York: Columbia University Press, 1994.

Yun, Shi. *Poèmes à chanter des époques Tang et Song.* Seyssel: Comp'act, 1987.

Studies

Aoyama, Hideo 青山宏. *Tô Sô shi kenkyû* 唐宋詞研究. Tokyo: Kyûko Shoin, 1991.

Bryant, Daniel. "The Rhyming Categories of Tenth Century Chinese Poetry," *MS* 34 (1979-80): 319-47.

Chinese Department, Hua-tung Normal University, ed. *Tz'u-hsüeh yen-chiu lun-wen chi (1949-1979)* 詞學研究論文集. Shanghai: Shang-hai Ku-chi, 1982.

___. *Tz'u-hsüeh lun-kao* 詞學論稿. Shanghai: Hua-tung Shih-fan Ta-hsüeh, 1986.

___. *Tz'u-hsüeh yen-chiu lun-wen chi (1911-1949)* 詞學研究論文集. Shanghai: Shang-hai Ku-chi, 1988.

Chu, Madeline. "Interplay between Tradition and Innovation: The Seventeenth Century *Tz'u* Revival." *CLEAR* 9 (1987): 71-88.

Egan, Ronald. "The Problem of the Repute of *Tz'u* during the Northern Sung." In Yu, *Voices,* pp. 191-225.

Fang, Chih-fan 方智范. *Chung-kuo tz'u-hsüeh p'i-p'ing shih* 中國詞學批評史. Peking: Chung-kuo She-hui K'o-hsüeh, 1994.

Fang, Chien-hsin 方建新. "*Ch'üan Sung tz'u* hsiao-chuan ting-wu" 全宋詞小傳訂誤. *Wen-shih* 40 (1994): 223-254.

Fong, Grace S. "Persona and Mask in the Song Lyric *(Ci).*" *HJAS* 50 (1990): 459-84.

Ho, Hsin-hui 賀新輝, ed. *Sung tz'u chien-shang tz'u-tien* 宋詞鑑賞辭典. Peking: Pei-ching Yen-shan, 1987.

Hsieh, T'ao-fang 謝桃坊. *Chung-kuo tz'u-hsüeh shih* 中國詞學史. Chengtu: Pa-Shu Shu-she, 1993.

___. "Tsai-lun Sung-tai min-chien tz'u" 再論宋代民間詞 *Kuei-chou she-hui k'o-hsüeh* 1987.2 (1987).

Jao, Tsung-i 饒宗頤. *Tz'u-chi k'ao* 詞集考. Peking: Chung-hua, 1992.

Liang, Jung-chi 梁榮基. *Tz'u-hsüeh li-lun tsung-k'ao* 詞學理論綜考. Peking: Pei-ching Ta-hsüeh, 1991.

Lin, Shuen-fu. "The Formation of a Distinct Generic Identity for *Tz'u.*" In Yu, *Voices,* pp. 3-29.

McCraw, David R. "*Yi kong wei zhong:* Interstanzaic Transition's Place in Soong Dynasty Lyrics." *JSYS* 24 (1994): 145-64.

Mo, Li-feng 莫礪鋒. "Lun Wan-T'ang Wu-tai tz'u-feng te chuan-pien—chien lun Wei Chuang tsai tz'u-shih shang te ti-wei" 論晚唐五代詞風的轉變一兼論韋莊在詞史上的地位. *Wen-hsüeh i-ch'an* 1980.5 (1980):.

Owen, Stephen. "Meaning the Words: The Genuine as a Value in the Tradition of the Song Lyric." In Yu, *Voices,* pp. 30-69.

Sargent, Stuart H. "Contexts of the Song Lyric in Sung Times: Communication Technology, Social Change, Morality." In Yu, *Voices,* pp. 226-256.

Wang, Shui-chao, *et al.,* eds. and trans. *Jih-pen hsüeh-che Chung-kuo tz'u-hsüeh lun-wen chi* 日本學者中國詞學論文集. Shanghai: Shang-hai Ku-chi, 1991.

Yu, Pauline. "Song Lyrics and the Canon: A Look at Anthologies of *Tz'u.*" In Yu, *Voices,* pp. 70-103.

___, ed. *Voices of the Song Lyric in China.* Berkeley: University of California Press, 1993.

Ziporyn, Brook. "Temporal Paradoxes: The Intersection of Time Present and Time Past in Song *Ci*" *CLEAR* 17 (1995): 89-109.

Tz'u-hua 詞話 (doggerel story)

Editions and References

Ch'en, T'ing-cho 陳廷焯 (1853-1892). *Pai-yü-chai tz'u-hua* 白雨齋詞話. Shanghai: Shang-hai Ku-chi, 1984.

Shen, Hsiung 沈雄 (*fl.* 1689) and Chiang Shang-chih 江尚質 (*fl.* 1689), eds. *Ku-chin tz'u-hua* 古今詞話. Shanghai: Shang-hai Shu-tien, 1987. Photolithic reprint of the 1689 *Pao-han lou* 寶翰樓 edition.

T'ang, Kuei-chang 唐圭璋, ed. *Tz'u-hua ts'ung-pien* 詞話叢編. 5v. Peking: Chung-hua, 1986.

Wang, Chung-hou 王仲厚, ed. *T'ang Sung tz'u-hua* 唐宋詞話. Hei-lung-chiang Chiao-yü, 1994.

Translations

King, Gail Oman. *The Story of Hua Guan Suo.* Tempe: Center for Asian Studies, Arizona State University, 1989.

Studies

Chu, Ch'ung-ts'ai 朱崇才. *Tz'u-hua hsüeh* 詞話學. Taipei: Wen-chin, 1995. *Ta-lu ti-chü po-shih lun-wen ts'ung-k'an,* 84. Reprint of a Ph.D. dissertation done on mainland China.

McLaren, Anne E. "Chantefables and the Textual Evolution of the *San-kuo-chih yen-i.*" *TP* 61 (1985): 159-227.

___. "The Discovery of Chinese Chantefable Narratives from the Fifteenth Century: A Reassessment of Their Likely Audience." *Ming Studies* 29 (1990): 1-29.

Tz'u-hua 詞話 (talks on lyrics)

Editions and References

Chang, Pao-ch'üan 張葆全, ed. *Chung-kuo ku-tai shih-hua tz'u-hua tz'u-tien* 中國古代詩話詞話辭典. Kweilin: Kuang-hsi Shih-fan Ta-hsüeh, 1992. Appends various bibliographical references and indexes.

Li, Fu-po 李復波, ed. *Tz'u-hua ts'ung-pien so-yin* 詞話叢編索引. Peking: Chung-hua, 1991.

Studies

Chang, Pao-ch'üan 張葆全. *Shih-hua ho tz'u-hua* 詩話和詞話. Shanghai: Shang-hai Ku-chi, 1983.

Wan-ch'ing-i shih-hui 晚晴簃詩匯 (**Poetry Collected at the Wan-ch'ing Studio**)

Editions and References

Wan-ch'ing-i shih-hui 晚晴簃詩匯. Hsü Shih-ch'ang (1855–1939), ed. 4v. Peking: Hsin-hua, 1989. Based on the 1929 edition.

Wang An-shih 王安石 (**1021-1086**)

Editions and References

Ch'iu, Han-sheng 邱漢生, ed. and comm. *Shih-i kou-ch'en* 詩義鉤沉. Peking: Chung-hua, 1982. Appends materials helpful in the study of Wang's writings.

Ch'üan Sung shih, 10:538-577.6474-6786.

Kuan, Shih-kuang 管士光, ed. *Wang An-shih hsiao-p'in* 王安石小品. Peking: Wen-hua I-shu, 1997.

Liu, Hsü-ch'i 劉須溪, *et al.*, eds. and comms. *Chien-chu Wang Ching-wen kung shih* 箋註王荊文公詩. Taipei: Kuang-wen, 1990.

P'ei, Ju-ch'eng 裴汝誠., ed. Wang *An-shih nien-p'u san-chung* 王安石年譜三種. Peking: Chung-hua, 1997.

Wang, Shui-chao 王水照 and Kao K'o-ch'in 高克勤, eds. *Wang An-shih san-wen hsüan-chi* 王安石散文選集. Shanghai: Shang-hai Ku-chi, 1997.

Yü, P'o 宇波, *et al.*, eds. *Wang An-shih ch'üan-chi* 王安石全集. 2v. Tsilin: Chi-lin, 1997.

Translations
Strassberg, *Inscribed Landscapes,* pp. 173-178.

Studies
Chiang, Mu 姜穆. *Wang An-shih ta-chuan* 王安石大傳. Taipei: Lien-ching Ch'u-pan, 1995.

Higashi, Ichio 東一夫. *Nihon chû kinsei no Ô Anseki kenkyû shi* 日本中近世の王安石研究史. Tokyo: Kazama Shobô, 1987.

Liu, Nai-ch'ang 劉乃昌 and Kao Hung-k'uei 高洪奎. *Wang An-shih shih-wen pien-nien hsüan-shih* 王安石詩文編年選釋. Tsinan: Shan-tung Chiao-yü, 1992.

Miura, Kunio 三浦国雄. *Ô Anseki* 王安石. Tokyo: Shûeisha, 1985. *Chûgoku no hito to shisô,* 7.

P'o, Che 朴哲. "Wang An-shih tz'u yen-chiu" 王安石詞研究. Unpublished Ph.D. dissertation, Ting-wu Ta-hsüeh, 1991.

Saeki, Tomi 佐伯富. *Ô Anseki* 王安石. Tokyo: Chûô Kôronsha, 1990.

Teng, Kuang-ming 鄧廣銘. *Wang An-shih chuan* 王庵石傳. Peking;Jen-min, 1998.

Wang, P'u-kuang 王普光. *Wang An-shih shih chi-ch'iao lun* 王安石詩技巧論. Sian: Shan-hsi Jen-min, 1992. *Chung-kuo ku-tai tso-chia yen-chiu ts'ung-shu.*

Wu-chou Wang An-shih Yen-chiu Hui, ed. 撫州王安石研究會. *Wang An-shih yen-chiu lun-wen chi* 王安石研究論文集. Wuchow: Wu-chou Wang An-shih Yen-chiu Hui, 1986.

Wang Ch'ang-ling 王昌齡 (*ca.* 690-*ca.* 756)

Editions and References
Huang, Ming 黃明, ed. and comm. *Wang Ch'ang-ling shih chi* 王昌齡詩集. Nanchang: Chiang-hsi Je-min, 1981. Rpt. Peking: Pai-hua-chou Wen-i, 1993.

Luan, Kuei-ming 欒貴明, ed. *Ch'uan T'ang-shih so-yin: Wang Ch'ang-ling chüan* 全唐詩索引：王昌齡卷. Peking: Chung-hua, 1997.

Li, Yün-i 李云逸, ed. and comm. *Wang Ch'ang-ling shih chu* 王昌齡詩註. Shanghai: Shang-hai Ku-chi, 1985. *T'ang shih hsiao-chi,* 1.5.

Yoshimura, Hiromichi 芳村弘道, ed. *Ô Shôrei shi sakuin* 王昌齡詩索引. Kyoto: Hôyû Shoten, 1983.

Studies
Hsieh, Ch'u-fa 謝楚發. "Wang Ch'ang-ling ch'i-chüeh mei-li ch'u-t'an" 王昌齡七絕魅力初探. *Chiang-han lun-t'an* 56 (1985): 50-55.

Hu, Wen-t'ao 胡問濤. "Lun Wang Ch'ang-ling te pien-sai-shih" 論王昌齡的邊塞詩. *Ssu-ch'uan Shih-yüan hsüeh-pao* 四川師院學報 1991.1 (1991): 75-81.

Huang, I-yüan 黃益元. "Wang Ch'ang-ling sheng-p'ing shih-chi pien-cheng" 王昌齡生平事跡辨證. *Wen-hsüeh i-ch'an* 1992.2 (1992): 31-34.

Li, Chen-hua 李珍華 and Fu Hsüan-ts'ung 傅璇琮. "T'an Wang Ch'ang-ling te 'shih-ko'" 談

王昌齡的詩格. *Wen-hsüeh i-ch'an* 1988.6 (1988): **85-97**.

Li, Hou-p'ei 李厚培. "Wang Ch'ang-ling liang-tz'u ch'u-sai lu-hsien k'ao" 王昌齡兩次出塞路線考. *Ch'ing-hai she-hui k'o-hsüeh* (1992): 75-80.

Okada, Mitsuhiro 岡田充博. "Ô Shôrei kenkyû bunken mokuroku kô" 王昌齡研究文献目録稿. *Nagoya Daigaku Chûgoku gogaku bungaku ronshû* 6 (1993): 39-53.

Wang, Ching-fen 王競芬. "Wang Ch'ang-ling sheng-p'ing hsing-i chi i-shih hsi-nien k'ao" 王昌齡生平行誼及遺詩繫年考. *Ssu yü yen* 25.1 (1987): 63-84.

Wang, Yün-hsi 王運熙. "Wang Ch'ang-ling te shih-ko li-lun" 王昌齡的詩歌理論. *Fu-tan hsüeh-pao* 1989.5 (1989): 22-29.

Wang Chi 王績 (585-644)

Editions and References

Han, Li-chou 韓理洲, comm. *Wang Wu-kung wen chi* 王無功文集. Shanghai: Shang-hai Ku-chi, 1987. Appends biographical information.

K'ang, Chin-sheng 康金聲 and Hsia Lien-pao 夏連保, eds. *Wang Chi chi pien-nien chiao-chu* 王績集編年校注. Taiyuan: Shan-hsi Jen-min, 1992.

Wang, Kuo-an 王國安, comm. *Wang Chi shih chu* 王績詩注. Shanghai: Shang-hai Ku-chi, 1985.

Studies

Chang, Hsi-hou 張錫厚. *Wang Chi yen-chiu* 王績研究. Taipei: Hsin-wen-feng, 1995.

Imaba, Masami 今場正美. "Ô Seki no denki" 王績伝記 *Gakurin* 14/15 (1990): 78-101.

Takagi, Shigetoshi 高木重俊. "ô Seki den ron: Ro Sai [ô Bukô bunshûjo] o megutte" 王績伝論：呂才「王無功文集序」おめぐって. *Kanbungaku ronshû* 1991: 359-390.

Wang Chien 王建 (751-*ca.* 830)

Editions and References

Luan, Kuei-ming 欒貴明 *et al.,* eds. *Ch'üan T'ang shih so-yin: Wang Chien chüan* 全唐詩索引：王建卷. Peking: Hsien-tai, 1995.

Studies

Naka, Junko 中純子. Chû-Tô kyûshi kô–O Ken kyûshi no miryoku" 中唐宮詞考–王建宮詞魅力. *Tenri Daigaku gakuhô* XLVII.1 (1995): 1-17.

Wu, Ch'i-ming 吳企明. "Wang Chien 'kung-tz'u' cha-i" 王建宮詞札迻. *Wen-hsüeh i-ch'an* 1982.4 (1982): 45-55.

Wang Fan-chih 王梵志 (early T'ang)

Editions and References

Chang, Hsi-hou 張錫厚, ed. *Wang Fan-chih shih chiao-chi* 王梵志詩校輯. Peking: Chung-hua, 1983. Appends a concordance to some of the terms used by Wang.

Hsiang, Ch'u 項楚, ed. *Wang Fan-chih shih chiao-chu* 王梵志詩校注. Shanghai: Shang-hai Ku-chi, 1991.

Translations

Tafel-Kehren, Dorothee. *Einige Gedichten von Wang Fan-chih: Übersetzungen von Texten aus*

Fonds Pelliot Chiois Ms. 3833. Bonn, 1982.

Studies

Chang, Hsi-hou 張錫厚, ed. *Wang Fan-chih shih yen-chiu hui-lu* 王梵志詩研究彙錄. Shanghai: Shang-hai Ku-chi, 1990.

Hsiang, Ch'u 項楚. "Wang Fan-chih shih-lun" 王梵志詩論. *Wen-shih* 31 (1989): 209–33.

Vetch, Hélène. "En marge de l'oeuvre de Wang le Zélateur: deux manuscrits inédits (P. 3724 et S. 6032) du volume sans titre." In *Contributions aux études de Touen-houang.* Michel Soymié, ed. Paris: L'École Française d'Extrême-Orient, 1988, pp. 155-193.

Wang Fu-chih 王夫之 (1619-1692)

Editions and References

Ch'uan-shan Ch'üan-shu 船山全書, ed. and comm. *Lung-yüan yeh hua* 龍源夜話. Changsha: Yüeh-lu Shu-she, 1992. *Ch'uan-shan ch'üan-shu,* 12.

___. *Shih ching pai-shu* 詩經稗疏. Changsha: Yüeh-lu Shu-she, 1992. *Ch'uan-shan ch'üan-shu,* 3.

___. *Shih kuang chuan* 詩廣傳. Changsha: Yüeh-lu Shu-she, 1992. *Ch'uan-shan ch'üan-shu,* 3.

___. *Tu T'ung-chien lun* 讀通鑒論. Changsha: Yüeh-lu Shu-she, 1988. *Ch'uan-shan ch'üan-shu,* 10.

Tai, Hung-seng 戴鴻森, ed. *Chiang-chai shih-hua chien-chu* 薑齋詩話箋注. Peking: Jen-min Wen-hsüeh, 1981. There is a Taiwan reprint published by Mu-to Ch'u-pan-she in 1982.

Translations

Wong, Siu-kit, trans. *Notes on Poetry from the Ginger Studio.* Hong Kong: The Chinese University Press, 1987.

Studies

Ch'ien, Chung-lien 錢仲聯. "Wang Ch'uan-shan shih-lun hou-an" 王船山詩論後案. In *Meng-t'iao-an Ch'ing-tai wen-hsüeh lun-chi* 夢苕庵清代文學論集. Tsinan: Ch'i-Lu Shu-she, 1983.

Li, Chi-p'ing 李季平. *Wang Fu-chih yü Tu T'ung-chien lun* 王夫之與讀通鑒論. Tsinan: Shan-tung Chiao-yü, 1982. Appends a *nien-piao.*

Liu, Ch'ang 劉暢. "Wang Ch'uan-shan shih-ko mei-hsüeh san-t'i" 王船山詩歌美學三題. *Wen-hsüeh i-ch'an* 1985.3 (1985): 101-09.

Liu, Ch'un-chien 劉春建. *Wang Fu-chih hsüeh hsing hsi nien* 王夫之學行系年. Chengchow: Chung-chou Ku-chi, 1989.

Liu, Heng-k'uei 柳亨奎. "Wang Fu-chih shih-p'ing ch'u t'an" 王夫之詩評初探. *Wen-hsüeh p'ing-lun* 8 (1984).

McCraw, *Chinese Lyricists,* pp. 41-62.

Wang, Chih-ch'un 王之春 (b. 1842). *Wang Fu-chih nien-p'u* 王夫之年譜. Peking: Chung-hua, 1989. Nien-p'u ts'ung-k'an. This Ch'ing dynasty work is annotated by Wang Mao-ho 汪茂和.

Yang, Sung-nien 楊松年. *Wang Fu-chih shih lun yen-chiu* 王夫之詩論研究. Taipei: Wen-shih-che, 1986.

Wang K'ai-yün 王闓運 (1832-1916)

Editions and References

Li, P'ei-ch'eng 李沛誠, comm. *Hsiang-chün chih* 湘軍志. Changsha: Yüeh-lu Shu-she, 1983.

Wang, K'ai-yün 王闓運, ed. *Pa-tai shih-hsüan* 八代詩選. 2v. Taipei: Kuang-wen, 1970.

Wang Kuo-wei 王國維 (1877-1927)

Editions and References

Fo, Chu 佛雛. *Kuang Jen-chien tz'u-hua* 廣人間詞話. Shanghai: Hua-tung Shih-fan Ta-hsüeh, 1990.

___. *Hsin-ting Jen-chien tz'u-hua* 新訂人間詞話. Shanghai: Hua-tung Shih-fan Ta-hsüeh, 1990.

Fo, Wei, ed. and comm. *Wang Kuo-wei che-hsüeh mei-hsüeh lun-wen chi-i* 佛維王國維哲學美學論文輯佚. Shanghai: Hua-tung Shih-fan Ta-hsüeh, 1993.

Hsi, Hsien-hui 滕咸惠, comm. *Jen-chien tz'u-hua hsin-chu* 人間詞話新注. Tsinan: Ch'i-Lu Shu-she, 1986.

Hsiao, Ai 蕭艾, comm. *Wang Kuo-wei shi-tz'u chien-chiao* 王國維詩詞箋校. Changsha: Hu-nan Jen-min, 1984.

Hsü, Tiao-fu 徐調孚 and Wang Yu-an 王幼安 comms. *Jen-chien tz'u-hua* 人間詞話. Taipei: Jen-min Wen-hsüeh, 1960. 4th reprint in 1982.

Liu, Kang-ch'iang 劉剛強, ed. *Wang Kuo-wei mei-lun wen hsüan* 王國維美論文選. Changsha: Hu-nan Jen-min, 1987.

Liu, Yin-sheng 劉寅生 and Yüan Ying-kuang 袁英光, eds. *Wang Kuo-wei ch'üan-chi: shu-hsin* 王國維全集：書信. Peking: Chung-hua, 1984. Chung-kuo chin-tai jen-wu wen chi ts'ung-shu.

Tu, Huan 杜環. *Ching-hsing chi* 經行記. Wang Kuo-wei 王國維, ed. and Chang I-ch'un 章一純, comm. Taipei: Shu-mu Wen-hsien, 1986.

Wang, Kuo-wei 王國維. *Shui-ching chu-chiao* 水經注校. Shanghai: Shang-hai Jen-min, 1984.

___. *Wang Kuo-wei i-shu* 王國維遺書. Shanghai: Shang-hai Ku-chi, 1993.

___. *Wang Kuo-wei hsi-ch'ü lun-wen chi* 王國維戲曲論文集. Peking: Chung-kuo Hsi-chü, 1986.

Yao, Kan-ming 姚淦銘 and Wang Yen 王燕, eds. *Wang Kuo-wei wen-chi* 王國維文集. 4v. Peking: Chung-kuo Wen-shih, 1997.

Studies

Bonner, Joey. *Wang Kuo-wei: An Intellectual Biography*. Cambridge, Massachusetts: Harvard University Press, 1986.

Ch'en, Yüan-hui 沉元暉. *Lun Wang Kuo-wei* 論王國維. Changchun: Tung-pei Shih-fan Ta-hsüeh, 1989.

Chou, Ming-chih 周明之. "Wang Kuo-wei te wen-hsüeh kuan" 王國維的文學觀. *Han-hsüeh yen-chiu* 13 1995.1 (1995): 239-80.

Fo, Chu 佛雛. *Wang Kuo-wei shih-hsüeh yen-chiu* 王國維詩學研究. Peking: Pei-ching Ta-hsüeh, 1987. Wen-i mei-hsüeh ts'ung-shu.

Hsiao, Ai 蕭艾. *Wang Kuo-wei p'ing-chuan* 王國維評傳. Hangchow: Che-chiang Wen-i, 1983. Che-chiang li-tai wen-hsüeh-chia p'ing-chuang ts'ung-shu.

Hung, Kuo-liang 洪國樑. *Wang Kuo-wei chih shih-shu hsüeh* 王國維之詩書學. Taipei: T'ai-wan Ta-hsüeh, 1984. Kuo-li T'ai-wan Ta-hsüeh wen-shih ts'ung-k'an, 66.

___. *Wang Kuo-wei chu-shu pien-nien t'i-yao* 王國維著述編年提要. Taipei: Ta-an, 1989.

Sun, Tun-heng 孫敦恆. *Wang Kuo-wei nien-p'u hsin-pien* 王國維年譜新編. Peking: Chung-kuo Wen-shih, 1991.

Suzuki, Yasushi 鈴木靖. "Ô Kokui no gikyoku kenkyû ni tsuite" 王国緯維の戲曲研究につい

て. *Hôsei Daigaku Kyôyôbu kiyô* 89 (1994).

Tsu, Pao-ch'üan 祖保泉 and Chang Hsiao-Yün 張曉雲. *Wang Kuo-wei ho* Jen-chien tz'u-hua 王國維和〔人間詞話〕. Taipei: San-min Shu-chü, 1993. *Chung-kuo ku-tien wen-hsüeh chi-pen chih-shih ts'ung-shu,* 65. Originally published by Shang-hai Ku-chi in 1978.

Wu, Tze 吳澤 and Yüan Ying-kuang 袁英光, eds. *Wang Kuo-wei hsüeh-shu yen-chiu lun chi* 王國維學術研究論集. Shanghai: Hua-tung Shih-fan Ta-hsüeh, 1983. *Chung-kuo shih-hsüeh yen-chiu chi-k'an.*

Yeh, Chia-ying. "Wang Kuo-wei's Song Lyrics in the Light of His Own Theories." In Yu, *Voices,* pp. 257-297.

Wang Po 王勃 (650-676)

Editions and References

Chiang, Ch'ing-i 蔣汪翊 (*fl.* 1883), comm. and ed. *Wang Tzu-an chi-chu* 王子安集注. Shanghai: Shang-hai Ku-chi, 1988.

Ho, Lin-t'ien 何林天, ed. and comm. *Ch'ung-ting hsin-chiao Wang Tzu-an chi* 重訂新校王子安集. Taiyuan: Shan-hsi Jen-min, 1990. *San-p'u ku-chi ts'ung-shu.*

Luan, Kuei-ming 欒貴明 *et al.*, eds. *Ch'üan T'ang shih so-yin: Wang Po chüan* 全唐詩索引：王勃卷. Peking: Chung-hua, 1992.

Shiomi, Kunihiko 塩見邦彦. *Ô Botsu shi ichiji sakuin* 王勃詩一字索引. Nagoya: Konron Shobô, 1986.

Wang, Kuo-an 王國安 and Wang Yu-min 王幼敏, eds. *Ch'u T'ang ssu-chieh yü Ch'en Tzu-ang shih-wen hsüan-chu* 初唐四傑與陳子昂詩文選注. Shanghai: Shang-hai Ku-chi, 1995. Chung-kuo ku-tien wen-hsüeh tso-p'ing hsüan-tu ts'ung-shu.

Translations

Mair, Victor H. *Mei Cherng's "Seven Stimuli" and Wang Bor's "Pavilion of King Terng:" Chinese Poems for Princes.* Lewiston: Edwin Mellen, 1988. Studies in Asian Thought and Religion, 11.

Strassberg, *Inscribed Landscapes,* pp. 105-110.

Studies

Chang, Chih-lieh 張志烈. *Ch'u T'ang ssu-chieh nien-p'u* 初唐四傑年譜. Chengtu: Pa-Shu Shu-she, 1992.

___. "Wang Po tsa-k'ao" 王勃雜考. *Ssu-ch'uan Ta-hsüeh hsüeh-pao (Che-she)* 1983.2.

Lo, Hsiang-fa 駱祥發. *Ch'u T'ang ssu-chieh yen-chiu* 初唐四傑研究. Peking: Tung-fang, 1993.

Nien, Wen-yü 聶文郁. Wang Po shih-chieh 王勃詩解. Hsining: Ch'ing-hai Jen-min, 1980.

Shen, Hui-yüeh 沈惠樂 and Ch'ien Hui-k'ang 錢惠康. *Ch'u-T'ang Ssu-chieh ho Ch'en Tzu-ang* 初唐四杰和陳子昂. Shanghai: Shang-hai Ku-chi, 1987.

Wang Shih-chen 王世貞 (1526-1590)

Editions and References

Koike, Kan 小池桓, ed. *Enen eibutsu shi* 弇園詠物詩. Tokyo: Kyûko Shoin, 1978.

Li, Yü-fu 李毓芙, ed. *Wang Yü-hsiang shih-wen hsüan-chu* 王漁祥詩文選注. Tsinan: Ch'i-Lu Shu-she, 1982.

Lo, Chung-ting 羅仲鼎, ed. and comm. *I-yüan chih yen chiao-chu* 藝苑卮言校注. Tsinan: Ch'i-Lu Shu-she, 1992. *Ming-tai wen-hsüeh li-lun ts'ung-shu.*

Wei, Lien-k'o 魏連科, ed. *Yen-shan-t'ang pieh-chi* 弇山堂別集. 100 *chüan.* 4v. Peking: Chung-hua,

1985.

Studies

Ch'en, Shu-lu 陳書錄. *Ming-tai ch'ien-hou ch'i-tzu yen-chiu* 明代前後七子研究. Nanchang: Chiang-hsi Sheng Jen-min, 1994.

Huang, Chih-min 黃志民. "Wang Shih-chen yen-chiu" 王世貞研究. Unpublished Ph. D. dissertation, Cheng-chih Ta-hsüeh, 1976.

Wang Shih-chen 王士禛 (1634-1711)

Editions and References

Wang, Shao-tseng 王紹曾 and Tu Tse-sun 杜澤孫, eds. *Yü-yang tu-shu chi* 魚洋讀書記. Chingtao: Ch'ing-tao Ch'u-pan-she, 1991.

Wang, Shih-chen 王士禛. *Hsiang-tsu pi-chi* 香祖筆記. Fu Hsüan-ts'ung 傅璇琮, comm. Shanghai: Shang-hai Ku-chi, 1982. Ming Ch'ing pi-chi ts'ung-shu.

___. *Ku-shih chien* 古詩箋. Annotated by Wen Jen-t'an 聞人倓 in the Ch'ing dynasty. 2v. Shanghai: Shang-hai Ku-chi, 1980.

___. *Wang Shih-chen nien-p'u* 王士禛年譜. Sun Yen-ch'eng 孫言誠, ed. and comm. Peking: Chung-hua, 1992. Nien-p'u ts'ung-k'an. This autobiography was originally entitled *Yü-yang Shan-jen nien-p'u* 魚洋山譜.

___, ed. *Wu-tai shih-hua* 五代詩話. Re-edited with commentary by Li Chen-hua 李珍華. Peking: Shu-mu Wen-hsien, 1989.

___. *Yen-po tz'u* 衍波詞. Li Shao-yung 李少雍, ed. Canton: Kuang-tung Jen-min, 1986. T'ien-feng ko ts'ung-shu. Appends materials for the study of Wang's life.

Translations

Strassberg, *Inscribed Landscapes,* pp. 297-302.

Studies

Bryant, Daniel. "Syntax, Sound, and Sentiment in Old Nanking: Wang Shih-chen's 'Miscellaneous Poems on the Ch'in-huai.'" *CLEAR* 14 (1992): 25-50.

Wang T'ao 王韜 (1828-1897)

Editions and References

Wang, T'ao 王韜. *Hou Liao-chai chih i ch'üan-i hsiang-chu* 後聊齋志異全譯詳注. 3v. Wang Pin 王彬, *et al,* comms. Harbin: Hei-lung-chiang Jen-min, 1988.

___. *Man-yu sui-lu Fu-sang yu-chi* 漫游隨錄扶桑遊記. Ch'en Shang-fan 陳尚凡 and Jen Kuang-liang 任光亮, eds. Changsha: Hu-nan Jen-min, 1982.

___. *Sung-pin so-hua* 淞濱瑣話. Liu Wen-chung 劉文忠, ed. Tsinan: Ch'i-Lu Shu-she, 1986. *Ch'ing-tai pi-chi hsiao-shuo ts'ung-k'an*

___. *Sung-yin man-lu* 淞隱漫錄. Wang Ssu-yü 王思宇, ed. Peking: Jen-min Wen-hsüeh, 1983. *Chung-kuo hsiao-shuo shih-liao ts'ung-shu.*

___. *Wang T'ao jih-chi* 王韜日記. Fang Hsing 方行 and T'ang Chih-chün 湯志鈞, eds. Peking: Chung-hua, 1987. *Chung-kuo chin-tai jen-wu jih-chi ts'ung-shu.*

___. *Weng-yu yü-t'an* 瓮牖餘談. Chengtu: Pa-Shu Shu-she, 1993. *Chung-kuo yeh-shih chi-ch'eng,* 49.

___. *Ying-juan tsa-chih* 瀛壖雜志. Shen Heng-ch'un 沈恆春 and Yang Ch'i-min 楊其民, eds. Shanghai: Shang-hai Ku-chi, 1989.

Studies

Chang, Hai-lin 張海林. *Wang T'ao p'ing-chuan* 王韜評傳. Nanking: Nan-ching Ta-hsüeh, 1993. *Chung-kuo ssu-hsiang-chia p'ing-chuan ts'ung-shu,* 34. Appends bibliographical references and a name index.

Chu, Ch'uan-yü 朱傳譽. *Wang T'ao chuan-chi tzu-liao* 王韜傳記資料. 3v. Taipei: T'ien-i, 1979.

Hsin, P'ing 忻平. *Wang T'ao p'ing-chuan* 王韜評傳. Shanghai: Hua-tung Shih-fan Ta-hsüeh, 1990.

Wang Ts'an 王粲 (177-217)

Editions and References

Han, Ko-p'ing 韓格平, ed. *Chien-an ch'i tzu shih-wen chi chiao-chu hsiang-hsi* 建安七子詩文集校注詳析. Changchun: Chi-lin Wen-shih, 1991.

Wu, Yün 吳云 and T'ang Shao-chung 唐紹忠, comm. *Wang Ts'an chi-chu* 王粲集注. Chengchow: Chung-chou Shu-hua-she, 1984. Appends biographical information.

Yü, Hsien-hao 郁賢皓, ed. *Chien-an ch'i-tzu shih chien-chu* 建安七子詩箋注. Chengtu: Pa-Shu Shu-she, 1990.

Yü, Shao-ch'u 俞紹初, comm. *Chien-an ch'i-tzu chi* 建安七子集. Peking: Chung-hua, 1989. *Chung-kuo ku-tien wen-hsüeh chi-pen ts'ung-shu.* Includes a section on the writings of Wang Ts'an.

Wang Wei 王維 (701-761)

Editions and References

Chao, Tien-ch'eng 趙殿成, ed. *Wang Yu-ch'eng chi chien-chu* 王右丞集箋注. Shanghai: Shang-hai Ku-chi, 1984.

Ch'en, K'ang 陳抗, *et al.*, eds. *Ch'üan T'ang shih so-yin: Wang Wei chüan* 全唐詩索引：王維卷. Peking: Chung-hua, 1992.

Ch'en, T'ieh-min 陳鐵民, ed. *Wang Wei chi chiao-chu* 王維集校注. Peking: Chung-hua, 1997. App ~nds selected biographical materials and traditional criticism of Wang's verse.

Ch'en, Wen-p'eng 陳文鵬. *Wang Wei shih-ko shang-hsi* 王維詩歌賞析. Nanning: Kuang-hsi Chiao-yü, 1991.

Teng, An-sheng 鄧安生, *et al.*, eds. and comms. *Wang Wei shih hsüan-i* 王維詩選譯. Chengtu: Pa-Shu Shu-she, 1990. *Ku-tai wen-shih ming-chu hsüan-i ts'ung-shu.* Reprinted in Taiwan as *Wang Wei shih* 王維詩 by Chin-hsiu in 1993.

Wang, Ta-chin 王達津, ed. and comm. *Wang Wei Meng Hao-jan hsüan-chi* 王維孟浩然選集. Shanghai: Shang-hai Ku-chi, 1990.

Translations

Barnstone, Tony, *et al.*... *Laughing Lost in the Mountains: Poems of Wang Wei.* Hanover: University Press of New England, 1991.

Carré, Patrick. *Les Saisons bleues: L'oeuvre de Wang Wei, poète et peintre.* Paris: Editions Phebus, 1989.

Chang, Wei-penn and Lucien Drivod. *Paysages: Miroirs du Cœur.* Paris: Gallimard, 1990.

Cheng, Wing-fun and Hervé Collet. *Wang Wei, le plein du vide.* 2nd revised ed. Millemont, France: Moundarren, 1986. Free, unannotated versions of more than 30 poems preceded by a short introduction.

Strassberg, *Inscribed Landscapes,* pp. 111-114.

Tsuge, Keiichirô 柘植敬一郎. *Ō I no fūi Shiga bunshû* 王維の風姿 詩画文集. Tokyo: Shoshi

465

Yamada, 1993.

Studies

Ang, A.C. 洪惜珠. "Taoist-Buddhist Elements in Wang Wei's Poetry." *Chinese Culture* 30.1 (1989): 79-89.

Chang, Ch'ing-hua 張清華. *Shih-fo—Wang Mo-chieh chuan* 詩佛—王摩詰傳. Chengchow: Honan Jen-min, 1991.

___. *Wang Wei nien-p'u* 王維年譜. Shanghai: Hsüeh-lin, 1988.

Ch'en, T'ieh-min 陳鐵民. *Wang wei hsin-lun* 王維新論. Peking: Pei-ching Shih-fan Hsüeh-yüan, 1990.

___. "Wang Wei sheng-nien hsin-t'an" 王維生年新探. *Wen-shih* 28 (1988): 185-94.

Ch'en, Yün-chi 陳允吉. "Wang Wei 'Chung-nan pieh-shu' chi 'Wang ch'uan pieh-shu' k'ao" 王維終南別墅即輞川別墅考. *Wen-hsüeh i-ch'an* 1985.1: 45-54.

Chin, Hsüeh-chih 金學智. "Wang Wei shih-chung te hui-hua-mei" 王維詩中的繪畫美. *Wen-hsüeh i-ch'an* 1984.4 (1984): 55-66.

Cleaves, Francis Woodman. "Additional Data on Sung Lien, Wang Wei, and Chao Hsün." Appended to "The 'Postscript to the Table of Contents of the *Yüan shih.*'" *JSYS* 23 (1993): 13-18 (1-18).

Dagdanov, G. B. "Vliianie chan'buddizma na tvorchestvo tanskikh poetov. Na primere Van Veia (701-761) i Bo Tsziu-ii (772-846) [The Influence of Ch'an Buddhism on the Writings of the T'ang Poets: The Cases of Wang Wei (701-761) and Po Chu-i (772-846)]." Unpublished Ph. D. dissertation, Institut vostokovedeniia Akademii nauk SSSR, 1980.

Liu, Ch'eng-chün 柳晟俊. *Wang Wei shih pi-chiao yen-chiu* 王維詩比較研究. Kweilin: Kuang-hsi Shih-fan Ta-hsüeh, 1997.

___. *Wang Wei shih yen-chiu* 王維詩研究. Taipei: Li-ming Wen-hua Kung-ssu, 1987.

Lu, Yü 盧渝. *Wang Wei chuan* 王維傳. Taiyuan: Shan-hsi Jen-min, 1989.

Kao, Ming 高明, *et al.*, eds. *Wang Wei* 王維. Taipei: Chin-hsiu, 1992. *T'ang shih hsin-shang*, 3.

Wang, Ts'ung-jen 王從仁. *Wang Wei ho Meng Hao-jan* 王維和孟浩然. Shanghai: Shang-hai Ku-chi, 1984. *Chung-kuo ku-tien wen-hsüeh chi-pen chih-shih ts'ung-shu*, 34. Reprinted in Taiwan in 1992.

Wang Wei Yen-chiu Hui 王維研究會, ed. *Wang Wei yen-chiu* 王維研究. Peking: Chung-kuo Kung-jen, 1992. Various articles on the life, thought and writings of Wan Wei.

Weinberger, Eliot. *Nineteen Ways of Looking at Wang Wei: How a Chinese Poem is Translated.* Mount Kisco: Moyer Bell, 1987.

Yang, Wen-hsiung 楊文雄. *Shih-fo Wang Wei Yen-chiu* 詩佛王維研究. Taipei: Wen-shih-che, 1988.

T'ao, Wen-p'eng 陶文鵬. *Wang Wei shih-ko shang-hsi* 王維詩歌賞析. Nanning: Kuang-hsi Chiao-yü, 1991. *Chung-kuo ku-tien wen-hsüeh tso-p'in hsüan-hsi ts'ung-shu.*

Wang Ying-lin 王應麟 (1223-1296)

Editions and References

Wang, Ying-lin 王應麟, ed. *Hsiao-hsüeh kan-chu* 小學紺珠. Shanghai: Shang-hai Ku-chi, 1990. *Ho-k'o pen lei-shu chi-ch'eng*, 2.

___. *San tzu ching* 三字經. Tsinan: Shan-tung Yu-i Shu-she, 1989.

___. *I chieh fu lu* 易解附錄. Shanghai: Shang-wu Yin-shu-kuan, 1935–37. Contains the commentary of Cheng Hsüan 鄭玄 (127–200).

Wang Yü-ch'eng 王禹稱 (954-1001)

Editions and References
Ch'üan Sung shih, 2:59-71.653-811.
Ch'üan Sung wen, 4:137-158.203-589.
Wang, Yen-t'i 王延梯, ed. *Wang Yü-ch'eng shih-wen hsüan* 王禹稱詩文選. Peking: Wen-hsüeh,
    1997.

Studies
Hsü, Kuei 徐規. *Wang Yü-ch'eng shih-chi chu-tso pien-nien* 王禹稱事跡著作編年. Peking: Chung-
    kuo She-hui K'o-hsüeh, 1982.

Wei Chuang 韋莊 (*ca.* 836-910)

Editions
Hsia, Ch'eng-t'ao 夏承燾, ed. and Liu Chin-ch'eng 劉金城, comm. *Wei Chuang tz'u chiao-chu*
    韋莊詞校注. Peking: Chung-kuo She-hui K'o-hsüeh, 1981.
Li, I 李誼, ed. *Wei Chuang chi chiao-chu* 韋莊集校注. Chengtu: Ssu-ch'uan Sheng She-hui
    K'o-hsüeh Yüan, 1986.
Tseng, Chao-min 曾昭岷, ed. *Wen, Wei, Feng tz'u hsin-chiao* 溫韋馮詞新校. Shanghai: Shang-hai
    Ku-chi, 1988.

Translations
Yates, Robin D.S. *Washing Silk: The Life and Selected Poetry of Wei Chuang (834?-910).* Cambridge,
    Massachusetts: Harvard University Press, 1988. *Harvard-Yenching Monograph Series,*
    26. Detailed scholarly study of Wei's biography, background and poetry followed
    by annotated translations of *shih* (110 poems) and *tz'u* (55).

Studies
Mo, Li-feng 莫礪鋒. "Lun Wan-T'ang Wu-tai tz'u-feng te chuan-pien-chien lun Wei Chuang
    tsai tz'u-shih shang te ti-wei" 論晚唐五代詞風的轉變-兼論韋莊在詞史上的地位. *Wen-
    hsüeh i-ch'an* 1980.5.
Yeh, Chia-ying 葉嘉瑩. *Wen T'ing-yün, Wei Chuang, Feng Yen-ssu, Li Yü* 溫庭筠韋莊馮延巳李
    煜. Taipei: Ta-an, 1992. *T'ang Sung ming-chia tz'u shang-hsi,* 1.

Wei Ying-wu 韋應物 (737-*ca.* 792)

Studies
Chiang, Kuang-tou 姜光斗 and Ku Ch'i 顧啟. "Wei Ying-wu jen Su-chou tz'u-shih shih te
    chien-shu ho wan-nien kai-k'uang" 韋應物任蘇州刺史時的建樹和晚年概況. *Su-chou
    Ta-hsüeh hsüeh-pao* 1986.4: 122-26.
Ch'u, Chung-chün 儲仲君. "Wei Ying-wu shih fen-ch'i te t'an-t'ao" 韋應物詩分期的探討.
    Wen-hsüeh i-ch'an 1984.4 (1984): 67-75.
Hsü, C.Y. "The Stone Drums." *Asian Culture Quarterly* 13.1 (1985): 87-109. A study of poems
    inscribed on ancient drum-shaped stelae and of Wei Ying-wu, Han Yü and other
    later poets' verses on them.
Jen, Li-li 任莉莉. "*Wei Su-chou chi* hsü-lu" 韋蘇州集敍錄. *Ku-kung wen-wu yüeh-k'an* 70-71
    (1989): 70: 128-33; 71: 130-37.
Lee, Oscar. "The Critical Perception of the Poetry of Wei Ying-wu (737-792): The Creation

of a Poetic Reputation." Unpublished Ph.D. dissertation, Columbia University, 1986.

Li, Shih-ying 李世英 and Hou Jun-chang 侯潤章. "Chin-nien lai Wei Ying-wu yen-chiu chih chien-lun" 近年來韋應物研究之檢論. *Lan-chou Ta-hsüeh hsüeh-pao* 1988.2: 100-5.

Lim, Chooi Kua 林水檺. "The Artistic Achievement and Style of Wei Ying-wu's Poetry." *Chinese Culture* 35 1994.3 (1994): 25-44.

Suzuki, Toshio 鈴木敏雄. "I Ôbotsu no zatsugishi ni tsuite" 韋応物の雑擬詩について. *Nihon Chûgoku Gakkaihô* 42 (1990): 125-140.

___. "I Ôbotsu gikoshi nijusshu kô" 韋応物雑擬詩二十首考. *Chûgoku chûsei bungaku kenkyû* 20 (1991): 159-78.

Tseng, Chao-min 曾昭岷, ed. *Wen, Wei, Feng tz'u hsin-chiao* 溫韋馮詞新校. Shanghai: Shang-hai Ku-chi, 1988.

Varsano, Paula M. "The Invisible Landscape of Wei Ying-wu (732-792)." *HJAS* 54.2 (1994): 407-35.

Wang, Hsi-yüan 王熙元, *et al*, eds. *Wei Ying-wu* 韋應物. Taipei: Chin-hsiu, 1992. *T'ang shih hsin-shang*, 8.

Yoshimura, Hiromichi 芳村弘道. "I Ôbotsu no shôgai" 韋応物の生涯. *Gakurin* 7-8 (1986): 7: 53-69; 8: 66-84.

Wen-chang pien-t'i 文章辨體 (Distinguishing the Forms of Literature)

Editions and References

Ho, Fu-cheng 賀復徵 (Ming dynasty), ed. *Wen-chang pien-t'i* 文章辨體. Taipei: Tai-wan Shang-wu Yin-shu-kuan, 1983. *Ching-yin-wen yüan-ko ssu-k'u chüan-shu*, 1402-1410.

Wen-hsin tiao-lung 文心雕龍 (The Literary Mind and the Carving of Dragons)

Editions and References

Chan, Ying 詹鍈, comm. *Wen-hsin tiao-lung i-cheng* 文心雕龍義證. 3v. Shanghai: Shang-hai Ku-chi, 1989.

Chang, Shao-k'ang 張少康. *Wen-hsin tiao-lung hsin-t'an* 文心雕龍新探. Taipei: Wen-shih-che, 1991.

Chia, Chin-fu 賈錦福, ed. *Wen-hsin tiao-lung tz'u-tien* 文心雕龍辭典. Tsinan: Chi-nan Ch'u-pan-she, 1993.

Chou, Chen-fu 周振甫, ed. *Wen-hsin tiao-lung chin-i* 文心雕龍今譯. Peking: Chung-hua, 1986.

___. *Wen-hsin tiao-lung chu-shih* 文心雕龍注釋. Peking: Jen-min Wen-hsüeh, 1980.

___. *Wen-hsin tiao-lung hsüan-i* 文心雕龍選譯. Peking: Chung-hua, 1980.

___. *Wen-hsin tiao-lung tz'u-tien* 文心雕龍辭典. Peking: Chung-hua, 1997.

Chu, Ying-p'ing 朱迎平, ed. *Wen-hsin tiao-lung so-yin* 文心雕龍索引. Shanghai: Shang-hai Ku-chi, 1987. Not a full concordance, this work contains an index of sentences, works cited, and literary-critical terms.

Feng, Ch'un-t'ien 馮春田, ed. and comm. *Wen-hsin tiao-lung shih-i* 文心雕龍釋義. Tsinan: Shan-tung Chiao-yü, 1986.

Hsiang, Ch'ang-ch'ing 向長清, ed. *Wen-hsin tiao-lung chien-shih* 文心雕龍淺釋. Changchun: Chi-lin Jen-min, 1984.

Huang, Shu-lin 黃叔琳 (1672–1756), ed. and comm. *Wen-hsin tiao-lung chi-chu* 文心雕龍輯注. Taipei: T'ai-wan Shang-wu Yin-shu-kuan, 1983. Based on the *Ssu-k'u ch'üan-shu* edition.

Li, Chen-fei 李蓁非, comm. *Wen-hsin tiao-lung shih-i* 文心雕龍釋譯. Nanchang: Chiang-hsi

Jen-min, 1993.

Li, Yüeh-kang 李日剛, ed. *Wen-hsin tiao-lung chiao-ch'üan* 文心雕龍斠詮. Taipei: Kuo-li Pien-i-kuan, 1982.

Lin, Ch'i-t'an 林其錟 and Ch'en Feng-chin 陳鳳金, eds and comms. *Tun-huang i-shu Wen-hsin tiao-lung ts'an-chüan chi-chiao* 敦煌遺書文心彫龍殘卷集校. Shanghai: Shang-hai Shu-tien, 1991.

Lu, K'an-ju 陸侃如 and Mou Shih-chin 牟世金, comms. *Wen-hsin tiao-lung i-chu* 文心雕龍譯注. 2v. Tsinan: Ch'i-Lu Shu-she, 1981.

Lung, Pi-k'un 龍必錕, comm. *Wen-hsin tiao-lung ch'üan-i* 文心雕龍全譯. Kweiyang: Kuei-chou Jen-min, 1992.

Mou, Shih-chin 牟世金, ed. *Wen-hsin tiao-lung ching-hsüan* 文心雕龍精選. Shantung: Shan-tung Ta-hsüeh, 1986.

Mu, K'o-hung 穆克宏, ed. *Wen-hsin tiao-lung hsüan* 文心雕龍選. Fukien: Fu-chien Chiao-yü, 1985.

Wang, Keng-sheng 王更生, ed. *Wen-hsin tiao-lung hsin-lun* 文心雕龍新論. Taipei: Wen-shih-che, 1991.

___. *Wen-hsin tiao-lung hsüan-tu* 文心雕龍選讀. Taipei: Chü-liu, 1994.

Yang, Ming-chao 楊明照, ed. *Wen-hsin tiao-lung chiao-chu shih-i* 文心彫龍校注拾遺. Shanghai: Shang-hai Ku-chi, 1982.

___, ed. *Wen-hsin tiao-lung hsüeh tsung-lan* 綜文心雕龍學覽. Shanghai: Shang-hai Shu-tien, 1995. An important reference divided into studies of research in various nations or regions followed by specialized studies of the author, editions, etc.

Yüeh, Chung-i 越仲邑, ed. *Wen-hsin tiao-lung i-chu* 文心雕龍譯注. Nanning: Kuang-hsi Chiao-yü, 1990.

Translations

Mekata,, Makoto 目加田誠. *Bunshin chôryô* 文心雕龍. Tokyo: Ryûkei Shosha, 1986.

Studies

Chao, Chün 趙俊. "Liu Hsieh te shih-hsüeh p'i-p'ing" 劉勰的史學批評. *She-hui k'o-hsüeh chi-k'an* 71 (1990): 75–81.

Chan, Ying 詹鍈,. *Liu Hsieh yü Wen-hsin tiao-lung* 劉勰與文心雕龍. Peking: Chung-hua, 1980.

Chang, Jen-ch'ing 張仁青. *Wen-hsin tiao-lung t'ung-ch'üan* 文心雕龍通詮. Taipei: Ming-wen Shu-chü, 1985.

Ch'en, Chao-hsiu 陳兆秀. *Wen-hsin tiao-lung shu-yü t'an-hsi* 文心雕龍術語探析. Taipei: Wen-shih-che, 1986.

Ch'en, Ssu-ling 陳思苓. *Wen-hsin tiao-lung i-lun* 文心雕龍臆論. Chengtu: Pa-Shu Shu-she, 1988.

Ch'en, Yao-nan 陳耀南. *Wen-hsin tiao-lung lun-chi* 文心雕龍論集. Kowloon: Hsien-tai Chiao-yü Yen-chiu She, 1989.

Chiang, Shu-ko 姜書閣, ed. *Wen-hsin tiao-lung i-chih* 文心雕龍繹旨. Tsinan: Ch'i-Lu Shu-she, 1984.

Chiang, Tsu-i 蔣祖怡. *Wen-hsin tiao-lung lung-ts'ung* 文心雕龍論叢. Shanghai: Shang-hai Ku-chi, 1985.

Chu, Kuang-ch'eng 朱廣成. *Wen-hsin tiao-lung te ch'uang-tso lun* 文心雕龍創論. Peking: Chung-kuo Kuang-po Tien-shih, 1991.

Chung-kuo Ku-tien Wen-hsüeh Yen-chiu Hui 中國古典文學研究會, ed. *Wen-hsin tiao-lung tsung-lun* 文心雕龍綜論. Taipei: Hsüeh-sheng, 1988. Contains a wide range of interesting studies by a variety of scholars.

Fang, Yüan-chen 方元珍. *Wen-hsin tiao-lung yü fo-chiao kuan-hsi chih k'ao-pien* 文心雕龍與佛

教關係之考辨. Taipei: Wen-shih-che, 1987.

Fu, Chih 甫之 and T'u Kuang-she 涂光社, eds. *Wen-hsin tiao-lung yen-chiu lun-wen hsüan* 文心雕龍研究論文選. 2v. Tsinan: Ch'i-Lu Shu-she, 1988.

Hsia, Chih-hou 夏志厚. "*Wen-hsin tiao-lung* ch'eng-shu nien-tai yü Liu Hsieh ssu-hsiang yüan-yüan hsin-k'ao" 文心雕龍成書年代與劉勰思想淵源新考. *Ku-tai wen-hsüeh li-lun yen-chiu* 11 (1986): 78-95.

Hsiang, Yün 降云, ed. *Wen-hsin tiao-lung yen-chiu lun-wen chi* 文心雕龍研究論文集. Peking: Jen-min Wen-hsüeh, 1990.

Huang, Wei-liang 黃維樑. "Ching Tiao-lung yü ching kung-weng–Liu Hsieh ho hsin p'i-p'ing-chia tui chieh-kou ti k'an-fa" 精雕龍與精工甕– 劉勰和新批評家對結構的看法. *Chung-wai wen-hsüeh* 18: 7 (1989): 4–20.

Jao, P'eng-tzu 饒芃子, ed. *Wen-hsin tiao-lung yen-chiu hui-ts'ui* 文心雕龍研究薈萃. Shanghai: Shang-hai Shu-she, 1992. A collection of articles selected from those presented at the 1988 international conference on the *Wen-hsin tiao-lung*.

Kral, Oldrich. "Tradition and Change–The Nature of Classicism in *Wen Hsin Tiao Long.*" *AO* 59 (1992): 181-189.

Li, Zhaochu. *Traditionelle chinesische Literaturtheorie: Wenxin diaolong, Liu Xies Buch vom prächtigen Stil des Drachenschnitzens (5. Jh.).* Dortmund: projekt, 1997. *Edition Cathay,* 25.

Miao, Chün-chieh 繆俊杰. *Wen-hsin tiao-lung mei-hsüeh* 文心雕龍美學. Peking: Wen-hua I-shu, 1987.

Mou, Shih-chin 牟世金. *Wen-hsin tiao-lung yen-chiu* 文心雕龍研究. Peking: Jen-min Wen-hsüeh, 1995. *Chung-kuo ku-tien wen-hsüeh yen-chiu ts'ung-shu.*

Mu, K'o-hung 穆克宏. *Wen-hsin tiao-lung yen-chiu* 文心雕龍研究. Foochow: Fu-chien Chiao-yü, 1991.

Pi, Wan-ch'en 畢萬忱 and Li Miao 李淼. *Wen-hsin tiao-lung lun-kao* 文心雕龍論稿. Tsinan: Ch'i-Lu Shu-she, 1985.

Shih, Chia-i 石家宜. *Wen-hsin tiao-lung cheng-t'i yen-chiu* 文心雕龍整體研究. Nanking: Nan-ching Ch'u-pan-she, 1993.

Shimizu, Yoshio 清水凱夫. "Chûgoku ni okeru 1980 nen ikô no Shô Kô *Shihin* kenkyû gaikan (2)-*Shihin* to *Bunshin chôryô* no bungakukan no idô ronsô o chûshin to shite" 中国における一九八〇年以降の鍾嶸「詩品」研究概観（二）-『詩品』と『文心雕龍』の文学観の異同論争を中心として, *Chûgoku bungakuhô* 45 (1992).

Sommardal, Göran. "The Literary Cosmology and the Literary Cosmos of the *Wenxian diaolong.*" In Joakim Enwall, ed. *Outstretched Leaves on His Bamboo Staff: Studies in Honour of Göran Malmqvist on His 70th Birthday.* Stockholm: Association of Oriental Studies, 1994, 247-68.

Sun, Jung-jung 孫蓉蓉. *Wen-hsin tiao-lung yen-chiu* 文心雕龍研究. Nanchang: Chiang-hsi Chiao-yü, 1994.

Ts'ai, Tsung-yang 蔡宗陽. "Liu Hsieh *Wen-hsin tiao-lung* yü ching-hsüeh" 劉勰文心雕龍與經學. Unpublished Ph. D. dissertation, National Taiwan Normal University, 1989.

Tsu, Pao-ch'üan 祖保泉. *Wen-hsin tiao-lung chieh-shuo* 文心雕龍解説. Hofei: An-hui Chiao-yü, 1993.

Tu, Li-chün 杜黎均. *Wen-hsin tiao-lung wen-hsüeh li-lun yen-chiu ho i-shih* 文心雕龍文學 理論研究和譯釋. Peking: Pei-ching Ch'u-pan-she, 1981.

Wang, Keng-sheng 王更生. "Liu Hsieh *Wen-hsin tiao-lung* feng-ko lun hsin-t'an" 劉勰文心雕龍風格論新探. *Shih-ta hsüeh-pao* 36 (1991): 139–157.

___. "Lun Liu Hsieh wen-t'i fen-lei hsüeh te chi-chü" 論劉勰文體分類學的基據. *Kuo-li pien-i kuan kuan k'an* 17: 1 (1988): 1–14.

___. "*Wen-hsin tiao-lung* t'i-hsi te ssu-hsiang yü li-shih chi-ch'u" 文心雕龍體系的思想與歷史基楚. *Fu-jen kuo-wen hsüeh-pao* 輔仁國文學報 1988.4 (1988): 131–149.

Wang, Peter B. "Classicism in Aristotle's 'Poetics' and Liu Xie's 'Wenxin diaolung.'"

470

Unpublished Ph.D. dissertation, University of Washington, 1990.

Wang, Yün-hsi. *Wen-hsin tiao-lung t'an-so* 文心雕龍探索. Shanghai: Shang-hai Ku-chi, 1986.

Wang, Yüan-hua 王元化. *Wen-hsin tiao-lung chiang-shu* 文心雕龍講疏. Shanghai: Shang-hai Ku-chi, 1992.

Wen-hsin tiao-lung hsüeh-k'an 文心雕龍學刊. Tsinan: Ch'i-Lu Shu-she. Published irregularly and edited by Wen-hsin tiao-lung hsüeh-hui 文心雕龍學會, this journal is devoted to studies of the *Wen-hsin tiao-lung.*

Wen-hsin tiao-lung yen-chiu. Peking: Pei-ching Ta-hsüeh. Established in 1995, this journal is devoted to studies of the *Wen-hsin tiao-lung.*

Yang, Ming-chao 楊明照. "Ts'ung *Wen-hsin tiao-lung* k'an Chung-kuo ku-tai wen-lun shih, lun p'ing chieh-ho te min-tzu t'e-sse" 從文心雕龍看中國古代文論史，論評結和的民族特色. *Ku-tai wen-hsüeh li-lun yen-chiu* 10 (1985): 1-9.

___. "*Wen-hsin tiao-lung yüan-tao-p'ien* wen chih wei te ye chü shih-chieh" 文心雕龍原道篇文之為德也句試解. *Wen-shih* 32 (1990): 282–311.

Yü, K'o-k'un 禹克坤. *Wen-hsin tiao-lung yü Shih-p'in* 文心雕龍與詩品. Peking: Jen-min, 1989.

Zhao, Heping. "*Wen xin diao long.* An Early Chinese Rhetoric of Written Discourse," Unpublished Ph.D. dissertation, Purdue University, 1990.

Wen-hsüan 文選 (**Anthology of Literature**)

Editions and References

Hu, Shao-ying 胡紹煐 (Ch'ing dynasty). *Wen-hsüan chien-cheng* 文選箋證. 32 *chüan.* Shanghai: Shang-hai Shu-tien, 1994.

Huang, K'an 黃侃 (1886-1935), comm. and Huang Cho 黃焯, ed. Wen-hsüan *p'ing-tien* 文選平點. Shanghai: Shang-hai Ku-chi, 1985.

Makizumi, Etsuko 牧角悦子, ed. *Monzen kenkyû ronsha mokuroku* 文選研究論著目録. Kyushu: Kyûshû Daigaku, 1986.

Sun, Chih-tsu 孫志祖, (1737–1801), ed. *Wen-hsüan Li-chu pu-cheng* 文選李注補正. Peking: Chung-hua, 1985.

Ting, Fu-pao 丁福保 (1874–1952), ed. *Wen-hsüan lei-ku* 文選類詁. Peking: Chung-hua, 1990.

Wei, Shu-ch'in 魏淑琴, Wu Ch'iung 吳窮, and Chiang Hui 姜惠, eds. *Chung-wai Chao-ming Wen-hsüan yen-chiu lun-chu so-yin* 中外昭明文選研究論著索引. Changchun: Chi-lin Wen-shih, 1988.

Translations

Chang, Ch'i-ch'eng 張啟成 and Hsü Ta 徐達, trans. and comms. *Wen-hsüan ch'üan-i* 文選全譯. 5v. Kweiyang: Kuei-chou Jen-min, 1990. Chung-kuo li-tai ming-chu ch'üan-i ts'ung-shu.

Ch'en, Hung-t'ien 陳宏天, Chao Fu-hai 趙福海, and Ch'en Fu-hsing 陳復興, eds. *Chao-ming Wen-hsüan i-chu* 昭明文藝譯注. 4v. V. 1-2, Changchun: Chi-lin Wen-shih, 1988; v. 3-4, 1992.

Knechtges, David R. *Wenxuan or Selections of Refined Literature. Volume Two: Rhapsodies on Sacrifices, Hunting, Travel, Sightseeing, Palaces and Halls, Rivers and Seas.* Princeton: Princeton University Press, 1987; *Volume Three: Rhapsodies on Natural Phenomena, Birds and Animals, Aspirations and Feelings, Sorrowful Laments, Literature, Music, and Passions.* Princeton: Princeton University Press, 1996. Contains closely annotated translations of the *fu* in *chüan* 7-12 and 13-19 respectively of the *Wen-hsüan* along with an excellent introduction, biographical Sketches, and bibliography.

Li, Ching-ying 李景溁. *Chao-ming Wen-hsüan hsin-chieh* 昭明文選新解. 5v. (of 6) Taipei: Chi-nan, 1990-2. Reproduces Li Shan's commentary; this modern-Chinese translation is not reliable.

Studies

Chao, Fu-hai 趙福海, ed. *Wen-hsüan hsüeh lun-chi* 文選學論集. Changchun: Shih-tai Wen-i, 1992.

Ch'en, Hung-t'ien 陳宏天, *et al.*, eds. *Chao-ming Wen-hsüan yen-chiu lun-wen chi* 昭明文選研究論文集. Changchun: Chi-lin Wen-hsüeh, 1988.

Ch'ü, Shou-yüan 屈守元. *Chao-ming Wen-hsüan tsa-shu chi hsüan-chiang* 昭明文選雜述及選講. Tientsin: T'ien-chin Ku-chi, 1988.

Kang, Ts'un-fan 岡村繁. "*Wen hsüan* yü *Yü-t'ai hsin-yung*" 文選與玉臺新詠. In Hsüeh-sheng Shu-chü, ed. *Ku-tien wen-Hsüeh ti-ch'i chi* 古典文學第七集. Taipei: Hsüeh-sheng Shu-chü, 1985, 209-226.

Kôzen, Hiroshi 興膳宏 and Kawai Kôzô 川合康三. *Monzen* 文選. Tokyo: Kadokawa Shoten, 1988. *Kanshô Chûgoku no koten*, 12. Appends maps and a *nien-piao*.

Obi, Kôichi 小尾郊一, Tominaga Kazutaka 富永一登 and Kinugawa Kenji 衣川賢次. *Monzen Ri Zen chûinsho kôshô* 文選李善注引書攷証. 2v. Tokyo: Kenbun Shuppan, 1990-1992.

Satake, Yasuko 佐竹保子. "*Monzen* kan ni 21 Ri Zenchû Shakureiki" 『文選』卷二十一李善注釈礼記. *Chûgoku bunka to sono shûhen* 13 (1992).

Takahashi, Tadahiko 高橋忠彦. *Monzen (fuhen) chû* 文選（賦篇）中. Tokyo: Meiji Shoin, 1994. *Shinshaku kanbun taikei*, 80.

Yü, Shao-ch'u 俞紹初. "*Wen-hsüan* ch'eng-shu kuo-ch'eng ni-ts'e" 文選成書過程擬測, *Wen-hsüeh i-ch'an* 1998.1: 60-69.

Wen-kuan tz'u-lin 文館詞林 (Forest of Writings from the Hall of Literature)

Editions and References
Wen-kuan tz'u-lin 文館詞林. Peking: Chung-hua, 1985.

Wen T'ing-yün 溫庭筠 (*ca.* 812-870)

Editions and References

Luan, Kuei-ming 欒貴明 *et al.*, eds. *Ch'üan T'ang shih so-yin: Wen T'ing-yün chüan* 全唐詩索引：溫庭筠卷. Ch'in-huang tao: Hsien-tai, 1994.

Liu, I-sheng 劉逸生 and Liu Ssu-han 劉斯翰, eds. and comms. *Wen T'ing-yün shih-tz'u hsüan* 溫庭筠詩詞選. Hong Kong: San-lien, 1986. *Chung-kuo hsien-tai shih-jen hsüan-chi*.

Studies

Kao, Ming 高明, *et al.*, eds. *Wen T'ing-yün* 溫庭筠. Taipei: Chin-hsiu, 1992. *T'ang shih hsin-shang*, 13.

Ku, Hsüeh-chieh 顧學頡. "'Hsin-Chiu T'ang shu' Wen T'ing-yün chuan ting-pu" 新舊唐書溫庭筠傳訂補. *Kuo-wen yüeh-k'an* (December 1947): 19-26.

Mou, Huai-ch'uan 牟懷川. "Wen T'ing-yün sheng-p'ing hsin-cheng" 溫庭筠生平新證. *Shang-hai Shih-fan Hsüeh-yüan hsüeh-pao* 1984.1 1984.

Rouzer, Paul E. "Wen Tingyun." Unpublished Ph. D. dissertation, Harvard University, 1989.

____. *Writing Another's Dream: The Poetry of Wen Tingyun.* Stanford: Stanford University Press, 1993.

Wan, Wen-wu 萬文武. *Wen T'ing-yün pien-hsi* 溫庭筠辨析. Sian: Shan-hsi Jen-min, 1992. *Chung-kuo ku-tai tso-chia yen-chiu ts'ung-shu.*

Yeh, Chia-ying 葉嘉瑩. *Wen T'ing-yün, Wei Chuang, Feng Yen-ssu, Li Yü* 溫庭筠韋莊馮延巳李煜. Taipei: Ta-an, 1992. *T'ang Sung ming-chia tz'u shang-hsi,* 1.

Wen-yüan ying-hua 文苑英華 (Finest Flowers of the Preserve of Literature)

Editions and References

An-hui Sheng Cheng-hsieh An-hui Chu-ming Li-shih Jen-wu Ts'ung-shu pien-wei Hui 安徽省政協安徽著名歷史人物從書編委會, ed. *Wen-yüan ying-hua* 文苑英華. Peking: Chung-kuo Wen-shih, 1991.

P'eng, Shu-hsia 彭叔夏 (*fl.* 1204). *Wen-yüan ying-hua pien-cheng* 文苑英華辨證. 10 *chüan.* Taipei: T'ai-wan Shang-wu Yin-shu-kuan, 1983.

Studies

Tosaki, Tetsuhiko 戸崎哲彦. "*Bun'en eika* no chûki no kaisôsei-shoshû no Ryû Sôgen no sakuhin o chûshin ni shite"『文苑英華』の注記の階層性-所収の柳宗元の作品を中心にして, *Hikone ronsô* (1994).

———. "*Bun'en eika* no chûki no kaisôsei–shoshû no Ryû Sôgen no sakuhin o rei ni tsuite" 文苑英華の注記の階層性-所収の柳宗元の作品を例について. *Hikone ronsô* 291 (1994): 17-42.

———. "*Bun'en eika* izen no 'Ryûshû' no shurui, tokuchô oyobi sono kankei, keitô o rei ni shite" 『文苑英華』以前の『柳集』の種類・特徴およびその関係・系統を例にして. *Hikone ronsô* (1994).

Wu Chia-chi 吳嘉紀 (1618-1684)

Studies

Chaves, Jonathan. "Moral Action in the Poetry of Wu Chia-chi (1618-84)." *HJAS* 46 (1986): 387-469.

Wu Ching-tzu 吳敬梓

Editions and References

Ch'en, Mei-lin 陳美林. *Ju-lin wai-shih tz'u-tien* 儒林外史辭典. Nanking: Nan-ching Ta-hsüeh, 1994.

Li, Han-ch'iu 李漢秋, ed. and comm. *Ju-lin wai-shih hui-chiao hui-p'ing pen* 儒林外史會校會評本. 2v. Shanghai: Shang-hai Ku-chi, 1984. *Chung-kuo ku-tien hsiao-shuo yen-chiu tzu-liao ts'ung-shu.*

———. *Ju-lin wai-shih yen-chiu tzu-liao* 儒林外史研究資料. Shanghai: Shang-hai Ku-chi, 1984.

———. *Wu Ching-tzu Wu Lang shih-wen ho-chi* 吳敬梓吳烺詩文合集. Hofei: Huang Shan Shu-she, 1993. *An-hui ku-chi ts'ung-shu.*

Translations

Inada, Takashi 稲田孝. *Jurin gaishi* 儒林外史. Tokyo: Heibonsha, 1994.

Studies

An-hui Sheng Chi-nien Wu Ching-tzu Tan-sheng Erh-pai Pa-shih Chou-nien Wei-yüan Hui 安徽省紀念吳敬梓誕二百八十周年委員會, ed. *Ju-lin wai-shih yen-chiu lun-wen chi* 儒林外史研究論文集. Hofei: An-hui Jen-min, 1982.

Chang, Kuo-feng 張國風. *Ju-lin wai-shih chi ch'i shih-tai* 儒林外史及其時代. Taipei: Wen-chin, 1993. *Ta-lu ti-ch'ü po-shih lun-wen ts'ung-k'an.* The author's Ph.D. dissertation done at Peking University in 1988.

Ch'en, Ju-heng 陳汝衡. *Wu Ching-tzu chuan* 吳敬梓傳. Shanghai: Shang-hai Wen-i, 1981.

Ch'en, Mei-lin 陳美林. *Hsin-p'i Ju-lin wai-shih* 新批儒林外史. Nanking: Chiang-su Ku-chi, 1989.

___. *Wu Ching-tzu p'ing-chuan* 吳敬梓評傳. Nanking: Nan-ching Ta-hsüeh, 1992.

___. *Wu Ching-tzu yen-chiu* 吳敬梓研究. Shanghai: Shang-hai Ku-chi, 1984.

Chung-kuo *Ju-lin wai-shih* Hsüeh-hui 中國儒林外史學會, ed. *Ju-lin wai-shih hsüeh-k'an* 儒林外史學刊. Hofei: Huang Shan Shu-she, 1988.

Li, Han-ch'iu 李漢秋, ed. *Ju-lin wai-shih yen-chiu lun-wen chi* 儒林外史研究論文集. Peking: Chung-hua, 1987. A selection of essays chosen from post-1949 scholarship on this novel and its author, followed by an extensive bibliography.

___. *Ju-lin wai-shih yen-chiu tsung-lan* 儒林外史研究縱覽. Tientsin: T'ien-chin Chiao-yü, 1992. *Hsüeh-shu yen-chiu chih-nan ts'ung-shu.*

Meng, Hsing-jen 孟醒仁 and Meng Fan-ching 孟凡經. *Wu Ching-tzu p'ing-chuan* 吳敬梓評傳. Chengchow: Chung-chou Ku-chi, 1987.

Wu Ping 吳炳 (d. 1646)

Editions and References

Feng-cheng wu 風箏誤. In Wang Chi-ssu 王季思, *et al.* eds. *Chung-kuo shih-ta ku-tien hsi-chü chi* 中國十大古典喜劇集. Shanghai: Shang-hai Wen-i, 1982.

Wu Wei-yeh 吳偉業 (1609-1672)

Editions and References

"Hai-pin wai-shih" 海濱外史. In Hsia Ssu 夏斯, ed. *Tung-ts'un chi shih-wai ssu-chung* 東村紀事外四種. Nantou: T'ai-wan Sheng Wen-hsien Wei-yüan Hui, 1993.

Huang, Yung-nien 黃永年 and Ma Hsüeh-ch'in 馬雪芹, comm. *Wu Wei-yeh shih hsüan-i* 吳偉業詩選譯. Chengtu: Pa-Shu Shu-she, 1991. Taiwan reprint by Chin-hsiu Ch'u-pan-she in 1993.

Li, Hsüeh-ying 李學穎, ed. *Wu Mei-ts'un ch'üan chi* 吳梅村全集. 64 *chüan.* 3v. Shanghai: Shang-hai Ku-chi, 1990. *Chung-kuo ku-tien wen-hsüeh ts'ung-shu.*

Studies

Chang, Kang-i Sun. "The Idea of the Mask in Wu Wei-yeh (1609-1671)." *HJAS* 48 (1988): 289-320.

Feng, Ch'i-yung 馮其庸 and Yeh Chün-yüan 葉君遠. *Wu Mei-ts'un nien-p'u* 吳梅村年譜. Nanking: Chiang-su Ku-chi, 1990.

McCraw, *Chinese Lyricists,* pp. 25-40.

Wu Wen-ying 吳文英 (*ca.* 1200-*ca.*1260)

Studies

Ch'en, Hsin 陳欣. "Wu Wen-ying tz'u lun-hsi" 吳文英詞論析 *Wen-shih tsa-chih* 1988.3.

Ch'en, Pang-yen 陳邦炎. "Meng-ch'uang tz'u ch'ien-i" 夢窗詞淺議. *Wen-hsüeh i-ch'an* 1984.1 (1984): 84-92.

___. "Wu Meng-ch'uang sheng-tsu nien kuan-chien" 吳夢窗生卒年管見. *Wen-hsüeh i-ch'an* 1983.1: 64–7.

___, *et al*, eds. *Wu Meng-ch'uang tz'u chien-i* 吳夢窗詞箋譯. Canton: Kuang-tung Jen-min, 1992.

Fong, Grace S. *Wu Wenying and the Art of the Southern Song Ci*. Princeton: Princeton University Press, 1987.

___. "Wu Wenying's *Yung-wu Ci:* Poem as Artifice and Poem as Metaphor." *HJAS* 45 (1985): 323-48.

Kao, Ming 高明, *et al*, eds. *Wu Wen-ying* 吳文英. Taipei: Chin-hsiu, 1992. *T'ang shih hsin-shang*, 14.

Lin, Shuen-fu. "Space-Logic in the Longer Song Lyrics of the Southern Sung: Reading Wu Wen-ying's Ying-t'i-hsü," *JSYS* 25 (1995): 169-91.

Wu Wo-yao 吳沃堯 (1866-1910)

Editions and References

Lu, Shu-tu 盧叔度, ed. *Wo-fo shan-jen tuan-p'ien hsiao-shuo chi* 我佛山人短篇小説集. Canton: Hua-ch'eng, 1984.

Wang, Li-yen 王立言, ed. and comm. *Hsin shih-t'ou chi* 新石頭記. Chengchow: Chung-chou Ku-chi, 1986.

Wei, Shao-ch'ang 魏紹昌, ed. *Wu Chien-jen yen-chiu tzu-liao* 吳趼人研究資料. Shanghai: Shang-hai Ku-chi, 1980.

Wo-fo shan-jen wen-chi 我佛山人文集. Canton: Hua-ch'eng, 1988.

Translations

Hanan, Patrick. *The Sea of Regret: Two Turn-of-the-Century Chinese Romantic Novels, Stones in the Sea by Fu Lin and The Sea of Regret by Wu Jianren*. Honolulu: University of Hawaii Press, 1995.

Liebermann, Marianne and Werner Bettin. *Daus Haus zum gemeinsamen Glück (Guanchang xianxing ji)*. Berlin: Rütten and Loening, 1964. Partial translations (636 pp.) with a postface by Werner Bettin.

Reclus, Jacques. *Crime et corruption chez les Mandarins; Chronique de la Chine impériale*. Paris: Fayard, 1979.

Studies

Nieper, Kai. *Neun Tode, ein Leben: Wu Woyao (1866-1910); ein Erzähler der späten Qing-Zeit*. Frankfurt: Lang, 1995.

Wu-Yüeh ch'un-ch'iu 吳越春秋 (Spring and Autumn Annals of Wu and Yüeh)

Editions and References

Chang, Chüeh 張覺, trans. *Wu-Yüeh ch'un-ch'iu ch'üan-i* 吳越春秋全譯. Kweiyang: Kuei-chou Jen-min, 1990; 1997. *Chung-kuo li-tai ming-chu ch'üan-i ts'ung-shu*.

Chou, Sheng-ch'un 周生春. *Wu-Yüeh ch'un-ch'iu chi-chiao hui-k'ao* 吳越春秋輯教匯考. Shanghai: Shang-hai Ku-chi, 1997.

Hsü, Nai-ch'ang 徐乃昌. *Wu-yüeh ch'un-ch'iu i-wen; Wu-yüeh ch'un-ch'iu cha-chi* 吳越春秋逸文，吳越春秋札記. Shanghai: Shang-hai Shu-tien, 1994.

Lau, D. C. 劉殿爵 and Ch'en Fang-cheng 陳方正, eds. *Wu-yüeh ch'un-ch'iu chu-tzu so-yin* 吳越春秋逐字索引. Hong Kong: Shang-wu Yin-shu-kuan, 1993. ICS ancient Chinese text concordance series.

Liu, Yü-ts'ai 劉玉才, comm. *Wu-yüeh ch'un-ch'iu* 吳越春秋. Taipei: Chin-hsiu, 1993.

Yang Chiung 楊炯 (*ca.* 650-*ca.* 694)

Editions and References

Hsü, Ming-hsia 徐明霞, ed. *Yang Chiung chi* 楊炯集. Taipei: Yüan-liu Wen-hua, 1983. Appends materials pertinent to the study of Yang's life.

Luan, Kuei-ming 欒貴明 *et al.*, eds. *Ch'uan T'ang shih so-yin: Yang Chiung chüan* 全唐詩索引： 楊炯卷. Peking: Chung-hua, 1992.

Studies

Chang, Chih-lieh 張志烈. *Ch'u T'ang ssu-chieh nien-p'u* 初唐四傑年譜. Chengtu: Pa-Shu Shu-she, 1992.

Lo, Hsiang-fa 駱祥發. *Ch'u T'ang ssu-chieh yen-chiu* 初唐四傑研究. Peking: Tung-fang, 1993.

Shen, Hui-yüeh 沈惠樂 and Ch'ien, Hui-k'ang 錢惠康. *Ch'u-T'ang Ssu-chieh ho Ch'en Tzu-ang* 初唐四杰和陳子昂. Shanghai: Shang-hai Ku-chi, 1987.

Yang-chou hua-fang lu 揚州畫舫錄 (**A Record of the Painted Boats at Yang-chou**)

Editions

Chou, Kuang-p'ei 周光培, ed. *Yang-chou hua-fang lu* 揚州畫舫錄. Yangchow: Chiang-su Kuang-ling Ku-chi, 1984.

Yang Hsiung 揚雄 (53 B.C.-A.D. 18)

Editions and References

Chang, Chen-tse 張震澤, ed. and comm. *Yang Hsiung chi chiao-chu* 揚雄集校注. Shanghai: Shang-hai Ku-chi, 1993. *Chung-kuo ku-tien wen-hsüeh ts'ung-shu.* Appends biographical materials.

Cheng, P'u 鄭樸 (Ming dynasty), ed. *Shu-wang pen-chi* 蜀王本紀. Chengtu: Pa-Shu Shu-she, 1993. *Chung-kuo yeh-shih chi-ch'eng,* 1.

Cheng, Wan-ching 鄭萬耕, ed. and comm. *T'ai-hsüan chiao-shih* 太玄校釋. Peking: Pei-ching Shih-fan Ta-hsüeh, 1989.

Han, Ching 韓敬, comm. *Fa-yen* 法言. Peking: Pei-ching Kuang-po Hsüeh-yüan, 1992.

Wang, Hsiao-yü 王孝魚, comm. and ed. *Fa-yen i-shu* 法言義疏. Peking: Chung-hua, 1987.

Wang, Jung-pao 王榮寶 and Ch'en Chung-fu 陳仲夫, ed. *Fa-yen i-shu* 法言義疏. 2v. Rpt. Peking: Chung-hua, 1997.

Yang Hsiung T'ai-hsüan ching chiao-cheng 揚雄太玄經校正. Hofei: Huang-shan Shu-she, 1995.

Translations

Nylan, Michael, trans. *The Canon of Supreme Mystery—A Translation with Commentary of the T'ai Hsüan Ching.* Albany: SUNY Press, 1993.

___. *The Elemental Changes, the Ancient Chinese Companion to the I Ching--the T'ai Hsüan Ching, Text and Commentaries.* Albany: State University of New York Press, 1994.

Studies

Tanaka, Masami 田中麻紗巳. *Hôgen—mô hitotsu no Rongo* 法言—もうひとつの「論語」. Tokyo:

Kôdansha, 1988.

Wang, Han 王菡. *"Yang-tzu Fa-yen li-tai chiao-chu pen ch'uan-lu"* 揚子法言歷代校著本傳錄, *Wen-hsien* 1994.3: 175-186.

Wang, I-hsien 王以憲. "Yang Hsiung chu-tso hsi-nien" 揚雄著作系年. *Hsiang-T'an Ta-hsüeh She-hui K'o-hsüeh hsüeh-pao* 湘潭大學社會科學學報, 1983.3.

Yang Shen 楊慎 (1488-1529)

Editions and References

Chang, Hsi-hou 張錫厚 and Wang Wen-ts'ai 王文才, eds. *Sheng-an chu-shu hsü-pa* 升庵著述序跋. Kunming: Yün-nan Jen-min, 1985.

Chang, Tsu-yung 張錫厚, ed. *Yang Sheng-an shih pai-shou* 楊升庵詩百首. Hsin-tu: Yang Sheng-an Po-wu Kuan, 1988.

Lin, Ch'ing-chang 林慶彰 and Chia Shun-hsien 賈順先, eds. *Yang Shen yen-chiu tzu-liao hui-pien* 楊慎研究資料彙編. 2v. Taipei: Chung-yang Yen-chiu Yüan, 1992.

___, eds. "Yang Shen yen-chiu tzu-liao hui-pien (Fu: Yang Shen yen-chiu lun-chu mu-lu)" 楊慎研究資料彙編 （附：楊慎研究論著目錄）. *Chung-kuo wen-che yen-chiu t'ung-hsün* 4 (1992): 96-105.

T'ao-ch'ing yüeh-fu 陶情樂府. Yangchow: Chiang-su Kuang-ling Ku-chi, 1980.

Wang, Chung-yung 王仲鏞, ed. and comm. *Sheng-an shih-hua chien-cheng* 升菴詩話箋證. Shanghai: Shang-hai Ku-chi, 1987.

Wang, Wen-ts'ai 王文才, ed. *Yang Shen hsüeh-p'u* 楊慎學譜. Shanghai: Shang-hai Ku-chi, 1988.

___, ed. and comm. *Yang Shen shih hsüan* 楊慎詩選. Chengtu: Ssu-ch'uan Jen-min, 1981.

___, ed. *Yang Shen tz'u-ch'ü chi* 楊慎詞曲集. Chengtu: Ssu-ch'uan Jen-min, 1984.

___ and Chang Hsi-hou 張錫厚, eds. *Sheng-an chu-shu hsü-pa* 升庵著述序跋. Kunming: Yün-nan Jen-min, 1985.

Yang fu-jen yüeh-fu 楊夫人樂府. Yangchow: Chiang-su Kuang-ling Ku-chi, 1980.

Yang Sheng-an fu-fu san-ch'ü san-chung 楊升庵夫婦散曲三種. 2v. Yangchow: Chiang-su Kuang-ling Ku-chi, 1980.

Yang, Wen-sheng 楊文生, ed. *Yang Shen shih-hua chiao-chien* 楊慎詩話校箋. Chengtu: Ssu-ch'uan Jen-min, 1990.

Studies

Feng, Hsiu-ch'i 馮修齊. "Yang Sheng-an yü min-chien wen-hsüeh" 楊升庵與民間文學. *Kuei-hu* 19 (1986): 50-51.

Huang, Pao-hua 黃寶華. "Yang Sheng-an shih-lun ch'u-t'an" 楊升庵詩論初探. *Shang-hai Shih-fan Ta-hsüeh hsüeh-pao* 1991.1: 1-7.

Schorr, Adam. "Connoisseurship and the Defense against Vulgarity: Yang Sheng (1488-1559) and His Work." *MS* 41 (1993): 89-128.

Wang, Wen-ts'ai 王文才 *and Chang Hsi-hou* 張錫厚, ed. *Sheng-an chu-shu hsü-pa* 升庵箸述序跋. Kunming: Yün-nan Jen-min, 1985.

Wang, Wen-ts'ai 王文才. *Yang Shen hsüeh-p'u* 楊慎學譜. Shanghai: Shang-hai Ku-chi, 1988.

Yang, Jih-ch'u 楊日初. *Yang Shen sheng-p'ing chi ch'i wen-hsüeh* 楊慎生平及其文學. Chia-yi, Taiwan: Hung-tou, 1987.

Yang Sheng-an tan-ch'en wu-pai chou-nien chi-nien ts'e 楊升庵誕辰五百周年紀念冊. Hsintu: Hsin-tu Hsien Yang Sheng-an Tan-ch'en Wu-pai Chou-nien Li-tao Hsiao-tsu, 1989.

Yang Sheng-an Po-wu Kuan 楊升庵博物館, ed. *Yang Sheng-an yen-chiu lun-wen chi* 楊升庵研究論文集. Hsintu: Yang Sheng-an Yen-chiu Hui, 1984.

Yang Wan-li 楊萬里 (1127-1206)

Editions and References

Chan, Chih. *Yang Wan-li Fan Ch'eng-ta tzu-liao hui-pien* 楊萬里范成大資料彙編. Peking: Chung-hua, 1964; 1985.

Chang, Ch'u-fan 章楚藩, ed. *Yang Wan-li shih-ko shang-hsi chi* 楊萬里詩歌賞析集. Chengtu: Pa-Shu Shu-she, 1994. *Chung-kuo ku-tien wen-hsüeh shang-hsi ts'ung-shu.*

Liu, I-sheng 劉逸生, ed. and Liu Ssu-han 劉斯翰, comm. *Yang Wan-li shih hsüan* 楊萬里詩選. Hong Kong: San-lien Shu-tien, 1991. Chung-kuo hsien-tai shih-jen hsüan-chi.

Yü, Pei-shan 于北山, ed. and comm. *Yang Wan-li shih-wen hsüan-chu* 楊萬里詩文選注. Shanghai: Shang-hai Ku-chi, 1988.

Translations

Cheng, Wing-fun and Hervé Collet. *Le son de la pluie.* Millemont: Moundarren, 1988.

Studies

Chou, Ch'i-ch'eng 周啟成. *Yang Wan-li ho Ch'eng-chai t'i* 楊萬里和誠齋體. Taipei: Wan-chüan-lou T'u-shu Kung-ssu, 1993. *Chung-kuo ku-tien wen-hsüeh chi-pen chih-shih ts'ung-shu,* 50.

Yang Wei-chen 楊維楨 (1296-1370)

Editions and References

Tso, Chih-fang 鄒志芳, ed. *Yang Wei-chen shih chi* 楊維楨詩集. Nanking: Chiang-su Ku-chi, 1994.

Yüan Yang Wei-chen hsing-shu chen-ching yen-mu lu-shu chüan 元楊維楨行書真鏡庵募緣疏卷. Peking: Wen-wu, 1982.

Yao Nai 姚鼐 (1731-1815)

Editions and References

Yang, Jung-hsiang 楊榮祥, ed. and trans. *Fang Pao, Yao Nai wen hsüan-i* 方苞姚鼐文選譯. Chengtu: Pa-Shu Shu-she, 1991. *Ku-tai wen-shih ming-chu hsüan-i ts'ung-shu.*

Yeh Hsieh 葉燮 (1627-1703)

Editions and References

Yüan shih 原詩. Peking: Chung-hua, 1963.

Studies

Ch'eng, Fu-wang 成復旺. "Tui Yeh Hsieh shih-ko ch'uang-tso lun te ssu-k'ao" 對葉燮詩歌創作論的思考. *Wen-hsüeh i-ch'an* 1986.5 (1986): 86–94.

Chiang, Fan 蔣凡. *Yeh Hsieh ho Yüan-shih* 葉燮和原詩. Shanghai: Shang-hai Ku-chi, 1985. Taiwan reprint by Wan-chüan-lou T'u-shu Kung-ssu in 1993.

___. "Yeh Hsieh 'Yüan-shih' te li-lun t'e-se chi kung-hsien" 葉燮原詩的理論特色及貢獻. *Wen-hsüeh i-ch'an* 1984.2 (1984): 39–46.

Huo, Sung-lin 霍松林, ed. *Yüan shih* 原詩. Peking: Jen-min Wen-hsüeh, 1979.

Pohl, Karl-Heinz. "Ye Xie's 'On the Origin of Poetry' (Yuan shi), A Poetic of the Early

Qing." *TP* 78 (1992):1-32.

Yeh Hsien-tsu 葉憲祖 (1566-1641)

Studies
Min, Hui-ying 閔惠映. "Yeh Hsien-tsu tsa-chü chih yen-chiu" 葉憲祖雜劇之研究. Unpublished M.A. thesis, Taiwan University, 1992.

Yen Chi-tao 晏幾道 (1030-1041?-1106 or 1119?)

Editions and References
Ch'üan Sung shih, 38:1644.535-536.

Studies
Chung, Ling 鍾陵. "Erh Yen chia-shih shih-chi pu-pien" 二晏家世事跡補辨. *Nan-ching Shih-ta hsüeh-pao* 1986.2 (1986).
Li, P'ei-ken 李培根. "Lüeh-lun Yen Chi-tao te tz'u" 略論晏幾道底詞. *Ning-hsia Chiao-yü Hsüeh-yüan hsüeh-pao* 1988.1 (1988).

Yen Chih-t'ui 顏之推 (531-*ca.* 590)

Editions and References
Utsunomiya, Kiyoyoshi 宇都宮清, trans. and comm. *Ganshi kakun* 諺氏家訓. 2v. Tokyo: Heibonsha, 1989–90. *Tôyô bunko,* 511 and 514.
Wang, Li-ch'i 王利器, comm. *Yen-shih chia-hsün chi-chieh* 諺氏家訓集解. Shanghai: Shang-hai Ku-chi, 1980. Appends biographical information on the author.

Translations
Ch'eng, Hsiao-ming 程小銘, trans. *Yen-shih chia-hsün ch'üan-i* 諺氏家訓全譯. Kweiyang: Kuei-chou Jen-min, 1993.
Huang, Yung-nien 黃永年, trans. and comm. *Yen-shih chia-hsün hsüan-i* 諺氏家訓選譯. Chengtu: Pa-Shu Shu-she, 1991.
Utsunomiya, Kiyoyoshi 宇都宮清, trans. *Ganshi kakun* 諺氏家訓. Tokyo: Heibonsha, 1994.

Studies
Shu, Ta-kang 舒大剛. "*Yen-shih chia-hsün chi-chieh* pu-cheng er-tze" 諺氏家訓集解補正二則. *Wen-shih* 39 (1994): 146–175.
Yu, Ya-tzu 尤雅姿. *Yen Chih-t'ui chi ch'i Chia-hsün chih yen-chiu* 顏之推及其家訓之研究. Unpublished Ph. D. dissertation, National Taiwan Normal University, 1991.

Yen Fu 顏復 (1854-1921)

Editions and References
Niu, Yang-shan 牛仰山 and Sun Hung-ni 孫鴻霓, eds. *Yen Fu yen-chiu tzu-liao* 顏復研究資料. Foochow: Hai-hsia Wen-i, 1990. *Chung-kuo chin-tai wen-hsüeh yen-chiu tsu-liao ts'ung-shu.* Appends various bibliographic indexes.
Wang, Shih 王栻. *Yen Fu chi* 顏復集. 5v. Peking: Chung-hua, 1986. *Chung-kuo chin-tai jen-wu*

wen-chi ts'ung-shu. Appends information valuable for the study of Yen's life and writings.

Yen Chi-tao shih wen ch'ao 顏幾道詩文鈔. Taipei: Wen-hai, 1969. *Chin-tai Chung-kuo shih-liao ts'ung-k'an.*

Studies

Ma, Yung 馬勇. *Yen Fu yü-ts'ui* 顏復語萃. Peking: Hua-hsia, 1993. *Chung-kuo erh-shih shih-chi ssu-hsiang wen-k'u.*

Ou-yang, Che-sheng 歐陽哲生. *Yen Fu p'ing-chuan* 顏復評傳. Nanchang: Pai-hua Chou Wen-i, 1994. *Kuo-hsüeh Ta-shih ts'ung-shu,* 11.

Shang-wu Yin-shu-kuan 商務印書館, ed. *Lun Yen Fu yü Yen shih ming-chu* 論顏復與顏譯名著. Peking: Shang-wu Yin-shu-kuan, 1982.

Yen-shan wai-shih 燕山外史 (The Tale of a Yen-shan Scholar)

Editions and References
Ch'u, Chia-wei 褚家偉, ed. *Yen-shan wai-shih* 燕山外史. Shenyang: Ch'un-feng Wen-i, 1987.

Yen Shu 晏殊 (991-1055)

Editions and References
Ch'üan Sung shih, 3:171-173.1940-1949.
Ch'üan Sung wen, 10:397-398.176-209.

Translations
Landau, *Beyond Spring,* pp. 62-74.

Studies
Chung, Ling 鍾陵. "Erh Yen chia-shih shih-chi pu-pien" 二晏家世事跡補辨. *Nan-ching Shih-ta hsüeh-pao* 1986.2 (1986).

Kao Ming 高明, *et al,* eds. *Yen Shu* 晏殊. Taipei: Chin-hsiu, 1992. *T'ang shih hsin-shang,* 5.

Yeh, Chia-ying 葉嘉瑩. *Yen Shu, Ou-yang Hsiu, Ch'in Kuan* 晏殊歐陽修秦觀. Taipei: Ta-an, 1988. *T'ang Sung ming-chia tz'u shang-hsi,* 2.

Yen Tan-tzu 燕丹子 (Prince Tan of Yen)

Editions and References
Lau, D. C. 劉殿爵 and Liu Fang-cheng 劉方正, eds. *Yen Tan-tzu chu-tzu so-yin* 燕丹子逐字索引. Taipei: Shang-wu Yin-shu-kuan, 1994. ICS ancient Chinese text concordance series.

Yen Yen-chih 顏延之 (384-456)

Studies
Ch'en, Mei-tzu 陳美足. *Nan-chao Yen Hsieh shih yen-chiu* 南朝顏謝詩研究. Taipei: Wen-chin, 1989.

Chou, T'ien-ch'ing 周田青. "Shih-lun Yen Yen-chih te wen-hsüeh chuang-tso" 試論顏延之的

文學創作. *Ssu-hsiang chan-hsien 96* (1990): 39–45; 83.

___. "Yen Yen-chih shih-wen cheng-wu erh-tse" 顏延之詩文證誤二則. *Wen-shih* 34 (1991): 46–117.

Huang, Shui-yün 黃水雲. *Yen Yen-chih chi ch'i shih-wen yen-chiu* 顏延之及其詩研究. Taipei: Wen-shih-che, 1989. The basis of this study is Huang Shui-yün's unpublished M.A. thesis, which was completed at Wen-hua University in 1988.

Shen, Yü-ch'eng 沈玉成. "Kuan-yü Yen Yen-chih te sheng-p'ing ho tso-p'in" 關於顏延之的生平和作品. *Hsi-pei Shih-ta hsüeh-pao* 62 (1989): 3–8.

Yin K'eng 陰鏗 (*fl.* mid-sixth century)

Editions and References

Chang, Shu 張澍 (*fl.* 1821), comp. *Yin Chang-shih shih-chi i-chüan, shih-hua i-chüan* 陰常侍詩集一卷，詩話一卷. Lanchow: Lan-chou Jen-min, 1987. *Li-tai Kan-su tso-chia tso-p'in hsüan-chu ts'ung-shu.*

Liu, Kuo-chün 劉國珺, comm. *Yin K'eng chi chu* 陰鏗集注. Tientsin: T'ien-chin Ku-chi, 1988. *Han Wei Liu-ch'ao wen-shih ts'ung-shu.*

Wang, Hui-shao 王會紹, *et al.*, comms. *Yin K'eng shih chu* 陰鏗詩注. Lanchow: Kansu Jen-min, 1987. *Li-tai Kan-su tso-chia tso-p'in hsüan-chu ts'ung-shu.*

Yin Shu 尹洙 (1001-1047)

Editions and References

Yin, Shu 尹洙, ed. *Wu-tai ch'un-ch'iu* 五代春秋. Chengtu: Pa-Shu Shu-she, 1993. *Chung-kuo yeh-shih chi-ch'eng,* 4.

Yin Yün 殷芸 (471-529)

Editions and References

Yin, Yün 殷芸, comp. *Shang Yün hsiao-shuo* 商芸小説, Shanghai: Shang-hai Wen-i, 1991.

Yu-chi wen-hsüeh 遊記文學 (travel-record literature)

Editions and References

Ch'en, Hsin 陳新, ed. *Sung-jen Ch'ang-chiang yu-chi* 宋人長江遊記. Shanghai: Hua-tung Shih-yüan Ta-hsüeh, 1987. Contains Lu Yu's 陸游 "Ju Shu chi" 入蜀記 and Fan Ch'eng-ta's 范成大 "Wu-ch'uan lu" 吳船錄.

___, *et al*, comms. *Li-tai yu-chi hsüan-i* 歷代遊記選譯. Peking: Pao-wen-t'ang Shu-tien, 1987. *Chung-kuo ku-tien wen-hsüeh p'u-chi ts'ung-shu.*

Fei, Chen-kang 費振剛, ed. and comm. *Ku-tai yu-chi ching-hua* 古代遊記精華. Peking: Jen-min Wen-hsüeh, 1992. Chung-kuo ku-tien wen-hsüeh ching-hua ts'ung-shu.

Ni, Ch'i-hsin 倪其心 *et al.*, eds. *Chung-kuo ku-tai yu-chi hsüan* 中國古代遊記. Peking: Chung-kuo Lü-yu, 1985.

Translations

Strassberg, Richard E. *Inscribed Landscapes: Travel Writing from Imperial China.* Berkeley: University of California Press, 1994.

Studies

Ch'en, Su-chen 陳素貞. "Sung-tai shan-shui yu-chi yen-chiu" 宋代山水遊記研究. *Shih-ta Kuo-wen Yen-chiu-so chi-k'an* 31 (June 1987): 623-740.

Riemenschnitter, Andrew. "Zwischen Himmel und Erde: Die chineische Reiseaufzeichnung als kosmographisches Genre, Beiträge zu einer Poetik der chinesischen Kultur, dargestellt anhand von ausgewählten Beispielen des 15. bis 19. Jahrhunderts." Unpublished Ph. D. dissertation, University of Göttingen, 1997.

Yu T'ung 尤侗 (1618-1704)

Editions and References

Yu, T'ung 尤侗. *K'an-chien ou p'ing* 看鑑偶評. 5 *chüan*. Revised by Li Chao-hsiang 李肇翔 and Li Fu-p'o 李復波. Peking: Chung-hua, 1992. *Hsüeh-shu pi-chi ts'ung-k'an.*

___. *Liang chai tsa-shuo hsü-shuo* 良齋雜説續説. 10 *chüan* Revised by Li Chao-hsiang 李肇翔 and Li Fu-p'o 李復波. Peking: Chung-hua, 1992. *Hsüeh-shu pi-chi ts'ung-k'an.*

Studies

Hsüeh, Jo-lin 薛若鄰. *Yu T'ung lun-kao* 尤侗論稿. Peking: Chung-kuo Hsi-chü, 1989.

Zeitlin, Judith T. "Spirit Writing and Performance in the Work of You Tong (1618-1704)," *TP* 84 (1998): 102-135.

Yu-yang tsa-tsu 酉陽雜俎 (Assorted Notes from Yu-yang)

Editions and References

Tuan, Ch'eng-shih 段成式. *Yu-yang tsa-tsu* 酉陽雜俎 10 *chüan*. Taipei: Hsin-hsing Shu-chü, 1988. *Pi-chi hsiao-shuo ta-kuan,* 9.1.

Yü Chiao Li 玉嬌梨 (Third Book of Genius or The Universal Marriage of a Pair of Beauties)

Editions and References

Han, Hsi-to 韓錫鐸, ed. *Yü Chiao Li* 玉嬌梨. Shenyang: Ch'un-feng Wen-i, 1981. Ming-mo Ch'ing-ch'u hsiao-shuo, 1.

Yü Hsin 庾信 (513-581)

Editions and References

Shu, Pao-chang 舒寶璋, comp. and comm. *Yü Hsin hsüan-chi* 庾信選集. Chengchow: Chung-chou Shu-hua-she, 1983.

Translations

Hsü, I-min 許逸民, trans. and comm. *Yü Hsin shih-wen hsüan-i* 庾信詩文選譯. Chengtu: Pa-Shu Shu-she, 1991. *Ku-tai wen-shih ming-chu hsüan-i ts'ung-shu.* Taipei reprint by Chin-hsiu, 1993..

Studies

Ami, Yûji 網祐次. "Yu Shin ni tsuite" 庾信について. *Ochanomisu Joshi Daigaku Jinbun Kagaku kiyô* 16 (1963): 1-40.

Chang, Kang-i Sun 長孫康宜. "Yü Hsin: The Poet's Poet." In *Six Dynasties Poetry*. Princeton: Princeton University Press, 1986, pp. 146–184. See also the important review by Donald Holzman in *HJAS* 48 (1988): 244–49.

Ch'en, Ch'ang-ming 陳昌明. "Lun Yü Hsin te ku-erh i-shih" 論庾信的孤兒意識. *Chung-wai wen-hsüeh* 14.8 (1986): 96–115.

Chiu, Shu-chen 邱淑珍. "Yü Hsin shih yen-chiu" 庾信詩研究. Unpublished M.A. thesis, Tung-hai Ta-hsüeh, 1991.

Chung, Yu-min 鍾優民. "'K'u-mu ch'i t'ien hai', 'Ch'ing-shan wang tuan ho'–Lun Yü Hsin tso-p'in yü jen-ko" 枯木期填海,青山望斷河–論庾信作品與人格. *Wen-hsüeh p'ing-lun* 1988.1 (1988): 143-51.

____. "Lun Yü Hsin te wen-hsüeh ch'eng-chiu" 論庾信的文學成就. *Chi-lin Ta-hsüeh she-hui k'o-hsüeh hsüeh-pao* 81 (1987): 72–77.

____. "Yü Hsin wen-hsüeh ssu-hsiang ch'u-t'an" 庾信文學思想初探. *She-hui k'o-hsüeh chan-hsien* 36 (1986): 258–265.

Hsü, Tung-hai 許東海. *Yü Hsin sheng-p'ing chi ch'i fu chih yen-chiu* 庾信生平及其賦之研究. Taipei: Wen-shih-che, 1984.

Jao, Tsung-i 饒宗頤. "Lun Yü Hsin 'Ai-chiang-nan fu'" 論庾信哀江南賦. In *Chung-yang Yen-chiu-yüan kuo-chi han-hsüeh hui-i* 中央研究院國際漢學會議 Taipei: Academica Sinica, 1989, pp. 831–838.

Kôzen, Hiroshi 興膳宏. "Yu Shin no daiga no shi ni tsuite 庾信の題画の詩について." *Tôyô geirin ronsô* (1985): 579-597.

Li, Kuo-hsi 李國熙. *Yü Hsin hou-ch'i wen-hsüeh chung hsiang-kuan chih ssu yen-chiu* 庾信後期文學中鄉關之思研究. Taipei: Wen-chin, 1994. Wen-shih-che ta-hsi, 75.

Liu, Wen-chung 劉文忠. *Pao Chao ho Yü Hsin* 鮑照和庾信. Shanghai: Shang-hai Ku-chi, 1986. 1991 Taipei reprint by Kuo-wen T'ien-ti Tsa-chih.

____. "Yü Hsin ch'ien-ch'i tso-p'in k'ao-pien" 庾信前期作品考辨. *Wen-shih* 27 (1986): 219–230.

Tomikhai, Tamara Khinchevna. *Iui Sin*. Moscow: Izd-vo Nauka, 1988.

Yang, Ju-pin 楊儒賓. "Lung-men chih t'ung pan-ssu pan-sheng–yu t'i-ts'ai, chu-t'i yü piao-hsien fang-shih: Lun Yü Hsin wan-ch'i tso-p'in suo chan-hsien te ching-shen shih-chieh" 龍門之桐半死半生一由體裁，主題與表現方式，論庾信晚期作品所展現的精神世界. *Yu-shih hsüeh-chih* 20.1 (1988): 39–79.

Yü Hsüan-chi 魚玄機 (844-868)

Editions and References

Ch'en, Wen-hua 陳文華, comm. and ed. *T'ang nü shih-jen chi san-chung* 唐女詩人集三種. Shanghai: Shang-hai Ku-chi, 1984. Collects poems by Yü Hsüan-chi, Hsüeh T'ao 薛濤 and Li Yeh 李冶.

Studies

Kuhn, Dieter. *Yu Hsüan-chi. Die Biographie der T'ang-Dichterin, Kurtisane und taoistischen Nonne.* Privately printed by Habilitationsvortrag, Heidelberg, 1985.

Yü-t'ai hsin-yung 玉臺新詠 (New Songs from a Jade Terrace)

Editions and References

Ishikawa, Tadahisa 石川忠久. *Gyokudai shin'ei* 玉台新詠. Tokyo: Gakushû Kenkyûsha, 1986. Chûgoku no koten, 25.

Mu, K'o-hung 穆克宏, ed. *Yü-t'ai hsin-yung chien-chu* 玉臺新詠箋注. 2v. Peking: Chung-hua, 1985. Based on the 1774 revisions by Ch'eng Yen 程琰 and contains the commentary by Wu Chao-i 吳兆宜.

Translations

Birrell, Anne. *New Songs from a Jade Terrace: An Anthology of Early Chinese Love Poetry*. Rev. ed.; Middlesex, England: Penguin, 1986 (1982). Contains J. H. Prynne's "Chinese Figures" which originally appeared as a review of the first edition in *Modern Asian Studies* 17 (1983): 671-704.

Studies

Chou, Chien-yü 周建渝. "Hsü Ling nien-p'u" 徐陵年譜. *Chung-kuo wen-che yen-chiu chi-k'an* 10 (March 1997): 105-182.

Kang, Ts'un-fan 岡村繁. "*Wen hsüan* yü *Yü-t'ai hsin-yung*" 文選與玉臺新詠. In *Ku-tien wen-Hsüeh ti-ch'i chi* 古典文學第七集. Hsüeh-sheng Shu-chü 學生書局, ed. Taipei: Hsüeh-sheng Shu-chü, 1985, pp. 209-226.

Nakasuji, Kenkichi 中筋健吉. "Kyûtaishi to *Gyokudai shin'ei*" 宮体詩と玉台新詠. *Nippon Chûgoku Gakkai hô* 41 (1989): 92-106.

Yen, Chih-ying 諺智英. "*Chao-ming Wen-hsüan* yü *Yü-t'ai hsin-yung* pi-chiao yen-chiu" 昭明文選與玉臺新詠比較研究. Unpublished M. A. Thesis, National Taiwan Normal University, 1991.

Yüeh, Chin 躍進. "*Yü-t'ai ying-yung* pan-pen yen-chiu" 玉臺新詠版本研究, *Chung-kuo ku-chi yen-chiu* 中國古籍研究. V. 1. Shanghai: Shang-hai Ku-chi, 1996, pp. 303-337.

Yü-yen 寓言 ("lodged words" or allegory)

Editions and References

Pao, Yen-i 鮑延毅, *et al.*, eds. *Yü-yen tz'u-tien* 寓言辭典. Tsinan: Ming-t'ien, 1988.

Studies

Chang, Kang-i Sun. "Symbolic and Allegorical Meanings in the *Yüeh-fu pu-ti* Poem Series." *HJAS* 46 (1986): 352-285.

Ch'en, P'u-ch'ing 陳蒲清. *Chung-kuo ku-tai yü-yen shih* 中國古代寓言史. Taipei: Lo-to, 1987. Lo-to ts'ung-k'an, 11.

___. *Yü-yen wen-hsüeh li-lun li-shih yü ying-yung* 寓言文學理論歷史與應用. Taipei: Lo-t'o Ch'u-pan-she, 1992.

Hartman, Charles. "Literary and Visual Interactions in Lo Chih-ch'uan's *Crows in Old Trees*," *Metropolitan Museum Journal* 28 (1993): 129-167.

___. "Poetry and Politics in 1079: The Crow Terrace Poetry Case of Su Shih," *CLEAR* 12 (December 1990): 15-44.

Liu, Ts'an 劉燦. *Hsien-Ch'in yü-yen* 先秦寓言. Shanghai: Shang-hai Ku-chi, 1988. Reprinted in Taipei by Kuo-wen T'ien-ti Tsa-chih She in 1990.

Liu, Wan. "Poetics of Allusion: Tu Fu, Li Shang-yin, Ezra Pound, and T. S. Eliot." Unpublished Ph.D. dissertation, Princeton University, 1992.

Liu, Xiaolian. "The Odyssey of the Buddhist Mind: The Allegory of 'The Later Journey to the West'." Unpublished Ph.D. dissertation, Washington University, 1992.

Spring, Madeline. *Animal Allegories in T'ang China*. New Haven: American Oriental Society, 1993. *American Oriental Series*, 76.

___. "Roosters, Horses, and Phoenixes: A Look at Three Fables by Li Ao." *MS* 39 (1990–91): 199-208.

Tan, Ta-hsien 譚達先. *Chung-kuo min-chien yü-yen yen-chiu* 中國民間寓言研究. Taipei: Mu-to, 1982. *Chung-kuo wen-hsüeh hsin-shang ts'ung-shu,* 3.

Yüan Chen 元積 (779-831)

Editions and References

Luan, Kuei-ming 欒貴明, ed. *Ch'uan T'ang-shih so-yin: Yüan Chen chüan* 全唐詩索引：元積卷. Peking: Chung-hua, 1997.

Wu, Tai-ch'ing 吳在慶. "Chin shih-nien Yüan Chen yen-chiu shu-p'ing" 十年元積研究述評. In *T'ang-tai wen-hsüeh yen-chiu nien-chien, 1992* 唐代文學研究年鑑, 1992. Kweilin: Kuang-hsi Shih-fan Ta-hsüeh, 1993, pp. 219-232.

Wu, Ta-k'uei 吳大奎 and Ma Hsiu-chüan 馬秀娟, comms. *Yüan Chen Po Chü-i shih hsüan-i* 元積白居易詩選譯. Chengtu: Pa-Shu Shu-she, 1991. *Ku-tai wen-shih ming-chu hsüan-i ts'ung-shu.* Chin-hsiu Ch'un-pan-she in Taipei reprinted this work under the title *Yüan Chen, Po Chü-i shih* 元積，白居易詩 in 1993.

Ying-ying chuan 鶯鶯傳. Tsinan: Shan-tung Wen-i, 1987. Contains pieces of prose and poetry related to the story.

Yü, Ch'ing 余慶近. "Chin-nien lai kuan-yü 'Ying-ying chuan' te tao-lun tsung-shu" 近年來關於鶯鶯傳的討論總述. In *T'ang-tai wen-hsüeh yen-chiu nien-chien, 1992* 唐代文學研究年鑑, 1992. Kweilin: Kuang-hsi Shih-fan Ta-hsüeh, 1993, pp. 246-249.

Studies

Chou, Chen-fu 周振甫. "Tu 'Ying-ying-chuan' hsien-i" 讀鶯鶯傳獻疑. *Wen-hsüeh i-ch'an* 1992.6 (1992): 60-65.

Fan, Shu-fen 范淑芬. *Yüan Chen chi-ch'i yüeh-fu-shih yen-chiu* 元積及其樂府詩研究. Taipei: Wen-chin, 1984.

Huang, Chung-ching 黃忠晶. "Tui Ch'en Yin-k'o hsien-sheng 'Tu Ying-ying-chuan' te chih-i" 對陳寅恪先生讀鶯鶯傳的質疑. *Chiang-han lun-t'an* 1989.8 (1989): 51-59.

Hwa, Lily. "The Poet-statesman: His Poetical and Literary Career." Unpublished Ph.D. dissertation, University of Illinois at Urbana-Champaign, 1984. Chapter three, "The Birth of Literary Giant in Exile" (pp. 93-132) contains most of the discussion on Yüan's oeuvre and the literary milieu of the times.

Ikas, Ludger. *Der klassische Chinesische Vierzeiler: Das Beispiel Yuan Zhen (779-831).* Frankfurt am Main: P. Lang, 1995. A revised version of his dissertation (Bonn University, 1994).

Kominami, Ichirô 小南一郎. "Gen Haku bungaku shûdan no shôsetsu–'Ôôden' o chûshin ni shite" 元白文学集団の小説ー「鶯鶯伝」を中心にして. *Nippon Chûgoku Gakkaihô* 47 (1995): 63-74.

Lee, Yu-hwa. *Fantasy and Realism in Chinese Fiction: Tang Love Themes in Contrast.* San Francisco: Chinese Materials Center, 1984.

Liao, Mei-yün 廖美云. "Yüan Chen shih-wen yung yün k'ao" 元積詩文用韻考. Unpublished M.A. thesis, Tung-wu Ta-hsüeh, 1993.

___. *Yüan Po hsin-yüeh-fu yen-chiu* 元白新樂府研究. Taipei: T'ai-wan Shang-wu Yin-shu-kuan, 1989.

Liu, Ying 劉瑛. *T'ang-tai ch'uan-ch'i yen-chiu* 唐代傳奇研究. Taipei: Lien-ching, 1994. Study of "Ying-ying-chuan" on pp. 443-56.

Pien, Hsiao-hsüan 卞孝萱. "T'ang-tai tz'u-yün shih wei Yüan Chen shou-ch'uang k'ao" 唐代次韻詩為元積首創考. *Chin-yang hsüeh-k'an* 37 (1986): 93-95.

Shang, Yung-liang 尚永亮. *Yüan-ho wu ta shih-jen yü pien-che wen-hsüeh k'ao-lun* 元和五大詩人與貶謫文學考論. Taipei: Wen-chin, 1993. *Ta-lu ti-ch'ü po-shih lun-wen ts'ung-k'an.*

485

Tung, Nai-pin 董乃斌. "Yüan Chen ch'i jen" 元積其人. *Wen-shih chih-shih* 1985.1 (1985): 75-80.

Uchiyama, Tomoya 内山知也. "'Ô ô den' no kôzô to shudai ni tsuite 鶯鶯伝の構造と主題について." *Nippon Chûgoku Gakkai hô* 42 (1990): 156-68.

Wang, Meng-ou 王夢鷗. *T'ang-jen hsiao-shuo chiao-shih* 唐人小説校釋. Taipei: Cheng-chung, 1983. Commentary on "Ying-ying-chuan" on pp. 81-103.

___. "Ts'ui Ying-ying te shen-shih chi-ch'i ku-shih kou-ch'eng te nien-tai" 崔鶯鶯的身世及其故事構成的年代. In Wang's *Ch'uan-t'ung wen-hsüeh lun-heng* 傳統文學論衡. Taipei: Shih-pao, 1987, pp. 271-82.

Wang, Shih-I 王拾遺. *Yüan Chen chuan* 元積傳. Yinchuan: Ning-hsia Jen-min, 1985.

___. *Yüan Chen lun-kao* 元積論稿. Sian: Shan-hsi Jen-min, 1994. *Chung-kuo ku-tai tso-chia yen-chiu ts'ung-shu.*

Wang, Ta-chin 王達津. "Lun 'Hui-chen-chi'" 論會真記. *She-hui k'o-hsüeh chan-hsien* 28 (1984): 257-60.

Wang, Yün-hsi 王運熙. "Yüan Chen te shih-ko p'i-p'ing" 元積的詩歌批評. *Kuei-chou Ta-hsüeh hsüeh-pao* 貴州大學學報 1992.2 (1992): 25-31.

Wu, Tsai-ch'ing 吳在慶. "Yüan Chen jo-kan wen-t'i yen-chiu kai-shu" 元積若干問題研究概述. *Pei-fang lun-ts'ung* 1993.3 (1993): 62-66.

Wu, Wei-pin 吳偉斌. "'Ying-ying-chuan' hsieh-tso shih-chien ch'ien-t'an" 鶯鶯傳寫作時間淺探. *Nan-ching Shih-ta hsüeh-pao* 1986.1 (1986): 95-100.

___. "Yüan Chen yü Yung-chen ko-hsin" 元積與永貞革新. *Wen-hsüeh i-ch'an* 1986.5 (1986): 48-53.

___. "Yüan Chen p'ing-chia tsung-lan" 元積評價縱覽. *Fu-tan hsüeh-pao* 1988.5 (1988): 65-70.

Yüan Chieh 元結 (719-772)

Editions and References
Katô, Satoshi 加藤敏. *Gen Ketsu shi sakuin* 元結詩索引. Tokyo: Tôhô Shoten, 1993.

Luan, Kuei-ming 欒貴明, ed. *Ch'uan T'ang-shih so-yin: Yüan Chieh chüan* 全唐詩索引：元結卷. Peking: Chung-hua, 1997.

Translations
Strassberg, *Inscribed Landscapes,* pp. 115-120.

Studies
Hsü, Ch'uan-sheng 徐傳勝. "Chung T'ang shih-jen Yüan Chieh" 中唐詩人元結. *Wen-shih chih-shih* 1989.8 (1989): 71-75.

Huang, Ping-hui 黃炳輝. "Tz'u-shan k'ai tzu-hou hsien-sheng shuo" 次山開子厚先聲説. *Hsia-men Ta-hsüeh hsüeh-pao* (1986): 129-36.

Li, Chien-k'un 李建昆. *Yüan Tz'u-shan chih sheng-p'ing chi-ch'i wen-hsüeh* 元次山之生平及其文學. Taipei: T'ai-wan Shang-wu Yin-shu-kuan, 1986.

Nieh, Wen-yü 聶文郁. *Yüan Chieh shih-chieh* 元結詩解. Sian: Shan-hsi Jen-min, 1984.

Sun, Ch'ang-wu 孫昌武. "Tu Yüan Chieh wen cha-chi" 讀元結文札記. *She-hui k'o-hsüeh chan-hsien* 1985.3 (1985): 292-99.

Wang, Ch'i-chen 王綺珍. "Lüeh-lun Yüan Chieh tui T'ang-tai ku-wen yün-tung te kung-hsien" 略論元結對唐代古文運動的貢獻. *Chiang-hsi Chiao-yü Hsüeh-yüan hsüeh-pao* 1988.2 (1988): 23-29.

___. "Lun Yüan Chieh te fu-ku chu-i shih-lun" 評元結的复古主義詩論. *Wu-han Ta-hsüeh hsüeh-pao* 1986.3 (1986): 73-79.

Yüan Hao-wen 元好問 (1190-1257)

Editions and References

Chiang, Chen-shan 蔣枕山, ed. *Yüan I-shan shih-chi chu-chien* 元遺山詩集注箋. Taipei: Kuang-wen Shu-chü, 1973. Includes the commentary of Shih Kuo-ch'i 施國祁 (1750–1824).

Chung, Hsing 鍾星, ed. *Yüan Hao-wen shih-wen hsüan-chu* 元好問詩文選注. Shanghai: Shang-hai Ku-chi, 1990.

Ho, Hsin-hui 賀新輝, ed. *Yüan Hao-wen shih-tz'u chi* 元好問詩詞集. Peking: Chung-kuo Chan-wang, 1987. Contains biographical and bibliographical information.

Ho, Shu-hou 郝樹侯, ed. and comm. *Yüan Hao-wen shih-hsüan* 元好問詩選. Peking: Jen-min Wen-hsüeh, 1983.

Liu, I-sheng 劉逸生, ed. and Ch'en Chih-chai 陳沚齋, comm. *Yüan Hao-wen shih-hsüan* 元好問詩選. Hong Kong: San-lien Shu-tien, 1984. Chung-kuo li-tai shih-jen hsüan-chi. Appends a *nien-p'u.*

Yao, Tien-chung 姚奠中, ed. *Yüan Hao-wen chüan-chi* 元好問全集. 2v. Taiyuan: Shan-hsi Jen-min, 1990.

Yüan, Hao-wen 元好問. *I-shan hsien-sheng hsin yüeh-fu* 遺山先生新樂府. 5 *chüan*. Nanking: Chiang-su Ku-chi, 1988.

Translations

Cheng, Li-min 鄭力民, trans. *Yüan Hao-wen shih hsüan-i* 元好問詩選譯. Chengtu: Pa-Shu Shu-she, 1991. Ku-tai wen-shih min-chu hsüan-i ts'ung-shu.

Strassberg, *Inscribed Landscapes*, pp. 235-244.

Studies

Li, Yüan-min 李元民. "Yüan Hao-wen shih-lun te min-tsu t'e-se wen-hsüeh i-ch'an" 元好問詩論的民族特色. *Wen-hsüeh i-ch'an* 1986.2.

Liu, Tse 劉澤. *Yüan Hao-wen lun-shih san-shih shuo* 元好問論詩三十説. Taiyuan: Shan-hsi Jen-min, 1992.

Lu, Kuo-yao 魯國堯. "Yüan I-shan shih-tz'u yung yün k'ao" 元遺山詩詞用韻考. *Nan-ching Ta-hsüeh hsüeh-pao* 1986.1.

Shan-hsi Sheng Ku-tien Wen-hsüeh Hsüeh-hui 山西省古典文學學會, ed. Yüan *Hao-wen yen-chiu wen-chi* 元好問研究文集. Taiyuan: Shan-hsi Jen-min, 1987.

Ts'ai, Hou-yüan 蔡厚元. "Yüan Hao-wen te shih-lun" 元好問的詩論. *Fu-chien lun-t'an* 1987.1.

West, Stephen H. "Chilly Seas and East-flowing Rivers: Yüan Hao-wen's Poems of Death and Disorder." *JAOS* 106 (1986): 197-210.

Yüan Hung-tao 袁宏道 (1568-1610)

Editions and References

Chang, Ming-kao 張明高 and Fan Ch'iao 范橋, eds. and comms. *Yüan Chung-lang chih-tu* 袁中郎尺牘. Peking: Chung-kuo Kuang-po Tien-shih, 1991.

Translations

Strassberg, *Inscribed Landscapes*, pp. 303-312.

Studies

Butz, Herbert. *Yüan Hung-tao's "Regelment beim Trinken."* Frankfurt: Haag & Herchen, 1988. *Heidelberger Schriften zur Ostasienkunde*, 12.

Chaves, Jonathan. "The Expression of Self in the Kung-an School: Non-romantic

Individualism." In *Expressions of Self in Chinese Literature*, Robert E. Hegel and Richard C. Hessney, eds. New York: Columbia University Press, 1985, 123-150.

Chou, Chih-p'ing. *Yüan Hung-tao and the Kung-an School.* Cambridge: Cambridge University Press, 1988.

Yüan Mei 袁牧 (1716-1798)

Editions and References

Chou, Ko-min 周舸岷, ed. and comm. *Yüan Mei shih-hsüan* 袁牧詩選. Hangchow: Che-chiang Ku-chi, 1989.

Hsü, Ting-pao 徐定寶, ed. *Sui-yüan nü-ti-tzu shih-hsüan* 隨園女弟子詩選. Nanking: Chiang-su Ku-chi, 1993. *Yüan Mei ch'üan-chi,* 7.

Hu, Kuang-tou 胡光斗, trans. and comm. *Hsiao-ts'ang shan-fang chih-tu chien-shih* 小倉山房尺牘箋釋. Taipei: Kuang-wen Shu-chü, 1978. Han-hsüeh hui-pien.

Ku, Hsüeh-chieh 顧學頡, ed. *Sui-yüan shih-hua* 隨園詩話. Peking: Jen-min Wen-hsüeh, 1982.

Shen, Meng 申孟, ed. and comm. *Tzu pu-yü hsüan-chu* 子不語選注. Peking: Wen-hua I-shu, 1988. *Pi-chi hsiao-shuo.*

Wang, Ying-chih 王英志, ed. *Hsiao-ts'ang shan-fang shih-chi* 小倉山房詩集. Nanking: Chiang-su Ku-chi, 1993. *Yüan Mei ch'üan-chi,* 1.

___, ed. *Sui-yüan shih-hua* 隨園詩話. 16 *chüan.* Nanking: Chiang-su Ku-chi, 1993. *Yüan Mei ch'üan-chi,* 3.

___, ed. *Yüan Mei chuan-chi tzu-liao* 袁牧傳記資料. Nanking: Chiang-su Ku-chi, 1993. *Yüan Mei ch'üan-chi,* 8.

___, ed. *Yüan Mei ch'üan-chi* 袁牧全集. 8v. Nanking: Chiang-su Ku-chi, 1993; 1997. Appends a *nien-p'u* and various biographical and literary information.

___, ed. *Yüan Mei p'ing-lun tzu-liao* 袁牧評論資料. Nanking: Chiang-su Ku-chi, 1993. *Yüan Mei ch'üan-chi,* 8.

Translations

Li, Ling-nien 李靈年 and Li Tse-p'ing 李澤平, trans. and comms. *Yüan Mei shih-wen hsüan-i* 袁牧詩文選譯. Chengtu: Pa-Shu Shu-she, 1990. *Ku-tai wen-shih ming-chu hsüan-i ts'ung-shu.* 1993 Taipei reprint by Chin-hsiu Ch'u-pan-she under the title *Yüan Mei shih-wen.*

Louie, Kam and Louise Edwards. *Censored by Confucius: Ghost Stories by Yuan Mei.* Armonk, N.Y.: M.E. Sharpe, 1996.

Seaton, Jerome P. *I Don't Bow to Buddhas: Selected Poems of Yüan Mei.* Port Townsend, Washington: Copper Canyon Press, 1997. Translation of a number of poems with an Introduction (pp. xi-xix) to Yüan Mei as poet.

Strassberg, *Inscribed Landscapes,* pp. 403-412.

Yuet, Keung Lo. "New Wonder Tales of Qi: Excerpts." *Renditions* 37 (1992): 77-85.

Studies

Chien, Yu-i 簡有儀. *Yüan Mei yen-chiu* 袁牧研究. Taipei: Wen-shih-che, 1988. *Wen-shih-che hsüeh chi-ch'eng.*

Eggert, Marion. *Nur wir Dichter; Yuan Mei: ein Dichtungstheorie des 18. Jahrhunderts zwischen Selbstbehauptung und Konvention.* Bochum: Brockmeyer, 1989. *Chinathemen,* 42.

Fu, Yü-heng 傅毓衡. *Yüan Mei nien-p'u* 袁牧年譜. Hofei: An-hui Chiao-yü, 1986.

Yen, Chih-chien 閻志堅. *Yüan Mei yü Tzu pu-yü hsüan-chu* 袁牧與子不語. Shenyang: Liao-ning Chiao-yü, 1993. *Ku-tai hsiao-shuo p'ing-chieh ts'ung-shu.*

Yüeh-chüeh shu 越絕書 (The Book of the Culmination of Yüeh)

Editions and References

Lau, D. C. 劉殿爵 and Ch'en Fang-cheng 陳方正, eds. *Yüeh-chüeh shu chu-tzu so-yin* 越絕書逐

字索引. Hong Kong: Shang-wu Yin-shu-kuan, 1993. ICS Ancient Chinese text Concordance Series.

Li, Pu-chia 李步嘉, comm. *Yüeh-chüeh shu chiao-shih* 越絕書校釋. Wuchang: Wu-han Ta-hsüeh, 1992.

Yüan, K'ang 袁康 and Wu-p'ing 吳平. *Yüeh-chüeh shu ch'üan-i* 越絕書全譯. Yü Chi-tung 俞紀東, trans. and comm. Kweiyang: Kuei-chou Jen-min, 1997. *Chung-kuo li-tai ming-chu ch'üan-i ts'ung-shu.*

Yüeh-chüeh shu ch'üan-shih 越絕書全釋. Kweiyang: Kuei-chou Jen-min, 1990. *Chung-kuo li-tai ming-chu ch'üan-i ts'ung-shu.*

Yüeh-fu 樂府

Editions and References

Chang, Ya-hsin 張亞新, ed. and comm. *Liu-ch'ao yüeh-fu shih-hsüan* 六朝樂府詩選. Honan: Chung-chou Ku-chi, 1986. *Ku-tien wen-hsüeh hsiao ts'ung-shu.*

Ho, Ch'üan-heng 何權衡, ed. *Liang-Han yüeh-fu shih hsin-shang* 兩漢樂府欣賞. Chengchow: Chung-chou Shu-hua She, 1983. *Ku-tien wen-hsüeh hsiao ts'ung-shu.*

Li, Ch'un-hsiang 李春祥, ed. *Yüeh-fu shih chien-shang tz'u-tien* 樂府鑑賞辭典. Chengchow: Chung-chou Ku-chi, 1990. Covers 468 poems by 243 poets; appends a bibliography and a list of tune titles (explicated).

Yeh, Kuei-kang 葉桂剛 and Wang Kuei-yüan 王貴元, eds. *Chung-kuo ku-tai yüeh-fu shih ching-p'in shang-hsi* 中國古代樂府精品賞析. 2v. Taipei: Pei-ching Kuang-po Hsüeh-yüan, 1993. *Chung-kuo ku-tai wen-hsüeh ching-p'in shang-hsi ts'ung-shu.*

Translations

Birrell, Anne. *New Songs from a Jade Terrace, An Anthology of Early Chinese Love Poetry.* Rev. ed.; Middlesex, England: Penguin, 1986 (1982). Contains J. H. Prynne's "Chinese Figures" which originally appeared as a review of the first edition in *Modern Asian Studies* 17 (1983): 671-704.

___. *Popular Songs and Ballads of Han China.* Honolulu: University of Hawaii Press, 1988.

Studies

Allen, Joseph Roe III. "From Saint to Singing Girl: The Rewriting of the Lo-fu Narrative in Chinese Literati Poetry." *HJAS* 48 (1988): 321-361.

___. *In the Voice of Others: Chinese Music Bureau Poetry.* Ann Arbor: Center for Chinese Studies, University of Michigan, 1992. *Michigan Monographs in Chinese Studies,* 63.

Cai, Zongqi 蔡宗齊. "Dramatic and Narrative Modes of Presentation in Han *Yüeh-fu.*" *MS* 44 (1996): 101-140.

Chang, Yung-hsin 張永鑫. *Han yüeh-fu yen-chiu* 漢樂府研究. Nanking: Chiang-su Ku-chi, 1992. *Chung-kuo ku wen-hsien yen-chiu ts'ung-shu.*

Holzman, Donald. "Songs for the Gods: The Poetry of Popular Religion in Fifth-Century China." *AM, TS* 3 (1 1990): 1-20. A translation and study of the eighteen popular religious poems which comprise chapter 47 of the *Yüeh-fu shih-chi* 樂府詩集. As a group, these poems are known as "Shen-hsien ko" 神弦歌.

___. "Folk Ballads and the Aristocracy." *Études chinoises* 13 (1994): 345-360.

Hsiao, Ti-fei 蕭滌非. *Han Wei Liu-ch'ao yüeh-fu wen-hsüeh shih* 漢魏六朝樂府聞學史. Peking: Jen-min Wen-hsüeh, 1984.

Kamatani, Takeshi 釜谷武志. "The Early Bureau of Music." *Acta Asiatica* 70 (1996): 37-53.

___. "Gafu setsuritsu nendai kô" 樂府設立年代考. *Mimei* 未名 11 (1993).

___. "Kan Butei gafu sôsetsu no mokuteki" 漢武帝樂府創設の目的. *Tôhôgaku* 84 (1992): 52-66.

Levy, Dore J. *Chinese Narrative Poetry. The Late Han through T'ang Dynasties.* Durham and London: Duke University Press, 1988. One of the few Western-language monographs on the *yüeh-fu* genre

Rouzer, Paul. "Watching the Voyeurs: Palace Poetry and *Yuefu,*" *CLEAR* 11 (1989): 13-34.

Wang, Ju-pi 王汝弼. *Yüeh-fu san-lun* 樂府散論. Sian: Shan-hsi Jen-min, 1984.

Wang, Lan-ying 王蘭英. *Han yüeh-fu min-ko shang-hsi* 漢樂府民歌賞析. Huhehot: Nei Meng-ku Jen-min, 1987.

Wang, Yün-hsi 王運熙. *Yüeh-fu shih shu-lun* 樂府詩述論. Shanghai: Shang-hai Ku-chi, 1996.

___ and Wang Kuo-an 王國安. *Han Wei Liu-ch'ao yüeh-fu shih* 漢魏六朝樂府史. Shanghai: Shang-hai Ku-chi, 1986. *Chung-kuo ku-tien wen-hsüeh chi-pen chih-shih ts'ung-shu.*

Yang, Sheng-chih 楊生枝. *Yüeh-fu shih shih* 樂府詩史. Hsining: Ch'ing-hai Jen-min, 1985. Covers from the origins to the end of the T'ang.

Yao, Ta-yeh 姚大業. *Han yüeh-fu hsiao-lun* 漢樂府小論. Tientsin: Pai-hua Wen-i, 1984.

Yüeh-fu shih-chi 樂府詩集 (Collection of Music Bureau Songs)

Studies

Holzman, Donald. "Songs for the Gods: The Poetry of Popular Religion in Fifth-Century China." *AM, TS* 3 (1 1990): 1-20. A translation and study of the eighteen popular religious poems which comprise chapter 47 of the *Yüeh-fu shih-chi* 樂府詩集. As a group, these poems are known as "Shen-hsien ko" 神弦歌.

Yün-chi ch'i-ch'ien 雲笈七籤 (The Bookcase of the Clouds with the Seven Labels)

Editions and References

Chiang, Li-sheng 蔣力生 *et al.*, eds. *Yün-chi ch'i-ch'ien* 雲笈七籤. Peking: Hua-hsia, 1996. Modern punctuated edition with some annotation.

Yün-chi ch'i-ch'ien 雲笈七籤. Compiled by Chang Chün-fang 張君房 (*fl.* 1008–1025). Tsinan: Ch'i-Lu Shu-she, 1988. Photolithic reproduction of the Ming Taoist Canon (*Cheng-t'ung Tao-tsang* 正統道藏).

Translations

Fukui, Fumimasa 福井文雅. "*Unkyû shichisen* kan 6 'Sandôkyô kyôbu.sandô hinkaku' kunnyaku 『雲笈七籤』卷六「三洞經教部，三洞品格」訓譯. *Waseda Daigaku Daigakuin bungaku kenkyûka kiyô* 42.1-4 (1995).

Yung-lo ta-tien hsi-wen san-chung 永樂大典戲文三種 (Three "Play-texts" from the Eternal Joy Grand Repository)

Editions and References

Ch'ien, Nan-yang 錢南揚, coll. and annot. *Yung-lo ta-tien hsi-wen san-chung chiao-chu* 永樂大典戲文三種校注. Rpt. Taipei: Hua-cheng Shu-chü, 1980 (Peking Chung-hua, 1979).

490

Studies

Akamatsu, Norihiko 赤松紀彦. *"Chô Kyô jôgen* gibun ni tsuite" 張協状元戯文について, *Chûgoku bungakuhô* 50 (1995), 97-107.

Table of Contents for *The Indiana Companion to Traditional Chinese Literature, Volume I*

494

497

498

501

502

503

Errata and Corrigenda

I want to especially thank Daniel Bryant, Glen Dudbridge, Volker Klöpsch. Y. W. Ma, and William Schultz who sent general lists of errata as well as the various individual contributors who noted corrections needed in their entries. Colleagues Bryant, Dudbridge and Schultz provided especially detailed lists.

Page	Line	Error	Correction
xi	17 up	Christa	Krista
xiv	11-12	insert GK George Kao 高克毅	
xv	14	癈	廢
xv	13 up	李培瑞	李培德
xv	2 up	Dartmouth University	Dartmouth College
xvi	7	Dartmouth University	Dartmouth College
xvii	4	WS	WSp
xxi	3 up	*hsüeh-k'an*	*yüeh-k'an*
xxiii	18 up	學述研究	學術研究
xxvi	20	"T'u-shu fu-k'an"	"Tu-shu fu-k'an"
xxvii	13	*Wen-hsüeh i-chien tseng-k'an*	*Wen-hsüeh i-ch'an tseng-k'an*
xxix	18 up	Chien, *Sung-shih*	Ch'ien, *Sung-shih*
xxxi	20 up	*Shih-shuo hsin-y*	*Shih-shuo hsin-yü*
xxxi	7 up	小川陽	小川陽一
xxxii	7 up	Yagisawa, *Gekisakuka*	Yagisawa, *Gekisakka*
xxxv	28	*Chuang-wen ch'i-kan*	*Chung-wen ch'i-k'an*
2	3	*peng-ch'i*	*pen-ch'i*
	6	*Cheng fa-jua ching*	*Cheng fa-hua ching*
	30	d. 285	d. 385
3	16	*Ching-kang ching*	*Chin-kang ching*
	16 up	Avatamasaka	Avataṁsaka
4	1	folklores	folklore
5	11	best-translated	best translated
6	3	Chi-p'an	Chih-p'an
	14 up	Ch'an-jan	Chan-jan
	9 up	Mâdhyimaka	Mâdhyamika
7	5	*ch'uan-ch'i*	*ch'üan-chi*
8	13	among Chinese masses	among the Chinese masses
	23	suit compiled	suit and compiled
9	2	*yün-wen*	*yün-wen,*
	3 up	*shihshû*	*shinshû*
10	5	(53-54), catalogues	(53-54), and catalogues
	12 up	renunciation of household	renunciation of the household
11	18-19	absorbed in	absorbed into
	Editions	Mizuno, Kogen	Mizuno, Kôgen 水野弘元
12	7 (left)	Hirano, Kenshô	Hirano, Kenshô 平野顯照
	19 (left)	*chiao-lu*	*ch'u-lu*
15	28	enconium	encomium
16	9	of	on
18	19	*yin-chu*	*yin-chü*
	22	*chien-tu*	*ping-hu*
19	11	Hsiao-chuan	Hsiao-ch'uan
23	24	editions	versions
27	1	works	words
	5	*cheng-yin-p'i*	*cheng-yin-p'u*
28	23 up (left)	*Gikyokushu*	*Gikyokushû*

	20 (right)	tz'u	tz'u
29	10 (left)	*Das Yüan-fu*	*Das Yüeh-fu*
	12 (left)	*un*	*und*
	15 (left)	*ch'u*	*ch'ü*
	27 (left)	*Choku*	*Chûgoku*
	28 (left)	*kinkyu*	*kenkyû*
	10 up (left)	Theater	théâtre
	26 (right)	*Shou hsi-ch'ü*	*Shuo hsi-ch'ü*
33	25	Ch'ih-po-tzu	Ch'ih-p'o-tzu
34	17 up	*yen-fu*	*yen-fen*
	10 up	*ying-hsuing*	*ying-hsiung*
36	3 up	thus whether	thus not whether
37	20 up	*pao-chuan*	*pao-chüan*
38	14 up	quanitity	quantity
39	7	清	青
	17	contempory	contemporary
41	5 up	reason	reasons
42	28	century,	century.
	7 up	*Shih Nai-an*	Shih Nai-an
43	15	of the the novel	of the novel
	17	editer	editor
46	3	indispenable	indispensable
	11	continiuation	continuation
	13 up	answer is the affirmative	answer is in the affirmative
50	12	Chi	Ch'i
53	19	Meng Yü-ch'ing	Meng Yün-ch'ing
54	1	*Feng-yeh*	*Feng-yüeh*
	20 up	after "Yang Wan-li's" add:	*Ch'eng-chai shih-hua* 誠齋詩話
56	5-6	Ch'in Kuan	Ch'in Kuan 秦觀
	2 up, text	*ts'ung-p'ing*	*ch'ung-p'ing*
	last line	批評	批評史
57	17 (left)	*hsi-ch'u*	*hsi-ch'ü*
	25 (left)	*poésie a*	*poésie à*
	4 (right)	*yashchuoi*	*yashchnoi*
	6 up (right)	Chicago, 1962.	Chicago.
	4 up (right)	London, 1975.	London.
58	29 (left)	Shih-jua	Shih-hua
	32 (left)	Liang Ch'i-chao	Liang Ch'i-ch'ao
65	12-13	when when literate	when literate
69	19 up	*Yü-tai hsin-yung*	*Yü-t'ai hsin-yung*
72	2	*ni-ku* 公安	*ni-ku* 擬古
	2	*kung-an* 擬古	*kung-an* 公安
73	1 (right)	Fei, Pu-hsien 斐	P'ei, P'u-hsien 裴
74	6 up (left)	*Rokucho*	*Rokuchô*
75	10 up	dialectical	dialectal
76	14	Yüan drama	Yüan dramas
81	22 (right)	*dentô*	*densetsu*
	22 (right)	伝説研究	伝説の研究
	7 up (right)	*Chü-i*	*Ch'ü-i*
82	2 up (left)	*Handworterbuch*	*Handwörterbuch*
	5 up (right)	王會泳	于會泳
84	4	*t'ieh-chi-erh*	*t'ieh-ch'i-erh*
	23	Wu Song	Wu Sung
86	11 up	*Hou-lang*	*Huo-lang*
89	24	turmoil	turmoils
	29	was not	were not
90	7 up	*K'eng*	*Keng*
	6 up	*K'eng*	*Keng*
91	11-12	T'ang Cheng-pi	T'an Cheng-pi
	3 (right)	*Chung-wei*	*Chung-wai*
92	22 up (left)	*Chü-i*	*Ch'ü-i*

	8 up (left)	Shih-liang	Shih-ying
	25 up (left)	*Bôken*	*Môken*
95	1	*hsi*	*hsi* 橄
96	20	add Chinese for	*tui-wen* 對文, *kao* 誥, and *yü* 喻
97	6	inscription	inscription,
	28	*chi-wen*	*ch'i-wen*
100	3	*Ch'u-tzu*	*Ch'u-tz'u*
101	28	鳴	明
103	9 up	Registered Lands	the Ceremonial Field
	6 up	番	審
104	12	Chou Yü	Chou Yung
	18 up	kan	an
105	5 up	Converted	Corrected
108	9	*ch'i*	*ch'i* 奇
	16	Weng	Wen
114	15	Ch'ien-teng	Chien-teng
115	17	*Ku-wen kuan-chih*	*Ku-wen kuan-chih**
	19	*T'ang-shih san-pai shou*	*T'ang-shih san-pai shou**
116	10 (right)	桐城文派評述	先秦散文選注
119	11 (left)	*K'uei-ssu ts'un-kao*	*Kuei-ssu ts'un-k'ao*
120	13 (left)	Wang Jao	Wang Yao
122	6 up	"Shuo-nan"	"Shui-nan"
123	10	*Jung-tsai*	*Jung-ch'ai*
	18	Liang Chang-chu	Liang Chang-chü
	4 up	adapt	adopt
	last line	commemmorates	commemorates
130	18	hyopophora	hyopophera
	16 up	north to the	north of the
131	15	tugged	tagged
	24	anatanaclasis	antanaclasis
	13 up	inversed	inverted
132	#15	*Ching-tse*	*Ching-ts'e*
	#16, 1	*Ying-ch'eng*	*Ying-ch'en*
	#16.b	*Tui-cheng*	*Tui-ch'en*
	#17	antanoclasis	antanaclasis
133	#18, c, 9	of basic	of the basic
	#18, c, 9	or metaphoric	or the metaphoric
	#20.b	remove Chinese after Jade Pool	
135	#29.c.iii		
	line 3	歸	婦
136	Bibliography		
	10 (right)	Hsü, Chin-t'ing	Hsü Ch'in-ting
137	11 (left)	*lin-wen*	*lun-wen*
	5 (right)	*Tu-chu*	*Tu-shu*
	4 up (right)	*K'uei-ssu ch'un-k'ao*	*Kuei-ssu ts'un-k'ao*
140	20 up	*Lo shu*	*Lo t'u*
146	23	*yan*	*yen*
147	3 up	Meng An-pai	Meng An-p'ai
148	17	elixir	elixir *huan-tan*
149	12 up	Pai Lu-chüng	Pai Lü-chung
	8 up	Wu Ch'eng-tzu	Wu-ch'eng tzu
	8 up	*Yü-ch'i ch'i-chien*	*Yün-chi ch'i-ch'ien*
	5 up	numberous	numerous
150	8	Lagerway	Lagerwey
	7 up	*Chung-chien wen*	*Hsiang-chien wen*
151	Bibliography		
	L, Ofuchi, 1980	*modurokuhen*	*mokurokuhen*
	19 up (left)	1096	1906
	16 (right)	Lagerway	Lagerwey
	17 (right)	*siécles*	*siècles*
	Robinet (right)	revelation	révelation
152	last line (left)	revelation	révelation

	4 up (right)	袄	佛
	last line (right)	*IP*	*TP*
153	6 up	(Boltz, 1984)	(Boltz, forthcoming)
156	26	ofthe	of the
157	18 up	*ch'un-hsien*	*ch'ün-hsien*
158	23	Shih Ch'en	Shih Ts'en
160	20	Ch'en T'ien	Ch'en Yin-
160	7 up	皇 is printed upside down	
172	Bibliography		
	2 (left	*kenyû*	*kenkyû*
	7 (left)	ue	jô
173	Bibliography		
	12 (right)	1962	1963
173	L, Loon, line 3	*Festscrift*	*Festschrift*
	R, Schipper		
	1966, line 3	of a manuscript	of manuscript
178	14	Lu K'an	Lu K'un
179	3	Ching	Ch'ing
180	3 up	*K'uei-ssu*	*Kuei-ssu*
181	14 up	陳文述	女兒國
182	18 up	add Chinese character for *pi* 比	
184	2	add Chinese character for *piao* 表	
185	9	*tzu*	*tz'u*
	7 up	*ko-ch'u*	*ko-ch'ü*
186	16 up	絕句	陸羽
187	7 up	Hsü	Ch'ang
193	L, Chou Shou-		
	ch'ang, line 3	Peng-lai	P'eng-lai
	2 up (left)	*te yen-chiu*	*yen-chiu* (i.e., delete *te*)
	11 up (right)	Lieh nu	Lieh nü
193	7	add 花 after 天雨	
199	15 up (left)	Tung	T'ung
200	15 up (right)	K'uao	K'uai
201	20 up (left)	*Zen Nogoroku*	*Zen no Goroku*
203	3 (left)	Yanagita	Yanagida
	12 up (left)	Hsiang-chou 襄陽	Hsiang-chou 襄州
	11 up (left)	Hsiang-yang 襄州	Hsiang-yang 襄陽
204	13 up (right)	史壕史	史壕吏
206	10 up (left)	four *ch'uan-chi*	four *ch'uan-ch'i*
207	11 (left)	Kei	Ku
208	L, Bibliography		
	Studies, line 1	Altier	Altieri
	Studies, ll. 13-14	sheng-hou	sheng-huo
209	L, Chang Cho		
210	1 (left)	*kenkô*	*zenkô*
	12 (left)	*shien*	*hsien*
212	24 (left)	Ssu-ch'iu	Ssu-ch'ou
215	L, Bibliography		
	Studies,		
	last entry	*Soshi kenkyu*	*Sôshi kenkyû*
		To Godai Hoku hen	*Tô Godai Hoku Sô hen*
	2 up (right)	について	について
	R, Bibliography		
	Editions, ll. 1-2	*cheng-chi*	*cheng-ch'i*
217	6-7 up (left)	Ho Chih-chang*	Ho Chih-chang
	6 up (left)	Wang Ch'i-jung	Wan Ch'i-jung
218	14 up (right)	Kuang-fuhui	Kuang-fu hui
	13-14 (right)	T'ung-menghui	T'ung-meng hui
219	7 up (left)	文始	文史
	1 (right)	*Kou-ku*	*Kuo-ku*
221	20 (left)	Yan Hung-tao	Yüan Hung-tao

	13 (right)	"Ch'i-i-shih"	"Ch'i-ai-shih"
222	7 up (left)	Shansi	Shensi
224	13-14 (right)	owner held it in his mouth	owner fondled it,
226	8 (right)	*P'ai-yü-chai*	*Pai-yü-chai*
	10 up (right)	–KISC	–KIC
228	22 up (left)	Ta-hsien	Ta-hsin
232	L, Bibliography		
	Editions, line 2	*Lung-chuan*	*Lung-ch'uan*
	Same	add 澄龍川文集	
	Same, line 6	教淺	校箋
	Same, line 7	濤	燾
237	11 up (right)	–RH	–RMH
240	8 (right)	out of the Past	out of the Pass
	15 (right)	*chang-an chieh*	*Ch'ang-an chieh*
	29 (right)	further credited for	further credited with
241	L, Bibliography		
	line 11	T'ao-ch'ang-ssu	T'ai-ch'ang-ssu
	lines 11-12	chao-ch'ing	shao-ch'ing
	line 16	ch'en-chia	Ch'en-chia
	line 20	*Gekisakuka*	*Gakisakka*
242	16 (right)	Ch'eng En-tsi	Ch'eng En-tse
243	R, Bibliography		
	Studies, line 4	*DMB*	*ECCP*
245	L, Bibliography		
	Studies, line 6	*DMB*	*ECCP*
	6 up (left)	*Lei chüan*	*Lei ch'üan*
	4 up (right)	*Lei chüan*	*Lei ch'üan*
246	6 up (left)	*I-yin*	*I Yin*
	2 up (left)	I-yin	I Yin
	6 up (right)	*San-shih-chungsan-shih-chung*	
247	2 (left)	*Hsin-chün*	*Hsin-chün*
	4 (left)	*I-yin*	*I Yin*
	15 (left)	*Hsin-chün*	*Hsin-chün*
	19 (left)	*k'ang*	*k'an*
	22 (left)	*I-yin*	*I Yin*
	11 up (left)	*I-yin*	*I Yin*
248	19 up (right	Way I heard Them	Way I Heard Them
	13-14 up (right)	for Again on the North Short of River Luan	
		read Sequel to the North Luan Shore Collection	
249	18 up (right)	盧	羅
254	9-10 (right)	add Chinese characters 弔屈原	
255	34 (left)	汪	江
	5 (right)	*pu-tzu*	*pu-tz'u*
260	L, Bibliography		
	Studies, line 1	Caudlin	Candlin
261	Chiang-hsi shih-p'ai		
	line 7	Hung	Huang
	lines 9-10	(*fl.* 119)	(1084?-1145)
	line 10	*ts'ung--p'ao t'u*	*ts'ung-p'ai t'u*
263	18 (left)	add Chinese characters 張炎	
	26 (right)	words	works
	27 (right)	poets this tradition	poets in this tradition
	4 up (right)	blossom	blossoms
268	L, Bibliography		
	Studies, lines 1-2	delete pp. 444-505	
	3 (right)	*Chiao-fang-chi*	*Chiao-fang chi*
269	L, Bibliography		
	Studies, line 4	*yin-y eh-shih*	*yin-yüeh-shih*
272	17 up (left)	祕	秘
	15 up (left)	祕	秘
	last line (left)	*wen-tun*	*wen-lun*
	7 up (right)	祕	秘

273	6 up (left)	索	李
274	11 up (left)	ming-ts'e	ming-tz'u
275	14 (right)	(1341-1427,	(1341-1433,
276	12 (right)	delete 東州	
	29-30 (right)	Ph. D. dissertation	M. A. thesis
277	14 (left)	animates	animate
	7 up (left)	Tung-ch'ing	Tung-ch'eng
	9 (right)	delete 錢	
283	R, Bibliography		
	line 4	tales	Tales
287	L, Translations		
	line 2	shôsuke	Shôsuke
291	5-6 (right)	小野忍	金瓶梅考證
	22 (right)	謝肇的	謝肇淛的
294	mid (left)	Ch'en, Teng-y an	Ch'en Teng-yüan
302	23 (right)	Fujiwara no Michinzane	Fujiwara no Michizane
	3 up (right)	*Nihonkou*	*Nihonkoku*
304	24 (right)	*yakubun Taisei*	*yakukambun Taisei*
	same	国訳文大成	国訳漢文大成
	28 (right)	*kokuyakubun*	*kokuyaku kambun*
	29 (right)	読国訳文大成	続国訳文大成
	20 up (right)	*zenshu*	*zenshû*
	18 up (right)	*Shinyaku*	*Shinshaku*
315	L, Bibliography		
	Editions, line 2	add Chinese characters 阮元	
	26 (right)	delete one Seraphin	
	4 up (right)	Robert James	James Robert
321	13 (left)	*Shou-chi*	*Shuo-chi*
322	23 (right)	*tsung-shou*	*tsung-shuo*
330	1 (left)	*I-y t'u-chih*	*I-yü t'u-chih*
334	19 up (left)	shiao-tiao	chiao-tiao
345	16 up	范仲淹	曲江池
349	L, Editions		
	line 8	Huang Hsing-tsu	Hung Hsing-tsu
	line 13	Huang Hsing-tsu	Hung Hsing-tsu
359	L, Bibliography	add Chinese characters 張友鶴	
	4 up (right)	*T'ang-jen*	*T'ang-jen hsiao-shuo yen-chiu* 唐人小説研究. 4v. Taipei, 1971-1978.
368	L, Bibliography		
	Editions, line 2	typeset	offset
370	L, Bibliography		
	Studies, line 2	Chin-ling	Ching-ling
	line 16	Kôjiô	Kôjirô
	line 18	Chin-ling	Ching-ling
373	15 up (right)	*ken kyû*	*kenkyû*
380	8 (left)	*tirees*	*tirées*
383	R, Studies, Ch'ien Nan-yang		
	line 2	han chai	kan Chai
386	L, Studies, line 4	add 封神演義	
387	L, Bibliography		
	Editions	replace line 6-9 with the following	
		Hai-fu shan-t'ang tz'u-kao 海浮山堂詞稿. Shanghai, 1981.	
		add: The best, most accessible text of Feng's *ch'ü*, based on the collation of all early editions	
391	L, Studies, line 10	Chien, Chung-wu	Chien, Tsung-wu
	2 up	Torao	Toraô
	same	*taiyo*	*taiyô*
397	16 up (left)	Ichiro	Ichirô
399	R, Editions		
	Hartman, line 2	Sung Edition	Sung Editions
400	26 (left)	Kan Go	Kan Yu

		Kan Go	Kan Yu
	1 (right)		
403	22 up (right)	治	治
407	11 up (left)	Konan, Ichiro	Konan, Ichirô
	same	*Sai keizakki*	*Saikei zakki*
	10 up (left)	伝承者	伝承者たち
409	9 (right)	*shipyosei*	*shinyosei*
410	13 up (left)	*hsi-hsiang*	*hsi-hsiang*
	8 (right)	*Saishô*	*Seishô*
	10 (right)	*Saishô*	*Seishô*
	12 (right)	*Saishô*	*Seishô*
	15 (right)	*Saishô*	*Seishô*
412	5 (left)	figa no nomdai	jida no mondai
414	10 up (left)	*shi-ni [o]*	*shi-ni [o] chuan*
417	last line (right)	141-911	141-191
428	17 (right)	"Chuang-cheng fu"	"Chuan-cheng fu"
429	18 up (right)	Rei-un	Reiun
	15 up (right)	Ho	Hao
	8 up (right)	めくって	めぐって
430	11 (left)`	Rei-un	Reiun
	15 (left)	Rei-un	Reiun
431	28 (left)	Hsiang	hsiang
	R, Editions line 11	Ho	Hao
440	6 (right)	bibiographical	bibliographical
445	1 (right)	___.	Lévy, André.
	4 (right)	Lévy, André. ___.	
	17 (right)	すける	おける
448	7 up (left)	yang	ying
452	5 (left)	redo 洪北江	
	22 up (right)	fiction treatise	fictional treatise
455	6 (right)	*chia-shu*	*chia-hsü*
	12 (right)	Feng Ch'i-jung	Feng Ch'i-yung
456	13 up (left)	also his preface	also his prefaces
	1 (right)(	(Ch'ien Hsing-ts'un 錢杏村)	(Chou Shao-liang 周紹良 and Chu Nan-hsien 朱南銑)
	23 (right)	New Jersey,　Princeton,	
	3 up (right)	利	刊
463	1 (right)	redo 例*	
464	8 (left)	poltical	political
471	20 (left)	uncharactertistic	uncharacteristic
472	20 (left)	，木入斗問題	，'木入斗'問題
	23 up (right)	T'ao Chün-ch'i	T'ao Chü-ch'i
475	5 up (right)	脩	修
476	17 (left)	Zenuyû	Zenryû
	26-29 (left)	move Wright, Arthur F. entry to p. 476, line 3 (right) '	
477	21 (left)	*K'ung-t'i*	*Kung-t'i*
	27 (right)	"Kôteki	"Kô Teki
	35 (right)	陽	楊
	21 up (right)	add Chinese characters 新刊關目好酒趙元遇上皇	
484	16 (right)	老老	姥姥
487	25 (right)	楊	陽
	last line (right)	delete 古逸詩	
490	last line (right)	Sui Sen-shu 隋森樹	Sui Shu-sen 隋樹森
492	2 (left)	wai-chih	wai-shih
493	18 (right)	*Wan-ching*	*Wen-ching*
494	20 up (right)	Sun Cho	Su Cho
	same	孫	蘇
495	8-9 (left)	add Chinese characters 捕蛇者説	
	22-23 up (right)	(see *Hsi-k'ung*	(see *Hsi-k'un*
	19 up (right)	add Chinese character 窮	
	18 up (right)	add Chinese character 工	

511

497	22 up (left)	Yao	Yüeh
	same	姚	樂
	20 up (left)	Yao	Yüeh
	11 (right)	"Hou Chih-pi fu"	"Hou Ch'ih-pi fu"
499	10 (left)	Liu Fen-sui	Liu P'an-sui
	14 up (right)	Bols,	Bol,
500	7 (left)	Chung-chu	Chung-shu
	14 up (left)	Yüan Chien	Yüan Chieh
	7 up (left)	Ryu	Ryû
501	16 up (left)	*Ku-wen-tz'u lei-ts'uan*	*Ku-wen-tz'u lei-tsuan*
	14 up (left)	*chüan*	*chuan*
	13 up (left)	纂	纂
	12 up (left)	*ts'uan*	*tsuan*
502	27 (left)	*lei-ts'uan*	*lei-tsuan*
	12 up (right)	*lei-ts'uan*	*lei-tsuan*
503	10 up (left)	*lei-ts'uan*	*lei-tsuan*
	2 (right)	*lei-ts'uan*	*lei-tsuan*
	5 (right)	*lei-ts'uan*	*lei-tsuan*
	25 (right)	*lei-ts'uan*	*lei-tsuan*
	20 up (right)	Liu Shu*	Lin Shu*
	34 (right)	*lei-ts'uan*	*lei-tsuan*
504	6 (left)	*lei-ts'uan*	*lei-tsuan*
	7 (left)	*lei-ts'uan*	*lei-tsuan*
	10 (left)	*lei-ts'uan*	*lei-tsuan*
	24 (left)	Yü, Hsin-hsiung	Yu, Hsin-hsiung
506	5 up (right)	*Kagaku*	*kagaku*
509	9 up (left)	Hung-chou	Hang-chou
510	9 (right)	*shôhai*	*shôgai*
	17 (right)	Sung kao-seng chuan	Sung *Kao-seng chuan*
512	21 (left)	backwood	backwoods
520	9 up (left)	Chang Ch'ao	Chang Ch'iao
525	11 up (left)	Lan ts'ai-ho	Lan Ts'ai-ho
	6 up (left)	tenmemt	tenment
528	14 up (left)	along	alone
529	6 up (left)	*Ch'üan-t'ung*	*Ch'uan-t'ung*
531	14 (right)	*Li Chia*	*Li Chiao*
	R, 2 up in text	*pan*	*p'an*
532	26 (right)	*(Fu-yüng-t'ing*	*(Fu-yung-t'ing*
539	20 up (right)	woud	would
541	27 up (right)	Gekisakuka	Gekisakka
	20 up (right)	*Gekisakuka*	*Gekisakka*
	12 up (right)	耑	顓
542	2 up (left)	is	in
545	L, Bibliography		
	Studies, line 11	Kou	Kuo
	1 (right)	add Chinese characters 王貴苓	
547	11 (right)	Sui-kit	Siu-kit
550	22 up (left)	add Chinese characters 月下獨酌	
551	20 up (left)	Shigenyoshi, Obata	Obata, Shigeyoshi
552	6 up (left)	Chu Ho-ling	Chu Hao-ling
553	13 (left)	*Ri Shô-in*	*Ri Shôin*
	26 (left)	*luan-ai*	*lien-ai*
555	L, Bibliography		
	Studies, line 1	*ECCP*	*DMB*
556	L, Translations		
	line 1	*Leider*	*Lieder*
	4 (right)	常州	長州
	4 (right)	(northwest of Soochow)	(alos in Su-chou prefecture)
560	Liang Ch'i-ch'ao		
	line 1	Chou-ju	Cho-ju
	16 (right)	literati	literatus
561	6 (right)	Hsing-ts'an	Hsing-ts'un

	7 (right)	ch'ing	Ch'ing
	13 up (right)	Ryô keichô	Ryô Keichô
562	1 (left)	Chiang-chih	Ching-chih
	20 (right)	Chin-i	Chih-i
564	L, Editions line 3	Chang Yu-ho	Chang Yu-hao
	7 (right)	Lu Ta-fang	Lu Ta-huang
	13 up (right)	dandei	kankei
566	4 (right)	inspires	inspired
	12 up (right)	add Chinese character 贊	
568	12 up (left)	Ch'un-yu	Ch'ün-yu
573	24 (right)	add Chinese characters 詩集考編	
	25 (right)	Konami, Ichirô	Kominami, Ichirô
578	21 up (left)	between 719," 20 insert *HJAS,* to read 719," *HJAS,* 20	
	16 up (left)	nesisiche	nesische
580	22 (left)	Dolezelova-Velingerova	Dolzelová-Velingerová
	Liu E, line 1	Tieh-yün	T'ieh-yün
582	22 (left)	Liu Hou-tsu	Liu Hou-tzu
	L, Bibliography Editions, line 3	Collected	Corrected
	3 up (right)	Rôzan yuki	*Rôzan yuki*
584	19 up (right)	*Chung-shan Ta-hseh*	*Chung-shan Ta-hsüeh*
588	8 (left)	*ch'uan-chi*	*ch'üan-chi*
	22 (left)	ch'uan-chi	ch'üan-chi
	25 (left)	ch'uan-chi	ch'uan-chi
591	30 (right)	Lyo	Lyou
592	7 up (right)	230	280
593	7 (right)	Ogawa,	Ôgawa,
594	5 (right)	(1956-1918)	(1858-1918)
	12 up (right)	T'ang, Kui-chang	T'ang, Kuei-chang
597	8 up (left)	Ch'ih Yün-ch'ing	Hsi Yün-ch'ing
	last line (left)	劉開揚	顏文選
	22 (right)	*Early,*	*Early T'ang,*
	28 (rght)	yon-	shi-
599	29 (right)	speach	speech
601	23 (right)	an	no
	11 up (right)	yon-	shi-
602	13 (right)	trough	through
	18 up (right)	Ho	Hao
603	8 (left)	Liu, Wei-ch'ing	Liao, Wei-ch'ing
604	R, Lu Kuei-meng entry, line 10	add Chinese character 邈 to read 孫思邈	
607	6 up (right)	Chia-yu	Chia-yü
611	21 (left)	Ogawa	Ôgawa
612	9 (right)	Chih-yuan	Chih-yüan
615	25 (left)	春秋世語	春秋事語
	same	(Tales of the World the	(Events and Speeches of the
617	28 (left)	Kao, Hen 高孚	Kao, Heng 高亨
620	19 up (left)	Chang-tai	Chang-t'ai
	27 (right)	Yagisawa, *Gekisakuka*	Yagisawa, *Gekisakka*
625	6 up (right)	Hung Tsu	Huang Tsu
631	19 (left)	*pieh-tsai-*	*pieh-ts'ai-*
633	20 (right)	delete *Mu T'ien-tzu chuan hsin-chu* 穆天子傳新注	
	8 up (right)	Tkei	Tôkei
638	11 up (left)	Sui Shu-san	Sui Shu-sen
641	23 (left)	O Yôshū	Ô-yô Shû-
647	15 up (right)	Chung Tung	Chung Jung
648	17 (right)	Tiao wang shih	Tao wang shih
649	13 up (left)	459	460
	8 up (right)	Hôshô	Hô Shô
	5 up (right)	Hôshô	Hô Shô
	2 up (right)	Hôshô	Hô Shô

513

650	10 (left)	Hôshô	Hô Shô
	13 (right)	Ts'ai	Ts'ui
	23 (right)	Ts'ui, Ling-chin	Ts'ui, Ling-ch'in
	same	add Chinese characters 崔令欽	
656	11 up (left)	楽府歴	楽府の歴
	3 up (left)	Ogawa	Ôgawa
658	5 up (left)	add Chinese characters 徐陵	
661	10 (left)	he Story	The Story
	27 (right)	*Hsüan*	*Hsüeh*
663	13 up (right)	Hsin-chen	Hsin-cheng
665	10 (right)	*kekyû*	*kenkyû*
	16 (right)	Hakushi bunshû	*Hakushi monjû*
	33 (right)	1945	1949
670	15 up (left)	add Chinese characters 諸葛亮	
	25 (right)	Ogawa	Ôgawa
	9 up (right)	Ogawa	Ôgawa
671	3 (left)	をおぐ,	をめぐって,
677	20 up (right)	*T'ang*	*Early T'ang*
682	12 (left)	rikuchô	Rikuchô
686	16 up (right)	*Wen-ching mi-fu lun.* *	*Wen-ching mi-fu lun* (i.e., *Bunkyô hifuron* *).
687	24 (right)	*cheh-ch*	*chüeh-chü*
689	18 (right)	*unterbrochener*	*ununterbrochener*
692	14 up (left)	Hong Kong, 1971.	2v. New York, 1961.
	12 up (left)	Hong Kong, 1974	Rpt. Hong Kong, 1974.
693	15 up (right)	*Shikei*	*Shikyô*
694	8 (right)	Hsiang-	Hsing-
696	8 up (right)	Jade Splinter	Jade Splinters
698	25 (left)	the translation by Volker Klöpsch is selective, not complete	
703	11 up (right)	She Ping	*Shr Pin*
709	6 up (left)	*Shui-hui*	*Shu-hui*
710	9 (right)	1653	1953
729	3 (left)	add Chinese characters 養才	
730	21 up (right)	add Chinese characters 中江	
740	6 (r9ght)	abriging	abridging
744	23 (right)	Chinese characters for *wen* 文 and *wu* 武 need to be reversed	
745	2 (right)	Tz'u-ch'i	Tz'u-chi
	13 (right)	dan	dans
751	3 up (right)	Chang Chu-cheng	Chang Chü-cheng
752	3 (left)	Yu-ming T'ang	Yü-ming T'ang
754	15 up (left)	*Gekisakuka*	*Gakisakka*
759	13 (left)	唐才子伝研究	唐才子伝の研究
762	14 up (left)	yü Ch'ien Chien-i	yü Ch'ien Ch'ien-i
763	29 (left)	*tsu*	*tzu*
766	4 (left)	1962	1963
768	13 up (right)	1984	1983
769	18 (left)	Bunjiro	Bunjirô
	20 (left)	–MC	–WMC
	last line (left)	complete	incomplete
	6 up (right)	profilic	prolific
770	14 up (left)	P'ei-yuan	P'ei-yüan
	9 up (left)	inedit	inédit
	7 up (left)	*Melanges*	*Mélanges*
	6 up (left)	a	à
	same	*Demieville*	*Demiéville*
	9 (right)	"Setsuru Ku"	"Setsuru kô"
771	7 (left)	theatre	théâtre
	25 up (left)	*kiyo*	*kiyô*
773	15 up (right)	Le Shih	Yüeh Shih
774	1 (left)	Chui	Chiu
	11 (right)	*chuan-ku*	*chuang-ku*
781	13 (left)	*Li Siécle*	*Le siècle*

	3 (right)	*hsueh*	*hsüeh*
	7 up (right)	*shou-hui*	*shuo-hui*
782	1 (left)	*mü*	*mu*
	8 up (left)	*Tôhôkakuhô*	*Tôhôgakuhô*
	10 up (right)	元雑劇 題材	元雑劇の題材
783	20 (left)	*Gekisakuka*	*Gekisakka*
	15 (right)	themes	theme
	18 (right)	*ch'ui*	*ch'iu*
786	8 (right)	chou	shuo
790	9 up (left)	generaic	generic
794	11 (right)	*chi-tsao*	*chih-tsao*
796	12 (right)	*Wei-wu fu*	*Nei-wu fu*
	16 (right)	Chun-chih	Shun-chih
	5 up (right)	1730	1703
799	10 up (left)	Nankano,	Nakano,
	7 (right)	*Mogols*	*Mongols*
800	13 (left)	烈	列
801	9 up (right)	Chia-ping	Chia-pin
808	15 (right)	Ting-i 定一	Tsung-i 宗一
811	12 (right)	Pao's	Mao's
812	14 (left)	Juan Yüan's 嚴焦	Juan Yüan's 阮元
	19 (left)	Yen Chieh 阮元	Yen Chieh 嚴杰
	3 (right)	Tan Ying	T'an Ying
	13 (right)	*tu*	*t'u*
818	11 up (left)	*To shih*	*To shi*
819	2 up (right)	ho	huo
821	7-8 up (right)	Former Shu 蜀)	Former Shu 前蜀)
824	15 up (left)	Edouard. *Li*	Édouard. *Le*
837	3 up (left)	*chu*	*chi*
840	L, *T'ung-Kuang T'i*		
	line 6	add Chinese characters for 陳衍	
841	2 up (right)	Wan-chih	Wan-chin
843	17 up (left)	auch	such
844	10 (right)	*Etudes*	*Études*
	11 (right)	*litterature*	*littérature*
848	21 (left)	Hung-Tso	Hung-tso
	2 up (right)	Hoffman,	Hoffmann,
851	12 (right)	seventh	seventeenth
	10 up (right)	*o megutte"*	o megutte"
852	5 (left)	indent: tz'u-hua shu-k'ao	
855	12 up (left)	, ed. Taipei,	(1160-1224), ed. 1st printed 1214; rpt. Taipei,
862	15 up (left)	*Li-tai fa-pao chih*	*Li-tai fa-pao chi*
866	17 (left)	*chang-an*	*Ch'ang-an*
	23 (left)	*chang-an*	*Ch'ang-an*
	24 up (right)	*chang-an*	*Ch'ang-an*
874	R, Studies		
	line 1	yon-	shi-
875	13 (left)	add Chinese characters for 藝苑巵梔＊言	
876	11 up (left)	add Chinese characters for 子貞	
	4 up (left)	add Chinese characters for 新成	
877	3 (right)	believed	believe
880	2 (left)	add Chinese characters for 應劭	
888	20 up (right)	chuan" , *Kuo-*	chuan" 傳, *Kuo-*
	13 up (right)	辨	辨
890	26-28 (right)	for 劉勰にこれる美の理念をめぐって：文心雕龍文学 read 文心雕龍文学原理論の諸問題： 劉勰にこれる美の理念をめぐって	
	14-15 up (right)	"Bunshin chôryû to shihin	"Bunshin chôryû to Shihin
	12 up (right)	*kenen*	*kinen*
894	6 up (right)	his	this

515

897	7 up (right)	18. *Shu* 疏	18. *Shu* 書
	6 up (right)	19. *Shu* 書	19. *Shu* 疏
909	29 (right)	*Untern*	*Unteren*
910	15 (right)	yon-	shi-
913	L, Bibliography Editions, line 4	*Yang Tzu-yüan*	*Yang Tzu-lang*
925	19 up (left)	takuchidusu	takuchikusu
	3 (right)	extraordinary	extraordinnaire
929	5 up (right)	pressd	pressed
936	6 up (right)	*bungoku*	*bungaku*
941	39 (left)	imtimate	intimate
942	6 (left)	Sactifices	Sacrifices
945	9 up (right)	It	it
	2 up (right)	Hsü Ling (*tzu*,	Hsü Ling 徐陵 (*tzu*,
946	24 (left)	考異	玉臺新詠考異
	2 up (left)	*chi kuan pen*	*hsi kuan pen*
	7 (right)	Torao	Toraô
	same	*shu*	*shŭ*
947	18 (left)	*to*	*t'o*
	15 (right)	passge	passage
	16 (right)	Ch'in	Chin
948	middle (right)	*Alieniloguim;*	*Alieniloquium*
950	21 (right)	*ch'uan-chi*	*ch'uan-ch'i*
958	13 up (left)	Beli-	Bel-
	12 up (left)	gique	gium
962	6 (right)	Fan Ch'in	P'o Ch'in 繁欽
964	10-11 (left)	中唐詩人藥府	楽府の歴史的研究
965	25 (left)	collectiion	collection
	3 up (left)	on	no
966	19 (left)	are	is
	20 up left	*Tuan-chieh:*	*Tuan An-chieh:*
	11 up (left)	–YHC	–WO
971	3 up (left)	Ch'an-jan	Chan-jan
974	L, Ch'in Kuan	(1049-1100), 234	(1049), 56, 234
980	R	move "Le Shih, 773" to p. 991, 3 up (right) as "Yüeh Shih, 773"	
993	30	*Cheng-fa-jua ching*	*Cheng-fa-hua ching*
995	27	*Chih-yen chai ts'ung-p'ing*	*Chih-yen chai ch'ung-p'ing*
1001	14	*tsung-shou*	*tsung-shuo*
1008	24	*Ku-wen-tz'u lei-ts'uan*	*Ku-wen-tzu lei-tsuan*
	7 up	*K'uei-ssu lei-kao*	*Kuei-ssu lei-kao*
1009	22 up	*Lei chüan*	*Lei ch'üan*
1011	7	"Liu I" by Shen Chi-chi	"Liu I" by Li Ch'ao-wei
1016	16 up	*San-tung ch'un-*	*San-tung ch'ün*
1020	19 up	*Ta-Ch'ing i't'ung chih*	*Ta-Ch'ing i-t'ung chih*
1021	28 up	*T'ai-tzu jui-ying peng*	*T'ai-tzu jui-ying pen-*
	3 up	*shih-ni*	*shih-ni chuan*
1026	13 up	*Wan-ching yüan-yang hui*	*Wen-ching yüan-yang hui*
1031	2 up	*Zen Nogoroku*	*Zen no Goroku*

Name Index

A

Ah Ying 阿英 (Ch'ien Hsing-t'un 錢杏囤, 1900–1977), 75, 77

Ai-na Chü-shih 艾衲居士 (Buddhist Layman Artemisia-Cassock), 158

Amitabha (Amitofo 阿彌陀佛), 118

An-ch'eng 安成, Prince of, 45

An Chi 安驥, 27, 28

An Ch'i, 29

An Hsüeh-hai, 30

An Lu-shan, 152

B

Berkowitz, Alan, 9

Boccaccio, 161

Brecht, 30

Buddha, 119, 151

C

Cao, Weiguo, 103, 149

Cha Li 查禮 (1715–1783), 84

Cha Shen-hsing 查慎行 (1650–1727),* 85

Cha Shih-piao 查士標, 196

Cha Wei-jen 查為仁 (1694–1749), 84

Chai Hao 翟灝 (1736-1788), 170

Chang Chi 張機, 121

Chang Chien-feng 張建封 (735–800), 106

Chang Chih-tung 張之洞 (1837–1909), 5

Chang Chin-feng 張金鳳, 27, 29

Chang Ching 張景 (970–1018), 101

Chang Chün 張俊 (1086– 1154), 3

Chang, Emperor 章 (r. 76–88), 91

Chang Fan 張璠, 40

Chang Hen-shui 張恨水, 31

Chang Heng 張衡 (78–139),* 10, 110

Chang Hsiao-hsiang 張孝祥 (1129 or 1132–1166), 43, 84

Chang Hsieh 張協 (d. 307), 10

Chang-hsien 章獻, Empress Dowager (969-1033), 151

Chang Hu 張祜 (791-854), 145

Chang Hua 張華 (232–300),* 7, 8, 109, 135, 187

Chang I (or Chang Chi) 張揖/楫 (fl. 227), 166

Chang Ju 張濡, 3

Chang Lei 張耒 (1054–1114),** 1, 2, 13

Chang Nan-chuang 張南莊 (fl. 1880), 76

Chang P'u 張溥 (1602–41), 9, 49, 195

Chang Pi-ying 章必英, 62

Chang Ping-lin 章炳麟 (1868–1936),* 64

Chang Shih-ch'eng 張士誠 (1321-1367), 185

Chang T'ing-yü 張廷玉 (1672–1755), 67

Chang Tai 張岱 (1599– 1684),* 186

Chang Tuan-i 張端義 (fl. 1235), 84

Chang Tzu 張鎡 (1153–after 1211), 3

Chang Tzu-lieh 張字烈 (1564–1650), 169

Chang Yen 張炎 (1248–ca. 1320),** 3-4, 43, 86

Chang Yen 張綖 (fl. 1513), 175

Chang Ying 張瑩, 40

Chang Yu 張有 (b. 1054), 167

Chang Yü-niang 張玉娘, 115

Chang Yü-shu 張玉書 (1642–1711), 169–170

Chang Yüan-kan 張元幹 (1091–1161), 43

Chao Erh-sun 趙爾巽, 67

Chao Ching-shen 趙景深, 77

Chao Hsin 趙信, 86

Chao Meng-fu 趙孟頫 (1254–1322), 128

Chao Ting 趙鼎 (1085–1147), 43

Chao Ying 趙塋 (d. 943), 152

Chao Yü 趙昱, 86

Ch'ao 晁 family, 53

Ch'ao Liang 晁梁, 54

Ch'ao Pu-chih 晁補之 (1053–1110), 1, 11, 13, 44

Ch'ao Ssu-hsiao 晁思孝, 53–54, 56

Ch'ao Yüan 晁源, 54

Chaucer, 161

Che-tsung 哲宗 (r. 1086–1100), 13, 14

Chen, Bingmei, 45, 176

Chen-chu 珍珠, 55

Chen-ko 珍哥, 54

Chen Pingyuan [Ch'en P'ing-yüan] 陳平原, 82

Chen Zhi, 3, 18, 123, 154

Ch'en Ch'ung 陳充 (fl. 1004–1007), 17

Ch'en Chi-ju 陳繼儒 (1558–1639), 50

Ch'en Chih-kuang 陳芝光, 86

Ch'en Chin 陳錦, 196

Ch'en Heng-k'o 陳衡恪 (1876–1923), 7

Ch'en Hung-shou 陳洪綬 (Ch'en Lao-lien 陳

517

Name Index

Name Index

519

Name Index

Name Index

Huan Wen 桓溫 (312– 373), 150
Huan-pi Chu-jen 環碧主人 (The Master of the Surrounding Green), 53
Huang Ch'ao 黃巢 (d. 884), 66, 113
Huang Feng-ch'ih 黃鳳池, 126
Huang Kung-wang 黃公望 (1269-1355), 196, 197
Huang Mo-hsi 黃摩西 (1866–1913), 78
Huang T'ing-chien 黃庭堅 (1045–1105),* 1, 2, 5-6, 13
Huang Tsun-hsien 黃遵憲 (1848–1905),* 5
Huang Tsung-hsi 黃宗羲 (1610–1695),* 11
Huang Yü-chi 黃虞稷 (1629-1691), 67
Huang Yüan-chieh 黃媛介, 186
Hughes, E. R., 64
Hugo, Victor, 76
Hui-ch'ung 惠崇 (d. 1018), 17
Hui 惠, Emperor (r. 290–307), 103
Hui 徽, Emperor (r. 1101–1125), 43
Hui, King of Liang 梁惠王 (370–319 B.C.), 21
Hui-lin 慧琳 (737–820), 168
Hui-tsung 徽宗, 14
Hung Ch'eng-ch'ou 洪承疇 (1593–1665), 50
Hung Chün 洪鈞 (1840–1893), 79
Hung Liang-chi 洪亮吉 (1746–1809),* 11, 90

I

Idema, W. L., 117
I-hui 奕繪 (1799–1838), 68

J

Jan-li Tzu 燃藜子 (Master of Burning Pigweed), 53
Jen Ch'ing 任青, 2
Jen 仁, Emperor (r. 1022-1063), 152
Jen Fang 任昉 (460–508),* 99, 155, 179
Jen Ku 任谷 73
Joyce, 24
Juan Chi 阮籍 (210–263),* 8, 23, 51, 72
Juan Yü 阮瑀 (ca. 165–212),* 163
Juan Yüan 阮元 (1764–1849), 170

K

Kan Pao 干寶 (fl. 320), 73, 173
K'ang-hsi 康熙 emperor (r. 1662-1722), 189 196

Kant, 79
Kao Ch'i 高啟 (1336– 1374),* 184, 185
Kao I-wei 高一葦, 62
Kao, Karl S. Y., 31
Kao Ming 高明 (ca. 1305-ca. 1370),* 18, 19
Kerr, Janet Lynn 林珍, 121
Knechtges, 9
Ko Hung 葛洪 (283–343),* 73
Ko Shou-chih 葛受之, 53
Ko Tsai 戈載 (fl. 1807), 169
Ku Ch'un 顧春 (1799–after 1876),** 68, 69, 140 see also Ku T'ai-ch'ing 太清, vol. 1
Ku Jung 顧榮 (ca. 260–ca. 322), 109
Ku K'uang 顧況 (ca. 725–ca. 814),* 70
Ku Lung 古龍 (Hsiung Yao-hua 熊耀華, 1936–1985), 191
Ku T'ai-ch'ing 顧太清 (1799–after 1876), 140 see also Ku Ch'un
Ku Yeh-wang 顧野王 (519–581, 169
Kuan Hsiu-ku 關秀姑, 31
Kuang-wu, Emperor 光武 (r. 25–57), 60, 98
K'uang Chou-i 況周頤 (1859–1926), 52, 68, 69
Kung, King 恭 of Lu (r. 154–ca. 129 B.C.), 187
Kung Tzu-chen 龔自珍 (1792–1841),* 68
Kung-sun Hsia 公孫夏, 173
Kung-sun Ni-tzu 公孫尼子, 193
K'ung Hsi-hsien 孔熙先, 39
K'ung Jung 孔融 (153–208),* 163
K'ung Ling-ching 孔令境, 77
K'ung Ying-ta 孔穎達 (574–648), 192
Kuo Chen 郭震 (656-713), 100
Kuo Hsiang 郭象 (d. 312), 21, 22, 25
Kuo Mao-ch'ien 郭茂倩 (fl. 12th c.), 104
Kuo Mo-jo 郭沫若 (1892–1978), 49, 193
Kuo P'u 郭璞 (276–324),** 71-74, 166
Kuo Shao-yü 郭紹虞 (1893–1984), 6

L

Lady Bamboo, 2
Lao Lai-tzu 老萊子, 150
Lao-mu 老母 (Venerable Mother), 118
Lao Tan, 148 see also Lao-tzu, Lao Tzu
Lao Ts'an, 79
Lao-tzu, 148, 150
Lee, Leo, 76

Name Index

Name Index

Name Index

Name Index

Name Index

Name Index

Wang Jung 王融 (468–493),** 178–80

Wang Kuo-wei 王國維 (1877–1927),* 44, 78, 79, 175

Wang Ling 王令 (1032–1059),** 181–82

Wang Mang, 60

Wang Meng 王蒙 (1301–1385), 196

Wang Meng-chi 王夢吉, 158

Wang Pi 王弼 (226–249), 110

Wang Pi-chiang 汪辟疆 [Wang Kuo-yüan 汪國垣] (1887–1966), 6

Wang Pien 王抃, 196

Wang Seng-ju 王僧孺 (465–522), 45

Wang Shih-chen 王士禎 (1634–1711),* 6

Wang Shih-min 王時敏 (1590–1680), 196

Wang Ssu-jen 王思任 (1575–1646), 185

Wang Tao 王導 (276–339), 72, 150

Wang Tao-k'un 汪道昆, 128

Wang Ts'an 王粲 (177–217),* 104, 163

Wang Tuan 汪端 (1793–1839),** 184–85

Wang Tuan-shu 王端淑 (1620/21–ca. 1701),** 69, 185–186

Wang Tun 王敦 (266-324), 72

Wang T'ung 王通 (584–617), 100

Wang Tzu-lan 王子蘭 (1803-1824), 184

Wang Wei 王維 (701–761),* 104, 197

Wang Wei 王微 (ca. 1600–ca. 1647), 109

Wang Wen-fu 王文夫, 62

Wang Yen-shou 王延壽 (ca. 124–148),** 187

Wang Yin-chih 王引之 (1766–1834), 170

Wang Ying-lin 王應麟 (1223–1296),* 11, 32

Wang Yü-ch'eng 王禹偁 (954–1001),* 12, 122, 123

Wang Yüan-i 王遠宜, 115

Weaver Maiden, 133 see also Chih-nü

Wei Ao 韋敖, 143

Wei Chuang 韋莊 (ca. 836–910),* 175

Wei Chung-hsien 魏忠賢 (1568–1627), 113

Wei-feng 惟鳳, 17

Wei Hsiu-jen 魏秀仁 (Wei Tzu-an 魏子安, 1819–1874), 80

Wei 韋, Master, 144

Wei Shu 韋述 (d. 757), 105

Wei Yeh 魏野 (960–1019), 16

Wei Ying-wu 韋應物 (737-ca. 792),* 145

Wei Yüan 魏源 (1794–1857), 6

Wen-chao 文兆, 17

Wen 文, Duke of the Chin (r. 636–628 B.C.), 11

Wen 文, Emperor of the Liu Sung 劉宋 (r. 424–453), 39, 45, 135

Wen K'ang 文康 (ca. 1798–1872), 26, 28–30, 81, 190

Wen T'ien-hsiang 文天祥 (1236–1283), 49

Wen T'ing-yün 溫庭筠 (ca. 812-870),* 175

Weng Fang-kang 翁方綱 (1733–1818), 6

Widmer, Ellen 49, 185, 187

Wilhelm, Helmut, 65

Wolff, Ernst, 68

Wong, Shirleen S., 86

Wu Chien-jen 吳趼人 (1866–1910),* 75, 79–80, 82

Wu Chih-k'uei 吳志葵, 50

Wu Ching-tzu (1701–1754), 127

Wu Chiung 毋煚, 66

Wu Cho 吳焯, 86

Wu Chün 吳均 (469–520),* 45

Wu, Emperor (r. 502–550), 156

Wu 武, Emperor of the Han (r. 140–87 B.C.), 173, 193

Wu 武, Emperor (r. 482–493), 178

Wu 武, Emperor of Ch'i 齊, 180

Wu 武, Emperor (r. 265–290), 109

Wu I 吳易 (sometimes given as Wu Yang 吳易, 1612–1646), 50

Wu 吳, King of, 160

Wu Ling-yün 武凌雲, 139

Wu San-kuei 吳三桂 (1612–1678), 115

Wu Shan 吳山, 186

Wu Sheng-chao 吳勝兆, 50

Wu Shih-ch'ang 吳世昌, 44

Wu Tao-ming 吳道明, 34

Wu Tsao 吳藻, 140

Wu Tse-t'ien 武則天, 189

Wu Tzu-hsü 伍子胥 (d. 484 B.C.), 99, 114

Wu Wen-ying 吳文英 (ca. 1200–ca. 1260),* 4

Wu, Yenna, 58, 162

Wu Yüan-chi 吳元濟 (d. 817), 142

Y

Yamada Katumi 山田勝美, 91

527

Name Index

Title Index

Title Index

Title Index

Title Index

Title Index

533

Title Index

Title Index

Title Index

536

Title Index

Title Index

Title Index

Title Index

Title Index

Title Index

Subject Index

A

Academia Sinica web site, 136

advanced placement examination, 144

albums–album-anthologies, 126; albums of illustrations, 128

allegory, 23, 55, 56, 146, 155, 156

allusions, 3, 86, 133-134, 143

ancient style poetry (*ku-shih* 古詩), 148

"ancient-style prose movement"–see *Ku-wen yün-tung* 古文運動

anthology of Ming poetry, 108

anti-Manchu sentiment, 112, 196

artists, 195, 196

audiences, discerning and sophisticated, 128

autobiography, 76, 98

B

background narrator (see also "foreground narrator"), 161

ballads, 182

biographers, 154

biographies, 2, 153, 159; of the Perfected, 155; idealized, 144

block printing Buddhist charms, 125; as a means to standardize the Confucian texts, 125; process of, 125

book collecting, 129

book illustrations, 128

book printing–see "printing"

bookbinding, 129

bookshops in the Han capital, Lo-yang, 124

Bodhisattvas, 117

Buddhas, 117

Buddhism, scriptures 117; "three banners" (form, emptiness, contemplation) of, 150; patrons of, 156

C

calligraphy, 128, 195

"canon" of traditional Chinese literature, 95

censorship, 67, 161

ch'an-wei 讖緯 prognostication texts, 60, 177

Ch'ang-chou tz'u-p'ai 常州詞派,* 44

characterization, 56

Che-hsi tz'u-p'ai 浙西詞派 (Western Chekiang School of Lyrics),* 44, 85

Chekiang School, 85

cheng 正, 129

cheng-shih 正史, "official" or "standard histories," 64, 134

chi chuan 紀傳 (annals and biographies) format originated by Ssu-ma Ch'ien, 135

chi 紀 (annals), 135

chi 記 (records), 101

ch'i 七 (sevens),** 9-11, 47, 91

Chiang-hsi shih-p'ai (江西詩派), 5

chiang-t'i tzu 匠體字 (craftsman) style of characters, 128

chieh 偈 (gatha), 117

Chien-an literature, 163; poetic innovations in, 163

chih-jen 志人, 124

chih-kuai 志怪 (records of anomalies),* 23, 70, 124, 189

children's literature–see *Erh-t'ung wen-hsüeh* **

children's songs, 35, 36

chin-shih examinations, 1, 5, 13, 88, 100, 141, 147, 181; Sung Ch'i yielding to elder brother in, 151; sponsors for, 141

chin-t'i shih 今體詩 (recent-style verse), 174

Chinese characters, traditional analysis of, 167

ching 經 (scripture), 117

ching-che-chuang 經摺裝 (sutra-binding), 129

Ching-chi chih 經籍志, 66 (see also *I-wen chih* **)

Ching-ling pa-yu 竟陵八友 (Eight Friends of Pa-ling), 179

Chiu-seng t'i 九僧體 (Nine Monks Style),** 16

Chu-lin ch'i-hsien 竹林七賢 (Seven Worthies of the Bamboo Grove), 151

chü-jen 舉人 examination, 84

ch'ü 曲 (arias),* 18-20, 84, 169

ch'ü-p'ai 曲牌, 117

chuan 傳 (biographies), 101, 106

ch'uan-ch'i 傳奇 (romances), 19, 62, 114, 126, 196; literati plays in,127

ch'uan-ch'i 傳奇 (tales),* 18, 23, 112, 116, 142, 144, 189; tied to politics and political expression, 146; as first consciously created fiction in China, 146

chüeh-chü 絕句, 35, 36, 47

543

Subject Index

Subject Index

hu-tieh-chuang 蝴蝶裝 (butterfly binding), 129
hua-pen 話本* stories, 142, 189
Hundred Days' Reform Movement 百日政變, 5, 75

I

I-wen chih 藝文志 (Records of Classical and Other Literature),** 63-67, 166
Immortals, 73
imperial library, in the K'ai-yüan era, 66
innovations in poetry characterize Chien-an times. These developments

J

Japanese Restoration, 78
ju-hua 入話, 142

K

ko shih 歌詩 (songs and *shih* poetry), 65
ku-shih 古詩, 35, 51
Ku-wen yün-tung 古文運動 (Ancient-literature or Ku-wen Movement),* 95, 96, 97, 100, 102, 105, 106, 146, 153; in the early Sung, 147
kuan-hua 官話 or "Mandarin," 93–see also "Mandarin"
kung-an hsiao-shuo 公案小説 (court-case novels), 189
kung-sheng degree, 112
kung-t'i shih 宮體詩 (palace-style poetry),* 90

L

late Ch'ing fiction,** 75–81; as a drastic change in Chinese narrative tradition, 77; beginning of, 78; novels often referred to as *hsia-i hsiao-shuo* 俠義小説 (novels of chivalry and righteousness), 189
Late T'ang Style, 16, 122
lei-shu 類書,* 126–see also "encyclopedias"
lexicography, 171; deficiencies of traditional Chinese methods of, 171
li 理 (principles of things), 2
lieh-chuan 列傳 (memoirs or biographies), 152
lien-chu 連珠 (strung pearls),** 89-91
Ling-yin Monastery 靈隱寺, 196
literary Chinese,** 92-94

literary criticism, history of 111
literary history, creative periods in, 82
literary supplement, 75
Liu-li-ch'ang 琉璃廠, bookstores at, 127
liu-shu 六書 (six categories of script), 167, 169
Loyang-party, 13
lü-shih 律詩 (regulated verse), 35, 47, 96

M

magazine editorials, 78
Maitreyan mythology, 118
man-tz'u 慢詞, 14, 42
Manchus, 68, 69, 115, 196; conquest of China, 127
Mandarin (at that time based on the language of Nanking), 171
Mao-shan 茅山, 155; Taoism at, 156
May Fourth, 81; scholars in, 78
meng-shu 蒙書 (children's primers), 32
metaphor, 72
Ming-Ch'ing succession, turmoil during, 195
Ming dynasty, collapse of, 158
modern Chinese children's literature movement (1921-1927), 37
modern Chinese fiction, 77
modernity, 76
moral tales, 144
multiple narrators, 159
music, 61, 193, 195; and literature, 192; influence on listeners, 193
musical treatises of the later dynastic histories, 194

N

National University (T'ai-hsüeh 太學), 147
nature, poetry of, 197
new music (*hsin sheng* 新聲), 60
New Party, in the Sung dynasty, 1
newspapers, 75; editorials in, 78
Nine Monk's poetry, 17–see also *Chiu-seng t'i***
Northern plays, Hao-fang style in, 114

O

official histories–see *cheng-shih* 正史
Old Text School, 176-177

545

Subject Index

Subject Index